Child Care
Parent Care

Child Care
Parent Care

A COMPREHENSIVE
SOURCEBOOK OF MEDICAL,
PRACTICAL, AND COMMONSENSE
ADVICE ON CARING FOR
YOUR CHILDREN AND YOURSELF
DURING THE PARENTING YEARS

MARILYN HEINS, M.D., AND
ANNE M. SEIDEN, M.D.

Doubleday & Company, Inc., Garden City, New York
1987

Illustrations by Mark Pederson

LIBRARY OF CONGRESS CATALOGING-IN-PUBLICATION DATA
Heins, Marilyn.
Child care/parent care.
Includes bibliographies and index.
1. Children—Care and hygiene.   2. Child rearing.
I. Seiden, Anne M., 1936–   .   II. Title.
[DNLM: 1. Child Care—popular works.   2. Child Rearing—
popular works.   3. Family—popular works.   4. Parent-
Child Relations—popular works.   WS 105.5.F2 H471c]
RJ61.H3826   1987   649'.1   85-20535
ISBN 0-385-17991-X
ISBN 0-385-17990-1 (PBK.)

For our children and yours.

MH
AMS

Contents

PREFACE   ix

ACKNOWLEDGMENTS   xvii

INTRODUCTION   xxiii

Part One
PARENTING IN GENERAL   1

  1. Basic Realities of Parenting; Our Philosophy of Parenting   3

Part Two
ONGOING ISSUES IN PARENTING   29

  2. Biosocial Rhythms: Integrating Children's Biological Clocks and Yours   31
  3. Socialization—More Than Discipline   46
  4. Special Events and Stresses in Family Life   93
  5. Safety First, Safety Always   123
  6. Helpers in Child Care   183

Part Three
DEVELOPMENTAL ISSUES IN PARENTING   219

  7. Children's Growth and Development   221
  8. Parents' Growth and Development   285

Part Four
PARENTING AT DIFFERENT AGES AND STAGES   313

  9. Getting Started: The First Few Days   317
  10. Getting Settled: The First Weeks (up to 12 weeks)   347
  11. Getting Going: Life with a Babe in Arms (3 to 6 months)   373
  12. Getting Careful: Life with a Crawler (7 to 14 months)   389
  13. Getting On: Life with a Toddler (15 to 23 months)   409
  14. Moving Outward: Life with a Two-Year-Old   433
  15. The Three-Year-Old—Now More Social   455
  16. The Four-Year-Old—Now More Verbal   480
  17. The Five-Year-Old—On to Kindergarten   506

Part Five
CHILDHOOD HEALTH AND ILLNESS   523

    18. Health Maintenance   525
    19. Choosing Health Professionals for Your Child's Care   602
    20. Symptoms of Illness in Children—and When to Call for Help 628
    21. Care of the Sick Child at Home   671
    22. How Illness Affects Children and Parents   704
    23. Emergencies   721

Part Six
THINGS THAT COULD BE DIFFERENT   767

    24. Different Kinds of Parents   769
    25. Parenting Non-biological Children   786

Part Seven
THE FUTURE OF PARENTING   809

    26. Parenting and Society   811

AN AFTERWORD   815

    CHAPTER REFERENCES AND SOURCE MATERIAL   817

    INDEX   865

Preface

How Did We Come to Write This Book?

Child-rearing books proliferate in a society where expert and not-so-expert opinions abound, where the roles of parents and the tasks of parenting are rapidly changing, where parents are often confused and troubled by their children's actions, and where there are no easy answers to questions.

Why another book on parenting?

Anne remembers being pregnant with her first child at the end of her internship, just before she started a residency in psychiatry. En route from California to Chicago with her husband driving, she had time to read Dr. Spock's book, *Baby and Child Care*, aloud from cover to cover. She was dismayed by its overly cheerful tone about the psychological side of things—and terrified at how time-consuming the practical advice appeared. Marilyn, by contrast, always loved Spock's breezy way of writing, which she felt alleviated anxiety in a very anxiety-prone population: young parents. Both of us appreciated his help but thought we could add something of our own.

For example, Spock's many pages on how to give the daily bath made it sound like a ritual requiring an hour or more. Anne wondered if she would be able to do all this *and* keep up with the demanding job she had committed herself to. Several hundred pages later she came to the chapter on how to raise twins. Among other practical suggestions, Spock suggested bathing the twins on alternate days, mentioning that babies don't need a daily bath. Why hadn't he mentioned that in the earlier chapters, she wondered? The mother whose job was raising two infants was getting advice that wasn't there for the mother whose job was raising one infant and holding down a job outside the home.

When a pregnant friend, a social worker, was advised by her obstetrician to quit her job a month before the baby was due, Anne wondered about this advice. She had never heard of doctors advising a healthy pregnant woman whose strenuous job was caring for older children to quit caring for them a month before the baby was due!

Parents are caught in a bind. They want and need the best advice that experts can give about the physical, psychological, and practical aspects of pregnancy and child rearing, but sometimes that advice doesn't fit the situations in which most children are raised today.

When Anne asked Marilyn if she knew a pediatrician in the Chicago area to join the project, writing a book was the farthest possible thing from Marilyn's mind. But as she learned more about Anne's ideas and the scope of the book,

PREFACE

she was intrigued. For many years mothers had told Marilyn in the clinic, or after talks she had given to parent groups, "You explain things well, why don't you write a book?" Marilyn realized there were many things she wanted to tell parents about child rearing based on her work as both a pediatrician and a mother.

Thus, a pediatrician from Tucson joined a psychiatrist from Chicago in a seven-year collaborative effort.

More About Us

Marilyn received her M.D. from Columbia University College of Physicians and Surgeons in 1955. She interned in pediatrics at New York Hospital and completed a residency in pediatrics at Babies Hospital in New York. She has practiced pediatrics, served as the Director of Pediatrics at Detroit General Hospital and Associate Dean for Student Affairs at Wayne State University in Detroit, and is now Vice Dean and Professor of Pediatrics at the University of Arizona College of Medicine. She is a member of the Editorial Board of the Journal of the American Medical Association and a member of the National Board of Medical Examiners. Her special interests in pediatrics include helping parents parent and teaching medical students and residents how to help parents parent.

Marilyn has been married for twenty-eight years to a veterinarian. Her daughter of twenty-seven is a resident in internal medicine and her twenty-five-year-old son is a musician. She has two grown stepsons, a stepdaughter-in-law, and three stepgrandsons.

Anne studied architecture and did graduate work in psychology, filling all Ph.D. requirements except the dissertation. She received her M.D. from the University of Chicago in 1964 followed by a rotating internship at San Francisco General Hospital and a residency in psychiatry at Michael Reese Hospital in Chicago. She worked in community psychiatry, served as Director of Research at the Institute for Juvenile Research in Chicago and is currently the Chairperson of Psychiatry at Cook County Hospital there. She has served on two National Institute of Mental Health committees which evaluate research projects for funding. She is an Associate Professor of both Psychiatry and Public Health at the University of Illinois. She is also in the practice of psychiatry and on staff at Michael Reese Hospital. Anne has an interest in the psychological and physical aspects of maternal and child health and the psychology of women. She is an active member of the women's movement and was a founding board member of the National Women's Health Network. She is a feminist and a health consumerist. For eight years she was the first elected representative of women psychiatrists to the Assembly of the American Psychiatric Association.

Anne has been married for twenty-four years to a scientist who serves as Professor in the departments of Pharmacological and Physiological Sciences, and of Psychiatry at the University of Chicago. He does research in psychoactive drugs and trains young scientists. They have a twenty-one-year-old son in college, an eighteen-year-old daughter and a ten-year-old son.

We are both middle-aged physicians and mothers. We became physicians before we raised our children, and we began our parenting before the contemporary women's movement was on the scene. We were both lucky enough to have wonderful, supportive husbands who were ahead of their time. When we began our parenting it was still considered unusual for women of our generation to have a full-time, demanding career *and* to raise children.

Working full-time while raising children wasn't unheard of, but it wasn't common. We both had to do a lot of thinking and soul-searching about it. There were people, including some family members and respected mentors, who told us it couldn't be done. Others gave us every encouragement. There were absolutely no books to read on how to combine motherhood and a career because all the books were written for full-time mothers. There were a few scattered sources of practical advice, which we had to piece together on our own. We read child care books and magazines, some of which helped us, and some of which outraged us (some did both). We consulted various doctors, seeking advice for ourselves and our families, and we were sometimes very satisfied with them and sometimes not.

Like all parents, we both had anxieties, guilts, depressions, and doubts. Our babies had diaper rash too. Our children had many common—and some uncommon—problems. Our children had many common—and some uncommon—triumphs and successes. As we write this, some of our children are fully grown and some are not. At these very moments of writing, Anne is dealing with the sometimes too-constant interruptions of a rambunctious ten-year-old and Marilyn is dealing with the too-rare contact with grandchildren in a distant city.

In one sense this book has been fifty years in the making, because it is the product of our whole lives. It is our own very personal attempt to put together what we both have learned as children, students, women, citizens, physicians, feminists, consumers, parents, and friends and relatives of other parents. No doubt, were we to live so long as to rewrite it in another fifty years, there would be a good deal that would change, as well as much that wouldn't.

As we look back, we made many mistakes in our parenting. There are many things we would both do differently if we had it to do over. (And, no doubt, there are many things yet to be discovered that would lead us to do still *other* things differently.) In a sense, we are writing a "wish book." This is the book that we wish someone else had written earlier for us to read! Even though it has been fun learning things about children and parenting from a wide variety of sources, it's also been a lot of work, and all too often we learned things later than we wished we had.

As parents, both of us have had the same mixed satisfactions and dissatisfactions with advice-givers that most parents have had. But as physicians who have done research and who are involved in the education of physicians, we have both developed some firm ideas about different kinds of advice and their relative worth. Not all professional advice is based on sound research. Experts can and should share personal opinions as well as validated data, but we think it's important to be clear about the difference.

Because we have each had to make our own synthesis of what we have learned and experienced, both as parents and physicians, we haven't always put it together in the same way or with the same priorities. Part of the tremendous fun and excitement of writing this book together has been the chance we had to challenge each other's assumptions and hammer out how we would put it together.

We don't always agree. Most often we can speak with one voice, but sometimes we can't. As you read along, we'll let you know where we disagree. We think the fact that we disagree is healthy. It helps us convey that, in many areas, both parents and experts legitimately differ in what they believe is the best approach.

Perhaps the most important thing about us is that we are women who are both mothers *and* health care professionals. We have struggled to find ways to meet our own needs and other parents' needs as well as the needs of our own children and other people's children in a rapidly changing society.

As authors we combine the perspectives of medical and scientific expertise, with personal practical experience as mothers. Not only do we have seven children and three grandchildren between us but we have compared notes on child rearing with friends, fellow professionals, our own parents and grandparents, sisters, brothers, cousins—and our own children. We talked to many other parents both in the course of our work and socially.

In addition to our scientific training, we have absorbed both traditional and current sources of child care information and opinion. We grew up with our own traditions and memories; we have been influenced by our times. Both as professional women, in our specialties of pediatrics and psychiatry, and in our personal roles as friend and family member, we have counseled many parents. We also teach medical students and other young health care providers and have listened to their voices. But most important, we can write about parenting with special fervor and knowledge, because *we have been there.*

Why Do People Read Books on Parenting?

By and large, people read books on child care because they can't rely entirely on their past experiences or instincts to raise children successfully and happily. We agree. We couldn't either.

Like other parents, we consulted standard how-to-do-it child care books in our own parenting. But we were often dissatisfied. Although child-rearing books are numerous, many of the books are written by purported experts but their advice is often conflicting.

Some books focus on only special aspects of child rearing such as a single age in the child's life. Some books place an emphasis upon child-rearing philosophy without providing information and techniques on day-to-day child-rearing issues. Many books fail to separate scientific knowledge from opinion. Books written before the end of the 1970s take a sexist approach to child rearing, making the assumptions that mothers are always homemakers, or that girls and boys require different and stereotyped child-rearing practices. Most books state or imply that the mother will not work outside the home, although some allude to practical problems of combining work and child care. Most books imply that the parents are in their twenties.

Some books fail to consider that parents as well as children have needs and almost no books give enough attention to the needs of the parent in the parent-child equation. Almost all of these books write about children and parents as though the parents had no other interests or commitments in life.

Few books on children are comprehensive, or combine a feasible child-rearing philosophy with a critical approach to the scientific study of parent-child relations. Even fewer translate philosophy, science, and good sense into practical techniques for managing the daily problems and issues of raising children.

Few child care books are written by women who are themselves mothers as well as professionals. Thus, they rarely have the desired combination of valid but practical knowledge, good common horse sense, and empathy with the mother who struggles with the daily tasks. One can sense that many of these authors haven't tried to get a screaming child away from the gum counter in a supermarket, while shopping for dinner guests that night, worrying about getting to work on time the next day if the sitter is late again, and being concerned right then about whether her menstrual tampon is leaking through.

How This Book Is Different

Clearly, there was a need for a book which separated fact from opinion, and helped the parent-reader become a more sophisticated consumer of parenting advice from whatever source. We decided to write it.

We realized that no book written at one point in time can have the last word on every topic important to parents. Therefore, we don't just tell parents "how to do it," but we also help them evaluate advice from multiple sources—scientific and traditional.

Because we think the reader is entitled to know what is behind our advice and recommendations, we include references on relevant scientific evidence, where it exists. We try to separate fact from opinion by reexamining those "facts" which have been religiously repeated by the experts, but which have little or no scientific basis. Although we present a good deal of factual information, there are many important areas where there are no absolute answers. Therefore, we share our own opinions with the readers while making clear that they are only opinions.

We have written the book as if we were talking with friends, much as we shared this information with each other and with the parents who came to us for help.

We may be professionals but we have laughed, and cried, and agonized over our own children and our own parenting. By sharing our knowledge and experience with parents, we believe we can help make parenting a more satisfying, less anxiety-ridden activity—and, as it should be, one of the great joys of life.

This book is a *comprehensive guide to parenting*, which realistically approaches the changing and often difficult context in which parenting occurs today.

Although the publisher would not permit us to produce a book that weighed more than a baby, we wanted to make this book *comprehensive*. Thus we include normal physical, cognitive, and social development and childhood illness, as well as practical daily care and issues of discipline. The family that purchased only one child-rearing book for reading and reference could rely on this one.

By *guide*, we mean a practical, down-to-earth, how-to-do-it book that does not just discuss ideas and attitudes, but in fact gives parents concrete advice when they need it, and can serve as a reference in an emergency.

By *parenting*, we mean this is not just another book on child care. We feel strongly that one of the chief barriers to good child care is lack of systematic attention to *parents'* needs in the reciprocal mutual parent-child process that is parenting. Children are very vulnerable when their parents' needs are unfulfilled, either as persons, partners, parents, or members of the general community. Parents cannot effectively give to children what they do not have to give. When parents are too stressed, or too unfulfilled, or too guilty to take their own needs into account, the children suffer. *Good care of yourself is an intrinsic part of being able to care for your child.*

The approach of this book has two important dimensions. First, we try to be intellectually honest and secondly, we try to be realistic about parenting. Far too many books present a "rosy-glow," romantic view of child rearing, implying that all will be well if only the child is loved, or respected, or nutritiously fed. This does parents a disservice, because it tends to increase their feelings of having done wrong whenever they have to cope with some of the inevitable difficulties in parenting.

Also, this book takes into account changing family structures. With the increase in single parenting and maternal employment, most parents cannot use a book which assumes full-time mothering. The book also acknowledges changing attitudes toward professional expertise. With the growth of the health-consumer movements, many parents are properly skeptical of some established medical advice and approaches.

The continuity in essential child-rearing issues, even across superficially different parenting situations, is a core part of our message. In today's world as never before, no family can be an island. The neglected child down the block may be the one who steals your child's bicycle—or worse. The fact that parents are happily married today could change tomorrow. Even the fact that you are not a parent at all does not insulate you from concerns about children—as a taxpayer and a citizen. Children are, and must be, everyone's concern.

We worked very hard to make this book as accurate and current as possible, but medical information changes rapidly. There is much health and medical advice in the book which we hope will be useful, but this advice should never replace individual medical advice about your child. *Questions about your child's health and illness should always be addressed to a physician.*

ACKNOWLEDGMENTS

Writing a book of these dimensions is a paradox. Each author is alone when writing but we were far from alone during this five-year project.

Marilyn speaks: In looking back, I realize I was generously afforded help in three domains—all important in the completion of this book. As a matter of fact, without these helpers and their support, the book would never have been completed.

First of all, I asked many questions of many competent experts in their respective fields. Sometimes the questions and answers were in the form of a brief telephone conversation. In other instances, the experts reviewed drafts of whole chapters or sections. Their critiques were invaluable in helping me produce the manuscript in its final form. The experts called upon were not only physicians or psychologists. Some experts were parents who read and critiqued drafts from the parents' point of view. To these experts of all persuasions, I offer a heartfelt "Thank you."

Many of these experts are faculty of the University of Arizona College of Medicine. They include: Hugh D. Allen, M.D., Professor, Department of Pediatrics; William Banner, Jr., M.D., Ph.D., Assistant Professor, Department of Pediatrics and Pharmacology, and Adjunct Clinical Assistant Professor, Pharmacy Practice; Alan D. Bedrick, M.D., Assistant Professor, Department of Pediatrics; Helen L. Britton, M.D., Clinical Assistant Professor, Department of Pediatrics; M. Paul Capp, M.D., Professor and Head, Department of Radiology and Director of Clinical Radiology; George D. Comerci, M.D., Professor, Department of Pediatrics and Department of Family and Community Medicine; Stanley W. Coulthard, M.D., Clinical Professor of Surgery; Burris R. Duncan, M.D., Professor, Department of Pediatrics; John L. Ey, M.D., M.P.H., Associate, Department of Pediatrics, and pediatrician practicing in Tucson; Peggy C. Ferry, M.D., Professor, Department of Pediatrics; Ronald S. Fischler, M.D., formerly Assistant Professor, Department of Family and Community Medicine and Department of Pediatrics; Gregory G. Gaar, M.D., formerly Clinical Instructor, Department of Pediatrics; Gail G. Harrison, Ph.D., Professor, Department of Family and Community Medicine, Associate Professor, Department of Nutrition and Food Science, Department of Anthropology, and Associate Professor, Department of Pediatrics; Kenneth V. Iserson, M.D., Associate Professor, Department of Surgery; Noel D. Matkin, Ph.D., Professor, Speech and Hearing Sciences, Surgery; Harvey W. Meislin, M.D., Professor, Department of Surgery and Director, Emergency Services; Eskild A. Petersen, M.D., Associate Professor, Department of Internal Medicine; William D. Rappaport, M.D., Clinical Assistant Professor, Department of Surgery; Daniel F. Reardon, M.D., Clinical Professor, Department of Pediatrics; Kathleen M. Rest, M.P.A., formerly Project Coordinator, Department of Family and Community Medicine; Lewis S. Shenker, M.D., Professor, Obstetrics and Gynecology; Catherine M. Shisslak, Ph.D., Clinical Associate Professor, Department of Psychiatry and Adjunct Assistant Professor, Psychology; Lynn M. Taussig, M.D., Professor and Head, Department of Pediatrics, Director of Pediatrics and Assistant Director, Respiratory Sciences; Louis Weinstein, M.D., Associate Professor, Department of Obstetrics and Gynecology; Rickey L. Williams, M.D., Assistant Professor, Department of Pediatrics; James M. Woolfenden, M.D., Professor, Department of Radiology; Alayne Yates, M.D., Professor, Department of Psychiatry and Associate Professor, Department of Pediatrics, and Chief, Psychiatry Section.

Other experts include: Karen S. Anderson, Ph.D., Associate Professor, History Department, University of Arizona; Margaret R. Dunlap, Ph.D., Psychologist, Children Evaluation Center of Southern Arizona; Laurence Finberg, M.D., Chair, Department of Pediatrics, State University of New York, Downstate Medical Center, Brooklyn; Lori Fischler, formerly Assistant to the Director, Arizona Poison Control Center; Marjorie Ford, formerly Executive Director, Planned Parenthood; Katherine Kilbourne, Associate Director, Food Services, University Medical Center; Patricia Nolan, M.D., Director, Pima County Health Department; Kitty L. Peyton, Ph.D., formerly Assistant Professor, School of Home Economics, University of Arizona; Martha Rothman, Executive Director, Tucson Association of Child Care; Janice Stevenson, Tucson Association for Child Care, Education & Support; Sheila Tobias, formerly Visiting Lecturer, Political Science Department, University of Arizona; Frank R. Williams, Th.D., Family Life Specialist, Cooperative Extension Service, School of Family and Consumer Resources, University of Arizona.

The Arizona Health Sciences Library, under the able direction of Thomas Higdon, deserves a special word of thanks. Every librarian consulted was a helpful expert. There was no book or reference I needed that they did not find. I commend and thank them all, especially the reference librarian Nga Nguyen and Zo Deane Knipe of the Interlibrary Loan Department.

Encouraging and helpful parents included: Judith Braslow, Washington, D.C.; Betsy Bolding, Tucson; Dottie Burks, Tucson; Barbara Fischer, attorney, Tucson; Mary Jane Heacox, Tucson; Amber Jones, Vice President, Albany Medical College; Jane Ruggill, Tucson; Mona Signer, Chicago; Nancy Schlossberg, Washington, D.C.; Jennifer Schneider, M.D., Tucson; Gloria and Bobby Smith, Tucson.

The second category of help I received is called "clerical." How anemic a term to describe the caring and energetic help given me in putting the manuscript together! These helpers include: Mary Ellen Benoit, Cheryl Bernth, Lynn Bonamy, Betty Curran, Ruth Isakoff, Anne McCutchin, Joanne McGinnis, Maria O'Regan, Gloria Smith, Carol Tenney, Janet Tupper, Dawn Vandenberg, and Donna Vandenberg.

All these women cheerfully transcribed, word-processed, and edited the manuscript in all of its stages. Every one of these women worked on the manuscript, as I did, in their spare time. They worked weekends and evenings, digging into time for their own families and their own respite from work. Special thanks go to Gloria Smith who served as my assistant. There is no way I can properly thank her for all of her help.

All of these women provided spirit and we made up a team. When the manuscript was finished, the team was tired but proud. We had gone through a five-year gestation period together. (During this time, by the way, two women were delivered of their own babies and still found time to help!) I will be forever grateful.

The third category is that of personal support and encouragement to the author, as distinguished from the project. Some of these people also helped as experts but are mentioned here because of their personal support. First, Vincent Fulginiti, M.D., former Head of the Department of Pediatrics at the University of Arizona College of Medicine, who provided encouragement from the beginning. A group of warm and loving friends supported me through this project: Betsy Bolding, Judith Braslow, Myra Dinnerstein, Martha Rothman, Sheila Tobias, and the late Judy Tyree. My sister, Judith Leet, listened to my anguished phone calls about whether the manuscript would ever be completed and always managed to be encouraging. She lovingly helped with the final editorial decisions.

My children suffered twice, first from my ignorance when they were growing up because I did not have this book to read; second, from my neglect of them over the past years when I was so busy writing.

My husband, Milton Lipson, has been supportive of every goal of mine, even when—as in the case of this book—it interfered with his own goals. He is proud of my accomplishments. I am proud to have his love and support—and grateful for both. I humbly tell him here that I am merely the reflection of his belief in me.

Anne speaks: I am grateful to the people who taught me about parenting, about interpreting scientific data, and to those who helped specifically with this project.

About parenting. Thanks first to those who taught me the most, our children Alex, Effie, and Sam—always lively, assertive, loving, and interesting people both when tiny and bigger. Next, to my husband Lew, who always shared his love, his feelings, his own memories of childhood, and our common efforts to balance the needs of our children and our other commitments to life and to ourselves. And to his mother, Dorothy, who has been so much a part of our family life. Thanks next to my parents, who were pioneers in their parenting, in their conviction that if you treat children as you do other people, you and they will be doing the best that's possible, whether life is easy or hard. And thanks to my siblings, Susan, Jane, and Hugh; among us we've spent many hundreds of hours thrashing out our own versions of our parents' vision of parenting. And to many other relatives who shared this process, especially Linnea and Mary, the innermost part of our extended family.

Parenting involves head as well as heart and hands; there's a bewildering mass of scientific and professional knowledge which can be difficult to sort and sift. I am grateful to my teachers: in architecture at North Carolina State in the late 1950s, where we learned that creativity can be stimulated to blend science, technology, aesthetics, and what is now called human engineering and environmental psychology. Later in psychology at the University of Chicago in the early sixties where every graduate course began with several weeks of philosophy of science, that is, how well do we know what we think we know? How does science sift reliable findings and useful theories from those which are contaminated by the wishful thinking of the scientists? Medical school was counterbalancing, and in many ways more like parenting: there may or may not be the reliable scientific knowledge one wants, but one has to act with the knowledge and the crisis of the moment. Psychiatric training at Michael Reese under Daniel Offer's direction added intellectual tools and rich experience with human problems, almost always interacting in some way with family life. I am also grateful to my teachers at the Institute for Psychoanalysis in Chicago, who demonstrated the renewed relevance of psychoanalytic thinking to infant research and to parenting, and to my teachers at the Harvard School of Public Health, who provided valuable critiques of common medical practices. I am profoundly grateful to my first research mentors, Morris Stein, Morton Lieberman, and Sheppard Kellam, and later to Israel Goldiamond for his seminars in behavior analysis.

Of the thousands of books on parenting, I am particularly grateful to three authors: Benjamin Spock, Betty Friedan, and Thomas Gordon. Spock pioneered in bringing the pediatric and psychiatric knowledge of his day to ordinary parents. Friedan brought a welcome and needed skepticism to the idea that parenting and family alone should define a woman's life. And Gordon put into print what my own parents had grasped at—a way of interacting with children—as with loved adults—with workable, mutual respect and assertiveness. The women's health movement fleshed out all three themes. I am grateful to Pauline Bart for many things, especially for introducing me to a feminist application of the sociology of knowledge—that is, the systematic study of the ways in which where we are in the social system influences what we want to believe and how we interpret data. Participation as a founding board member of the National Women's Health Network introduced me to many creative women who were critically evaluating health care philosophy and health care delivery. Among them, special thanks to Belita Cowan, Doris Haire, Michelle Harrison, Mary Howell, Barbara Seaman, and the wonderful women of the Boston Women's Health Book Collective. Their groundbreaking book, *Our Bodies, Ourselves,* was the inspiration for this book. Nada Stotland and Susan Fisher were two other inspiring colleagues who take seriously the task of bringing responsible criticism to bear on medical practice in women's health and child rearing.

I am grateful to many colleagues and helpers who contributed to this particular book. They are too many to name them all in this book, but I thank them all, and owe special mention to Victoria Schauf and Merilyn Salomon, who participated in early versions of the concept of this book; to Shiomay

Young, then an outstanding research assistant and now a social scientist in her own right; to Carol Sakala, who took time from her own research to assist in research for this project; to the entire research and clinical staff of the Institute for Juvenile Research who, under Frank Rafferty's leadership, studied topics ranging from damaged infants to adolescent development and delinquency, and family life. At Cook County Hospital I am grateful for the endless opportunities to learn from human problems and from the staff who try to help with them, most particularly for this project, Karin Krueckeberg and Alice Dakin in child psychiatry, Jaime Trujillo, Betty Shamley, Joseph Hermes, and Suzanne Cooperman for their work with adolescent and older mothers, and two medical directors, Rowine Brown, for her knowledge of child abuse and medico-legal issues, and Agnes Lattimer for her commitments to quality care for children and adults, and to the people who provide that care. Without dedicated administrative assistants, Joanne Kent and Terry D'Sousa, I could not have finished the daily job in time to go home at night and write. Without wonderful secretaries, the endless versions of the outline and manuscript would not have been possible: especially Estelle Marvel, Harriet Hammond, Eileen Rider; and Jacquie Washington, who keeps the office running. Special thanks are due to Martin Harrow and Bruce Bonecutter for administrative wisdom and personal and professional support on this, and many projects. Special thanks also are due to Deepak Kapoor and James Newman, who provided expert psychiatric coverage during my working vacations—and also shared valuable insights and experiences from family life.

Judy Farquahar has played a most complex role: from cross-cultural insights to practical parenting to nitty-gritty suggestions. Many others helped by reading parts of the manuscript; I am grateful to all.

Special thanks are due to Andrew May and Effie Seiden for expert and diligent help in last-minute manuscript preparation. And I also want to add my thanks to Gloria Smith for her superb talents and great commitment to every aspect of this project.

A book on parenting is a book about living, and almost everyone with whom I crossed paths in the last twelve years of writing has had an impact: our children's teachers, parents of our children's friends, and other parents in the community, many of whose names I may never know. The list is endless and the gratitude profound. I hope readers will write with critiques or suggestions to improve future editions, and in advance, I want to thank you too.

Introduction

Parenting Is Everybody's Business

Because the children of a society are that society's future, parenting is everybody's business.

This book is written for parents, those thinking about becoming parents, those about to be parents, and those who want to help parents professionally or as friends and citizens.

This book addresses the concept of parenting at all ages, concentrating on children from newborns to kindergartners. We speak to stepparents, foster parents, and child care workers of all persuasions. We speak to those who help parents in all of the human services professions such as medicine, psychology, social work, and nursing. We speak to trainees in these fields as well as the clergy and others who counsel and advise parents. We speak to those preparing for parenthood, not only prospective parents in prenatal classes, but also those studying child development in junior high school, high school, or college. We speak to social planners concerned with family policy and the impact of society on family life. We speak to politicians and government workers who make decisions and carry out policy affecting children and their parents.

We were told that the easiest way to start writing a book is to picture the reader in your mind. This is a bit difficult for us because we picture many different readers. Some are pregnant women, waiting for their first child. Some are couples debating whether or not to have a child. Some of you have more children than the two of us combined! Some of you are grandparents or great-grandparents and are older and wiser than we are. Some of you have Ph.D.'s in child development or in nutrition or in sociology and have more knowledge about your field than we do. Others may not be as highly educated, but may have much family or cultural wisdom about child rearing that we lack.

How can we write a book that is helpful in some way to all of you? We have decided that the one thing all readers of this book will have in common is *concern about their child or about children in general.*

We have written this book for the *concerned* parent or parents. We know your goal is to do the best job you can in raising your child and also in living your own life.

Some of you may be anxious about parenting in general or feel helpless because parenting is a new role, and no one has taught you how to prepare yourself for this new job or even given you a job description. Therefore, we have written this book as simply and straightforwardly as we could. We designed the book so that those of you who already know, perhaps better than we do, what we are talking about, can go on to another section to meet your needs.

We present data that are scientifically defensible on which we base our advice but we recognize that you are in charge of your actions as a parent. You can choose to take our advice—or anyone else's for that matter—or to ignore it. We will make it very clear in those few areas in which we feel there is *only one way to go,* why there is only one way, and how to find that route as quickly and easily as possible.

Though we are both professionals, we have been pregnant, we have been new mothers, we have been anxious parents, we have made mistakes, we have learned from them, and, in some instances, have not yet learned from them! We know what an awesome responsibility parenthood is. We hope this book can help make your role as parents or grandparents or substitute parents as easy and pleasurable and self-fulfilling as possible.

Unlike many other parenting books that assume the parent is always the mother (or specific parent books addressed to the father or the stepparent), in this book we talk to the person who is parenting—mother or father, grandmother or grandfather, stepmother or stepfather. In those occasional sections where we are talking to a parent of a specific sex, we say so.

How to Use Parenting Advice—Including Ours

It's important to understand that advice from "experts" is not always the same as "expert advice." Experts can get their information from many sources of varying reliability. Information may be based on well-researched findings that have stood the test of scientific peer review. Peer review means that fellow scientists scrutinized both the methodology of the study and the rigor of the statistical measures applied to the data. However, the fact that the information is based on good scientific evidence does not mean it will always apply nor does it mean it will apply to a given child.

Furthermore, scientific evidence is not always conclusive, which can lead to controversy rather than consensus among experts.

Some child-rearing advice is based on folk wisdom. Folk wisdom, by definition, is unsubstantiated by scientific research. That doesn't make it either right or wrong. Some advice which has been continued for centuries, especially if found in many different cultures, is likely to be pretty safe since there has been time for bad consequences to be discovered. For example, the Bible advises a pregnant woman not to drink alcohol although it was not until 1977 that the National Institute on Alcohol Abuse and Alcoholism advised limiting alcohol in pregnancy, and 1981 before pregnant women were advised to avoid it altogether. On the other hand, several primitive cultures advocate treating the umbilical stump with cow dung. There is no known benefit to this practice, which carries with it a high risk of frequently fatal tetanus infections. Also we can't wait for folk wisdom to help us with new hazards such as the automobile.

Folk wisdom and gut instinct say hold your infant in your arms for safety. Accident research proves unequivocally that your baby is safe only in an infant car seat.

Professional advice is not always based on scientific data. The convenience of medical personnel may determine advice or practice. For example, giving birth while lying down rather than upright is more convenient for the doctor though probably not as convenient for the mother.

One of the things we deplore in some of our professional colleagues is their failure to communicate the differences between well-researched areas that have yielded scientific consensus and areas where the expert is speaking as an individual giving an opinion.

For example, when a pediatrician recommends a schedule of immunizations, it's based on the current recommendations of the Committee on Immunizations of the American Academy of Pediatrics. Periodically this committee reviews all available evidence on the safety and efficacy of available immunizations, and balances that data against the national and international statistics on the frequency and seriousness of the illnesses to be immunized against. This data is based on large-sample studies, far beyond the scope of any single office practitioner to conduct.

On the other hand, when a pediatrician advises a parent to encourage babies to go to sleep by "crying it out," this advice is not based on any research on human infants. Such advice is not scientific medicine, but rather is "clinical folklore." Writing this kind of advice as a standard recommendation for all babies without clearly indicating that there is no scientific evidence to support it is an example of abuse of the expert role.

Similarly, when a psychiatrist tells a patient that antipsychotic medication plus psychotherapy and rehabilitation is the most effective treatment for schizophrenia, this represents a consensus arrived at from many well-designed research studies. But if the same psychiatrist tells parents not to allow a child to sleep in the parents' bed, this is an opinion unsupported by research.

Doctors advise patients on all kinds of issues, sometimes giving advice and sometimes just speaking as an interested person trying to help, much as a caring friend or relative might. We don't think there's anything wrong with this at all; in fact, we quite frequently do it ourselves! But the parent or patient too often takes *all* the expert's advice as being equally sound. We think doctors should clearly make a distinction between data and opinion.

On our part, we'll try to let you know when we're presenting the best available scientific knowledge, and when we're offering "household hints" based on our own clinical/personal experience and folklore. When our folklores are different, we'll tell you that too.

Format and How to Use This Book

Part One entitled *Parenting in General* includes the history of parenting and child rearing, and the basic realities of parenting today.

Part Two entitled *Ongoing Issues in Parenting* has five chapters: *Biosocial Rhythms: Integrating Children's Biological Clocks and Yours; Socialization— More Than Discipline; Special Events and Stresses in Family Life; Safety First, Safety Always;* and *Helpers in Child Care.*

Part Three is devoted to both aspects of developmental issues in parenting, with a chapter on *children's* growth and development and one on *parents'* growth and development as both parents and people.

Part Four, entitled *Parenting at Different Ages and Stages,* deals with children from the first few days of life through kindergarten.

Part Five is devoted to *Childhood Health and Illness.*

Part Six is called *Things That Could Be Different.* The chapter on different kinds of parents looks at the older parent and the employed mother, while the chapter on parenting non-biological children views parenting adopted children and stepchildren.

Part Seven is entitled *The Future of Parenting.*

We doubt that many of you will read this book from cover to cover. Indeed, some chapters are designed to be reference chapters, to be used when you have something to look up.

There is a lot of repetition because we don't expect you to read every word. For an example, we discuss safety as a chapter, *Safety First, Safety Always.* We also discuss safety in each chapter devoted to a specific childhood stage. We talk again about results of accidents in the chapter *Emergencies.*

We have made each section reasonably complete for browsers but we refer frequently to other sections for the explorers among you. Additionally, you can use the Index to find what you want.

Every chapter ends with a section entitled Suggested Readings and Resources, which provides an annotated bibliography of books we feel may be helpful to you, as well as sources of help for special problems. We hope to be complete enough in what we say so you need not go to the literature, but the references and source material we used in researching this book are available at the end of the book if you wish to read further or gain more information.

We called this book *Child Care/Parent Care* because we believe strongly that there's a vital balance between children's and parents' needs. In this book we talk a lot about marriages. Obviously, not all parents are married, but most are during part or all of the child-rearing years. Though half of marriages end in divorce today, half do not, and most people who divorce remarry eventually. Stresses of parenting are often cited as a reason for divorce, which we consider sad.

Our goal in this book is to make every suggestion we can to decrease parental stress. Accordingly, in almost every chapter, we make suggestions about maintaining your marriage while parenting. Some of this may be jarring or painful to single parents, or to parents who are partnered without having decided about a permanent commitment. Please read between the lines. Where we say spend time with your spouse, if you don't have one, read it to suit *your* situation. What we mean is, spend time on the couple relationship you have (if you do) or on seeking one (if you want) or on your needs for friendship and mutual support if you are not interested right now in seeking a couple relationship. The basic point is, *take care of yourself and the human network that works for you* to keep yourself and your family in balance.

Often throughout this book we are prescriptive, not because we know all the answers—far from it—but because we want to make our suggestions clear. *We never mean to imply that parenting is easy—it's not.* However, the rewards are great.

We wrote this book to be useful to parents. If any readers have suggestions on how such a book can be made *more* useful, please contact us through the publisher. We are both very much interested in the general question of how communications between professionals and parents can be improved.

Part One

PARENTING
IN GENERAL

1

BASIC REALITIES OF PARENTING;
OUR PHILOSOPHY OF PARENTING

Scope of Chapter

This chapter begins with a brief overview of the biology and history of parenting, touching on animal vs. human parenting as well as the human family. The next sections deal with the politics of parenting: the family and the state; historical views of parenting; parenting in the context of today's world; why parenting is so hard today; children's and parents' needs; and the bottom-line realities of parenting. The last section presents our personal philosophy of parenting, which evolved from our experiences as parents as well as doctors.

Introduction

Is parenting harder today than in the immediate and distant past? In many ways it's obviously easier. More mothers and babies survive birth and infancy. Today people can exercise choice about when they will have their children, and how many and how widely spaced they will be. There are useful formal resources for problems in parenting—medical, social, and legal. Much has been learned about obstetric, medical, and psychiatric illnesses affecting parents and children, and research to gain further knowledge continues.

Yet in several ways parenting is more difficult today. First of all, because of medical advances, parents *expect* every child to live and be physically and mentally healthy. These expectations may outstrip our knowledge and power. Second, economic and social changes have rapidly changed the natural support systems people could depend on before—stable marriages (whether happy or not), extended families, a community of friends and neighbors with shared values. Third, society holds parents responsible for their children whether or not they have enough help and support in raising them.

What are some of the special difficulties parents face today? Why is it often so hard for parents to get the kinds of practical help and emotional understanding they need in order to be good and happy parents? Why do some people say they never want to be parents? Why do some raise their children in neglectful or abusive ways?

Parenting is a major issue for our whole society, not just for parents. But in our highly individualistic culture, much of the responsibility for children is left to the parents alone. As individual human animals, we do not always have reliable instincts to handle all the problems of our children. Not only that, but our social system is not organized for optimal child care. In fact, Vance Packard has called our children an endangered species, because of our society's lack of commitment to them![1]

BIOLOGY AND HISTORY OF PARENTING

Animal vs. Human Parenting

Humans are an unusual kind of animal. We are social animals in that almost all of us live in groups. But most other social animals live in societies rigidly organized by class or gender to care for their young as well as perform other functions. Ants and bees, for example, have a single "queen," which lays the eggs, and separate classes that care for the young, collect food, or serve as "warriors." Other social animals have highly predictable divisions of labor around child care. Cattle live in herds, but nursing is done by the individual mother until the calf can eat adult food. With some ape and monkey species child care is done entirely by the mother; in others the males or other females participate in feeding and protecting the young.

Reptiles, fish, and amphibians hatch from their eggs and move off alone to search for food, but all mammals and most birds and social insects need parenting.

Among birds, some species are "precocial" and some "altricial." "Precocial" means mature (as in the word "precocious" for a child who matures early intellectually). Precocial birds, like chickens, are feathered at hatching and can see and feed themselves. "Altricial" means immature. Altricial birds, like house finches, have no feathers when hatched and must be fed and warmed by their parents.

Among mammals, altricial ones like kittens have closed eyes at birth and can crawl to find the mother's teats but are otherwise immobile. They must be kept in a "nest" and require very intensive maternal care. This care tapers off with a fairly early weaning, after which the young can survive without the mother. By contrast, precocial mammals such as buffalos or wild horses are born in the open, with open eyes, and have the ability to walk at birth. They have an extended nursing period, during which they become self-sufficient and socially integrated into the herd.

Primates, including monkeys and chimpanzees, as well as humans, have some features of both altricial and precocial mammals. The human infant *can* open its eyes at birth but cannot even crawl. It must be lifted to the breast or it will not survive. Today most of us wean our infants at an early age before they can feed themselves, but we must keep them around us for a very long time in order to socialize them into *our* herd. Since humans, even in primitive societies, need parental care for a long time, it is not until after puberty that children usually take an equal place alongside the adults of the tribe.

In complex societies, parental care is needed for an even longer time. Today's educational expectations, and the prolongation of adolescence, mean that children require parental care for many years. The mother cat has six weeks of kitten care for any given litter, but humans actively parent for at least twenty years and worry and care about their children for a lifetime.

As with altricial birds, either human parent is capable of doing all the tasks of parenting (except for breast-feeding) and, of course, other adults or older children can substitute for the parent in many of these tasks.

Two robins can provide worms and warmth for a small number of nestlings for one summer. One mother cat can care for a litter by herself for six weeks. A mother chimpanzee nurses one infant for four or five years, until the half-grown creature can forage for itself. But the mother will not go into heat and conceive another chimpanzee until that happens. The human mother might have a second child in ten months and usually has responsibility for their care for two decades or more.

Human Parenting—Families and Their Backups

No human society has ever relied entirely on the biological parents alone to provide everything that children might need, for a quarter of a century, without some form of backup help. Too many things can happen in that span of time, such as parental illness or incapacity. The extended family or community has always had to care for orphans.

The family is the way we provide lengthy care to the human infant and child. All human cultures have either families or family-like groupings, but the "rules" of what constitutes a family vary enormously among cultures. Anthropologists find that in most cultures one can identify a "nucleus" of mother, father, and child—what the Hindu extended family calls "the divine triangle." But this nucleus has usually been embedded in a larger extended family, a kinship system, or tribe. The wider family serves multiple purposes: pooling of economic resources in good times and bad, support in illness and disaster, sharing in child rearing and the care of the aged, stabilizing adult personalities, and passing on of values and traditions.

Extended families provided social security, but had many features that would seem like disadvantages to many of us today—less autonomy, for example. Full-grown adults remained subject to the orders of elders and the rules of tradition.

Probably one reason that Americans today are so fiercely individualistic is that our country was mostly settled by people who left or were torn away from their extended families. We Americans usually don't want our adult personalities "stabilized" by our parents, or our child-rearing practices dictated by our mothers-in-law. But we can never completely free ourselves from the need for the help of others. However, it's often unclear what the rules are. Whom can we count on for help? To whom do we owe help? Whom can we count on for advice and how much do we have to follow it?

Very few people today can be sure that relatives or friends could or would carry them through a catastrophic illness, or even recurrent minor ones. In case of real adversity, many people might have to turn to impersonal government or private agencies for much of the help they and their children might need.

A Look Back in History

Surprisingly, it is only fairly recently that the history of childhood has emerged as a field of scholarly study, with major books, a journal, and systematic advance of knowledge in the field.

Philippe Ariès wrote one of the major books in this area, published in 1965.[2] He pointed out that childhood (at least after infancy) was not always viewed as a special period of life, with special needs, characteristics, and developing abilities. Children in Western and other civilizations did not usually wear clothing distinctive from that of adults until about the nineteenth century. They did not have special institutions like compulsory school instead of work, a different level of responsibility for crimes, and a separate juvenile justice system.

Childhood has not always been viewed as primarily a period of preparation for adult life. In other times and places the responsibilities for getting the daily work done and caring for the smallest children were divided up among children, adults, and the elderly on the practical basis of who could do what. Ariès viewed this more fluid line between childhood and adulthood as having been beneficial for children. Other historians, such as deMause,[3] emphasize that children were often exploited and their special needs ignored.

No society can survive and reproduce itself if there is not fail-safe societal responsibility for the care and rearing of its children. But human societies have differed a great deal in how that responsibility is shared, monitored, and evaluated, and in availability of resources when there is a breakdown in parenting.

Some of the ways in which human societies have handled child care responsibility include:

1. The "mother-alone" model. The mother pretty much has the sole responsibility for children until they are able to take over responsibility for themselves. Others in the tribe or community might have varying degrees of responsiveness to the mother's or the child's needs, but little or no enforceable responsibility for doing so, and little control over how she does it. This model

works for our close relatives, the chimpanzees, as Jane Goodall eloquently describes.[4]

However, in human societies, this pattern is rarely, if ever, seen in pure form. It won't work well when the climate is cold enough to require accumulation of personal wealth in order to eat, keep warm, and survive; when fertility patterns are such that a mother is likely to have more than one child of an age requiring close supervision and care; or when the physical and social environment is such that there are many dangers requiring adult protection of children beyond their early childhood years. In all these situations, mothers need help— usually male as well as female labor for economic survival.

2. "Extended-family" or "tribal" models. Here the mother lives with, or close to, other people who have a firm responsibility to help support, care for, and socialize her child and herself. In some such societies, the mother continues to live with the family into which she was born. Her mother, sisters, and, sometimes, brothers and other relatives continue to stay in the family home, accumulate property there, and share in the child rearing. Her husband may join them for a lifetime, or for a brief period, depending on the duration of his relationship to her. If their relationship breaks up, he will return to his mother's home, taking only a few personal possessions, and leaving the children and any accumulated wealth with the children's mother and her family. These societies are called "matrilineal" by anthropologists, when inheritance is through the female line, and "matrilocal" when the family lives in the mother's home. They may or may not be "matriarchal" (meaning ruled by a mother), since the real power is sometimes wielded by the oldest woman, but sometimes by the oldest man in the grouping. The younger male partners of the young women may or may not have incentive to do significant economic work, since they have no permanent claim to the wealth which may be accumulated.

In other extended-family societies, a young woman is married (by choice or by arrangement), and leaves her home and family to join that of the extended family into which her husband was born. There she lives by their rules, and under their direction and protection. Most likely her husband's mother or grandmother will have a great deal of responsibility and direction for how she rears her children. Rarely does she have the opportunity to return home permanently, even if she is unhappy with the family or the relationship with the husband. Such a patrilineal, patrilocal, and patriarchal family has been relatively common in human history. While such an arrangement was often an unhappy one for women, especially young ones, it may have survived because of its success in harnessing and channeling the energies of males into economic activity which created and accumulated material wealth.

3. Family community models. With the rise of class societies, wealthy families often maintained and increased their wealth by clustering other subordinate families around them. The medieval manor shared some of the characteristics of a village as we know it today and some of the characteristics of a large extended family. But for the subordinate families, the governance came from neither the wife's family nor the husband's, but from the dominant family.

Children were often apprenticed or placed in domestic servitude at quite young ages, so that much of the child rearing, socialization, and education was done on the job rather than by parents or immediate family.

4. Isolated nuclear families. Although the family nucleus of mother, father, and child can always be identified in the middle of any kind of extended family, much as the nucleus of a cell is in its middle, rarely in human history does one find it standing alone. To see this nucleus separate, both from the extended family and the place of work, is quite new. Such families have existed in great numbers only since the Industrial Revolution, so that the long-term stability of the isolated nuclear family is not yet clear.

A number of economic resources are needed in order for the isolated nuclear family to work. Examples include alternative resources for the care of the aged, enough industrial productivity so that the society can forgo economic production by women during the years that children are small, and enough wealth to purchase transportation systems between home and workplace.

The isolated nuclear family may appeal to many persons raised in the American individualistic tradition, because there are no other adults in the home who express their views about lifestyle, child rearing, and the marital relationship. On the other hand, the absence of other adults seems to intensify the emotionality of the marital relationship and, indeed, the stability of marital pairings seems to have been declining in recent years.

The isolated nuclear family model was highly celebrated in the so-called "togetherness era" of the 1950s, during which suburbia exploded and became a norm for those who could afford it. Mothers were expected to stay home with the small children, at least until they were in school all day. Fathers were expected to earn money at work in the city, but also to share at least a "hobby" interest in child rearing during their "off" hours. Family outings, Little League, and other father-child leisure activities were encouraged.

But in practice the realities of suburban life did not always match the dream. Many fathers took second jobs, worked overtime, or occupied themselves with buddies outside the family. Many mothers described themselves as "trapped." They were either overly isolated from adult companionship, or unhappy with seemingly trivial "kaffeeklatsch" substitutes. Betty Friedan's The Feminine Mystique[5] called attention to the sociology of suburbia for women, and Marilyn French's novel The Women's Room[6] describes this period and its dissatisfactions very well—as well as some of its satisfactions.

Suburbia, by definition, was middle and upper-middle class. In the 1960s, young adults raised in this model began to question certain social inequities. Many of the traditional values of middle class life were seen as hypocritical or obsolete.

Also, as divorce became more common, the model shifted. More mothers began to raise their children alone as fewer women took their children back to their own mothers' homes. Fathers were supposed to visit and provide child support, but many did not. The isolated nuclear family has often broken down into the mother-alone family, usually with a hope that a new nuclear or "blended" family would be reconstituted by remarriage.

5. Community responsibility for children. Social reform movements since the late 1800s have recognized that children are vulnerable in a complex industrial society in which only their parents have legally enforceable responsibility for their care. Thus there have been attempts to augment family responsibility with a commitment of the society as a whole toward its children. Today there is less likely to be personal help from neighbors. Rather, help, if any, is provided by various social and medical agencies, such as protective service teams, departments of child and family services, and foster parents. These agencies are often overworked and underfunded, and of course can only serve families brought to their attention.

There have been some attempts to form clusters of families or communes in which many adults would share at least backup responsibility for all the children. But in contemporary America, at least, such communal arrangements have generally not lasted longer than many marriages do, and the adults have no lasting legal responsibility for each other's children.

POLITICS OF PARENTING: THE FAMILY AND THE STATE

Just as societies differ in family structures for child rearing, so do they differ in views about the ultimate authority for final decisions about children. For example, in many so-called primitive societies, tradition dictates most decisions, severely limiting parents' freedom of choice. In some societies, a child might be killed if it were born to too young a mother, or were one of twins, or born under other circumstances considered to be inauspicious.

Under Roman law, there was a highly developed and codified system of family law on a patriarchal base. The Roman father had the absolute authority to decide whether a child should be reared or exposed to die. He could also order an older child put to death for disobedience. By law, the father could make these decisions regardless of the wishes of the mother or other family members.

As the Catholic tradition developed, authority was vested in religious law, which became increasingly codified, limiting the family's decisions. Infanticide and abortion after "quickening" were considered murder and, after the Middle Ages, abortion was forbidden altogether. For the family to exert any choice about number or spacing of children was suspect at best but, if exerted, could be done only through abstinence. In practice, the abstinence decision was left to the man, since a wife could not refuse her husband. Children's obedience to parents, and wives' to husbands, were absolute religious duties, modeled on everyone's duty to obey God. "Godparenting" was not an empty ceremony, but a solemn vow obligating the godparents to raise the children in a godly manner should the parents become unable to do so. As the Church grew and became more organized, convents came to offer some support to homeless children and sick persons—the origins of institutional orphanages and hospitals.

With contemporary separation of church and state, both policy about children and backup arrangements for their care began to be seen as the responsibility of the community and state. For example, some countries have laws attempting either to favor or inhibit fertility. Such laws are based on the country's perceived over- or underpopulation, and often relate only coincidentally to any perceptions of the individual needs of children or their parents. Underpopulated countries have passed laws allowing extremely liberal maternity benefits to encourage childbirth. Conversely, in India, laws have been passed providing enforced sterilization or jail terms for parents who have more than the legal number of children. The People's Republic of China has developed fairly effective small-group social pressures to ensure compliance with national goals of population control, but has recently added other strong legal and social incentives to favor the one-child family.

In the United States, there is a growing consensus that every child should be a wanted child. To achieve this goal, society promotes use of morally acceptable contraceptive measures by every sexually active person. Given that contraceptives are available, there is concern about the rising numbers of unwanted births to young teenage mothers and considerable controversy over what society should do about this.

There seems to be a consensus that most families can be trusted to decide for themselves when to have children and how many, but there is considerable controversy about whether abortion is an acceptable method to achieve that goal. The Supreme Court has held that a woman cannot be forced to continue a pregnancy against her will. But it has also held that citizens who oppose abortions cannot be forced to use their tax dollars to pay for them. The law has had great difficulty dealing with more complex moral and interpersonal dilemmas of abortion, such as what to do when there is a disagreement about an abortion—between woman and man, or between a young teenager and her parents.

The state has a potential interest in the number of children born and the outcome of their rearing. Vast over- or underpopulation affects everyone, not just parents. The state also has a fiscal responsibility to children whose parents cannot afford their care. Children who are seriously abused or neglected by their parents evoke our sympathies and may become dangerously antisocial. We generally want the state to have the power to prevent or remedy those wrongs. Parents who cannot control their own children may want the help of the courts in doing so. Yet most state systems are expensive, slow, cumbersome, and sometimes of debatable effectiveness or quality.

As a society, we subscribe to the value that our children are, in part, the whole society's responsibility. We also subscribe to the value that all children should be wanted, and that it is desirable to have a smaller number of children, well cared for. But, at present, finding workable means for making these values a reality is still a problem. Thus, in practice, childbearing decisions and child rearing are still largely the responsibility of parents, who may need more help in parenting than is generally available.

Why, despite the avowed concern of our society for children, is it so hard for parents today to get the kinds of help and understanding they need in order to be good and happy parents? In the first place, children are a dangerously low priority in our society. Children are not voters, and many parents in their child-rearing years are too busy to be politically active. There is not always a strong enough political constituency to get the laws and social programs needed to help children and parents. The Disabled American Veterans and the Gray Panthers, for example, lobby for effective political action. There is no effective children's lobby.

Non-parents have their own agendas, political and otherwise. In our society where everyone is heavily invested in "getting ahead," most people are likely to be busy doing just that, or feeling worried if they are not doing so. Not only do non-parents have their own agendas, but they may also feel that non-involvement in the parenting of others is a good idea.

The modern notion holds that parenting is for the parents and that grand-parents, uncles, aunts, and neighbors should "MYOB," as Ann Landers says (it stands for "Mind Your Own Business"). Others may fail to understand or re-spect the real demands of parenting. A new parent may have many friends who are not parents. Any worker may have a boss who is not a parent, or one who has left parenting to his or her spouse. Families are smaller now, and many of us have not had to care for younger siblings or cousins. Small children are rarely cared for in the workplace. For these reasons, the minute-by-minute realities of child care may be a vast unknown for many otherwise well-informed adults.

It seems as though many people no longer respect the bearing and rearing of children. There is a new social pressure against children and their parents. Buying new cars is seen as good, because it stimulates the economy and provides jobs (though it also leads to higher taxes for roads, policing, and other services). Having more children is somehow suspect, because it means more schools and medical care, thus raising taxes (although also providing jobs and stimulating the economy). Antichild and antiparenting sentiments are not entirely rational, but they are astonishingly prevalent. For example, some landlords and condominium associations do not allow children—sometimes not even for a visit to Grandma and Grandpa.

People are often afraid of children and the feelings that children can evoke in them. Whether they recognize it or not, the dependency and demands of children pose special emotional problems for almost all adults—sometimes more strongly so for non-parents, who do not have the daily opportunities we parents do to come to terms with these feelings. For example, hearing children's cries touches off strong emotions in almost all adults—including those who are not their parents. Non-parents may respond to a crying child with pain, anger, a wish to shut the cry off or escape from it, or to escape from the memories of their own helplessness as children.

Some adults handle these feelings by staying away from children, or at least young children. This not only isolates children from the mainstream of community life, but also isolates their parents or other caretakers from other adults.

People are often destructively critical of parents. As parents we may get criticism about when or how we have our children, and how we rear them. We can be criticized for having too many children, too few, or an only child; for having them too close together, or too far apart; for bearing them too young, or too old, or while not married, or in an unstable marriage. We can be criticized for having them while too poor, so that they may become a public expense, or when too rich, so they may become spoiled. We can be criticized for being too strict, too lenient, too little involved, or too overinvolved. Virtually whatever we do as parents will be seen as wrong in somebody's eyes!

Until quite recently, our society and its institutions have assumed that the "normal" parenting constellation consisted of a housewife, an employed husband, and their children residing in a single household. Yet the typical "Dick and Jane" family represents fewer than 10 percent today. However, schools in some communities still send children home for lunch to the "housewife mother," who may not be there because she works full-time. Conferences with teachers are often scheduled during the day so that a working mother either loses a day's pay or is criticized for disinterest in her child. Even pediatricians may not have office hours which working parents can make without missing work—although this situation is improving.[7]

Expertise and experts are revered too uncritically. Child-rearing advice is available from an immense number of highly vocal sources, ranging from family and friends to religious, psychological, and medical "authorities." The problem is that these authorities often disagree. Yet all strongly present the case that their advice is correct, and that dire consequences will follow from neglecting it. This is especially dangerous today. In traditional societies, not only was advice consistent but it changed very slowly when at all. Whatever "mistakes" were embedded in the advice were at least predictable, and often remedial measures were built into the traditions. Societies or religions which induced excessive guilt, for example, usually developed means of expiating it. Currently, the advice changes so frequently that there is insufficient time to develop remedial measures.

A particularly troublesome problem with experts in the recent past has been the tendency to attribute all problems in children to faulty parental child-rearing practices. While it is true that parents can be given knowledge which will prevent *some* problems that once were unavoidable, it is also true that some problems are neither attributable to faulty parenting nor amenable to a change in parenting. "Experts" have caused a great increase in parental anxiety, guilt, and fear. Some parents have even been made to feel that good parenting would prevent all daily conflicts and all mental illnesses. Thus, parents of children with problems have often received blame instead of sympathy and help.

Furthermore, parents, especially women, are often isolated. If women are not lucky, or careful, or both, child rearing can be a lonely business that separates them from the mainstream of adult life.

Society places enormous responsibility on parents, but doesn't always give them confirming confidence in their ability to carry out their responsibilities. Nor does society usually give parents ready access to the kinds of real support that would help them.

VIEWS OF PARENTING

There are many views of parenting but we found five persistent themes.

The Instinctive View

Some writers imply that parents naturally and spontaneously know how to parent. Such writers suggest that parents will automatically know what to do with their children if they only relax and overcome their hang-ups and anxieties, and perhaps learn to ignore the intrusive advice of well-meaning experts.

Parental instincts are supposed to be foolproof and provide us naturally with both parenting skills and parenting satisfactions.

Joann Grohman[8] and Alice Bricklin[9] have written beautiful books in this vein, and much of what they say about a simpler and more natural approach to child care is compelling and valuable. Jane Goodall said she learned much about how to parent from observing chimpanzee mothering, which was predictable enough to be called instinctive in chimpanzees, and felt comfortably natural to her.

These writers imply that much of the problem posed by "civilization and its discontents" can be solved by being less civilized and thus less discontented in at least our early nurturing. There is a strong counterculture attitude in this view of parenting, often combined with a spiritual or religious tradition, particularly around birth. Instinctive mothering is valued, and fathering is viewed as something to be achieved by weaning men away from the competitive values of a materialistic society.

The Nostalgic View

Many people feel that things are terribly distorted nowadays, with regard to most aspects of childbearing and child rearing, and that they were far more ideal in some distant, natural past. Parenting would be no problem if only people could get back to the good old days, which are seen by its adherents as either more indulgent or more authoritarian or both. Unlike the instinctive view, the nostalgic one holds that we have lost parental instincts and must return to the "old" ways. This view includes the belief that children were more obedient and well behaved in the past, although writers as far back as the ancient Greeks expressed the same nostalgia about *their* past.

The Romantic "Traditional" View

Many people view parenting as an ideal time, full of love and happiness for the parents as well as the child, at least if all goes well. Many words have been written about how women are supposed to find their deepest fulfillment in the gentle guiding of little feet and (a little less often) about how men discover the satisfactions of true manliness in "husbandry."

When *McCall's* magazine, in the 1950s, referred to itself as "The Magazine of Togetherness," it was celebrating a romantic view of family life. Men could be participants in the business world, but women were responsible for making the hearth and home an erotically romantic setting for couple relationships as well as parenting. The magazine published advice from various professionals about new ways to achieve these old ideals. Expert advice was offered on home decorating, patios, fashion, beauty, and cooking as well as child rearing. Books like *The Total Woman* advised women how to be childlike partners to men while being solo daytime parents to children.[10]

The Pessimistic View

Betty Friedan noted the many illusions in the romantic view of family life in *The Feminine Mystique.* Other writers, many of them mothers, have called our attention to the "trapped young mother syndrome" *(Redbook* magazine had a whole series on that syndrome in the late 1950s). Feminist sociologists like Jessie Bernard[11] pointed out how marriages are advantageous to men—perhaps to the detriment of children as well as women. Men's-movement sociologists like Joseph Pleck[12] taught us that men were emotionally limited by "traditional" families—made into "work objects" and cut off from tenderness with their children. Some observers point to the rising incidence of child abuse and juvenile misbehavior as evidence that something is going terribly wrong in the relationships between parents and children today.

Other social scientists have shown that the presence of children is *not* correlated with life satisfaction. Also parents of preschool children, especially mothers, are less likely to describe themselves as happy than are non-parents.[13,14] By contrast, Marilyn, in a study of women physicians, found that those who had children rated themselves as high in quality of life as those who did not.[15]

The Realistic-Eclectic View

Our own view of parenting falls into what we call the realistic-eclectic view. Most parents have children both because of biological pressures and specific expectations. Parents expect their children to bring them immortality and more immediate special joys, hard to find in any other way. Parents also know that children bring special problems which aren't found in most other relationships.

Because of the great imbalance in power, responsibility, and maturity between parents and children, parents expect to feel some "instinctive" responses to children's needs and behavior. But parents need knowledge also. As parents ourselves we know that the parts of parenting we haven't observed, experienced, or anticipated can be overwhelming. Being realistically aware of what to expect from parenting helps us to notice, experience, and cherish the joys of parenting as well as to anticipate the problems, roll with the punches, and know when to get help.

THE CONTEXTS OF PARENTING

How well we can manage the frustrations and experience the joys of parenting depends a good deal on the context of parenting, which has three main dimensions:

1. The individual context. The context of me, myself, as a parent and person. How satisfied am I with myself and my life? How much awareness do I have of my own needs and when they are being met? How well can I tell when my frustration is building up, and my ability to parent effectively is correspondingly going down? How well have I learned to cope with frustrations when they aren't avoidable, and to problem-solve when possible? How well have I learned to assert my own needs and empathically respond to the needs of others? How well do I fit my parenting and the rest of my life together?

2. The family context. How involved are my spouse and my family/social network in parenting our child? How helpful are they, how sensitive are they to their own needs, to my needs, and our child's needs? How capable are they in problem-solving, in handling frustrations, in sharing joys?

3. The environmental and social context. What is the environment in which I am trying to do my parenting? Do I have the resources I need— economic, social, and intellectual? Certainly isolation, overcrowding, too much work, or too much poverty can all affect my ability to parent, often in ways beyond my control.

PARENTING IN A CHANGING SOCIETY

Today's world is a different and changing place. Children have always
needed to be fed, clothed, sheltered, and loved. But some parenting issues are
very different in today's world and, of course, today's world isn't the same world
for every member of it.

Marked changes in the way people live have had a tremendous impact on
families. In just a few generations we have moved from a subsistence agricultural
economy to an expanding industrial one and now, for many of us, to a contracting, stagnating, or restabilizing industrial economy. Some of us have become richer in these processes; some poorer. Many of us have moved far from
our old roots, and most of us have found our families becoming smaller than
families used to be. In one generation there has been a doubling of the divorce
rate, just when extended families became less dependable. The chances are great
that our futures and our children's futures will differ from what we grew up
expecting. Our children's friends will also come from a wide variety of family
structures and parenting situations.

The geography of parenting—where parenting takes place—has been
changing rapidly over the last few generations as most people now live in towns
or cities, many of which have become seriously overcrowded, with impaired
essential protective services. Suburbia may provide better schools and safety, but
it also changes family life by making children dependent on the automobile for
normal social activities.

Family structure has changed, very much, very recently. Just a few years
ago, a child-rearing book would assume that you, the reader, must surely be a
young, married housewife, and that your children's friends would come almost
entirely from similar families. Today you, the parent reader, might be a mother
or a father, in your teens or your forties, married or single. The children you
parent may be stepchildren or grandchildren. Your own biological children may
be in your custody or someone else's.

Things changed before you picked up this book, and are likely to change
much more before your parenting experiences are over. Parenting used to be
regarded as one of the great stabilizing forces in society. But today, parenting is
changing at least as much as the rest of society, if not more so. The expectation
of change is more of a reality than most traditions today.

REALITIES OF CHILDREN'S NEEDS

Children have always had the same material needs as adults for food, clothing, and shelter. But for a prolonged period they are totally dependent on
parents to provide these things. Parents are responsible for filling their material

needs. Parents may or may not have help in providing these needs but the needs remain and cannot be wished away. Parents are on call twenty-four hours a day, for twenty years, often without vacation.

Children have the same basic emotional needs we do, for love, belonging, attention, understanding, approval, and feeling "special" to someone. But their total dependency, in combination with their very limited autonomy, results in a greater emotional demand on parents. There is a greater need for parents to recognize and meet their emotional needs. Children depend on us to fill their physical and emotional needs in the face of their initially limited capacity to express their own needs, understand our feelings, or control their emotional expression and behavior. This can be emotionally exhausting for parents.

Children's needs and capacities, of course, change dramatically with their age and development. (See Chapter 7, Children's Growth and Development, p. 221.) It can be challenging, to say the least, to keep up with this—not to expect too much of them when they are little, or to expect too little of them when they are older.

Children become socialized and civilized, only slowly over time, and to varying degrees. Infants, from birth, loudly and immediately demand that their needs be satisfied now. They can't see very far into the future, and can't always understand that help is on the way if it hasn't arrived yet. It was thought for a while that such immediate satisfaction could "spoil" young children, but the evidence is just the opposite. Immediate comfort and help are good for them, though perhaps draining on us. Slowly they learn to wait, compromise, and negotiate.

At different ages and times, and to different degrees, children become sensitive to the needs and priorities of others. It takes a long time to learn how to fill their needs. And children certainly aren't born with the knowledge that they can often get better parenting when they learn to understand their parents' needs and feelings too—though even small children often make touching attempts to comfort a distraught parent.

Children need protection. They can be actively and dangerously destructive to themselves and others, and to possessions. They run in front of cars, break their favorite toys, or our favorite things, and make messes. Sometimes children need protection from their parents, because this whole process of waiting for and encouraging them to become civilized can take so long that parents can become frustrated and enraged.

Besides the needs that all children share, children have special individual needs of their own. A second child, for example, may have different needs from the first—either because of being second, or because of inborn differences in temperament. What you learned about how to meet the needs of the first child may not be enough to help you meet the needs of the next.

REALITIES OF PARENTS' NEEDS

Parents are people, like anybody else. We have our own needs in addition to, and independent of, our children's needs from us. We too need material things. We have bodily and social needs for peaceful meals, enough sleep, exercise, and recreation. We have relationship needs for friends, family, lovers, co-workers, neighbors, and a sense of community. We need respect and self-esteem. We need a sense of relative success and meaningfulness in life as well as a sense of personal growth which validates that we are "getting somewhere" in life's journey. Today's American culture emphasizes the need for a personal identity, separate from family roles. We want to be identified as ourselves, not as Kim's child or Terry's spouse or Joni's parent.

Our needs for self-development and personal growth cannot, for most of us, be met solely through raising children. This is true for both housewives and house husbands, as well as for employed parents.

Parenting occurs at a definite time in the life cycle, the very time there may be other special needs. Some of us are just getting jobs or careers started, or we may be in the midst of the crucial years of career development or job advancement. We may have just moved, which breaks old relationships and creates special time demands to make new ones. Our parents may be retiring or aging, or advancing and moving. Our brothers and sisters may be leaving our parents and may be struggling with their own growth and/or their own children. And, in the middle of all this, we continue to have normal social needs for friendships.

All in all, the parenting years are likely to be the same years that are full of many other demands—having nothing to do with parenting, but competing for our investment of time and energy.

As parents, we need specific things from our children:

1. Love. Parents almost always have children hoping to have someone to love, and to love them. But the kind of love children can give may be very different from the kind of love we want, or need, or imagine. Even tiny infants can love strongly in the sense of being warmly attached to us. But it takes a long time for children to develop reliable empathy or caring about our needs or about us as separate persons.

2. Ties to others. It is unusual to think of having a child without imagining how the child will affect ties to others. We often hope that having a child will bring joy to our parents, or make them see us as grown-ups. We may hope that a child will strengthen our marriages or give added depth to our relationships with our partners. Others do indeed share an interest in our children. But it's rare that having a child solves problems that stem from other causes. And the new child can bring conflict with other relationships instead of enhancing them.

3. Pride. All of us hope to be able to be proud of our children. But the kinds of things that make us, as parents, proud may be very different from the

natural capacities of a particular child. And many of these hopes, even when fully achievable, lie far in the future and are uncertain rewards during early childhood.

4. Self-esteem. All of us want to be able to feel proud of ourselves as parents, even in the face of the inevitable challenges and frustrations of parenting. We *want* to be good parents, we want our children to consider us good parents, and we want the world to acknowledge that we are good parents.

5. Appreciation. Parents, whether we admit it or not, generally feel we do a lot for our children and, naturally, want gratitude and appreciation in return. We may get a "thank you" for a cookie, but it takes *years* before our children can appreciate all that we did for them or express this appreciation.

As parents, we also have needs because of our children. During pregnancy, birth, and the breast-feeding period, women need health care and extra support from others. Throughout the parenting years, we may need the help of others as people and as parents. Sometimes we need to learn how to ask for help and support.

Men often need extra support for the new emotions and responsibilities that occur with parenting, but may find it hard to ask for this. Some men today are taking on new roles and responsibilities in child care and may feel deep needs for thanks and appreciation. They may need help in recognizing and filling these emotional needs, which weren't formerly recognized as masculine.

During the early child-rearing years, parents often have special needs for the companionship of other parents who are facing similar situations. Our usual friends, if not engaged in child rearing, may not fill these needs and may not even understand them. Parents need people who understand both that there are times when we need to get away from our children, and also that there are times when we need to bring them along while doing other things like working, shopping, and socializing.

Parents need understanding and sharing of our parental emotions. When the little daily joys of parenting occur—the cute things the child said, the first step, the first smile—we need to share our feelings about these moments with other adults who don't think our feelings are silly or trivial. When our children have problems, or create problems for us, we have strong feelings—anger, fear, hurt—and have great needs for sharing those feelings with others who understand that what we feel is both legitimate and powerful.

RECIPROCAL NEEDS

Our needs as parents and our children's needs from us may be in conflict. For example, you may need peace and quiet just when your child needs rambunctious horseplay. Or your child may need to play with friends when it's hard for you to find time to provide transportation. Or you might need things your child can't supply, like adult companionship or a change of scenery, when your child wants you home. Some mutual accommodations always have to be made. It's healthy for children to learn to accommodate to our needs, just as it's healthy for us to accommodate to theirs. Striking a good balance of reciprocal needs is the main goal.

As parents we need to have the feeling we are in charge of our own households. Reciprocally, children need to have a clear feeling that their voice and viewpoints are heard and respected. And we also have to accept the fact that we cannot control, or be totally responsible for, all the behavior of our children. Children's behavior results from their developmental stage, their innate temperaments, the peer groups they enter, and a host of other factors.

Most of us as parents try to find styles of parenting that suit our own personalities, and our religious, ethnic, and family backgrounds. We hope our children's temperaments fit our own personality styles. It's harder to raise a hyperactive child in a compulsively neat or wildly chaotic home, for example, than in a moderately structured one.

It is also true that there is more than one way to be a good parent—in fact, there are lots of ways to be a good parent, and no way is the perfect one. What works in your family may not work in your neighbor's, and vice versa. Our children need our help, not only in learning our values, but in learning how to negotiate in a world in which values differ.

Can people do anything to make parenting better? Vance Packard ends his alarming account of our "anti-child society" with an optimistic chapter of possibilities. In doing so, he moves back and forth between the needs of children, parents, and society, because indeed all are interrelated.

"The authentic human community," he says, "is one in which the social groupings are small so that a sense of belonging is almost automatic."[16] Children can walk or bike to see their friends; parents develop a sense of community; knowing the parents of your children's friends does not require special effort. He talks of inspired architects and city planners—and of young couples in shirt-sleeves who rehabilitated inner-city neighborhoods. He talks of flex-time employment for adults, of rethinking compulsory education for adolescents—or offering work-study programs for them. He recommends assistance to parents who are starting families, and using the elderly with parenting experience as "emergency grannies."

He offers an interesting summary of "nine adult skills that help children thrive," which can be paraphrased:

1. Make it clear that you are crazy about your child. He quotes the social psychologist Bronfenbrenner: "The child needs at least one person who has an irrational involvement with him, someone who thinks this kid is more important than other people's kids."

2. Do a lot of interacting with the child, especially verbal interacting—laughing and talking, rocking and smiling with infants, and lots of conversation with older children every day.

3. Work to help the youngster develop high self-esteem. Be a good listener and always treat the child with respect.

4. Condition children to do well: get them started in habits like persistence, planning, and achievement. Don't let them feel oppressed: make a challenge out of any oppression that may exist.

5. Encourage children to be explorers and encourage curiosity as a lifetime adventure.

6. Give children a strong sense of family solidarity, including aunts, uncles, cousins, as well as the nuclear family (whether there is one parent, two, or stepparents in the family).

7. Become adept at moving children from parent discipline to self-discipline, so that self-discipline becomes part of the child's developing sense of competence and self-esteem—rather than the kind of discipline based on fear, which the healthy child mobilizes to resist.

8. Guide children toward a clear system of values. Make values a solid source of pride for the child.

9. Help children experience plenty of responsibility. Provide challenges which children can master, adding to their self-esteem and sense of self-worth and accomplishment. Give them pride in growing up and in giving to others with skill and compassion.

These suggestions are an interesting mix. There is room in them for all the expertise our highly developed society can provide—in architecture and city planning, public health and individual health care, business management and fiscal policy—and lots of room for every individual parent to take action. Parents don't *need* to be alone in the terrors that parenting can bring, and parents don't *want* to be alone in the adventures of parenting. When people don't separate parenting from the rest of their lives—and don't separate ideas of public policy from the needs of families—they have the groundwork for lifetime nurturance of everybody from infants to the elderly.

BOTTOM-LINE REALITIES OF PARENTING

1. *Knowledge.* We may like to think that parenting is instinctive, but it isn't purely instinctive for humans, nor even for our nearest animal relatives. Harlow showed that monkeys tend not to parent well if they haven't learned social interaction from normal parenting and peer play in infancy and early childhood.[17] Human parents have even more things to learn in order to care for their children's needs—from how to feed and bathe a baby to automobile safety and how to negotiate with a teacher about school goals for older children.

2. *There are many teachers.* Obviously, if we don't instinctively know how to parent, we have to learn. We learn from recalling our own memories of childhood, from observing our children, or from watching other adults raise children (though chances to observe that intimately are rarer today). We can read books, or go to classes, or call the university extension service. Today there are parenting newsletters, parenting workshops, and programs for working par-

ents—all providing advice. Whatever we do, we can expect to be presented with many points of view. Assimilating the advice of all the "parenting teachers" is a creative and formidable challenge for parents today.

3. *Who is an "expert"?* Today, many professionals, including physicians, social workers, psychologists, teachers, and researchers in child development and anthropology, have definite ideas about child rearing. But it is obvious that the experts disagree among themselves quite often and, indeed, change their collective minds every few years. When Anne was growing up, her mother prided herself on being "modern" in her child rearing. Today it wouldn't even be clear what "modern" is, if indeed one should try to do it! It's hard for parents to find a clear path among all this advice. It's hard to know how to sort out what advice is useful from that which only provokes useless anxiety.

And it's easy to feel "put down" or intimidated by it all. When the elders were the main parenting teachers, people could at least look forward to becoming respected elders themselves. Today we get much of our advice from people who may outrank us for a lifetime.

4. *Outside control of parenting.* Parents never have had full control over the destiny of their children. In times past, one's own parents, extended family, or the elders in the community had much influence, and could bring much pressure to bear on parents. It may not have been welcome pressure, but at least it came from people who shared basically similar values. Today, anonymous and powerful strangers from social agencies can make major decisions for us—such as whether we are fit parents.

5. *Realities for women have changed.* Women usually have enduring ties to their children, and these ties can be exploited by employers, fathers, and by society in general. Today if there is a divorce, it may be assumed that women can earn as much as men (which usually isn't true) and therefore shouldn't expect alimony, which used to compensate for their lesser earning ability. Women may be awarded child support payments, but the majority of such payments are not actually made. Yet, at the same time, women can be made to feel guilty for working to support their children!

6. *There are also changing parenting realities for men.* The workplace doesn't fully recognize that many men now take active roles in parenting. Single fathers, especially, may or may not find any available or reliable parenting support network. (See chapters on Different Kinds of Parents, p. 769, and Parenting Non-biological Children, p. 786.)

Besides all of the normal and predictable kinds of difficulties described above, things can go seriously and unpredictably wrong. A child can have a serious accident or illness and require a lifetime of care; or a child can be physically or emotionally handicapped or otherwise unable to fulfill our parental hopes and ambitions; or unexpected problems and even catastrophes can occur to parents: illness, accident, financial or marital stress, wars, depressions, unemployment, deaths.

In sum, the decision to have a child is like signing a blank check against the future. We sign up for twenty-four-hour-a-day responsibility, seven days a week, for at least twenty years. The extent of the demands our children will make on us (or we will make on them) cannot possibly be predicted. The amount of help we need can be planned for but cannot be ensured. Children come with no guarantees and, if not satisfactory, cannot be returned for a refund. For some, this uncertainty is a challenge and an adventure; for others it is terrifying. For most people, it is some combination of adventure and terror.

OUR PHILOSOPHY OF PARENTING

It goes without saying that we would not have undertaken this book (or our own medical specialties) unless we loved children. It is a continual source of wonderment to us both that every baby who is born is totally unique—there has never been another exactly like that baby and never will be. Every one of those unique human beings needs the loving care of parents.

This is a parenting book called *Child Care/Parent Care*, because parenting is a mutual process. Our advice to parents is analogous to the advice given on airplanes to parents traveling with small children. Flight attendants will tell you to put the oxygen mask on *yourself first* if there is a sudden drop in cabin pressure. There is a very important reason for this advice. If you have oxygen you can stay conscious and give it to your baby, but the baby cannot give oxygen to you. To parent successfully, you must be in good enough shape to take care of your child.

Most child-rearing books talk about "child-proofing" your home to make it safe for your child. This means locking up medicines and toxic household products, removing sharp antique letter openers from the coffee table, and placing your crystal somewhere above the child's reach. The purpose of child-proofing is to make an environment suitable for a child so that the child may thrive and grow in an atmosphere uncluttered by objects that may be dangerous to the child, distressing to the parents if damaged, or both.

Our philosophy of parenting dictates that the home of every parent should be *"parent-proofed."* Actually, not so much your home, but your *life.* Prior to having your first baby, you should think very carefully about how you are going to parent-proof your life so that even after your child comes, your home (or a corner of it) remains an environment where *you* can thrive.

We both urge you to do this for your children: It's hard for a child to thrive if the parent is not thriving. We don't mean that you are supposed to be happy all the time—no one is. But we hope you *can* feel reasonably happy and secure in your role as a parent. You and your child are both cheated if you just grit your teeth and bear it for twenty years, although many parents have done just that.

What suggestions do we have for parent-proofing your life?

1. First of all, create an *environment for you,* apart from the baby. You should have a place where you can get away, where you can have a beloved

object or two and be able to enjoy a few moments of peace and quiet and be yourself.

Be sure you know what you want to do in that environment. Don't get so involved with the baby that there is no "you" left. It doesn't matter what things you choose, but they should be for *you*. Even if you are a working parent and have a private office downtown, you still need, in your home, a place that is yours where you can be defined as You, not Parent.

2. Create an *environment for your relationship*, a place where you and your spouse can be lovers and friends, not just parents. You need a place where you two can argue, hold hands, or make love. Such a place should be truly yours, where you can be together without fear of intrusion. There is nothing wrong with locking your bedroom door for a while. (We are not terribly concerned about the adverse effects on the child who may find you in the act of lovemaking. We *are* concerned that you and your spouse have a place to enjoy lovemaking without interruption.)

3. Your life must have *time for you*. We know, because we have both been there, that there are some days when you have a sick or cranky child or lots of problems at work when you may be on your feet (and on your toes emotionally) for twenty-four hours. But whenever possible each day, set aside some time for yourself. Once again, as a person—not just as a parent.

4. Parent-proofing also means finding *time for friends*. Everybody needs time for friends and other relatives. The most successful families we both have seen have always had room for friendships—both as couples and individuals.

5. In your parent-proofed life, there should be *no* room for martyrdom. We all make sacrifices for our children from trivial (we take them for a walk when our feet hurt) to thundering (we do not take a fantastic job in a distant city because our children do not want to move). But continued martyrdom is not healthy for children *or* us.

6. Pay attention to *your own health*—not just the health of your children. This includes your mental health.

7. Most important of all keep your *own* future in mind. Although you will be a parent all your life, for most of us the tasks of parenting will end roughly two decades after the birth of the last baby. Whether employed now or not, don't ignore your own future. Even if full-time parenting thrills you every moment, all babies will grow up, move out of the house, and most will have babies of their own. Then you will be "unemployed" as a parent. Think about your future as a person after your parenting tasks are done.

8. Finally, parenting works best for your children when you *pay attention to yourself*. Parents sometimes fall into the trap of thinking only about their children and putting the children first in all considerations. The best parent has a *clear sense of self*. Good parents give good "I" messages because they are in touch with internal feelings. When a parent knows how to use "I," some of the other "I's" fall into place: *I*ntelligent thinking about parenting: *I*nsight into their children's "I," *I*ngenuity, *I*nventiveness, and *I*nstincts, which you can trust.

Many years ago, in her humorous book *Please Don't Eat the Daisies,*[18] Jean Kerr told parents having trouble disciplining their kids to remember two things: You're bigger than they are, and it's your house! She was on the right track, but we think that being bigger has nothing to do with it. We rephrase this to: You're in touch with *yourself,* you value yourself, your opinions, and your thoughts. And somebody has to be in charge.

Remember that only by being in touch with and valuing yourself are you a good role model for your children.

We think that parents who feel good about themselves are usually good parents, while parents who are worried and guilty all of the time may not be. How do you learn to feel good about yourself? Try a *KISS.* "K" for knowledge, which we hope this book imparts; "I" for insight into your own behavior and what you can do about it; "S" for self-confidence, and "S" for support, which means you are able to ask for help and seek support systems.

One woman told Marilyn that when she looks back she realizes she hated parenting: "I was smiling but hating every minute of it." She went on to say she did her job, her children became responsible adults, and mother and children are good friends now. But the tasks and responsibilities of parenting made those years of her life very difficult for her. We suggest that you try to enjoy parenting. But don't expect to enjoy every minute of parenting any more than you enjoy every minute of anything else. And please remember, there's nothing wrong with you if you're *not* enjoying every moment.

9. We also suggest that you *accept some guilt.* We know about parenting guilt ourselves. When we look back, sometimes we were stupid, sometimes society gave us wrong information, sometimes we did things we regret but we couldn't help ourselves because of where we were at the time. There are no perfect parents. Part of parent-proofing includes *accepting yourself and your imperfections.*

During the entire twentieth century our society has piled guilt on parents. The two models of parental influence delineated so clearly by Skolnick *both* foster guilt.[19] The Freudian theory presupposes the *vulnerable child* who is easily damaged during the early years when parents have the most influence. The behaviorists tell us the child is *malleable* so that parents totally shape the child. Both models imply that parents—and parents alone, forgetting about the genetic endowment of the child—determine all outcomes.

Nonsense! Parents *are* important. We all do the best we can. Excessive guilt about how you parent is destructive to you—and your child. Minimize guilt by recognizing parenting in its true context, by accepting yourself and your child for what you are as individuals, and by seeking help if your guilt is excessive. Expect to feel some guilt, as society will imply that whatever goes wrong is your fault. Use healthy guilt to motivate changes you *can* and *need* to make, and shake off such undeserved guilt the way a dog shakes off water!

SUGGESTED READINGS AND RESOURCES

Ariès, Philippe. *Centuries of Childhood: A Social History of Family Life* (Robert Baldick, tr.). New York: Knopf, 1965.

Interesting reading.

Boston Women's Health Book Collective. *Ourselves and Our Children: A Book by and for Parents.* New York: Random House, 1978.

A series of warm, personal, useful essays on parenting from considering parenthood to being parents of grownups. Realistic and thoughtful.

Caine, Lynn. *What Did I Do Wrong?* New York: Arbor House, 1985.

One thoughtful woman's story about her own parenting experience and the role guilt played. She has an upbeat message we share: stop blaming yourself.

Cosby, Bill. *Fatherhood.* Garden City, N.Y.: Doubleday, 1986.

A humorous look at parenting by a famous father.

Degler, Carl N. *At Odds: Women and the Family in America from the Revolution to the Present.* New York: Oxford, 1981.

A historical look at women and families in America.

Erikson, Erik H. *Childhood and Society,* 2nd ed. New York: Norton, 1963.

A classic. Trained as a psychoanalyst, Erikson is also an expert in child development.

Greenberg, Martin. *The Birth of a Father.* New York: Continuum, 1985.

A personal account of fatherhood written by a psychiatrist. Some useful suggestions for new and about-to-be fathers.

Hardyment, Christina. *Dream Babies: Three Centuries of Good Advice on Child Care.* New York: Harper, 1983.

A fascinating history of advice on child care from 1750 to 1981.

Keeton, Kathy, with Baskin, Yvonne. *Woman of Tomorrow.* New York: St. Martin's, 1985.

A glimpse at the future of women at home and at work.

LeMasters, E. E., and DeFrain, John. *Parents in Contemporary America: A Sympathetic View,* 4th ed. Homewood, Ill.: Dorsey Press, 1983.

This book has both good information and a sympathetic voice.

Margolis, Maxine L. *Mothers and Such: Views of American Women and Why They Changed.* Berkeley: University of California Press, 1984.

How views of American women have changed over the years. The author points out how the basic society we live in shapes our roles.

Pizzo, Peggy. *Parent to Parent: Working Together for Ourselves and Our Children.* Boston: Beacon Press, 1983.

An important book that points out the "power" of parents who join together in parent groups. There is a history of parent activism, an analysis of the resourceful parent, and an outline of what parent groups provide and can accomplish. There are excellent chapters on how parents can change institutions and laws.

Stinnett, Nick, and DeFrain, John. *Secrets of Strong Families.* Boston: Little, Brown, 1985.

A slim book with lots of good ideas about making *your* family strong.

NEWSLETTERS

Practical Parenting. 18326 Minnetonka Blvd., Deephaven, Minn. 55391. (Yearly subscription, $6.50.)

Sesame Street's Parents Newsletter. P.O. Box 2889, Boulder, Colo. 80322. (Monthly Newsletter, $15.00.)

Growing Child. 22 N. Second St., P.O. Box 620, LaFayette, Ind. 47902. (For twelve issues send child's birthday or expected birth date and $11.95.)

Part Two

ONGOING
ISSUES
IN PARENTING

Introduction

Some of the basic issues in parenting are pertinent all or most of the time, regardless of how old the child is. These chapters are about the basics of parenting and offer advice you may be able to use at any or all of the ages and stages of parenting.

The first chapter, *Biosocial Rhythms,* deals with the fact that our children's biological clocks and our own may be in different time zones. The next chapter is called *Socialization—More Than Discipline.* This chapter looks at social aspects of parenting—and culture—which transform a newborn into an adult. A chapter on the special events and stresses of family life follows. Next is a chapter which covers the vital issues of child safety. The last chapter in this section, called *Helpers in Child Care,* helps parents find good helpers when they are needed.

Ideally, you will read through these chapters before you start the individual age chapters. These chapters set the stage for parenting and impart the information and the philosophies we both have found useful in parenting.

2

BIOSOCIAL RHYTHMS:
INTEGRATING CHILDREN'S
BIOLOGICAL CLOCKS AND YOURS

Scope of Chapter

This chapter will deal with biological activities that occur daily and regularly on a rhythmic basis: eating, sleeping, and elimination. The child's very life depends on fulfilling these biological needs in the right amounts and at the right time. The family's physical, emotional, and social comfort, in turn, depend on reconciling the child's needs with the needs of the rest of the family.

We describe the intricate dance between parent and child that adjusts the biological rhythms of the one to the other. The chapter won't deal with such matters as specific nutritional needs at different ages, or specific diseases that could interfere with these rhythms. Rather this chapter covers what is currently known about the biology of these rhythmic needs, and the philosophical and practical issues for parents in addressing them.

Introduction

These seemingly different biological rhythms—the basic cycles of our lives —have a number of things in common. They are compellingly important for health and survival. These are not optional parts of parenting! You can't decide to feed or not feed your child on the basis of whether you feel like it, for example. However, with most babies and children you have some latitude in how you fill these needs. The very contrast between the obvious importance of the needs, and the wide choices about how parents fill them, has led to reams of advice for parents in both folklore and books.

There is a potential for conflict between parents and babies in these areas. The baby is born requiring a frequency of feeding and diapering and sleeping that is *very* different from usual adult schedules. Parents obviously wish to help the child fit into the parents' rhythms as smoothly and quickly as possible. If the baby resists, there can be conflict. There are rich opportunities for parental rage or guilt over these conflicts. In fact, episodes of child abuse are often triggered by "biological" events such as a child spitting up, soiling the pants, or waking at night just one more time than the parent can stand. Also parents can have painful guilt over the natural resentment they feel when the child's perfectly normal need for feeding or comforting at night interferes with the parents' perfectly normal need for sleep.

The same biological rhythm issues can potentially get parents into conflict with other people. If another mother proudly says her three-month-old sleeps peacefully through the night, and yours doesn't, you can easily feel both competitive and unworthy. "Why is my child less mature than hers?" "What is she doing right that I am doing wrong?" If parents settle into a pattern of comfortable indulgence of a baby that seems to work well for them, a mother, sister, neighbor, or even a pediatrician can make the parents feel guilty for "spoiling" the child.

There are strong religious and cultural values around these issues. Sayings like "Cleanliness is next to godliness" can make a parent feel that dry pants at an early age are not just a convenience for parents, but almost a religious duty. The idea that children can be "spoiled rotten"—that is, ruined forever at an early age by too much indulgence of their bodily rhythms—has actually been linked to religious doctrine. Actually, no mainstream religion specifically requires rigorous training of infants, but some parents whose religion emphasizes rigorous self-control for adults may misinterpret these requirements as applying to even tiny infants. A few religious cults have extreme ideas about punishment and discipline even for infants.

Our culture values "independence" very highly and also seems to view achieving "maturity" as though it were a race to be won. Children who reach some landmark later than other children (say, they are slower to stay dry or give up the bottle, or eat with a fork) may be called "immature" in a way that implies they are either defective or morally reprehensible.

All cultures and all parents have to deal with the fact that the infant comes into the world as a little animal, with intense demands for immediate filling of frequently recurring needs. Obviously, adults who acted like infants would be intolerable in society. Parents are expected to socialize the little animal into a grown-up person who has learned to behave responsibly. The question is, how soon, and by what means? Society has an interest in whether the child is being properly socialized, as well as the parents.

Nobody is fully rational in dealing with diapers and spit-up and sleep issues. We have a visceral revulsion toward material that has been spit up from the stomach or expelled from the bowels that is probably not just a product of our own cleanliness training.

Dogs can be housebroken and cats train themselves. However, no amount of training will "housebreak" a horse or a monkey. This seems to be based on the evolutionary history of the animal. You can housebreak a dog because it has an "instinct" not to foul its own den. The training capitalizes on that instinct and directs it. Horses evolved on ranges where their excreta did not spread disease among them; they just moved away from it. Monkeys evolved in trees where their droppings could fall safely to the ground. Humans, like dogs, have always had caves or homes where a buildup of excretions would endanger health.

Revulsion for the products of excretion helps motivate us to keep healthily clean. People use excretory language like "shit" to apply to anything repulsive or to express strong emotions about almost anything, showing how deeply we feel about products of excretion. We could use the word "tears!" as we are more likely to cry than defecate due to strong emotions—but we don't.

After some years of reasonably well-regulated adult existence, it can be a shock for new parents to discover what little animals babies are. But it's not just babies. Most parents expect a baby to have animal needs. The shock for many parents is how long it lasts. At five or six your child could still be wetting the bed, or waking up at night with nightmares that need comforting, or just be unable to "Sit still and be quiet!" when you desperately want some peace and quiet. It doesn't make it any easier when other adults start blaming you, or you start blaming yourself, figuring that something wrong in your child-rearing practices caused one or more of these common developmental delays.

FEEDING

In the newborn period, the rhythms of feeding and eliminating, activity and sleeping are closely linked. The baby wakes most often with hunger, often excretes after eating, and is likely to fall asleep soon after satiation.

Let's look first at breast-feeding new babies the way it is done in non-industrial societies in warm climates. There's good reason to believe that this is closest to the "natural" conditions under which humans evolved, for which bodily rhythms are most attuned. It will sound romantic, and not all of it fits the conditions of a cold climate or an industrial society.

Anthropologists point out that there is no such thing as a "noble savage," and very few cultures that can really be called "primitive." Humans everywhere have language, culture, and very complex customs. Some of the most complex customs surround such inherently problematic issues in human existence as sexuality, childbirth, breast-feeding, and child rearing.

The rituals and customs surrounding basic child care in non-industrial societies may actually be far more complex than ours. Before we had refrigeration, and chemical processes to modify cow's milk for human infants, the very survival of infants depended on breast-feeding. The absence of safe alternatives meant all cultures had to start from the same place. The rituals helped assure that the rhythms of infant and mother came into phase with each other.

Niles Newton defined the "transition period" as "the period between delivery of the infant and the establishment of its total physiological separateness," which corresponds roughly to the duration of breast-feeding.[1] In non-industrial societies, the transition period is long. However, in modern cultures it could be modified or essentially non-existent, as when there is no breast-feeding. There are four main characteristics of the non-modified transition period:

1. Throughout the day, mother and baby remain in close physical contact,

often skin to skin, and they sleep together at night. During the day the infant is held vertically against the mother's body, usually on her hip or back, instead of horizontally in cribs.

2. Mothers are very sensitive to infant crying, immediately putting the baby to the breast, or anticipating hunger and offering the breast before crying begins.

3. Breast-feeding is continuous (many times a day) and prolonged by our standards—two, three, occasionally four or more years.

4. Conscious child-spacing for at least that period of time is attempted, relying on the contraceptive effect of frequent breast-feeding alone or supplementing it with ritual sexual abstinence.

Obviously, such rhythms of feeding and sleeping are very different from what is customary in America today. It is in fact customary to organize the feeding of new babies around another biological rhythm, namely that of parental sleep. For many years the goal was to get the infant onto a "schedule" as quickly as possible, a pattern very different from the one described above. Scheduled feedings were usually given at three- or four-hour intervals, and as soon as infants would tolerate it, they were encouraged to miss one of the nighttime feedings so as to "sleep through the night," which was regarded as a great developmental achievement.

Solid foods were added early, even within the first few weeks of life outside the womb. Quite often the stated rationale was that solid food, being slower to digest, would help the infant sleep through the night. Actually, there is precious little evidence this is true and good evidence that early solids interfere with iron absorption.

Books encourage mothers to remember that not all crying means hunger. If the baby cries within a short interval after a feeding, the mother is often advised to pick up the baby, look for another cause of crying, and distract the baby in the hope that it will go back to sleep without expecting food so soon again. We do not know about the possible effects of such wide-spaced feedings on infant feeding difficulties, milk production or colic. But we do know that successful initiation of nursing can be impaired by such scheduling.

Solid foods were needed as a source of iron for bottle-fed babies before iron was routinely added to infant formulas, because iron from cow's milk is absorbed less readily than from human milk and cow's milk can cause gastrointestinal bleeding. In the period during which bottle-feeding became common in this country, the early introduction of solid foods also became common, and many breast-feeding mothers were also encouraged to introduce solids at an early age. Earlier child-care manuals offer suggestions on organizing the solid food pattern into "meals" resembling the three main meals a day which are customary for adults in this culture.

Later, after the bottle has perhaps been given up, parents are reminded that children need "juice or a snack" between meals. The question then, of which feedings are defined as "snacks" and which as "real meals," is a curious cultural distinction. Parents are admonished to make the snacks nutritious also, a tacit recognition that "meals" are supposed to be serious nutritious food, not necessarily preferred by the eater, and that other foods called "snacks" are permissively exempted from nutritional expectations. Since adults also snack as well as eating "real meals," the pattern of socializing the child into the meals-plus-snack rhythm is clearly one of adjusting the child's feeding rhythms to those characteristic of adults—or tolerating a different pattern in the child.

Parent-child conflicts over eating take many forms. How can parents get children to accept unfamiliar foods? How can parents get children who are perceived as having poor appetites to eat more? How can parents get children who are perceived as too fat to eat less? How can parents get children to eat more of foods which are considered nutritious? How can parents get children to eat less of foods which children like but which are perceived as bad for them, such as candy, pop, and other "junk food"? How can parents prevent children from eating too much between meals and spoiling their appetite for meals? How can parents get children to eat what's on their plate and not waste food? How do parents get children to exhibit proper table manners?

It is obvious that such conflicts are complex mixtures of practical problems (no one wants to pick up food the child has willfully thrown on the floor), medical-nutritional problems (poor nutrition is known, in some cases, and believed in others, to cause disease), and human-relations concerns (anyone who has "slaved over a hot stove" wants admiration and appreciation for his or her cooking).

In addition, people have deep moral feelings about food. All major religions have something to say about food and meals. Gratitude and reverence expressed in grace before meals is a good example. In the Christian religion, the fall of mankind from an original state of grace was attributed to eating a "forbidden" food. The major restitutive ritual, Communion, is a sacred meal. Observant Jews obey dietary laws, and the High Holy Days include fasting and feasting. Most religions have food rituals or prohibitions.

Many adults feel deeply, almost religiously, that wasting food is wrong. When one is conscious that there are millions of starving people in the world, serving lavish enough meals to create waste can seem sinful. The fact that little children may play with food, throw it on the floor, or change their minds about what they want to eat, can be deeply disturbing to adults. Although these behaviors are classified under "table manners," the values involved make the issue feel more important than just manners.

For that matter, manners are *not* trivial for most people. Eating with care and delicacy and restraint is one of the things that makes people human instead of animal. Watching someone eat grossly is repulsive to most people. Parents don't want their children to eat repulsively in front of them and don't want them to grow up eating in a way that would ostracize them socially. Since mealtimes are likely to be the times parents comment on their table manners, family mealtimes can become an ordeal for children in many families.

We both have learned approaches—which are discussed later—to help avoid parent-child-food conflicts. For example, in infancy baby-centered feeding starts you off meeting the baby's needs in ways easiest for parents. You don't need to feed solids until your baby is old enough to reach for what you are eating out of curiosity and imitation. Feed young children separately when they are too young to be mannered eaters. Also don't waste gourmet food on the young when they are delighted with crumbled hamburger every night. Let tasting adult food be a special treat—Mikey may like it! When the children are older and join you at the table, we suggest you start our important parent-centered rule. Simply stated this rule is: Eat what was prepared or, if you don't want it, help yourself to cereal. Both Marilyn and Anne's children thrived on this approach.

SLEEP

The sleep-wakefulness rhythm is the first one you are likely to encounter in a new baby, even before feeding. The very first time you hold your baby, you'll notice at once whether the baby is quietly asleep, "fussy-awake," or in the "quiet-alert" state in which babies can return your gaze with open eyes.

Sleep-wakefulness is a fascinating rhythm in itself, and it's also a pretty good model for the other biological rhythms that are part of life. In recent years a great deal has been learned about sleep which is both interesting and useful to parents.

There are several distinct stages of sleep, ranging from light to deep, and each is manifested by distinct patterns of electrical activity in the brain. The stage in which adults and older children report dreams has an added feature: rapid movements of the eyeball occur behind the closed eyelids. You can see this if you watch a sleeping child or adult during the Rapid Eye Movement, or REM, phase of sleep. Not only do children sleep more than adults, and babies sleep more than children, but the younger the child, the higher the proportion of sleeping time spent in REM sleep. Premature babies sleep more than full-term ones, and spend an even higher proportion of sleep time in REM sleep. It's fascinating to think about what a newborn baby could be dreaming of, or what the "dream pictures" would be like before birth in a fetus whose eyes have never seen the light of day.

In adults, sleep usually occurs in one episode for about eight hours, with five or six episodes of REM sleep concentrated later in the night, and deep sleep concentrated earlier in the night. Newborn infants have many shorter episodes of sleep, and many short episodes of wakefulness. Gradually over the first year of life, both the sleep episodes and the waking ones become longer, with fewer of each, until the early childhood pattern of a night's sleep plus one or two naps is established.

Most adults are pretty well able to make their sleep-wake cycle fit into the twenty-four-hour day, a phenomenon that sleep researchers call "entrainment" of the biological rhythms of sleep-wakefulness to the twenty-four-hour day. Along with this, a number of other biological rhythms are affected. Body temperature drops during the usual sleep hours, and rises during the usual waking ones—so do heart rate and breathing rate. Feeding and elimination in adults usually occurs during waking hours, and even the kidneys' output of urine is less during sleep. These rhythms become so tied into the twenty-four-hour day that even adults who go into a lasting coma continue to vary their body temperature, heart rate, and breathing rate in the same rhythm that suited their previous wakeful hours.

Rhythms that more or less correspond to the twenty-four-hour day are called "circadian rhythms" (from the Latin *circum dies* or "around the day"). People's circadian rhythms don't always precisely correspond to twenty-four hours. Some people have a long circadian rhythm of twenty-five to twenty-six hours, and have particular difficulty entraining their sleep rhythms to the clock. Such people tend to go to bed late and have difficulty getting up in the morning. They don't get fully "warmed up" intellectually or muscularly until late in the day and may work or play far into the night. These nocturnal people are called "owls" by sleep researchers. Other people, called "larks," tend to get up with the sun and have their best hours early in the day.

Interference with the circadian rhythm—by jet lag, changes of shift at work, or being awakened by children—can all make adults irritable, inefficient, and less clear in thinking and performing. When a new parent's circadian rhythms are disrupted by a baby's very different body rhythms, the adult can be fatigued and irritable for a prolonged period of time.

Sleep patterns also tend to vary with age. Many adolescents and young adults have an owl pattern. They can work or party all night, tend to sleep late if they can get away with it, and are very hard to wake up in the morning. Most young children, especially those around one or two, are irrepressible larks, and wake at six o'clock or so regardless of what time they went to bed—and regardless of how badly their parents want to sleep. Some show their adult pattern very early—others are larks when young and become owls later.

At birth, most babies don't show a very pronounced circadian rhythm. This is interesting because before birth they were certainly affected by the mother's circadian rhythm. The composition of the nutrients in the blood reaching the baby through the umbilical cord changed with the mother's rhythms of eating and digestion.

In newborns, the sleep-wakefulness cycle is very closely tied to the feeding cycle. This makes clear biological sense in a breast-fed baby. Initially, the baby's gut is not very well practiced in absorbing fluid and nourishment from food although there was some gut activity during intrauterine life when the fetus swallowed amniotic fluid, absorbed the liquid and some of its contents, and gave the kidneys practice in making urine out of the extra fluid and wastes. Correspondingly, in phase with the baby's unrehearsed gut, initially the mother's breasts put out only colostrum—a watery liquid containing proteins, minerals and immunologic factors, but little fat or carbohydrates. Then small amounts of milk are produced that increase over time with increasing stimulation from sucking. Small and frequent feedings suit the biological needs of both the baby and the nursing mother.

Gradually milk production increases, the baby's capacity to handle a larger feeding increases, and the time between feedings can correspondingly increase. The baby stays alert for a longer period of time, can suck longer, and also begins to take time to look around and absorb more of the visual, auditory, and tactile world. The sedative effect of a full stomach lasts longer when the stomach is filled with more milk, and the baby quite naturally begins moving into longer periods of sleep, and longer periods of wakefulness.

After the first few months, other cues than hunger-satiation begin to determine sleep-wakefulness. As the infant gets attuned to environmental stimulation, the light and activity of the days entrain more wakefulness, and the dark and relative quiet of the nights entrain more sleep. This process occurs naturally but it can be influenced—either enhanced or inhibited—by what the environment provides to the baby.

Hungry babies cry, and crying takes a lot of effort. If feeding doesn't occur, exhaustion does. A hungry, crying baby will eventually fall asleep even if not fed. Parents who are eager to have the baby sleep through the night as soon as possible have been encouraged to ignore a little crying at night. And often enough, the baby does stop crying and fall back asleep without a feeding.

It's interesting and important to think about how the baby would organize that experience. Does light—day—come to be reassuring as a time when hunger will lead to being fed? Does dark—night—come to be frightening, as a time when hunger will not be fed? Could this lead to, or contribute to, fear of the dark in later childhood? We don't really know. In so-called "primitive" cultures the mother is always next to the baby, night and day. In our culture, the tiny baby is likely to be in a crib night and day, picked up when crying signals that the baby is awake and hungry. Does it make a difference whether the mother is a "crying-person" or a "hungry-person" as opposed to a "constant-person"? We don't really know.

One thing we *do* know is that parents are people with their own needs and rhythms. A parent who is already a "lark" is less likely to be bothered by a baby's early morning awakening than one who cherishes late morning sleep. On the other hand, a parent who is an "owl" is less likely to be bothered by a 2 A.M. feeding—that's still part of the "day." However, it seems likely that a baby might have a little trouble with sleepy parents at one or the other end of the day, whatever happens—unless one parent is a lark and one an owl.

Marilyn was an owl who luxuriated in both staying up late and staying in bed in the morning until she had her first baby. For some strange reason, she then became a real lark. Now her eyes droop at 9 P.M. and she wakens in the predawn hours ready to go. One of her children is an owl. He works nights and stays in bed until early afternoon. Her other child, who is a resident at a busy hospital, is currently sleep-deprived and might go either way, to larkhood or owlhood, when her residency is over.

Anne describes herself as an owl, given to working late hours. All her children had periods of night wakefulness quite as regularly as they had daytime naps, on into the preschool and early school years. This was a rather precious time to interact with her children and she probably encouraged night wakefulness in a form of entrainment. After early childhood, one of Anne's children became a lark, and two are clearly owls.

It's interesting how children learn to recognize that they are tired. Almost all children can self-regulate eating within rather broad limits, but not all children know when they are tired. The very disorganization that comes from fatigue may prevent some children from recognizing that fatigue is what the problem is. Larks seem to know when they are tired and larks voluntarily go to bed but owls often don't know when they are tired even though their fatigue and fussiness may be apparent to everyone else.

Why do so many children, who know quite well when they are hungry or thirsty, not know when they are tired? Our simpleminded guess is that for all the millennia of human evolution, children needed to know when they were hungry and express that knowledge or they would have starved in infancy. But for most of the same millennia, children didn't really need to know whether they were tired or not. After the last meal of the day and after dark, most families probably gathered around the fire for a while, with not enough light to do much other than sing songs and tell stories. These activities to this very day are sedative for most children. Without too much to distract them, children probably listened for a while, watching the hypnotic flames, until they fell asleep in their mothers' arms, or lying next to them. Remember, candles and lamps, let alone electricity, are relatively recent in human history. Some of the mindless content of evening TV may attract more viewers because of the hypnotic flickering light—like a campfire substitute—than because of its interest value!

Under those more primitive conditions we just described, there wouldn't be a conflict between parents and children about the children's bedtime as both parents and children relaxed at the same time and fell asleep on their own. Even today, families that have nightly bedtime hassles with their children often have no problem on a camping trip. The children are physically active during the day, physically tired at night, and enjoy the campfire and the talk around it. The children are free to lie quietly watching the fire, and drift off to sleep whenever it overtakes them. If the parents need sleep less soon, they stay awake longer for more talk and stories.

Parenthetically one might ask how is it biologically adaptive for parents and infants to have such different sleep rhythms? How could nature have allowed little babies to need to feed at a frequency that can wreak havoc with their parents' need to have a good night's sleep? One possible answer, of course, is that it wasn't nature that arranged for the infant to sleep in a different room, or be bottle-fed.

When the bottle-fed baby in the next room gets hungry, the baby has to wake up enough to cry loudly enough to wake up mother or father. That person needs to wake up, get out of bed, perhaps find a robe and slippers in the dark, go pick up the baby, carry the now squalling infant to the kitchen, get a bottle from the refrigerator, heat the bottle, test the temperature, perhaps cool it if it over-heated, and, finally, feed the baby and put the baby back to bed. The baby might not even go back to sleep right away, because in the light of the kitchen, the baby may be further aroused and now want to play. This scenario takes considerable time and energy, and can be a serious disruption of sleep because not all parents fall back asleep easily.

By contrast, the nursing baby sleeping next to the mother in the traditional way begins to stir in sleep as hunger begins to be felt. The sleeping mother begins to stir as she feels the baby's stirring and the increasing engorgement of her own breasts. She can roll over and nurse the baby before the baby ever cries, and can do it in a drowsy state without fully waking up. As the baby's hunger is satisfied, so is the mother's breast engorgement relieved. Both can drift back off to sleep with no serious disruption.

Common signs of fatigue in the older child include:

1. *Hyperactivity.* Unlike adults, who tend to slow down when they're tired, children tend to become *more* active in a frantic disorganized way.

2. *Irritability.* The tired child will pick fights, make mountains out of mole-hills, exhibit stubbornness, insist on something that would be more negotiable with a non-fatigued child.

3. *"Bugging you"*—the tired child has no energy to self-entertain. All these signs mean that the higher brain centers are not working well anymore. It's very hard to reason with a tired child. Saying "You're tired" is likely to elicit an angry, "I'm not!" However, sometimes saying, "We're both tired—let's lie down on the floor and take a break together" will work.

Parental exhaustion when the child is still going strong can result in a real conflict of interests. Parental exhaustion when the fatigued child *thinks* he or she is going strong is even worse. The child becomes more obnoxious and the parent more strained by the minute. Placing an overtired toddler forcibly in a crib and closing the door may not be welcomed by the child, but it is certainly preferable to more violent forms of child abuse.

Parents can't safely meet the emotional and physical needs of demanding infants and children without considering their own needs as well. Parents, married or single, need self time and "couple time" together in the evening for talk, sex, or whatever, and parents have a right to time alone. Because children need their parents' relationship to work, it is important to the *children* that you take this couple time.

Fortunately your child will have an average night sleep time of eleven hours or more until age six. This is nearly half of your twenty-four-hour day and is, on the average, three hours more than *you* will sleep. Thus, there *is* some time for you and your spouse or partner.

Most parent-child conflicts about sleep probably stem from the following practices. In infancy, parents encourage their children to sleep through the night without feedings as soon as it can be achieved, which could, in some children, introduce unnecessary tension into the sleep situation. In childhood, parents try to get children to go to bed while there are still many interesting activities going on. Children hate to tear themselves away from adults and their fascinating environment. When parents insist, the children feel deprived at best and, at worst, rejected. The parent knows that fussiness and obnoxious behavior are a sign of fatigue and the need for sleep, but the child interprets being put to bed when fussy as a punishment for being bad. Some parents use the child's room as a place of punishment and "Go to bed" gets mixed up with this. Some children today do not get enough physical exercise to discharge emotional tensions and make them physically tired and emotionally calm by bedtime. Some older children build up a lot of emotional tension in the evening, due to homework, mealtime conflicts about table manners, or other heavy family issues.

Many children, and parents, are really getting too little sleep, or too little margin to cover needs for extra sleep. Perhaps using an alarm clock means that you can't be sure that your body will have had enough sleep to wake naturally at the time you need to meet your commitments.

Most parents cherish the time alone together, which they only get at night after the children are asleep. Some children may actually sense that you want to get them out of the way to be alone with each other—and that can heighten the child's sense that bedtime means competition for attention and love.

At certain ages, children fear sleeping alone. Most children have nightmares or disturbing dreams during some periods of childhood—often when the child is going through an important developmental phase which means there is a lot to process. Dreams do process disturbing daytime events, but they don't always fully succeed in that function. If the clouded, sleepy mind of the child awakened by a dream tries to deal with the hazy residue of disturbing events, the child may be frightened, confused, and lonely. Fear of the dark is usually a fear of the *thoughts* that occur in the dark—it can erupt, recede, and reemerge several times in any one childhood. Some cultures do not expect anyone, of any age or marital status, to sleep alone. We both have always thought it somewhat sad that, at the very age when children have fears and need comforting and closeness at night, they are asked to sleep alone while adults sleep together.

Modern Western society seems almost designed to produce sleep difficulties in children. Sleeplessness in children, as well as crying at night, may actually be a learned behavior which parents unwittingly reinforce.[2] Certainly these behaviors are seen in many children and are often carried over into adult life. Sleeping pills were the most commonly prescribed medications until tranquilizers overtook them—and both tranquilizers and alcohol are heavily used by adults as aids in getting sleep.

What can parents do about sleep issues? First, you need to recognize that the problem can be tough. If you have bedtime conflicts with your children, it doesn't mean you are bad parents with faulty child-rearing styles. Rather, it's because the conditions and customs of modern industrial society make it extremely difficult to find harmonious sleeping patterns for children and adults. Parents who achieve it with ease are probably lucky—they have a child who parallels their own sleep patterns, or have hit on a combination of approaches that work for them.

Some families use a no-nonsense, rather rigid approach with a fixed-by-the-clock bedtime preceded by a bedtime ritual. Other families are ultrapermissive. The parents wait for the children to get sleepy and go to bed on their own. The child eventually falls asleep this way, perhaps on the living room floor.

Most families have a pattern somewhere in between. There *is* a bedtime but it is modifiable on special occasions. The only really enforced rule is that once the child is in bed, the child should be quiet—although a light, books, or radio are all permitted—so the parents can meet their needs for time alone.

The most important point we want to make is that it's not in your power to make your child fall asleep. All you can do is set up facilitating conditions.

ELIMINATION

Many adults have quite regular rhythms of elimination. Going to the bathroom to urinate during coffee breaks (or intermissions at plays or half-time at football games) is common. In fact, the length of time work or recreational activities last without a break is partly tied to the interval you can expect adults to go without a bathroom break. Some adults have a definite time of day when they expect to have a bowel movement, often with an elaborate reading ritual built around it.

Newborn infants, obviously, do not have any such pattern of elimination. They have no daily schedule. The infant's kidneys put out urine at a fairly regular rate, although the kidneys can shut down the urinary output if the baby becomes dehydrated. When the bladder becomes full enough to exert some pressure, a reflex is stimulated which causes the bladder to contract and empty. This happens many times throughout the day and night.

As the infant grows, several things change. The bladder becomes larger, and is capable of holding more urine before emptying. The baby begins to develop a circadian rhythm like that of adults, with longer sleep at night, and longer wakefulness during the day. The kidneys begin to develop the adult pattern of making more urine during the day and less at night.

There are similar changes, although not quite as simple, in the maturation of bowel rhythms. Contraction of the bladder almost always expels urine. The bowel, on the other hand, is contracting continuously, rhythmically moving its contents on down toward the colon, whether defecation occurs or not. Many factors affect the rate and strength of bowel contractions, including diet, irritants, and emotional factors. Diarrhea occurs when an irritant speeds up the bowel and pushes the food along faster than it can be absorbed. Irritants can be bacterial toxins as in gastroenteritis, foods to which the child has an allergy, or a whole variety of other substances. Most medicines which are taken as laxatives are irritants to the bowel. Also every adult is familiar with the sensation of "butterflies in the stomach" that accompanies anxiety, or the sudden "clutch in the gut" that you can feel with an unexpected emotional shock. These sensations are due to the reflex contractions of the gut that occur with such emotions.

The reflexes that move food out of the stomach and on down the small intestine, where most of the nutrients are absorbed, are somewhat different from those that empty the colon in elimination. Otherwise, toilet training wouldn't be possible without profoundly upsetting digestion. The colon does tend to contract when food enters the stomach (this is called the gastrocolic reflex). Adults often feel an urge to defecate during or after eating, but the urge is not usually so strong as to be overpowering.

Newborn babies vary a great deal in the frequency with which they produce bowel movements. This is much more variable than the frequency of urination. Some infants have many small bowel movements a day; others a few. Some breast-fed babies have bowel movements only every several days, because human milk is so completely digested that very little residue reaches the colon. Over the first months, as the baby develops a day-night cycle, bowel rhythms become adjusted to the cycle. Bowel movements at night become less frequent. Gradually the child comes to have a predictable time or times of day when the bowel movement is likely to occur.

But before the child can learn to be toilet trained, the nervous system must undergo a great deal of maturation. Toilet training does not appear to be neurologically possible until the child is able to walk with some smoothness. There are reports of some societies in which infants are trained at a very early age. This is a different kind of training from what we normally do in our society. The baby wears no clothing over the bottom, and the child lives in a dwelling with a dirt floor or other surface which can be wet or soiled. The mother learns to recognize subtle cues that the infant is about to urinate or defecate in time to hold the baby away from her body and let the baby eliminate on the ground. Apparently very young babies can learn a momentary delay of urination and defecation under such circumstances. It sounds like a great way to prevent diaper rash, but is not very practical in a culture and climate in which children must be kept clothed and in which floors and furnishings need protection from products of elimination.

Toilet training has received a great deal of attention in the psychiatric literature, because it is a potential source of severe conflict between parents and children. Oddly enough, bedtime and eating conflicts are less thoroughly discussed, even though they can be just as much or more stressful for some parents and children.

There are a number of reasons why conflicts can occur around elimination. As children become neurologically ready to withhold their stool, and to exercise voluntary choice about pushing it out, they usually become more aware of their stool. Reflex evacuation is just another biological process—but the ability to hold in, or push out, a stool when the child wishes to do so is a new skill. All children "play" with new skills as they develop them—the drive to play is the expression of the drive to master new skills. As a matter of fact children sometimes play for hours with new skills like standing up and plopping down.

But the child who has just pushed out a stool can't repeat it until the child has another stool to push out, which may not be until tomorrow. What the child can do is continue the play by squeezing it with the hands, smearing it around, and so on. Not all toddlers become fascinated with playing with their stools, but many do. Putting the stool into a toilet and flushing it away may be as unappealing to the toddler as taking away any new toy just when the toddler wants to play with it. To adults, on the other hand, the idea that the child wants to play with something so dirty may seem like the height of perversity. Many children experience their first really severe scoldings for playing with and smearing stools.

Parental discretion is advisable around a toddler's stool play. Obviously, for both aesthetic and hygienic reasons, you don't want stool smeared all over the house. On the other hand, some stool play may be a valuable developmental step as it means your child has developed stool awareness, a vital first step in toilet training.

Our suggestions about toilet training are elaborated on page 422. The main thing to remember is not to make toilet training coercive, because you can't coerce another person's body. Biology and instinct are on your side. Humans, like dogs and unlike monkeys, have an instinct not to foul their lairs, as soon as they are mature enough to avoid doing so. Don't attempt serious toilet training until the child indicates readiness. Signs of readiness include being able to walk, sit down, stand up smoothly; being able to handle some clothing independently (like pulling underpants and jeans off and on); and being aware of when a stool is about to be passed.

This chapter has discussed biological rhythms—your child's and yours. Every human being has these biological rhythms and associated needs. These needs are legitimate. Your needs, as a parent—whether your need for sleep, or your need to have a bite to eat or a moment to defecate without being disturbed by a child—are also legitimate.

Parents truly *want* to meet their baby's needs and most do so. There is some evidence that babies whose needs in infancy are met may be better adjusted as adults. However, you will not always be able to meet every need engendered by your baby's biological rhythms at the exact moment that need is expressed. And your baby's rhythms and yours will not coincide for a long time —if ever.

Remember, it's okay to let a baby wait once in a while. It's okay to put a cranky child in a playpen once in a while in order to meet your own needs. If possible, we recommend the playpen rather than crib if you need to confine a cranky child in a safe place away from you. This is because you want bed to be perceived as a pleasant place for sleep rather than an unhappy, lonely place of confinement or punishment for a cranky mood.

With each passing day, your child will become more mature. This means your baby will grow up and no longer interrupt your rhythms as often as he or she did as an infant.

Hang in there!

SUGGESTED READINGS AND RESOURCES

Brazelton, T. Berry. *Infants and Mothers: Differences in Development.* New York: Dell, 1983.

A neat book which traces the development and caretaker interactions of three different babies ("average," "quiet," and "active") through the first year of life. Interesting reading (and a few good hints) about parenting different ways with different babies.

Erikson, Erik H. *Childhood and Society,* 2nd ed. New York: Norton, 1963.

A classic. Trained as a psychoanalyst, Erikson is also an expert in child development.

Lansky, Vicki. *Getting Your Baby to Sleep (And Back to Sleep).* New York: Bantam, 1985.

Helpful hints on getting your baby to sleep.

Schuster, Clara Shaw, and Ashburn, Shirley Smith. *The Process of Human Development: A Holistic Approach.* Boston: Little, Brown, 1980.

A wonderfully readable, incredibly comprehensive book looking at human development from conception to senility. A great resource.

3

SOCIALIZATION—MORE THAN DISCIPLINE

Scope of Chapter

This chapter deals with *socialization,* the social processes by which we help our babies mature into adult human members of a social community. We cover philosophies of guidance and discipline, basic goals of socialization, principles of guidance, and methods of guidance. We also look at socialization of children by influences other than parents. Further, we cover special areas of socialization: sex, aggression, sibling relationships, child-orienting the home and getting organized, helping children further their own socialization, and finally manners.

Introduction

This chapter is one of the most important in the book, in terms of parental concerns. After we are sure that we have fed, clothed, and sheltered our children, and attended to their safety and health, "bringing them up right" is usually our main concern. Many parents unnecessarily fear they can "spoil" a baby and that it will affect future behavior.[1]

The chapter deals with all the things we do as parents to help transform the little human mammals who are born to us into socialized human beings who hopefully will be responsible and happy citizens. In one sense, whether we are successful parents or not cannot be determined until our children have grown up and are functioning as mature adults and good citizens. The biological definition of a successful parent is a parent whose offspring survive and reproduce. A social definition of a successful parent is one who does one's best, since many good parents have less than perfect outcomes for reasons beyond their control.

This chapter covers much of the ground that is also covered in chapters on biosocial rhythms, body care, safety, and development. But the focus of this chapter is a little different from those. In this chapter we will focus on those things that parents *do, purposefully* or *automatically,* to shape their children's behavior, stimulate their minds and spirits, and help them learn to experience and use their emotions instead of being overwhelmed by them. We will also see how socialization builds on development, attachment, stimulation, communication, consequences, and gradually, self-discipline. It is not accomplished by parents alone although parents are the most important socializers. Parents, inevitably, are models that the children will imitate and follow.

Parents really worry about socializing their children. It's almost as though we have an "instinct to socialize" perhaps based on evolution. Children who were best socialized into the tribe might have been the best survivors.

For several generations, parents have labored under too great a burden of anxiety about socialization. Parents are bombarded with books, magazine articles, and TV "evidence" that they are always to blame if the child isn't socialized properly. Several generations of mental health professionals believed that major mental illnesses were usually caused by faulty child rearing, and also believed that teaching parents good child-rearing techniques would prevent major mental illness.

Today it is recognized that the most serious mental illnesses usually have a biological basis. Parents are not the cause of such tragedies, though when they occur, there is much that parents can do to get treatment for the illness and lighten the burden for the patient and family alike. Furthermore, many children reared under the most painful and chaotic circumstances have proved to be hardy "survivors" who went on to make good adult lives for themselves.

A frightening and painful burden has been lifted from the shoulders of parents. We parents can approach socializing and guiding our children with confidence, doing the best we can to make family life harmonious and constructive. We now understand that we do have an impact on our children's emotional, social, and intellectual development—an impact of which we can be proud—without suffering undue worry that *everything* rests on us.

There are perhaps three desirable outcomes of socialization: 1. The development of self-love, self-esteem, sensible self-discipline, and a healthy respect for one's own needs and safety. 2. The development of a healthy respect for others' needs and feelings. 3. The development of reasonable knowledge and social skills with which to express these attitudes—that is, what used to be called "knowing how to do."

At advanced levels, there are other aspects of guidance, all moral ones: 4. A reasonable understanding and respect for conventional morality—that is, respecting the need for appropriate authority. 5. A higher goal, not always achieved in early childhood, if ever: principled living. By virtue of this, one can solve, or at least struggle reasonably with moral dilemmas, resist peer pressure when appropriate, or even break one rule on the basis of a higher one.

Socialization begins with rapport and attention and mutual playfulness—catching the baby's eye, smiling and smiling back, moving toward and away from each other, just playing together—all those "baby games" like Peek-a-boo. It progresses to imitation, when babies and parents play games of imitating each other's sounds and behavior, and converge on learning baby talk together. Socialization proceeds through virtually full-time watchful guidance (as with the toddler) to beginning self-guidance until the child is ready for reliable self-guidance and self-discipline.

Although socialization is the biggest parental job—the one that's hardest to delegate, and the one that parents have the most worries about—children do get socialized. Beginning with playfulness, adding empathy, and using available knowledge, we can make socialization a mutually rewarding adventure with our children.

PHILOSOPHIES OF DISCIPLINE AND GUIDANCE

Controversies About "Discipline"

Most parents have some pretty intense feelings about discipline. Some people think of "discipline" as a dirty word. Others think of it as one of the noblest goals of child rearing. Many feel completely confused about the subject, and may behave quite erratically about it. People tend to be ambivalent about "discipline" because it makes them think of "punishment." Yet almost everyone considers *"self-*discipline" a positive concept, referring to being goal-directed and well organized, useful traits for children and adults alike.

Obviously, all of us were subjected to some disciplinary maneuvers by parents, teachers, and other authorities. Some of these actions aroused resentment. Some of us react by wanting to repeat the same training we received; others want to try something very different.

In traditional societies, there is usually one "right way" to bring up children. Parents are expected to have learned it from their own childhood training and to apply almost exactly the same kind of rearing and training to their children. Other adults will help by using the same methods and approaches. In fact, this is one of the main things people mean when they talk about a "traditional society."

Our society, by contrast, offers many choices to parents in child rearing. It is not that we are entirely without traditions. In fact, as a heterogeneous collection of immigrants from many countries, we Americans have a diversity of traditions to draw on, as well as new combinations and innovations to invent. But very few traditions in contemporary American culture seem right to everybody, as is the case in an isolated, traditional, homogeneous culture.

Western culture for the past several centuries has enjoyed a lively debate about the philosophical and theological foundations of discipline for children. The far right extreme in this debate is sometimes explicitly based on the theological doctrine of Original Sin. Children, if left to themselves, are and would grow up to be evil, aggressive, and dangerous. In this view, parents should observe their children carefully for evidence of bad habits or impulses, and root those out with forceful punitive discipline. The far left extreme in this debate is explicitly based on a doctrine of romantic naturalism. Children, if left to themselves, are innocent, loving creatures who would grow up to be just fine if they were allowed to develop naturally, undistorted by the expectations and pressures of a corrupt society. Parents, in this view, should be as permissive and unintrusive as possible, so as not to distort their children's natural good impulses.

The problem with this debate in its extreme form is, of course, that it is too abstract and unrealistic. Children left to themselves do not grow up either good *or* bad; they do not grow up at all.

All children who have ever grown up have had some kind of care givers (see p. 186 for why we use this term) in infancy, and the care givers are inevitably people with needs and ideas of their own. Child rearing very heavily involves the process of mutually adjusting the child's and the care giver's needs to each other, and in that process a great deal of mutual "discipline" occurs. If we correctly view discipline as teaching, children and parents are constantly teaching each other, whether either side likes the lessons or not.

Another problem with the great debate on discipline is that often it does not take into account the different ages of children. To indulge a newborn infant at the moment it feels an impulse of hunger may lead to blissful repose. For an adolescent to indulge a sexual impulse at the moment it is felt could lead to a charge of rape. We are all aware of the fact that sometime, well before adulthood, we need to have considerable control over our impulses. But it is not at all clear that early and rigorous *external* control of impulses is the best way to help the child develop reliable *internal* controls. Nor, on the other hand, is it proven that early and complete gratification of impulses *automatically* leads to a friendly wish to inhibit them when necessary later on.

Furthermore, children are individuals. Some thrive on a very predictable environment where they know just what to expect. Others fight anything resembling a rule.

Experimental evidence unfortunately isn't very conclusive about how to guide normal, healthy children. There are many experimental studies dealing with various treatment approaches for psychiatrically ill or "problem" children. One can compare, for example, a behavior modification program with an expressive psychotherapy program and see whether the one or the other helps with certain kinds of problems. But it is very risky to generalize from children with serious problems to healthy children. There are no longitudinal studies, say, comparing spanked with non-spanked children after twenty years. Anthropological studies of other cultures also may not be too helpful. One culture may spank and another not, but there are too many other variables to conclude that spanking makes a difference. So "expert" advice on discipline, including our own, is based on opinion and observations rather than solid experimental evidence.

Parents *can* learn some useful ideas about child guidance and discipline by looking at cross-cultural studies. Modern Americans are far less indulgent of infants and very young children and far more permissive with older children than is the case in most cultures. Also, we try to teach courtesy and inhibit aggression at very early ages and often by very discourteous and aggressive methods. For example, "Don't hit your sister!", followed by a *smack.* By this example children learn that they are not supposed to hit when aggravated by a younger child's behavior, and that this rule is enforced by their being hit by an older person. One could logically generalize that bigger people hit smaller people but not if a still bigger person is present who is protecting the smallest person (a constant theme in children's TV shows and movies). However, one wouldn't learn not to hit. As a result, or perhaps coincidentally, American adults are less reliably courteous than those of many other cultures, and we have a high rate of domestic and civil violence. By middle childhood, many of our children have an extensive repertoire of verbal and physical rudeness, whether they use it frequently or not.

Asians, by contrast, tend to indulge small children and expect courtesy and deference as a mark of *maturity* rather than a demeaning obligation for the young only. In fact there is an Indian saying, "Treat your child like a king till he's five, like a slave till he's fifteen, and a friend after that."

Anne vividly remembers her culture shock at seeing how a Korean woman handled a three-year-old's temper tantrums. This woman often cared for Anne's son on Saturdays, in her own home with her son of the same age. When Anne came to pick up Sam, it was late in the day. Sam was still enjoying his playmate, but he was tired and fussy and didn't necessarily want to stop and come home at the precise moment Anne stopped by. Often he'd throw a *royal* fit—and Mrs. Yi responded by treating him like *royalty!* Before Anne had a chance, like a typical American mother, to be embarrassed and try to *stop* Sam's behavior, Mrs. Yi quickly and deftly moved right in—virtually kneeling to get at his eye level and catch his eye. She would engage his attention respectfully and say something like, "Oh, Sam! What have we done? Are we making you so unhappy? Please let me *help* you finish the game—or get the toys together—or find the coat," as the case might be. It worked!

Spontaneous Learning vs. Planned Teaching

Parents expect young children to learn some things spontaneously, while other things are taught. Parents expect children to learn to sit, stand, talk, walk, and run without "teaching." We may offer a helping hand and are likely to spontaneously reward or "reinforce" their new skills with our pride and delight. We parents also respond to our toddlers' early attempts at talking with delight, not correcting or criticizing.

However, with regard to courtesy and control of aggression, parents don't have the same confidence that children will pick these up. Most of us don't assume that our children will learn "Please" and "Thank you" as readily as they will learn other words and language customs. We tend to assume that this has to be taught explicitly, by rewards and punishments. "I want a cookie." "Say please" (hold up cookie). "Please." "Okay, here's the cookie."

In fact, if we parents are liberal in the use of these courtesies and social graces with our children, most children pick them up by imitation as naturally as they learn the language. A little gentle coaching may be needed to back up imitation.

Who's the Boss?

Traditional approaches to child rearing usually emphasize training children to know that the parent is the boss. In some modern homes children seem to be the bosses. Neither approach seems comfortable to most parents. Is there an alternative?

Thomas Gordon, who has developed the well-known Parent Effectiveness Training program (P.E.T.), points out that most parents think of parent-child conflicts in terms of someone winning and someone losing.[2,3]

> Most parents see the whole problem of discipline in childhood as a question of being either strict or lenient, tough or soft, authoritarian or permissive. Because they are locked into this either-or approach to discipline, they see their relationship with their children as a power struggle, a contest of wills, a fight to see who wins—a *war.* Today's parents and their children are literally at war, each thinking in terms of someone winning and someone losing.

Gordon points out that parents are very concerned about power, and usually use one or two methods of allocating power or, as a third alternative, an unfortunate combination of the first two methods:

Method 1. Authoritarian. Parents are bosses and try to win all conflicts. They insist that children obey and may use drastic methods to achieve this. Consequences of authoritarian discipline include low motivation for children to carry out parental solutions to problems, resentment toward parents, and diminished or no opportunity for children to develop self-discipline. The consequences for parents may include difficulties in enforcement, a sense of failure if authoritarian rule is not obeyed, and a sense of harshness and distance from children if it is.

Method 2. Permissive. Children are bosses and win most conflicts. The parents go along with what the children want. Consequences include children who are impulsive, unmanageable, self-centered, demanding, and "spoiled," and parents who feel powerless or exploited.

Because so many parents today are uncomfortable with the disadvantages of either authoritarian or permissive child rearing, Gordon finds that a "combination of methods" is the most common approach. Today's parents are likely to oscillate between Method 1 and Method 2. The parents act permissively until they can't stand it any more, then suddenly revert to authoritarian Method 1. The children then get surprised and angry, and when parents can't stand *that* any more, they revert to permissiveness. Both basic methods and the combination are similar in that someone wins and someone loses, while the consequences of the oscillation approach can include the worst features of both authoritarian and permissive methods. Adolescents raised by authoritarian, permissive, or oscillating parents may become particularly undisciplined when their increasing independence deprives parents of the ability to rely on rewards and impose punishments.

P.E.T. teaches Method 3, which is a "no-lose method" of *healthy mutual assertiveness.* You sidestep power struggles and concentrate on effective problem solving. Parents are encouraged to firmly express their feelings when they are unhappy with children's behavior, and thus model and help children to express their feelings when *their* needs are not being met.

Method 3 requires that you make a careful distinction about *who owns the problem.* If the parent is unhappy with the child's behavior, the parent owns the problem. In this case, you use "I-sentences." "*I* am unhappy because you left your coat in the hall and I had to pick it up." If the child is showing signs of being unhappy, the *child* owns the problem. In this case you use sympathetic active listening—"you-messages"—to help the child discuss the problem. "*You* look upset. Would you like to talk about it?"

Both P.E.T. books offer many practical suggestions on how to be an effective, active listener who can encourage communication from your children. These techniques are also useful for communication with spouses, friends, and people at work, since P.E.T. is fundamentally based on the premise that children are not so different from other people.

This approach makes family life much happier by avoiding a large number of unnecessary power struggles. Classes are available in learning this approach. If Anne had her way, P.E.T. courses would be as common a preparation for child rearing as Lamaze classes for childbearing. P.E.T. classes usually meet for eight three-hour sessions, and parents can take a refresher course if they need to—but most don't. Parents who become enthusiastic about the approach can take a further training course to become instructors. As with Lamaze training, it is best to take a course, and have the benefit of discussion with other parents and a leader. But if courses are not available in your community, you can learn a great deal about the method from reading the books.

BASIC GOALS OF SOCIALIZATION

What are the main goals in socializing children anyhow?

1. As parents we want our children to gradually adjust their biological rhythms to those of adult society (eating, elimination, sleeping/rest/activity patterns, and sexuality). This adjustment to adult society depends mostly on maturation and a bit on training.

2. We want them to increase the number of things they can do for themselves, like dressing and feeding, and no longer need the total care that infants need. This depends on maturation, imitation, and training.

3. We want them to become concerned about their own safety, and not

take undue risks of accidents, illnesses, or injuries. This depends on maturation, imitation, training, and also on cognitive knowledge and attitude development.

4. We want them to learn language and gestures and customs, so they can communicate harmoniously and skillfully with others. This depends a lot on maturation, experience, knowledge, and imitation.

5. We want them to learn to integrate their needs with those of other people. We want them to accept and deal with the fact that somebody else might have conflicting wants. We want them to learn how to negotiate as needed, to get along with others. We also want them to see that even their own wants could conflict with each other, and that some of their own wants have to be deferred or modulated in order to satisfy other wants. We want them to slow down, modulate, and control raw hunger, aggression, greed, sexuality, and need for attention, for their own sakes, not just to please others. These areas take lots of maturation, imitation, experience, attitude development, and understanding.

6. We want them to develop empathy—the capacity to be sensitive to others' needs and feelings, so that they respond not *just* out of rules for proper behavior, but out of genuine understanding and caring. This is more likely to occur when *they* feel loved and receive empathy.

7. We want them to develop a love of honest work so that they can support and take care of themselves without being exploited or exploiting others.

8. We want them to feel and act on loyalties to the groups they belong to, without being slaves to group opinions which might be unfair or unwise.

9. We want them to develop morally to the stage of thoughtfully evaluating, rather than blindly following *or* rebelliously rejecting the rules of one group or another.

10. And in all of these areas, by late childhood or at least by adulthood, we hope that they will be able to behave smoothly, gracefully, and courteously. Well-socialized persons perform the "social dance" effortlessly as though they have learned the steps, hear the music, and have mastered the performance well enough to innovate a bit.

There are also some goals we'd best *avoid* in socializing:

1. Trying to make the child a copy of ourselves or somebody else when that doesn't fit the child's natural gifts and temperament.

2. Trying to make the child an *opposite* of somebody else: "Your father was an irresponsible rat and I don't want you to be like him."

3. Trying to use children to fill our unfulfilled dreams, instead of letting them develop their own dreams, and doing what we can to fulfill our own.

HOW DO FAMILIES SOCIALIZE CHILDREN?

How do children become socialized? Where does guidance or discipline come in?

Families handle socialization in different ways. Some have a lot of "rules" which are explicitly stated, which children are expected to obey. Others hope that their children will learn to have cooperative attitudes, or can be "reasoned with" so as to learn to understand the expectations of others. Most use some mixture of rules and reasoning, but lean more heavily to the one side or the other.

Regardless of whether an individual parent prefers the use of rules or reason, however, children tend to pick up both. Children infer rules even if they are not stated (as they infer the basic rules of grammar of the language, just from experience in hearing and speaking it). And children, when they are old enough, usually figure out that there are reasons behind the rules, even if only the rules were stated. Still later, they naturally want to participate in negotiating the rules.

Children learn to be socialized in *interaction* with others. There is every reason to believe that children learn socialization *much* better from people they are attached to and love, than from strangers or uncaring others. Effective self-discipline starts with love, and attachment, and all those "baby games" that help attachment blossom. There's a big difference between external imposed "discipline"—i.e., making the child do what *you* want—and internal discipline which has become a part of the child. External discipline only works as long as there is someone watching the child to ensure that it is followed. Self-discipline goes with children wherever they go.

Children *can* and do internalize rules and make them their own. But rigid rules may work only for the situation they were designed for. You may be able to teach a young child not to run into the street but the child also has to be careful in driveways and become aware of all possible automobile hazards. You can (usually) teach children to go to bed at the bedtime you have set. But that rule alone won't teach them how to later balance their own need for sleep with their work requirements. You can teach children how to show respect for authority to an extent that may leave them helpless if they later have a boss who says, "I don't want a 'yes-man.'"

Our society is changing too fast for parents to generate rules that will cover all the situations our children will find themselves in. That's why we like the term "guidance," which is a broader concept than "discipline." You guide by nurturance, which fosters attachment. By respecting your own needs *and* your child's, you can guide and model a kind of healthy mutual assertiveness which helps children fit well into modern society.

The best guidance techniques do not humiliate children, but rather raise children's self-esteem. The parents' behaviors communicate clearly the message that guidance is an expression of the parent's love and respect for the child rather than the reverse. Parent-child attachment and love are the important first steps which ensure the child's acceptance of guidance, and stimulate the growth of self-discipline.

SOME BASIC SOCIALIZATION TERMS

Socialization begins with a parent providing the baby with survival needs. While babies are being fed and cleaned and clothed, they are also learning that a *person* or *people* do these things for them. Daily care is a socializing process through which the baby learns *basic trust* in the dependability of the social world, and experiences healthy sensuality from being fed, bathed, and cuddled. Smiles, eye contact, and playing games develop *social responsiveness* throughout infancy. Indeed, small infants need daily care in a playful way, with social interaction cued to the individual infant's needs and expressions. This is "baby-led play" like "baby-led nursing" (see p. 326), and it provides lots of touching and cuddling.

Communication

Communication refers to the ways in which one person interacts with another—by making eye contact, moving toward or away, speaking, playing games, taking part in shared projects, making love, or working together. From the moment of birth, human infants live in a social world. Other people are almost always present or nearby, and even a hermit can't escape the traces of other people's expectations and teachings. People who interact skillfully with other people are more likely to have a rewarding life. Children whose basic temperaments are unusually shy or aggressive need to learn communication styles which not only suit their temperaments but also work with others.

Attachments

Attachments refer to those special relationships which make particular individuals intensely important and not readily replaceable by others. Infants normally become attached to their parents and other care givers, and vice versa. Children become attached to "best friends." Adolescents and adults in love become attached to their loved ones. Most people also become attached to groups, ideals, and even abstract ideas of great importance. Indeed, people seem to develop their sense of self and identity out of their attachments as much as any other single factor.

Early attachment of parents to children is today referred to as "bonding"— a term derived from the animal research literature. It is based on the fact that some animal mothers either form an immediate and strong attachment bond to their young at birth, or not at all. With humans, the circumstances of birth may play an enhancing or inhibiting role in forming attachments, but humans can bond to a child long after birth even though animals cannot.

Empathy

Empathy refers to understanding. This is more than just sympathy when you express *your* sorrow at another's misfortune, but rather is the ability to share another's feeling of joy or anguish from their perspective as *they* feel it—"walking a mile in their moccasins" as the old saying goes. "Sympathizers" tend to give lots of advice, but "empathizers" give lots of warm, close, active listening, with sometimes a look, touch, or hug to convey both that they understand how it feels and that they care.

Stimulation

Stimulation refers to those things care givers do to infants, and infants later do for themselves, to help them take notice, play, think, and communicate. Stimulation fosters attachment because it is such vivid interaction. One doesn't bond to a wet noodle. Stimulation of the senses and the mind go together, right along with stimulation of emotions and fostering of attachments. Later on, intellectual stimulation, as well as attachments to teachers and to parents who love learning, forms the basis of love of learning in school.

Guidance

Guidance refers to those things that parents do to and for children, that help *organize* the child's behavior and the child's world. Many people call this "discipline," but as noted above, this is a confusing word because it means so many different things to different people. Guidance also has two meanings. First of all, it means being the kind of guide your child would *want* to follow (the attachment dimension). Secondly, being a "guide" means *going somewhere*— having goals in mind. We like to think of "guidance" as what the *parent* provides, and "discipline" as the "self-discipline" the *child* gradually develops over the course of a lifetime.

Self-discipline

Self-discipline is built on growth and development in three main areas. First, it requires biological maturation of the child's body and development of emotional experience. Babies begin to experience love, attachment, fear, anger, calm, and happiness, as increasingly distinguishable states of being. Second, it requires social development. Babies interact with other people, initially primary care givers, learning to enjoy their company while gradually recognizing that these others have needs too. Third, it requires intellectual development—learning to think and communicate. Learning to *understand* why a parental "no" might make sense requires intellectual maturity.

The *"self-discipline triangle"* involves three parts: recognizing *one's own needs*, recognizing the *needs of others*, and recognizing *general rules and expectations*. All three are needed, and the balance between them is complicated. People who too rigidly follow rules and expectations without sensitivity to their own and others' needs are likely to have a compulsive, joyless life, pleasing neither self nor others. People who do not understand rules and expectations at all, even with the best of knowledge of their own and others' needs, have to keep rediscovering the wheel, and are unable to take advantage of cultural wisdom. People who try to please only others are not likely to achieve even that. People who try to please only themselves are not likely to achieve that either. There is no mature love unless one cares about the loved one's needs. Humans are social animals, and cannot be happy as isolated people without attachments of some sort.

All children bring their own temperaments into the self-discipline process. Parents, too, bring their own temperaments, needs, and values to bear on the process. Parents can actually interfere with children's development of self-discipline, or we can assist. Some of us find it easy to provide the kind of coaching our children need. Others find it difficult, while some find it easy with one child and hard with another. For example, a very well-organized parent who likes to keep things neat may have a lot of difficulty with an active, rambunctious child who has little bent toward order. Another parent may have the same temperament as the child, and get along very well.

GENERAL PRINCIPLES OF GUIDANCE

The general structure of the household can exert a calming influence on children. Many infants and young children adjust readily to well-established routines. A household in which everything is negotiable, including dinnertime and bedtime, may seem fine to an adult, but young children, who do not have as advanced negotiating skills as adults, may paradoxically find the very sort of environment which is freeing to grown-ups is tyrannical and unmanageable, or confusing, to them.

There are some natural hierarchies of priority. For example, children's safety is more important than how neatly they are dressed. At almost any age, family happiness and cohesion is more important than having a perfectly tidy house.

A terribly important principle in helping children become self-disciplined is the parents' awareness of their *own* needs. Sometimes parents need peace and quiet, or time alone away from the children. After the "baby honeymoon" is over, parents need to pursue some of their own interests and friendships. After infancy, parents need to receive gradually increasing respect and empathy for their own needs from their children.

If you do not stop to figure out what you need and how to get it, your children's needs may interfere too much with your own. Then it's tempting to view a child's perfectly natural behavior as "bad." Children who get the message that they are "bad" may give up on trying to be "good." This is one way children lose their self-esteem, which is one of the worst things that can happen to a child. Other children who come to feel that their natural childish spontaneity is "bad" make a too-desperate effort to act "good." Outwardly, they behave with precocious maturity and are seen as "good"—but inwardly their self-esteem is impaired because they believe their true feelings are "bad."[4]

In order to teach empathy and respect for others, we as parents need to confidently assert our own needs. Some of us find it easy to assert our own needs, but others (because of our own temperament or upbringing) find it difficult to do so, and may even feel guilty. As parents, we need to relearn *awareness* of our own needs before we can guide children well. The fact that parenting forces us to relearn new awareness of our own needs can be one of the ways it helps us as parents to grow and develop as people. (See Parents' Growth and Development.)

THE MYTH OF CONSISTENCY

Parent advisers, mental health workers, and child care professionals are forever telling parents that they ought to be "consistent." This is a word we wish could be stricken from the child care literature, in part because it is impossible to achieve, and in part because the very word "consistency" is so inconsistently used.

Part of the confusion about consistency arises because the word "consistency" is used to handle what are really other more complex parenting problems. A parent who usually lets the child do whatever the child wants to do, with mounting resentment, and then occasionally gets upset and demands 100 percent compliance may be called inconsistent. True, but the inconsistency is that the parent is oscillating between authoritarian Method 1 and permissive Method 2, as described earlier. The real problem is that what the parent needs is not abstract consistency, but practical help in learning mutually assertive Method 3. With this method, parents can be more assertive about what they need from their children, and more sensitive to their children's needs all along, before problems or tensions build up.

Sound advice about being consistent is that parents should not confuse children in such a way as to make it impossible for them to exert their natural wishes to please their parents. So don't make rules you don't plan to enforce. The following are perfectly *acceptable* examples of inconsistency:

• Most parents can live in some tolerable degree of disorder most of the time, but want to clean up when they are having a party.

• Most parents can tolerate a certain amount of the normal noise and exuberance of healthy children, but on a day when they have a headache, they cannot.

• Most parents might be willing to handle a certain amount of non-compliance in children by reasoning with them most of the time. But if today happens to be a pressured day, you might have to say, "Do what I tell you; I'll explain later."

• Parents are different from each other. One parent might have a greater need for peace and quiet than the other. What parents really want from the child is not consistency about the decibel level at all times, but the sensitivity to respond to different people as individuals.

• A baby-sitter, day care center, or teacher might have different standards from yours. It is not necessary to have consistent standards over all situations, but to be up-front about the fact that different people have different standards and teach that to the children.

• Parents might suddenly realize that something they have been permitting is more dangerous than they realized. For example, if you have been letting your teenage daughter spend a lot of time in an unstructured way with friends, you may come to learn that the group is involved in unsafe activities. A change of expectations is better than consistently following the old ones!

Gerald Nelson makes a couple of important points about two situations where he feels consistency is important: If you are using specific rewards or punishment to control specific behaviors, consistency counts.[5] Also, consistency between two parents is needed to the degree that children understand what the parents expect. For example, when the parents differ over a discipline issue, they should resolve it directly with each other, not use the children to fight parental battles. Couple counseling (or using some of the P.E.T. methods of direct confrontation with each other) may help. Two other books which help describe constructive conflict resolution skills to be used between adults are *The Intimate Enemy*[6] and *Getting to Yes.*[7] (See Special Events and Stresses.)

We feel that when there is a genuine difference of feeling about an unimportant behavior (for example, one parent can't stand children picking their noses, and the other couldn't care less), it's easy to request the child not to do it around the parent who can't stand it.

If the problem is one of goals or priorities—one parent wants to make a scholar out of the child, and rewards homework, while the other rewards athletics or socializing, for example—discussion and soul searching are needed, not more parental "consistency." Is the child a natural athlete, scholar, or socialite who needs or wants to invest considerable time to develop outstanding talents? Is the child way behind in one of these areas, and does he or she need to invest time to catch up with at least minimal skills? Is one of the parents trying to fit the child into a mold that doesn't suit that particular child? How does the child feel about it? Does the school have some useful input?

METHODS OF GUIDANCE

Techniques for helping children develop self-esteem, empathy, and self-discipline will be different, depending on where the children are developmentally, and indeed where the parents are developmentally. Much interaction with children is spontaneous and requires no special techniques—what Gordon calls the "no-problem area."[8] Most approaches to guidance deal with what to do when your children are doing things you do not like, or when they appear unhappy. What do you do then? Ignore the child's behavior? Reason with the child? Give advice? Scold? Spank? Isolate the child? All of these techniques might have their place for different ages or different kinds of problems.

Automatic Methods

MODELING

The best form of guidance is Golden Rule guidance. Treat the child the way you'd like to be treated yourself—with empathy, respect and loving attention most times, and with clear respectful feedback when you expect or need something you aren't getting from them. Use requests often and orders rarely.

What do you do when someone you love is angry at you? How would you want to be treated? Wouldn't you want quick, specific, direct feedback coupled with a strong emotional reassurance of how much that person still loves you? Wouldn't you want as clear as possible an idea of what made them angry at you?

When you're angry at your child, you can give the child a good model of how you'd like children to handle *their* anger. You could say, for example, "I'm *really* mad because you said you'd be home at six and now it's nine. I was really worried—[pause]—I love you and I know you are the kind of child who usually keeps your promises," followed by a hug.

This approach is the essence of Gerald Nelson's *The One-Minute Scolding.*[9] He gives wonderful examples of the constructive use of anger, and explains his theory about how this kind of modeling promotes bonding and attachment as well as acceptable behavior. The one-minute scolding is good modeling because it is an honest expression of strong emotion, which comes from care and concern for the child's behavior and the parents' feelings, coupled with a genuine boost to the child's self-esteem, one which is honest and comes from the heart. With a little practice this technique easily becomes automatic, precisely because it is so honest and direct.

The One-Minute Father[10] and *The One-Minute Mother,*[11] derived from Nelson's ideas, emphasize using "one-minute praisings." These too can be good modeling if they are honest expressions of strong parental appreciation for the child's behavior which pleases the parent. With practice, praising can become more automatic, honest, and direct.

Also, modeling alone won't cover all guidance issues, but it is the basic method, because it is completely automatic: *whatever* you do is a model for the child. If you are dissatisfied with your own behavior, either for its own sake or as a model, you have the option of making changes in your behavior which will automatically modify what you are modeling.

ENVIRONMENTAL CONTROL

Guidance and discipline can be greatly simplified by reducing the number of things you have to give guidance about. When you "childproof" and/or "child-orient" your home, there are many fewer things you have to exert discipline about. When the valuables are on a high shelf, you don't have to do something every time the child reaches for them. When the child's study environment is comfortable and well organized, you don't have to push the child so much to get homework started. When the child's room is organized in such a way that it's easy to put toys and clothes away, much less coaching in cleaning up is required.

GIVING INSTRUCTION

Giving instruction can become automatic, but it is astonishing how often parents forget the simple step of clearly *telling* the children in advance what they expect.

Young children can't read your mind and don't always know that parents may expect different behavior in an unusual situation—a wedding or funeral or formal restaurant meal, for example. Often, telling them in advance, and even coaching or acting out what will be expected, can help.

You would probably automatically tell your spouse in advance if a seemingly casual social event was really an important business dinner. With a little practice you can make it equally automatic to tell your children in advance when the situation they are about to encounter is going to make you want different behavior from them. Gordon calls this a "preventive I-message" and has many useful things to say about it.[12] You can also *ask* your children if there's anything you can do to help *them* behave in a new situation.

SIMPLE IGNORING

Simple ignoring is another astonishingly easy technique in child rearing, which can be built into your automatic approach. It saves a lot of time and trouble to ignore minor problems like spilling milk. Many of them will be handled by the child's maturation anyhow. However, remember we're talking about ignoring a behavior. We are *not* talking about ignoring the child by withdrawing attention as an open or disguised form of punishment.

SIMPLE ENJOYING

Simple enjoying of young children's childish behavior is another automatic method which has much to recommend it. Some parents feel a duty to start training the child out of behaviors which will be unacceptable later, even though they are adorable now. You can save yourselves a lot of energy, conflict, and grief by just enjoying the behavior as long as it is still adorable.

Mutual Assertiveness Methods

Mutual assertiveness methods, of which Parent Effectiveness Training is the best known example, are based on certain practical but philosophical assumptions: 1) a serious belief that children are people and deserve respect; 2) a serious belief that parents are people too, and deserve respect; 3) an attempt to cultivate a climate of mutual respect; and 4) an expression of these values through empathy, attachment, and genuine caring, as well as communication skills, negotiation skills, and problem-solving skills. Naturally, such an approach helps *build* empathy in children because it gives the children a model for how to communicate *their* feelings and needs too. As few rules as possible are set up unilaterally by parents. Instead, emphasis is placed on decisions hashed out to mutual satisfaction. The rules that are set tend to be seen as matters of mutual respect, convenience and order, like traffic regulations. Rules that are simple and obvious, or jointly negotiated, are more respected by both parties than unilateral rules—because once you've helped make the rule you have a stake in making it work. Children respond to this, just as adults do.

What does this method have going for it? The main thing is that it is a rewarding way to live, and a rewarding way to relate to other people, as well as one's children. And it also helps children learn and model a rewarding way in which to relate to other people in the outside world. In the long run, it saves time and energy and also preserves love and harmony.

However, there are potential pitfalls in this approach. First of all, children are not born democratic; they are born autocratic. Some of their early methods for controlling *your* behavior are coercive and demanding. They put out punishing noises (like crying) before they learn to dispense rewards (like smiles). Children are not born with immediate respect for your property, your feelings, or your needs.

In short, children are not born civilized. But children are born appealing, and eager to make contact. They are born with a capacity for communication from Day 1, in ways which tend naturally to correspond to our needs as parents. We can't *control* newborns, any more than they can fully control us, but we can *meet* them. In feeding, holding, smiling, and talking we can experience what active communicators our newborn babies are. As the baby molds itself into our arms, we are making contact. Civilization can wait. The early mutuality of communication is earthy contact—body contact, eye contact, functional contact—in meeting the baby's needs and responding to the baby's at first diffuse emotions. We can't really spoil newborns, but trying to "spoil" them can be mutually rewarding.

Mutual assertiveness with infants and young children may seem difficult when their assertiveness is so clear. But we are assertive too. It meets our own needs as well as the baby's when a crying baby is comforted and sleeps, or is fed and catches our eyes for play. As the early weeks pass, it becomes very clear that both we and the baby have a mutual interest in the baby's comfort. We meet our needs as well as the baby's by helping entrain the baby's biological rhythms —feeding when hungry, soothing when fussy, controlling the level of stimulation so that more play is encouraged in daytime, with a quicker return to sleep at night. Play can be mutual from the beginning, since the first toy is the care giver's face.

Our other needs—such as those for enough sleep, for responding to our other interests—are best met by asserting our needs for the help of others, sometimes to do some of the baby care, preferably to take over some of our other responsibilities.

As young children grow, we can recognize and respect their feelings and provide words for them. This helps them understand that needs and feelings are valued. We also provide a good model by behaving in ways that show we value our own needs as well—the "non-verbal I-message" of putting a squirming toddler down, or restraining a little hand from hurting our eyes. Much of the push for mutuality initially comes from us.

With older children, mutuality can be further built into play—making games rather than power struggles out of new challenges like solid foods, playing with household objects, choosing which clothes to wear.

The constant theme is recognizing the legitimacy of needs that sometimes conflict. The child's wish for our full attention isn't "bad"—but neither is our wish to give attention to other matters. Mutual assertiveness comes from a respect for both parties' needs and honest acceptance of conflicts as inevitable, resolvable, and growth-producing.

Power Methods

1. *The mildest form of coercion is unilateral assertiveness.* You simply say very clearly and forcefully what you want to happen, and why you want it to happen, including the consequences it has for you and the feelings you have about it. It is essentially the "I-sentence" method, which is described thoroughly in P.E.T. It is a no-blame technique, which simply lets the child know clearly the impact of his or her behavior on you. All parents have power in the relationship with their children and it's *not* wrong to exert this for your own benefit or

your child's safety. Indeed, you have an obligation to prevent your toddler from playing with matches, for example.

2. *Persuasion* (or what in parent-child relationships is often called "reasoning with"), is stronger and more unilaterally assertive. Reasoning with children has a lot to recommend it. "I want you to do this *because*," or "I want you to stop doing this *because*," and giving the reason, helps the child learn that there are reasons behind your requests, and conveys respect for both your needs and the child's intelligence. There are certain circumstances in which you won't have the time to work through complex reasons. In any case, "reasonings" should always be as brief as you can make them. Young children tune out after about half a minute.

3. A still stronger example of unilateral assertiveness is the "one-minute scolding." Nelson, who developed this technique, points out that "scolding plus emotion, affection, and re-affirmation" techniques were first used with very difficult children in foster homes, children who had never had enduring attachments which made them feel loved and developed their self-esteem. Only later was it discovered that these same techniques worked well with all children, and even with adults in work situations.

The one-minute scolding works because it is brief, immediate, covers one point forcefully, and conveys love as strongly as scolding. This way parents can briefly convey disapproval, induce guilt about a specific behavior if needed, while avoiding unnecessary guilt and damaged self-esteem. The elements of the one-minute scolding are: 1) scolding the *behavior*, not the child; 2) a moment of transition; 3) positive reaffirmation of the child's worth; 4) a quiz about the behavior; 5) a hug.

The parent first very forcefully engages the child's attention, holding or touching the child, and making eye contact. The parent scolds the child for a specific misbehavior (such as breaking a household rule, or failing to obey a significant order). The parent looks and acts as upset as he or she feels: mild irritation if that is the case, or considerable anger if that is the true feeling. The parent gives the reason for the scolding, explains the rule or expectation, and continues until the child responds with signs of feeling ("a tear, a sad face, a quivering lip"). *But the parent does not continue to scold more than thirty seconds.* (Nelson adds that with very young or extrasensitive children, even that much scolding time is too long.)

Then in the transition time parents *pause*, get control of their feelings, and remind themselves how much they love the child. At this point the entire attitude is changed. Suddenly, an angry, scolding parent switches to a loving, nurturing parent. The expressive part is best expressed in Nelson's own words:

> Initially, the second half of the scolding is the more difficult to produce. Even though she has been very upset and angry, maybe even rageful, the parent must reassure the child of his worth. The child needs to know beyond a doubt that he is loved, that he will not be abandoned, that he is capable of changing and learning how to behave, and that he will be helped consistently. Everything about

the way the parent expresses confidence and tenderness is felt in tone of voice, body language, and touch:

You're a neat, delightful fellow.

A positive statement is followed by a feeling statement about him:

I love you so much!

And the child hears how he'll be able to behave properly:

I'll help you. I want to be a good mama, so every time you forget and hit your sister, I'll scold you. Soon you'll remember that we don't hit. Even if you forget, I'll just keep reminding you. You're such a nifty brother and it's not necessary to forget . . . etc.

The parent is reassuring, warm, and in control.

With this positive affirmation, most children feel relieved and reassured of their parents' love. Then the parent checks to see if she has been a clear and effective teacher with a quiz:

Why am I scolding you now?

Because I hit my sister.

Right! Some praise rewards the child for knowing what this scolding is about.

And why must I scold you every time you make a bad mistake?

Because I'm not supposed to hit my sister.

Right! And because I love you so much! What are you supposed to do when you feel mad with your sister?

Come to you for help if I can't handle it.

Right, etc.[13]

The parent ends the scolding with a hug to reinforce how much love he or she has for the child and to indicate that the scolding is over.

It is easy to see why this method would work better than conventional scolding. Conventional scoldings are usually too long and generally include many problems at once. They often involve calling the child a number of bad names such as "bad, lazy, clumsy," etc. A one-minute scolding, by contrast, is *brief*, handles one fresh issue at a time, and links strong, honest emotionality about the specific behavior with equally strong honest emotionality about your love for the child. Instead of impairing self-esteem or inducing despair, it can enhance self-esteem through linking your love and your expectation of acceptable behavior in the future. It also *works*, while kids "tune out" long tirades or scoldings.

4. *Behavior analysis and behavior modification.* In dealing with children's unacceptable behavior, it certainly pays to try to figure out what the kid is getting out of it. This is technically called *behavior analysis* and it is needed before trying *behavior modification*. Behavior modification is a systematic application of rewards and punishments applied to get someone to do what you want him or her to do.

The steps in behavior analysis are:

a. *Precisely identify the behavior* that is the problem. Is it "playing in the mud"? Or is it "playing in the mud with your good clothes on"? Or is it "playing in the mud just when we're about to go somewhere"? Just "playing in the mud" is not the problem, because under certain circumstances or at certain times, that would be perfectly acceptable.

    b. Identify the *reinforcer*—what is the child getting out of this behavior? Is it fun in itself? Does the child get attention (negative attention is still attention)? Is the child doing it to avoid doing something else? Is the child getting excitement and relief from boredom? If the child is doing it, the child must be getting something out of it.

    c. Find an acceptable way (for both you and the child) in which the child can get the reinforcer that the child wants and is looking for. For example, if the bored child is getting excitement by picking a fight with his/her siblings, think of some more acceptable pastimes for the child—having a friend over, or playing a game with the child. Suggest reading or an absorbing task that needs doing.

    d. With verbal children, pay particular attention to clearly explaining what you *do want* from them, not just what you *do not want*.

    5. *Time-outs.* Behavior modification professionals generally use the term "time-out" to refer to any situation in which the child's activity is interrupted, and the child is required to stay in a specified, not very rewarding place, as a means of interrupting the rewards from unacceptable behavior. A chair can be used, for example. "Go stand [or sit] in the corner" was a classic technique used by schoolteachers in the past. Today, from day care to elementary school, children go to the designated "time-out" place, which almost never is the corner and is designed not to be humiliating in front of peers. You can also use this in a home setting. It is feasible and proper to take or send a child who is out of control, or about to become out of control, to your home "time-out" location until the child calms down and can behave acceptably.

    Time-outs are usually a form of mild punishment from the child's perspective, but most teachers and parents who use them do so as a relatively benign preventive measure to keep things from getting further out of hand. It avoids escalation of conflict, and possibly more serious punishment, when the child persists in an unacceptable behavior and does not accept your request or command to stop the behavior in question.

    6. *Isolation* is the technique of taking or sending children off by themselves when their behavior is obnoxious to you. In many families, if children are misbehaving at dinner, they are sent away from the table. Or children who are losing their tempers or being generally obnoxious are told to go to their rooms, for a specified period of time or "until you calm down" or "until you're ready to behave youself."

    Karin Krueckeberg, head of child psychiatry at Cook County Hospital, emphasizes that, while this is a technique initially used by the parent to control the child, the parent's language can emphasize the child's potential self-control.[14]

        "I like to point out to parents that going off to a room, while you simmer down before you lose you temper, is a technique that children can use for the rest of their lives if necessary—after all, it's something that we as adults use ourselves.

If we are losing our tempers or are too upset about a situation to think clearly, and don't want to respond immediately until we have regained control of ourselves and can think clearly, this is often exactly what we do. By using this method, it can be presented to the child as a means of learning a useful self-control skill, not just a punishment."

Dr. Krueckeberg recommends that if a young child is truly enraged and out of control, you use the "holding technique." Just hold the child firmly and warmly until the rage subsides. This is better than sending the child to his or her room, for three reasons: an enraged young child may have a feeling of disintegrating, and may need the safety of being held tightly; an enraged young child may be terrified of destroying the world, so the security of parental control can be very reassuring; and the child is protected from self-injury.

Strong Power Methods

Strong power methods are also based on the parent's greater power over the child. Parents have more power than children. For most years of their children's childhood, parents are stronger, earn more money, have more knowledge and ability, and have sharper verbal skills.

Though virtually all parents will on occasion use strong power methods, either to protect the child from sudden danger or because the parents lose their temper, we think these methods should be used very sparingly.

PHYSICAL POWER METHODS

Spanking, hitting, or shaking children are forms of physically coercive punishment. They are very limited in their usefulness because they basically say that a bigger person can coerce a little person, regardless of mutual needs. These techniques can backfire. They breed resentment, and teach the wrong message. Fear of parents is not what you fundamentally want to achieve. You want your children to learn acceptable standards of behavior, whether you are around to coerce them or not.

All parents will lose their tempers once in a while and swat. (We both have met some parents who boast they never spanked but usually on further questioning they said they never *meant* to spank so it was not their modus operandi.)

Because all parents occasionally lose their temper, using physical means occasionally shouldn't cause parental guilt. Everybody has lapses. We need to give up our wish for parental perfection, and accept our own imperfections without undue guilt, in order to be patient with our children and maintain our own self-respect.

What about spanking as a regular means of guidance? Both the American Public Health Association and the American Academy of Pediatrics have formally stated their opposition to the use of planned corporal punishment. There are some compelling reasons for this opposition. First, hitting or spanking conveys a very undesirable message to a child—namely, that might makes right. If you hit a child as punishment for disobeying you, it is illogical not to expect the child to hit a younger sibling. Second, there is a distinct possibility that the custom of hitting children as a means of discipline contributes to the prevalence of other forms of domestic violence. You will convey the message that, while hitting is not generally acceptable among adults, it is okay among those you love. Third, the parent who habitually and purposefully hits may be at greater risk of serious child abuse. Statistically, families in which child abuse and wife abuse occur are much more likely to be families in which physical punishment is a regular means of discipline.

Most important of all, *spanking doesn't work*. The best thing you as a parent have going for you is your child's *strong desire to please you*. If you spank, you run the risk of diminishing this desire because the child may feel angry and vengeful toward you, or lose respect for you when you hit, or both.

On the other hand, some authorities, like Forehand and McMahon, do advocate the cautious and sparing use of spanking as a backup to time-out procedures.[15] They suggest placing the child in a chair as a "time-out" and telling the child to sit there for three minutes, for example. If necessary, tell the child that leaving prematurely will result in a spanking. They claim that with this method it is rarely necessary to spank the child more than once or twice before the "time-out" chair will be adhered to.

Occasionally, you may be confronted with a situation such as a squirming toddler who needs your help in dressing, but is kicking or moving in such a way that it is impossible to dress the child. It may be necessary to say something like, "Look, you've got to hold still so I can dress you. I really don't want to have to spank you, but if you can't cooperate, I'm going to have to."

If you must spank, use only your hand, and only spank on the buttocks. Hitting around the face can be physically dangerous, and has another disadvantage; it impairs the dignity of *both* parties. However, if you do lose your temper and hit your child's face, it's not the end of the world. As soon as you calm down, apologize for hitting. Stress the "I-message"—"I lost my temper because I expected you to do . . . [whatever it was]. I'm sorry I hit you, but I still expect . . . [whatever it was]. I get angry when you don't do that."

Hitting a child with an object like a hairbrush or a belt is dangerous and never acceptable. Shaking children may *seem* milder than spanking, but actually is extremely dangerous, particularly in young children, because it can cause whiplash injuries which could be fatal.

VERBAL POWER METHODS

It's easy to think that if you aren't hitting children, you aren't hurting them. But words can hurt more than blows. Using "put-down" words like "clumsy," "stupid," "careless," or "bad" can make children feel very bad about themselves. This method can seriously backfire. Children may believe what you say, decide that they are hopelessly bad, and give up on trying to be good. This can have lasting effects on both their self-esteem, and on their wishes to please you and others.

Other words that imply that your child is losing your love can be even more frightening. Cold stares and "not-speaking" techniques can have the same effect. If children lose hope of pleasing you, you have lost your strongest tool in guiding their behavior.

Another non-recommended verbal power method is yelling. In the first place, unless it is used extremely rarely, it loses any effect. Of course, almost everybody yells occasionally to blow off steam. However, you could find yourself in a situation where you yell at your children frequently. You fall into this pattern: you make a request, the child does not do it, you repeat it, yelling. If this vicious circle is occurring, back off and look at what is happening. Your child is routinely tuning out any of your requests or commands the first time they are stated in a normal voice, which is the opposite of what you want to achieve. It is better to reduce the number of requests and commands, and make a clear distinction between requests and commands.

In general, a *request* to a child should be like a request to an adult—i.e., something you are *asking,* and you *hope* they will do, but if not, you will accept their refusal. On the other hand, a *command* ought to be something that you really mean, and are prepared to back up. Anne occasionally had to say to her children, "Look, I don't give many orders, but this one is an order, not a request." We both learned the importance of *being sure you have the child's attention* before making any request or command. Say the child's name, and get an acknowledgment; catch the child's eye. *Then* make your request or command.

A particularly dangerous form of yelling is the prolonged, loud, adult temper tantrum when a large adult hovers over a small, terrified child, screaming rage and insults at the child. Parents can easily underestimate how terrifying an experience this can be for a child, and how long the effects can last. Some parents feel relieved—"at least I didn't hit"—but Anne has seen adult patients in psychotherapy who still suffer from that memory of terror years ago. The child, recognizing that the parent is out of control, cannot know what to expect next. In many cases they actually fear that the parent is going to kill them, or develop the belief that they are so bad that they ought to be killed (and may indeed become suicidal later).

If you find yourself having an adult temper tantrum, *you* need a time-out. Back off as quickly as you can, and find a means to calm down. Go to your own room. Apologize to the child very briefly, and say you'll explain later. Call a friend, cry, have a cup of tea, or whatever works for you. When you are calm, tell the child that you want to explain. Pick the child up with a hug and reassure the child of your love. Explain that grown-ups sometimes have temper tantrums too, that you are sorry, and that you want to control your tantrums just as you want your children to control theirs.

You may also want to examine what triggered your rage. If it was a minor transgression on the part of your child, you can overlook it. If it was a serious matter, you have to convey two points: 1) the child was not responsible for your terrifying tantrum—you accept responsibility for that, but 2) the serious misbehavior of the child was the *trigger* for your tantrum. Don't let that fact go completely unacknowledged. Otherwise, your child may become skillful in provoking you into tantrums which direct attention away from the child's behavior.

Violence between siblings is one of the commonest triggers for parental verbal—and sometimes physical—violence. Their cruel or violent behavior itself is contagious, and often touches off strong feelings in us. Other common triggers are children spilling things, making messes, or acting "careless" in ways in which parents have to repair the damage. Cleaning up messes is hard and endless work, for which you don't get enough credit. If you feel unappreciated already, one more mess can be a last straw. You may need to get more help or more appreciation, or both.

Parental loss of control is quite common. *All* of the parents in an interview study of two-parent families reported hitting, and 90 percent reported yelling. Forty-three percent of families reported loss of control, which was defined as treating the child with a greater degree of physical or verbal aggression than the parent found acceptable.[16] However, no child is going to be damaged for life by an occasional parental temper tantrum, particularly if restitutive measures like those we recommended above are taken.

However, if you find yourself losing your temper often, and resorting to either verbal or physical violence, we think you need help, either practical or professional—or both. Such behavior means you are being stressed beyond your limit. Maybe you need to sacrifice some purchases and hire some household help. Perhaps your youngsters should be placed into a playgroup. Perhaps you need more rest and less isolation for yourself. Some housewives arrange to do some of their housework together to avoid isolation, or take turns taking the children for each other. Sometimes a treatable illness like depression causes irritability and a short fuse, in which case a psychiatrist can help. Losing your temper and yelling frequently at children is likely to be damaging to your *own* self-esteem, as well as your children's. You need some assistance for your own sake, not just your children's, if this is happening to you.

OUTSIDE CONTROL

Very occasionally, in extremely conflicted and dangerous situations with teens or young adults, guidance may be beyond parental control. You could need to use social supports including, if necessary, the legal system. Parents vary in their willlingness to do this, even when their youngsters engage in genuinely delinquent behavior. One extreme is to "let the child take his or her own medicine" and face legal consequences. The opposite extreme is to do everything possible to protect youngsters from the legal consequences of their behavior. We think a balanced approach is best.

There can be extreme situations in which police are needed for the protection of the youngsters, others, or yourselves. The fact that you need outside help in controlling their behavior doesn't need to mean the end of your love—any more than when you need outside help from a hospital to regain health when you have a serious illness. Using firm measures to protect yourselves while continuing to express love for difficult children requires some kind of counseling or support system as well. One example of a support system is the "Toughlove" approach, which may be useful in extreme situations in adolescents.[17] However, counseling for yourself—if not for the child—is necessary in such situations.

*   *   *

We can best summarize our socialization suggestions for parents with a brief list of *Do's* and *Don'ts*. *Do* model the behavior you want. *Do* decide which behaviors and rules are important. *Do* clearly communicate your expectations. *Do* make rules specific, understandable, and enforceable. *Do* reward good behavior. *Do* give the child a lot of earned and spontaneous praise (to balance the times you will be giving actual or implied criticism). *Do* strive for reasonable consistency. *Do* take a "time-out" yourself if you need one. *Do* use the child's desire to please you. *Do* acknowledge and encourage developing maturity. *Do* give choices when you can. *Do* listen to the child's "side of the story." *Do* make any necessary punishment fit the behavior. *Do* touch, hug, and cuddle your child and say, "I love you" often.

If possible *Don't* spank. *Don't* engage in "verbal spanking" (put-down words, threats, sarcasm, yelling, etc.). *Don't* say the child is bad (only the behavior is bad). *Don't* expect a behavior before the child is developmentally ready or able to do it. *Don't* be afraid of your child. *Don't* say "I don't (or won't) love you." *Don't* expect perfect consistency (or any other kind of perfection) from your child or yourself.

SOCIALIZERS OTHER THAN PARENTS

Play and Friendship

It is through play—first with the mother and other care givers, then with other children—that social relations with others begin. Play teaches children *how* to interact with others so that their needs are met, they can meet the needs of others, and understand the concept of sharing, giving and taking.

Young monkeys all need rough-and-tumble play with other young monkeys to grow into normal, healthy adult monkeys. Children need rough-and-tumble play too. It used to be thought that before school age, children needed only home and family, and not peers. We now know that parallel play (when two young children play in the same area, but independently, without much interaction with each other) is an important stage in developing the ability to play together mutually.

Play is an important socializing experience. Children are interested in other children and want to relate to them, even at young ages when they are quite selfish about toys. The experience can help them balance their selfish interest in wanting what they want, against the other child's similar interests. Children get both rough-and-tumble play and give-and-take experiences from playmates, and other children can provide this far more easily and naturally than parents or other adults can.

Thus, children from toddler age on need to play with same-age children for at least an hour or two a day, several days a week. This can be easily achieved at day care or nursery school or in neighborhoods with lots of children. However, isolated families need innovative ideas to provide friends for their children.

The Media

Books and magazines are still very important socializers for children, even in this TV era. Children love picture books even before they are verbally able to name the pictures. They love to be read to over and over again and may memorize their favorite books. Some even learn to read by connecting the printed words with the words they have memorized.

Feminists have done us all a service by pointing out how seemingly innocent children's books carry a picture of the world which parents may or may not agree with. Boys are portrayed as active and girls as passive in too many children's books. There was a time when all the children's books portrayed white children, or if they showed children of other races and nations, did so in very stereotypic and deprecating ways. In recent years, publishers have become sensitized to these issues, and more balanced children's books are available.

Older children's literature, like Grimm's fairy tales, for example, includes some frightening themes of witches, deaths, spells, being put to sleep by magic potions, and so on. Children often incorporated these frightening ideas into their nightmares. There was a period of time during which children's literature was "sanitized." It was made unduly cheerful, and even bland, in an attempt to avoid frightening children. It turned out, not surprisingly, that children had nightmares anyhow. Nightmares come from the normal fears and anxieties of childhood, children's learning to come to terms with their own strong emotions.

Today we recognize that even quite frightening themes in books can be good for children. They get the idea that their fears are not purely their own, and are given a language which helps structure their fears. There are also an increasing number of children's books which deal realistically with special problems children might face—like going to the hospital, parental death or divorce, and sexual maturing. Good bookstores and children's libraries usually have booksellers and librarians who keep up with this expanding and useful literature.

Many children enjoy books about people-like animals as much or more than books about children. Children can identify with animals as living things who are not humans, but have problems and feelings and goals and achievements. The fact that the central character is presented as an animal gives the child a certain freedom to identify or not.

Even in today's world with very sophisticated television productions, children enjoy the personal touch of being read to as much as ever. Reading is often the last bedtime ritual, as well as a wonderful springboard for discussion. As older children first learn to read, they often enjoy reading to a parent, or alternating reading different pages. This window to the world is still a miraculous one, not to be missed.

Preschoolers often enjoy making their own books, if you show them how. Cut-and-paste pictures from magazines, of the child's own choice, can be woven into stories, and the child can also draw pictures. You can choose with the child whether to write the story, or whether just to tell it. Now that relatively inexpensive Polaroid cameras are available, even quite young children can take their own photographs of things around the household that interest them, and with a little help make their own books out of their photographs. You can "bind" the book by stapling or sewing pieces of paper together—or by starting with a blank bound book or notebook.

Parents do not necessarily approve of some of the ways in which their children's horizons may be "broadened" by TV. A feminist might not be happy having her children exposed to a lot of sitcoms in which very stereotypic gender roles are portrayed. A sexually conservative parent may be very unhappy with the alternative lifestyles that are portrayed on TV. Almost everybody is concerned about the amount of violence, and the inference that violence is a standard means of solving problems. More than other media, such as books and magazines, TV portrays characters who are believable, and children often take what they see on TV as a realistic portrayal of life, rather than adult fantasies about life. Needless to say, this is a legitimate cause of much parental concern (see p. 594).

TV can also provide a variety of cultural experiences. For example, children can see a ballet or a symphony at ages at which they would have trouble sitting still in a symphony hall. On TV, they can watch but can also come and go. Thus they get introduced to concerts without having to sit still too long.

There is much that is good and much that is problematic about TV, and parents may find it hard to balance these things out. That is partly because television's role as an electronic baby-sitter is in conflict with its role as a window to the world. As a baby-sitter, it is used to occupy children's time and keep them amused when parents have something else they need to do. As a window to the world, parents can sit with children, looking out the same window as the children are, in order to discuss it with them. When parents are watching television with their children, or as a family group, there is another potential problem: one family member may want to converse, while another may want to listen uninterrupted.

What is a parent to do about TV as a socializer? Try to watch TV with your children when they are watching, so that if there is something portrayed that you like, you can expand on it, and if there is something portrayed that you do not like, you are there to say why—much in the same way that you can stop and discuss any issues that are raised if you are reading a book to a child. There is a lot to be said for a videocassette recorder, which can be bought for a little more than the price of a second TV set. With regular TV you have to accept what is broadcast on its own time frame. With a VCR, you can record programs. You can also rent a movie that you want to watch with your child. The wonderful thing about having the show on tape is that you can stop the tape to discuss something. This gives you the same control over TV that you would have with a book. It makes TV watching a much less passive experience.

Values: Cultural and Religious

We have another job—helping our children develop their values. Most organized religions have Sunday schools for young children and youth groups for adolescents. These groups provide wholesome social opportunities while making a serious attempt to translate the major values of the religion into precepts suited to the developmental stages of youngsters. This is a tremendous asset for us as parents, because it is very hard to do that entirely on our own. The Sunday school programs of major denominations have given as much careful thought to developing age-appropriate curricula as have educators in the better school systems.

Organized religious groups can be especially valuable during adolescence, when it is developmentally normal for our youngsters to expand their horizons and question parental values. To become the kind of independent adults which our society expects, adolescents need to be able to compare different value systems. However, since the separation of church and state forbids the school from providing any organized teaching of religious values, our youngsters may be left with few alternatives for learning values other than those of their peer group and the media.

Religions tend to be organized around the moral dilemmas faced by adults. How does one make sense out of the tragedies of life? How does one deal with the imperfections in others, or in oneself? In childhood, children should be introduced to a moral framework for resolving adult dilemmas, whether they face them yet or not. Of course they do face many of the same issues. Just like adults, children have opportunities for stealing, cheating, lying, and betraying or blindly following friends.

Sunday school is a socializer which can be a good antidote to the materialistic consumer-oriented or violence-and-revenge-oriented "TV model" of life. Some parents hesitate to use Sunday schools because as adults they do not fully believe in all the tenets of their faith and fear it is hypocritical to expose children to Sunday school if they are not believers themselves. Ironically, some of the same parents feel free to expose children to books and TV, when they cannot possibly fully believe in all the values portrayed in these socializers.

In times past, religious groups were an important part of the social system, providing support in crises, as well as ceremonies for life transitions, and added socialization for children. People belonged because they got something out of it, and gave something to it, whether they had the time, education, or inclination to critically examine the belief system or not. A majority of Americans still do so. Those parents who feel critical of belief systems in some religious groups (including the one you may have been brought up in) can "shop around" for a group for their children which they can accept enough to support. If you really do not want them to go to any religious group, at least consider other values-oriented group activities like Scouts or the "Y." As parents, you *can* teach values, but it is good for children to be exposed to other adults and peers who care about values and spend some time thinking about them.

Most holidays are either religious or patriotic in their original concept, and involve a celebration of an important event. In our country, most school systems celebrate Christian holidays and allow time off for Jewish children to celebrate Jewish holidays, but do not notice other major religions like Islam, Hinduism, and Buddhism.

Parents should help children appreciate why the day is designated a holiday. The Fourth of July is not about firecrackers; it is a celebration of the birth of our country and of a new definition of political democracy. Christmas is not just presents and Santa Claus; it celebrates the birth of a unique person, who commanded the reverence of many subsequent generations. Easter got mixed up with rabbits—a fertility symbol, an ancient pagan celebration of spring as a sign of rebirth—but it commemorates the terribly painful dilemma of someone who died defending his beliefs, and had a major impact on other people in doing so. Important religious holidays were designated to commemorate events that are important to adults. The form of the celebration is designed to get children interested so that at later ages they will have fond memories of the celebration and want to know more about its deeper meaning. Unfortunately, that does not always happen.

Other Organized Groups

School, of course, is the main outside socializing force in our children's lives. Indeed school is the only outside socializer which is required for children by law.

In middle childhood, groups other than home, school, and religious organizations become available to children. Athletic groups like Little League, and other interest groups centered around artistic, musical, or play activities, provide chances for social participation and in turn impart values to children. The very fact that these groups are optional, instead of compulsory like school, adds importance. There is a "menu" of such groups from which you can choose for your children based on their needs and preferences. And of course, as they get older, they will begin to choose for themselves. Optionally chosen group activities help blend the child's individuality with social needs and skills.

SPECIAL AREAS OF SOCIALIZATION

Sex

Early sexual experience, for the infant, isn't separate from the sensual, daily body care experiences of being cuddled, fed, and cleansed—and the seductive interpersonal experiences of learning to catch a care giver's eye and play games. The body's sexual apparatus works in infancy also. Tiny boys get erections when being bathed and cleaned, and sleep studies show that they get erections during dreams as girls get vaginal engorgement and lubrication. Linking these sexual reflexes up to sexual fantasies and later sexual experience is a developmental task which for most people continues over a lifetime but definitely begins in infancy.

By middle childhood most children masturbate in privacy, although some girls do not. Sex educator Jessie Potter[18] points out that care givers automatically encourage boys to handle the penis as a part of toilet training—when they teach them to aim for the potty instead of the wall! Girls are quite likely to miss out on comparable encouragement. Sex researchers as far back as Kinsey[19,20] have pointed out that some women do not discover masturbation until *after* becoming sexually active with partners, whereas the vast majority of boys discover masturbation as a pleasure in childhood, with increased frequency in adolescence. Harriet Lerner points out that many girls don't even learn the words for their genitals, like vulva, clitoris, vagina.[21] It is easy and natural to teach these words while bathing these parts of the little girl. A casual acknowledgment by the parent that it "tickles" or "feels good" when bathing the genitals gets across the message that sexual privacy doesn't mean sex is bad—on the contrary, it feels nice to have private pleasures.

Masturbation in privacy is an important part of sexual self-discipline. First, it feels good. Second, people who know how to please themselves sexually are better able to help their later sexual partners please them—leading to a better sex life. Third, it probably helps associate partner sex with love. Young adults who can satisfy their sexual needs themselves don't have as much need for sex with partners until they find a partner they love and care about.

Many children masturbate or at least clutch their genitals when anxious (just as others may suck their thumbs in the same circumstances). It's best to help the child identify and solve the source of the anxiety if possible. Common stresses include life events such as a new school, a new baby in the family, a move to a new house or other change in family circumstances, a parent's loss of job or return to work, or family problems like illness or parental conflict. The child may need extra attention and support to master such stress.

A child who hasn't yet learned the conventions can be gently told, "That isn't considered polite in public." You can offer to hold the child's hand, or hold the child during moments of anxiety.

Masturbation in public after early toddlerhood is likely to be a sign of some stress or problem. Some children from very liberal homes may do so because their parents haven't taught them the usual social conventions. A child who persistently masturbates publicly despite being taught conventional behavior needs some evaluative attention. Is the child under stress which hasn't been recognized and dealt with? Is there family tension which has so far been ignored? Is the child stressed by overstimulation, or bored by not enough to do, and not enough playmates? (Children, like adults, have fantasies while masturbating, and often the bored or lonely child enjoys imaginary companionship from masturbatory fantasies.) Is the child retarded?

Children's sex play with peers (often called "playing house" or "playing doctor") is normal for young children. Parents who are *very* bothered by this can usually distract the youngsters, but we think it's healthier to let them do it, and give them some privacy. A very few children whose sexual curiosity isn't satisfied this way may at a later age try to satisfy it with younger sibs or other children, which can be *seriously* disturbing to the younger child and must be stopped. On the other hand, if you happen to encounter your child and another child of about the same age and dominance involved in some sex play, and they both seem to be comfortable, our best advice is to excuse yourself to give them the same privacy you'd expect of them if they happened to come in on your sexual activity. If they do it conspicuously in front of you, the chances are they are somewhat uncomfortable with it, and are non-verbally asking for your reaction.

Parental sexuality and its effect on children have been the subject of much discussion. When Freud rediscovered childhood sexuality, and attempted to explain it to a Victorian society which was in some ways sexually repressive, it seemed logical to avoid overstimulating children sexually. It was believed, for example, that it was inevitably traumatic for children to discover their parents making love. It's easy to see that it *could* be upsetting to suddenly discover parents engaging in an activity that they can't or won't discuss with their children. And it is true that children can feel jealous or "left out" of parental intimacy—just as they can feel "left out" if parents monopolize the dinner table conversation, or have long phone calls with other adults. However, throughout most of human history, whole families have lived in one-room shelters, and it's obvious that occasional observation of parental sex must have been a part of the fabric of daily (or nightly) life.

Most adults want privacy for their sexual lives, and if children enter the room, will stop. If a toddler asks, "What are you doing?" it's simple enough to say, "Making love." If the child asks, "What's that?" you can either explain or offer to explain later, and attend to whatever need brought the child into the room in the first place. However, interruptions are distracting to most parents so you might consider locking the bedroom door, not to protect the children but to protect *your* privacy.

The best way to ensure your child's happy, healthy sexuality is to have a satisfying sexual relationship yourself. Neither of us advocates making a display of sex in front of the children, but warm, spontaneous affection like hugs and kisses between parents is a healthy thing for kids to see. There is nothing wrong with the child's seeing you go into your bedroom and close the door. A newspaper column listed seventh-graders' suggestions for parents' romance. The tone was pretty much "Go ahead and do it," and "Don't be afraid to tell us to get lost."[22] The kids wanted their parents to express their love and be romantic.

We are often asked about parental nudity. Family styles and individual feelings play a big role here. Some "experts" have told us that parents should parade their nudity in front of the children in order to help them grow up uninhibited about their bodies, and others have said the opposite—that parental nudity causes dangerous stimulation and should be avoided. For the most part, life is easier for children if their parents are pretty conventional. Our answer to the question, "When should I stop changing clothes or undressing in front of my child?" is the age at which you would feel uncomfortable in front of a neighborhood child.

Victorian advice about answering children's sexual questions was to tell them fables: babies were "left by the stork" or "found in a cabbage patch" or later "brought by the doctor" as medicine replaced midwifery. Today's standard advice is to answer questions honestly, in a way that fits the child's developmental level. There is the classic joke about the boy who asked his mother, "Where did I come from?" She told him an elaborate story about the birds and the bees, leading up to human sexuality, and at the end he said, "That's interesting. The boy in front of me came from Cleveland."

Today's advice about sex education is sensible, but not easy for everybody to follow. People usually talk about sex more freely with sexual partners than with anyone else. The same taboo that keeps the majority of people from sexually molesting their children may make it difficult for them to talk about sex with their children. Some parents need help in making the distinction between sexual talk with partners, and informational talk with children. The questions children ask about sex—and the answers parents give—are both age specific. We discuss these in appropriate age/stage chapters but wish to make a few points here. Children learn a lot about sex before nursery school. They learn about sensual pleasures, they learn about their parents' attitude toward sex, and they learn whether their parents consider sex shameful or not.

Wise parents answer their children's questions about sex in an age-appropriate way, giving accurate information and conveying the pleasure one can get from sex as well as the responsibility one needs to exert.

Some kinds of sex education may be more palatable to adolescents from adults other than their parents, just as they sometimes learn how to drive more comfortably from a teacher than from a tense parent. As they are beginning to experience themselves as young adults, sexuality and driving are both areas in which it can be uncomfortably obvious that their parents have many more years of experience than they do. Explicitly recognizing this, in some cases, makes them feel too much like children at an age when they are tenuously trying to feel more like adults.

In today's world, children get a great deal of sexual information from TV, movies, books, and peers. Their knowledge may be extensive, but spotty. There may be gaps in their knowledge even when they know many isolated facts. Putting this all together into a coherent picture of adult sexuality may be difficult for growing children. By middle childhood and adolescence, when they are eager to be seen as grown-up (but insecure about it), they may not talk comfortably about sex with their parents even if their parents are comfortable in talking with them. Their age-appropriate needs for sexual information are best met in a peer-group setting in which they can feel more equal.

We feel this is an area in which parents must bravely forge ahead even if they feel somewhat uncomfortable doing so. Sex is really without shame, as Yates states in her book, although people may do shameful or exploitative things in the name of sex.[23] Children should readily be *helped* to experience the pleasure of their sensuality and should never be made to feel ashamed of their bodies or feelings. If this suggestion makes you feel ill at ease, we suggest bibliotherapy. Read some of the sensitive and thoughtful books on child sexuality (see Suggested Readings and Resources). Try to get in touch with your own feelings about sex and remember how you were helped to understand your sexuality. If necessary, get counseling to increase your own comfort if your hangups are making you anxious about your child's sexuality.

Please do *not* think we advocate irresponsible sex or promiscuity. We don't. In fact all the evidence we can find points to what might seem paradoxical. Children who are helped to accept their own sexuality are more, not less, likely to engage in responsible, not exploitative, sex. Indeed, the child who is free to masturbate may be freer to defer entering the world of partner sex. The promiscuous young people we pity tend to be those who were not taught about sex or helped to understand the power of their sexuality—or who feel unloved or unworthy in other ways.

The other area we implore you to work through has to do with sex stereotyping. Many parents, even those who consider themselves enlightened, unconsciously expect their sons to be masculine (which to them means tough, manly, macho) and their daughters to be feminine (which to them means non-assertive, compliant, and deferential). Parents may be severely threatened by a son who wants to play with dolls (perfectly normal in preschoolers) though they are less threatened by a tomboy daughter.

Do all you can to avoid sex stereotyping. Remind yourself that most qualities stereotyped to one sex or the other are *human* qualities found to a degree in healthy people of both sexes.

Read books like *Growing Up Free.*[24] Talk to other parents and support groups and get counseling if you need it. But don't imprison your child's life by sex stereotyping.

Marilyn's grandson, who knows his grandmother is a pediatrician and who is cared for by a woman pediatrician, said, "I want to be a doctor when I grow up." He paused and added, "I have to be a *man* doctor." Perhaps his grandson will live in a world without sex stereotyping. Then our world will be one where all human beings can reach their potential regardless of their gender.

Aggression

Interestingly, most well-run nursery schools deal with young children's aggression more easily than most parents do in homes. If a child starts to grab or hit, a nursery school teacher will say calmly, something like, "We don't hit here," and if necessary hold, restrain, or distract the child from the fight. Usually the child is soon interested in some other activity. Because fighting isn't allowed to continue, fighting isn't modeled for the child.

At home, it is harder. Just as we parents "let down our hair" at home, children also tend to do so. They are more apt to use physical and verbal aggression, yelling, whining, and tantrums. Parents have a harder time keeping calm about these behaviors than nursery school teachers do, partly because more of these behaviors occur at home, and partly because we are more emotionally involved with our own children. Parents want children to grow up well socialized, and are terrified that the children may continue this kind of behavior for life if the parents don't do something to eliminate it.

It helps to remember that you don't want to *eliminate* aggression in your children. Rather, you want to help them deal with aggression and move into more sophisticated successful assertiveness techniques. Of course, adult bullies don't usually do well in life. But neither do passive "patsies."

Crude aggressive behavior in children is like the "baby talk" of assertiveness. It is the early step in learning a "language" of protecting oneself and solving interpersonal conflicts. Children eventually should become people who can stand up for their own rights and those of others.

No parent can stand a lot of raw aggression very long. It's best to convey: 1) respect for the child's strong feelings about whatever the problem is; 2) patience with the immature ways young children have in communicating those feelings; 3) gradually increasing expectations that children use words to communicate dissatisfaction and solve problems. In the meantime, use mutual assertiveness techniques or "time-outs" if raw aggression gets out of hand. Modeling is an important part of guidance, because the children *will* observe how you stand up for yourself and solve interpersonal problems, even if they can't do it that way yet. There are other methods useful for discharging aggression in children—or adults—such as pounding pillows. (See p. 586.)

Playful "pretend" fights and wrestling with toddlers and young children can be fun, and a good means of modeling how to negotiate instead of fight. This helps accept the playful aggression while gently helping the child structure and channel it into more mature expressions, and appropriate times and places.

It is interesting to watch other young animals, like kittens, engage in playful "fights" in which it is quite clear that this is play rather than war.

If we had our way, schools would also teach socialized "aggressiveness." Skilled teachers would hold age-appropriate discussion groups looking at issues that lead to aggression which every child confronts, like "How do you handle jealousy?" "What do you do when you're angry at your brother?" It's not enough for parents and teachers to say, "Don't hit your brother!" That's only one tiny piece of the issue. The far larger piece is how do people deal with anger, aggression, and jealousy.

Many times parents want or are advised to do their own fighting in privacy, away from the children. But as Bach and Wyden[25] point out, this deprives children of the opportunity to observe how adults resolve disputes maturely. *Serious* parental fighting (of predivorce proportions) is probably best done away from the children, if possible, as are fights about issues whose complexity children will not understand (such as sexual issues or intricate financial problems). But ordinary daily hashing out of issues, such as who is cooking dinner or why the bank account is overdrawn, can be helpful modeling for children. Also, it's very difficult to fight *away* from the children. In most households, any loud argument is likely to be overheard, and any ongoing emotional tension is likely to be picked up. Preschoolers and early school-age children are likely to make the assumption that parental tension stems from the children's own "bad" behavior. It is much better to explain candidly *why* you are fighting.

Sibling Relationships

Most children have siblings. Only 5 percent of the adult population were "only born" children. Each child—even one of a pair of identical twins—is different and is treated differently in a family. As Schuster says, "No two children are ever born into the same family."[26] By the time a second child is born, the family has changed.

Sibling relationships are very important ones. Children learn how to interact with others by interacting with family members. It's easy to understand why we talk so much about sibling rivalry. The firstborn child *is* displaced from a throne of unshared parental attention. Time with, and touching by, the parents both decrease. Rivalry occurs as a result of this competition for attention and the perceived loss of affection. Children between one and one-half and three and one-half years both feel and express sibling rivalry with a newborn which can include avoiding contact with the baby, verbally rejecting the baby, or even abusing the baby.

Most parents today are quite aware of sibling rivalry and prepare the older child by talking about the baby ahead of time and involving the child in preparations for the new family member. After the baby arrives, involving the older child in simple tasks and finding some time for that child alone both help to diminish rivalry. Wise family members and friends bring a "sibling" present as well as a baby present.

Most adults have affection for their siblings although some have little or no contact by choice and do not speak well of their siblings. Although people usually say it was something in adult life that caused the rift, it's quite possible that the real problem is unresolved, and perhaps unconscious, early sibling rivalry.

In the home environment, fights often occur between siblings. There are many reasons for this. An older child is likely to be especially intolerant of behavior in a younger child that was only recently mastered by the older child. It takes a long time for children to understand development. Children are *always* ambivalent about their siblings. Some children would be perfectly happy to have their siblings drop off the face of the earth although if it actually happened, of course, they would feel tremendous guilt and loneliness as well. In most cases intense rivalry in childhood abates and the bickering stops.

Parents can help by 1) accepting sibling conflict as natural, 2) making sure that it doesn't get out of hand, to the extent of causing bodily injury or severe verbal cruelty, and 3) finding ways to spend some time alone with each child.

When a mother is pregnant, the earlier child is likely to be fascinated. This is a good chance to talk about both the positive and negative sides of having a new baby. It *is* genuinely interesting to have a new tiny baby in the home, but it also is going to be a pain in the neck for the older child who has to share your attention. As in all life situations which can be anticipated, it helps to prepare children for this. Such preparation can be quite low key, just pointing out casually that, "Yes, it's going to be exciting to have a new baby, but you may not enjoy every moment of it. There are going to be times when I am going to be busy with the baby and we will need to find some other children you can play with."

Sibling love and admiration can be as real as sibling rivalry, and has somehow received much less attention in the literature. In families of three or more children, an older child may be rivalrous with the next but in turn quite nurturant to the one after. Younger sibs often admire the skills of older sibs and want their attention, even when they are treated rather rudely by the older sibs. Often the older sib will take some genuine interest in the younger one, especially when the older sib's friends are not around. The younger sib's wish to "tag along" can be very irritating to the older one, however.

In some situations, particularly if you are a single parent, you may genuinely need the help of the older child as a baby-sitter. Children often respond to these situations with good grace. You can be quite honest about the economics of the situation, the cost of hiring a sitter, and what the family would have to sacrifice to do that. Usually some payment to the older child who is sitting is a good idea. Be careful not to exploit a "too-good" older child whose own legitimate play needs may be forgotten. They would do better to complain a bit.

By the way, parents sometimes worry about having an only child. It used to be thought that only children were handicapped by the lack of sibs, but there is no evidence that this is true. Indeed, some studies have shown that the only child may have greater self-esteem and self-reliance than a child with siblings. Families have become smaller, so that many of today's children have no siblings. Our advice for parents of "onlys" is simple. Provide experiences for play and interaction with other children, starting from early toddlerhood. Also, avoid spending too much time with an only child. Parental attention is great, but too much parental attention can be smothering.

Child-orienting the Home

Child-proofing is a matter of safety; child-orienting, by contrast, is a matter of style and convenience. It means rearranging the household to *fit*, rather than camouflage, the fact that children live there.

Let us give you an example: Plastic cups and dishes, kept on low shelves instead of a high cabinet, can be reached by even a toddler. If juice is in a small pitcher on the lowest shelf of a refrigerator, and paper towels for wiping up spills are nearby, the toddler can take pride in getting a drink years before children in other families stop whining for help. Helping fix meals and setting the table are real sources of pride for toddlers. Unfortunately, many homes are arranged in such a way that the child is not physically able to help until well beyond the age at which psychological interest in helping has peaked.

We have some suggestions for child-orienting:

1. Put the daily dishes and cereal under the sink and toxic cleaning compounds high in the china cabinet which the child can't reach.

2. Keep silverware in a caddy with the dishes, instead of a high drawer, which in turn can be saved for the sharp knives.

3. Use oriental rugs instead of carpets. Anne's mother did as anything spilled would get lost in the pattern.

4. Child-orient only *some* rooms. (Marilyn and Anne both converted the dining room into a room-sized playpen with toys and a child-sized table and chairs for snacks and drawing. Marilyn used gates and a sofa to block the door between dining room and hall, on the one side, and the kitchen on the other, and did not purchase any dining room furniture until the children no longer needed a play room next to the kitchen. Anne more or less child-oriented the whole first floor, with gates at the stairs. Only the parents' studies were off limits.)

5. Provide easy, natural places for children to put things down or put them away. (Anne's youngest was spending hours each week searching for his shoes. She tried to get him to put them "away" in his room when he took them off, but that was too much trouble to be realistic. She had better luck in training him to always put them on the stairs as soon as he took them off—bottom of the stairs if he was downstairs, top if he was upstairs. It was a natural spot because he often sat on the stairs to take them off.)

A major source of conflict between parents and children is the organization of possessions, space, and time. Make it easy for the child to organize things. Provide low shelves for toys, and low hooks for coats (or baskets).

Stephanie Winston points out the awful nature of the usual "toy box."[27] Toys are hidden away from adult view. The apparent "order" hides the fact that the toys are jumbled so the child can't easily get the pieces together to play with them.

Don't buy a toy box. If somebody gives you one, use it for a blanket chest or for *large* one-piece toys like stuffed animals, or one large multipiece toy like a large set of blocks. (Beware of toy boxes with heavy lids.) Use separate boxes (dishpans, shoeboxes, or refrigerator boxes with lids) to keep all the relevant pieces of small multipart toys like Lego blocks together. If the boxes are transparent plastic, it will be easy for the child to find the toys. You want your children to learn that organizing toy parts and putting them away makes later play easier and thus benefits *them* not just you.

Parental time in small, frequent doses can help children put their things away—right after they've finished playing, if possible. We suggest a five-minute cleanup at bedtime and a longer time over the weekend to really get things into shape. Children, like adults, *hate* looking for lost objects. Help make it easy for things not to be lost. Try to have "a place for everything" which is *easily and logically related to where it is used or taken off.*

Coat storage needs to be near the door if you have much hope of getting coats put away. You can have several baskets for dirty laundry, one in the children's room or bathroom, if that's where they take the dirty clothes off. You need toy storage near the place the child uses the toy, or at least a temporary storage place: for example, baskets at the side of the dining room if children play in the dining room. Then at bedtime the baskets can be carried to the child's room if that is the permanent storage place for toys. Once again, if you use parental *brain* power to make organization easy, you need less parental *muscle* power.

Plastic laundry baskets in the hall are a good solution for winter boots, mittens, jackets, and scarves. The solid bottom of the basket holds dripping water off the rug and catches some mud—the open sides let air circulate enough for things to dry by the next day. This solution wouldn't work in homes with a small hallway—but even laundry baskets in the living room might be more pleasant than boots strewn all over it.

6. Keep the noise levels down! Noise tolerance varies among people, just as pain tolerance does. Many men in particular are sensitive to needs for "peace and quiet" at home, whether the noise is from infants' cries or adolescents' rock music. Many particularly bitter family power struggles center on attempts to get the children to shut up. Children being "seen but not heard" represents a rather authoritarian approach to this problem, but the noise of children does *not* go away by itself. Over the long haul, sound insulation can be cheaper than tranquilizers, or pitched battles and lost tempers.

You can use lots of things in your home to absorb sound: rugs, carpets, (both with the heaviest possible pads underneath), curtains and draperies, filled bookshelves rather than hard flat walls, soft surfaces and upholstery, plants all help. The principle is that sound reverberates when there are big flat hard bare surfaces. Sound waves are absorbed by anything soft, rough, complicated in texture.

One can use things that block the transmission of sound—such as doors that close, even if it is necessary to add cork and weatherstripping to the door. One can also use things that mask sounds—music of your own choice (as opposed to someone else's choice), air conditioners, fans, or running water.

The child-oriented lifestyle does not mean everything is a big mess. A messy house is not particularly good for children's developing sense of orderliness. The look is more likely to be comfortably casual, something like a summer cottage or a dude ranch.

Carol Eisen, a writer who applied a penetrating philosophical mind to the analysis of daily problems of housekeeping, pointed out that there are three values in housekeeping: ease, elegance and economy.[28] One can never have all three at once; you have to choose. One could have elegance and ease—at the sacrifice of economy—by hiring a good maid. One could have elegance and economy by working one's fingers to the bone—at the sacrifice of ease. Or one could have relative ease and economy by sacrificing elegance. We recommend the latter. Most of us have our children at a time in our lives when we haven't enough money to purchase much elegance anyhow. *And,* our children are guaranteed to prefer the child-oriented home to the elegant one!

Helping Children Deal with Their Problems

All children encounter problems in daily life, just as adults do. They will have fights with friends, experience hurt feelings, find themselves not doing well in either academic or athletic skills, or both. It's important for parents to learn to listen, and not be too hasty in offering advice.

The parent's goal should be to provide emotional support and encouragement to children so they can develop their own ability to master these problems. Parents can't solve their children's interpersonal problems for them, but they can do more by listening than by giving advice.

Some problems can be anticipated, and parents' greater ability to anticipate can help their children. Preparation for stressful events, like illnesses, deaths, or separations, as well as positive events that require adaptation (a new child in the family, changing to a better school, going off to summer camp for the first time) starts with telling the child about it. Sometimes parents wish to protect children from both stressful events and positive challenges. However, in children, as with adults, unexpected demands for adaptation can be more unsettling than expected, and even rehearsed, ones.

Some children will have or develop problems serious enough that professional help is desirable. Since all children have some problems, it can be hard to know when help is needed. You don't want to overreact and get unneeded help for a problem that the child will spontaneously solve, but you don't want to underreact and postpone getting needed help either. Comparing notes with other parents and discussing the child's behavior with teachers, pediatricians, and other adults who see your child in different settings are all helpful. Nevertheless, if you have nagging doubts about the normality of a child's behavior, it's wise to have at least a consultation with a mental health professional skilled in evaluating children. Parental "gut feelings" on these matters are very important. Conversely, if teachers or others persistently tell you that your child has problems not manifested at home, take this seriously. Children are often quite protective of parents and if they are having emotional problems, they may only display them elsewhere.

Parents can help encourage communication about problems by appropriately communicating some of their own. You should convey the idea that everyone has some problems in life, and other people can help. Show your child that friends and family can help by listening. Point out that adults use a whole variety of other helpers with special skills like lawyers, doctors, teachers, or counselors of various sorts. Convey that there is a continuum of problems and that problems, for the most part, are solvable. Tell your child that the key to the solution is talking about the problem, admitting you have the problem, and getting help for the problem.

Manners

Although the world now is a much more casual place than it was, manners remain vitally important.

The dictionary defines manners as polite conventions or polite ways of social behavior. We define manners as the delicate language of human communication—a language based on love, concern, and empathy—all human characteristics.

We're not hung up on where to place the oyster fork—we don't own oyster forks. But we do feel children who learn the basic social conventions are advantaged.

Human beings are complex social animals. Their polite conventions and social graces prevent people from hurting each other as they interact.

We feel manners start with an awareness and love of *self*. Until or unless this is present, there can be no genuine sensitivities to *others' selves*.

Table manners, thank-you notes, "pleases," and "thank-you's" are all ways of showing others we are aware of their selves, which mirror our own in wants and needs. These social graces can be learned gradually in moments of warm and sincere appreciation, not as a grudging burden.

Because the world is so complex and because parents never know where in the world their child will end up, we feel an important goal of parenting is to prepare children for any place in this complexity. Basic good manners are not an elite class concept; they are welcome everywhere.

We guess the best way to say this is that when you're "through" as a parent your child should be able to enter any door on earth and feel *comfortable* and self-confident. Unless your child feels at ease and comfortable, the social interaction on the other side of that door may not be smooth.

These may seem like old-fashioned words in an era of ultracasual interactions between people. Casual is fine—unless it becomes callous or uncaring. Human communication is too important to be left to chance and possible breakdown.

A Concluding Word

We've talked a good deal in this chapter about what parents should do because we get so many questions from parents about the area of socialization.

But we must point out a very important concept: *resiliency*. Even traumatic childhoods can result in well-functioning adults. Biology—the child's—plays at least as important a role in shaping our children as we do. And, further, mistakes that we make can be compensated for by many things in our children's lives including our own insights and changing behaviors. As Kagan says, "Rarely will there be a fixed consequence of any single event—no matter how traumatic—or special set of family conditions."[29] Stella Chess echoes this sentiment: ". . . we now have a much more optimistic vision of human development. The emotionally traumatized child is not doomed, the parents' early mistakes are not irrevocable and our preventative and therapeutic intervention can make a difference at all age periods."[30]

Do not despair of mistakes in discipline. Rather try to find methods that achieve the goals of socialization while preserving your sanity and your child's self-esteem.

SUGGESTED READINGS AND RESOURCES

Alexander, Martha. *Nobody Asked Me If I Wanted a Baby Sister.* New York: Dial, 1977.

A dear little book to read to a preschooler whose mother has had—or is about to have—another baby.

Ames, Louise B., with Haber, Carol Chase. *He Hit Me First: When Brothers and Sisters Fight.* New York: Dembner, 1983.

Ames gives a good discussion of sibling conflicts and how parents can handle them at different ages, although her book is a little thin on the positive feelings that siblings often develop.

Arent, Ruth P. *Stress and Your Child: A Parent's Guide to Symptoms, Strategies and Benefits.* Englewood Cliffs, N.J.: Prentice-Hall, 1984.

A useful book, especially for parents who have difficulty setting limits or for parents in specific stressful situations.

Bank, Stephen P., and Kahn, Michael D. *The Sibling Bond.* New York: Basic Books, 1983.

An interesting book covering many practical aspects of sibling relationships, not just day-to-day conflict, but concentrating more on the early years and discussing the positive side of sibling relationships.

Briggs, Dorothy Corkille. *Your Child's Self-Esteem: The Key to Life.* Garden City, N.Y.: Doubleday, 1970.

A wonderful book that analyzes the steps parents can take to help their child develop self-esteem and the missteps that can lead to lack of self-esteem. A classic—not to be missed.

Caney, Steven. *Kids' America.* New York: Workman, 1978.

Activities, projects, stories, recipes, etc., all uniquely American. A good way for a child to learn about this country and have fun at the same time.

Carlson, Dale, and Fitzgibbon, Dan. *Manners that Matter, for People Under 21.* New York: Dutton, 1983.

Suitable for sixth-graders and up through high school. Concentrates on important manners including—along with the traditional issues—contemporary examples such as how to get home from a party if your date is drunk, and how to write a letter to inquire about a Rolling Stones concert.

Dodson, Fitzhugh. *How to Discipline with Love.* New York: New American Library, 1978.

A sensible book that defines discipline, points out how counterproductive certain forms of discipline are, and teaches parents how to use productive disciplinary techniques. Don't miss the "Parents Have Rights Too" chapter.

————. *How to Parent.* New York: Signet, 1970.

A classic. Somewhat verbose but a helpful and useful book worth reading.

Durkin, Lisa Lyons. *Parents and Kids Together.* New York: Warner, 1986.

A fun book about having fun while helping your child learn.

Elkind, David. *The Hurried Child: Growing Up Too Fast Too Soon.* Reading, Mass.: Addison-Wesley, 1981.

We don't always agree with the author, but appreciate his calling attention to the "hurried child" in our fast-paced, complex society.

Ernst, Cécile, and Angst, Jules. *Birth Order: Its Influence on Personality.* New York: Springer-Verlag, 1983.

A highly technical but fascinating book debunking all our mythologies about birth order.

Faber, Adele, and Mazlish, Elaine. *How to Talk So Kids Will Listen and Listen So Kids Will Talk.* New York: Avon, 1980.

A good "how to" book dealing with optimal ways parents communicate with children. Scenarios and suggestions are both informative.

Gibson, Janice T. *Discipline Is Not a Dirty Word: A Positive Learning Approach.* Brattleboro, Vt.: Lewis, 1983.

The author uses the old-fashioned word "discipline" but she is quite modern in her approach to parental guidance of children from infancy to adolescence.

Ginott, Haim G. *Between Parent and Child.* New York: Avon, 1985.

A classic in that it was one of the first to teach parents how to use "I-messages" to children instead of the usual scolding or nagging. Somewhat dated in parts.

Goldsmith, Sharon. *Human Sexuality: The Family Source Book.* St. Louis, Mo.: Mosby, 1986.

A well-written, easy-to-read book on human sexuality in question-and-answer format. Can help parents' relationship with each other and help parents teach their children about the joys of responsible sex.

Gordon, Thomas, with Sands, Judith Gordon. *P.E.T. in Action.* New York: Bantam, 1978.

The all-time classic approach to warm, mutually assertive techniques for solving family problems and avoiding either a laissez-faire permissiveness or painful dictatorship (by parent or child).

Johnson, Spencer. *The One-Minute Mother.* New York: Morrow, 1983.

———. *The One-Minute Father.* New York: Morrow, 1983.

Both books are worth reading.

Joslin, Sesyle. *What Do You Do, Dear?* New York: Harper, 1961.

———. *What Do You Say, Dear?* Reading, Mass.: Addison-Wesley, 1958.

These two books use fantasy (and great illustrations by Maurice Sendak) to teach very young children what to say and do in common social situations. Great to read to preschoolers.

Kiley, Dan. *Keeping Parents Out of Trouble: A Modern Guide to Old-Fashioned Discipline.* New York: Warner, 1982.

A real "get-tough" antipermissiveness book. The author believes tough discipline is the key to happy children as it gives them confidence, frustration tolerance, and impulse control. We don't always agree but there are some useful suggestions for dealing with specific issues.

Kliman, Gilbert W., and Rosenfeld, Albert. *Responsible Parenthood.* New York: Holt, 1983.

A modern psychoanalytic look at the "six-year pregnancy" from conception through age five, encompassing both the biological pregnancy which produces the baby and the psychological pregnancy which produces the *person.* The book stresses *prevention* of psychological disturbances in childhood and later life.

Krumboltz, John D., and Krumboltz, Helen Brandhorst. *Changing Children's Behavior.* Englewood Cliffs, N.J.: Prentice-Hall, 1972.

A behavior-modification handbook. Many vignettes to illustrate the ways parents or care givers can encourage the behavior they want rather than behavior they don't want. Some useful hints such as setting an alarm for 1 A.M. in the front hall. The teenage daughter who makes it home by curfew turns off the alarm so parents sleep instead of waiting up.

Leman, Kevin. *Parenthood Without Hassles (Well, Almost).* Irvine, Calif.: Harvest House, 1979.

A series of essays to do with parenting. Not a "how to" book but there is a good chapter on teaching responsibility.

McCoy, Elin. *The Incredible Year-Round PlayBook.* New York: Random House, 1979.

A delightful book with suggestions for children to play (and learn) in the sun, sand, water, wind, and snow. An imaginative, clever book for parents to use when their own ideas about outdoor play have been used up.

Main, Frank. *Perfect Parenting and Other Myths.* Minneapolis, Minn.: CompCare Publications, 1986.

One of the latest in a series of "cute" books written to help parents deal with socialization. Big on natural and logical consequences.

Martin, Judith. *Miss Manners' Guide to Excruciatingly Correct Behavior.* New York: Warner, 1983.

———. *Miss Manners' Guide to Rearing Perfect Children.* New York: Penguin, 1985.

Guides to living with each other and behaving toward each other in a civilized way. Very person-centered. Some suggestions for children's behavior may sound a bit elitist but they are "right on" to prepare them for our complex world.

Nelson, Gerald E. *The One-Minute Scolding.* Boulder, Colo.: Shambhala Publications, 1984.

The original "one-minute" method of effective communication. Nelson's idea was adopted by Blanchard and Johnson for the one-minute manager, mother, and father books. The only hard part is staying within the time line when you are really angry! Every parent should read this.

Parish, Peggy. *Mind Your Manners.* New York: Greenwillow, 1978.

Very comprehensive—tells why having manners is important.

Pitt, Valerie. *Let's Find Out About Manners.* New York: Franklin Watts, 1972.

Provides understandable definitions of etiquette. This could be read to preschoolers or enjoyed by fourth- or fifth-graders on their own.

Pogrebin, Letty Cottin. *Growing Up Free: Raising Your Child in the 80's.* New York: McGraw-Hill, 1980.

An imporant book for today's parents who wish their children—both sons and daughters—to grow up free from the effects of sexism.

Rosemond, John K. *Parent Power: A Common-sense Approach to Raising Your Children in the Eighties.* Charlotte, N.C.: East Woods Press, 1981.

This book has a radical title but a rational point of view: parents are people. The author advocates that parents be "benevolent dictators," which he defines as being in control of authority tempered with "exercises in democracy," which parents gradually increase as the child grows older. The author is more enamored of the "well-done spanking" than we are, but the book is well written and thoughtful, although the author makes everything seem easy and implies that all children will respond to his methods.

Scharlatt, Elisabeth L. (ed.). *Kids, Day In and Day Out.* New York: Simon & Schuster, 1979.

An anthology of ideas, instruction, and innovations—all to do with children. Especially good sections on books for children and games children can play.

Schulman, Michael, and Mekler, Eva. *Bringing Up a Moral Child: A New Approach for Teaching Your Child to be Kind, Just and Responsible.* Reading, Mass.: Addison-Wesley, 1985.

A thoughtful, carefully written book by two psychologists who give workshops on a family-based program for moral development.

Sisson, Edith A. *Nature with Children of All Ages: Adventures for Exploring, Learning and Enjoying the World Around Us.* Englewood Cliffs, N.J.: Prentice-Hall, 1982.

A very informative book, though designed for teachers, camp counselors, etc., to show children how to learn about nature and our world. Parents will pick up many hints that can enhance the whole family's enjoyment of the outdoors.

Statham, June. *Daughters and Sons: Experiences of Non-Sexist Childraising.* New York: Basil Blackwell, 1986.

A wonderful, comprehensive, up-to-date book about gender roles and non-sexist child rearing. Well worth reading.

Stewart, Betty. *Growing Up Before Your Children Do: An Insightful Approach to Parenting.* Evanston, Ill.: Haven Corp., 1981.

Some insightful suggestions for parents written by a family therapist. Good chapters on troublesome areas like lying and cheating, which all children do at one time or another.

Trelease, Jim. *The Read-Aloud Handbook.* Wheaton, Ill.: Tyndale, 1983.

A wonderful book for parents who want to encourage their children to read books by reading to them—from the time they are born! Useful suggestions about reading aloud plus a 100-page bibliography of books suitable for reading aloud.

Tureki, Stanley, and Tonner, Leslie. *The Difficult Child: A Guide For Parents.* New York: Bantam, 1985.

A psychiatrist and the father of a "once difficult child" offers some useful suggestions for parents. We don't always agree with them but still recommend the book if you have a temperamentally difficult child.

Waitley, Denis. *Seeds of Greatness: The Ten Best-Kept Secrets of Total Success.* Old Tappan, N.J.: Fleming H. Revell, 1983.

Although this is a self-help book for adults, it's not a bad idea to plant some of these "seeds" in your children as they are growing up.

Weiss, Joan S. *Your Second Child: A Guide for Parents.* New York: Summit, 1981.

An interesting book covering many practical aspects of sibling relationships, not just day-to-day conflict, but concentrating more on the early years and discussing the positive side of sibling relationships.

Yates, Alayne. *Sex Without Shame: Encouraging the Child's Healthy Sexual Development.* New York: Morrow, 1978.

A book designed to encourage your child's healthy sexual development.

PARENT EFFECTIVENESS COURSES

Parent Effectiveness Training. Trained leaders conduct groups. Information about local groups may be obtained from telephone directories or by writing Dr. Thomas Gordon, Effectiveness Training, Inc., 531 Stevens Avenue, Solana Beach, Calif. 92075. Phone 619-481-8121.

STEP (Systematic Training for Effective Parenting). Information may be obtained from local community groups or by writing STEP/PECES Coordinator, American Guidance Service, Publishers' Building, Circle Pines, Minn. 55014. (PECES refers to a Spanish version of the program.)

How to Talk So Kids Will Listen: Group Workshop Kit. Adele Faber and Elaine Mazlich. Audiotapes, workbooks, and a leader's guide enable parent groups to conduct their own six-session self-led courses. Suggestions for followup are included. Information available from Negotiation Institute, Inc., 230 Park Avenue, New York, N.Y. 10169. Phone 212-986-5555.

Active Parenting. Developed by Dr. Michael Popkin. Videotapes, workbooks, and a leader's guide are available, as well as one-day leader-training seminars. Active Parenting, 4669 Roswell Road, N.E., Atlanta, Ga. 30342.

4

SPECIAL EVENTS
AND STRESSES IN FAMILY LIFE

Scope of Chapter

This chapter covers the special events in family life—both the joys and the jolts that life brings us all. We included this in Ongoing Issues in Parenting, because family life has a kind of rhythm. It oscillates between times which are pretty routine, and times when that routine is broken. Finding the balance between the two is an ongoing issue in parenting. Too much routine, and family life can become boring and disappointing. Too many changes too often, and family life can become chaotic and exhausting. Although none of us controls life's disasters, we *can* control the way we and our family deal with special occasions. We *can* start our own traditions. We can also understand what stress does to families and how to minimize its effect on us.

We will briefly discuss those happy special events of families and include suggestions for handling these in today's world when most parents are so busy. We cover birthdays, milestone ceremonies, outings and vacations, and special achievements.

Next we look at the darker side of family life. We list the common stresses inherent in all families as well as special stresses that befall some families. In each instance, we suggest ways to recognize when you or your family might need help and how to find it.

JOYFUL EVENTS

Birthdays

Some parents celebrate their child's *real* birth day—a new ceremony in our culture. What fun to pack a present for the new person you haven't yet met while you are getting ready to go to the hospital! Perhaps you will be allowed (or will smuggle in) champagne to toast this new, unique person you have created. Every time we think of the miracle of birth we get dewy-eyed. Never before—

and never again—will this particular bundle of human genes come together into a person. Also when we think of all that goes *right* in most pregnancies and births, certainly this new unique human being deserves a toast and a present!

Most of us begin to celebrate our child's birth twelve months later. Of course you'll buy a cake, one fat candle (and one for good luck!), and presents. You'll take pictures to share with grandparents and other relatives. And, of course, your baby won't appreciate anything—except perhaps licking frosting off his or her fingers.

We are both ardent believers in really *celebrating* each child's birthday. A birthday party, however modest, is a marker of each child's individuality. It notes another step along the road to maturity. It celebrates the growth and development the child has achieved.

Every child, even in large families, deserves special attention from—and time with—the parents. A birthday is one of these special times.

The custom is one child guest for each year of age for young children. Cake is a necessity, with candles to blow out and make a wish on. Presents? Of course. Special presents from parents and grandparents are customary, plus a gift from each child who comes to the birthday party. Each guest in return gets some sort of "favor" (party hat or snapper) plus a little gift to take home.

None of these favors has to be elaborate. A coloring book or small toy are both fine, depending on age. Marilyn's daughter's tenth birthday party in the month of May ended on a happy note when each guest took home a potted pink geranium. A package of seeds to plant would be another good idea in the right season.

We don't feel the elaborate productions with pony rides, magicians, etc., are necessary, but if you can afford them, and if it's your way of saying, "You're special to me!" to the birthday child—great!

You may not have money or time for a fancy party, but don't skip it altogether. Even if you're moving cross country at the time, buy a cake and cut it at a highway rest area!

Let your child help plan for the party. It's a great way to show children how we plan, how we make lists, how we decide what has to be done first (like order the cake), and how to remember important things (like writing a checklist with both candles *and* candle holders).

Ask the child what he or she wants for a present. Even if the child asks for the moon when all you can afford is a balloon—the fantasy is fun. Fantasize together. Tell the child what *you* want that you can't get—at least for now.

Let the child decide who to invite. Teach fairness—shouldn't a child who invites nearly everybody in the class invite the other two as well? Teach expediency. If you can only afford to feed and provide favors for six, explain why and help the child choose.

For busy mothers and fathers, party planners in many communities will do the whole party for a fee. Both of us left out lots of things we might (or should) have done with our children, but we always did the birthdays ourselves—because we *wanted* to.

As children get older the go-to-a-restaurant-and-an-event party becomes popular. You can get tickets to a hockey game or a popular movie or the circus if your child's birthday coincides (or comes close) to one of these.

Restaurant birthday parties can be a bit tricky. It's best to order one meal for all. Sometimes the restaurant provides the cake but often you must arrange to bring your own cake and candles. Most restaurants are happy to provide plates and forks.

Marilyn's son wanted his eighth birthday party at a special restaurant. He invited six friends to meet at the family boat. Marilyn borrowed child-size life jackets from her boating friends, and she and her husband took these somewhat rambunctious children to a waterfront restaurant noted for its crowded bar and *great* hamburgers. When the cake she brought was put on the table, all the restaurant's patrons joined in singing "Happy Birthday" and a slightly inebriated barfly gave her son a dollar, to his delight!

Holidays

Holidays definitely both enhance and disrupt family life. Where holidays fall on this scale depends largely on adults—but, alas, many aspects of holidays are beyond one's control. Our generic advice when things are beyond your control is simple. If you can't fight or flee, flow—just roll with the punches!

We will look briefly at the big holidays and offer our suggestions, which are, as always in this book, both parent-centered *and* child-centered. We'll point out the pitfalls and offer practical suggestions.

CHRISTMAS

Everyone knows Christmas is commercialized and hectic but it's still beautiful. It seems as though the whole world is decorated. There's a camaraderie that exists in late December that is never that intense at other times during the year. You feel it all over the world—in Mexico and Paris and London and Toronto. Christmas can bring people close together, which, God knows, we need.

Of course, we all get sick of the media hype and we both deplore the fact that the Halloween costumes are still on the living room floor when the stores fill with Christmas wrapping paper and Santa Claus appears everywhere. Also, some non-Christians feel left out at Christmas time.

Our parent-centered suggestions for Christmas, which can help make this a happy holiday for all, are:

1. Keep it simple. Joy does not have to be complicated. Children enjoy simple pleasures and festivities more than fancy ones. Actually, too many new toys or events all at once can be overwhelming.

2. Establish family rituals early. It gives children a great sense of continuity and contentment to know they can count on the fact that everyone's stocking

will be hung on the mantel on Christmas Eve or that everybody goes to Grandma's for supper that night.

3. Give your child the most precious gift of all. Teach the child the joy of giving. Help your child to make lists, plan, make, and wrap little gifts. Teach the child that giving a gift always implies some pondering of the wants, and needs, and tastes of the receiver. This pondering is a part of communication and your children will need these communication skills all their lives.

4. Involve your child in special family preparations like gift wrapping, cooking special foods, etc.

5. Work out family tugs-of-war about who goes where. A sad, but common, remark heard in our culture: "My son and the grandchildren always spend Christmas with *her* folks." Try to avoid falling into that trap. Learn the joy of alternating or bringing the whole extended family together (each family brings its own card tables, chairs, silverware, and dishes as a matter of course). If you live far from your extended family, invite other families or friends who live alone.

6. Don't expect too much from the children until they are grown. Children will act their age—or a bit younger—at holidays. Holidays are very stimulating, which wears young children out. Expect them to whine and act childish. Learn to whisk them away before the crying crisis happens if you can. If not, carry lots of tissues.

7. Don't expect too much of yourself! Stresses are always high at holiday time, probably because everybody is doing too much. Most people add the holiday tasks to their routine tasks. Whenever possible, *omit* routine tasks. (It took Marilyn many years to realize the time to clean house is *after* a party, not before!)

8. Let relatives spoil your children on Christmas. One day out of 365 won't make a difference.

9. Don't forget some self time for you and your relationship. Don't do everything for the children, so that the only pleasure for you is vicarious. Holidays are not just for kids; they're for parents too!

10. Last, but not least, don't ignore or forget safety rules. Holidays are a "danger" time. (See p. 163.)

FEAST DAYS

We're ecumenically lumping together Thanksgiving, Easter, Passover, and other holidays when the whole family meets to eat a special and traditional meal.

Try to avoid overburdening one family member. If everyone goes to the biggest house (which makes sense), divide up the food preparation and assign people to the cleaning up. Bring children into the preparation and helping as soon as they are old enough. Read books to young children ahead of time so they're prepared for the symbolism of the Passover or Easter meal and understand why we eat turkey on Thanksgiving. Don't expect too much of the young ones, but use the occasion to model and bring out good manners in older children and to celebrate "holiday best."

MINOR HOLIDAYS

Be prepared for some of the unexpected demands these holidays make on families. Your son may tell you on February 13 that he needs a valentine for every one of the thirty-six kids in his class or your daughter may tell you it's her turn to bring a treat to school. We both tried to buy cards and goodies ahead of time for this sort of crisis.

Halloween means costumes and trick or treat. We've both just about decided that between the dangers of children walking in the dark with masks on and the crazies who put cyanide in candy that today we would say "No" to trick or treating and substitute a home or school party instead. However, if this is still a custom in your neighborhood there are some simple precautions. Always accompany young children and only visit folks you know. Be sure the children are car-wise before they are allowed out alone. Check the candy before your child eats it, and discard anything that appears suspicious.

Ceremonies Marking Milestones

These ceremonies include First Communion, Confirmation, and Bar or Bat Mitzvah. All of them demand something of a child—arduous preparation for a Bar Mitzvah, for example—but give something in return. This type of ceremony tells a child, the family, the congregation, and the world that the child is maturing and has accomplished something. What a lovely kind of ceremony!

The guidelines for all milestone ceremonies can be the same. A simple party is all the child needs. If you can afford (both in *time* and money) the elaborate party, go ahead but remember the planning takes an emormous amount of energy.

We feel quite strongly that *manners* are important here. Every gift deserves a thank-you note. From the time the child is able to print his or her own name, the child should help with the thank-you notes. For example, a picture of the child with the child's own printing of the name can accompany the note you are sending to Grandma or Mrs. Jones.

By Bar Mitzvah or confirmation age, the child should keep his or her own list of gifts (you may have to show the child how), write each note, address it, stamp it, mail it, and check it off the list *before* spending any of the money or using any of the gifts.

Why make such a fuss? Rituals give us the opportunity to *focus* on giving and receiving, on the meaning of picking a gift, and the importance of acknowledging one. Don't miss this opportunity with your child. By the way, there are several good books on manners for children. (See Suggested Readings and Resources.)

A wedding is a beautiful ceremony marking the start of the most stable organizational structure in the world—the family. Every culture has families and, as far as we can figure out, has always had families.

Some preschoolers are asked to be in the wedding ceremony as flower girls or ring bearers. Explain to children *in advance* what they have to do, including wearing unfamiliar clothes, following directions, and being "on stage" in front of lots of people. Explain where you'll be at the end of the long walk down the aisle so the child won't be anxious. By the way, some three- and four-year-olds are too shy to accept the honor. Allow them to say no.

Whether to invite or take the children to weddings is a perennial topic in advice columns. Some weddings and some families are casual, cordial, and open. Everybody is welcome, even babes in arms. Their cries at a crucial moment bring smiles to all except perhaps the baby's mother, who may be mildly embarrassed. Some weddings and families are more formal and structured with a place at a table for only the specific guests invited. There really is no room for uninvited guests—even small ones. Let these differences guide your family both in whether to invite youngsters to weddings (and other ceremonies) and whether to bring them.

If you are invited to a wedding or any other formal occasion, unless the invitation says "and family" or names your children individually, we suggest that if you would like to bring them you always ask for permission to do so.

Theoretically a baby or child can always be brought to the ceremony in the church or synagogue, but ask yourself why you would want to do this. The baby won't remember it and might interrupt the ceremony by voicing his or her own legitimate, but out-of-place, needs.

There are young couples today who make a habit or tradition of *never* going anywhere without their babies. This may result from lack of money for sitters, inability to find a sitter the parents feel confident in, or a true desire to be with their children at all times.

We get a bit nervous about this for two reasons. As we said earlier, parents *must* pay attention to their own needs in order to be good parents. We worry about a couple that never go out for a meal alone or for a hand-holding walk or to a party with adult friends. Parents must develop too—their relationship and themselves. (See Chapter 8, Parents' Growth and Development, p. 285.) Also, children are often happier in their own house with a favorite sitter and a peanut-butter sandwich than at a formal dinner where the food is not to their liking and their squirming upsets their parents.

As both of us get older we appreciate ceremonies and acknowledge the "cementing" effect they have on families and relationships. Some blasé teen-agers scorn all the fuss about family dinners and milestone ceremonies. Later they often get more in tune with the cycle of life and the connections between the old and young, and find gatherings with extended families to be treasured occasions.

In summary, enjoy ceremonies—you *and* your children both. Teach your children the meanings of ceremonies. Teach them the joy of *connection* with their kin, teach them the manners of family life. Praise them for their endurance (a long dinner is tough on kids) but also recognize when they need a break and provide it.

Have fun—all of you!

Special Achievements

Graduations are important ceremonies. However, some children don't wish to attend. Usually they can be encouraged to get into the spirit of the occasion if you talk it up. If the child gets presents for a graduation he or she should write thank-you notes promptly (with your help for pre-writers).

School plays or athletic events in which our children participate are important. Always try to attend, even if it's only kindergarten and your child is playing a pumpkin with no lines. Anxiety is common on the big occasion, if your child has the lead in the play or is the team's star. This should be acknowledged, talked about (if your child wishes), and sympathized with. Incapacitating anxiety needs treatment, but usually rehearsal at home will help prevent it.

Outings and Vacations

The whole family is going to a restaurant, or the beach, or everybody is going to Disneyland for the family vacation! Everyone's going to have a great time, right? Not necessarily!

On the positive side, outings are likely to bring a sense of fun and adventure just because they are a break from the usual routine. Many trips and outings provide chances to master new skills, see new people and places, visit old friends and relatives, make new friends, and thus generally expand horizons. A friend of Marilyn's once said, "I love to travel because I can store up new memories."

Trips and holidays can be not only stimulating but also reassuring to the parents as the children are with them all day long. And it is always fun to share your children's exciting anticipation of an upcoming event.

We feel that it's important to foster a sense of family "togetherness" by doing things in which the whole family participates. But inevitably some family outings are less fun than anticipated.

Children of different ages have different interests and time-pace. It may be more rewarding to take a toddler and a ten-year-old to the Museum of Natural History separately. Both parents can take the children to the museum but split up with plans to meet at the cafeteria. Two-family trips with the assorted children of both families can be fun and there are more possible groupings for forays followed by a get-together.

It's ironic to find that a vacation—which is "supposed" to be a happy time for all concerned, often is just the opposite—and truly brings out much of the worst in the family. Parents may put a lot of effort and money into family vacations, and get complaints from the children instead of gratitude. Parents anticipate a rest but find themselves working harder than ever. They are busy settling quarrels between children (which tend to increase when everyone is in close quarters), tending to basic needs in unfamiliar surroundings, and dealing with unexpected problems—like car troubles and losing the family dog.

Some suggestions for *vacations:*

1. You don't have to go somewhere every time. Sometimes it's more relaxing to take a vacation at home. Explore short outings in your own community. Spend extra time with the children on projects you don't normally have time for. Spend the time and money you might have spent on travel on helping your daughter fix up her room, for example.

2. Consider separate vacations with one child at a time. A one-child-at-a-time vacation—even if it's only overnight—often provides a chance for deeper communication than is usually possible in the ordinary hustle-and-bustle of daily family life. Marilyn treasures memories of trips she and her daughter took to New York for an outing of theaters and museums. To avoid fatigue they did not eat dinner before the theater. They substituted a feet-up-on-the-bed picnic in their hotel room with yogurt, fruit, cheese, etc., purchased at a nearby deli. The kind of conversation a parent and child can have when they are out of their family setting and therefore out of their usual roles is remarkable.

By the way, outings with one child at a time should not just occur at vacations. Families today have a tendency to "mash" the family together (it's easier because you know where everyone is). However each child is unique and has a unique relationship with each parent. All of you will profit by time spent alone with each other. This can be a walk, a quiet game, or a shopping trip, as well as a special vacation together.

3. Start planning early so there's time for everyone to share ideas on how each one would like to spend the family time and money. The discussion itself can be part of the fun. Learn what each other's vacation fantasies are. Whatever you plan, don't make it such a tight schedule that everyone is exhausted and there is no time for rest or impulsive side-trips.

4. Make lists of what you plan to take. Teach children to make their own lists. Even prewriters can tell you what they plan to take so you can write their list for them.

The children have to know the rules. For example, if you're all flying somewhere, you will all travel light. Even a three-year-old can be helped to understand there's no room for a tricycle in a suitcase.

5. One of the older children can be taught to keep a travel diary as you go along, listing places you stopped at, and so on.

6. Loading and unloading the car, keeping track of one's own possessions, not wandering off, and obeying safety rules are all to be expected of children in age-appropriate ways.

Some suggestions for *eating in restaurants:*

Family restaurant meals should always be fun, right? After all, nobody has to cook or clean up, and everyone gets a chance to eat something of his or her choice. Not always! Unfortunately, restaurant meals can turn into a horror, with crying children, spilled milk, and parental indigestion.

The trick to eating out with children is to pick the right kind of restaurant. This doesn't just mean McDonald's, although we have to admit that McDonald's caters nicely to the young. The food is ready quickly and there are places for the children to play while they are waiting.

For those parents whose palate demands a bit more than fast food, what do we suggest? In most communities there are restaurants that will serve children reasonably quickly. Sometimes these are neighborhood bars with limited menus but the hamburgers are usually good. "Family" restaurants need to be checked out in advance. Some of them—even those famous for catering to kids—have quite slow service. Cross the slow-service restaurant off your list even if they have children's menus.

Marilyn didn't figure out how to solve the Sunday night "Where are we going for dinner?" dilemma until just before the children went off to college. Instead of arguing about who wants to go where, give each person (parents included) a turn. Mom picks tonight, Sally next Sunday, and so on. No griping when it's not your turn.

There are a couple of tricks we always used. If the child is really hungry, ask for crackers or rolls right away. Marilyn never left the house to go to a restaurant without something in her purse that would keep the kids busy. She always carried crayons and some paper (although the back of a place mat works fine). Our children were also initiated quite early into word games such as Ghost and Botticelli (sometimes called Buddha) in order to keep them occupied. Marilyn's family played a version of Twenty Questions in which the person whose turn it was had to give the letter something began with and the color it was. When her son was about five he said, "I'm thinking of something that begins with 'P' and comes in black and white." He stumped everybody. The answer was "People"!

When do you let children order from the menu? They have to be able to read—both words and *prices*, as most of us do not care to have our kids order caviar and lobster too frequently. We feel children should be encouraged to choose and to explore new foods, but some of you may feel more strongly that they should order what they will eat.

Travel with Children

Car travel is a problem with some babies and children who are prone to motion sickness. Because so many of us spend so much of our lives in a car, it's a good idea to recognize that the child has this problem and use Dramamine. We have seen parents who are so against drugs that they refuse to use anything, but Dramamine can make the difference between a miserable child in a smelly car and a happy child in a clean car. It may make the child a little sleepy but it doesn't matter—the child's not driving. Dramamine is given half an hour before the car trip and you should feed the child lightly. For children over two follow directions, for babies under two ask your doctor.

Most of us learned to keep little bags of things the children can do in the car to keep themselves amused. Puzzles, games, coloring books, and crayons are all good. A clipboard with paper, self-adhering stickers, a tape recorder with cassettes of familiar songs, cards, and small books are all fun. It's also a good idea to take pre-moistened towels and plastic bags for organizing games and for litter.

As soon as the children are old enough, teach them how to read maps and guidebooks. Let them pick out the interesting side-trips, calculate mileage, decide what town will be "there" at lunch time, etc. By the way, when they're old enough to want their own music, we suggest headsets. Marilyn had a rule of no eating in the car unless absolutely necessary. Yes, eating keeps the kids quiet, but it makes a terrible mess. Anne handled this problem by packing non-sticky food and beverages. We suggest taking water to drink, especially if it's summer. Boxed juices with straws are also good. Besides, we think it's better to stop every two or three hours to let the kids get out to play. You can all eat then. We also believe in exercise for the kids every time you stop. All of you can jog around the rest stop or parking lot (be careful of cars). You can also stop at municipal parks or pools.

Further travel hints include: Be sure to count heads after every stop. We suggest driving early or during nap time. Another trick is to pick motels with playgrounds and pools. Picnics, instead of restaurants, are fun and give the child more running-around time.

Airplanes are a great way to travel with a child. Marilyn remembers carrying her six-week-old baby along with the diaper bag, flight bag, and pocketbook. When she put all of this down to change the baby in an airport restroom it was difficult to get loaded up again. However, the trip was over in a few hours and she thought to herself, "How much easier this was than it would have been by covered wagon!"

The toddler taking his or her first plane trip should be told what to expect (seat belt, noise, etc.). Don't forget the child's own flight bag with a favorite book, toy, and snack. Be careful about airplane food, which is often very hot. Bring a safe snack to use when peanuts are handed out.

Parents often ask us about ear pain. Seasoned travelers learn how to clear their eardrums by swallowing hard or chewing gum when the plane is changing altitude. Usually ear pain will occur on landing rather than on takeoff, although young babies often cry on takeoff because of the noise. A wise mother will nurse or offer water or formula to the baby when the captain turns the seatbelt sign on for landing.

Motion sickness on planes can usually be handled easily by Dramamine. If you have children that sometimes get sick in cars, they may or may not get sick in planes, so it's worth waiting to see. However, children who suffer from severe motion sickness in cars will probably need some Dramamine in planes as well. This should be given a half hour before boarding the plane.

What about the screaming baby that simply won't be comforted? Marilyn once put a few drops of scotch in her baby's milk with a little sugar added to make it palatable. It worked. You don't need a prescription, and scotch is usually on board.

By the way, children suffer from jet lag, too, although sometimes because babies sleep and eat on demand rather than on a routine basis, it may be milder than their parents' jet lag.

If you have any questions about children traveling alone on airplanes, there is a good booklet "Fasten Your Seat Belt" (available from Cowles Syndicate, Inc., P.O. Box 4994, Des Moines, Iowa 50306-4994) which tells you how to prepare your child for independent air travel. Marilyn's daughter went by plane alone to visit her grandparents when she was eight. Her brother decided to do the same when he reached that age, as did Anne's children. It's a good way to give a child a little dose of independence.

Parents often ask about foreign travel. How do I find out about shots for my child? What shots are safe? Where is the water safe? How do you know when food is safe? How do you know when milk is safe for the baby?

Our federal government has published a good book on immunizations for foreign travel.[1] Shots necessary for foreign travel to developing countries may give a baby or child some fussiness and fever, but these reactions are usually mild.

Smallpox vaccination is no longer needed for many countries. However, there are still some countries that require proof of smallpox vaccination, which means that your baby will have to have be vaccinated.

Most travel agents will tell you where water and food are safe, because customers who come home sick are not likely to travel with that agent again. When in doubt, in the case of a very young baby, we would recommend taking a food supply. Breast milk is perfect and prepared formula is easy to transport, although you will have to boil the water. A portable instant coffee boiler makes this easy—one with adapters for international electrical outlets.

Hygienic conditions vary and, even in reasonably civilized countries, may not be very good. Dairies are often not as clean as the ones here. If you are on a short trip, you may want to let your children switch to bottled carbonated beverages and catch up on milk when they get home.

Marilyn took her small children to Mexico many times. They were instructed not to drink any water but bottled water. Bottled water was even used for brushing teeth. Milk, raw vegetables, unpeeled fruit, and "street" food (for example, shaved ice with syrup) were avoided.

If you are going to *live* in a Third World country, be sure you immunize your child before you go (or make arrangements to do so there if your baby is too young). In addition to regular immunizations, your child may need special shots, like typhoid, typhus, yellow fever, etc. When you are going to such a country, an injection of gamma globulin just before you leave is somewhat preventive against one form of hepatitis. Ask your doctor.

By the way, check with your child's doctor and take medicines you may need when you are abroad. An antibiotic to prevent or treat traveler's diarrhea *(turista)* is a good idea along with Pepto-Bismol, which also can be helpful. Marilyn always carries aspirin or acetaminophen, Dramamine, Benadryl, antibiotics, bacitracin ointment, Tums, Band-Aids, Ace bandages, steroid cream, and sunscreen, plus whatever specific is needed, such as antimalaria medicine in endemic areas.

Leaving the Children Home

Most parents want a vacation from the children once in a while. Also, these days, many parents are required to travel in their business or professional careers.

We are both strong believers in couples finding time alone together to concentrate on their relationship. Yes, this means leaving the children at home occasionally. Every couple must make its own decision about when to leave the children, where, and with whom. Many mothers, either because they are breast-feeding, concerned about whether they should leave an infant with a sitter, or so much in love with their new baby they don't want to leave, do not consider vacations away from home for the first year. Or the couple takes the baby with them on vacation and arranges for sitters at their destination so they can have a dinner or two out.

There is nothing wrong with leaving a young infant for a few days if the parents—or a single parent—must be away. The ideal is a sitter or grandparent the baby is familiar with, in the baby's own home. Taking the baby to Grandma's house is a bit more disruptive but many babies do quite nicely. During the stranger anxiety months (see p. 395), it is wise to have the sitter spend time with the baby before the parents go.

Older children whose parents travel a good deal often prefer college-age sitters. Marilyn often asked medical students or nurses whom her children knew to move in while she and her husband were gone. She restricted vacations with her husband to a week or two until the children were in their early teens. Also, for every vacation alone, Marilyn spent a vacation with the children.

By the way, young career couples today often have to do a fair amount of business travel. The ideal is to arrange their schedules so one parent is in town when the other is gone.

We are very firm believers in "reaching out to touch someone" very frequently when a parent is away a lot and the "someone" is a young child, even one too young to talk. Marilyn called several times a day to tell her children where she was, what she was seeing, and to ask what their day was like. She also sent a daily postcard or letter and always brought home trinkets and special presents from the city or country she was visiting.

JOLTING EVENTS

Catastrophes

Family life can be devastated by a catastrophic event such as a death, learning of a fatal illness, or the birth of a defective baby. Divorce and job loss—or not being able to find a job at all—fall in the non-lethal, but definitely catastrophic, category. Some homes are devastated by a fire or natural disaster.

All of these events affect the persons involved *and* the family. We all have ties to our family members that make us value them and want to help them (these are important in an evolutionary sense as such ties encourage us to support our family to maintain our gene pool). This means that the illness or sadness of a family member will deeply affect us.

Children are *always* affected by these jolts. The important principles to remember are to tell them what is happening, to be honest with them, to allow them to express their feelings, and to recognize that children do not always show grief in the same way we do. Indeed, children may appear to breeze through a death in the family only to have their reaction affect their school performance or peer relationships down the line.

When we suggest how to parent-proof your life (see p. 23), we point out how important it is to care for yourself so that you have the strength to parent. Try to remember this advice, if you are unfortunate enough to have a catastrophe occur.

Moving

One "jolt" to everybody, that is especially hard on children, is a *move*. Even a move to a new house in the same town is stressful, a distant move more so. A move to a new school district ranked as a high stress in a study of school children.[2]

Next to a death in the family, moving is probably the most traumatic event to befall a child. Children—sometimes without knowing when or why it is going to happen—suddenly are taken out of their own room, their familiar surroundings, their neighborhood, their school. They can't see their friends anymore.

This is a big loss. The child doesn't necessarily appreciate that the family is moving to a bigger house or that a parent has received a big promotion. The child just experiences the loss.

Some families must move frequently. Parents in such families should learn to roll with these stressful punches and help their children to follow suit. Other families have relative stability, which means, if a move comes, no one is prepared for it.

Marilyn's children had lived in one house all their lives. They were both quite jolted, at ages seventeen and nineteen, when their parents moved across the country. Marilyn's son graduated from high school before the move and started college in the new state. Many think that this is a good time for a move. Marilyn and her son disagree. It meant her son had no friends at home when he came back from college and very few ways of making friends during vacations. Both children still feel a bit "homeless."

Although we are far from moving experts, having each done it only once since we were married, we do have some suggestions for parents and for children. Everyone tells you to make lists. Marilyn suggests that the first list be what you *don't* have to take with you. Some things can be sold (garage or moving sales glean an amazing amount of money), others given away, and lots of junk should be *thrown* away. It's ridiculous to pack, move, and unpack junk. Don't ever close a carton without labeling it—and not just "pictures" but "framed photos of kids from Bill's study."

Do as many of the recurrent things you have to do—like dentist and doctor appointments—*before* you leave. That means you have time to find new professionals to take care of you. Don't forget to take your *old* address book and a telephone book (including yellow pages) from your old city. Then if you need a finial for a favorite lamp you bought in Old City, you can call or write that shop. Get all records (schools, doctors, etc.) before you leave and pack them in a safe, retrievable place.

As for the children, there are two schools of thought. Many will advise you to move, if you can, at the end of the school year so your child can start in fresh and make new friends. However, this can lead to a lonely summer as it's hard for children to make friends in some neighborhoods outside of school. Some feel moving *during* the school year helps your child adjust to the new school and neighborhood. If possible, show your child the new house and school before you move.

Prepare your children for the move. Even two-year-olds can be introduced to the concept when you read them children's books about moving. Make the new environment look as close to the old one as possible. This is *not* the time to buy a new crib. Move the old one. Take a flight bag on moving day with your child's favorite toys so they're available before the movers come or before you unpack.

Warn your children far in advance about the move and, if possible, take them to see the new city and house. Let them keep in contact with old friends and arrange for visits if possible. (Teach them to keep their own address book and phone numbers. Some long-distance calls to old friends are worth the cost.) Involve them in the packing and moving and unpacking and let them decorate their new room.

We have been talking about long distance moves in pretty stable families. Things can be worse when a divorce or death is involved. It can also be rough when family fortunes suffer reversals and the child moves to lesser material comforts than in the past. However, children are resilient, especially if they see their parents bounce back.

Any move, even to a house around the corner, can be disquieting to a child. Preverbal children are often quite upset on moving day and afterward. Not only their routine, but their familiar surroundings are gone. If possible, have someone familiar stay with the baby on moving day and set up the baby's crib (with its same toys and covers) first thing.

By the way, another stress to the family that falls in the category of good, rather than bad, news is a promotion at work. Even when no move is involved and there is a substantial raise, the family can be stressed. The parent generally has more responsibility and often will spend more time at work. Alternatively, the parent spends lots of "home time" worrying about the new duties and whether he or she is doing a good job. This means there's less time for family. Almost always this sorts itself out but remember, if you or your spouse get a promotion, some family stress may be expected.

FAMILY STRESS

Stress Is Part of Everyone's Life

Stress is a part of every family's life, even though not all of us will have all of the same stresses, or necessarily any of the worst ones, and few of us will have severe stress all of the time.

Stress is acknowledged to have a relationship to psychiatric and medical illness. *Anything* that poses any adaptational demand is stressful. Thus, things that we think of as bad events (like a death or losing one's job), and things that we normally think of as good events (like the birth of a new baby or a promotion at work), are all stresses. Divorce is a stress, but so is marriage, because both events require *changes* in lifestyles, giving up some old ways of doing things and learning some new ways of doing things.

Life without any stress is an impossibility. Also such a life would be non-productive, and probably rather boring. A little stress is good. We need to "rehearse" our physiological responses of flight and fight to be ready for a big stress if it comes. It is when we experience lots of stress without any breather that we are adversely affected.

The effects of stresses build up over time. A few stresses can be challenging; more can be tiring, and too many, overwhelming. Holmes and Rahe developed a well-known scale of major life events to which they assigned point values.[3] There is a statistically significant relationship between such events in people's lives and the risk of coming down with a physical or mental illness within the following year or two.

Life events in four groups of children were studied by Coddington.[4] Teachers, pediatricians, and pediatric mental health workers were surveyed and asked to rank a child's adjustment to a list of life events which could occur in childhood. As would be expected, death of a parent, followed by divorce and separation of parents, ranks highest. Serious illness or death in a sibling and birth of a sibling were lower but still high. Near the bottom was loss of a job by a parent and change in parents' financial status.

Recent research has come up with a Hassle Scale. The Life Events Scale doesn't take into account how well people *cope* with the life event—but just adds them up. Further, the scale doesn't help us understand how events translate into daily living. More important, life events emphasize the impact of change. Lazarus[5] points out that stress also comes from chronic, unchanging situations like a poor relationship, loneliness, boredom.

Hassles also have an impact on physical and mental health based on their frequency, duration, and intensity. The way people reporting their hassles react to them is probably of prime importance. Lazarus says, "Psychological stress resides neither in the situation nor the person; it depends on a transaction between the two. It arises from how the person appraises an event and adapts to it."[6]

Some of the hassles described by middle-age respondents included concern about weight, health of a family member, rising prices, home maintenance, too many things to do, misplacing things, yard work, investments/taxes, crime, physical appearance. The hassles differ in different groups so college students provide a different list. Hassles correlate better than life events with health outcomes, especially short-term outcomes.

"Uplifts" were also tabulated. These are pleasant or satisfying experiences, like relating well with important people, feeling good, getting enough sleep, completing a task, etc. They serve as rechargers when our psychological batteries are run down. However, the study did *not* show that uplifts buffered the negative effects of hassles to the degree predicted, especially in women.

Sometimes when Marilyn and Anne were feeling overwhelmed we would add up our *own* units on the Life Events Scale. It was comforting to realize we had a right to feel so overwhelmed when we scored high! In fact, people should learn to respect that feeling of being overwhelmed. It is nature's way of telling us to avoid any further stresses in our lives until we have coped with the ones that are bothering us now.

When we are already stressed, even the smallest of stressful events can cause us to blow up, lose our tempers, or otherwise react strongly. Folk wisdom refers to "the straw that broke the camel's back." Others may think we are overreacting, particularly if they have no knowledge of where we're at in our lives. They may not be as sympathetic as we would like them to be. Worse than that, we may not even be sympathetic with ourselves. ("It's terrible for a grown-up to make a big fuss over such a small issue.")

Stress is built up by discrete units. Remembering this can help us preserve our self-esteem by recognizing that we are not overreacting to the last small stress, but rather reacting normally to the whole batch of them.

Sometimes we can explain this to other people and get needed support and sympathy. Sometimes we can feel our breaking point approaching, and should do everything in our power to reduce our stress. Even fairly small children can understand that we're frazzled and need to be left to ourselves for a while.

Common Stresses in Family Life

Some stresses in family life come from children's normal development, and the demands that poses on us.

Infants can stress us with the totality of their demands, frequent feedings and diaper changes, and the sleep deprivation they cause in us. *Toddlers* can stress us by getting into things, and exposing themselves to dangers so that they need constant watching. *School children* can stress us by being big enough to take care of themselves, but not always doing so. They are smart enough to talk back, know our weak spots, and purposely make us angry. They can also stress us by not achieving in school. *Adolescents* can stress us by demanding more freedom and independence than we feel they are ready for. Particularly in early adolescence, they can stress us by being critical of us, our lifestyles, and our parenting techniques. *Adult children* can stress us by being so autonomous we never hear from them—or conversely, by being dependent on us after we thought they were old enough to take care of themselves.

We all have *worries* as a constant background for stress. Money can be a problem. Unemployment can severely stress the entire family. There are common stresses in everyone's family life, like relationships, in-laws, mealtimes, sick children, or kids who are acting up.

One of the common worries of couples is fighting in front of kids. One school of thought holds that parents should *never* allow their children to see any marital discord. This is obviously impossible. But even if a couple *could* hide all their feelings and appear to agree all the time, they would be modeling a totally unrealistic view of marriage. They would also not give their children the opportunity to see models of inevitable disagreement and how they are resolved between two adult people.

We suggest really heavy stuff not be discussed (or argued about or fought over) in front of the children—or in front of anyone else, for that matter. A public place is not appropriate for private issues. On the other hand, it has been suggested that the couple who never fight in front of the children but split anyhow add an element of "they don't have any reason to get a divorce" to their children's burdens. Real violence (including vicious screaming and name calling) upsets children.

All of us have spats with our loved ones. Most of the time these occur when one or both partners is tired or frustrated. We both have found that if we have the strength to take an internal "time out" to ask ourselves "what's really bothering me, and how can I reduce the tension I feel?," spats can often be avoided. If the children see you bickering, let them also see you kiss and make up. You can even use your fight as a lesson by explaining that the fight would not have occurred if you were in touch with your feelings and took your "time out" before you opened your mouth.

Sometimes in the pressure of busy family life there's not enough attention to go around. Everybody knows about sibling rivalry, especially with younger children who usually need and get more parental attention than the older child. Parents also have rivalry with their children. Fathers often feel envy of and rivalry with their new baby, who takes too much of the mother's attention. But children also feel rivalry with parents who take time and space with each other away from the children.

Oedipal rivalry is the term that is given specifically to the little boy's envy of the father's special and sexual relationship with the mother (and the little girl's envy of the mother's special place with the father as his woman and sexual partner). The sexual aspects of Oedipal rivalries have been emphasized in the psychoanalytic literature, but probably the special attention which parents (or stepparents) pay to each other is also a source of tension—especially if the child feels left out.

Almost all family members have rivalries over "turf issues" and material possessions. Biologically, living beings have an "inward compulsion—to possess and defend" their space, which ethologists call territory.[7] Humans, too, are territorial animals. We stake out property, chase off trespassers, and go to war to defend our territory. Children, even at an early stage, want their own territory.

All children want some space where the sibling can't enter; they want their siblings to leave their possessions alone. Enforcing this, particularly with younger children, can be difficult. As parents, we gave up some of our "turf" when we "child-proofed" our home or large areas of it. Most of us prefer to put our cherished possessions out of a young child's reach, and wait for the child to develop enough maturity to understand which of our toys they can play with and which they cannot. Children don't want *any* of their things touched—and have no intention of giving up any of their turf. After all, it's not *their* baby!

Sexuality

Sexual feelings, both parental feelings and those between parents and children, can be sources of stress in family life. Almost no sexual relationship is perfect all the time. It is ironic that the very children who result from our sexual activity can have a complicating effect on it. Some women experience a prolonged period after childbirth before sexual interest returns—either because of fatigue, hormonal factors associated with nursing, or just being so wrapped up with a new infant that temporarily romance is displaced. Many couples find that having children around interferes with their sense of sexual privacy. Some romantic or erotic things that childless couples enjoy doing—like making love impulsively in the living room instead of the bedroom, or wearing provocative clothing or no clothing around the house—can be inhibited in the presence of an audience.

We both believe that parents should not only have a bedroom of their own but preferably one with a lock. From an early age, children can be told that when the door is locked their parents don't want to be disturbed, except in a dire emergency. Lovemaking in other parts of the house will have to wait for those wonderful occasions when the children are at Grandma's or off at camp.

Many parents wonder about locking their children out or hinting that the privacy they seek is for sexual reasons. It's perfectly okay to both lock and hint. We now know it's healthy for children to realize their parents love each other and have sexual lives apart from the lives they have with their children. Notice we say *apart*. Marilyn feels that sex or nudity in front of the children is not a good idea. Anne says, "The issue is our need for our own lives. If children inadvertently come in on us making love, it won't hurt them though it may interrupt us. We can just ask them to leave. Children who repeatedly come in to interrupt probably need more attention in non-sexual areas."

SEXUAL ABUSE

Our children are sexual creatures even when quite young and can arouse sexual feeling in us and other adults who are relatives or close friends. In fact, current studies estimate that as many as a third of all women and a tenth of all men had some unwelcome sexual contact with an adult in childhood or adolescence.[8] This always upsets the children, who often are warned not to tell anyone about it—sometimes with frightening threats.

Sexual abuse of children is defined as "the involvement of dependent, developmentally immature children and adolescents in sexual activities that they do not fully comprehend, to which they are unable to give informed consent, or that violate the social taboos of family roles."[9] One study showed that, contrary to popular opinion, most sexual abuse of children was perpetrated by family members or persons known to the child, generally the father. Most children in the study were chronically abused—often for many years.[10] The child may not realize at first that the behavior is deviant, or it may even be pleasurable. Most adults who engage in this behavior threaten children with reprisals if they tell anyone. Sometimes special gifts or favors are offered if the child complies and does not tell. Injury, venereal disease, and pregnancy can all result.

Most child molesters—four out of five offenders—were themselves abused as children. The perpetrators would fall in the to-be-pitied category, except for the fact they do such terrible things to helpless children.

Incest is the specific term given to sexual relations (including fondling, genital contact, and actual intercourse) between persons too closely related to marry.[11] Father-daughter and stepfather-stepdaughter incest constitute over 75 percent of the cases. The true incidence is unknown but estimates range between one to five thousand cases per million people. Incest occurs in some families as part of a generally chaotic lifestyle with multiple problems like alcoholism, physical abuse, and mental illness. However, incest also occurs in what appears to be a stable family—not known to the courts or social agencies. The incest is usually hidden—as is the family pathology. The marriage is usually dysfunctional with sexual estrangement between husband and wife. Often, to preserve the marriage, the wife consciously or unconsciously feels compelled to deny the situation.

If you suspect or realize your partner is sexually abusing your child, get help! We know that sexual abuse is quite common and ranges from molesting the child to having the child watch the sexual act and forcing the child to perform oral sex or have intercourse. Sexual abuse is very destructive to a child and must be stopped. Call your doctor, a social agency, or a child protective agency at once.

Many mothers look the other way (they need help too), are afraid to say something, or are unable to believe such a thing could happen so they doubt their own suspicions. For the sake of your child, yourself, and your marriage (yes, some offenders respond to therapy), *do* something.

Molestation of children by strangers is much less common than sexual abuse by a family member or friend, but there are child molesters in our society. Whether children are approached by someone known to them or by a stranger, children should learn a very important lesson early. Children should be told their bodies are their own and no one should touch them where they don't want to be touched or in a way that is upsetting to them.

Loving grandparents sometimes want to force a kiss on a young child who doesn't want it. It's better to restrain the relative with a hug of our own, and a reminder—"She loves you and I bet she'll kiss you later." Forcing children to accept unwanted kisses is something we would never do to adults, and something which is dangerous for children. It gives them the idea that familiar adults have a right to intrude on their bodies—a potential setup for abuse by other relatives or friends—and unpleasant even if it goes no further.

There are also deranged people in the world who abduct children and rape and/or murder them. What the FBI calls "assertiveness training for kids" is as important as teaching children they have the right to say "No!" to an adult *(Newsweek* suggested teaching your children their full address, including state, and phone number, including area code).[12] Teach your child that a stranger is somebody you don't know very well and "bad strangers" ask a child to go somewhere with them or want to give them a present. Tell your child that grown-ups don't ask children for directions—and not to go near cars with strangers. Children should be taught to run toward a public place and yell "Help!" if they are bothered by strangers, not to run toward a deserted place. They should be taught to get help by phone (by dialing 911) and never to say they are home alone to a stranger on the phone or at the door.

Unfortunately, recent media publicity has frightened some children. Gloria reported that her six-year-old son was upset when she talked to a stranger next to her in the market checkout line. It is difficult to reach the balance between blind trust in and blind fear of all strangers, but we must all try.

It now appears that the statistics on missing children have been misinterpreted. Most of the missing children are teen runaways or children abducted by a custody-fighting parent, *not* children kidnapped by a deranged stranger. Many pediatricians are concerned today about the effects of scary publicity on children.[13] After all, every milk carton a child sees can have a picture of a missing child. Children may worry about when they will be abducted. It's probably a good idea not to overemphasize this problem, to answer all the child's questions truthfully, and to reassure your child that you, and other responsible adults, protect children.

This is not a pleasant subject to read about—or to write about. Obviously children need to know something about molesters and kidnappers in order to protect themselves, but they also must learn that many more people protect children than hurt them. We all have to be careful not to raise a generation of children so concerned about strangers that they cannot relate to anybody.

Child snatching by a parent can be devastating to the child.[14,15] This usually occurs within two years of a divorce and usually results from a parent's attempt to get revenge or to use the child as "hostage" for property settlement negotiations. The kidnapped child is often told that he or she will be going on a vacation and will return. Often the abducting parent subsequently tells the child the other parent doesn't want him or her anymore or has died. Children can have serious anxieties, fears, and school problems as a result of this. No child should ever be used by any adult—especially a parent—for that person's own gain.

Aggression

Aggression is often stressful for parents to deal with. Infants and small children display normal but unsocialized aggression: crying, yelling, and striking out in a disorganized way. This aggression becomes organized as tantrums when the baby reaches toddlerhood, which is actually a step forward. At any age, frustration triggers aggression, a biologically normal response directed at removing the frustration, or the frustrater. Most of us gradually learn that it helps to *use* our anger, but in a sophisticated, targeted, effective way called assertiveness.

Most social animals have dominance hierarchies among adults—the so-called "pecking orders"—and will use aggression to establish a dominance hierarchy. It is rare for aggression to explode into dangerous violence against a member of the same species in other animals, most of whom display surrender gestures which establish the dominance hierarchy, and cut off further aggression. Unfortunately, as humans, we do *not* have automatic behaviors which cut off the behavior of aggressors. We have to learn means of controlling our own aggression and protecting ourselves from others.

In recent years public attention has focused on domestic violence as a major social problem. Some have estimated that violent aggression against children, between spouses, or even against the elderly occurs in as many as a quarter of American homes. Accurate statistics are hard to come by because, in many families, both the aggressor and the victim are embarrassed and ashamed of the violent behavior. The aggressors feel guilty for having lost control while the victims often feel that they must have done something bad in order to have deserved violent treatment.

There is a very thin line between corporal punishment and the acceptance of domestic violence.[16] We seem to believe that those who love you can hit you. Families may tolerate hits, slaps, even kicks, between siblings, which if a neighbor's child perpetrated on their child might lead to a charge of assault and battery.

WIFE ABUSE

Battering of wives, a cultural phenomenon that has recently come "out of the closet," is quite common. A national survey published in 1980 revealed that 16 percent of married people admitted they were subjected to physical violence by their spouse during the survey year.[17] It is estimated that 2 million women are beaten by their husbands each year.

Women (and occasionally disabled men) may feel that they have to tolerate violence from someone on whom they are economically dependent. Maria Roy has described the cycle of violence that often occurs in homes in which men batter women.[18] There is first a period of rising tension, followed by a triggering event which may be minor, then the actual violence, and then a period of remorse and making up on the part of the aggressor. The man typically becomes very tender, promises never to do it again, and during this period many women become so hopeful that things will become better that they stay in the relationship. By the time the tension mounts again, the women who know what to expect may find the tension so unbearable that they may actually do something to provoke the violence just to get it over with.

Wife battering is not healthy for the wife, the spouse, or the children. No human being has to tolerate physical abuse. There is nothing a woman does which deserves physical abuse. Abuse of wives is rarely a one-time-only phenomenon. Rather, wife abuse is a repetitive pattern which destroys people and families. Often the beatings start in pregnancy or after the birth of a baby because of jealousy over the loss of attention. If you find yourself in such a situation, *get help!* If you feel your life—or your child's life—is in danger, call the police. If you must leave the house and have no resources, call the YWCA. Many Y's have shelters or can advise you where to go. Shelters as well as counseling, legal advice, child care, and job counseling are available in many cities for abused women. Look in the yellow pages or see social service directories.

CHILD ABUSE

Physical child abuse can be defined as non-accidental physical attack or physical injury, including minimal as well as fatal injury, inflicted upon children by persons caring for them.[19] Although infanticide and harm to children by their care givers has been around from the beginning of recorded history, the term became firmly fixed in our culture thanks to the landmark work of C. Henry Kempe, who organized the first national conference on the "Battered Child Syndrome" and published an article on this subject in the *Journal of the American Medical Association* in 1962.[20] Within a few short years, all fifty states enacted legislation requiring professionals to report suspected cases of child abuse and neglect, and in 1974 a National Center for Child Abuse and Neglect was established.

The incidence of child abuse is high. It is estimated that between 1.2 and 2 million children a year are abused, or one out of every hundred children.[21] Physical abuse is the leading cause of death in babies between six and twelve months and represents 25 percent of emergency room visits in children under one year, and 10 percent in children from one to five.

In a culture that accepts corporal punishment and a hierarchical social structure both within families and outside of families, those stresses that occur in *every* family can lead to abuse. These stresses can be engendered by the child, the social situation, or the parent. Ray Helfer of Michigan State University notes there are three components to child abuse: potential for abuse in the parent, a special kind of child, and a crisis or series of crises.[22]

Although some people abuse children because they believe that it is their right, or even religious duty, some child abuse can be explained on a cumulative stress basis. Lifelong factors which place people at risk for abusing children include a history of having been abused as children and a discipline pattern that relies heavily on punishment, particularly physical punishment, like spanking, hitting, and shaking.

Whatever one's personal history of being abused in the past and using physical punishment in the present has been, the single most important factor in avoiding dangerous abuse is *awareness of our own feelings*. We may not always have control over how much stress life brings us, but we can learn to *recognize when we are approaching our breaking point*.

The "I can't stand much more of this" feeling should be taken very seriously. When we feel this way we need to communicate this message to someone who can help. In an emergency, place a small child in a crib or playpen or place a larger child in a bedroom with the door closed. Then you can back off and simmer down. An older child can be told, "I feel like I'm about to lose my temper and I don't want to hurt you. Stay in this room for your own protection until I calm down."

At times like this, parents need to get help and get it quickly. Ask your spouse for help. If you are a single parent, call a relative or a friend. Work out a "buddy system" with another parent who lives close by so that when parental stress gets to be too much for either one of you, you can spell each other for a while by taking each other's kids.

Parents Anonymous (PA)—a self-help group for child abusers—has emergency hot lines for telephone support in many cities. There are over a thousand chapters which are listed in the telephone directory. A toll-free number (1-800-421-0353) will put you in touch with PA and you will be assisted in finding the closest source of help. PA also provides group meetings for abusive parents who learn about ways to defuse stress before it spills over onto the children.

PA points out that abuse can occur when you are reminded of something from your own childhood that still hurts, or when a present need is not being met, or something stressful is happening. Their goal is to increase the parents' self-esteem as well as to teach them how to prevent an abusive episode. Members can call another member at any time if they feel abuse is likely to occur or they feel out of control.

It helps to be aware of high-risk times for triggering abuse. Katherine Vedder, former head of the Protective Services Team at Cook County Hospital, talks about oral-anal triggers for child abuse. "Oral" triggers are not eating, spitting up, or making a mess with food—either spilling it on the floor or clothes. "Anal" triggers are soiling the pants or clothes one more time than the parent can stand cleaning up—particularly when the child has just been dressed up and/or there is time pressure to get the child somewhere like church, or school, or a party. There is also some evidence that abused infants are more often retarded in mental and motor development.[23]

Triggers in older children include making a mess, spilling things on clothes or furniture, breaking things, getting into fights with siblings, or disobeying parents who require instant obedience to meet their own needs. It is obvious that these are normal childhood behaviors, but they *do* result in extra work for parents. They are irritants at any time, but much more likely to act as triggers for abuse at times when parents are overstressed, or have too much to do in too little time.

Child abuse can be fatal or can cause permanent brain damage. The emotional consequences are also grave. The child believes he or she is so terrible that the abuse is deserved. The abused child often becomes an abusing adult, which means your *grandchildren* can be abused. If you are an abuser, or think you might become one, do something about child abuse, now!

Almost every community has a Child Protective Services or similar agency. If you are abusing your child, *call now!* They provide help which includes temporarily removing your children from the home if this step is needed. They provide counseling for you or may refer you to Parents Anonymous. Two techniques are most effective in helping the abuser: teaching problem-solving skills and teaching stress management techniques.

All of us get furious with our children. Marilyn and Anne go as far as to say if you haven't felt very angry impulses toward your child, you aren't involved enough with your child, nor do you have enough of yourself invested in the child, to be parenting properly! Many parents, especially in times of stress, hit or slap their child harder than they really meant to. They wonder, "Is this child abuse?"

Theoretically, any slap can be termed "physical attack" even if there is no sign of injury. Bruises, fractures, and bleeding are all physical injury. Is reddening of the skin injury? Whether it is or not, even repeated light slaps can be emotionally abusive because the child can come to feel he or she deserves the parents' wrath. This is incompatible with the self-esteem every child needs to become a well-functioning, happy adult.

We said more about this in the chapter on Socialization, but ideally no parent should hit a child. We all learn better when we feel good than when we feel bad. However the slap across the bottom seems culturally ingrained in most of us. We were spanked, we model our behavior after that of our parents, we spank. It's as simple as that. To say you should never hit a child is equivalent to saying you should never have a car accident. It's almost inevitable that some degree of both will happen. We can do our best to avoid it, to limit the extent, to pick up the pieces later, and get help if needed.

However, when our stress level is high, our control is likely to be low. Marilyn remembers being so angry at her children she didn't dare raise her voice or spank as she knew she'd be out of control. She admits she spanked her children on occasion and screamed at them as well. She wishes she had not done so. If she had another chance, she would now know how to avoid this kind of behavior. Marilyn used to think that being a good mother meant paying attention to her children. Now she knows, as does Anne, that a successful mother pays attention to *herself* and her own needs in order to parent well.

Alcoholism

It is beyond the scope of this book to dwell on every chronic problem that befalls families, but alcoholism must be mentioned. We now know that alcoholism has a genetic component. Some people cannot tolerate alcohol, and addictive abuse of this substance occurs when they drink. The "clues" as to whether you are an alcoholic are well established. This disease should be suspected if drinking is making your home life unhappy, if you lose time from work due to drinking, if you drink every day to excess, if you cannot get started in the morning without a drink, if you drink alone, if you have blackouts when you can't remember anything due to drinking, or if others complain about your drinking.

Alcoholism is destructive to the individual, to the spouse, and to the family. If you suspect it, get help. Alcoholics Anonymous (the first—and most successful—self-help group) is listed in the phone book. Alcohol treatment and counseling centers are springing up in many communities and are also listed under Alcoholism in the phone book.

If you are an alcohol abuser, you should not drive. Driving while intoxicated is a major killer. Blood alcohol concentrations of twenty- to thirty-four-year-old drivers involved in fatal motor vehicle accidents were higher than in drivers of other ages.[24] Many parents are in that age range; do not subject your child to the hazards of driving with you if you are intoxicated. Call a cab—or get a sober friend to drive.

Marital Stress

All marriages have stressful moments. There is no such thing as a perfect relationship. Most marriages provide the partners with more joy than grief, so that the spouses are willing to put up with the bad days, the occasional fight, or those minor, but insoluble, differences that can be nerve-wracking, especially when we're upset.

Sometimes the fighting and the differences are so great that the marriage begins to crumble. Though it doesn't always work, we are strong believers in marriage counseling and almost always suggest giving it a try. Even if the marriage ends, counseling or mediation can help achieve a fairer, more amicable settlement that makes co-parenting better for children and parents both.

Depression

A real stressor of families is depression in one of its members. Depression is very common. It is estimated that 30 percent of women and 20 percent of men have symptoms of a clinical depression sometime during their lifetime. Sometimes people are clinically depressed for an obvious reason—the death of a loved one for example. However, sometimes the reason people feel so down is not easily apparent and, indeed, feeling so bad without a reason is part of why depression is so horrible.

Depression can be a killer. Sometimes a person feels so bad that suicide seems the only way out. But depression is treatable. If you or your spouse or child are depressed, *get help!* Ask your doctor for the name of a psychiatrist or call your local mental health clinic or go to an emergency room. Even when there is an obvious trigger—such as a loss—if severe depression persists, get help.

Problems with a Child

Family stress over a child who has a problem can be very severe. A physical or mental illness, delinquency, running away, hyperactivity, retardation—all can lead to personal stress in the parents and siblings and can put a strain on even the best of marriages.

Sometimes the child does not exhibit any of the above but, nonetheless, is a problem to the parents.

Some children seem to be in the same "channel" as their parents are. They have the same temperaments, energy levels, wake/sleep cycles, etc., as do the parents. Raising such a child is easy.

Some children are in a very different channel. From early on they are in conflict with their parents because of different temperaments. Later their goals and values may be very different. This is not to say their channel is "bad," just that it is *different* from that of their parents. It's hard for the parents and such a child to communicate; they don't understand each other.

We have both seen families fall apart because of this kind of a child, one who does nothing wrong but who also cannot do anything right as far as the parents are concerned. Once again, if you feel you and your child are not communicating or you and your spouse are constantly arguing about how to deal with a child—get help!

In Summary

All families experience stress; most of it goes away by itself, most issues are resolved, and most problems get solved. However, chronic stress can be debilitating.

One feature of family stress is that parents are stressed at the same time as children and, therefore, have less emotional energy, time, and ability to give at the very time when the children need support the most. Parents should not blame themselves for that, but should recognize that it is a problem.

Sometimes supportive adults who understand about the effects of stress can help your child when the family is under stress. Many teachers can be helpful to the children. At the very least, teachers should know if there is a lot going on in the family. Children under stress may be disorganized in school and may not be doing their work. Parents sometimes hesitate to tell teachers about private family problems. All you have to say is that "There is a high stress situation at home which might be affecting Billy's performance in school. The nature of the problem is something that I prefer to keep private just now, but I wanted you to know that if Billy has some difficulties for a while, it may be a result of this."

Learn to get help for *yourself*, if it's needed. As a matter of fact, concentrate on yourself first. As long as you are the responsible person, your first priority must be getting the support to make you able to stay responsible. Second, recognize that to keep yourself afloat, it may be unrealistic for you to provide more support for the children than you can realistically do. Sometimes the children need to leave the home for a bit. Sometimes they are better off going to a grandparent's home or the home of a friend. It is helpful to give them as much choice and control as possible, since children in the middle of big stresses quite often feel helpless. Let them know how to reach you by phone.

Tell your children something about your problems. It is a mistake to pretend that everything is normal when it is not. This upsets children because they can perceive something is wrong and if you do not give them any information, their fantasies may be worse than the reality.

One doesn't need to share *everything* with the children. You can leave out details. However, be realistically open about everything that is going to have a direct impact on the children's lives, as soon as you know what that impact is. For example, if the family is going to have less money to spend, tell your children.

We have repeatedly used the phrase "Get help!" We mean it. We feel fortunate to live in a time when help *is* available. More than ever before in history, there are trained professionals to help people understand themselves, put their problems in perspective, get along with the important people in their lives and, most important of all, help people realize they are not alone. Every community has sources of help in the form of social agencies, mental health clinics, or private psychiatrists or other mental health professionals. The church or synagogue can also offer help for many problems. Your doctor can point you in the right direction.

Years ago everybody had to suffer in silence. People were ashamed to talk about their problems or those of their family because they felt it showed weakness. We all know everything we've talked about in this section can happen to *any* of us. The stigma of seeking help from a mental health professional (which used to be kept a big secret) is fortunately diminished. People are more apt to be stigmatized by not being smart enough to seek help before a personal or family disaster occurs. Be grateful we live in an era when there are so many caring and helpful people available to us.

Many of you will figure out what is stressing you and clear up that problem by yourselves. That's great! You will grow and your relationships will strengthen in your growth. George Vaillant did an important longitudinal study of college students to analyze factors in adapting to life. His book, which is called *Adaptation to Life,*[25] listed five ways successful people adapted to the vicissitudes of life: Suppression ("I won't think about this problem right now"); Anticipation ("My mother always says those upsetting things, I'll be ready for it"); Sublimation ("I'll pour myself into my work"); Humor ("I'll find a way to laugh about this"); and Altruism ("I'll do something for somebody else no matter how bad I feel"). This list makes an acronym—SASHA. You may want to remember this— they are all useful, self-coping strategies.

In these ways, stress can be a growth experience. As you learn to cope, you can begin to feel pride in the very coping. You also model for your child the coping mechanisms you have learned. The children profit by seeing you, too, get hurt and cry and then get over it. They learn first hand that adults can cope— and how they do so even when it's hard.

SUGGESTED READINGS AND RESOURCES

MOOD

Burns, David D. *Feeling Good, The New Mood Therapy.* New York: Morrow, 1980.

Although not all psychiatrists may agree with this therapy modality, the checklists and suggestions can be very helpful to persons who are feeling down and discouraged.

MANNERS

Joslin, Sesyle. *What Do You Do, Dear?* New York: Harper, 1961.

————. *What Do You Say, Dear?* Reading, Mass.: Addison-Wesley, 1958.

These two books use fantasy (and great illustrations by Maurice Sendak) to teach very young children what they say and do in common social situations. Great to read to preschoolers.

Martin, Judith. *Miss Manners' Guide to Excruciatingly Correct Behavior.* New York: Warner, 1983.

————. *Miss Manners' Guide to Rearing Perfect Children.* New York: Penguin, 1985.

Guides to living with each other and behaving toward each other in a civilized way. Very person-centered. Some suggestions for children's behavior may sound a bit elitist but they are "right on" to prepare them for our complex world.

Parish, Peggy. *Mind Your Manners.* New York: Greenwillow, 1978.

Very comprehensive—tells why "having manners" is an important thing to practice.

Pitt, Valerie. *Let's Find Out About Manners.* New York: Franklin Watts, 1972.

Provides understandable definitions of etiquette. This could be read to preschoolers or enjoyed on their own by fourth- or fifth-graders.

ABUSE

Back, Susan. *Spouse Abuse Yellow Pages,* 2nd ed., 1981. Write: Ms. Bonnie Moul, Social Systems Research and Evaluation Division, Denver Research Institute, University of Denver, P.O. Box 10127, Denver, Colo. 80210, or Call (303) 871-3963. Cost is $9.00.

Davidson, Terry. *Conjugal Crime: Understanding and Changing the Wifebeating Pattern.* New York: Ballantine, 1978.

A useful book about the problem of wife beating. An excellent chapter on guidelines for wives, children, friends, and even wife beaters who want to stop.

I Am a Parents Anonymous Parent. Parents Anonymous, Inc., 1981. Main Office: 6733 South Sepulveda, Suite 270, Los Angeles, Calif. 90045. Telephone: 1-800-421-0353. Executive Director: Margot Fritz.

Kersey, Katharine. *Helping Your Child Handle Stress.* Washington, D.C.: Acropolis, 1986.

Some useful suggestions on helping your children with possible problems.

Lerner, Harriet. *The Dance of Anger.* New York: Harper, 1985.

A look at anger in women.

Sanford, Linda Tschirhart. *The Silent Children: A Book for Parents About the Prevention of Child Sexual Abuse.* Garden City, N.Y.: Anchor Press/Doubleday, 1980.

A comprehensive book about sexual abuse in childhood. It is written for parents to help them prevent sexual abuse in their children but has enough data to make it useful for professionals. There is a very good section for parents of special children like the handicapped, or parents of different ethnic groups.

Star, Barbara. *Helping the Abuser: Intervening Effectively in Family Violence,* 1983. Family Service America, 44 East 23rd Street, New York, N.Y. 10010.

Programs that work.

Straus, Murray A.; Gelles, Richard J.; and Steinmetz, Suzanne K. *Behind Closed Doors: Violence in the American Family.* Garden City, N.Y.: Anchor Books/Doubleday, 1980.

The results of a survey of families in 1976 indicate that in 28 percent of families at least one violent act occurred between spouses; 82 percent of children were violent toward a sibling in the previous year, and 73 percent of parents report violence against the child. Highlighting our predilection for violence, it makes for depressing but interesting reading.

Wachter, Oralee. *No More Secrets for Me.* Boston: Little, Brown, 1983.

Stories designed to help children recognize and deal with sexual abuse. Low-keyed, but the dual message gets across: Say "no" and tell somebody.

5

SAFETY FIRST, SAFETY ALWAYS

Scope of Chapter

This chapter will provide knowledge you need to be a protective parent. After a few words about accidents in general and a section on the parent's role in accident prevention, we present information about child safety four ways.

First, we talk about safety by stages. This section roughly parallels the chapters in Part IV: stages of looking at children in the first year of life, toddlerhood (roughly ages one to three), preschool years, and early school years. We tell you about what the child *can* do developmentally, what accidents might happen as a result, and how you can prevent these accidents from occurring.

Second, we present safety information again by highlighting certain specific *hazards*, looking at accidents conceptually by type. This section is useful for those people who like to think about things this way.

Third, we present safety instructions by alerting you to special situations you have to be careful of.

Fourth, we highlight the hazards a child is likely to encounter in each *room* in the house or *area* the child might be in.

A section on consumer product safety follows, looking especially at baby equipment and toys.

Last we touch on the parents' role in not only teaching the child to become an adult responsible for his or her own safety but also in preventing the child from being a fearful adult always worried about safety.

In addition to this chapter, there is a section in each age/stage chapter entitled Safety which will highlight accidents likely to happen to the child of that age, and once again will emphasize the parents' role in prevention.

Introduction

How lucky you are if you have just had a baby! Your child has a life expectancy of over seventy years! In the year 1800, two hundred out of every thousand children born died in infancy. By 1930 the death rate in infancy was sixty per thousand and it is currently less than twenty. You gave birth to your child in the United States, which has a health care system that, though far from perfect, is still the best in the world. Thanks to improved sanitation and living conditions, safe water supplies, available immunizations, antibiotics, and research in infectious disease, we have conquered most of the contagious diseases that were once fatal to children.

If anything untoward is going to happen to your child, chances are it will result from an accident. More than half the children who die in this country die from severe injuries.[1] However, if protected from accidental injury, a child born in the eighties can expect to live to the year 2060!

Parents used to live in fear that their children would catch dread diseases which they could not prevent. Today parents *can* prevent most accidents. Indeed, parents *must take the responsibility to protect their children from accidents* which are the chief killers and maimers of children today.

We will present lots of warnings in this chapter and list many possible hazards. We do *not* want to scare you. Our goal is to show how you can incorporate principles of safety into your life. We want safety to become second nature to you—not an issue of fear and anxiety and extra work. Indeed the "work" we suggest you do, such as child-proofing, actually saves you a lot of work and anxiety because you can relax when your crawler or toddler moves through a child-proofed home while you *cannot* do so in a dangerous home. Once general safety rules are followed you can become more relaxed.

After reading this chapter, which presents a lot of information in several different ways, you may feel a bit overwhelmed. "How will I ever remember all this?" "Do I have to memorize the list of dangerous plants?"

The answer is a resounding "No." What you should do is simple. When baby starts crawling put *all* plants out of reach. Little ones can reach up high but hanging plants are very popular today. If you have a large ficus or palm you have been nurturing since you moved into your first apartment before you even got married, move it to an "off-limits" room that baby can't get into. The reason we list the dangerous plants is so you can quickly look it up if baby *does* accidently grab and chew on a leaf.

You may still feel that safety rules are overwhelming. "How can I learn all these principles?" Remember how difficult learning how to drive seemed? You wondered how you could ever remember to do everything at once—shift gears, steer the car, watch for pedestrians, etc. But armed with knowledge and practice you became a skilled driver. Now you don't even think about the tasks. Driving has become second nature.

Safety will become second nature to you as well. Start by reading—and perhaps rereading—this chapter. Next put yourself down to your child's level (both in height and motion skills). As you crawl around the house look for possible hazards. Finally modify your house so those hazards are no longer a danger to baby.

WHAT IS AN ACCIDENT?

We call traumatic injuries "accidents" encompassing the concept of "bad luck" or an "act of God." The first dictionary definition of accident is "an event occurring by chance or arising from unknown causes." The second definition is the one we should use in the context of child safety: "an unfortunate event resulting from carelessness, unawareness, ignorance or a combination of causes."

Sometimes an injury or fatality results from what really seems "accidental" —a plane crash, for example, that the parent could not foresee or prevent. But for the most part, injuries that occur in childhood are preventable. Knowledge can help anticipate and avoid such injuries.

Scientifically, physical injury results from interaction between an agent that can do harm, a vector which carries that agent, and the host—the child involved.[2] The agent that causes injury is always *energy transfer;* the energy transferred to the child can be electrical, ionizing (radiation), mechanical, and/or thermal (heat or cold). The extent of injury depends on the rate and amount of energy transferred to the host. Preventing contact between the agent (the harmful energy) and the host (the child) is the way to prevent injury.

How can we reduce interaction between the child and the various types of harmful energy? Some ways to do this involve commercial and regulatory decisions and cost money. For example, society could prevent some hazards by not manufacturing minibikes or handguns. The *amount* of the hazard could be reduced by reducing the top speed of automobiles or enforcing drunk driving prohibitions.

Most of the ways of preventing interaction between the child and the energy can—and should—be carried out by the parents. Parents can reduce the amount of scalding water in their home by lowering the thermostat on their hot water heaters. They can separate the child from the hazard by not allowing the child to play in the roadway. They can interpose a barrier between the child and the automobiles' energy by fencing the yard.

Accident prevention also can be considered in the light of three policy evaluation criteria: efficiency, freedom of choice, and equity.[3] Efficiency is the effectiveness per unit cost of a strategy to reduce accidents. Cost cannot be calculated without assessing risk, and both probability and severity are essential components of risk.

Our culture actually praises and values risk takers. Everyone knows what Lindbergh did and thrilled at Armstrong's walk on the moon. Some have gone as far as to say that parents should *not* discourage risk taking in order to help the child develop autonomy.[4] Most people *underestimate* the probability of death due to the automobile, swimming, and handguns.

What about freedom of choice? Should each of us have the right to go without seat belts, for example? If we say no, we may be in conflict with liberal beliefs that each of us should make our own decisions. Carrying this to its logical conclusions one could say that individuals are responsible for the accidents they have. However, that leaves out the agent and the environment which, along with the host, *all* play a role in the accident. In the last analysis an individual can act completely voluntarily *only* if he or she can fully assess the risk and have the ability to act to lessen the risk, if so desired.

Children *cannot* assess risks and the stage of their physical development prevents them from taking steps to reduce their own risks. Equity then, demands that parents must take over this risk assessment and reduction role until children have the maturity to safely do so on their own.

Legislation and community action, enforcing safety practices, and safety education *can* make a difference.[5] For example, child-proof caps on aspirin and other medicine bottles have reduced accidental poisonings considerably. A reduction in deaths from falls in New York City occurred after the health department made available free, easy-to-install window guards. Legislation in Honolulu requiring fencing around private and public pools reduced drownings. Parents who care about children may wish to get involved in political action to develop community safety laws and practices.

In summary, an accident is not just "bad luck" or "chance." Most accidents are preventable. Children need protection from accidents, which must be provided by parents. Children also deserve safe products and passive protection sometimes, but not always, mandated, such as smoke detectors and pool fences. A combination of parental vigilance, public health measures, and governmental regulations are all needed to make this world a safe one for our children.

WHAT IS THE MAGNITUDE OF THE PROBLEM?

Unintended injury is the leading cause of mortality (death) and morbidity (pain, suffering, and handicap) of children between the ages of one and fourteen. Almost ten thousand children a year die as a result of an accident. Motor vehicle crashes, drownings, and burns are the leading causes of accidental deaths in children.[6] Injury rates per hundred thousand children have not changed or worsened over the past twenty years.

Accidents rank second only to acute infections in reasons for children to visit doctors and one quarter of all visits to emergency rooms and one sixth of all admissions to pediatric hospitals result from accidents. Each year three out of every ten children are restricted from their normal activities for at least a day because of an injury. Some children are incapacitated for life because of spinal cord injuries.[7]

PARENTS' ROLE IN ACCIDENT PREVENTION

Obviously accident prevention is part of the care you give your infant and child. Your protective role as parents depends a bit on where you live. If you are an Aborigine living in the bush, you protect your child from snakes and wild animals. If you live in Chicago or Scottsdale, you protect your child from the automobile and all of the dangerous consumer products that can harm your child.

What can parents do to ensure safety for their children? First of all, as we have already said, educate yourself as to the possible hazards in your child's environment. Unfortunately, you have to do something even broader than recognizing and remembering dangerous objects and practices. You must develop a "safety attitude." One author calls it a "safety reflex."[8] By this he means you become so tuned in to possible hazards and methods of prevention that you *automatically* do what is safe. You automatically turn the pot handle in—even if the pot is cool. You automatically set a good example for your child by buckling up your seat belt. You automatically "speak safety" to your children as, for example, when you check the smoke alarm you remind your children what to do if they hear the alarm in the middle of the night.

Most parents queried *after* an accident had befallen their child recalled that the accident happened because they figured it could *never happen to them.* The parents were either unaware of the potential danger (they never realized baby aspirin could kill a baby if enough orange-flavored pills were chewed up and swallowed) or they were unaware that their child *could* or *would* do the specific dangerous thing which caused the injury. Sometimes parents were unaware of the developmental capacity of their young child. "I never dreamed he could climb up to the medicine cabinet," or they didn't realize how imitative young children are. If children see Mommy swallow pills, they may try some; if Daddy jumps into the swimming pool, they may try it too.

Parents often expect *too* much from their children in terms of development. "He is so bright, he won't do that!" But they forget the importance of *experience* as part of the intelligence needed to protect yourself.[9] For example, a young tree climber may not realize fragile branches break. A child may have partially learned a rule like "Don't go in the street," but when lured by a rolling ball may forget the rule because it is not yet completely internalized.

A developmentally oriented safety survey of parents teaches us some interesting things.[10] Parents were asked to fill out a multiple choice questionnaire asking about their safety practices with children in four age groups from infancy to adolescence. For example, "Do you put the crib sides up when you leave the baby alone?" Parents could circle "always," "sometimes," or "never." Forty percent of all the responses indicated the parents' practice left the child at risk. Two areas in which parents seemed especially unaware of hazards were burn prevention and automobile safety—two major causes of death and injury in childhood. Parents seemed well informed about certain hazards like keeping small objects away from babies or not leaving babies alone in the tub. They didn't allow small children to play with bows and arrows or eat wild mushrooms. These safe practices are commendable but the wild mushroom is much less likely to harm your baby than the wild Corvette.

As we have already said, accident prevention education is not always a success and not all accidents can be prevented. Indeed even when free car seats were dispensed at birth, less than three out of ten babies were crash protected at age two to four months.[11] Non-protectors have the "It won't happen to me" attitude or rationalize, "I'm only going a few blocks to pick up Johnny at school." In fact, contrary to popular opinion, most car accidents occur not on interstates but on roads within a few miles of the victim's home.

Even armed with a "safety attitude," you can be at risk when you or your family experience an illness or crisis. As we discuss later under Special Situations, extra vigilance is needed at the very time you may not feel like doing anything, let alone anything extra.

Parents have an additional task beyond vigilance and protection. They must teach their children eventually to be responsible for their *own* safety. Parents know they will not be around forever to protect their child. How do we teach *responsibility* to children? Briefly, you start by being responsible yourself.

You begin by showing your newborn that you are reliable and loving. Your behavior serves as a role model to your child that grown-ups are reliable and loving. As your child gets older, the use of your responsible "No!" must be coupled with your vigilance so you can swoop the child away if the "No" is ignored. Young children need to be taught cause and effect of their actions by experience. Thus one of your tasks is to reinforce cause and effect. We would never suggest you deliberately burn children to teach cause and effect. That's cruelty. But if toddlers burn their hands on the toaster, you explain that they are hurt because of touching the hot toaster. You also teach what other things are hot and should be avoided. You remind them when they reach for the toaster again that they'll get burned.

You also begin to teach toddlers responsibility at an early age—it starts with picking up toys before someone trips over them. Preschoolers develop responsibility by pleasing their parents, who are very important to them. Children will tend to do what you have praised them for and begin not to do what you disapprove of, even if you aren't there. But this development of conscience takes a long time. So during this period you must teach and watch at the same time.[12]

In summary, parents should not overestimate the young child's ability to follow safety rules. Safety rules should be non-negotiable and should always be enforced. Safety rules should be explained. When you forbid daredevil activities, suggest safe substitutes. Don't overplay the sympathetic parent role when the child does have an accident. Children sometimes do it again for the attention.

Some parents have told us that they believed strongly in teaching self-reliance, autonomy, and independence to their children. They felt safety admonitions fostered dependency and retarded the development of their children. There is no evidence that this is true. There is a strong likelihood that children interpret the casual approach, perhaps somewhat accurately, as evidence of non-love or non-caring on the part of their parents.

Still other parents have a casual lifestyle. They themselves pay very little attention to safety rules. They tend to lead disorganized lives—some by choice and some because of their burdens. They are the fast drivers, the heavy smokers, the non-seat-belt wearers. We have seen casual *households* but we never have seen casual *grief* after something happened to a child. We've both heard anguished cries of "Why didn't I?" or "Why did I?" in the hospital emergency room.

Education is not enough. We know that parents go through several stages before they develop new *practices* even after they have acquired knowledge.[13] First they become *aware* of a hazard. Then they begin to have an *interest in taking precautions*. A *trial period* with the safety practice follows. Finally *full adoption of the safety practice* occurs.

Knowing this pattern, perhaps you can speed up the process. One trick is to figure out how the new practice can be done *easily* in your household, because if things are hard to do we don't do them. For example, if you have come to realize that drain cleaners and dishwasher detergents are dangerous, decide whether it is *easier* for you to move all cleaning products to the top shelf and put the crackers and cereals under the sink or whether it is easier for you to install a locking gadget on your undersink cabinet.

You must make an *effort*. Reading this chapter is not enough. It has been shown that education does not result in behavioral changes to any appreciable degree. Indeed, because of the limited success of educational programs, legislation may be one answer.[14]

There is another cost here. We come smack up against a conflict with an ideal very precious to Americans: individualism, freedom, and free will. Rules, regulations, exhortations, pleadings can all be met with the counter-argument: It's my *right* to decide for myself whether or not to use a seat belt. Many parents feel quite strongly about this right.

Marilyn has been in the practice of pediatrics long enough to know that *no* parent regards his or her individual freedom highly enough to avoid feeling both grief and guilt when something happens. They *all* say, "If only I had put his seat belt on," or, "If only I had not left her alone," or, "If only I had locked the pool gate."

Marilyn feels quite strongly that parents, in a larger societal sense, have no right to place their child in a hazardous situation, even if they maintain that right for themselves. She would try everything: fines for parents who allow their child unrestrained seating in cars, rewards for those who buckle up, shame and embarrassment, like publishing a list of parents who don't care enough about their child to buckle the child up. She even has walked up to total strangers who are buckling in their child and said, "It makes me happy to see you love your child enough to use the car seat!"

One word of caution to parents. Many have told us they "watch their child every minute." No way! It's impossible! Even if you could do it, you would harm your child in the attempt. A child *must* explore and reach out in order to learn. A better approach is to child-proof your house.

One last word for parents. Even in the twenties and early thirties—the ages of many of our readers—accidents are the leading cause of death for both men and women, although the rate is higher in men. Take care of *yourselves.* Your children need you.

SAFETY BY STAGES

If you can anticipate what is likely to happen to your children at a given stage of their development, you can do much toward preventing most accidents from occurring. The following tables look at *what can happen* to a child in each of six childhood stages, *why* these events can occur, and *what you can do to prevent it.* For an expanded discussion of the child's developmental stages, please turn to the relevant chapter on that particular age/stage.

We feel strongly that forewarned is forearmed and that all parents should read these six Safety by Stages tables *before* and during the stage their child is in. However, we must point out that there is no way to predict with certainty which child is going to have an accident. You cannot completely rely on the stereotype of the crawler getting into the poisonous products under the kitchen sink or the two-year-old climbing on the toilet and taking a dangerous drug out of the medicine cabinet. If you stereotype too much you may feel it can't happen to you beause your child doesn't fit the stereotype. Accidents can happen to any child!

Although it used to be thought that accident repeaters were overactive and impulsive daredevils,[15] this is not universally true. A major study compared children who had had one accident with those who had two or more or no accidents. There were no variables that distinguished these groups. As we can't identify the child likely to be accident prone, we must consider *all children to be at risk.*[16]

TABLE 1

FIRST YEAR:

What Can Happen	Why	How You Can Prevent It
1. Falls	1. Even newborns wiggle. Your baby can begin to turn over or crawl right now, even if yesterday he or she couldn't.	1. Keep the crib sides up. Don't leave the baby on a bath table or any surface except the floor. Always keep the baby strapped in an infant seat or a high chair. Keep the infant seat on the floor. Be careful of baby walkers near stairs.
2. Suffocation	2. The baby can't move its head off a soft pillow; can wiggle into bad places, such as between crib and mattress; can inhale bad things.	2. Keep the baby on a flat surface only. Be sure you have a safe crib. Do not cover the mattress with a plastic bag. Do not use a pillow. Keep powder away from where the baby can knock it over and inhale it. Small objects like diaper pins and toys should not be kept near babies. Eliminate strangling hazards (cords on toys, window shade, etc.). Do not prop the baby's bottles. Do not give food the infant can choke on.

TABLE 1 (Continued)

FIRST YEAR:

What Can Happen	Why	How You Can Prevent It
3. Burns	3. The baby is helpless in a fire.	3. There should be smoke detectors in every home. Never leave the baby alone in the house. Keep the baby far away from radiators and other hot surfaces. (Remember out-of-reach definition.) Do not leave vaporizers within reach. (Cold vaporizers are preferable.) Prevent scalds—keep hot water under 125° F. Check bathwater before putting the baby in. Use electric plug guards. Be careful of the sun—it burns babies! Don't let the baby touch a seat belt buckle heated by the sun. Don't drink hot liquids or smoke while nursing or feeding the baby.
4. Drowning	4. Helpless in water.	4. Never leave the baby alone in the bath. Put a towel in the bottom of the bath so the baby can't slip. Don't use bath oils in the bath. Use little bits of soap and always keep the soap out of the tub so the baby can't slide on it.

TABLE 1 (Continued)

FIRST YEAR:

What Can Happen	Why	How You Can Prevent It
5. Poisonings and swallowings of small, indigestible objects	5. The baby can use pincer finger movement. The baby can reach. The baby can pull.	5. No medicines, soaps, powders, oils, vitamins, or any such product should be within reach of the baby. Keep away from the baby all small objects that can be swallowed. Be careful of toys with small parts. (See below in products section.) Keep plants out of the baby's reach.
6. Automobiles	6. The baby is helpless in an automobile or under an automobile.	6. Always use appropriate car restraints. Do not let the baby crawl in a driveway.

TABLE 2

TODDLERS (Ages 1 and 2):

What Can Happen	Why	How You Can Prevent It
1. Falls	1. The child becomes a walker. The child becomes a climber. Curiosity begins! Thinking begins! (The child can pull a chair over and climb upon a counter to get a cookie or anything else he or she wants.)	1. Be aware of the child's capabilities. Provide gates and good lighting on stairs; pick up clutter on stairs. Child-proof your home so that the child cannot climb on objects unattended. Remember that children don't fly and can be hurt even falling out of a one-story window. Screens must be on windows, and windows must be kept closed. Give your child nonslip shoes; keep the shoes tied; do not let the child run about in socks; clothes should be short enough so the child won't trip. As the child starts to walk faster, guard against slipping. There is no need to scatter rugs about when the child is toddling. Don't wax the floor slickly; mop up spills. Skid-proof your bathtub.

TABLE 2 (Continued)

TODDLERS (Ages 1 and 2):

What Can Happen	Why	How You Can Prevent It
2. Ingestions	2. The child puts everything in his or her mouth.	2. Most parents are aware that medicines can be hazardous to children. The problem is that many parents are completely unaware of what else can be poisonous, like the cigarette butt in the ashtray and almost the entire contents of the cabinet under your sink where you keep all your cleaning supplies, etc. Child-proof your house. Keep household poisons out of sight and out of reach; especially hazardous ones should be locked up. See to it that your child cannot climb to reach dangerous objects. Use child-proof containers. Discard old medicines. Store products in their original containers away from food. Don't tell children medicine tastes like candy. Have your local Poison Control Center number at hand. Have syrup of ipecac on hand and travel with it. Beware of visitors' purses and suitcases, which may contain poisonous substances.

TABLE 2 (Continued)

TODDLERS (Ages 1 and 2):

What Can Happen	Why	How You Can Prevent It
3. Burns	3. The child is helpless in a fire and helpless when exposed to scalding water and other liquids.	3. Smoke detectors should be in every home. Teach your child the meaning of "hot." Keep pot handles turned in. Keep matches and lit cigarettes out of reach (preferably out of the house). Be careful of vaporizers. Do not let the child go near the faucets in the tub where the child can turn on the water. Turn the hot water off first so that if water drips it will be cold. Do not let the child run around the house unless you know that the radiators are not hot. Remember that the child is helpless with electricity and likes to poke at things. Cover electrical outlets. Keep electrical cords turned away so that the child can't pull coffeepots over and be hurt by them. Repair frayed cords. Unplug appliances when not in use. Do not let electric wires be chewed by children. Don't overload electrical circuits. Use a fireplace screen. Do not let adults smoke near toddlers (eye burns can occur).

TABLE 2 (Continued)

TODDLERS (Ages 1 and 2):

What Can Happen	Why	How You Can Prevent It
4. Drowning	4. The child is helpless in water.	4. Protect a child in the tub and in a pool. Never let a child be unattended near a pool. Even a covered pool can have enough water in the cover to drown a child. If you have a pool, lock the pool and have the child "pool-proofed" (learn to float on the back). Protect the child from any water (ditch, puddle, well, toilet bowl, etc.).
5. Automobiles	5. It is very hazardous for a child to play in driveways, since the child is usually crawling or sitting down and people backing out literally do not see the child. Children and automobiles cannot coexist peacefully in driveways.	5. No child should be alone at this age out of doors unless confined to a carriage or a playpen. An appropriate car restraint is essential. Do not let the child play in driveways or garages.

TABLE 3

PRESCHOOL (Ages 2, 3, and 4):

What Can Happen	Why	How You Can Prevent It
1. Falls	1. Remember, a child can open doors and can run.	1. Keep doors locked, screens on windows. No horseplay or running with food or objects in the mouth should be allowed. Never leave the child in a cart unattended.
2. Ingestions	2. A child likes to look into closets and open drawers.	2. Keep your house child-proofed (see Table 2).
3. Burns	3. A child is helpless in a fire.	3. Smoke detectors should be in every home. Be careful about matches and cigarette lighters. Rehearse house evacuation.
4. Drowning	4. A child is helpless in water (even a child who can swim is far from a strong swimmer).	4. Never leave an unattended child in the pool. Do not trust water wings or arm floats (use them only if you are present at the pool).
5. Automobiles	5. A child can't win in an automobile-child collision.	5. No child should be alone outside until the child is old enough to walk to school alone. Teach the child pedestrian safety, but do not trust the childs's judgment until the child is of school age. Teach the child to keep his or her tricycle out of the street and to watch out for cars in driveways.

TABLE 4

EARLY SCHOOL YEARS (Ages 5 to 9):

What Can Happen	Why	How You Can Prevent It
1. Automobiles	1. Automobiles are always a hazard.	1. Teach about seat belts by example and rule. Reinforce pedestrian safety. "White at night."
2. Bicycle accidents	2. A child can ride, is daring.	2. Teach the child techniques and bicycling rules. Bike lights and reflectors at night.
3. Drownings	3. Is daring.	3. Teaching swimming skills especially "drownproofing."
4. Burns	4. Not safety-conscious.	4. Teach child how to summon aid in a fire. Do not permit playing with matches (teach safe use). Firecrackers should be a "no-no."
5. Firearms	5. Not safety-conscious.	5. Keep firearms locked up. Keep ammunition locked up separately.
6. Cuts	6. Not safety-conscious.	6. Teach safety with knives. Teach about broken glass. Use safety glass on patio doors.

TABLE 5

PREADOLESCENT (Ages 10 to 13):

What Can Happen	Why	How You Can Prevent It
Motor vehicles	Preadolescents have strenuous physical activity needs.	Teach pedestrian safety.
Drowning		Teach bicycling safety.
Burns	The need for approval of preadolescent-age mates leads to daring.	Teach water safety, including frozen-water safety.
Firearms		Instruct in the safe use of firearms.
Falls		Provide recreational facilities.
Bicycle accidents		Prepare for automobile driving by setting a good example.

TABLE 6

ADOLESCENCE:

What Can Happen	Why	How You Can Prevent It
Motor vehicles	Peer pressure	Efforts in this regard should be started earlier than adolescence, but the child must be apprised of the dangers of automobiles, bicycles, and recreational drugs.
Drowning	Risk taking	
Bicycle accidents	Depression	Brief outlets for risk taking should be provided.
Ingestions (recreational drugs and alcohol)		Vigorous safe physical exercise should be encouraged.
		Boat safety should be taught.
		Responsibility as a baby-sitter should be taught.

SPECIFIC HAZARDS

Falls: The Height of Gravity

One of the first safety issues you have to worry about when you bring your newborn baby home is preventing a fall. When Marilyn visits a mother and her newborn baby in the hospital, she likes to do her examination of the baby in front of the mother. The last thing Marilyn does in examining the baby is to elicit a Moro reflex. This reflex (see p. 319), which is also called the "startle" reflex, occurs when the baby is stimulated by a loud noise or a sudden change in position (such as would occur after a sharp slap on the mattress). The Moro reflex consists of the baby jumping (sometimes literally off the mattress), extending all four extremities, and breaking out into a cry.

As the mother is comforting the baby, Marilyn points out that this reflex is something her baby was born with and it will remain with the baby for the next several weeks. "Let's imagine together a scenario in which you leave the baby on the bath table and go to get a diaper from the next room. If the door slams or another loud noise occurs, it is possible that the baby can jump enough to fall off the table to the floor." In point of fact, Marilyn knows of no baby that has Moro-ed from the bath table to the floor but she takes the trouble to point out this reflex to mothers in order to show that a newborn baby is *not* an inert lump of clay. Though newborn babies don't move much, they *do* move and cannot be left unattended on any high surface.

In addition, as the child matures and starts wiggling or making creeping movements, falls become more likely. Remember, though your baby cannot roll over today, he or she may do so tomorrow. (Marilyn's daughter did and fell— fortunately to the carpet from a bed—but Marilyn still feels guilty, stupid, and scared that she left her on the bed though it was only for the usual "moment.")

So, to prevent the first type of accident that occurs to infants, never leave the child unattended on an unprotected surface. Remember always to use a strap in baby tenders, high chairs, strollers, and in carriages. Never leave crib sides down.

Newborns should not be left on a bath table or *any* surface except the floor. Learn always to keep one hand on the baby while you are reaching for a diaper or the soap. Before you put your baby on a bath table or any surface above the floor, plan ahead. Place all the things you'll need within reach. If you can't reach an object, then take the baby under your arm to get it or put the baby on the floor while you get it. Don't worry about the floor being dirty. A little dirt is far better than a fall. By the way, be careful of stairs yourself when carrying your baby.

As the child gets older, falls continue to be a problem. High chairs are *high*.

This is to make feeding the baby easier for the parent, but it is not safe for babies. If the tray isn't locked, babies can push it and themselves on the floor. Unstrapped babies can slide out the bottom. Because many high chairs are equipped with flimsy straps, for safety's sake use a harness to keep your child safely in the high chair. All baby seats, whether they are jump seats, swings, baby tenders, infant seats, etc., are safe only if the parent does two things. First, purchase safe equipment. Second, always strap the baby in properly. When babies are big enough to climb out of the playpen, take it down. The same holds for crib sides.

When your baby begins to crawl in preparation for walking, you have some additional preparation for accident prevention. Gates or closed doors must guard every stairwell. Avoid scatter rugs, don't clutter stairs with objects, and be sure lighting is adequate.

As an eloquent article entitled "Children Can't Fly" attested, falls from windows are, unfortunately, almost always fatal. Upper-story windows *must* be child-proofed.[17] You can use tricks like only opening the top window. You can also prevent the bottom window from opening more than two or three inches by installing window burglar locks. Handles can be removed from windows that swing in or out. *Never* rely on a window screen; a child can push against the screen and both can fall. Don't place "climbing steps" of furniture near windows.

Be careful not to seal off windows which might be used for exit in a fire. All the gadgets you install for the baby's safety must be easily opened by an adult.

Be especially careful with balconies. Many apartment buildings are built for adults, and balcony construction can permit a small child to roll underneath the rail or crawl over a low rail.

There are two especially dangerous places where children fall: the bathroom and near the patio door. Prevent slips in the tub with safety strips. Keep soap in the soap dish (not on the floor) and don't use glass containers in the bathroom. Patio doors break into glass daggers when broken, especially if the glass is annealed rather than tempered or laminated safety glass. We recommend metal guards over the glass and repeated reminders to running children not to run near or through the door—even if it's open!

Most falls occur on level surfaces. These can be minimized by careful attention to floor surfaces (no scatter rugs, no holes in the carpet, no slick wax, no banana peel or other garbage on the floor, and a minimum of clutter) and by paying careful attention to your child's footwear. Avoid slippery shoes. Also don't allow a child to walk around in socks. They are slippery, especially on wooden floors. Either put the shoes on or take the socks off.

Your yard can be a prime location for falls. Clean up grease on the driveway, remove snow and ice, and make the yard trip-proof by removing or relocating hazards such as rakes. A tree and a ladder are both invitations to climb so don't leave ladders standing. Teach your child to climb a tree safely. Also remove dead or weak limbs that might break under a child's weight. Playground equipment such as swing sets should be sturdily built with swing seats made out of lightweight material so that no child can get hurt if conked on the head by an out-of-control swing. These sets should be set up on grass or soft dirt rather than concrete.

One piece of what we consider unnecessary play equipment causes lots of injuries from falls. This is the skateboard. About a hundred thousand injuries resulting in emergency room visits occur annually.[18] If your child must have a skateboard, insist that it be used on clean, smooth surfaces away from cars and non-skating people.

The Awful Automobile

The most horrible pictures we have ever seen showed automobiles that were involved in minor fender-bender accidents in which infants *lost their lives.* You may have taken your baby home from the hospital in a way that subjected the child to a tremendous amount of risk. Your husband drove and you sat in the front seat of the car with the baby in your arms. If the car stopped very suddenly, *even if it did not hit another car,* your arms would have opened involuntarily. Your baby, a very light object, could have flown forward and bashed his or her head on the dashboard. Many infants die this way every year.

The figures are staggering. In 1980, 2 million of us were injured in motor vehicle accidents and more than 52,000 were killed. Almost 250,000 injuries and 4,100 deaths involved children under fifteen.[19] It has been estimated that 2 out of 100 children born in this decade will *die* in a traffic accident and two thirds of all infants will be so injured! Young children, especially those in urban environments, are more likely to be killed in a pedestrian rather than a passenger accident. Children account for half of all bicycle fatalities.

Research has taught us lots about kids and cars—a bad combination in an accident. Children riding in front seats are at higher risk. Children under six months of age have the highest passenger death rate, higher than any other age group even though they travel less often. Half of the passenger fatalities in children occurred at speeds under fifty-five miles per hour. The child, because of its large head, becomes a missile in a sudden stop; in a crash, the child held in an adult's arms weighs hundreds of pounds and will force the adult's arms open. Also, the weight of the adult's body will crush the child (who becomes a human air bag) against the dashboard.

We also know that the risk of a motor vehicle accident occurring increases at high speeds or on poor roads, especially two-lane roads. Small cars are more dangerous than big ones. Young drivers are more dangerous than older ones, with the death rate of eighteen-year-olds higher than that of any other age group and higher in boys than in girls. Ten percent of all fatalities involve sixteen- and seventeen-year-olds.[20] Paradoxically, eliminating Driver Education courses cuts *down* the number of sixteen- and seventeen-year-old drivers and this in turn cuts down the number of teenage crashes.[21] Alcohol is a factor in accidents and cigarette smokers are also more likely to die, perhaps because of lighting up or perhaps because of the effects of carbon monoxide on drivers.[22]

The most important factor, because you can do something about it, is *restraint*. The ratio of child passengers not killed to those killed in motor vehicle accidents was 1 out of 227 in crashes of unrestrained children and 1 out of 3150 of restrained children.[23] To phrase this another way, 6,300 or 16 percent of 39,500 children involved in a crash were restrained and only two of these died. Of the 33,200 children *not* restrained, 146 died. Car restraint could have resulted in 93 percent *fewer deaths*. In another study, of 89 children killed, only three were restrained, one improperly.[24]

Children are killed in *non-crash* accidents. They fall out of the car or are fatally injured in sudden stops or swerves. All of these deaths can be *completely* prevented with the proper use of restraints. Proper door locks are an added protection.

We know which parents are likely to use car restraints. They are generally from a higher socioeconomic group, show a great interest in preventive health, and have a family dentist.[25] Another reason to persuade you to wear *your* belt is that your health risk in general is correlated with whether you wear a seat belt. If you don't, you are not only a poor role model for your child but also may not be around to raise the child as you are more at risk yourself.

The American Academy of Pediatrics has launched a new campaign called "Every Ride—A Safe Ride" as a successor to a 1980 campaign called "The First Ride—A Safe Ride."[26] This new campaign will stress continued use of restraints beyond infancy and will try to reach teenage drivers. Car seat rental programs that hospitals provide increase the use of restraints of the newborn leaving the hospital from 15 to 70 percent.[27]

State legislation to *mandate* the use of restraints for children has also been effective. Tennessee passed the first law requiring that children under four be properly restrained.[28] All states now have a child restraint law. Injury rates decreased 30 percent while death rates decreased 55 percent between 1978, when the law was passed, and 1981. Today most states have a child restraint law but some state laws do not have any teeth; the car is stopped but the drivers are only warned. One community decided to use the carrot approach: drivers will be monetarily rewarded if children are safely restrained.

One of the most heart-rending statistics we know has been included since 1982 in the *Morbidity and Mortality Weekly Report* published by the Centers for Disease Control in Atlanta. This is called "Potential Years of Life Lost by Cause of Death." The measure is derived for persons from one to sixty-five by taking the number of deaths in each age category and multiplying by the difference between sixty-five and the age at the midpoint of the category. The figure for auto accident deaths is incredible. In 1975, 665,497 potential years of life were lost by 12,884 children under nineteen killed that year.[29] This is higher than the number of potential years of life lost for *all* ages in 1980 due to many diseases we think of as killers such as heart disease, diabetes, or emphysema.

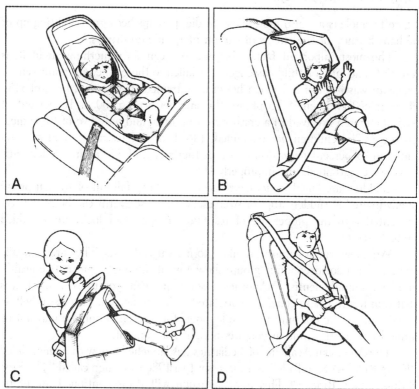

Car restraints: A. infant car seat; B. toddler seat, harness-type; C. toddler seat, shield-type; D. booster seat.

Have we convinced you? Good, then let's help you implement car safety. Start by buying the proper car restraints for your child. (See illustration; see Tables 7, 8.) Always place your child in the appropriate-for-age restraint. Always follow the manufacturer's directions for safe use. Always use your own seat belt so you can be a good role model.

There is only *one* safe way to transport an infant in a car. The baby should be placed in an approved infant car seat strapped to the car with the seat belt.

TABLE 7

Type of Restraint	The Child to Be Protected		
	Infants up to 9 months	Children 8 or 9 months up to 4 years	Children 5 years or older
Infant Car Seat	Yes		
Child Car Seat	No	Yes	

Child Harness (Installed in center of rear seat)	No	Yes	
Vehicle lap belt	No	No	Yes*
Vehicle shoulder belt (worn only with lap belt)	No	No	Yes*

* Car pillows should be used as necessary to raise child up from vehicle seat so that safety belt will not restrain against child's abdomen.

Reprinted by permission and adapted from Harmon, Murl. *A New Vaccine For Child Safety*. Safety Now Co., Inc., Jenkintown, Pa., 1976.

TABLE 8

National Passenger Safety Association
Safety Seats—1986

All of the seats listed have been certified by the manufacturer as meeting the current federal motor vehicle safety standard (No. 213) in effect as of February 1986. They provide a high degree of protection if used strictly according to manufacturers' instructions.

Name of seat	Manufacturer or Distributor	Comments
INFANT SAFETY SEATS *Use from Birth to 20 Pounds; Rearward Facing Only*		
Cuddle Shuttle	Collier-Keyworth	1 harness position
Dyn-O-Mite	Evenflo	2 harness positions
First Ride	Cosco	1 harness position
Infant Car Seat 570	Century	2 harness positions
Infant Car Seat 580	Century	2 harness positions; Seat removes from base for use as household carrier
Infant Carrier	Ford, Chrysler	(Same as Infant Love Seat)
Infant Love Seat	Century	2 harness positions
Infant Safety Seat	Evenflo	2 harness positions
Rock 'N Ride	Kolcraft	1 harness position
TODDLER SEATS *Over 20 Pounds; Use facing forward*		
Bobob	ZB Sales	5-point harness; comes with replacement belt
Britax	Evenflo	20–80 pounds; designed for handicapped children
E-Z-On-Vest	E-Z-On Products (formerly Rupert)	harness for toddlers & large children; suitable for handicapped; installed with tether systems
Honda Safety Seat	Honda	5-pt. harness; tether (same as Century Child Love Seat)
Safe Guard	Evenflo	5-point harness

Name of seat	Manufacturer or Distributor	Comments
AUTO BOOSTER SEATS *30–70 pounds; (NPSA suggests that a convertible or toddler safety seat be used until a child outgrows it or weighs at least 30 lbs.)*		
Booster Car Seat	Evenflo	adjustable small shield; belt through base
Child Cushion	Volvo	Use only with lap/shoulder belt
Click N' Go	Pride-Trimble	adjustable small shield
Commander	Century	adjustable small shield
Co-Pilot II	Collier-Keyworth	adjustable small shield
Explorer	Cosco	adjustable small shield; seat height adjustable
Flip 'N Go II	Kolcraft	adjustable small shield
Quick Click 605	Strolee	adjustable small shield
Tot Guard	Ford	large shield; adjustable seat height
Tot-Rider Quik-Step	Kolcraft	adjustable small shield
Voyager	Collier-Keyworth	adjustable mini-shield; belt through base
Wings	Evenflo	adjustable mini-shield
CONVERTIBLE SAFETY SEATS *Birth–43 Pounds; Rearward Facing for Infant; Forward Facing for Toddler*		
Bobby-Mac Deluxe II	Evenflo	3-pt. harness, separate shield
Century 100	Century	5-pt. harness
Century 200	Century	3-pt. harness/body pad
Century 300	Century	5-pt. harness; armrest
Century400XL	Century	3-pt. harness/shield; straps adjust easily
Century 1000 STE	Century	5-pt. harness; straps adjust easily
Century 2000 STE	Century	3-pt. harness/body pad; straps adjust easily
Chrysler Child Seat	Chrysler	same as Century 200
CK Classic	Collier-Keyworth	harness/shield
Commuter	Cosco	harness/shield
Concor V	Aprica	5-pt. inertia reel harness; broad buckle forms body pad; 3 shoulder strap positions
Fisher-Price Car Seat	Fisher-Price	3-pt. retractable harness locks tight when body pad is buckled
Formula 1	Collier-Keyworth	3-pt. harness/shield
GT 1000	Graco	5-pt. harness
GT 2000	Strolee	improved version of GT 1000
Guardian 635,640,650	Gerry	retractable 3-pt. harness/ body pad
Hi Rider XL2	Kolcraft	5-pt. harness; armrest

Name of seat	Manufacturer or Distributor	Comments
Infant/Child Safety Seat	Nissan	retractable 3-pt. harness/body pad
One Step	Evenflo	3-pt. harness/shield
Pride Ride 820 series	Pride-Trimble	5-pt. harness
Pride Ride 830 series	Pride-Trimble	5-pt. harness; armrest
Roundtripper	Collier-Keyworth	5-pt. harness
Safe & Snug	Cosco	3-pt. harness/shield
Safe & Easy	Cosco	5-pt. harness
Safe-T-Seat	Cosco	5-pt. harness
Seven-Year Car Seat	Evenflo	Adjusts to fit from birth to 60 pounds; 3 pt. harness/adjustable shield
Sprint	Collier-Keyworth	5-pt. harness
Travel Tot	Welsh	5-pt. harness; separate shield
UltraRide	Kolcraft	5-point harness
Wee Care 609,612,614	Strolee	5-point harness; 609 is compact version
Wee Care 610,618,620	Strolee	5-point harness; armrest; 610 is compact version
Wonda Chair 810	Babyhood	5-point harness

Reprinted by permission from the National Passenger Safety Association, Washington, D.C., 1986.

As your child gets older and wants to sit up in a car, you can choose among several of the specially made child restraint seats that are approved by the National Highway Traffic Safety Administration. These car seats are expensive but well worth it. Cheap car seats with metal bars that hang over the back of the front seat are *not* safe in a collision.

By the time a child weighs forty pounds, he or she can be placed in a regular seat belt. Whether the child will start a lifetime of "buckling up for safety" depends on the example *you* set.

As the child gets older, he or she may want to stand in the car or, heaven forbid, ride in a truck or open car unprotected. You are making a great mistake if you permit this. *Every time a child is in any moving vehicle the child should be securely strapped in a car seat or seat belt.* Many children open the door and fall out while the car is moving, with disastrous consequences.

Children who ride in car seats exhibit safe behavior while those left loose are apt to show dangerous, distracting behavior (standing, climbing, crying or screaming).[30] Remember, if you are in a carpool, you need restraints for each child.

Some parents are concerned that strapping or seat-belting a child is risky because if the car is in an accident that involves fire, or if the car is submerged in water, the child will be trapped. Statistically, these two accidents occur so infrequently that you need not have much concern. There is no question that the use of safety belts is lifesaving, *especially* in children. As we have already pointed out, the child is so light that the child will fly forward in the car at a *greater* rate of speed than a full-sized adult. Thus, the injuries will be greater.

Never leave your child alone in a car. Toddlers have been known to put a car in gear or even start a car but they are absolutely no good at stopping one. A stolen car is bad enough but if your child is in that car you have a nightmare on your hands.

A most common car hazard parents may not think of is *heat*. In the summer (or in warm climates) when car doors and windows are closed, (often to keep the child safe inside the car) the car's temperature rises to an unacceptable level for a child within fifteen minutes.[31] In most climates windows must be half opened (which means a crawler could fall out) for temperatures to approach safe levels, but temperatures in Arizona might reach hazardous levels even with the windows open all the way. Children can become victims of fatal heatstroke within an hour or two and burns due to contact with seat buckles and plastic upholstery have been reported. *Always take your children with you when you leave the car, even for a moment.*

As the child gets older and begins to explore outdoors, the automobile becomes a modern-day dragon slaying our children. There is a "no-contest" situation in any collision between a child and a car—the child will *never* win. Be especially vigilant about children playing in driveways, especially small toddlers.

No child should be left out of doors alone before he or she is ready to walk to school alone. Mothers sometimes say, "I am watching the child from the window." Not good enough. Do not take this risk. We cannot approve of three- and four-year-olds playing unsupervised outdoors in the street. Many parents tell us their children even at two or three are trained "to stay on the sidewalk," but we know that this practice is not safe. A child of that age is not capable of being trusted. We *do* feel by the time the child is four it is very important that the parents practice teaching the child to cross the street safely, looking both ways. Then by the time the child is ready to go to school, he or she is able to do so safely.

We are absolutely convinced that no child under school age should play outdoors alone, unsupervised (except in a safely fenced yard).

When the child is old enough to play outdoors, running out from between parked cars becomes a hazard. Both parents and teachers must constantly remind children not to do this. All drivers should (although they don't) *slow down* on residental streets with parked cars and should *stop* when they see a ball roll into the street.

Many pedestrian-car accidents surprisingly occur to older children at night. The usual child pedestrian accident involves a boy whose mean age is 7.3, crossing the street between intersections between 2 to 7 P.M.[32] Children who are walking or playing outdoors at night must wear white or light-colored clothing. Use reflector materials and arm bands for additional safety. The most hazardous time is twilight—the time many children are coming home for supper. Urge them to be careful.

Bicycles and cars are also asymmetrical adversaries—the car will always win.

Five hundred children between ages five and fourteen are killed yearly on bicycles.[33] Most accidents involving young children are the child's fault: the child rushes into traffic or goes through a stop sign. Marilyn lived in a community where children under twelve had to ride bicycles on the sidewalk—a sensible law.

The risk-taking ten-to-twelve-year-old boy who decides he wants to drive a car is another special hazard. The teenager who doesn't use seat belts and drives at high speeds to show off (to himself and others to prove he is not afraid) or who uses alcohol or recreational drugs while driving is one of our biggest worries. Teamwork (parents, teachers, and police) is needed to stop the epidemic of teenage motor vehicle deaths.

Teenagers and motorcycles are another bad combination. If your teenager does use a motorcycle be sure he or she uses a helmet. Repeal of helmet laws has definitely increased mortality.[34] Also insist on long pants and long-sleeved shirts made out of a sturdy material. Do not allow a small child whose feet don't reach the foot pedals to ride as a passenger. The child who is big enough to ride as a passenger must wear a helmet and sturdy clothing.

Another hazard is *parental use of alcohol or recreational drugs. In addition accidents have been caused by parents' emotional instability. Do not drive* when you are upset; the distraction can be deadly.

School buses are the safest ground transportation. Sixty pupils were killed in 1982 but only ten were passengers. Over half of the children were struck by the bus after leaving. Instruct your child in school bus safety. Buses are not generally equipped with seat belts but buses built since 1977 have high seat backs and better padded seats for safety. Your child should always sit in the seat —not run around the bus or engage in horseplay.

One last word. To protect your child completely, you have to prevent your child from coming in contact with a drunk driver. You may have heard about MADD (Mothers Against Drunk Drivers), SADD (Students Against Drunk Drivers), and RID (Remove Intoxicated Drivers). All these, and other community action groups, are worthy of your support. The intoxicated driver is a public health menace far worse than Typhoid Mary.

The Complications of Crawling: Child-proofing

As your child gets older you must become aware of the accidents likely to befall crawlers and toddlers. First of all, crawlers not only develop active leg muscles but also develop those wonderful muscles that enable every human child to make a pincer movement between the thumb and the forefinger. As children crawl along they now can pick up little objects from the ground. These little objects might be nails, glass, coins, buttons, batteries, pebbles, or just about anything. The child will lift up the head, look at the object, and immediately put that object in the mouth. Therefore, when you have a creepy crawler, you must see that the floor is kept clean of all hardware and other small or noxious objects no child should ingest.

This is also the time when you have to worry about children lifting themselves up and pulling heavy or dangerous objects (glass, ashtrays, coffeepots containing scalding liquid) down on themselves.

Now is the time you must absolutely child-proof your house. You must inspect every surface that the child could possibly reach. Remove things like glass bowls and coffeepots and put them where the child cannot reach them—or their dangling cord.

We have heard mothers say, "I don't want to do that. I want my child to learn how to live in a house with these nice antiques," or "I will watch my child every minute." Wrong! You have plenty of time to teach your child to appreciate fine antiques and, as we said earlier, you *cannot* watch your child every minute. Indeed, if you never allowed your child to explore, you might be seriously handicapping the child's ability to learn to take risk and accept anxiety— both requisites of growing up.

The sensible thing to do is child-proof your house. Marilyn suggests that parents get down on their hands and knees and crawl around the house. Then they can see what the child might see or reach from that vantage point and remove all dangerous objects or hazards.

The Perils of Poison

Our civilization leads to yet another hazard: accidental ingestion of poisonous substances. In the bush, poisons tend to be live: plants or animals. In cultures like ours, there are over 250,000 different products manufactured and sold—many, if not most, of which are potentially harmful to children.

What do we know about poisonings? We know that children between one and five are most vulnerable, and that medications are the chief offenders, followed by household products and plants. Paracelsus was supposed to have said centuries ago that all substances are poisonous and the only difference between a remedy and a poison is the dosage.

We know epidemiologically that certain factors lead to a poisoning incident. Poisoning is likely to occur if poisonous products aren't put away right after use, if they are stored in food or drink containers, or if empty product containers are not properly disposed of. We know that stress in the family or a change in household routine, whether caused by Christmas or flu, can lead to poisoning incidents.

Over 5 million children will put something potentially poisonous in their mouths each year!

In both kitchen and bathroom, the average American home is perfectly designed to encourage poisoning. The cabinet under the kitchen sink is where nearly every household in America keeps its cleaning supplies. Cleaning supplies may be great for dishes and clothes but are not good for the inside of a child's esophagus or stomach. As children crawl along they can easily open this cabinet and ingest the bleach or the dishwasher detergent (which is very caustic) or the drain cleaner (which can be fatal or terribly crippling to a child). Do not be deterred by the fact that the substance tastes terrible. Children will, at this stage, ingest anything. Do not be deterred by the fact that the container says "Poison." Your child cannot yet read.

You have two choices. You can put *all* cleaning supplies in the cabinet *above* sink level where the child cannot reach, and put your cornflakes and other cereals down below. Or you can get a lock for this cabinet, and any other cabinet or drawer your child can reach which contains hazardous substances. Marilyn used a simple lock that was made for a screen door which had a little extra loop on it that had to be pulled back before the lock could be lifted. By the time a child is five or six, he or she can open such a lock, but the one- or two-year-old cannot. This lock made both the medicine cabinet and the cabinets underneath the sink perfectly safe from exploring young children.

The bathroom is another room in the house well designed to trap the toddler, especially the bright, energetic, exploring one. This child crawls onto the top of the toilet seat, crawls onto the top of the toilet tank, and then can easily reach the medicine cabinet above the sink. In your own house look at how your bathroom resembles steps for toddlers. Once again, bathroom cabinets should either contain only harmless substances (almost no bathroom product fits in this category) or should have a lock.

It is important to point out that there are things in every medicine cabinet in America that are not ordinarily thought of as harmful. Aspirin, for example, before it was put in child-proof containers, used to kill three thousand American children a year. The number of fatalities has gone down considerably, but nonetheless aspirin and non-aspirin analgesics are still hazards. Colognes, aftershave lotion, cold remedies, etc., are often not considered poisonous but all can harm a child.

One should not put absolute trust in child-proof containers, because many children figure out how to open them. A child-proof container is a deterrent but not an absolute one. The safest way to go is to lock all medicine cabinets from the time the baby is born (this gets you in the habit), until the child is old enough to obey and reason (school age).

Babies can get *poisoned* while being diapered! Two percent of all calls to a Poison Control Center were for a poisoning incident that occurred during diapering.[35] Most incidents were inhalations of powders that the child grabbed, but babies also ate ointments, baby wipes, acetaminophen (Tylenol), alcohol, and baby shampoo. *All* of these products are potentially hazardous. Though you may need them during a "change," don't place them where your baby can grab them!

We offer some other hints to help you avoid a poisoning incident. Don't let your child see you take medicine, don't tell your child the medicine tastes like candy, or use vitamins that look like cartoon characters.

Another hazard is your purse. Grandmother's or Mother's purse should never be left where a child can reach it. There have been deaths reported from Grandmothers' visits, (Grandmother puts her purse on the coffee table and the child ingests her digitalis and blood pressure pills). It would be pretty hard to be a happy grandmother after such an accident.

It is also important to remember that the elderly often have arthritis so that they bypass or booby-trap child-proof containers. Therefore, when your child is visiting Grandmother or Grandfather, please ask them to poison-proof their home.

Poisonings can occur when products—ordinarily safely locked up—are in use. When you are cleaning the bathroom or washing the kitchen floor, if you have to leave to answer the phone or doorbell take either the buckets and bottles or the baby with you.

Because lead can be so deadly to young children—it causes fatal or crippling brain damage—be sure your child is not exposed to this poison. Exterior paint and plaster in houses built before World War II both can contain lead, so do not allow your child to chew on such surfaces—ever.

One other poison we must mention is deadly and both odorless and colorless: carbon monoxide. Be sure your car exhaust system is in good working order. Do not use space heaters unless the area is properly ventilated. If you use a space heater, always open the window. Clean chimneys and flues before you start the furnace in the fall. Do not ever use hibachis or grills inside the house, garage, camper or tent (better to be rained on or eat cold hot dogs than to get asphyxiated). By the way, escaping gas used to heat houses can also harm a child, not because it is poisonous, but because it displaces the oxygen the child needs and can explode. Prevent your child from reaching or turning on handles of gas valves or stove burners. If you smell gas—get out of the house and *don't* turn on any switches.

Table 9 shows how to poison-proof your house. For more information about syrup of ipecac, which every home should have on hand, (see p. 687 and p. 725).

TABLE 9

POISON-PROOF YOUR HOME

KITCHEN
- Household cleaning products stored in *locked* cabinet
- No medicines on counters, refrigerator, windowsills
- All cleaners, household products, and medications out of reach
- All cleaners, household products, and medications in original safety-top containers

BATHROOM
- All medicines, sprays, powders, cosmetics, mouthwashes, etc., stored out of reach in locked cabinets
- Medicine chest cleaned out regularly
- Old medications flushed down toilet
- All medicines in original containers

BEDROOM
- No medicines in or on dresser or bedside table
- All perfumes, cosmetics, powders out of reach

LAUNDRY AREA
- All bleaches, soap, detergent out of reach
- All products in original containers

GARAGE/STORAGE
- All products out of reach
- All products stored in original containers with safety caps
- Insect spray and weed killers in *locked* area
- Gasoline and car products in *locked* area

- Turpentine, paints, and paint products in *locked* area

GENERAL HOUSEHOLD
- Alcoholic beverages out of reach
- Plants out of reach
- Ashtrays empty

GENERAL PRECAUTIONS:
- Never tell children medicine "tastes like candy"
- Give medicine only to person doctor has prescribed it for
- Don't leave a child and a poison alone even "for a second"
- Don't take or give medicines in the dark or without reading **the label**
- Keep syrup of ipecac on hand

Reprinted by permission from the Arizona Poison Control System, University of Arizona Health Sciences Center, Tucson, Arizona.

Some especially hazardous medicines include aspirin, acetaminophen (Tylenol), iron, Catapres, Afrin, Visine, narcotics, Clinitest tablets, Darvon, and Isoniazid (INH).

Some especially dangerous household compounds are those containing hydrocarbons such as furniture polish, kerosene, gasoline or lighter fluid; button batteries (which can lodge in the esophagus and cause severe damage); lye products (which can destroy the esophagus); rubbing alcohol, nail polish remover, mothballs (naphthalene), dishwasher detergents, disinfectants, ammonia, bleach, solvents, and some fire extinguisher liquids. One thing that might surprise you is the hazard of baby powder. Inhalation can be fatal.[36]

Table 10 shows commonly ingested household items that are usually *nontoxic*, but this table can only serve as a *guide*. If your child has swallowed poison, you don't have time to read this table—get help! On the other hand, it can be reassuring to find that makeup is usually harmless if your toddler appears with a mouthful of lipstick. *Always call your Poison Control Center if your child has ingested any substance you are not SURE is safe.*

One word about household plants. As a rule of thumb no plants or pieces thereof should be ingested by children. Many are potentially serious or fatal, including the castor bean, oleander, chinaberry, jimsonweed, and dieffenbachia. Also, your baby can choke on a plant leaf.

Table 11 shows the safe, and not so safe, plants likely to be around the house or yard.

TABLE 10

NON-TOXIC (HARMLESS) MATERIAL COMMONLY INGESTED

Abrasives
Antacids
Antibiotics
Baby product cosmetics
Ballpoint pen inks
Bathtub floating toys
Body conditioners
Calamine lotion
Candles (beeswax or paraffin)
Carboxymethylcellulose
Chalk (calcium carbonate)
Clay (modeling)
Corticosteroids
Cosmetics
Crayons (marked A.P., C.P.)
Dehumidifying packets (silica or charcoal)
Deodorants
Deodorizers (spray and refrigerator)
Elmer's Glue
Etch-A-Sketch
Eye makeup
Fishbowl additives
Glues and pastes
Glycerol
Golf ball (core may cause mechanical injury)
Greases
Gums
Hair products (dyes, sprays, tonics)
Hand lotions and creams
Indelible markers
Ink (black, blue)
Kaolin
Lanolin
Linoleic acid

Linseed oil
Lipstick
Lubricant
Lubricating oils
Magic markers
Magnesium silicate
Makeup (eye, liquid facial)
Newspaper
Paint—indoor or latex
Paraffin
Pencil (lead—graphite, coloring)
Petroleum jelly (Vaseline)
Play-Doh
Polaroid picture-coating fluid
Porous-tip ink-marking pens
Prussian blue (ferrocyanide)
Putty (less than 2 ounces)
Rouge
Sachets (essential oils, powder)
Sesame oil
Shoe polish (most do not contain aniline dyes)
Silica
Silly Putty (99 percent silicones)
Spackles
Suntan preparations
Sweetening agents (saccharin, cyclamate)
Teething rings (water-sterility?)
Thermometers (mercury)
Titanium oxide
Toothpaste (without fluoride)
Vaseline
Water colors
Zinc oxide
Zirconium oxide

Reprinted by permission from Rumack, B. H. ed. Poisindex 44th Edition. Englewood, Colo: Micromedex, Inc., 1985.

TABLE 11

THESE PLANTS CAN BE DANGEROUS

They can cause severe symptoms and even death, if eaten.

Azalea leaves, stems, berries, flowers, leaves, seeds
Bird of paradise
Bleeding heart, any part
Boxwood
Bull nettle
Buttercup
Castor bean
Cherry leaves, twigs
Chinaberry tree
Crocus
Daffodil bulb, narcissus bulb, hyacinth bulb, crocus bulb
Deadly nightshade
Dieffenbachia
Dumb cane
Foxglove
Glory-lily
Ground cherry
Hemlock
Holly
Horse chestnut
Hydrangea
Indian tobacco
Iris, any part
Jimsonweed (stinkweed)
Lantana
Larkspur, any part
Lily of the valley, any part

Marijuana
Mayapple
Mescal bean
Mexicantes
Mistletoe
Morning glory
Mountain laurel
Mushroom (eighty kinds)
Night-blooming jasmine
Nightshade
Nutmeg
Oleander, any part
Peach leaves, twigs
Philodendron
Poinsettia
Poison ivy
Pokeweed
Poppy
Potato leaves
Privet berries
Rhododendron leaves, stems, berries
Rhubarb leaves
Spurge laurel
Sweet pea, any part
Tomato leaves
Water hemlock
Wisteria pods, leaves, stems, berries
Yew berries, foliage

THESE PLANTS ARE NOT DANGEROUS

African violet
Aluminum plant
Aralia
Baby tears
Begonia
Bird's-nest fern
Bloodleaf plant
Boston fern
Bridal veil
Coleus (painted nellie)
Coleus (trailing queen)
Corn plant
Devil's-walking-stick

Dracaena
False aralia
Fiddle fig (fiddleleaf)
Gardenia
Hibiscus
Inch plant
Jade plant
Norfolk Island pine
Parlor palm
Patient lucy
Peacock plant
Peperomia
Piggyback plant

Prayer plant	Schefflera
Pregnant onion	Silver tree
Purple passion	Snake plant
Pyracantha (shrub)	Spider plant
Rosary vine	Swedish ivy
Rubber tree	Variegated wandering Jew
Dwarf schefflera	Velvet plant

Reprinted by permission and adapted from *Safety Guide for Poisoning*. Arizona Poison Control System, University of Arizona Health Sciences Center, Tucson, Arizona.

Just in case: Keep the number of your local Poison Control Center at every telephone.

Practically every city has a local or regional Poison Control Center available. Call them before you take any action on your own. *Don't* induce vomiting before consulting your pediatrician or Poison Control Center—you may be doing more harm to your child. Be cautious of the "what to do" advice on labels, which is often wrong. Never use fingers, salt water, or mustard to induce vomiting.

Ancient and Modern Hazards: Fire, Water, and Glass

1. Fire! This is a fearful hazard. Playing with matches is a "no-no" for the child and leaving matches where the child can reach them is a "no-no" for the parent.

Every child old enough to understand should know fire safety rules, including safe ways of exiting from the house in a fire, what to do if your clothing catches fire (cover your face and roll on the ground), and how to call for help. Wearing flame-resistant clothing decreases the risk of severe burns. Polyester (100 percent) is naturally flame-resistant, which means the fabric will shrink away from a flame and melt rather than burst into flames (but the melting causes burns).

The best way to ensure survival in the case of fire in your home—a dreaded occurrence to us all—is to install smoke detectors in your home. There are several types on the market. The type of detector you install is probably not as important as the place of installation. There should be a smoke detector on every level of your home. The detector should be installed close to bedrooms so you can hear the alarm even if the door is closed. Smoke detectors should be installed on the ceiling or high on the wall because smoke and heat rise. Check them monthly to be sure they work, and replace batteries annually.

There is probably no better way of ensuring your child's safety in a fire than by installing and maintaining a smoke alarm system. An alarm is a real lifesaver —and is cheap! Many municipal fire departments provide them at cost.

Rehearse what you will do when the alarm goes off in the middle of the night. How will you escape? Does everyone know the route? Does everyone know the rules? Don't open a door without feeling it, don't open a window until everyone is near it, stay down on the floor with your nose and mouth covered, and go to the designated meeting place.

One word of caution. Deadbolt locks are great to deter burglars but terrible on kids when the house is on fire. *Everyone* must know where the key is—and it must be near the door.

Electrical injuries in children, in addition to causing fatal electric shock, can also cause severe burns. Prevention of electric injury in children includes such commonsense measures as eliminating frayed cords, not overloading circuits, properly using three-pronged appliance cords in proper outlets, keeping dummy plugs in all outlets not in use, keeping electrical appliances such as razors, toothbrushes, and hair dryers away from sinks and bathtubs, and instructing children about the hazards of electricity in water. In addition, children must be instructed about the dangers of high-tension wires and what to do in a lightning storm to avoid being struck (avoid being near any structure that extends into the air higher than its neighboring structures).[37]

We can see no earthly reason for young children to play with firecrackers. Even sparklers can burn a finger.

Scalds are a special hazard to children and account for 40 percent of all burned children and 75 percent of all burned children under age four.[38] Scalds can be prevented by keeping hot water in heaters at temperatures less than 125° F. (a good energy-conservation measure as well). Many scalds result from children pulling at coffeepot cords or pot handles on the stove. Cords and pot handles should be kept out of reach. There is room on every stove to accommodate turned-in pot handles; there is no need to let them project out where a toddler can grasp them. Use back rather than front burners when you can. If your toddler has figured out how to turn on the stove, remove the knobs. Do not use hot vaporizers—the cold steam ones are safer.

2. Water is a hazard for children. A child can drown in bodies of water ranging from buckets of wash water to oceans, from swimming pools to large puddles, and from lakes to toilet bowls. All such bodies of water and children should be firmly separated, or an adult should always be present to watch the children.

Seven thousand drownings occur each year. This accident ranks second only to the automobile in accidental deaths from age five to forty-four. Near drowning (the child may live but be permanently brain damaged) is another horror and it is estimated that most diving accidents result in permanent paralysis.[39]

A child should be taught water safety, drown-proofing, and lifesaving techniques at an early age. Ninety-five percent of drownings or near drownings occur in pools, bathtubs, or at beaches where children are not supervised. We are not saying that babies only a few months old should be taught to swim, but we do feel that no child should graduate from junior high school without passing a swimming and water safety test. "Drown-proofing" skills can be taught to school-age children and "pool-proofing" is currently being successfully taught to toddlers in Tucson but *no child* can be considered "drown-proof." Adults must supervise all children near water.

Swimming safety rules are common sense. Never allow anyone to swim alone, including adults (a good role model doesn't model dangerous behavior). At social gatherings assign one person to watch the children. Do not swim during an electrical storm.

Wading pools are cool and pleasant but they are probably not a good idea as ideally children should be taught to approach water as though it is *always* over their heads. In any case, children should not be allowed in a wading pool without adult supervision.

We do not approve of floating devices like water wings because every child has to learn that his or her own body is what prevents sinking in water. However, always use flotation devices like Coast Guard approved life jackets for children while boating.

For those of you with home pools, fences are a must. Self-latching locks on gates which the child cannot reach help keep toddlers out. Be sure that there are no chairs or tables near the fence over which the child could climb. The pool should be clearly visible from the house. An alarm system which sounds when someone falls in the water is additional security. Every pool needs a pole and/or flotation device handy at *all* times. Remember to keep all pool chemicals and testing kits away from children.

Two other words about the dangers of water. Many drowning accidents occur in youths who hyperventilate before they dive into the water in order to be able to swim farther. This dangerous practice has actually been *taught* to youngsters by some swimming coaches. It works in the sense that it decreases the carbon dioxide tension in the blood, which decreases the blood flow to the brain, so that swimmers are less conscious of low oxygen tension in the blood and don't feel the need to surface to breathe. *But* some swimmers—even good ones—dull their consciousness to the degree that they drown. Don't let your child (or yourself) do this.

The other danger is diving into unknown waters, whether diving into shallow water or diving from a great height (i.e., the roof of the house into the deep end of the pool). Not only can the child hit the deck instead of the water but the child will go down deeper if diving from such a height and may hit the bottom of the pool.

Diving—under safe conditions—is fun and promotes coordination. Diving into unknown waters has left many a youth paralyzed for life. One grandmother we know, whose grandson is a quadriplegic because he dove into the pool from a motel roof at his high school graduation party, cried when she said, "He only made one mistake in his life—but what a tragic one!"

3. A modern hazard is the glass patio door. About a quarter of a million persons are injured annually in America by accidently walking into or falling against glass patio doors or shower enclosures. About half of these are children under fifteen. Children should be taught *never* to run near these areas. The glass

in every patio door should be marked (with tape if necessary) so the child knows there is a door there. Children have been known to run headlong into a glass door with disastrous results. Be sure the glass in your doors and windows is approved by the U.S. Consumer Product Safety Commission.

Problems With Pets

Some of our 25 million dogs bite half a million people every year![40] Two thirds of these bites are taken out of the bodies of children under fifteen. Most take place in the summer and 90 percent are inflicted by a "friendly" dog—the family pet or a neighbor's dog.[41] One study showed that 43 percent of dog bites required a visit to the doctor and 17 percent needed stitches.[42] Children under four most often get bitten at home, on the head, face, and neck.[43] The dogs that bite the most are the German shepherd, chow chow, poodle, Italian bulldog, and fox terrier.[44]

Fatalities can occur. A recent study identified seventy-four deaths from dog attacks, twenty-three in infants under a year.[45] Most attacks were by pet dogs who were not considered vicious and there was no history of provocation by the victim. Disfiguring injuries can also occur. Marilyn remembers a once beautiful four-year-old girl whose cheek was torn off by the family's pet boxer, *which had attacked her before.* We suggest you be especially careful with big dogs around children.

Marilyn's husband is a veterinarian who loves animals and makes a living caring for household pets. But he says dogs and infants are a poor combination. If a dog has been the only "child" before a baby is born, jealousy can lead to dangerous situations. Therefore, do not let a dog near a newborn unless you are there to protect the baby. When toddlers begin to crawl they often poke the dog or pull its ears until the dog is provoked to bite—understandable behavior on the part of both baby and dog but often with bad results.

Marilyn's husband feels that ideally you should not own a dog until your child is at least five so that the child can not only be protected from the dog but also can be taught proper handling of pets.

How can you prevent dog bites? First of all, don't have a dog—especially a big dog—around small children. Teach your child to respect all dogs (they all have teeth), especially while the dog is eating, sleeping, or defecating. Tell your child never to startle or mistreat or tease a dog. Tell your child never to approach a strange dog or hold the face close to a dog. Don't let your small child try to lead a large dog. Don't let your child skate or bicycle in front of a strange dog; the dog sometimes gets frightened and attacks.[46]

Cats also bite and scratch and should be kept away from exploring crawlers. About fifty thousand people a year seek attention for cat bites.[47] Twice as many females as males are bitten or scratched by cats. Though they do not suck the breath out of babies, cats can cause allergies in a susceptible child.

Both cats and dogs should sleep in their own beds—not your child's! Diseases can be passed in both directions.[48] Do not let your child eat or mouth a flea collar—poisonous!

The dog roundworm can infect children who eat the eggs, and an illness known as toxocariasis can cause serious symptoms of rash, fever, and cough. This parasite can also involve the eye. The dog hookworm can cause an itchy skin eruption. Cats can pass another parasite, toxoplasmosis, to children. To prevent these problems your pet should be treated for worms by the veterinarian, dog feces should be removed from the lawn or play area, and cat boxes should be cleaned daily.[49]

Exotic animals also cause problems. A ten-year study of wild or exotic animals kept as pets showed that many of the injuries from such creatures, in which the age was recorded, occurred in children.[50] Keep your child and your ferret, monkey, rattlesnake, or other exotic pets away from each other. By the way, skunks and raccoons are carriers of rabies. They should *never* be kept as pets.

Firearms

Marilyn and colleagues once wrote a sad article on gunshot wounds in children—all preventable.[51] As with the automobile, kids don't stand a chance with a gun. If you keep guns in your house and also have a child, remember the guns should be locked up and the bullets should be locked up *separately.* If you have children, never keep a loaded gun under your pillow or under your bed or in your coat pocket or in your car. Many people do this for "protection" but your first responsibility as a parent is to protect your child from an accidental gunshot wound. Gun safety should be taught but most hunting accidents occur to those who *have had gun safety training* so this is obviously not enough.

Beware of the air rifle and BB guns. Do not be misled into thinking they are harmless. They can cause serious injuries especially to the eye, face, head, or neck.[52] One study reported seven potentially lethal air rifle injuries.[53] Air rifles require the same safety rules (keep away from young children and instruct in safe usage) as do real guns.

We both would like a world without guns, even toy guns, but realistically we know that boys like to play with guns. However, don't let the following tragedy occur in your house. A four-year-old boy who had just killed his two-year-old brother with a .38-caliber pistol he found under the bed told Marilyn, "I will never do that to him again!"

As we said before, don't let children play with firecrackers. They are all potentially dangerous.

Sports Hazards

Sports, athletics, and physical fitness are all great for kids and other living things. Injuries, however, are all too common. The figures are astounding. In 1981, the following injuries which resulted in an emergency-room visit occurred: 550,000 bicycling, 470,000 baseball; 442,000 football; 433,000 basketball; 96,000 soccer; 47,000 skiing; 38,000 racquetball or squash; 28,000 tennis; 19,000 golf.[54] These numbers are for people of all ages but give you an idea of the relative hazards and exposures. And remember, there are many other painful injuries which are treated at home or in a physician's office so no visit to an emergency room occurs.

The general rules for sports are simple: expert training, good equipment, a period of warm-up, stop when fatigued.

The bicycle deserves a special word. Most accidents in children involve boys, within five blocks of their home, and between 4 and 8 P.M.[55] Stunt riding, speeding, or a problem with the surface are the common precipitators. Bicycle safety rules are important. The rules are simple: good equipment in good repair; the right size bike for the child; teach (and quiz) the child safety rules. These include: always drive with the traffic in single file; watch for grids, potholes, loose sand, or gravel and car doors opening; use hand signals; never hitch a ride on a truck; no bike riding at night without lights and reflectors; be sure the bike has spoke and chain guards; only one child to a bike. Disobedience of bike safety rules should result in suspension of riding privileges just as disobedience of traffic rules can lead to suspension of driving privileges. Helmets are almost never worn but should be.[56]

We hate to categorize riding an ATV (all-terrain vehicle) as sport but whatever you call it, if your child has access to one, beware! There are over 2 million ATV's in use. Unfortunately thousands of injuries occur each year. Cases of paralysis resulting from spinal cord injury have been reported in children.[57] The American Academy of Pediatrics suggests limiting the use of ATV's to those over sixteen.[58] Remember these are *not* toys, though they are small and may look harmless.

SPECIAL SITUATIONS

Anything that throws the family out of its normal everyday routine is apt to be hazardous for the baby or child by increasing the risk of accidents. An accident is more likely to occur when one of the following takes place:

1. A new baby is brought into the home
2. Moving day (moving is emotionally traumatic too)

3. A death in the family
4. A visit from grandparents or other house guests
5. Holidays, like Christmas
6. Vacations
7. Illness in a parent or sibling

Special situations call for special awareness which should lead to special attention and special vigilance during these occasions.

Special child-proofing of the house in anticipation of special hazardous situations is also important. When children go to visit grandparents and other adults who aren't used to having youngsters around the house, be sure the grandparents make that house safe.

Christmas is an especially dangerous time for two reasons: you have lots of stuff around the house not ordinarily there and you may be tired from the holiday hustle and bustle. Beware of holly and mistletoe, snow sprays (don't inhale), tree ornaments, button batteries, and falling or pulled over Christmas trees.

Halloween trick or treat night used to give parents only one thing to worry about: small children in costumes and masks, walking around in the dark, in competition with the automobile. Now we have *two* things to worry about. Crazies may be putting dangerous things in candy. Most families have eliminated or sharply curtailed trick or treating and have neighborhood Halloween parties instead. We think this is a good idea. Children don't need all that candy anyway.

If you do allow your children to go out on Halloween night, use flame-resistant costumes which reflect light, do not allow masks that obscure vision (use makeup instead), tell children to go only in groups to lighted houses, and not to eat the treats until you have examined them.

Studies have shown that when the family Life Events Score (which measures personal stress) is high, children are more likely to be involved in an accident.[59] This underscores the need for increased vigilance at these times.

But, you may ask, how can a parent be extra vigilant when, by definition, he or she is already frazzled to the max? As we discuss elsewhere, the secret is to ask for help. Recognizing you are frazzled because of your life stresses, and recognizing the resultant need to be even more careful of your child's safety is all *you* have to do. Then ask friends or relatives to take over your protective functions until you are back to normal.

A Special Word About the Newborn

When your baby is born, remember it is not an inert lump. The infant not only has a startle reflex but can also wiggle when on its stomach. Some babies are very active wigglers.

Though newborns are not inert, they are quite helpless and need your complete protection and vigilance, without which they cannot survive. *You* will have to be careful about falls. *You* have to be careful about products such as cribs, toys, pacifiers. *You* have to recognize the bath is a hazard. *You* must remember older siblings can hurt the newborn as can animals in the house. *You* have to recognize that the automobile is the number-one killer of America's young.

Scientific studies have shown that a newborn, when placed face down, will move its head to the side provided the child is neurologically intact. However, you must have a hard surface to do the experiment. Don't do it with a soft pillow. Indeed, the baby should have no pillow. Do not use plastic sheets, which could fall over a wiggly baby and cause smothering. You must be sure that the crib does not permit the baby's head to get wedged either between the mattress and the slats or between the slats.

A Special Word About Household Chores

We think by the time a child is ten he or she should know how to survive in a house when Mom is not available. This means being able to heat soup, make cocoa, fry an egg, etc. It also means knowing how to do this *safely* and how to *clean up afterward*. This means parents have to give cooking and safety lessons in the early years. (There are children's cookbooks to help you do this but mostly you show your child how to do what you do.)

Even young children have to be taught that stoves are dangerous and that pot handles and cords of electric appliances should be turned inward. When they are through cooking, they have to turn everything off. Garbage disposals can be hazardous to little fingers. Don't leave knives in soapy water.

Microwave cooking in one sense is safer, because there are no pots of boiling water with handles that can be pulled down and there are no open flames. However, microwave cooking can be dangerous. Children have to be taught you can't put metal in the microwave. You should not stand close to or stare at the microwave while the food is cooking. Do not microwave anything in a small container like a baby food jar. When something is covered with a cover or plastic wrap you must be very careful opening it so that the steam escapes without burning you. Hot food can spatter when you add ingredients or stir with a spoon. Containers can get quite hot in the microwave so pot holders should be used.

Although we think children should learn about adult chores early, we suggest power equipment be forbidden to any child under ten or eleven and we suggest strict supervision when the child starts using power tools like saws. Power lawnmowers can be surprisingly injurious to young children and fatalities have been reported.[60]

A Special Word About Boys

Boys suffer more injuries than girls, to a significant degree, from age two on. By the time boys are between thirteen and eighteen they experience 90 percent more injuries than girls. Boys have more lacerations, concussions, and sports equipment injuries. Boys use bicycles more than girls and for more hours, which means some of these higher rates in boys can be explained by exposure. However, this is not the only factor. Boys with greater motor skills might actually be expected to have *fewer* accidents. Behavioral differences may play a role: boys are more inventive and manipulative than girls.[61] It is postulated that the greater incidence of accidents in boys may be related to sex stereotyping of behavior. We may *expect* boys to take more risks. If we do, we should also expect them—and help them—to be more careful!

A Special Word About Occupational Hazards

Because of your occupation, you may run the risk of subjecting your child to special hazards. People who work with asbestos, lead, cadmium, beryllium, and certain other heavy metals should change clothes before coming home from work. Farmers and crop dusters have to be especially careful about organic phosphate insecticides on their clothes or around the premises. Policemen and others who use firearms in their work and who, further, are required to have their guns with them even when they are not on duty, have to be extra careful when small children are around.

Hobbyists also should keep their workrooms locked. Almost every craft uses potentially harmful substances.

A Special Word About Things Most People Consider Safe

Be careful about exploding *soda pop bottles.* Buy plastic or cans and don't let your children shake glass bottles.

We ordinarily think of food as safe—not always. The *peanut* is a killer. When Marilyn is feeling dogmatic she says, "No peanuts until age five." An alternative directive was suggested by Marilyn's favorite Poison Control Center director: "No peanuts—or plums or cherries, because of the pits—until the child chews well, is under observation, and is given only a small quantity at a time."

Don't let any child run with food in the mouth. Aspiration (inhaling food in airway) is always bad; it's terrible with peanuts because the peanut oils damage the bronchus where the peanuts get stuck. Don't give *peanut butter* to babies. Globs of peanut butter have asphyxiated babies.

The following should never be given to babies or children until they are really good chewers: hot dogs (the biggest killer), nuts, candy with nuts, popcorn, raw carrots, crisp bacon, or chewing gum.[62] Also avoid bones, apples, raisins, and grapes. Three things we usually associate with happy children—*marshmallows, bubble gum,* and *balloons*—have all killed babies by sticking in their windpipe. Do not give such things to babies or put them where a baby can reach them.

Young children should be supervised when eating. Always cut things *completely* through and be sure each piece is completely separate. Even so, feed a small amount at a time because the child can fill his or her mouth too full for safety. Be careful about toothpicks, which are usually considered harmless and are often located in food.[63]

Christmas bow pins have killed babies (they inhale the pin) although a new design is less lethal because air can get around it.[64] However, it's best to keep these things away from babies. Who wants to go to the emergency room with a choking baby on Christmas Eve?

SAFETY—EVERYPLACE

This section consists of tables only. The tables (12 to 22) cover *places* where a child is likely to be exposed to hazards. We list not only the common areas all of us recognize but also the hidden hazards some of us don't think can harm a child. Suggestions for safety parallel each hazard listed.

We start with the kitchen and follow with the living areas, bathroom, bedroom, utility room/basement, garage, hobby room, yard, playground, shopping sites, and the great outdoors.

We don't want you to think, after reading these pages, that the only safe place for your baby is in your arms or under a rock. Instead we want to sharpen your *safety instinct* by pointing out some things you may never have realized.

TABLE 12

KITCHEN

Hazard	Safety Hints
1. Stove	1. Turn pot handles in. Be careful carrying hot liquids. Keep child (and clothing) away from open flames.

Hazard   *Safety Hints*

Keep fire extinguisher handy.
Keep child from turning knobs on gas stove.
Don't let fingers get pinched in oven door.

2. Microwave

2. Protect child from spatters of overheated food.
Be careful opening lids or plastic wrap —steam is very hot.
Use only approved cookware.

3. Knives (and other sharpies like food processor blades)

3. Store safely.
Teach child how to handle and hand.
Do not leave in soapy water where they can't be seen.

4. Appliances

4. Keep cords from dangling.
Do not let child play with food processor or blender.
Unplug when not in use.

5. Floor

5. Food and water both slippery. Mop up.

6. Cabinets

6. Contain hazardous substances like drain cleaner, furniture polish, dishwasher detergent. Keep locked or high up.

7. Dishwasher

7. Beware of pinched fingers.
Don't let child eat the detergent in the machine door.

8. Garbage Disposal

8. Beware of lost fingers.
Install switch above counter level.

9. Electric Can Opener

9. Do not leave sharp-edged lid attached to magnet.

10. Trash Can

10. May contain can lids, containers with poisonous drugs, etc. Beware!

11. Food

11. Peas and beans can be inserted in small noses.
Extracts contain alcohol.
Guard against food spoilage.

12. Trash Compactor

12. Do not allow baby to crawl in one of these.

TABLE 13

LIVING AREAS

Hazard	Safety Hints
1. Furniture with sharp edges	1. Do not let toddler run near these.
2. Knickknacks	2. Can be sharp, breakable, or filled with poison (ashtrays). Put away.
3. Fireplace	3. Screen safely (watch that crawler doesn't pull screen down). Keep poker, etc., away from baby. Logs have splinters. Long fireplace matches look like colorful lollies but aren't.
4. Bar	4. Alcohol is a poison; drain dregs, put away. Bottles and glasses break. Peanuts are a special hazard.
5. Dining Table	5. Tablecloth can be pulled down.
6. Floor	6. Scatter rugs slip; beware of frayed carpet.
7. Lighting	7. Lamps are pull-downable. Do not overuse extension cords. Cover all plugs.
8. Greenery	8. Many household plants are poisonous.
9. Christmas Tree	9. Can tip over. Can catch on fire. Baby can eat pine needles or ornaments.
10. Wastebasket	10. Could contain cigarettes, small objects, etc.

TABLE 14

BATHROOM

Hazard	Safety Hints
1. Medicine Cabinet	1. Lock it. Keep all medicines (including non-

Hazard	*Safety Hints*
	prescription drugs) in original container. Discard old medicines.
2. Other Cabinets	2. Toiletries and makeup can be poisonous. Do not let baby drink shaving lotion or shampoo, etc.
3. Bathtub	3. Guard against slipping. Guard against scalding (remove hot water handle if you can't lower water temperature). Do not leave child unattended in tub (baby should be last thing brought to the tub and first thing taken out).
4. Toilet	4. Keep lid down (toddler can drown). Avoid seat smashing down on fingers and other parts of little boys. Be careful to lock up toilet bowl cleaners and drain cleaners.
5. Floor	5. Mop up water. Use bath mats. No soap on floor.
6. Appliances	6. No hair dryers, radios, or other high voltage appliances used or stored in bathroom.
7. Razors	7. Store and dispose of blades properly.
8. Wastebasket	8. No razor blades or old medicines.

TABLE 15

BEDROOM

Hazard	*Safety Hints*
1. Bed	1. Guard against falls.
2. Furniture	2. Keep baby from pulling drawers out.
3. Drawers	3. Do not allow baby to get into scissors, cosmetics, headache pills, etc.
4. Makeup Table	4. Powder and perfume can be hazardous.
5. Closets	5. Do not let baby pull down clothes. Be careful of plastic cleaner bags. Don't let baby get locked in. Don't let baby eat mothballs.

Hazard	Safety Hints
6. Windows	6. Prevent falls.
7. Electric Fan	7. Only use fans with screen or cover fan with screen yourself (put screen on inside of screen guard).
8. Sewing Corner	8. Sewing machine should not be left on. Keep small objects like needles, scissors, buttons, etc., away from child.

NOTE: Bedrooms are where we sleep; most home fires occur at night when we're asleep. Therefore, install smoke detectors outside of bedrooms and rehearse exit plans.

TABLE 16

UTILITY ROOM/BASEMENT

Hazard	Safety Hints
1. Washer/Dryer	1. Children have been known to crawl in. Keep doors closed.
2. Cabinets	2. Hazards from bleach to furniture polish —store away from children.
3. Iron/Ironing Board	3. Avoid dangling cord. Ironing boards can collapse or be pulled down.
4. Furnace/Hot Water Heater	4. Often can see flame, which attracts babies. Sometimes sides get hot, so keep baby away.
5. Trash Cans (Cans, broken glass, razors, old medicines, plastic dry cleaner bags, etc.)	5. Keep baby away! Always dispose of glass or razors safely (wrapped up). Discard medicines in toilet; oil and other poisons at an approved dump.
6. Storage	6. Beware of old trunks or refrigerators baby could get trapped in. Remove refrigerator doors and lock trunks. Avoid fire hazards. Look at *all* stored objects with a "safety eye." Is it sharp? Poisonous? Can it be pulled over?
7. Tools	7. Keep out of reach. No nails or washers on floor.

Hazard	Safety Hints
8. Power Tools	8. Do not allow child access to any of these.
9. Guns	9. Lock up guns and ammunition separately.

TABLE 17

GARAGE

Hazard	Safety Hints
1. Automobile	1. Lock so child can't get in (power windows work when key is turned on even if motor isn't). Never leave keys in car. Never allow children to play in car.
2. Gasoline	2. Do not store gasoline or store only in approved containers away from child.
3. Home Repairs	3. Everything is hazardous—tools, power tools, paints, etc. Keep away from child.
4. Trash Can	4. Always contains hazards—keep children away!
5. Power Tools and Appliances	5. Lawn mowers and snow blowers are particularly dangerous.
6. Garage Door	6. Lock remote control in car. Be sure manually operated doors will not fall on child.
7. Household and Automotive Supplies	7. Lock up paints, oils, glues, pesticides, gasoline, turpentine, car waxes, charcoal lighter fluid, etc.

TABLE 18

HOBBY ROOM

Hazard	Safety Hints
1. Hunting	1. Guns, ammunition, bows and arrows, knives all must be locked up.

Hazard	Safety Hints
2. Fishing	2. Hooks hurt—keep them away from kids.
3. Gardening	3. Watch out for fertilizer, pesticides, etc. Seeds are often treated with fungicides, etc. Do not let child eat them. Be careful of pruning shears, etc.
4. Sewing	4. Pins and needles can be swallowed—clean up floor with a magnet.
5. Arts and Crafts	5. Watch out for paints, glues, etc., as well as knives.
6. Golf	6. A golf ball if punctured *really* explodes —keep away from kids.
7. Photography (Other hobbies using chemicals)	7. Keep away from children.
8. Use of CO_2 cartridges (rockets, etc.)	8. Dangerous to use; dangerous when punctured.

TABLE 19

YARD

Hazard	Safety Hints
1. Driveway	1. Keep children out of driveway if possible. Some people back into the garage so they never have to back out. Remove hedges, etc., that obscure vision of driver.
2. Power Tools/Appliances	2. Do not let small kids operate lawn mower, trimmers, or snow blower. Keep children away when you are using them—they often hurl stones like missiles.
3. Ladder	3. Do not keep upright—too tempting.
4. Trees	4. Teach kids safe climbing. Remove weak limbs.
5. Pool	5. Pool safety important. Do not leave baby unattended in any pool—even a wading pool. (Flowerpots or garbage cans can collect lethal amounts of rainwater.)

Hazard	*Safety Hints*
6. Greenery	6. As lots of outdoor plants are poisonous, do not let child eat them. Do not plant bad ones like oleander.
7. Dirt	7. Don't let child eat—can contain parasites.
8. Outdoor Paint	8. Can contain lead; do not let baby chew on porch rails.
9. Live Creatures	9. Protect child from dogs, bees, mosquitoes. Do not let cats or dogs use child's sandbox.
10. Playground Equipment	10. No hard swings. Install on grass, soft dirt, or sawdust to cushion falls.
11. Barbecue	11. Be careful of flames and heat of grill. Lighter fluid is poisonous. Some grills are tippable—do not let children near them until charcoal has cooled. Keep portable grills high up.
12. Clothesline	12. Be sure young baby can't get tangled.
13. Trampoline	13. An atttraction to neighbor kids but *must* only be used under supervision.

TABLE 20

PLAYGROUND

Hazard	*Safety Hints*
1. Playground Equipment	1. Check for hard swings, stability, surface placed on.
2. Pool	2. Water safety at all ages.
3. Sandbox	3. Check sanitation.

TABLE 21

SHOPPING SITES

Hazard	*Safety Hints*
1. Shopping Cart	1. Prevent falls, pinched fingers. Do not let child stand up. Don't let child get into dangerous household products. Never leave child unattended.
2. Stacks of Groceries	2. Prevent child from pulling or knocking these down.
3. Crowds	3. Keep very young baby away from crowds.
4. Poisonous or Dangerous Products	4. Do not leave child unattended to open drain cleaner or pull heavy lamp on head.
5. Parking Lots	5. Pedestrian safety rules must be enforced. (People drive slowly in parking lots but are often distracted.)
6. Malls and Department Stores	6. Prevent lost children; watch yours. Watch child on escalators; do not permit horseplay on escalators.

TABLE 22

THE GREAT OUTDOORS

Hazard	*Safety Hints*
1. Camping	1. Watch out for knives, hatchets, etc. Remember camp fires throw sparks; do not let children run near an open fire. Guard against lost children. Teach children survival skills. Teach children about bears, snakes, and other possibly unfriendly creatures. Avoid poison ivy, etc.
2. Boating	2. No child aboard without an approved life jacket.

Hazard	*Safety Hints*
	Non-slip shoes. No horseplay on deck. Be careful of outboard motors and props. Watch the boom when sailing! Teach canoe safety. Obey water skiing safety rules.
3. Hiking	3. Safe shoes (not sandals). Most trails have no guard rails—watch children carefully. Always carry water and matches. Always carry a compass and map. Always carry rain gear (giant-size garbage bags are fine in a pinch).
4. Swimming	4. Don't let child swim alone. No diving in strange waters. Be careful of fins/masks (only capable swimmers should use them—the mask can fall off and the fins can give a child a false sense of swimming strength).
5. Sledding	5. Do not permit sledding in the street. Do not permit sled to be pulled by a vehicle. Snow saucers cannot be steered and should be used only on gentle slopes.
6. Skating	6. Do not permit skating on soft ice, salt water ice, ice near open water, sunken ice, or ice with air spaces underneath. Allow skating only when there are four inches of blue or clear ice. Teach child how to pull out a playmate safely.
7. Visiting the Farm	7. Avoid cutting machinery. Permit riding only on equipment with a passenger seat. Do not permit kids to drive farm equipment.
8. Construction Sites	8. Too dangerous (cave-ins, equipment, toxic chemicals) to permit play there.

DANGEROUS CONSUMER PRODUCTS

In an affluent society such as ours, product injuries will be more common than bites from wild zebras. Three aspects of product safety are needed to provide protection for children. First of all, parents must become informed so that they can be wise purchasers and users of products. Second, the manufacturers themselves must be vigilant about child safety. Third, there is a need for government regulations to mandate safety and ban unsafe products. We have several federal programs that have been lifesaving to many children: the Poison Prevention Packaging Act, Flammable Fabrics Act, Refrigerator Safety Act, Federal Hazardous Substance Act, and the Consumer Product Safety Act. Useful addresses are listed under "Sources of Consumer Information" at the end of this chapter.

Parents can act to protect other children if they recognize a hazardous consumer product. The USCPSC (United States Consumer Product Safety Commission) has a hot line (800-638-2772) to receive complaints. Any person can petition the USCPSC to rule on a potentially hazardous product. Write to the Office of the Secretary, USCPSC, Washington, D.C. 20207. Within 120 days the government must grant or deny the petition.[65]

The list of possible hazards is long: cribs, toys, infant seats, walkers, high chairs, baby powder, bicycles, tricycles, etc. Because the list is so long, you must become a vigilant parent in order to keep hazardous products and your child far apart. Do not buy or use hazardous products. Examine products carefully so you can be your own vigilante.

Let's start by discussing baby equipment. Since crib safety regulations were issued in 1974, crib-related injuries have been reduced, but they still happen. The most serious injuries and deaths occur in very young babies who get wedged in a crack between the mattress and the crib, or catch their heads between the slats. Because cribs can be lethal if the slats are so far apart the baby can wedge his or her head in and strangle, crib slats should be less than 2⅜ inches (6 cm) apart and the sides should be 26 inches (66 cm) above the mattress. The mattress must fit firmly so the baby cannot get wedged between the sides and the mattress. Older babies and toddlers are most likely to be injured when attempting to climb out of the crib. When the baby starts climbing out, it's safest to lower the crib sides and pad the floor with pillows. Never fill the crib with toys that could be used as steps for climbers.

Cribs that have posts higher than ⅝ inch are hazardous, as children can hang themselves. If you have an older crib with such posts, saw them off and sand the rough area smooth. "Questor" cribs manufactured between 1970 and 1982 have dangerous mattress-support hangers and have been recalled.[66]

Walkers can be very hazardous. Half of the infants in one study had an accident (either a tip over, a fall down stairs, or finger entrapment).[67] Both the circular- and X-frame types have been implicated. Because this is an absolutely non-essential bit of equipment, we suggest not buying one. If you do buy a walker, get a stable one, don't let the baby get near stairs, and keep the walker on only one surface (they can tip going from carpet to floor).

In order to be safe, high chairs need a stable wide base, a good strap, and a guard lock to prevent collapse. Many people use sassy seats (hook on tables) instead of high chairs.

Playpens come in two varieties: slats and mesh. When shopping look for a design which has no sharp edges or protrusions and no pinching potential at the hinges. The sides should be at least twenty inches above the pad. Large mesh can snare fingers or buttons on clothing. Do not leave mesh sides down as a young baby can roll into the space between the mattress and the mesh and suffocate.[68] Also agile babies can use large mesh openings as toeholds. Do not put toys or pillows that can be used as stepping stones in with the child. Remember playpens are for *little* ones. Do not use them for children taller than thirty-four inches or over thirty pounds. One other warning: Babies can bite off pieces of vinyl on the top railings of many mesh-type playpens and choke. Watch babies who are chewing on these. V-shaped accordion gates are hazardous and they are no longer being manufactured or distributed.

Three products we usually think of in connection with a happy baby are also dangerous. Never use a nipple stuffed with cotton as a pacifier, as the nipple can separate from its collar and strangle the baby.[69] Beware of small rattles used for cake decorations or favors; they can be swallowed. Disposable diapers can catch fire and babies can choke on pieces of diaper they bite off; take precautions to prevent both hazards.

Strollers must have hinges that safely protect your baby's fingers, and no sharp edges. Brakes must lock. The stroller must be stable enough to not tip backward when a baby stands up. The restraining device must hold the baby at both waist and crotch.

Toys can be a hazard. In 1984 more than 588,000 children with toy-related injuries required emergency treatment and thirty-one children died.[70] The Child Protection and Safety Act was passed by the federal government in 1970 specifically to keep unsafe toys off the market and the Consumer Product Safety Commission periodically lists toys banned for safety reasons. However, there are still unsafe toys on the market, both those manufactured here and those imported from abroad.

The most common reported injuries were cuts and bruises from being hit by or falling off a toy. Aspiration of small toys, or insertion into the nose or ear, was also a common problem.[71] The balloon has killed eighty children since 1983, who suffocated on an uninflated balloon or pieces of balloon. When the child takes a breath while the balloon is in the mouth, the balloon can be drawn into the throat. Children under six should *not* play with uninflated or broken pieces of balloons.[72]

By the way, there has been some concern about potential hearing loss from noises emitted by toys such as squeaking toys, moving toys, stationary toys like a toy drill, toy weapons, and firecrackers.[73]

Parents must obey certain basic safety rules when buying toys. Be sure fabric and stuffing are not flammable. Be sure there is no lead in the material or paint. Watch out for detachable parts that might be swallowed or aspirated, like removable small squeakers, beads, or buttons. Check for sharp edges and points. Avoid toys that, when broken, have sharp edges. Be sure long strings and cords are safe (very young babies have strangled). There was a recent recall of Johnson

& Johnson crib toys (Soft Triplets, Triplets Marching Band, and Piglet Crib Gym) because babies can get caught by the neck or the strings.[74]Always avoid cheaply constructed toys. Be cognizant of age appropriateness. For example, plastic building sets with thousands of small pieces are great for six-year-olds but unsuitably dangerous for infants.

When buying toys you have to take your child's development into account. Some two-year-olds can enjoy toys designed for older children, while others are better off with those made for younger children. Marilyn shares this story about her three-year-old son, who asked for a bow and arrow set. She checked for safety: the "arrow" came with rubber suction disks to stick on the target, the bow had very little power. However, one day she found her son, who had pried off the suction disk, sharpening the arrow in the pencil sharpener! He created a real weapon which had to be confiscated.

Hinged toy chests are also dangerous, as both fingers and heads have been caught. We recommend plastic laundry baskets instead.

There are certain products which though manufactured "correctly" lead to risk taking (usually on the part of boys) that seems unwarranted. The youth of America could reach adult status without skateboards, slingshots, or minibikes. However, these items are all popular. Parents have one of two recourses. They can forbid the use of the product by their child or they can work to have the product banned.

It has been suggested that parents think ahead for safety when purchasing a toy.[75] Will there be a safe place to use it? Do you have a place to keep toys for older children (a chemistry set, for example) away from the tots? Are you buying safe equipment instead of a cheap article that won't protect your child, like a toy football helmet? If the toy or equipment requires supervision (like a trampoline), who will provide it? Does your child really need the hazardous toy?

For those of you who have further questions about these or other pieces of equipment, we refer you to *The Complete Baby Book,*[76] which has a large consumer guide for baby products and toys, as well as government pamphlets.

Some products homeowners don't think of as dangerous have killed children. For example, an automatic garage door is a wonderful gadget but children playing to "beat" the door have been seriously injured when they didn't make it. Automatic car windows have strangled children, so we repeat, never leave children alone in a car and keep your car doors locked when the car is in your garage.

There is a long list of "ordinary" products which are especially dangerous to children. Disposable cigarette lighters, for example, are often discarded still containing lighter fluid and children have been injured. Recliner chairs have killed babies who were crawling on the leg rest and were trapped between the chair and leg rest when their weight forced the leg rest down.[77] A bunk bed mattress killed one two-year-old when it fell on the child, and a child's head can be caught between the guardrail and the mattress.[78] It is recommended that mattress supports be screwed into the frame and that boards be added between the guardrail and mattress if there is a space larger than 3 1/2 inches.

Another dangerous item found in every home is a window blind or drapery cord. Do not leave young children in cribs or playpens where they can reach the cord. Do not let cords dangle near the floor where your crawler can reach them. Babies have been found strangled in this innocuous-looking product.

Button batteries are very prevalent today in this era of digital watches, calculators, cameras, etc. Ingestions can be fatal or can cause severe tissue destruction if inserted in the ear or nose, so keep calculators, cameras, *and* spare batteries locked up.[79]

Parents often ask us about the safety of microwave ovens. If your microwave was built after 1971 and has no damage to door hinges, latch, or seals, leakage is not a cause for worry (see p. 165 and p. 592).

HOW CAN YOU KEEP FROM BEING A FRIGHTENED PARENT AND RAISING SCARED CHILDREN?

We want our children to survive, but we also want our children to become functioning adults, not people who are afraid of everything. Our real objective is to teach our children to *care* for themselves, to *love* themselves, and, therefore, *to be careful.* The thing to teach is: *I am important to myself and to my parents. I will be careful and I will be in control.*

By helping your child realize his or her own self-worth, you can minimize risk taking and maximize courage. You teach self-worth by loving your child, recognizing the child's uniqueness, and praising the child as often as you can. It is not an easy task but it can be done.

Safety rules are extremely important. Disregard of safety rules should be the most important—and non-negotiable—area of child discipline. But you do not have to create fright in order to teach the child to obey safety rules. As with many things in life there is a balance between the importance of the safety rules and the effect they may have in making the child fearful. Marilyn's daughter claims that she was fearful about learning how to drive because her mother was always so insistent on automobile safety. However, she became a willing as well as a careful driver. Given the choice, all of us would rather have a live child with a mild phobia than no child.

The whole purpose of this chapter has been to alert parents to awareness of some of the potential hazards that can befall their children. We have pointed out the importance of parental protection which must be maximal at infancy, but must also continue, in modified form, through adolescence.

The way you yourself think and act about safety in front of your child may be the most important aspect of safety. The way you treat your child in terms of his or her value and the way you treat yourself in the terms of your value are also important.

We hope this chapter has given you the "safety reflex." This reflex can become automatic, easy, and lifesaving.

IF YOUR CHILD IS INJURED

Please remember that *every* child will be hurt or injured while growing up, nearly always severely enough to require medical attention. Don't feel guilty, and do help your child not to feel inappropriate guilt. Instead, *learn* from the incident. If the accident could have been prevented, be sure it is prevented in the future. Warn other parents.

SUGGESTED READINGS AND RESOURCES

Arena, Jay M. *Your Child and Household Safety*. Washington, D.C.: Chemical Specialties Manufacturers Association, Inc., 1986.

Pamphlet worth writing for.

Gillis, Jack, and Fise, Mary Ellen R. *The Childwise Catalog: A Consumer Guide to Buying the Safest and Best Products for Your Children*. New York: Pocket Books, 1986.

A recent book on safety products from cribs to clothes. Lots of useful information.

Harmon, Murl. *A New Vaccine for Child Safety*. Jenkintown, Pa: Safety Now Co., 1976.

Dated but still helpful.

Urquhart, John, and Heilmann, Klaus. *Risk Watch: The Odds of Life*. New York: Facts on File, 1984.

A very clearly written book that explains what risk is, suggests new ways of measuring risk, simplifies epidemiology and health risk statistics, and analyzes the effect of the media on our perceptions of risk. Useful for parents who want to know more about the interpretation of health risks in their children.

*   *   *

U.S. Consumer Product Safety Commission, Washington, D.C. 20207, phone 800-638-CPSC or 800-638-2772.

Pamphlets and fact sheets on toy safety are available.

SOURCES OF CONSUMER INFORMATION

American Academy of Pediatrics
Committee on Accident & Poison
Prevention
141 Northwest Point
P.O. Box 927
Elk Grove Village, Ill. 60009-0927
  Areas of safety: Many.
  312-869-9327

American Automobile Association
8111 Gatehouse Rd.
Falls Church, Va. 22047
  Areas of safety: Cars and traffic.
  703-222-6000

American Camping Association
Bradford Woods
Martinsville, Ind. 46151

Areas of safety: Organized camps.
317-342-8456

American Medical Association
Pamphlet Order Department
535 North Dearborn Street
Chicago, Ill. 60610

Areas of safety: Many. Ask for
"Publications List", a listing of
available materials.
312-645-7168

**National Fire Protection
Association**
Batterymarch Park
Quincy, Mass. 02269

Areas of safety: Fire prevention and
escape planning, baby-sitting. For
50 cents will send "Sparky's Fire
Department Membership Kit."
1-800-344-3555

Physicians for Automotive Safety
16 Hobart Gap Road
Short Hills, N.J. 07078

Areas of safety: Automotive baby
care.

Toy Manufacturers of America, Inc.
200 Fifth Avenue
New York, N.Y. 10010

Areas of safety: Toys, games.
212-675-1141

**U.S. Consumer Product Safety
Commission**
Washington, D.C. 20207
Regional field offices are located in
Atlanta, Boston, Chicago, Cleveland,
Dallas, Denver, Kansas City, Los
Angeles, Minneapolis, New Orleans,
New York City, Philadelphia, San
Francisco, and Seattle.

Areas of safety: All areas of
consumer safety.
1-800-638-2772
Toll Free—National Office (except
Alaska and Hawaii)

U.S. Food and Drug Administration
Ms. Mary Ball, Director
Office of Consumer Inquiries, HFE-88
5600 Fishers Lane
Rockville, Md. 20857

Areas of safety: Food, poisoning,
general health. Prepares monthly
FDA Consumer, annual subscription
costs $8.55.
301-443-3170

6

HELPERS IN CHILD CARE

Scope of Chapter

Parents need helpers in order to care for children. Some helpers are family and friends. Some are paid child care workers. All of these helpers have a natural and understandable tendency to exact a price for the help they provide—money, respect, love, or time spent with them in meeting some of their needs.

This chapter will cover what kinds of help parents need, where to obtain it, and how to evaluate its quality and price.

Introduction

You can't do it alone!

Medieval Madonna and Child paintings depict a mother holding an infant in loving embrace. The child is usually clothed in nothing more than a halo or a wisp of fabric—certainly nothing so prosaic as a diaper. The happy pair look complete unto themselves, with no apparent needs.

The real care of ordinary human infants by ordinary human parents is *not* like this, except for an occasional, fleeting blissful moment. Infants and children have almost unremitting needs, which are not portrayed in Madonna pictures. Their needs are even greater in times of sickness. Parents also have needs, both our own needs apart from the child, and those necessary to care for the child. Parents, too, have illnesses and problems.

There are two major kinds of help parents need. The first is advice; the second consists of helping hands ranging from a friend minding your baby to a paid housekeeper.

When families were larger and less mobile, and when family life was simpler and more governed by tradition, most advice and help in parenting came from family and neighbors. Grandmother knew how and when to start feeding adult food to babies and she was close by, either in the same house or village. Grandmother or a neighbor or midwife knew how to attend a birth and prepare traditional remedies for sick children. An older child could hold an infant while

Mother worked at cooking or in the fields. Early lessons in "how to help" were learned at home.

Today, of course, fewer helpers are likely to be family or old friends, and more are likely to be professional or institutional "expert" sources of care and advice. Certainly much good has come from these changes, but there are some drawbacks as well, as we will discuss.

HELP IN THE FORM OF ADVICE

Experts have professional knowledge and can often provide scientifically validated child care advice. However, they are less likely to give personal, loving care and concern. And, sometimes the expert's well-intentioned advice about our children's needs does not take into account our own needs. And experts may not realize how demanding it could be on a parent to carry out their advice. Experts may also be overspecialized and give advice in one area which might interfere with another. On the other side of the coin, medical or psychiatric advice for *parents* sometimes overlooks the effect on children.

Even worse, much supposedly expert advice is *not* solidly based on scientifically validated knowledge. We all have heard of "old wives' tales" as a put-down term, but there are "old doc's tales" and "old teacher's tales" as well.

For example, only a few years ago, many pediatricians encouraged mothers to give up breast-feeding at the first hint of any problem, substituting artificially formulated feedings instead. The fact that these formulas were mathematically calculated gave pediatricians a sense of confidence in the newly developed science of infant nutrition. Parents began to feel that formulas were technologically or scientifically advanced, while breast-feeding appeared "old-fashioned." More recently, scientific research has demonstrated many advantages in human milk which were not known by previous pediatricians. Paradoxically, a grandmother or "old wife" who urged breast-feeding was giving advice which today's evidence shows to have been scientifically sounder than the *seemingly* scientific medical advice of the earlier day.

Similarly, only a few years ago, psychiatrists were busy forecasting all sorts of dire consequences if mothers were employed at anything other than the full-time care of their own young children. This advice was based on then-recent findings about emotional damage which occurs in children completely separated from their families and placed in impersonal institutions. But the experts, we now know, overgeneralized from their findings. They forgot how recent it has been in human history that any substantial number of people could afford to remove able-bodied women from the workforce during their reproductive years. And the experts often confused the dire consequences of wartime separations, poverty, or desertion which forced women unwillingly into the workplace, usually at ill-paid and exhausting jobs, with the benign consequences of chosen work. The advisers caused needless guilt and anxiety in women who *had* to work, and led many who *wanted* to continue their employment to abandon it, for fear of harming their children. Paradoxically today, when newer research has demonstrated the mental health benefits of employment for mothers who want it, those who choose not to be employed outside the home may feel pressured and guilty!

Educators also rapidly change the "expert" advice which they give. In one generation, "phonics" is the only proper way to teach reading; a few years later, the "look-see" method is felt to be the only way; today, back to phonics again. Actually, it appears that some children learn best with one method, some better with the other, and the vast majority can learn either way. At one time, mastery of school skills was considered the only criterion for promotion in grades; at a later time "social promotion" became a valid concept; now we seem to be back to "mastery learning." But at any given time, the current thinking of the experts tends to be presented to parents as though it were the absolute and only truth.

Some educational dogma had *no* scientific or measured validity. For a while teachers were down on coloring books because having to "stay within the lines" was supposed to stifle creativity. To our knowledge, no one ever measured creativity or the effects thereon of coloring within the lines. Actually it probably improves eye-hand coordination.

Clearly, accepting advice from advice givers requires some means of evaluating the soundness and appropriateness of the advice received. This is more true today than ever before, because there are so many more potential sources of advice.

Our advice to you about advice follows. Any advice which doesn't feel right to you should be reevaluated. You may need second and even third opinions. Some good sources are 1) Experienced parents—especially those who have the same parenting situation you have (i.e., both parents employed, if that is true in your case). 2) The older generation; grandparents have a valuable perspective. 3) Books. Obviously *we* wouldn't be writing a book if we didn't think books could help. But don't rely on just *one* book—all authors have their biases, including us. Compare what others have to say. 4) Magazines. *Parent* magazine and *Medical Self Care* offer pretty much what their names imply. Articles in women's magazines like *Woman's Day, Family Circle, Ladies' Home Journal, McCall's,* and *Working Mother* generally have high editorial standards today. They often give references to the professional literature which you can read or call to your doctor's attention. 5) Professional advisers like doctors. (See chapter on Choosing Health Professionals for Your Child's Care.) 6) Groups. From Lamaze classes to La Leche to Parent Effectiveness Training, parent-training and self-help groups abound. 7) Teachers (and other child care workers) know a good deal about children because they spend so much time with them.

It's apparent, from looking at this long list, that advice givers differ in one important respect vis-à-vis *your* knowledge. Some of them, like medical or legal specialists, have far more knowledge and experience in their areas than you do, and many degrees and certificates to prove it. Some of them, like neighbors, may have far less knowledge and experience than you do. The important thing to remember is that *you* have to decide whether to take anyone's advice.

CHILD CARE HELP

There are some basic characteristics you should look for in child care givers. One author says this term is preferable to baby-sitter—you don't want the person just sitting there—or caretaker—because she (or just possibly he) is not taking but rather *giving* care.[1] For the most part, we will refer to care givers as "she" because today almost all of them are women.

The most important characteristic of a good care giver for young children is an *interest* in caring for children. This means the care giver finds children fascinating, enjoys spending time with them, and conveys the feeling that children are interesting people. However, it doesn't mean being a doormat for children. Rather, it means liking and responding to their maturing independence and expecting growth and good behavior from them.

Some people are interested in children because they raised their own—that was their main career—and now their own have grown up or are in school. Some people are interested in children because they *didn't* have their own, and feel they missed something valuable in life. Some young people, who hope to have children of their own in the future, enjoy a child care job in order to learn more about it.

Experience in child care is helpful, of course, but an intelligent *interested* person with no experience may do better than an experienced person with fixed ideas. Just as an inexperienced first-time mother can do a good job but will need more advice than an experienced one, an inexperienced child care helper will need more supervision.

Some people are great for an hour or two, and can be excellent if their tolerance is not exceeded. For example, many teenagers make excellent evening or afternoon baby-sitters, but lack the stamina or interest needed for day-in-and-day-out care. Many elderly helpers are great, but lack the energy for full-time child care.

Others have both the energy and tolerance for all-day care, but will need to pay attention to their own needs for respite care, the company of other adults, social and intellectual stimulation, and rest. The best asset for an all-day child care giver is one which is important for parents too: enough sensitivity to self to permit honest empathy to the child's needs and honest respect for their own needs.

Even quite small children delight in having someone in their environment who resonates with a special talent or preference or interest of the child—such as a helper who brings the child's favorite chewing gum, or who especially likes to enjoy music with a musical child—or who gives a back rub in a special way. The thing that makes this so precious to children is the often unspoken sense of

"I'm me, I'm special, I'm not just any old kid, and caring for me is not just any old job."

Age is important. The very young may not have the judgment you require and the very old may lack the energy to do the job. A child care giver should be able to speak the language properly and frequently to your child. What about foreign-speaking care givers? We are not concerned about accents but some foreign-speaking care givers don't talk much at all because they feel embarrassed about their accent, while children *need* to hear speech. It goes without saying that child care givers must be competent in child care and understand child development. This doesn't mean a master's degree in child development, but rather a feeling of what to expect from children at different ages. The most important thing is a liking for children and being comfortable with children. Not everybody is.

CHILD CARE: WHAT ARE THE ISSUES?

Children's Needs

Infants need constant care every hour of every day. Lots of verbal as well as non-verbal interaction is important from infancy on, even before the child can talk back. Toddlers may feed themselves, but they need constant supervision because of the accident-proneness of that age, and they also need continual guidance because of their rapid motor, language, and social development. Older children need more unobtrusive supervision, which meets their physical and emotional needs and gives them freedom of movement while the care giver stays close enough to notice any problems.

Parents' Needs

Parents have the needs that any human being has at any time—these do not disappear during parenting. Economic, social, and intellectual needs and needs for intimate and/or sexual pairing are constant throughout the life cycle. Parents have need for rest and sleep, despite the fact they may have an infant or several young children, or sick children to care for. Parents also have needs for new information and often new skills, at all new stages of parenting.

For all of these reasons, it is silly, if not downright dangerous, to assume that routine daily care can be provided by only one person. It simply cannot be done.

Some parents take great pride in never leaving their young child with a baby-sitter. This may seem like the ultimate emotional support for the young child, but there are some cautions for both the child and the parents. What would you do if the child so raised had to be hospitalized—or a parent did? Children are emotionally safer if they have had some experience with other care givers—even if only at multiple family picnics where other parents tie their shoelaces. Children are emotionally safer if they know from experience that there are a *number* of trustworthy adults who can care for them. They are emotionally safer if they have had the opportunity to master mild degrees of "separation anxiety" than if they meet it for the first time in an overwhelming dose. Parents, of course, need time off from parenting just as all workers need time off from their jobs in order to return to them refreshed.

The Myth of the Ideal Care Giver

You've probably heard it said that the ideal care giver for young children would have certain personality characteristics: intelligence, common sense, warmth, loving nurturance, emotional sensitivity to others, maturity, patience, playfulness, humor, ability to be disciplined and to discipline, and consistency. But no human being has all of these qualities, certainly not all of the time. Some people generally have some of these qualities more than others. Most of us temporarily "lose" some of these qualities when we are tired or overworked or ill. Too many mothers have felt undeserved guilt because they lacked some of these qualities or, worse, because they left their children with care givers who lacked some of them.

The principle of *balance* is important here. A parent who is emotionally warm but disorganized might actually benefit the children by finding a sitter who is more disciplined (remember Mary Poppins?). Parents who are strong on discipline and low on indulgence often correct the balance by leaving their children with more permissive people such as the proverbial indulgent grandparents. Children themselves can make balancing choices. In a large family, a cohesive neighborhood, or a nursery school with several teachers, they can choose which adult to turn to at which time for which need.

The principle of consistency has been much overrated in child care advice. (This is more fully discussed on page 58 in Chapter 3, Socialization.) It's true that your child needs to get clear cues about how to please you and others, so as to have the satisfying feeling of being a "good child." But, in all honesty, parents' needs are not always consistent. Even very small children can learn that parents have different moods. They can also easily learn that different care givers have different strong points. One may be great for games and giggles; another may nurture in a more structured way, like baking a cake together.

ROUTINE DAILY CARE:
WHO IS TO PROVIDE IT?

The usual options for child care are yourself only; yourself and spouse only; parents plus occasional sitters; regular full-time alternative care by relatives, housekeepers, day care homes or centers. All of these options have advantages and disadvantages.

Yourself only. As noted above, the advantages include the fact that continuity is assured (unless you or the child need to be hospitalized), and you do not have to worry about having control over the quality of care provided by someone else.

The disadvantages include the possibility of your becoming overworked, especially with a difficult or ill child. A solo care giver can also become over-isolated and begin to suffer from "cabin fever" in the absence of adult company. There are also disadvantages for the child: a lack of exposure to other adults and children and no opportunity to master mild degrees of separation anxiety. The child must put up with you alone even on your "bad days." And you, in turn, will have to keep the child with you at all times, even on errands.

Yourself and spouse only. We have known couples who arranged their lives so that one or the other of them was always with the children; no outside sitters were used at all. The advantages of this arrangement are the continuity of care it provides, at least if your spouse has the same philosophy of child care as you. In addition, there is a little more chance for each partner to get out and do something away from the children. The main disadvantage is that you and your spouse won't be able to do that together. Most couples need some time alone together, away from the children, to "have a date" and nourish their sense of themselves as a couple. And the disadvantage to the child is the lack of exposure to other adults besides Mommy and Daddy.

You and/or spouse plus occasional sitters. This is the arrangement that, until recently, was most common. Fathers were employed and mothers provided most child care, but sitters were used occasionally so that parents could go out for shopping, errands, and social events. The advantage of this arrangement is continuity for the children, the parents' sense of general control over child rearing, and some opportunity for "respite care."

The disadvantages stem largely from the possible effects on young children of separations which are not predictable and routine. The sitter may not always be the same person, or may not be there often enough or regularly enough for the children to have a solid relationship with him or her.

Family care. Historically, raising children meant sharing their daily care between mother and other members of the extended family—grandparents, aunts and uncles, older children—who would watch the child for part of every day. Such people loved the child almost as much as the parents did, were familiar to the child, and usually shared the same philosophy of traditional child rearing that the parents had.

For those few of you who can arrange it now, these advantages still exist. Some of us live in three-generational households; some of us will be lucky enough to live close to relatives. Unfortunately, familial expectations are different now. There are also money issues: "If I am employed and my mother or sister is not, how much of my income should I share with her in return for child care which makes my employment possible?" There are control issues because both personal and generational differences between parents and grandparents do exist. Grandparents, or your sister, may be more indulgent, or expect more discipline than you do. Family members may be less willing to take "orders" from you than from an employer. Friction with a family member can be more disturbing than friction with an employee, because there is a lifetime relationship which you care about. It is difficult to "fire" a relative even when irreconcilable issues interfere with the child care you want for your child. On the other hand, there could be less friction since there may be more agreement about general philosophy of family life.

Child care in your home. Full-time hired housekeepers are likely to be an expensive solution. Housekeepers may be the most difficult group in which to evaluate quality of care since, unlike day care centers, they do not have to meet licensing requirements. Sometimes there are cultural differences which make communicating your child care philosophy difficult.

However, a housekeeper certainly provides other advantages. She cares for your child in your child's familiar environment. A sick child can be cared for at home. There is someone at home to answer the door for the plumber. There are some disadvantages. If the housekeeper is sick herself, you may have to arrange substitute care on short notice, whereas day care centers have their own arrangements for substitutes just as schools do.

In-home child care can be part-time. Some mothers ask a weekly cleaning woman to watch the baby. Some parents who both work are on different shifts so one or the other is home except for an hour or two. Some excellent people who are not available for full-time work, such as high school or college students, or older people who are semiretired, can be hired to watch the child for a short time.

Day Care Centers. All states require that day care centers be licensed. Licensing requires that a day care center be under the direction of someone with special education and knowledge of early childhood educational and care needs. The center also has to meet code requirements for fire safety, sanitation, and other health and safety issues, and has to have a specified ratio of adults to children. What licensure does not guarantee is the staff's emotional warmth and genuine interest in caring for children.

Day care homes, or "informal day care," are arrangements in which someone, with or without children of her own, cares for a small number of children in her own home. These homes generally do not have to meet any licensing standards. In some communities they are monitored. For example, the Tucson Association for Child Care certifies day care homes and monitors on a quarterly basis with at least one to two unannounced visits. The purpose of monitoring is to assure that homes maintain a certain prescribed level of safety and quality care.

In a sense, every time you leave your child with a neighbor while you shop, or let her leave her child with you for the same reason, you are using an informal, unlicensed day care home. Some experts on early childhood care disapprove of the existence of unlicensed day care homes but, in fact, this is the *most common* form of alternative child care in America. If you choose this approach, you should talk to other parents who have used the same home. However, *you* will have to evaluate both the safety of the environment, and the emotional quality of the care yourself. Your child's response is an important piece of information.

Your own day care home. Some mothers who have one or two children, and prefer to care for them personally, may still have some extra energy and need some extra income. There is a great need for more home day care centers, and providing one is a valid option to consider. A good book by Frances Alston, *Caring for Other People's Children*,[2] gives a very complete how-to-do-it guide, covering everything from whether to get licensed or not, to how to handle the business side of running such a small business, as well as how to provide nutritious meals and creative play, and how to respond to medical emergencies. She also gives suggestions on the special needs of children who are in afterschool day care, instead of all-day care. In fact, her book is so good that it could be useful to a conscientious parent who does not want to start a family day care home but just evaluate the one she's using (and perhaps give the care giver a copy if she doesn't have one).

We add a few suggestions of our own:

1. In many communities, there are networks of family day care centers. The network office can help you get set up, refer clients, give advice on problems, and help you meet licensing requirements. In some cases they even maintain lists of emergency substitutes if you become ill or need extra help.

2. Consider enrolling enough children that you can afford to employ at least a part-time person to help play with the children—perhaps a retiree. Young children adore contact with elderly persons but, in today's world, they often have too little chance for it. Similarly, many elderly persons who could not run a center on their own have much to offer young children in your center.

3. Be sensitive to your own children's feelings about other children in the home. As a person running a small business, you can't "play favorites" during business hours, but your own child does need to know that he or she is your true favorite. Some special time together after the workday may be even more important for the day care mother and her child than for the mother who works outside the home and has a reunion with the child after work.

HOW DO YOU DECIDE ABOUT
CHILD CARE OPTIONS?

Think honestly about *your* needs first. The needs of most young children are fairly similar. By contrast, you as an adult have had many years to develop your own individualized needs and preferences. The saddest mothers are those who quit work that they really love because they think they "ought to" be a full-time mother (rather than wanting to), and those who are forced by economic needs to stay in jobs they hate, when they'd really prefer to be with their children full-time.

If you are a gregarious person, and love to be with other adults, you should hesitate to be a full-time mother unless you can work out ways to share mothering with others, such as setting up play groups, "library schools," or acting as a playground mother. If you are working now and hate your job, it may be that staying home for child care is just what you want to do. On the other hand, it could be that what you really need is *both* a child and a more satisfying job. The decision to stay home or not might also depend on how supportive your spouse is. Not surprisingly, both choices—working or staying home—are much easier with a supportive and cooperative spouse.

The "house-husband" option was almost unheard of until recent years, although there have always been husbands who managed the home during temporary periods of unemployment if their wives were employed. Most data on this option seems to come from men who wrote about their experiences, either during the time they were doing it—in which case they'd have to be described as a writer working from home as well as house-husband—or after they'd stopped, in which case they'd have to be described as a temporary house-husband. Not too many men stay on as house-husbands permanently, though increasing numbers are successful single parents.

It's obvious that the kind of child care you arrange will largely depend on what you can afford. Trade-offs (like room and board) can sometimes substitute for money but not always. Certain employed parents get a partial tax credit for child care.[3] The most costly single expense of child rearing is child care.

Despite economic needs or personal preferences, some parents still feel lingering guilt about using day care or housekeepers, and feel their relationship with the child will be impaired. Clarke-Stewart[4] has thoroughly reviewed the evidence on this point and is convinced it isn't so, other things being equal. She has studied excellent university-run programs, more typical community ones, informal home care, and child care programs in a number of countries. It turns out that children in day care, either centers or homes, have temporary advantages in social skills and vocabulary over children reared at home alone. However, home-reared children do catch up in these skills, so those of you who want to raise your own children shouldn't feel guilty either! Choose what is right for your family or what is best among the available alternatives.

BABY-SITTERS

Once in a While

This form of alternative child care is used by almost everyone as a substitute for the primary care giver. Most parents need baby-sitters from time to time, even if they have full-time housekeepers or work as full-time homemakers.

Baby-sitting is by definition part-time work. The people who do it are generally people outside the regular workforce—teenagers, college students, retired or widowed older persons. However, a few regularly employed people do evening and weekend baby-sitting to supplement their income.

Almost any kind and reasonably intelligent person who likes children and has some experience with them can be an occasional baby-sitter for a few hours at a time. The amount of experience, skill, and judgment required increases with the length of time you'll be away, and whether you can be reached in an emergency.

Having teenagers as baby-sitters benefits the teenager and society as well as you, because it gives young people experience in child care, which is often lacking in today's small nuclear families. Society as a whole would benefit if all young parents had had more experience in child care than most have had when they become first-time parents. At the same time, you have to be sure that your child doesn't suffer from the teenager's lack of experience.

It's best to have one or two regular baby-sitters, if possible, so that they are familiar to your child. It's also best to begin with a new baby-sitter in early infancy, if you can, before stranger anxiety sets in. We don't recommend that inexperienced young teenage baby-sitters care for a very young infant. However, a responsible girl of fourteen or so, especially if she has younger siblings whom she has cared for, could meet your needs. Begin by asking her to work as a "play-sitter" for a few hours in the afternoon, or early evenings or weekends, while you are present but working on other tasks. Then you can answer any questions she has, and have a chance to personally observe how she interacts with your baby and how she performs child care tasks like changing diapers.

Most parents select teenage baby-sitters on the basis of knowing the child's parents, or on a recommendation from a friend. If you don't personally know the sitter, you have to ask for references. References should include information on how good she is with children, honesty, reliability, etc. Also, always ask: 1) Were there any problems? 2) Do you still use, or would you rehire, this sitter?

The first time you employ a new baby-sitter, if it's not a "play-sitter" in your presence, it's best to do so on a social occasion where you can be reached by phone. No matter how hard you try to anticipate questions, there are likely to be some things you forget to think of. We cover how to instruct baby-sitters on emergencies in the chapter dealing with emergencies on p. 724.

Before you leave, be sure to tell the sitter the house rules about snacks, TV watching, bedtime, etc. We always wrote those down. Also, be sure to tell the sitter where she can find snacks for herself and what you expect in the way of *her* behavior. For example, it's not a good idea to let the sitter invite friends over as she can get distracted from her child-watching duties.

It may seem sexist to keep referring to the baby-sitter as "she." In fact, however, far more teenage girls than boys seek work as baby-sitters. This is partly because, at this age, girls are physically and emotionally more mature than boys, and partly because of sexist stereotypy. It would be good for society, as a whole, if more young potential fathers had baby-sitting experience in their teen-age years. We would be less likely to use a male baby-sitter for an infant unless the boy in question is emotionally mature and has had a lot of experience caring for younger sibs. However, teenage boys can make great sitters for preschoolers and school-age children. They are energetic, like to play vigorously, and have more interest in sports and games than is still true of many girls.

Overnight and Vacation Baby-sitting

Occasionally parents may want or need a night or a weekend, or a longer vacation, away from the children. The kind of responsibility that is required for this job is considerably greater than when parents are gone only for a few hours. The qualifications are really those of a housekeeper, rather than a baby-sitter. In addition, the child's anxiety about being left is likely to be greater because you won't be returning after a few hours.

Barring serious emergencies, we personally wouldn't leave an infant or a child too young to telephone, with a stranger for any extended time. We would consider a responsible relative or neighbor whom the child knows or a person qualified in infant care who has some opportunity to become familiar with the child before the trip occurs. Otherwise, we'd postpone the vacation, or take the child along and hire sitters at the vacation site. Anne did this often for profes-sional trips—making sure in advance that the hotel had baby-sitters. Marilyn used pediatric nurses from the hospital she worked at, coordinating her vacation with their time off from work. The children knew the nurses and Marilyn had assessed both their competence and their caring abilities.

Older children may be better off staying in a playmate's home. You may be able to find a playmate whose parent will do this for you, in return for your offer to reciprocate when they want to do the same. Sometimes you can arrange for the kids to go to their grandparents' house and get household help for *them*, or trade off with your sister or brother and their children.

Emergency Sitters

A single parent, or a married parent whose spouse is out of town, can become suddenly incapacitated. If you have sympathetic and available relatives, neighbors, or friends, any of them may take your child or children into their home.

If you cannot make such arrangements, but have an unexpected need for a reliable person and no time to check references, there are resources you should know about. Almost every community large enough to have hospitals has nurses' registries listed in the Yellow Pages. These agencies provide registered nurses, licensed practical nurses, and homemakers. Such agencies take considerably more responsibility for checking the qualifications and abilities of their people than do ordinary employment agencies. Needless to say, personnel of this caliber cost more than ordinary sitters, but when you don't have time to check out references, the added cost is probably worth it for your peace of mind.

For older children, many neighbors or relatives are willing to "look in" on your children provided they aren't required to be there all the time. However, we do not recommend leaving children alone for a prolonged period of time or overnight until they are well into their teens.

REGULAR CARE: HOUSEKEEPERS

The Perfect Housekeeper

We'll start with housekeepers, even though this is not the commonest form of alternative child care as it's too expensive for many families. However, the housekeeper alternative most clearly illustrates the problems involved when women try to reproduce the kind of care they would provide if they were full-time housewife/mothers at home. Also, there are many books written on day care, but few on housekeepers.

Keeping a child in his or her own environment can be less disruptive to the child (and you as well). Your child will bask in the attention of a care giver whose major job is caring for him or her alone. On the minus side, an at-home care giver may offer less stimulation, supervision, companionship, and socialization than the child would receive in a group situation.

Many of us have a fantasy of the ideal housekeeper which is startlingly close to the fantasy that a sexist man might have of the ideal wife (except for sexual relations)! This paragon would love my children, care for them in a way that keeps all of the daily hassles off my back. She would exercise considerable autonomy and independence in caring for my children and home. She would make lots of decisions by herself—but they would aways be the same decisions that I would make! If it turned out that we had a different view about some major policy issue like how to discipline, or whether a clean kitchen or clean clothes was the highest priority, then she would immediately and lovingly realize that of course I was right, and do it my way thereafter. She would work long hours and enjoy every minute of her work. She would never complain, although she would also be tactfully open about any problem that was occurring, and always manage to give me the feedback I needed in the very way and at the very time that I wanted to receive it. Although housebound, she would be mentally alert, in touch with current events, and able to intelligently discuss my children's homework with them. She would be knowledgeable about children and child development and provide loving age-appropriate stimulation for my children, just as I would.

A working woman might add: although as mentally alert as I am, she wouldn't feel bored by being housebound, as I might. She would be creatively challenged by the task of being a homemaker. She would give my husband some of the little attentions he'd love to receive on coming home. Of course, she wouldn't be in sexual competition with me for his attentions. In fact, she'd give me some of the *same* little attentions when I got home from a busy day at work.

Problems with this fantasy are obvious. If she had all my qualifications and attributes, probably she'd be after my job and looking for a housekeeper herself! But another problem with the fantasy is a bit more subtle. If my fantasy about what I want in a housekeeper is unrealistic, I may feel guilty about expecting too much and settle in turn for expecting too little.

Employer Difficulties

For a number of years, Anne puzzled about why it was easier to supervise staff at work than housekeepers at home, and easier to hire (or if necessary, fire) staff at work than at home. She has thought about her feelings and realizes that guilt has been an issue for her. Because of racism, or immigrant status, or a background of poverty or illness, intelligent women applied for housekeeper jobs because they simply weren't eligible for the higher-paying, higher-status jobs such as Anne's. Anne realized that she was not personally responsible for their bad luck, or society's exploitation of them, but that she did benefit from it. In hindsight, she realizes that on several occasions she let housekeepers exploit her.

Also at work, in the outside world, personnel policies are pretty clear, and not up to the employer alone. The job description is usually written, as are severance policies. A job in the workplace is usually fairly circumscribed whereas a housekeeping job is very different. Outside jobs have set standards and limited demands and hours, but home jobs have an infinite capacity for expansion. This is tough on a housekeeper with high standards she can't meet, and also tough on a working mother whose housekeeper cannot or does not meet standards of the household.

There is a shortage of people wanting to do domestic work so changing housekeepers is usually much more difficult than changing employees on the job. Finally, if your children have formed an attachment to her, as you would hope they would, you will be incurring a loss for them. All these factors put you in a poorer bargaining position than you may be as a supervisor at work.

Marilyn adds that 1) Most women today grew up in "servantless" homes and have no modeling experience of how to deal with domestic help; 2) Our individualistic culture says we should be capable of doing things ourselves whether it's housework or yard work, and *especially* child rearing. Americans are inherently suspicious of nanny-raised children even when they turn out to be a Winston Churchill!; 3) Many parents are concerned about leaving their children with someone who might not transmit their values and culture as they would; 4) Many mothers do housework unconsciously and don't realize how much or what they do, so that writing a job description or schedule is *hard work;* 5) Many of us have trouble setting our own priorities or deciding what's important around the house, so it is difficult to tell others.

Marilyn did not have guilt about having household help. She always accepted her own status as a professional and her own need for help. She always paid well (both salary and fringes) and felt she was a good employer. She was exploited far more than she exploited (housekeepers leaving without notice, drinking on the job, etc.).

If you've decided to seek a full-time housekeeper, remember the following: 1) You need to be realistic—no housekeeper is perfect, just as no parent is perfect. 2) You should pay attention to what the housekeeper's reasons are for wanting this job, and be prepared to make mutual adjustments. 3) You need to remember that you are ultimately responsible for your children and, in this employer-employee relationship, you are the boss, hopefully a friendly and kindly one. 4) Don't exploit; give her the best pay and working conditions you can afford. 5) Don't allow the housekeeper to exploit you.

Live-in Versus Day Housekeepers

If you have room, you might want to consider a live-in full-time housekeeper. You need to have a room for a housekeeper, preferably with a bath. Most expect their own TV set and radio and a comfortable area for sitting.

There are many advantages to the live-in arrangement. It more closely duplicates the extended-family situation. The housekeeper is more likely to be like a member of the family. If she has a minor illness she can probably still care for the children while leaving the laundry until she feels better, just as you would. You know that she's there if you have to be late getting home.

On the other hand, you have to recognize that she might get overloaded, and feel she's on duty twenty-four hours a day. You need to build in some protection against burn-out. Every housekeeper needs both days off and "off hours" on working days when she won't be disturbed. Some housekeepers live in during the week, and go elsewhere weekends. This arrangement gives them a highly desirable change of pace.

Financially, if you pay a weekly wage, the live-in housekeeper conventionally gets as much as the by-day housekeeper. She gains financially because she gets room and board with you. However, she might wind up working longer hours, or get called on in more weekend emergencies. We recommend a weekly wage for specified hours with extra pay for extra hours of work. You should also pay extra for household guests, dinner parties, and anything else that makes extra work.

The biggest problem with live-in help—unless you have the right kind of floor plan—is privacy. Many working mothers would like live-in help but do not wish to sacrifice privacy. Marilyn was so desperate for help in getting the children ready in the morning that she sacrificed privacy for live-in help. (In retrospect, she should have realized in advance that she would need live-in help and bought a house which would have allowed privacy for both parents and housekeeper. She was too hung up on the "You're supposed to care for children yourself" myth to do so.) Some working women we know have help for two "shifts." Perhaps one woman to feed and dress the children in the morning and another to come in after school for housecleaning, evening meal preparation, and baby-sitting, if needed.

If you know you are going to need help, we suggest you 1) get a home which accommodates a live-in housekeeper, or 2) get a home on a bus line. If not, your housekeeper will need her own transportation—many do not—or you have to pick her up.

With a day worker, you need to arrange for a backup if she can't come. She should give you as much notice as possible but all of us can get taken ill suddenly. Marilyn had backup help she paid "on retainer" to be available if the regular housekeeper became ill. At another time Marilyn had a cleaning woman *and* a housekeeper. If the housekeeper was ill, the cleaning woman could provide emergency help and she knew the house *and* the children. You should make it clear that a day worker who baby-sits at night will be paid extra.

Some day workers want to bring their own child to your home. This can work out nicely if she can handle all the children concerned and avoid favoritism or neglect of her own child. There may also be liability implications if the worker's child is injured at your home.

Finding and Keeping Helpers

IDENTIFYING NEEDS

You probably know what kind of help you need. It's also wise to think about needs a helper might have and how you could meet those, ranging from dollars to a place to live. A relationship built on reciprocity has a better chance of surviving.

THE SEARCH AND SELECTION

Once you've identified what kind of housekeeper you need, the next step is the search for candidates. We'll discuss specifics of advertising, agencies, etc., below. Selection is more complicated than just finding a person you like. You should always check references and, further, hire on a trial basis (and always keep the names of runners-up).

NEGOTIATING THE CONTRACT

Almost always, you have in your head some expectations of what the helping relationship is going to be like, and so does the helper. Writing a job description or contract may seem artificial, but it can be clarifying and helpful to both parties.

EVALUATING SATISFACTION WITH THE HELPER AND THE HELP

Despite the best selection and contracting you do, there can be dissatisfaction. We recommend a definite probationary period. It's important to sort out major from minor dissatisfactions. The following issues are major for Marilyn and Anne: competency; safety instincts; warmth and kindness to children; openness to questions and possible criticism; and ability to communicate her own concerns.

CONFLICT RESOLUTION

Conflicts are inevitable in helping relationships. In trying to resolve them, remember to state your feelings to your helper as a fact, rather than an accusation, using "I-sentences." For example, "Sally, I am confused because we keep running out of clean socks for Sam, and I thought we had enough. Do we need to buy more or is there some problem with doing the laundry on time?"

If there is a serious problem which is going to require some time to discuss, it's a good idea to let your housekeeper know in advance that you plan to do that, so that she can get her thoughts in line about it too.

ENDING RELATIONSHIPS WITH HELPERS

Helping relationships do end. Most ideally, this is because the need for it has passed, both parties are pleased, and each is ready to move on to other things. But, of course, on other occasions helpers quit.

How do you prevent quitting? Some reasons why perfectly satisfactory housekeepers quit are beyond your control, of course. They may have personal reasons, get offered better jobs, decide to go back to school, or whatever. But sometimes perfectly good people, especially housekeepers, quit because of "helper burn-out." This usually occurs in excellent people who work very hard, are very eager to please, and who feel that their efforts are unappreciated. With very competent people, it's especially easy to overlook their need for expressed appreciation. Some people with the greatest need for appreciation have the least ability to verbalize that need.

You can try during the "contract-making" and orientation phase to emphasize that you want to hear about any unsatisfactory job conditions *before* the helper gets so dissatisfied she wants to quit. This doesn't always work. Often the helper doesn't want to bother you or is the kind of person who is reluctant to complain to anybody.

Sometimes one can detect early burn-out, even if the housekeeper can't verbalize it. Diminished enthusiasm for the work, and increased complaints, particularly non-specific ones that don't seem to point to anything that can be changed, are frequent signs. Sometimes, if you get an "early warning" you can see if the job can be redesigned to make it more appealing. Sometimes a combination of job redesign and a vacation can prevent quitting. But often it can't. With luck, you will get two weeks' notice, which should be in the contract. Of course, you'll give a better reference if she keeps her bargain.

Sometimes you have to fire a housekeeper. It makes sense to give warning but, in the case of child care, you may have to dismiss your helper at once. You have an obligation to give notice of two weeks or whatever was agreed upon, but you may have to give two weeks' pay as severance and get emergency help in the meantime. This is especially true if the safety or well-being of your children is concerned. If the situation is serious enough to fire someone, it may be even more dangerous to rely on that helper after you have given notice.

Defining the Job

After a lot of experience with different housekeepers, Anne evolved the following approach:

Treat the job in the same businesslike way you would treat any other job, but add the personal friendly note which makes some well-qualified people prefer home work over office or factory work. Usually this includes being on a first-name basis, spending some time indicating personal interest in the housekeeper as a person, not just the care given for your children. (Marilyn doesn't agree on the first-name basis. She feels first names could prevent the businesslike relationship from succeeding. She used liberal doses of praise and gratitude as well as financial rewards like raises/bonuses to add the "friendly note." Anne notes that the housekeeper may have a strong preference about what she is called.)

Provide a *written job description.* Which jobs are part of the housekeeper job? Which are chores that the children are expected to do? Who enforces it if the children don't pull their share of the load? What are the hours on duty? What are emergency requirements? What holidays are paid? (We both said, a minimum of three weeks' paid vacation per year, one week at a time of the housekeeper's choice, two or more weeks at times when we were on holiday.) Is sick leave paid or not and, if so, how many days per year? Do you want housekeeping done on specific days of the week or is that left up to the housekeeper's judgment? What are the priorities between child care and cleaning?

Marilyn wrote a detailed job description with daily, weekly, and monthly chores listed, including which furniture polish was to be used for the dining room table. When the children were small the list included hourly tasks as well! However, she told the housekeeper she wanted to consider her as, and treat her as, a professional and always wanted to know if the housekeeper had a better way to do things.

Wages and Benefits

What about wages and benefits? Some housekeepers want to be paid in cash without reporting income to the IRS. If you do this for an employee who works more than fifty hours per quarter, you are in violation of the law (so is she, but you are more vulnerable to financial and legal penalties). Legally, Social Security must be deducted and paid every quarter and W-2 forms must be filed for every household employee. However, a child care worker is *not* an employee if she is sent by, and works for, an agency, or can be defined as an independent contractor. After several experiences with housekeepers who had serious illnesses and no insurance, Anne decided that she would offer health insurance, individual plan, as a benefit after one year's satisfactory service. One housekeeper took that benefit, another one requested the privilege of taking the premium equivalent in cash and taking her chances.

Workmen's Compensation insurance laws vary by state. If you are not required to carry Workmen's Compensation, you should be sure that your household insurance will cover any injuries incurred on the job which might be considered the result of your negligence.

The Search

Occasionally you hear of a wonderful person by word of mouth. More often, you will have to go to employment agencies, read the want ads, or advertise.

Employment agencies are supposed to make some attempt to understand your requirements and exercise selectivity in sending only applicants who meet them. Our experience is that they really don't do that. In the first place, agencies in many communities do not handle domestic workers. Those agencies that do often have the same difficulties finding good help that you have.

Some communities have domestic employment offices as part of welfare programs. We have found the women who sign up here are likely to want day cleaning work rather than a weekly job as many have their own children. But, it's worth a try. The unemployment office sometimes has names of those willing to do child care, but not often.

Newspaper advertising should stress what you expect, and what are the special assets of your home. Housekeepers are scarce and hard to find, so it's a good investment to pay for a somewhat longer and more distinctive ad that makes your job seem attractive. Obviously, the words "top pay" in an ad can help. Also, be very specific, for example: "age 35–50," "local references a must," "a minimum of three years' experience," "non-smoker," or whatever your requirements are. Ideally, your ad will have a box number so you can receive a written letter describing qualifications. Often, however, you won't have the time to do that.

You should consider placing an ad in ethnic, foreign language, or neighborhood newspapers either in your own neighborhood or one where help is likely to be found. Check if neighborhood churches have bulletins or newsletters that will take an ad. You might try posting your ad on a community bulletin board like those at supermarkets. Always read the "situation wanted" ads in these same newspapers or bulletins—and read the bulletin boards!

We also suggest creativity, as both agency and advertising routes may not work. Call local hospitals to see if a nurse is about to retire. Ask clergy in neighborhood churches whether they know of anyone who wants a job. Call volunteer offices to see if a volunteer worker has mentioned that she needs to find a job. Call local colleges, community colleges, and nursing schools. Quite often, class schedules can be arranged around your schedules, especially in the case of graduate students doing independent study.

Some working mothers want to import a nanny or a woman from a foreign country who wants to work for room and board and the opportunity to be in this country. Recent changes in immigration laws have made this formerly difficult task downright impossible. The Immigration and Naturalization Service (INS) and the Department of Labor (DOL) require you to advertise and check unemployment rolls before you import a foreign worker. You need a DOL certificate stating that no unemployed American will take your job before the INS will allow your "import" to enter the country. You have to promise year-round employment and are responsible for the worker if she becomes ill.

You may want to consider an *au pair* girl. This is a French term referring to part-time help, generally from Europe. They are usually young women who want to learn English and travel in exchange for part-time child care and light housework. This kind of help is also tough to come by today. If they enter the country as students, they cannot work unless they can prove they have a previously unforeseen economic problem. If you import an *au pair* girl you must go through the steps outlined above for employing a foreign worker. In both cases, the biggest drawback is that you do not have a chance to interview and meet the person in advance.

Our last suggestion is to always talk about your need for a housekeeper at work, socially, etc. Sometimes a secretary will know of somebody in her neighborhood who needs work or a friend's mother who just mentioned she wanted to find a job.

Interviewing and Selection

You can cut down the number of interviews by doing part of the interview by telephone. First of all, many people won't have read the ad carefully and may not fit your needs. Take their employment history, ask about references, and describe the job so that they can see if they want it. Marilyn always checked references *before* giving her address.

It's hard to evaluate people from interviews alone. Someone can interview well when sober, but drink heavily on the job. Some people who are shy may be great on the job, but interview poorly. Some people who come across as very competent in the interview turn out to be overbearing and bossy on the job.

Always say that the first two weeks are probationary, and let your second and third choices know that you valued them very highly and, although you've chosen someone else, you'll keep their names and phone numbers on file in case the person you chose doesn't work out.

Be sure to have the children present in an early part of the interview and get a feel for how the applicant interacts with them. If they are old enough, have the children interview the applicant independent of you. (If the applicant is offended by this, she may be too rigid and authoritarian for you.) Your children have a much stronger incentive to try to get along with the new housekeeper if they have participated in the selection process. If the children like or don't like the applicant, you don't have to be *bound* by their impressions, but you certainly should take them into account.

At the interview, ask—and record—answers to specific questions. Besides age, marital status, children, address, phone number, transportation, experience, etc., you have a legitimate interest in their health history. Always ask if they have been hospitalized and why, whether they have or have had any infections (hepatitis, TB, etc.). If the answer is "yes," ask if you can check with their doctor. Marilyn insisted on non-smokers and always asked about alcohol but never ever had an alcoholic tell her she was one! We also suggest you ask about her own children and their health, including whether she lost any and how. If there were any infant deaths, be sure there was a plausible cause.

At the time of the interview, outline the job requirements (and provide her with your written job description) and go over expectations, wages and benefits. Show her the house so she can see whether there are too many stairs for her liking. Always ask about child-rearing practices and philosophy—"How would you handle it if Joey took a toy from his baby sister?" "What do you do if a baby is choking?" "What do you do if the baby won't stop crying?" Ask about safety practices and knowledge and try to get some idea if she has sufficient awareness of child development to have realistic expectations of your child's needs and accomplishments. Most important, get a sense of whether you and the applicant communicate well so you can work out the problems that will inevitably arise.

Checking References

Most people applying for a housekeeper position will not have a written résumé. Therefore you must ask what jobs they have held for the past five or six years, what the reason for leaving each job was, and the reasons for any gaps in employment. If the applicant refuses to allow you to use any recent employer as a reference, she should have a pretty good explanation. It's acceptable for her to say, "This person will probably not give me a very good reference, because we had many disagreements. She complained whenever the living room was messy, even though I thought it was more important to play with the baby." When you call you may be able to sort the problem out. A reason such as "They have left the country and can't be reached" should be viewed with suspicion. It may be true, but it may also be an attempt to hide a bad reference.

By the way always *call* references even if the housekeeper brings an out-of-state written reference. A long-distance call is a very small price to pay for more information. Be cautious about phone references in the same neighborhood as the applicant. Sometimes a friend is told to pretend she was an employer and give a superior reference.

There are two kinds of references: character references from a minister or teacher and work references from an employer. Ideally, both are obtained. When you ask a previous employer about the prospective housekeeper, be specific. How well did she care for your children? Was she reliable? Did you have any problems with her? Why is she no longer with you? Would you rehire her? Would you recommend that I hire her to care for my two-year-old child (or my six-week-old infant) while I am at work? In the case of a young girl or a never-employed widow you may decide to go with just the character reference especially if each has had experience with children at home.

Alcoholism is a frequently concealed reason for being fired from previous jobs and is, of course, a serious problem in housekeepers who work unsupervised for many hours of the day. Anne vividly remembers the very first professional trip she took out of town. Her husband came home for dinner to find the housekeeper passed out on the dining-room floor, surrounded by cigarette burns on the rug. Apparently, she'd put the children down for their afternoon naps and begun drinking heavily. The fact that she was unconscious was bad enough, but the fact that she could have burned the place down was even more frightening.

We both believe in rehabilitation but would not employ a recently symptomatic alcoholic if the job involved unsupervised care of infants only. We also would be hesitant to have *both* parents out of town with the children in the care of an alcoholic sitter. Marilyn tried to rehabilitate an alcoholic housekeeper that everyone in the family loved, using AA, the church, locking up the alcohol, assistance from family members. There were several close calls. Once she and her husband were out of town at a meeting and their nightly call home reached the six-year-old who said: "Lucy is lying on the floor saying bad words and we're hungry." They arranged for neighbors to care for the children and flew home at once. They finally had to discharge Lucy with great reluctance.

Other handicaps to avoid are untreated mental illness, retardation severe enough to handicap judgment, deafness such that she can't hear the child, language barrier too severe to use the telephone, uncontrolled epilepsy, use of drugs, and infections like hepatitis, tuberculosis, or syphilis.

Starting the Job

If at all possible, arrange an overlap—several days to a week—when you (or your previous housekeeper) can work along with the new one. That way you can demonstrate your routines, show where things are kept, observe the new employee in action with the children, and make suggestions. Marilyn often asked the new housekeeper to start on Saturday and Sunday and paid double time for this.

While not being overly critical, be firm from the beginning about anything you see which you won't be happy with unless it's changed. Most people are eager to please at the start of a new job, and less malleable later on.

Be sure to schedule enough time in the morning or evening to go over any difficulties or questions. Always ask the housekeeper to make suggestions about doing things. At least at first, you can't have her arrive as you are leaving, and vice versa, or there will be no communication time. We suggest you start out with an extra hour on either end of the day (which you pay for). During the early days, call home several times a day. Even though we could both take phone calls at work, we *always* called home frequently to keep in touch.

Try to split supervisory responsibility with your spouse. Ideally, perhaps you can shift your working hours a bit so that one of you can overlap an hour with the housekeeper in the morning, and one in the evening. Don't be embarrassed to watch her work and her interaction with the children, particularly if your children are too young to talk. You may need to repeat your priorities—that you really think it's more important to spend play time with the children than to keep the place spotless.

Our own bias is that when you hire a competent person to do a job for you, it's to your mutual advantage to let her do the job her way. But, if some item of philosophy or priority really bothers you, then it's vitally important to discuss it. It's important to find some time, away from the kids, to hash out issues. The busier you are and the less time you have to talk things out, the more you are going to have to assume that she will do things her way. In effect, you have delegated a large part of your parental responsibility to someone that you want to know well and feel you can trust. (This is rather similar to what some men, who worked long hours and had housewife wives, have always done.)

However, while the *style* is up to the individual, the *priorities* and *essentials* are your decisions.

A big help is a three-ring notebook with tabs which you can create, called a "Household Procedure Manual." The first section is telephone numbers—parents at work, doctors, other emergency numbers (plumber, furnace, appliance repair, etc.). The second section is the written job description. The third is a schedule such as daily and weekly tasks, taking into account things like the children's school schedules.

The fourth section is information—appliance repair policies, children's medical records—your signed authorization for emergency medical treatment, health insurance cards. Another section can be reminders such as calendars—a list of planned vacations, trips out of town, etc.

Anne thought when she started the household notebook that it was primarily for the housekeeper's benefit. She was astounded how quickly the children started using it. Within the first week the youngest child was adding phone numbers. The next week the oldest child, who already had some credit cards, bank accounts, Social Security and draft registration numbers, produced a Xerox copy of all his important information (even a copy of his eyeglass prescription), and asked that it be put in the notebook. The school directory, with phone numbers of the children's friends and teachers, no longer got lost because the children could see it was to their advantage to put it back into the pocket of the looseleaf household notebook.

Even with a good household notebook that is kept up-to-date, you will need a mechanism for last-minute instructions if you leave before the housekeeper arrives or you pass each other at the door. We suggest you leave notes in the same spot every time—under the bread box or on the refrigerator door. We also use yellow note stickers on or near the object in question. For example, you might leave one on your daughter's blouse stating she spilled spaghetti sauce on it and the blouse will need stain-removing attention before being washed.

Handling Children's Complaints About the Housekeeper

First of all, expect them! If you were the care giver, they'd have complaints about you. Let the children know that you hope they can settle things with the housekeeper but if they can't you want to hear about it in the evening (and, of course, you want to be called at once in any emergency). If you have several children, the housekeeper may be drawn into some of their conflicts and, if she tries to settle them, may be considered unfair by at least one child.

There may also be some real favoritism. Many housekeepers have a stronger attraction to the baby or youngest child—although sometimes if they've been with you from the beginning, the first one is forever "their baby." While you can't legislate love, you can insist on fairness to every child.

Rarely, a housekeeper is downright cruel to a child and may even intimidate that child into not telling you. You need open communication time with each child to encourage the child to speak about these things if they are occurring. Watch for unexplained bruises or accidents as frank abuse can occur. We are somewhat more worried about emotional neglect as it may be harder to spot in an infant. If your baby seems apathetic, your housekeeper could be neglecting your child. Observe how they interact.

Relatives as Housekeepers

Some of us are lucky enough to have nearby relatives who will exchange baby-sitting with us. Sometimes one sister who is a housewife will care for the children of another who works outside the home. Sometimes a relative moves into your home and takes over the same responsibilities that a housekeeper normally would.

One young couple Marilyn knows were both physicians with the wife still in residency training when their first child was born. The husband's widowed mother came to help out when their first son was born, and never left. She moved, found a new job, and became a surrogate mother.

Just before this writing, Anne's most recent housekeeper was her first cousin. Anne says, "This was far and away the best housekeeping arrangement I've ever had, for me and for the children. It's wonderful having someone around who is genuinely part of the family, shares childhood memories with me, has a fairly similar philosophy of life, and even makes potato salad the same way we always did in our family. My good luck here, in finding her, partly came from her bad luck. She had raised her own child, gone back to college, and prepared for a career which has diminished opportunities in today's job market. She was in the midst of many job interviews without success at a time when our previous housekeeper abruptly left for personal reasons. I wasn't sure she'd want to work for us, but it seemed only fair to offer her the chance. We thought of it as a perhaps temporary arrangement that would permit her to go on job interviews during the hours our children were in school but, in fact, it lasted over two years until she remarried."

What are the differences between a relative and an unrelated live-in housekeeper? There are obvious advantages to a relative. She is someone who already loves you and your child, has had a previous relationship to you before the job and almost certainly will continue to have one long after she's left it, and brings a continuity to family life which outside housekeepers can't provide.

You should provide the best possible working conditions, pay her fairly, and treat her well. A housekeeper who is a relative is more likely to feel like a social equal and to let you know things she is dissatisfied with. Conflict resolution can be easier, because conflicts are more likely to be brought up early before they become major. On the other hand, some conflicts can be more complicated than with a purely "hired hand," because you have a lifetime relationship which you want to preserve.

It's important for the relative-housekeeper to have as pleasant a room as possible, and that it be clearly her own territory. This is, of course, true for nonrelative housekeepers, but children feel freer to intrude on a family member. Also she cannot be a part of every moment of your family's life. If she has moved from another city to work with you, she may need some assistance from you in making friends of her own.

DAY CARE CENTERS

About 2 million children are in formal, licensed day care centers and an additional 5 million three- to five-year-olds attend nursery schools or kindergartens serving as day care centers.[5] Organized day care is a necessity for working or single parents. We are one of the few industrialized nations lacking a national day care policy. Proprietary operations, like Kindercare, are becoming quite common but most of America's children are cared for in unlicensed homes which may or may not be safe or adequate. Licensed day care centers can be found by word of mouth, in the Yellow Pages, or in advertisements. You can just look around the neighborhood, especially at churches, which often have day care centers. A very few institutions such as hospitals, universities, and factories have on-site day care centers for the children of their employees, but there are only about six hundred such centers today. The United States Senate just set up a child care center for the children of its employees and four other federal agencies have established such centers.[6]

Some public schools offer free half-day programs for four-year-olds and some are extending kindergarten to full day. Some employers are offering a subsidy to day care centers as a substitute for on-site care. Other corporations purchase a service for working employees which provides information about day care and, in some instances, emergency sick child care. The National Association for the Education of Young Children provides information about both starting and choosing early child care programs. The Children's Foundation advocates a Child Development Associate Credential (CDA) to upgrade child care workers' skills and status. Also, a National Academy of Nannies has been started to train young women for highly paid child care work.[7]

Consider only a licensed day care center. However, licensing does not guarantee that the environment will be emotionally satisfying and creatively stimulating for your child. You will have to evaluate that by a visit. Friends who have had children in the same center could be a good source of advice, but your own observation is important. Do the children look happy and well cared for? Are they overregimented? Or is the environment chaotic? Are the children reasonably clean? Does the staff seem to understand child development and treat children appropriately? When the children get into conflicts with each other, does the staff seem to handle it in a constructive rather than punitive way? Is the environment safe? Is there a sufficient diversity of indoor and outdoor play equipment and supplies? Is there a "quiet corner" for a child who wants to be alone for a while? Is there a comfortable provision for taking naps, including a chance for a child to nap a little longer than the others if necessary? Are the toys used or just on the shelves? Is there a TV? If so, is it used for special shows only, or are the kids watching it too much rather than playing or interacting?

Another important consideration is how happy the staff look. If they don't enjoy their jobs, they will have a hard time providing a warm atmosphere for children. Many day care centers are open for as long as twelve hours to accommodate parents who have both early and later work hours. If so, there will be some shift changes. Do the children have a chance to say good-bye to a worker they've been with during the morning? Are shift changes staggered, or is there one major change of shift and, if so, what happens to the children during the transition? If possible, take the child to visit the center several times before you begin to leave the child there on a regular basis, so you can monitor many of the above concerns yourself.

One of Marilyn's friends whose job is to evaluate day care centers says the biggest problem is how the centers screen their help. They must check references carefully, screen for health problems, prison records, etc. Most licensed centers do this conscientiously and well, *but* in an emergency, they may use substitutes who are not carefully screened. Most day care center problems with abuse or neglect can be traced to substitute help.

You should know that most people in the child care field recommend at least two qualified workers for each group of four to six babies and toddlers. However, some states require only a 1:8 ratio of workers to babies, 1:10 for toddlers up to age three, and 1:15 or 1:25 for children from ages three to six.

Thus, you may need to have stricter requirements than the licensing agency if you want a more favorable staff ratio.

If your child is too young to talk about the day care center, you need to be extra careful in evaluating it. Are there sufficient staff to play with the babies, rock them and sing to them, not just give bottles and change diapers? Are feeding and diapering records kept and available to parents? Do the staff seem to be people who genuinely love babies, as opposed to people who just can't get other work? Is the environment stimulating with crib mobiles, toys, music boxes, and the like?

What happens if a baby becomes sick during the day? Is there adequate provision to try to deter spread of infection to other babies? Is there provision for hand washing between diaper changes? This is critical for very young infants, under three months, who do not have well-developed immune systems. In fact, it is so important that many pediatricians would discourage day care under three months if at all possible, although in France it is customary to start at about six weeks.[8]

How are the babies fed? Are babies held for feedings, or are bottles propped? If your baby is on some special formula or feeding program, is the center set up to individualize feedings and be sure your baby's needs aren't mixed up with someone else's? If you want to provide your own expressed breast milk, can they provide refrigeration for it? Can they accommodate to your wish to breast-feed the baby at reunion time at the center?

Are you free to visit at any time and check on things? A well-organized center, like a well-organized school, has a right to expect not too many intrusive unscheduled visits by parents. However, you have the right to see for yourself what things are like when they aren't expecting parents. An occasional unannounced drop-in, to leave, for instance, the child's forgotten mittens, can be done quietly enough not to disrupt their routine, but in such a way as to reassure yourself that the quality of care doesn't change drastically once the parents have dropped off the children.

There is no question that both day care centers and home care facilities have an increased incidence of certain infectious diseases. These include gastrointestinal diseases like diarrhea and parasites, hepatitis, respiratory infections, and skin infections or infestations.[9] Diarrheal disease is more common in day care centers with young, diapered children and staff that both diaper babies and prepare food.[10,11] The prevalence of day care centers has actually changed the incidence and patterns of infections in children.[12] Children are now exposed to and acquire certain infections at a younger age than formerly.

Attention to hygiene and use of simple soap-and-water hand washing cuts down the incidence of diarrheal diseases. It was found that the use of disposable diapers, using covered containers for soiled diapers, locating changing areas next to a sink and away from food preparation areas, and cleaning surfaces where diapers are changed all help reduce the incidence of diarrhea.[13]

You may hear about an increased incidence of Hemophilus influenzae type b disease in young children[14] attending day care centers. A vaccine for young children is now available.[15] It is currently recommended that if a child is exposed to H. influenzae in a day care center, prophylactic antibiotics should be given. Ideally your day care center will be informed by the doctor about this infection in the sick child and will inform you so you can call *your* doctor. People are terrified of AIDS today. Official recommendations for preschool children infected with the virus which causes AIDS is that they be cared for in settings that minimize exposure of other children to blood or body fluids, and specific guidelines for handling these fluids have been promulgated.[16] However, to date there is no evidence that AIDS is spread by any means other than sexual contact, transfusions, or reuse of hypodermic needles in drug addicts.

Do not consider a well-run day care center a pesthouse—most are not. We suggest you ask about hand washing between babies and whether food preparation and diapering chores are given to separate workers. Your pediatrician is the best guide we know on how to prevent and treat infection and exposure.

A recent concern of parents is the possibility of physical or sexual abuse of young children in a day care center or house day care. Such horrors are always newsworthy and get immediate and sustained attention in the press. The actual incidence is not known but it is not as high as the media would make you think. Your best defense against abuse is to drop into the center unannounced at varying times of the day. As we have already said, be wary of a center where this is not permitted. Check your child for unexplained bruises. Always believe your child if sexual fondling or molestation is mentioned. *Young children do not make such things up.*

A friend of Marilyn's suffered terribly when her infant was abused at a day care home. The child had to be hospitalized for head injuries, but fortunately recovered. Dianne prosecuted the woman in order to get publicity to warn other parents, not for revenge. It came out in the trial that the day care home operator had abused one of her own infants. Always remember to ask about the care giver's own children, whether they are all living and, if not, what they died of. We would never take our child to a day care home unless we got a recommendation from a mother whose child, the same age as ours, had received satisfactory care. We also would not take our child to a newcomer in the community without carefully checking references.

The substitute help problem alluded to earlier continues to plague day care centers. Many of the people hired out of desperation because *someone* is needed to care for the babies turn out to be alcoholics, mentally ill or retarded persons, or general ne'er-do-wells. Some of these people may be physical or sexual abusers of children, though unfortunately seemingly stable people may also be abusers. On balance, *most* people working in day care do so because they love children and prefer that job to other alternatives such as factory or supermarket work.

We are convinced of two things: 1) The risk is small, especially if you check out the center or home and pay attention to your child. 2) Until government subsidy of day care occurs, as in other nations, the problem will continue.

Mothers of infants and young children who use day care always have four questions. 1) *Will this harm my baby?* We can be reassuring: day care of reasonable quality has not been shown to be harmful. Babies in day care are *different* from babies at home.[17] For example, they cried more when separated from their mothers, but this could be considered adaptive coping behavior and even a sign of earlier maturing. Also, babies in day care are better at interacting with peers and tolerate frustration better than home babies. 2) *Will my baby know I'm its mother?* The answer is a resounding yes. Babies, even those with multiple care givers, will relate to you as mother. 3) *Is it true my baby in day care will get sick more often than if the baby were at home?* The answer is yes, but rarely is this increased incidence of infectious diseases a serious problem for the baby. However, it might be a problem for the employed mother, who may not be able to afford sick child care so must lose time from work. 4) *How old should my baby be before starting in day care?* Obviously if you have to work when your baby is a few weeks old, day care is better than no care. Many "experts" say a mother and baby should have four to six months together before the mother goes to or returns to work. Brazelton makes a good case for the mother and baby going through four stages of attachment together before the mother goes to work.[18] In the first stage, which takes ten to fourteen days, the baby learns to be attentive to the mother and the mother learns cues from the baby about being both ready and tired for attentiveness. The second stage, which lasts eight weeks, is the stage of playful interaction when the mother learns how to recognize the baby's non-verbal cues and helps the baby maintain the alert state. The third stage, from the tenth week to the fourth month, is when the mother and baby learn to play games together. In the fourth stage, which occurs in the fourth month, babies rapidly learn about themselves and their world. Thus Brazelton suggests that a mother, when possible, spend the first four months with her new child.

We are not experts, as we know there are no answers. We both went back to work when our infants were only a few weeks old. Many women must go to work, out of economic necessity, when their babies are much younger than four months. Every mother must make her own decision. If your job permits, consider returning half-time at first.

Those mothers who go to work when the baby is very young should not feel guilty. There is no evidence you are harming your baby. We do worry a bit about the mother, however, because she may miss some precious moments. So we advise you to spend as much non-work time as possible with your baby—for your own sake.

INFORMAL DAY CARE

In this common type of child care, you simply leave your child in another home where one woman cares for one or several children, often in addition to her own. You hear about such people by word of mouth, advertising, or grocery store bulletin boards. Or, you can advertise for such a home. Usually, such homes are not licensed. In some communities they are screened and certified by a child care agency. But always you will need to evaluate the safety and warmth of the environment yourself.

A suggested checklist follows: Safety (fire exits? windows? safety rules obeyed in home? cabinets locked? etc.); Size (it's unlikely that one woman can care for more than two infants, three toddlers, or four preschoolers without added help); Length of day (if the day care mother is working too many hours, she is likely to become exhausted and be unable to give high quality care); Backup (what do you do if she, her child, or yours gets sick?); Toys (are there enough? are they the right kind?); Hygiene (is the home clean? are hygiene rules like washing hands after diapering obeyed?); Pets (are there unsupervised pets? odor?); Smoking (does she, or do other members of the household, smoke?); Yard (is it fenced? clean? safe?).

Suggestions for how to evaluate child rearing values and attitudes come from a recent book, *The Working Parents' Guide to Child Care.*[19] Bring your child to the home and watch the child interact with the care giver. Ask how long she's been working with children, how and why she got into that kind of work, and what kinds of children she likes caring for or finds most difficult.

You might follow these with specific questions about how the care giver helps a new child adjust, what she does when a child cries for the mother, how she feels about demand feedings, bottle weaning, toilet training, and pacifiers.

In addition to your questions, we suggest you look around and *observe*. What are the other children doing? Do they seem happy? How does your child react to the care giver? Is the TV used as a baby-sitter?

The answers to your questions and your observations should let you make a conclusion about whether the home is the one you want your child in and whether the worker has the intelligence, skills, and warmth to care for your child.

Some working mothers are beginning to set up their own child care. They form a partnership, hire a care giver, and rotate houses. This is a great idea but you need a contract drawn up between the partners including what they want the child care worker to do, whose house will be used when, who will serve as backup if she is sick, and how to define a sick child who must be cared for at home. You also need a contract with the hired care giver.

CHILD CARE FOR OLDER CHILDREN

With school-age children, a full-time housekeeper may be unnecessary. Yet, for children to come home to an empty home can be lonely, or even dangerous. At the very least, it may lead to more afternoon TV watching than most parents consider desirable.

It's best to avoid the "latch-key" child situation if you can. However, when the full-time housekeeper comes to seem obsolete, a family conference might brainstorm alternatives. Maybe the older child would like to earn part of what the housekeeper formerly did, by contracting to start dinner after school and watching over the young ones. Children should be involved either in creative, athletic, or social activities, or some kind of responsible work after school.

In smaller communities, children often gather spontaneously at a house or neighborhood field for several hours of after-school sports and games. A working mother may be able to arrange for (and offer to pay) a neighbor to be "in charge." Your child knows to call her if there is a problem.

Some schools offer structured after-school play, or homework labs. Some children prefer to do their homework and get it out of the way, leaving the evening free for other activities. Some prefer structured athletic or artistic activities. Others prefer active play of a free-for-all nature. A good program should be able to provide some individualization.

After-school jobs are another opportunity for older school children and teenagers to use time constructively, earn money, and learn to keep commitments. Some housekeepers love a three to seven job. They "pick up" the house, look after the kids, and cook dinner—especially if they're paid well for the unusual hours.

EMERGENCY AND INSTITUTIONAL HELP

Everything can be going swimmingly—until! Your housekeeper can become ill or your child can get sick and need you. What's a working mother to do? Many stay home with the child, which can cause financial problems if they are "docked" or use up their sick leave. Some trade off with their spouses ("You stay home this time with the ear infection; I stayed home with the sore throat").

Some communities have an emergency child care agency that, for a fee, sends a worker to the home if the child is ill. This can be expensive but cheaper for the mother than losing her job.

Nobody likes to think about it, but things could happen that make normal child care arrangements insufficient. In two-parent homes, if one parent is ill, the other can usually fill in the gaps. But single parents can also become seriously ill. Social agencies sometimes provide homemaker services: the doctor or hospital treating the illness can usually refer you to a social worker who knows which community resources are available. Sometimes your health or disability insurance will pay for homemaker services. Sometimes church congregations can help out. Sadly, sometimes children need to be in a foster home because of parental illness, disability, or incapacity.

Boarding schools can be considered and some take quite young children. Boarding schools, even in the absence of an emergency, can be an excellent experience for children. A good one can provide superior educational opportunities and practice in independent living as well as an opportunity to increase a child's circle of friends. Marilyn recommends boarding school for certain selected teens who: 1) are unhappy in their neighborhood high school, 2) need a challenge, or alternatively, extra help in school work, 3) are showing early signs of antimotivation or antisocial behavior. It's not for everyone, but it can work wonders.

SUMMER CHILD CARE

Many parents can "manage" during the school year because, in fact, during the school day they are receiving "free" child care. However, the summer brings three months without this care.

What suggestions do we have for working parents? First of all, summer school isn't just remedial anymore. Some school systems have enrichment courses in languages or computers. There may also be a private school nearby with enrichment courses. Though you can't afford year-long tuition, perhaps you can manage summer school. Many communities have day camps, Bible schools, play schools, or sports camps to teach a child a specific sport like tennis. These generally last only a week or two so you will probably need to find child care help around these. However, the most important reason to arrange these for your child is to prevent a terminal case of boredom. The summer is too long a chunk of unstructured time for most children.

We are great believers in sleep-away camp. As nursery school prepares your child for school, camp prepares your child for living away from home. It not only teaches your child specific skills like swimming, but some very important social lessons like living with other children in a group, relating to adults other than parents, *and* learning how to live apart from parents. Camps also provide summer jobs for older teens (counselors-in-training). Some camps charge for this, but others provide room and board. The experience may be valuable for getting a camp counselor job later.

By the age of ten, most children are ready for one or two weeks away at camp. From the time the child is eleven or twelve, many of them are ready for one month or even a whole summer away. Both Marilyn's children worked up to two months away but as they got older they wanted only one month at camp so they could spend time at home with friends.

The *New York Times Magazine* section, available in many parts of the country, advertises camps and categorizes them by boy or girl camp or special interest camp, like sailing or scuba. There are also published directories of camps. But we think the best way to find out about a camp, like the best way to find a doctor or a dentist, is to ask people who have been there. First of all, decide what kind of camp, what part of the country, how much you are willing to spend. Try to talk to people who have sent their children to that camp. Talk to *both* the children and the parents.

What do you do if your child wants to come home the day after arriving at camp? Tell your child this is not a good idea. There are exceptions, of course, but even at a relatively young age children can learn that when they make a commitment they keep it and camp is a good place to start. Acute homesickness usually passes quickly.

Marilyn served as a camp doctor once and she watched a new arrival cry for forty-eight solid hours. The camp nurse held the girl on her lap most of this time. Two weeks later the child was the lead in the camp play and had a marvelous time. We think it would have been a shame if she had not had the opportunity to grow up beyond her tears.

When her children were young and still quite dependent on an adult for transportation, Marilyn hired a summer "driver." She paid this young woman a retainer to be available to drive the children to swimming lessons, summer school, etc., and also be available for outings to places like the zoo (Marilyn's treat).

*   *   *

We have pointed out that all parents need helpers in child care. Most parents want to spend as much time as they can with their children, and everyone has heard the phrase "quality time."

A group of parents recently asked Marilyn what "quality time" means. She defines quality time as time when you are *not* doing anything else: You are *attentive* to your child (either *looking at* or *holding the child;* you're at the *child's level* (literally, like on the floor, and, figuratively, at the child's developmental level). The time you spend is *personalized* (doing what the child personally likes to do). Often during quality time you are *instructing,* both showing the child how to do something and modeling how to be a caring parent. Each sibling needs and deserves some quality time alone with each parent. Providing lots of toys, indulging in every whim, or "giving in" are all guilt time—*not* quality time.

Anne agrees and adds: Often during quality time you are learning and seeing the world through your child's eyes—one of the great delights of parenting!

SUGGESTED READINGS AND RESOURCES

Alston, Frances Kemper. *Caring for Other People's Children: A Complete Guide to Family Day Care.* Baltimore: University Park Press, 1984.

    Readable, thorough and helpful.

A Parent's Guide to Day Care. U.S. Department of Health and Human Services. Washington, D.C.: Publication No. (OHDS) 80-30254, March 1980.

    A government pamphlet with good, easy-to-fill-out checklists.

Brazelton, T. Berry. *Working and Caring.* Reading, Mass.: Addison-Wesley, 1985.

The latest Brazelton book on working mothers and their babies. Well worth reading.

Conley, Diane, ed. *Summer Opportunities for Kids and Teenagers.* Princeton: Peterson's Guides, 1983.

A great directory for summer camps, both traditional and special (travel, computers). Includes information about camp jobs. Easy to use.

Endsley, Richard C., and Bradbard, Marilyn R. *Quality Day Care: A Handbook of Choices for Parents and Caregivers.* Englewood Cliffs, N.J.: Prentice-Hall, 1981.

One of the early books on day care. Three good checklists for evaluating day care centers: a list you can use on the telephone, an observational list, and a parent involvement checklist.

Glickman, Beatrice Marden, and Springer, Nesha Bass. *Who Cares for the Baby? Choices in Child Care.* New York: Schocken, 1978.

A carefully crafted, thoughtful book which looks at the realities for today's working mothers. Well worth reading as it raises all the questions, and answers many of them.

Long, Lynette, and Long, Thomas. *The Handbook for Latchkey Children and Their Parents.* New York: Arbor House, 1983.

A rather sad book which, in the best of all possible worlds, would not need to be written. Ideally there would be no latchkey children, but for parents of the estimated 5 million unsupervised children this book contains useful instruction.

Margolis, Maxine L. *Mothers and Such: Views of American Women and Why They Changed.* Berkeley: University of California Press, 1984.

A thoughtful historical analysis of the role of the American housewife-mother—and why society likes her that way.

Meyers, Carole T. *How to Organize a Babysitting Cooperative.* Albany, Calif.: Carousel Press, 1976.

Brief, practical, useful guide.

Scarr, Sandra. *Mother Care/Other Care.* New York: Basic Books, 1984.

A readable account of the mother's dilemma: my care or other care. Well worth reading.

Siegel-Gorelick, Bryna. *The Working Parents' Guide to Child Care.* Boston, Mass.: Little, Brown, 1983.

A thoughtfully written book on the modern dilemma: How can I find good care for my children while I work? Many useful and practical suggestions.

Sotelo, Jo; Stevenson, Janis; and Williamsen, Jean. *Consumer's Guide to Child Care.* St. Meinrad, Ind.: Abbey Press, 1983.

A short but comprehensive pamphlet, well worth reading.

Swan, Helen L., and Houston, Victoria. *Alone After School: A Self-Care Guide for Latchkey Children and Their Parents.* Englewood Cliffs, N.J.: Prentice-Hall, 1985.

A guidebook to self-care with many useful suggestions for parents—and for children who are home alone. The book concentrates on safety, what to do in emergencies, and coping with loneliness and boredom.

*   *   *

National Association for the Education of Young Children, 1834 Connecticut Avenue, N.W., Washington, D.C. 20009. Phone 800-424-2460.

Part Three

DEVELOPMENTAL
ISSUES
IN PARENTING

7

CHILDREN'S GROWTH AND DEVELOPMENT

Scope of Chapter

This chapter is an overview of what we know about human development—focusing on the development of the child. We start with a brief description of developmental theories. The next section highlights *kinds* of development from physical development to development of morals. Developmental tables follow in order that parents can see at a glance what to expect at all ages/stages. We then discuss the parent's role in child development and give specific suggestions for optimizing your child's development. Finally, we discuss deviations from normal development in several areas, stressing how parents can pick up significant clues.

We not only feel that developmental information is important but also that parents can well understand ranges of ages and differential developmental rates. Some professionals have been concerned that parents will "overcompare." We believe that parents can better learn to deal with anxiety about their child's development *with* specific knowledge than without it.

Introduction

The dictionary definition of development is "to grow into a more mature or advanced state." From the moment of conception your baby not only is growing physically but also is *developing* into a more organized, advanced, and mature state of being. It was once thought that development started at birth and ended when adulthood was reached. Now it is known that neurological and intellectual development take place in the *fetus* and several stages of *adult* development have been recognized.

Probably the most fascinating thing about children is their *capacity for growth*—physical, intellectual, social, cultural. Marilyn has fantasized about a time lapse photography movie which would start with pictures of a baby emerging from the mother's womb and show that same baby at each stage of development. We both love to look at photographs of babies and parents and grandparents to see how they come to resemble each other. And even if one isn't a parent, one could spend several lifetimes observing how babies and young children in different environments and cultures grow into adults.

When your baby is born, you can become an observer of your own baby's exciting growth and development, like a scientist doing a longitudinal study. That is, a study that looks at the same subject or subjects over a long period of time. The following is excerpted from a paper published in 1877 by a scientist who observed his own baby. "During the first seven days various reflex actions, namely sneezing, hickuping, yawning, stretching, and of course sucking and screaming, were well performed by my infant. On the seventh day, I touched the naked sole of his foot with a bit of paper, and he jerked it away, curling at the same time his toes like a much older child when tickled. The perfection of these reflex movements shows that the extreme imperfection of the voluntary ones is not due to the state of the muscles or of the co-ordinating centres, but to that of the seat of the will. At this time, though so early, it seemed clear to me that a warm, soft hand applied to his face excited a wish to suck. This must be considered as a reflex or an instinctive action, for it is impossible to believe that experience and association with the touch of his mother's breast could so soon have come into play. During the first fortnight, he often started on hearing any sudden sound, and blinked his eyes."[1] You will see in Chapter 9 when we talk about what the newborn can do, that all of the observations this man made of his own son were extremely accurate. The writer was Charles Darwin.

We personally loved to watch the miracle of innate and interactive development in our children and the children of others. We hope you will enjoy this unfolding drama in your child, as much as we enjoyed the "show" in our children.

Two apparently opposite comments from the popular press best sum up the attitude parents need to develop toward the issue of child development. One author pointed out that babies know exactly how old they are; his son always did what he was supposed to do from fuss to spit up to sleep sixteen hours a day.[2] George Will wrote a column about the "new" evidence that the boy Einstein was brilliant, not seemingly retarded.[3] Mr. Will, to his dismay, noted that when Einstein's father gave his four-year-old son a compass, Einstein figured out then and there that if the needle always points in the same direction, space is not empty. Because lots of compasses given to lots of four-year-olds will *not* produce an Einstein, Will offers the following aphorism: "Parenting is a science of single instances." We agree—that's what makes it so interesting and such fun!

Development is so important it will be covered in several places in addition to this chapter. Each chapter devoted to a specific age and stage will include information about development in that period. Each age/stage chapter will provide key developmental information in the following areas: biophysical (appearance, size, shape, reflexes, etc.), cognitive, language, and personal-social (interaction). We will tell you not only what the child can do at that specific stage but also what the parents can start *looking forward to* in the near future. We will also suggest what parents can do to make their child's environment optimally stimulating for development at each age/stage.

THEORIES OF DEVELOPMENT

In order to better enjoy observing your baby along his or her own wonderful trajectory of becoming a person, you may want to take the time to learn more about human development. This is a complicated subject; there are many theories of how and why human development takes place. None of these theories are proven, nor do they completely fit all stages or aspects of human development. A theory by definition is not completely proven—it's a way of looking at things and organizing observations. Also, theories are developed by *people* who are affected by their own geography, culture, and time in history. Nonetheless, a theory is useful because it helps us relate certain facts and observations.

A good example of how theories depend on the person developing them is found in the theories of Freud. Many of the things he said about women, for example, are far from universal. His writings were, however, for the most part accurate observations of middle-class intellectual Jewish families in Vienna in the late nineteenth century. Freud, like everyone else, made mistakes because of where he was in time and space. For example, he could not believe that the childhood incest reported by his adult patients could have occurred so often—so he assumed these reports were fantasies.

To look at theories of development, we have to start with theology, although neither of us is a theologian. According to the Doctrine of Original Sin, which theologians relate to Adam and Eve's fall from grace, sin was felt to be inborn. Those base appetites, instincts, and strivings a child was born with must be "educated" out of the child before they led to sinful conduct. The belief that evil was inborn in a child culminated in the Calvinist doctrine which stated that children should be regularly whipped in order to get rid of the evil and become moral adults.

Locke, the English philosopher who lived in the 1600s, disagreed with this point of view. He felt that infants are born with what he called a *tabula rasa,* or a blank slate. He said that all we possess in the way of our behaviors comes to us from the world. The blank slate concept posed a great burden to parents who were obligated to educate their children from the moment they were born because it was the environment supplied by the parents (and by society) which would make the child grow into a moral person. The emphasis was clearly on the environment rather than heredity.

Rousseau (1712–78) felt that man is by nature good and is born good. His educational philosophy was not to "teach" things to the child, but to draw out what was already there in order to allow maximum development of human potential. Interestingly enough, this was not really permissiveness because Rousseau's idea of freedom was submission of the individual to "the general will." He defined the general will as that which one would *choose* for the general good.

According to this rather optimistic philosophy Rousseau said, "Freedom is obedience to a law of reason which is self-imposed." We wish!

In our own country, the early behaviorists took a direct line of reasoning from Locke in their belief that all the tendencies and behaviors of a baby would be shaped by the environment. Behaviorists feel the child's behaviors elicit responses from the environment which modify the child's behavior by positive or negative consequences. Obviously, behaviorists paid little attention to heredity or what attributes the child was born with. They also paid very little attention to the maturational stage of the child.

The early behaviorist school reached its height with the social learning theories of J. B. Watson in the early part of the nineteenth century. Watson strongly believed that *all* behavior arose from conditioning. He felt that even emotions were learned and that even the most complex forms of behavior were nothing more than reflexes and conditioned responses.[4] He stressed that parents had an obligation to develop positive behaviors and characteristics in their child. Watson went so far as to say in 1925, "Give me a dozen healthy infants, well-formed, and my own specified world to bring them up in and I'll guarantee you to take any one at random and train him to become any type of specialist I might select—doctor, lawyer, artist, merchant, chief and, yes, even beggarman and thief, regardless of his talents, penchants, tendencies, abilities, vocations, and race of his ancestors."[5]

Popular child-rearing books of the twenties and thirties accepted Watson's theory. Emmett Holt, a renowned pediatrician of his day, did. He, and later his son, wrote a leading textbook in pediatrics called *Diseases of Childhood and Infancy* originally published in 1892 and still used, though new editions are now called simply *Pediatrics.*

Marilyn has a 1929 edition of Holt's *Care and Feeding of Children* first published in 1894.[6] This book, which her mother used when Marilyn was a baby, is written in question-and-answer style. Several answers suggest feeding babies no more often than every four hours. One question reads: "What is the most certain way of causing a child to develop the crying habit?" The answer is, "By giving him everything he cries for. This will soon do it even in one with the most amiable disposition." "How is such a habit to be broken?" "By never giving a child what he cries for." Holt goes on to say if the child is comfortable [by which he means the baby's hands and feet are warm and the diapers not wet], the child should simply be allowed to "cry it out." Marilyn's mother confesses she didn't always follow Holt's guidelines. Anne's mother tried to with one child, as the doctor advised. Then with more experience as a parent, she ignored such unnatural advice.

Freud, who wrote much of his work in the early part of this century, felt that children are born with instinctual sexual energy, which he called "libido,"[7,8] as well as instinctual aggressive energy. As the child matures, libido is invested in different areas of the body. For a newborn baby, it is the mouth—hence the first libidinal stage is termed the "oral stage." In the toddler, the libidinal area during the toilet-training stage is the anus. In the phallic stage, the genital organs are invested with libidinal energy. Freud felt that at each of these stages there is a conflict between what the baby wants and what society wants, i.e., the baby is inherently asocial or even "demonic."[9] The baby wants non-stop breast-feeding to continue; society weans. The baby wants to hold on to the feces; society demands they be deposited in a specified place. The baby has erotic attachments to the mother; society calls this incest, which is the strongest possible "no-no"—a taboo. Freudian theory holds that if these conflicts are not resolved, either because of parental overindulgence or underindulgence, the child will fixate on the conflicted stage or regress to an earlier stage for gratification. Oral fixations are habits which involve the mouth, such as smoking, alcoholism, or obsessive eating. Anal fixations, based on withholding, include compulsiveness and aggression. Freud thought phallic fixations led to homosexuality, chauvinism, arrogance, and narcissism.

One of the most troublesome things about classical Freudian theory is that it's all over by the time the child goes to school. Freud believed that all major tasks of development were completed by age six. In fact, that was what made the child academically educable at around age six. School years were termed the "latency" years in which the libidinal forces of the child stayed at a relatively low level until puberty and adolescence. Problems in later years were felt to result from repetition of unresolved problems of early childhood.

In recent years, contemporary psychoanalytic self-theorists have provided interesting modifications of Freudian theory about drive development.[10,11,12] They believe that the infant and child are social from birth and gradually develop a coherent sense of self by internalizing parts of interactions with care givers. While filling infants' needs, responding to their emotions, and showing pride in their development, care givers also do something else. These attentions give infants the experience of an *other*, which simultaneously reflects the child's dawning sense of *self*—like a mirror. The developing self, in Kohut's terms, organizes itself around these internal pictures of others whose role is to provide vital psychological functions for the self. These are objects to admire, to resemble, to support and empathize with one's own feelings.

We all, adults and infants, need real people to provide these functions and images to keep our self-esteem and coherent sense of self. These functions correspond to our lifetime need for validation of our feelings, a sense of kinship or similarity, and for guiding ideals. Adults who lose these functions feel empty, or "not together"; at times of stress we need to restore them with new self-objects (which for adults can be people, achievements, or abstract principles). In early infancy, interaction with care givers supports infants' dawning realization that they *have* a self.

In later infancy, as the infant becomes aware of the strength and nurturance of care givers, the care giver is perceived as an object of admiration—the "idealized other." The seemingly magical ability to control these powerful others, when recognized, gives rise to "infantile grandiosity." Later, as crawling and walking begin, the baby's self is expanded by a sense of tremendous achievement, and infantile grandiosity becomes tempered with pride in this personal accomplishment. Similarly, the admiration by and of loved care givers adds to the strength of the sense of a personal self.

Kohut proposes that the raw libidinal and aggressive drives of, say the Oedipal period in Freud's theory, appear as such only if the sense of self fragments and can no longer contain the drives. This fragmentation happens if there is a lack of both real people in the present, and stable internal images from past experience, performing these self-integrating functions. In toddlers, frustration can lead to a lack of perceived integration of the self (interruption of "narcissistic balance,") which in turn leads to aggressive fragmentation—a tantrum. In Oedipal children, impairment of the stable sense of self and self-objects leads to exaggerated lust and aggression. This is the Oedipal *complex* which Kohut contrasts to normal Oedipal development—a time in itself of increased affection and assertiveness which does not have to be particularly conflictual. In older childhood and adulthood, particularly at times of major transitions or other stresses, the lack of narcissistic balance from good self-objects can lead to depletion and depression, "narcissistic rage" (adult temper tantrums), or chronic inability to admire appropriate others, see others' points of view, and give empathy.

Gesell, who wrote in the forties and fifties, felt that the child played the crucial role in development. His maturational theory held that there are *predetermined maturational stages*—children will develop when they reach certain stages. Specific behaviors are only seen when the child is "ready" for those behaviors. In other words maturation of the neuromuscular system is the determinant of behavior at specific ages. The environment thus is seen as less important because the emergence of the child's behavior is innate and determined from within the child.

Gesell spent his life observing many infants and children and describing their behaviors in several categories: motor, personal-social, language, and cognitive. One of his most important talents was his ability to use the English language well—he describes different stages beautifully. Here is Gesell on adaptive behavior in a twenty-eight-week-old: "Although eyes are still in the lead, eyes and hands function in close interaction, each reinforcing and guiding the other. Whereas the 16-week-old infant is given to inspection of surroundings, the 28-week-old infant inspects objects. And if the object is within reach it is usually in his busy hands. Head became versatile in the previous trimester; hands become versatile in this one. Directly he sees a cube he grasps it, senses surface and edges as he clenches it, brings it to his mouth, where he feels its qualities anew, withdraws it, looks at it on withdrawal, rotates it while he looks, looks while he rotates it, restores it to his mouth, withdraws it again for inspection, restores it again for mouthing, transfers it to the other hand, bangs it, contacts it with the free hand, retransfers, mouths it again, drops it, resecures it, mouths it yet again, repeating the cycle with variations—all in the time it takes to read this sentence."[13]

Gesell's writings introduced the concept: "The child is just going through a stage and he'll outgrow it" into our language. Though not always correct, this phrase has been reassuring to several generations of bewildered parents dealing with the sometimes frustrating behaviors of their children.

According to Gesell, the role of the parents in development presupposes that parents recognize the child's self-regulation of growth. Parents need to have consideration (Gesell used the phrase "alert liberalism") for each individual child. Children are seen as *"people."* Each individual, whether one year or ninety years, must be regarded as important in his or her own right. This supreme regard for the individual is the basis of democracy.[14]

Erik Erikson was trained by Freud's daughter, Anna. Erikson, whose first important book was published in the sixties, went beyond Freud's psychoanalytic theory to recognize eight stages of development: infant, toddler, preschooler, school-ager, adolescent, young adult, middlescent, and older adult. Erikson describes each developmental level as having a basic task and a negative counterpart that occurs if this task is not completed. The basic virtue of each task is achievement of that level and the ability to go on to the next level. The infant has to learn basic trust, the toddler must achieve autonomy; the preschooler, initiative; school-ager, industry; adolescent, identity; the young adult, intimacy; the middlescent, generativity; and the older adult, ego integrity. Table 23 shows these levels, basic tasks, negative counterparts, and basic virtues. Erikson does not like to ascribe an age range to these levels as children and adults possess individual rates of development. He acknowledges that both genetics and environment affect the rates of development.

Erikson says that development results from the resolution of the forces within each developmental phase. Failure (or delay) to go on to the next phase can retard development. However, he points out that positive circumstances in life may lead to successful resolution later even after the usual age for that stage has concluded chronologically. The most important difference between Erikson and Freud is the emphasis Erikson places on the way individuals feel about themselves as social beings and as individuals. In his view, this outweighs the libidinal forces and fixations or "hang-ups."

Maslow based his developmental theory on basic human needs.[15,16] He conceptualizes these needs as based one upon the other (like a pyramid) but does not divide these developmental stages by age as the human organism needs all of these at every age. The most basic needs are *physiological* (food, warmth, oxygen), for which the infant is totally dependent on adults. The next need is *physical safety*, ranging from a safe place to play, if you are a toddler, to a crime-free environment, if you are an adult. The third need is for *affection*—lifelong. The next need is *self-esteem*, followed by *prestige* and *self-actualization*, which means other needs are met and the person is in satisfactory homeostasis with self and the physical and social world.

Havighurst, an educator who first published his book on development in 1948, saw development as a series of tasks to be mastered.[17] His understanding was that development depends on cognitive learning. For example, the infant must learn to talk, walk, control elimination, etc. In early adulthood, the person must "learn" to select a mate, live with a marriage partner, manage a home,

TABLE 23

PSYCHOSOCIAL DEVELOPMENTAL LEVELS

Developmental Level	Basic Task	Negative Counterpart	Basic Virtues
1. Infant	Basic trust	Basic mistrust	Drive and hope
2. Toddler	Autonomy	Shame and doubt	Self-control and willpower
3. Preschooler	Initiative	Guilt	Direction and purpose
4. School-ager	Industry	Inferiority	Method and competence
5. Adolescent	Identity	Role confusion	Devotion and fidelity
6. Young adult	Intimacy	Isolation	Affiliation and love
7. Middlescent	Generativity	Stagnation	Production and care
8. Older adult	Ego-integrity	Despair	Renunciation and wisdom

Reprinted by permission and adapted from E. H. Erikson, *Childhood and Society,* 2nd ed. New York: Norton, 1963. In *The Process of Human Development, A Holistic Approach,* by Clara Shaw Schuster and Shirley Smith Ashburn. Copyright © 1980 by Little, Brown and Co.

start a family, find an occupation, assume civic responsibility, and find a congenial social group.

    Piaget (1896–1980) spent a lifetime studying cognitive development in the child. He divides development into four stages: a *sensorimotor* period (from birth to two); a *preoperational* period (from age two to seven) in which the child is able to use not only language, but also symbols; a *concrete operations* stage (seven to eleven) when the child is able to find logical solutions to concrete problems; and a *formal operations* period (eleven to fifteen) when abstract thinking begins. Table 24 shows Piaget's stages in detail. Piaget looks at mental development as beginning at birth and feels that all people acquire cognitive skills in the same way, though at different rates. At each of his levels, previous levels must be incorporated and integrated.

TABLE 24

LEVELS OF COGNITIVE DEVELOPMENT

Period	Age	Characteristics
Sensorimotor	0–2 years	Thought dominated by physical manipulation of objects and events
Substage 1	0–1 month	Pure reflex adaptations No differentiation between assimilation and accommodation

Period	Age	Characteristics
Substage 2	1–4 months	Primary circular reactions Slight differentiation between assimilation and accommodation Repetition of schemata and self-imitation, especially vocal and visual Reflex activities become modified with experience and coordinated with each other
Substage 3	4–8 months	Secondary circular reactions Differentiation between assimilation and accommodation; still overlap Repeat action on things to prolong an interesting spectacle Beginning to demonstrate intention or goal-directed activity
Substage 4	8–12 months	Coordination of secondary schemata Clear differentiation between assimilation and accommodation Application of known schemata to new situation Schemata follow each other without apparent aim Beginning of means-ends relationships
Substage 5	12–18 months	Tertiary circular reactions Ritualistic repetition of chance schema combinations Accentuation and elaboration of ritual Experimentation to see the result, find new ways to solve problems
Substage 6	18–24 months	Invention of new solutions through mental combinations Primitive symbolic representation Beginning of pretense by application of schema to inadequate object A symbol is mentally evoked and imitated in make-believe A symbolic schema is reproduced outside of context; thus, transition between practice play and symbolic play proper
Preoperational	2–7 years	Functions symbolically using language as major tool

Period	Age	Characteristics
Preconceptual	2–4 years	Uses representational thought to recall past, represent present, anticipate future Able to distinguish between signifier and signified Egocentric, uses self as standard for others Categorizes on basis of single characteristic
Intuitive	4–7 years	Increased symbolic functioning Subjective judgments still dominate perceptions Beginning ability to think in logical classes Able to see simple relationships Able to understand number concepts More exact imitations of reality * Limitations to Preoperational Thinking: Child does not understand nature of classes Child uses syncretism (links unrelated ideas) Child juxtaposes ideas Child engages in animism (attributes life to inanimate objects) Child engages in artificialism (people cause natural events) Child is egocentric
Concrete Operations	7–11 years	Mental reasoning processes assume logical approaches to solving concrete problems Organizes objects, events into hierarchies of classes (classification) or along a continuum of increasing values (seriation) Reversibility, transitivity, and conservation skills attained * Limitations to Concrete Operations thinking: Child cannot solve hypothetical problems because of focus on here and now Child cannot generate all possible combinations in a system Child uses only inductive reasoning
Formal Operations	11–15 years	True logical thought and manipulation of abstract concepts emerge

Period	Age	Characteristics
		Hypothetical deductive thought Can plan and implement scientific approach to problem solving Handles all kinds of combinations in a systematic way

Reprinted by permission and adapted from J. Piaget, *The Psychology of Intelligence*. Translated by M. Piercy and D. E. Berlyne. Totowa, N.J.: Littlefield Adams, 1973; and *Play, Dreams and Imitation in Childhood*. Translated by C. Gattegno and F. M. Hodgson. New York: Norton, 1962. All rights reserved. Also from Flavell, J. H., *The Developmental Psychology of Jean Piaget*. New York: Van Nostrand, 1963.

In *The Process of Human Development, A Holistic Approach*, by Clara Shaw Schuster and Shirley Smith Ashburn. Copyright © 1980 by Little, Brown and Co.

* Source: Kitty L. Peyton. Piaget for Pediatricians: Cognitive Development of Children. Talk given at the University of Arizona College of Medicine, May 17, 1985.

It is apparent that there are many different theories of child development and that none of them completely explains all stages or all ages. Some of the theories are not widely accepted or proven and obviously, some theories emphasize one domain of development at the expense of others. However, most of the theories are based on fairly sound evidence and on rather extensive observations. Thus each of them contributes to understanding what happens to the child in the wonderful journey from infancy to adulthood.

Although for centuries the argument raged as to whether the genes or the environment determined development and behavior, over the past quarter century an interactional model has been proposed—and is largely accepted. Today both behavioral and biological attributes are looked at as reciprocal each with the other. Thus early life experience is important but not decisive for later development; psychological development occurs by both continuity and change; development continues throughout the life cycle; and no one factor (child's innate attributes, parents, or society) determines disturbed psychological development.[18]

Further, the concept of consonance (goodness of fit) and dissonance (poorness of fit) between the child and the environment—both the microenvironment of the family and the wider community—is paramount. The environment's expectations or demands should fit the child's own attributes and behavioral style.

KINDS OF DEVELOPMENT

What kinds of development are there? Briefly there are several kinds: biological, cognitive, language, moral, social, and psychosexual.

Biological Development

Biological development is the neurological development of the brain and nervous system and the development of the muscles and glands. The brain rapidly develops in the fetus and young child and by the time the baby is a year of age, much of the brain growth has occurred. There is a rapid increase in the number of synapses (connections between nerve cells) in the cortex of the growing infant's brain. According to Lewis, between ages one and two, the baby actually has as many as 50 percent *more* connections than the adult has. The density of synapses decreases from age two until about age sixteen and then stays at that level until about age seventy-five.[19]

Parts of the baby's cortex (outside portion of the brain) develop at different times. The motor area develops first and the parts of the brain which serve the arms develop before those which govern the legs. Visual areas develop before auditory ones do.

Myelinization is the process whereby some nerve cells in the brain and peripheral nervous system become coated with a covering called the myelin sheath. When myelinated, the nerve is functionally mature, and transmits impulses more rapidly. Myelinization occurs rapidly in infancy but continues at a slower rate through adolescence. The white matter in the cortex, which is the part of the brain that integrates sensation and motor activity and maintains attention and consciousness, is not completely myelinated until after puberty, and the process may continue into adulthood.[20]

The patterns of the baby's electrical brain waves as measured by an electroencephalogram (EEG) also develop in specific ways. Immature patterns disappear earlier in the premature infant than in the full term, probably because of interaction with the environment after birth. A change in EEG pattern occurs at about three months of age and also at about age two, six, and eleven years, all of which coincide with times of important cognitive development.

We know that genetic factors are important in biological development. Temperamental characteristics such as activity level, rhythmicity, adaptability, mood, and attention span tend to be similar in identical twins.[21]

Cognitive Development

Cognition pertains to *knowing* and includes perceiving, recognizing, conceiving, judging, sensing, reasoning, and imagining. Complex cognition is what distinguishes humans from lower mammals. Unlike simple reflexes which can occur without consciousness, thinking is the highest level of human behavior. The brain of a human being can sort out stimuli from within and from outside the body and access stored memories before a response occurs—often quicker than a computer can.

Our conscious mind is pretty wonderful. One scientist stated: "At the highest levels of integration, the phenomenon of consciousness allows the widest possible range of information to be brought to bear in analyzing sensory input and selecting appropriate behavior. At this level, states, percepts, memories, and action strategies can somehow be experienced by an inner awareness that totally eludes biological description. The evolutionary purpose of this aspect of the organization of our behavior may lie in the *competitive edge provided by the ability to try out behaviors on models of the world in our minds before we use them on the real world outside.* The more sophisticated behaviors made possible by the capacity for this mental activity, such as verbal language and scientific experiment, have carried us to the point where *we can attempt to understand ourselves*" (italics ours).[22]

Incredible as it may seem we are accumulating evidence that fetuses can and do learn. One research study showed that babies at birth distinguished their mother's voice from other women's voices by a measurable sucking pattern. The next step was to have the mother read *The Cat in the Hat* aloud to the fetus during the last few weeks of pregnancy. The babies showed evidence of reacting in recognition to a tape recording of the mother reading that story![23]

From the moment of birth your child has the ability—provided the environment is supportive—to develop into a thinking, reasoning human being.

It is truly amazing what *learning* can take place from the moment of birth. Although newborns are limited by their developmental and neurological immaturity, they can accomplish almost unbelievable feats. The newborn can *decide* what to pay attention to in the environment. The newborn can shut out a noisy environment and respond to a soft voice. Babies learn this quickly because they come into the world programmed for certain choices.[24]

One experiment showed that babies can quickly learn that when a bell rings, if they turn the head to the right they will get sugar water; when the buzzer sounds, they won't turn the head because there will be no sugar water. In addition, if the sequence was reversed so the bell meant, "Don't turn your head," while the buzzer got them sugar water, the babies quickly adapted to the reversal![25]

Language Development

Though adults raised in different countries speak different languages, the pattern in which *all* human infants acquire language is identical, as is the age at which language develops. Complex language acquisition is unique to the human species, though chimpanzees can learn to use sign language for communication. A "language acquisition system" located in the brain has been postulated by

Chomsky and others, and the exciting new field of developmental psycholinguistics is studying how children learn and use language.[26]

The newborn can discriminate between sounds and, at birth, the human infant is programmed to respond to the human voice. Crying is the infant's first "language" and rapidly differentiates into cries of hunger, pain, etc. Cooing begins early and rapidly turns into vowel sounds. Next consonant sounds develop in all humans and talking in words follows. Nouns, verbs, adjectives, and adverbs appear in that order. Somewhere between two and four, children have quite complete command of their entire language and its syntax.

One of the most remarkable things about the human infant is that it learns human language in a very short period of time. Grammatical speech ("See ball") does not begin until about age one and a half; yet by three and a half, a short two years later, the child has acquired spoken grammar. Before understanding what a word is, let alone a sentence, children extract rules of language from what they hear and apply them. Even some of the "mistakes" a young child makes in speech are based on following a rule where an adult uses an exception. For example, a child may say "sheeps" as the plural of "sheep."

According to de Villiers, language starts long before speech does.[27] The newborn baby is preprogrammed to discriminate between speech sounds of the human voice and can discriminate speech from non-speech sounds. Thus infants *pay attention* to the human speech of their parents and *listen* to the rhythm of language. They are prepared for *alternation* in speech (first I talk, then you talk) by playing games like peek-a-boo where first one person and then the other is active.

The first speech sounds, called babbling, begin at three or four months and peak at about nine to twelve months. Some babies stop babbling when they acquire words but others continue to babble using the *intonation* of sentences though not real words for several months. Children rapidly adapt their babbling to the rhythm and sounds (phonemes) of their native language. Thus they learn the melody of the language before they learn the words. Marilyn's eighteen-month-old daughter was invited to the birthday party of the school-age girl who lived next door. In the middle of the party she stood up in her high chair and, with eyes sparkling, gave an animated, though totally unintelligible, "speech"!

Children in all cultures babble the same sounds and even totally deaf children begin to babble at the same age as normal hearing children though they cease to vocalize shortly thereafter. Babbling is innate—speech requires *hearing* spoken language. Normal hearing babies born into deaf mute families start human speech sounds as do babies in families where words are spoken. However, if a child is not in an environment of stimulation, speech acquisition is slowed considerably. All normal babies communicate with meaningful gestures as well as words; children born to deaf parents who use sign language pick up the gestural "words" as quickly as other children learn speech or more so.[28]

Children have the ability to comprehend and respond to words before they can say any. The first words they learn name the objects or events in their world: the people important to them, the foods they like, the events of their day—like bath and potty. Next come animal names and sounds. Children learn the names of objects at what de Villiers calls an intermediate level of generality. For example, they learn flower before rose or tulip and long before they understand that flowers, along with trees, are all plants. Parents, in their speech to young children, intuitively cue this because they name objects in this way. In a sense children and parents mutually teach each other "baby talk"—a simplified language easy for the child to grasp.

Children learn the rules of language in a specific way as sentences begin. First they learn word order ("me fall" not "fall me"), next possession ("my bear"), location ("spoon in cup"), recurrence ("more milk"), and non-existence ("soup all gone"). Children start to make sentences with simple noun phrases. They next add adjectives to nouns. Verb tenses are used before verb auxiliaries like can or will. Children hear "gonna," "hafta," "wanna" as words before they learn to say "going to."

Negatives are an early concept. Children understand that a negative is a discrepancy between what someone wants and what actually is, and that the discrepancy must be present before we can make a negative statement. Although there are millions of sentences we could utter about things that are not true, rules of conversation say that we don't utter these unless someone believes the opposite. (We don't say—unless we're being funny—"You don't have three eyes.") We say a negative *after* someone declares the opposite or acts as if it were true.[29]

Questions come into being first with the use of intonation, next with the use of question words like "where?" and "why?" The young child asks many "why" questions, sometimes continuously according to parents. Parents, however, ask the child many "false" questions to which they know the answer ("What color is this?"). It is not until the parent realizes that the child's level of understanding permits answering a true question that a true question is asked.

Parents play an important role in the language acquisition of their children. The way in which parents speak to the young is very different from adult speech. Mothers talk to their one- to two-year-olds in simple sentences which refer to concrete objects and events and are grammatically correct. Words are stressed and intonation exaggerated. There are pauses between sentences and a good many of the sentences are repetitions.

Not only parents but *all* people unconsciously adopt this pattern of speech when talking to the young (as well as to pets and lovers). The speech of the care givers both provides the baby with names of objects and helps control the baby's behavior. As the child gets older, parents begin to request information from the child or explain things to the child about the world.

Interestingly enough, acquisition of a new language does not occur after puberty in the same way that it does before. A child brought to a new country rapidly learns the language without an accent, but an adult needs formal teaching and then almost always retains an accent.

It is fascinating to us that this picture is true in all cultures. We now know that the child does more than *imitate* language. A child almost miraculously comes into the world with the ability to abstract language relationships so that an infinite number of sentences can be constructed. A truly amazing, truly human, feat.

Moral Development

Moral development is cultural and depends on intelligence and self-esteem, as well as the capacity to anticipate the future, to empathize, and to control impulses and fantasies.[30] Young children fear punishment for wrongdoing and, according to Piaget, think rules are sacred because they are handed down from adults ("morality of restraint"). By middle childhood, rules are seen as having a rational basis and children in playing games, for example, can make "local ground rules" to suit specific situations. By age twelve or so, internal guilt serves as the monitor of behavior ("morality of reciprocity").

Kohlberg clarified for us six stages of moral judgment which are developmental in that they are sequential and age-dependent.[31,32] In Stage 1, (two- and three-year-olds) the child has a punishment-obedience orientation. Fear of punishment determines what is right or wrong so that if children think they will be punished for an act, it is wrong. Stage 2 is the morality of the four- to seven-year-old. These children conform out of self-interest or because of what others can do for them (rewards). These early stages are called "preconventional morality."

Stages 3 and 4 are termed "conventional morality." Stage 3, which is termed the good boy/good girl morality, is the stage of mutuality based on seeking and gaining approval of others—important to the school-age child. The child does the right thing in order to avoid disapproval. At ages ten and twelve, Stage 4 (maintenance of social order and deference to authorities) begins. Children do their duty and accept the need for authorities like teachers and police, to whom they show respect. At this age respect for authority is based on the child's ability to abstract the concept of social order, whereas earlier the child listened to the teacher out of self-interest (conforming feels good).

"Postconventional morality" (Stages 5 and 6) can begin in adolescence. Stage 5 is the social contract stage, which explicitly recognizes the reciprocal rights of self and others. Moral teenagers understand they can't get something for nothing and they can't take without giving or belong without producing.[33] Reciprocally, they also recognize that they have rights. This is what a "social contract" means. In the sixth or highest stage, individuals are moral for self-motivated reasons. They do what they think is right even if others think differently, but would not violate a moral principle except on the basis of a higher principle such as draft resistance in an unjust war, or civil disobedience to correct a social injustice.

Sullivan, in an important paper on "Can Values Be Taught?" found that a high proportion of adolescents and adults *never* reach Stages 5 and 6.[34] Educational programs *could* facilitate learning or developing Stages 5 and 6 (and some adolescents do this on their own or with parental help). School systems often prefer to keep youngsters at the conventional, non-questioning stages because it makes life easier for the school. Parents can compensate for this by encouraging questioning.

Carol Gilligan studied identity and moral development in women and men, and found a difference in the ways they tend to look at moral dilemmas.[35] Women's moral identities are based not on the masculine hierarchical structure of defining justice but rather on reciprocity and balancing human needs. Thus, women tend to see moral problems as ones of care and responsibility in relationships while men tend to see morality as a matter of rights and rules. To a man, responsibility means not doing what he wants to do because he is following the rules. To a woman it means doing what others are counting on her to do regardless of her own wishes. Women also are more likely to believe that non-violence is the way to resolve moral conflicts.

Obviously, development of morality depends on parental warmth and acceptance, which promote identification with and adoption of parental values. Cognitive factors also play a role. One must have a basic level of intelligence in order to perceive the abstractions of moral thought. Bright children can learn the expectations of their culture quicker and can more easily move on to critiquing their culture's expectations and perceiving the behavior needed for success in their world.

Fortunately, we do not have to wait for advanced stages of moral reasoning to get moral, mannerly, or socialized behavior from our children. Norma Haan and her associates have recently shown that practical moral behavior—that is, how people solve actual moral dilemmas in daily life—develops differently from the Kohlberg descriptions of development of abstract verbalization about moral choices. Even four-year-olds, who can't verbalize about reciprocity, can use reciprocity, show empathy, and negotiate fairness in games with peers.[36] And Robert Coles describes courageous, moral behavior by young children whose ideals were taught and supported by parents, churches, or their community.[37]

Psychosocial Development

Social development begins at birth. Infants are *programmed* for interaction with care giver adults without whose attention they will die. The baby's behaviors are "designed" to encourage the immediate attachment to the mother which we call *bonding*. The infant responds to—and becomes attached to—the mother's face. Attachment is an affectional tie which is discriminating and specific; bonding is attachment which is maintained even when contact is interrupted.[38] The baby is born with innate abilities to establish human relationships. Babies can gaze at a face and prefer a human face (or its salient features). The baby can make facial expressions which are identical to expressions of adults although the baby does not necessarily "feel" the way the adult does who has the same expression.

There is a nice fit between the baby's repertoire and that of the care givers.

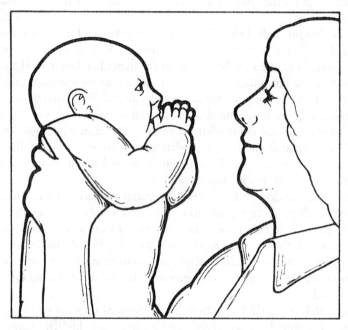

En face *position.*

Everybody in *every* culture seems to approach babies in much the same way. They use exaggerated facial expressions of moods—surprise and frowning. They vocalize to a baby in a special way—simple grammar, short length of utterance, nonsense sounds, repetitions, and a high pitched voice. Speech is also slowed down with long vowel duration and there is a longer pause between each utterance. Mothers and babies *gaze* at each other for thirty seconds or more though adult people do *not* gaze into each other's eyes without speech for over ten seconds "unless they are going to fight or make love or already are."[39]

It is interesting that care giver behaviors are elicited by the baby from almost *everybody* from grandparents to strangers in the street. These behaviors usually are somewhat stronger in women than men, but they don't depend on puberty or go away after menopause. This gives the human infant a great advantage because it brings *flexibility* into the infant care system.

What triggers this care giver repertoire in people is their response to "babyness," which we all like in humans and in puppies. Babyness consists of a large head, compared with the body, a large forehead, compared with the face, large eyes and round protruding cheeks.[40] By the way, girls begin to prefer baby faces (human and animal) at about ages twelve to fourteen while boys show this tendency about two years later and to a lesser degree. Even children as young as six (both boys and girls) show care giver behavior toward live babies and live baby animals. They raise the pitch of their voice, repeat vocalizations, use baby talk, and engage in a prolonged gaze. Children do not show these behaviors as much in doll play, which is rather a task-oriented imitation of parenting (feeding, bathing, scolding).

A baby starts out with social responsiveness which is not discriminating. There is predictable response to stimuli (visual, auditory, etc.) but the baby will show this response to any person providing the stimulus. By three months the baby begins to discriminate in social responsiveness. By eight months the baby *knows* the mother, other familiar care givers, and all non-familiar people (strangers). The baby definitely prefers the mother! This is true whether the baby is in day care or raised by a nanny.

There are several elements which affect the psychosocial development of the infant, but interactions between the mother and infant are of prime importance. These two have lived in the same body for nine months but they are different individuals with different genetic makeups and personalities, and interactive styles based on these.

We find many young parents do not know about the remarkable differences between babies *from birth*. Many young parents think all babies act and can be reacted to and treated the same way. Brazelton, in his excellent book *Infants and Mothers: Differences in Development*, traces three babies through infancy, each of whom has one of the three "behavior" types he identified: "average," "quiet," and "active."[41] Throughout all the stages of development these babies behaved differently from each other and the parents had to respond to each baby in a specific way to "match" the baby.

Margaret Mahler talks about the "psychological birth" of the baby that occurs when infants recognize the separateness of their own body from that of the care giving mother. The separation begins at about five months when the baby distinguishes between self and non-self. The baby touches and explores the mother's face; babies mold themselves to the mother's body. Early differentiation leads into the "practicing" phase. Babies touch, taste, and smell everything they can; they crawl away from—and look back to—the mother.

Separation continues in toddlerhood. What Mahler calls "rapprochement" is seen between eighteen to twenty-four months. Children walk away, but they want the mother to share all their new skills. So the child moves away—and runs back, both literally and figuratively.[42]

Erikson teaches us that infants who have developed a basic trust in the primary care giver can begin to predict and control events. The baby is learning like crazy—motor skills, language, social skills—and each mastery helps the baby differentiate and separate self from his or her primary care giver.[43]

Toddlers, in a safe environment which enables them to explore and master age-appropriate skills on their own, develop awareness of self and autonomy. The trick for parents is to allow the child to develop a sense of self-control without losing self-esteem during this stage when children need so desperately to *try* to do everything on their own but must be protected from lack of knowledge and experience to do so wisely.

The negativism expressed by toddlers is a result of frustration with their lack of autonomy. When toddlers get older they learn socially acceptable ways to get what they want. Although this stage has been termed the "terrible twos," this term is an error according to Frances Ilg. Marilyn called her to ask where the term came from. Dr. Ilg said that it should really be the "terrible two-and-a-halfs" because twos and threes are in a relatively calm stage. The expression was a misunderstanding. The tantrum of the toddler indicates development of the child's will as he or she becomes independent of the mother. This is progress in development! Incidentally "terribleness" is a judgment not a description and is not inevitable at two and a half. Parents in our culture often enhance conflict because they expect too much and try to add obedience and respect to the already enormous tasks that these children face at this age.

Toddlers also develop language to express their autonomy, learn to control their bowels and bladder, learn how to play with others, and can begin to learn self-control. Spitz described the developmental sequence of self-control.[44] The young infant passively accepts frustration and is usually quiet when confronted with a "no." As the child matures, temper tantrums and saying "No!" to everything are the responses to frustration. Children may tell themselves "No!" when they are about to engage in a forbidden activity. Physical aggression toward others or objects is the next stage, followed by verbal aggression with name-calling and four-letter words. Socially acceptable behavior begins when children realize they can control events through verbalization, and altering of goals follows. Children learn they can get their way—much of the time—by these means. Finally, the child learns cooperation, which is truly the epitome of self-control—and also implies understanding of the needs of others. This is an important aspect of maturity but it takes a long time. As noted above, an understanding of reciprocity between one's own needs and the needs of others is rarely achieved before adolescence—if then.

School-age children undergo social development in an arena other than the home and spend much of their time with people other than their families. The child's tasks are many: acquiring intellectual skills, the development of self-concept and independence, and learning interrelationships with peers, adults outside the family, and the community. Erikson calls these years the industry versus inferiority age. Most of the child's energies go into mastering the cognitive and social skills needed by an adult in our complex society. The child also develops mastery of his or her body. As Havighurst points out, now the child works hard to become competent at games and sports.

Psychosexual Development

FREUDIAN THEORY

Freud felt that sexual pleasure was the focus of personality development and that drive or libido (psychosexual energy) is linked to all behavior. The first stage of psychosexual development is the *oral phase* in which virtually all of the infant's activities (eating, talking, exploring) are centered around the mouth. Sexuality starts at birth with the pleasure the newborn feels from sucking. Freud thought that satisfaction or dissatisfaction with early feeding led to dependency or aggression later. Erikson felt basic trust, without which autonomy cannot occur, developed in this stage. The infant feels contiguous with the mother and part of her during this phase.

The toddler begins to feel separation and autonomy about the same time as sphincter control is acquired. In fact it would be hard to achieve sphincter control before gaining some sense of autonomy and separation. Freud termed this the *anal phase* and attributed behavior in later life such as generosity (giving up the stool) and frugality (holding on) to the child's integration of toilet-training experiences.

The preschooler becomes curious about his or her own genitals and the sexual differences between people. This is called the *phallic phase*. Negative parental attitudes toward masturbatory activity could, according to Freud, affect later sexual adjustment. During this phase Freud noted two phenomena. Boys may suffer from castration anxiety ("If she doesn't have one maybe mine will be cut off") and girls may have penis envy or even a fantasy that they once had a penis which had been lost. In addition, Freud thought the three-year-old boy falls in love with his mother and is jealous of the father (Oedipal complex) while girls fall in love with the father and try to compete with the mother (Electra complex). The "Oedipal" love a three- or four-year-old boy has for his mother can be extraordinarily strong. When the toddlers realize they cannot possess their parent of the opposite sex but that they can grow up and have a replacement partner, they can then identify with their own sex in order to develop those characteristics and behaviors they will need to possess a love object of the opposite sex.

Latency is not, as some have said, asexual. Rather children between six and twelve place most energy on learning and organization and spend most of their time with same sex peers consolidating their knowledge of their own sex. Puberty and adolescence bring renewed interest in genital sex and the beginning of adult kinds of intimacy.

SEXUAL IDENTITY

Young children know whether they are boys or girls before they can always speak the words clearly. Often by the time the child is eighteen months of age if you say "What a cute boy you are!" to a girl, she laughs or shakes her head. This knowledge is called core gender identity and is firm by age three.

Core gender identity is the basic identification of self as male or female. *Gender role* refers to behaviors or characteristics that are attributed to one gender or the other. Many of these are culturally determined. By ages three to four, children assign gender roles to dolls according to sex role stereotypes, which means the way we raise our children in our culture encourages the development of stereotyping very early.[45]

Early in history gender roles were assigned according to the appropriate physical attributes needed for survival. Thus the woman—the only one who could bear and nurse the child—was assigned agrarian tasks. The male's greater strength was appropriate for hunting and family protection. Today, technology enables women—or men—to artificially feed infants, and modern transportation ensures that everybody can easily depart from and get back to the home. The protective physical strength of men can be replaced by technology from guns to electronic surveillance devices.

Gender role stereotypes emerge when *other* human characteristics, which *either women or men can have*, become linked to biological differences and are actually seen as though they were just as absolute. If society believes that girls and women are (or should be) nice and compliant, and boys and men are (or should be) tough and aggressive, these messages become imbedded in our children which can constrict their childhoods and ill prepare them for adult life.

Sexism includes sex role stereotyping, but goes beyond it. This is the idea that there is a natural hierarchy, and that in it, men are supposed to come out on top. We are just beginning to learn how damaging this can be to healthy personality development of *both* girls and boys. Far too many girls have grown up with the basic idea that they really shouldn't learn to be too competent, but concentrate on marketing skills needed to capture a man who would take care of them. Far too many boys have grown up with the idea that adult life would make constant demands on them for competence, dominance, aggressiveness, and emotional control. They have learned to hide their feelings, and possibly even worse than that, learned to hide areas in which they felt weak, rather than learning to get appropriate help. They have learned that they are "not supposed to hit girls" but are often encouraged to hit each other ("Don't start a fight but if he starts it, fight back!").

Even parents who are trying hard to raise their children in non-sexist ways, who want both their girls and boys to experience their full potential as human beings, are often startled to see their young children seemingly take a rigid view of gender role behavior. Even daughters of women doctors may say that women are nurses, not doctors. There is a story about very modern parents who bought a truck for their daughter and a doll for their son for Christmas. They tiptoed into the playroom and found the girl cradling the truck in her arms and the boy going "vroom—vroom" with the doll on the floor!

Children learn sexist attitudes in a variety of ways—from parents, other relatives, peers, teachers, mass media, and other influences from the society as a whole. Such attitudes may be taught *consciously* by authorities who genuinely believe that male authority is a proper foundation for society. Many religious groups have explicitly held such beliefs in the past—and some still do.

Unconscious sexist attitudes can be transmitted by, for example, a husband who claims to feel equal with his wife but puts his career commitments ahead of hers, and his family commitments behind hers. A wife may claim to feel equal to her husband but in practice put his needs above hers, defer to his point of view, and so on.

Not all sexism in young children is cultural. A child's first conception of gender roles is very simpleminded and narrow, just like first conceptions of language and everything else. These conceptions develop into more sophisticated ones as children try them on, try them out, and continue to observe. Parents should not be surprised if at first young children try out exaggerated, oversimplified versions of their sex role. The idea of sex differences fascinates young children. Sometimes sex differences are more problematic for boys, who can see clearly that women become pregnant, have babies, and nurse them, but have a less clear picture of what is special about adult male sexuality. Exaggerated copying of sex-typed male behaviors may be a way of coming to terms with this and may account for the small boy's fascination with toy guns.

Although some feminists would want us to believe there are absolutely no inherent behavioral differences between the sexes, most feminists believe this is neither true nor desirable. As we accept physical differences, we also recognize psychological and behavioral differences. Many of these are culturally influenced and may change as our cultural norms change and sex role stereotyping decreases. But viable feminism means celebrating differences not denying them— just as "black is beautiful" is a healthier response to racism than looking for skin fade cream.

Only four gender-related behaviors have been substantiated through research. When measured by sophisticated tests, females on the average do have greater verbal ability. Males on the average have better visual-spatial skills and mathematical skills, and score higher on measures of aggression. All the other characteristics attributed to masculinity or femininity are probably culturally imposed. Also, it's important to remember that these four behavioral differences are averages, not fixed individual characteristics. Fewer girls may have outstanding ability in math but the ones who have it may be great mathematicians. Fewer men may have great verbal ability but there are many great writers who are male.

Gender role stereotyping is very pervasive in our culture even today. Although overt sexism is not only illegal but is deplored by all thinking people, covert and unconscious sexism persists. We are a nation divided when it comes to issues like the ERA—possibly the most misunderstood and maligned twenty-three-word amendment ever put before the states. The ERA simply gives women the same constitutional rights as men.

How can we guard against stereotyping and sexism? A non-sexist approach to child rearing requires that we have more equal *expectations* about the adult roles of men and women. Girls should not be given "double-bind" messages: i.e., you can train for work outside of the home, but your real and only purpose and goal in life is to become a mother and wife. Nor should boys be encouraged to believe that "bringing home the bacon" is synonomous with fathering. Boys and girls should be provided with situations (and rewards) for developing both expressive (i.e., nurturing emotional qualities) and instrumental (action, goal-oriented) activities. Parents should evaluate and modify both the degree to which they share family and parenting tasks and the degree to which they behave according to rigid sex role stereotypes. Educational and social networks (e.g., media) should not promote sexist attitudes and behavior.

The *real* changes will come slowly. Not until we raise our *sons* differently— in a non-sexist way—can we expect our daughters to enter a non-sexist world. Thus under the best of circumstances, without backlash and with a true societal commitment, this will take at least a generation.

We do *not* advocate raising children as though they were *sexless* or *unisex*. Gender identity is basic and important to the individual as well as to the human race. There is even evidence that stereotypes are useful to a degree for young children. Stereotypes help very young children code and remember information, especially important because children must learn so much about their world all at once. Stereotypes also may reduce anxiety about gender differences and provide a guide for children's behavior until their gender identity is merged with their other identities such as body image, family and group membership, sense of personal self, morality, and sense of cognitive self.

We know that both men and women suffer from stereotyping and being forced by their gender into roles they do not desire. Many males want to be able to express tender or nurturant behavior without being seen as deviant. Women want a life free of social or occupational restrictions. We advocate elimination of destructive stereotyping and discriminating societal practices.

DEVELOPMENTAL TABLES

For physical growth and development refer to the tables or text in each age/stage chapter. Normal tooth development is shown in illustration opposite.

Tables showing Developmental Highlights (Table 25), Motor and Social Behavior Development (Tables 26 to 34), and Language Development (Table 35) follow.

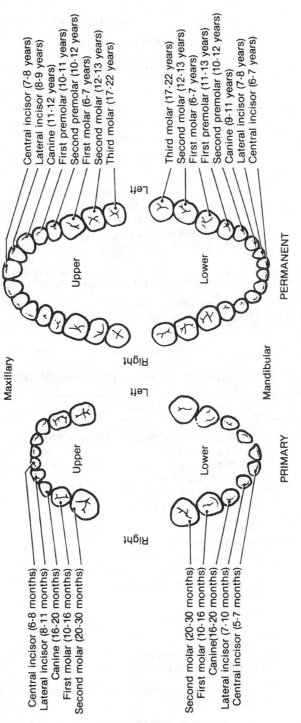

PERMANENT

Maxillary

Left
- Central incisor (7-8 years)
- Lateral incisor (8-9 years)
- Canine (11-12 years)
- First premolar (10-11 years)
- Second premolar (10-12 years)
- First molar (6-7 years)
- Second molar (12-13 years)
- Third molar (17-22 years)

Left
- Third molar (17-22 years)
- Second molar (12-13 years)
- First molar (6-7 years)
- First premolar (11-13 years)
- Second premolar (10-12 years)
- Canine (9-11 years)
- Lateral incisor (7-8 years)
- Central incisor (6-7 years)

Upper

Lower

Right

Mandibular

PRIMARY

Left

Left

Upper

Lower

Right

Right
- Central incisor (6-8 months)
- Lateral incisor (8-11 months)
- Canine (16-20 months)
- First molar (10-16 months)
- Second molar (20-30 months)

Right
- Second molar (20-30 months)
- First molar (10-16 months)
- Canine (16-20 months)
- Lateral incisor (7-10 months)
- Central incisor (5-7 months)

Normal tooth development.

TABLE 25

DEVELOPMENTAL HIGHLIGHTS

1 month—smiles
2 months—coos
3 months—gains head control
4 months—reaches with the arms
5 months—rolls over
6 months—sits alone
7 months—crawls
8 months—demonstrates a pincer grasp
9 months—pulls self to standing
10 months—stands alone
11 months—walks holding on to furniture
12 months—walks alone

These are the approximate ages each developmental highlight appears. All of these depend on neural myelinization which gives the maturation needed for each task. Myelinization proceeds from head to foot.

Reprinted by permission and adapted from Brown, Marie Scott, and Murphy, Mary Alexander, *Ambulatory Pediatrics for Nurses*. 2nd ed. New York: McGraw-Hill, 1981.

TABLE 26

MOTOR AND SOCIAL BEHAVIOR DEVELOPMENT

Infant: Newborn

GROSS MOTOR	Symmetrical random extremity movements Pronounced head lag Prone: turns head to side and draws knees under abdomen Symmetrical, full Moro reflex Strong, symmetrical tonic neck reflex Walking (or stepping) reflex

FINE MOTOR	Tight hand grasp
	Hand predominantly fisted
	Face—Eyes follow to midline
	  Head and eyes move together (by 1 month)
	  Attracted to object with eyes
	Rooting reflex
	Sucking reflex

LANGUAGE	Cries.
LOVE	Beginning development of a one-to-one relationship with mother. Likes to cuddle, to be held close.
FEARS	Dislikes being uncovered, held loosely. May dislike bathing. Dislikes loud noises.
PLAY	Knows nothing of sharing and giving; infant very taking at this stage. Play consists of someone else doing something to child—stroking, cooing, cuddling.

Infant: Newborn (continued)

DEPENDENCY	Depends entirely on someone else for meeting basic needs—feeding, clothing, cleaning, shelter, stimulation.	
MORALITY	Has no idea of right or wrong.	
SELF-IMAGE	Knows no difference between self and mother (symbiotic relationship).	
HABITS	*Eating:*	Frequently (every 2 to 4 hours) from bottle or breast. May cry when hungry and fall asleep when satisfied.
	Bowels:	Frequent movements. Shows no knowledge of activity.
	Sleeping:	Generally most of 24 hours. Most sleep in spaces of 50 minutes with rapid eye movements.
	Dressing:	Taken care of entirely by mother.

TABLE 27

MOTOR AND SOCIAL BEHAVIOR DEVELOPMENT

3-month-old

GROSS MOTOR	Symmetrical random extremity movements Little or no head lag Prone: Holds head at 45 to 90° angle and keeps legs outstretched Symmetrical, full Moro reflex (but fades by 5 months) Weak, asymmetrical tonic neck reflex Walking reflex begins to fade	

FINE MOTOR	Little or no hand grasp
	Hands predominantly open, but will grasp rattle
	Face—Eyes follow object 180°
	  Smiles responsively
	  Attracted to and watches own hands
	Rooting reflex begins to fade
	Sucking reflex begins to fade	

LANGUAGE	Cooing, one-syllable vowel sounds: "ah."	
LOVE	Loves to be held. Smiles socially.	
FEARS	Loud noises are disturbing.	
PLAY	Looks at mobile. May have found thumb.	
DEPENDENCY	Still entirely dependent.	
MORALITY	No idea of right or wrong.	
SELF-IMAGE	Beginning to learn mother is separate.	
HABITS	*Eating:*	Bottle or breast at about 4-hour intervals.
	Bowels:	2 to 3 per day.

3-month-old (continued)

Sleeping: Sleeps 16 hours.
Dressing: Mother's care.

TABLE 28

MOTOR AND SOCIAL BEHAVIOR DEVELOPMENT

6-month-old	
GROSS MOTOR	Reaches with arms Sits with support comfortably—in chair alone briefly Prone: Supports upper chest with arms Scoots effectively Rolls over, stomach to back Creeping begins
FINE MOTOR	Crude palmar grasp Can hold small block momentarily Transfers small objects (around 7 months) Bangs objects (5 to 7 months) Face—Eyes follow object 180° horizontally Attracted to small object: reaches, grasps, and puts in mouth
LANGUAGE	Consonant sounds ("mm"), babbling, vocalizes pleasure and displeasure.
LOVE	Has established a one-to-one relationship with mother (or mother substitute). Responsive to looks, gestures, verbalization. Lots of smiles.
FEARS	Dislikes loss of support, loud noises, strangers (around 6 to 9 months).
PLAY	Likes games of Peek-a-boo, Pat-a-cake, Soo-big. Will play games alone or in response to someone else.
DEPENDENCY	Still dependent on mother for most activities. Can control some of own movements—rolling over, sitting, reaching.
MORALITY	Must be totally controlled by external forces (mother and environment). Knows self is different from mother.
SELF-IMAGE	Knows mother is different from other family members.
HABITS	*Eating:* Likes to feed self crackers, but mostly sucks on them. Likes the feel of food oozing between the fingers. Will sit in high chair for a meal. *Bowels:* Bowel movements and voidings less frequent. *Sleeping:* Sleeps more at night and less during day. *Dressing:* May struggle against holding still long enough to be dressed. Diapering often awkward because of rolling, crawling.

TABLE 29

MOTOR AND SOCIAL BEHAVIOR DEVELOPMENT

9-month-old

GROSS MOTOR	More control over reaching with arms Sits alone Prone—crawls on hands and knees, crawls with one hand full Rolls over completely when desires
FINE MOTOR	Effective pincer grasp for small objects Explores objects with hand and mouth Learns to squeeze, slide, push, pull, rip objects with hands Can turn small object over
LANGUAGE	"Da-Da," "Ma-Ma," responds to name and "No!"
LOVE	Prefers mother.
FEARS	Fear of strangers, separation anxiety.
PLAY	Beads, blocks.
DEPENDENCY	Holds own bottle.
MORALITY	None yet.
SELF-IMAGE	Looks at face in mirror.
HABITS	*Eating:* Drinks from cup, finger foods, may try spoon. *Bowels:* 1 to 2 per day. *Sleeping:* Sleeps through night plus 1 to 2 naps. *Dressing:* More cooperative.

TABLE 30

MOTOR AND SOCIAL BEHAVIOR DEVELOPMENT

12-month-old

GROSS MOTOR	Can twist within sitting position Prone—may walk on hands and feet like a dog Walking holding onto furniture Can pivot standing alone Throwing—deliberately drops or lets go rather than real throw Stepping—climbs on chairs, sofas, beds
FINE MOTOR	Mature grasp—can reach for, pick up, and give back block (used to initiate social contact)
LANGUAGE	2 to 8 words, babbles short sentences.
LOVE	Still absorbing a lot of love and returning little. Learning to give love pats, hugs, kisses.

12-month-old (continued)

FEARS	Strange people and places; dislikes separation from mother.
PLAY	Can give and take in game of "give-it-to-me" with block or ball. Likes games with more action—push, pull, run.
DEPENDENCY	Becoming more independent because of motor control (walking, running, sitting). Tries to do some things for self (feeding, removing clothing).
MORALITY	Needs constant external limits and watching.
SELF-IMAGE	Can function emotionally as an individual as long as mother is physically present in room.

HABITS		
	Eating:	Feeds self cracker, getting most of it in mouth. Drinks from a cup. Likes to be with family at mealtime but may need to be fed separately.
	Bowels:	May squirm or complain when diaper soiled.
	Sleeping:	Probably sleeps through night, plus 1 or 2 daytime naps.
	Dressing:	Can remove some garments. Helps to dress self by sticking out appropriate extremity.

TABLE 31

MOTOR AND SOCIAL BEHAVIOR DEVELOPMENT

Toddler

GROSS MOTOR	*Walking*	Even smooth gait by 2 years
	Stepping	Can stand on one foot momentarily
		Climbs up stairs on hands and knees (12 to 15 months)
		Climbs up stairs, upright, holding on, one foot at a time (1½ to 2 years)
	Throwing	Rigid, underhand toss
		Begins to throw overhand (around 2 years)
		Cannot catch ball
	Running	Unsteady
		Smooth rhythmical run (2 years) but can't stop quickly
	Jumping	Broad jump with two feet (2 years)
FINE MOTOR		Does not distinguish right from left side
		Holds pencil and scribbles
	Writing	Scribbles marks in all directions rapidly
		Scribbles in patterns (2 years)
		Likes to touch, handle, manipulate objects (and name them)
LANGUAGE		200 words (by 2 years), names pictures in book, gives name.

Toddler (continued)

LOVE		Wants and needs love from mother. Can tolerate short separation from mother (across room or in next room with frequent visual and verbal checks on her presence).
FEARS		Thunder, dogs, darkness.
PLAY		Beginning awareness of ownership—"my toy," "my coat," etc. Solitary play. May have imaginary playmates. Will look at pictures in a book momentarily.
DEPENDENCY		Strives for independence and control (learns one way is to say "no"). If handkerchief is held, can blow own nose. Likes to have a choice.
MORALITY		Beginning self controls (may say "no" while reaching for forbidden object). Still needs many external controls.
SELF-IMAGE		Can show and name some parts of body—eye, ear, nose.
HABITS	*Eating:*	Uses a spoon without spilling. Holds and uses a cup but may drop it or throw it when finished. Can suck through a straw. Eats with family, but cannot sit through entire meal.
	Bowels:	May show an interest in urges, but not reliable. May not fuss at being placed on potty chair, but may have no action.
	Sleeping:	Daytime naps may disappear or become times of quiet play rather than sleep. Bedtime can be a struggle.
	Dressing:	Can put on simple garments. Likes to remove all clothing.

TABLE 32

MOTOR AND SOCIAL BEHAVIOR DEVELOPMENT

Preschooler

GROSS MOTOR	*Walking*	Tandem walk a line (3 years) Without watching feet (3 years)
	Stepping	Climbs up stairs alternating feet (3 years) Climbs down stairs alternating feet (4 to 5 years) Hops down 3 steps on one foot (3½ years) Hops down 4 to 6 steps on one foot (4 years) Crude skip (5 years)
	Throwing	Throws overhand with ease Begins to shift weight when throwing

Preschooler (continued)

		Catches ball stiffly with extended arms (3½ years)
		Catches ball with hands (4 years)
	Running	Adds smooth arm action
		Adds speed
	Jumping	Can broad jump a longer distance

FINE MOTOR — Knows there is a right and left side but cannot distinguish (4 to 5 years)

       Writing   Recognizes and draws complete circle (2 to 3 years)
Draws crude cross (2½ to 3½ years)
Draws crude 3-part figure (3 to 4 years)
Recognizes and copies crude square (4 years)
Combines 2 simple geometric forms (4 years)
Can combine more than 2 geometric forms (aggregates) (5 years)

LANGUAGE — Can have 1,000-word vocabulary, learns 50 words a month, uses pronouns.

LOVE — Parents represent the strength and wisdom in child's life (they can do no wrong).
With enlarging world, there are beginning attachments for persons outside immediate family.

FEARS — Worries about own body (skinned knee, hangnail, bumps, bites—needs bandage and kiss).
Worries about outside world (ghosts, bad men, the doctor's office).

PLAY — Parallel play (3 to 4 years).
Shared play (4 to 5 years).
Everything becomes a game.
Tries new roles.
Imaginary play ("let's pretend" situations and playmates).
Likes games of tag, hide-and-seek, dress-up.
Learns to play simple sit-down games (checkers, card games, Parcheesi) but hates to lose and will change rules and cheat to avoid it.

DEPENDENCY — Rapid transitions from dependence to independence.
Needs security objects for times of stress—thumb, blanket, favorite toy, mother's hand.
Strives for independence with "Let me do it."

MORALITY — Can control some of own urges.
May invent imaginary friends to take the rap for own wrongdoing.
More aware of others in body and feeling (how they are the same or different).

SELF-IMAGE — More interested in doing activities within own sex role (girls want to be feminine, boys masculine).

HABITS — *Eating:*   Can control and pour from a small pitcher.
May be able to sit and eat with family if able to leave when finished.

Preschooler (continued)

	Likes to serve self.
Bowels:	Completed day and night dryness (3½ to 4 years).
	May still announce the event.
	May still need help in cleansing and clothing.
Sleeping:	Only at night.
	May have nightmares.
	Begins to understand that dreams happen while sleeping.
Dressing:	Does own buttons.
	Will dress self if clothing laid out.

TABLE 33

MOTOR AND SOCIAL BEHAVIOR DEVELOPMENT

School-age child

GROSS MOTOR	*Walking*	Can walk a balance board
	Stepping	Smoother hop/skip (6 years)
		Can hop on one foot up to 10 seconds
		Can hop longer distances with more rhythm
	Throwing	More bodily motion and more accuracy at target
		Catches ball with hands and body
		Greater distance throw (8 to 10 years)
	Running	Adds speed
	Jumping	Longer-distance broad jump
FINE MOTOR		Knows and can distinguish right from left side (6 to 7 years)
	Writing	Can draw crude figure with up to 6 parts (5 to 6 years)
		Copies diamond (6 years)
		Can tie shoes
LOVE		Learns parents can be wrong.
		Sometimes can be disillusioned with own parents and would like to trade them in or is certain he or she is adopted.
		Learns to share some of own thoughts only with peers.
		Parents and home a place to return to for some companionship, comfort, and security.
FEARS		Is superstitious. Fears ghosts and elements.
PLAY		Games show superstitions, teasing, insults.
		Cooperative play—baseball, jacks, hopscotch.
		Peers of same sex important.
		Collections—a type of hoarding.
DEPENDENCY		Rejects some ideas of parents and tries own ideas, but usually returns to home base.
		Reduces need for dependency by using rituals—bedtime, mealtime, bathtime.

School-age child (continued)

MORALITY	Thinks of own needs first and is out to satisfy them. Can think of relationship between the act and following consequences. Begins to develop an idea of what it means to live by a label (good boy, good girl, bad boy, bad girl). Peer group begins to influence morality with fixed rules and rituals.
SELF-IMAGE	Begins to see self within a label given by world (boy, girl, mean, nice, bully, cute, etc.).

HABITS

Eating:	Eats meals with family and can sit through entire meal. Has definite likes and dislikes, but may change suddenly. Has rituals around mealtime—same location at table, same silverware, same food.
Bowels:	Needs no help from adults.
Sleeping:	May spend night away from home.
Dressing:	Can decide on own clothing and dress self. But may ask for help and then ignore it. Can comb own hair.

TABLE 34

MOTOR AND SOCIAL BEHAVIOR DEVELOPMENT

Adolescent

GROSS MOTOR	Increasing physical strength and endurance Increasing motor ability Increasing coordination
FINE MOTOR	Same as adult—coordinated, controlled, deliberate movements
LOVE	Vacillating and expanding. Within home: parents wonderful, wise, understanding, and deceitful, dishonest, and stupid. With peers: relationships intense and unstable. With world: idealistic and shallow.
FEARS	Worries about loss of identity (bodily, emotionally). Worries about failure (in school, career, friendship). Is uncertain.
PLAY	Develops skills in individual and group play (games, sports, activities). Joins clubs, groups, sports. Cliques important—involve peers of same sex but with activities associated with opposite sex.
DEPENDENCY	High ambivalence between wanting limits and freedom. Discovers responsibility that comes with freedom.

Adolescent (continued)

MORALITY	Begins to see that own actions affect a large group of individuals rather than just self. Beginning logical thought about own principles, rights, justice as compared with rest of community.
SELF-IMAGE	Learned through group contact. Desires to be just like everyone else but more so. Tries on many different roles. Hypochodriasis (excessive worry over body and bodily functions).
HABITS	*Eating:* Many food fads. Constant eating. Worry over bodily functions leads to fad diets to correct specific problems. Would rather eat with peers than family. *Sleeping:* May get so wound up in activities that adolescent sleeps very little. May have trouble going to bed and getting up in morning. *Dressing:* Conformity with peers—clothing, hair, makeup, jewelry.

Reprinted by permission and adapted from Brown, Marie Scott, and Murphy, Mary Alexander, *Ambulatory Pediatrics for Nurses.* 2nd ed. New York: McGraw-Hill, 1981.

TABLE 35

LANGUAGE DEVELOPMENT

Approximate Age	Baby Says
Birth to 4 weeks	Crying
4 to 16 weeks	Coos and makes "laughing" noises. Vocal play produces vowels and some consonant sounds involving tongue and lip activity. May engage in vocal dialogue with mother.
20 to 24 weeks	Vocalizes when comfortable. Vowel-like cooing and considerable babbling, with consonants modifying the identifiable vowel. Makes some nasal sounds (m, n) and some lip sounds.
6 to 7 months	Babbling now includes self-imitation. Many of the sound productions resemble one-syllable utterances that may include ma, da, di, do.
8 to 9 months	Considerable self-imitative sound play. Is also likely to imitate (echo) syllables and words that others say.
10 to 11 months	Repeats the words of others with increased proficiency. Responds appropriately to many word cues for familiar things and "happenings." Precocious child may have several words in vocabulary.

Approximate Age	Baby Says
12 months	Still likely to imitate the speech of others, but so proficiently that he or she seems to have quite a lot to say. First labeling words for most children.
By 18 months	Vocalizations reveal intonational (melody) pattern of adult speakers. May begin to use 2-word utterances, 25 percent intelligibility.
24 months	Understands hundreds of words and sentences. Has a speaking vocabulary of 50 or more words. May begin to use 2-word combinations, 50 to 70 percent intelligibility.
30 months	Vocabulary growth is proportionately greater than at any other period. Many, though not all, of the child's sentences are grammatically like those of the adults in the child's life. Understands most of what is said if it is within the child's experience. Almost total intelligibility.
36 months	Speaking vocabulary may exceed 1,000 words. Syntax almost completely "grown up." Can say what he or she thinks and make intentions clear.
48 months	Productive vocabulary between 1,500 and 2,000 words; understands up to 20,000 words. Grammatically, has acquired much of what he or she is likely to acquire.

Reprinted by permission and adapted from McMillan, Julia A.; Stockman III, James A.; and Oski, Frank A., *The Whole Pediatrician Catalog.* Vol. 2. Philadelphia: Saunders, 1979.

THE ROLE OF THE PARENTS IN CHILDHOOD DEVELOPMENT

Now we come to the bottom-line question. What do parents *do* about their child's development? Do parents have any role in the development of the child?

First of all, as we've said before, enjoy observing your child's development —the most fascinating show on earth! You will find that even when you are cross or tired, when your baby does something new, it will be a turn-on (most of the time!). And your excitement is communicated to the child, rewards the new behavior, and helps develop self-esteem.

Keep in mind that there is a continuum of development. There are some major rapid breakthroughs—yesterday the child did not have a social smile, today the baby has the basis for that social smile (a functioning body and nervous system and stimulation from the environment so the baby has something to smile to) and baby smiles! However, much development is more gradual and may wax and wane (dry one night—wet the next!).

It makes sense for a parent to *know* factual information about child development for several reasons: 1) to be able to watch the show intelligently; 2) to appreciate deviations from the norm, especially serious ones; and 3) to know what *can* be done to foster optimal development.

You have learned your baby is *not* a blank slate. On the other hand, you as a parent are not totally responsible for all your child will become. What role will you as a parent play in your child's development?

There is some new and fascinating data on identical twins reared apart from infancy. When such twins are examined in later life, they not only look alike but they act and think and feel alike on a wide variety of psychological and personality tests and questionnaires about their behavior. Indeed, the degree of concordance (agreement) between the behaviors of identical twins reared apart and those of identical twins reared together is high, which makes it look as though John Locke was dead wrong.[46] But it is important to remember that even twins reared apart are usually reared in the similar middle-class environments which adoption agencies favor so their environments in general may have been similar.

However, these twin studies, which demonstrate the importance of heredity, provide very little evidence that the environment plays *any* role! This can be rather discouraging to new parents who have just bought a crib mobile, a complete set of the Beatrix Potter books, and a stereo so they can play Mozart in the nursery. As with so many issues, the answer to the question of the relative importance of genes and the environment is that both play a role.

The importance of parents to the development of children has been looked at in a new way by Kaye, who hypothesizes that the role parents play in the development of their baby is that of master to apprentice.[47] The master provides protected opportunities to practice selected subtasks, monitors the growth of the apprentice's skills, and gradually presents more difficult tasks. Further, parents are preadapted to this role.

Kaye, influenced by self-theory, points out that every human takes a remarkable journey from the moment the egg and sperm unite to the unique person with a mind (more than a brain) and a sense of self. He feels a brain alone could not bring about a mind, which arises from communication. Symbols of language and thought could not emerge without a preadapted fit between adult and infant.

Babies and adults communicate *before* the baby has a mind, in the adult sense. True, the infant is endowed with some intrinsic cognitive abilities but communication with adults that fosters learning requires only that the infant have certain reactions which parents *interpret* as meaningful long before they are. The biological imperative for the human infant is not to recognize the mother, as the baby duckling must do to survive, but to ensure that the *mother* recognizes and cares for her infant. Included in this care are her preadapted behaviors which foster social learning in the baby.

All mothers in all cultures talk to their babies in the same way: high pitched voice, many repetitions, simple grammar. Kaye would have us believe that this is an innate characteristic of human parents. Because we are the most helpless of mammals and require the longest period of parenting, it is to the advantage of the species to preadapt to the type of parenting that ensures the pair will stay together for this period of learning. Humans can thus adapt to a variety of conditions (Kaye calls us an "opportunistic" species) because so much of our adaptation is left to learning and cultures. We rely much more on learning than genetic transmission of traits, but without the innate disposition to learn (on the part of the baby) and to teach (on the part of the parents) our species would not have evolved as it did.

We know without question that a child's behavior will change as the child develops. We know that the speed and direction of early development is preprogrammed in the human baby. We know that the child cannot be molded exactly as the parent wishes.

Probably the most important thing parents provide is the creation of the best possible *environment* for physical growth, development, and learning. It is a long road to maturity. Some never get there because of lack of endowment. Sadly, some endowed with a good deal do not achieve a fulfilling adult life because they lacked adequate parental care and support. During the time the child is in your care, you, as a concerned parent, *can, should,* and *will* make a difference.

Play and learning are the major occupations of the child. Indeed these are the only things the child does, apart from fulfilling physical needs. Developing and learning are *fun* for the young child and one of the major sources of joy in childhood. Sharing this fun with the child is one of the many joys of parenting.

Stimulation

Adults can foster or inhibit love of learning in a number of ways. Inhibition of learning can occur both when children are understimulated and overstimulated. The work of Spitz, Bowlby, and others has shown that children in institutions whose physical needs were met but who were not talked to or cuddled or picked up had gross alterations not only in their development but also in their physical growth.[48,49] They had what is called "failure to thrive" and many of them died. Sadly, this happens today and in homes, not institutions, usually when parents are overstressed or undersupported.

One of the earliest experiments on infants was designed by King Frederick II, Holy Roman Emperor, in the thirteenth century. He theorized that ancient languages might have a hierarchical order and that newborns, if not spoken to, would first speak Hebrew and then ancient Greek or Latin before speaking their own tongue. To prove his theory, he forbade nurses and foster mothers to speak at all when caring for a group of infants. Unfortunately, without the attention of speech, all the infants died so we will never know if Hebrew would have come out first.

The now famous expression "TLC" ("Tender Loving Care") came into being when doctors and nurses realized that a hospitalized child who was not doing well required a special medicine: liberal doses of tender, loving care. When "TLC" was written in a baby's chart, the nurses knew this meant the baby needed especially large doses of cuddling, being talked to, being picked up, etc. in addition to the other treatments ordered.

Can understimulation occur in a home as well as in a hospital? Yes, it can and with most serious results. Sometimes parents, especially young parents, don't realize that a baby needs to be picked up and cuddled and talked to. Some may not realize how important it is to spend time looking closely at your baby in what's called the "en face" position. This means the baby's face is right in front of your face, about eight inches away, so that you both can make eye-to-eye contact. (See illustration p. 238.) Parents may not realize the importance of talking to a baby because the baby cannot talk back. But parents should talk to their baby—lots of talking, every chance they get. Remember King Frederick! Besides, babies will respond—with sounds or movements or attention—even if not with words. Their responses make parents *want* to talk and sing to their babies.

Some parents may have retained from their own childhood the mistaken notion that a child must be disciplined from birth in order to avoid spoiling the child. Such parents are convinced they must let the child "cry it out." They may be well-intentioned parents who are meeting the physical needs of the baby and who love their baby. However, they may be listening to their own fears of "spoiling" the baby and not recognize that the crying is a signal that the baby wants and needs something. Not only does the baby need food, but also stimulation and human contact and holding and cuddling. These are important needs. Don't be afraid of spoiling babies—they love receiving our ministrations and we can love doing it without guilt.

The child whose needs are not met, especially needs for loving human contact, may become depressed and stop eating. Most serious of all, such a baby may stop crying—the child gives up. Then the parent feels there is no reason to spend much time with the child because the child is considered to be a "good" baby. Such children can actually stop growing as, in their depressed state, they do not take in enough calories for growth.

Some parents actually neglect their babies and parental neglect is a form of child abuse. *Psychosocial separation* is the term we give to the physical loss of the mother, but it may not lead to loss of mothering as maternal care can be given by the father or a surrogate mother. *Psychosocial deprivation* is the emotional loss of *any* warm, loving relationship.[50]

For whatever reason, neglectful mothers do not relate well to their baby. They do not bond to the child, have no real interest in the child, and do not care for the child. Interestingly enough, this can occur with one baby while other children are treated well. Doctors used to be fooled by this. They thought there could be no problems in parenting because other children in the family were thriving. Therefore, if such a baby failed to thrive doctors believed there must be a physical reason for the problem.

Failure of bonding with one baby is usually related to things going on in the parent or family—perhaps an illness or a life crisis which ties up all the emotional energy so the parent has none left to invest in the infant. In some cases, loving mothers or fathers may become depressed themselves or be physically or mentally ill and may not be able to offer the child the emotional nourishment or even the care all children need. It may also be related to there being something wrong with the baby like prematurity or autism. If you feel you truly have no interest in your baby or want to hurt the baby, get help! Tell your own doctor or the pediatrician at once. You probably need more nurturance yourself. Most doctors recognize this and can find help for you.

What about overstimulating? Can this occur? It really can. We have seen a baby's crib stuffed so full with toys and mobiles that the baby had no room to move. Sometimes a child's room is so filled with toys that the child has no room to play. Marilyn has actually seen a mother turn her tiny infant's head toward the television set to see "Sesame Street," even though the baby was too young to see clearly beyond a few inches. Other parents spend hours teaching their toddlers, who can barely grasp a crayon, how to print their names.

Generally, this kind of overstimulation occurs for good motivations. Parents truly want to foster their child's cognitive development. Sometimes the motivations are more selfish. Some parents—for their own reasons—want each child to be an infant prodigy. Statistically, prodigies don't come along very often. Besides, it's not healthy for parents to live only through their children.

Another kind of overstimulation parents fall into with young babies is *physical overstimulation.* Active games like bouncing, swinging, or moving babies rapidly are fun for most babies but only for a brief time. A frantic or disorganized baby needs slow, rhythmic motion, like rocking or holding with massage.

What, then, is optimal stimulation? Stimulation should be *responsive to the child's own signals, as in "baby-led nursing."* Parents should be able to recognize when their baby is ready or open for stimulation. A child whose eyes catch yours, perhaps while feeding, is generally ready for human contact. A child who has had enough turns the face or eyes away—"gaze aversion."

Any caring parent can learn from the baby how to be responsive. Such signals as turning away, crying, irritability, or anger indicate that the baby needs rest from stimulation. Usually parents learn their child's individual signals quite early. We hear many mothers use the expression "My child is overtired." This well describes a situation when the child spent the day in lots of exciting play. Such a child is physically tired, irritable, and emotionally drained although often the child's behavior is aggressive and provocative. Such a child needs nothing more than the *absence* of stimulation, as wise parents recognize.

Parents also have to recognize that a child who shows excessive withdrawal may need a very special type of stimulation. The very placid infant, the infant who sleeps most of the time, or the child who is truly withdrawn needs to be evaluated by a pediatrician.

Parents can also foster or inhibit their children's development and learning by not recognizing conflicts with the *parents' own needs.* In early toddlerhood, a child's exploratory learning may conflict with the parent's needs in several areas. The child must explore the world but that can cause broken dishes. When the child starts exploring the world, parents are fearful that: 1) Something will happen to that child without their eternal vigilance, and 2) Their role as parents is diminishing because they no longer have complete control of the child. These are understandable feelings, but they have to be dealt with.

From the time your baby is born, let yourself enjoy contact with the baby. Spend time face to face. Talk. Invent games. Sing songs. Play records. As the baby gets older start reading (first picture books, then read with the child, then read aloud to each other).[51]

In sum: Enjoy your baby! Let your baby enjoy you! It looks as though the mother's *responsivity* to the baby—which is different from stimulation—is the key.[52]

Play

One of the most important things a parent can do is recognize the importance of *play* and provide an age-appropriate milieu for optimal play. Play is vital to all mammals. Chimpanzees spend half their time playing and captive dolphins will play with objects tossed into their tank.

What is play? It is easier to list the characteristics of play than to define it. Play of mammals and children is similar to adult activity and is exuberant or boisterous as though the animal or child has excess energy. Play is often vigorous exercise with contact with partners. Play is pleasurable, has no extrinsic goals, is spontaneous and voluntary, and involves active engagement of the player.[53] Play thus differs from other pleasures or organized sports and differs from just lounging around or daydreaming, all of which have some but not all of the above characteristics. There is another characteristic, which is that play has a systematic relationship to non-play. Play is linked to learning, to creativity, and to development of social roles. Play in this context has been described as "behavior in the simulative mode," which is buffered from normal consequences as in the fighting play of young mammals. Some have stressed the antic quality of play.[54] Playfulness often seems to involve a high degree of concentration.

Piaget wrote about three stages of play.[55] *Sensorimotor play* (infancy through year two) consists of repeating and varying lots of motions as children learn control over their bodies and relate sensations to movement (hence the term, sensorimotor). From ages two to six, children engage in *symbolic or representational play*, which occurs when the child can encode experience into symbols and can remember events. The child will fill a pan with mud and describe it as baking a cake. The third stage of play, called *games with rules*, starts in the school years. Our language is perceptive, as play governed by rules or conventions is called a "game" rather than play. The child who plays games understands cooperation and competition as well as the abstraction of rules, all of which require a degree of cognitive and social maturity.

There are different kinds of play. "Rough and tumble" play is seen in animals as well as nursery school children. It is "actually a shorthand term for a number of action patterns that are performed at a high pitch of activity usually by a group."[56] In children it consists of running, jumping, falling over, chasing, wrestling, hitting at, laughing, and making faces. It usually occurs out of doors and breaks out spontaneously after a period of structure (i.e., during recess after a morning of schoolwork at desks). Rough and tumble play usually is engaged in by a group of same sex children and is more vigorous among boys than girls. It is found in every culture and, as the children mature, will evolve into culture specific games or activities with rules. "In most human cultures play with motion does not disappear with approaching maturity, although it does come increasingly under the influence of social constraints and conventions that specify how, when, where, and by whom and in what garb the more boisterous and active types of play can be indulged."[57]

There is some evidence that certain young mammals deprived of rough and tumble play do not develop normally. It can be inferred that this play fills an important developmental need for the human mammal as well.

Play with objects helps the child find out what things are and how they work. Children can use objects to express themselves and for social interaction with other children and adults. The child when confronted with an unfamiliar object goes through exploration, familiarization, and eventual understanding—all of which will help the child in dealing with the world.

The baby needs both the eye and then the hand working together to play with objects. The baby will develop "object permanence," which is the recognition that an object exists even when it is out of sight. The baby learns to imitate what actions *others* take with objects and even has delayed imitation (i.e., the baby can remember what another did with an object in the past and imitate it).

Other types of play include play with language (rhyming, word play, nonsense words), play with rules, and make-believe play (dramatic or thematic play). Pretend play doesn't start before age three and diminishes (or becomes daydreaming) before adolescence. Pretend play includes pretending roles, action stories, and pretense about objects and settings. The most common roles are family ones—generally stereotyped and assigned to the actual sex of the child. Other roles are fictional—from books or TV—like Hansel and Gretel or the Cookie Monster. Children engaged in pretend play construct action plans which they carry out without saying ahead of time what they will do. One of the most common plans in most cultures is averting threats. The children pretend there is a monster and defend themselves or let the monster get them. Other plans include taking a trip, sleeping, cooking, eating, and telephoning.

Pretense is very important to child development. Children seem to pretend as a prelude to developing abstract thought. Children with a high level of fantasy tend to be better at concentrating on tasks, have more self-control, and are divergent thinkers, which means they come up with new rather than stereo-typed responses to problems. This type of thinking is found in creative persons.

Play with rules starts with the first team of infant and adult—games like Peek-a-boo. Cooperative games with peers, like Ring-Around-a-Rosy, come next. Actually some "games" start quite early but are better called "routines." This social play between toddlers or between a toddler and a parent doesn't last very long and the rules change often. But these interactions *are* shared activity and turns are taken. Older children play games with rules to test the limits of their own skills and what others will tolerate.

Why is play so important? Play equals learning. An anthropologist said, "Play helps animals become better monkeys or wolves or whatever creature they are."[58] And play helps babies become human creatures. Species that need to learn a lot, like the higher primates and humans, play the most. Animal play is exaggerated action without any goals—like a lamb gamboling. Rarely do animals hurt each other even when they snort, bite, or claw at each other like bear cubs or kittens. Animals signal they want to play. We've all seen a dog "bow," i.e., drop down on its forelegs, which is the signal for play in that species. Human mammals, especially when young, must play. Play is vital to the learning which must take place for this human creature to survive in this complex world.

What does play "do" for the child? Play aids physical development and enhances cognitive and social development. Pretend play helps the child learn how to think metaphorically. Emotional development is fostered by play, which provides the child with an outlet for energy and helps the child decide what's real and what isn't. Social development starts with eye contact and continues through pretend play, which lets the child "try on" roles.

Play has another important function. It is the child's way of becoming encultured to his or her particular society. Play integrates new members of a culture into the group which stabilizes that culture. Play also helps modern cultures change by helping teach how to adapt. "What comes only with intense, eye-glazing study to the anthropologist comes easily to people born and reared in that society. But people who are born in a society have a tremendous advantage over the anthropologist. For them learning about their culture is, quite literally, child's play."[59]

Toys

Parents and children are bombarded with commercials and advertisements for toys, most of which seem to be overpriced, made out of plastic of question-able durability, or need four batteries to work.

Before you head for the store let us share our experiences. When Marilyn's daughter was about a year old, her very favorite game was sitting in a cardboard carton in which her father pulled her through the house. Her second favorite toy was a pot and cover. Anne's children loved to play with pots and other household objects. The moral of this story is that parents do not have to spend lots of money to provide play materials for their young children. Be creative with what you have around the house. At later ages, if the child wants a fairly expensive toy, "try before you buy," if possible. Notice what your child enjoys playing with at nursery school or with playmates. If your child has a sustained interest in the toy, it may be worth the investment. All too many toys are packaged to be appealing, but after purchase are unused.

By the way, you don't have to feel guilty if you don't spend hours playing with your children. Some playful interaction between parent and child is vital, especially in the early months. However, as the child gets older, the parent can step back a bit. Of course you provide the space, the play materials, and the encouragement for the child to play on his or her own. When the child seems bored or in need of you, by all means play and enjoy. But your role is parent, not constant playmate!

Effective Parenting

Parent and care givers *do* make a difference. One study looked at "competent" and "non-competent" six-year-olds. Competent children starting school can get and maintain the attention of adults and use adults as resources in socially acceptable ways; lead and follow peers, express both affection and anger to their peers and compete with them; express pride in their own actions or possessions, and act out an adult activity. Such a child also has language competency, age-appropriate intellectual competency, and "executive abilities"[60] meaning the ability to plan and complete an activity which has two or three steps.

Effective parents (as measured by their competent six-year-olds) had done three things differently in their children's early years:

1. They designed the child's world to allow safe exploration and access to people and things which encouraged and satisfied their child's curiosity.

2. They were available to the child, responded to the child, spent time with the child, and used language at or slightly above the baby's comprehension. This time was *not* continuous. Rather it was numerous, brief (twenty- to forty-second) interactions many times daily.

3. These parents always set limits, though they praised and loved a lot too.

Competent children had more social experience. They spent more time as infants looking at objects and people and were talked to much more. The non-competent child spent more hours in "empty time," for example, in a playpen scanning with their eyes or doing nothing.

Many have interpreted Burton White's stress on the importance of parents in early development to mean that the mother, and mother only, should be with the child constantly during the important first three years of life.[61] This has caused conflict in the minds of many mothers who work by choice or by necessity when their children are small. We agree that the first three years of life are very important. We also feel that parental needs are important. Our interpretation of White's data is that a child from birth to three (and later) needs the loving attention of *care givers* who understand the importance of their frequent interaction with the child, who can tolerate an environment designed for children, and who can set limits.

The mother of the brightest two-year-old girl we know went back to work when Melissa was a few days old. Melissa is cared for by her grandmother one day a week, a sitter in her home two days a week, and goes to a sitter's house two days a week. Her loving and attentive parents—*both* of them—also pay lots of attention to her on weekends and at night. Melissa has five loving adults to help her develop—what richness!

Creativity

Parents sometimes wonder how to encourage or help develop creativity in their child. The genius of a Picasso or Mozart is inborn and can be fostered, but not created, by the child's environment. However, creativity and self-expression are fun—all of us should make attempts to do something creative be it painting, singing, cooking, knitting, or whatever.

One suggestion is to encourage your child's experimentation with materials, like crayons, marking pens, paints, food dyes, clay, and even mud. Let the child "paint" on not only paper but on eggs, paper bags, etc. Windows and mirrors can be fun to paint on. We suggest you use only washable stuff and discourage drawing on your walls (though some parents, including Anne, allow and encourage wall drawing in the child's own room).

An artist suggests graduating to quality material. Good crayons, poster paints, and watercolors are not terribly costly. Use "recycled" paper like computer printouts. Don't forget artist's sketch pads for traveling.[62] Remember your child is painting, not making a painting. Praise and enjoy the efforts. Early drawings are a rich window into the child's view of the world. Remember to hang them up on the refrigerator and other sites. One cartoon said, "Today the Amana Gallery, tomorrow the Louvre!"

Creativity can also be fostered by the parents in another way—by encouraging the child's imagination. When you read to the child, make up stories by putting in your own variation, in a familiar story—for fun. Then ask the child to make up his or her own variations or entire stories. Encourage dress up, putting on shows, telling fantastic tall tales, and even playing with an imaginary playmate.

Sometimes parents ask about specific creative learning for their children such as music, art, or ballet lessons. At what age should these start? Should such lessons be part of school or extracurricular? Certainly, musical instrument lessons at school are a great way to introduce a child to music. These lessons are often group lessons, which foster a very important aspect of music—playing together. However, Marilyn feels if your child exhibits musical talents, or if music is important to you and you really want to encourage it in your family (and fantasize about a family string quartet!), private lessons are in order, usually not before school age except for special programs like Suzuki violin or Orff-Kodaly music classes, specially designed for the preschool child. Further, the better the instrument and the more skilled the teacher, the more likely the receptive child is to learning and playing. If you can afford it, usually dollars and quality correlate in this area. If money is a consideration, we suggest renting a piano or other instrument until you are sure of your child's interest.

Overly coercive attempts to rule the child's practice will almost certainly backfire but music is an art which does require practice. Only the very talented child will be able to play without practicing, and then only for a short time in the beginning.

We suggest that parents do the following about music lessons: be sure there is a level of interest on the part of the child or, alternatively, be willing to try lessons for six to twelve months and equally willing to stop them if your child either hates it or refuses to practice; work out a structured practice time each day, five days a week (everyone is entitled to a sabbath break); keep practice times short (ten to twenty minutes to start); ask the child's teacher if you should supervise or help the child (if you play, your reinforcement of the teacher's instructions can help); and as quickly as possible, have fun with the child and the music (sing along when the child plays, etc.). The most important thing you can do is love music yourself, play yourself, and be a musical role model *before* you start your child at music lessons.

The same principles of good teaching and equipment apply, of course, to art lessons, ballet lessons, etc. (They also apply to sports but we are talking about creativity rather than athletics just now.)

Learning to enjoy the creativity of others is also an important developmental task. Many parents want their child to grow up with an appreciation of culture. This won't happen by itself. Schools do have field trips to museums or concerts, but parents who really love the arts will want to expose their child to the theater, musical performances, or the visual arts more often than the school will. Marilyn believes in early exposure. She was taken to concerts and operas very early in life. She remembers seeing the Met's *Hansel and Gretel* when she was not quite four. It made an incredible impression on her. To this day when she hears the overture she can vividly visualize the stage. She remembers wondering how the chorus of angels walked up to heaven (an invisible staircase). The wonder of that performance will never leave her. Marilyn first took her children to theater, ballet, and concerts when they were between three and four. Obviously, parents have to pick the specific performances carefully. Many cities have special children's concerts or dance programs. A children's museum— whether it be the arts or science variety—is a good way to introduce a child to the world of displayed wonders.

Your own interest in the arts—either a lifelong interest as Marilyn had—or a newly awakened interest because you want your child to appreciate the arts more than you did as a child—will be sensed by the child. Enjoy together!

Educational TV can be a great way to introduce young children to the arts —in small, comfortable doses at home. There are also age-appropriate books in all areas of the arts.

Creativity includes much more than the arts. You can be creative in cooking—and teach your child this as well. Don't just make stuffed celery, but rather celery boats, perhaps with a carrot stick mast. The ultimate in creativity is finding new and successful and imaginative ways to get along with people. This is a sort of *creative empathy.* By teaching your children how to creatively put themselves in others' shoes, you encourage this sort of creativity—and provide the basis of a happy life for your child because of the child's enhanced interpersonal skills.

HOW YOUR BABY BECOMES A SOCIAL PERSON

The human infant is a social creature. As we said earlier, there is evidence that a newborn baby is preprogrammed toward the human face and will respond to the human face preferentially almost at the moment of birth. In turn, the adult *responds* to the baby's response. Even as early as thirty-six hours after birth the baby can come close to imitating exaggerated expressions (surprise, frown, and smile).[63] This ability is important for the survival of a mammal as helpless as a human baby. If the infant can get the adult care giver to pay attention to it, this ensures the infant's survival. Unlike other mammals who have a very short period of infancy, human mammals need care and nurturing for a long period of time. They are born very helpless, neither able to crawl to the breast nor to get the breast to come to them except by *social* means: crying and smiling. Babies can and do literally seduce an adult into loving and caring for them.

The first relationship is the mother-child one but other adults are readily seduced into loving and caring. Surprisingly soon, relationships with other babies, children, and peers become very important. The earliest interaction with other babies—say a group of crawlers in one room—consists of each baby crawling to the other and exploring the other as an object. A baby around one year of age begins to understand that another baby is a peer who can react to the initiation of social contact and can imitate it.

Friends

Parallel play is the term used for young children playing next to each other, often engaged in the same action, but not *with* each other. However, toddlers who are given frequent opportunity to see each other can develop "friendships" and spend a good deal of time interacting rather than playing alone. By the time a child is two, he or she seems to understand what a friend is: "A familiar peer from whom one expects particular responses and with whom one engages in a distinctive and enjoyable set of activities."[64]

As infants become toddlers, it is important that they have opportunities for play and interaction with other children. It used to be thought that play with other children was not important for a child before nursery school age, because few collaborative games were played. We now understand that "parallel play" leads to interactive play and that through both, children learn social, communicative, and survival skills.

With school, friendships start in earnest. Selman describes three stages of childhood development of social awareness. In Style 1 (between six and eight) the child thinks of friendship as a one way relationship. A friend pleases you but reciprocity is not yet important. Between nine and twelve, Stage 2, friendship is understood to go in two directions but reciprocity is based on specific incidents rather than on the friendship as a continuing social relationship. Selman calls this "fairweather cooperation." In Stage 3, which occurs in late childhood or early adolescence, children are able to perceive mutuality and intimacy as part of a continuing relationship.[65]

A study of "popular" children revealed that the children classmates enjoyed playing with were those who paid attention to other children, praised them, listened and acceded to their requests, and showed affection. Simply, the child who includes and accepts gets included and accepted.[66]

Children are attracted to those children similar to themselves. Friends are usually the same age, sex, size, level of intelligence, and physical maturity. In addition, they have similar interests, social values, and like to do the same things. Interestingly, race is not important to young children unless they learn that message from their parents. Children are overjoyed when they find another child who likes the same things they like, probably because it validates their own likes and dislikes. Often the members of the friendship pair are "complementary" to each other and each brings something to the friendship from which the other can learn. Thus an adventurous child and a quiet one may become friends.

Conflict with a friend, especially when the child is in Stage 2, is interpreted as the end of the friendship. A quarrel or some negative vibes—lead to the statement, "I'm not Johnny's friend any more." Of course, the next day they may be friends again. Children lose friends mostly as a result of moving, though some friendships end because the children change at different rates, especially at puberty.

Most children's friends are the same sex and age, as are the school groups (clubs, gangs, or informal cliques) they belong to. Cross-age friendships do exist and are healthy, especially in our society, which is very much into age segregation of its children. Adult intervention has led to successful tutoring programs in which older children help preschoolers or first-graders, for example. Cross-sex friendships also exist and are healthy.

Although siblings get to tolerate and even love each other as they get older, they rarely become friends as children. Rubin speculates that sibling rivalry, though always present, is not the reason.[67] Age segregation probably plays a greater role.

As children get older, the peer group of children they play with fills a most important need. However, we do not feel that children should be left out of doors unsupervised until they are around five when they are able to understand traffic and other dangers. We do feel that playing alone with other children (or under reasonably casual supervision, such as a mother glancing out from the window), is desirable at an earlier age if it can be safely arranged. Whenever possible, encourage other children to play near your house under your supervision or in your enclosed yard. Ideally, other parents will reciprocate.

What about parental guidance in developing social skills? How much of sharing and assertiveness is learned by the child from peer interaction without parental influence or interference? When and how is parental help needed in negotiating social interactions? Our feeling is that supervised play, which will become increasingly less supervised as the child gets older, gives the parent the opportunity for comforting children when they are hurt, and for making suggestions when things are getting tense about sharing. Preaching doesn't help but you *can* point out to children that sharing means they'll have their own turn. Sometimes when the children are getting fussy, parental interference can "break up the game" by providing juice or water or offering to read everybody a story.

Parents should make every effort to provide other children for their children to interact with. In many current neighborhoods and lifestyles, this can be difficult. In the past, child rearing was carried out in a more public arena. In a village children were likely to observe other mother-infant pairs. Young children then moved naturally into peer play on their own initiative as their motor and social skills developed. Today, children are often reared in a home or an apartment where they may be the only child of that age around. In addition, the environment outside that home may not be safe for children, especially because of the automobile but also because of other hazards such as crime. Children reared this way must move abruptly when they enter school or nursery school from a social environment composed mainly of one attending adult to an environment with many other children and no one adult focusing primarily on them. Such discontinuity in social structure may pose a problem for some children.

Parents can avoid this problem by making a real effort from the time their child is a year old to provide other children to play with. This can be done by inviting parents with other children over to your house, or inviting yourself to theirs. You can invite children for special social situations (birthday parties, etc.). You can arrange to meet mothers with children of the same age in public places such as playgrounds and parks. You can set up informal neighborhood play schools whereby one or two mothers (or housekeepers) in rotation take all the children in their home or yard for an hour or two.

Because many children are reared today in single homes without other children around, nursery school is more important than ever. Marilyn has even gone so far as to say even a mediocre nursery school is better than no nursery school. We both feel it is vital that opportunity for social interaction occurs before school starts. Play schools or nursery schools provide this, in addition to providing an environment for learning some of the basic early school skills. It doesn't matter whether you take the child to Sunday school one day a week, to play school twice a week, or to a learning nursery school five days a week. What is vital is some kind of social interaction in a setting with non-parental adults and other children.

The best way to gauge the "social" development of your child as well as the child's willingness and ability to give up dependency in age-appropriate ways is found in Table 36.

TABLE 36

MILESTONES OF INDEPENDENCE

When	Child Should
By 6 months	be left with baby-sitter while parents have evenings out.
By 2 years	be left home, while awake, with baby-sitter.
By 3 years	experience being left somewhere other than own home.
As soon as ready	be allowed to feed, dress, and wash self.
By 3–4 years	be allowed to play in yard by self.
By 5–6 years	be allowed to play in neighborhood by self.

Reprinted by permission and adapted from Schmitt, B. D., *Pediatrics* (1971) 48:433. In *The Whole Pediatrician Catalog*, Vol. 1, by Julia A. McMillan, Phillip I. Nieburg, and Frank A. Oski. Philadelphia: Saunders, 1977. Copyright American Academy of Pediatrics, 1971.

What about the child that is being reared in *really* childless environments? How do you deal with your children's social development when you live on a ranch—in the wilderness areas of Arizona, for example, where there are no other children within miles? This is where parental ingenuity is important. Usually there is a church with a Sunday school within driving distance. Contrive lots of trips to town at a time when you have arranged for interactive play. Take camping vacations to campsites where many children run around free as in primitive villages. Consider importing cousins to stay with you for the summer. Children raised in childless environments profit from camps and boarding school, sometimes at slightly younger than usually recommended ages.

What of children's friendships with adults? By all means such friendships and interrelationships should be encouraged because many children today are not fortunate enough to have grandparents in their home or community. "Adopted" grandparents can be very important. A special relationship with an older person in the neighborhood can be very fulfilling. Some teenagers without younger siblings "adopt" a sibling child and spend time with the child for their own pleasure, not just for baby-sitting.

Values

The parents' role in the development of values and an ideology—usually but not always a specific religion—is paramount. Every culture must "sensitize the representatives of the younger generation to the expectations that extend and enhance the operation of that culture."[68] As children learn which behavior is approved so they feel good, and which is disapproved so they feel bad, conscience develops—an internalization of parental and cultural expectations.

Parents don't teach values just by talking about them. Values develop over a long period of time during which the child first performs—and then understands—behaviors consistent with the culture.[69] High self-esteem—which presupposes parental love, respect for the child, a low level of permissiveness, and accountability—is vital to the development of self-discipline and ultimately the acquisition of caring values.

All children will have questions like, Where did I come from? Why am I here? What happens after life? These questions are often answered within the context of a religion. The way each of us conceptualizes the Deity is culturally determined, but all humans seem to need some concept of what life means. The tendency of humans to congregate and appeal to stronger individuals or a superhuman force to help them is universal.

Religion gives children a sense of belonging to a group wider than the nuclear or extended family. Organized religion (Sunday school, etc.) provides the young child with knowledge about the family's ideology, exposure to peers of the same group, and the sense of "congregating." We recommend children be exposed to a religion. We recognize that some parents do not belong to a church or synagogue or are non-believers. Often parents left their religion as they became adults and they value their newfound sense of freedom. They are concerned that their child will be overcoerced into an ideology they may have struggled to escape from. However, we feel all children can benefit from the sense of community that a religion brings and that all children have the right to "escape" on their own when they grow up.

Parents often ask us about the seeming hypocrisy of sending their children to Sunday school if the parents don't go to church. We recommend saying something like, "I went when I was a child to learn. As an adult I do not feel I need church but you may feel differently when you grow up," or "I didn't go to Sunday school as a child and I feel I missed something other children had."

DEVELOPMENT IN SCHOOL CHILDREN

When a child is in school, there may be troublesome moments for some parents. The child may question cherished beliefs. Conversations may touch upon areas of value conflict or sexual embarrassment. The wise parent learns to deal with such matters by dealing with his or her own feelings.

How can parents help during the school years? There is a good deal of negative talk about our schools: "Schools aren't doing their job," "Schools should go back to basics," "Children graduate from high school but don't even know how to read or write," "There are too many frills," "There are not enough frills—every child should have music and art, we should teach more languages." Some of these concerns are obviously contradictory. From our point of view, there *are* problems with the educational system. There *have* been numerous changes in school systems, teachers, and teaching philosophies in recent years. It is true that discipline may be a problem in some schools. We know that many children are not being optimally educated.

The ideologies are complex and contradictory. Some groups of parents feel very strongly that schools should be basic, disciplinarian, and authoritarian; others feel that a school should be a place that nurtures a child's development, as Rousseau suggested two centuries ago. The common ground is that *all* parents want their children educated well. Education must include cognitive knowledge, life skills, and social interactional skills which one needs to survive in our complex world. In addition, we add that schools should provide some of the aesthetics that one needs in order to escape from this complex world!

There is a practical as well as ideological conflict for parents. Should we leave the school alone to do it all? Should we play a role in our children's education? Should we push the child to do extra work if no homework is assigned from the school? Should we provide educational toys or outside lessons for the child who seems to be bored? Should we provide tutoring for the child who seems behind? All of these are valid questions and there are no easy answers.

We both feel that the most important thing parents can do is to view learning as fun. This may be a problem because some parents will not have perceived learning as fun in their own school days, and it is hard to impart something that you didn't experience or you don't truly believe. However, we think it possible for even those parents who hated school to recognize that school has changed, and to recognize the importance of the child's starting school with positive, not negative, feelings.

It has been said that pushing a child is bad; parents should not insist that their children get good grades; they should not foster a sense of competition. Generation after generation of immigrant children were sent to school *with* these parental demands and did quite well in terms of negotiating a space for themselves in American society. So we don't think "push" is always a dirty word —especially if it's done gently and cleverly. However, never compare your child unfavorably with a child—whether a sibling or a friend—who's getting better grades. That sort of push backfires.

From the very beginning parents can impart to their children that an important part of life is a sense of *self-pride in a job well done*. Indeed, most children in the stage of what Erikson calls "industry" (during the middle school years) are so anxious to learn and to do a good job that adults really have to work to prevent learning! The child's pride in his or her accomplishments starts at home. Not only do we suggest you display your children's early art work, but also hang up their first efforts to print their name, make a chart with a gold star for every book they read, and share your pleasure in their achievement, as well as praise, or even reward, the child for good grades. Shared pleasure is a *much* stronger motivation than praise, but children need both.

We believe in parents working closely with the school. Marilyn also believes quite strongly that parents who are able to do so should provide children with outside opportunities for learning. This does not mean forcing things on the child, but just making opportunities available. If parents have the financial resources to open doors for their children, they should do so. As you know, this is a complex world. Knowing *about* many things, knowing *how to do* many things, and knowing *how to appreciate* many things all can provide the child with resources needed to deal with a complex world.

So if you can afford it and it is available in your community, by all means provide outside sports, or dance or art lessons. If your child has talent in specific areas, foster that talent. If not, consider outside lessons and opportunities like a Chinese menu where you select from each column. Make available lots of different things so that your child may find something he or she likes.

Anne feels more casual about these matters. She feels outside activities are meant to be optional and she would leave it up to the child in most cases.

Let the children know what is available. Is it healthy to rush from school to ballet lessons, to art lessons, to the soccer game? Can you overprogram your child? Sure you can, but the answer to most questions in life based on a possible conflict of ideals is *balance*. Remember when we talked about overstimulation and understimulation of the infant and pointed out that optimal stimulation was the answer? With older children, optimal exposure to extracurricular activities is best. All children need time for themselves in order to play and to be with other children. Also, your children need time away from you, and your values, so that they can develop their own. But there still is time for pleasurable enrichment.

Some shy children need parental encouragement and help in finding comfortable activities. Some ambitious children enter into more activities than they can handle, and need your help in setting priorities.

What about the parents' interactions with the schools? What do principals and teachers wish parents would do? Several teachers and principals we talked to have said the following. First of all, avoid excess TV (more about that later). Second, read to and with your children from an early age. It is important to model reading (both oral and silent). This means that children *hear you read* to them and also *watch you read*. Let them read to you as soon as they can. Incorporate reading into all home activities. Read aloud recipes, directions, and signs. Teach your child to recognize stop signs by their shape and the color of the letters even before your child can read.

Children *do* model reading. When Marilyn's children were two and four, they were sitting together in a big chair looking at a picture book of songs. The younger one said, "Let's sing Clementine." They both tried to find the Clementine song by turning the pages to find the picture of the miner's daughter. The older one said, "I know! Let's look in the index!" which she proceeded to do. She found the index all right, but a wail followed: "I can't read!"

Third, communicate with school personnel. Assume that teachers and administrators are accessible, willing to listen, and act in the child's best interest (if they don't, there are other avenues, but start there). Talk with the school personnel about concerns, hopes, expectations, disappointments about the school. Fourth, let the teacher know about any changes that may affect the child (grandparents coming to live in the home, a new sibling, parents' separation, illness, moving, etc.). Fifth, support school policy—everything from arrival time and playground time to reasonable discipline. If you disagree with something, talk to the teacher or principal. Also be honest with the child: "I don't agree with that policy but it's important for you to get along in school by following the school's policies." Sixth, provide assistance when requested in activities in teaching, if you can. If you are not employed and have the time to do so, get involved and be a classroom helper. Be willing to go on field trips or other activities. If you are a busy working parent, offer to spend one hour sharing some special expertise you might have. Have you taken a trip to China? Offer to show your slides of Chinese children. Are you a stamp collector? Share some of your collection with the students. Seventh, understand and support school expectations for educational outcomes. This means things like structuring home environment for study. Does the child have a quiet place? Are books available? Is there a dictionary? When the teachers assign homework, Marilyn would encourage the children to complete it and expect the children to do it, but not do it for them. Anne would not get involved unless a definite problem emerged, or the child asked for involvement.

Finally, help make education the number-one priority in the child's life. Let your child know that this is his or her job, which should be done well, as you do yours well. There are two contracts your child has: one with the school, one with the home. Both are concerned with the child's development into a functioning, autonomous adult.

Anne's number-one priority is good character; second is emotional responsiveness and being an empathic, assertive human being. Education is her third priority, flowing naturally from the first two and from children's spontaneous love of learning.

Anne adds, you can convey your belief that education is one of your high priorities for your children's lives. You can convey without question your assumption that school is their job, which you assume they will do as well as they can, just as you do your job. Too much intrusion by parents on the child's relationship with the school can convey a lack of confidence that your child can manage that relationship—which could become a self-fulfilling prophecy.

What do teachers expect from children? An age-appropriate level of responsibility and independence which parents should both recognize and encourage. For example, a kindergartener should be able to spend three hours at school without needing mother, a nap, or constant individual attention. Fifth-graders should be able to anticipate the consequences of behavior and therefore should be able to complete assignments. Junior high students should get to school on time by themselves, turn in assignments without any outside help, and handle their own lunch arrangements and money. Teachers also expect children to have a socially acceptable moral and ethical code for behavior and conduct and to abide by those of the school or accept the consequences.

One teacher feels strongly that the measured decline in American schools has resulted from changes in cultural values which have been occurring since the sixties.[70] He feels that parenting has changed (more divorce, more employed mothers), television and video games pull children away from books and study, and hedonism has become a way of life. Children—and adults—prefer instant pleasure to postponed gratification. Parents, on the other hand, often blame schools and the teachers for not maintaining discipline in classrooms, not assigning homework, etc. We do not want to get caught in the middle. Both parents and teachers have to work at the education of America's youth.

Lots of learning takes place in children outside of school. They learn about becoming socialized from playing outdoors and indoors with other children. They learn athletic skills in school, in play, and in organized athletics like Little League. They learn how to care for a home by modeling after mother and father and doing chores. They learn mechanical skills by modeling and chores as well as from hobbies like building airplanes. They learn aesthetics from being encouraged to look at the world around them, by going to museums, and reading. They learn about nature by playing outdoors, having a pet, going hiking with the family. They learn a lot about our culture and its stereotypes from TV.

There's lots to learn. These are the learning years. Give your child a rich menu of learning experiences, not just TV.

Don't forget summer learning. Many schools offer summer enrichment courses as well as remedial ones. Parents can offer learning enrichment if schools don't. For example, if your school doesn't give enough writing assignments, you can help your children learn those skills by writing thank-you notes and letters to friends and relatives.

Day camps and sleepaway camps are good for athletics, crafts, and social learning. Most communities have special summer programs ranging from art to computers to Bible study. Libraries often have summer reading programs. Many children love sports lessons (like tennis or swimming) or cultural ones (ballet or drums) during the summer. Visits to grandparents' house (especially alone) can also be important learning experiences. Summer can be lonely and boring for children who don't have some structured activity.

ABNORMAL DEVELOPMENT

Parents want to assure themselves that their baby is developing normally. They dread the thought that the baby might be retarded or damaged in some way. Even when they suspect something is wrong, they often deny their thoughts.

Parental assessment of the development of their child has been found to be quite accurate.[71] Parents with developmentally disabled young children were able to estimate their child's level of function, which closely corresponded to the actual measurement of that child's function by a trained professional. Parents' descriptions of their children's behavior and development are usually correct, although the parents may have an inaccurate *interpretation* of the behavior. "He's spoiled" or "He's lazy" may be how they explain why a child doesn't do a particular task. The retarded is thought of as "He won't" rather than "He can't."

Parents' interpretations of what is going on with a developmentally disabled child also are colored by the process of denial. They often cannot face the fact there is something wrong with their baby so they pretend to themselves that all is well.[72] Sometimes one parent is more realistic than the other, which leads to conflict.

Most parents are not terribly familiar with the fine points of developmental milestones. But most parents, even young and inexperienced ones, know that a child around one year of age begins to walk and to talk. In our opinion, denial is a more important factor than ignorance, except in the case of the overly placid baby who may be considered "good" instead of retarded.

Alas, pediatricians can be deny-ers, too. It was shown many years ago that pediatricians tended to overestimate the IQ of the children of parents who were concerned about retardation in children or those brought to the doctor's office when the parents wondered if the child was slow in developing.[73]

Some pediatricians may not refer "slow" babies for diagnostic developmental assessment by a team specially trained in child development as early as they should. Besides denial, the feeling that nothing can be done may pervade. But we feel every child suspected of retardation, deafness, or an attention-deficit disorder deserves an assessment and diagnosis. All parents deserve to know what, if anything, is wrong and what they can expect in the future both for that child and future children. Besides, many special programs for early stimulation are available today which appear to help some children maximize their development if started in time.

Assessment of a child's development includes a thorough history, vision and hearing tests, physical and neurological examinations, and whatever diagnostic X-rays or laboratory tests are indicated. In addition a battery of psychometric tests is usually done. These include both tests that assess aptitude and those that assess achievement. General aptitude tests include measurement of intelligence (IQ tests). Specific aptitude tests involve vocabulary, language, memory, visual perception, attention span, and other such parameters. Standard achievement tests like the Iowa Tests of Basic Skills and the California Achievement Tests are given in school. There are also special diagnostic tests to measure reading and arithmetic.

Retardation is reasonably common—about 2 to 3 percent of the population has an IQ below 70, which is outside of the normal range of 70 to 130.[74] An IQ of between 50 and 70 is considered mild retardation and under 50 is severe. This means about 7 million people in the United States are retarded. Many of these cases are familial in that when retarded individuals were studied, over a quarter of their close relatives were retarded. However, many things can cause retardation in a child born into a normal family. A small percentage of those cases are preventable or modifiable if diagnosed and treated in time. For example, infants born with hypothyroidism (low amount of thyroid hormone) if untreated will become profoundly retarded; if treated early they can be normal in intelligence. Even when the basic condition cannot be treated, individualized schooling and social experiences can help achieve normality of social development and thus ability to use the intellectual capacity that is there.

"Red Flags"

These are certain developmental milestones that, if not met at the appropriate time, indicate an abnormal pattern of development. Table 37 shows these. If your child does not do these things at the age mentioned, tell your doctor and insist on an evaluation.

TABLE 37

**INDICATIONS FOR FURTHER EVALUATION
FOR DEVELOPMENTAL DELAY**

At 3 Months	Does not react to sudden noises
	Does not appear to listen to speaker's voice
	Does not try to find speaker's face with eyes
	Has not begun to vocalize sounds
	Has been left to lie in crib for hours without visual or auditory stimulation
	Does not raise the head when lying on stomach
At 6 Months	Does not turn to the speaking person
	Does not respond to being played with
	Is not visually alert
	Never laughs or smiles

**INDICATIONS FOR FURTHER EVALUATION
FOR DEVELOPMENTAL DELAY**

Is not babbling
Does not reach for or try to pick up toy
Is not learning to sit up
Does not appear to be gaining weight
Does not arch back when lying on stomach
    and raising head

At 1 Year   Has not been responding to Pat-a-cake,
                       Peek-a-boo, or other baby games
                   Is not imitating a variety of speech sounds
                   Is not saying two or three words such as bye-bye,
                       ma-ma, da-da
                   Is not pulling up to standing position

At 18 Months   Is not yet beginning to feed self with spoon
                   Does not imitate speech or vocalize in jargon
                   Is not moving about to explore
                   Does not give eye contact
                   Has not or does not spontaneously squat when picking
                       up objects

At 2 Years   Is not naming a few familiar objects and using a few
                       two- or three-word phrases
                   Is not noticing animals, cars, trucks, trains
                   Is not beginning to play symbolically with
                       housekeeping toys, little cars
                   Is not moving about vigorously, running, climbing,
                       exploring
                   Avoids eye contact
                   Does not seem to focus eyes on large picture
                   Engages in rocking or head banging for extensive
                       periods of time
                   Is not walking up stairs

At 3 Years   Does not seem aware of other children, of adults,
                       of the weather, traffic, etc.
                   Uses little or no speech
                   Does not engage in imitative play symbolic of adult
                       activities
                   Avoids looking at pictures or pointing to pictures
                       of familiar objects
                   Does not follow simple directions
                   Engages for long periods of time in repetitive
                       behaviors like flipping pages of a magazine, or
                       spinning a wheel on a little truck, head banging, etc.
                   Cannot ride tricycle if given plenty of opportunity
                       to do so

At 4 Years   Does not have at least partially understandable
                       speech with sentences
                   Uses echolalic speech or frequent, bizarre,
                       meaningless sounds
                   Does not focus visually on pictures

INDICATIONS FOR FURTHER EVALUATION
FOR DEVELOPMENTAL DELAY

Does not seem interested in listening to a simple
  story
Repeatedly tests all limits
Is so quiet and conforming that never
  tests or tries anything new
Has pronounced fears and phobias
Frequently engages in flapping of arms or
  flipping of hands to express excitement
Runs about from one thing to another every minute
  or so without getting fully involved in an activity
Is still untrained in toileting (occasional slips
  do occur at this age)
Does not draw some sort of representation of human
  beings (at least a head and a few features), if
  crayons or pencils have been available
Stays on the periphery of playroom, paying no
  attention to other children for some weeks, after
  most children have overcome shyness and have begun to
  play with or near other children
Avoids eye contact
Engages in head banging or rocking
Cannot tolerate change or frustration without
  frequent two-year-old type tantrums

Reprinted by permission and adapted from Young, Alice, and Schliecker, Isabel, *Daycare and Early Education*, New York: Human Sciences Press, May–June, 1977. McMillan, Julia A.; Stockman, James A. III, and Oski, Frank A. *The Whole Pediatrician Catalog.* Vol. 2. Philadelphia: Saunders, 1979.

Because language is so important to comprehensive learning and school performance, language delays are important to recognize. Table 38 shows condensed guidelines for expressive language development and guidelines for referral in the case of speech delay. If your child is not doing the things listed by the time indicated, tell your doctor. Language delays *can* be due to hearing problems, some of which are curable or modifiable. If a child is severely hearing impaired, early special training is needed to prevent irreversible problems with learning. A human without language cannot learn normally. Early treatment makes normal, or close to normal, intellectual development possible. Delay may make it very hard to ever catch up.

TABLE 38

Condensed Guidelines
of Expressive Language Development

Age	Vocabulary	Syntax	Intelligibility (unfamiliar listener)
12 mo.	2	"Ball"	25%
18 mo.	10	"Want Ball"	50%
24 mo.	200	"Ball, all gone"	70%
36 mo.	600	"Gimme my ball"	80%
48 mo.	1,200	"I gotta big ball for Christmas"	90%

Referral Guidelines
for "Speech" Delay

12 mo.	No differentiated babbling or vocal imitation
18 mo.	No use of single words
24 mo.	10 words or less
30 mo.	100 words or less; no evidence of 2-word combinations; unintelligible
36 mo.	200 words or less; no use of kernel sentences; clarity of 50% or less
48 mo.	600 words or less; no use of simple sentences; clarity of 80% or less

Matkin, Noel D., Ph.D., Professor, Audiology, University of Arizona, 1982.

School Problems

Sometimes a child appears to be developing normally until school starts. Early school reports then say "not ready" or "poor attention span" or "impulsive." Sometimes early reports are fine but when fourth grade rolls around demands increase and the child can't keep up. Sometimes the child seems fine but can't learn to read.

If a child is not doing well at school, hearing and vision *must* be checked. Psychometric and neuropsychological tests should also be considered. Achievement tests at school aren't enough; the child should be evaluated by special aptitude tests either by the school psychologist or a private educational psychologist. Clinical psychologists or psychiatrists are fine for emotional problems but may not be skilled in developmental testing.

There are some early warning signs of school failure.[75] Poor selective attention is one. We have to concentrate in order to learn. Children with an attention deficit are often described as hyperactive, fidgety, or impulsive. They are distractible, do not finish assigned tasks, often have emotional liability (with swings of mood) and instability. Some children with attention-deficit disorders, especially girls, may be quiet, not hyperactive, but do poorly at school. Language disability is another early sign. Language is more than speech; it encompasses coding and organizing ideas and concepts.

What is called temporal-sequential disorganization is another problem. This means the child doesn't understand concepts of time and serial order. This makes it difficult for the child to follow directions. Some children have visual processing weakness and cannot deal with spatial relationships, like size and position. Such a child may do poorly at copying shapes early on, and go on to letter reversals. Children with poor motor coordination, both large muscle (clumsy in athletics) and small muscle (poor finger control as in writing) may have school problems.

Children with any of these early warnings should be carefully and completely assessed by a battery of tests as well as a complete neurological examination. Early diagnosis can help the child. In the first place, diagnosis of the child's *strengths* as well as weaknesses can be made. Also special educational techniques can be used. The goal, if possible, is to keep the child at or above grade level, using compensatory methods rather than letting the child fall behind. When that happens, self-esteem is shattered which adds an emotional burden to the existing problem. It is also very important that parents know Johnny can't read yet because his brain has a problem which makes him perceive letters in reverse. If they don't know this they may berate him for being lazy or dumb. A study of fourth- and sixth-grade students showed that they are remarkably accurate about their dysfunctions in school performance.[76]

Parents, along with teachers, must pay attention to the development of the child through the important early years of school. Early diagnosis and intervention are paramount.

*   *   *

In conclusion, development of your child is a thrilling show to watch and participate in. Indeed, watching growth and development is heartwarming not only in our own children and grandchildren, but in all human beings. Development, growth, and changes take place (or should) throughout the life cycle. The adult who can say at every birthday "I learned and grew last year" is blessed.

The following beautiful poem written by Pamela Sims when she was twelve expresses our feeling about the wonderful, wondrous, and inevitable patterns of human life.[77]

Born
Cute, Little
Laughing, Crying, Loving
Small, Happy, Growing, Maturing
Living, Loving, Learning
Wrinkling, Graying
Aging

SUGGESTED READING AND RESOURCES

Brazelton, T. Berry. *Infants and Mothers: Differences in Development.* New York: Dell, 1983.

A neat book which traces the development and caretaker interaction of three different babies ("average," "quiet," and "active") through the first year of life. Interesting reading (and a few good hints) about parenting different ways with different babies.

Caney, Steven. *Kids' America.* New York: Workman Publishing, 1978.

Activities, projects, stories, recipes, etc., all uniquely American. A good way for a child to learn about this country and have fun at the same time.

Cunningham, Cliff, and Sloper, Patricia. *Helping Your Exceptional Baby: A Practical and Honest Approach to Raising a Mentally Handicapped Child.* New York: Pantheon, 1978.

A useful handbook for parents of retarded children. Has extensive checklists for assessing the child's development at several ages, as well as many useful suggestions for enhancing development also arranged by ages.

de Villiers, Peter A., and de Villiers, Jill G. *Early Language.* Cambridge, Mass.: Harvard University Press, 1979.

A very informative book about language acquisition which many parents will enjoy.

Garvey, Catherine. *Play.* Cambridge, Mass.: Harvard University Press, 1977.

A book which takes a serious and scientific look at what we all take for granted—child's play.

Gesell, Arnold. *The First Five Years of Life: The Preschool Years.* New York: Harper, 1940.

Gesell, Arnold; Ilg, Frances L.; and Ames, Louise Bates. *The Child from Five to Ten,* Revised ed. New York: Harper, 1977.

Gesell, Arnold; Ilg, Frances L.; and Ames, Louise Bates. *Youth: The Years from Ten to Sixteen.* New York: Harper, 1956.

Although the first two Gesell books are out of print, they're worth a trip to the library. Wonderful, informative reading.

Greenspan, Stanley I., and Greenspan, Nancy Thorndike. *First Feelings: Milestones in the Emotional Development of Your Baby and Child.* New York: Viking, 1985.

A look at development from the emotional point of view. Covers ways parents can best support infants of differing temperaments.

Hofer, Myron A. *The Roots of Human Behavior: An Introduction to the Psychobiology of Early Development.* San Francisco: Freeman, 1981.

A bridge between neurobiology and psychology. Not easy reading, but the book is an exciting synthesis which will be of interest to some.

Kaye, Kenneth. *The Mental and Social Life of Babies: How Parents Create Persons.* Chicago: University of Chicago, 1982.

For parents who want to delve deeper into the amazing way babies become persons. Technical but fascinating book.

Kohut, Heinz. *Self Psychology and the Humanities.* Charles B. Strozier, ed. New York: Norton, 1985.

The best available summary, for the thoughtful general reader, of Kohut's contributions to making psychoanalytic theory newly relevant to today's parents and citizens.

Lickona, Thomas. *Raising Good Children: Helping Your Child Through the Stages of Moral Development—from Birth Through the Teenage Years.* New York: Bantam, 1983.

An easily read book which serves as a handbook for parents. It delves deeply into the child's styles of moral development and provides suggestions for enhancing moral development at each stage.

McCoy, Elin. *The Incredible Year-Round PlayBook.* New York: Random House, 1979.

A delightful book with suggestions for children to play (and learn) in the sun, sand, water, wind, and snow. Great creative blueprints for sand sculpture: good ideas for cooling off with water when you don't have a swimming pool. An imaginative, clever book for parents to use when their own ideas about outdoor play have been used up.

Morris, Larry A. *Teach Me.* Tucson, Ariz.: Aztex Corporation, 1982.

A wonderful book that tells parents what they can expect from a baby at a given age and also outlines what they can do with the baby in terms of play, toys, language, etc., from birth to fourteen months.

Rubin, Zick. *Children's Friendships.* Cambridge, Mass.: Harvard University Press, 1980.

An in-depth look at what we know about friends and friendships in childhood.

Scharlatt, Elisabeth L., ed. *Kids: Day In and Day Out.* New York: Simon & Schuster, 1979.

An anthology of ideas, instruction, and innovations—all to do with children. Especially good sections on books for children and games children can play.

Schuster, Clara Shaw, and Ashburn, Shirley Smith. *The Process of Human Development: A Holistic Approach.* Boston: Little, Brown, 1980.

A wonderfully readable, incredibly comprehensive book looking at human development from conception to senility. A great resource.

Schwartzman, Helen B. *Transformations: the Anthropology of Children's Play.* New York: Plenum Press, 1978.

A highly technical and scholarly but fascinating treatise on children's play. Good information on cross-cultural aspects of play.

Sisson, Edith A. *Nature with Children of All Ages: Adventures for Exploring, Learning and Enjoying the World Around Us.* Englewood Cliffs, N.J.: Prentice-Hall, 1982.

A very informative book, though designed for teachers, camp counselors, etc., to show children how to learn about nature and our world. Parents will pick up many hints that can enhance the whole family's enjoyment of the outdoors.

Sparling, Joseph, and Lewis, Isabelle. *Learningames for the First Three Years: A Guide to Parent/Child Play.* New York: Walker, 1984.

An illustrated play book that gives specific ideas on what activities to do with children along with the "whys?"

Tomlinson-Keasey, Carol. *Child's Eye View: A New Way at Understanding the Development and Behavior of Children.* New York: St. Martin's, 1980.

An easy-to-read book explaining child development from birth through the pre-school years from the child's point of view. Useful suggestions for dealing with the behavior after you understand why the child is doing it.

Trelease, Jim. *The Read-Aloud Handbook.* Wheaton, Ill.: Tyndale, 1983.

A wonderful book for parents who want to encourage their children to read books by reading to them—from the time they are born! Useful suggestions about reading aloud plus a hundred-page bibliography of books suitable for reading aloud.

8
PARENTS' GROWTH AND DEVELOPMENT

Scope of Chapter

This chapter focuses on ways parents develop as persons in response to the parenting experience. After all, parenting is a mutual enterprise—as parents we have effects on our children and they have effects on us. How we develop as parents and as persons while we are parenting affects not only ourselves, but also our spouses, and our entire lives. Although parental development and "care of the care giver" are central points of this book and will emerge in each chapter, this chapter is one in which we concentrate on them. This chapter covers stages of parenting as well as parental growth in response to stages of children's growth. We emphasize what we as parents get out of parenting and how we can enhance our own development through parenting.

Introduction

Until three decades ago, the study of human development was mostly the study of child development. However, recently, researchers have begun to study how people develop and change throughout the life cycle.

The "mid-life crisis" is now a commonly used term, referring to the time when people come to a collision between what they'd expected from adult life and what they've actually gained from it. Books like *The Seasons of a Man's Life* and *Passages* called our attention to the fact that people continue to grow and to develop psychologically after reaching adult years.[1,2]

Almost all parents feel that their lives are affected by the parenting experience in important ways. Parents speak of two kinds of changes: the temporary changes that occur while child rearing is going on, and more permanent changes —the ways in which parents become different persons because of the experience of raising children.

Many parents are young adults—barely out of adolescence if not still in it —when child rearing begins. Some wait until they are well established as adults before having children. Most parents are more or less middle-aged by the time their children leave home, and some may even be elderly by then. It's almost certain to be at least two decades, maybe three or more, before the active parenting of any one child is over. With several children widely spaced, parenting could occupy a good part of one's adult years.

Parents thus spend a number of years growing along with their children. The fact that parents are growing, developing, and maturing right along with the children is often overlooked. Almost everybody hopes to continue to grow. Everybody wants to become wiser, more mature, and a better person. And most people indeed fulfill that hope, whether they have children or not. How much growth is due to the experience of child rearing as such? How much would have happened anyhow, just from accumulated life experience without parenting? How much do children help parents, or even perhaps hinder parents, as they attempt to further their own growth?

These are not easy questions to answer. Some of them are almost new questions—unique to the special circumstances of raising children in late twentieth-century America. Few studies have been done in which individual people were followed over time through their development as parents and adults compared with non-parents. Thus much of what we say in this chapter is based on our own observations and speculations.

PARENTAL DEVELOPMENT—THEN AND NOW

In most traditional societies, there was little distinction between maturing as an adult and maturing as a parent. Almost all adults became parents, except for those few who were unable to—and they were pitied or disparaged. Under the guidance of one's elders, one learned parenting tasks and roles as one learned other tasks and roles in society. With years and with practice, one became one of the elders. For both men and women, the more children one bore and reared, the more one was perceived as potent and capable and trustworthy. While individual abilities certainly carried much weight in deciding who of the elders would be most respected, having larger numbers of children and more experience rearing them did not hurt.

And in many traditional societies all adults treat children pretty similarly. Any adult would offer about the same indulged amusement at normal and "cute" young-child behavior, and the same guidance to get an out-of-control older child back in line, as the child's own parents would. Any adult can act in a "parental" role with a child. In fact, this is one of the things that we mean when we refer to a traditional society. When this uniformity of child-rearing begins to break down, we talk about a society losing its traditions, because child-rearing traditions are among the most important ones societies have.

For many parents today, long years of formal education are part of adult growth and development. Having children at a young age is often seen as a terrible sacrifice of opportunities for personal growth or career advancement, rather than as a mark of early maturity.

People today tend to be fiercely individualistic, take pride in independent thinking, and do not tolerate other adults telling their children what to do. Many today want to develop their own style of parenting, much as many write their own marriage contracts.

American society is usually described as being both "individualistic" and "youth-oriented." The mix is not necessarily an easy one. Adult individualism does not guarantee that the needs of youth will be well met. In return, individualism among the young does not guarantee that elders automatically receive respect—far from it! Today the things one learns as a parent do not automatically translate into higher prestige in the outside community.

STAGES OF PARENTING: GROWTH THROUGH PARENTING

Growth as parents compares in some ways with growth and development during childhood. Parents experience (1) overall growth as parents, which is interwoven with growth as persons, and (2) different stages *with each individual child* in response to the *child's* developmental stage.

Overall Growth of Parents as People

First, there is "fantasy parenting," which starts in childhood play, in which one enacts being a parent. Traditionally, girls have been encouraged to do this with dolls. Yet both boys and girls play-act parent-child relationships with dolls, teddy bears and pets, as well as dramatic games in which the child pretends to be the parent while the parent, a doll, or another real or imaginary child takes the role of child. Young children reenact a crude version of what they've experienced: spanking their dolls or bears, putting them to bed, giving them "medicine" if they are "sick," and the like.

Children often satisfy sexual curiosity and express their understanding of adult sex in "playing house" or "playing doctor." Children also play out the problematic or painful experiences in the child-parent relationship and in so doing learn to master those painful experiences, play the parent's side of the conflict, and begin to practice identifying and empathizing with the parent.

In middle childhood, children observe how other children and parents interact and begin to develop an ability to criticize their parents' parenting, just as they learn the rules of other games. In later childhood and in adolescence, youngsters may do a great deal of comparing parents, picking up one "ideal trait" from one family and another from another—Jane gets to stay out as late as she wants—Sally gets a bigger allowance than I do—Bill's parents come to the basketball game whenever he's playing—and so on. The overt language criticizes the actual parent. The latent message is that these children are beginning to think for themselves about what they think parenting should be like.

Usually, parenting, like most issues in life, is seen pretty idealistically by teenagers. They assemble in their minds the best traits of all parents, and may have unrealistic views of what real parents can realistically provide. Their typical view is that if parents handled things right, there wouldn't be much conflict.

Teenagers may or may not realize that criticizing parents is part of image-building for their own parenting. But behind every criticism lies an ideal image. Some of those ideals are likely to conflict with others. For example, an ideal of being "always patient and understanding" might conflict with "being a person in one's own right."

As we've said before, in traditional societies, the picture of parenting can be called "replicating": parenting one's own children is as good a copy as possible of how one was parented oneself. In our society today, many young adults develop an inner image of "restitutional parenting": doing for my children what I wish my parents had done for me; or maybe even "oppositional parenting": doing the exact opposite of what my parents did.

Parallel to the development of an idealized fantasy self as parent, future parents develop the picture of an idealized child—often an image of how they think they might have turned out had they been ideally raised! This is part of "restitutional parenting" and is a powerful motive for many people to have children. Often the idealized child in each parent's mind is of the same sex: "the boy I would have wanted to be"; "the girl I would have wanted to be." Since the actual child will be of a different sex from one of the parents, and different in many personal attributes from both parents as they wished to be, giving up some of this dream is part of coping with parenting.

Most people with reasonable self-esteem as individuals feel that their parents must have done at least a few things right. However, most people also have at least a few ideas about parenting that contrast with the way in which they were raised. The need for restitutional or oppositional parenting can be so strong that making peace with one's actual parents becomes an important part of coping with one's own parenthood—either before or during the parenting years.

Every actual pregnancy occurs after many years of fantasy parenting. During these years, as Ellen Galinsky points out, there is a lot of anticipatory thought about how it will be to be a parent.[3] During pregnancy, anticipation thoughts are "images" because the actual child isn't here yet. Most images are positive, romantic, even unrealistic: a preparation for "falling in love with the baby." Yet, just as with falling in love with an adult partner, reality doesn't always fit the idealized images.

Real-life parenting is different from images of parenting. No one can know fully what their parenting is going to be like. Many parents complain bitterly that "Nobody told me what it would be like." Others say just the opposite: "I expected to enjoy it, but I couldn't have imagined just how terrific it is." These statements are often related to whether the parent got a temperamentally easy baby or a difficult one.

When real-life parenting comes along, people find themselves doing things that are very different from their fantasy picture of parenting. People move from trying to be the "idealized parent" to resigning themselves to being "actual parents." Finally, they become "self-accepting parents," who have real pride in having done one's imperfect best. While this book will try to encourage self-acceptance as parents, as authors we would be idealizing and exaggerating what can be done with one book if we expected to give the reader "instant" self-acceptance. In fact, to a certain extent many parents don't achieve self-acceptance until they see their children safely launched. Today parents feel that they get "graded" by how well the children turn out. Parents are often too anxious or involved with the *outcome* to enjoy the *process* as much as they could.

Throughout this book we offer a constant message in behalf of parental self-acceptance. It's inevitable that you won't follow all well-meaning advice, including ours! But we repeat often: love yourself as the imperfect person and parent you are and it will be much easier to love your children as the human and imperfect people they are!

PARENTS' GROWTH IN RESPONSE TO CHILDREN'S STAGES OF GROWTH

Three of the major theorists of child development discussed in the last chapter highlights aspects of childhood that have specific impact on parents.

Piagetian Stages of Development

THE SENSORIMOTOR STAGE

Seeing the infant as a sensual person, who reacts and relates before using words, helps parents get in touch with their own non-verbal selves. Adults predominantly use words to communicate. Most parents find it immensely delightful and enriching to take up the task of communicating with a new person—all through body language. Parents and babies have rich body communication through touch and eye contact along with soothing and playful nonsense sounds. This experience feels wonderful to parents perhaps because a part of them "remembers." Parents don't consciously remember their own preverbal experience, but do feel their lives are enriched and rounded out by experiencing this part of life again through a baby's eyes. Becoming able to comfort a crying baby by touch and rocking because the baby can't explain things can give parents an enormously rewarding feeling of basic competence.

Later, as the baby begins to crawl, parents learn constant vigilance. Keeping another person constantly in mind, even when parents are in the middle of other tasks, can be burdensome. But it can also add to parental empathy, and their ability to concentrate on more than one thing at a time.

THE PREOPERATIONAL STAGE

As children's speech becomes more complex, they can put ideas together, and begin to have some understanding of symbols and causality. Constant "why?" questions can become tiring—but are also very stimulating. When children ask "why?" about something parents have long since come to take for granted, parents are stretched by having to come up with answers. Parents have a new opportunity to see aspects of the world they have forgotten to notice anymore. Simultaneously, children make parents feel younger, as parents share the children's fresh view of the world—and older, as parents recognize that they have the wisdom and life experience to answer many questions.

THE CONCRETE OPERATIONS STAGE

As schoolchildren begin to think logically and solve concrete problems, their mastery over the world increases enormously. As this is the level of thinking which adults most commonly use (when not engaged in solving abstract problems), parents can now have adult-type conversations with children. Since the children are in this stage for a relatively long time (on the average between ages seven to eleven), parents' responses are likely to vary over time. Initially, parents almost always experience pride at their child's new intellectual growth. Later, parents often feel a bit uneasy as the children increasingly use their cognitive skills to argue logically for something they want. Children learn the rules of the social game and can use the rules to argue a point against the parents—and sometimes win.

STAGE OF FORMAL OPERATIONS

When adolescents suddenly display their ability to think abstractly about complex questions, parents again experience a sense of amazement. Children now struggle with abstract problems, perhaps some that parents haven't solved themselves. Now parents realize that they have reared someone who may in some ways surpass them. This can give parents a sense of awe, and an expanded sense of self—"I brought this person into being who will take up the challenge of life and carry it forward, even after I am gone." This adds to the parents' sense of immortality in a way that is larger than just the hope of having children. Children now also challenge parents to think, to explain, to support their own values. They expand their parents' minds.

Freudian Stages of Development

Each of the classical stages of libidinal development evokes parental emotions and stirs the parents' conscious and unconscious memories of passing through that stage themselves. Parents generally have strong feelings remaining from each stage and with their children have a chance to reexperience these feelings. Parents can not only be enriched by recognizing how strong their feelings are, but can even have a new opportunity to master old feelings by reexperiencing them through a child's eyes.

ORAL STAGE

Feeding and comforting a hungry and frantic infant surely reminds parents of their own frantic unfulfilled feelings. Adults tend to be ashamed of such feelings, and often deny their intensity. In one sense, it is reassuring to experience them with a child. As parents empathize with the frantic fear of a tiny person who cannot know if its needs will be fulfilled, they can learn to empathize with their own frantic feelings.

ANAL STAGE

The toddler who is ready for toilet training is also big enough to have quite definite ideas about many things. Learning about others' property and developing some respect for a sense of order are quite as much a part of this stage as learning to use the potty, and for much the same reasons. Adults who have learned social graces—and perhaps have even learned to be less assertive than they should be—often experience amazement that such a little creature can be so tough and stubborn and insistent. Parents can be thrilled to share the child's rapidly expanding sense of self and personal will.

Toilet training itself is the child's first experience of a clash between personal wishes and society's demands. Since this is a constant theme throughout life, reexperiencing its beginning can be both fascinating and enriching. For those parents who had unpleasant experiences around these issues, there is a wonderful opportunity for restitutive parenting. Guiding children gently toward compromise between their own wishes and those of others—in ways that help the children feel "big" and proud as they slowly learn to get along—can be a self-esteem booster for parents as well as children.

PHALLIC STAGE

Children's discovery of specific genital masturbation as opposed to generalized good bodily feelings often stimulates strong feelings in parents. The fact that such a young child can act sexual, in an "adult" way, is amazing or disturbing, depending on one's point of view. Certainly in the past, parents as well as religious and medical authorities thought masturbation should be prohibited.

Some children did indeed stop; others learned to do it only when not observed. But now that masturbation is considered both healthy and normal, parents need not feel guilt or alarm, or feel any responsibility other than to teach the child the social conventions about when and where masturbation is acceptable. Since parents barely remember (if at all) their own early sexual feelings, this too is an opportunity to reexperience forgotten aspects of one's self.

OEDIPAL STAGE

Parents often have strong feelings about Oedipal children, especially boys (around age four). Children of both sexes regularly insist that they will grow up to marry the opposite sex parent. For the girl, this represents a beginning recognition that Daddy also could offer something special beyond just being a nurturant caretaker. Girls' flirtations with fathers are likely to seem quite adorable to both parents, since mothers usually feel confident of daughters' continued love. Boys, however, can disturb the whole family with the intensity of their wish to exclusively possess Mother. A mother would have to be pretty unresponsive not to be flattered and deeply gratified by this undiluted love. Fathers can be quite shaken. Just when the little guy is getting big enough to throw a ball, and Father anticipates doing some specifically symbolic "boy" things with him, the boy may quite openly express his wishes that Father would drop dead and quit intruding on his relationship with Mom. This occurs even in homes where parents are trying hard to drop gender stereotypes—because children at this preoperational stage think very stereotypically.

If there are tensions in the marriage—and what marriage doesn't have its tensions?—mothers can bask in the new love affair and genuinely turn away from fathers. Fathers who feel left out can emotionally turn away from both wife and son. Some fathers become angry and seize this opportunity to insist on rigid authoritarian discipline (thus confirming the boy's belief that he'd be happier without the old man around). Some older siblings may insist that the boy is "spoiled" and needs to "shape up." But parents who understand what is happening can enjoy it, and take pleasure in seeing a preview of the child's future adult sexuality, and future capacity for falling in love. In gently reaffirming the strength of their tie to each other, so the child understands its strength, couples can renew their own experience of their own bonding, adding resilience to the marriage.

It is generally believed that the impact of Oedipal feelings is intensified in small nuclear families, in which all parties concerned have fewer adults and children at home to relate to. It should be noted however that many of the Viennese families in which Freud first described Oedipal matters employed wet nurses and nannies, and had large households. So it shouldn't surprise us to find these feelings emerging with classical force even in large families and in those in which both parents share equally in employment and child care.

LATENCY STAGE

Freud believed that once children resolve the Oedipal conflict, by recognizing that parents aren't available sexual partners, they accept the idea that they must wait until they grow up to find partners of their own. At that point sexuality becomes latent until puberty. In the meantime, children turn their attachments and interest to peers and school. The age at which this happens is roughly the same as the age at which Piaget observed the emergence of concrete operational thinking, with attendant interest in classifying things and learning rules of the social and physical world. Parents are likely to have mixed emotions about their children's investment outside the home. For most, pride predominates when parents see their children master friendships and school tasks. Yet there's often some sense of loss. Mothers especially are likely to wonder aloud, "Where did my baby go so quickly?"

What parents can gain during this period is a comfortably gradual separation, as the children become progressively able to avoid hazards and take care of themselves. Parents gradually replace initial pride in themselves for being able to take care of all the children's major needs with an empathic pride in the children's increasing ability to care for themselves. Parents feel increasing trust in their children's common sense while the children correspondingly feel increasing pride in their competence.

Eriksonian Developmental Stages

On page 228 of the chapter on Children's Growth and Development, there is a table of Psychosocial Developmental Levels, as described by Erikson. Each of eight developmental stages of life, in this scheme, is associated with a "basic task" (like "basic trust" for the infant), a negative counterpart ("basic mistrust"), and basic virtues ("drive and hope").

Erikson's scheme has been widely accepted, because it is useful, descriptive, and organizes things in a way which is helpful to clinicians treating troubled people at various stages of life. Erikson felt failure to grow and progress in a given stage leads to the negative counterpart and mental illness.[4] Some adult developmental studies support the concept that mastery of one stage is necessary before mastery of the next can become easy, if indeed possible.

Parenthood, in Erikson's scheme, is covered under "generativity," a characteristic of the adult or "middlescent" years. But one can experience "generativity," or the wish to give life to the next generation, by charitable activities, or by being nurturant to young people at work, or in the family and neighborhood.

The last chapter pointed out a few examples of how parents can help children in their mastery of these basic stages, or notice if children are not mastering developmental tasks. The chapters on stages and ages will give much practical detail for parents on how to be helpful with children of different stages.

This chapter uses these stages as a way of organizing *what children and the parenting experience can do for parents' own growth* as each individual child develops and matures. As Kaye points out with regard to infancy, experienced as well as inexperienced mothers pass through many of the same stages with each new child.[5] Experience, and familiarity with the parent role, may lower anxiety, but each new child is a fresh experience. Relating to every new infant is a new developmental experience for every parent—a new opportunity for growth.

INFANCY

The infant's basic task is trust vs. mistrust and the basic virtues are drive and hope. The corresponding care giver tasks are providing *attachment and reliable care,* making it safe and fun to be a baby. Developmentally, parents achieve the following:

- A realization of having produced a new human being who never existed before—a source of mystical feelings for many parents, which can permanently expand their horizons.
- A feeling of "completeness," of "filling in a gap" in their experiences of themselves. "Did I used to be that little and cute myself?"
- Reaching biological adulthood, whatever one's achieved or recognized degree of social adulthood. Giving birth, by definition, is the act of an adult. Even in very young parents the act of birth often leads to a mature desire to care for the baby, even if it was unplanned or unwanted.
- Experiencing new sides of oneself. For parents raised in gender-stereotypic ways, this can have profound consequences. A woman raised to be "dependent and deferent" finds the baby's needs elicit development of responsibility. A man raised to be "tough" may find the baby elicits an experience of a tender and nurturant side of himself he didn't know he had. (Some young fathers, not yet secure in their success in the work world, may have this experience with later children rather than the first.)

TODDLERHOOD

The toddler's basic task is autonomy vs. shame and doubt and the basic virtues are self-control and willpower.

The corresponding care giver basic tasks are *watchfulness* and *admiration.* Shame and doubt become hazards for the child if the parents cannot see beyond the surface aggravations of willpower and self-control, to admire these tremendous developmental steps. Autonomy becomes a hazard if care givers don't exert watchfulness about safety hazards. Developmentally, parents can gain the following from this stage:

- By avoiding power struggles with the toddler, parents can learn negotiation skills which will be critical to effective parenting in later years—

particularly adolescence—when physical power over the child becomes limited.

- The ability to maintain self-esteem in the face of interpersonal conflict can be learned. Parents may have been able to avoid interpersonal conflict in other relationships, but toddlers are unlikely to leave them that option!
- Those parents who were taught as children to deny the intensity of their needs in general, and their needs for autonomy in particular, have a rich opportunity to reexperience the world from a toddler's viewpoint. Toddlers want what they want when they want it! Many parents have learned through experience that we do not always get what we want, and sometimes in the process have taught ourselves to pretend we didn't care. Seeing the world through a toddler's eye reminds us that we do care very much.

"PRESCHOOLHOOD"

The basic task is initiative vs. guilt and the basic virtue is direction and purpose.

The corresponding care giver tasks are *stimulation* and *continued admiration and watchfulness*. Guilt impairs initiative for the child if the expanding activities the child initiates are seen as "bad." Yet from the adult's perspective, these activities can cause messes, or dangers, and extra work. Developmentally, parents gain from the increasing challenge to their own initiatives.

- Parents can get back in touch with their own playfulness when they provide play experience for their children. Few adults use finger paints who don't have a preschooler. Most of us have forgotten how much fun finger paints can be!
- Parents, constantly challenged, can learn to be good sports and develop senses of humor and balance.

Anne remembers that at about age four she learned to write her name and a few other words. Proudly she wrote her name in large letters on the living room wall. Surprisingly to her, her parents did not applaud this—they even attempted to induce a little guilt. Wanting to continue showing off her writing prowess, the next time she was more careful. She took a pin and scratched her little sister's name on the dining room table, thinking the sister would be blamed, and forgetting the minor detail that everyone knew the one-year-old sister couldn't write. To her parents' credit, instead of rage, they collapsed in laughter at Anne's mixture of maturity in writing and immaturity in solving the problem of where to write. They went out and got her a very dramatically large tablet of newsprint paper. The scratch marks on the table were shown off to all the family friends, with appropriate laughter but also with a clear message that in the future Anne would use paper.

SCHOOLHOOD

The basic task is industry vs. inferiority and the basic virtues are method and competence.

The corresponding care giver tasks are *admiration, and when needed, respectful, unobtrusive help.* Industry, as applied to the school tasks and home chores of the school years, is a natural extension of the initiative and curiosity of the preschool period. *Completing* organized tasks, small or larger ones, is what makes industry out of it. Developmentally, parents can gain:

- A special and very important kind of patience, as they learn to separate and balance their needs from those of the children and from the children's needs in the outside world. Parents *can't* do their children's homework for them if the children are to accomplish their tasks of these years. Parents *can* help their children in setting structure, helping them learn such methods and competencies as breaking large tasks down into small doable components.
- Parents learn how to let their children go, trusting their competence while unobtrusively assuring themselves that they are letting go at the right time in the right way. Parents even have to learn when to stop saying, "Be careful!" inasmuch as they must begin to trust their children to be careful *themselves.*
- Parents learn new ways of intimate communication with their children. They are no longer communicating through touch and baby talk but rather through meaningful two-way verbal interchange.

ADOLESCENCE

The basic task is identity vs. role confusion and the basic virtues are devotion and fidelity.

The reciprocal care giver tasks are *respect, admiration, and patience with the sometimes confusing behavior of rapidly shifting roles* which adolescents assume as they try out their various versions of their identity.

Developmentally, what do parents gain?

- Some parents gain a great deal of pleasure just by sharing adolescence with their youngsters. It's fun to watch the children wear some of your clothes, and start to take part in the kinds of parties and amusements that adults enjoy. Parents can relive the fun parts and hope to make up for some of the painful parts of their own adolescence.
- However much parents worry about potential problematic sexual behavior of their adolescents, there's a fundamental sense of pride in seeing that one's children have the capacity to reproduce.
- Parents can gain negotiation skills—sometimes greater than they thought themselves capable of.

YOUNG ADULTHOOD

The basic task is intimacy vs. isolation and the basic virtues are affiliation and love.

This phase is a poignant one for most parents. Their children are at the same stage of their lives at which they became parents. Yet, paradoxically, just when parents have a new potential source of identification with them, it is the time in the children's lives when parents' corresponding tasks are *separation and relinquishment of control.*

What parents usually gain in their own development include:

- Independence from the children.
- Pride in the children's independence or at least mastery of anxiety about how the children's lives go on from here.
- Learning to give up control, which can be liberating. In some families, control is the only possible parenting role, and though some adolescents will submit, very few young adults will.
- If there are grandchildren, learning to give support and advice when needed, without overdoing it or underdoing it.

MIDDLESCENCE

The basic task is generativity vs. stagnation and the basic virtues are production and care.

Parents can gain the following from these years:

- Quiet pride if all is going well with their children.
- Pride in their ability to still be helpful if there are problems.
- Novelty of experience, as adult children bring experiences that were never expected.
- Freedom from the tight "bonding" aspects of generativity as it's experienced in earlier years. As parents grow older, they often detach a bit from their own children and can begin to care about all or other children. They can satisfy their grandparenting needs in part by being nurturant to other young children, if their own don't provide grandchildren, or are distant. Foster parenting is one possibility.
- The fact that older parents continue to have important roles in the lives of their adult and middle-aged children is quite overlooked in our society. Sometimes a very tender rapprochement is a valuable part of this stage of life. As children become adult and middle-aged, they quite often become more understanding and forgiving of parental foibles and mistakes. Mark Twain, in a famous saying, commented on how foolish his father looked to him when Twain was a youngster and young man, and how with each decade the old man became wiser and wiser. While no doubt the old man was continuing to accumulate wisdom, the point of the story was that the son was accumulating appreciation and empathy. As parents and children grow older together, quite often children

forgive parental mistakes (having recognized some of their own), and admire parental virtues (having taken them for granted before). As their responsibilities for "production and care" increase, they quite often come to understand more what their parents' difficulties were in mastering that stage when they were younger. At this age, they often want to "make peace with their parents" if they have not done so before.

OLDER ADULTHOOD

The basic task is ego-integrity vs. despair and the basic virtues are renunciation and wisdom.

A few parents will live to be parents of children who are older adults themselves. An amusing story is told of a seventy-year-old man who was hospitalized for a short illness. As the social worker began making plans about which nursing home to send him to, he insisted that his mother would come to pick him up. The psychiatry professor on rounds used this as an example for the medical students of how older people often regress into childish fantasies—until the ninety-two-year-old mother and her ninety-four-year-old sister arrived to pick the patient up and take him home!

The parental tasks in most cases will involve:

- learning to accept old age with probable illnesses and infirmities
- learning to handle dependency on children
- cherishing the good memories and accepting the bad ones
- maintaining an ability to keep friendships and make new ones so as not to be totally emotionally dependent on children

PARENTING—EFFECTS ON MARRIAGES

Shared Project—Shared Joys

There is no doubt that having children together is a shared project. Compared with other hobbies or interests which couples might share, parenting is richer, more complicated, more ever-changing. Marriages are usually built on some combination of "what we have in common" and "what's different and intriguing between us." Parenting can maximize both.

Sharing the joys of parenting brings parents closer together. Almost no outsider cares as much about the little joys—whose eyes and hair and nose the baby has, the first tooth, the first word. Sharing the caring can bring parents together in a specially intimate way.

Mastery of Stress

There is also no doubt that parenting is stressful. Parents worry about whether the baby is all right; they worry about illnesses and safety, and about an older child's behavior. They worry about their child's vocational choices and choice of mate. Sometimes it seems as though the worries never cease.

Probably not enough has been said about the positive side of mastering parental stresses together. Many parents recognize that having children and raising them helps put other worries into proportion. Some things they used to worry about—like the perfection of home decor or precisely where they stand in some adult pecking order—just don't matter so much. This can be liberating.

Dilution of Intimacy

There is no doubt that caring for children takes time. Often this time comes from time parents would otherwise have spent alone with each other. This can be experienced as diluting marital intimacy—having to share both home and heart with the children. While this is often spoken of as a negative, here too the positive sides have sometimes been neglected.

An enduring question in marriages is what happens when the honeymoon is over? Either the marriage is transformed into a more solid realistic daily life together, or there is a sense that the honeymoon is ended and a concern about what is left. The ever-changing experience of having children together can provide a continued infusion of the unexpected. If this is approached with zest and adventure, the marriage grows.

Especially for Women—Identity Gained and Lost

Everyone wants and needs to feel "I'm somebody." Being a baby's mother really can add to that feeling. There is nothing like having a small child to make one feel important and needed. Some women say this feeling of being the needed mother of a helpless baby is the *best* "I'm somebody" feeling. Nothing else in their lives before or afterward reached this peak.

At the same time, many women today complain, "I want to be somebody in my own right—not just my husband's wife or my child's mother."

Both feelings are valid. In the fifties when there was great emphasis on "togetherness," the concept implied gaining one's identity from family life. In the sixties and seventies, feminism gave strong support to women's needs for an individual identity apart from the identity gained from family roles. In the eighties, women's identity needs continue to be recognized. There is a growing recognition of pressure on women from multiple roles. Individual and family identity are *both* important.

Today's society is oriented around education and prestigious careers. In the past, when most men worked at farming, laboring, or factory jobs, a man's identity included being a good father who supported and helped guide the family. Jobs didn't necessarily give men the same sense of importance as family roles. In fact, the job was considered important *because* it supported a man's role within the family and home so that one could say "A man's home is his castle."

Some social theorists have made more of role divisions than probably existed in practice. Talcott Parsons, for example, felt that men were naturally the "instrumental" or task-oriented leaders in home life, and women the "emotional" leaders.[6] Yet many people experienced their fathers as intensely emotionally involved with family life and their mothers as very much involved in instrumental, task-oriented issues.

The point is that almost all parents experience the state of parenthood as an important part of their identities. And few parents, male or female, experience parenting as the only thing important about them as people. In fact, being a parent affects identities in other roles—which brings us to the next section.

PARENTING AND THE "FAMILY LIFE CYCLE"

Family theorist Jay Haley has been quoted as saying that the relationship with in-laws is the major characteristic which distinguishes humans from all other forms of life.[7] Other animals may have enduring ties between a mating couple, or between parents and offspring, usually mother and child. Only for us do mating and child rearing both create new nuclear families and forge lasting links between two extended ones.

Family theorists have been interested in drawing parallels between the development of an individual's life cycle, and that of a family. A nuclear family does have a beginning, a youth, maturity, and finally an end. Just as children are born, grow, age, and die, nuclear families form, raise children, mature, and are ended by death. By contrast, an extended family can go on forever, even though new members are born into it and old members die. Many people, with enough diligence, can trace their roots back many centuries. In having children, and caring about nieces and nephews, people can anticipate sending the branches forward into an indefinite future.

The word "family" refers to very complex systems of relationships. There are multiple generations, and multiple branches of extended families. Unlike business firms, from which one can be fired or quit, or friendships, which can be changed, relatives are relatives for life. Even if people choose to "cut off ties" with certain relatives, what is left is *cut* ties, not no ties. As McGoldrick and Carter point out, people often act as though they can choose membership and responsibility in a family system, when in fact there is no choice.[8] Children cannot choose whether to be born, and only recently could adults choose whether or when to have children. Even the freedom to choose whom to marry is a rather recent option, and the decision to marry is much less freely made than people believe at the time they marry.

Further, an increase in the freedom of individuals to choose whom to marry and when to have children decreases the freedom of their *parents* to decide when to have children-in-law and when to have grandchildren. In-laws are added to families without one's choice. We have no choice about gaining or losing nieces, nephews, cousins, and other family members, let alone siblings, and the future spouses and children of all these people. Yet all of these people will influence our lives, and we theirs. One can choose to end a marriage but one cannot end the relationship of "ex-spouse." Ex-in-laws continue to be important in many people's lives, either because of direct mutual ties between the adults or because the adults are forever linked in concern for the children.

The most obvious effect of parenting on families is that the birth or adoption of the first child creates a new nuclear family. Though society increasingly accepts couples who choose not to have children, in everyday speech they are tellingly called a "couple" rather than a "family." And the birth of a first child creates a recognized unit, even in cultures which emphasize the extended family.

The nuclear family grows and develops as it passes through time. McGoldrick and Carter have provided a table of what they regard as normal stages, analogous to Erikson's stages for individuals (see Table 39). Their observations are that tensions can arise at any of the transitions between stages.

TABLE 39

Family Life Cycle Stage	Emotional Process of Transition: Key Principles	Second-Order Changes in Family Status Required to Proceed Developmentally
1. Between families: the unattached young adult	Accepting parent-offspring separation	a. Differentiation of self in relation to family of origin b. Development of intimate peer relationships c. Establishment of self in work
2. The joining of families through marriage: the newly married couple	Commitment to new system	a. Formation of marital system b. Realignment of relationships with extended families and friends to include spouse

Family Life Cycle Stage	Emotional Process of Transition: Key Principles	Second-Order Changes in Family Status Required to Proceed Developmentally
3. The family with young children	Accepting new generation of members into the system	a. Adjusting marital system to make space for child(ren.) b. Taking on parenting roles c. Realignment of relationships with extended family to include parenting and grandparenting roles
4. The family with adolescents	Increasing flexibility of family boundaries to include children's independence	a. Shifting of parent-child relationships to permit adolescents to move in and out of system b. Refocus on mid-life marital and career issues c. Beginning shift toward concerns for older generation
5. Launching children and moving on	Accepting a multitude of exits from and entries into the family system	a. Renegotiation of marital system as a dyad b. Development of adult to adult relationships between grown children and their parents c. Realignment of relationships to include in-laws and grandchildren d. Dealing with disabilities and death of parents (grandparents)
6. The family in later life	Accepting the shifting of generational roles	a. Maintaining own and/or couple functioning and interests in face of physiological decline; exploration of new familial and social role options b. Support for a more central role for middle generation c. Making room in the system for the wisdom and experience of the elderly; supporting the older generation without overfunctioning for them

Family Life Cycle Stage	Emotional Process of Transition: Key Principles	Second-Order Changes in Family Status Required to Proceed Developmentally
		d. Dealing with loss of spouse, siblings, and other peers, and preparation for own death. Life review and integration

Reprinted by permission from McGoldrick, Monica, and Carter, Elizabeth A., The Family Life Cycle. In chap. 7 of *Normal Family Processes*, edited by Froma Walsh. New York: Guilford Press, 1982.

The Transition to Independent Young Adulthood, or the "Between Families" Stage

To the individual issues of the Eriksonian stages, the family-development viewpoint adds the importance of resolving and renegotiating relationships with the family of origin. Renegotiation has elements of both separation (as emphasized by individual personality theorists) and reunion. This means an individual has to separate from the family sufficiently to become his or her own person *and* has to reunite in order to maintain adult-type kinship ties. Getting "stuck" at this stage can impair moving on to form one's own family, or conversely can mean an unduly complete separation. Having children before completing this transition can mean raising them either as a part of a new extended family of origin, or conversely raising them without being free to turn to grandparents for needed help.

Transition to Marriage

Forming a marriage involves not only commitment to intimacy between two people but a realignment of old relationships with family and friends to include the spouse, and a realignment of the couple relationship to include the extended family. Sometimes when couples live together without or before marriage, it is precisely because they want to emphasize the relationship with each other, and not embroil the rest of their families.

Transition to Parenthood

A stage which is particularly relevant to this book is the third stage, which is the family with young children. This shift involves moving up a generation to become care givers to the younger generation. *Moving up a generation* is the telling phrase here. Thinking of oneself as a member of the "older generation" is a big shift for all of us, and probably much harder in a youth-oriented society which highly values the individualistic freedom of the unattached young adult, and doesn't automatically give the new parent generation enough added respect to compensate for the added responsibility. Mastering this shift involves developing *pride* in parenting, and enjoyment of responsibility. In most marriages, this requires appropriate sharing of responsibility.

Sometimes in today's family only the husband "grows up." He is the responsible authority; the wife is more like a child or dependent young adult. In fact, in the classical Christian marriage ceremony, the father gives the bride to the husband, whom she promises to obey. In other instances only the wife "grows up." The husband may work and earn money as he has since childhood, but responsible child rearing is left up to the wife. He perhaps resents the transformation of his carefree young wife into a responsible mother, and experiences loss rather than growth. The wife experiences him as one more demanding child. Sometimes neither "grows up." Either there is a dangerously chaotic child-rearing situation, or some member of the third generation (often the grandmother) makes decisions, gives directions, and takes responsibility for the children.

We have been delighted and gratified to see the pattern in our own homes —that of shared child rearing—become more common. Today father and mother take childbirth preparation classes together, are together during the labor and birth, may share rooming-in accommodations or even decide to experience a home birth together—and both participate fully in the child's early care. Thus, they move up a generation *together* and help each other through the transition.

Transition to Parenthood of Adolescents

In the wider family system, this transition does not just involve parents' dealing with an individual adolescent's growing and shifting independence. Adolescence involves realignment of many other family roles. Extended family members tend to scrutinize and criticize parents' parental behavior in a way they haven't since infancy, because infancy and adolescence are the two times in the child's life cycle when parenting is most controversial and everybody has opinions about what's "right."

Just when the adolescents are developmentally ready for more independence, parental fear of being criticized for their youngsters' behavior can make it difficult for the parents to let go. Any misbehavior or maladventure of the adolescent can be very public (car accidents, sexual misadventures, drug-related problems, etc.). The wider family and society want to know how the adolescents are turning out: Graduating? Getting into the desired colleges? Socially successful?

In the traditional family, when childbearing begins in the twenties or thirties, the adolescence of children coincides with parental mid-life marital and career concerns, as well as with grandparental retirement and aging. Parents, in the so-called "sandwich" generation, may look forward to a coming freedom from daily child care while anticipating possible care of their own parents. One's adult siblings become important in a new way as parents wonder whether those siblings will share any responsibilities for the older generation. If the grandparents are living, the very contrast of the youth and vigor of the adolescent children points out the vulnerability of the grandparents. If they are not still living, parents may begin to wonder how long they themselves will live.

Transition to Parenting Adult Children

When adult children become independent, parents face the task of maintaining a sense of family with them and trying to develop adult-to-adult relationships with them. The family expands to include the new people their adult children bring into it: their partners, their children, and to some extent the extended families of their partners. Some families start having family reunions around this time. Large extended families may provide enough weddings and funerals that special reunions are not needed. Even quarrelsome families may pick up old quarrels with new zest, fighting being one way to stay involved!

If you remain married to your original partners—and fully half of us do, despite increased divorce rates—you face a family at home which is constricting although your child's family may be expanding. Becoming just a couple again is more often than not enriching, but fantasies of a second honeymoon may or may not materialize in the ways expected. Traveling together, shopping together, just choosing your own TV channels without competition from the kids can be richly rewarding. Maintaining a sense of adventure and novelty is a great asset.

Those who have lost partners through death or divorce have the same challenges of learning to live alone or creating a new family. With the children gone, you may have more time and energy to look for new partners. Alternatively, you may organize your life around work, friendships, and enjoying time alone.

Family Transitions to Old Age

Those who retire from work face a major identity crisis, especially if their work has meant a good deal to them. Being a member of a family and community takes on new importance. The extended family is likely to consist of descendants rather than elders, and nieces and nephews become important family contacts.

PARENTING—DEVELOPMENT AS WORKERS AND CITIZENS

Parenting and Work

In our country, most women who are not housewives work in settings where it is difficult to bring children along. In many countries (such as China), it is normal to have a child care center on the job, where a mother can breast-feed a baby at lunch and on coffee breaks.[9]

There's an old saying, "When you're pregnant you suddenly notice pregnant women everywhere." The number of other pregnancies hasn't increased, but your awareness of them has. In many jobs, the way you approach the job changes after you contemplate parenthood. One is more likely to think of matters such as the feasibility of on-the-job child care, or protection from toxic reproductive hazards. In manufacturing, or sales, or human services jobs, the bulk of the customers are usually parents—and you are more likely to understand their needs and preferences when you have experienced parenthood. Thus the parenting experience could actually make you more valuable on your job.

There was an old idea that married men with children made the best employees. They were thought to be more responsible and mature on the job, not just because their families depended on them, but because fatherhood in itself was maturing. Anne can remember, as recently as 1969, a work situation in which a promotion was announced, justified specifically on the grounds that "Now that Joe is becoming a father, he is ready to be a supervisor." Actually, Joe's supervisory skills had been evident for some time, but his new status as a father was thought in the work setting to be logically related to a promotion.

Today selecting someone of either sex for a promotion at work solely on the grounds of their personal parenting experience could be grounds for a discrimination lawsuit. Yet the old idea probably did contain some truth. Most parents do find that they learn something from bearing and rearing their children that carries over into the work situation.

Parenting and Civic Life

While one certainly does not need to be a parent to recognize the importance to *everyone* of providing adequate schooling and health care for children, one's priorities and attitudes toward these matters can be influenced in either direction by actual experience. Liberals, for example, believe in taxing themselves for a variety of human services which aid the health and welfare of families, but may not spend much time and money supporting action in that direction. Having children, and belonging to a PTA, can be the stimulus required to expend time and energy collecting campaign funds and votes for a school bond issue. A very few people change their political and civic values as a result of parenting experience—their own, or that of someone close to them. For example, some people who have always assumed that most families on public assistance are to blame for their plight may become more sympathetic when bad luck forces them or a family member to rely on aid.

Parenting and Family and Friendship Roles

Parenting can both bring us closer to some people and isolate us from others. In the novel *The Women's Room,*[10] Marilyn French very powerfully portrays the ways in which a group of suburban housewives were drawn to each other by sharing their concerns about the development of their children and their marriages. Yet these women felt isolated from the outside world. In the vast majority of families in which both parents are employed, women devote more off-the-job time to child care and other family responsibilities than men do, and may have less time than desired to spend with extended family and friends. On the other hand, the fact of having less time to spend with friends can be a reason for being more selective, making firm decisions about whom to spend time with rather than drifting into friendships as a matter of convenience.

Just as with marriages, parenting tends to strengthen good family relationships, and further strain tense ones. Mother-daughter and sister-sister ties have traditionally been strengthened by the shared experience of mothering. However, when you have different ways of parenting from your mothers and sisters, their criticism can be both more painful and more freely given than that of outsiders. In-law relationships can be even more strongly polarized. Grandparents normally care deeply about how well their grandchildren are raised. Sometimes they interfere little with a young couple's lifestyle before children come along, but for either good reasons or bad, cannot keep silent when children are at stake. As with other aspects of parenting, mastering these relationships can be either a source of personal growth or an added stress.

Some of you will have the bittersweet experience of seeing your father take a greater interest in your children than he seemed to take in you as a child. Many men missed out on fathering, because they divorced and lost touch, were too busy with work, or did their fathering as young and immature men at a time when our culture didn't encourage active fathering. As more mature men, they realize what they missed.

Some grandfathers may be able to take a genuine interest in a grandchild, but are not up to handling, or even acknowledging, old guilt about having neglected their own child. Recognize that children can have a valuable relationship with grandparents and parents who don't get along, just as they can have valuable individual relationships with parents who don't get along with each other.

HOW TO ENHANCE PARENTAL DEVELOPMENT

We assume that you want to grow during parenthood. We are convinced that parents have developmental needs just as children do. We are further convinced that being in touch with yourself so that you know what those needs are is an important first step. As McBride says, ". . . parenthood is a role you *grow into* by understanding your own behavior and by learning how to handle your own needs."[11]

Brazelton feels that preparing for parenthood forces self-evaluation.[12] The anxiety of pregnancy—will I be a good parent?—helps unwire the old connections to one's own parents and frees up the couple for new connections. He sees the pediatrician as playing a crucial role in the mother's development. For example, if she feels dependency on the pediatrician, this can free the mother for healthier acceptance of her child's dependency. As she works through her anxieties and fear about child rearing, her growth helps her sense of self-confidence.

One can also look at parenthood as a series of developmental tasks of adult life[13] in which the parent changes as well as the child. The ability to grow with the child into the next stage is a major parental task, but parents may reexperience an earlier developmental stage of their own which can interfere with or facilitate this growth.

We have come to the conclusion that there are three elements of the relationship between parents that promote individual and couple growth and development. They all begin with "C." First you have to *care*. This means care about each other and the children. Second you have to *communicate*. This doesn't just mean asking your spouse to pass the salt. It means open communication that is based on getting in touch with your own feelings and having the courage to state your feelings. The third element can be *counseling*. If you ever feel "stuck" as a person or as a partner, try counseling. It can help though the choice of the right counselor is important. Indeed a major part of parental development is *relationship* development. The couple that learns how to make decisions together is well on the way to caring communications. One psychologist lists five guidelines to cooperative couple decision-making. You start by asking for what you want. You listen to the other person. You agree to avoid power plays. You agree not to rescue, i.e., save the other person from disappointment. You seek creative solutions.[14]

One couple Marilyn knows always asked for what each wanted on a scale of one to ten. If she wanted to go to the movies and he wanted to stay home, they would find out how intensely each felt. If she *really* wanted to see the Ingmar

Bergman movie at a score of eight, and he wanted to stay home only at a four level, they went to the movies.

One question parents ask us frequently has to do with fighting in front of the children. We think observing conflict between parents is not only inevitable but desirable in that it helps teach children about how humans interact with each other. However, repeated replays of old arguments which are unresolved are hurtful to you and to the children. Marilyn remembers unsettled conflicts in her marriage. She now knows she should have "fought" harder to settle the issues—with counseling if necessary—and then forgotten about them.

A SPECIAL WORD ABOUT FATHERS

Although the father is known to be crucially important to the development of the child, the biological basis of the father-child bond is poorly understood and even denied. What binds the father to his children results from complex biosocial and cultural processes. Fathers, like mothers, respond to the appeal of "babyness" but fathers, like mothers, are dependent on socialization and induction into the role of parent if they are to enjoy this responsibility and perform it adequately. This socialization, which in the past many fathers did not have, is critical to the father-child bond.

Rituals and rites of most cultures indicate preference for a male child. It's been thought that a father—especially a new father—identifies more easily with a son whom he sees as carrying on not only his genes but his personality.[15]

What binds the father to his children results from complex biosocial and cultural processes. This means that fathers are dependent on "proper socialization and positive induction" into the role of parent if they are to perform this responsibility adequately. This sets up the possibility that the father-child bond may not be as dependable as the mother-child bond.

The father tends to be rather ill-prepared for the role. Few boys baby-sit, for example. Courses in child development are apt to be taught in home economics, which boys often don't take. However, in today's world where men attend childbirth preparation courses, this seems to be changing. We haven't heard a mother say that her husband refuses to change diapers for a long time. Also today's father has more leisure so that he can spend more time with the baby. Thus today the American father is more than a breadwinner.

And today a million children are being raised by their fathers alone. Also a small but growing minority of men elect to be full-time house-husbands and, as such, are the primary nurturers in the family.[16]

The world expects mothers to be naturally nurturant or to become so when the baby is born. The father is less thought of as a nurturant figure. However, especially today, many men develop into "active" fatherhood and become nurturant fathers, which is healthy for their children's development and also stabilizing for their marriage.[17]

Many men became freer to consider themselves primary nurturers with the rise of feminism. They turn toward active parenthood for the same reasons some women turn away: a loosening of rigid sex roles. Sometimes a man, who prior to fatherhood acted stereotypically macho, finds that the new baby brings out his nurturant side. Thus parenthood can give men a chance to develop into a new and fulfilling role.

One writer looked at the nature and functions of the father role. The father, of course, provides half the genetic makeup of the child. He is a primary support person for the mother during her pregnancy. After birth the father can continue to support the mother, can serve as mother surrogate, have a primary fathering and socialization role, and serve as a role model to sons.[18]

Just as the father is important to the development of the child, the role of fathering is crucial to the psychological adult development of the father. Appleton points out that as fathers grow and change, their daughters relate to three phases of their father's life.[19] The daughter who is a little girl knows one father; as an adolescent, she knows another; and as a woman, still a third. At the time of a father's mid-life crisis, the adolescent daughter may very much need him. When the daughter is ready to separate, the stable father has developed to a stage in his life when he can help "push her out."

*   *   *

In summary, parents grow and develop as do children. Both the wondrous joys and the enormous tasks of parenting are determined, in part, by the fact that all the characters in the play are changing. Your baby changes—and you change. What an absorbing drama to watch and experience!

SUGGESTED READINGS AND RESOURCES

Benedek, Therese. "Parenthood During the Life Cycle." In Anthony, E. James, and Benedek, Therese, eds. *Parenthood: Its Psychology and Psychopathology*. Boston: Little, Brown, 1970.

A psychoanalytic look at parenting. One chapter is devoted to parenthood during the life cycle including grandparenting.

Birren, James E.; Kinney, Dennis K.; Schaie, K. Warner; and Woodruff, Diana S. *Developmental Psychology: A Lifespan Approach*. Boston: Houghton Mifflin, 1981.

A well-organized, readable textbook of developmental psychology that some parents will find useful.

Bloomfield, Harold, with Felder, Leonard. *Making Peace with One's Parents*. New York: Random House, 1985.

A useful book.

Galinsky, Ellen. *Between Generations: The Stages of Parenthood*. New York: Berkley, 1981.

A useful section entitled "The Departure Stage" may be of help to parents with adult children.

Helfer, Ray E. *Childhood Comes First: A Crash Course in Childhood for Adults.* Denver, Colo.: Kemper National Center, 1978.

A book about "remedial" development for adults whose childhoods were less than optimal in nurturance.

Lenz, Elinor. *Once My Child, Now My Friend.* New York: Warner Books, 1983.

A thoughtful analysis of your parental role when the children are adults. Good suggestions on how to phase out the parent and phase in the friend.

Lidz, Theodore. *The Person: His or Her Development Throughout the Life Cycle.* New York: Basic Books, 1976.

Psychoanalytic in orientation, this thoughtful book traces human beings through the life cycle. Well written and readable.

Littwin, Susan. *The Postponed Generation: Why America's Grown-up Kids Are Growing Up Later.* New York: Morrow, 1986.

A look at adult development today: how the baby-boomers are faring.

Offer, Daniel and Sabshin, Melvin, eds. *Normality and the Life Cycle: A Critical Integration.* New York: Basic Books, 1984.

Theoretical but very readable. A new classic.

Schuster, Clara Shaw, and Ashburn, Shirley Smith. *The Process of Human Development: A Holistic Approach.* Boston: Little, Brown, 1980.

One of the best overviews of human development we've read. Well organized and written. A good way for parents to learn more than parenting books have space for.

Part Four

PARENTING AT DIFFERENT AGES AND STAGES

Introduction

This section of the book covers parenting of children from the newborn to the kindergartener.

We talk about ages and stages for a reason. A stage roughly corresponds to an age, but not exactly. Children may reach certain developmental *stages* at different *ages*.

Each of the nine chapters has a similar format. First the *Scope of Chapter* specifically and clearly indicates the age we are dealing with. Next comes a short *Introduction* highlighting what makes this particular age and stage different from the others.

The first main section of each chapter deals with *Key Information*, when that information is pertinent to that age/stage, in the following format:

   I. Key Information
     A. Biophysical Information
       1. size and shape
       2. body function
       3. motor skills
     B. Language/Cognitive Skills
Cognitive is the adjective form of *cognition,* which the dictionary defines as

the act or process of knowing. Therefore, cognitive describes the process whereby knowledge about one's world is obtained and used through perception, reasoning, and symbols. Cognitive skills are learning and problem-solving skills, and they appear long before the school years and include much more than reading and arithmetic.

    C. Social Skills

Social skills include all of the interactive skills with other people ranging from the primary care givers to the community.

    D. Emotions/Feelings

    E. Developmental Warning Signals

These are developmental landmarks which, if not attained, are predictive of a delay in development. There are a few critical developmental mileposts which a normal child will always reach by a specific time. For example, if you see that your baby does not raise the head when lying on the stomach by age three months, you have noticed a critical developmental delay. It is vital to find out the cause of the developmental delay, which means telling your baby's doctor about this delay right away. Often a comprehensive developmental workup, which can only be done in a university hospital or clinic, is needed.

The entire *Key Information* section of each age/stage chapter presents specific facts about the typical child of that age ranging from how much such a child weighs to what specific developmental achievements can be expected. We must emphasize, as we said before in the chapter on child development, that *every child is different and each child develops at his or her own pace.* Nonetheless, we wanted to make each age/stage chapter as helpful as possible to those parents who want to find out all they can about a child of this age. Thus, we present *Key Information* about age two as though there *is* a prototypic two-year-old. The information we give you is about such a mythical child.

In order to present Key Information we use *averages* and *normal ranges.* Generally the range used means 90 percent of all children at a given age will fall between the two measurements listed. Thus the average girl baby weighs 7.4 pounds at birth. The range is 6.2 to 8.6, which means 90 percent of all girl babies fall within those weights at birth. If your baby falls within the normal range, your baby is "normal" for that measurement. If your baby is outside of the normal range this usually means you should consult your baby's doctor to find out why.

Marilyn remembers a well-known professor of pediatrics of the previous generation warning his students *not* to tell parents too much about child development because they would "overcompare" and get nervous if their baby didn't do a specific thing at a specific time. Anne also was surprised at hearing this kind of advice from her pediatric professors. Most pediatricians today, and certainly both of us, feel quite strongly that knowledge is never harmful. Ignorance is harmful, as is misinterpretation of knowledge, but not knowledge. Therefore, we give you as much information in each age/stage chapter as we have room for in the format we designed. We try to make it easy for you to learn what you want to know about your child. We depend on you to interpret the data correctly, which means you must never lose sight of the fact that we are writing about a mythical prototype while you are dealing with your own unique child.

The next sections of each chapter list *Care Giver Tasks, Health Care,* and *Safety* for each age/stage (where that section is meaningful for a particular age or stage):

    II. Care Giver Tasks
        A. Basic Care
            1. feeding/nutrition
            2. cleaning/grooming
            3. sleep/activity
            4. exercise
            5. stress management
            6. emotional "nutrition"
            7. care of the care giver
        B. Socialization Tasks
            1. play/stimulation
            2. fostering cognitive growth
            3. discipline/guidance/values
    III. Child Care or School
    IV. Health Care
            1. medical care
            2. dental care
            3. environmental health
    V. Safety

In these age/stage chapters we generally refer to the primary care giver as the mother ("she") for simplicity. However, except in the case of very specific instances such as breast-feeding, which only females do, all other tasks can be done by any care giver, including the father. Thus when we say "You should burp the baby halfway through the feeding"—"You" can refer to Father as well as Mother.

You will note that these chapters vary in length. Sometimes there are more things to say about a particular age than about others. The section also has a good deal of cross-referencing. Because of the overlap in children's development and needs, certain big issues are placed in a specific chapter and cross-referenced. For example, we cover nursery school in the chapter on the three-year-old because it seems most appropriate there. But we tell parents reading the chapter on two-year-olds where to look for information about such schools in the next chapter.

Despite cross-referencing of the big, easily identifiable issues, there is a good deal of repetition in these chapters. We have deliberately done this so that a parent can read a specific chapter and be reasonably confident that we have covered the major points on that age/stage.

One final suggestion: It's probably a good idea to read "around" the age/ stage you need. If you are starting to read this book because you have a three-year-old, read the chapters on Two and Four as well. Thus, you will see where Three was coming from and where Three is going.

9

GETTING STARTED: THE FIRST FEW DAYS

Scope of Chapter

This chapter deals with the first few days of life after birth. During this time you'll get started on the basics—feeding, diapering, adjusting to the baby's sleep rhythms.

Introduction

The first week or two with a new baby is a *momentous* time. Your first concerns will usually be quickly answered: Is the baby ok? Am I ok? After that, you'll be concerned about two potentially conflicting themes: the baby's need for care and your need for rest and recuperation. Both needs can be balanced if you give first priority to them and let everything else take second place. During the first few days, you will get to know your baby as the new little person who just entered your family.

KEY INFORMATION

Biophysical Information

SIZE AND SHAPE

The average weight at birth is 7½ pounds. Baby boys are a little heavier on the average, ranging between 6.3 and 9.1 pounds while girls range between 6.2 and 8.6 pounds. Black babies tend to be slightly smaller on the average than white ones.

Babies lose about 6 to 10 percent of body weight within the first few days of life. This is because they are born with extra body water which sustains the baby until nutrition is well established. Birth weight normally is regained within about a week, although it may take a bit longer in breast-fed babies.

The average length is just under 20 inches (19.9). Males range between 18.9 and 21 inches; females between 18.8 and 20.4 inches.

The neck is short and head is large, relative to the rest of the body. The average head circumference is 13.8 inches, ranging between 12.8 and 14.8.

The skull is relatively soft, and has two "soft spots" or "fontanelles." The front ("anterior") fontanelle, on the top of head near the front, is bigger, about 1-1/2 inches long and 1 inch wide; the back one is smaller, about fingertip size. These soft spots are present because the skull bones are not fully joined together before birth, making it possible for the baby's head to adjust to the mother's pelvis during birth.

The vertebral column is very flexible, also an advantage during pregnancy and birth, and it will not firm up until the baby is ready to begin upright posture. This extra flexibility has a sensual advantage for parents as it adds to the softness and cuddliness when you hold your baby in your arms.

The chest is more rounded than in adults, with an average circumference of 13.7 inches.

The abdomen is very rounded compared with older children and adults. The baby has no waist at all! This is because the infant chest and abdominal organs, such as lungs and liver, are large relative to the size of the chest. It will take some years of growth before the chest becomes large enough for the liver to move up to its adult position tucked under the lower ribs.

The skin is normally covered at birth with a white, lanolin-like, greasy or "cheesy" substance (technically named vernix caseosa). This serves as a protective coating for the skin before birth when it is constantly moist. There may be downy, fuzzy hair called lanugo over the back and cheeks. The skin itself may be reddened and/or scaly after the vernix caseosa is wiped off and the skin is often wrinkled from the constant prenatal moisture. Until the oil glands of the skin start functioning, the skin may look dry and peeling. The baby may have blisters on the upper lip, or marks on the wrist or thumb caused by prenatal sucking.

There may be either no hair or dark, thick "birth hair" covering much of the body, which will soon fall out. The head hair at birth, or that which grows in early infancy, may or may not be the same color hair that the child will have as an adult. Some babies of dark-skinned parents have lighter-colored skin at birth than they will have later. Most babies have lighter eye color at birth than they will later develop.

BODY FUNCTION

REFLEXES

The sucking, swallowing, and gag reflexes are all present at birth. The baby also has a "rooting reflex," which is related to sucking. When the cheek is stroked, by finger or nipple, the baby will turn its head and mouth to that side. (That's why trying to *push* the baby's head toward the nipple is counter-productive as the push activates the rooting reflex and makes the baby try to turn its head *toward* the push instead of away from it.) The "gastrocolic reflex" is also present from birth: food entering the stomach makes the gut contract and tend to expel stool.

Other reflexes present at birth include the startle or Moro reflex (when startled by loud noises or a sudden change in position which simulates falling, the baby stiffens, thrusts the limbs out, and cries); the stepping reflex (if a baby is held in a standing position, the legs extend and partially support the body); and the grasping reflex (the baby will make a fist when palms are stroked). At birth, the grasping reflex is so strong the baby can support its own weight by the strength of its grasp. Later this reflex is weakened, and not until toddlerhood can children once again suspend themselves from their hands like little monkeys.

Babies also have many adult reflexes. They can sneeze, cough, yawn, hiccup, and stretch as well as cry (but maybe without tears for the first few weeks, since tear glands are often not fully developed at birth). Babies can withdraw an arm or leg from painful stimuli. Also a baby who is placed face down on a firm surface can rotate the head into a position permitting breathing.

SENSORY FUNCTIONS

Your baby can make eye contact with you right after birth (if you were not sedated during labor and/or the baby was not given eye drops first)—a big thrill for most parents. Newborns can focus their eyes on objects about eight inches from their eyes. They can fixate their vision on, and visually follow, a close object. Even at birth, babies prefer the human face to other stimuli. Babies will stare at light and windows and prefer to look at patterns and shapes rather than solid colors.

As soon as the amniotic fluid has drained out of the ears a baby can hear. Babies can turn their heads to a sound and respond to loud noises with startle reflex. They prefer human heart sounds and high pitched vocal sounds (and correspondingly, most adults "instinctively" use a higher pitched tone of voice in talking to babies).

Taste and smell are also well developed. Newborns prefer sweet to plain water and can distinguish the odor of their own mother's milk from other mothers' milk by a few days of age.

Touch is also well developed. Newborns love physical contact—especially being held. Some babies are soothed by being wrapped firmly in receiving blankets during the first days of life (simulating the firm pressures previously experienced inside the womb). This is called swaddling and can be a useful technique for calming some fretful babies.

SPECIAL CHANGES IN ADJUSTING TO LIFE OUTSIDE THE WOMB

For the baby, life after separation from the mother's body is very much a continuation of life as it was before—and, at the same time, an enormous change. There are some momentous changes in physiology, and some issues of recuperation from the birth process itself.

Breathing and Circulation

For many months before birth, the baby made breathing movements, but obviously there was no air in the lungs. The first breath that is drawn in expands the lungs as they take in air for the first time, which has become the legal definition of a live birth. As the lungs expand, blood is drawn into their arteries. For the first time the lungs return large quantities of oxygen-rich blood to the heart. The two openings (ductus arteriosus and foramen ovale) that formerly bypassed the lungs in favor of placental circulation are closed by the higher blood pressure in the lungs and pulmonary blood vessels. As the placenta stops pulsing oxygen-rich blood through the umbilical vein, the baby's source of oxygen changes forever.

These remarkable changes in circulation and breathing happen rapidly and silently. The first cry is the dramatic moment but the first breath has already occurred or there would be no first cry!

In many babies, the new circulation takes a little while to get fully regulated. Their hands and feet may be a little cool, bluish, or mottled for a day or two. This is the body's way of making sure that vital organs get enough oxygen, and is a normal variation if everything else is all right.

Regulating Temperature

Before birth, the baby did not need or get practice in keeping just warm enough, since the mother's body maintained temperature for both. Newborn babies have difficulty keeping their temperature regulated for a period of time immediately after birth, probably partly because of lack of practice. But temperature instability is also related to the fact that body temperature is affected by many other circulatory and metabolic processes which change rapidly during the first few hours and days. Small or thin babies have difficulty for a longer period of time because of the absence of an insulating layer of fat. Premature babies have special difficulty because of both thinness and immaturity, which is why incubators are used.

Feeding and Elimination

Before birth babies make sucking movements and even suck their thumbs, swallow amniotic fluid, urinate, and have some activity of bowel muscles. Actual fecal elimination is uncommon before birth, except in cases of fetal distress, because the bowel contents are slight (they consist mostly of early cells of the digestive tract itself, which are sloughed off as the tract matures). Most babies will pass a first stool and will urinate for the first time within hours after birth— some almost immediately—but a few normal babies may not pass urine for up to six hours, or stool for up to forty-eight hours.

The first urine looks like all urine—after all, the baby has been passing it for some time. But the first stools are distinctly unusual, and may look alarming to parents who don't know what to expect. They are black or greenish black, very sticky, and stain clothing. They are called "meconium stools" and give way to more mature baby stools of a brown or yellow color as the first colostrum and/ or milk winds its way down the digestive tract, over the first few days. Colostrum has a laxative effect which assists this process, as does frequent feeding.

The baby has been swallowing amniotic fluid during pregnancy, but has had no experience digesting a complex fluid like milk. Although breast milk does not mature from colostrum to "mature milk" for several weeks, most formula-fed babies tolerate an imitation of mature human milk as soon as they are given it, and can digest and absorb it, though not as completely as breast milk.

Regulation of Activity

The baby's sleep rhythms may be initially disrupted by labor and birth. Before birth, babies adjust their activity to such environmental stimuli as the mother's activity and position, and they startle to loud external sounds. After birth, both external and internal stimuli affecting activity are stronger and more changing. Hunger/satiation, dark/light, noise/quiet, cold/warm are all variables which will affect the baby's sleep/wakefulness cycles.

Right after birth unsedated babies have an initial period of "quiet alertness" for about an hour, during which they can make that first eye contact which is so incredibly moving to parents. Human mothers predictably touch their newborn infant's hands, feet, and body and then establish eye contact.[1]But soon thereafter the baby becomes very sleepy. In fact, some babies can't stay awake long enough to nurse for more than a short period of time in the beginning.

The distribution of REM (dreaming) and non-REM sleep (see pp. 36 and 572) is normal on the first day after birth. On the second day, it is temporarily changed, with progressively less deep sleep, less REM sleep, and shorter sleep periods—while the percentage of time spent crying increases and peaks on the third day. The fragmented sleep and variable degree of fussiness shown in the first few days may be the baby's equivalent of the "baby blues" which mothers, to a variable extent, experience at the same time.

Hormones

Many mothers never realize how many ways their own bodies helped regulate physiological functions for the baby before birth. Yet babies' bodies are designed to take over their *own* hormonal and physiological regulation after birth, very smoothly in most cases. Even those few babies born with a major thyroid or adrenal insufficiency appear perfectly normal at birth, because the mother's hormones met all of the baby's requirements until birth. Babies of both sexes may have swollen breasts and genitalia for a few days from the lingering effects of maternal hormones. Girls may even bleed slightly from the vagina as these hormones subside, and the breasts of girls and boys occasionally secrete small amounts of milk in the first few days.

Language/Cognitive Skills

Although newborns can't speak, they *can* communicate. Crying tells you the baby is experiencing some discomfort—an empty stomach for example. Even at this young age your baby attends to sounds and prefers your voice and high-pitched voices in general. One study showed that if you repeatedly read the same story to your baby before birth, or play the same music, the baby remembers and reacts favorably.[2]

A newborn can learn! A complicated series of experiments have shown that babies can be "taught" to recognize that an auditory signal means milk will be available and will turn the head to the nipple.[3] Babies can also imitate the mother's facial expressions at a very early age. Mothers learn too! They can identify the odors of their own babies by three or four days, and recognize the cry of their own infant soon after birth.

All the little games of rocking, smiling, face-gazing, eye contact, and imitating, as well as your singing, speaking, and smiling—tend to cement your relationship to the baby, and add joy to your life—and your baby's!

Social Skills

Even at birth your baby is a social creature. Socialization—the process whereby the newborn eventually becomes the adult human who functions in the social world of the family and the community—begins at birth.

Your newborn is receptive to stimuli like your face and begins to interact with you. The baby is programmed to attract your attention and love by crying or gazing into your eyes. You, in turn, are programmed to respond to your baby. As a matter of fact *everybody* is so programmed. Even young children respond to the "baby face" of mammals, both human and animal. Everybody likes to look at young creatures including kittens and puppies as well as human babies. The big eyes and big cheeks which all young mammals possess are universally appealing. Almost everybody who sees a baby instinctively uses a high-pitched voice and talks in "excited" baby talk.

This programming in both baby and adult ensures survival of the baby. In the event the mother is not able to care for the baby, another member of the human tribe is more likely to do so if the baby is appealingly attractive—or if the cry is persistently annoying.

CARE GIVER TASKS

Basic Care

WHO ARE THE CARE GIVERS?

Before birth, only the mother carries and nourishes the baby. Afterward, other people can do these tasks. In most societies, close friends and relatives assist the mother in the most immediate care of the newborn.

Birth gives fathers, grandparents, other children, and devoted friends a chance to do more for the baby than just feel it kicking through the mother's belly. This adds to their attachment to the baby; every baby is better off having a network of attached potential care givers.

FEEDING/NUTRITION

BREAST-FEEDING

The breast is prepared to make milk by the same hormones that are secreted during pregnancy, and the shifts in hormones that occur after birth. To deliver the milk, all that is needed is the stimulation of suckling and environmental support.

Lactation has two phases: milk production, which occurs in the little sacs at the back of the breast, and milk "let-down," which is the process by which milk is released from those sacs into the ducts that open into the nipple, and thus becomes available for the baby. (See illustration on p. 324.) The amount of milk production is controlled by the amount of sucking, which both empties the breast and stimulates more production.

How do the breasts "know" if you need to make more milk for your baby? The baby gets hungry more often, sucks more often, and empties the breasts fully. This stimulates the production of more milk. How do the breasts "know" if you are producing more than your baby needs? The baby falls asleep or stops sucking before fully emptying the breasts, and the pressure of remaining milk signals the breasts to cut down on production. This system accommodates to your baby's increasing needs with growth, and can even accommodate to twins, triplets, or wet-nursing another infant in addition to your own. Later, when babies take other foods as well as milk, the baby will suck less, and the breasts adjust the supply downward to suit the baby's intake of milk.

As you know, in the first few days, what is secreted is not mature milk, but *colostrum*, a thin, clear, watery-appearing liquid. Since it doesn't look like real milk, it was formerly thought to be deficient milk, and mothers were not particularly encouraged to feed their babies with it. Actually, the opposite is true.

Remember that before birth the only thing the baby swallowed was the

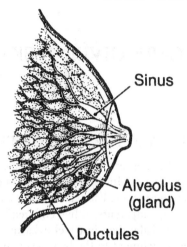

Lactating breast.

amniotic fluid, an even thinner, more watery fluid than colostrum. Colostrum is a transition fluid, well suited to help the baby's stomach and intestines prepare for mature milk. Recent research has shown that frequent, ad lib nursing during the colostrum period helps the intestine loosen and expel the sticky meconium, thus helping prevent the gut from absorbing too much bilirubin, which could cause jaundice.[4]

More important, the colostrum contains some unique immunologic factors which can help protect the baby against infection. Even if you plan to switch to formula later, you can benefit your baby during the newborn period by feeding colostrum. There is some evidence that breast-feeding protects babies younger than three months of age from serious infections.[5]

How to Start Breast-feeding

Be sure your baby is awake, as a sleepy baby nurses poorly. At first it's usually easiest to lie down in a comfortable position with several pillows under your head, and plenty of room beside you for the baby. (Later you may prefer a rocking chair, with something to put your feet up on.) Cradle your baby's head close to your breast, using the arm on the same side as the breast being used. Brush the breast against the baby's cheek, to stimulate the baby's rooting reflex. You can use two fingers of the other hand to make more of a "point" with the nipple. Move the nipple toward the mouth as the "rooting" baby is moving toward your nipple. When the nipple is fully in, it will be far at the back of the baby's mouth, with the mouth gumming the areola rather than just the nipple itself. This is important because in breast-feeding the baby actually gets the milk, not by sucking, but by rhythmic pressure on the ducts in the areola (just as a person milks a cow by manual pressure around the areola behind the nipples themselves). (See illustration p. 325.)

First feedings are often erratic. Some infants wake a lot and nurse frequently; others less often, particularly during the first day or two. If the mother was given medications during labor, residual sedative effects in the baby may persist longer than in the mother, because the baby's system excretes them more slowly. The sedated infant may nurse less often and less vigorously, but this will gradually wear off.

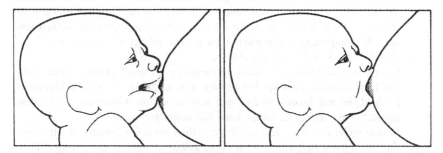

Position of baby's mouth at breast.

Most advisers recommend brief feedings at first, to avoid nipple irritation, defining "brief" as not more than three minutes at each breast. But often, especially with a first baby, the mother's let-down reflex takes a few days to condition. It may take three to four minutes of suckling to achieve let-down. If so, you will need more than five minutes nursing to empty the breast. How can you tell when let-down occurs? There is a "tingly" full feeling in the areola, usually of *both* breasts. While the baby is on one breast some milk will often drip from the other one.

After a few days, "transitional milk" comes in. Most women experience some degree of breast engorgement now. The breasts feel heavy, tight, and sometimes hot. Frequent brief suckling at this time helps relieve pressure and gets nursing started naturally. Engorgement is greater when babies are fed on a rigid three- or four-hour schedule than when they are constantly with the mother and fed on demand—usually every hour or two for a few minutes. Frequent suckling *before* engorgement sets in helps to prevent or at least diminish it. Frequent manual expression of small amounts of milk also helps prevent marked engorgement if the baby can't or doesn't suck often enough to do so. (See below.)

Different Styles of Suckling in Babies

Babies are individually different in their approach to early feeding. Lawrence[6] cites Barnes and colleagues saying:

> Infants have been aptly classified by their feeding characteristics as barracudas, excited ineffectives, procrastinators, gourmets or mouthers, and resters.
> *Barracudas.* When put to the breast barracudas vigorously and promptly grasp the nipple and suck energetically for from 10 to 20 minutes. There is no dallying. Occasionally this type of infant puts too much vigor into his nursing and hurts the nipple.

Excited ineffectives . . . become so excited and active at the breast that they alternately grasp and lose the breast. Then they start screaming. It is often necessary for the nurse or mother to pick up the infant and quiet him first, and then put him back to the breast. After a few days the mother and infant usually become adjusted.

Procrastinators . . . often seem to put off until the fourth or fifth postpartum day what they could just as well have done from the start. They wait till the milk comes in. They show no particular interest or ability in sucking in the first few days. It is important not to prod or force these infants when they seem disinclined. They do well once they start.

Gourmets or mouthers . . . insist on mouthing the nipple, tasting a little milk and then smacking their lips before starting to nurse. If the infant is hurried or prodded, he will become furious and start to scream. Otherwise, after a few minutes of mouthing, he settles down and nurses very well.

Resters prefer to nurse a few minutes and then rest a few minutes. If left alone, they often nurse well, although the entire procedure will take much longer. They cannot be hurried.

These classifications are interesting, but a mother who had never read any of these descriptions could do well by simply following the La Leche League's classic advice: practice *"baby-led nursing,"* at least at the beginning. Keep the baby close to you, and nurse whenever the baby indicates interest, following the baby's "style."

Mothers' Nursing Styles

Oddly enough, though infants' approaches to breast-feeding have been classified, we haven't run across a classification of the obvious differences in mothers' approaches. We offer the following:

Determined and committed. This mother is medically and psychologically convinced that breast-feeding is best, and determined to let nothing stand in the way. She is aware of the possibility of some difficulties, determined to overcome them, is knowledgeable about resources, and willing to use them. She is likely to be disappointed if nursing doesn't work, but since she doesn't give up without a strong reason, she can understand the problem and be satisfied that she did what was best.

Romantically committed. This mother is convinced that breast-feeding is right because it is the most natural thing in the world, following pregnancy as naturally as pregnancy follows conception. She may be unaware of the possibility of minor difficulties, and allow them to escalate into major ones, since she is so sure that there can never be a problem with something so natural. She may not recognize the need for prompt help or support in some cases, and may be bewildered as well as heartbroken if there are major difficulties.

Casual. This mother hadn't thought about it one way or the other, but when she seemed to have milk, it seemed right to give it to the baby. Her general lack of anxiety may help breast-feeding go very well, but if any difficulties crop up, she is tempted to stop as casually as she started.

Skeptical and Anxious. This mother doesn't think she can do it, either because she knows others who tried and failed, or because she is afraid that breast-feeding will be uncomfortable or incompatible with her other commitments.

If you are a skeptical/anxious mother, it would be difficult to try to convert you to a committed one, but you might want to try a casual "wait and see attitude." The fact that the milk is produced, regardless of your anxiety, is sometimes a source of unexpected pride. Your body really *will* make milk. Some skeptical women really want to breast-feed more than they can admit to themselves, but are deeply anxious about failure. Although the let-down reflex may initially be inhibited by anxiety, the inhibition can be released by a number of kinds of support. Sometimes instruction in manual expression helps, so you can feel the difference between production and let-down when the baby is not around, before trying it with the baby.

One anxious mother said, "My mother-in-law kept telling me I didn't have enough milk, and the baby was failing to regain its birth weight. I now think her anxiety was adding to mine and interfering with let-down. Well, anyhow, during manual expression one day (necessary because my breasts were making *plenty* of milk, and were uncomfortably full), I happened to express a stream so full and strong that it shot across the room and hit her in the eye. She walked to the bathroom to wipe it off, and I never heard one more word from her about my not making enough milk. I realized I had a 'let-down' problem, and went off quietly alone with the baby for the next few feedings. Once we'd got our rhythms adjusted, we were able to nurse anywhere."

Downright Opposed. This mother says, for example, "I'm returning to work soon," or, "My husband wants to share fully in the care of the baby," or, "I don't want to be tied down," or, "I somehow just find the idea distasteful."

We encourage trying the more casual wait-and-see approach, at least through the colostrum phase. Fathers can share in baby care in many ways other than feeding. Many are enraptured by watching breast-feeding with their two loved ones together. One doesn't have to be tied down by a nursing baby. It might help to discuss your feelings with a successful nursing mother, because sometimes the "downright opposed" feeling stems from some unrecognized anxiety which can be assuaged by talking it over with someone who's done it— preferably in a situation similar to your own.

Tried It and Didn't Like It. This mother, despite all the talk about the joys of breast-feeding, simply doesn't find it rewarding—because of inverted nipples, painful nipples, embarrassment, or other reasons.

If you try breast-feeding and find you don't like it, consider getting the help you need for any specific problem like inverted nipples; and seeking support from La Leche—especially La Leche members whose initial experience was difficult.

If this fails to help, do what's *right for you.* You and your baby will be happier if feeding times are mostly joyful times. If you discover that breast-feeding isn't joyful for you, and you can't make it rewarding even with help and support, then take pride in making the decision that's right for you. In times past the only alternatives to breast-feeding were to hire a wet nurse or to let your baby starve. Today you can retain the joy and closeness of feeding your own baby with bottles. *Don't feel guilty.* Many fine healthy people have been raised on bottles, and for a while in this country, the majority of babies were.

However, whatever your ultimate feeding style will be, during the getting started period it's usually safer, easier, and more natural to let the baby have the colostrum and early milk. You can always decide later how long you want to continue. Even if you didn't plan to breast-feed, and didn't do any nipple preparation, you can change your mind and breast-feed, or at least give it a try, with no preparation at all. If you do, you'll want to be extra careful about following the usual advice, such as keeping the initial feedings brief and frequent.

It's even possible to change your mind if you were given medication right after birth to suppress lactation. Those medications are not strongly effective and do not remain in your system very long. Their effects can be overcome by the nipple stimulation involved in suckling.

Overcoming Problems

PROBLEMS WITH LET-DOWN

In preindustrial countries in which almost every mother breast-feeds, it is customary to keep the baby with the mother at all times and offer feedings whenever the baby seems to want it—even every hour or two. Though you may not be feeding this naturally and frequently later, it is still a good way to begin, both for you and the baby. Your nipples get frequent stimulation for only short periods, which is the best way to build them up. After all, if you took up jogging, you'd start with short jogs and build up to longer ones. It's also best for the baby, who hasn't had prior experience with concentrating on any task for prolonged periods of time.

Access to frequent feeding at "baby-led" intervals is one of the most important reasons for a "rooming-in" arrangement, if you're in a hospital. Anne had her first child in a conventional obstetric unit, where the babies were brought out every four hours for nursing or bottle-feeding. The four-hour interval was too long for the baby. At each feeding it was evident that he was either overly hungry and frantic, or had passed beyond that stage into exhaustion and sleepiness. Nursing didn't go too well in the hospital, and two days after coming home she developed cracked nipples and a breast infection. The obstetrician advised tetracycline and putting the baby on a bottle. If she had it to do over again, she'd have called La Leche or a pediatrician or obstetrician with special commitment to supporting breast-feeding.

For her second child, Anne had signed up for "rooming-in," but at the time she gave birth, all the "rooming-in" rooms were taken, and the baby was brought from the nursery on the same four-hour schedule. She signed herself and the baby out of the hospital after twenty-four hours, and the breast-feeding went fine for six months. She had her third baby at home, and the breast-feeding proceeded with such satisfaction that she continued nursing until the toddler gradually weaned himself at a little over two years old.

By the way, if you are planning to return to work soon after birth, you *can* still successfully breast-feed. A study of employed nursing mothers showed that women who expressed breast milk nursed longer than women who missed feedings. Many women managed to breast-feed until the baby was over a year—and continued to work.[7]

NIPPLE PROBLEMS

These can often be avoided by frequent short feedings in the first days of life, particularly before the breasts become engorged.

In the early days it is wise to keep the breasts open to the air as much as possible between feedings. Wear nothing over them, or only a very loose soft gown. After engorgement sets in, this may be painful when you are not lying in bed. A possible solution is simply to lie in bed. The worst possible thing to do, during the early days, is to wear a nursing bra with nursing pads and a plastic lining. This guarantees that the nipples will be constantly moist, their most vulnerable state. If your breasts are engorged, your nipples tender, and you want to or have to get up and walk around, use the Netsy-type nipple shield worn inside a sturdy bra. These are a double-layer plastic "doughnut." The inner layer fits against the breast, holding back the engorged breast and areola, and letting the nipple protrude through the "doughnut" hole. The outer layer is solid, and holds the clothing away from the nipple. A hole at the top lets the air inside exchange freely with the room air (so no moisture builds up). Any milk which leaks is caught in the bottom part and can be emptied as often as you like. The plastic cup can be easily opened, emptied, washed, boiled, and it can be worn inside any bra that is large enough (maybe a size or two larger than your usual ones). You can buy these nipple cups at some drugstores, obtain them from La Leche, or mail-order them. If you can't get them locally and are ordering them, a temporary expedient recommended by La Leche is an ordinary dimestore tea strainer, with the handle removed, worn inside an ordinary cotton bra. This keeps the clothing from rubbing against the nipples and allows free flow of air to the nipples. The bra holds the strainer in place.

Lawrence[8] advises health professionals to suggest the following for prevention or treatment of cracked nipples: Look for any source of tenderness in the breast or anxiety in the environment; conduct prefeeding manual expression; carefully position infant on breast; nurse on unaffected side first, with affected side exposed to air; apply expressed breast milk to nipples, and let it dry on between feedings; apply dry heat for twenty minutes four times a day with a sixty-watt bulb, eighteen inches away. If necessary, use nipple shields while nursing. (We would question this advice, since nipple shields apply suction rather than the baby's usual "gumming" action, and can cause more pain than they relieve. But if it works for you, use it.) Rarely, temporarily stopping the nursing on the affected side and replacing it with manual expressing or pumping, may be indicated. If necessary, give aspirin or codeine in short-acting preparations just after nursing. (We think this advice should be carefully reviewed with a doctor familiar with successful breast-feeding, since these drugs get into the milk. Aspirin especially in the first few days could be dangerous because of its anticoagulant effect.)

Notice that Lawrence does not recommend the careful washing of nipples which some other authorities do. In fact, she advises *against* it, because washing removes protective skin oils. The bacteriostatic activity of early milk is more effective than that of soap and water, and is less irritating. Use soap and water to wash your hands before handling the nipple, so as to cut down on extraneous bacteria, but leave the nipple itself alone except for spreading some of your milk on it.

WHAT IF YOU CAN'T BREAST-FEED THE BABY AT FIRST?

Despite everything we said about the importance of colostrum (see p. 323), don't worry if there is a problem with the baby requiring immediate medical intervention which delays breast-feeding. First things come first. In the old days when everyone breast-fed, some babies died from conditions that can now be corrected with intensive care or surgery.

If for some temporary medical reason, the baby can't nurse now, but will be able to in future, your own comfort and the maintenance of the milk supply require some simulation of nursing. Otherwise, your breasts will "interpret" the unrelieved fullness as a signal that they are producing too much milk, and cut down production. Eventually this completely stops the supply, which is how natural weaning occurs. Simulated nursing can be provided by a breast pump, manual expression if you can learn the trick of it, or a cooperative husband who is willing to suck like a baby.

Breast pumps vary. The "suction type," available at any drugstore, is close to useless; the mechanical type, which more closely imitates a real baby's action, is expensive, but can be rented from most hospitals or La Leche.

Manual expression, once you've learned to do it, requires no equipment and can be done almost anywhere. (See illustration on p. 331.) Although manual expression is a relatively easily learned skill after nursing is well established, it may be difficult at the beginning. Try to get an experienced person to show you. Start off with gentle but firm massage of one breast, using both hands with the thumbs up, cupping the breast at its outer perimeter against the chest wall. Slowly slide both hands toward the center, making a circle with the hands, until you reach the areola. Repeat the massage several times, keeping the pressure even and moderate. An engorged breast might feel some discomfort at this point, but not pain.

After the massage you are ready to start the actual expression, or "milking" of the milk. If you are removing milk from the left breast, support it with the right hand. Use the left hand to encircle the part of the breast just behind the areola, and gently roll the fingers forward, compressing the lactiferous sinuses. Repeat this procedure several times, rotating your thumb and fingers around the

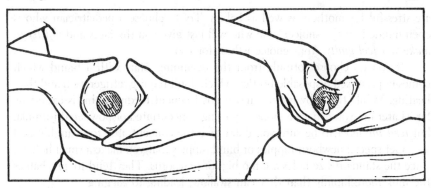

Manual expression.

breast so that all of the sinuses are equally compressed. Then repeat the whole process with the other breast. If you are expressing milk just to relieve pressure, you can discard it. If you plan to give it to the baby later, Riordan notes that it keeps thirty minutes at room temperature, twenty-four hours in a refrigerator, one to two weeks in the freezing compartment of a refrigerator, longer in a separate freezer.[9] Freeze breast milk in plastic containers and thaw under running water. Do not refreeze.

Mothers are often concerned about whether certain foods they eat will get into the breast milk and upset the baby. Generally, what is in the mother's diet makes no difference to the baby. But certain foods (spicy foods, cabbage, onions, chocolate, strawberries, tomatoes) occasionally will cause distress in the baby. By the way, although it has been assumed that increasing the mother's fluid intake increases the volume of milk produced, this does not seem to be true.[10] The best way to increase the volume of your milk is to nurse more frequently.

Bottle-feeding of Breast-fed Babies

We'd strongly urge you not to bottle-feed during the getting started period, not even water unless there is some good reason for giving it, such as to prevent dehydration if the weather is very hot during the early days when the milk flow is lighter. La Leche recommends that the baby not be exposed to *any* intrusion of a rubber nipple until well after nursing is established. The baby's mouth movements in sucking from a rubber nipple are different from those of "gumming" the areola, and a baby who is just getting the nursing habit established can apparently be confused by the difference.

BOTTLE-FEEDING

If you elect bottle-feeding during the getting started period, we offer the following suggestions:

Carefully review the pros and cons for *you,* with your pediatrician. If, for example, you were anticipating that bottles might be more convenient, the opposite could be true if you have a strong family history of allergies. Bottle-feeding may seem simpler and more convenient, but some of its complications are stressful for mothers as well as babies. Try to choose a pediatrician who is open-minded on the subject, one who will just give you the facts and *not try to make you feel guilty.* Your choice is best for you.

If you do choose formula from the beginning, start with a brand which comes in premixed disposable bottles, which don't require refrigeration and then heating. While the baby is tiny, and needs frequent feedings, this is easiest by far. (Later on, you can save money by using concentrated or powdered formula, but *read the label* to be sure you don't give the concentrated form undiluted.)

Get special newborn nipples or blind nipples that you make a small hole in, since the standard-size holes are too big for newborns. They tend to give babies the milk more rapidly than they can swallow, leading to gagging.

You don't need to take medications to "dry up your milk." Milk production will stop by itself after a few days of engorgement. Some women find it comfortable to wear a firm bra or firmly pin a folded towel as a binder around the breasts during this period. Some find aspirin or ice packs helpful.

Hold the baby close to you while giving the bottle, so that both of you can enjoy the same intimate closeness you would if you were breast-feeding.

If you are in an emergency situation like a revolution or unexpected home birth during a blizzard or tornado and cannot get formula, try to breast-feed because it's the safest supply of sterile good milk for a baby. Don't use water that hasn't been boiled. Don't ever give regular cow's milk—whole or skimmed —to a newborn baby. If no milk or formula is available, a temporary expedient is the medieval "sugar tit." Mix water and whatever form of sugar is available; boil the mixture; saturate a sterilized (boiled) cloth tied into a nipple shape and give it to the baby to suck. The proper proportion of sugar to water will taste "mildly sweet" to an adult rather than "syrupy." Boiled sugar water or formula can also be given by sterilized spoon or eyedropper, if bottles are not available.

BURPING

All babies swallow some air when sucking, whether they are breast- or bottle-fed. When they do, the air bubble distends the stomach, causing discomfort and sometimes spitting up of milk. Therefore, after feeding you have to help the baby get the air out.

There are several methods for burping babies: 1) Hold the baby upright over your shoulder and pat the baby's back. 2) Slowly raise the baby to a sitting position. 3) Rest the baby, tummy down, across your knees and pat the baby's back. You can alternate these methods until you hear the burp. If there is no burp after a few moments, you can stop—unless the baby is fussy. Breast-fed babies often swallow less air, and if the baby falls asleep at the breast, burping can certainly be omitted. Fathers often enjoy doing the burping, especially when the baby is breast-fed.

Spitting up a little milk, with or without burping, is very common in small babies. For this reason, protect your clothing with a diaper as you hold the baby after feeding, or while burping. Immediately after feeding, if you put the baby down to sleep, do so tummy down or half-sitting in an infant seat. Then, if there is any spit-up, the baby won't inhale it.

CLEANING/GROOMING

At birth

Shortly after birth it's customary to clean, diaper, and clothe the baby. Babies can be either washed with a face cloth or bathed. A controlled study showed that the method of cleaning made no difference in the infection rate, but more infants cried when they were washed. Bathing seems to be calming and to cause less loss of body heat and it does not increase risk of infection.[11]

After cleaning, clothing the baby is vitally important. The baby has been used to a surrounding temperature of 98.6 degrees, much warmer than adult humans tolerate if they have a choice. The baby will have difficulty maintaining normal body temperature at first. Even when the baby is against the mother's body, some clothing or covering on the side away from the mother will be needed. Most people "instinctively" try to keep babies covered, tending if anything to overcover and overdress them.

In most hospital nurseries, babies are dressed in very loosely fitted infant diapers (so as not to rub too tightly against the umbilical cord stump) and short-sleeved knitted cotton shirts. The air in the nursery itself or the isolette is kept warm enough so that no other clothing is necessary. When the babies are brought out for feedings they are wrapped in cotton receiving blankets. (Opening the blanket for a few minutes to look at the whole baby will not cause undue chilling!)

In home births, or if you take the baby home a day or two after birth, careful attention to warmth and clothing is needed. The same loose shirt and diaper used in the nursery are a good base, but the baby will need as many additional layers as adults need to feel comfortable. On a hot summer day when you feel like wearing shorts, a diaper and shirt are enough for the baby. In spring or early fall when you'd wear underwear, a shirt, and a sweater, give the baby the same number of layers. A cotton receiving blanket is the equivalent of your shirt, and a shawl or blanket is the equivalent of your sweater. Or the baby can wear gowns, stretch suits, and sweaters.

If it's *really* cold indoors—which is not the best situation for newborns—either go to bed with the baby under the number of quilts it takes to keep you comfortably warm, or carry the baby next to your body in a Snugli-type carrier *under* the sweaters or coats it takes to keep you warm. The same sweaters or loose coats or capes that you wore as maternity clothes will cover the newborn baby in a Snugli. Be sure to put a cap over the baby's head.

This same clothing also works if for any reason it is necessary to take a baby outdoors in very cold weather during the first days of life. It's likely to work better than snowsuits or buntings, because when you take the baby indoors, you can remove your clothing without disturbing a sleeping baby. If you are traveling by car, you need a zippered bunting bag with separated legs, so the baby can be placed in the safety car seat. Sweaters and *several* layers of blankets will do well also in a pinch—again, as thick as the coat you'd need to wear for comfort. Don't forget a warm cap.

BATHING

Bathing the baby is *not* part of getting started. You will postpone it until after the cord stump drops off and the belly-button heals, in order to reduce risk of infection.

What babies *do* need is frequent cleansing of the skin-fold areas: the diaper area, the neck, and around the arms or wherever you notice a crease. This can be done with clear water on soft cloths or cotton, or with baby lotion. Soap can remove the natural skin oils which protect the skin, without replacing them. Many babies are able to tolerate washing with soap, and some soap may be necessary to remove sticky residue of bowel movements, especially the first meconium ones. Baby lotion dissolves some of the skin oils, but tends to replace them with a more or less similar material.

Baby *oil* is petroleum-based, not a natural skin substance, and it tends to clog sweat glands. We don't recommend it. "Baby wipes" contain some baby oil along with other ingredients, but they are safe for most babies and certainly a great convenience, especially when traveling with a baby. Nor do we recommend any kind of powder. It's not necessary, and if inhaled can be dangerous.

If your baby boy was circumcised, healing will occur within ten days. Don't worry about a bit of blood oozing once in a while (although if it persists tell the doctor). Doctors recommend placing a bit of Vaseline on the tip at each diaper change.

Uncircumcised foreskin is easy to take care of. The genitals should be washed in an uncircumcised baby but you don't have to retract the foreskin to wash under it. Skin cells from the glans of the penis are shed and will work their way to the top. This is called infant smegma. If you see it oozing, clean it away with soap and water. The glans of the penis and the foreskin develop together. They will separate sometime between birth and age five. The American Academy of Pediatrics recommends that parents *not* retract the foreskin—a change from advice that used to be common. They summarize care of the uncircumcised penis by simply saying, "Leave it alone."

DIAPERING

Today most parents choose disposable diapers, which are convenient and do not require pins. About 15 billion diapers are used per year, mostly disposables. Disposables for a newborn cost several dollars a day; buy in quantity if you can.

Diaper service diapers come prefolded. For those of you who are using unfolded diapers you wash yourself, don't worry about neat folding. Any way you fold the diaper that fits your baby is fine. Always use *diaper pins*, not just big safety pins, as they are safer because they are less likely to open.

The diaper area requires very careful cleaning, particularly in our culture where diapers are constantly worn. Diaper rash is very common, and it can cause discomfort for the baby, and in extreme cases, infections. It is caused by a combination of vulnerable skin plus a warm moist environment, which favors the growth of bacteria or fungi.

The ways to avoid diaper rash are to keep the area dry and clean, prevent breakdown of the natural protective mechanisms of the skin, and avoid adding irritants to the area.

A simple and natural approach is: 1) Let the baby have as much time as possible every day with the diaper area exposed to open air. You can just lie the baby on a folded diaper. 2) Use soft and comfortable, non-irritant diapers (best are cotton from a diaper service). 3) Change the diaper as soon as possible after it's wet. 4) Don't use soap on the skin. 5) Rinse with clear water or baby lotion. Most babies will survive violation of some of the above suggestions without developing diaper rash, but we wouldn't recommend ignoring them all.

If diaper rash begins to develop, the chances are that you can clear it up with home remedies quickly applied: 1) Leave the baby's bottom nude, exposed to the air, at least part of the time, and every few hours if possible. 2) After the air exposure, apply Desitin ointment to clean dry skin before reapplying the diaper. 3) Avoid disposable diapers until after the rash is well healed. 4) Use soft cotton cloth diapers, from a diaper service if possible since their equipment rinses more thoroughly than home equipment. If a diaper service is not feasible, rinse the diapers twice in the washing machine. This is to remove even trace residues of potentially irritating detergents, and residue of the ammonia-causing bacteria. You can also boil hand-washed diapers in a pot on the kitchen stove if you don't have a washing machine, or if it breaks down. Hand washing alone will not remove bacteria because the water isn't hot enough.

During the getting started period, your newborn will wet or soil eighty to one hundred diapers a week. This is far too much laundry for any new mother to do! If you don't have a diaper service or someone else to do the laundry, we'd recommend using disposables, with careful attention to the other ways of preventing diaper rash.

SLEEP/ACTIVITY

Initially newborn babies wake up after every sleep cycle. In the early days this coincides with a need for nursing. Later, during the getting settled period, the baby will be taking larger feedings, and will begin to consolidate sleep cycles so as to wake less frequently. But don't expect that during the newborn period!

In the days just after birth, as the baby is learning to integrate sleep and feeding rhythms, sleep may be quite erratic and fragmented. The irritability and increased crying, which tend to peak on the third day, are natural phenomena, *not* a result of poor caretaking, insufficient milk, or inadequate soothing of the baby—though it can be quite frustrating to the mother who doesn't expect it. If the third-day peak of crying coincides with bringing the baby home from the hopsital, the mother could easily feel that she was doing something wrong. Not to worry. The baby will smooth out the sleep cycle very soon.

EXERCISE

Exercise is not something you need to be concerned about during the getting started period. Newborn babies provide themselves with all the exercise they need, by sucking, stretching arms and legs, turning necks and heads in ways that they didn't have room for inside the womb.

STRESS MANAGEMENT

In the early days of life this comes naturally from the rhythms of basic care. All you have to do is feed frequently; keep the baby warm and clean and dry; and avoid extremes of heat or bright light or loud noises (which are stressful for you as well). Taking good care of yourself, and reducing unnecessary stress on yourself, makes it easier for you to soothe the baby. Sleep when the baby sleeps, feed when the baby is hungry. If, after feeding, the baby seems restless and doesn't fall asleep easily, try burping, rocking, or walking the baby. Some babies in the early days sleep more comfortably if they are swaddled by wrapping in a cotton receiving blanket, making a little confined space like the womb they have been used to.

EMOTIONAL "NUTRITION"

During the period of "getting started," the rhythms of basic care provide all the emotional nutrition a baby really needs. But many parents enjoy from the first day doing the things that will be important emotional nutrition later, like talking or singing to the baby and trying to catch the baby's eye.

CARE OF THE CARE GIVER

YOUR RECUPERATION FROM LABOR AND BIRTH

Fatigue

It's said that it takes a major league football player eight days to fully recover physically from a strenuous game. Giving birth is at least as athletic as a football game, and may last many hours longer. You will need time and extra rest to regain energy. Common energy-stealers include excitement about the new baby, which can put you on an emotional "high" and blunt your perceptions of your own needs for rest and sleep. Family and friends may be so eager to call and congratulate or visit you and the new baby that you spend too much energy on them now. Older children and husbands may feel left out and demand extra attention just when you have less energy to give (even the family dog may feel neglected!). You may have enough energy for the baby, but not for the laundry the baby creates.

Your Obstetric Recovery

The physiological changes as your body returns to the non-pregnant state are in many ways quite as complex and fascinating as the changes which developed as pregnancy began.

UTERUS AND CERVIX

The uterus shrinks with remarkable speed, so that by about twelve days after birth it normally cannot be felt above the pelvic bone. Its average weight is about two pounds after birth, only half that a week later, half of that by two weeks, and only about three ounces by six weeks.

Abdominal size returns to that of prepregnancy more slowly. Weight loss is achieved more easily if you are breast-feeding, since many calories go into the making of milk. Later, you may want to do exercises to help the stretched abdominal muscles tighten up. Sit-ups, or leg-raising as you lie on your back, will exercise your abdomen when you are ready to do it. There is no hurry.

The cervix is quite open right after birth, closes to an average of 2 cm in a week, to 1 cm by two weeks, and is just a closed slit, the usual non-pregnant configuration, by six weeks. There is some discharge, called lochia, for two to four weeks. For about the first four days it is red, usually somewhat heavier than a normal menstrual period. From about days five to nine it is paler, pink or brown, and from about days ten to fifteen it becomes more creamy or greenish, with occasionally a slight bloody tinge for as long as three weeks. Pads are recommended rather than tampons because the secretions are alkaline, and infectious organisms can grow more readily than in the acid vaginal secretions of ordinary cycles. Two complications are rare, but serious if they occur. Sudden or persistent fresh red blood could mean that some of the placental fragments remain in the uterus; severe hemorrhage could occur. Any foul odor from the discharge suggests infection, which could spread rapidly if not treated promptly with antibiotics. Either bleeding or foul odor requires prompt medical attention.

THE BREASTS IF NOT BREAST-FEEDING

The oldest and simplest method of stopping lactation is to bind the breasts rather firmly with a firm bra or a towel, avoid nipple stimulation, and wait for lactation to stop. About half of women trying this will experience engorgement, pain, and some leakage of milk, usually for about two to three days. Aspirin and ice packs are sometimes used to reduce pain and engorgement. A variety of drugs can speed the suppression of lactation, but unless there is a specific reason, why not use the simpler methods?

Your Emotional Recovery

Many women experience some kind of heightened emotionality during the postpartum period, moving easily from ecstasy to tears. The "baby blues" peaking around the fifth day are common enough to have been given that name. Nada Stotland[12] has suggested that a tendency toward crying may be adaptive as loved ones are likely to respond to a mother's tears with sympathy and help, and give the mother some of the "babying" and support she needs.

Women who don't know about the "baby blues" may fear there is something wrong with them, or even may imagine that they are going crazy when they're not. What psychiatrists call "transient situational [stress] reactions" may occur after childbirth and probably are your psyche's way of telling you you need more rest and more emotional and/or practical help than you are getting.

There *is* such a thing as postpartum depression and/or psychosis. Though those are very rare, they do occur, and can be very serious. Symptoms include a severe immobilizing depression, suicidal thoughts, delusions (false beliefs), hallucinations (hearing voices or seeing things that are not there), or thoughts of harming the baby. This is a psychiatric emergency; tell someone you need treatment and be sure to get it.

THE BABY HONEYMOON

In the first few days and weeks you have new practical tasks and new emotional experiences in caring for and getting to know your new baby. You have needs of your own, including taking care of your body, getting enough sleep, and having enough time and freedom to experience and deal with your emotions.

Emotionally, this is a time for a honeymoon, getting to know and fall in love with the new little person who came into your life. A new mother needs some time and space away from the outside world to do this—to concentrate on firming up a new relationship which is bound to hold surprises.

It's odd how our culture supports the need for a marital honeymoon, even though the couple have chosen each other, had some chance to get to know each other, and maybe even lived together before finalizing a marriage. You'd think the need for a "baby honeymoon" would be all the more recognized as an important time. After all, you may have chosen to have a baby, but you didn't specifically choose *this* one, and you two haven't met before birth. You and your baby need time to get to know each other and fall in love. Even though your bodies and behaviors are programmed to bring you two together, you need time and space and freedom to do it with smoothness and joy.

Many mothers experience the first days or weeks at home with the baby in a kind of dreamy fog—waking when the baby wakes, feeding and changing diapers, and going back to sleep. Some experience little desire to eat—others are ravenously hungry. Gradually the mother catches up on her rest, and the baby stays awake for longer periods, seeming to "wake up and take notice" of parts of the world around. The baby feeds for longer periods, takes larger amounts, and usually sleeps for longer periods.

Getting started means getting the basic rhythms of sleeping and feeding smoothly integrated, with the least possible stress to the parents. Everything that's non-essential should be deferred. That leaves time and space for rest, for play with the baby, for experiencing the joy of the baby rather than a sense of pressure or anxiety.

Mothers vary enormously in what they consider essential—not only among themselves, but between one baby and the next. You may want to spend prime time reading a story to an older child. Most mothers want their husbands and/ or other children to share in the honeymoon. Getting out of the house to avoid going stir-crazy may be essential to some of you or the last thing in the world that others want. Spending some time in person or on the phone with good friends may be essential for some; others prefer being alone with the baby and family at first. Keeping in touch with work or studies is important for many, though most like to take at least a brief baby sabbatical.

This is a time to indulge your *own* needs as much as you can, both for your own sake, and because you are much calmer and happier in meeting the baby's needs if you do. Your own individual needs may include doing some of your usual work, or reading, or housework. But be sure to ask yourself if this is something you *want* to do right now, or something you think you *ought* to do. If you are normally a "superwoman" with high standards at home and work, this is a time to lower standards on non-essentials, and use the captured time to indulge yourself and enjoy your baby.

Some practical suggestions for enhancing the honeymoon follow:

- Have rooming-in preferably round the clock.
- When you get home have someone else provide the personal services nurses provide in a hospital. Someone can bring you the clean diapers and baby clothes and take away the dirty ones; someone can make your bed with nice clean sheets every day (since you'll be sleeping frequently, and probably dripping some milk). You need someone to hold or watch the baby while you take a shower, a nice long bath, a walk, or whatever most relaxes you when you want to get away from the baby for a few minutes.
- Have your favorite foods cooked by somebody else, and brought to you when you want them. Have your favorite juices on ice by your bedside, or brought to you when you like.
- Have someone who loves them play with your other children, indulge and pamper them a bit, and bring the children in to see you and the baby at a time when the children are feeling good about themselves and the baby.
- Pamper yourself and be pampered in a way which indulges your needs and whims, while you are spending *your* energy on relating to this baby and providing the pampering the baby needs and enjoys.

This may sound like an expensive and luxurious approach, far out of reach of most families. It doesn't have to cost much to fly in Grandma for a few weeks, or hire a housekeeper to help out during the same time. Maybe a friend can help, or a new-mothers' support group can provide suggestions or help, which you can later reciprocate. Such support groups are proliferating and can be located through the La Leche or the Self-Help Center (see Suggested Readings and Resources).

If you can't get this kind of help from family or friends, and can't afford to hire it, then of course you will adapt to reality. Just drop every non-essential task in order to save energy for yourself and your baby. And don't spend a moment feeling guilty if you find it hard to do it all yourself. Instead congratulate yourself on your stamina in doing as well as you are!

A WORD FOR FATHERS

We applaud the "new" man of the eighties who has a deep interest in fathering and nurturance. Many of you went to childbirth classes, attended your baby's birth, developed attachment to your baby, and now want to participate in the baby's care. Don't be ashamed or anxious if you still find baby care a bit frightening or difficult for you.

Animal studies have shown that, except for the just-delivered mother, other care givers need an induction period of close contact with the young in order to display parenting behavior.[13] This does not mean that males are not meant to care for babies. Indeed, we know that *all* humans respond to a baby's smile and cry. One experiment with monkeys showed that if the monkey fathers were left with infants without the mother, after a few days the males groomed and played with the infants as the mothers did.

You are not a monkey, but this study can teach you that prolonged, frequent contact with your baby will provide the "induction" to parenting you need. When the baby is nursing, you may have to make a special effort to be with the baby. We suggest the three "C's": cuddling, crooning, changing.

Socialization Tasks

PLAY/STIMULATION

Over this and the next two stages, socialization starts with the development of "basic trust." The baby experiences that his or her needs will be met, any discomfort will be soothed, any distress will be attended to. These experiences provide the basis for the trust the baby will develop. On the one hand, remember that you can't spoil a baby. On the other hand, be reassured that almost all babies have their "fussy times" when you cannot relieve distress.

Play actually starts at birth. Out of the mutual experiences of feeding and burping, being picked up and put down, being cleaned and dressed, an intimate "dance" of mutual attention develops between baby and care givers. It advances rapidly over the first week or two. Play and recognition of the mother develop mostly in the "quiet-alert" state, which is increasingly "entrained" to her attentions, remarkably soon.

Though the first quiet-alert hour at birth is followed by sleep, babies return to this state, so there are lots of other opportunities for interaction. These quiet-alert moments are fleeting during the first days, averaging only three minutes an hour during the day, and less at night. But this doubles over the next few weeks, and is increasingly synchronized with the mother's activity. The chance that a baby will be in an alert state while being held by the mother increases from 25 percent of the time on the second day to 57 percent of the time on the eighth day.

Klaus and Kennell, who are widely known for the research that they have done on first-hour attachment, cite two studies which asked mothers, "When did you first feel love for your baby?"[14] In one study 41 percent said during pregnancy; 24 percent at birth; 27 percent in the first week; and 8 percent after the first week. In another study, 25 percent of the experienced mothers and 40 percent of the first-time mothers felt indifference on first holding the child, though most went on to develop affection during the first week. (Delayed onset of affection was more likely if labor had been painful, or the membranes were ruptured artificially, or the mothers had been given a large dose of Demerol.)

Unfortunately, there has been so much recent emphasis on the experience of early attachment, that some parents fear that all is lost if they miss that first hour. This simply isn't true. If for some reason immediate separation is required, there are many later opportunities to resume the process of attachment. And, of course, adoptive parents experience attachment also.

It can be distressing to new mothers when some aspects of the interactive dance with the baby do not go smoothly at first. But the increased entrainment of the baby's alert states to your interventions brings you closer together, allows for more eye contact, and strengthens the development of affection over the first weeks and months.

In early breast-feeding, the infant often appears to drift off to sleep before having taken "enough," and mothers instinctively "jiggle" the baby just a little to restore the alert state. Too much jiggling can disrupt the nursing, and apparently overstimulate the infant; too little is ineffective.[15] Over the first two weeks the vast majority of mothers entrain their jiggling to the baby's alertness, just as the baby entrains alertness to the mother's interventions. Mother and baby together establish the dance of interaction. Even experienced mothers have to learn the dance anew with each new infant; thus the intimacy of the dance is a new creation with each mother-infant pair. New babies need *brief* periods of play and eye contact. They signal when they've had enough by turning the eyes and head away (called gaze aversion). When this happens, please don't feel hurt and rejected, or try to regain the baby's attention by extra stimulation. Respect the baby's sense of what is enough for now, and look forward to the next play period.

HEALTH CARE

The vast majority of babies do just fine in the getting started period. The first pediatric well-baby checkup is usually made within the first twenty-four hours of life to be sure the baby has made a successful transition to extrauterine life and was born with no rare conditions. Ideally, it's nice for both parents to be present when the pediatrician makes this examination, although in some hospitals this is difficult to arrange logistically. Being present gives you a chance to get more familiar with how your pediatrician handles your baby. This helps cement the three-way relationship between parents, pediatrician, and baby.

Many pediatricians will do a Brazelton developmental evaluation of a newborn baby in your presence, and parents normally find it quite thrilling to see all the many reflex and social responses which tiny babies can make in this situation. The Brazelton Neonatal Assessment Scale is more than a neurological exam. It examines not only reflexes but also the baby's skills in organizing these reflexes, the baby's reactions to the environment, and the way the baby reacts to distress and stimulation.[16]

In subsequent days, you'll make many observations of your baby. You may worry whether certain findings indicate a problem. As you can see below, usually they don't.

Below is a list of some common findings in newborns. Many of the conditions are self-limiting and no cause for concern. When there is cause for concern we tell you so. It is especially important for you to observe your baby carefully if your baby was born at home or has had *early discharge* from the hospital.

Parents often feel embarrassed to call the doctor when they are not *sure* that the baby is ill. However, signs of illness in very young babies are not clear-cut, even to doctors. If you are concerned, it is better to call than to worry.

Head. The head may be slightly swollen or out of shape just after birth, from pressure exerted against the mother's pelvic bones during labor. The head will spontaneously resume its usual shape over the next few days. Sometimes a baby's head has bruises or swellings filled with blood (cephalohematomas) from pressure of birth itself, or forceps. These will be absorbed within six weeks and need no treatment.

Circulatory system. Persistence of cool extremities, and blue or mottled color of hands and feet, is normal in the first few days. If it persists longer than that call it to the attention of your doctor.

Muscle tone and reflexes. A limp baby is not normal; careful evaluation is needed. Transient limpness can result from medications given to the mother during labor, and will resolve within a day or two but the baby should be under careful observation until this resolves. Sudden onset of limpness is an emergency.

Excretions. If the baby doesn't wet a diaper within six hours, or pass a stool within forty-eight hours, evaluation for possible blockage is needed.

Vomiting is a different proposition from spitting up. It's sometimes called "projectile" because the force of the vomiting projects the stomach contents away from the body (the way adults throw up), in contrast to some dribbling of stomach contents out of the mouth as in spitting up. It is potentially serious, as repeated vomiting in the newborn period could mean an obstruction somewhere in the baby's intestinal tract.

If the baby lost more than 10 percent of birth weight in the first few days, or requires more than ten days to regain birth weight, an evaluation is needed. Weight loss first shows itself as dehydration: fewer than four to five wet diapers a day, sunken eyes, and absence of tears when crying in a baby who previously had tears. Lethargy, a weak suck, or lack of interest in sucking are also likely in the case of abnormal weight loss.

Absence of adequate milk production by a nursing mother is almost never a cause, but absence of sufficient milk "let-down" could be. Continued weight loss in a breast-fed baby is just as serious as in a bottle-fed baby; both need prompt evaluation. It is possible to be so committed to breast-feeding as the "natural way," that one overlooks the possibility of weight loss.

Frantic interest in nursing followed by distress in nursing and breast refusal could indicate sore gums. Rarely, the baby dislikes the taste of the mother's milk because of strong-flavored foods in her diet. Intolerance to formula could cause weight loss, but would likely be accompanied by diarrhea and abdominal pain.

Skin. Rashes and/or small white pimples (milia) may occur as infant skin makes the transition from a fluid to dry environment. These resolve spontaneously. You may notice Ebstein's Pearls in your baby's mouth. These are white and shiny spots on the baby's palate. They are of no concern and disappear within a few weeks. "Birth marks" or areas of darker pigmentation are common. The "mongolian spot" over the base of the spine is quite common and doesn't mean anything. It looks like a purple or blue bruise which recedes in color and disappears as the baby gets older. "Strawberry birthmarks" consist of an unusually large number of tiny capillary blood vessels near the skin in one particular area. They pose no problem at all to the baby, and most of them disappear spontaneously. Rarely, a baby develops a cavernous hemangioma. These are larger birthmarks, which grow after birth. However, they begin to recede in growth when the child is about eight or nine months old, so surgery is not indicated unless there is bleeding or the hemangioma is in a "bad" spot where it causes pressure. A "stork bite" birthmark consists of flat, red coloration on the midline of the face, often the eyelid or just above the nose. These get darker when the baby cries, but will go away spontaneously after about six months of age.

Many babies have some puffiness of the eyelids, or irritation of the eyes, for a few days after birth. Most commonly this is a result of sensitivity to eye drops given after birth, to prevent infections. Pus emerging from the eye suggests an infection, requiring prompt evaluation.

Jaundice is a yellow coloring of the skin and whites of the eyes caused by high levels of bilirubin in the blood. New red blood cells are constantly forming, and old ones being broken down, in newborns just as in adults. But newborns are born with a high number of red cells so they have extra red blood cells to break down, and a less mature liver to excrete the bilirubin which is a by-product of this breakdown. Also more bilirubin is reabsorbed from the gut, before the meconium is replaced by mature stool. The combination of more bilirubin to dispose of, and a less mature liver to do it with, results in a temporary increase in the bilirubin level of all infants' blood.

Many normal infants will have bilirubin levels high enough so that the skin and white of the eyes become noticeably yellow within a few days after birth. This is called physiological jaundice, and requires no treatment. If jaundice appears earlier than thirty-six hours or is rapidly increasing, the baby needs prompt medical attention. The blood bilirubin level must be checked, because high and rising levels could cause permanent brain damage. Exposure of the skin to ultraviolet light helps the blood break down excess bilirubin; but this needs to be done by trained personnel who can carefully regulate the exposure and protect the baby's eyes under the bright light.

Breast-fed babies may have higher bilirubin levels than bottle-fed ones. Physiological jaundice was formerly considered a reason to discontinue breast-feeding. It has recently been discovered that babies who are breast-fed frequently from the beginning (more than eight times a day) have lower bilirubin levels than babies fed the more usual six or eight feedings which are typical hospital routines.[17] The frequency of feeding rather than the amount of fluid taken was what made the difference. Presumably, this is because each feeding stimulates the gastrocolic reflex which stimulates the expulsion of meconium, allowing less time for bilirubin to be reabsorbed from the gut.

Most *congenital abnormalities* such as malformations are obvious soon after birth, but a few congenital metabolic diseases do not show up in the newborn period, and are therefore routinely tested for. These most commonly include hypothyroidism (which occurs in 1 baby in about 4,000); phenyketonuria ([PKU] 1 in 14,000); and galactosemia (1 in 40,000). These tests are not fully reliable until at least three or four days after birth and therefore if done early will need to be repeated at a first pediatric visit.

Any suspicion of *infection* should be checked with the baby's doctor. The most common symptom of infection is refusal to nurse. The baby could also have lethargy, irritability, signs of pain or distress. Fever is rare in the newborn.

Before we leave the subject of health care, be sure the baby's arrival is on record at your health insurance office. Also, don't forget to add the baby to your list of dependents when you do your taxes this year! It's a good idea to apply for baby's social security number as well in order to get that chore out of the way.

SAFETY

You will note we use pretty strong language when it comes to safety in this —and subsequent—age/stage chapters. That's because safety is so important.

Although the newborn can't move much, your baby *does* move. Some are quite talented at "scooting." Never leave the baby unattended in a crib with the sides down or on a bath table. If you are carrying your baby and *must* put the baby down, use the floor.

Be sure you have a safe crib and never use plastic bags to cover the crib mattress. Do not use baby powder. Never prop bottles.

Always use an approved infant car seat. This should be the first present you buy for your baby—it's an important part of your gift of life.

Because the baby cannot regulate body temperature well, another *must* protection is against extremes of heat and cold. Unprotected exposure to direct sunlight must also be avoided. Don't permit anyone to smoke in the presence of your baby—not even yourself; there is no question the baby is affected by passive smoking and by nicotine in breast milk.[18]

The baby's helplessness also warrants protection from loving but exuberant older siblings and pets.

*   *   *

Getting started wasn't so hard, was it? Or if it was, you *are* started and can go on to getting settled.

SUGGESTED READINGS AND RESOURCES

American Academy of Pediatrics. *A Gift of Love: Breast Feeding.* (1984) Publications Department, P.O. Box 927, Elk Grove Village, Illinois 60007.

A booklet from the American Academy of Pediatrics about breast-feeding.

Balter, Lawrence, with Shreve, Anita. *Dr. Balter's Child Sense: Understanding and Handling the Common Problems of Infancy and Early Childhood.* New York: Poseidon, 1985.

Another TV and radio expert who offers some good ideas. Easy reading.

Brazelton, T. Berry. *On Becoming a Family: The Growth of Attachment.* New York: Delacorte, 1981.

A beautifully written, easy-to-read-book about newborns and attachment under favorable conditions, and when there is a problem like prematurity.

————. *Infants and Mothers: Differences in Development.* New York: Dell, 1983.

A neat book which traces the development and care giver interactions of three different babies ("average," "quiet," and "active") through the first year of life. Interesting reading (and a few good hints) about parenting different ways with different babies.

Brewster, Dorothy Patricia, *You Can Breastfeed Your Baby . . . Even in Special Situations.* Emmaus Pa., Rodale Press, 1979.

A very comprehensive and helpful book, including suggestions for travel, work, maternal or infant illness, twins, prematures, etc.

Burck, Frances Wells. *Babysense.* New York: St. Martin's Press, 1979.

Another baby book using hints supplied by five hundred parents. Great section on baby toys you can make at home.

Eagan, Andrea Boroff. *The Newborn Mother: Stages of Her Growth.* Boston: Little, Brown, 1985.

An analysis of the process by which a woman becomes a mother—after the birth of the baby. Vignettes of new parents make interesting reading.

Gesell, Arnold. *The First Five Years of Life: The Preschool Years*. New York: Harper, 1940.

Although this Gesell book is out of print, it is worth a trip to the library. Wonderful, informative reading.

Kelly, Paula, ed. *First-Year Baby Care*. Deephaven, Minn.: Meadowbrook Press, 1983.

Excellent photos and illustrations to show you how to care for your new baby. Worth looking at.

La Leche League. *The Womanly Art of Breast-feeding*, 3rd ed. New York: New American Library, 1983.

The classic book of breast-feeding. Supported by an international organization, with chapters in many cities, providing individual and group support to breast-feeding mothers.

Messenger, Màire. *The Breastfeeding Book*. New York: Van Nostrand, 1982.

A recent British book on breast-feeding. Well written and nicely illustrated.

Pryor, Karen. *Nursing Your Baby*, 2nd ed. New York: Pocket Books, 1974.

A revised edition of a classic, basic, beautifully written guide.

Stern, Loraine, and Mackay, Kathleen. *Off to a Great Start!: How to Relax and Enjoy Your Baby*. New York: Norton, 1986.

Another book to help you get started.

Stoppard, Miriam. *Day-by-Day Baby Care Book: An Owner's Manual for the First Three Years*. New York: Ballantine, 1985.

A truly comprehensive, fully illustrated, step-by-step handbook on a range of child care activities from infancy to age three. This very good book examines everything from equipment, clothing, holding, and handling, to aspects of development.

White, Burton L. *The First Three Years of Life*. Revised ed. New York: Prentice-Hall, 1985.

A comprehensive summary of Dr. White's extensive research on children in the first three years of life. The book is organized around aspects of the young child's environment which White has bound to the development of competence in relating to the world. Readable language.

*   *   *

La Leche League International, P.O. Box 1209, Franklin Park, Ill.: 60131-8209; Phone 312-455-7730.

Self-Help Center, 1600 Dodge Avenue, Evanston, Ill.: 60201; Phone 312-328-0470.

Provides referrals to a variety of self-help groups for people with problems in common around the country.

10

GETTING SETTLED:
THE FIRST WEEKS
(UP TO 12 WEEKS)

Scope of Chapter

This chapter discusses babies from one to twelve weeks old. It deals with the process of getting settled down with the baby. You are now dealing with parenting the "arm baby" as the old southern expression goes.

Introduction

The first three months of life after birth are sometimes referred to as the "fourth trimester of pregnancy." In the first weeks after birth, infants are still very much newborns. But by the end of three months they are *babies!* It takes about twelve weeks for the average healthy newborn to make the transition. Parents make the parallel transition of settling into life with a baby and a baby-led routine. But in between birth and three months or so, almost anything can happen!

By now, you know how to pick up the baby, how to feed and burp, how to put diapers on and take them off, how to clean the baby's behind, and how to put the baby down to sleep. But just learning how to do these things may have taken all of your time and energy up until now. Getting settled is the stage of getting these activities into some routine and beginning to integrate baby care with the rest of your life.

On the baby's side, learning how to nurse, sleep, wake, cry, and regulate breathing and temperature—in short, learning how to achieve some homeostasis (or stability of the baby's internal environment) with your assistance—was also a full-time job. During the getting-settled stage, babies spend more time awake, even when not crying or feeding. This is the quiet-alert state we talked about on p. 321, in which babies can respond socially to you and the world.

During the first three months, the *tasks* of baby care become more and more familiar and automatic. *Play* with the baby becomes an increasingly important and varied part of parenting, as the baby becomes more responsive. There are lots of exciting "firsts": smiles, gurgles, laughter, and communicative sounds

348							CHILD CARE/PARENT CARE

and gestures. You will start providing toys and using objects in the environment as toys, though you are still the baby's most important toy!

With a few very easy babies, parents get settled almost as soon as they get started. With more difficult babies one may despair of *ever* getting settled! But with the average baby, the first three months are a time of increasing parental comfort with parenting.

KEY INFORMATION

Biophysical Information

SIZE AND SHAPE

The most important aspect of growth in this stage is a steady gain of weight. The average weight gain is a little over 1 ounce per day, or about 2 pounds per month. Birth weight is usually regained by ten days, and is usually doubled by three to five months. So a baby who weighed 7 pounds at birth would be expected to weigh about 9 pounds at one month; and about 13 pounds at three months. See Table 40 for weight and length ranges.

TABLE 40

AVERAGE WEIGHT AND HEIGHT TABLE

	Average Weight in Pounds	Range	Average Height in Inches	Range
Age Four Weeks				
Boys	10.0	8.5–11.5	21.2	20.2–22.2
Girls	9.7	8.0–11.0	21.0	20.2–22.0
Age Eight Weeks				
Boys	11.5	10.0–13.2	22.5	21.5–23.5
Girls	11.0	9.5–12.5	22.2	21.5–23.2
Age Twelve Weeks				
Boys	12.6	11.1–14.5	23.8	22.8–24.7
Girls	12.4	10.7–14.0	23.4	22.4–24.3

The head circumference grows about 1/2 inch per month. By twelve weeks, 96 percent of both girls and boys have a head circumference between 14.4 and 16.4 inches. A head much larger than this, or one that is enlarging more rapidly, should be checked immediately for possible hydrocephalus. This is rare but in many cases the sooner diagnosed, the more effectively treated. The anterior fontanel (front soft spot) may enlarge for the first few months, but the posterior one (back soft spot) closes. This process is usually completed by about four months. The average chest circumference is 16.2 inches, or only slightly larger than the head.

The baby's posture is "growing up" too. In the early weeks the head is in the midline. By about four weeks, as the baby begins to rest with the head turned to the side, the hands are now held loosely clinched or open.

BODY FUNCTION

Reflexes. The Moro (startle) reflex is still present. Sudden sounds will cause the baby to "jump" and "clutch up" with all four limbs. This response takes a different form if it is evoked while pulling gently on the infant's hands. When both the Moro and palmar grasp reflexes are evoked at the same time, the infant grasps and clings with hands, arms, and legs—just what an infant monkey would do while clinging to its mother if some sudden movement threatened dislodgment.[1]

The tonic neck reflex or "fencing" reflex will begin to fade at about eight weeks. If you turn the baby's head, the baby extends the arm on the side the head is turned to, and bends the opposite arm. The tight grasp reflex which was present at birth is also beginning to fade by twelve weeks and voluntary grasp control replaces reflex grasping. This makes it possible for the baby to hold a rattle or your finger—a big delight for parents as well as babies.

The stepping reflex is still present and the baby will "walk" or "step" when supported by arms with feet against a firm surface. The rooting and sucking reflexes persist but by twelve weeks are beginning to fade, as sucking is more under the baby's voluntary control.

Smell and taste. By a few days of age, the baby can discriminate the smell and taste of its mother and its mother's milk, and the smell of other familiar persons. The baby may notice taste changes in the breast milk when the mother has eaten strongly flavored foods.

Hearing. From birth, babies are often calmed by repetitive, rhythmic sounds: heartbeats, motors (car, air conditioner or fan), and soft soothing music like lullabies. Conversely, in the early weeks, though hearing is quite good, a sleeping baby apparently is able to ignore sounds which will wake an older child. In the first month, while awake, the baby may learn to distinguish one or a few people by their voices. In the second month, babies show obvious interest in sounds, and in the third month, respond to them with their own sounds.

Seeing. Newborns can focus their eyes at close range, usually about eight inches, preferring to focus on the human face from birth. The closeness of this range encourages you to bring your face close to the baby's. By two months babies will look at moving objects or people. By about three months babies can visually track a slow-moving object, explore a room with their eyes, and search for the source of a sound. Babies show preferences for colors and brightness. Normal infants are occasionally "cross-eyed" (that is, not coordinating eye movements) for brief periods at first. This doesn't require any evaluation unless it is frequent and persistent after the first several months.

Activity. In the first month, most babies sleep a lot and are alert for only a few brief spells each day.[2] By two months a sleep pattern begins to emerge, and by six to eight weeks babies usually sleep for longer periods at night than during the day. While awake the length of their quiet-alert periods increases steadily, up to forty-five minutes at a time by three months. This vastly increases play opportunities, both alone and with others.

Immune System. This system's function is increasing rapidly, but during the early part of this period is still immature.

MOTOR SKILLS

Head control develops rapidly. In the first month, babies can lift their heads very briefly when lying on the stomach, but otherwise they have no head control. In the second month, they can raise their heads for longer periods and have a little unsteady head control in a sitting position. By three months they can easily lift their heads while lying on their stomachs and sit supported for a few minutes with good head control. Thus they become a "lap baby" not just an "arm baby."

Hand control. From the first month, some babies comfort themselves by mouthing and sucking fists and fingers; in fact many do this before birth. In the second month, grasp control begins and they become able to hold an object for a few minutes. By the third month, they usually reach for objects with both hands and feet and bat or swipe at interesting objects within reach to see if they move.

Body control comes a little more slowly, but by two months many babies can turn from side to side—and thus could roll off a bed or table. A very few are precocious in rolling over and can surprise you by falling. Thus use of a restraint or a barrier from the *beginning* is an important safety habit.

Language/Cognitive Skills

Young babies respond to attention by smiling, cooing, and active movements of the arms and legs, from about two months on. Usually the baby smiles at you by four weeks and by about twelve weeks smiles spontaneously. Babies begin to link listening and looking, and show curiosity by active exploration with eyes, hands, and mouth at two to three months. Babies also begin to be able to entertain themselves for brief periods, watching their own hand movements for example.

Body language increases rapidly over the second and third months. Babies, with increasing skill, will catch your eye, smile, wiggle, and arch their bodies toward when you lift them. When held in your arms, they don't just lie there but rather actively "mold" their bodies into yours, as though at one with you. Mahler calls this the stage of infantile symbiosis in which she believes that the baby feels the care giver and self are like two halves of one whole being.[3]

Different behavior systems become coordinated: eye and hand, for example. Babies start intense looking, at parents, at other moving objects, and at patterns. Looking and searching replace passive watching. They develop complex ear-eye-head-turning responses to sounds. Infants use gestures and body language in a communicative way before they can communicate with words.

Speech begins with gurgling sounds, and playing with sounds made with saliva in the first month or two. Babies make vowel sounds like "oo" at around eight weeks, then "bubble sounds." The first consonant is usually "mm." By around twelve weeks babies produce socially responsive cries and sounds. The average baby begins to recognize that crying gets a response, and thus begins to control the social environment. In fact the baby now may begin with only a gentle whine or whimper, and save full-blown crying for times when the earlier signal isn't responded to promptly.

Social Skills

At this age social skills are very closely linked to the development of language. Long before babies learn specific words, they learn the social contour of a conversation. They catch your eyes, make a sound, stop while you make sounds, then resume babbling in "reply."

Babies seem to differentiate familiar voices from those of strangers by two months. They respond preferentially to the female voice rather than the male from birth. Both women and men often use a special high pitched voice and exaggerated inflections with babies that they don't use for other people. Babies form special relationships with primary care givers by two to three months as by then they can associate people with certain events (like mother with breast-feeding, father with his own characteristic kinds of care and play, siblings with their own kinds of play).

Hearty laughter, especially in response to tickling, can be seen by three months. Smiling and laughing are usually enormously pleasurable to care givers. These responses give you a feeling that your baby is happy, which makes the work of care-giving more rewarding and strengthens your falling in love with the baby.

Over the next few months you can expect increasing exploration of produced and receptive sounds and more frequent giggling and laughter.

Emotions/Feelings

Babies begin to display different emotions and moods by two to three months. They use clearly different cries and movements for different needs; show fear, not just a startle reflex, in response to loud noises or falling; show rage in response to strong discomfort or frustration; and learn to direct the care-giving environment by purposeful cries and noises.

When mothers were asked to keep a "crying" diary for three months, crying per twenty-four hours averaged sixty-one minutes at one week and rose to eighty-four minutes at five weeks, but declined to forty-two minutes by thirteen weeks. Crying was related to "motor maturity" and mother's description of infant fussiness.[4] Thus, normal babies *do* cry. However, even at the rate of one and a half hours per twenty-four hours, you have twenty-two and a half hours of non-crying baby.

The baby's temperament is the single most important factor in how readily the baby and the household get settled.[5] Some babies are placid and therefore "easy." They feed with few problems, fall asleep easily, wake when they are hungry again, and do relatively little fussing in between.

Other babies are more "difficult." They can't quite get their act together about feeding, they fall asleep before they've had enough milk, wake again soon, or seem to fight sleeping. They have trouble adjusting their biological rhythms to the environment. Still others are "slow to warm up"—withdrawing from new stimuli but adjusting well after more experience. Leach describes "miserable babies," "jumpy babies," "sleepy babies," and "wakeful babies" as four kinds who are hard to settle down.[6] She recommends extra stimulation for the sleepy baby, and a slow, unstartling approach for the jumpy baby. Both the wakeful baby and the miserable baby need lots of human contact—in a Snugli awake or asleep for the miserable baby, and being around someone rather than left in a crib for the wakeful one.

There was a time when pediatricians and psychiatrists thought that anxious mothers caused babies' difficulties in getting settled. But now we recognize that it's more likely to be the other way around. Obviously a few weeks of walking the floor night and day, trying to console a difficult, colicky, or inconsolable baby, is enough to make any parent anxious and irritable.

We still don't know what causes these differences in babies' temperaments, but we do know that there are genetic factors in temperament. Parents who were hyperactive as children, light sleepers, late to achieve bladder control—are all more likely to have children with the same pattern. All of these traits are different aspects of adjusting biorhythms to the environment. Different babies, like different adults, adjust at different rates and with different degrees of ease. A child can be slow in one aspect of development and average or advanced in other areas.

About one fifth of small infants have *colic*. They demonstrate continuous loud crying for many hours, usually late in the day, with drawn-up feet and evidence of abdominal distress. Sometimes the face is flushed. Often the baby does *not* stop crying when picked up. The causes aren't always clear, but it can result from cow's milk allergy. This wasn't previously recognized because breast-fed babies get colic as well as those fed formula. But recent studies have shown that cow's milk in the *mother's* diet may be associated with colic in the baby.[7,8] Colic went away in half the babies of the mothers who gave up cow's milk for a week (and returned in two thirds of the babies if the mothers resumed drinking milk).

Mothers with a colicky breast-fed baby and a family history of allergies should avoid eating common allergens, such as cow's milk, wheat, eggs, and peanuts, and any food to which she or any immediate member of the family may be allergic. Temporary colic can be observed in some breast-fed infants after their mothers eat such foods as garlic, onions, cabbage, turnips, broccoli, beans, rhubarb, apricots, and prunes. If you have a difficult or colicky baby, it is worth exploring dietary adjustments. Of course, if cow's milk is eliminated from the mother's diet, other calcium sources are needed; it's possible that milk processed as cheese or yogurt can be tolerated. Colic after feeding has also been related to parental smoking.[9]

Colicky or "difficult" babies can be soothed by other means also. No medications really work in colic. You can try frequent burping, walking the baby, rocking, or long drives in a car (don't forget the car seat). A dark, quiet room for the baby, with soft music, may help. A bottle-fed baby may need smaller holes in the rubber nipple, to prevent overly rapid gulping. Some recommend liberal use of the Snugli-type carrier, a windup swing (be sure you get a safe one and stop using it when the baby grows out of it), massaging or rubbing the baby's tummy, and laying the baby on your lap on a hot water bottle covered with a towel (be sure the baby cannot get burned).[10] In any case, remember that this stage will pass. In one study colic lasted an average of nine weeks and was over in three fourths of the babies by three months, in almost all by four months.

In one study crying in colicky infants actually decreased to the levels of crying in non-colicky infant controls when parents were taught appropriate responses to the infants' crying.[11] The most important advice to parents was *not* to let the baby cry but rather to pick the baby up and ascertain why the baby is crying (hunger, need to be held, boredom, fatigue).

If you do have a difficult baby, for whatever reason, and the tension is getting to you, you need some respite. Get someone else to care for the baby for at least an hour or two every day, maybe even twice a day. Get out of the house or away from the baby by taking a walk or a break of some sort. You can try to get friends or relatives to take the baby to their house while you have a nap. Pay attention to your own needs. Get respite *before* you get to the point of resentment and anger at the baby.

If you really feel you are at the end of your rope, GET HELP! You can't leave an infant alone in the house but if you must get some rest or relief and can't find a relative or friend to help, call your pastor or pediatrician. If you are really about to explode, call Child Protective Services and *tell them so.*

Remember that if you have a baby with an easy temperament, it's likely to continue. But if you have a baby with a difficult temperament, it will require more time to get settled. But the early difficulties *will end,* usually by three months. You will be able to get uninterrupted sleep and get on with your life.

Babies who have colic experience a great deal of distress from it—and transmit that distress very clearly to parents. Remember, even if your attempts at soothing do not succeed, the baby at least will see that the care giver cares.

With babies, as with most adults, being alone in distress is more terrifying than being with someone who tries to comfort.

Developmental Warning Signals

If the baby at three months doesn't react to sudden noises, doesn't appear to listen to your voice or try to find the speaker's face with the eyes, this is developmental delay. Inability to fix the eyes and follow a moving object within nine to twelve inches also deserves prompt evaluation. Children with impaired vision or hearing may suffer greatly during the phase of active sensorimotor learning. Also, if the baby does not raise the head while lying on the stomach or has no head control when held, this must be called to the doctor's attention.[12]

CARE GIVER TASKS

Basic Care

FEEDING/NUTRITION

BREAST-FEEDING

If you are breast-feeding and your milk is forming copiously and letting-down easily, and the baby takes it skillfully, the two of you are already well started. Don't be discouraged if this process takes longer than a week, however! It's quite normal to take up to three weeks for the process to get going and two to three months before you feel like a real expert.

A prolonged starting phase is especially common with first babies, thin-skinned fair women (who may have more initial nipple problems), and mothers who for whatever reason are experiencing stress or anxiety which can interfere with milk let-down.

If things aren't yet going smoothly, refer back to the section on breast-feeding in the last chapter and to some of the books and resources recommended there. Get support and suggestions from experienced successful breast-feeding mothers. La Leche League can help you make contacts if you don't have friends and relatives to encourage you. Avoid giving up too easily and using supplemental bottles or pacifiers before nursing is well established. However, if you did give up during the stress of the immediate postpartum period, and then regret it, the milk supply can sometimes be restarted. Get one of the good books covering the subject (e.g., Brewster[13] or Pryor[14]), get support from a La Leche leader experienced in relactation, and work closely with a pediatrician who will both support your efforts and be sure that the baby is getting enough nutrition during the initial phases.

A surge in appetite and increased frequency of demand for feeding is common at two to three weeks. The baby is now well stabilized after the birth experience and already beginning to increase alertness. Some breast-fed babies will demand feeding as often as hourly during much of the day. Going along with this is the quickest way to increase your milk supply to match the baby's increasing needs.

Most babies who are fed when they seek feeding will soon begin to settle into at least some approximation of a schedule, but it won't necessarily be very regular. Breast-fed babies usually want feeding every one and a half to three hours at first since breast milk is very quickly digested and absorbed. (Bottle-fed babies usually feed at longer intervals since formula is not digested as quickly as human milk.) Feeding when the baby wants it is easy and natural. But if the care giver needs or prefers a more predictable schedule, by two to three months most babies can be eased into a three- or four-hour schedule. The comfortable way to do this is gradually. Always pick a crying baby up. A baby who wakes and cries very soon after a feeding may need more burping rather than more milk. Try a little walking, rocking, or play before immediate feeding. A baby who sleeps more than five hours during the day can be gently awakened and will usually take some milk when fully awake, and after a little walking, talking, and play. Babies wake and want at least one nighttime feeding for at least three to five months. If you want to get your own sleep, you can often ease the baby into your schedule by waking the baby at 11 or 12 P.M., just before you go to bed.

There is now evidence that exclusively breast-fed babies may have significantly slower rates of growth than bottle-fed babies.[15] Health and absence of infection may be more important than rapid growth, but we want to point out that if your baby is not gaining weight, loses weight, or appears not to be growing to you, tell the doctor. Although rare, some exclusively breast-fed babies do not get enough nutrition.

Early Weaning. If you are a mother planning transitional nursing with early weaning, the baby will have received most of your colostrum by now, and you can start phasing in formula in whatever schedule is convenient—for example, night feedings at first, or alternate feedings. Soon you can breast-feed briefly after a bottle feeding. The baby should take just enough milk to reduce any painful engorgement and the remaining fullness in your breasts will give them the signal to produce less milk until it eventually stops as in any weaning. But don't be surprised if you enjoy nursing so much that you change your mind, nor feel guilty if you stick to your original plan.

BOTTLE-FEEDING

If you are bottle-feeding, you and the baby probably have your feeding techniques well mastered. Getting settled will involve a gradual increase in the amount the baby takes at any feeding, and a gradual decrease in the frequency with which the baby insists on feeding.

Many parents do not continue using prepared disposable formula bottles after the getting started period as they are much more expensive than concentrated or prepared formula. Formulas made at home from condensed milk are the cheapest of all, but are so much more work that few find it worth the savings, especially since the result is a poor imitation of human milk.

Undoubtedly you will have discussed which brand of formula to use with your baby's doctor. Most of the standard brands are based on cow's milk which has been modified to make it more similar to human milk in its basic composition. Infant formulas based on goat's milk or soybean "milk" are also available. These are more expensive, and most doctors will not recommend them unless the baby seems to be poorly tolerating cow's milk-based formula, or unless there is a strong family history of allergies to cow's milk.

Most formulas are fortified with iron and vitamins. It is important to discuss with the same doctor which formula you will choose and which if any vitamin drops you will give, to avoid overdosing or underdosing with vitamins. If you have to change brands for a few feedings (say because your grocery or drugstore was out of your usual brand) there is no cause for concern. But if you permanently change brands you should be sure that the formula and any vitamin drops you are using are complementary.

Read the label carefully to ensure that you know whether you have purchased the full-strength formula (needing no added water), the concentrated form (usually needs to be mixed half and half with water), or the powdered form (usually needs the contents of a scoop which is provided for each eight-ounce bottle of water). It's very important to measure accurately and not guess at the amounts, since infant kidneys cannot handle formula which is too concentrated. Conversely, thinning the formula too much will result in malnutrition.

Most doctors no longer recommend sterilization of water in formula. You must be sure that the water supply is safe and that you always scrub the bottles and nipples with hot soapy water and that you make up only one bottle at a time. Also, never leave unused formula in the bottle until you can get around to washing it. Always pour it out, fill the bottle with cold water, and let stand. When you have time, do the scrubbing.

All you have to do is mix tap water and concentrated or powdered formula in a clean bottle. A clean bottle is one which has been scrubbed (bottle brush) with soap and hot water. Some mothers like to scrub first and then put bottles through the dishwasher cycle. Nipples do not go in the dishwasher. You can also use disposable bottles which are sterile and time-saving.

Formula which is in an unopened container is sterilized and therefore does not require refrigeration. Opened cans of powdered formula do not require refrigeration if you are careful not to let anything which is not sterile into the powder. If you keep the scoop in the can, wash your hands before handling it. If you keep it outside the can or use a tablespoon, wash the spoon or scoop carefully with soap and hot water. Formula which has been made up by adding concentrate to water needs to be refrigerated if it is not taken right away. If the baby has taken part of a bottle and not finished it, the remaining milk can be refrigerated and offered at the next feeding, but should be discarded if it is not taken at that time.

Prepared formula, like expressed breast milk, keeps fresh for only a short time at room temperature, twenty-four hours if refrigerated, less if in a thermos or insulated travel container. If you are traveling, it's safest to take prepackaged single-bottle feedings.

Choice of bottles and nipples. Glass or plastic bottles must be scrubbed each time they are used, and glass can break. It's slightly more expensive, but easier, to use presterilized plastic inserts which slip into a bottle-like container. Then you need only scrub the nipples in hot, soapy water. The Nuk and Playtex types of nipples are designed to give the baby's mouth a nipple shape more closely resembling the breast.

Warming of bottles. Most of you will make up one bottle at a time and feed it directly to the baby. Those of you who are making a batch of formula will have to refrigerate the day's supply of bottles. Refrigerated formula is customarily warmed by placing it in a pan of hot or boiling water for several minutes. Shake and test temperature by putting a drop on your wrist. If it feels cold, it needs more heating; if it feels more than the slightest bit warm, you have overheated it and need to cool it by placing it in a pan of cold water. In your first tries you will overshoot, but with a little practice, if you always use the same pan with the same amount of water, you will be able to estimate how many minutes of warming are needed. You can also hold the bottle under hot tap water to take the chill off. Some babies don't seem to mind being given cold formula right from the refrigerator. If yours accepts it and seems comfortable, obviously this is a great timesaver. Prepackaged unopened bottles can be given at room temperature. You need only add a clean nipple.

Solid Foods

Adding solid foods in the first three months of life was a fad that has largely been discarded. It was based on the idea that babies might sleep longer after a feeding if their stomachs were fuller. It is now recognized that early addition of solid foods gains nothing and risks causing iron-deficiency anemia and allergies. Also, small babies don't have the muscular coordination to refuse unwanted food, except by extrusion. Force-feeding is not a happy way to start feeding. The simplest advice is to add no solid food until the baby is big enough to sit in your lap at the table and reach for it. This occurs at around five to six months, definitely after the getting settled period is over.

Vitamins and Minerals

Vitamin and mineral supplements are added to infant formulas and the question arises whether breast-fed babies need them also. Virtually all writers on the subject emphasize that the milk of healthy well-nourished mothers is all that *most* babies need. Anything else is a precaution, and the importance of precautionary supplements has been controversial. Iron, vitamin D, and fluoride have been the main issues, as well as vitamin B_{12} for vegetarian mothers.

Iron deficiency is rare in breast-fed babies because iron is more readily absorbed from breast milk. Formulas based on cow's milk cause microscopic blood loss into the gastrointestinal tract, so extra iron is added to these formulas to compensate. If you give both breast milk *and* supplemental formula or solid foods in the early months, your baby may need added iron because the proportion of iron added to formulas is based on the assumption that the baby is entirely formula-fed. Thus solid food or supplemental formula could cause some blood loss without providing enough iron to fully compensate for it. Infant multivitamin drops with iron are also needed if you make formula at home from condensed milk.

Human milk has low levels of vitamin D, though higher than previously recognized. (It is carried predominantly in the watery rather than fatty portion of the milk where researchers first looked for what is normally a fat-soluble vitamin.) In tropical climates, babies, like mothers, make their own vitamin D when they are exposed to the sun. In northern climates, a few breast-fed babies become deficient and develop rickets.

The American Academy of Pediatrics recommends precautionary vitamin D supplementation for breast-fed infants, since they occasionally get rickets.[16] There is great variability of vitamin D content in breast milk and the efficacy of supplementing the mother's diet rather than the baby's has not been proven or disproven. The combination of greatest risk for developing rickets is the coupling of a mother with low vitamin D levels, a baby with dark skin, and little exposure to sunlight. There's some question about whether to supplement *all* babies for something a *few* may need. Anne didn't bother; Marilyn did and always prescribes supplementation with vitamins for breast-fed babies as the American Academy of Pediatrics recommends. She feels to take the risk of rickets today is either silly or sinful, depending on your point of view.

Fluoride levels measured in human milk are low. Since tooth decay is one of our most prevalent childhood diseases, the AAP has recommended fluoride supplementation in breast-fed babies from birth, while noting that one can just as well wait until six months.[17] The latter seems more natural, since by six months a child may be taking some solid food and drinking more water. Many breast-fed infants have done without fluoride supplementation and have had no adverse dental problems, but the decision about whether to supplement should be made individually, based on family dental history and on the local level of fluoride in the water. Marilyn recommends fluoride drops from birth in breast-fed babies.

CLEANING/GROOMING

Skin care is important for babies. It will be quite a while before they can wash themselves, or even let you know where their skin hurts or itches. The navel, the diaper area, and the scalp need special attention.

NAVEL CARE

The dried umbilical stump usually drops off in about ten days. After the cord falls off, clean the stump with a little rubbing alcohol. A slight amount of bleeding is no problem. Some babies' navels (like some adults) are "outers," which protrude; others are "inners," which retract. An "inner" can collect discarded skin cells, which sometimes become green, gooey, and infected at first. Very gentle wiping with rubbing alcohol on a Q-tip should help remove this material. Avoid bathing the area and keep it dry until complete healing has occurred. A few babies develop a granuloma of the navel. This is an accumulation of heavy, red scar tissue which looks like a serious wound but isn't. A pediatrician can easily remove it with silver nitrate. After the navel heals, it needs no more or less care than adult navels do, that is, virtually none.

THE DIAPER AREA

Careful cleaning after every stool is important to prevent diaper rash. (See p. 334.) Babies vary a lot in how much a dirty diaper bothers them. At this age, most don't seem to notice unless there is a diaper rash, or the stool is irritating (as sometimes happens after introducing a new food when you start doing that), or the sheets and clothing are wet and clammy. A baby who is uncomfortable will fuss. There is no need to wake a sleeping baby for a diaper change unless you are changing frequently to treat a diaper rash.

Until the penis of the circumcised baby is healed, apply Vaseline with each diaper change. After it heals don't bother.

BATHING AND SKIN CARE

How often to bathe? Every day, if you enjoy it and the baby does—it's a great form of play. If you don't have time, or if you or the baby don't enjoy it, babies don't need a daily bath. They need bathing when they look or smell dirty. Some babies with sensitive skins may even be irritated by daily removal of the natural skin oils. This is more often seen in families with light hair and eyes and a tendency to easy sunburning and dry skin. If you and your family fit that description, and your baby's skin is dry, bathe the baby less often. Try rinsing only, without using soap, especially in winter when indoor air is dry. Or rinse with water and cotton balls only the face, neck creases, hands, and diaper area— a process Leach calls "topping and tailing."[18]

A baby who looks or smells dirty or sour clearly needs to be rinsed or bathed. Anne didn't start bathing her entirely breast-fed third child until he began solid food at around eight months. Then his smell changed, and it was obvious he needed bathing. Before that time, she used baby lotion on a soft tissue to rinse off the diaper area, face, and the creases around the neck. He was the only one of her three children who never had any diaper rash, prickly heat, or other skin problems. Marilyn's babies were bathed daily—a source of great pleasure for Marilyn, her husband, and the children.

When to bathe? In a few weeks, many babies will develop an alert period before or after a midmorning feeding, when they enjoy play and attention. This is a good time for a bath. Some families prefer an evening bath time so both parents can participate, and some mothers who are employed outside the home enjoy an evening bath ritual as a special time with the baby.

Where to bathe the baby? A Bathinette, an infant bathtub on a changing table or kitchen counter, or the kitchen sink: all will do. You can fit a sponge into the tub or sink to make it more comfortable. The Gerry Company produces a special infant tub which holds the infant in a semireclining position, with the head entirely out of the water. You can also give a sponge bath on your lap (using a waterproof apron to protect your clothing), or you can use the same surface you use for diaper changing for a sponge bath. Don't use an adult bathtub. It is too dangerous and difficult for an infant unless you are in the tub with the baby, in shallow water (one to two inches).

How to bathe? Assemble everything you need before you start, since you can't safely leave the baby in water for even a second. Babies should be the last thing to put in the water and the first thing to take out. As a precaution, put an extra towel on the floor, so that if you have to leave the baby for a moment, you can place the baby on the floor where there is no risk of a fall. Make a decision in advance whether you will answer or ignore the phone or doorbell, so that you won't have to be flustered deciding what to do if there is a ring.

You'll need a couple of towels, a washcloth, and soap or shampoo if you are using them. Get out the clean diapers and clothes with which you'll dress the baby, and the baby lotion if you use it.

Powder is no longer recommended. Its purpose was to keep the diaper area dry—which is better accomplished by giving the baby some undiapered "air time" when needed. Powder is easily inhaled, and can do serious damage to infant lungs.

The room in which the baby is bathed should be comfortably warm and not drafty. The water should be a bit warmer than body temperature. Babies do not tolerate as wide a range of bath temperatures as we do. The temperature should feel comfortably warm to your elbow (not your hand, which may be accustomed to hotter water).

The slipperiness of a wet baby is the hardest thing for inexperienced baby-bathers to get used to. But you can maintain a reliable grip by resting the baby's head on your left wrist and forearm (if right-handed) and gripping the baby's left shoulder between your thumb (on the baby's shoulder) and your fingers (in the baby's armpit). If this doesn't feel natural to you, practice with a dry baby until you find it easy, before trying it on a wet and slippery one! Or get an experienced baby-bather to show you. If you feel uneasy at first with trying to bathe a new baby, your baby can certainly get by with sponge bathing of the diaper area and skin folds, until you become more used to handling the baby or can get someone to help you with first baths. A towel in the tub also helps prevent slipping.

Shampooing as a special routine isn't usually necessary during the early months, except for those babies with very thick hair. The scalp can be sponged with a wet washcloth like the rest of the skin. Some babies develop cradle cap, a thick, oily, crusty-appearing form of infant dandruff. This is absolutely harmless and in most cases will go away by itself as the baby's skin gets more used to extrauterine life. Washing with mild soap and water on a soft terry washcloth will remove the looser flakes. Don't hesitate to shampoo a crusted scalp as vigorously as you would your own—but don't use fingernails to remove the flakes. Your baby will let you know by squirming or crying if your rubbing is so strong that it is uncomfortable—most of them like it.

FINGERNAILS AND TOENAILS

The newborn's tiny adorable fingernails are so thin that they are very sharp. Early arm movements are clumsy and babies often scratch their faces—some even do this before birth. But babies dislike being held still for nail-clipping. The easiest way is to clip the nails while the baby sleeps, using an ordinary adult nail clipper which will not easily cut skin, or a pair of special baby nail scissors. Since even the cut surface of these tiny nails can be sharp, nightgowns with flip-over mittens may be needed during the early weeks. Or you can pin infant socks to the sleeves of any garment, temporarily. In just a few weeks, babies coordinate sensory and motor skills enough to stop scratching themselves.

CLOTHING

The getting settled period continues to be a time to keep things simple. Babies this age are growing rapidly, so stretchable knit sleepwear and undershirts, in a six-month or even one-year size, will soon fit. Ease of washing and changing clothes are the main considerations. You'll need light sweaters if the room is cool, or for going out in the summer. In the winter blankets or buntings are much easier than fitted garments.

SLEEP/ACTIVITY

During the getting settled period, sleep rhythms are closely related to feeding rhythms. The newborn feeds, burps, and usually falls asleep quite easily—in your arms, by your side, or in a crib or carriage. Light and noise and external events continue to make little difference during this period for most babies.

Newborns sleep a lot and are alert for only a few brief spells each day. By two months a sleep pattern begins to emerge, and by six to eight weeks babies usually sleep for longer periods at night than during the day. While awake, the length of their "quiet-alert" periods increases steadily, up to forty-five minutes at a time by three months. This vastly increases play opportunities, both alone and with others.

Over the first three months, alert periods develop during which the baby is neither feeding nor sleeping nor crying, but awake and open to play. When feeding is no longer the stimulus for sleep, the baby begins to experience fatigue as a separate state. After an alert period, instead of drifting off to sleep, the baby may become fussy and start to cry. It takes experience and some experimentation with your own baby to tell when crying means hunger and a need for more feeding or when it means fatigue and a need for rocking or singing or cuddling and massage to ease the transition to sleep. Infants do not always know when they are tired. They may fight sleep, just like many older children and even adults.

An old saying has it: "Babies cry for four reasons, two at each end. They need feeding or burping, or have a dirty diaper or a diaper pin sticking them." But some crying is not easily explainable. Some babies cry out of boredom and frustration. They have finished feeding, but are not ready to go back to sleep. They want to play but have insufficient means to do so alone. Babies are only just learning self-entertainment and, at least before discovering the thumb, may need social interaction for entertainment and learning.

"Fussiness" typically increases between two and six weeks from almost an hour to three hours a day. This can be a point of despair for care givers but it's reassuring to see it as an achievement. It is a sign of the baby's increasing wakefulness and need for stimulation. This is a good time to bring out the Snugli, or infant seat, and get the baby involved in daily activities. The crying infant should be picked up, played with, or engaged in some activity.

There used to be a widespread belief that babies should be "trained" to be quiet by allowing them to "cry it out," but this is nonsense. You can't spoil a baby. In fact, everything generally referred to as spoiling is just what the baby needs. Infants whose cries are responded to very promptly cry less often and less long than those who are forced to cry it out. And they learn more about their environment.[19] When fussiness comes from boredom, picking them up gives them more of an opportunity to observe a changing environment. Increased carrying actually reduces infant crying.[20]

When fussiness results from fatigue, the baby may need help in inducing sleep. Rhythmic motion and noises are soothing to many babies (and older children). Walking the baby, rocking, rhythmic massage, a car ride, music, the hum of a fan or air conditioner, are all methods which have been accidentally or purposefully used to lull babies into sleep. Be careful of overly cool drafts on the baby with fans or air conditioners. These methods don't always work, but are worth trying.

After prolonged crying, babies will eventually fall asleep from sheer exhaustion, but doing this regularly leads the baby to associate sleep with unpleasant rather than comfortable bodily states. Trying to comfort a crying baby feels more natural to most parents than letting the baby cry it out alone. Nevertheless, if occasionally you are unable to comfort a tired baby by any of these methods, you may just have to let the baby cry.

Regardless of what you do, sometime during the first three months or so your baby will fall into more "settled" daily rhythms of sleeping and feeding. Alert periods will naturally be longer during the daytime, because that is when you are more alert to play with the baby. Alert periods will be shorter at night-time and the baby will gradually learn to fall back to sleep alone.

Babies, like adults, do not have unbroken sleep throughout the night. Rather, they have definite sleep cycles which include brief periods of light sleep or awakening roughly every ninety minutes. Apparently a few babies learn to entertain or soothe themselves and fall back asleep without awakening parents, if they are not hungry or frightened and if wet diapers don't bother them. But don't let some parents tell you their infant "sleeps through the night." It's a myth. What they mean is their baby lets them sleep uninterrupted, by being self-sufficient about handling nighttime sleep cycles. Most likely their baby has an "easy" temperament as well.

EXERCISE

As babies become more coordinated over the first three months, they begin exercising arms, legs, and necks on their own. The fact that this is developmentally defined as the early sensorimotor period underscores the fact that sensory and intellectual growth and development are closely linked to muscular exercise now.

Eye-hand coordination gives exercise to the arms and hands also. At first, babies learn to visually follow a moving bright object. Soon they learn to bat at it with a fist or hand, and reaching to grasp it follows next. By lifting and turning their heads, babies strengthen their neck muscles. When you activate the "stepping reflex" by holding the baby upright against a bed or floor, the reflex stepping movements strengthen the legs in preparation for later voluntary stepping. When you push a hand against the sole of the baby's foot, the same reflex makes the baby push back. Gradually over the course of the first three months, the baby will smile or giggle and make a game out of this exercise if you do. In fact, almost everything that is discussed under "play" is a form of exercise for the baby.

STRESS MANAGEMENT

Stress management is relatively straightforward in the first three months. It is largely a matter of getting into a smooth routine. The main stressors are hunger, fatigue, and skin discomfort—too much heat or cold, dirty diapers, or a diaper rash.

Pacifiers, as the name implies, are the classic stress-reducer for young babies. Many babies either don't get their sucking needs satisfied by feeding, or they like the comfort of extra sucking—either of thumb or pacifier. If the baby *generally* needs more sucking in the early weeks, you can give smaller more frequent feedings and, if using bottles, try newborn nipples with tiny holes. If the baby *specifically* needs sucking at times of stress—in unfamiliar places, going to sleep, for example—pacifiers are fine after nursing is well established.

Don't put honey on pacifiers—honey can cause severe or fatal botulism in babies under a year. Don't put pacifiers on a string around the baby's neck—babies can strangle that way. The main trouble with pacifiers is that older babies can drop them, losing them or getting them dirty. As soon as the baby has enough muscle control for thumb sucking, we recommend taking the pacifier away. The thumb has a great advantage in that it can't be dropped. A thumb is an always-available form of comfort, the only one which is under the baby's own control. A baby whose thumb is *constantly* in the mouth is probably bored and needs more social stimulation—rocking, being carried around, and played with. Other than that, the baby's capacity for thumb comfort in the early months is a blessing.

Putting a baby to bed with a bottle is *not* a good substitute for thumb or pacifier. We feel strongly enough to say, "Never do it." The baby can become dependent on it for sleep. Later, when teeth come in, the drip of milk against the teeth as the baby is falling asleep leads to rapidly developing cavities and defects in tooth enamel.

EMOTIONAL "NUTRITION"

Emotional nutrition is built right into physical nutrition and body care at this age. Babies feel loved the same ways adults do from personalized attention, cuddling and other soft touching, eye contact, sweet talk, and playfulness. Cats lick their kittens in cleaning them; you caress your babies' skin with your hands, and their minds with your voices. You catch their eyes in feeding them, either at the breast, or by holding a bottle-fed baby close while feeding, as though at the breast. Most parents spontaneously speak, coo, and sing to their babies.

Consoling a distressed baby is another form of emotional nutrition, which conveys that life provides emotional as well as physical comfort. At a later age they begin to learn to comfort themselves. At this age they can get the idea of comfort only from what you do for them. The fact that you are there, and trying to help, obviously means a great deal to babies. Why else would they, over the next few months, develop the attachment that they do to their primary care givers?

CARE OF THE CARE GIVER

TAKE CARE OF YOURSELF

In most age/stage chapters this section is fairly brief. The reason it is so long here is that care giver needs are greater in the beginning. Unless you're lucky enough to have helpers, you have to take good care of yourself while getting settled, not only for your own contentment but so that you can care for your baby.

If you haven't yet worked out an easy-natural nighttime feeding routine, or if you have a baby who cries a lot, your basic recovery from birth exhaustion may be quite naturally delayed. Fathers, too, can be exhausted from the excitement of birth and loss of sleep.

Usually during the latter part of the first month you may realize just how tired you are, if excitement masked your fatigue earlier. Many mothers "crash" during this period. Almost everyone experiences heightened emotionality—either higher highs than usual, lower lows, or both. A few mothers experience a delayed version of the "baby blues" now. Fathers can also experience such feelings, particularly if they are trying hard to share in nighttime feedings, or provide the emotional support and practical help a new mother may need—and perhaps trying to do it on top of normal or even increased work commitments.

What to do about those feelings? First, don't try to fight them. As we said earlier, they are an adaptive mechanism designed to elicit help from those who are close to you. If you need to cry, cry. And try to find someone who will be emotionally and practically responsive to your tears and their sources.

Second, if you're tired, continue to go to bed with the baby and sleep when the baby does. If you're breast-feeding, this is no problem. If you're bottle-feeding, keep prepackaged sterile prepared formula bottles by the bed. Unless the bed is low to the floor or against the wall, use pillows or some other barrier so the baby won't roll over and off.

As we said earlier, don't cook. Don't wash anything, clean anything, or do anything that someone else can do for you, or that can wait, until you feel convinced that things are comfortably settled down with the baby and you are *ready* to undertake new activities or resume old ones. Take positive pleasure from this excuse for dropping other tasks.

Give yourself every opportunity to continue as much of a "honeymoon" with the new baby as possible. Some women are lucky, have easy babies and lots of energy, and don't need the above advice. If so, enjoy. We talk about the possible difficulties because the prevailing mythology makes women think they should be more independent than is reasonable. The very woman who needs extra support, help, and fussing over, may be the most vulnerable to feeling guilty about her needs.

YOUR OBSTETRICAL RECUPERATION

Although the most dramatic recuperation already has occurred during the first week or two, there remain a few issues to discuss.

Your abdomen will remain soft and large since the muscles are still stretched out. Some women enjoy, others are bitterly disappointed in, the fact that maternity clothes are more comfortable than tight-waisted ones for a while after the baby is born! In the Middle Ages, the rounded abdomen of a woman who had borne children was considered desirable and womanly. Today there is a cultural preference for flat abdomens. If your postbaby look bothers you, be assured that there are exercises which will help flatten your tummy and some degree of flattening will occur just from normal moving around in the first few months. You can do exercises if you wish to hasten the process; ask your doctor when to begin. You stored extra fat during pregnancy, as nature intended, for a reserve food source to draw on during nursing. Most women lose most of this weight within a few months.

The uterine discharge (lochia) will persist in decreasing amount, for two to four weeks. Normally it requires no attention other than the use of pads.

Because the open cervix could possibly permit uterine infection, in the past many obstetricians have recommended not resuming sexual intercourse until six weeks after birth when the cervix is normally closed. The six-week delay was advised because, though infection was rare, if it did occur in a preantibiotic era, it could be life-threatening. Nowadays, many birth attendants will recommend resuming intercourse when you feel like it, probably after the lochia has become thin and you have no further pain from episiotomy or stitches if they were done.

Kitzinger recommends a realistic approach.[21] Start lovemaking in a general affectionate and cuddling way as soon as you feel like it. Don't attempt to have intercourse at first, and don't try to *prove* anything to yourselves. Take time to have several exploratory sessions in lovemaking, until you feel ready, confident, and passionate enough to try complete intercourse. Rushing it could lead to unexpected discomfort, which would leave you tense the next time, and in turn cause more pain. If you have diminished vaginal lubrication, many writers suggest an artificial lubricant such as K-Y jelly (which is water-soluble, not Vaseline, which is greasy).

Since you have a scheduled six-week postpartum visit with your doctor, Kitzinger sensibly recommends that you try having intercourse before that visit. If you are experiencing any pain, tell your doctor where and when the pain occurred. You will need a method of contraception, probably condoms, even if you are breast-feeding. Women have been known to conceive within two or three weeks of giving birth.

THE OUTSIDE WORLD

One of the ways you can tell that things are getting settled is that it will seem natural and comfortable to rejoin the outside world. You won't think of taking the baby on visits or walks, or doing optional shopping, until things have settled down into enough of a routine that you are getting enough sleep, feel confident about providing basic care, and have caught up on whatever backlogs were created by the birth.

Some of you are now thinking about the outside world in terms of when to go back to work, others in terms of resuming social activities, some both (although it's rare in the first year to have enough time and energy for a new baby, a demanding job, *and* a full social life). New mothers' employment is more a part of what we have called Getting Going, the next chapter, than of Getting Settled. However, some women do go back to work during the first three months, particularly if it is possible to bring the baby along to work. If you are going back to work at this point, or thinking of it in the near future, you might want to reread the chapter on helpers and be thinking ahead. It can take a surprisingly long time to find competent help, and planning ahead is easier when you allow enough time. Brazelton recommends a four-month maternity leave if at all possible, so that you can fully experience the "getting settled" period as your honeymoon with your baby, and *your* achievement, not your helpers'[22] (see p. 212).

FATHER'S NEEDS

The getting settled period can be a difficult one for fathers. Many fathers today are excited about participation in birth and the first few days of the baby's life, and increasing numbers of fathers take paternity leave or vacation at this time. But during the getting settled stage, fathers are generally eager to return to life as it was before the baby and commonly return to full-time work. On his daily return home, it may be hard for the mother to tell—or the father to hear— just what kind of a day it was at home.

Some fathers feel displaced by the baby and many think that they will never have their own wife or life again. But the getting settled period is *not* a permanent way of life. It only takes around three months. The parenting marriage is different from the couple alone marriage, but it can very positively master the natural crisis of getting started and settled.

SIBLINGS' NEEDS

Older children can get decidedly *unsettled* during the baby's getting settled period, as if they intuitively sensed the crisis nature of the getting started period and didn't act up then. The "image-making" process described by Galinsky for parents occurs in siblings also.[23] A two-year-old may have thought that the new baby would be a playmate. A child who is getting parental praise for maturity may be shaken to see that *no* amount of mature behavior elicits as much parental attention as the infant's infantile behavior.

Common problems parents have in caring for older siblings during this period include thinking you can avoid sibling rivalry and overemphasizing the maturity of the older child. Maturity is a legitimate source of pride, but the older child needs the balance of being able to "play baby" too.

We suggest you get the older child involved in helping you care for the baby (which is a genuine source of pride and pleasure for the older child). Be mindful of safety; a four-year-old is too distractable to watch the baby on a changing table. You can also ask the child to do things for *you* (bring you your nightgown for example). Pay special attention to transition times—like tucking the older child into bed or greeting the child on return from kindergarten or school. Get someone to take the child to a favorite place like the playground. Also, from time to time get a sitter for the baby and do something special with the older child.

Socialization Tasks

PLAY/STIMULATION

Infants are fascinated with things that move. They gaze for increasingly long periods of time at the shifting shadows cast by leaves on a tree outside the window, or a mobile in their crib. As they gain motor control, they begin to enjoy batting and kicking at things and trying to grasp them. The ways in which objects respond to noise or touch or expression is fascinating to babies, and they quickly grasp the distinction between inanimate objects which respond mechanically to touch and animate objects like you who respond to their sounds and facial expressions. Imitations of facial expressions and gestures fascinate young infants. They have exchanges of laughter and giggles as soon as they can do so.

It seems that mothers are more likely to play face-to-face and verbal games, or games involving simple toys, with babies, whereas fathers are more likely to play active games like tossing the baby. Whether this is a biological difference or a cultural one isn't clear, but it is clear that babies enjoy both kinds of play.

In early infancy, it is as important to stick with the principle of "baby-led play," as it is to provide baby-led nursing. The "quiet-alert" periods are relatively short, and even though they lengthen over the first three months, they can end quite abruptly. Babies can only play when *they* are ready to. An infant who has had enough active play will signal that by averting the eyes and then acting irritable. Such a baby now needs quiet soothing, not further stimulation. It is possible for an inexperienced infant care giver to misread the signs of irritability, and feel rejected or think that the baby needs still more active play. This can be overstimulating and disorganizing for the baby.[24,25]

During the first three months, special toys are not needed, but well-timed sensory stimulation is important. The best "toys" are the people with whom the baby interacts. Interactions with parents are a foundation for later more complex play. From responsive care the baby learns basic trust (that the world is dependable), and basic playfulness (that one can enjoy smiles and giggles while getting basic care).

After mastering sucking, babies become increasingly alert while feeding, and their visual control increases. They begin to look around the room, catch your eye, and increasingly notice objects. Visual toys like crib mobiles now become very absorbing. Babies will spend more time in the visually alert state if their visual environment is varied. Talking and singing to the baby provides a rich auditory environment. When the baby starts to coo and babble, most parents are enchanted with cooing and babbling back—a kind of playful "conversation" long before the baby uses real words.

It's good to place babies on the stomach periodically during the day, to encourage head-raising and allow for different visual exploration. If you do this on a floor quilt, you can lie down also and catch the baby's eyes face to face.

Games we suggest are touching various textures of fabric and fur or fake fur; "Peek-a-boo;" "Mousie, Mousie" (to encourage giggling and tickling); "Flying High" (done gently); "Going to Get You!" The best toys are brightly colored mobiles, a stainless steel mirror about seven to nine inches above baby's head, crib devices suspended close enough to be touched as well as seen by the baby, and easily grasped rattles.

There are some toys to be cautious about. Any stuffed animals with easily detachable eyes, any toys with long cords, or any toys with small parts which could be swallowed become dangerous as the baby learns to pick things up and swallow them.

DISCIPLINE/GUIDANCE/VALUES

Infant guidance is simple. There is only one value your infant can learn at this age: basic trust. This means that a reliable care giver will be there and respond. Without any conscious effort, parents automatically lay the foundations for later guidance as a by-product of daily care. You give a sense of order in the universe through the rhythms of feeding and grooming, night and day, play times and sleep times. You lay the foundation for a sense of reciprocity in catching each other's eyes, and imitating each other's sounds.

HEALTH CARE

Medical Care

The American Academy of Pediatrics recommends the first well-baby visit at eight weeks for a full-term normal baby but between two and four weeks for a low birth weight baby or any baby who had other problems at birth. Some doctors want to see all newborns between two and four weeks. And some parents want the reassurance of a well-baby check before eight weeks.

A routine examination at this age includes: assessment of nutrition, general appearance, and development; a careful physical examination; and weighing and measuring the baby's length and head circumference. The doctor should also discuss feeding, vitamins, daily care, and safety as well as ask you what questions you have.

Current AAP recommended immunizations at this age are the initial DPT injection and oral polio.[26,27] If parents have not been immunized, giving them inactivated polio immunization before the baby gets oral polio vaccine will protect against parental illness from the live virus in the oral vaccine which can be more severe in adults than in babies.

Slight fever or inflammation of the DPT injection site may result. Any serious adverse reaction to DPT should be described to the doctor. A very small minority of children (about 1 in 310,000) have adverse responses to the pertussis component and they need to avoid it in subsequent immunizations to prevent severe reactions (see p. 614).

The next well-baby checkup is usually scheduled for four months of age. Most new parents have questions about when to call for medical help between well-baby checkups. In general our advice is call if you are concerned. You should discuss this question with your doctor in prenatal and first postnatal visits. Many doctors and HMO's have handouts to help you decide when to call.

If the baby ever looks sick, loses energy or alertness, refuses to feed, stops wetting diapers, or vomits more than the normal spitting up, call the doctor.

Anytime something "doesn't look right" to you, call. The baby's doctor is your doctor too and you are entitled to discuss *anything* that worries you.

Dental Care

Since babies this age have no teeth, dental care, if you are breast-feeding, consists only of getting adequate calcium and fluoride yourself. Avoid taking drugs like tetracycline which can damage preerupted teeth. If your doctor has prescribed fluoride drops for your baby, give them regularly.

Environmental Health

Good environmental care is relatively simple. Cigarette smoke irritates the lungs of infants and children and moderately increases their susceptibility to respiratory infections. If you or other household members must smoke, at least pick a smoking room, keep it well ventilated, and keep the baby out of it.

Noise, especially loud and/or unfamiliar noise, becomes an environmental issue during this stage as the baby begins to drop the "stimulus barrier," increasingly knows what noises to expect, and becomes more sensitive to unexpected ones. It's a good idea to use the getting settled period for the baby to become accustomed to normal household noise. Some families who don't know about the early stimulus barrier get things backward, and for the first few weeks tiptoe around the new baby in a way that is incompatible with normal family life after the novelty wears off. Then they return to normal activity at about the time the baby becomes sensitive to the unexpected noise. It's much better to let the baby get accustomed to normal household noise from day one. In fact, the baby's ability to get used to normal sounds may be one of the reasons noisy humans evolved babies with an initial stimulus barrier.

SAFETY

In a small tribe nearly everyone has been exposed to the same diseases. In large tribes this isn't true. In crowds, the possibility of the baby's being exposed to an illness which the mother hasn't had is high and babies' ability to resist illness with their own antibodies is low. Most pediatricians discourage exposure of babies under three months to large crowds for this reason. If you have to take your infant out, use a Snugli-type baby carrier as it discourages hand-to-face touching and face-to-face contact with well-meaning but possibly infectious adults.

After congenital illnesses, the leading cause of serious damage and death in young infants is car accidents. Even minor accidents, from which adults walk away, can cause death or permanent brain damage in young infants. Never let a baby ride in a car unless in an approved car seat (see p. 146).

Occasionally parents are tempted to leave a settled baby alone or with a young sibling "for just a few minutes" during a predictable nap period. The hazard of fire makes this a most unsafe practice—as does the possibility of a sudden eruption of sibling violence.

Always be on guard against falls. Be sure the crib is safe (see p. 177). Observe bath safety precautions at all times. Keep your young baby out of bright sun, especially in the summer or in warm climates.

*   *   *

At the end of the getting settled period, you and your baby are having fun together. Enjoy the playful interactions. They are not only fun for babies but help them develop.

SUGGESTED READINGS AND RESOURCES

Barber, Lucie W., and Williams, Herman. *Your Baby's First 30 Months.* Tucson, Ariz.: H. P. Books, 1981.

A chronologically arranged, easily read guide to positive child rearing in the first thirty months. Photographs and charts are used well, and diary space is provided to help you follow your child's development.

Brazelton, T. Berry. *Infants and Mothers: Differences in Development.* New York: Dell, 1983.

A neat book which traces the development and care-giver interactions of three different babies ("average," "quiet," and "active") through the first year of life. Interesting reading (and a few good hints) about parenting different ways with different babies.

Burck, Frances Wells. *Babysense.* New York: St. Martin's Press, 1979.

A baby book using hints supplied by five hundred parents. Wonderful section on baby toys you can make at home.

Dunn, Judy. *Distress and Comfort.* Cambridge, Mass.: Harvard University Press, 1977.

An informative book about why babies cry.

Eagan, Andrea Boroff. *The Newborn Mother: Stages of Her Growth.* Boston: Little, Brown, 1985.

An analysis of the process by which a woman becomes a mother—after the birth of the baby. Vignettes of new parents make interesting reading.

Gesell, Arnold. *The First Five Years of Life: The Preschool Years.* New York: Harper, 1940.

Although this Gesell book is out of print, it is worth a trip to the library. Wonderful, informative reading.

Stoppard, Miriam. *Day-by-Day Baby Care Book: An Owner's Manual for the First Three Years.* New York: Ballantine, 1985.

A truly comprehensive, fully illustrated, step-by-step handbook on a range of child care activities from infancy to age three. This very good book examines everything from equipment, clothing, holding, and handling to aspects of development.

Weissbluth, Marc. *Crybabies, Coping with Colic: What to Do When Baby Won't Stop Crying.* New York: Berkley, 1985.

A pediatrician's guide to colic written by a man whose first child had colic. Practical advice. Lots of information packed into a thin, easy-to-read book.

White, Burton L. *The First Three Years of Life.* Revised ed. New York: Prentice-Hall, 1985.

A comprehensive summary of Dr. White's extensive research on children in the first three years of life. The book is organized around aspects of the young child's environment which White has bound to the development of competence in relating to the world. Readable language.

11

GETTING GOING:
LIFE WITH A BABE IN ARMS
(3 to 6 MONTHS)

Scope of Chapter

This chapter deals with the lap baby—who today is as likely to be found in an umbrella stroller or Gerry backpack as on someone's lap. The age is three to six months; the stage is the period from sitting, at least assisted, until crawling.

Introduction

These particular months of infancy are generally an easy stage for all. The infant survival issues of getting started, and the family survival issues of getting settled, are now for the most part accomplished. And parents don't yet have the moment-by-moment anxieties they will have with a crawler and toddler of "What will the baby get into next?"

However, just as parents become confident that they can meet the baby's needs for basic care and get a little peace and rest when the baby sleeps, suddenly they discover that the baby wants much more from them than just basic care! As Penelope Leach puts it: "Two related specters can ruin this period for both mother and child. The first is the infant's boredom. The second is the mother's fear of spoiling him."[1]

KEY INFORMATION

Biophysical Information

SIZE AND SHAPE

The average weight gain is less rapid now, about 1-1/4 pounds per month or 2/3 ounce per day. See Table 41 for weight and length ranges.

TABLE 41

AVERAGE WEIGHT AND HEIGHT TABLE

	Average Weight in Pounds	Range	Average Height in Inches	Range
Age Three Months				
Boys	12.6	11.1–14.5	23.8	22.8–24.7
Girls	12.4	10.7–14.0	23.4	22.4–24.3
Age Four Months				
Boys	14.0	12.5–16.2	24.7	23.7–25.7
Girls	13.7	12.0–15.5	24.2	23.2–25.2
Age Five Months				
Boys	15.0	13.7–17.7	25.5	24.5–26.5
Girls	14.7	13.0–17.0	25.0	24.0–26.0
Age Six Months				
Boys	16.7	14.8–19.2	26.1	25.2–27.3
Girls	16.0	14.1–18.6	25.7	24.6–26.7

The head circumference in both boys and girls is between 15.9 inches at three months and 17.0 inches at six months, and the rate of head growth is slowing now. The back soft spot (posterior fontanel) is closed, although the front one (anterior fontanel) typically closes between nine and eighteen months, as the period of rapid brain and head growth ends.

Teething begins from the center of the mouth outward with the lower set erupting first. The middle bottom teeth (central incisors) erupt first, usually between five to seven months. Next the upper middle teeth erupt, between six to eight months. (See illustration p. 245.) Babies vary greatly in how much teething bothers them. Some drool a lot and are fussy as the teeth are beginning to erupt. Although almost every symptom imaginable has been attributed to teething, a controlled study concluded that all that healthy teething causes is daytime restlessness, increased finger sucking, gum rubbing, drooling, and loss of appetite.[2] Fever is not one of the symptoms and a temperature over 100 degrees F should not be attributed to teething.

BODY FUNCTION

Bowel function matures, so that by the end of this stage, solid foods can be safely added to the diet if the baby indicates interest. Some babies develop predictable times of day when they are likely to have bowel movements by six months. They may give visible cues of grunting, squirming, or straining when about to have a bowel movement. (This of course does not mean the baby is ready for toilet training.) Smell and taste become more highly developed in lap babies, as the baby becomes ready for solid foods and new taste experiences.

Lap babies have well-developed binocular vision. Their eyes can converge and accommodate to near or distant objects. Babies now intently stare at very small objects. They perceive colors and can discriminate colors. Some enjoy looking at picture books while sitting in a parent's lap. One can expect this interest to grow over the next few months as the baby increasingly recognizes the names of common objects and can recognize a picture as a representation. Lap babies begin to discriminate sounds as words, and to understand some simple instructions. They may scare themselves by making a loud squeal.

MOTOR SKILLS

At three to four months, babies lying on the stomach can lift both head and chest off a surface, using the arms to help. By about four to six months they can roll from stomach to back or side, or vice versa, and sit briefly with the head held steady. Naturally, these increased abilities to move around carry an increased risk of falling off surfaces like a bed or changing table.

By the fifth month, babies can move voluntarily by rocking, rolling, twisting, and kicking, and can easily be pulled to a standing position. They can support a large amount of their own weight in standing, and will bounce actively in a supported stand or parents' arms.

By the sixth month, they can sit supported by their hands and even sit unsupported for short periods with the hands free, which provides increased play opportunities. They can change the orientation of the entire body in order to reach for a toy or some desired object.

By six months, babies can oppose their thumbs against their palms in grasping objects, but they do not yet have a fully developed "pincer" action of thumb to finger, which permits picking up small objects (food or otherwise) and putting them in the mouth.

By the seventh month, they can pivot and may creep or begin to crawl, backward at first.

Language/Cognitive Skills

Now hearing begins to support language development, and babies recognize their own names and the word "no." These "automatic" words are more easily recognized because parents use a different tone of voice with them, conveying stronger emotions of love and alarm. In fact, as everybody knows, even pets who will not go on to produce human speech learn to respond to their own names and simple commands like "no."

Gestural language becomes active—for example, waving "bye-bye." Lap babies begin to imitate all sorts of gestures and body movements. Speech imitation is more difficult, but is starting. Interestingly, in families where the parents are deaf and communicate through sign language, babies pick up some of the signs at an earlier age than most babies produce spoken words.[3] This shows that the baby's understanding of symbolic communication develops more rapidly than the ability to use words to articulate it. You can see by the way baby responds to "No" that understanding precedes speaking.

Lap babies learn to produce sounds by repetition. By the third month they make responsive sounds to talking and singing, and also smile spontaneously (which means smiling without any external cause). By the fourth month they begin babbling and practicing sounds, and they laugh distinctly. By the fifth month they make "social sounds," babbling to themselves, to toys, to a mirror image, or to other persons to get attention. They also show emotions of fear, disgust, and anger by making combinations of sounds.

They watch the mouths of others closely, and try to imitate both sounds and inflections. Soon after that, they will learn to say several syllables and use different ones in the same breath. They may vocalize at you, with you, or alone. They may make lots of repetitive sounds, especially before dropping off to sleep. They are able to scare or soothe themselves with their own vocalizations.

Lap babies explore the world through looking, touching, and manipulating objects (Piaget's sensorimotor stage; see p. 228). This is a good age to use a playpen near the care giver (in the same or next room), since the baby can sit or lie down and look out through the bars, manually explore the toys in the play-pen, and visually explore the world outside.

Social Skills

Socially, lap babies become intensely interested in people, especially famil-iar care givers. They want to smile, laugh, talk, and play. Endlessly they practice their new abilities trying to sit up, roll over, and reach for things to look at, touch, mouth, and get to know. But almost all of these new abilities require adult help. The baby reaches for a toy and drops it, or in trying to turn over gets caught on the toy. When babies can't do what they try to do, they can get frustrated and fussy; almost invariably, being picked up and played with will make them happy.

It's common for care givers or others to say, "The baby just wants atten-tion," as though attention were not a legitimate need in the same way that hunger or sleep is. Some adults do fear that the lap baby will be spoiled by being given so much attention. The opposite seems to be the case. Given lots of attentive, responsive, socializing play at this stage, the soon-to-be crawler will be off into new spatial explorations.

Mahler has coined a quaint term for this remarkable transition between the seemingly self-absorbed newborn and the socially interactive lap baby.[4] She calls it "hatching" from the symbiotic fusion with the mother. Leach calls the stage "discovering people."[5] Both authors stress the ability of the baby at this age to form firm attachments to one or more people who love and are involved with this individual baby and who experience reciprocal delight in response to the baby's delight in them.

The lap baby's smile acts as a social catalyst, eliciting responses from others from four months on. Now babies are increasingly responsive to the emotional tone of social contacts and at about the end of this stage, will clearly respond to facial expressions. They adore mirrors and will reach for and pat their own image in mirrors.

By around four to five months, they show a much more differentiated sense of self and others, and around six months, they begin to demonstrate differentiation by touching and playing with the care giver's body, face, nose, eyeglasses, and jewelry. They maintain "a certain new look of alertness, persistence, and goal-directedness" according to Mahler. They demonstrate a clear preference for their familiar primary care givers by four to six months, and may begin to show anxiety around strangers. As they get older, they may resist being separated, as when going to bed. They may also show abrupt mood changes.

The fact that this is a sensorimotor period of development means that social, cognitive, sensory, and muscular development are all very much interwoven. These babies become highly curious about the environment and will explore as much as possible, first visually, then tactilely as they develop more hand control.

Emotions/Feelings

Besides being able to express specific emotions, babies continue to have an overall emotional style which is part of their temperament. With newborns and arm babies, temperament affects parents most strongly by its impact on practical problems like the ease or difficulty of getting settled. With lap babies, temperamental differences are now seen as part of the baby's evolving personality.[6] Since much of temperament involves how one deals with changes and novelty, this age of intense curiosity highlights temperamental differences.

Now specific temperaments are likely to be more obvious. The degree to which a given baby meshes with parents' temperament may become a serious issue. Babies who fall easily into a schedule are delightful for parents with scheduled days, but may be difficult for parents who like to pick up and go somewhere with the baby when the spirit moves the parent. Placid babies delight many parents who are calm themselves. Demanding babies may delight dominant parents, as "a chip off the old block," or stir up anxiety in parents who fear that the child will become uncontrollable. Babies of the "slow-to-warm-up" temperament enjoy games and new experiences as much as other babies—but need more repetitions of a new experience before enjoying it. Placid babies need the care giver to initiate activities in order for the baby to get enough stimulation for intellectual development.

Developmental Warning Signals

Suspect delayed development and seek medical evaluation for infants of six months who fail to smile, do not respond to being played with, are not visually alert, do not babble, do not turn to the speaking person, and do not localize attention to a soft sound on either side. Failure to reach out for or pick up a toy is also a problem, as is persistent squint, or failure to fix the eyes and visually follow both near and far objects through an arc of 180 degrees.[7]

CARE GIVER TASKS

Basic Care

As before, the best guide to daily care is to keep it simple, and eliminate all non-essentials that are not meaningful to you. A continuation of the "easy-natural" approach of the earlier periods still makes sense, augmented with much increased opportunities for satisfying play with the baby. Lap babies are great playmates. Much of daily care can be incorporated into games and sprinkled liberally with words.

FEEDING/NUTRITION

MILK

Milk, breast or bottle, is still the only nourishment that is needed. In many parts of the world, children are breast-fed for several years, with very gradual addition of solid food and no non-human milk at all. Most American mothers, even enthusiastic breast-feeders, will at least occasionally use baby-sitters between three and six months, and many go back to jobs. While one certainly can both breast-feed and work, the question of either backup formulas or weaning is likely to come up. A recent study showed no difference in milk production between employed and non-employed mothers.[8] Ordinarily whole cow's milk is still not well tolerated by most babies of this age, and 2 percent milk presents too many solutes (salts) for the baby's kidneys to tolerate well. Continued breast- or formula-feeding is safest and best tolerated, and certainly by three months nursing is well enough established that breast and formula by bottle can be alternated. If the quantity of breast milk seems to be decreasing, one can restore it quickly by eliminating the formula or any solid foods, and encouraging the baby to suck frequently for a few days.

Let the baby's appetite be your guide as to how much to offer. You don't need to worry about the amount taken at any given feeding if the baby is comfortable and maintains a steady weight gain of about a pound a month. Water isn't usually necessary in exclusively breast-fed babies unless the baby is losing extra water by sweating during a fever or excessively hot weather. Boiled water is not necessary unless local water supplies are contaminated.

SOLIDS

Generally, solids are added during the lap baby stage. Adding solids doesn't need to be a hassle as there are some simple guidelines which help get early feeding off to an easy and natural start.

Don't start any solid food until the baby is about six months old. Remember that if the baby is getting adequate milk, iron, and vitamins, there is no *nutritional* need for solid food before the first birthday. This means that you will have a full six months during which food is for *tasting, experimentation, pleasure, and play.* You do not have to worry if the baby doesn't like a particular food, or any food. Just wait a few days, pick a time when the baby seems interested, and try a taste of the same or another food.

If there is any family history of allergy, offer only one new food at a time and wait two to three days before offering something else. Then, if there is an allergic reaction, it will be obvious what it came from. Some common nutritious foods which are frequent allergens are cow's milk, eggs, and wheat. Chocolate is also a frequent allergen and has no particular nutritional benefit. Avoid any specific food to which a close relative has a food allergy.

The easiest way to make a transition to solid foods is to let the baby make it. A six-month-old baby who is big enough to regularly sit comfortably on your lap will do so at some mealtimes too, and will begin to be interested in imitating what you are doing with the food. The baby's increased intellectual growth and curiosity, as well as increased fine-muscle skills, will lead to reaching out for spoons or for food on your plate at this stage or the next. Giving small tastes of good food, for pleasure, is a natural way to start happy, healthy eating patterns. "Playing" with food, which parents object to in older children, is exactly what you want to see at around six months. Babies of five to six months may also enjoy sips of fluid from a cup.

There is no need for parents to be anxious about how quickly or slowly the child takes to the new game of sampling new tastes and textures of food. By giving small tastes only as the baby wishes, and not trying to make a meal out of it, you also avoid some of the spills and messes which are inevitable in the course of feeding babies before they are old enough to handle food and tableware.

Early table feeding illustrates a good general principle of child rearing. Whenever possible, it's pleasant to make a new issue a *playful* one before it becomes an *essential* one. You can do with food what you will do with reading. Parents read stories to their children for pleasure long before it is essential for the children to read. If you waited until it was essential, you'd add stress and difficulty to a new experience which is stimulating and unstressful when it is a game.

What to feed for first foods? You can't safely give just anything off your plate. Avoid anything which requires chewing, since the baby could choke on it. But, it's surprising how many things you eat that the baby can share provided the consistency is very soft: mashed potatoes, mashable vegetables and fruits (especially bananas), mashed cottage cheese, mashed egg yolk, cooked cereals or dry cereal flakes as a finger food. You can offer sips of juice or water from your cup as soon as the baby is able to handle it with assistance.

There are a whole variety of special baby foods, either commercially purchased, or made in your blender, which can be given at this age, but why bother? Anne's experience is that the only special baby foods that were worth buying were some of the finger foods for older infants, such as baby sausages and teething biscuits. Marilyn found the jars convenient. Both Marilyn and her husband enjoyed feeding the children well-balanced meals from jars in addition to letting the children reach for table food.

If you do make special baby food with a blender or food processor, for convenience you can freeze portion-sizes in an ice cube tray and thaw them—a cube at a time—in a plastic bag in hot water or in a microwave oven (be careful! see Table 12; pp. 165, 548). Don't add extra salt, sugar, or spices. Babies don't need them and will enjoy the natural tastes of food.

Despite the fact that early feeding and nutrition can be very simple, many parents feel anxious about the topic. If you have anxiety about any topic connected with feeding, take time to discuss it at your four- and six-month well-baby pediatric visits. You will be pleasantly surprised at how simple and reassuring the advice is today for healthy babies.

CLEANING/GROOMING

The diaper area continues to need careful care, more so as additional foods are added, since the stool may become more irritating. Mild diaper rash can be handled with exposure to air and Desitin.

The skin folds, as always, need wiping and sponging. As the baby begins to add solid foods other than breast milk, the baby's sweat may take on an offensive odor, or appear irritating to the baby's skin. The daily (or almost daily) bath takes care of this.

Dressing the lap baby needs to reflect the baby's increasing activity. Shirts and diapers are fine in hot weather. Stretch suits or jerseys and pull-on pants are popular. Blanket sleepers may become necessary at night for the baby who sleeps alone and kicks the covers off.

Most parents start to differentiate day and night clothing at this stage with pajamas for nighttime sleep and daytime clothes in the morning. There is no need to rush this, unless it is a source of parental pleasure. Some sleepy babies are stirred up and reawakened by changing into night clothes. Others incorporate the body contact of changing clothes into the bedtime ritual. At this age it makes absolutely no difference, so do what works best for you and your baby. You will find it more convenient to let the baby sleep in clothing which permits easy diaper changing when the baby wakes at night.

SLEEP/ACTIVITY

During this period, sleep time decreases from around sixteen hours to twelve hours, but is quite variable for individual babies. Babies stay awake for increasing periods of time—up to three quarters of an hour at three months and, by four months, at least an hour at a time, with increased and sustained interest in details of their environments. By the fifth month, they can easily stay awake for one to two hours at a time, resisting interruptions in play. By the sixth month, they more clearly show individual differences in activity level, the amount of sleep required, and how it is distributed between nighttime sleep and daytime naps.

As lap babies mature, they organize their days into wakefulness punctuated by naps, usually one morning and one afternoon nap. Similarly, they begin to organize their nights into sleep, usually punctuated by one or occasionally two periods of wakefulness long enough to awaken their parents with a demand for food and/or play.

Sleep at night starts to become an entirely different proposition during this stage than it was in the newborn period. Sleep rituals begin to become important now, as the baby no longer automatically drops off to sleep after feeding. Older infants, like older children, do not necessarily recognize their own need for sleep as readily as they recognize hunger. They may get overtired and crabby, but still not want to give up consciousness. Their longer awake times are very precious to them at this age. There is so much of the world that they want to experience! Soon they are aware that we may still be awake when they go to sleep, and they don't want to leave us or miss anything.

Don't frustrate yourself trying to *put* babies or children to sleep, which isn't within your power. Rather do what you can do, which is to join them in finding ways to gain confidence and relaxation so that they can *fall* asleep. Bedtime rituals and prebedtime wind-down activities differ for different ages but have a common theme. They emerge at this stage because this is the first time during which children are awake for lengthening periods (punctuated by naps), and sleeping for prolonged periods.

Some parents use the bedtime bottle as a go-to-sleep ritual, carried over from infancy, when sleep followed feeding almost automatically. This has been criticized as a hazard to the baby's teeth (which it is), but the real issue is that of helping the baby differentiate sleep as a different need from hunger, which babies are increasingly ready to do. Parent-child collaboration in going to sleep becomes a very delicate and interesting part of the parent-infant dance. Rocking, singing, and dependable sleeptime rituals are better than the bottle at this age. Often the baby would like to have the same person (usually the mother) always perform the ritual. But it may be a good idea to vary this a bit. Babies who are normally *always* put to sleep by Mommy may find it very hard to go to sleep if Mommy suddenly isn't there.

Be careful not to overstimulate the baby just before bedtime. Fathers sometimes interrupt the evening wind-down time by coming home from work and playing actively with the baby. In some homes the mother does this too. If both of you work, we suggest you adjust the baby's bedtime accordingly—an hour or so after you have a satisfying playtime for all.

Lap babies are much more sensitive to the external environment now. Noises, especially unfamiliar ones, may waken them, even though just a few weeks before they would have slept right through the noises. Because they are intellectually organizing the world, they have a better picture of what to expect, and more concern if something loud and unfamiliar occurs.

Night lights are a subject of controversy in some homes. Some babies sleep easily in the dark, but many do not, and fear of the dark will increase over the next several years as the child's imagination increases. Babies are definitely not spoiled by a night light, and may be much reassured by one, especially if they sleep alone. Having the level of light visibly less than that used for waking hours is enough to help make the day/night difference clear.

Developing a nap time schedule is more a matter of consolidating daytime wakefulness, and dropping some naps, than of starting to take naps. Typically, identifiable napping evolves pretty naturally from the early infant pattern of frequent short sleeps. Instead of napping for two or three hours after a feeding, around the clock, the older infant stays awake after some feedings, and starts to separate fatigue from a full stomach as a cue for sleep. Separating sleep from feeding is an important developmental landmark, and babies differ in the speed with which they achieve it.

It's interesting that some older infants easily fall asleep for naps in the daytime, while having trouble going to bed at night. Perhaps they sense that naps are short and casual, but that nighttime sleep may involve a long separation from parents and the interesting outside world. Parents also may make nap time easy by being more casual about it, for example, letting the baby nap anywhere, and without changing clothes or darkening the room and otherwise upsetting the baby's routine daytime expectations.

Usually babies pick their own times for naps and clearly signal that they are tired. They need only a little help from you to accept the need for sleep. A little rocking, singing, lying down with them, putting them in bed or the playpen or infant seat, or whatever place they have associated with napping, is enough. Many will nap anywhere you let them (of course, you must pick a safe place from which they can't fall or be hurt). Flexibility about the place is helpful since you want your babies to be able to sleep comfortably if nap time comes when the baby is away from home. Almost all babies will nap easily in a car seat in a moving car.

EXERCISE

Most exercise comes naturally from play at this stage. Lap babies are active and curious enough that little parental attention is needed to ensure they get enough exercise. Usually parents are enchanted by their baby's attempts to roll over, sit up, and reach out for objects. You will be fascinated by the "scooting" movements they develop just before beginning real crawling. Most of us find ourselves spontaneously doing the things that help babies develop muscle strength and coordination: bouncing them on our laps, helping them sit, or holding them in a standing position, for example.

The only exercise "equipment" necessary for babies at this stage is some safe free floor space on which they can practice scooting and later crawling on their own initiative, and a crib or playpen in which they can practice pulling themselves up when they are ready to.

STRESS MANAGEMENT

Most of the techniques for stress management of lap babies are the same as those for arm babies. When stressed, they "regress" or act like younger babies. At that time they may need walking, rocking, massage, or singing as parental soothing methods. Some will start soothing themselves by rocking movements. Most will suck a thumb, a pacifier or, soon, the edge of a favorite blanket or stuffed animal. Starting around this age and for the next several years, the child who has a favorite object will develop a strong attachment to it, and may show real grief with difficulty sleeping if it is temporarily or permanently lost. Hugging the favorite object becomes especially soothing in times of stress—going to sleep, traveling to strange places, visiting the doctor, or being left with a baby-sitter, for example.

EMOTIONAL "NUTRITION"

Emotional nutrition is easy at this stage. It comes as a by-product of good care, lots of talk and interactive play (with some opportunities to play alone), and help as needed with stress management. The fact that it comes easily does not mean that it is unimportant! On the contrary, this time when the baby is "hatching" from early infancy self-absorption is a critical time in which to develop and deepen attachment to care givers and family.

CARE OF THE CARE GIVER

In some ways, there are fewer anxieties for parents in this stage than before or after. Smiles, laughter, verbalizations, and gestures are so engaging that many people find babies this age quite irresistible. Some fathers, for example, who couldn't relate well to a baby in arms—"too much like a fragile doll"—find the lap baby intriguing. However, boredom can become a serious issue for the mother who spends most of her time with the baby.

At this time, parental needs emerge which can seem to conflict with baby care. For example, many mothers plan to go back to outside employment at around three months when the baby is expected to be settled. Once the baby is clearly settled, all parents experience a "coming up for air" phenomenon. Some former activities begin to look awfully good again. A movie or a party that wouldn't even have been appealing a month ago (when you'd rather have slept if you had the time), now seems like fun. Most of you are more secure in parenting now, and a little more able to take the baby for granted. So you have psychological as well as physical energy to invest in other things.

It can be disturbing to find that some of your support systems may have rapidly evaporated now. Your spouse may have been extraordinarily helpful when he could see that you and the baby had overwhelming needs—but he may disengage and go back to "business as usual" now. If you have older children, they may have been extremely patient as you lavished time on a crying baby that clearly needed rocking to get to sleep—but now they may very well feel that they have postponed their own needs quite long enough.

You will feel many pressures suggesting that it's time to get back to normal —whatever your family's version of normal is. Now you need to give time and attention to yourself and the rest of the family, and gradually begin to get the baby integrated as a more regular, less special member of the family.

It's almost impossible to expect that your spouse relationship—sexual and otherwise—will go back to being just like it was before. The challenge is making the relationship better and richer. Psychologically, you have a new lover—the baby. Integrating your love for your partner with the love that you have for the baby is a developmental task somewhat like one's first experience of falling in love. You did not stop loving your parents when you experienced a new love— but having two kinds of love at once (sometimes with conflicting demands from each loved one) does require some adaptations—different in every family.

Socialization Tasks

PLAY/STIMULATION

Play is the lifeline of communication between parents and children at this age. The baby is eager to play games and make games out of routine aspects of daily care. Soon the baby will be able to exhibit a sense of humor by "teasing" purposeful non-cooperation with activities like dressing and feeding.

Almost all household objects which the child can grasp can become toys, if they are not dangerous. Once the baby can sit, banging pots and pans, or spoons against them, is fun. Nesting plastic containers with lids enable the child to put one inside the other. Alternatively, you can put a large wooden spool inside one and the baby can rattle it. The toys you might want to buy in the store include baby "gyms" and "baby boxes," teething rings, Roly-Polys, high chair toys with a suction base, soft balls to squeeze and roll, and soft washable animals and dolls.

Children who can stand if supported, and bounce, often seem to love that activity for a longer period of time than parents have energy for it! Bouncer chairs are great for babies who enjoy them. The kind of "walker" which the child can move around with foot movement on the floor while sitting on the seat is fun for some babies—but very dangerous if anywhere near stairs. Also, some of them are tippable.

The playpen is useful at this age, as the babies can begin to scoot and crawl and pull themselves up. It is also a safe place to put the baby while you answer a telephone, doorbell, or go to the bathroom alone. If you want your crawler to accept the safety of a playpen, you will have to introduce it as a cheerful play environment, *before crawling begins.* Make it a rich play environment which the baby enjoys for a while every day. When your baby is ready for crawling, the playpen will have to be alternated with supervised free exploration time.

Some adults seem to delight in tickling an infant past the point of enjoyment, to the point where the baby wants to stop, protests, and then falls into helpless disorganization. Once one has observed this behavior, it should be clear when the infant or child really wants to stop. The child's response changes to a forced, frantic tone of voice and body. If you are playing with your child and observe this frantic laughter, *stop* the game. Your baby has had enough. Do not let any other adult do this to your baby either.

DISCIPLINE/GUIDANCE/VALUES

The lap baby can now expand basic trust to include the wider universe. Stranger anxiety, which can appear in a mild form at four to five months and in a strong form, on the average, around eight months, might seem to be a loss of basic trust, but really it's the opposite. The baby appropriately trusts familiar persons and experiences some anxiety or caution about unfamiliar ones. This will be a foundation on which parents can help children build appropriate caution and self-protection in later years.

You don't have to do anything special to develop independence; that will grow gradually with time. If the baby wakes and cries and wants you at night, feel free to provide nurturant care. Some babies at this age want long play periods in the middle of the night, when parents are tired. You *can* let babies this age "cry it out" if you want sleep, once you are sure that the baby is fed, changed, warm, and well. But you don't have to if it feels unnatural to you. If the baby can see that household activity has stopped and there's nothing to be missed, tucking the baby back into its bed or yours can facilitate going back to sleep.

Discipline is mentioned at this age only to recommend ignoring the concept. You can't enhance your child's later self-discipline by trying to impose discipline now. In fact, you could make things harder for yourself and your baby by trying to impose more control than is realistic, over such things as sleep, toileting, feeding, and moving around. Instead, start child-proofing the household (see Chapter 5, p. 123) before the baby gets big enough to get into hazards. Provide guidance by nurturance, and by following the baby's natural biorhythms, and your own. When the baby's needs for sleep and play come at different times from yours, you can help the baby shift toward yours more easily if you do it gradually. For example, put the baby down for a nap a few minutes earlier each day.

As the growing lap baby approaches the crawler age, the focus of potential conflict will change from sleep schedules to potential hazards. Even precrawlers can pull lamps off tables, spill powder (a good reason not to use it), and swallow or choke on small objects. At this age babies can learn to understand the meaning of a short "No!" as you remove a hazardous object and distract the baby. "No" will be much more meaningful and much less conflictual if you don't have to say it too often. The use of a playpen and baby-proofing means that you and your active lap baby can have some hours free of "No!" every day!

TRAVEL AND TRIPS

Most lap babies adore trips in strollers. Now the baby, if carried, wants to look around. Use a Snugli-type carrier on the back or a Gerry type backpack once the baby has firm head and back control to provide a wide view.

Travel is still relatively easy. We recommend prepared formula bottles and small jars of baby food, neither of which have to be refrigerated before opening. If the jar isn't used up, discard it. Anne, who traveled close to twenty thousand miles with Sam during his first year or two, never bothered with baby food and let Sam move to regular table food naturally while continuing to breast-feed.

HEALTH CARE

Medical Care

Pediatric well-baby visits during this age are normally scheduled at four and six months. In these visits, the pediatrician will weigh and measure your baby, assess the baby's nutrition and general appearance, do a careful physical examination including testing vision and hearing, and assess the child's developmental status.

Usual immunizations are a second and third DPT at four and six months and oral polio at four months.

You can expect nutritional advice, suggestions that liquids can be given by cup at six months, and advice about vitamin, iron, and fluoride supplementation to be individualized according to your baby's individual diet.

You can also expect safety advice: caution that the baby will soon be mobile, crawling, then walking.

Dental Care

It's good to start the toothbrushing habit as soon as the baby has teeth. You can wipe the teeth gently with gauze or use a *very* soft-bristled infant toothbrush and, like everything else that's new, get the habit started initially in a playful way, at whatever time of day is convenient. It is not terribly important to get the first baby teeth thoroughly cleaned, because the front incisors have fewer crevices and thus are not as decay-prone as the molars, which erupt later. Rather, you are introducing another important grooming task at a time before it's critical and when babies are more adaptable to new things because of the inherent curiosity of the age. Toothpaste is optional at first; you can try it like you do new foods. (If you use fluoride toothpaste, only use a tiny amount.) If the baby objects, wait a few days before trying again.

Environmental Health

During the three- to six-month period, the baby's environment is likely to expand greatly as babies are taken outside the home environment. Toxins in the environment become increasingly important. As lap babies become creepers and crawlers, they can pick up tiny objects—flecks of lead-containing paint, for example. Cigarette smoke in a closed environment (home or car) is a lung irritant and some babies will eat cigarette butts from an ashtray.

SAFETY

Safety issues for lap babies are closely tied to their play patterns, as discussed above. As voluntary grasping begins, everything goes into the mouth. Falls are more of a risk as babies become more mobile. Car hazards are no different from earlier, though the active lap baby may protest more about using car seats (just be firm until the idea is automatic). Upstairs windows will soon be a hazard as the baby becomes a creeper, crawler, and climber, and can easily go through a loose screen. Details of baby-proofing the house for a crawler are discussed in the next chapter, but read ahead! Most parents are surprised by the suddenness with which a lap baby becomes a crawler.

*   *   *

Now your lap baby becomes a crawler—but your lap will be wanted and needed for many years.

SUGGESTED READINGS AND RESOURCES

Barber, Lucie W., and Williams, Herman. *Your Baby's First 30 Months.* Tucson, Ariz.: H. P. Books, 1981.

A chronologically arranged, easily read guide to positive child rearing in the first thirty months. Photographs and charts are used well, and diary space is provided to help you follow your child's development.

Brazelton, T. Berry. *Infants and Mothers: Differences in Development.* New York: Dell, 1983.

A neat book which traces the development and care giver interactions of three different babies—"average," "quiet," and "active"—through the first year of life. Interesting reading (and a few good hints) about parenting different ways with different babies.

Burck, Frances Wells. *Babysense.* New York: St. Martin, 1979.

A baby book using hints supplied by five hundred parents. Wonderful section on baby toys you can make at home.

Gesell, Arnold, Ph.D., M.D. *The First Five Years of Life: The Preschool Years.* New York: Harper, 1940.

Although this Gesell book is out of print it is worth a trip to the library. Wonderful, informative reading.

Stoppard, Miriam. *Day-by-Day Baby Care Book: An Owner's Manual for the First Three Years.* New York: Ballantine, 1985.

A truly comprehensive, fully illustrated, step-by-step handbook on a range of child care activities from infancy to age three. The book examines everything from equipment, clothing, holding, and handling to aspects of development.

White, Burton L. *The First Three Years of Life.* Revised ed. New York: Prentice-Hall, 1985.

A comprehensive summary of Dr. White's extensive research on children in the first three years of life. The book is organized around aspects of the young child's environment which White has bound to the development of competence in relating to the world. Readable language.

12

GETTING CAREFUL:
LIFE WITH A CRAWLER
(7 to 14 MONTHS)

Scope of Chapter

This chapter deals with life with babies who are beginning to get around under their own steam. It covers ages seven to fourteen months. The key characteristics of this age are crawling and exploring, especially exploring objects that can be picked up and looked at or mouthed.

Introduction

Up to now you always knew where your baby was—probably in the crib but definitely where you last left the baby. The relative ease of parental care which characterized your baby's infancy now comes to a halt. The primary reason for this quite dramatic change in your baby, and also in your parenting, is the baby's emerging motor skills. Maturation of the large muscles of the body gives the baby independence. Now that babies are able to get up on hands and knees, they are no longer content to be confined to crib or playpen, but prefer crawling freely about the house.

Movement becomes crucially important to the baby now, not only for movement's sake, i.e., to practice and master motor skills, but also to reach and explore all those interesting objects which the baby has up to now been forced to observe from afar!

Coupled with the capacity for independent movement comes an insatiable curiosity to explore, discover, and find out about things. What the baby learns through these new experiences of touching, tasting, seeing, hearing, and smelling will form the groundwork of knowledge about the world and the basis for the developing cognitive system.

Now you must pay very careful attention to the way you design the baby's environment. Not only must it be safe, but it also must be an environment which encourages exploration.

The period between seven to fourteen months also signals your baby's increased interest in, and attachment to, you. Your interactions with the baby will be instrumental in teaching the baby language and in teaching the baby how to love. Burton White goes so far as to say that the quality of these interactions at this age are so important that they will have a lot to do with your child's later development.[1] Daniel Stern describes this as the time when the baby develops a *sense of a subjective self* which opens up the *domain of inter-subjective relatedness*—i.e., attunement to feelings and motivations of others.[2]

KEY INFORMATION

Biophysical Information

SIZE AND SHAPE

The rapid growth rate of infancy leads to some dramatic changes in your baby's size in the seven-to-fourteen-month age period. By one year most babies have tripled their birth weight. Table 42 shows weight and length averages.

TABLE 42

AVERAGE WEIGHT AND HEIGHT TABLE

	Average Weight in Pounds	Range	Average Height in Inches	Range
Age Seven Months				
Boys	18.9	16.5–21.6	28.0	27.0–29.2
Girls	17.6	15.2–20.2	27.2	26.2–28.5
Age Ten Months				
Boys	21.5	18.5–24.5	29.7	28.5–31.0
Girls	20.0	17.3–23.0	29.0	28.0–30.2
Age Twelve Months				
Boys	22.2	19.6–26.2	30.7	29.5–32.0
Girls	21.2	18.4–24.5	30.0	28.7–31.5
Age Fourteen Months				
Boys	23.7	20.9–27.0	31.0	29.5–32.5
Girls	22.0	19.0–25.0	30.0	28.9–31.5

Although your baby is still gaining weight and growing in length during this period, you will notice that the rate of change is somewhat slower now than it was in earlier infancy. The appetite begins to diminish and the baby will gain only about 5 pounds between age one and two. The pudginess of earlier infancy disappears during this period. The baby also develops mild lordosis (protruding abdomen and concavity of lower back), which will disappear by the early school years.

Your baby's head circumference at one year ranges between 17.3 to 19.3 inches and will increase less than 1 inch in the next year. The brain has reached about two thirds of adult size at one year of age. Chest circumference at one year is now about 18.3 inches and the chest has elongated.

By ten months your baby should have four upper and four lower teeth. These teeth, the upper, lower, and lateral incisors, are used for biting. Molars for chewing appear at about one year.

BODY FUNCTION

Your baby's heart rate is now down to about 115/minute. A gradual decrease in this rate will occur over the years to come. At one year of age normal blood pressure is 96/65.

Visual acuity is about 20/100, which means the baby can identify an object from twenty feet away which those with normal vision can identify from two hundred feet. Your baby is less farsighted now than in earlier infancy and can visually examine quite tiny objects which are close.

Bowel movements are down to one or two per day. By about a year the baby may let you know the diaper is soiled by squirming, or other evidence of discomfort.

MOTOR SKILLS

By the age of seven or eight months, the baby has already learned to control the neck muscles to hold up the head, the muscles in the back and shoulders to sit up unassisted, and the arm muscles to pull up to a standing position. Your baby has probably already been *creeping*, which is scooting along on the belly. The motor skills which emerge during this period involve maturation of the leg muscles. The first of these is *crawling*, which begins as follows: In the course of play, the baby will learn to get up on the hands and knees and rock back and forth. The muscle strength created by this activity eventually enables the baby to move forward. What an accomplishment!

We remember how our children enjoyed the newfound mobility of crawling. They also loved feeling new textures like different carpets and *grass* with their hands, which caused crows of delight.

A second motor skill acquired during this time is *climbing*. The first stage of this skill occurs early in the period and involves climbing very small heights, usually no more than 6 inches. The second stage occurs around eleven or twelve months and involves the ability to climb about 12 inches. Like crawling, climbing lets the baby explore and investigate the environment. At the same time, the baby's ability to make a 12-inch climb means that the baby can get from a kitchen chair to the top of a kitchen counter and within reach of kitchen cabinets. This means you must remove dangerous products from all areas which the baby can reach by climbing.

By about nine months of age babies can pull themselves to a standing position in the crib or playpen. Some will be able to pull up on other furniture like chairs or sofas. This is the time you must be sure that all objects the baby can possibly pull up on are sturdy and will not fall over on the child. (See chapter on safety.)

The next motor skill acquired in this developmental period is *cruising*. This activity usually occurs by eleven months of age. The baby holds on to a supporting object, such as a piece of furniture, and carefully slides the feet sideways. Cruising is the precursor of unaided walking, which occurs at about twelve to thirteen months of age. The mean age of walking alone is slightly over fifty-two weeks for white children and slightly under fifty weeks for black children, who have a slight but consistently accelerated motor development when compared to white children from eight weeks on.

The baby's first unaided steps are definitely an event to be celebrated! Walking is followed by running and the ability to straddle small wheel toys at about thirteen or fourteen months. Running well is an age-two accomplishment.

By about twelve months of age babies can pull themselves to a sitting position and twist around while sitting to reach for a toy or look at their mothers, in response to being called by name. This permits both more play and more social interaction.

One of the most fascinating things to watch now is your baby's learning of new skills. Most of the baby's behavior at this age is practicing newly found skills. Some babies spend as much as an hour pulling themselves up on the crib bars. They are totally absorbed in such tasks and show joy at mastery.

Your baby's ability to reach for and secure small objects is now much improved over earlier hand activity. In the past the baby attempted to pick up objects by making sweeping motions of the hand. By eight months these movements are replaced by more precise thumb-finger actions. By ten months the baby's use of the pincer grasp (thumb and forefinger) is excellent and the baby can dexterously pick up tiny objects like pills or thumb tacks from your floor. (Be careful about what's on that floor!) During this time the baby begins to manipulate objects in earnest. The baby can squeeze, push, pull, rip, slide, and of course, explore with the mouth.

Most often objects are picked up and put into the mouth, but the baby also holds objects in the hand to look at them. The baby now can use the two hands for different purposes. Usually, one hand explores and the other hand holds. Earlier in infancy, if you offered a toy when the baby already held one, the baby would drop the first and reach for the second. By ten months, the baby will reach for the toy you offer while still holding the first in the other hand. If a third toy is offered while both hands are full, the baby will drop one or both toys before reaching for the third. By twelve months the baby will hold one toy in one hand, place the second in the crook of the arm—or even in the mouth!— and reach for the third with the free hand.

By twelve months your baby's visual and muscular control will be coordinated sufficiently to stack blocks. Once this skill is acquired, the baby will spend a lot of time stacking blocks and watching them fall down. The hand that is used for stacking the blocks is nearly always the preferred or dominant hand. Don't try to change your child's dominant hand. Little good is accomplished by always placing toys in the baby's right hand to make the baby right-handed. Your baby will determine by experience which hand works best. *You* can learn your baby's handedness by observation.

Language/Cognitive Skills

How do babies learn? And how do they learn so much so quickly? According to Piaget, cognitive development has its beginnings in the child's formation of basic schemata or organized behavioral patterns. These schemata are used to organize the child's understanding of the world. Looking schemata, hearing schemata, and touching schemata all help the infant examine each new thing that is encountered. This examination helps the baby interpret the meaning of the object and put it into some perspective in relation to previously examined things.

Throughout early infancy, the child's application of schemata to stimuli in the world was severely limited by the child's inability to move around and to retrieve and manipulate objects. All the young baby can do is look at an object placed in front of the eyes or bat the object with the hand. With the motor skills acquired by eight months or so, two exciting things happen. The baby now has the ability to crawl *and* to pick up and manipulate objects. The more opportunity the baby has to apply basic sensory schemata (looking, hearing, feeling) and variations on these schemata (pulling, pushing, rotating, dropping) to objects and later to events in the world—the more the baby will learn.

Early in the seven-to-fourteen-month period of development, the baby will apply these schemata *singly* to objects. In other words the baby will pick up an object, stare at it, turn it, bang it, squeeze it. But by about ten months, a significant milestone in cognitive development takes place. Your baby now begins to *combine* schemata in order to achieve a particular goal in relation to objects. For example, envision this scenario. The baby is in the crib and sees a toy lying on the dresser. The baby reaches through the crib bars, picks the long, slender toy up, and pulls the toy horizontally toward the crib. Unfortunately, the toy will not fit through the crib bars. Prior to the age of ten months, the baby would be stuck at this point. Unable to get the toy through the crib bars using the single-scheme repertoire, the baby would probably become frustrated and cry or would give up and drop the toy. At ten months, however, the child has advanced cognitively to the point of mentally combining and coordinating schemata. The baby's approach to this problem is first to pull the toy toward the crib, then *rotate* the toy (a separate single schema previously learned in play) to the point where it will fit through the crib bars. The baby has solved a problem! What a great accomplishment!

The switch from playful to purposeful or intentional manipulation of objects is a highly significant feature of this period. A baby who begins to combine schemata to solve problems has clearly made a great leap forward in developing intelligence.

Babies will also begin to understand that they can *cause* things to happen in the world. You will see your baby reproduce those actions discovered by chance or those the baby has seen you do. For example, if babies make a noise by accidentally hitting a rattle, they will repeat the act purposefully to produce the noise. After seeing you stack blocks, the baby will try to imitate you. The ability to *learn by imitation* is a very important intellectual accomplishment. By this stage your baby can already imitate Pat-a-cake and wave bye-bye. You will be delighted when you see this. Show your delight by praising the baby for trying to imitate you. This helps establish a good pattern of learning.

Another feature of this age/stage is the child's acquisition of the concept that objects continue to exist even when they are no longer seen. Prior to this time, when the baby dropped a toy, it simply ceased to exist. Now, the fact that the baby searches for the toy after it drops reveals an understanding of the fact that the toy continues to exist. This is called "object permanence" and has important implications for the baby's relationship with people as well as things. Peek-a-boo games help the baby learn that an object no longer seen still exists.

Once babies' mental picture of the mother, based on visual and auditory schemata, reaches the point where babies understand that the mother continues to exist even though not seen or heard, they may become very demonstrative when she leaves! Now it becomes more difficult to leave the baby with a sitter or another adult. Your baby will need many experiences of seeing you disappear and come back again before feeling secure about your leaving.

A significant amount of language learning goes on during this period of development. By ten months babies know their names and have a core of words, mostly related to familiar objects, which are well understood even though not yet spoken. The baby is able to respond correctly to commands, such as "Come here!" and answer simple questions, such as "Where's your nose?" by pointing. By fifteen months the baby can also communicate needs and wants by pointing.

Babies "jargon" quite a bit during this period. This means they begin to make sounds when alone at play or "talking" with other people that have pitch and varying inflections. "Jargon" sounds much like speech, and indeed rapidly reflects the rhythms and sounds of the baby's native language. This reflects the fact that babies are attentive to the rhythms, patterns, and styles of conversation long before they are able to articulate words.

Sometime around the first year, the baby will speak the first word, (besides the "ma-ma" "da-da" syllables which appeared earlier at about ten months) and by fourteen months or the end of this period of development, may have a vocabulary of three to twelve words. You would think vocabulary acquisition would proceed rapidly once the child began to make the connection between an object and the auditory symbol (word) that the object is called by. But this is not the case. Vocabulary acquisition does not begin to accelerate rapidly until after the eighteenth month. This is probably related to neuromuscular development and the fact that the baby's repertoire of familiar objects and experience is still fairly limited until that time.

Social Skills

Your baby's social orientation is decidedly more selective now than it was earlier. At younger ages, the baby would establish eye contact, smile, and vocalize in response to the presence of *any* adult. Your baby would also accept being held and comforted by any person. Now there is an increasing orientation toward the primary and familiar care givers.

This is because of the cognitive growth which has taken place. The baby has now formed a consistent mental picture of Mother. Not only can the baby recognize the difference between Mother and other people, but the baby prefers to be with her rather than with others. This starts a new phase in the attachment process which we discuss further below.

The motor acquisitions of crawling and walking play a significant role in the baby's social activity now. Prior to this time, the baby had to await social contact passively. Now the baby can actively seek out people. A baby at this age is very affectionate and friendly and likes to hug and kiss. Meet these early attempts at interaction with encouragement and a positive response. The baby learns from primary care givers whether or not interaction with people is good, as well as how interactions take place. In fact, the approach a preschooler has to other children (friendly, withdrawn, or aggressive) has been shown to correlate with the parents' approach to the baby at this state of development.[3]

Although now babies actively initiate contact and interaction with Mother and other familiar people they will probably actively avoid or protest contact with strangers. In fact, the baby may suddenly cling to Mother and hang on tightly to her neck whenever a stranger appears. This shy or withdrawn behavior, which is very common between six and eighteen months, is called *stranger anxiety*. Most likely it occurs because the baby does not have a secure mental picture of these strangers. Although this is a sudden change in the baby's previously friendly behavior, don't let it worry you. It is a normal reaction during this age/stage. It does make leaving the baby with "strangers" a bit of a problem for a while.

We suggest you allow the baby time to get to know strangers before being left alone with them. Some babies this age will cry at being left with strangers, or cry *every* time Mother leaves, until object permanence is learned. A single baby-sitter instead of a variety of sitters may help. Most babies stop crying soon after the mother leaves—if that's any consolation to you. It is beginning to look as though babies who "get used" to sitters or day care early in infancy may have somewhat less stranger anxiety than those who have been with a single care giver up to now.

The baby's whole orientation now reflects growth toward increasing independence of movement and action. Babies can now help in dressing by appropriately moving parts of the body and can feed themselves finger foods and drink from a cup. The baby at this age loves all exploratory activities and particularly enjoys water play so that the bath is a treat. Ball play is another joy as the baby loves the interaction with the ball thrower.

Emotions/Feelings

Pleasure is probably the easiest of infant emotions to distinguish. Very young infants demonstrate pleasure through smiling, which is at first fairly indiscriminate, appearing in response to any high-pitched voice or face. Later, the smile is more selective, appearing in response to the face and voice of the mother or other family members. During months seven to fourteen, the child's expression of pleasure greatly expands to include other gestures of affection, including hugs and kisses. These expressions are given both spontaneously and on request. By the end of the first year, babies will develop a rudimentary sense of humor. The baby will laugh when tickled, when shown funny faces, when listening to unusual sounds, and when playing Peek-a-boo.

Pain in early infancy is a result of hunger, cold, colic, or other physical distress and is manifested by crying. The older infant begins to demonstrate distress for reasons other than physical pain. By eight months, separation anxiety causes distress. It's important for parents to both recognize and accept this new emotional need.

Anger is another emotion which becomes common during the seven-to-fourteen-month period. Anger usually results from frustration. Because babies love the new independence of moving about, they may be terribly frustrated when restricted. Especially when they are tired or unable to accomplish a task, small frustrations sometimes escalate into tantrums. Tantruming behavior is discussed in a later section of this chapter (see p. 400).

The emotional development of children is tied to the quality of the relationship between the child and the primary care givers. Starting at about eight months, this relationship enters a new phase. Now the child needs to experience responsiveness from the care givers in the routine activities of the day. Babies watch the care giver's actions, use her as a haven in distress, use her for assistance, learn from her what they can and can't do, and learn about her disciplinary style. Babies need to have many experiences of consistent, responsive nurturing. Receiving these, the baby will learn to trust other people, develop the sense of security necessary for exploring the environment, and begin to feel how good it is to have close relationships with others. Failing to receive these, the baby is more apt to be fearful and suspicious of others.

Developmental Warning Signals

If by one year of age your child does not respond to Peek-a-boo or Pat-a-cake, does not imitate speech sounds, does not say two or three words like "Mama," "Da-da," and does not pull self to a standing position, your child is suffering from a developmental delay which warrants a workup to find out why.[4]

CARE GIVER TASKS

Basic Care

NUTRITION

The baby can be given a balanced diet of baby food or appropriate table food at this time, but foods that could cause difficulty chewing and swallowing should be avoided. Items in this category include small foods like raisins and nuts, hard foods like carrots and celery, and sticky foods like peanut butter (unless spread very thinly).

Now that the baby has improved use of the small muscles of the fingers and hands, self-feeding starts in earnest. Provide foods that can be picked up with the fingers. Only give a small amount at one time so that the baby doesn't get too much in the mouth at one time. Appropriate foods include chicken, hamburger or meat cut into *very* small pieces, scrambled eggs, tiny cubes of cheese, large curd cottage cheese, small pieces of fresh or canned fruits (without rind or pits) small pieces of cooked vegetables, pasta like macaroni shells, soft bread (preferably whole grain), and crackers or cookies. Be sure meat is completely cut through in very small pieces, especially hot dogs, which are a common cause of choking.

By the time the baby is walking, three small meals a day and a morning and afternoon snack will be the usual pattern. It's normal for the baby's appetite to change from day to day, so don't worry if eating patterns vary. Though mothers often want to continue feeding what they feel the baby should eat, it's best to allow the baby to self-regulate daily food intake.

Messy as it is, food play is important and should be overlooked if not encouraged. Squishing fingers through mashed potatoes before licking them is, for the baby, an aesthetic, exploratory, and learning experience as well as a nutritional one.

Avoid foods that contain excess sugar and salt. (See pp. 535 and 553.) Vitamins are not necessary if the baby is receiving a well-balanced diet.

Weaning to cup from either bottle or breast can easily be accomplished at around one year. Some babies this age still want a bottle, especially at night, but most are willing to give it up in lieu of the new skill of drinking from a cup. We don't recommend giving the baby a bottle to go to sleep with. A cuddle and song session in the rocking chair is better and not destructive to the teeth.

One question many mothers ask when their child reaches this age is, "Should we stop breast-feeding?" Note we used the word "we" to point out that the decision is a mutual one. The baby participates in making the mutual decision about continuing breast-feeding by the strength of interest that he or she shows in breast-feeding. Many babies at this age, others at a later one, will clearly show that they no longer care about the breast very much. Their horizons and activities have expanded so much that they are content with a hug from you or a game together and are no longer interested in spending time at your breast.

At the crawler age, most babies level off in the rapidity of their growth, and begin to take noticeably less food. This is normal and desirable, as overfeeding at this age could lead to excessive fat if intake exceeds the now diminished growth requirements.

Mothers who are breast-feeding may not be aware of a change in appetite since the baby just naturally takes less milk. However, some mothers will experience a decrease in milk supply below what the baby needs, especially if the baby is eating a large amount of solid foods and nursing at prolonged intervals. There may not be enough sucking to keep the breasts adequately stimulated. If this occurs, it may be remedied by cutting back on other foods and nursing more often for a few days. On the other hand, if you want to wean now, add formula or whole cow's milk, preferably in a cup, to enhance the baby's new skills further. This will diminish the amount of your milk the baby takes, and nature will take its course. (Note that pediatricians do *not* recommend whole milk before one year of age because whole milk can cause gastrointestinal bleeding and iron deficiency anemia.)

Some mothers feel that they *ought* to wean at this time because the baby is getting "too big" to nurse. There is something sensual about nursing someone who can look you in the eye and talk to you! In fact, the very sensuality of the experience is probably what makes some mothers uncomfortable with prolonged nursing and it also may make other people uncomfortable in watching.

In primitive societies, breast-feeding is usually continued well into the second year, for good reasons. The water supplies are not safe, and babies can die of diarrheal infections which older children and adults survive. Continuing to breast-feed an older baby can be a source of great pleasure to mother and baby. The "regression" to more infantile behavior that is natural to all children when hurt or frightened can be soothed most naturally in this way.

Some mothers stop breast-feeding at this time because they plan to work or have a more active social life. However, keeping some breast-feeding going can be a pleasant way of making reunion with your baby at the end of the day.

CLEANING/GROOMING

Daily bathing and shampooing become more important during this period particularly as the baby is handling lots of food in early self-feeding efforts. Sometimes more food lodges in the baby's hair than in the mouth! Most babies enjoy bath time tremendously. Water toys enhance enjoyment of this daily routine even further.

The baby is too large for a plastic bathtub now, and you will probably have to switch to the adult tub. If your baby is frightened by the size of this new tub, you can help make the transition by placing the small tub inside the large tub until the baby becomes accustomed to it. It's also a good idea to take the baby out of the tub *before* you pull the plug. Not only are the gurgles frightening to hear, but the baby may fear he or she will slip away with the bathwater.

Though the baby can now sit up well, never leave the baby alone in the bath. Also, don't let your baby stand up in the tub without your support. A baby can easily slip and become hurt or frightened.

Shampooing becomes necessary now as the hair is usually too long just to wash the head with a cloth. Babies of this age will clearly remember getting soap in their eyes, and may learn to hate the shampoo process. Although baby shampoo is much less irritating to the eyes than regular shampoo, it is still uncomfortable for some babies. We find that most babies hate the tugging on the hair and water pouring down the face as much as they hate the shampoo.

It helps to keep the hair cut short so the shampoo will take less time. Use the smallest amount of shampoo required to do the job so less rinsing is needed. Try bathing the baby in the tub with you, with only about two inches of water in it so you can rest the back of the baby's head against the bottom of the tub between your legs. Use one hand to pour water from a plastic cup over the hair, while the other is poised with a dry washcloth to quickly wipe any water or shampoo off the face before it gets into the eyes. For postshampoo combing, try No More Tangles, which is pretty effective. Marilyn's daughter so hated having her hair combed that she learned at an early age to do her own. Controlling the tug herself was easier than letting Mother wield the comb.

Continue to cut toenails and fingernails as needed and to brush the baby's hair with a soft-bristled brush.

Dressing the baby is in some ways easier and in some ways harder than earlier. Babies will now be able to assist you somewhat during dressing, since they can now move parts of the body on request. This accomplishment is as much a physical-motor acquisition as it is a language acquisition. By now muscular development and coordination and the ability to comprehend words that are names of objects, such as arm and leg, have occurred. That's the good news.

The bad news is that the baby is skilled enough in wiggling to make dressing a difficult time. The baby *hates* to hold still or be confined. Be very careful about falls from bath tables at this age. As a matter of fact, we recommend dressing all squirmers on the floor.

SLEEP/ACTIVITY

The baby's need for sleep begins to decrease at this time, but most will still need one or two daytime naps lasting anywhere from one to three hours. Generally the morning nap is the first to go. Babies usually need about ten to twelve hours of sleep at night. Some babies this age wake early but are generally content to play in the crib if some safe toys are around.

By the time nine months rolls around you may notice that your baby is able to keep himself or herself awake at times, even when really tired. This behavior is closely tied to the separation anxiety and object permanence which we spoke of earlier. The baby doesn't want to lose you! There are times when a baby becomes so overtired and tense that sleep actually becomes impossible. This behavior will decline as the baby becomes more secure in the relationship with you. Meanwhile, you can lie down together while the baby falls asleep.

Night waking is still fairly common during the second half of the first year. In one study, boys, infants with a history of colic, and snorers or mouth breathers had a higher incidence of night waking.[5]

EXERCISE

Exercise needs during this period are met by the child's natural expenditure of energy on trying and mastering motor skills, such as crawling, climbing, walking, and running. Interest in these activities results in *incessant* activity. It is important that the baby be given maximum access to the living area of the home (after it has been child-proofed) so that the capacity for exercise can be facilitated and curiosity nourished.

STRESS MANAGEMENT

Frustrations which arise from the baby's feelings of helplessness are the major producers of stress in this period. Some of the frustration arises from physical helplessness. Although babies are acquiring many new motor skills and can move about considerably more independently, they are still limited in physical capabilities. The baby may be able to stand alone, but not sit down again without help! The baby may be able to climb, but balance is only marginal, and judgment as to where the behind will land when turning to sit is not very good. Consequently, babies may be frustrated by frequent falls.

Other frustrations arise from language helplessness. Although the baby is acquiring the rudiments of a language pattern, can comprehend many words, and can perhaps speak a few words, the baby cannot yet make all wants or needs clear. These frustrations may lead to strong expressions of emotion which the baby has little power to control.

Particularly if the baby is tired, frustrations may result in a *tantrum*. The baby screams, bangs the head, and/or moves the arms and legs violently. We think the best response to this behavior is to stay with the baby rather than leave the room and ignore the tantrum. Calm the baby by your presence. Place your hand lightly on the stomach or chest. As the baby calms down try a gentle back rub or a rock in the rocking chair. Although the tantrum may be disturbing to you, try to realize that it occurred because the situation had become totally unmanageable for the *child*. Stay calm and loving as you wait these episodes out. Try to prevent the tantrums from recurring by reflecting on what caused the frustration, watching your child's signals, and altering possible environmental instigators.

Of course, tantrum behavior can become a learned response when children have observed that an emotional outburst will get what they want. Don't allow this strategy to become successful by giving in to something the baby wants, for which your best judgment is "No."

Stress can also arise when a baby of this age has a sibling not much older who feels and shows resentment toward the baby. The older child may hit the baby now and again, push the baby down, or take toys away. It is generally true that the closer in age the two siblings are, the more frequent and intense the hostile behavior from the older to the younger child will be during the seven-to-fourteen-month period. The baby may learn how to cope with the older sibling, but it may be at the expense of learning how to behave like the aggressor does!

Anticipate sibling rivalry and learn how to deal with it. Three guidelines for dealing with the older child which can considerably reduce the stress experienced by the younger child are pertinent here. First, *be firm* in not allowing aggressive behaviors toward the baby. When such actions occur, physically restrain the older child from the action. Try cuddling and giving reassurance that you love the older child but won't allow the child to hurt the baby. Second, give the older child some private time with you each day, free from distractions and away from the younger sibling. Third, stimulate the older child's interest in other activities.

EMOTIONAL "NUTRITION"

As we have previously pointed out, a new phase in the ongoing development of attachment began in your baby at about eight months of age. Your baby now has a close, demanding relationship with you and doesn't want to share you with anyone. This first experience of real affection will delight you but a baby clinging to your leg while you're cooking dinner for company or dressing to get to work on time can be a bit much. Obviously this new human's affection should be accepted and responded to. By your positive responses, your child learns that it is good to have close relationships with others and that others can be trusted. On the other hand, no mother can—or should—devote her entire day to the demands of her crawler. You—being older and wiser—will have to strike a balance between your baby's legitimate need and yours. It will not hurt babies to be left to their own devices once in a while. It also won't hurt the baby if you are indulgent when crankiness prevails or the baby's need to play seems very urgent.

It's a striking fact—and a reassuring one—that babies cared for all day by even the most nurturant care giver still show the same demanding attachment to their mothers as do mother-reared children. It may be exhausting for the mother who's come home from a busy day's work, but it's a welcome sign of the baby's love.

CARE OF THE CARE GIVER

Care givers of crawlers have one potential problem: exhaustion! Up to now, the babies were often content to be placed in a crib after the basic needs were met by your care. *Now* it seems as though you are chasing an active explorer all the time. Our suggestion is simple: Find a way to get some rest between all this baby chasing. Try napping or relaxing during the baby's naps. If you have a very active crawler, perhaps you can pay a neighborhood ten- to twelve-year-old child to substitute for you one hour a day.

Socialization Tasks

PLAY/STIMULATION

The basic feature of play in the seven-to-fourteen-month period is exploration of play objects. Early in the period babies spend lots of time manipulating objects or trying to produce action with objects. This is the age of banging and bouncing objects because the babies enjoy both the motion and the sound which results from their actions. The entire nature of each object, i.e., the object's size, shape, hardness, taste, sound, etc., can be learned only through the child's sensation of the object. We have already said that exploration of objects in the environment is crucial to the child's continued cognitive development.

When babies begin to coordinate schemata and exhibit what we have termed intelligent, goal-oriented behavior, they begin to play differently. By twelve months, babies go beyond the sensory examination of objects and try to figure out what they can *do* with objects. Hence, the baby tries to dial a telephone and talk through it or tries to stack a set of plastic doughnuts.

Although play behavior is clearly related to cognitive development in the seven-to-fourteen-month-old child, parents do not need to invest in all the latest toys. Precious few of these are actually worth their cost. Children of this age profit from interaction with almost any objects which are in their environment, provided that the objects are unbreakable, free from sharp edges, and do not have removable pieces which might be swallowed.

One enjoyable homemade toy for this age is a "collection" of ten or twenty objects of different sizes and shapes (such as plastic containers and lids) in a large container (such as a one-gallon plastic ice cream tub). Another great toy is a string of wooden sewing spools. Babies also love to crawl into big cardboard cartons set on end.

One commercially available toy which is valuable for children of this age is a ball (eight- to twenty-four-inch diameter is best). Balls can be moved in an interesting and unpredictable fashion with very little effort on the part of the child. They provide the child with practice of motor skills which will be perfected in the next age/stage.

Toys and games that enhance your child's small motor skills are best for babies at this age and are best liked as well. Plastic hand "tools" like hammers and scissors are fun even if they don't really work. The baby will love fitting things together like blocks and puzzles. Nesting plastic food containers are great now for putting inside each other and will be useful later for holding small toys. Crayons and pencils are fun to hold even before the baby is ready to draw.

When it comes to toys, babies have no sense of "mine" or "yours" yet. They think that the whole world and all its toys belong to them, which can upset older siblings who *know* which toy is theirs. However, babies now can begin to develop an attachment to a special object like a stuffed animal or blanket.

You can facilitate your child's language learning at this time by talking in natural conversations while you are feeding, bathing, or dressing the baby. You can point out objects the baby sees while on a walk or ride. You can also deliberately name every object you are using or giving to the baby. Verbalize safety rules ("Stove! Hot! Don't touch!").

You can also facilitate language learning by reciting nursery rhymes over and over again and by singing songs. A time-honored game is naming and touching parts of the body. Find heavy cardboard picture books at your local library or bookstore, and spend some time each day "reading" the book to the baby, and talking about the pictures. Initiate games by asking, "Where's the doggy?" First you, and then your child, find and point to the doggy in the picture. You will be amazed at how many objects the baby can point to—after your coaching—before speaking the words. All your efforts will be rewarded as the baby begins to use language more expressively in the months to come.

You can also call attention to sounds (how a clock ticks or a kitten purrs) and play the game of "Doggy goes bow-wow!" The baby can be made aware of smells (bread baking or Daddy's shaving lotion) and "feels" like feathers or ice.

A safe environment for crawling will enhance the baby's large motor skills. So will "equipment" that helps the baby move, like rocking horses and walkers. Games you play with your baby like nonsense songs, Peek-a-boo, etc., all help communication skills. The more you talk to your baby, the easier it will be for your baby to learn to talk to you.

As babies near the end of this age/stage, you can play a role in helping them relate to other people. You can introduce the baby to the mail carrier or friends coming to visit. Baby may be shy at first but should quickly learn to smile and wave—at least "bye-bye!"

A WORD FOR FATHERS

Play is important to your crawler, and fathers are great play instigators at this age. One study showed that fathers were more likely to pick up babies for play than for care-giving tasks.[6] Fathers are also more apt to engage in physically active games with babies than are mothers and do more bouncing and tossing.

Those fathers who found it difficult to relate to a newborn often find that interaction with a crawler is more to their liking. Some fathers like to crawl on the floor with the baby and play Horsey with the baby riding on Dad's back.

DISCIPLINE/GUIDANCE/VALUES

Setting limits for the baby and seeing that these limits are carried through is an important new concern for parents during this stage. Now that babies can crawl, pull themselves up on furniture, walk, and climb, they need to learn some restrictions. These limits are for their own safety, because the baby has no judgment yet on which to base safe behavior.

This is a good time to begin a pattern of solid and effective discipline. It's easy to say you should to adopt a style that is firm, but at the same time loving. But it's not always easy for parents to maintain a proper balance between firmness and lovingness. Parents often fear that being firm and denying what the baby wants will make the baby love them less. This is not the case. It actually looks as though a child who has not been dealt with firmly during late infancy may be considerably less well prepared to cope with life situations than one who has.

Some basic rules for effective guidance of the seven-to-fourteen-month-old include the following:

1. Set limits by stating clearly, and in a manner that babies can understand, what they may or may not do.

2. Allow the baby to experience a consequence for not complying with the limits you have set. For example, physically remove the baby from a dangerous situation quickly and firmly. A physical approach is the best one, because a baby at this age can't possibly profit from discussions and explanations. Don't keep saying "No" and letting the child do it. Follow through with a consequence when the behavior does not stop.

3. Use distraction when possible.

4. Set as *few* limits as possible.

The best way we know to minimize the number of limits is to design the environment so that the baby's activities within the environment are safe. For example, if the baby insists on climbing the stairs and cannot be continually supervised, place a gate across the third step from the bottom and allow the baby to climb these steps. Similarly, if the baby insists on opening lower cabinet doors and pulling out the contents of the cabinet, either place a lock on the cabinet or replace the items in the cabinet with items that are safe and that you do not mind being pulled out and played with (Tupperware, for example).

Although some limits will clearly be necessary, the more limits you place on a very explorative crawler, the more times you will have to say "No!" and remove the child from the tempting object. Constant "No! No's!" are unpleasant for both you and the baby. This can lead to hostile, frustrated feelings on the part of the care giver, and doubtful, mistrustful feelings on the part of the child. The worst thing that can happen is that the child feels that exploring and being curious are not good. Such feelings do not help the child's motivation to learn.

Babies of this age often start biting—and their teeth and jaws are strong enough to inflict pain on another child or on you. Not all children do this, but those that do seem to do it for a while. We do *not* recommend biting back; it doesn't work. We do recommend preventing the bite when you can. React to a bite by saying "Ow!—No!" and turning the baby away from you. Give the baby a plastic doughnut or other safe object to bite. Do not put the baby in the crib or playpen except as a last resort. You don't want your baby to think of crib or playpen as a place of exile.

Another habit of this age is playing with or eating feces. This is a normal part of exploring the world which at this age includes feeling, smearing, and mouthing even one's own stool. It will not hurt the baby in any way. Try not to overreact; just clean up the mess and forget about it. The baby will forget this habit too—usually very quickly.

Thumb or finger sucking is still common in babies this age and should not cause parental worry. Finger sucking at night is much preferable to a bottle as it does not cause dental caries.

What about playpens at this age? Many parents recognize that a safe place to put the baby is essential and yet express concerns that at the very age when exploration is so important to the baby's learning, it is not right to restrict this exploration. Playpens can be used in moderation for parental convenience and child safety, provided playpen time is balanced by exploration time. One alternative if you can arrange it is to gate an entire room. Marilyn used her dining room which did not yet have any furniture, for this purpose. The room was carpeted and had a sofa across one door and a gate across the other. The room contained a child-size table and chairs, lots of toys, and two children who happily crawled and played next to the kitchen where the activity was. Anne also used her dining room as a playroom, which had both sturdy adult and child furniture.

By now, the baby's needs without question can be met by another care giver, so you and your spouse can go out and enjoy yourselves alone—if you have not already done so. If just the time when you feel ready to leave the baby with a sitter coincides with the development of stranger anxiety in your baby, you have our sympathy. It's too late to suggest you start leaving the baby with one sitter at a much earlier age so the baby becomes familiar with the sitter before the onset of stranger anxiety. We *can* tell you that the baby will stop crying soon after you leave, and that soon the sitter will not be a stranger. We feel parents' needs are important and, although we sympathize with the fact that the baby has to learn you will return the hard way—by experiencing it—we advocate going ahead with your plans despite the tears.

HEALTH CARE

Medical Care

The baby will see the doctor at least once during this period often at the routine one-year checkup. At this examination, the doctor will weigh and measure the child, assess general appearance and nutrition, check on vision and hearing, and conduct a developmental assessment. A skin test for tuberculosis, which you will "read" and report to the doctor, may be administered. The doctor may order a hemoglobin or a hematocrit test to determine whether anemia is present. No immunizations are needed at this time unless makeup shots are in order. A measles, mumps, rubella (MMR) immunization is needed at fifteen months.

Babies this age are prone to respiratory infections, especially colds and ear infections, and diarrhea, which may need medical attention. These infections are more common in infants in day care.

Dental Care

Brush the baby's teeth with a soft, baby-sized toothbrush and a pea-size amount of fluoride-containing toothpaste. Brush your teeth in front of the baby first to show the baby how to spit out the toothpaste. Although you have to do the brushing for the baby, many like to play at this game and like to put their own toothbrush in their mouth.

It is not a terribly serious matter to get the first baby teeth thoroughly cleaned, because the front incisors have fewer crevices and thus are not as decay-prone as the molars, which erupt later. What's important is that you introduce another important grooming task at a time when it isn't yet critical, and when babies are more adaptable to new things because of their inherent curiosity.

SAFETY

In view of the child's emerging array of motor skills, it is clear that the key to safety lies in child-proofing the environment. Basic guidelines for accomplishing this task follow.

Lock up or place well out of reach *any* substances that might be hazardous to your baby if put into the mouth. This includes both toxic substances and small objects. Fill all electrical outlets not in use with blank plugs (these may be purchased at a hardware store). Remove all appliance cords from the baby's reach. Check all TV and stereo controls that are within the baby's reach to be certain they will not produce a shock, and check all knobs to be sure they do not come off easily and cannot be swallowed (they should be larger than 1½ inch breadth). Remove all plants that the baby could eat or pull over. Lock all medicines in a small lockbox, or keep them well out of the child's reach. Use a gate across stairs and do not permit the baby access to open windows.

The car seat is always essential. By this age most babies will want to sit up strapped in the toddler-type car seat so they can look out.

Although the task of child-proofing your home may seem to be a troublesome one, you must remember that a child between seven and fourteen months of age *cannot* be expected to use any good sense when it comes to safety. The measures you take to make the environment safe substitute for the child's safety sense until it develops.

* * *

Crawling is over. On to toddlerhood!

SUGGESTED READINGS AND RESOURCES

Barber, Lucie W., and Williams, Herman. *Your Baby's First Thirty Months*. Tucson, Ariz.: H.P. Books, 1981.

A chronologically arranged, easily read guide to positive child rearing in the first thirty months. Photographs and charts are used well, and diary space is provided to help you follow your child's development.

Brazelton, T. Berry. *Infants and Mothers: Differences in Development*. New York: Dell, 1983.

A neat book which traces the development and care giver interactions of three different babies ("average," "quiet," and "active") through the first year of life. Interesting reading (and a few good hints) about parenting different ways with different babies.

Brooks, Jane B. *The Process of Parenting*. Palo Alto, Calif.: Mayfield Publishing, 1981.

A parenting handbook which spans development of children from birth to adolescence. The book also covers special topics such as working parents, single parents, and stepparents.

Church, Joseph. *Understanding Your Child From Birth to Three*. New York: Pocket Books, 1982.

An excellent source of knowledge for parents desiring information on the psychological development of the child. The book includes chapters on children's fears, sex differences, discipline, and individual differences in personality.

Divas, Mireille. *I'm a Year Old Now*. Englewood Cliffs, N.J.: Prentice-Hall, 1983.

A translation of a book by a French psychoanalyst. Written from the point of view of a year-old child in the form of friendly suggestions and admonitions to his parents. A bit dated in its advice to working women, though it was written in 1983.

Gesell, Arnold. *The First Five Years of Life: The Preschool Years.* New York: Harper, 1940.

Although this Gesell book is out of print it is worth a trip to the library. Wonderful, informative reading.

Leach, Penelope. *Babyhood,* 2nd ed. New York: Knopf, 1983.

A stage-by-stage look at babies from birth to age two, including how they develop physically, emotionally, and mentally. Summaries of development and behavior are given at three months, six months, and one year.

Mueser, Anne Marie, and Liptay, Lynne M. *Talk & Toddle.* New York: St. Martin, 1983.

A very readable book about child care in the first three years, arranged alphabetically by topic for easy consultation as the need arises.

Sparling, Joseph, and Lewis, Isabelle. *Learningames for the First Three Years: A Guide to Parent/Child Play.* New York: Walker, 1984.

An illustrated "play" book that gives specific ideas on what activities to do with children along with the "whys?"

Spock, Benjamin, and Rothenberg, Michael B. *Dr. Spock's Baby and Child Care.* New York: Pocket Books, 1985.

The latest revision of one of the best-known and most widely circulated of child care books.

Stoppard, Miriam. *Day-by-Day Baby Care Book: An Owner's Manual for the First Three Years.* New York: Ballantine, 1985.

A truly comprehensive, fully illustrated, step-by-step handbook on a range of child care activities from infancy to age three. The book examines everything from equipment, clothing, holding and handling, to aspects of development.

White, Burton L. *The First Three Years of Life.* Revised ed. New York: Prentice-Hall, 1985.

A comprehensive summary of Dr. White's extensive research on children in the first three years of life. The book is organized around aspects of the young child's environment which White has bound to the development of competence in relating to the world. Readable language.

13

GETTING ON:
LIFE WITH A TODDLER
(15 to 23 MONTHS)

Scope of Chapter

This chapter deals with the child from fifteen to twenty-three months. The dictionary defines a toddler as one who toddles, i.e., walks with short unsteady steps, as a young child. Indeed, your child will toddle at the beginning of this age/stage, but with increasing agility.

Introduction

This period is one of increasing competence for your child in a variety of areas. Your toddler has even more advanced motor skills than those your baby achieved in the seven-to-fourteen-month period. Toddlers begin to run, climb, and jump with considerable speed and agility. More complex cognitive skills will enable the child to, for the first time, construct mental pictures of objects. These mental pictures assist the child in organizing the world and in beginning to *think out* problems. Language development makes it possible to hold conversations with key people in the child's world. Children also begin to feed and dress themselves now. Unfortunately, all these competencies result in strivings for independence which can make your life difficult at times. On the other side of the coin, you will delight in your toddler's accomplishments!

KEY INFORMATION

Biophysical Information

SIZE AND SHAPE

Table 43 shows the weight and height averages at these ages.

TABLE 43

AVERAGE WEIGHT AND HEIGHT TABLE

	Average Weight in Pounds	Range	Average Height in Inches	Range
Age 15 Months				
Boys	24.1	20.9–27.7	32.0	30.5–33.5
Girls	22.8	19.1–26.5	31.5	30.0–33.0
Age 18 Months				
Boys	25.3	22.0–28.5	33.2	31.7–34.5
Girls	24.1	20.8–28.0	32.7	31.2–34.2
Age 21 Months				
Boys	26.5	23.1–30.5	34.2	32.7–36.0
Girls	25.3	21.3–30.0	33.7	32.2–35.2
Age 23 Months				
Boys	27.5	23.9–31.0	34.0	32.9–36.0
Girls	26.0	22.5–29.5	33.9	32.5–35.5

Because the rate of growth is still decreasing when compared with the rapid growth of infancy, your child will gain only about five to six pounds during the coming year and will tend to grow about four inches. Girls will grow somewhat faster than boys.

Your child will acquire all twenty of the primary teeth during this period. The addition of molars (beginning at about one year) to the incisors will provide the potential for trying a variety of foods heretofore not edible because they require chewing.

BODY FUNCTION

Due to maturation of the organs and muscles associated with elimination, bowel and bladder control may be partly achieved during this period. Toddlers begin to make evident their urges to defecate though they are far from reliable.

Toddlers also may complain when wet or soiled and want to be changed. (Toilet training will be discussed in a later section in this chapter.)

Toddlers can blow the nose if you hold the tissue. Convergence of the eyes, which is the coordinated movement of the two eyes toward fixation of the same near point, enables the toddler to see better. In addition, more accurate depth perception is acquired.

MOTOR SKILLS

The sensory and motor areas of the child's cortex are developing rapidly now. This development will result in the child's attempting increasingly complex motor behaviors during the fifteen-to-twenty-three-month period. The child "toddles" well, i.e., walks alone, but with a wide-based, irregular gait. The child will learn to walk more smoothly, to walk backward and sideways, and to walk up stairs one at a time while holding on. The child will run stiffly at first, later more smoothly. Next the child will develop good control over starts and stops. This is a significant accomplishment since running requires much more coordination of the trunk and limbs than does walking. Sufficient coordination will not occur during this period for the toddler to make turns while running, but this skill will soon follow. For now, when toddlers want to change direction, they stop running—or fall!

Jumping is a new acquisition of this period. Your toddler will jump with both feet, as sufficient coordination has not yet occurred to enable jumping on one foot. Straddling is another accomplishment of this developmental age. Toddlers enjoy sitting astride a small-wheeled vehicle and propelling it forward with their feet. Although a toddler may be able to sit on a small tricycle, the child is not yet developmentally ready to operate one. The muscle strength required to push the pedals and the coordination required to push the pedals and to steer at the same time are simply not present. This means you can wait until the child is two before purchasing a tricycle.

Initial attempts at releasing objects, which began at the end of the crawler period, will be mastered now. A toddler can release several pellets into a bottle, put several cubes into a cup, build towers (using three blocks at seventeen months and six blocks at twenty-four months), and throw a ball on request. This throw is a rigid underhand toss at first, but by about two years, the toddler begins to throw overhand. The toddler can't catch a ball, though.

Continued control over the small muscles in the hands and fingers, as well as coordination of eye and hand movements, will enable the toddler to string large wooden beads, scribble circularly, imitate horizontal and vertical pencil lines, and put a key in a lock. This developing control and coordination will also enable the child to develop self-help skills related to feeding. Significant improvements in the way your child handles a spoon and a cup will become evident during the fifteen-to-twenty-three-month period. For example, at fifteen months, your toddler fills the spoon with food poorly and may turn the spoon upside down before getting it to the mouth. At eighteen months, the toddler can fill the spoon well, but still has difficulty getting it to the mouth and may spill a considerable amount of the food that was on the spoon. By two years, however, the child is able to insert the spoon in the mouth without turning it, and may spill only a small amount.

A similar progression is noted relative to the toddler's use of a cup. At fifteen months, the toddler can hold a cup by the handle with the fingers, but the cup is very likely to tip. At eighteen months, the child lifts the cup to the mouth and drinks well, but may drop the cup. By two years, the child handles the cup very well, lifting it, drinking from it, and replacing it safely on the table. The choice of a dominant hand, which may have appeared in the seven-to-fourteen-month period, will be clear by two years, and can be readily observed in the way the child handles feeding utensils. Toddlers can also learn to draw liquids through a straw and many love this "game."

As we mentioned earlier, development of motor skills not only increases the complexity of the child's behavior, but also brings the child into wider contact with the environment, which has many ramifications for cognitive growth and learning. This statement is perhaps truer for the fifteen-to-twenty-three-month period than for any other stage of development.

Language/Cognitive Skills

Recall for a moment how your child's cognitive activity has centered, to date, on the physical manipulation of objects. The purpose of this manipulation was to find out what objects are alike, i.e., what their characteristics are. Your child performed endless physical actions upon objects: banging them, dropping them, mouthing them, squeezing them, etc. The child even became capable, at about twelve months, of performing combinations of actions upon objects in a goal-oriented way. However, up to now the child has not had complex internal ideas about objects. The significant feature of the latter stages of sensorimotor intelligence is that the toddler develops these internal ideas.

This is an extremely busy time! Toddlers actively seek new and interesting things. Everything is explored: wastebaskets, objects on coffee tables, knobs of TV's, etc. All new objects that the child encounters are examined to see if they fit into his or her current conception of the world or whether the object will require the child to alter that conception. For example, the child's conception of the world might include the understanding (based on physical moving of objects) that balls are round and smooth. But if, in the course of continued, active exploration of objects in the environment, the toddler comes across a ball that is not smooth, but is *textured* like a tennis ball, this discovery enlarges the child's conception of the world, at least as far as balls are concerned! The internal idea about balls which the child is in process of developing must now be changed to include the understanding that balls may be smooth or textured. In the course of the cognitive growth throughout the next few years, children will add to their conception of balls the notions that balls may be small or large, red or blue, striped or polka-dotted, vinyl or rubber, etc. Children's internal ideas of balls will preserve the basic characteristic of balls while allowing for the fact that balls can be quite different in appearance and in texture.

The *development of internal ideas of objects* is the most significant feature of the fifteen-to-twenty-three-month period. These ideas allow the child to enter a qualitatively new style of intelligence that features *mental manipulation of objects* in addition to overt physical manipulations. The child increasingly begins to think out solutions to problems rather than just perform a series of trial and error physical actions. You will notice that by the time children are eighteen months old, they will indicate by momentary hesitations and by eye movements when confronted with a "problem," that they are engaging in mental trial and error. A good example is when the toddler puts together a simple puzzle. At fifteen months, the toddler may pick up every puzzle piece availiable and try, in a trial and error way, to fit it in the puzzle. After eighteen months, and increasingly as the child moves toward twenty-four months, the child looks at the cut-out space, then looks at the pieces, *mentally* manipulating them in the mind until spotting the one that will fit. Then the child selectively reaches for that piece and puts it in the puzzle. An enormous achievement!

You will also notice that your child begins to *anticipate consequences*. For example, after rolling a ball toward the couch and seeing it disappear, the child goes to look behind the couch for it.

The fact that the toddler begins to manipulate objects mentally during this period does not mean, however, that he or she will stop physically manipulating them. Toddlers need and want both forms of manipulation: physical *and* mental. So toddlers will engage in constant exploration of the world. The child will form new internal ideas and alter those already formed in order to make them more accurate and useful (like the idea of balls we discussed earlier).

Imitation is a behavior that will be particularly noticeable during this stage. In the past, your child could imitate some actions, but only if they involved movements that were very much like the movements the child was already capable of making, like waving bye-bye. At this stage, however, the toddler is capable of much more accurate imitation. You may notice that your child uses gestures or facial expressions that the child has observed others in the family use. The child scolds the dog in the same way that you do or engages in a temper tantrum after observing another child have one. This behavior is made possible by the child's ability to form internal ideas.

As you might expect, the incredible amount of cognitive development which occurs at this period is related to increased language capability. The more opportunity the toddler has to manipulate objects physically, to develop internal ideas about them, and to hear the words that are used to label them, the more language will be learned. As Stern notes, the child now gains a *sense of a verbal self* which opens the whole rich domain of *verbal relatedness*.[1]

In language comprehension, the toddler will recognize anywhere from a hundred and fifty to three hundred words, including the names of individuals in the child's world. Recognition of words is evident from the fact that the child points accurately to parts of the body, to people, and to pictures of named objects.

By fifteen months most toddlers will say "Thank you" (or at least "Ta-ta") and can follow simple commands ("Come here"). By eighteen months the toddler can carry out two directions ("on the table," "to Mother") and two-word sentences begin.

Up to around eighteen months, the toddler's speaking vocabulary will typically include about ten to twelve words, which are used for the most part to name familiar objects. After eighteen months, the child's speaking vocabulary will increase dramatically. The toddler will also begin to use two-word sentences which are called telegraphic sentences because they contain only the essential words needed to convey a message. Telegraphic sentences might seem to be a very limited form of speech, but you will find that your toddler uses them to specify a great variety of kinds of communication. For example, the child specifies *identification* ("See kitty"); *possession* ("Daddy truck"); *negation* ("No milk"); *recurrence* ("More milk"); *non-existence* ("Milk allgone"); *location* ("Kitty there"); *attribution* ("Coat pretty"); and *questions* ("Kitty allgone?"). The toddler can also specify and request subject-action combinations ("Mommy throw"). By the end of this age/stage, the toddler will have expanded telegraphic sentences into fairly complete sentences that include some prepositions (to, with, on), some pronouns (I, mine, yours), and plurals.

You will find, of course, that *your* toddler's language development is not the same as the toddler who lives next door or down the street. There are often very big differences in the vocabularies of toddlers of the same age and in the complexity of their sentences. For one thing, toddlers appear to have different strategies in learning words. Some spend a lot of time listening to words but not trying to produce them until they feel they understand enough words and can talk well. Others may try to produce many words early on. Also girls excel in the quantity of expressive language development from about twelve months on, although the difference is slight.

There are also individual differences in the time and order in which patterns of speech emerge. It has been suggested that these differences reflect variations in the child's personality and orientation to the world. Children may develop different kinds of vocabularies for the same reason. For example, some will have strongly referential vocabularies; i.e., words to name objects or people in the environment ("See doggy," "See kitty"). Others will have vocabularies which are more interpersonal; i.e., words used to create a bond with others ("Love you," "Me help"). Still others may utilize instrumental vocabularies; i.e., words to gain an end ("More cookie," "Want dog"). You might find that it is fun to keep a diary of *your* child's early vocabulary to notice if the child uses words in a particular way and how this matches the child's personality and other behavior.

Social Skills

Toddlers can tolerate separations from their mothers but have to run back to check on them often. There is an "independency-dependency crisis" at this age, particularly with respect to the primary care giver. On the one hand, the toddler is very involved with Mother or care giver and spends a large part of each day making contact with her, socializing with her, seeking her assistance, expressing affection to her, and seeking her approval. On the other hand, the toddler spends a great deal of time opposing her will, testing the limits she has set, and refusing to comply with her requests. This latter activity is termed *negativism* and frequently characteristic of a child around one and a half.

The abrupt change in your toddler's behavior may lead you to believe that a terrible breach has occurred in your relationship with your child. However, this is not the case. Most children go through negativism at this age. The behavior seems to reflect the child's need to move away from total dependency on the care giver, and develop independent opinions and behaviors. (Interestingly, the second stanza of this song occurs in adolescence.) While it can be a frustrating time for both parent and child, this negativism will not last forever. Usually by the time of the child's second birthday, the negative behaviors have subsided considerably. Wait it out and handle it as playfully as possible. Have *pride* in your toddler's developing assertiveness while not caving in to more negative displays. Also avoid any tendency you might have to overfeed your child in an attempt to stop the negativism. Offering crackers or cookies to distract or bribe your child can lead only to lifelong distortions in the child's association between anxiety and food.

As we said earlier, toddlers can feed themselves with a spoon or fork at this stage, and are also learning to use a cup. Mastery of these skills will be fairly well achieved by the second birthday. Toddlers are also able to assist in dressing and undressing themselves, though undressing is much easier!

While most of the toddler's pursuits are non-social during this period, some unique social abilities emerge. One of these involves more sophistication in the child's ability to get and hold the attention of adults, which is the earliest acquired social skill of babies. Another social skill involves getting an adult's assistance in a task that is too difficult. These skills enable the child to have many good social interactions with adults. These interactions will give the child the opportunity to experience being responded to and to realize that adults will help—most of the time.

We do not recommend that you give your toddler your undivided attention every moment of the day. The child needs to experience the real world, which does not revolve exclusively around himself or herself. Parents who pay *too* much attention to their children may do them a disservice by preventing them from learning ways of getting and holding someone else's attention. Parents may also do their children a disservice by giving them help automatically every time it is asked for even when help is not really needed. Respond to your toddler frequently, and allow the child to feel that help is available *most* of the time, but also allow the child opportunities to learn that family and society have their own agendas which will sometimes result in personal frustrations for the toddler.

Play experiences with other children should be fairly short in duration during this period and should be well supervised. The toddler is not yet old enough to share toys with others, and generally responds by hoarding toys and not allowing anyone else to touch them. This behavior is very expectable and normal in a child who has only recently acquired the notion of object permanency (see p. 394). However, while this behavior is normal, toddlers may harm each other in their attempts to guard their possessions. Supervision is essential.

Emotions/Feelings

The fact that toddlers are more explorative, more independent, and more definite in sense of self during the fifteen-to-twenty-three-month period, means that you can expect to see them express themselves in a much more assertive way. As we already said, there will be frequent refusals to do what you want the child to do, and your child will insist on doing things without assistance. Assertion often leads to frustration and/or anger during this period, as the toddler faces the fact that adults intervene to alter "refusals." Toddlers can't always accomplish what they set out to do. The temper tantrums which result from these frustrations will, fortunately, decline with age and the development of language, general ability, and more mature assertiveness skills.

In spite of the negativism displayed at this age, you will see many signs that attachment to the mother is still important. We have previously discussed the toddler's displays of affection to the care giver and the strong desire to keep her attention. These overtures of affection are appealing and should be responded to and reciprocated. The reason is simple: the stronger the emotional tie between the toddler and care giver, the freer the child will feel to leave her for brief periods to explore the world and to establish other relationships. The kind of relationship the child has with the mother in this period of life is an excellent predictor of the kind of preschooler he or she will become. Securely attached toddlers become outgoing preschoolers who are well liked, sympathetic to others, self-directed, goal-oriented, and eager to learn new skills.[2]

Empathy is a relatively new emotion which emerges at this time. At ten to twelve months, your baby tended to respond to another child's distress by crying. After one year, however, the baby developed the ability to respond to another's distress by touching, cuddling, or rubbing the injured party. By eighteen months, the toddler will indicate understanding of the emotional distress of others by mimicking facial expressions of pain. You can facilitate the development of empathy in your toddler by being a model of kindness and concern for others when they are hurt, and by simultaneously expecting and guiding your child to control aggression, by pointing out how it hurts the other person.

Aggression may be more prevalent now, especially if the toddler has an older sibling who has been aggressive toward the younger child, or if the child is placed in a situation where there is a need to compete for toys and attention with other children. Aggression must be patiently, but firmly and consistently, channeled.

Fears become more prevalent in this period. You may find that your child is afraid of thunder, the dark, being left alone, animals, or imaginary monsters. Don't try to talk your child out of these fears, and don't try to make the child ashamed by saying, "Big boys aren't afraid of the dark." Children's fears are *very real* to them, and need to be dealt with on a real level. Try to structure the child's environment so that he or she has the ability to exercise some control over the things feared. For example, children who are afraid of the dark are helped by a night light. As the toddler becomes older, and has more facility with language, your explanations will be more helpful in causing fears to subside.

Developmental Warning Signals

You already know that children develop at their own pace. But there are some key "danger signals." If by age eighteen months your child does not feed self with a spoon, does not "jargon" or imitate speech, does not move around to explore, does not give eye contact, or does not squat down to pick up objects, your child is suffering from a developmental delay which warrants a workup to find out why.[3]

The above signs are red flags. They require action on your part but do not necessarily call for panic. Start the process by going to your pediatrician. Tell the doctor about these developmental red flags. Often a comprehensive developmental assessment, which can be done only in a university hospital or clinic, is in order.

CARE GIVER TASKS

Basic Care

NUTRITION

Your child's nutrition during this period will be mainly supplied by the same table foods you provide for the rest of the family. Molars now give the toddler the capacity to chew, so you can introduce more foods, and you can also stop mashing and chopping them as much. However, you must continue to completely cut meat, especially hot dogs, into small bites to prevent choking. For safety's sake serve small portions and always supervise your toddler's meals and snacks.

Since the toddler's stomach size is still small, the child needs to eat frequently during the day. As a result, you need to provide snacks which furnish adequate calories in a nutritious form but do not contribute to tooth decay. At this age, try fresh fruits and vegetables, cubes of cheese, peanut butter or cheese sandwiches with whole grain bread, and fruit juice. Try to avoid giving your child those commercial snack foods which are highly refined and processed and contain few nutrients. Because the toddler loves to imitate, if *you* get in the habit of nutritious snacks rather than junk food, your toddler will likely eat what you eat.

Be sensible, too, about the kinds of food you provide at mealtime. Ideally, meals will include a well-balanced diet of meats, fruits, breads, and vegetables that the toddler likes. Provide small amounts and let toddlers point or say "More" when they want more. Don't feed too many desserts and other foods containing sugar to avoid introducing a lifelong habit which can lead to both tooth decay and obesity.

CLEANING/GROOMING

A daily or almost daily bath should normally be part of the child's routine at this age, since toddler's explorations get them sticky and dirty. Toddlers will probably want to wash themselves, which should be encouraged, but you will need to go over most areas. You, of course, still need to cut the nails.

Washing hands is a task the toddler can learn very early, and one which the child will enjoy if you wash your hands at the same time. The toddlers should be helped to do this before meals, after sitting on the potty, and after playing with pets. Toddlers can also be taught to wash their own faces, especially if you provide a special sponge which is softer on the skin than a washcloth.

Toddler girls are prone to urinary tract infections probably for two reasons: a short urethra and incorrect wiping after toileting. When cleansing your daughter's bottom always wipe down, from front to back—away from the opening to the bladder. As she learns toileting herself, teach her the correct direction to wipe.

Toddlers will probably show interest in brushing their hair, and in dressing and undressing (most toddlers can take off clothes earlier and better than they can put them on). You can assist these early attempts at dressing by buying clothes that are easy to get on. We recommend pants that have an elasticized waist, and loose pull-on shirts with big necks. To encourage the child's interest in dressing, you might try putting an item only partly on and letting the child complete the task. Be careful about what's on the toddler's feet. Running in socks is dangerous, especially on wood or vinyl floors; bare feet or shoes or sneakers with non-skid soles are safer.

SLEEP/ACTIVITY

Most toddlers still take daytime naps, lasting anywhere from one to three hours, and sleep an average of eleven hours each night. Close to the end of this period your child will probably make the transition from two naps to one. Unfortunately, as Spock says, "There's a stage in a baby's life when two naps a day are too many and one is not enough."[4] During this stage you may have a cranky child on your hands during the day and an overtired one at night. It usually doesn't take long for the child to equilibrate, however.

Sleep will be facilitated if you take the time to make bedtime a happy time, with special routines including cuddling, reading, and/or singing. Average toddlers will wake up two or three times a night but usually will go back to sleep on their own. However, about a third of toddlers will cry and want to be cuddled or changed. We both found that a soft night light and toys in the crib helped our children drift back to sleep most of the time. When they really seemed to need us—for whatever reason—we took them in bed with us or slept with them for a while. Most families do the same.[5] We have always deplored the fact that at the age children most need to be close to someone, our culture tries to make them sleep alone! There is only one thing wrong with taking young children to bed with you. They may interfere with the parents' rest or important togetherness times. Our bottom-line advice is that it's *your* bed; you decide who sleeps there!

Your child may begin to climb out of the crib during this age/stage. This activity should signal your child's readiness for a single bed, low to the floor or equipped with safety rails. Most toddlers are proud of a "grown-up" bed. It also lets you comfort the child by lying down together until the child falls back asleep.

EXERCISE

Toddlers will need more opportunities to exercise their emerging motor skills in this period than was necessary in the seven-to-fourteen-month period. Now that the child can run fairly smoothly, jump, and use small-wheeled vehicles, the child will need more space than was required earlier and will also need lots of outdoor experiences. A trip to the park or a daily walk is in order if outdoor play space is not available at home. In rainy climates, we think it's a good idea to provide some indoor climbing apparatus such as a small slide.

STRESS MANAGEMENT

The greatest amount of stress in this age/stage results from conflicts with authority and difficulties over the establishment of habits, such as eating, bathing, and bedtime. Stress may also result when the toddler's striving toward independence becomes frustrated. Toddlers want to feed themselves, but the spoon keeps turning upside down and spilling its contents before it gets to the mouth! Toddlers want to dress themselves, but the buttons on the shirt will not work! Toddlers want to play with the water in the toilet, but Mother not only takes them out of the bathroom but shuts the door! The frustrations toddlers feel are often expressed in the form of emotional outbursts. Tantrums actually peak during this period of life. Refer to page 400 for suggestions on dealing with temper tantrums.

Although all of the frustrations which the toddler experiences cannot be avoided, many of them can be minimized. One of your most important caretaking tasks at this period is the management of the child's environment with an eye toward minimizing frustration. We have already suggested that you buy clothes that are easy to get on. We also suggest that you provide toys that are within the child's skill level, and put away those that are too complex. In short, try to use *preventive* rather than corrective methods of controlling frustration.

In addition to managing the environment, you can minimize your toddler's frustration by the way that *you* interact with the child. First, praise your child's initial attempts at trying new behaviors without waiting for successful completion of the task. Second, make your requests of the child simple and your limits or demands few in number.

Stress may arise from the presence of an older sibling in the family who reacts aggressively toward the toddler or a younger sibling—a new baby who competes for attention. Each child needs some individual time.

EMOTIONAL "NUTRITION"

As a result of the many frustrations that toddlers experience during this period, they will need lots of physical nurturance and affection. It is through holding, cuddling, kissing, etc., that toddlers receive the message that they are lovable people. All primary care givers need to give this message. The message needs to be given not only at "pleasant" times of the day, but also after your child has been disciplined for some "transgression." These times require special reassurance. Don't hesitate to let toddlers know that they are good. Remind your child how much love you have for him or her, especially when you have had to stop or limit your child's behavior.

As the primary organizer of the child's environment and activities, establish —and follow through on—some basic daily routines. Security at this age is best maintained through the orderliness of the toddler's routines.

Toddlers are quite likely to form attachments to a "transitional object" like a blanket or stuffed animal, if they have not already done so. The transitional object has been described as the "first *not-me* possession." The child will carry the object everywhere, turn to it when stressed, and get *very* upset if it's lost. This phenomenon is especially common in middle class children who sleep in a room by themselves where the incidence of attachment to a transitional object (most often a blanket or favorite stuffed animal) is 77 percent.[6] The attachment is normal and the child will eventually give up the object.

CARE OF THE CARE GIVER

As with parents of crawlers, if you're a full-time care giver, your biggest problem could be energy depletion caused by chasing your active, exploring toddler from early morning to late at night, seven days a week. In some instances you only have one hour off—when the toddler naps.

We urge you to arrange for "respite" care for yourself. As we said earlier, try to find a neighborhood child who wants a regular "job." Payment for toddler-chasing varies from neighborhood to neighborhood but ten-year-olds in our neighborhood start at fifty cents an hour—a small price to pay for your physical and mental health. Don't forget to instruct your helper in your safety rules and limits. Part- or full-time day care can also provide a toddler-friendly environment and respite for the mother.

Socialization Tasks

PLAY/STIMULATION

Play, at this stage of development, as we have already pointed out, is largely non-social. Even in situations where toddlers are placed together, they really don't interact much. Their "play" is termed parallel and is characterized by children playing independently beside one another. Nevertheless, they gain a great deal from experience with another child.

For the most part, play still involves exploratory behavior in relation to objects in the world. Your toddler will practice skills endlessly upon objects, including dropping and throwing them, swinging hinged objects back and forth (doors, books, etc.), opening and closing them, placing them in an upright position, knocking them down and replacing them, putting them together and taking them apart, putting them through openings, and pouring them into and out of containers. As we have already pointed out, the toddler needs to engage in this exploratory behavior to develop internal ideas about objects. Your job is to provide a safe and stimulating environment where the toddler can carry on the explorations.

By toddlerhood there are observable differences between boys and girls in play and toy preferences. This seems to be independent of whether the children are reared in traditional homes (girls in pink; boys in blue) or homes with a modern orientation toward children where efforts are made to avoid sex stereotyping. Girls at this age are more apt to choose quiet toys while boys run around more with their toys. We feel that parents should accept these differences, which are real, and allow each child to play the way he or she wants to. At the same time parents should avoid excesses of sex stereotyping by encouraging girls to climb and to get dirty while playing and by allowing boys to have dolls or teddy bears to hug.

Parents are an important part of their toddler's language learning. You can greatly facilitate the development of your child's verbal ability by talking to the child often in language that is slow, distinct, and natural (don't use too much baby talk), by asking questions, and by responding to what the child says. You can also assist language development by reading storybooks to your child and talking about the pictures, and letting your child listen to conversations between adults.

Remember that language development will be slower if an older sibling is allowed to "talk for" the child, or if the child is waited on constantly, and thus has no need to make requests.

DISCIPLINE/GUIDANCE/VALUES

With the onset of "negativism" in the fifteen-to-twenty-three-month period, the issue of discipline becomes increasingly salient. We recommend that you handle negativism as firmly and consistently as is needed, but also that you avoid power struggles and yield to the child when the stakes are high for the child and not very high for you. Keep in mind that "negativism" is just a reflection of the child's growing desire to be independent and that it will pass as maturation brings more independence. Nobody ever hastened the departure of negativism by slapping, yelling, nagging, or shaming a child. In fact, nothing will hasten the departure of this behavior except time and pride in the positive side of the child's assertiveness. If you respond in a loving, understanding way, if you set and enforce essential limits, and if you *praise desired behavior*, you will find that your child's reaction to discipline is positive. Your toddler will want to please you. In fact Anne didn't experience any serious degree of negativism at this age with any of her children.

In the preceding stage, a major value your child eagerly pursued was the desire to please you. This value isn't lost during toddlerhood, though it can seem to be submerged because the toddler is developing a new and very important value: a sense of *self* as an autonomous person who also deserves self-assertiveness and being pleased. The child plays with this new value as with any new skill. The details can be very exasperating: if every time you say "up" the child says "down," or if when you choose the red shirt the child arbitrarily wants the green one. But if you keep your eye on the big picture, this phase is fascinating. The autonomy to resist blind obedience to your wishes lays a foundation for later independent thinking and ability to resist blind obedience to peer pressures in adolescence or bad situations in adulthood. Admire the value, even though in the details you may have to model some firm assertiveness of *your* needs.

TOILET TRAINING

If you want to start a heated discussion, ask a group of mothers and grandmothers, "At what age should toilet training begin?" or "How does one go about it?" The answers may be quite varied. You might hear everything from: "My child was trained at six months; I just put her on the potty every twenty minutes," to "I don't think a child is really trained until three or four," and "Children train themselves—they don't need any help!"

When we lived in sod cabins or covered wagons without easy means of heating or washing, early bladder and bowel control were important both for the baby *and* the mother. Today most of us have the ability to keep our baby warm, so being wet is not as hazardous as it was formerly. We also have the ability to launder our baby's diapers with relative ease—or we can afford disposables.

You might think that mothers would automatically opt for later training. Yet some mothers feel an awesome responsibility to train early because training is the first "visible" socialization they do and they want the world to know they succeeded. Other mothers are pressured by *their* mothers to start "early" because they did. One young woman told Marilyn some mothers want to complete training early so they can brag about it because they consider this an example of high intelligence in their baby. However, there is no correlation between age of training and intelligence in the baby.

Some time between eighteen months and two, the average toddler will begin to show awareness of bowel movements. When play has become well enough organized that the child has to stop playing in order to bear down and push the stool out, it is not likely to escape the toddler's attention. With verbal children, you can talk about what is happening. Baby-talk words for the bowel movement like "pooh-pooh" seem natural, probably because pursing the lips and then blowing out to make the "pooh" noise are rather like the grunting the child may naturally do in expelling the stool. When the child notices the occurrence of the bowel movement, and can talk about it, this is a natural time to introduce the idea of putting the pooh-pooh in a potty.

Your toddler has a lot to learn about toileting. The child must understand what adults expect the child to do with their excretions. They have to realize what it feels like just *before* they have to go. They have to know how to get to the potty or a toilet. They have to learn to remove clothing quickly and sit on the potty. They have to learn to relax the sphincter muscles and let the urine or feces out. It's easy to see why the child has to be *ready* to learn this complicated, sequential pattern.

How and when should you start toilet training? First, you will look for signs that your child is physically and emotionally ready to be trained at this time. You will notice that your toddler has an interest in the toilet, and wants to imitate adult behaviors related to the toilet. You will also notice that the child has an awareness of when he or she has wet or soiled, or when he or she is about to do so. (The physical warning signals that accompany bowel movements usually come before the actual urge to defecate. Unfortunately, the physical warning signals for urination are almost immediate with the urge to urinate.) And of course your child has mastered running and walking, and is able to sit and play quietly for a period of time.

CHECKLIST FOR POTTY TRAINING READINESS

Marilyn has had this checklist in her files for quite a while—so long she doesn't know whom to credit. It's a good list. When you can answer "yes" to these questions, your child is ready.

My child frequently stays dry for several hours at a time.

My child knows when he or she is ready to urinate, and indicates this by holding himself or herself or by some facial expression.

My child walks easily from room to room and *sometimes* runs.
My child can pick up small objects easily.
My child understands simple requests.
My child can communicate his or her needs to me.
My child can regularly attend to a task for five to ten minutes.

The *parent's* checklist may include the fact that the parent is sick of changing diapers or can think of better uses for a five-dollar bill than disposable diapers; the preschool that the parent wants for the child is unwilling to take children until they are toilet-trained; or the mother feels if one more person asks her if Susie is trained, she will scream.

The most important thing Marilyn learned about toilet training (both from her own two children and from hundreds of mothers and children in her practice) was that the longer you wait to train your child, the shorter and easier the process is.

There is good evidence that reliable daytime control of bowels and bladder occurs at about ages two and a half to three while nighttime control is usually achieved between ages three and four. Boys are slower than girls to achieve control.[7] These numbers hold true *whether training was started at nine months or two years.* So early starting does not mean early finishing—far from it. All an early start means is a longer time spent at the task, and possibly unnecessary conflicts. If you are lazy—and don't like long tasks—or if you are efficient—and don't like long tasks—or if you achievement-oriented—and don't like long tasks—take our advice and *wait.* Besides, early training is *Mother training*—the child will achieve control when he or she is ready.

We know from working with many mothers that the need to socialize the child is very strong in parents. Parents feel an awesome responsibility. This need to socialize may even be in our genes because as we evolved perhaps those children who learned to be socialized were better equipped to survive in a tribe. Toilet training can be thought of as an important socialization task. Parents are often anxious they won't succeed or will do something wrong. Not true—you will *all* succeed or rather *all of your normal children eventually will achieve bowel and bladder control.* We guarantee this. (By the way this is one of the few guarantees children come with!)

The first thing you do is teach your child—if you haven't already done so—the words you will use for feces and urine. "Pooh-pooh" and "wee-wee" are fine. Later your child will pick up the adult terms for both of these body excretory products from peers or from you.

Next you provide your toddler with a potty chair. Or you can buy a potty seat that fastens to the regular toilet. Most children balk at the toilet seat and feel uncomfortable or fearful on it probably because it is high off the floor and is also attached to the noisy flushing "motor." Occasionally a child will balk at the potty chair and prefer the potty attachment, probably because it's more like what Mommy and Daddy use. By the way, Brazelton suggests[8] you *not* use the urine deflector on the potty. Your little boy can get hurt climbing on or off. Boys very quickly—and with delight—learn to deflect the urine stream themselves when they realize that peeing in the pot makes a noise!

Marilyn offers parents three simple steps: Prepare, Place, and Praise.

1) *Prepare* the child by showing him or her what grown-ups do with their stool and urine. 2) *Place* the ready child on the potty—first with clothes on, then off. 3) *Praise* the child when he or she performs.

Let's look at these steps in more detail. Why *prepare?* Remember your child has been in diapers since birth. The child has to recognize that feces and urine come out of the body and that people don't like them lying around just anywhere so they deposit them in a special place.

What's the best way to prepare? Let the ready child watch you. Mothers are followed into the bathroom anyway by a crawler or toddler who wants to be with you. Don't just sit there, tell your child what you are doing and why you are doing it. Show the child what you have "made." Let the child flush and watch. This frightens some toddlers—if so, wait a few days or weeks before flushing in front of the toddler or asking the child to flush for you. While you are changing the toddler's diapers tell your child what he or she made. Show your child it is the same product you made and it goes in the same place.

Fathers: make a special effort to teach your son how and where men urinate. We think it's a good idea to show your son that you can also sit down to urinate and hold the penis down so the urine goes into the toilet. You can say that little boys start that way (because they often will urinate while having a bowel movement on the potty) and then learn to stand up, stop, and start as grown men do.

Place. Start by placing your ready child on his or her own potty chair. First introduce the child to the chair and say what it is for and that when the child is ready you'll help him or her learn how to use it like a big person does. Let the child get used to the chair being around and then place your clothed child on the chair to get used to it.

Brazelton suggests seating your clothed child on the potty once a day at a routine time and using a cookie to reward the child for sitting down. It helps if you can get an older child to show your child what is supposed to happen. The next step is to take the child back to the potty a second time each day after the child has had a bowel movement in the diaper. Together, drop the stool into the potty. This is usually followed by the child performing in the potty within a few days or weeks. (In Brazelton's series of 1,170 normal children, 80 percent began to perform on their own by age twenty-seven months using this method.)

When the child tells you what he or she has done—in the diapers—the child is ready for the next step: place the child on the potty chair *without* clothes. Tell your child he or she is ready to try to do what grown-ups do. Pick a good time for placing the child on the potty, like after meals or when you notice the pants have been dry for two hours or so. Don't ask the child if he or she wants to use the potty, but say instead, "It's time to use the potty . . ." "Use the potty; then you can . . ." Keep the child on the potty for just a short time like five minutes. Don't ever strap the child or force the child to sit there. If the child is unhappy let the child get off.

We believe in "going for broke." When you are ready to train in earnest, take the diapers off—at least when the child is up and about though you can still use diapers for nap and nights. The reason for this is it signals to a ready child that *you* think he or she is ready. It also gives the child maximum independence in toileting. The child can pull down the training pants quickly but cannot get out of a diaper without your help or a lot of time-consuming wiggling, by which time it's too late. If the climate and your house permit, bare bottom is even better than training pants for the few days or weeks of training.

Obviously you must be prepared to accept accidents. You must also treat accidents very casually. "Susie, you wet your pants. Take them off and put them in the hamper. Take a dry pair and put them on yourself. Next time try to pee in the potty. I'll remind you. Okay?"

Praise. Marilyn, a staunch believer in rewards for good performance, provided a tiny candy when the potty was correctly used. She did the same thing when housebreaking her dog and it worked for both the puppy and the children!

Training is a form of behavioral modification and this works best with rewards. One day your child will perform when you have placed him or her on the potty. With lavish praise—and a reward—your child will realize the performance was a good one. After a few of these place—perform—praise cycles the child will be able to make a connection in his or her mind and realize that there is *control* over the performance. "I can do it myself!" Learning to wipe takes a bit longer.

Please remember the total process can take several months. Also remember there can be as long as a year between daytime and nighttime control so don't throw away the diapers yet. If the child is in substitute child care, it is extremely important to communicate with the provider, so that all the adults involved can work together. This allows the child the security of consistency and reinforcement.

By the way, one price we pay for the luxury and hygiene of flush toilets when we have toddlers around is a plumbing bill if the toddler flushes a teddy bear or any other non-flushable object down the toilet. Recognize your child's fascination when the stool disappears with a rush of sound and swirl! The curious child will want to see if this magic occurs again—perhaps with something different. This is the place for firm "No's!" Keeping the seat down and the door closed works but may delay the development of learning how to get to the toilet when necessary *without* calling Mother. However, if your child seems to be going through a period of utter fascination with the swirling waters it's probably best to keep the doors closed except when you can be there—perhaps to let the toddler flush toilet paper repeatedly until tired of the game. The fascination is usually temporary and, shortly, your child will learn that only excretory products and toilet paper are allowed in the toilet. In the meantime, you could leave the child's potty seat just outside the bathroom door.

Remember to give your child time to learn this complex skill. If you find that your child is not particularly successful at toilet training, consider that perhaps he or she isn't ready to be trained. Stop your efforts without shaming the child, and try again in a month or two.

Try not to start toilet training if your child is in a highly negativistic period. The negative behavior may worsen and you may wind up in a battle of wills. Waiting out the negativism before toilet training begins is far better and easier.

Keep in mind that even when the toddler is able to stay dry during the day, your child will not stay dry through the night. Nighttime control is rarely established before thirty-six months and often not until much later. Camp directors and military boot camps are aware of the fact that some otherwise normal kids —especially males—may continue to have nighttime enuresis into middle childhood or even into their teens. Medical evaluation is worthwhile (see p. 652). The use of medication (imipramine) and training devices (bell and pad) is controversial.

Meanwhile the laundry problem remains. We have two hints:
1) Have the child sleep with a heavy bath towel tucked over the sheet. The child who wets in the night can just pull the towel off, throw it on the floor, and put it in the laundry hamper in the morning. No fuss, no blame.
2) Water beds, unlike conventional mattresses, do not become urine-soaked and smelly.

If ordinary training methods fail, Azrin's book *Toilet Training in Less Than a Day* is full of practical suggestions.[9] He has applied his methods successfully even with severely mentally retarded children, who are especially difficult to train.

DAY CARE

The majority of mothers today find it necessary or preferable to work outside the home when their children are young. We have covered substitute child care in the chapter on helpers, and we want to say a few words here about care at this age.

Toddlers need both loving care and "space," both physically and psychologically, to achieve that degree of independence they are capable of. The key care giver, in whichever of the possible child care options you choose, should be a person whose qualifications for child care and concepts of child development are acceptable to you. Be certain that this person can love your child and will be able to meet his or her needs.

If you choose family day care or center day care, you must find out the ratio of children to adults in that setting. It is our belief that while one adult can handle three or four older youngsters, she can't meet the needs of more than two toddlers (and not more than six children in all). You may also want to ask questions such as the following:

Exploratory Behavior. Will there be opportunities for exploring or will my child be confined all day?

Discipline. What are the limits here and what type of consequences will ensue if my child breaks a limit? How is aggression handled? How is negativism handled?

Consistency of Care. Are the people who will give care to my child here on a regular basis, or are the care givers volunteers who are here sporadically?

Safety. How carefully will my child be supervised in daily activities? How hazard-free does the environment appear?

Be certain to visit the home or center where your child will be cared for before making your choice about substitute care.

After you begin to work, keep in close touch with the individual (or individuals) who is caring for your child. Consider that person to be a partner in the child's growth and development, and a source of information for you about the child's experiences.

Above all, continue to provide your baby or toddler quality time with you when you are at home, giving the child attention. It's important that *you* play, talk, and cuddle your child when you two meet after a day's work. It is the quality of time you spend with your child, not the quantity, that will be crucial in the ongoing development of an attachment to you, and in proper adjustment to others.

We sympathize with mothers of young children who are employed full-time and don't always have the energy to provide quality time when they come home from work. We've been there! Part-time work when the children are young helps as does eliminating virtually everything from your household duties, except absolute essentials. If there's ever a choice between cooking dinner or fast food and time for your baby, choose the latter.

Marilyn, who worked full-time when she had two toddlers, remembers dropping to the floor when she arrived home to spend time with the children on their level. She and her husband ate with the children, bathed them, and sang songs in the rocking chair until bedtime. *Then* Marilyn opened the mail. She remembers what a luxurious feeling it was when the children were older, had friends or other amusements when she came home, and barely said "Hello." She could look at the mail when she first came home!

HEALTH CARE

Medical Care

Toddlers should see the doctor at least once during the fifteen-to-twenty-three-month period. At the fifteen-month checkup, the doctor will weigh and measure the child, assess nutrition and general appearance, and do a careful physical examination. The examination will include a vision, hearing, and developmental assessment. The measles, mumps, and rubella (MMR) immunization will be given at this time.

Your child may be quite fearful of doctors at this age. As stranger anxiety peaks it's a good idea for your doctor to do as much of the examination as possible while the toddler is in your lap. The toddler doesn't like being undressed or appreciate being touched or handled by strangers. The wise pediatrician shows the toddler on a doll, or on himself or herself, everything that will happen (how the stethoscope and otoscope are used, for example).

Dental Care

Give your child a soft toothbrush and help the child to use it after meals, especially once the molars have emerged. Use a pea-size amount of fluoride-containing toothpaste. Your child will probably be interested in brushing his or her teeth now, but some help from you will be required to do an adequate job. Children should be taken for their first visit to the dentist when they have acquired all twenty primary teeth.

Environmental Health

As said earlier, the most important environmental care for the toddler is to make the environment both stimulating and safe for exploration. This is a "danger age" for TV. The child watches the screen as things are happening there— albeit in only two dimensions. Parents are often exhausted running after the toddler all day—and plopping the child in front of the TV set is *so* tempting. We've already explained that TV is not a good baby-sitter but we appreciate parental exhaustion. Marilyn suggests you limit TV to no more than thirty minutes. Anne would go by the child's interests and the quality of programming up to an hour or two a day if the child enjoys some quiet viewing time. Another suggestion is to hire a neighborhood ten- to fourteen-year-old for that tough hour before dinner to give you a "toddler break."

SAFETY

The continued development and refinement of the toddler's motor skills during this period make child-proofing very critical. The toddler opens doors and drawers, takes things apart, and can open bottles easily. Your toddler not only has the curiosity but the motor and thinking skills to pull over a chair in order to climb into the cabinet in order to get something. The toddler has a much easier time exploring the environment than younger children because of these advancing motor skills. Your child also has a much easier time picking up objects and putting them into his or her mouth. In fact, the first act the toddler is likely to perform when encountering something new and interesting is to put it in his or her mouth, gum it, and swallow it, if possible. This applies to objects that are solid as well as liquids in bottles or containers. Remember your toddler has well mastered the art of drinking from a container.

The most dangerous aspect of toddlerhood is the impulsivity of children at this age and the speed with which they can "get into things." The large number of accidental poisonings each year in this age group is related to the fact that toddlers do not pause to test the odor or the taste of substances which they swallow. Poison-control centers report that toddlers even swallow such foul-smelling and foul-tasting substances as gasoline and cleaning fluid. This is clearly an area where the powerful curiosity of a child can have extremely harsh consequences.

Eighteen months is the *peak* time for exploring drawers, wastebaskets, and cupboards, both those near the floor and those that can be reached by climbing. Child-proof your house accordingly! (See Chapter 5, p. 123.)

Also, toddlerhood by definition means walking, but not yet well. Prevent dangerous falls (stairs, porches, patio glass doors, etc.) and remove sharp-edged furniture. Be especially careful in the kitchen as the toddler can now reach for pot handles or appliance cords and cause hot liquid to spill. Watch out for your own coffee cup—keep containers with hot liquid well inside the table or stove.

Children play with a greater variety of toys at this age and have greater access to their siblings' toys. These toys and other objects, particularly metal cars, need to be examined for sharp parts and parts that are small enough to be swallowed.

In hot climates where backyard swimming pools are prevalent, children at this age must be the particular focus of pool safety. Lock doors that yield access to the pool, and *maintain absolute vigilance.*

When baby starts toddling, feet should either be clad in shoes or should be bare, as socks are slippery. One doctor suggests that leather shoes are safer than sneakers as toddlers fall less when wearing shoes.[10] When you are holding a toddler by the hand do *not* lift the baby up (as over a curb). You could injure the baby's shoulder.

*   *   *

Toddlerhood brings both fun and fears—*for the parents.* At the end of this period your child is on the way to becoming a walking, talking individual person.

Babyhood is over!

Remember, children at this age *move more quickly* than they did at previous periods. At the same time, they *do not comprehend danger* and they *do not have a realistic sense of their own capabilities.*

SUGGESTED READINGS AND RESOURCES

Azrin, Nathan H., and Besalel, Victoria A. *A Parent's Guide to Bed Wetting Control: A Step-by-Step Method.* New York: Pocket Books, 1981.
Azrin, Nathan H., and Fox, Richard M. *Toilet Training in Less Than a Day.* New York: Pocket Books, 1981.

Two practical books on toilet training based on the authors' experience with both normal and difficult situations such as with retarded children.

Barber, Lucie W., and Williams, Herman. *Your Baby's First Thirty Months.* Tucson, Ariz.: H.P. Books, 1981.

A chronologically arranged, easily read guide to positive child rearing in the first thirty months. Photographs and charts are used well, and diary space is provided to help you follow your child's development.

Beebe, Brooke McKamy. *Tips for Toddlers.* New York: Dell, 1983.

A collection of tips from parents. Covers toddlers from toilet training to starting nursery school. Easy to read, many good ideas.

Brazelton, T. Berry. *Toddlers and Parents.* New York: Dell, 1976.

This book has much information that is appropriate for this age child. It details the struggle of the striving for independence from both the child's and parent's view. By using actual families, many behaviors and specific problems are dealt with. Brazelton helps parents analyze their child's temperament.

Brooks, Jane B. *The Process of Parenting.* Palo Alto, Calif.: Mayfield Publishing, 1981.

A parenting handbook which spans development of children from birth to adolescence. The book also covers special topics such as working parents, single parents, and stepparents.

Church, Joseph. *Understanding Your Child from Birth to Three.* New York: Pocket Books, 1982.

An excellent source of knowledge for parents desiring information on the psychological development of the child. The book includes chapters on children's fears, sex differences, discipline, and individual differences in personality.

Gesell, Arnold. *The First Five Years of Life: The Preschool Years.* New York: Harper, 1940.

Although this Gesell book is out of print, it is worth a trip to the library. Wonderful, informative reading.

Leach, Penelope. *Your Baby and Child: From Birth to Age Five.* New York: Knopf, 1978.

From birth through the preschool years. Lovely drawings and photographs.

Mueser, Anne Marie, and Liptay, Lynne M. *Talk & Toddle.* New York: St. Martin's, 1983.

A very readable book about child care in the first three years arranged alphabetically by topic for easy consultation as the need arises.

Rubin, Richard R.; Fisher, John J., III; and Doering, Susan G. *Your Toddler.* New York: Macmillan, 1980.

Another toddler book—well written and charmingly illustrated with photographs of children in this age group.

Sparling, Joseph, and Lewis, Isabelle. *Learningames for the First Three Years: A Guide to Parent/Child Play.* New York: Walker, 1984.

An illustrated "play" book that gives specific ideas on what activities to do with children along with the "whys?"

Spock, Benjamin, and Rothenberg, Michael B. *Dr. Spock's Baby and Child Care.* New York: Pocket Books, 1985.

The latest revision of one of the most well-known and widely circulated of child care books.

Stoppard, Miriam. *Day-to-Day Baby Care Book: An Owner's Manual for the First Three Years.* New York: Ballantine, 1985.

A truly comprehensive, fully illustrated, step-by-step handbook on a range of child care activities from infancy to age three. The book examines everything from equipment, clothing, holding and handling to aspects of development.

White, Burton L. *The First Three Years of Life.* Revised ed. New York: Prentice-Hall, 1985.

A comprehensive summary of Dr. White's extensive research on children in the first three years of life. The book is organized around aspects of the young child's environment which White has bound to the development of competence in relating to the world. Readable language.

14

MOVING OUTWARD:
LIFE WITH A TWO-YEAR-OLD

Scope of Chapter

This chapter deals with the two-year-old—the child in transition between toddlerhood and childhood. You no longer have a baby—but you don't have a grown-up either. Far from it!

Introduction

Age two is a transition year. Many milestones are already achieved—crawling, walking, and first words—but the more mature three-year-old is not yet here.

Before age two, children are described as being six months old, eighteen months old, twenty-one months old, etc. But the two-year-olds are called two until they are three—not twenty-eight months old, or thirty-three months old. No doubt our way of describing age reflects certain attitudes and expectations. Parents rejoice when their baby achieves a milestone and look forward to the next one a few months later. Now that the baby is two, it's a long way until three!

During the long year, questions arise from others or in the parent's own mind: "You mean she *still* isn't toilet-trained?" "Does he *still* need a bottle?" "Can he put two words together yet?" "Has she started to do puzzles?" Some parents begin to worry about whether their child is "learning"—colors, numbers, letters, etc. Parents may fall into the trap of focusing on where their children are going, instead of where they are.

In addition, during this year the child may enter a difficult stage. Some children go through a negative assertive period before age two, but most enter such a period at about age two and a half. This negativity makes some parents doubt their ability in parenting. The techniques that "worked" when their child was younger may now seem ineffective. Parents look at their demanding, seemingly less flexible child and wonder what is happening.

As in other stages of transition between equilibrium and disequilibrium, which seem to occur about every six to eight months, there can be difficult moments or weeks. But it is during these times that some of the most exciting developmental breakthroughs occur. Often just before a child learns to walk or talk or enters a new stage of perceiving/thinking, there is a disequilibrium, which represents an internal struggle. Parents can view this struggle either as a stage to "get through" or as an exciting, challenging time. Usually, reality includes both. The jump in language skills, improved motor skills, bowel and bladder control, improved memory, and the appearance of new fears all are part of this year, which is a powerful time of growing.

The two-year-old continues the ambivalence of toddlerhood—asserting independence one moment and needing the security of parents the next. The development of self-control, along with assertiveness and a sense of self, makes this year one of the most important in the child's life.

This stage with all its accompanying ambivalence has been compared with the adolescent stage. Parents might want to remember what their own teen years were like and realize that a two-year-old has less language, less experience, and no peer support to help him or her through this period. Understanding parents have a marvelous opportunity to help their child grow this year!

KEY INFORMATION

Biophysical Information

SIZE AND SHAPE

The average two-year-old girl weighs 27.1 pounds (range 23.5 to 31.7) and the average boy weighs 27.7 pounds (range 24.7 to 31.9). Children will gain four to five pounds during this year.

The average boy will be 34.4 inches tall (range 33.1 to 35.9) and the average girl will be 34.1 inches (range 32.3 to 35.8). Adult height will be about double the two-year height and growth during this year will be between 2½ and 3½ inches.

It is no longer necessary to have frequent height and weight checks as in the first year of life but measurement at least twice yearly is probably a good idea. If height does not rise perceptibly over a nine-month period, you should check with a pediatrician.

Somewhere around two, parents look at their child and realize "the baby is gone—and much of the toddler, too." The child looks more like a little boy or girl. The child has better motor coordination, a walk has replaced the toddler waddle, and chubbiness starts to disappear. Children this age are often even more physically beautiful than before—maybe nature's plan to help parents through difficult periods!

By age two, all twenty primary teeth will have erupted. The two-year-old still has a relatively large head (the average head circumference is 19.2 inches), accounting for nearly one quarter of the total height, but this disproportion will even out during the preschool years.

BODY FUNCTION

By the end of this third year of life, many children can control their bowels and will have achieved daytime bladder control although nighttime bladder control is still a way off.

At two the child may be exposed to more children and therefore more colds. Many are in day care or play more often with other children—with a resulting exchange of respiratory viruses. Bronchitis may be a complication of a cold. Earaches continue to be a problem for some. Because of the vast language learning occurring now, parents should monitor ear infections and have the child's hearing checked if necessary.

MOTOR SKILLS

How exciting to watch the child at age two develop motor refinements! The child's activity level is still high. Most adults would be exhausted if they tried to mimic every movement of a two-year-old for a day. Skills are practiced over and over until perfected, and then the child moves on to a new area to master. Two-year-olds delight in each new accomplishment.

Twos use their new ability to move in an upright position in order to cover distances quickly. The two-year-old can run well. For many children, running is their means of locomotion—even for short distances. They may still have difficulty stopping and starting quickly, or in changing directions. (Check your child's "raceways," for furniture corners or other hazards, in case of falls from accelerated speeds.) Twos also enjoy experimenting with walking backward, sideways, and on tiptoe.

Climbing is a continued adventure! Small ladders, stools, furniture, and large cubes are all challenging. Some children who were slow to develop motor coordination may shy away from climbing. Others don't have a sense of fear about climbing and can slip or fall—especially when they are tired—so supervision is in order.

Twos begin to alternate feet going up stairs, but alternating feet going down steps comes later. Twos can also open doors. They delight in jumping up and down and jumping from low objects and will begin to jump *over* objects this year. A two-year-old loves a rocking horse or chair. By the end of the year a two-year-old will throw a ball with a sense of purpose, kick a stationary ball, bend over from the waist to pick up objects, turn a somersault, push a toy with good steering, and learn to ride a tricycle. Children this age crave movement and both need and want the time to develop large motor skills.

Small-muscle activities also develop considerably this year. Two-year-olds play with blocks more purposefully and can build a tower of six blocks. Twos also string large beads, pound pegs, take apart and put together snap toys, turn pages of a book, unwrap small objects, manipulate clay, turn doorknobs (Beware!), and do simple form puzzles. Twos use crayons and pencils and can do circular scribbling and imitate a horizontal stroke. They can also fold paper once in imitation.

Language/Cognitive Skills

Although language development is remarkable at this age, it is important to remember that the range of "normal" speech acquisition is quite wide. Some children who have spoken very little all the way to two and a half or even later, end up talking in marvelous sentences by three. Some children speak amazingly well by age two.

Most children will have a receptive vocabulary (words or phrases they understand) of hundreds of words, even though they cannot speak most of them. At the beginning of this period they will often speak just ends of words with two or more syllables or the last word of a phrase you say. By the end of the year they usually have a speaking vocabulary of over two hundred words, many of which still need parent interpretation, however.

New words are gained daily and practiced over and over—almost as chants. When a friend's child first learned "pizza," he repeated it fifty-four times (she counted).

Twos often lapse into a babbling or jabbering when playing alone or with others. You can hear the intonations of adult sentence patterns but cannot pick out any words. We think it must be a relief to children to speak as quickly as they want even if it's not in adult words! Twins may even develop their own language.

At first the child's language is primarily self-initiated, but by two and a half language is often spoken in response to an adult and sometimes to peers. The two-year-old can speak simple three-word sentences with a pronoun, verb, and object. The pronoun most often used is "me." Sentences are not always "correct" according to adult standards. "Me go" or "Want book" gets the child's point across, however, and correction of words or grammar is counterproductive at this time.

The child has a genius for learning a whole language system in a relatively short time. As children listen to adults around them, they will self-correct automatically. Parental emphasis on correct pronunciation or sentence structure may actually retard the child's spontaneous efforts by making the child self-conscious. Parents should be patient while listening to the child's communication efforts and should not hurry the child. Hurrying could prolong stuttering, which is a developmental stage most children go through. During the preschool years, children may pass through temporary periods where they *appear* to be stuttering. They probably are trying to get thoughts out that come faster than their physical ability to speak them.

The "communication crisis" of wanting to communicate but not having the words causes much frustration for toddlers, which still continues at times in the two-year-old. However, during this year, the child will learn words and phrases to help express feelings.

Because this age is so important for language growth and its accompanying intellectual development, what can parents do to facilitate this development?

Talking to and with the child may seem too simplistic an answer, but it is a very powerful help. Sometimes this is forgotten by busy parents as children begin to speak on their own. We suggest you point out things while riding in the car, ask for help on shopping trips, describe tasks as you work together or get dressed. This helps children gain new vocabulary and hear good language modeled. Review shopping trips or family experiences: "First we went . . . Then we saw . . . Then we . . . And then we went home" helps develop sequencing, memory, and even a story sense.

Reading favorite books and reciting rhymes are enjoyable and also provide another opportunity to hear language. Pattern books (with rhymes, repetition, and predictability) are all fun for children—and also provide positive modeling for reading.

Helping two-year-olds learn to follow directions is helpful both for the present and for later school experiences. Such activities can be game-like. Start out with simple requests and increase to two or three steps as the child is ready. "Put the car under the table"; "Put the doll on the chair and give her a bottle." The games also help children understand prepositions—on, under, near, below, behind, etc.

Counting in the beginning is done by rote, without a real concept of numbers. Children can, however, begin to deal with one-to-one correspondence as they make sure each doll or animal has a cup at their tea party.

Because this is such a critical time for language and cognitive development, it is important that parents monitor any signs that would indicate hearing loss. If your child frequently does not respond to simple requests or questions, look around when called from behind or from another room, respond to new sounds, or does not begin to say single words or repeat your words, it would be wise to have the child's hearing checked by a professional. A deaf child needs to learn sign language at this age for normal development of language and thinking.

Language growth and motor activities are not separate from but rather are heavily interrelated with cognitive development. What seems like play at this age is context for the child experiencing his or her world. This is where real cognitive growth occurs and the basis for problem-solving skills, creativity, memory, etc., starts now. Children this age are naturally curious and creative. They are early problem solvers as they move, build, put together, and take apart.

Twos are still egocentric and see the world through their own eyes. But they begin to pretend and imitate. Also they begin to think through problems, rather than just act quickly. The sensorimotor period of earlier years shifts to preoperational. (See p. 228.) It is fascinating to see the child's memory improve so the child can remember small details from one-time visits or experiences.

Two is an age when the child responds best to order and regularity. As two-year-olds struggle to make sense of their world, they get so hooked into the way things are "supposed to be" that they often seem rigid or inflexible. This new phase can be seen as both positive and negative from the parent's point of view. It can be maddening when you can't find the cup your child *always* uses, or when the child screams at being interrupted while engaged in any activity he or she doesn't feel is completed. At the same time parents can use this stage to help the child develop responsibility and the earliest stages of classification and logic. If it hasn't been done before, organize your child's room. ("Blocks go here"; "Your jacket is hung here"; "Animals go here"; "Socks go in this shoe box in the drawer.") Containers can be labeled with pictures and a word, so the child can also help maintain this order. Show your child how to help put away groceries or silverware to reinforce this organizing skill.

As children gain language and communicate more easily, it is easy for parents to forget *how* differently children perceive the world. Twos' egocentricity may cause them to think that they cause everything to happen. Children's focus on one dimension of a problem may distort the reality. Also, reality is distorted by the child's inability to appreciate conservation. If two balls of playdough that are the same size and shape are rolled into a long skinny snake and a short fat snake, the child will say the long snake has more dough in it. Two feels that objects that move are alive—including windup toys or a book falling off a shelf. Children of two compare objects with themselves and feel the object has their own characteristics.

Twos' concept of time is also different. They can remember specific details from the past that will surprise you, but chronological order is difficult. Tomorrow or next week doesn't have much meaning except that it isn't now and a two-year-old lives in the present. Imagination, as we use the word, means pretending —involvement with something not real. The child at two has a good deal of difficulty separating fantasy from reality. Some of the fears children express which seem so illogical to parents are *real* to children. A parent who understands how the child perceives his or her world is much more likely to be in tune with and to appreciate what the child is thinking.

Social Skills

The toddler who declared independence last year is really developing into his or her own person. Parents can learn much about their child by stepping back and watching. What role does the child take when other children are around? How does the child approach strangers? What happens when the child can't get his or her own way? Such information will be useful in knowing how best to interact with the child.

Twos may begin to play well alongside others. Some even begin to watch other children's activities and copy them. At two and a half the child may become both bossy to peers and possessive. A sense of "mine" and "yours" develops. Since language is still limited, the child may resort to pushing, biting, and grabbing.

The two-year-old can remove clothes (unless they're tight or intricate), shoes, and diapers. Twos are beginning to be more interested in dressing themselves, but must have the right kind of clothes to do so. Having access to larger clothes (especially an older sibling's) is fun for two-year-olds and good practice for total self-dressing, which comes later. Twos can wash and dry various body parts and brush the teeth with supervision.

Two-year-olds really enjoy imitating adults and can even be helpful to adults. A busy parent may not find the child's actions actually helpful, but trying to help is satisfying to the child and important groundwork. At this age the child is building self-esteem and when allowed to help (wiping a high chair tray or cleaning up a spill) self-esteem blossoms. It is important to allow enough time, show the child a "how-to" technique, and not to redo the task—at least not in the child's presence. Parents who express frustration later when children *never* help often did not start early enough or take the time to "teach" helping to accept the child's early spontaneous helping.

Children *need* to feel a sense of connectedness with others and a sense of self-worth. Even though two is an age of independence, it is also an age needing connectedness, which allows the courage to be independent.

Emotions/Feelings

Erikson describes this age as the stage where youngsters wrestle with the polarities of autonomy versus shame and doubt.[1] The internal nature of the child at this age demands that he or she establish a sense of self by exploring and manipulating all alone. However, two-year-olds still need parents who establish limits in firmly reassuring ways. If parents are too coercive, too authoritarian, too punishing, or too shaming, the child may feel the loss of self-esteem, doubt his or her competence, and experience shame. Overprotection may also lead to loss of self-esteem as the child is not able to establish autonomy.

When parents calmly help a young child work through his or her feelings, they are positively contributing to the child's personality in a way that will never be possible or quite the same again. When you feel especially frustrated by your two-year-old, maybe it will relieve your frustration to remember just how important your help can be.

It is important to remember that this striving for independence is as powerful (and as normal) as was the will to walk. The child is not rejecting the parent or being naughty. The child is just being and growing. Remember how far the two-year-old has come in achieving this autonomy and independence from total helplessness in twenty-four short months!

As the child's sense of separateness and autonomy develops, the child will begin to establish ways of identifying with or relating to others. Imitation is, of course, a primary way. Early on, two-year-olds of both sexes identify a great deal with their primary care giver (usually the mother). As the year goes on, there is more identification with the same sex parent and more imitation of that parent. In homes where both fathers and mothers do care-giving and household tasks, sex role stereotyping may be minimized.

Depending in part on how open parents are with nudity, the child becomes aware that he or she is more like one parent than the other in terms of genitals —even though grown-ups are "different" from children. It is important that children learn to name their body parts—including the genitals. If the genitals are left out, a message comes across that something is wrong with these parts. It is also important that you say males and females have some different body parts —not that females are missing a penis or that males lack the ability to get pregnant. Otherwise, boys may fear that they could "lose" their penis, or girls feel "less than" because they are missing something, or boys could fear that they are unimportant because they can't have a baby.

Playing with the genitals often becomes more pronounced with toilet training and the release of the diaper encasement. Masturbation at this age is a positive, private achievement that can be ignored—except for a gentle reminder that it not be done in public (see p. 76).

The same sense of separateness and autonomy that is such an achievement for a two-year-old may also lead to new fears. The child's sense of self is closely related to the body. When a two-year-old is injured, there is often an exaggerated preoccupation with a scratch or cut. Because the child may not feel "complete," the child will tell you about the hurt again and again! A bandage, even if not truly needed, usually helps the "scare" go away. Just as some children hate to see feces (a part of themselves) flushed away, some Twos (with limited logic) fear blood from a cut as a "loss" of self. A Band-Aid keeps the child's essence from escaping out of the body.

The child may react to other fears—even those handled well six months ago—thunder, the dark, being alone, animals, vacuums, water, and on and on. This is not a good time to encourage or force the child to deal with such a "silly" fear on his or her own. Two-year-olds need a loving, calm, supportive parent and perhaps a special blanket, night light, or back rub in order to grow through these fears, which often disappear as quickly as they arose.

Developmental Warning Signals

If by two years of age your child avoids eye contact, head-bangs for long periods, does not name a few familiar objects nor use a few two- or three-word sentences, does not notice animals, cars, trucks, etc., does not play symbolically with cars or housekeeping toys, does not move about vigorously and explore, does not focus the eyes on a large picture, or does not walk up stairs, your child has a developmental delay which warrants a workup to determine why.[2]

CARE GIVER TASKS

Basic Care

NUTRITION

Knowing about what constitutes good nutrition is one thing, getting a typical two-year-old to eat is another. We had better start by saying we *guarantee* that your child will not starve despite the marked decrease in intake which peaks at this age. Your child has both decreased the rate of growth (which results in a decreased appetite) *and* has newfound autonomy (which results in some very decided food habits). Relax and avoid power struggles with your child over eating. Here are some hints for feeding your two-year-old.

- First of all, if your child is growing, is not sick, or has no more than the usual illnesses, is energetic and curious, and is developing on schedule, your child is eating enough. So don't worry.
- Start with *smaller* portions at meals. Try only two tablespoons (one tablespoon for each year of age) of each item to be served. Some parents start with foods the child is least interested in, while the child is the hungriest, and then add other foods or seconds.
- Allow a two-year-old to help with a food snack or meal preparation, whenever possible. Twos are more likely to taste what they've helped prepare (even if it's just a couple of stirs, or putting the forks in place).
- Finger foods are easier to handle.
- Imaginative breakfasts can be tried, if the child balks at traditional ones. Peanut butter on toast, homemade pizza on an English muffin, hamburger or vegetable soup are nutritious and may be more to some children's liking than the usual breakfast food. Some children also would rather eat cereal or eggs in the evening. It doesn't matter!
- Avoid casseroles or dishes with sauces where things are "mixed" up. Keep ingredients separated for the two-year-old when you are cooking.
- Milk can be disguised in puddings or comes already packaged as a cheese slice.
- Don't nag your child about food; if the child doesn't eat what you put down at meals, try a "no-cook" substitution. (For example: if your two-year-old is not eating the cubes of roast beef, offer a slice of cheese. If the child eats neither, take both away and don't worry about it.)
- Don't reward nutritious eating with desserts. The habit you start may be hard to break!

Parents are often concerned about protein for growth in a young child who is not eating much. High protein foods include eggs, cheeses, yogurt, and peanut butter, as well as meat, fish, and poultry. Store-bought cheese spreads, some macaroni and cheese mixes, pot pies, canned soups, cream cheese, bacon, and processed meats have very little protein.

Two-year-olds should not have the following foods because of the danger of choking (remember both the molars and the ability to chew are new and have not had much practice): grapes, peanuts, raw carrots, seeds, popcorn, and hot dogs unless completely cut through into tiny pieces.

A two-year-old is likely to go on food jags and eat only one or two things. Snacks are still important, because of high energy expenditure, but it is better if snacks are two hours away from meals.

Power struggles at eating times should really be avoided during this year. Mealtime has many possibilities for becoming a battleground: how much the child eats, worries about nutrition, messes, manners, etc. It has been stated that a child can use two bodily openings for power—the anus and the mouth! Parents cannot really force compliance in either toilet training or eating, so don't even try.

Even though a child can use a spoon and fork fairly well by two, finger foods are still easier. Because early Twos are still going through the toddler "groping" and sensorimotor stages, the desire to touch food is high. They should have many opportunities, apart from mealtimes, to satisfy this "groping" urge, (finger painting, mustard in a seal-meal-bag, mud, sand, and water play). But they probably should not be allowed to finger-paint with mashed potatoes on the table. However, let the child use the hands when the goal is to carry food to the mouth. Later, as two-year-olds become more skilled, they will use the table utensils to make roads in the mashed potatoes and ponds for the gravy. Don't worry about this either; the habit is given up long before high school!

Language is now used to assert independence, so Twos may say "No" even to foods they like! It is so delightful to have the power to say "No!"

One study of healthy middle class children revealed that 85 percent of the babies at six months had appetites described as "good" or "excellent" by their mothers.[3] Between two and three years of age, only 10 to 20 percent were thought to have "excellent" or "good" appetites; 60 percent were "fair"; and 20 percent, "poor." After the children started school, their appetites increased and, most important of all, these children stayed healthy. Girls' appetites start to decrease a few months sooner than boys'.

Ninety-five out of a hundred children cut down on their milk consumption during the preschool years, and milk intake may be at the lowest level between the ages of two and three. If you are concerned, add more milk to food in cooking and use more milk products. Only fill the child's glass a quarter- or half-full and let the child ask for more. Some children delight in being able to pour their own milk from a small toy pitcher and are more likely to drink it after doing so.

Children also vary a great deal in their best and worst periods during the day both in terms of eating and general "being." Many parents think supper hour is the worst. Children *and* parents are apt to be both tired and hungry at that time of day. When both parents work, this hour may be even more stressful. Everyone involved needs to relax.

We suggest taking time to relax before supper, perhaps with juice for the children and *very* small snacks—whatever kind of relaxing suits you and your child. Supper may be a bit late, but may proceed more easily. Alternatively, one can make the snack into the last meal for the children, like English high tea. Adults can have a real meal later.

One more comment about two-year-olds helping with food preparation. It is marvelous for language development when the parent talks non-stop about what is happening. So many wonderful concepts and words to share, whether the child is actually helping or merely sitting up where he or she can see: mixing, hot, cold, frying, blending, first, next, scrambling, tearing, cutting, boiling, pouring, baking, measuring, shredding, food names . . . and on and on.

CLEANING/GROOMING

Twos' attitude toward bathing or washing up can vary considerably from week to week (or day to day). Most are fascinated with any water contact and thoroughly enjoy a bath. The problem comes in getting them out! Others balk at a bath either as part of asserting power, or out of a fear of water.

The more children this age are involved in tasks, the more likely they are to cooperate. Set up a bath ritual/routine to help two-year-olds with problems getting in or out of the bath. First the child gets the soap, then the special bath toys, then the towel and washcloth, and then fresh clothing, while the parent runs the water. If the child is fearful of water, run the water gently without the child present and use a small amount of water. Another approach is to bathe along with the child for a while. For those two-year-olds who hate to get *out*, try a kitchen timer. There's something magical about the authority a kitchen timer has—when it goes off, it's time to get out!

Some two-year-olds become resistant to the shampooing of hair. A shampoo does not need to be a daily event. Try letting the child have a *small* amount of shampoo (no-tear variety) in the hand to "help." They will be fascinated with the bubbles they make by rubbing their hands. Or just rinse the hair without shampoo if it isn't greasy or sticky.

Parents quickly learn the best time for a bath by observing the child's behavior after the bath. For some children the bath is calming and for others it is stimulating. If your child is stimulated, avoid a bath before bedtime.

For safety's sake a parent must monitor bath time. The parent must both prevent falls and the turning on of hot water. In addition, bath time is a great time for learning to take place. You can teach body-part names and pouring skills as well as personal care skills. You will also have to continue cutting toenails and fingernails.

Dressing a child this age can be an ordeal—at least some of the time—especially for busy working parents. Try "fun" clothes for the child with animals or characters that the child likes. Try clothes children can put on by themselves (you may need to buy a larger size and take up hems). Try giving two-year-olds two choices of what to put on.

SLEEP

Most Twos only nap once a day—some try to cut down to none. The average child sleeps nine to twelve hours. Daily and evening routines pay off where rest is concerned. We recommend setting up bedtime rituals—reading books, rubbing backs, getting special blankets and animals, getting water. One word of caution—as they become more locked into rituals, two-year-olds will insist on the completion of the *whole* ritual. We suggest you have a simple ritual without too many steps so that you can do it without resentment! See the section in the chapter on three-year-olds, which deals with quiet, close times before bed.

Children this age may begin to wake with night fears or night wandering. Real nightmares can occur at this age. The child may sit straight up in bed screaming but is really not awake and may need help in waking up first before going back to sleep. When this happens go to the child immediately. Calm the child, rub the back, and let the child go back to sleep. Children need the reassurance that someone is there when a nightmare occurs. Some parents lie down with the child until the child falls alseep. There is nothing wrong with letting the child come into the parents' bed.

If nightmares are frequent, evaluate the child's day as the day may be too "full." Try to establish restful, stressless, close times during the day with a predictable routine.

How you wake the child is as important as how you put the child to sleep. Children taking very long naps that will interfere with bedtime sometimes need to be wakened. Working parents may have to wake up children to meet their work schedules. Think about how you would like to be wakened from a sound sleep. Touch the child gently first, talk softly, and then lift up the child while continuing to talk softly.

If the child is in day care, we suggest parents always ask about the child's naps that day. Then the parents will know what to expect in terms of their child's sleep needs for the rest of the day.

EXERCISE

Parents may laugh at the thought of their active two-year-old having exercise needs. But look at your child's day. Does the child have an opportunity for longer walks, or space to run distances? Does the child spend time outside nearly every day? Are there chances to balance, climb, jump, and explore? Does the child get a chance to throw and kick?

Exercise is important but parents should help the child pace the day. Intersperse high activity times with quiet times.

STRESS MANAGEMENT

We have already mentioned ways parents can help reduce stress for their children: help the child establish routines, pace the child's day, and help the child meet developmental needs such as the need to move and to establish independence. Children feel more stress when they don't know what their limits are or when limits are inconsistent. Children also experience stress when they feel out of control. A parent can help a child get control by helpful rather than punitive actions. Take away an object being misused, remove the child to a quiet area, or cuddle a cranky child *before* the tantrum.

Even when as young as two, your child will imitate your manner of handling stress. Like all children, two-year-olds will pick up on and react to the parent's emotional mood. Thus think of ways to reduce your own stress.

A mixed message is conveyed when a parent *yells*, "I want a quiet house!" or whacks a child and says, "You may not hit your brother." A parent who feels out of control can either escalate the situation or model how to act when angry. The latter is better! A parent should be able to express anger—at the child's action, not at the child's self. The way in which the parent expresses anger will model a way for the child to express anger.

Child abuse sometimes occurs for the first time at this age. Understanding what is "normal" behavior for this age child and what the child is going through in this stage can be helpful to parents. But sometimes, for reasons in their own life, parents do not feel in control of their actions. If, at any time, you sense yourself reaching the "breaking" point with your child, take a "time-out" and reach out—not with embarrassment, but with pride in your good sense—to the many agencies that can help. There are free counseling services or parent classes which teach about ways to deal positively with children and give parents a chance to share with others and support each other (see p. 115).

EMOTIONAL "NUTRITION"

At two emotional nurturance is very much needed. Although the two-year-old is active and independence-seeking, the child still needs to be cuddled a lot. At times two-year-olds will want to be treated as though they were younger. It's okay!

Here are some practical tips on dealing with feelings at age two:

- Don't make an issue of things you don't really care about just to prove who is boss. There will be plenty of times when you have to take a stand. Set limits only for those things that are really important.
- When possible, avoid situations and activities that you know produce tantrums.
- Be sensitive to those times of the day when a child is tired. Take steps to work around this time or come up with a creative way of managing this time positively. (One mother found when she came home from work she was anxious to get dinner going and thought she'd spend time

with her two-year-old while dinner was cooking. This turned into a disastrous, fussy, hectic time for both the mother and the two-year-old. Just taking a half an hour to cuddle and read, or watch "Sesame Street" together, changed the whole evening—for both.)

- Reduce the number of requests you make as these can all be a setup for "No." State facts simply: "It is time . . ." "Put this here . . ."
- Help children by controlling the kinds of experiences they are having. If the child is having a good deal of frustration or negative feelings, try to involve the child in positive, favorite, successful activities.
- Children may throw a tantrum because it is the only way they know to express a feeling. Physical outlets for anger (punching pillows, banging clay) allow for another type of expression. The tremendous growth in language this year will be another tool for the child. Parents can help the child learn to express feelings. Teach your child to say, "I feel angry," "I'm scared." What a relief to a child to be able to talk!

CARE OF THE CARE GIVER

Parents who live with a two-year-old need plenty of nurturing themselves and self-time to renew their own energy level. Just as it is important for the child to have a routine and appropriate activities for peak and low energy times, so is it important for the parent. The parent will not have the necessary patience and love to give if tired, depleted, and empty.

As parents, you should care for yourselves the way you care for your child: good nutrition, exercise, relaxation techniques, etc. Hurried parents often cheat themselves in a way they never would a child. It's better to think, "I am taking care of me so I can be there for my child because I am important for myself *and* for my child."

Find quiet spaces for yourself during the day (relaxing in a bath, learning to meditate, reading a favorite book, walking or jogging). Parents of two-year-olds need *time alone,* and also *time alone with their mates.* In the case of working parents, real creativity is needed to find such time, but it is important to do so. Remember the importance of a baby-sitter so you and your spouse can be alone even if your budget only permits you to take a walk together.

Socialization Tasks

At this age socialization occurs through the opportunity to observe, time to talk about what's happening, and through play and play materials.

PLAY/STIMULATION

Some parents have the tendency when their child turns two, to begin to focus on formal learning—naming colors, shapes, letters. And indeed, some two-year-olds delight in this experience, whether with parents or Sesame Street.

However, since two-year-olds are still in the sensorimotor or preoperational stage, rote kinds of learning are fairly meaningless, unless related to personal experience.

Children this age need to handle their environment. Two-year-olds learn much more when they are touching as well as seeing and hearing. Twos also learn best when the concept is meaningful and in a real context. On the way to child care every day, a friend's two-year-old son recognized that they turned at the Circle K store sign. He soon recognized Circle K on the milk and began to say "K" every time he saw one. The same thing happened with "STOP" (from the sign) and his name, which was always on his lunch bag. Learning was built on the child's own day and his interests.

There are many natural, meaningful ways children can learn while playing or just experiencing, as parents talk about what is happening. "Hand me the red block." "This is your biggest truck." "Let's make circles." Even while playing totally alone with sand or water, while stacking or moving toys, or when building or creating, children are learning concepts, scientific ideas, discrimination skills, problem-solving skills, divergent and convergent thinking.

Children will learn—naturally and easily—when four components are present:

1. The *opportunity* to play and to experience their environment.
2. The *materials* and *environments* to explore.
3. *Parents* and *care givers* to help talk through what is happening and to provide a "push" when needed, or encouragement and praise.
4. *Modeling* by adults—the child experiencing adults who talk and read and write, and who are curious and interested.

It is important to note how TV can work against the above components— the child may sing along or talk back, but often does not; there is often no adult talking and sharing; and the behavior modeled by an adult glued to the TV is a passive one.

Children this age are like sponges and can learn incredible amounts, but do not need to be sat down and taught to "learn." Actually that can be a negative experience because the child may be robbed of important experience time handling objects and learning concepts. The child may not have an interest or see meaning in what the adult is trying to teach and may begin to form a negative reaction to learning that is force-fed in the "school sense."

Children this age enjoy playing around other children, and usually welcome this—especially if the parent is present or they are in familiar surroundings. Sharing and taking turns are still difficult and adult intervention, redirection, or modeling is often necessary. Since children are learning languages so quickly, adults should supply the words children need to solve disputes or to express their feelings: "I want your ball"; "You can play next"; "I'm angry"; "Play with me."

Children this age are more concerned with process than with product. They love to pound clay, scrub a paper with a paint brush until it's covered and brownish gray, build a tower and smash it down. They have little interest in the final product—if any. The experience is what is important to the child.

DISCIPLINE/GUIDANCE/VALUES

Some conscientious parents, aware of how much their children are beginning to say or understand, try to "reason" with a two-year-old who is misbehaving. At age two, children understand no abstract concepts and few generalizations. Also, two-year-olds *must* test to find boundaries and limits from experience—not just words. Parental *action* is more necessary than a speech, especially if a child is in a dangerous situation. But action is also appropriate when a child is "out of control" or doing a great deal of testing in an area unacceptable to the parent. If a child throws food on the floor at mealtime, prompt removal from the chair or high chair is appropriate along with: "Food needs to stay on the tray or in your mouth," or simply, "Stop!" If it feels right in a few minutes or seconds, the parent can allow the child to return, but should remove the child again if the behavior recurs.

If one child hits another child, removal is necessary—to a chair or separate area. (Not to bed—a negative feeling about bed or bedrooms is the last thing the two-year-old and parent need!) The way the parent acts is important. The action and voice should be firm and definite, but do not have to be loud and angry. The child actually feels relief in knowing that limits are clear because Two is still sorting out the world and limits help do that.

Be positive with two-year-olds. This builds self-esteem in the child, and besides Two says "No" enough for everyone. One study showed that in home environments with poor parent-child interactions, the negative comments outweighed the positive 300–1. In homes with average interactions, the negatives outweighed the positive comments 30–1. In homes with good interactions, the negatives outweighed the positives only 3–1. Being positive with children, especially in the early years, takes real effort and practice on the part of parents but pays off in good parent-child interactions.[4]

Here are some examples of ways words usually said can be changed to a positive mode. The positive phrases in a soft voice tell a child what the parent *does* want instead of saying "No."

What's Happening	What's Usually Said	What Could Be Said
Pushing or hitting	"Stop that now!"	"Be gentle." (demonstrate)
Taking toys	"Don't do that!"	"Ask for the toy" or "That's Allison's, here's yours."
Throwing a toy	"You may not do that."	"Use the toy this way."
Screams or shouts	"You stop screaming!" (usually said in a near-screaming voice)	"Talk softly indoors." (whispered firmly)

| Throws clothes | "Don't you know where the clothes go?" | "The clothes belong in the basket." |

Two will begin to model your positiveness, although it takes work on your part and much repetition.

Marilyn knows a mother who says "Non-negotiable" when she definitely takes a stand. Her children know this is firm and not worth testing. Mother has taken a stand. Even though her two-year-old child doesn't know the real meaning of "non-negotiable," he understands because of his mother's consistency and action.

Since two-year-olds imitate parental behavior, striking a two-year-old in any manner is a way of saying "Hitting is okay." We don't think it is (see p. 67).

The key words for discipline at two are: *prevention* (encouraging and praising helpful behavior, gearing activities and environments to meet the child's needs and energy level); *respect and modeling* (treating the child the way you expect to be treated and the way you expect him or her to treat others); *expressing love* for the child even when angry with the child's behavior (individual attention, anger at the act done—but no withdrawal of love from the child); *reinforcing* the child's appropriate behaviors and kindness, and lots of *touching*.

VALUES

Parents' modeling actions just mentioned are the most powerful way to convey values. Parents' warmth and self-respect allow children to feel free to express themselves and their love, and to learn that even loving parents don't let themselves be pushed around.

Even at this early age, children are absorbing important information about human interactions. How their parents relate to each other is absorbed, as is how their parents relate to other people in their world when the child is around. It is an important time for parents to evaluate what picture of their interactions their children are going to carry and generalize later about men, women, and families.

As mentioned before, children this age are imitative and into routines. Family traditions, whether it be simple prayers at meal or bedtime, holding hands around a table quietly, or making family poems or songs will stick with the child and can start now. Even if the specific activity isn't remembered, the feelings of warmth and togetherness will be.

TOILET TRAINING

Some parents who have been patient with toilet training and willing to "follow" their child's lead and the steps outlined in the Toddler chapter begin to worry if the child is not trained at this age. This pressure is more intense if a new child enters the family, if friends' children seem to be trained well, or a child who seemed to have achieved control suddenly starts having more accidents. If at two your child has not started toilet training, read the section on training in the Toddler chapter. If a previously trained child is having accidents remember the average age of daytime success is 27+ months. You may have started too early; stop for a while. This will do your child no harm. You can start over in a month or two.

DAY CARE

Parents who need or want day care for two-year-olds should first read about nursery school selection in the chapter on the three-year-old child (see p. 471). In addition, there are some special considerations to think about when choosing child care for a two-year-old. The discussion in this chapter on play and on the developmental needs of the two-year-old are reminders of what two-year-olds need. Whether a parent chooses a family day care home or a center or a relative, there are three areas the parent needs to evaluate: the environment, the materials, and the adult/child interactions.

THE ENVIRONMENT

- Is the environment *safe?*
- Will the environment be comfortable for the child? Is the facility clean from a health standpoint, but with a "lived-in look" where children obviously play and live and learn?
- Is there a safe outside play area?
- Would sand or water play be possible?
- Are there soft areas and private spaces for children?
- Does each child have his or her own place for napping?

THE MATERIALS

- What is available for large motor development and movement? (space to run, jump, climb; objects to go over, under, through, and around, push and pull toys)
- What building materials are available?
- What materials to develop small muscles are there? (puzzles, stacking and nesting toys, miniature toys, toy dishes, clay, writing and coloring materials, art supplies)
- What opportunities are there for social interaction? (housekeeping area, dress-up clothes, music toys, puppets, dolls, trucks)
- What opportunities are there for language learning? (large picture books, puppets, records)

ADULT/CHILD INTERACTION

This is probably the most important area to look into. First, does the child care provider understand two-year-old children, how they are developing, and what they need? Secondly, does the provider's philosophy basically reflect or complement the parent's attitudes about child rearing?

How can a parent find out? Obviously the best way is to observe the provider with other two-year-olds. This is easier to observe in a child care center than in a day care home. If there aren't any other two-year-olds, a parent can still watch how the provider interacts with her own children or other day care children.

The adults' attitude is a critical factor: whether they truly see each child as an individual, whether they get down to the child's eye level when talking to the child, how easily they touch and hug children, and their general tone of voice and ability to listen. Just as important is whether there is *opportunity* for adult-child interactions. In a day care home, are there so many other children that it will be difficult for the child to get individual attention? The parent can also ask questions like:

- "What is your daily schedule like?"
- "How do you handle toilet training?" (or naps, tantrums, biting, or fighting)
- "What if a child won't share?"
- "What kind of responsibilities do the children have?"
- "Why do you want to do child care?"

Certainly, these questions don't need to be "fired" one after another, but all or most of the topics should be discussed. A parent, after a visit and an interview with the provider, will have a "gut" feeling about the care situation. It should be trusted. The initial reaction is usually accurate, even if a parent can't logically explain the feelings.

Two-year-olds in day care are not as verbal as older children in being able to talk about all that happens during their day. It is critical that parents make good choices about day care and continue to monitor the care situation. We suggest dropping in unexpectedly and taking time to visit off and on. Previsits to child care options are important. References or recommendations from other parents who have used the child care or referrals from a reputable community agency are essential.

HEALTH CARE

Medical Care

After the fourth DPT and fourth polio immunization at eighteen months, many pediatricians used to say they would not need to see the child until age three. However, Hib immunization is now recommended at age two (see p. 614). Besides, it is a rare child who has no cause to see a physician for a year and a half. Even if the child does stay healthy, a well-baby check somewhere in this year makes sense—for height and weight checks, and a general physical examination.

Dental Care

We believe in the first visit to the dentist at two, or at the latest three when all the first teeth are in. Ideally, your community will have a dentist who specializes in children's dental care. It is important that a child's first visit to the dentist be positive.

The routine of brushing after meals and snacks can be helped by a step stool at the sink.

SAFETY

This is a time when the parents' role becomes a supervisory one—a *careful* supervisory one! Because of the child's fast mobility and curiosity, lack of knowledge of consequences, and determination to do things alone, the two-year-old is at a precarious stage.

Two-year-olds have been known to climb to amazing heights, secure things off high shelves, unlatch "child-proof" locks, swallow rather large objects, and disappear from "secured" backyards. It is nerve-wracking for parents to keep a continued eye on this fast-paced child, but imperative.

Take this checklist and go through your own house if you have a two-year-old. Don't ignore something because your child has never touched it before. It only takes once—a two-year-old is *so* curious!

— medicine and vitamins under lock and key
— cleaning supplies under lock and key
— paints, varnishes, craft supplies in locked cupboard
— laundry supplies out of reach and locked
— cosmetics out of reach
— no poisonous plants
— sharp knives out of reach
— sewing supplies and scissors out of reach
— no plastic bags in reach
— all windows and doors latched in a way the child can't maneuver
— outside areas padlocked
— dangerous tools locked
— outside area safe
— bathroom able to be locked and unlocked from outside
— hot water temperature turned down so it can't scald child if turned on by mistake

— unused electric plug outlets capped
— no extension cords in reach
— no appliances or cords in child's reach
— matches and other combustibles under lock
— the home equipped with smoke detectors and a fire extinguisher
— no water left in small pools
— swimming pool fenced and locked from the rest of the yard

Even with these precautions, the two-year-old needs to be supervised. Even with supervision a parent can be one foot away from the child and an accident or near miss can occur.

At this age, children test limits. Some may begin to balk at car seats as they realize other family members don't have one. This is an area where parents can say "Not negotiable" and not move until children are belted in their car seats.

* * *

In looking back over this chapter, we may have dwelled too much on the negativity which can be part of this age. Don't be disheartened. During this year, parents will see some of the most exciting growth they will ever see. Parents will enjoy the emergence of their son's or daughter's own personality, and experience some of the most tender expressions of their child's affections. Two is a *very* special year!

SUGGESTED READINGS AND RESOURCES

Ames, Louise Bates, and Ilg, Frances L. *Your Two-Year-Old: Terrible or Tender.* New York: Delacorte, 1976.

A book all about two-year-olds written by Ames and Ilg of the Gesell Institute. A nice discussion of whether two's are terrible along with suggestions for parenting a child of this age.

Barber, Lucie W., and Williams, Herman. *Your Baby's First 30 Months.* Tucson, Ariz.: H. P. Books, 1981.

A chronologically arranged, easily read guide to positive child rearing in the first thirty months. Photographs and charts are used well, and diary space is provided to help you follow your child's development.

Braga, Joseph, and Braga, Laurie. *Children and Adults: Activities for Growing Together.* Englewood Cliffs, N.J.: Prentice-Hall, 1976.

This book is divided into chronological age groups, with specific activities for both physical and mental development listed for each age level. Many of the activities can be conducted during your routine process of interacting with your child.

Brazelton, T. Berry, *Toddlers and Parents.* New York: Dell, 1976.

This book has much information that is appropriate for this age child. This book details the struggle of the striving for independence from both the child's and parent's view. By using actual families, many behaviors and specific problems are dealt with. Brazelton helps parents analyze their child's temperament.

Cole, Ann; Haas, Carolyn; and Weinberger, Betty. *I Saw a Purple Cow and 100 Other Recipes for Learning.* Boston: Little, Brown, 1972.

Activities and games for preschool and older children using common household materials and everyday experiences. Includes things to make and things to do; simple, easy-to-read format with lots of illustrations.

Gesell, Arnold. *The First Five Years of Life: The Preschool Years.* New York: Harper, 1940.

Although this Gesell book is out of print, it is worth a trip to the library. Wonderful, informative reading.

Gregg, Elizabeth, and Boston Children's Medical Center Staff. *What to Do When There's Nothing to Do.* New York: Dell, 1984.

Six hundred and one easy-to-do imaginative play ideas for babies, toddlers, and two-to-six-year-olds. Ordinary household items such as milk cartons, corks, cereal boxes, pots and pans, and paper bags can all be used.

Sotelo, Jo; Stevenson, Janis; and Williamsen, Jean. *Consumer's Guide to Child Care.* St. Meinrad, Ind.: Abbey Press, 1983.

This small, inexpensive guide helps parents decide about whether to use child care, what kind of care situation would meet their needs, and how to help their child. Checklists are included.

Sparling, Joseph, and Lewis, Isabelle. *Learningames for the First Three Years: A Guide to Parent/Child Play.* New York: Walker, 1984.

An illustrated "play" book that gives specific ideas on what activities to do with children along with the "whys?"

Stone, Jeanette Galambos. *Guide to Discipline.* National Association for the Education of Young Children, Washington, D.C., 1978.

A handy guide for care givers of children in groups (available from NAEYC for $1.50). Actual words are given to use with children in a variety of situations that set limits while upholding the child's sense of self-esteem.

White, Burton L. *The First Three Years of Life.* Revised ed. New York: Avon, 1985.

A comprehensive summary of Dr. White's extensive research on children in the first three years of life. The book is organized around aspects of the young child's environment which White has bound to the development of competence in relating to the world. Readable language.

15

THE THREE-YEAR-OLD—
NOW MORE SOCIAL

Scope of Chapter

This chapter deals with the three-year-old. Babyhood is definitely over and childhood firmly at hand.

Introduction

The three-year-old has come a long way from the baby you first held in your arms—and still has a long way to go. In many ways preschoolers are fun to parent because they are now *real children* instead of babies or toddlers. But Three is far from grown up.

The three-year-old is less trouble than the two-and-a-half-year-old was. At two and a half, negativity seemed *so* prominent and growing up seemed *so* far away. But a two-and-a-half-year-old does grow into a three-year-old and becomes —almost magically—a person parents can both relate to and deal with, albeit a *little* person.

What leads to this "magic"? The amazing development of skills which has occurred and which continues to occur makes the difference. The three-year-old has the verbal skills necessary to act like and to be recognized as a verbal, thinking person. Three not only has a vocabulary and can talk but also *thinks* in words, which is such a large part of how we think as adults. The child also has developed "little monkey" skills and can run, walk, and climb with surprising ease. Three is really liberated from your arms now.

According to the *Whole Pediatrician Catalog*, the word which best characterizes age three is "trusting."[1] Three-year-olds are more organized and coordinated, try to do what is expected, love accomplishments, and love pleasing people. They are cooperative and easygoing. As Gesell says, "Three tends to be in good equilibrium with people and things around him perhaps because he is in better equilibrium within himself."[2] On the whole this is a settled year although three and a half often brings a bit of insecurity and disequilibrium.

KEY INFORMATION

Biophysical Information

SIZE AND SHAPE

The average three-year-old weighs about 30 pounds and is about 3 feet tall —conveniently easy to remember as it's all threes. The average weight for boys is 32.2 pounds (range 28.7 to 36.8). The average weight for girls is 31.8 pounds (range 27.6 to 37.4). The average boy is 37.9 inches tall (range 36.3 to 39.6) and the average girl is 37.7 inches tall (range 35.6 to 39.8). Although the head is still relatively big (19.6 inches in circumference), the child now has a trunk because the protuberant belly of babyhood has flattened as growth made room for abdominal organs.

Your child is still growing at a fast clip but growth is slowing down relative to the growth rate of infancy. Between ages three and four your child will gain about 4½ pounds and grow about 2½ inches. The plumpness of babyhood will turn into the leanness of childhood even when growth is right on target. Children at three—especially those destined to grow up tall and thin—can look very leggy and their *relative* thinness bothers some parents who consciously or unconsciously feel that plump equals healthy.

The head circumference at three is very close to that of adult size and most of the brain cells in the white matter of the cerebral cortex have become myelinated. The frontal sinuses are formed or will be shortly.

BODY FUNCTION

By age three bowel control is usually established. The child learned to stop and start the urine stream at about age two and a half, so at three daytime bladder control is pretty good. However, nighttime control is less likely. In order for the child to stay dry through the night the bladder must be big enough to hold about ten to twelve ounces.[3] Many children will not yet have achieved this bladder size by age three.

The child still has relatively small breathing passages and may get as many as six to nine colds a year, which often "settle" into the chest or the ears. However, the child has begun to cope with illness better. For example, fevers are not generally as high as in earlier years. A three-year-old can usually understand a minor illness and be less frightened or overwhelmed by it. The three-year-old's average pulse rate is about 100 and the average blood pressure is 90/60.

MOTOR SKILLS

Wow! The three-year-old has learned a lot in thirty-six short months! Now the child walks easily without watching the feet and with good posture. At three your child can tandem walk along a line and run well, including stopping suddenly or dashing around the corner without falling. Threes can also rise to tiptoes; stand on one foot, and leap and hop a few steps; climb up and down a jungle gym; go up stairs alternating feet though usually walking down two feet to a step; walk backward a few steps; jump from a height of eighteen inches; ride a tricycle; build a tower of nine blocks; imitate building a bridge of three blocks; throw a ball (but the child tries to catch a ball with the arms held out in front of the body, not adjusting to where the ball is going to come).

Small-muscle skills have also mushroomed. The three-year-old can copy a circle and imitate a cross. Three holds a pencil well and some can even print their own first name in block letters—especially if it's a short name! When you ask a three-year-old to draw a person, the child is usually glad to comply, but as Gesell says, the drawing has to be labeled or no one *knows* it's a person. There may be a circle with appendages or an attempt at a face. Or, more likely, the child may just scribble and say proudly, "That's a person."

Parents should know that, although the motor skills we described are present at this age, later on the child may appear to be a bit less well coordinated or fearful of falling. Some children, at about ages forty-two to forty-eight months, may avoid climbing or running. This usually lasts only a short time and may be related to the child's increasing understanding of danger. On the other hand, many three-year-olds like tough challenges such as balancing on a balance beam and don't exhibit fearfulness even when it is appropriate. This makes close supervision of play still a must.

By age three and a half the child will begin to skip and will hold a pencil correctly, trace along a line, and draw a crude three-part person.

Language/Cognitive Skills

By age three the average child has a vocabulary of at least a thousand words and three-word sentences are well established. The child can count three objects correctly (this will increase to four during the year), and can repeat three numbers or a six-syllable sentence. Three uses plurals and asks rhetorical questions (lots of them!). By this age, children definitely know what sex they are and their full name and by age three and a half children can tell you how many there are in their family. Three loves to have stories read and reread (and will recognize and object to any skipping or changing of words!).

There are some misarticulations in speech, such as "dis" instead of "this" and "wide" instead of "ride" (Marilyn's daughter at this age referred to herself as Wachel Ezizabeth instead of Rachel Elizabeth). Stuttering, which is present in about half of young children, may now appear. Usually the whole word is involved and generally stuttering first occurs when the child begins to put words together in sentences, so the onset peaks around two and a half or three. Stuttering will tend to disappear and reappear in some children until they are five and parents need not be concerned about it nor try to correct this developmentally "normal" speech pattern. In fact, some say emphasis on it can make stuttering worse.

Language is now reciprocal. The child responds to the comments and questions of another. In addition, children talk to themselves ("I'm climbing up the slide"). Language is used to communicate needs and to learn about the needs of others.

Language is now used to obtain things like objects and information, to direct the child's own activities ("I climb up"), to control feelings ("Mommy is going bye-bye"), to control others ("Stop that!"), to get attention ("Look at me climb!"), and to create imaginary situations. All of these are incredibly complex communications skills to have developed in three short years.[4]

Three is the age of "Why?" which means the child has matured enough to understand relationships between things in a more sophisticated, causal way. Three wants to know the reasons things happen. A three-year-old child has both intense curiosity and imagination.

Piaget recognized that children perceive and interpret things differently from the way adults do and also reason differently. He noted that the development of intelligence occurs in stages and must do so because children start out without any concept of time, space, sequence, cause, and effect—all of which adults take for granted.

The three-year-old uses preoperational thinking (see p. 228). This means that the child can now use language symbolically but cannot yet use language abstractly or do any abstract thinking. By definition, preoperational thinking means the child cannot use deductive logic. Instead the child makes judgments based on the child's own perception of experiences or events. The child may relate things by juxtaposition—because parts are close to each other even though they are not related—or by centration—the child concentrates on only one aspect of a changing relationship.[5] The child by now can use representational thought to recall the past and to anticipate the future. Some children delight their parents by discussing memories from an earlier time when they couldn't speak.

A three-year-old is *egocentric* (which is not to say selfish, although this may be true as well). Rather, appropriately for their stage of development, they see themselves at the center of the universe. Identification with another comes later —with maturity. A three-year-old also *overgeneralizes*. Though the three-year-old has learned the names of many objects and has learned about differences in temperature, size, shape, texture, etc., of objects, the child cannot yet grasp the fact that a substance retains the same mass when it changes shape (conservation). This leads a three-year-old to insist that the *same* amount of liquid poured into a skinny glass is more because it looks taller in the skinny glass than in a wider shallow glass.

Three-year-olds can count long before they understand numbers. However, they don't yet understand that counting is the way to get an answer to the question "How many?" By three, time is pretty well understood and children can begin to anticipate. Three-year-olds have learned what a *day* is. The concept of tomorrow follows, then the day before yesterday, and finally the day after tomorrow.

Logic begins with classification, which even a three-year-old can begin to do. Threes understand that toys have categories; cars are different from blocks. Three-year-olds can sort things before they understand the next level of abstraction, which is to understand what class the objects are in. For example, a three-year-old may be able to sort things by color (put all the red blocks in one pile). Threes can also sort apples in one basket and oranges in another, but they may not yet understand that apples and oranges both belong in the fruit category. Three-year-olds may not seem to have a good grasp of cause and effect, but they do understand that causes happen before events and before the consequences of the event.

The three-year-old is at a primitive stage of moral development because subsequent stages require a higher level of abstraction than the child possesses. The child thinks it is bad to break something even if it was an accident because the fact that the object is broken is what is bad. Consequences or punishment are what the three-year-old thinks determines whether an act is right or wrong. If Three thinks, "I'll be punished for it!" the act was wrong! Three-year-olds can also believe that objects such as matches have the power to punish.

Social Skills

Three-year-olds can play simple games in parallel with other children, wash their hands, pour from a pitcher, feed themselves with little spilling, brush their teeth with supervision, put on their own shoes, and unbutton front and side buttons.

At three both solitary play and cooperative play with others are important. Solitary play includes imitation of the tasks adults do and also often includes an imaginary playmate. The child practices motor and imaginative skills in this play —often over and over again.

Play with others no longer is exclusively parallel. Children interact with each other in many ways. They may play with the same toys. They may engage in rough-and-tumble play together. At this age, generally two children play better than three or four or more.

By the time your child is three and a half, most play is cooperative. Cooperative play continues through childhood, and becomes more elaborate with more players. Friendships are stronger and sometimes children are excluded because they are not liked or are seen as "different".

At age three, everything the child does becomes a game. Three loves new roles because of the newly developed imitative skills. Dress-up and imaginary play are both great fun.

The three-year-old begins to be able to play sit-down games like checkers and simple card games but hates to lose and will change the rules or blatantly cheat to win. This is a normal developmental behavior—it does *not* mean your child is on the way to a life of crime and dishonesty! You and the child can make temporary "ground rules" which give the child a chance to win.

Children at this age understand about turns, are willing to take turns, and are generally cooperative and obedient. They take great joy and pride in completing a project such as a painting (and love to have it exhibited) and have a great interest in combining play objects to make other things—like making a bridge or a garage out of blocks. Three-year-olds usually take responsibility for using the toilet but still announce it and often wait till the last minute. Many Threes begin to sleep through the night without wetting or waking up.

A three-year-old is very ritualistic in both play and dressing. You can take advantage of this and involve the child in cleaning up. The child is *not* too young to learn how to put toys away. Marilyn's daughter, responding to Marilyn's complaint that it was dangerous to come into the bedroom to kiss her daughter good night because so many toys were on the floor, cleared a neat path between the door and her bed. Marilyn realized that a child who could do that could be more regularly involved in cleaning up! Anne had a similar experience and took delight in the compromise.

Later on in the third year, at about three and a half to four, children tend to become more oppositional, especially in dressing and meals. Your three-and-a-half-year-old is not *quite* back to the terrible two-and-a-half stage although parents may sometimes think so. Three-and-a-half-year-olds have a new appreciation of their own preferences much as two-and-a-half-year-olds do. Parents who value instant obedience may find this age frustrating. Try to appreciate your child's growing individuality. Don't have power struggles about minor matters, but be "non-negotiable" about important areas like safety. You cannot yet expect a child of three and a half to appreciate *your* needs—this comes later as your child matures.

Emotions/Feelings

The three-year-old, despite all the new skills which lead to independence from parents, still needs them and their love very much. The child has already learned that he or she is separate from Mother. Now the child becomes more keenly aware of sense of self and makes new strides in the long process of developing autonomy. The autonomy/dependency duality will continue for a long time—and for some will last a lifetime if certain feelings about parents are not resolved.

As far as sexuality is concerned, a three-year-old child has been aware of his or her own gender for quite a while. Three-year-olds learn, if they didn't before, that there is not only a verbal difference between "boys" and "girls" but also a genital difference. Sexual curiosity is great at this age. The child who has not yet seen genitals of the opposite sex generally has the opportunity to do so at nursery school. This leads to a surge of curiosity about who has what kind of genitals, where the girl's penis disappeared to, etc. This knowledge is part of learning mastery of one's own body. Children can be helped to understand that their body belongs to them and to no one else, a parent task discussed in the chapter Special Events and Stresses in Family Life. Masturbation may start or continue—and requires no action except gentle reminders to do it in private.

Children at three are very aware of conventional male/female roles. Indeed three-year-olds are great stereotypers probably because they are trying concretely to firm up their gender identity. Don't worry that this age-typical stereotyping means your child will be sexist—this won't happen unless you reinforce it. Avoiding sexism means teaching your child to respect and value human attributes regardless of the sex of the person who has them. (See p. 242.)

There may be fewer anxieties at age three than at two, because the child has a firmer grasp of the universe and what to expect. If there are fears and anxieties, they are likely to be of a more sophisticated sort: fear of death, illness, or bodily damage. The three-year-old is very worried about staying in one piece. Threes now know that toys and cookies break and suspect that there are threats to their own intactness. Three-year-olds may also express fear of more prosaic things like the dark, dogs, or noises (Marilyn's son was afraid of a vibratory noise that occcured when the wind blew and air got in between the storm windows and the regular windows. This made a loud buzzing sound which her son called "The Bzzzz" and which absolutely terrified him. Anne's children were all frightened by the noise of vacuum cleaners).

By three, the child can conjure up monsters and "control" them by making up a story. Three can now tell lies, which *really* shows how intelligent your child has become! To the question, "Who spilled the juice?" Three may say, "The dog did it!" and mean it. Three is the peak time for imaginary playmates—and many three-year-olds have them.

Children this age love parents so much that they intensely want to be just like them. They like to dress up as their parents. At this age they don't just imitate actions of their parents but actually identify with them. They want to use the same words and do the same things. This is especially true of three-year-old boys and their identification with men's stereotypic clothes and toys like boots and guns. Boys, as well as girls, at this age also identify with mothers and may enjoy dressing up in women's clothes or makeup and may even use a pillow to pretend to be pregnant.

Most three-year-olds are quite ready for nursery school. (See p. 472.) *All* Threes need the experience of rough-and-tumble play, along with opportunities for games, stories, creative activity, and imaginative play with other children. A few, particularly if they have had little experience with other children earlier, may be frightened by children in large groups. But every effort should be made to find same-age children for them to play with. It's not too late to make up for play experiences that have been missed.

Some three-year-olds are rather shy and dependent. It was once thought that all shyness-dependency problems were caused by anxieties and insecurities in children. Further, parents assumed they did something wrong which "caused" shyness. Current research suggests that some shyness is an inherited temperamental characteristic of the child. Just as some children take longer to talk than others, some move more slowly into developing enough "outgoing-ness" to play socially with other children. A shy child may need a year or two more experience with a daily "play group" where there are other familiar children, and the mother or care giver is present, before becoming ready to be left in a large nursery school setting where the children are more rambunctious. Such a child may play more comfortably with younger children or with nurturant older ones.

Three-year-olds have specific "tensional outlets"—as the Gesell Institute calls them.[6] Sometimes these behaviors are thought of as bad habits and, if present, parents feel 1) their child is maladjusted, and 2) they should do something about their child's behaviors. Gesell has wisely pointed out that, like adults, children have tensions which are *normal*. There are age-specific ways of relieving these tensions—which are also normal. Children grow out of these behaviors as they mature to the next set.

One such tensional outlet is thumb sucking, which persists in some (though at three the child will allow you to remove the thumb during sleep). Many threes still want a transitional object like a blanket or teddy bear with them all the time and may rub this while they suck their thumb. Thirty-nine percent of all three-year-olds have an attachment to a special object.[7] This is a *loving* behavior to be cherished. Later your child will outgrow it—no need to worry that the teddy bear will be carried to high school.

At three and a half, tensional outlets increase both in the number exhibited and the frequency of those seen. Children this age may stutter and exhibit nose picking or fingernail biting. Whining becomes prominent and reaches its peak at three and a half.

The overall incidence of behavior problems in three-year-olds was 11 percent in one survey; a sleeping problem was the most common.[8] Many children begin to have bad dreams and nightmares at this age as their more sophisticated thinking permits more complicated anxieties. Having to sleep alone is still sometimes a source of anxiety, and you shouldn't hesitate to comfort the child at night.

Developmental Warning Signals

If by age three your child does not seem aware of other children or adults, has little or no speech, doesn't imitate adults in play, doesn't follow simple directions, can't ride a tricycle, doesn't point to pictures of familiar objects, or engages in repetitive activities for long periods like spinning wheels on a truck or head banging,[9] your child is suffering from a developmental delay which warrants a workup to find out why.

CARE GIVER TASKS

Basic Care

Unlike those children in the baby age/stages, three-year-olds are reasonably independent in many aspects of physical care. Almost all can feed themselves, though they are not very skilled at cutting meat. Food likes and dislikes are pronounced, but we swear on a stack of Bibles that your child will eat enough of a variety of foods to ensure proper growth and nutrition. The only exception to this is when food and autonomy/dependency needs get mixed up so that food becomes the center of a battleground where parents and child fight it out. Power struggles over food are a needless source of pain, but if you find yourself in one, see the chapter on socialization, p. 46.

NUTRITION

Your task as a parent is to provide your child with nutrition to fuel his or her body. Nutrition needs can generally be easily met at this age. Special food preparation is no longer needed. The three-year-old can eat about everything you eat, although meat still needs to be cut in small pieces (be especially careful with hot dogs) and dangerous substances like peanuts should still be avoided.

Three-year-olds should be well on the way to choosing a "happy, healthy diet" for themselves (see p. 549). This is a balanced diet with lots of protein for growth, relatively little in the way of saturated fats, little refined sugar. The diet contains lots of grains, fruits, and vegetables and the child drinks at least one pint of milk a day. Some pediatricians suggest limiting fat at this age, accomplished by using 2 percent milk, lean meat, poultry and fish, and margarine instead of butter. Most, including Marilyn, do not limit eggs at this age because the egg is such a good source of protein. If your child is eating food from all four food groups and taking a pint of milk a day, multivitamins are not necessary.

Three-year-olds *need* snacks. Their energy (calorie) requirements are large for their size and their little stomachs do not hold large quantities of food so they can't meet these requirements eating three meals a day as we can. The trick is to avoid "gooey" snacks, which hurt teeth, and "empty calories," which replace nutritional calories in the child's diet. Wise parents stock what Leach calls "I'm hungry" foods.[10] These should be readily available to anyone in the family who is hungry and can't wait for the next meal—including a three-year-old. You can fill an old-fashioned cookie jar with soda crackers or graham crackers or keep a box of these on a low shelf. Try filling sandwich-size plastic bags with a handful of raisins, small cubes of cheese, or slices of apple or orange.

Some sugar is needed by three-year-olds for energy. Fruits provide it but they may also need sugar found in plain cookies, simple cakes, etc. The key is to minimize sugar as a percentage of your child's diet. Also, for the sake of their teeth, avoid sticky sugars and encourage them to rinse or brush after sweets and after meals.

Saccharine, sorbitol, and aspartame have no place in the diet of three-year-olds unless prescribed for some reason like diabetes. What, you may ask, about chewing gum? It's easy to say gum is not essential, so don't permit it. But though gum has no positive nutritional value—and may have a negative impact on teeth if it contains sugar—it is so much a part of our culture that forbidding it is probably cruel. Indeed the day a child learns that gum is to be chewed, but not swallowed, is a milestone rite of passage into childhood from babyhood. Marilyn used sugarless gum for her kids although the latest evidence is that sorbitol may not be much better than sugar. In any case, the sugar in gum is rapidly whisked away by the saliva and swallowed so it doesn't have the lasting effects on the teeth of a caramel, for example. By the way, a slogan Marilyn used about gum was, "In your mouth or in the trash—*never* in your hands." This prevented the gum-on-the-upholstery problem.

We offer a few basic suggestions to help keep you cool in the task of providing nutrition to your child. As you know, you no longer *feed* a three-year-old. Three eats—most often what and when Three wants. 1) Present the child with a balanced diet, paying reasonable attention to the child's likes and dislikes. 2) Make it clear that if the child doesn't like what's being served for supper there is always cereal or peanut butter or something else that Mommy doesn't have to *cook*. 3) Give the child only small amounts. 4) Make an adventure out of taking a tiny taste of new foods but respect the child's right to say "Ugh." 5) We don't believe in artificial rules at the table—like "Clean your plate" or "Eat all your vegetables before you get dessert." 6) We *do* believe in not allowing snacks to substitute totally for meals. Snacks can certainly provide nutrition (an apple with a peanut butter sandwich or crackers and cheese is perfectly good nutrition). But poorly timed snacks may interfere with family meals, which generally occur three times a day. We feel the social value of sharing food at mealtimes is nearly as important as the nutritional function.

We also believe in modeling and encouraging table manners from the start without making a big deal over this. Granted, nearly everyone's lifestyle has become more informal through the years. However, on the nights you are using candles and a tablecloth, three-year-olds can and should be gently instructed in the appropriate manners to go with this. Formal meals can actually be fun for children when both parents and child look on them as a treat and celebration. For the children it can be like the dress-up games of this age when they enjoy trying on your fancy clothes. Adult socialization includes being able to eat formally. Obviously, three is too young an age to expect much, but it is fun to start the game.

After each meal three-year-olds can clear their plates and even scrape them and, with a little help, rinse their hands. Marilyn used to tell her children to hold their sticky hands together until they got to the bathroom to wash them. This prevented traces of food from adorning the walls. It's also a good idea to follow hand washing with tooth brushing or at least rinsing ("swish and spit" or "swish and swallow").

We also think restaurant manners are important—even at age three. Parents must be clever enough to pick an appropriate restaurant, however, as no three-year-old can be expected to sit through a six-course gourmet dinner. Many "family" restaurants have children's menus and play materials. Be prepared if they don't and always take along some crayons or pencils. Paper place mats can be colored or turned over to draw on. Children cannot be allowed to run around in a restaurant—it's hazardous (hot coffee, etc.) and disturbing to other patrons. Even in a fast-food establishment manners can be stressed: stay at your table and dump all food and paper into the trash can.

CLEANING/GROOMING

Hygiene is pretty simple at three. Although a daily bath is not essential, an active three-year-old generally is dirt-covered by the end of the day and enjoys soaking or scrubbing off the dirt. A simple hair-do needs shampooing only once or twice a week but you will not harm the child's hair if you shampoo daily.

A three-year-old child is much too young to take a bath or shower alone. However, the child can be responsible for some of the scrubbing up and can even learn to run a sponge around the bathtub when the water is draining thereby starting the cleaning process. You still will have to supervise, do the shampooing, and clean the ears. For obvious safety reasons, never leave a three-year-old alone in the tub or shower.

A three-year-old can brush the teeth but will need some supervision to make sure that the teeth are getting clean. Use a fluoride-containing toothpaste. Many dentists recommend occasional use of a disclosing agent so that the child can "see" that all the color was scrubbed off.

You, of course, will still cut toenails and fingernails but three-year-olds can begin to use an emery board and can clean their own nails with an orange stick.

Dressing a three-year-old can be blissfully easier than dressing a two-year-old who resembled an excited octopus *or* it can be a time-consuming battle about what to wear. Most three-year-olds are capable of dressing themselves provided you see to it that the clothes are easy-off, easy-on (T-shirts, both long- and short-sleeved, and pull-on trousers, for example), and that you tie shoes or get Velcro sneakers and avoid back buttons. Some three-year-olds may want more help from us because they still enjoy the body contact. This is usually manifested by dawdling—generally at the time we are most harried!

Expecting Threes to dress themselves, helping them choose what to wear the night before, and placing those clothes where they are accessible all will help these children begin to take responsibility for self-dressing.

Outside clothes should be easy for the child to put on. Lightweight, quilted jackets are the best but a three-year-old will not be able to manage the zipper. Mittens should be fastened on or they will vanish. Boots should be slip-on. Slip-on or Velcro-fastened shoes give three-year-olds maximum independence as they cannot yet tie shoelaces.

SLEEP

Getting the child of this age ready for bed is often a challenge. Nearly all Threes will be in a bed rather than a crib. We think that the "youth" bed is a waste of money. Go right from crib to a twin or full bed, depending on the size of your child's bedroom.

We believe in early development of independence, thus we recommend a sturdy lamp by the bed that children can turn on by themselves if they are unhappy in the dark. A radio can also give children control over their environment and they *can* be taught to keep it at low volume.

Some children of this age unwind with a pre-bedtime romp but most need quiet play at this time. A warm bath followed by lap time in the rocking chair with Mom or Dad works for many three-year-olds. Marilyn used to put both children on her lap along with a big book of folk songs and they would all sing songs together. They would start with lively songs and end with a quiet lullaby. Some threes are overly stimulated by playing in the water and should bathe at another time.

Continue or establish a bedtime ritual with your child: pajamas, toilet, wash hands, brush teeth, say prayers, pop in bed, have a story, for example. It's the idea of a dependable ritual which is soothing; the specifics aren't important.

Children are not always sleepy at the time when they should go to bed to prevent morning crankiness. Alas, our world has a chronology to which most of us must adapt. Try an "early warning system" like an alarm clock or kitchen timer which rings a few minutes before the child needs to start getting ready for bed. Let the child take toys or books to bed. One warm suggestion came from a mother-doctor who snuggles under the covers with her child before saying "Good night!"[11] As she points out it warms up the bed and gives both mother and child a special feeling of closeness and relaxation. Anne's Swedish grandmother said it was unnatural to send young children to bed alone. She felt someone should lie down with and cuddle them until they drift off to sleep.

Three-year-olds are prone to nightmares and also can frighten themselves by conjuring up imaginary monsters. This is related to the fact that at this age they become very afraid of their own angers. (Marilyn can still remember how a pile of clothes in her room resembled a witch and terrified her when she was very young.) We find nothing wrong with a night light or even a full room light for the child who dislikes the dark. Where is it written that everyone has to sleep in the dark, just because most adults prefer it? Babies sleep in the daytime and young children nap then. Associating sleep with the dark takes years to establish. By the way there are useful books to help three-year-olds conquer their fear of bedtime. (See Suggested Readings.)

EXERCISE

Exercise needs are generally met by the normal activity of the three-year-old. However, the child who prefers sedentary play may need encouragement. Walks and runs with parents are usually fun. Threes also need "rough and tumble" play with their own size people.

Three is not too young to get started in the sports the family loves. We've seen three-year-olds on skis and horses, for example. Obviously they need careful teaching and close supervision to follow all safety rules and commonsense precautions.

STRESS MANAGEMENT

Although after a day of chasing a three-year-old, the *parent* is likely to need stress reduction, the child also gets cranky and out-of-sorts. Often parents forget this child was a baby only a short time ago and that he or she still needs cuddling and rocking chair time. Generally, fatigue is an important factor in the three-year-old's stress, which, in turn, causes those behaviors that give parents a good deal of stress. Parents can often predict, and thereby prevent, situations that lead to fatigue. Try to avoid taking a three-year-old grocery shopping if the cart is too confining and walking too tiring. Try to maintain a *quiet time* midday even when the three-year-old refuses to nap any longer. Balance hectic days (company, special outings) with quiet play-at-home ones.

Anger is a very early emotion. We can recognize anger in infants—the red face, the eyes screwed tight, the fists clenched, and the loud cry. Anger in a three-year-old is even more recognizable. Three-year-old children have become intelligent enough to hit another child rather than flail their arms in a wild tantrum as was the pattern at age two. Angry three-year-olds usually jump up and down, cry loudly, and turn red in the face.

Learning to handle anger is a lifelong task for some. Help teach your child safe and sensible ways to use and vent anger effectively. Ideally, no human being should hurt another, either physically or verbally. Practically speaking this means taking the child's hands and physically not letting the child hit another child—or you.

As you know tantrums are due to anger or frustration. In three-year-olds as well as in adults, physical activity can discharge a good deal of anger and aggression. It truly "gets it out of your system." When anger strikes, try to encourage non-hurtful physical activity, such as banging a drum, pounding a pillow, or marching around the room shouting a song. After the child is calm, you can ask the child why he or she feels angry and try a bit of interpretation. Always remember to say that anger is okay—it's hurting ourselves, other people, or objects that is unacceptable.

By the way, you *will* get angry at three-year-olds, furiously angry at times. Just when you think it's safe to consider your former babies to be more mature children, they act like babies again! Learn how to cope with your own anger. Beware of abusive actions (see p. 115).

Teach your child, by example, that anger can be a *good thing*—not just something to get rid of. Anger, like pain, hurts, but it also communicates distress when important needs and wants are frustrated. As adults, we can use anger as a motivator to try to change an unacceptable situation. We can use our young children's anger as an important signal that *they* feel frustrated and helpless. Whenever possible, we can help them solve the problem. When it can't be solved, we can help them learn ways to tolerate frustration, discharge anger and, ultimately, problem-solve.

EMOTIONAL "NUTRITION"

Besides feeding and cleaning, another important mammalian task is *touching*. Cats provide needed touching for their kittens by licking; monkeys groom. Humans cuddle and hold and croon and speak lovingly. Three-year-olds still need lots of this even though they seem quite big and independent. All of us need emotional nurturance all of our lives.

Parents have the very important task of *self*-nurturance as well. You have to love *yourself* so you can love *your children* so they can love *themselves*—probably this is the most important message in this book.

Self-esteem is very important to a three-year-old. In this regard, it's perfectly okay to let the child win at easy games. You can set the game up so the child wins or give hints. There's plenty of time for your child to learn about the tougher rules of games and life.

Three is an age when many children become siblings. The birth of a new baby is a major event in the life of an only child. Sibling rivalry is discussed in the chapter on socialization, but it's especially easy to get fooled by a three-year-old who is a *child* by now, not a baby in the parents' eyes. When the new baby comes, many three-year-olds have a to-be-expected, normal regression. This can disturb parents who expect too much of a three-year-old. We suggest involving the child in the care of the baby (in a supervised, sharing way), and spending some you-and-me-alone time with the older child.

Three is also an age when Mother is apt to resume work or become more involved in non-employment, out-of-the-home activities. Three-year-olds can definitely understand that Mother will be coming back, but will need some special time when she does, especially if she's been at home full-time up to now. Threes generally tolerate sitters quite well when parents go out in the evening. The same sitter should be used whenever possible. If parents plan to be away on a trip, introducing sitter and child before you go is important.

Remember, Three is still small enough to be swept into your arms for a cuddle, to be rocked, to be sat on your lap for a quiet talk. Three still needs to have a chance to play baby again.

Socialization Tasks

PLAY/STIMULATION

For three-year-olds play is learning—play is actually their job. As parents we need to provide a safe and stimulating environment for this play to take place, and to enhance play and learning experiences for our children.

As far as the learning aspects of play are concerned, parents should provide both an atmosphere which encourages learning and the materials, such as toys, books, paints and paper, puzzles, etc., which are used in learning. Such an atmosphere encourages *curiosity* and *activity* as opposed to the passivity of too much TV. Parents should find the time and energy to answer questions, praise acquisition of skills and knowledge, and they can nudge the child a bit beyond where he or she is—in a loving way. Saying to a three-year-old, "Next year you'll be able to start piano"—or take ballet—or learn to catch a ball like the big kids —is a good idea. Remember these are important learning years and your child lives to learn as he or she learns to live in the grown-up world.

Learning materials are easily available and relatively inexpensive. Lists of age-appropriate toys, games, sports equipment, and books are readily available in books which your library will have. If you go easy on the plastic "junk" toys, you'll have money for pads of drawing paper, crayons, puzzles, etc. (Junk toys are easily recognized because they are encased in plastic so your child can see them in the supermaket. They are also widely advertised on television and they come in series so that every child wants all twenty!) Since threes love to imitate, toy household tools (like hammers) and equipment (like irons and ironing boards) are much appreciated.

By the way, praise your child's pictures (and other artistic endeavors). Refrigerator magnets or masking tape make it easy for you to display pictures. If your offspring has produced a real masterpiece you want to save permanently, don't put it in a drawer somewhere. Instead write the date on the back and frame it in an inexpensive "diploma" frame. This preserves the picture even if you don't have room to hang it. You can store a child's best productions in a box under the bed until you do have wall space.

Incidentally, children's art is great for bathrooms, hallways, and kitchens. Anne's husband had one of their daughter's paintings professionally framed for his office and both Marilyn's office and library have framed paintings and papier-mâché sculptures done by her children as far back as kindergarten.

DISCIPLINE/GUIDANCE/VALUES

Although life with a three-year-old is easier than life with two and a half, soon three and a half will be here.

Probably the best advice we can give here is 1) don't expect too much, and 2) enjoy every pleasant moment. We can all get fooled by how civilized a child is one minute and how babyish (clinging, demanding, fearful, etc.) the next. The best way to handle this is to demand little, but demand the essentials with firmness, self-respect, and reasonable consistency so that your behavior is predictable for your child.

Although guidance and discipline are discussed in depth in Chapter 3, p. 46, we have a few suggestions for the three-year-old. Because threes like to please it's very important to make your rules both realistic and clear. Threes especially need face-saving whenever possible. Apologize if you blame the child for something he or she didn't do, for example. This also models the art of apology.

By the way, don't be concerned with "lying" in your three-year-old. When Three says that the imaginary playmate did it, the child is well on the way to developing a conscience. Three blames another precisely because the child has learned the behavior is wrong, which was your goal. Three also needs to preserve a self-image as a well-behaving child, which is also your goal.

Remember that it is normal for a three-year-old to handle his or her genitals. Don't panic. All you have to say is, "It's not polite to do that in front of other people" and provide a hug if the child seemed to be doing it out of anxiety. Three is the peak year for sexual curiosity. All three-year-olds want to know where babies come from, and most of them will ask you. Our suggestions are simple: answer the questions honestly in an age-appropriate manner. Threes will generally want to know how the baby gets in and out of the mother but do not need graphic descriptions of intercourse. As long as they find out there is a special place for the baby (and that it's not connected to food, urine, or feces) they'll be satisfied. It doesn't hurt to say that parents start the process by making love, and that helps reassure boys that they'll have a part in the future.

Although we have stressed repeatedly in this chapter that three-year-olds are barely out of babyhood, we want also to point out how eager they are to please and how completely they want to identify with their parents. What this means is that while you should not demand too much, you *can* ask for a bit more sometimes in the way of grown-up behavior. Let your three-year-old stretch to his or her maximum. It won't do any harm once in a while. Marilyn remembers her father saying, the day after each birthday, "A big girl like you, almost [the next age] years old already, can do it!" He always had an encouraging smile on his face and it always made her *want* to do whatever it was. Loving and wanting to please are wonderful learning motivators.

A three-year-old can't make a bed with neat hospital corners—and neither can we. But a three-year-old wants to imitate you and you can take advantage of this. Show both girls and boys how to make beds. It's easy and fun if you use down quilts that just need shaking. But a three-year-old can even do some traditional bed making, smoothing down sheets and blankets, provided you overlook the lumps.

All three-year-olds can put dirty clothes in a hamper, put jackets and boots in proper places, hang up pajamas and towels, and pick up toys. The use of child-friendly storage for toys helps. We recommend baskets or plastic bins for easy sorting (dolls in one, trucks in another). Plastic bins with compartments are also useful as are clear plastic shoe bags, both hung at child level for toy storage.

Threes can also help sweep floors and put books and magazines on a shelf or rack. They can carry groceries from sacks to shelves, put silverware and pots away, and, if you arrange your kitchen properly with dishes on low shelves and use unbreakable dishes, empty the dishwasher. It can be fun for them—and good for you!

VALUES

Parents inevitably teach their children their ideas about values, morals, and God. When a child is three, parents are the main teachers, although some organized religions start three-year-olds in religious nursery schools, which is fine. Actually values are absorbed from birth on—caring, nurturance, assertiveness, self-respect. Most values are taught unconsciously: the child models our actions, hopefully moral ones. It is amazing how early children pick up on parents' words and actions. Marilyn tiptoed into her three-year-old son's room one night after she thought he was asleep. She gently kissed him and whispered, "God bless you, my son." He sat bolt upright with a look of surprise and said, "I didn't sneeze!" He didn't have a clear-cut picture of religion, but he knew that God was mentioned when a person sneezed!

By three a conscious effort to teach humanism ("I care for others") can begin. Wise parents will instruct gently, avoid pushing, and remember that the essence of morality is respect for the feelings of others—even others as young as three.

NURSERY SCHOOL

WHO SHOULD GO?

Nursery school is good for most three-year-olds. When Marilyn's children were growing up it was "acceptable" to send three-year-olds to a "play school" two or three mornings a week—but no more. Day care was almost unheard of. Five-day-a-week nursery schools for three-year-olds were virtually non-existent, except that in some cases special arrangements could be made by working mothers or mothers who were ill to send their child to the two-day-a-week session *and* the three-day-a-week one. By age four it was considered permissible to let the child attend preschool five mornings a week.

Our world has changed. Not only are more mothers working but there are fewer children in our neighborhoods. We know that vital socialization cannot take place unless the child has peers to interact with. Five-day-a-week nursery school was already available by the time Anne's first child was two and a half, and was routine for three-year-olds when her others reached that age.

We both have always advocated nursery schools. We both feel the age a child should first attend nursery school is variable. Today many children are in day care as infants and most have some nursery school experience by three. Indeed many go to nursery school by two or two and a half. However, three is the age at which most children start. And there are good reasons for that.

The three-year-old has both the skills and the needs for nursery school. The *skills* include independent motor skills such as feeding, talking, and (usually) toileting. The *needs* include a peer group of same-age children to interact with, as every child needs to learn how to get along with similar creatures. Learning to get along with parents—while a magnificent accomplishment—is not enough. The child also has to learn how to relate to grown-ups other than the parents.

The child needs exposure to new games and toys in a setting with other children so as to learn how to share and to communicate feelings. Children will also benefit from being taught specific skills such as printing their name, but these skills are less important than the social skills. They also learn how to put away toys more easily than in most homes, since nursery schools are organized for this.

Some parents, reluctant to lose or alter the special relationship they have with their child, are dubious about nursery school. They are tempted to think they can "teach" their child what a nursery school teacher does. But the major learning at nursery school comes from interaction with other children, strangers at first. This interaction occurs in a safe setting which permits lots of rough-and-tumble play under the supervision of a non-parental adult. This cannot be provided at home unless the neighborhood has *lots* of other three-year-olds.

WHO IS READY?

Our belief that all children should have a nursery school experience does not blind us to the basic fact that no two children are alike. Some are ready at age two; others not quite mature enough at four. The following list of questions may help. You should be able to answer "Yes" to most of them.

Is your child able to take care of toileting with no or little help? This means no diapers during the day as well as being able to go to the bathroom alone or at least tell an adult he or she needs a bathroom.

Is your child able to play alone—at least for a while?

Is your child able to tolerate frustration—at least to the point that temper tantrums are mostly a thing of the past?

Is your child used to being away from you for a while?

Is your child able to understand simple adult commands or suggestions and communicate needs and wants verbally?

Is your child in pretty good health? As we discussed in the last chapter, exposure to lots of children does increase the number of infections the child will have that year—although it probably decreases the rate of infections later. (We used to see lots of respiratory infections in kindergarten—now we see more in nursery school—and probably fewer in kindergarten.)

The child who has a handicap and is not ready for regular nursery school may especially profit from a special one such as those for learning-impaired or motor-impaired children.

HOW DO YOU PICK A NURSERY SCHOOL?

As in choosing day care, the most important things for the child all begin with "s": the attitudes of the *staff* toward children and the *safety* and *suitability* of the *surroundings* for children. Important factors for the parents are location, hours, and cost.

An excellent discussion about choosing a nursery school can be found in Rubin and Fisher's *Your Preschooler.* [12] They suggest checking on licensure and choosing only a licensed school. Many communities have a child care agency that dispenses information about day care centers and nursery schools. If your community doesn't have such an agency, rely on word-of-mouth information from parents who feel the same way about children that you do. You can also use the Yellow Pages to get names and call to ask about licensure (if you have any doubt about whether you are told the truth, call the agency in your state or community which issues the license). Also ask the school for names of parents you can talk to.

Rubin and Fisher have a suggested checklist—and we have added to it. Parents are the ones to determine whether a particular nursery school is suited to their own child.

1. Assess the schools' basic philosophy, which means finding out about whether the program is structured for intellectual growth (like a Montessori school) or concentrates on entire growth, whether it is sectarian, whether it fosters creativity and the arts or physical prowess.
2. Assess the schools' policies about eating problems, naps, toilet accidents, and discipline.
3. Find out about how the school handles accidents and illness. What happens, for example, if you get hung up in traffic when you are supposed to pick your child up and you are late?
4. Assess the physical surroundings. Does the school look safe? Clean? Is there enough space both indoors and out for play? Is there a suitable place for meals and naps?
5. Check the equipment. Is the play equipment safe? Are there suitable toys? Are there enough toys, books, and supplies for the children? Is there a variety of materials for learning, like puzzles, musical instruments, nature materials, sandboxes, water play, etc.?

6. Assess the staff:
   a. Are there enough staff to provide an acceptable ratio for your child? (At age three at least one adult for ten children is recommended.)
   b. Is the health of the staff assessed before hiring and is staff health monitored?
   c. Does the staff have a nurturing attitude and behavior?
   d. Does the staff exhibit understanding of children and their behavior?
   e. Does the staff have the knowledge to guide your child appropriately in games, arts, crafts, etc.?
   f. How does the staff handle misbehavior or conflicts?
   g. How does the staff handle the shy or withdrawn child?
   h. Does the staff seem willing to talk with you about your child?
   i. Does the staff seem to enjoy their work?
   j. Can you visit at any time? It's been recently noted that schools which seriously abuse children have restrictive visiting policies.
7. Consider a co-op nursery school. Some nursery schools have regular staff and also require a parent or care giver to come twice a month to help. This both reduces the cost and gives parents a wonderful chance to see their own children in their natural peer environment (as well as monitor its safety). Anne and her husband each took one day a month of their vacation time for this purpose and wouldn't have missed it for the world.

HOW DO YOU PREPARE YOUR PRESCHOOLER?

The best way is to talk about nursery school for a long time. The first time you take your toddler to the park to swing you can mention that when he or she goes to nursery school there'll be a swing set. Start talking specifically about *the* school a few weeks before it starts. Ask how your child feels about nursery school.

It's a good idea to take your child for a visit beforehand and point out all the fun things, especially all the children having (hopefully) a good time playing together.

It's also helpful to anticipate both questions and anxieties. There will be a teacher to help point out where the bathroom is, etc. You can tell your child that you understand feeling a bit scared because you did when you first started school.

Most parents stay—and the schools permit this—the first few hours or days. Some schools start a new child and mother off at snack or mealtime.

WHAT IF YOUR CHILD CRIES WHEN YOU LEAVE?

Some children never look back; they love every minute of school. Others find it very difficult to be left. Usually such children are the somewhat shy, more sensitive tots who are frightened by the fact their mother is leaving and also frightened by the other children.

Probably, after a warming-up period, it's best to make up your mind you're going to be a brave parent and leave after a firm and loving "Good-bye, I'll be back." Spock points out (and we feel he's right) that there is often a connection between overdependence in the child and overprotection by the parents.[13] Overprotective parents tend to be very devoted to their children, very soft-hearted, and more likely to want their child's tears to stop now rather than consider the child's future. They often feel guilty that they are not better able to meet *all* of their child's needs and they are unable to admit or tolerate any resentful feelings they have toward the child. The overdependent child also can't face the bad thoughts he or she has toward the mother. So both cling— one in actuality, the other unconsciously. The mother wants to stay close to the child to protect him or her from exaggerated dangers. She looks anxious when she leaves and the child who fears something will happen to *her* if she leaves is convinced from looking at her face that it will.

If you and your child are caught in this cycle, *you* are the one who needs to sort out your feelings. Often, just making up your mind to leave cheerfully works, as 90 percent of children are easily and quickly distracted by a skillful teacher and the excitement of school. Each day that you return and your child masters the fears makes the child feel more grown up. The pathologically fright-ened child, who is truly terrified and does *not* get distracted, needs—along with the parent—some professional help.

REACTION TO NURSERY SCHOOL

Some children play so hard they're exhausted and need some cuddling and quiet play when they come home until they regain their energy levels. They generally also need a snack—many come home *starving*.

Occasionally, after a good adjustment period your child may no longer want to go to school. What the child says about school is always worth listening to, but rarely do you have to *do* anything except listen to the child and talk with the teacher. Sometimes something disturbing has happened which your child hasn't verbalized. For example, a favorite friend moves or there's a new teacher who does things differently.

You'll be amazed at how soon a child as young as three in a play or nursery school setting begins to care about how other children feel. Threes begin to share toys, to play cooperatively, to model their behavior after the adult (if a child wants their toy, they will try to persuade that child that another toy is preferable just as the adult does).

In summary, as adapted from Ames and Ilg, nursery school does the follow-ing:[14]

• Helps the child to learn to play with other children, to share, to take turns, to adapt to a group, and to use aggression in effective and socially accept-able ways.

• Provides equipment, toys, and materials that the usual household does not and exposes the child to art, music, and stories different from the ones at home.

    • Provides a situation where a child is less the center of attention than at home.

    • Gets the child used to the idea of being away from the family, and lets the child begin a life of his or her own.

    • Gets the child away from a troublesome home situation if one exists.

    • Gives the child a chance to become close to adults other than parents and relatives.

    • Gives the child's mother a teacher with whom to discuss the child in terms of behavior both at home and at school.

If you absolutely can't afford a nursery school or there is none near you, start a play group. Find same-age children for your child to play with; their parents become non-parent adults for your child to interact with.

Usually three to five children make a good group. Parents have to decide how often to meet, how long, where (taking turns at each other's house is a good idea), how to structure the group in terms of play, stories, etc., what snacks to serve, etc.[15] These groups can be fun for all and can serve as good substitutes for nursery school or as an introduction to nursery school.

HEALTH CARE

Medical Care

We have already discussed the important *preventive* aspects of health care at age three: nutrition, exercise, stress reduction. Threes should see the doctor at least once this year for the "three-year checkup" at which time the doctor will weigh and measure to chart the child's growth, do a careful physical examination, check blood pressure, and do vision and hearing screening. Doctors often order a urinalysis at age three, especially for girls, who are prone to urinary tract infections. A skin test (or patch test) for tuberculosis is usually applied. There are no immunizations scheduled for this checkup.

Your child will not need to see the doctor more than once a year except for illness. Three-year-olds are still prone to respiratory infections and ear infections. Those in nursery school may also get diarrhea or skin infections. However, serious medical problems are rare at three. Those problems which could be made worse by delay in diagnosis and treatment include hearing impairment, speech delay, or not using one eye (which can be diagnosed by visual screening).

Dental Care

From now on, children should see a dentist yearly, to have the teeth examined, and to have topical fluoride applied. The child of three is now ready to begin to be taught by dental professionals how to take care of the teeth (see p. 571).

Environmental Health

For a more complete discussion see p. 588. We just want to remind you about two major and potentially harmful household pollutants: cigarette smoke and excessive television. Studies have definitely shown that young children who live in a house with smokers have more severe respiratory infections. TV can be in the environment, but judiciously, as three is an age when TV can become a habit hard to break. As we've said before, TV should not be used as a "baby-sitter" to keep children quiet or out of the way. These are important learning years and learning is best when it is active. Much of television is repetitive and all of it is passive.

SAFETY

The "little monkey" needs a safe environment to run and climb and play. Because your child has advanced motor skills, and moves fast, the child is now at great risk for injuries from falls, burns, and pedestrian/car accidents. At three children's motor skills exceed their common sense. Three really doesn't know what is dangerous and can't be trusted to remember you have said "No!"

Be sure the child can't slip out of doors unsupervised. Patios need safety glass doors which are well marked so the child knows there is a door. Be careful about falls from windows. Screens should be secure and you should not open windows wide enough to permit your three-year-old to get through. Three-year-olds must be constantly reminded not to run with objects or food in their mouths. In a fall the object can cause mouth cuts while the food can cause choking.

Ingestions can still be a problem so the locks you put on cabinets when your three-year-old was a crawler still should be in place. A three-year-old is so independent we often forget the child may not have much sense when it comes to toxic substances. Three also is a great imitator. For example, a hungry three-year-old may want to slice an apple to dip the slices in cinnamon and sugar. Be sure your sharp knives are *not* accessible and that your children come to you for such tasks even as they take pride in being able to get the apples, cinnamon, and sugar together all alone.

Now that your child has some independence it's especially important to child-proof your house to take this into account. For example, Threes can wash their own hands and turn faucets so you must be sure the hot water temperature in your heater is low enough to prevent scalding. See p. 167 to review hazards room by room. Look at these rooms through a three-year-old's eyes by actually crouching down to the child's level.

Matches and flammable clothing can cause a disaster in a three-year-old. Matches should be locked up in a cupboard! A three-year-old should be taught two things about fire. First, what to do if they or their clothes catch on fire (teach your child to drop to the floor, covering the face with the hands). Second, how to get out of the house if the house is on fire or filled with smoke. Buy clothing which is flame-resistant.

Even a three-year-old who can swim needs continuous supervision around water. Never rely on water wings or air floats.

The three-year-old must also learn car safety skills. Threes should always be in an approved car seat. Threes should never be allowed to play on the sidewalk unsupervised and should be constantly reminded to keep themselves and their tricycles out of the street and to watch for cars in driveways.

*   *   *

In summary, three is a good year for both child and parent. The reason we both enjoyed our own three-year-olds so much is that three is truly the first year of childhood. Babyhood is now largely over. Watching a child develop verbal and social skills at this age is great fun! Enjoy!

SUGGESTED READINGS AND RESOURCES

Ames, Louise Bates, and Ilg, Frances L. *Your Three-Year-Old: Friend or Enemy.* New York: Delacorte, 1976.

A 1976 book by those experts from the Gesell Institute who know a good deal about young children. The authors beautifully describe the characteristics of Three and offer some sound advice about how to deal with three-year-olds.

Bonsall, Crosby. *Who's Afraid of the Dark?* New York: Harper, 1980.

Useful for the three-year-old.

Brazelton, T. Berry. *Toddlers and Parents.* New York: Dell, 1976.

This book has much information that is appropriate for this age child. This book details the struggle of the striving for independence, from both the child's and the parents' view. By using actual families, many behaviors and specific problems are dealt with. Brazelton helps parents analyze their child's temperament.

Church, Joseph. *Understanding Your Child from Birth to Three.* New York: Pocket Books, 1982.

An excellent source of knowledge for parents desiring information on the psychological development of the child. The book includes chapters on children's fears, sex differences, discipline, and individual differences in personality.

Gesell, Arnold. *The First Five Years of Life: The Preschool Years.* New York: Harper, 1940.

Although this Gesell book is out of print, it is worth a trip to the library. Wonderful, informative reading.

Hoban, Russell. *Bedtime for Frances.* New York: Harper, 1960.

Rice, Eve. *Goodnight, Goodnight.* New York: Puffin, 1983.

Both books are useful for the three-year-old. The child can model appropriate bedtime behavior after the characters in the book.

Sparling, Joseph, and Lewis, Isabelle. *Learningames For the First Three Years: A Guide to Parent/Child Play.* New York: Walker, 1984.

An illustrated "play" book that gives specific ideas on activities to do with children along with the "why's?"

Spock, Benjamin, and Rothenberg, Michael B. *Dr. Spock's Baby and Child Care.* New York: Pocket Books, 1985.

The latest revision of one of the most well known and widely circulated of child care books.

Watson, Clyde. *Midnight Moon.* Cleveland: Collins/World, 1979.

Another good bedtime book.

White, Burton L. *The First Three Years of Life.* Revised ed. New York: Prentice-Hall, 1985.

A comprehensive summary of Dr. White's extensive research on children in the first three years of life. The book is organized around aspects of the young child's environment which White has bound to the development of competence in relating to the world. Readable language.

16

THE FOUR-YEAR-OLD—
NOW MORE VERBAL

Scope of Chapter

This chapter deals with the four-year-old child—a stage characterized by some as the Frustrating Fours. We characterize Four as exuberant and energetic, both physically and emotionally.

Introduction

Parents who have spent the first years of their child's life building the child's self-esteem now may begin to wonder if they have overdone it! They hear their four-year-olds boss others around, brag a lot, issue ultimatums (even to parents), and overestimate what they can do. Parents who have encouraged curiosity and creativity in their child now must face hundreds of questions and perhaps cope with an imaginary playmate.

Fours are "doers." Four is speedy and changes from one activity to another fast enough to make your head spin. Like Two, Four has high levels of physical energy, but unlike the two-year-old, the four-year-old has more chances for success—especially where small motor skills are concerned. Four is also warm and exuberant. The child's world is opening up to new experiences and new people outside the home. These new situations bring about even more questions, more new words, and, unfortunately, more new fears.

At the same time the four-year-old refuses parental requests with "No!" and "I won't!" the child is using the parents as the final authority with others ("My mommy said . . ."). Peers become an important part of the child's world, and cliques may begin when children consciously include or exclude others from play. Even with increasing peer interaction, one of the four-year-old's strongest fears is separation from the parents. There is a very strong attachment to the mother or the primary care giver at this age.

Some four-year-olds seem to be out of bounds at times, which is why some people talk of the "Frustrating Fours." As in the case of the so-called "Terrible

Twos," when parents realize what is happening within the four-year-old they can begin to assist the child in growth and focus on the positive, imaginative, curious, adventurous, loving child. This can occur best if parents recognize the seemingly negative behavior as part of an important normal development.

KEY INFORMATION

Biophysical Information

SIZE AND SHAPE

The average four-year-old boy weighs 36.4 pounds (range 32.1 to 41.4) and is 40.7 inches tall (range 39.1 to 42.7). The average four-year-old girl weighs 36.2 pounds (range 31.2 to 43.5) and will measure 40.6 inches (range 38.4 to 43.1). Fours are usually about double their birth length. They will grow approximately 3 inches in the next year, and gain 4 pounds.

The child's body has definitely slimmed down. Four looks more like a "grown-up" boy or girl, except when the child cuddles up in the parent's lap for a hug, and the posture and little hands remind the parent of what a short time has elapsed since babyhood.

BODY FUNCTION

Visual acuity is nearly 20/20 and there is good convergence, i.e., the muscles of the eye permit focusing on small close objects. Bladder and bowel control are usually well established by this age. However, accidents at night can still occur, and active four-year-olds who are very involved with peers in play may put off using the toilet until it is too late.

As children are exposed to other children, colds and flu may be common, but many four-year-olds get fewer ear infections.

At four, children can tell their parents what symptoms they have. They can say, "My throat is sore" or, "My stomach hurts."

MOTOR SKILLS

Even though four-year-olds are able to think and to express thoughts, they are still very body-oriented. These children are continually testing their bodies and trying activities which involve new motor skills. They feel successful when they master a skill or perform a new task, but also feel failure when they don't perform the way they think they should. Fours think and learn best when their bodies are also involved and feelings are expressed through body actions.

What large muscle skills does a four-year-old have? A four-year-old can balance on one foot (four to eight seconds), walk up and down stairs alternating feet, catch a bean bag with the hands only, run with control even when changing directions, throw a ball with accuracy, hop on one foot, ride a tricycle or big wheel, and climb well. Four can also bounce and catch a ball and jump forward and backward as well as over objects. Skipping may be attempted, but for many four-year-olds this complex skill is not yet present. Children of this age are interested in daring challenges and need to be monitored and advised often about safety rules.

Along with the many large motor accomplishments, small muscle skills are developing rapidly. However, there is a real range in abilities at this age. Because of developmental reasons, environmental opportunities, or the child's own interests, some fine motor skills are like second nature for some children but a real challenge for others.

Many four-year-olds will be able to make clay shapes (putting together two and three parts), cut with scissors, draw a human figure and recognizable pictures, fold paper, button large buttons, and copy geometric shapes and letters even though the proportion and slant may not be correct. Some Fours can print their names or copy simple words. Art projects (painting, pasting, constructing) have more purpose, and the product more closely resembles what the child had in mind (unless he or she is a perfectionist).

Language/Cognitive Skills

Most four-year-olds have an extensive vocabulary. The speaking vocabulary can be as high as two thousand words, and the child can produce sentences containing up to five or six words. Fours talk a lot and are said to average four hundred words per hour (many parents feel this is a conservative estimate!). Questioning is at a peak—up to hundreds a day. Their curiosity, manifested in lots of "why" questions, reveals they are very much in touch with their environment. Simple explanations usually suffice and children pass on this information with confidence in the "authority" who gave it to them.

The child of four can understand up to twenty thousand words, and syntax is very adult-like. In addition to speaking, most four-year-olds can carry a tune and play simple musical games. They can recite poems and some songs from memory, relate fanciful tales, play with nonsense words, invent words, and try out new relationship words like "even," "almost," "how," "something," "like," and "but."

Although the child's language is becoming fairly sophisticated, words may still be misused in terms of meaning, mixed up order, and mispronunciations. We suggest the parent ignore these errors without criticism. You can repeat the statement correctly without any fuss, if you like, but overcorrection could make the child hesitant to speak.

Speech is now nearly 100 percent intelligible to both the primary care giver and the unfamiliar listener, although some developmental misarticulations persist including s, z, r, l, and some s blends like sh, str, sl, and spl. Children vary a great deal in speech ability. However, you should check with a speech and hearing specialist if your child can't be understood very well at all, carry out two simple directions in a row, recount an experience, carry on a simple conversation, hear you from another room, or if your child needs the TV on very loud.

The four-year-old is fascinated with meanings, reasons, and explanations. This accounts for the innumerable "how," "what," "where," and "why" questions. The drive to talk is great—during baths, while eating, while sitting on the toilet, in the car—wherever! If no one is listening (and it's hard *always* to listen), Fours will often continue talking to themselves or to a pet, toy, or a younger sibling. New words, large words, and silly words all have an attraction. Because the four-year-old is learning about the power of language and its impact on others, the child takes a *special* delight in rude, frank, or "dirty words." Four is fond of elimination swearing and, if angry, is likely to refer to a friend as a "pooh-pooh"—or worse.

Although four-year-olds operate in the preoperational phase described by Piaget, which means they need less immediate sensory input and think more symbolically than earlier, their thought processes are still concrete and fairly self-centered. Their views are likely to be half fact and half fanciful—still a long distance from adult logic.

Egocentrism, centration, inability to follow transformation, and irreversible thought, as identified by Piaget, all help prevent preschoolers from thinking with adult logic.[1] The four-year-old is becoming more sympathetic to others' moods and feelings, but egocentrism still makes it difficult to see something from another's point of view. When an adult says to the child who takes a toy, "You know how it feels when someone takes your toy, return it," the child may return the toy sensing the parent's tone, but not because he or she spontaneously thinks about how the other child feels.

Centration describes the child's ability to focus on how something *seems* to be, not on how it actually is—centering their attention on one dimension of an object or event, instead of all the dimensions simultaneously. For example, lobsters in a tank are viewed as "bugs taking a bath."

Preoperational children also cannot follow transformation—where one state is changed to another (e.g., the blocks mentioned above are spread out). The child concentrates on one state (the end result). Lack of reversible thought means the child can't go back easily to where the blocks were to begin with. Whatever is *now* is what *is.*

To understand the four-year-old's kind of logic, it is helpful to look at some other ways children this age tend to think. To these children, the bigger the other person is (in relation to themselves), the older that person is. Although Fours can now talk about where they have been or where they are going, the concept of space or distance is still somewhat distorted. Distant cities or states have little meaning, though a four-year-old recognizes local paths and space sequences amazingly accurately. Memories of landmarks allows Fours to alert parents whenever they are within blocks of their favorite fast-food restaurant or toy store.

The four-year-old's concept of time is different from that of adults. Because these children focus so on themselves, they are able to think about when they were babies ("I was too little to . . .") and about their next birthday or next major milestone ("When I go to school . . ."). These children still find it difficult to think of their parents being babies or growing older. Indeed, the child may believe that he or she will "catch up" with the parents. Even though children use words like "yesterday" and "tomorrow" or "next Christmas," they lack real comprehension of the meaning of these words and the words may be misused.

The four-year-old's ability to remember activities and events symbolically is evident as the child plays out ideas in the mind. Art reflects these ideas, as do the child's stories. A combination of egocentrism, creativity, and imagination brings about a "magical" year.

Imaginary friends and playmates often appear now—people or animals. This is a delightful, truly creative production which the child may want to share or keep secret. These imaginary creatures serve a purpose and usually disappear by age five.

Tall tales abound at this age. There's really no point in worrying about "lying" when the child creates tales of fantasy. You can respond by saying, "What an interesting story!" or "You think you saw that?" or "Is that what you were pretending?" If the child persists in wanting the parent to "believe" what is said, one can go along with the game of just saying, "I hear you." By the way it's fun to record the stories on tape or in a journal. You and your child will enjoy them later.

By four and a half or five, the child is more in touch with the difference between fact and fancy, and may begin to use the words, "I'm pretending . . ." or "Listen to my story . . ."

Dramatic play now involves more complicated scenarios. The child loves to "try on" different adult roles and attitudes. The role the child likes best is being the parent. Parents can learn a great deal about how they are coming across and responding to their children by observing the child's dramatic play. Through your child's play action you may see yourself in ways you don't really like. You may even learn something that leads you to change the way you act!

Children this age are intent on "fairness" and rules, and may focus on these characteristics as they role play and try to make sense of their world. It doesn't mean that they only think of parents as rule-makers. On the other hand, it is encouraging to parents to see their children ask questions of others kindly, give choices, and show patience with others in the same way the parents do.

Because of their egocentric nature, fours feel they are the power that causes things to happen—wishing can make things so. This power can relate to minor things like wishing the ice cream truck to drive by, or to much more serious happenings like "causing" a divorce or injury of a sibling, or even a death.

Even though the four-year-old child recites the "rules" of the house to anyone who will listen, the child is just at the very beginning stages of moral development. Fours act "properly" most often out of imitation or fear of punishment because they can't yet really put themselves in another's place or see the "bigger" picture. They just know what happens if they don't act correctly. Some fours don't seem concerned about punishment as they go through a stage of testing. They are checking out their power in order to find out what is "okay" and "not okay," before leaving the close world of their parents and family and heading out into the world of school and other adults.

Social Skills

Four-year-olds play well with other children and can even work on projects with others. Some of them feel more comfortable with a single friend than in a larger group. Four-year-olds are more likely to show affection, approval (or disapproval), and sympathy for others than they did at three. They have extreme—but harmless—behaviors like loud laughing or crying.

Four-year-olds seem less responsive to praise. The desire to please, seen in many three-year-olds, is less than it was. As four-year-olds begin to relate to and enjoy peers more than adults, they may become more selective about going along with authority. Fours are often argumentative to test parents. Giggling and disruptive behaviors while adults are trying to organize an activity are not uncommon. With consistency and effort on the part of adults, Fours can learn not to interrupt the play or conversations of others.

The child may now be able to use words instead of physical action to deal with negative feelings in a group. However, parents who observe the child's play group may be disturbed to observe name-calling, bossiness, or exclusion of some child. Cliques can form, although they can change almost from minute to minute. As Fours are exposed to more children, they become aware of physical differences for the first time and they learn children may come in different races, handicaps, sizes, and abilities. It takes sensitive adults to help children deal positively with others who are different from themselves. It's not too early to forbid cruel name-calling or behaviors and to model respect for all humans.

Fours seem quite self-sufficient. These children can feed and dress themselves (except for using a knife or tying shoes). Naps may be shorter, only two or three a week, or gone altogether. Brushing their own teeth and bathing themselves make Fours feel grown-up. Most four-year-olds sleep through the night and have their toileting habits under control.

Although by age four the mature child can be cautiously and gradually allowed to play outdoors alone, provided there is little traffic and the environs are child-friendly, you *cannot* trust an early four-year-old to stay on the sidewalk, so the child must be supervised.

Emotions/Feelings

Emotions at this age lie close to the surface with behavior tending to go to extremes—very angry at times, laughing or crying loudly at other times. The child may appear self-confident, boastful, and sometimes argumentative. Argumentativeness is both to test parental reaction and to experience new verbal activities like lying and strong language. However, many parents find their children basically positive, enthusiastic, and appreciative at age four.

Four-year-olds can be quite aggressive toward other children and are unpredictable with siblings. They are sometimes provocative to older siblings and, though often gentle with the younger ones, they can also be mean or even dangerous.

Because Fours are so language-competent now, they can learn a variety of feeling words to express what is going on inside. Along with simple feeling words like "happy," "sad," or "angry," they begin to use words like "proud," or "excited." These are sophisticated words, and some subtleties of meaning may somewhat escape four-year-olds. However, it is surprising how accurately they can use them. When you reach this age it must be a great relief to be able to verbally communicate to someone else how you are feeling.

With Four's awareness of the environment and other persons, two fears may become more prominent than they were before. One is fear of bodily injury, the other is fear of death. When four-year-olds see a handicapped person —especially another child—or hear of another's illness, they can become preoccupied that the same thing might happen to them. The child often asks questions when noticing these problems. We encourage you to talk with children about fears, with just as much information as they can handle. There is no way the parents can promise children that they will never be ill, but children can know that their family does many good healthful things to take good care of themselves and that adults will always be there to take care of them. Fours need this reassurance. Some cruelty to the handicapped comes from fear or ignorance and can dissipate with reassurance and explanations.

Because children at this age have a strong interest in their bodies, this is a natural time to share simple books about the body or even take trips to the museum where there are displays of body workings. It is important that the parent stay nearby to help the child understand what is seen and to be sure the exhibit is not frightening to the child.

Children who have not already done so will now ask more questions about the physical differences between the sexes and where babies come from. The parent should welcome these questions, be proud of developing curiosity, and answer with simple, straightforward answers. It is not necessary, or possible, for a child of this age to attain a full understanding of the processes of birth, intercourse, or the moral issues of sexuality. There is plenty of time for the parents to answer further questions as the child matures. Four's main interest is usually in the anatomical features of each sex (especially the opposite sex), and how babies originate. The parent should use correct terminology and not cloak the explanation in symbolism, lest the whole process take on a mystique and bring about distorted curiosity or misconceptions on the part of the child. Libraries have many good children's books to help, as well as references for parents. (See p. 76.)

Because of the child's need "to know" about everything, sexual exploration at this age is common and normal—usually under the guise of "playing doctor" or some other pretend game. This interest will subside at around five years of age if the child has received the necessary information.

Modesty may begin around this age—seemingly overnight—and is actually a sign of sexual self-consciousness. First the child becomes shy with non-family members and then later with family members. Girls usually go through this stage around age four and boys around age five. Even in homes where family nudity is common, children will go through this modesty stage. In families with older siblings, or if the children are exposed to other children, as in nursery school, modesty may occur sooner. Parents can, and should, talk about privacy, in a positive way, even before this age. This includes being able to use the bathroom in private, knocking on a family member's bedroom door, and not infringing on a sibling's private space. All family members deserve privacy and it is an important concept to teach.

One more note about children's sexuality at this age. Around age four, the child usually becomes very attached to the opposite-sex parent. It is the child's first, safe attempt at establishing a romantic relationship. Parents should not make the child feel guilty or embarrassed about this attraction, or tease about it. At the same time parents need to avoid any seductive behavior that exploits these feelings. The feelings of the child should always be accepted as a stage of development, even when the little boy announces he will grow up and marry Mommy, or the little girl flirts outrageously with Daddy.

Similarly, the other parent need not feel left out. By six, the focus will be on the same-sex parent. Children at four are doing important homework that will help them later develop relationships with other adults. If the child lives in a single-parent home where the parent is of the same sex, this is an important time to seek out one or more opposite-sex adults for the child to relate to.

The intensity of the love a child of four has for the opposite-sex parent is very great. Marilyn says a woman is never loved as completely and unreservedly by anyone in her life—not husband or father—as she is loved by her four-year-old son.

Now, back to the fear of death. Many adults don't have a clear idea about what death means and struggle internally for answers. The young child wants to know where the person went and why. The child has a difficult time believing the person or animal won't come back. When children hear someone has died they may begin to worry that their parents might die or that they themselves might. Sometimes the child's questions come a long time after an incident.

Parents can explain that most people don't die until they are very old—a long, long time from now. Beyond that, parents need to take into consideration the child's questions, the child's level of development, and their own religious beliefs. It is unwise to say things like, "Auntie Ellen went to sleep" (the child may stay awake for days—so as not to get "caught" while asleep), or "Grandma Dora was such a good person, God took her" (the child may be afraid to be too good, for fear of a similar "reward"). If the death occurs to someone close to the child, the child should be encouraged to verbalize feelings (often anger at being left) and be offered a lot of reassurance that he or she will always be cared for.

Children this age still have occasional nightmares, but they remember their dreams better and can talk about them. Encourage the child to talk about the dream if the child *wants to* but don't push if the child wants to forget. Sharing dreams in daylight over the breakfast table can be fun and can also help children to realize that adults too have dreams that are scary, funny, or just interesting.

Four-year-olds may be afraid of monsters, the dark, strange sounds, or shadows. Night lights, rearranging the room to rid it of shadows, and soft music may help, as well as monitoring TV and the films the child sees. It also helps to see that the child sets a reasonable pace during the day with enough calm spaces.

In general, even though four-year-olds can seem very independent and bright, they still very much need to know that the parent is always there when needed.

Developmental Warning Signals

If your child at four years does not have understandable speech with sentences, does not focus on pictures, does not seem interested in listening to a simple story about his or her experiences, repeatedly tests all limits, is very quiet and conforming to the degree of never trying anything new, has pronounced fears or phobias, frequently flaps the arms or hands to express excitement, runs from one activity to another, does not draw a figure with a head and a few features, does not play with other children, avoids eye contact, engages in head banging or rocking, cannot tolerate frustration without frequent tantrums, or is not toilet trained (don't worry about an occasional accident), your child has a developmental delay.[2] Problems emerging at this age are more likely to be minimal brain damage or emotional disturbance than retardation.

If your child has a vocabulary of six hundred words or less, does not use sentences, and only 80 percent of words are understandable, a speech and hearing workup is in order.

CARE GIVER TASKS

Basic Care

"I can do it myself," which parents heard, at least non-verbally, at age two is now made perfectly clear in words by the four-year-old. In fact, lots of things are made perfectly clear to the parent now—what foods the child likes, which clothes, etc. As with the two-year-old, the parent must decide which issues are important and which ones aren't. It's not worth the energy to argue every point. Besides, it's exciting to watch the child make choices and to really allow the child to have input. Children at four can take quite a lot of responsibility for their own care. Daily care routines help avoid hassles.

NUTRITION

By now, the four-year-old has a pretty good idea of what foods the family "allows" and what foods are good for you. Mandy combined her four-year-old inventiveness with her knowledge of nutrition. She explained that her mother didn't have to worry about giving her junk food because an alligator (small) was living in her stomach and eating all the bad foods, so they wouldn't hurt her!

TV and peers go a long way toward influencing fours about foods. Fortunately today so many parents are concerned about nutrition that they support each other. Fours, like other children, will go on food jags. If the food is vaguely nutritious, the parent should probably go along with it. This stage will pass and won't hurt the child.

Several good learning activities for Fours revolve around food. You can have the child participate in menu planning. Even if you don't usually write a menu, it's a good time to start. There are three positives here: the child sees words written down, which helps set the stage for reading; the child helps make food choices and *may* be more likely to eat the selections; and the child increases awareness of foods that include the necessary nutrients for a balanced diet.

Another related food activity is to have the child help make up a shopping list. At the grocery store, the child holds the list and pencil and the parent tells where to check off each item. This prevents too many requests from the child because you can say "It's not on the list." It also makes reading meaningful, and helps the child feel grown-up and important.

A third food activity is having the child assist in the preparation of meals and snacks. Real involvement can happen only when there is lots of time, because children both can't be rushed and need instruction. However, when Four does simpler tasks like mixing, gathering materials, and setting the table, this can actually be a help to you if you're in a hurry. Children this age can often prepare their own snacks, sandwiches, and cereal and they should be encouraged to do as much for themselves as is possible. This helping can include cleaning up.

A garden, or container planting, is a fantastic learning experience, and many children have learned to like vegetables and salads as a result of enjoying their harvest.

The four-year-old's personality may spill over into mealtime—literally "spill over" for some of them. Even though they have developed fairly good dexterity in handling utensils, their high energy level may lead to glasses toppling or dishes dropping. Save yourself grief by resorting to plastic ware and, without fuss, teaching children to wipe up spills by themselves.

Because most Fours like to talk, they may attempt to dominate the conversation at mealtime or use some of their more shocking language or far-out stories to gain attention. Parental guidance can tap into the child's sense of fairness that everybody should have a chance. If you find the language issue too important to ignore, the child can be dismissed from the table after fair warning that parents require a different level of "table talk."

Usually four-year-olds like the experience of eating out. They may be so much into behaving correctly that they will take younger children to task for embarrassing them with bad manners. Since Fours love to role-play, parents can pretend at home that the family is at a restaurant. Children can practice taking orders and serving.

CLEANING/GROOMING

Fours vary a great deal from one another when it comes to cooperation in performing routines—and they themselves vary from week to week. The issue is not whether they *can* do the tasks, but whether they *choose* to and how they view them. If the child sees these tasks as "grown-up," part of their independence, part of a set routine, and not in competition with other more fascinating activities, there are less likely to be problems.

The child still needs training in the complete sequence of the bath and needs to have within reach all necessary equipment. Given this, Fours can be allowed as much independence as they can handle. Some of them demand privacy in the bathroom but we feel four is too young an age for bathing alone behind closed doors. However, if the bathroom has been safety-proofed, a four-year-old can be left alone as long as you are near to monitor if things get too quiet or there are unusual noises.

Since some Fours resist shampooing, parents may find showers work better. Playing beauty shop is a treat for some; cream rinse helps avoid tangles; short hairstyles may sponge clean; or you can try shampooing together with your child.

Independence is a key word at age four. It is difficult for children to put away clothes if hangers are out of reach or drawers are too heavy to pull. If there is a well-established organizational plan for clothing and toy storage, it is easy for the child to keep things put away or in order.

Many parents are amazed at how early some fours become "clothes-conscious." They have very strong opinions about what they will or won't wear. Taking them shopping, although less efficient, is helpful (stay out of the designer clothes sections). Buy in the child's color choices and always shop with comfort and ease of dressing in mind.

SLEEP

By age four many children go to bed more easily. Some Fours are even able to say, "I'm tired and I'm going to bed." For some children—especially the active ones—a calming-down period before bed is essential. Some four-year-olds will still be dealing with (or going through for the first time) bedtime problems such as procrastination, nightmares, and bedtime rituals.

The time before bed can be a special close time for parents and children. We suggest back and foot rubs (children can learn to do this for their parent first, and then it's the child's turn to receive relaxing treatment), the rocking chair, telling stories without a book (then the four-year-old can tell some too), quiet talks reviewing the day or planning for tomorrow, closing your eyes together and imagining scenes of happy places—real or pretend.

One parent we know suggests going back into the room about twenty minutes after the child is asleep to talk softly to the child—especially if the parent and child have had a discordant day or the child is experiencing lots of fears. She told us her child had been waking terrified that something was chasing him. She went in several nights in a row and said softly to her still-sleeping child, "You are sleeping peacefully and relaxed. You are safe. You are in your bed in our house and safe. We are here. We love you very much. We are so happy to be sharing life with you." The nightmares stopped.

When parents and children have rough days, this technique seems especially positive, as parents feel calmer and reconnected with their youngster. It also makes it easier to say these words aloud the next day. The words always need to be *positive*, stated in the present tense, reassuring, expressing confidence in the child, and said with love. The words should never focus on the problem area nor should the technique be used for controlling behavior.

The four-year-old's bedroom should be a special place. The child is likely to take friends there now and in general spend more time there. The room should be comfortable with books and favorite small toys within reach of the bed, soft animals and dolls (for boys too), a radio, a light, pictures of friends and family (of the child's choosing) and art work the child has done. The bedroom that is used as a place for isolation or punishment is not likely to have a pleasant connotation and may lead to bedtime problems.

Children this age vary in whether they benefit from naps, as do parents' reasons for wanting children to take naps. Some parents want a break themselves during the day. Working parents would like their children up a little longer in the evening, so they can spend time with them. Still other parents want early bedtime for children, so that the parents have some alone time. You can't *make* a child nap but you can insist on a quiet time.

EXERCISE

Four is extremely active, but parents must make sure the child has adequate chances to move and develop the way he or she should. Parents may have to turn off the TV, take the child to a park or schoolground, and plan family sporting or outdoor activities.

Parents play two important roles in the area of exercise and physical development—one unconsciously and one more consciously. Children this age are either already involved with other children or soon will be. Many children are sensitive around other children if they don't have some of the physical skills that others do. Some children are reluctant to try skills in group situations where they perceive "everyone else" has the skills. We are not suggesting that parents work with young children to begin early training for competitive sports. However, time spent exposing children to appropriate skills with patience and encouragement is not only helpful for the overall physical development of the child, but also allows the child to feel more comfortable with peers, which builds self-esteem.

The other, less conscious, role parents play is providing a role model for exercise. Children who see their parents spend long hours at the desk or in front of the TV and rarely see them go outdoors or be active participants are likely to be the same way. "Do as I say, not as I do" works about as well here as it does in any other area—not very well.

STRESS MANAGEMENT

There may be a temptation (or provocation) to get into power struggles with your four-year-old. When the child says "No!" or "I won't," a red flag will go up inside most adults. The same red flag can go up when a parent sees the child acting bossy or hears the child asking "Why?" for the five hundredth time. Thus there may be hundreds of times the parent and child have the opportunity to get into struggles or negative confrontations which cause stress. Parents should both monitor the number and kinds of these confrontive situations and try to circumvent them, or think of creative positive ways to deal with them. Some parents stressed by the child who "pushes the parents' buttons" will profit by dealing positively, calmly, and firmly with situations (or even removing themselves psychologically). Less stress within themselves means less stress in the child.

Four's emotions, including negative ones, often lie just below the surface. Parents need to ensure that children are rested, eating well, and are helped in pacing themselves. Most importantly, the family needs to have play time together—time to laugh, to go *off* schedule, to sing, to roughhouse, and to touch.

Children, even by age four, can be encouraged to talk through their thoughts and feelings when they or their family are experiencing a life crisis or stresses. The child may be experiencing the situation very differently from what the parent imagines. Children often feel that they have caused distressful circumstances. In a divorce, children may focus on parents' earlier disagreements that related to the child, or the fact that he or she was "bad" at times. Because children want their parents together so badly, they feel something is wrong with them when they can't make their "magic" work to bring their parents together. These same dynamics can occur when there is a death.

Four-year-old Mandy, tired of a demanding grandmother's visit, said to her mom, "I wish Grandma would go away," and then, as an afterthought (and remembering that the adults had said Grandma was having health problems), she added, "I mean back to Chicago, where she lives." She was protecting herself in case something worse should happen.

During normal sibling rivalry and disagreements, one child is often so angry, he or she wishes (inside) that the other child would disappear or at least have some ill fortune. If something bad happens to the other child at a later time, the sibling can go through real anguish—again, because of egocentrism and belief in his or her own power.

Although these are tough situations for parents, they need to encourage the child to verbalize feelings, and give simple explanations and assurances.

EMOTIONAL "NUTRITION"

Independent four-year-olds can only be truly independent when they are sure the parent is really there for them. Whether the needed hug is because someone called them a mean name, or they're afraid of strange shadows, or there's a new baby in the house, the need is real. When they leap out into the world of others, they still want to be able to turn at any moment and see their parents not far behind.

Because the four-year-old is so language proficient, the child can say, "I'm angry," or "I'm frustrated." Fours can also learn to say to parents, "I love you," "I want to hug you," "I want to help you," "I'm glad you're my dad [or mom]." These positive expressions are both nurturing to parents, and positive for the child. Teach your child to give, as well as receive.

Socialization Tasks

Up to now in the age/stage chapters, we called the first section under Socialization, Play. This section is now called "Play and Fostering Cognitive Growth" for good reason. Although play is part of cognitive learning in early life, by age four, parents can be more directive with the child to help prepare the child for the learning which will take place in school.

PLAY AND FOSTERING COGNITIVE GROWTH

Before we talk about specifics, we want to remind you that parents can help with their child's development in three ways—through encouragement, opportunities, and awareness of the child's learning style. Parents can appreciate and praise the child's accomplishments; they can point out to the child the small intermediate steps, as well as the major leaps, in development. If a child hasn't had the opportunity to catch a ball, or use crayons, or put together a puzzle, these skills will develop slowly. The parent can provide the materials, the environments, and the times for the child to explore new skills. As children are self-motivated, very little else is necessary.

Parents who have taken the time to observe their child know, by the time their child is four, a good deal about that child's learning style and temperament. From the very beginning, some children hang back and observe for a while before attempting a skill. Other children try everything immediately, then retreat and surge forward again.

Each child has a pattern of behavior which parents will learn to recognize. This will help parents know how to approach their child in any learning situation—when to step back, when to push gently. Parents can then express confidence in their child knowing that the child *will learn* or that a *given stage will pass*. Transmitting this sense of belief in the child is a very powerful contribution to building healthy self-esteem.

The social four-year-old is acquiring experiences and trying on roles at a rapid rate. The child is busy classifying people and things to make order out of the world. Fours are intent on figuring out how they fit in the world, what is expected, and why things are the way they are. Even though they talk about ideas more, can recognize some symbols, and have some ability to deal with abstractions, they still learn best when they can touch and experience objects and events.

SOME WAYS PARENTS CAN ENHANCE LEARNING AT HOME

Language—(reading, writing, listening)

Because of the early rich language experience provided by parents and TV, many Fours today are already able to read their name and some words, recognize letters, or even read books. Parents don't have to do formal teaching. All they have to do is capitalize on their child's interests. Here are some activities that help children become aware of words and reading:

- Label items in the home ("David's room," "table," "closet," "blocks," etc.)
- Write notes to answer children's questions ("Yes," "No," "kitchen," "Dad")
- Label (with one or two words) pictures in a special photo album for the child (Mom, Eli, zoo, dog, Ann's car)
- Point out familiar product names or signs in magazines, on products, while traveling.
- Make simple books for the child. Pieces of cardboard covered with the child's choice of contact paper or construction paper can be the covers; staple blank pages inside. (Libraries have books on bookmaking, if more elaborate products are desired.) You can "write" a book based on

illustrations, or photos. Ideas include baby animals, ways to travel, my family, superheroes, friends, my favorite places to go, my wish book, a book about red things or growing things, a number book, a book about space, when I grow up, a vacation, trucks, cartoon characters, my favorite foods (or toys). Let the child suggest ideas. The book can include a single word or phrase (based on the child's abilities) as well as pictures.

• Read to the child—often. Use rhyming or patterned books where the child supplies words or phrases as the parent pauses.
• Read part of a new book and let the child guess the ending or make up different endings. Have the child retell familiar stories.
• Make up your own stories; then ask your child to make up a story.
• Keep magnet letters on the refrigerator for the child to use.
• Encourage the child to write, even if it is still scribbling.
• Have the child dictate messages for cards and letters.

Math

Children have lots of natural opportunities to think about number concepts and counting. Parents can help children see the world of numbers around them —on letter addresses, house numbers, clocks, speedometers, calendars, book page numbers, thermometers, rulers, TV channel listings, recipes, and newspaper ads. Children can begin to learn number names as well as learn to recognize the symbol.

Children at four can also learn the meaning of first, second, third, etc. "We do this first . . ." (Lining up blocks, cars or dolls)—"Hand me the second block." "Bigger," "longest," "tallest," "smallest,"—words expressing relativity are all concepts that are important to math and science as well as reading.

Children have lots of chances each day to count and calculate. Dad says, "I need four spoons for the table." Or "We need two big chairs and one little chair. How many is that all together?" "You have two grapes; how many will you have if I give you two more?" Or "There are three socks on the floor. How many will you have if I put two away?" There are also simple commercial games involving counting. Some children like simple card games that involve math skills.

The beginning of fraction understanding is second nature to four-year-olds, who are interested in fairness. Let the child divide a piece of cake, M & Ms, or a banana—such precision! If you want some fun, ask a four-year-old to divide a bag of popcorn.

Setting the table, planning a party for a certain number, or packing a picnic lunch give fours a chance to apply counting to a real-life situation.

Science

Play and a rich environment for experimentation can really help a four-year-old develop scientific awareness. The given activity may not be as important as the scientific processes that are being developed. The real payoff is the *scientific attitude* the child is developing. A child this age is naturally curious, full of wonder, testing, absorbing, drawing conclusions, and then testing again—already a little scientist! One good adult role is to "stay out of their way." You just have to provide materials and environments for experimentation, and an occasional motivating question, lend a willing ear to listen to the child's observations and excitement, and teach the new words the child needs to express his or her findings.

What kinds of materials and environments lend themselves to "scientific" exploration? Boxes, sand, mud, water, art materials, blocks, any building equipment, magnets, a box of junk, old items to take apart, a set of safe tools, a backyard, the park, the woods, the beach—any new outdoor environment. To maintain interest, items can be rotated by the parent. As you observe your child at play, you will begin to see the child's real interests and will get ideas for other activities/materials and for later toy purchases and gifts.

With these materials the child can experience things like weight, volume, erosion, cause and effect, proportions, balance, measurements, properties of air, and gravity. The child will be hypothesizing, planning, experimenting, questioning, drawing conclusions, and testing again—all good scientific skills.

The ability to classify, to see patterns, and make order of the world is also a scientific attitude. Fours love to have little collections of rocks, space figures, dolls—whatever. These collections not only meet their need to have something private that is especially their own, but collections will enhance their ability to classify. "All the red rocks here"; "all the sparkly rocks in this box"; "all the smooth rocks here."

The parent also has a chance to build on the child's natural curiosity by asking questions that begin, "I wonder what would happen if . . . ?" "Why do you suppose that is . . . ?" "How did that happen . . . ?" "Do you think that would happen if you . . . ?"

It is not important at this age for the child to give scientifically accurate answers—or for the parents to give them, for that matter. The process and attitude are what count. You have to remember that at this age the child still believes in "magic" and may give a magical explanation to a scientific question.

Creativity

The reason we list creativity as a separate area is because as children get older, they are expected to conform more and more. In school, children primarily use the left hemisphere of the brain, which is more literal and less creative. This emphasis is like educating half a child—encouraging only half the potential.

A creative person can function more effectively in life. We are not talking only about creating paintings, poems, dance, etc., (although these art forms allow expression, which is important for all human beings). The creative child (or adult) will be a risk taker, producer of ideas, flexible person, synthesizer, and a high-level thinker and learner who looks at patterns and solutions. Many of the science activities listed above are opportunities for children to enhance their natural creative abilities.

Parents have already observed their children create: new words, fantastic structures, new uses for objects, new ways of doing things, new songs and dances. Your role is to provide the opportunities and materials, not to "teach" your child to be creative.

The child should have creative materials in reach and have an adult demonstrate the safe and appropriate use of tools (rounded scissors, glue, tools, paints). The products the child wishes to save should be displayed and valued. As with early science experiences, the establishment of a creative *attitude* is more important than any given activity in the child.

It is almost easier to say what parents can do to *discourage* creativity in a child. They can focus on "correct" answers, not allow children chances to make decisions or have choices, be concerned with products instead of processes, never allow the child to make messes or experience creative constructing, compare youngsters, point out mistakes until the child is afraid to take risks, pass on prejudices so the child thinks there is only one way to be, and never take the child to art museums or theaters.

Children who have the chance to brainstorm solutions to problems, make decisions, see their parents model flexibility, openness, and creativity have a great head start in creativity.

Creating stories is second-nature to Fours. Stories are still fanciful or disorganized, but the skill is being rapidly developed and should be encouraged. A young woman told us her grandfather, who always had time to listen and play, developed two games for his grandchildren. He put lots of single words on slips of paper into a hat. The children took turns drawing out a slip with a word on it, and made up a good story. At first the words were: "clowns," "rabbits," "puppy," "nighttime," etc. Later the words were more difficult: "astronaut" or "friendship."

Anne's favorite story game as a young child goes as follows. The child is asked to think of three things to tell a story about, as unrelated as possible: say, a dog, a rock, a tornado. The adult invents a story including all three elements. At a later age the child can play the opposite role.

Another good game to encourage creativity is to start a story and have the children add on and on in turn.

Of course lots of four-year-olds' time is spent in pure play. They love to play with others but also enjoy playing alone. Appropriate toys at this age include dress-up clothes (you can create exciting costumes out of grown-up discards), a blackboard or easel, Tinkertoys, play stove and sink, toy dishes, and a doctor kit.

A WORD FOR FATHERS

Soon your child will be going out into the world. Your sons and daughters both need your help in introducing them to the world that has hitherto been seen as male. Though one day we may have a less sex-stereotyped society, today, in many areas like sports, carpentry, automotive mechanics, etc., men are more at home than women. Children of *both sexes* should be taught enough about an arena so that they are comfortable and feel neither left out nor ignorant when that arena is mentioned. Also, it can be *fun* for a father to teach his daughter carpentry, for example.

Fathers also should do their sons a favor and teach them—or encourage them to learn—those sex-stereotyped household tasks *formerly* associated with women. This is especially true for what we call survival skills. A boy should know how to cook well enough to feed himself when grown, how to clean *all* rooms of the house well enough so he doesn't get evicted from an apartment when an adult, how to sew a button on a shirt, and how to shop for food and clothes. We appreciate that some traditionally brought-up men find this a difficult task, but their sons may find it an *impossible* world later if they lack these skills.

DISCIPLINE/GUIDANCE/VALUES

Parental "consistency" and positivity have already been discussed but there are a few ideas that seem especially relevant at age four.

Logical consequences—The gist of this concept—and the reason it appeals to the four-year-old's sense of fairness—is that the consequence of any misbehavior makes sense and fits the situation. (For a thorough discussion of this method read *Children: The Challenge* by Dreikurs and Soltz.)[3]

The Act	The Consequence
The child spills milk	The child cleans up (instead of being yelled at or sent to his or her room)
The child dawdles over dinner	The child misses the story that occurs after the table is cleared because he or she is still eating (instead of being yelled at to hurry up)
The child didn't put the favorite shirt in the basket and wants it *today*	The child must chose another shirt (instead of Mom or Dad washing it separately or lecturing about irresponsibility)

Because the consequences fit the child's act, the parent can act decisively and without anger. The child is more able to see the connection, and take responsibility for his or her part.

Giving choices—This concept is closely connected with the philosophy of logical consequences. It is especially appropriate because four-year-olds want to be "grown-up" at the same time they are resistant at times to directives from parents.

The Choice	The Directive
"You can go to your room and hear one more story before bed or play with two	"You need to go to bed now."

more puzzles and then go to bed."

"You can choose the clothes tonight that you will wear to Grandma's."	"Here, hurry and put these on. You have to wear this shirt and pants."
"Help me decide what would taste good with chicken . . . peas or corn?"	"David, you have to eat vegetables; these are good for you."

The choices should be something the parent can live with. Some parents see this as a needless game because they feel their child needs to do what is required—period. It is important for children to begin early to make choices. It will save hassles because the child will have some say in what is happening. Choosing gives the child a sense of self-esteem—even though he or she ultimately does what the parent wants. As children grow, there will be more and more choices they need to make—many times with no parent in sight. Learning to make choices should start early.

"Logical consequences" carries a risk if it is done in a phony way. For example, it's *not* a logical consequence that a child who doesn't enjoy the dinner should go to sleep hungry. That's a parental coercive decision. It might be a logical consequence that the child select or fix a substitute meal.

Family meetings—Even if the family has just one parent and one child, family meetings can begin by the time the child is four. A set time each week is reserved for these meetings, which are used for solving problems, planning menus and special family events, voicing complaints or appreciation, or whatever is important to the family. Each member can put something on the "agenda," and *each* person needs to be given a chance to be heard. You can teach your child to practice problem-solving: defining the problem, brainstorming solutions (even the far-out ones), evaluating solutions, compromising, and planning actions. Parents who approach these meetings with openness and respect for each child (not just a chance to lay down the law) will find children looking forward to the meetings even into their teen years, and remembering them years later when they themselves are adults.

Rules—Even though we have spent a good deal of time on logical consequences, giving choices, and family meetings, every four-year-old needs to know what the rules are in his or her household. One of the biggest needs of the four-year-old is to know boundaries and limits.

It is easy for parents to spout rules. We know there could be a "rule" for nearly every behavior. Eventually our children might know and remember them all. However, this won't happen at four.

We suggest the following "rules" about rules.

1. Decide what issues are *really* important. Only make rules covering these areas.
2. State rules clearly and simply.

3. Where possible involve children in setting the rules (possibly in a family meeting).
4. Include the "whys" for rules—a brief explanation given once, not preached over and over again.
5. Enforce the rules consistently, positively, and firmly.
6. Make consequences clear and fair.
7. Set a good example.

The real reason for most rules is to allow a family to live together in harmony, and to allow everyone to meet as many needs as possible. The goal of socialization is to have children develop the inner ability of self-discipline—they will not always have a parent around to make decisions for them. Remember this long-range goal.

SOME SPECIFICS

Although Fours usually do not know the meaning of four-letter words, they pick them up, and when they see the reactions of their parents (or others), they use them to test limits and get attention. We think you should ignore such language. If you feel strongly about your child not using these words or the behavior persists, we suggest saying firmly you don't like the words and why— and give alternative expressions. Parents should also evaluate their own language to see if they are giving a mixed message to the child. If parents use the words themselves while telling the child these words are "bad," the child can be confused. Children may also avoid the use of these words in the parent's presence, but say them away from home or wait until a really special time—like when Great-Aunt Alice visits.

Fours often are quite insulting to parents as well as to playmates. Ames and Ilg suggest playing "Insult" with four-year-olds.[4] You can hurl epithets like, "You're a toasted marshmallow!" or "You're a squashed potato chip!"

The child's honesty with language can be disconcerting to a parent. Four may say to a relative, "Don't you know smoking is bad for you?" or "That lady is really fat," in a voice loud enough for the person in the supermarket to hear. Fours also tell "personal" things to others like "Daddy came home drunk last night. Boy, was my mom mad! He had to sleep on the couch!"

Some four-year-olds who are misbehaving respond to a role-playing game. "You are the guest here—and guests don't run in the house," for example.

There is lots of embarrassment at this age when bladder accidents occur— especially in front of peers. When accidents occur at home, the four-year-old can take responsibility for cleaning up, including putting the wet clothes in the laundry basket. The episode needs to be handled matter-of-factly and with understanding. A four-year-old needs to know that other children have this problem. The parent can help the child in many ways by reminding the busy child to go to the bathroom. As far as bedwetting (enuresis) is concerned, we suggest waking the child once in the night, putting up a night light, protecting the mattress and putting a large towel on the bed which the child can remove if it gets wet, and most of all demonstrating patience and the belief that the child can handle the situation. Bed-wetting seems to run in families, suggesting some inherited maturational cause and it is more common in boys (see p. 652). At any rate, it is a rare child who doesn't master dryness at night in his or her own time.

VALUES

Parents will have a ready "mirror" available because four-year-olds will reflect the parents' values through word and deed. "Why did you tell Grandma we were going out today. Aren't we staying home?" "Why did Mommy call in to work and say I was sick? I'm not sick!" Four will tell it like it is. Fours have had rules given to them for four years; they see things as either black or white. The subtleties of "white lies" or extenuating circumstances are beyond them.

Adults compromise and allow the ends to justify the means. A four-year-old will call this behavior to your attention. Maybe this is a good time to do some reevaluating. At the very least, try some family discussion about values. Explain to your child the social importance of "white lies" ("It would hurt Grandma's feelings if we said that . . .").

PRESCHOOL

Some four-year-olds will have already been in day care for three years, and will be experienced at being out of the home. For others, this year could be their first venture into an organized preschool experience. The majority of children today have some out-of-home experience before kindergarten. A few school districts across the country have even began to offer programs for four-year-olds in their schools—either full- or part-day. For many parents who have struggled to afford child care, these free full-day or extended-day programs are a blessing.

Selecting good child care environments is covered elsewhere, beginning on pages 450 and 473. As you evaluate a program for your four-year-old, keep in mind the temperament of your child, your own child-rearing techniques, and your expectations about educational programming.

Both the parent and the child should have a good inner feeling about the environment they observe, but most important about the primary care givers and teachers the child will have. Does the teacher encourage the "scientific attitude" mentioned previously? Is the provider energetic, curious, and interesting? Remember, this adult will be the model for the child a good number of hours each day. Does the provider understand this age in terms of development? Is the provider comfortable with different kinds of children and respectful of individual children? Does the care giver provide environments, materials, and activities you think are important? Does the teacher give choices, allow children to take on responsibilities and plan, help children work positively through difficult situations, and give and receive affection easily?

Actually, it would be a very special adult who possessed all these capabilities and qualities. But seek out the best child care givers you can find.

HEALTH CARE

Medical Care

Four-year-olds should go to the pediatrician for an annual checkup. Between four and six years of age the child needs the fifth DPT shot and fifth polio immunization. Vision and hearing testing are done each year.

How fortunate are the parent and child with an understanding pediatrician who takes time to answer the four-year-old's many "why" questions and to reassure the child when ill. The pediatrician can reinforce the parent's advice on how important rest, good food, and exercise are for the child to stay healthy.

Dental Care

Periodically, children should use a disclosing agent (ask your dentist) to see how well the toothbrushing has worked. The child's toothbrush and cup need to be in reach and a brushing routine established. Observation of a parent who brushes and flosses regularly helps, as children model parental behavior.

The four-year-old should certainly have been to the dentist by now. If this is the year of the first visit, we have a suggestion. Since Fours enjoy role playing so much, you can play "dentist" with your child ahead of time so the child will have a general idea of what to expect. As we said earlier, an annual visit to the dentist is in order.

Environmental Health

The child's environment is no longer confined to the family's dwelling and yard. The four-year-old is in preschool, other children's homes, dance or art class, and even out in the neighborhood. More than ever, parents realize they have less and less control over the child's environments and the influences affecting them.

Four has some fears, but also an amazing sense of confidence. Parents can capitalize on the child's enjoyment of role playing to act out situations that might be dangerous for the child. "Pretend all the kids decide to go to the store across that busy street you aren't supposed to go near." Give children a chance to think of actual words they can say or actions they can take so they will be more likely to do so if the situation occurs. But, remember, children this age don't generalize well from situation to situation. It takes lots of work and lots of specific examples.

Fears parents have of child abduction or molestation need to be dealt with in a positive way. Fours need to know how to protect themselves with specific actions they can confidently take. Parents can gain good information from community groups about ways to talk with children about molestation.

SAFETY

One of the dilemmas parents face with the active independent four-year-old is when to stand back and when to intercede.

When any four-year-old first approaches a new physical apparatus or play experience, you should go over the rules for use. This is true whether it's a bike, a swing set, a climbing apparatus, or a pool. When children violate the rules they need to be "retrained" or even removed for a while. Adults need to be especially careful when Fours are playing with others who are teasing or challenging children to new "heights." At this age children are likely to throw caution to the wind.

Children this age are too young to be left unsupervised for any length of time. They *cannot* be left home alone. Fours also should not handle machinery or mechanical devices alone. They are fascinated by these but lack the sophisticated sense of how machines work and what the dangers are. Be careful of swimming pools; Fours can both climb over a fence and unlock latches. It goes without saying that a four-year-old should never be around a pool alone.

There should be no hassle about car seats: the car doesn't move until eveyone's belt is clicked into place. Speaking of cars, Fours are likely to be fascinated with how a car works and may have learned a great deal observing the parent drive for several years. Keys should not be left in automobiles and cars should be locked when parked. Children have been known to get in a car in a driveway and shift it into reverse so that the car rolls into the street.

Ingenious Fours also are pretty good at taking off "child-proof" medicine and vitamin tops. They have been found doing scientific experiments with household cleaning supplies. Anything potentially poisonous still needs to be under lock and key (and not with the key hanging next to the shelf, as the child probably has learned to unlock a lock with a key from watching you).

Because Fours run a lot, falls are common. It is important to forbid horseplay while running, or running with food or objects in the mouth. Matches and cigarette lighters are still dangerous. Four is old enough to use them but is helpless in a fire. Knives and scissors should be carried point down if at all.

*   *   *

Summary: A mother of a four-year-old was asked to describe her child in a few words. She said: "Inquisitive, aware more of others' feelings, frustrated easily, somewhat impatient, doesn't listen too well, talks a lot, really wants explanations, a little actress. She's always trying on new roles, and is so smart! She amazes me with how much she knows!"

This is a good summary. It's an exciting year for both parent and child. It's also the last year before kindergarten. Four is still your preschooler. Most of the time you'll be grateful. You may on occasion wish your child were not around all day, but age five is right around the corner.

SUGGESTED READINGS AND RESOURCES

Baratta-Lorton, Mary. *Workjobs for Parents.* Reading, Mass.: Addison-Wesley, 1975.

A variety of manipulative activities designed to help children develop language and number skills, eye-hand coordination, observation skills, using easy-to-find materials. Each activity is clearly outlined and illustrated.

Belliston, Marge, and Belliston, Larry. *How to Raise a More Creative Child.* Allen, Tex.: Argus Communications, 1982.

Ways parents can help their child be more creative.

Braga, Laurie, and Braga, Joseph. *Learning and Growing: A Guide to Child Development.* Englewood Cliffs, N.J.: Prentice-Hall, 1975.

A practical, readable guide to understanding children's development, birth through preschool. Many suggestions for parents to help stimulate growth in the areas of language, independence, physical development, etc.

Briggs, Dorothy Corkille. *Your Child's Self-Esteem: The Key to His Life.* Garden City, N.Y.: Doubleday, 1970.

An excellent, readable discussion of developing self-esteem in children of all ages. Many examples of ways to handle children's feelings, and ideas for positive discipline.

Dreikurs, Rudolf, and Soltz, Vicki. *Children: The Challenge.* New York: Dutton, 1964.

Based on forty years of pediatric practice, a consistent approach to discipline covering: logical consequences, talking with children, giving choices, behavior changes, etc.

Gesell, Arnold. *The First Five Years of Life: The Preschool Years.* New York: Harper, 1940.

Although this Gesell book is out of print, it is worth a trip to the library. Wonderful, informative reading.

Goodwin, Mary T., and Pollen, Gerry, 2nd ed. *Creative Food Experiences for Children.* Washington, D.C.: Center for Science in the Public Interest, 1980.

A comprehensive resource providing ideas of food experiences in which children are active participants.

Samples, Bob. *The Metaphoric Mind: A Celebration of Creative Consciousness.* Reading, Mass.: Addison-Wesley, 1976.

Helps parents see their child from a holistic perspective. The book discusses right- and left-brain capabilities and helping children to reach their full potential.

Spock, Benjamin, and Rothenberg, Michael B. *Dr. Spock's Baby and Child Care.* New York: Pocket Books, 1985.

The latest revision of one of the most well known and widely circulated of child care books.

THE FIVE-YEAR-OLD—
ON TO KINDERGARTEN

Scope of Chapter

This chapter is about the age of five. Up to this age we have described children mostly in terms of their own individual growth and development. Now we must consider the calendar of the outside world—the school year. Thus the chapter is titled, "The Five-Year-Old—On to Kindergarten."

Introduction

Following the previous year's expansion of achievements, your child now embarks on a course of smoother, steadier growth and development. Five is more poised and controlled in physical abilities, more reflective in thinking, and more discriminating in speech. Five-year-olds are also quieter and behave more like adults, imitating them in play and in daily activities. Best of all, perhaps, Five, like Four, desires to please people, especially parents—and to be "good."

There can be a bittersweet quality to the kindergarten year. This is the last year that our children are ours alone—the last year that we can legally make *all* the decisions. Children may or may not go to kindergarten, but next year, and for many years to follow, the child legally must go to school.

Within the family, this is a special year too. Those of us who have indulged our children pretty much up until now have to recognize external requirements. Even without school and the outside world looming ahead, the five-year-old is big enough that his or her behavior would be intolerable to us if not regulated. At the same time, five-year-olds are big enough, bright enough, and verbal enough to understand most of the reasons behind what we ask of them.

Five-year-olds can be very much like adolescents, for similar reasons. They are at the threshold of a major life transition, just about to leave the bosom of the family. They are poised to look and act in both directions, forward and backward.

KEY INFORMATION

Biophysical Information

SIZE AND SHAPE

The average kindergartner weighs 41 pounds and is about 43 inches tall. For boys, the weight range is 35.5 to 46.7 pounds, and for girls, 34.8 to 49.2 pounds. The height range is somewhat less variable. For boys, height varies between 40.8 to 45.2 inches and for girls, height varies between 40.5 to 45.4 inches. The average chest circumference is 22 inches. During the next year the child will gain about 6 pounds and about 2.5 inches.

Growth in several areas accounts for the fact that your child no longer looks at *all* like a baby. The legs continue to lengthen, the abdomen becomes much less prominent, and the muscles continue to become firmer. In addition, growth and placement of the teeth affect the shape of the jaw and mouth, making the face appear more angular. The child's appearance is usually "healthy" with bright eyes and lots of vitality.

The body proportions of children are still considerably different from those of adults. The child's head at age five has attained 91 percent of its mature size, while the body height is less than 75 percent of its adult size. The surface area of the child's head at age five accounts for 13 percent of the total body surface, while that of an adult accounts for only 8 percent. So the head at five is still relatively large in proportion to the body. By age five the brain will have reached about 75 percent of its adult weight.

BODY FUNCTION

At the age of five or six there is a rapid increase in muscle growth, which accounts for the major portion of the weight gain at this age. No new muscle fibers develop, but those that are present grow in length and breadth, and there are also changes in composition that greatly expand the functional usefulness of the child's muscles. The bones also will begin to undergo change at this time, both in size and in composition.

The maturing digestive system will have fewer upsets over the next few years and will allow the child to retain food for longer periods of time. Bowel movements generally occur once a day, usually following a meal. Ear infections are less likely to occur than during earlier years. Visual acuity continues to improve as the eyeball grows and modifies its shape.

MOTOR SKILLS

Between the ages of four and five, your child's motor coordination increased tremendously. By five, the child is much more poised and controlled in large motor activities. Five really loves to be in motion and doesn't stay still for long.

Five-year-olds are, or will become, adept at a variety of new motor skills including roller skating, jumping rope, acrobatics and trapeze tricks, walking on tiptoes and on stilts, and skipping. Fives can stand on one foot for more than eight seconds and can catch a bounced ball. The child of five can ride a small two-wheeled bicycle if taught how. The child's extreme flexibility and suppleness are due to the muscle growth we have already described, and to the fact that the ligaments are not yet firmly attached to the bones.

Five-year-olds are more adept at small motor skills than they were at four. Fives can fasten buttons that they can see (but not those on the back of clothing), use a writing instrument to copy circles, crosses, and squares as well as letters and numbers, and use the hands to cut, paste, trace, and draw. Drawings of human figures now contain a head, eyes, nose, and mouth, as well as a distinct body and legs. Many Fives can also tie a bow, which means they can tie shoelaces. The child's approach to objects, as well as the grasp and release of them, is now very precise and accurate. Toys are now used more skillfully and purposefully.

Handedness is well established at this age. Your child will use the preferred hand in activities like writing or drawing, but will use both hands in activities like block building.

The acquisition of age-appropriate motor skills becomes crucially important at this age. Starting at five, there tends to be a strong relationship between motor skills and competence among peers. Although your child's pleasure in movement will usually be sufficient motivation to practice motor skills, you can strengthen this motivation by providing space and opportunity for such practice to occur, and by being genuinely interested in motor accomplishments.

Language/Cognitive Skills

Language development proceeds at a very rapid rate during the kindergarten year. In speaking, your child will now use *complete* sentences of five to six words with adjectives, adverbs, prepositions, conjunctions, pronouns, and proper nouns. Five will also begin to use the articles "a" and "an" more frequently. You will find that five-year-olds understand sentences containing dependent clauses beginning with "if," "because," and "when," and that they can respond to three requests (even unrelated ones). Fives can also talk pretty clearly, as most words are now well articulated. Most baby talk and infantile articulations are behind the child now. Some children who lisp will need speech therapy in school but generally for only a short time.

Five-year-olds can name most parts of the body and at least four colors. They also can name a penny, nickel, and dime. Five has a concept of numbers and can count up to ten correctly. Some five-year-olds can add up to their age with or without the help of their fingers and can copy numbers or write numbers from dictation. By five and a half, the child can count up to twenty objects.

Children of five are great talkers and often overrespond when questions are asked. They ask questions about what words mean. You will notice the questions are fewer and more meaningful than at age four. Five-year-olds use the answers to these questions to build up an impressive store of information, which they categorize (somewhat ineffectually as we will see below when we talk about cognition) and can subsequently recall quite remarkably.

Five-year-olds love being read to and love to "read" alone. As a matter of fact, they spend a considerable amount of time looking at books, tending to prefer books that show occurrences in the lives of children, and in which animals act like humans. Many five-year-olds can read some words and some may even be able to read.

Early readers are more likely to be girls, to have lived in a home where parents read a lot, to have been exposed to many books, and to have spent a good deal of time being read to by an adult or older child. By five and a half most children will recognize all the letters of the alphabet and can "read" preprimers.

Thinking and reasoning do not progress nearly as fast as language acquisition in this period. Although five-year-olds are progressing in cognitive ability, they are still subject to many of the characteristics of what Piaget has termed preoperational thinking. For example, Fives still think transductively (rather than inductively or deductively as adults can), and therefore link events in a cause-effect fashion that should not be linked, or fail to see the connection between events that should logically be linked. One preoperational five-year-old we know who was in a minor car accident with her mother at a particular street corner told her mother that she shouldn't drive by that corner anymore. The child was illogically linking the street corner and car accidents as if the first caused the second. A preoperational thinker would also fail to understand that if he has a brother, his brother must also have a brother.

Other characteristics of preoperational thinking are the tendency to attribute lifelike qualities to inanimate objects (animism), the tendency to be unable to see the world from any point of view other than his or her own (egocentrism), the inability to classify effectively, and the inability to mentally reverse thinking.

Let us explain a bit further. You may hear a five-year-old make comments like "The clouds are angry today," or "The bus shouldn't have left without us; it knew we wanted to get on." The child might also ask you why the sun keeps following us around all day. These verbalizations result from the limitations of animism and egocentrism. They are examples of very normal five-year-old thinking and will persist until the cognitive system becomes more fully developed and organized after the age of seven.

Most Fives believe in Santa Claus and the Tooth Fairy. They believe in God, in a childlike way, and are beginning to conceptualize death as finality (though most still think death is reversible).

Children will make statements at this age which reflect their difficulty in classifying objects and events in their world. Five-year-olds can make simple classifications that involve putting together things that serve the same purpose —e.g., a spoon and fork go together because you eat with them. However, classifications made on the basis of more abstract qualities, like *attributes* of objects, are much more difficult for the five-year-old to make. This is especially difficult when an object can belong to more than one category at a time; e.g., the object is long as well as shiny.

The ability to classify effectively is a cognitive acquisition that will greatly facilitate the mobility and flexibility of thought. Your child needs continued opportunities at play to discover and classify attributes and properties of objects. Parents can help the development of classification skills by playing games where they gather a number of objects and then ask the child to put together, for example, first the round things, then the striped things, and finally, the things that are round *and* striped.

Your child may show that the ability to reverse thinking; i.e., take it back to its point of origin, is limited. Fives believe that changing the shape of something, like flattening a ball of playdough or a pile of mashed potatoes on the dinner plate, increases the amount of playdough or mashed potatoes. Being able to reverse thought would enable the child to see the ball of playdough as it originally appeared and would help the child understand that the wide appearance of the flattened ball was just a result of substituting wideness for highness. You can help your child learn how to reverse thinking by play with objects that can be changed from one form to another—and back again—like clay or cookie dough.

Although logical thought in your five-year-old will be restricted by the aspects of preoperational thought we have just discussed until about age seven, Five is definitely more cognitively advanced than was Four. You will be delighted to watch as your five-year-old begins to think in more complex ways.

At five, the child begins to give more thought to judgments and decisions. The attention span lengthens and the child now has good memory for sequences of numbers and letters that are concretely presented. Fives can also differentiate much more clearly between fantasy and reality. They can name the days of the week and know how they are ordered. Five-year-olds have a keen interest in calendars and in the clock and most can tell time. Even those who cannot always read a clock to tell what hour it is can tell that it is bedtime when the little hand is in such-and-such a place. Some prefer digital watches because they can understand numbers more easily than a place on the dial.

Social Skills

Like the three-year-old, the five-year-old is in a state of equilibrium with respect to orientation to the world. Unlike the three-year-old, Five is independent and pretty secure in this independence. Because of both equilibrium and independence, the kindergarten period is a very pleasing one for both your child and *for you!*

Your child likes familiarity at this period. Five-year-olds are most comfortable when in their own home with their own things, following their familiar schedule of activities. Fives tend to be quieter than Fours were, and to think and behave more like adults, imitating them in play and in daily actions. As a result, five-year-olds often achieve independence in self-care activities.

Fives also love to help Mother and can be trusted to do a pretty good job at simple tasks. They are careful to attempt only what they can achieve, but proudly do it "alone." Spontaneous activity is also under good control, and the child often asks for permission to engage in activities before starting them. Being good and being "big" are very important at age five. For this reason, daily events, like bedtime, that caused difficulty at age four tend not to be a problem now.

The five-year-old's developing conscience is very much in evidence. Fives usually answer questions honestly and understand that there are rules defining right and wrong behavior, but do not generally understand the principles behind them. Five has no idea that subjective intentions often enter into moral decision making, so the child's conscience tends to be very rigid and to be expressed in extremes. Most five-year-olds believe that a particular behavior is either all right or all wrong. In the child's mind, breaking a rule is always wrong, even if the reason for breaking the rule was to help someone.

Socially, five-year-olds tend to be shy with people, but will slowly build up steady relationships. They are increasingly aware that what they do affects other people. As a result, Fives have a greater ability to play with others. Although Fives get along with siblings (and both boys and girls can be protective and mothering to younger siblings), they get along better with peers outside the family. The five-year-old child seems to play best with children of the same age, and plays better outdoors than indoors.

Your child's entrance into kindergarten for at least two to two and a half hours a day at some point during this period of development will provide the perfect opportunity for social interaction with a wider group of age mates. Play experiences will now be largely *cooperative*, as opposed to parallel or associative, which we discussed in relation to younger children. Now children tend to play and work together with a common goal in mind. They will share toys, ideas, and labor. Usually a leader will emerge from the group who will assist in assigning roles to the other players. In kindergarten, children tend to play in groups involving both sexes. Friendships are fluid, and "best friend" attachments are not usually sustained for long periods.

Emotions/Feelings

Five has a wide range of emotions and feelings which are easily (and frequently) expressed. Among these feelings are joy, affection, anger, shyness, and jealousy. Five is in contact with wider circles of people at this time, and is becoming more adept at interpreting feelings of others.

At five and a half another disequilibrium phase may appear, usually not as severe as earlier ones but, on the other hand, you have had it so good you may resent having problems again. Five and a half is less inclined to be good, is more self-centered, and begins to dawdle or be overdemanding at times. The child is emotionally more tense than earlier, especially at home, and may complain of stomachaches or headaches. Tensional outlets (especially hand-to-mouth ones like chewing a pencil or the fingernails) are common. The child is more restless and even seems to have less motor control than previously exhibited when grasping a pencil, for example. As you have already learned, disequilibrium phases occur when the child is getting ready for the next stage: in this case, school full-time.

Expressions of physical aggression are more controlled in this period than they were at age four for several reasons. First, your child is becoming much more aware than earlier that other people have their own points of view which differ from the child's own. Five-year-olds are noticeably less egocentric. Second, they are learning rules for right and wrong behavior. Third, they are at a stage where they really want to please adults and peers. Although physical aggression may be inhibited, verbal aggression may increase ("You're a pooh-pooh!").

Tensional outlets, such as thumb sucking or nail biting, may start or resume when the child enters school but this is not cause to worry. As the child grows more secure in the new environment these will usually be given up. In one sense Fives are smart enough to know they are feeling tensions and these tensions are relieved in a harmless way without hurting themselves or others.

In general this is not a fearful age. The anxieties and fears that do surface, generally caused by things like thunder, sirens, darkness, and mother's abandonment, tend to be temporary and concrete. The five-year-old is less afraid of things like witches and ghosts that have no basis in reality.

Occasionally, however, a five-year-old may have frightening dreams which cause awakening. For the most part, these nightmares contain frightening animals or strange or bad people, or may involve being near a fire or falling into water. In addition to being awakened by nightmares, they may also talk out loud in their sleep. The nightmares reflect their fear of real dangers or of their own anger, which they are mastering—albeit incompletely. You can help your child develop and maintain a healthy emotional attitude by making it clear that you value the child and respect his or her competence and feelings.

Fives know there is a difference between the sexes but are less interested in "showing." As a matter of fact most are modest about their bodies and about going to the bathroom. They know that babies grow inside the mother and are more interested in how the baby will get out than how it got in. But if they ask about getting in, you can just say that it's something that happens sometimes when parents make love.

Developmental Warning Signals

By now you have a pretty good idea about whether your child has developed normally in motor skills—both large and small muscle—and language skills. At age five if your child does not play with other children you should consider this a warning signal and tell your pediatrician. Another warning signal is truncated speech—speech with many word endings consistently missing.[1]

Be sure your child's vision is tested before school starts. Now you *must* be sure your child is using both eyes and has normal vision in both. If your child is only using one eye, the "lazy eye" is often treated by patching the other. It's very important to do this early before the other eye "gives up."

CARE GIVER TASKS

Basic Care

NUTRITION

The tremendous changes going on in your child's physical growth and development require that he or she receive a proper balance of nutrients during this period.

The child should drink between two and three cups of milk daily to meet calcium and riboflavin needs. The child needs meats, cheese, and legumes in order to meet protein needs and should eat egg yolk, greens, enriched or whole grain cereals, and liver to meet iron needs, and organ meats, oysters, egg yolk, beans, or nuts to supply the small, but necessary, amount of zinc. Finally, your child should receive a daily source of vitamin C.

Children this age like plain, simple cooking. They like meat, potatoes, raw vegetables, milk, and fruit, but gravies, casseroles, and even puddings may be too "complicated."

Although your child's appetite is generally well established by five, not all meals are uniformly well eaten. Fives can feed themselves well, but dawdling is quite common so they may be slower than the rest of the family in finishing meals. If they are not hungry, don't make them clean the plate.

CLEANING/GROOMING

Your child can now bathe almost completely alone, although he or she generally can't yet draw the water and an adult should always be nearby. Five-year-olds dress themselves much better than they did at four, handling all but back buttons, and only sometimes getting things backward.

Five-year-olds can lace their own shoes, and will probably learn to tie them during this year. Some help wiping after a bowel movement may still be required. Most five-year-olds will be dry at night (the exact figure is 85 to 90 percent). Of those who are not, all but 15 percent will achieve dryness during each following year.[2]

SLEEP

With the onset of kindergarten, those children who have not already done so give up naps completely. Occasionally a five-year-old will still need a nap after a hard day at school. Fives tend to go to bed early in the evening, and sleep through the night for about eleven hours.

EXERCISE

Opportunity for exercise at age five is crucial to adequate physical growth and development because of the rapid growth of muscles at this age. Lack of muscle use lowers muscle tone and results in more fatigue. Fortunately, most Fives are highly self-motivated to exercise and to practice motor skills. As their muscles become stronger, they experience a strong drive for muscular activity. They want to be on the go constantly and are restless when required to remain inactive. This drive is so intense that five-year-olds may overtax their strength to the point of fatigue or injury. For this reason, individuals who instruct young children in motor activities such as swimming or acrobatics must be aware of the child's capabilities and help prevent the child from overdoing it.

STRESS MANAGEMENT

Tensional outlets are most often observed in the child of this age just prior to bedtime. Your child may retrieve the special blanket or stuffed toy, suck the thumb, or ask to be rocked. Such outlets may also be used, however, when stressful events in the environment cause children to retreat momentarily from the world and regroup their defenses.

Don't worry when these tensional outlets seem like regressive behavior. On the contrary, not only is this stage usually temporary but it should be welcomed as a signal that your child knows he or she needs and can get extra assurance and acceptance at that moment. Indeed, five-year-olds should be permitted to have and show tensional outlets, which should be accepted and responded to.

Parents are often overly concerned about nail biting. Most nail biting starts around age five. About 60 percent of ten-year-olds bite their nails, then fewer children do so each year until college, when about 20 percent are nail biters; at age thirty about 10 percent still gnaw away.[3] More boys than girls are nail biters, at least after age ten.

Because almost all children stop nail biting and it's a reasonably harmless habit, we recommend you ignore this tensional outlet. If the child *wants* to stop and seeks your help we suggest promising to give your daughter a manicure when the nails are long enough or promise your son a special treat. Some children ask for the product that makes their nails taste bad so they'll remember (nail biting is a fairly unconscious habit). Hypnosis has become successful but it seems like using a cannon to kill a gnat.

EMOTIONAL "NUTRITION"

At this age you need an attitude and style of interaction with your child that facilitates growth and the development of independence, but at the same time is accepting, reassuring, and nurturing. Your child needs you to provide the support that he or she needs while facing the new demands of entering school, interacting with peers, and learning effectively.

CARE OF THE CARE GIVER

For those of you who have adored every moment you spent alone with your child, you may feel some pangs at having to share. We know mothers who feel this way; they really are wrenched when their child goes off to school. If you fall into this category, the time your child is in school is a great time to get in touch with your *other* feelings too. You now know you're a good mother and you love mothering. But you cannot stop the flow of time. Your child is out of the house for only a half day in the kindergarten year but soon will be gone all day. What *else* do you want to do? Is this a time to go to school, get a job, start volunteer work, etc.?

We suggest you begin to explore your needs the very first day your child starts school. Then you won't have time to feel lonely.

By the way, those of you who can't *wait* to have a half day for yourself— and know exactly how you will spend it—don't feel guilty. You have spent time with your child; now it's time for *you.*

Socialization Tasks

PLAY AND FOSTERING COGNITIVE GROWTH

Play now takes the form of cooperative small group efforts aimed at some goal-oriented activity, such as playing house or playing firefighter. Usually roles are assigned so that in a house-playing episode, for example, one child may be the mother, one the father, and several others, the children. Blocks are often an important part in this play, either for building houses or for constructing roads, trucks, bridges, tunnels, and garages for vehicles. Dolls are also an important part of play sequences. For the most part, five-year-olds can carry on play episodes without much adult intervention.

"Play-work" for your child will also involve considerable activity (both at home and at kindergarten) with paints, markers, paste, and scissors.

As we suggested earlier, there is a very strong interrelationship between play, the development of motor skills, and self-esteem at this age. As children play, their acquisition of motor skills is facilitated, and as they become competent in motor skills, they are held in esteem by their peers. Interestingly, children at this age (and increasingly through the elementary school years) are attracted to those peers who are physically competent. As early as age five, children know who among themselves is the fastest runner and who is the best climber. Children who are not well coordinated and who do not move well are, unfortunately, viewed as incompetent. Such children need extra help in developing motor skills, if possible, and if not, help with self-esteem by developing competencies in other areas. They may also need help in play experiences with other children, sometimes including younger and older playmates.

There is also a strong relationship between play and cognitive development at this age. The more opportunity children have for handling objects, observing cause and effect relationships between objects, and classifying them, the more opportunity they will have for constructing a cognitive system which eventually results in logical thinking.

Fives may develop a great love for a given activity and want to do it over and over again. Marilyn remembers a five-year-old child who loved fishing in the pond near his summer house. During the winter he repeatedly "fished" from the top of the basement stairs!

Fives can walk to school by themselves provided it is a safe route, and you teach the way, and you check out the child's performance. We are both on the cautious side with young children and suggest you arrange for an older child to walk with your child for at least half of the kindergarten year.

DISCIPLINE/GUIDANCE/VALUES

Throughout this book we recommend that parents guide their child in a firm but loving manner which takes into account the child's developmental characteristics and needs. Guidance at the kindergarten age is no different.

Five-year-olds need affectionate acceptance and understanding of their abilities. They need a chance to learn from mistakes. Five-year-olds also need a satisfying range of interesting things to do. At the same time, they need to learn that their wishes sometimes cannot be granted, that there are safety rules, and that others have needs. Parents are tempted to make many rules and limits, but it's best for all concerned to keep the rules few. Never make a rule that isn't important enough to you that you can and will enforce it consistently.

Because your child is at an age where pleasing others is important, for the most part, Fives will behave the way you want them to behave. Don't take such behavior for granted; the child still needs lots of praise for being "good." This helps the child want to continue to follow parental guidelines when older.

Your child is at an age where he or she is beginning to exercise more judgment and thought. Fives may balk at a limit you have set. When this happens, try to help them meet the limit in their own way. For example, a child who objects to bedtime when you call can set a timer to ring in ten minutes as a signal for bedtime.

Because Fives have the "maturity" to really get your goat despite the serenity to be good most of the time, you *will* have to discipline. Dodson points out that the modalities most used by parents (scolding, spanking, and restriction of the child's location or activity) are the least effective methods.[4]

If you have not already started an effective methodology, this is a good time because Fives tend to want to please you. Limit your "No's," mean what you say, use "time-outs" (not in anger but in a matter-of-fact way before you explode when a non-negotiable rule is infringed upon), and use positive rewards. Five is not too early to "contract" ("If you are quiet and don't disturb the baby, I'll play with you after the baby is asleep.").

Because of the five-year-old's increased awareness of others' feelings, this is a good year for suggesting empathy. For example, "How would you feel if — ——— did ——— to you?" More empathy with parents is possible: "Can you see this has been a bad day for me, and I'm upset?" Because of the five-year-old's verbal and cognitive abilities, the P.E.T. approach becomes particularly easy and natural (see p. 62).

KINDERGARTEN

Your child is now ready for and needs kindergarten, which gives five-year-olds a structured, half-day school program with other children of the same age. In this setting, the child will make great strides in cognitive learning, the mastery of motor skills, and the development of social relationships.

In our country, it is felt that children should enter formal education sometime between four and a half to six. Most school systems require that the child enter first grade by age six; almost all school systems recommend the child enter kindergarten the year before. More mature Fives who do not need an afternoon nap are often placed in the afternoon session while the less mature children are generally assigned to the morning session.

Kindergarten "readiness" involves good physical health, the emotional readiness to be separate from the parent for several hours and to interact with adults and children who are at first unfamiliar. Readiness also includes the ability to obey directions, an attention span that permits sitting still and concentrating on one task, the ability to wait for and take turns, and basic hand-eye skills needed for learning (pencil handling, turning pages, etc.).[5] One of the signs of "unreadiness" for regular kindergarten is not interacting well with other children, but such a child may need a special kindergarten or other experience to help.

Some children have a choice between entering kindergarten "early" or later because of the child's birth date. For example, a child might enter kindergarten at four years, eight months, or wait until five years, eight months. If your child isn't "ready" according to the above parameters it will not hurt to wait a year. One year in a child this age represents a fifth to a quarter of the child's whole life and a good deal of growth will occur in that year. On the other hand, the "ready" child should not be kept out of kindergarten for a year because the child is on the young side of five. Make the decision by studying your child, not the calendar.

Usually schools have an orientation program in the spring when the next fall's kindergarten children and their parents are invited to the class for short visits in small groups. This is an excellent way to prepare your child for kindergarten. The child needs to know what kindergarten is like, what a teacher is like, and how the children act in school before he or she can begin to anticipate the experience positively. If your school system does not have an orientation program, try making your own arrangements for such a visit.

Schools usually have a spring registration for all children planning to enter kindergarten in the fall. At this registration you will be asked to bring your child to the school, so that you can complete school enrollment papers. At this time your child may be asked to perform a few prearranged tasks as a means of globally assessing readiness for kindergarten. For an assessment of large motor skills, the child may be asked to throw and catch a ball, to skip, and to stand on one foot. For an assessment of small motor skills and eye-hand coordination, the child may be asked to copy predrawn shapes, such as a circle, a square, and a cross or may be asked to draw a person. For an assessment of cognitive awareness and readiness, the child may be asked to point to a color (when named) or to point to his or her name (among several which are visible).

As we have already pointed out, these are tasks which the five-year-old should be able to do. Educators recognize that, for different reasons, some children will not have had life experiences which have readied them to perform these tasks. In these cases, the results of the readiness "test" will not necessarily mean that a child cannot enter kindergarten, but may suggest that the child will need extra help in making a successful transition into the program.

The kindergarten day tends to follow a consistent routine to which your five-year-old will adjust easily. Usually the day begins with a free play period, in which the child can choose, for example, to build with blocks, manipulate puzzles, or play house. Following free play, there follows a music period, a snack time, a story time, rest, a teacher-directed activity period, and outdoor play. The exact arrangement of the routine is, of course, not as important as the fact that there is a routine and the child knows what to expect each day. Orderliness of routine is very important to five-year-olds.

Within the basic routine, your child will be introduced to a variety of subjects, including social studies, science, ecology, math, language arts, health education, nutrition, music, and art. Accordingly, the child will learn about people from other lands, conduct experiments with things that float and things that sink, learn to write his or her name in manuscript letters, use a calendar, learn songs, and develop readiness for reading.

The teacher in kindergarten will be crucial to your child's success in school. A kindergarten teacher should be a person who understands the physical, social, and emotional needs of the five-year-old, and can set up both the curriculum (mostly through play) and the environment to foster the child's development. The teacher should also be a person who can give affection and approval to children. Your child's achievement, positive peer interaction, and self-esteem, as well as later attitudes toward educational experience may well depend on the teacher's adequacy in performing these functions. Get to know your child's teacher. Seek out the teacher's important feedback about your child's learning needs and characteristics.

HEALTH CARE

Medical Care

Your child will need to see the doctor for a checkup prior to entrance into kindergarten. At this checkup, the doctor will weigh and measure the child and also do a careful physical examination. Vision and hearing are tested. A DPT booster and Polio booster are needed at this time.

The doctor will have to complete a health form, which is required by the school. This form allows the doctor to indicate any abnormalities of development that may be pertinent, to specify which immunizations your child has had, and to certify that the child is physically able to participate in a group program.

Your child's health at age five is generally good. The child may have fewer colds this year, as compared with the repeated colds he or she had at age four. Stomachaches at this age are frequently associated with the need for a bowel movement. Five-year-olds are still at high risk for contracting childhood diseases such as chicken pox.

Dental Care

Around age five or six your child's deciduous or baby teeth begin to loosen and shed. The going rate for a Tooth Fairy visit in our neighborhoods is a dollar, but obviously this varies with neighborhoods. This is one area where keeping up with the Joneses is not too expensive. Children of this age are preoccupied with their teeth falling out and talk about it.

Now that your child will soon have some permanent teeth, it is essential that your child have good teeth cleaning habits. Children below about seven or eight can't floss without help but can usually brush their own teeth in the morning and after meals without needing help—except a reminder. A yearly visit to the dentist is recommended, and the dentist can advise about flossing techniques.

Environmental Health

We have already discussed the need of the kindergarten child to have an environment with enough room for movement and for exploring both indoors and outdoors. We have also pointed out that this environment should be stimulating.

Since there is a rather broad feeling that educational television is stimulating to young children, let's talk about it. It is our view that while television has educational potential, it also has limitations which apply to the development of young children who are just putting their world together. The basic limitation is that it is a two-dimensional experience. Young children need *three-dimensional experiences* as well. Their sensory style of learning, which we have described in every chapter, requires that they touch, taste, see, hear, and smell to get the feedback they need for increasing their comprehension. We feel too much exposure to television can interfere with learning rather than enhance it. Ration the amount of time your child spends watching television in favor of three-dimensional experiences.

SAFETY

The major safety issue at this age is to ensure that the child learns safety rules commensurate with his or her increased physical independence. Your child must learn rules for walking in crosswalks and riding tricycles or bicycles safely. The child must also know how to react if approached by a stranger (Say "No!" and run away.) Your child should know how to give his or her name, address, and phone number to authorities should the child become lost. Teach your child how to locate houses on the street where the child can go in an emergency and in which adults can be sought when the child has a problem.

If your child has outgrown the car safety seat, be sure the child buckles up in adult seat belts. Remember that the five-year-old will want to act like you, so buckle up your own seat belt! Lifelong habits for car safety will be established at this time.

Because the automobile is always a potential hazard to a small child, pedestrian safety must be taught and enforced. Tricycle (and bicycle) safety is also a must. By the time the child develops the coordination to ride a two-wheel bike, sheer physical prowess leads to daring behavior and peer pressure reinforces this.

Parents must counteract this by strictly enforcing safety rules. If necessary, infringements (like riding in the street when that is forbidden) have to be punished by a no-riding-at-all edict for a specified time. But try "I-messages," "I care about your safety," "I don't want to have to take away the bike but I may have to."

Children usually play in groups at this age—and they play hard. Teach them to be careful near glass patio doors. Even a good swimmer at five needs supervision in and around water. Fire is a perennial hazard and five is an age when playing with forbidden matches or firecrackers often starts. A five-year-old has the coordination to strike a match but not quite enough sense to use a match safely, so make matches a real "no-no."

*   *   *

Although five and a half is often a disequilibrium phase, it is not as difficult a period of disequilibrium for either child or parent as two and a half may have been. The kindergarten year, as a whole, is a happy one for both child and parent. As Ames and Ilg say: "Five wants to be good, means to be good, and more often than not succeeds in being good."

Five is a fun year for your child and you. This is the last year before a home-reared child will spend more waking hours at school than at home.

It's a year full of looking both forward and backward—the last year of early childhood, just on the threshold of the new responsibilities that the school years will provide. The five-year-old's combination of playfulness and growing maturity is awesome.

Enjoy!

SUGGESTED READINGS AND RESOURCES

Gesell, Arnold; Ilg, Frances L.; and Ames, Louise Bates. *The Child from Five to Ten.* (rev. ed.) New York: Harper, 1977.

Although not a recent reference, this book provides classic information on normative trends in the growth and development of children. Very readable and informative.

Granger, Richard H. *Your Child from One to Six.* Washington, D.C.: U.S. Department of Health, Education, and Welfare, Publication No. (OHDS) 79-30026, 1979.

This paperback publication is a concise compilation of information which contains a comprehensive section on health care and safety precautions.

Spock, Benjamin, and Rothenberg, Michael B. *Dr. Spock's Baby and Child Care.* New York: Pocket Books, 1985.

The latest revision of one of the most well-known and widely circulated of child care books. The book includes a chapter on the child from three to six, and also features more general chapters on illness, first aid, schools, etc.

Part Five

CHILDHOOD HEALTH
AND ILLNESS

Introduction

As parents, the health of our children is a major concern. We want to know what to do when our children become ill, how to be sure our children are getting proper medical care, and what we can do to prevent or minimize illness in our children.

No matter how hard we as parents try to keep our children healthy, every parent will be confronted with a sick, cranky child at one time or another.

Some of us are lucky—our children will have very few illnesses. Others may have children who are born with, or develop, a chronic health problem. Some of us will, sadly, have a child who dies from an illness or accident. Fortunately, this is a rare occurrence today; the mortality rate of children is much lower than it was in the past.

When a child becomes ill (even if it's only one of the eight or so colds a child is likely to come down with every year), parents often assume that they have done something wrong. We as parents may blame ourselves instead of the respiratory virus. Sometimes we blame the child for getting sick at a time when it is most inconvenient.

Parents of sick children have justifiable complaints. The child needs care which makes unreasonable, and sometimes unfillable, demands on our time and energy. Sick children often regress—that is, act younger than their age. Sickness often brings on whining, irritability, or clinging. Regression is likely to give parents a feeling of "Oh no, here we are back to that stage!" at a time when they thought the child was beyond it.

Children often don't understand the natural causes of illness. They fear that being sick means they have done something wrong and are being punished. They may be irritable and angry or guilty and depressed. They may also suffer from impaired self-esteem if they have chronic illness or disability.

Other children in the family are affected by illness too. They fear they will catch the illness or they feel guilty about negative feelings toward an ill sibling who is getting increased attention. The sibling's attention-getting behavior (whining, misbehaving, etc.) usually occurs just when parents are most exhausted with care and worry over the sick child.

There is probably no area in parenting where factual knowledge is more helpful than in illness. Specific information helps parents understand and cope with illness in children and it also helps parents decide whether their children are getting the best possible medical care. Marilyn and Anne, as parents *and* physicians, found that factual knowledge helped combat unnecessary panic. Some of the most frightening-*looking* situations are fairly safe and some problems that don't look dangerous need prompt attention.

When we talked to parents about what they wanted in a parenting book, nearly all parents mentioned they wanted to know when to call the child's doctor. Thus we decided to devote a large portion of this book to health and illness. Further, we decided to provide parents with much more information than is usually contained in child-rearing books. Much of what we present in this section is technical. However, we worked very hard to explain things clearly. We also provide many references and suggestions for further reading so that the parent who wants or needs more information can easily find it.

This section contains six chapters on childhood health and illness. The first chapter is entitled *Health Maintenance*. This chapter talks about preventive maintenance of your child's body and includes what parents can do to enhance their child's capacity for health both now and in the future. The second chapter, called *Choosing Health Professionals for Your Child's Care*, deals with how parents can find competent and caring doctors and other health professionals. *Symptoms of Illness in Children—and When to Call for Help* will discuss these common symptoms which many parents will be confronted with. *Care of the Sick Child at Home* covers sick care at home including what to do before the doctor gets there—or what to do at home instead of getting medical help. Next is a brief chapter, *How Illness Affects Children and Parents*, dealing with the effects of illness on all family members. The last chapter in this section, *Emergencies*, points out what parents can do in emergencies and how to prevent some emergencies.

18

HEALTH MAINTENANCE

Scope of Chapter

This section on Childhood Health and Illness starts with health for two reasons: general good health is a goal in itself, and people with healthy bodies have more resistance to illness. There is no question that good nutrition, adequate sleep, enough exercise, and minimal levels of stress all help keep children (and adults) healthy. In addition, a happy environment in which a child feels comfortable, loved, valued, and appreciated contributes to physical health as well as emotional balance and happiness.

Maintaining health and trying to prevent illness is part of parenting—a vital part. This chapter provides information to help you promote health and prevent disease in your children. We talk about specifics in health maintenance starting with nutrition, then hygiene, sleep, exercise, and stress management. We also look at the child's environment and ways to keep that environment healthy.

Sometimes we discuss areas which are controversial. We present the scientific data which is available at this time and give you the best advice we can in areas where there are no "rules." This chapter does not contain many "recipes" for health. Instead it provides information to help you, as parents, make informed decisions about your family's lifestyle.

Introduction

When we look at the ability of the child's body to automatically maintain its own health, we are awed. The body's own homeostatic (equilibrium-seeking) mechanisms get most of us by, because we have evolved that way. We grow, digest, fight off most diseases, without much thought.

As millions of years of biological evolution have prepared our bodies, thousands of years of social and cultural evolution help us with preventive care. Our culture brings us clean water, traditional dietary habits, aesthetics of cleanliness and hygiene, and habits of exercise which serve us well for the most part. Individual parents and families do not have to rediscover the wheel.

On the other hand, modern life has brought some new problems, and health sciences have brought some new solutions as well as some new problems and decisions to make. The bodies of knowledge involved are fascinating in themselves; many people like to make a study of nutrition, or the physiology of jogging, or to gain knowledge about illnesses because the knowledge is interesting as well as practical.

This chapter contains quite a lot of information, for reading and reference. But don't get overwhelmed! Most children will be adequately fed and exercised from their own appetites and interests, whether or not their parents ever count calories, vitamins, or hours of exercise.

NUTRITION

Nutrition today is a paradox. In the United States, in many respects, nutritional health has never been better. There is a veritable cornucopia of available food which is free from spoilage because of preservatives, refrigeration technology, and an active packaging industry. Marilyn has not seen a child with food poisoning resulting from food spoilage in many years. Compared with children in less developed nations of the world, our children have a highly nutritious, highly varied, and relatively cheap diet available to them. The American family spends a much lower percentage of its income on food than do families in many other countries.

Yet on every side parents are made to feel at fault for not feeding their children a "proper" diet. Headlines scream that America's children are malnourished. Children will all become obese because they stuff themselves with junk food, loaded with "empty calories." Their brains are being destroyed by additives or residual insecticides. They are not eating "natural" foods and therefore will suffer from the effects of "chemicals." They are eating too much fat and will all have heart attacks at an early age. What is the truth? What are parents to do?

Not all parents, of course, feel the same way about food. Religious or cultural traditions, vegetarianism, or other values, as well as income, affect what parents eat and feed their children. For many parents *time* is an important limiting factor. Eating fresh, homegrown vegetables and fruits might make nutritional and gustatory sense but put intolerable pressure on a parent's lifestyle. Marilyn remembers a harassed woman doctor who felt she must feed her son "made from scratch" foods, which meant several hours of food preparation a day, which further meant dropping out of medicine. All parents have to decide how much trouble and time they can devote to food and how close they wish to come to nutritional perfection, if such a standard exists.

Yet it is probably a safe assumption that all of you want your children to be fed (and, almost more important, learn to eat) a soundly nutritious diet. This chapter will discuss how to do that as simply and easily as possible without more worry or concern than it is worth to you.

Let's start with the basics of nutrition. What follows will be a short review of what nutrition is and how nutrition can be translated into food shopping, preparation, and eating of food.

THE BASICS

Water

REQUIREMENTS

Nothing is more important than water to the human organism, except oxygen. It has been said that babies need water more than adults do. This is not entirely true. Deprivation of water can result in death in a matter of days for adults, sooner in babies. But water is more important to babies than it is to adults in the sense that the baby must take in more water per pound of body weight than an adult. However, the amount of water needed per one hundred calories expended is about the same in adults as in infants.

A three-day-old baby needs a total of 8 to 10 ounces (250 to 300 ml) of water daily. By the time the baby is six months old, it needs between 30 to 36 ounces (950 to 1,100 ml) of water per day. From one year of age when the daily requirement is about 38 to 43 ounces (1,150 to 1,300 ml), it goes up about 3 1/2 ounces (100 ml) each year until the child is six, when it then goes up about 1 2/3 ounces (50 ml) each year. The adult of eighteen requires between 64 and 96 ounces (2,200 to 2,700 ml) of water, which is between 2 and 3 quarts a day—from all sources.

Almost every food that you give your children contains some water. The diet of a baby, who needs relatively more water, is very high in water because the infant drinks rather than eats and foods like pureed fruit and vegetables have a very high water content.

We say this now and we will say it again: a young child's requirements for water will increase if the child is running a fever or has diarrhea. This can be a problem for parents because at the very time when your children need more water, they are sick and therefore may be less interested in drinking. This means you will need utmost creativity to encourage your sick children to take liquids.

We believe that all babies should be encouraged to take water. Ideally, breast-fed babies should not receive anything by rubber nipple until the breast milk supply is *well* established. But soon after that, offering water by bottle is one way to get the baby used to the rubber nipple in case bottle-feeding is needed in an emergency—or to enable the mother to go to work or out for some recreation.

La Leche advisers do not agree that breast-fed babies should be offered water. They feel that the best way to increase a nursing baby's water intake is to give the nursing mother extra water (which does *not* increase milk volume) and offer the breast more frequently (which *does* supply more fluids to the baby). The La Leche advice is based on an ideal principle that a baby should never taste a rubber nipple but rather should continue on the breast at least until ready for the cup. This principle is fine but may be impractical.

We strongly encourage teaching children to drink *water* when they are thirsty. Not pop, milk, or even fruit juice, unless the child needs the extra nutrients (mostly sugar) found in the fruit juice. If milk is used to relieve thirst, the intake of solutes and calories can be excessive.

PURITY OF WATER

As far as water safety is concerned, virtually every part of this country has a relatively bacteria-free, pure water supply. Infants can generally be offered any water which is safe for grown-ups (whether it be from a city system or a rural well), without boiling. For years it has been recommended that until the infant reached three months all water be boiled and placed in sterilized bottles. In most of the United States this is probably germ overkill, but before you decide to offer unboiled tap water to a newborn, it would be wise to look into the safety of your own water supply. If you have any questions about water safety, your local health department will be able to tell you about the safety of a well or a municipal water supply. In Chicago there have been recent concerns about high lead levels in water from lead pipes, ironically worse with new rather than old lead pipes. Local health departments can advise about this also. It is a good idea to run water for several minutes in the morning before drinking it, since minerals from pipes accumulate overnight.

Alas, more undesirable things than bacteria may lurk unseen in the water we drink. Environmental contamination of wells with toxic chemicals such as nitrites can be a problem. In Tucson, which is the nation's largest municipality using only well water, careless disposal of industrial wastes led to higher than acceptable levels of TCE (trichloroethylene) in certain wells, which had to be closed. Sometimes, local health departments will suggest that local water supplies are not safe for children or pregnant women. Heed local warnings.

CALORIES

Definition

A calorie is a measurement of the heat produced in metabolism. A large calorie or kilocalorie is the amount of heat it takes to raise the temperature of 1 kg of water from 14.5° to 15.5° C. When we say an apple has 75 calories, we mean 75 kilocalories, and that means that the potential heat produced in the metabolizing of the apple will raise the temperature of 75 kg of water 1° temperature centigrade.

We need calories for so-called basal metabolism, which is the amount of energy it costs us just to stay alive and keep our bodies warm and running (like a motor idling). We need additional calories for the expenditure of energy (work, exercise, etc.), and children need still additional calories for growth. Some calories are lost in the stool and not all calories from food are available for energy.

Requirements

In infancy, a baby needs about 50 calories per pound (115 calories per kilogram each day). This is five to six times more calories per unit of weight than the adult requires. Because this requirement drops steadily as the rate of growth slows, by the time children are adults, they need 40 calories per kilogram or 18 calories per pound on the average. (See Table 44.)

Although it is true that adolescents need more food during the pubertal growth spurt (some mothers have likened teenage boys at the dinner table to vacuum cleaners), calories required per pound drop steadily from infancy to adulthood. There is no real discrepancy here. After the growth spurt that occurs at puberty, the child weighs more pounds than earlier in childhood. The calories required per pound do not increase. Obviously an adolescent eats more calories per *day* than a baby. As Table 44 shows, the average one-year-old will take in about 1,300 calories per day. An adolescent boy might ingest as many as 3,900. Many adolescents become more physically active and stay up longer hours, both of which increase caloric requirements.

Girls need fewer calories at all ages, although pregnancy and lactation add caloric requirements. It has been estimated that it "costs" 75,000 calories to produce a full-term baby. The mother needs an extra 300 calories per day during pregnancy which, calculated on the basis of 250 days after the first month, comes to about 75,000 calories. These calories are used to "fuel" production of the baby as well as build the added tissues of the mother (bigger uterus, breasts, additional fat, etc.).

Lactation also costs energy. The fat which women gain during pregnancy serves as an energy reservoir so that fewer additional calories are needed by the mother per day in the first three months of lactation than during subsequent months.

In addition to gender and age, there are other factors involved in calorie requirements, including body size, climate, and activity. To move a big body around takes more energy than to move a little one, so that a tall person needs more calories than a short one. Fat people often compensate for their increased energy needs by decreasing activity. Living in a cold climate can cost extra energy either due to the extra weight of protective clothing or due to shivering,

TABLE 44

CALORIC REQUIREMENTS

Category	Age Years	Average Calories (Energy) Needed	Range		Average Calories (Energy) Needed	Range
Infants	0–½	kg × 115 (lbs. × 52)	(43–66)			
	½–1	kg × 105 (lbs. × 48)	(36–61)			
Children	1–3	1,300	(900–1,800)			
	4–6	1,700	(1,300–2,300)			
	7–10	2,400	(1,650–3,300)			
Males	11–14	2,700	(2,000–3,700)	Females	2,200	(1,500–3,000)
	15–18	2,800	(2,100–3,500)		2,100	(1,200–3,000)
	19–22	2,900	(2,500–3,300)		2,100	(1,700–2,500)
	23–50	2,700	(2,300–3,100)		2,000	(1,600–2,400)
	51–75	2,400	(2,000–2,800)		1,800	(1,400–2,200)
	76+	2,050	(1,650–2,450)		1,600	(1,200–2,000)
				Pregnancy	+300	
				Lactation	+500	

Reprinted by permission of the National Academy Press and adapted from Recommended Dietary Allowances, 9th rev. ed., Committee on Dietary Allowances, Food and Nutrition Board National Academy of Sciences, Washington, D.C., 1980.

which raises the metabolic rate. Physical activity in extremely hot weather raises the metabolic rate so more calories are required. Heavy work or vigorous exercise can raise calorie requirements by a factor of three. This is why exercise can be so important in the prevention and treatment of obesity.

Proteins and carbohydrates provide four calories per gram metabolized; fat provides nine calories per gram ingested. The well-balanced diet consists of 10 percent protein, 30 percent fat, 60 percent carbohydrates.

Too few calories leads to undernutrition or a state of being malnourished. Too many calories can lead to "overnutrition" or obesity. But people vary in how tenaciously their bodies absorb and store excess calories. What about "baby fat"? Interestingly enough, newborn male babies contain about 14 percent fat, which increases to 25 percent at about six months before decreasing to adult levels of 14 percent, so "baby fat" really exists![1]

BASIC FOODSTUFFS

If you think of the body as a living engine, food is the fuel or energy to run that engine. Like all energy available on this planet, food comes from the energy of the sun through that miracle of life called photosynthesis. All green plants which contain chlorophyll have the ability to take carbon dioxide from the air and hydrogen from water and, using the energy from sunlight, transfer these inert chemicals into organic ("living") compounds made up of carbon, oxygen and hydrogen. These compounds which plants create are called carbohydrates. We use oxygen to burn the fuel in food, which in turn releases the energy from the sun to power the cells of our body.

As you know, the three basic foodstuffs are proteins, fats, and carbohydrates.

Proteins

Proteins are made up of amino acids, which means that amino acids are necessary for the synthesis of body proteins. Amino acids are made up of carbon, hydrogen, oxygen, and nitrogen. There are twenty-four amino acids, nine of which are essential, which means they cannot be synthesized by the human body and must be ingested in food. There are two types of proteins. Animal protein is formed when animals eat plants. Certain plants (legumes like soybeans) which can fix nitrogen from the soil make plant protein.

Infants need close to two grams per kilogram of protein daily, while adults need slightly less than one gram per kilogram. This difference reflects the protein needed for growth.

Even when a person has stopped growing, however, there is a continued need for dietary protein. As tissues are broken down (for example red cells, which live about four months) some of the amino acids are used to make new tissues but some are either metabolized or lost in the stool, urine, and even the hair and nails. These amino acids must be replaced as the body doesn't have a place to store amino acids.

Pregnancy and lactation both greatly increase the need for dietary protein. Serious illness, such as infection or burns, increases the need for protein. In athletes, and others who perform strenuous physical activity, there is probably no increased requirement for protein, although there is an increased requirement for calories. During adolescence, males need more protein/pound than do females (because they are building a bigger body).

Too little protein can be disastrous for infants. Marasmus, or infantile malnutrition, results from deficiency of both protein and calories. These infants are *starving*. Kwashiorkor disease, seen in developing countries, occurs when toddlers ingest adequate, or close to adequate calories, but not enough protein.

Can too much protein be fed a baby? Definitely! Infants who are fed too much protein, especially when it is concentrated (as in boiled skimmed milk, which is dangerous for young babies, especially those with diarrhea), can develop serious kidney, metabolic, and brain problems. Human breast milk contains the least amount of protein per ounce when compared with the milk of any other mammal. It is interesting that long gestation, slow growth rate, and low protein content of breast milk are found in mammals with big brains.

Carbohydrates

Carbohydrates supply most of the calories, or energy, of a diet and much of its bulk as well. Sugars are simple carbohydrates; more complex carbohydrates are called starches. All carbohydrates are digested into glucose, the fuel which runs every cell in the body. If there is too little carbohydrate in the diet, there is not a large enough energy source for daily metabolism or for growth. Too much carbohydrate in the diet will be transformed into excess fat (i.e., obesity). Also, too much refined sugar promotes tooth decay.

Carbohydrate food, like whole grains and vegetables, also provides most of the bulk of the diet, which is needed for optimal digestion. Fiber is now considered important as a factor in preventing constipation, hemorrhoids, and even cancer of the colon. Fiber is not digested by the human gut so that most of it stays unchanged in the intestine and provides the bulk which the colon needs for proper functioning and stool production. Fiber decreases the time food stays in the gut and also increases the water content of the stool so that the stool is softer and easier to pass.

Fats

Fats come in two forms: saturated (fats without room for atoms of hydrogen to attach themselves) and unsaturated (fats with one or more places called double bonds where hydrogen atoms can attach). Unsaturated fats which are liquid at room temperature may be monounsaturated (olive or peanut oil) or polyunsaturated (corn, safflower, sunflower oil). Saturated fats are animal fats found in meat, butter and cream, or oils which have been artificially saturated as is done in making some margarine.

Contrary to popular opinion, fat is good for us and fats are essential to nutrition. Furthermore, one constituent of fat—a fatty acid called linoleic acid —is like an essential amino acid as it cannot be synthesized by humans or other mammals. It is recommended that infants have a diet in which at least 1 percent of the calories ingested are in the form of linoleic acid to prevent deficiency. This is rarely a clinical problem because breast milk and formula both have about 50 percent as many calories as fat.

SHOULD FATS BE RESTRICTED?

What about too much fat? It now seems apparent that the average American diet contains too high a percentage of calories derived from fat. Although there is still controversy, some good evidence has accumulated supporting the fact that a high fat diet is one of the causal factors in coronary heart disease. The Framingham study showed that apparently healthy males with high serum cholesterol levels (found in people who ingest lots of animal fat) had an increased risk of developing heart disease. The higher the cholesterol, the larger the risk. Cross-cultural studies have shown that people living in countries where the diet contains a high percentage of saturated fatty acids (animal fats) compared to the caloric intake have a higher incidence of coronary heart disease. The American Academy of Pediatrics recommends that half of the total fat ingested by children should come from plant sources. This reduces animal fat consumption but ensures that essential fatty acids are consumed.

Although the "prudent diet" recommended by the American Heart Association includes reduction of total fat and restricts eggs and whole milk, the recommendations are for adults. Pediatricians do not generally restrict eggs in children, unless they are allergic to them, as the egg is well tolerated and is a good source of protein as well as fat. Low fat milk is hazardous for babies (the protein content is too high for the kidneys to handle) and in older children can deprive the child of calories which are needed for growth *and* cause deficiency diseases due to lack of essential fatty acids.

We recommend not worrying about dietary fats until your child is five (unless your child has a familial hyperlipidemia—a congenital excess of lipids in the blood—in which case you need expert pediatric and nutritional advice).

After age five, a sensible goal is gradually to encourage children on the road toward the recommended adult diet. We use margarine, corn oil, and 2 percent milk in our own homes. Fish, chicken, or salad is the usual dinner for Marilyn and her husband, not red meat. However, she fed her children eggs and hamburger quite liberally when they were young as these foods are both eagerly accepted by children and are a good source of quality protein.

VITAMINS AND MINERALS

The Vitamin "Alphabet"

Vitamins are organic compounds necessary in minute amounts for cellular metabolism. They act as cofactors for essential enzymes. This means that essential chemical reactions in the body's cells can't progress without them. Without vitamins the body might have plenty of fuel but be unable to use it effectively. Vitamins must be present in the food because our bodies either cannot make them or cannot store them for a long period of time. Both deficiencies and excesses of vitamins can cause disease. Vitamins come in two varieties: water soluble (all the B's and vitamin C) and fat soluble (A, D, E, and K).

Vitamin A, which is found in yellow vegetables and fats, is necessary for vision, bones and teeth, and skin cell maturation.

There are several B vitamins which are found in milk, meats, vegetables, and whole grains. Thiamine (B_1) is necessary for carbohydrate and protein metabolism. Riboflavin (B_2) promotes energy release from metabolism. Niacin (B_3) is essential for cellular metabolism. Pyridoxine (B_6) is required for amino acid metabolism. Vitamin B_{12} is also necessary for cellular metabolism. Folic acid is essential for cell division. Other "B's" include pantothenic acid, choline, and biotin.

Vitamin C, found in citrus fruits and vegetables, is necessary for the formation of intercellular structural material, which means it is needed for wound healing. Vitamin D, found in fortified milk and fats and also synthesized in the skin by exposure to sunlight, helps regulate calcium and phosphorus metabolism. The role of vitamin E, found in germ oils and certain green vegetables, is not completely understood but it may be needed for muscle metabolism. Vitamin K, found in green vegetables, is necessary for blood-clotting.

VITAMIN REQUIREMENTS

Table 45 shows essential vitamins, their characteristics, effects of deficiency, effects of excess, and dosage. Although in the past, vitamin deficiency diseases such as rickets were common in children, today diseases of vitamin excess are more likely to be of concern. Vitamin D toxicity can lead to fatal hypercalcemia (too much calcium in the blood). Much of the food fed to an infant is fortified with vitamin D and most infant formulas contain twice the daily requirement of vitamin D. If vitamin-enriched cereal and vitamin drops are fed to a baby who takes large amounts of formula, toxicity could occur. Doctors no longer recommend supplemental vitamin drops for infants fed commercially prepared formula, provided the infant ingests twenty-five ounces of formula daily. Infants on evaporated milk formula need only vitamin C (or daily juice).

Although breast milk contains enough vitamins to have maintained our species through the centuries, the American Academy of Pediatrics suggests D supplement for exclusively breast-fed infants just to be sure. Rickets, though rare, *can* occur in exclusively breast-fed babies, especially if the mother's own vitamin D intake is suboptimal and if the infant has suboptimal absorption of sunlight due to a dark skin, northern climate, or little opportunity to be out of doors. Vitamin C levels of breast milk are just a tad below the minimum requirements recommended by the American Academy of Pediatrics.

Marilyn recommends vitamin D for exclusively breast-fed babies. The drops can do no harm (breast milk does not have enough vitamin D to "overdose" the baby) and are protective. Such supplements are *always* needed by prematures because of their rapid growth, which increases the requirements. After a child is a year of age, no vitamin supplementation is necessary provided the child eats a varied diet.

Minerals

Certain minerals are found widely in the body and are essential to all biochemical and physiological functions. These include sodium, potassium, magnesium, calcium, chloride, phosphorous, and sulfur. Ordinarily, dietary intake of these minerals is in a range which prevents either deficiency or excess. In illness such as diarrhea or malnutrition, sodium and potassium can be dangerously low, along with loss of body water. Some infants with diarrhea lose more water than sodium and may end up with dangerously high levels of sodium.

SHOULD SALT BE RESTRICTED?

There has been a good deal of interest in the salt content of the American diet. Salt is sodium chloride; it is the sodium that is of concern. The annual per capita consumption of salt in this country is seven pounds! In addition, processed foods contain other sodium compounds such as sodium bicarbonate (baking powder), and MSG (monosodium glutamate). Even diet soft drinks may contain sodium. Some families, and some individuals, heavily salt their food based on cultural and personal preferences.

A link between high sodium intake and hypertension (high blood pressure) has been established. Populations with very high salt intakes have high rates of hypertension. Many people voluntarily reduce their salt intake to prevent hyper-

TABLE 45

VITAMINS

Name	Characteristics	Effects of Deficiency	Effects of Excess	Daily Requirement	Food Sources
Vitamin A (retinol)	Fat soluble, needed for vision, integrity of skin, and bone tissue	Night blindness, dry cornea, poor growth, impaired resistance to infection	Hypertrophy of bone, hepatomegaly, alopecia, increased cerebrospinal fluid pressure	Infants—300 ug; adolescents—750 ug; lactation—1,200 ug	Milk fat, egg, liver
Biotin	Water soluble; synthesized by intestinal bacteria	Dermatitis anorexia, muscle pain, pallor (deficiency only with large intake of egg white)	Unknown	Unknown	Liver, egg yolk, peanuts
Vitamin B$_{12}$ (Cobalamin)	Slightly soluble in water, needed for red blood cell nutrition and nervous system	Pernicious anemia; neurologic deterioration	Unknown	1–2 ug	Animal foods, only: meat, milk, egg
Folacin	Slighty soluble in water, light sensitive, heat stable; some production by intestinal bacteria	Megaloblastic anemia	Only in patients with pernicious anemia not receiving cobalamin	Infants—50 ug; adolescents—40 ug; pregnancy—800 ug	Liver, green vegetables, cereals, orange

TABLE 45 (Continued)

VITAMINS

Name	Characteristics	Effects of Deficiency	Effects of Excess	Daily Requirement	Food Sources
Niacin (Vitamin B_3)	Water soluble, heat and light stable	Pellagra: dermatitis, diarrhea, dementia	Flushing, pruritus	6.6 mg/1,000 calories	Meat, fish, whole grains, green vegetables
Pantothenic Acid	Water soluble, heat stable	Observed only with use of antagonists; depression, hypotension, muscle weakness, abdominal pain	Unknown	Unknown; estimated at 5–10 mg	Most foods
Vitamin B_6 (Pyridoxine)	Water soluble	Dermatitis, glossitis, cheilosis, peripheral, neuritis. Infants— irritability, convulsions, anemia	Unknown	Infants—0.2–0.3 mg; adults—2 mg	Liver, meat, whole grains corn, soybeans

TABLE 45 (Continued)

VITAMINS

Name	Characteristics	Effects of Deficiency	Effects of Excess	Daily Requirement	Food Sources
Riboflavin (Vitamin B$_2$)	Water soluble	Photophobia cheilosis, glossitis, corneal vascularization, poor growth	Unknown	0.6 mg/1,000 calories	Meat, milk, egg, green vegetables, whole grains
Vitamin B$_1$ (Thiamine)	Absorption impaired by synthesis by intestinal bacteria	Beriberi: neuritis, edema, cardiac failure, hoarseness, anorexia, restlessness, aphonia	Unknown	0.5 mg/1,000 calories	Liver, meat, milk, whole grains, legumes
Vitamin C (Ascorbic acid)	Easily oxidized	Scurvy	Massive doses may lead to temporary increase in requirement	Infants—35 mg; adolescents—45 mg	Citrus fruits, tomatoes, cabbage, potatoes, human milk
Vitamin D	D$_2$ from diet, D$_3$ from action of ultraviolet on skin; needed to transport calcium across gut wall and to make and preserve bone	Rickets, osteomalacia	Hypercalcemia, azotemia, poor growth, vomiting, kidney stones	All ages, 10 ug (400 I.U.)	Fortified milk, fish, liver, salmon, sardines, mackerel, egg yolk, sunlight

TABLE 45 (Continued)

VITAMINS

Name	Characteristics	Effects of Deficiency	Effects of Excess	Daily Requirement	Food Sources
Vitamin E	Stored in fat tissue	Hemolytic anemia in premature infants; otherwise, no clearcut deficiency syndrome in humans	Unknown	Infants—4 mg; adolescents—15 mg	Cereal, seed oils, peanuts, soybeans, milk fat, turnip greens
Vitamin K	Fat soluble, synthesis by intestinal bacteria, needed for blood coagulation	Hemorrhagic manifestations	Hyperbilirubinemia	Newborn—single dose of 1 mg; thereafter, 5 ug/day; older infants, children—unknown	Cow's milk, green leafy vegetables, pork, liver

ug = micrograms
I.U. = International Units

Adapted from Barness, L. A.: "Vitamins in Nutrition." In *Practice of Pediatrics*, Vol. 1, rev. ed. Hagerstown, Md.: Harper, Chapt. 28, 1974; and Forbes, G. B.: In Hoekelman, R. A., Blatman, S., Brunell, P. A., Friedman, S. B., and Seidel, H. M., ed.: *Principles of Pediatrics: Health Care of the Young*. New York: McGraw-Hill, pp. 138–39, 1978. In American Academy of Pediatrics, Committee on Nutrition. *Pediatric Nutrition Handbook*, 2nd ed. Elk Grove Village, Ill., 1985. Copyright American Academy of Pediatrics.

tension, although some physicians feel it is unnecessary for all of the population to avoid salt as only 20 percent will become hypertensive. However, most physicians agree that the average American diet is excessively high in sodium.

There is no clear-cut evidence that links a high salt intake in infants with later development of hypertension but it is possible that future research will establish this. Certainly it can establish the habit of expecting salty flavor. Currently, some doctors suggest lowering the salt intake in children with a family history of hypertension. Infants should not be fed salted table foods because the capacity of the kidneys to excrete sodium is limited in the first year of life. Baby food is no longer salted and mothers should not add salt to commercial or home-prepared baby food because *they* think the food tastes too bland.

There is no question that newborns dislike salty liquids. Marilyn has seen videotapes of babies given a salty solution. They stop sucking, frown, cry, and push the nipple out of their mouths. Therefore, it is safe to assume that the liking for salty foods is *learned*. There is new evidence[2] that at age four a child's taste for salt depends on how much salt was fed in infancy. As too much salt may be harmful, why teach your child to like salt or to crave it?

What we do at our own homes is familiarize ourselves (and our children) with the high salt content of processed foods. Neither of us uses salt in cooking, although we made no attempt to restrict our children from adding salt to their taste.

TRACE MINERALS

Other minerals are vitally needed for enzyme function but only in very minute quantities, much as vitamins are. These are called trace minerals and include iron, copper, zinc, selenium, iodine, fluorine, silicon, nickel, arsenic, lead, manganese, molybdenum, chromium, cobalt, and vanadium. A normal diet will provide most of these.

Iron supplements are needed in prematures and rapidly growing babies. Although breast milk contains very little iron, it is efficiently absorbed from breast milk. Despite this, about one out of ten breast-fed babies will develop a low hemoglobin if on breast alone so we recommend iron-fortified cereal or iron drops be started at age six months.[3] If iron is started earlier, absorption of iron from the breast milk is decreased.

In areas with iodine-poor soil, iodized salt provides adequate iodine. Fluoride for dental enamel needs to be supplemented in deficient areas (see page 555).

FEEDING YOUR INFANT

What Kind of Milk—Yours or the Cow's?

We do not have to belabor the point that breast milk scores higher on all the parameters used to determine optimal infant feeding. In the first place, breast milk "worked" to maintain the human race for thousands of years before we domesticated cattle. In terms of safety, the match between the composition of human milk and the needs of the human infant, the presence of immune factors that may protect the human infant against infection, and the low cost and ease of administration, breast milk wins over formula. In addition, breast-feeding is emotionally satisfying. It is theorized that breast-feeding strengthens bonding between mother and infant, which theoretically could promote "optimal" socialization.

Are there any possible disadvantages to this superfood? Yes, there are. Infants on the breast generally do not grow as rapidly as formula-fed babies,[4] although rapid growth may not be normal, necessary, or desirable as long as growth progresses. Vitamin D, pyridoxine, thiamine, and B_{12} deficiencies can occur in exclusively breast-fed infants of mothers whose nutritional status may be compromised by economic factors or vegetarianism and, as we said above, exclusive breast feeding can result in iron deficiency anemia after six months of age.[5] Prematures may not grow at a rapid enough rate when fed mature human milk (they may need more protein than mature human milk provides though mothers of prematures produce a modified milk more suited to their needs).

Chemical contaminants, especially those that are concentrated in fat such as hydrocarbons, are excreted in the breast milk as are many drugs. The Committee on Drugs of the American Academy of Pediatrics has published tables of drugs that are contraindicated during breast-feeding, drugs that require temporary cessation of breast-feeding, and drugs that are compatible with breast-feeding but might cause symptoms in the baby.[6]

Always *tell* your doctor you are breast-feeding so he or she will not prescribe a medication which could harm your baby. Always *ask* your doctor before taking any non-prescription medication if you are nursing.

Fluoride is poorly excreted in breast milk.[7] Supplements are recommended even if the mother drinks fluoridated water. Therefore the American Academy of Pediatrics recommends fluoride supplementation for all breast-fed babies— and we concur.[8] Certain viruses are excreted in breast milk as are hormones and allergens (which the mother has ingested). In some babies physiologic jaundice can be exacerbated by nursing but frequent breast feedings may minimize this.

Breast-feeding failures *do* occur, especially with first babies. Occasionally, infants of young, inexperienced mothers, especially those without a family or external support system, may end up severely malnourished or dehydrated as a result of attempts to continue breast-feeding even when weight loss has occurred. Babies who nurse at will at night may even get "nursing bottle caries,"[9] which occurs when a baby who has teeth sucks on a bottle all night long—a practice we don't recommend.

What about the infant whose mother cannot breast-feed? "Humanized" formula-feedings (i.e., made similar to mother's milk) can be safely prepared and are nutritionally adequate. However, whole cow's milk can be dangerous for young babies (they may develop an intestinal obstruction from milk curds called a lactobezoar or they may develop diarrhea) and is not recommended. Some babies develop an allergy to cow's milk formulas. Also cow's milk (especially in large quantities) can cause intestinal blood loss, which adds to the iron deficiency in "milk-anemia" babies. The hazards of low fat and skim milk were discussed on page 532.

There is no question in our minds that optimal maternal-infant bonding can, and does, occur in the absence of breast-feeding. The mother who cannot (or does not wish to) breast-feed should not feel she is a failure as a mother and should not feel guilty. Formulas properly administered (in terms of correct preparation and amounts) as well as close body contact while feeding are known to be an effective replacement for the breast.

A survey[10] showed that between 1971 and 1981 the incidence of breast-fed infants ages three to four months quadrupled. Breast-feeding was most common in infants with highly educated, affluent mothers, but the greatest rate of increase was seen in less-educated mothers.

It is interesting to note that in 1979 the American Academy of Pediatrics named human lactation as a high priority for emphasis during the International Year of the Child. For Third World countries, this is laudable. In our country, however, more women are employed than ever before so that breast-feeding may be difficult for some. Also, some pediatricians may almost coerce mothers into breast-feeding, ironically at a time when consumer and patient rights have never been more important.

We support breast-feeding because it's easier, cheaper, more convenient, and pleasurable—for *most* but not all mothers. But you can raise a healthy baby with formula feeding. In fact, there have been some myths which exaggerate the benefits of breast-feeding. It is *not* true that babies who are breast-fed are less likely to die of Sudden Infant Death Syndrome; it is *not* true that breast-fed babies do not get infections, though they may get fewer ones; it is *not* true that breast-fed babies are protected from all allergies; it is *not* true that all breast-fed babies are well nourished (today a common cause of failure-to-thrive is inadequate nursing in the mothers who are pressured by their own feelings or by others into continuing breast-feeding when feeding failure is present); and it is *definitely not true* that only breast-fed babies become well adjusted or have close relationships with their mothers.

The decision is *yours*—it is your baby and they are your breasts and it is your lifestyle—not ours or your doctor's.

Our recommendations to a new mother are simple: Here are the pros and cons of breast- and formula-feeding. Make up your own mind depending on *your* feelings, schedule, and goals. We suggest "trying it" to the mother who is undecided for two reasons: the baby could benefit from colostrum, which contains factors that may help prevent infections, and the mother may find breast-feeding is acceptable or even enjoyable. See p. 323.

FORMULA

This book is not the place to discuss the specifics of commercially prepared formulas. All those on the market are safe and remarkably similar nutritionally.

The most convenient preparations (ready-to-serve) are the most expensive. If you are mixing prepared or evaporated milk formulas by yourself, follow directions carefully and be sure you have read labels correctly so you don't feed concentrated formula to the baby thinking it is ready-to-serve.

Formula you place in your own bottles need not be sterilized provided you make up one bottle at a time, are sure that the bottle is clean, and refrigerate the bottle if it is not to be used immediately.

When you are using formula, iron must be supplemented either by the use of formula containing iron or iron drops. There is no evidence that formula containing iron causes upset stomachs so we recommend its use.[11] With evaporated milk formula, vitamin C supplement is also needed.

Solid Foods: Why, When, and How

Until about 1920 American babies subsisted on breast milk or formula during the first year of life. The first supplements recommended were cod liver oil (to provide vitamin D) and orange juice (to provide vitamin C). Subsequently, cereals, vegetables, and fruits were recommended at age six months and as years went by more and more foods were offered to babies earlier and earlier. Doctors and mothers somehow became convinced that adding solids helped babies sleep through the night, although evidence for this was lacking.[12]

The Academy of Pediatrics divides infant feeding into three stages which overlap somewhat. These are: the nursing period, the transitional period, and the modified adult period.

In the *nursing period*, which lasts for four to six months, breast milk or formula is all that is recommended. The baby's anatomy and physiology are such that the baby can only suck and swallow liquids. (By the way, newborns don't really suck, they *suckle*. Sucking requires use of the muscles of the mouth and face and must be learned. Suckling is a behavior a newborn mammal is born with. It consists of lowering the jaw with the mouth closed, which creates a negative pressure, and moving the tongue forward on the nipple as the jaw is raised.) Also, the young baby's intestinal tract is unable to handle foreign proteins and the kidneys are too immature to handle a large protein or sodium load.

The *transitional* period starts by about four to five months with the disappearance of the extrusion reflex (thrusting out of the tongue when the lower jaw drops because a spoon is pushing it down). (See Table 46.) By five to six months of age the baby can sit up for feeding, can voluntarily open the mouth to get food or close it to say, "I've had enough," or "I don't like whatever is on that spoon." Feeding a baby before the transitional period has been likened to forced feeding, since the baby can't refuse. This is not desirable from either a nutritional or an emotional point of view.

TABLE 46

DEVELOPMENT OF FEEDING SKILLS

Age	Oral and Neuromuscular Development	Feeding Behavior
Birth	Rooting reflex	Turns mouth toward nipple or any object brushing cheek
	Sucking reflex	Initial swallowing involves the posterior of the tongue; By 9 to 12 weeks, anterior portion is increasingly involved, which facilitates ingestion of semi-solid food
	Extrusion reflex	Pushes food out when placed on tongue; strong the first 9 weeks By 6 to 10 weeks, recognizes the position in which he or she is fed and begins mouthing and sucking when placed in this position
3 to 6 Months	Beginning coordination between eyes and body movements	Explores world with eyes, fingers, hands, and mouth; starts reaching for objects at 4 months but overshoots; hands get in the way during feeding
	Learning to reach mouth with hands at 4 months	Finger sucking—by 6 months, all objects go into the mouth
	Extrusion reflex present until 4 months	May continue to push out food placed on tongue
	Able to grasp objects voluntarily at 5 months	Grasps objects in mitten-like fashion
	Sucking reflex becomes voluntary and lateral motions of the jaw begin	Can approximate lips to the rim of cup by 5 months; chewing action begins; by 6 months, begins drinking from cup
6 to 12 Months	Eyes and hands working together	Brings hand to mouth; at 7 months, able to feed self biscuit
	Sits erect with support at 6 months	Bangs cup and objects on table at 7 months
	Sits erect without support at 9 months	
	Development of grasp (finger to thumb opposition)	Holds own bottle at 9 to 12 months Pincer approach to food

TABLE 46 (Continued)

Age	Oral and Neuromuscular Development	Feeding Behavior
	Relates to objects at 10 months	Pokes at food with index finger at 10 months Reaches for food and utensils including those beyond reach; pushes plate around with spoon; insists on holding spoon not to put in mouth but to return to plate or cup
1 to 3 Years	Development of manual dexterity	Increased desire to feed self 15 months—begins to use spoon but turns it before reaching mouth: may hold cup, likely to tilt the cup rather than head, causing spilling 18 months—eats with spoon, spills frequently, turns spoon in mouth; holds glass with both hands
		2 years—inserts spoon correctly, occasionally with one hand; holds glass; plays with food; distinguishes between food and inedible materials
		2 to 3 years—self-feeding complete with occasional spilling; uses fork; pours from pitcher; obtains drink of water from faucet

Reprinted by permission from Suskind, Robert M., ed. *Textbook of Pediatric Nutrition.* New York: Raven Press, 1981.

During the transitional period, solids can be gradually introduced. Once again we have no hard and fast rules, just a few simple guidelines. Start with iron-enriched cereal. Follow this with strained fruits and vegetables, either from the jar or home blended (see below). Meats follow. The wise baby food shopper buys strained meats rather than the high meat "dinners" or combination food preparations. You get more protein and iron per ounce for your money when you purchase the more expensive strained meats. Juice is not recommended until the baby can drink from a cup, as juice from a nipple may cause "nursing bottle caries." Mashed egg yolk, moistened with milk or water can be offered. (Egg white, whole egg, or ice cream that contains whole eggs are deferred until later because many babies become allergic to the egg white.) Desserts are not necessary. (See Table 47.)

TABLE 47

FEEDING GUIDELINES

	0-2 weeks	2 weeks-2 months	2 months	3 months	4-5 months	5-6 months
Formula						
Oz. per feeding	2-3 oz.	3-5 oz.	4-6 oz.	4-6 oz.	5-7 oz.	5-7 oz.
Average total oz.	22 oz.	28 oz.	29 oz.	30 oz.	32 oz.	30 oz.
Number of feedings	6-8	5-6	4-5	4-5	4-5	4-5
Food texture	Liquids	Liquids	Liquids	Liquids	Liquids	Baby soft
Food additions						
Baby cereal, enriched						1-2 tbsp., B & S*
Strained fruits						1½ tbsp., B & S
Strained vegetables						2 tbsp., L
Strained meats						1 tbsp., L
Egg yolk or baby egg yolk						½ medium yolk or 1 tbsp.
Teething biscuit						½-1 biscuit
Oral and neuromuscular development related to food intake	Rooting, sucking, swallowing ————————————————→			Extrusion reflex diminishes; sucking becomes voluntary	Learning to reach hands to mouth; develops grasp	Chewing begins; can approximate lips to the rim of cup

TABLE 47 (Continued)

FEEDING GUIDELINES

	6–7 Months	7–8 Months	8–9 Months	9–10 Months	10–11 Months	11–12 Months
Whole milk						
Oz. per feeding	7–8 oz.	8 oz.	8 oz.	8 oz.	8 oz.	8 oz.
Average total oz.	28 oz.	28 oz.	24 oz.	24 oz.	24 oz.	24 oz.
Number of feedings	3–4	3–4	3	3	3	3
Food texture	Gradual increase ———→		Mashed table ———→			Cut fine
Food items						
Orange juice	4 oz. (cup)	4 oz.	4 oz.	4 oz.	4 oz.	4 oz.
Fortified cereal	⅓ c., B	⅓ c., B	½ c., B	½ c., B	½ c., B	½ c., B
Fruit, canned or fresh	4 tsp., B L & S	4 tsp., B L & S	2 tbsp., L & S	2 tbsp., L & S	3 tbsp., L & S	3 tbsp., L & S
Vegetables	1½ tbsp., L & S	2 tbsp., L & S	2 tbsp., L & S	2 tbsp., L & S	3 tbsp., L & S	3 tbsp., L & S
Meat, fish, poultry	1 tbsp., L & S	2 tbsp., L & S	2 tbsp., L & S	2 tbsp., L & S	2½ tbsp., L & S	2½ tbsp., L & S
Egg yolk or baby egg yolk	1 medium yolk or 2 tbsp.	1 medium yolk or 2 tbsp.	1 medium yolk or 2 tbsp.	1 whole egg	1 whole egg	1 whole egg
Starch-potato, rice, macaroni			2 tbsp., S	2 tbsp., S	2 tbsp., S	2 tbsp., S
Oral and neuromuscular development related to food intake	Begins using cup	Sits erect with support ———→ Without support	Feeds self biscuit ———→	Holds bottle	Picks up small food items and releases	Will hold and lick spoon after dipped into food; self-feeding

* one food at a time

Abbreviations used: B = breakfast, L = lunch, S = supper

Reprinted by permission and adapted from Suskind, Robert M. ed. *Textbook of Pediatric Nutrition.* New York: Raven Press, 1981.

One word to mothers of exclusively breast-fed infants. Iron absorption from breast milk (which as we have said contains little iron) is so efficient that iron deficiency is rare (although to be on the safe side we recommend iron drops be started at six months). Baby food *decreases* the absorption of iron, however. It is suggested that when baby foods are started, after you know the baby has tolerated several foods, put them together as one meal *without* breast milk. Then the meal will not interfere with iron absorption of the milk. This meal could ideally contain iron-rich foods like cereal, orange juice, or meat.[13]

Two words of warning. 1) Add *one new food at a time* at intervals of two or three days to make sure that, if an allergic reaction occurs, you will know which food did it. 2) Be careful of spoilage. Be sure the jars you buy and use are safe. If the seal is broken or the jar appears to have been opened, do not use it. If the jar doesn't "pop" when you open it (which breaks the vacuum), do not use it. Store jars in a cool, dry place and rotate so you use the ones purchased earlier first.

Place the portion to be eaten in a dish and refrigerate the remaining food in the jar after opening. You can easily warm the refrigerated portion in water in a saucepan. You can also use the microwave, provided you are *very careful* (baby food manufacturers do not recommend use of microwaves for heating baby food or formula).[14] Cover the dish loosely with a plastic wrap. Microwave on high for fifteen seconds for each ounce of food. Meats and other thick stuff may spatter so never put uncovered baby food in the microwave and be very careful when you uncover heated food. Do not heat baby food in the jar. *Always stir and test temperature* before feeding the baby, and beware of spattering. Microwave heated food gets *too* hot very quickly.

However, heating baby food or formula is old-fashioned. Most babies like food at room temperature. If you make up formula one bottle at a time, it does not have to be heated. Many babies do not seem to mind cold milk or baby food.

The *modified adult period* is the third period of infant feeding, when babies can eat what adults eat with a few exceptions. Here again the rules are simple. Attention must be paid to mashing or dicing food so that the baby can safely eat the food without choking. Chocolate is not recommended because it is highly allergenic. Certain aromatic vegetables like cabbage, broccoli, onions, and cucumbers are usually not given to babies as they are considered hard to digest. Home-prepared spinach and beets should be avoided because of the possibility of high levels of nitrites. Raw honey should not be fed to babies under a year because botulism spores can live in honey and the infant gut is vulnerable to them. Junior foods are generally not needed because it is so easy to mash what the rest of the family is eating. Anne saved a lot of hassle with her third child by following La Leche suggestions, skipping the transitional period, and feeding family food when the baby reached for it (starting about eight months). She never fed any baby food at all.

After the baby is two, except for peanuts and other "choke" foods or foods the baby has shown an intolerance for, anything goes. We do not recommend wine or beer, however, as babies do *not* need alcohol and *do* need milk.

MAKING YOUR OWN BABY FOOD

Making your own baby food is ridiculously easy and saves money. All you need is a blender, a fine strainer or a baby food grinder easily purchased for a few dollars. All you have to learn is a few simple rules. Your hands, the utensils, and the food should be clean. Everything but ripe banana should be cooked (simmered, steamed, or baked) until tender at a low temperature and in a very small amount of water to preserve vitamins. Do not add salt or sugar or spices—there is no need to as babies don't like or need seasoned foods. Also, don't use canned grown-up food because this is usually heavily salted or sugared or both. You can puree the same food you are preparing for the rest of the family by removing a small amount before you add seasonings.

Homemade baby food should be refrigerated or frozen as soon as it is prepared. Freezing in an ice-cube tray provides convenient small portions. You have added no preservatives and have not sterilized the food, so homemade baby food should not be taken on trips because of the danger of spoilage. Baby food in jars should be used for traveling.

You no longer have to make your own baby food to avoid salt or sugar, but you can help your baby become a young gourmet by feeding *fresh*, not overcooked food. Except for the foods babies should not be fed (see above) you can turn most foods into great baby food. For very young babies, especially if bottle-fed, we recommend using baby cereal rather than your own hot cereal because the baby variety is iron-enriched. By age two, most babies are on a varied diet so iron supplements are no longer needed and grown-up cereal is fine.

A HAPPY, HEALTHY DIET

We feel children should be fed, and should learn to eat, a *balanced* diet. A balanced diet consists of food from four major food groups.

1. Dairy products, such as milk and cheese.
2. The meat group, which includes protein food such as meat, eggs, poultry, fish, and peanut butter.
3. Fruits and vegetables. This must include those fruits high in vitamin C plus green or yellow vegetables.
4. The starch group, which includes cereal, grains, potatoes, rice.

In order to provide good nutrition for your child you should: 1) acquire the knowledge of what good nutrition is; 2) eat a balanced diet yourself; 3) not be a fanatic about food because eating should be pleasurable as well as necessary; 4) have the goals of training your child for a *lifetime of good eating habits*.

A concept that we endorse is what Marilyn used to tell her children: *Eat a happy, healthy diet.* Happy comes first, because such a diet makes you feel good. Even toddlers can be taught that what goes in their mouth may have something to do with how they feel. Also a healthy diet that isn't happy will be ignored by children as soon as they are out of your sight!

A happy, healthy diet is a diet that is balanced and that contains the necessary amounts of protein, only a small amount of saturated fat, little refined sugar, and provides lots of whole grains, fruits, and vegetables.

In 1977, the Select Committee on Nutrition and Human Needs of the U.S. Senate reviewed the then available data on diet. It was recommended that the typical U.S. diet should be modified to increase carbohydrate and unsaturated fat intake but to decrease *total* fat intake. Suggestions to accomplish this include the following: 2 percent milk, not whole milk; fish, poultry and lean meat, not fatty hamburger or luncheon meats; margarine, not butter; unsweetened fruit juices, not pop; complex carbohydrates, such as whole grains and potatoes, not simple sugars. In addition, a decrease in number of eggs/week (only two) was recommended. Present knowledge suggests this diet is probably the best and we recommend it for all *older* children and adults.

Some pediatricians have voiced concern about such a diet for young children, however. High bulk, relatively low calorie foods like grain and vegetables may not provide enough energy or essential nutrients like iron. Not everybody can afford high priced fish and lean meat. Hamburger contains fat, but also lots of protein and iron and it's cheap. In young, rapidly growing preschool children, hunger for sweets and fat may reflect their nutritional and caloric needs. In summary, don't worry too much about fat intake in young children.

Eating Habits

As parents we generally feel we should help our children develop good "eating habits" and consider this, rightly so, an important part of parenting. The human animal is omnivorous, which means humans can eat *all* foods as distinguished from carnivorous (such as lions, whose digestive system and metabolism are specialized to handle only meat) or herbivorous (such as cows, who munch only vegetable matter). The unspecialized nature of human eating gave humans the freedom to live anywhere on earth.

Omnivores are *taught* to eat—generally by the parents. When children are babies, parents have much control over their food intake. Parents decide by purchases, decisions, and recipes which foods, how much sugar, how much salt, etc., their children will eat. As children get older, these decisions become their own, although during the early years the way parents shop is a "control" because the four-year-old's decisions on what to eat for a snack depends on what food we have in the house.

We both believe strongly that there are two important meanings to the word "balance" used in reference to diet. First of all, there is the balance of foods that contain all essential nutrients. The other is the balance of the mind neither to overemphasize nor to ignore nutritional principles.

Some parents are extremely nutrition conscious, to a degree that can back-fire. Marilyn remembers one mother whose husband was a dentist. They never allowed their son to have candy. One day the child went to a birthday party and literally ate himself sick! Some parents are ideologically opposed to telling any-one what to do—including telling their children what to eat. Neither approach is balanced.

Of course treats can be given to a child. Who ever heard of a birthday without a birthday cake? But for the everyday snack, stick to things like crackers and carrot sticks. (See Table 48 for happy, healthy snack suggestions.)

TABLE 48

SUGGESTED SNACKS

apple, orange wedges, banana chunks (sprinkle with lemon or orange juice
   and store in plastic bag in refrigerator)
summer fruits: peaches, plums, grapes, etc.
dried fruits: raisins, prunes, etc. (limited amounts if these cause loose stools)
cheese cubes or prewrapped slices
yogurt (flavor your own with mashed fruit, applesauce, or honey)
reduced-sugar small cans of fruit (can be eaten right out of can)
toast and honey
popcorn*
low sugar cereals (small-size shredded wheat can be spread with peanut
   butter)
whole carrots* or carrot sticks*
raw vegetables* (cabbage wedges, celery, etc.)
cottage cheese on crackers
crackers (plain or spread with margarine, jelly, honey, or peanut butter)
non-gooey cookies (animal crackers, arrowroot biscuits, etc.)
granola mix* (rolled oats, nuts, raisins, carob bits)
fruit juice popsicles
snow cones (pour frozen juice concentrate over shaved ice)
peanut butter balls* (roll spoonful in granola or wheat germ)

* not for children under two because they can choke on or inhale these items

Snacks

Children *need* snacks. Probably most adults would feel better eating six small meals rather than three larger ones. However, the adult day is very much segregated into three meals and for the busy mother, three is quite enough to cook!

Many parents will hear themselves saying, just as their mothers did, "Don't eat that now, you'll spoil your supper." Sometimes this remark is justified, espe-cially if the child is about to substitute a piece of pie for the more nutritious meal that will be on the table in a few minutes.

We both feel that family mealtimes together are desirable. Ever since caveman days, eating together has been a pleasant, convenient time for people to communicate. Today mealtimes may be the only time busy members of a family get together. We also feel a parent should not have to prepare food and do dishes all day long—there are too many other important things to do in life! So, parents are justified in not handing out snacks just before mealtime.

We also know that most children want—and need—snacks, generally at midmorning, midafternoon, and before bedtime. Children cannot eat large enough quantities at mealtimes to meet their nutritional needs.

So why does snacking have such a bad reputation? Because the wrong kind of snacks can fill the child up, leaving no hunger for the nutritious and balanced diet you may have planned. You have probably heard the term "empty calories." Nutritionally "empty" foods like pop, candy, potato chips, doughnuts, rich cookies, and the like, could become the major part of the diet if children snack frequently and consequently either skip meals or sit at the table playing with their vegetables and baked potato.

Incidently, busy mothers employed or otherwise may have trouble finding time to make carrot sticks. But processed convenience foods are usually heavily salted or sugared. When children are old enough to use a carrot scraper they can be taught to scrape their own carrots (and also have some ready for Mother when she comes home!). Or they can just scrub the carrot well and eat it whole.

We both used other tricks. A wedge of cabbage or stalk of celery doesn't take much preparation. A prepared dip or mixture of ketchup and cottage cheese can be on hand for the children who want flavored vegetables. Even a busy parent can slice a pear or an apple into eighths and leave it in the refrigerator in a plastic bag. In Anne's house common snacks are fruits and leftovers like cold pizza or chicken.

Eating habits are personal and vary among people. Family and cultural patterns greatly influence what these habits will be, although there may also be individual genetic factors that determine whether people prefer sweets or pasta or potato chips.

A useful article highlighted *eating styles* of children, noting they are individual, probably both genetically and culturally determined, and reflect the age of the child.[15] For example, toddlers decrease their food intake and at the same time develop distinct preferences and aversions to certain foods—a fact that often drives parents wild! As the child grows and spends time in nursery school or at friends' houses, "social snacking" begins, which means that food intake is no longer under the control of the parents. Today when many mothers are employed, most of the waking day of the child may be spent with non-parent care givers, so that a mother may not know what her child has eaten. This makes "balancing" the child's diet difficult. However, mothers can try to keep track of the diet by talking with the care giver. Together, they can do the "balancing" act by agreeing on snacks, adding "missing" nutrients, and recognizing when the child has a "hungry period" so that nutritious foods can be offered then.

School-age children may avoid breakfast altogether (in many homes children fix their own breakfast, which they might dump down the disposal while mother isn't looking), not eat the nutritious portions of lunch at school, use allowance money to buy junk food at the convenience store on the way home, head for the soda pop and potato chips you bought for the party you are having tonight, and *not* eat the tuna casserole and salad at dinner because they aren't hungry! Adolescents can be involved in an even less nutritious scenario because adolescents have more money to use for junk food, and fast-food shops are socially important.

As "eating styles" are to a degree a product of the home environment, both of us paid attention to nutrition as our children were growing up. Because we realized that as parents we had some control over what foods were available to our children, we tried to shop and store foods wisely, to set a good example, and to encourage our children to seek—on their own—the "happy, healthy diet."

Our practical suggestions for the busy mother who wants to feed her children "right" but doesn't have much time include: 1) Plan for nutritious snacks when shopping. 2) Store these on low "snack shelves" in cabinets and refrigerator where children can easily get them. 3) As early as possible teach children how to prepare for themselves those nutritional snacks that require preparation.

In summary, children inevitably develop their own eating habits, based in part on what they are exposed to. You are not only feeding the child a balanced diet today but are teaching the child how to make lifelong choices. Don't make too many fusses at the table. Instead, teach children to value their bodies and therefore to pay attention to what goes into that body. Then children will eat a happy, healthy diet when they become adults because they *choose* to, and enjoy it.

Is Sugar Sinful?

A concern voiced about sweet snacks is that the child will develop a craving for them, whereas if not exposed to candy the child will prefer carrots. Dangers of reducing carbohydrate intake in the rapidly growing child have already been pointed out. On the other hand, there is no question that the average American diet contains too much refined sugar. In 1975 the per capita annual sugar consumption was 114 pounds (90 pounds of white sugar and 24 pounds of corn syrup and dextrose). It has been estimated that the per capita consumption in 1900 was somewhere between 20 and 60 pounds.

There is good evidence that newborns prefer sweetened to non-sweetened or salty liquids, a natural preference since human milk itself is sweet. By six months of age, the preference for sweetened liquid diminishes, but *less* so in babies who have been fed sweetened liquids. Thus, there may be some truth to the exposure theory for infants and children. Marilyn's son did not like sweet things (he prefers salty snacks) until he went to nursery school where the "No dessert until you finish your meal" litany was heard every lunchtime. *Then* he began to eat sweets, although he rarely does now.

In defense of tooth enamel (see below), there is no question that sugar promotes tooth decay. Highly sweetened snacks, especially those that stick on the teeth like caramels, are harmful as they can give children repeated attacks of the most common of human diseases: dental caries. Carbonated sweetened beverages are bad for teeth as the tiny bubbles carry the sugar right to the teeth. Fruits also contain sugar but the fiber in fruit has a natural detergent action that helps clean the teeth. Rinsing the mouth after eating sweets is not as good as brushing but is better than nothing.

The intake of sweets in children is often too high. In poor homes, sweets and starches prevail because they are cheap. Often in homes where food money is not a factor, parents are busy and—let's face it—packaged snacks are not only high in sugar but are convenient!

However, we were never fanatics about sugar. Our children are nutritionally okay and have all their teeth so you may wish to follow our example.

What we tried to do about sugar in our own households was to establish good lifetime eating habits by stocking our supermarket carts with nutritious snacks, by setting an example ourselves, by avoiding the overuse of sweets as a reward, and by acknowledging that eating is both a necessity and a pleasure and sometimes people *want* something sweet and comforting—and that's okay.

Has it worked? One of Marilyn's children eats a balanced diet but *is* a candy person (her father would kill for chocolate); the other almost never eats sweets. Anne's children are all snackers but eat relatively little refined sugar.

Artificial Sweeteners

Saccharine- and sorbitol-containing foods are not advisable for children. Saccharine is a cocarcinogen and a lifetime of exposure would not be healthy. Sorbitol can cause diarrhea. Avoid diet pop for children. They can make their own pop using fruit juice and club soda! We don't know enough about the latest artificial sweetener, aspartame (NutraSweet), to recommend its frequent use by children.

NUTRITION AND TEETH

What disease affects almost every child and adolescent? Dental caries! By age twelve, 90 percent of children have one or more cavities. Dental caries is the most widespread disease of humans. The American Dental Association estimates that there are 600 million unfilled cavities in the United States, which would cost $10.8 billion to fill!

We have learned a good deal about teeth and tooth decay in the past four decades and know nutrition is a key preventive factor. The preerupted teeth of children need adequate levels of protein. Vitamins A, C, and D, calcium, phosphorus, and fluoride. Generally, except for fluoride in some areas, the ordinary infant diet contains more than enough of these essential nutrients to nourish the teeth and help protect them from decay.

Fluoride Supplementation

Too little fluoride leads to tooth decay. Too much fluoride can mottle and discolor the teeth. If you live in an area where there is less than the recommended levels of fluoride in the water, fluoride supplementation is recommended by both doctors and dentists. This can be in the form of fluoride drops or the fluoride can be combined with vitamins. The dentists do not approve of the latter because: 1) Doctors may say the child no longer needs vitamins after infancy and dentists feel fluoride is needed until age fourteen. 2) In areas where there is some fluoride in the water, dosage adjustment is difficult because of the vitamins. Topical fluoride is also protective. Dentists apply fluoride directly to teeth after they have erupted, even when the local water has recommended levels. Ask your doctor about how much fluoride supplementation your child in your area needs.

Sugar and Dental Health

The effects of a high sugar diet on teeth are detrimental. What Aristotle observed over two thousand years ago when he noticed sweet figs and bad teeth were associated has now been proven. Studies have shown that, without question, sugar is the culprit responsible for tooth decay. We now know that *any* starch (if it contains a fermentable carbohydrate) can cause cavities because starches break down into sugar.

Sugar is bad for three reasons: sugar supplies food for the bacteria which live in everybody's mouth and cause cavities (brushing may reduce the bacteria count but it *never* removes all of them); it ferments under the action of bacterial enzymes to form organic acids that leach minerals out of the tooth; and it is an ingredient of the stored polysaccharide *dextran* that makes dental plaque sticky. Plaque, which is a collection of bacteria and salivary substances that forms on the teeth, provides a source of sugar food for bacteria when other sugars aren't in the mouth.

Everybody knows that refined sugar is bad. What about natural sugars? *All* sugars, including honey, molasses, fructose, lactose, and maltose, can nourish the cavity-causing bacteria that live in our mouths. Honey and molasses are more nutritious than table sugar because they contain vitamins but they still can rot teeth (although honey is much sweeter than sugar so less is taken). Dried fruits like raisins are worse than the original grapes from whence they came because the sugar is more concentrated and the fruit is sticky instead of juicy so the sugar stays in the mouth longer. Then why are raisins on our "snack list?" Because they are not "empty calories" but a highly nutritious food which provides a source of certain vitamins and iron. But to keep your dental bills down, teach your children to swish and swallow after raisins—and all other snacks and meals for that matter.

Studies have also shown that *when* the sugar is consumed is an important factor. Consuming sugar with meals leads to fewer cavities than eating the same amount per day between meals. One study showed that preschool children who ate *no* snacks scored 3.3 sick teeth compared with 9.8 in those who reported eating four or more sugar-containing snacks.[16] But, as we have said elsewhere, the rapidly growing preschooler *needs* snacks. Our compromise is nutritious snacks and rinsing.

Parenthetically, snacking here is an area where Anne and Marilyn agree completely but the experts are in conflict. The dentists recommend limiting snacks and avoiding snacks with sugar, while the doctors recognize the need for snacks.

By the way, one area in which the dentists are absolutely right—and the doctors agree completely—is in the prevention of "nursing bottle syndrome." Babies who are put to sleep with a bottle whether it contains milk, juice, or soda pop can develop a horrible and unsightly condition in which all of the front teeth (usually worse in the upper teeth) are decalcified and virtually destroyed by the acids that form when fermentable carbohydrates are broken down by mouth bacteria. The saliva flow slows when the child sleeps, so fermentation is enhanced. We personally, as well as other doctors and the dentists, are opposed to this method of feeding and this method of readying a baby for sleep.

Dentists also point out that sorbitol, mannitol, and xylitol, which are used to sweeten "sugar-free" or diet gums and candies, are not without risk. Though these substances are metabolized to sugar slowly so that the saliva can better buffer the action of the sugar, more work has to be done before we can substantiate the claim that these chewing gums are safe for teeth or prevent cavities. Gum isn't as bad as candy because the sugar is rapidly carried away by the saliva. So a stick or two won't add to your dentist bill much. Neither we, nor dentists, recommend giving children foods, gum, or pop artificially sweetened with saccharin or NutraSweet.

In summary, everybody has to eat and carbohydrates should form 50 percent of the diet. To protect teeth: reduce gooey snacks; pay attention to tooth hygiene such as rinsing after snacks and meals, brushing, and flossing, which really are protective; and use recommended fluoride preparations.

MILK

How much milk is good? You don't have to worry about breast-fed babies. They will regulate themselves without any difficulties. The bottle-fed baby may not be a good self-regulator and often ingests more milk than is really needed because it's so easy to get. We have all heard commercials advising us that everybody needs a quart of milk a day. Except under extraordinary circumstances, no one, except a rapidly growing baby under a year of age, needs a quart of milk a day. By the time a baby is close to a year of age, milk should be restricted to three eight-ounce bottles or cups a day, because milk is so filling that it may prevent the baby from getting other nutrients needed from solid foods.

We recommend that parents *not* permit a baby to suck milk down constantly. Some babies will take over two or three quarts a day. These so called "milk babies" are not only overweight but, in addition, may be severely iron deficient. Because they drink milk and milk only, they get no iron-containing foods, and because their sole food is cow's milk, they *lose* iron. It has been thought that milk is a perfect food. Milk is a remarkably complete food which contains high quality protein, carbohydrates, and fat along with great quantities of calcium. However, cow's milk does not contain enough iron in available form for human absorption.

Minimum Milk Requirement

If a child does not take at least twenty-four ounces of milk a day, the child will not get enough calcium. There are babies who seem to dislike milk and refuse to drink it. Sometimes this occurs after weaning from the breast and the baby never is happy taking milk from a cup. One of Marilyn's grandsons, who had received only breast milk, never cared for the cow's variety from a cup.

There are various methods for feeding calcium to a non-milk drinker. Chocolate or other flavorings can be tried, although the former adds both calories and sugar and the latter may add food dyes, which some parents wish to avoid. A few drops of vanilla and a bit of sugar added to milk and blended with ice creates a vanilla milk shake. Cheese is concentrated calcium. One ounce of Cheddar, brick, or Swiss cheese contains almost as much calcium as found in eight ounces of milk. Yogurt, ounce for ounce, is as good as milk as a calcium source. Milk can also be easily disguised when it is used as all or part of the liquid to make hot cereal, rice, soups, etc. Usually, between cheese and disguised milk, the daily quota can be met.

Currently it is recommended that children between one and ten take in 800 mg of calcium per day while adolescents between eleven and eighteen take in 1,200 mg. Twenty-four ounces of milk contains 894 mg of calcium. Any nutrition handbook can be used to calculate how much calcium is found in "substitute foods." High calcium foods include fish like canned sardines and salmon; leafy greens like broccoli, mustard greens, kale, and collards; and dried legumes like beans and peas. Corn tortillas made with bonemeal are a good source of calcium. As a last resort for milk avoiders (or those children who cannot tolerate any dairy product) a calcium supplement can be prescribed by your doctor.

Reduced Fat Milks

One word about reduced fat milks. Skimmed milk can be dangerous for young babies and should never be given to infants with diarrhea. Babies also *need* the fat in whole milk and we recommend its use. Even for an overweight baby, 2 percent milk should not be used before age two. Lower calorie milk just encourages the baby to drink more. If the baby needs any dietary restriction this should be done only with expert advice.

What About the Baby Who Cannot Tolerate Milk?

Are there any babies who cannot tolerate milk? Yes. A baby can be allergic to cow's milk, although true milk allergy is rare. Infants with eczema who worsen when milk is fed often improve when they are placed on a soy-based formula.

You may have heard of lactose intolerance, when milk or milk products cause intestinal symptoms in adults. There have been a few cases of congenital lactose deficiency described in which infants cannot tolerate either breast or cow's milk because both contain lactose, and the baby lacks the enzyme needed to digest this sugar. The usual kind of lactose intolerance, however, does not appear until ages four or five, or later. It is both hereditary and common in certain groups of people. Lactose intolerance is found in 75 percent of blacks but only 10 percent of whites, mainly of Mediterranean extraction. Symptoms are diarrhea and bloating, but avoidance of milk prevents symptoms. The only problem for parents of a child with lactose intolerance is to get good dietary advice so that proper substitute foods are used to replace the nutrients found in milk.

FOOD AMOUNTS

What about amounts? Too little food will lead to a scrawny baby—nobody wants that. Too much food? You get an obese baby and we are told this can lead to an obese adult with an increased risk of early coronary artery disease. What is a mother to do?

Most of the time children will regulate their own food intake. Indeed, in one experiment, when children were given free access to nourishing foods, over about a two-week period they took adequate amounts of a balanced diet.[17]

How can a parent be sure? How can parents tell if their child is properly self-regulating food intake? First of all, if you are worried you can write down what your child is eating each day over a period of several days. You can even go to the nutrition handbooks to calculate the exact amounts of the nutrients taken in. We don't think the calculations are necessary, however, because in this country, with our bounteous food supply, common sense and relaxation are better for "nutritional parenting" than compulsiveness. Sometimes when you *do* write down the intake you are pleasantly surprised to realize how much your toddler is actually eating over a day or week. And if your toddler is eating little, remember the rate of growth has really slowed down and less food is needed. Some toddlers eat smaller meals; others go through a phase of eating only one meal a day.

The child who is gaining weight steadily and has a healthy appearance and normal activity levels produces good evidence that the amount of food intake is adequate. There is *no* need to weigh a baby or child every day, of course, unless this is prescribed for a specific reason.

MEALTIME ATMOSPHERE

The happy, healthy diet becomes meaningless if mealtimes are unpleasant. Of course, occasional mealtime conflict is to be expected in any healthy, spirited family, but constant conflict is a problem.

There are many reasons the table becomes the arena for parent-child and child-child conflict. Children don't eat certain foods and don't eat at all at the table; table manners are gross; children are deliberately provocative because they use grossness to get the attention of parents; the parents are deliberately over-bearing because the child is a captive for the day's disciplinary words and actions. Children may fight with each other at mealtimes for various reasons: because it is safe (since parents are there as referees), to provoke parental attention, or simply because children, like adults, are irritable when hungry.

We feel meals should be as pleasant as possible and offer a few suggestions. 1) Serve small portions—children are really turned off by too full a plate. 2) Don't insist the child eat everything—all forced-feeding is a violation of human rights. 3) Don't worry about the child not eating enough, or not eating certain foods. If you relax about your child's eating habits, they often improve. 4) Don't worry about manners in young children. Encourage good age-appropriate manners but remember it takes a long time to become an adult with adult manners. 5) Don't make children stay at the table when they are finished. Let them play quietly in the kitchen or dining room until you are finished. 6) Don't insist that children wait for either parent to come home if the meal is going to be late. Feed the children early so parents can enjoy their meal together. 7) Don't expect your children to eat anything that you don't like, even if it is good for them. 8) Don't force children to eat what they don't like. We don't, however, feel that you have to fix a special meal for each child; children (or adults) who don't like what you fix can help themselves to cereal.

"NATURAL" FOODS

What about additives and preservatives? What's natural? What's organic?

Natural is a much misused word. There are "artificial" things that are good to eat and there are "natural" things that are not. An example of artificial things that might be good for you are Egg Beaters if you have a cholesterol problem. An example of something natural that is not good for you is a holly berry.

The term "natural" or "unprocessed" refers to foods which have not been processed and which do not have preservatives, emulsifiers, or other synthetic substances. "Organic" or organically grown foods are those grown without the use of chemical fertilizer or pesticides of any kind.

Whether food is organically grown or whether artificial fertilizer is used may make a difference to the farmer's pocketbook and may make a difference as to how much food is produced. However, it does not make any difference to the food, which takes in the nutrients it needs when it is a plant—from either natural or artificial sources. Pesticides and chemical fertilizers have saved the lives of many children by making food available to children who would otherwise have died of malnutrition. However, residual pesticides could be toxic, so fruits and vegetables should be thoroughly washed before eating or cooking.

Natural Milk

Generally, both "natural" and "organic" foods are more expensive than their supermarket counterparts but to those families who value "natural foods," they are certainly safe and acceptable for children with one exception. *Raw milk* (milk which is unpasteurized) can be hazardous for babies—and adults. This is true even for raw milk which is "certified" (certified means the milk when tested had fewer than ten thousand bacterial colonies per cubic centimeter—one thirtieth of an ounce—which is a lot in a whole bottle). Several epidemics of gastroenteritis with fatalities due to unusual bacteria have been caused by ingestion of raw milk. In Tucson in 1981, almost two hundred cases of enteritis were traced to a single raw milk source from a commercial outlet which was state-approved.

Pasteurization is a process which destroys most of the "bad" bacteria without denaturing the milk in any appreciable way, especially today with new "flash" pasteurization methods which preserve flavor and nutritional levels of the milk. It would be foolish to risk illness in your child because you feel strongly about "natural" milk, and after all, drinking cow's milk isn't "natural" in the first place. As one doctor said when describing the epidemic due to raw milk, "Mother Nature is cruel!"[18]

What about your own milk if you are a farmer? You can, of course, pay careful attention to barn and teat hygiene in your cows, but the epidemics described above occurred because bacteria which are normally present in the intestinal tract of cows found their way into the milk. As there is no way to completely prevent contamination of cow's milk with cow's bacteria, we would not feed raw milk to our own children and can't recommend it to others.

Fresh Foods

What about fresh versus frozen versus canned foods? Our transportation industry gets fresh fruits and vegetables to our markets before all the vitamins have disappeared. Freezing foods preserves essential nutrients. Canning may decrease levels of certain vitamins but does not decrease other nutrients to any appreciable degree.

Nothing tastes better than freshly picked, home-grown vegetables, but if your lifestyle is such that gardening is impossible, shop at your supermarket with the assurance that the food is nutritious. As a shopper you already look for the freshest fruits and vegetables because they are the best-tasting and the best buy (overripe fruit will probably be thrown out before it is eaten).

The greatest loss of vitamins will occur in your own kitchen. Store food carefully, rotate supplies so the first purchased is eaten first, and cook with as little liquid and at as low a temperature as possible. Try to use liquids that vegetables, fruit, or meats have been cooked in as they contain much of the vitamins. Serve potato skins—they are not only tasty but high in vitamins.

Additives and Preservatives

What about food additives found in processed foods but not in "natural" ones? What is an additive anyway?

An additive is defined by law as a substance added to a basic food through production, processing, storage, or packaging. There are natural additives such as spices, salt, or sugar. Almost three thousand food additives are now in use, which can be grouped into flavors, colors, preservatives, and texture agents. Almost a quarter of the two thousand flavor additives are natural but the rest are synthetic. Colors also come in natural and synthetic but synthetic dyes are preferred by the food industry because they are more stable and colorful than the natural ones.

Prior to the chemical age, people preserved food by drying, fermenting, smoking, souring, heating, and cooling. Now we also have many different varieties of chemicals to help in the fight against food spoilage which has both health and economic consequences. Antioxidants prevent fats from turning rancid; sulfur dioxide is used in the preserving of dried fruit; a variety of additives act against bread mold. Nitrates and nitrites are very effective in making bacon and sausage safe from bacterial toxins but, as you may have heard, may be transformed into cancer-causing agents called nitrosamines when the food is broiled or cooked at high temperatures. Nitrates are found in some foods naturally and, in the case of vegetables like spinach and beets, in large quantities. They are not toxic but they can become converted into nitrites, which can cause a condition called methemoglobinemia (the nitrite combines with hemoglobin to form methemoglobin in red blood cells, which then are unable to carry oxygen). To avoid this, well water should be tested for nitrites and large quantities of spinach shouldn't be fed to young infants. Drinking a large amount of the water in which spinach is cooked can be dangerous to children or adults.

The federal Food and Drug Administration (FDA) watches over the additives in our food and must rule on the safety of compounds before they are added to food. Toxicity tests which this agency performs include long-term animal testing, which is designed to provide a model of human lifelong exposure and is important to evaluate the carcinogenic potential of a substance. The Delaney Clause in the 1958 Food Additive Amendment stipulates that no substance which has ever been shown to cause cancer can be used as a food additive. However, many substances which were used as additives prior to 1958 have never been tested—and may never be. They were exempted from the legislation and are known as GRAS additives—standing for Generally Recognized as Safe. These substances can be removed from the GRAS list only if the FDA demonstrates a lack of safety.

In addition to actual toxicity and the cancer-causing potential of additives, some food additives have also been implicated in allergy. In very sensitive people, asthma or hives can occur, especially in those allergic to aspirin. Hence, after a sensitivity has been established, parents should read the fine print on the labels and avoid unlabeled processed foods.

Is Hyperactivity Caused or Aggravated by Food Dyes?

What about food dyes and hyperactivity? You may have heard about the Feingold diet. Dr. Feingold, a pediatrician and allergist, hypothesized that hyperactivity could be caused or aggravated in sensitive children by "salicylate"-containing foods. These foods are so described because they can cause sensitivity in those who are allergic to aspirin. His diet eliminates all synthetic colors and flavors and some natural foods like oranges, apples, grapes, and tomatoes. Dr. Feingold claims dramatic lessening of the symptoms of hyperactivity in two thirds of the children on his diet, especially the younger children.

Dr. Feingold's analysis of success was based on clinical observations by himself and parents or teachers who knew whether or not the child was on the diet. Diet crossover studies and specific challenge studies have both been done. Diet crossover studies place hyperactive children on the Feingold diet or a diet that looks like the Feingold diet but contains salicylates, artificial flavors and colors. The challenge studies feed known hyperactive children who have appeared to respond to the Feingold diet a challenge food test containing artificial food colors. The results of both types of studies have been inconclusive. Most children who improve on the Feingold diet do *not* respond to a challenge with increased hyperactivity. This has led some to question Feingold's claims and to wonder whether parental expectations for the diet affected their perceptions of hyperactivity in their children.

However, parents and teachers *have* reported a lessening of symptoms both in the literature and to Marilyn. The diet is nutritionally sound and can do no harm (except for adding another parental burden and possibly implying to a child the message that behavioral control is all external to oneself). If Marilyn had a hyperactive child she would consider trying the diet. If response occurred she would continue it, especially if drug therapy could be avoided or reduced in dosage.

NONTRADITIONAL DIETS

What about nontraditional diets like vegetarianism in children? We have serious concerns about certain nontraditional diets in children, especially young children. If you are a vegetarian and plan vegetarianism for your child (Marilyn could not recommend this) we suggest getting nutritional advice before doing so —from a physician and/or dietician who is knowledgeable about sound vegetarian diets (many are not).

Many people are vegetarians for reasons of health.[19] Vegetarian diets are lower in fat, cholesterol, and sugar than the diet of most Americans. They also contain less pesticides, which are concentrated in the fat of animals. Some people become vegetarians for ecological reasons, because it takes several pounds of grain to generate one pound of animal food. Vegetarian foods are cheaper than meat foods, so that economics is another factor. Some have religious (Seventh-Day Adventists) or philosophical concerns and do not wish to kill animals for food.

Herbivores (animals that eat only plants) are sometimes mentioned in support of vegetarianism, because they survive without animal protein and drink no milk after weaning. These mammals are quite different from humans, however.

Humans do not have the ability to ruminate. Bacteria in the rumen of the cow assist in the digestion of cellulose and manufacture both important B-complex vitamins and essential amino acids. This means the cow can do quite well on grass, whereas a human being cannot. The intestine of a human cannot handle a field of grass. Not only don't humans have time to chew their cud all day but as omnivores they have always been dependent on low residue, high quality foods, which include meat, milk, and eggs. Rabbits and rodents eat some of their feces, which results in less waste of essential nutrients and better intake of certain vitamins formed in the lower digestive tract. People don't do that either.

Vegetarianism has been established as safe and healthful in adults. Seventh-Day Adventists, for example, who do not eat meat (but do eat eggs and milk) have health comparable to the general population and lower blood pressures. Nutritional benefits of a careful vegetarian diet include the facts that obesity is rarely found and serum cholesterol is generally low. However, the word *careful* is important. A vegetarian diet is not a balanced diet by definition, and therefore must be carefully planned in order to ensure that all the essential nutrients are eaten. This can be done and, with the aid of certain books such as *Laurel's Kitchen,* can be done very successfully.[20]

However, totally vegetarian diets with no sources of animal protein can be difficult, if not dangerous, for children, because they are so high in bulk they may not meet caloric needs. Any diet more restricted than the milk-egg vegetarian diet would risk your child's ability to grow properly. Even adults on a total vegetarian diet must pay careful attention to protein content, including quality of protein in the diet. When one is using only vegetable proteins, each meal must provide essential amino acids in optimal ratios. This can be done by combining cereal grains which do not contain much lysine (an essential amino acid), with legumes that have adequate lysine but little methionine (another essential amino acid). The combination of rice and beans will do this and makes up a common diet in Third World countries where animal protein is not available to most of the people but, of course, this combination does not always prevent malnutrition. Another important principle in a vegetarian diet is to use a wide variety of foods to avoid deficiencies.

Vegetarians also must avoid excessive bran, which could lead to a transit time too short for absorption of needed vitamins. Good dietary planning can provide most of the vitamins. However, a vitamin B_{12} deficiency can occur because this vitamin comes only from animal products. Most vegetarians recognize this (because they are excellent nutritionists) and supplement themselves with vitamin B_{12}. However, there are some vegetarians who are opposed to taking vitamin pills who may develop a B_{12} deficiency.

Vegetarian Children

What about vegetarian children? How do they grow? There have been published reports of fifty-nine malnourished vegetarian children.[21] However, some of these malnourished children had disturbed parents or malnourished mothers and thus were leading highly atypical lives. Children on restricted vegan (only plant foods) diets were shown to be prone to rickets, and vegetarian children under three years grew more slowly than the norms and also had variable growth rates. Decreased growth velocity in vegetarian children is felt to be related to the limited capacity of the child to ingest an adequate volume of low caloric density food.

Generally, birth weights of vegetarian children in developed countries have been similar to non-vegetarians possibly because vegetarians tend to be more highly educated women who are careful to get an optimal vegetarian diet. However, low birth weight infants do result from macrobiotic diets in pregnancy.

A Dangerous Vegetarian Diet

One diet that can be extremely dangerous in pregnancy and for children is the macrobiotic diet.[22] This diet comes in different levels, both nutritional and spiritual, and the highest level diet is composed only of cereals. Strict adherence to this high level macrobiotic diet can result in scurvy, anemia, protein and calcium deficiencies, emaciation, and death. Because important brain as well as skeletal growth occurs early in life, pediatricians generally advise parents, even if they are on a macrobiotic diet themselves, to spare their children this nutritional hazard. After all, we expect our children to take many years to achieve high spiritual levels in other dimensions of life as well.

In summary, if vegetarianism is important to you as parents, if you are not opposed to using eggs and milk for your infants and children, and if you recognize the possible nutritional hazards and therefore get good advice (perhaps finding a vegetarian doctor or dietician, in addition to using the books we are suggesting), vegetarianism will not harm your children. If you are a vegetarian nursing mother (nursing is recommended as long as possible for children who will be fed a vegetarian diet), you must pay careful attention to your own diet and vitamin intake so that your milk will be nutritious.

HYGIENE

The word hygiene comes from the Greek "Hygeia," the goddess of health. Hygiene is defined as the science of the establishment and maintenance of health or the practice of habits conducive to health, such as appropriate cleanliness. Hygienic conditions are those which promote health.

In some parts of the world there is an enormous lack of hygiene. These countries have high infection rates, and children die from diseases transmitted by filth, impure water, and other unsanitary conditions. In this country we sometimes get complacent because most of us take clean water, sanitary conditions, and refrigerated or preserved foods for granted. We are lucky that it is usually possible to provide hygienic levels of cleanliness with relatively little effort.

Definitions of Dirt

Let's talk about a clean environment for our children. Most people instinctively feel that "dirt" is bad and that a clean child is somehow healthier and happier. But what is dirt? What types of dirt do your children have to be protected from? One type of dirt is sewage, which contains the fecal material of many human beings. Before it is treated, sewage can spread viral diseases, such as hepatitis, and bacterial infections, such as typhoid fever. People seem to understand about dangers from this "dirt." Even in primitive countries, defecation is done outside of the house and generally in specified places. In countries where plumbing is not widely available, such as in rural areas of Mexico, or where raw sewage is recycled for fertilization of crops, such as in China, many people *do* develop viral or bacterial enteric infections. Some die and the rest develop immunity. Tourists, both adults and children, visiting such places have to be extraordinarily careful not to contract an intestinal infection or hepatitis. They should avoid both unboiled water and raw vegetables.

Another kind of dirt is ordinary earth or soil, found in backyards, gardens, and playgrounds. It isn't always just "good clean dirt." Soil contaminated with horse droppings may contain tetanus spores, which can enter the body through puncture wounds and cause tetanus. The encysted eggs of dog and cat roundworms can live in soil for long periods. When eaten by a child these eggs can cause a disease called toxocariasis or visceral larval migrans which can cause serious skin, eye, and internal organ symptoms. The spores of certain fungal infections, such as coccidioidomycosis which causes valley fever, can live in soil. The old saying that all children will eat a peck of dirt before they are grown may be true but it is probably not desirable.

Once again we suggest parents be sensible. Backyard play is so important to a child we would never suggest you keep your child away from this soil. However, if your child is a dirt eater and plays in a yard which currently serves, or formerly served, as a bathroom for dogs or cats, it is probably a good idea to protect the child from the overzealous ingestion of dirt. This can be managed by keeping the child in a playpen during the dirt-eating years. A blanket can help but you will also have to watch the child and get as much dirt as possible out of the mouth when you catch the child munching.

Casual dirt-eating does not usually last very long. The child of fifteen or eighteen months much prefers food. Repetitive or habitual eating of dirt and other non-food substances, called pica, can be a problem, as it may both be a symptom of malnutrition and anemia and can lead to lead poisoning.

SANDBOXES

What about sandboxes? Backyard sandboxes are fun and a good place for toddlers to play, although a child can certainly grow up happily without one. If you have a sandbox, be sure cats do not adopt it for their own sandbox usage. Cat feces have been associated with toxoplasmosis, especially in pregnant women. If you have reason to believe a stray cat has used your sandbox (remember cats can climb over fences), we recommend replacing the sand with fresh sand. It's probably less trouble to keep the sandbox covered when not in use.

PETS

Speaking of pets, what about pets in the house? Are pets "clean" enough to be near small babies? Generally, yes. Do we recommend pets in the home? Certainly.

Pets can be great for kids and bring a lot of pluses. A pet generally loves you no matter what, even when you are feeling or acting ornery. Dogs can be good watchdogs. Some dogs even alert families if there is a fire (although smoke detectors are more reliable). Some wise dogs even watch the children when crossing the streets. Learning to care for a pet is a good way to establish responsible behavior in young children. Last but not least, pets are fun to be with and have around.

However, Marilyn's husband, who is a veterinarian, feels that dogs and children under four or five are not good household combinations. In the first place, the pet is at risk because young children can, without realizing that they are inflicting pain, pull tails or ears or gouge the eyes of pets. Of course a child below the age of five is too young to assume responsibility for the pet.

Marilyn's husband especially doesn't approve of the combination of large dogs and small children. The "friendly dog syndrome" has been described in the medical literature.[23] These "friendly" creatures are big-breed dogs who either lived in the home before the child was born or are brought into a home where there are young children. If provoked, such dogs may attack a child. This can happen with a small-breed dog too, but in that case a child doesn't usually get as seriously hurt. With a large-breed dog, whole cheeks or ears have been torn off and there have even been fatalities.

To be on the safe side, we recommend that small children and large-breed dogs not share a household. We know this can be hard on parents who have a beloved dog.

If you already have a dog that is potentially dangerous to newborns (those that have been aggressive to babies in the past, those that are aggressive in

568 CHILD CARE/PARENT CARE

general, and those that are predatory to small animals), a veterinarian has suggested ways to introduce a baby to a dog.[24] You start by teaching the dog to sit/stay, increase the time the dog will sit/stay while you are moving around, carry a doll around while the dog sits/stays. Then, and only then, do you introduce the baby to the dog gradually. Remember, no dog can be completely trusted, so a dog should never have unsupervised access to a new baby.

Some children are allergic to dander (animal dandruff) or bird feathers. Diseases can be transmitted from pets, including ringworm, the visceral larval migrans, and toxoplasmosis we just mentioned, and cat scratch fever, a rare viral disease which causes marked swelling of lymph nodes. Generally, however, reasonable attention to pet hygiene and disposal of pet fecal material are all that is needed, and the fun of a pet at the proper age far outweighs these dangers, which are quite rare.

We are often asked about whether dogs or cats should sleep in the child's bed or be allowed to eat out of family rather than dog dishes. If the child is not allergic to the pet there is no evidence that sleeping with a pet is bad. However, in those rare cases in which a disease is carried by a pet, more frequent contact makes catching the disease more likely. Aesthetically most people object to muddy paw prints on the sheets. A compromise might be a bed for the dog on the floor of the child's room. Dishes should be thoroughly washed after anyone —human or animal—has used them.

What about cats? Do they really smother babies? Cats do like to curl up where there is something warm. There have been reported cases of cats curling up on the chest of a newborn infant to be near the baby's warm breath, which could theoretically be dangerous. Cats are really not very childwise as they both scratch and bite with little provocation. Many cats, however, will avoid a baby because they don't like to get their tails pulled.

HOUSEHOLD DIRT

The last "dirt" we will discuss is household dirt and dust. How clean should a house be? Does it matter to a baby how often the carpet is vacuumed? Can general aesthetics prevail or should a house be especially clean for a baby? Should people believe the ads for disinfectant cleansers? Is it really important to scrub all the walls and baseboards of a house to get rid of the germs? Is it important to scrub the diaper pail daily? What about the bathroom?

It is hard to sort out reality from the rhetoric of TV commercials. "Germs" are all around us. Most of the disinfectant cleansers have such a low concentration of disinfectant that they probably don't do any more good than plain soap and water.

Dust and household dirt should be kept to the minimum, especially when there is an allergic child around, but many parents today are too busy to be able to maintain the standards of housekeeping that their parents did.

In an interesting book called *Never Done, A History of Housework in America*, Susan Strasser explains that society has come through a transition.[25] In the past, women not only cleaned and cooked and washed but also made or grew the products with which to do this work. The housewife of the past had a very long workday but she controlled it and was her own boss. Today, the sphere of work at home has shrunk considerably, more due to industrialization and urbanization than to the women's movement, but nonetheless many women today work outside the home where they have a boss who tells them when and where they must do things. We feel that employed mothers are better off parenting rather than spending the limited time they have at home cleaning compulsively. And women who are housewives today usually prefer parenting and creative or social activities to compulsive cleaning.

In our own households we wash our hands before food preparation and see that the children eat off clean dishes. We vacuum the carpets periodically in order to keep the dust down. We kept our children's rooms as clutter free as possible, without fancy drapes or bedspreads to make cleaning easier.

A reasonable degree of household cleanliness is all that a child—or even a newborn baby—needs.

CLEAN FOOD

Although we mentioned earlier in this chapter that food poisoning is rare today, it *can* occur. There are several types. Bacterial food poisoning due to salmonella or staphylococcus contamination of food causes vomiting, cramps, diarrhea, and even fever, usually a few hours to a day and a half after the food is eaten. Botulism is caused by toxin produced by spores growing in improperly sterilized preserved food. Although in rare instances this happens in commercially canned foods (never use the contents of a can whose lid has popped up), most cases result from home canning of low acid foods. Also, the spores are found in honey, so honey should not be fed to babies under one year. Trichinosis can result from eating under-cooked pork which comes from garbage-eating pigs.

By using reasonable hygiene and common sense you can protect your child from the hazards of food. Food should be kept hot or refrigerated promptly after cooking. If left at room temperature, certain foods like ground meat or custard pie can be unsafe to eat in four hours.

When in doubt about food safety (the food smells, looks, or tastes spoiled, or has been unrefrigerated too long) throw it out. Wastage is better than illness. Be careful on picnics, when camping, or when traveling in cars, especially in the summer. Inexpensive Styrofoam coolers keep a lunch safe when ice or sealed cooling containers are used.

Body Care

As parents, we are responsible for the protective body care of our baby's skin, hair, and teeth.

What about baths? Most of us feel better when our skin, hair, and teeth are clean—and those around us feel better too! The same is true for babies, but nowhere is it written that every baby has to have a bath every day or that a child's hair must be washed every day. The daily bath may be fun, relaxing, and it is certainly cleansing, but for busy mothers or babies who don't particularly like the water, a bath when the child is dirty is all that is needed.

The parts of the body that get really dirty like the bottom and skin folds can certainly be taken care of with sponge bathing or with cotton moistened with baby lotion.

As children get older and begin to play vigorously, dirt can really get ground into the skin, especially in boys but also in girls. Generally, it is easier to get this dirt off daily. One of the goals of a daily bath for older children is encouraging them to take responsibility for their own skin and body care. This means knowing where the dirt is and how to get it off, including the hard parts like the ears. It also means knowing how to get the dirt out of the bathtub. We are convinced that by the time children are in school they should be able to bathe or shower themselves (with the bathroom door open and an adult near at hand because of slipping and other hazards). They should also clean out the tub and hang the towels up to dry, but we should not expect perfection.

SHAMPOOS

The short hair of a baby can be washed easily with ordinary soap when you are washing the rest of the baby. As the child gets older and the hair gets longer, shampooing is generally done every few days or once a week. Washing one's hair at least once a week is probably a good idea as the oils which accumulate otherwise make the hair harder to manage. Older children may want to wash their hair daily, especially when they have the kind of haircut that requires blow-drying. There is no problem provided children do the hair care themselves. Parents have enough to do.

As far as we can determine, daily washing with mild shampoo does no harm to the hair, as all the oils are replaced by the oil glands of the scalp. Conditioners do no harm either and may decrease tangling of hair after shampooing (tangles are tough on little girls with long hair).

Be careful of blow-dryers. They are dangerous in the bathroom, because of the danger of electrocution. Blow-drying is safe in the bedroom. Some children will show hair breakage with daily blow-drying and will have to cut down the frequency.

TOOTH CARE

Teeth should be brushed frequently. Ideally, teeth should be brushed after every meal and snack. This is not generally practical, but certainly a good tooth scrubbing should be done at bedtime and after every meal at home. For the children who don't have a toothbrush handy after lunch or after snacks at school, swishing and swallowing is a good idea. Teach your child to take a mouth of water, swish it around, and then swallow it. This gets *some* of the food particles off.

The American Dental Association recommends cleaning children's teeth from the time the first tooth erupts. You can use a gauze pad or a clean washcloth to wipe the baby's teeth. When the child is old enough to stand, buy a soft child-sized toothbrush with end-rounded bristles. Show the child how you brush and let him or her imitate you. Then you take the brush and do it right. You will probably have to help or supervise brushing until your child is in first grade—longer for some. A fluoride-containing toothpaste should be used, but only use a small amount and be sure toothpaste is not accessible to the child. Remember to replace toothbrushes every three or four months. You don't *need* an electric toothbrush—ordinary ones work fine. But some kids like the electric kind and therefore do more brushing.

In addition to careful cleaning, protect your children's teeth with fluoride. Although fluoride works best as the tooth enamel is being formed, it also works on the teeth already in the mouth. So, dentists also recommend topical fluoride in toothpaste and in fluoride rinses, in addition to the fluoride either in the water or provided by one of the supplements we mentioned above. Dentists often prescribe a prescription fluoride bedtime rinse for children three to eighteen provided they live in areas where the natural fluoride content of the water is in the proper range so that the additional fluoride will not cause mottling of the teeth. You can also buy over-the-counter rinses. These can be safely used by children six and over provided they can be properly taught how to spit. These were not around for Marilyn's children but she would certainly use them now. As fluoride is toxic in higher than recommended amounts, *all of these products* (including fluoride toothpaste) *must be safely stored.* Dentists point out that no fluoride preparation will overcome the effects of a diet in which sugars are fed frequently.

Should parents floss children's teeth? A pamphlet published by the American Dental Association recommends doing this daily, after the child has teeth which are crowded together enough that the toothbrush doesn't reach between them. The purpose is twofold: to remove food particles caught between the teeth and thus prevent decay, and to clean the pocket where the gum encloses the tooth, thus removing plaque and preventing gum infections.

Marilyn would follow the current ADA advice if raising children now. Anne would individualize, based on the child's tooth and gum health, and the advice of the child's dentist, since children too young to floss their own teeth often do not appreciate parents doing this for them. If it seemed indicated for an individual child, she'd get the dentist to help her and the child work out a routine for doing it painlessly, which included helping the child learn how to do it personally as soon as possible.

GOING TO THE DENTIST

We recommend the first visit to the dentist by age two or even earlier if you see a cavity or if a tooth is injured. Try to find a pediatric dentist who specializes in making the first visit a pleasant experience for the child. (See

Chapter 19, Choosing Health Professionals for Your Child's Care, p. 602.) Marilyn's children couldn't wait for their next appointment.

If you were—or still are—frightened by the dentist, try to avoid frightening your child when you take the child to the dentist. We know how hard it is to pretend you're not frightened when you really are. We suggest you make an effort by rehearsing ahead of time what you will say and do, so you won't appear frightened to your child. This is one of those areas in which you should say, "Do as I say, not as I do," because you don't want your children to develop either your fear of dentistry or the neglect of the teeth that your fears may have engendered in you.

Anne adds, for parents who have a fear of dentists, taking care of yourself first helps you care for your child. Before your children reach the dentistry age, get yourself a good dentist who can treat you with painless, modern dentistry and help you lose your fears. Local or state dental societies, or the nearest dental schools, can refer you to a dentist who specializes in allaying dental fears and phobias. And for your child, all pedodontists specialize in allaying children's fears.

Today, dentists have a new method of preventing cavities—fissure sealing. Though expensive it is very effective. Dentists were asked how they prevented cavities in their own children.[26] They all used fissure sealing as well as topical fluoride and avoidance of snacks.

Subsequent visits to the dentist should be at least every year. Parents who live far from a dentist or who cannot afford dental care have a problem. We suggest that some visits are better than none if distance or finances prevent regular visits. A dental school usually has a clinic providing lower cost care. Careful attention to *preventing* cavities through fluoride, brushing, and flossing would obviously be especially important for families who can't see a dentist.

Parents who wish to know more about care of their children's teeth can write to the American Dental Association, 211 East Chicago Avenue, Chicago, IL 60611, for pamphlets and information.

REST AND SLEEP

Sleep in Children

A baby's need for sleep is great. The average newborn sleeps sixteen hours a day with a range from ten and a half to twenty-three hours.

We have learned a good deal about the scientific aspects of sleep over the recent decades. There are two kinds of sleep. REM (rapid eye movement) sleep is the lighter sleep that is associated with dreaming. In adults what is called non-REM (NREM) sleep, occurs in deepening stages and progresses to REM sleep. This happens in about five or six cycles during the entire night.

Babies are somewhat different. Before birth, babies have the same stages of sleep as adults, except that the younger the baby, the greater the percentage of sleep time spent in REM sleep. The baby's sleep rhythms may be initially disrupted by labor and birth. On the second day, the baby's sleep is temporarily changed, with progressively less deep sleep, less REM sleep, and shorter sleep periods. The percentage of time spent awake and crying increases with a peak on the third day. It may be that the baby has lost the circadian rhythmicity established before birth by the mother's activities and may need time to entrain activity to the extrauterine environment. Although in adults *all* sleep is either REM or non-REM, babies demonstrate active REM, quiet sleep, and indeterminate sleep. In term babies, indeterminate sleep makes up 10 to 15 percent of sleep while active REM sleep is 45 to 50 percent of sleep time and quiet sleep is 35 to 50 percent. Indeterminate sleep diminishes by three months of age. Very new babies seem to be able to sleep undisturbed by noises in their environment (they "sleep like a baby"). This is the so-called "stimulus barrier" of the very young. As the infant grows, this barrier diminishes.

As the baby gets older the proportion of quiet sleep increases and active REM sleep decreases until late childhood when the young adult pattern of 20 percent REM and 80 percent non-REM sleep is found. Also, as the baby gets older, the sleep cycle (i.e., the time it takes for all stages of sleep to occur) changes. The cycle in newborns lasts forty-five to fifty minutes, although it is shorter in prematures and babies born before thirty-four weeks do not seem to have any sleep cycle. Adults have sleep cycles of ninety to a hundred minutes.

Unlike adults who have a long period of non-REM sleep at the beginning and have most of the REM sleep toward the end of the night, the newborn's cycles are more regular. Also the day/night patterning of sleep differs in babies. Babies are generally three months old before they show daytime wakefulness and nighttime sleepiness.[27] By about eight months of age, there is sustained daytime wakefulness, usually punctuated with two naps, and an uninterrupted night of sleep. At least the parents' sleep is generally uninterrupted, as many babies wake after REM sleep and fall asleep again by themselves.

Studies have shown that there are wide age differences in sleep patterns during childhood. Two-year-olds fall asleep very rapidly, taking only ten to twenty-five minutes to pass from wakefulness into deep sleep, and REM sleep represents about a quarter of the cycle. REM sleep is often accompanied by muscle twitches, especially of the face. The child has five to eight sleep cycles and sleeps for about nine to twelve hours.

By the time the child is ten all stages of sleep are clearly recognizable and it takes thirty to forty minutes to reach deep sleep. The length of sleep varies between eight to ten hours. Adolescents between fourteen and eighteen become almost identical to adults.

Interestingly enough, position during sleep changes as the child gets older. For example, between the second and fifth year of life a child tends to lie on the right side. Many facial expressions can be noticed while children are asleep, ranging from pleasurable or ecstatic to aggressive or anxious. Motor activity and moving limbs are much more common in younger children.

By the way, "cosleeping" (the child and parent sleeping together) was found in 35 percent of white and 70 percent black families in a recent survey.[28] This means it is fairly common. Cosleeping children were likely to fall asleep in a place other than bed and to have both adult company and adult body contact at bedtime. In white families cosleeping was associated with a lower level of parent education, increased family stress, and disruptive sleep patterns in the child. The practice is not harmful but it may not be helpful either. Many parents instinctively sleep with an anxious child at a time of crisis, and both may find it comforting. An interesting book *(The Family Bed* by Thevenin) points out that in times past whole families regularly slept together.[29] In other cultures such as Japan, no one is expected to sleep alone. In our culture, a single parent who regularly sleeps with a child does run the risk of increasing the child's sense of displacement if the parent finds a new partner.

Sleep and Nap Hints

One of the biggest sleep problems we have noted in restless newborn babies is that they are overdressed or that the room is too warm. The baby needs the same number and kind of clothes and blankets you do.

Speaking of rooms, should a newborn baby sleep in the parents' room? Sure, if that is what makes you more comfortable. Is it all right for the baby to sleep in a room down the hall? Sure, provided you can hear the baby.

Sleep disorders do occur in children. According to their parents, 94 percent of children and adolescents sleep soundly and 86 percent are in good moods when they awake in the morning. However, 45 percent reportedly acted differently the day after a poor night's sleep.[30] In the six months prior to the survey parents reported sleep talking, restlessness, snoring, nightmares, tooth grinding, bed-wetting, insistence on sleeping with others, sleepwalking, and night terrors in decreasing order. Most of these behaviors were reported in young children, indicating that there is a developmental or maturational phenomenon.

Don't worry about noise; let your baby become accustomed to the noise level in your house rather than ask the world to tiptoe around the baby. Babies *do* sleep through most household noise and will get used to falling asleep with the usual decibel level of your home. There are some babies, however, who *are* very sensitive to noise and who do waken easily. Those babies usually do not fall back to sleep easily. It's best to keep the house quiet if you have one of those. They often settle down to sleeping through noise by three to six months. By the way, one study correlated the temperament of babies with sleep patterns. "Difficult" babies slept nearly two hours less per night than "easy" babies. They also napped one hour less per day.[31]

As toddlers get older they need less sleep. However, when children give up a nap there are sometimes problems. Parents say that they *know* if their children nap they are less cranky. There are suggestions and tricks for sleep enhancement although if you have an active non-sleeper you are probably not going to do much about it. One trick is to lie down with the child yourself. Children will usually lie down cheerfully when everyone else does, as they do in day care centers or nursery schools. You can also make a bargain that the child doesn't have to sleep but has to rest for one hour. Use an alarm clock.

We have found that children who learn how to, or never forget how to take naps are generally happier. They seem to self-regulate their bodies. They know when they are tired and take the appropriate action. Marilyn remembers one day when she was responsible for escorting Margaret Mead, then in her seventies, to several meetings in Detroit. At a luncheon held in her honor, Dr. Mead fell asleep for about five minutes as soon as she sat at the table. She awoke refreshed and ready to start the rest of her long day. She told Marilyn that she learned to do this on her many field trips because she never knew where her next bed was going to be and had to rely on "quick sleep." People who have the ability to do this (and not all of us can) manage to get refreshed when the rest of us stay crabby and tired.

If you can encourage this behavior in your child it may help later. One of the tricks to encouraging is to do it yourself. As a matter of fact, when there is tension between parents and child due to fatigue it is a good idea if the parent can recognize this and say, "We are both tired, let's stop what we are doing and go lie down for a few minutes." Lie down on the bed or even on the floor and set the alarm for five minutes. The trick is to learn (and to teach our children) that tiredness is what makes us cranky. The answer to tiredness is not better self-control but rest. By the way, quiet music is often a good antidote for crankiness, along with lying down.

Older children often exhaust themselves in school and other activities and this has to be guarded against. The goal is that children should learn to recognize their own fatigue and work out their own ways to prevent or alleviate it (going to bed early before the game, taking a nap after baseball practice, etc.).

There are great differences in sleep requirements, needs, and patterns. Some adults get along on three or four hours of sleep and others are miserable if they get less than eight. The world seems to be divided into night people (owls), and day people (larks). Generally, these are lifelong patterns that do not change; sleep biorhythms are established in childhood and remain for life.

It is important that parents recognize and allow children their own biologic rhythms. This is part of their wonderful uniqueness which you don't wish to change even if you could! However, until they reach adulthood when they may have some control over the hours they work and the hours they sleep, children live in a world in which people generally sleep at night and must get up early in the morning to go to school or work. There are no schools (with the exception of afternoon kindergarten sessions) that start late in the day even though there are some children who might learn better later in the day because of their own biorhythms.

For parents with a child who has difficulty going to sleep on time and getting up on time for school we offer the following suggestions: 1) As soon as possible give such children responsibility for getting themselves up. Show them how to set an alarm clock or clock radio. 2) Let the child have sleep-in time on weekends without any concern that it will cause the child to become lazy or slothful. 3) Help the child learn tricks on how to fall asleep early. One of the reasons that owls have such difficulty getting up in the morning is that their body rhythms do not permit them to fall asleep until very late at night. Sometimes this can be partially reversed when the parents figure out what promotes sleep in the individual child. 4) Find a way to avoid conflicts and fights about bedtime, since the conflict itself will stimulate the child, thus making sleep more difficult. 5) Most children (and adults) can stay up later on weekend nights and compensate by sleeping later Saturday and Sunday. However, a few severe owls are only able to stay entrained to a normal work or school schedule if they go to bed at the same time every night of the week. This is called Delayed Sleep Phase Syndrome and its victims suffer the symptoms of severe jet lag.

Generally, you will be lucky if you have the same sleep pattern as your child. If not there may be conflicts. Behavioral modification does help—theirs or yours.

Sleep Disturbances

Sleep disturbances in the preschooler tend to be quite common. Some children have difficulty going to sleep, others waken in the night, have nightmares, don't want to sleep in the dark, or extend their ritualistic presleep behavior. Most of these can be easily handled with a little extra cuddling and understanding and, of course, waiting for the developmental maturation that will occur.

A recent study confirmed the very ritualistic presleep behavior of preschoolers.[32] Bedtime routines usually involve diaper change or toileting, a drink, a song or story, good night kisses, etc. Sixty-six percent of preschoolers in the study sometimes took more than thirty minutes for this routine. Many children fell asleep with the light on and required a treasured object in bed with them. Curtain call behaviors, including requests for another drink or another good night kiss, are much more common among older preschool children than younger ones. Night awakening at least once a week occurred in over half of the preschoolers and about a third of children awakened at least once every night. Nightmares were rare until age three but nearly a third of the older children exhibited this behavior at least once every two weeks.

There is probably a neurophysiological basis for sleep pattern changes in the preschool years. In addition, bedtime rituals and delaying tactics, as well as nightmares, could reflect the child's conflicts over separation or individuation and the Oedipal phase of development. Anne's grandmother felt these behaviors represented adaptions on the part of young children to the "unnatural conditions" in which they are required to sleep, i.e., alone or between cold sheets. We both have felt sad that at the very time in life when one most needs to be cuddled and to have someone close, our culture dictates that the child should sleep alone. We both enjoy sleeping with our husbands and encourage our children to look forward to their adult life when they can have a permanent partner. In the meantime, Anne freely lets her children into her bed or joins them in theirs if they wake needing comfort and company.

There are some sleep disorders we should mention briefly. Night terrors, which are rare, are different from the ordinary nightmare or anxiety dream. The child with a night terror sits upright in bed, screams, stares at something and is in obvious distress. It can take up to ten minutes to fully waken and console such a child who then immediately falls asleep. There is very little dream recall; in the morning the child doesn't remember the attack.

Sleepwalking is not as rare as one might think. It is estimated that 15 percent of children between five and twelve have walked in their sleep at least once. It is more common in males than females. Some children just sit up in bed and appear glassy-eyed, others actually walk. The episode may last from a few seconds to a half hour or more and the child doesn't remember the event. Frequent sleepwalking can be a serious problem if the child walks into dangers or out the door. The danger can be decreased with an outside lock on the child's door, or, more controversially, with medications. Usually, as the child gets older the episodes disappear.

Enuresis (bed-wetting) is often considered a sleep disorder. Polysomnographic monitoring (a multiple-channel sleep record of brain waves, eye movements, and activity) shows what happens in an enuretic episode in a child. This usually occurs up to three hours after falling asleep, just before the child enters the first REM sleep period. The child demonstrates body movement, increased heart rate, an erection in males, and decreased electrical skin resistance (sweating) followed by urination. For several minutes after the start of the episode, children are difficult to awaken, do not remember the event, and do not report a dream. Developmental maturity cures most of these cases.

Just as we want mealtimes to be pleasurable, and give rise to pleasant interactions, most of us would love harmonious bedtimes. Presleep rituals, singing songs together, reading stories, rocking in the rocking chair, all can be pleasurable for both parents and child. However, there is often a great deal of parent/child conflict over sleep. Bedtime, especially when the parent as well as the child is feeling cranky or when individual rhythms are in conflict, can be less than fun. Once again, we have nothing but commonsense suggestions that you have probably already thought of yourself. The long-range goal is not to worry about the fact that the child is not getting to sleep on time tonight, but to see that children develop a certain sensitivity to the care of their own bodies, which includes noticing fatigue and getting enough sleep. In adults today, sleeping pills are among the most frequently used drugs, which suggests that many of us didn't learn to relax and sleep during childhood.

EXERCISE

No one had to worry about exercise during the time when all the children worked on the farm as soon as they could walk. Now fewer of us live on farms, child labor has been outlawed, and there are autos and buses to take our children everywhere. Many of our children do not get enough exercise for good physical fitness.

Physical fitness reflects the amount of physical work that you do. Physical work comprises all body movement—even setting the table and eating. Exercise is more vigorous physical work, and the more that we do, the more fit our entire bodies will be.

There is a physiological reason why exercise is good for us. The act of physical exertion obligates our bodies to get more oxygen, so we breathe more deeply and our hearts pump faster and harder. Both the lungs and the heart become "stronger" and more fit because they have performed more work. In addition, exercise keeps our joints limber and our muscles stronger. Exercise also benefits the mind. People who exercise report they sleep better, concentrate better, and have less emotional tension in their lives—or at least a better tolerance for it.

There are three kinds of exercise. One kind benefits the cardiovascular system by increasing the heart rate. This includes such things as fast walking, jogging, swimming, tennis. The second kind is specific muscle training, such as provided in calisthenics and weight training. The third kind is competitive athletics, which builds a competitive spirit and exercises the body.

Encourage exercise in your children! It is good for you too!

Can Babies Exercise?

You can, in fact, start "exercising" your baby very early. During the first few months of infancy, babies develop the reflexes and coordination they will use all their lives. First the baby gains control of the muscles of the eyes, then the neck muscles to control the head. With grasping comes the development of eye/hand coordination. Finally, the legs develop for crawling and walking.

The first thing that babies need to develop their muscles, interestingly enough, is human contact. Babies need faces and objects to look at so that coordination of the eyes and the head can start early and naturally. In order to strengthen kinesthesia, which is the ability to recognize body positions, it is recommended that the parents playfully hold the child in different ways, first in one arm, then the other, on the side, on the back, up in the air, and even upside down.

Proprioception is defined as perception of stimuli produced within an organism. Proprioceptors in our muscles tell us where that muscle is and what it is doing at any given time. A good place to help develop proprioception in your baby is in water. You can partially submerge your baby in warm water during the bath. Infants have an active swimming reflex until they are about four months old.

A good way to get babies to move their whole bodies is to avoid binding clothing. Another way is toys—baby jumpers are fun and help develop leg and back muscles. When your baby starts to crawl, the baby should be encouraged to crawl over and under and around objects. The same thing is true with walking. Expose the child to different surfaces such as inclines, declines, rough surfaces, etc. Kindergyms or exercise programs for infants and young children are held at Y's and at some good day care centers.

You may wish to look at *The Baby Exercise Book*, written by a French woman with a doctorate in the field of kinesiotherapy who runs a center for infant physical development.[33] The book shows you how to perform passive exercises to foster relaxation, "gymnastics," and preparation for walking. There are basic principles for infant exercises which are simple and fun. First, few or no clothes—let your baby move unencumbered by fabric. Second, the stroking, loving movements you probably instinctively made with your hands when you were introduced to your baby at birth can be extended to infant massage. Systematically stroke your baby front and back (baby lotion can be used but it is not necessary). Often this relaxes a tense baby. Since babies enjoy massage, it pleasurably helps them become aware of the whole body. Third, encourage your baby to reach and turn and crawl.

Exercise in Toddlers and Preschoolers

When your toddler begins to walk, all kinds of exercises can be built into daily life. The age of your child, of course, will determine what motor skills are in place. Creeping, standing, and walking are all achieved at specific times within fairly small ranges. True running occurs when the child can maintain balance without a foot on the ground. It is not until about age four that the "runner" can stop, start, and turn with any degree of smoothness. Jumping is not possible until about twenty-seven months, when the child can jump up and down on both feet or do a one-foot leap. Balancing while jumping—such as the standing broad jump—does not occur until about age four. Throwing a ball starts when the infant can release an object (about six months) but goes through four stages. It is not until between ages five and six when the child learns to shift weight bearing and "follow through" that a good throw develops. A real overhand throw doesn't occur until six or later—and girls sometimes never develop this.

Encourage "rough and tumble" play among toddlers. It is good for them. Indeed, there is evidence that the young monkey who has been deprived of an opportunity for rough-and-tumble play with other young monkeys does not develop into a well-adjusted adult monkey.

Walk and run with your child; teach your child the fun of jumping, hopping, and skipping. Body image is important and it is fun to dance or try dance movements in front of a mirror, especially to music.

Balancing is essential to exercise. You don't need a gym as you can always find a place where the child can walk along a narrow low rail or line to practice balancing. By three a child can walk the length of a line for ten feet. Until a child is about five, however, skiing and skateboarding are too difficult because the child doesn't have the muscle strength, though the beginning balance skills are in place.

Because running skills are important to all sports, run with your child and make a game out of stopping and starting and running fast or slow. Climbing should be encouraged while paying attention to safety. Throwing and catching are important in many sports so that playing with a ball is both fun and helpful to future activities. Help the child develop coordination. A jump rope can be introduced when the child is three and a half, by lettting the child jump over a rope held low to the ground. With two people holding the rope, the rope is moved from side to side as the child approaches, then the rope can be circled completely over the child's head.

Exercise in Older Children

As the child gets older, family participation in games is helpful. Such exercise both provides a good example and helps teach children new ways of using their bodies. Have a family fun run, go on walks together, swim at the local pool, etc. Encourage early participation in *your* sport. If you love tennis, by all means buy your child a racquet. If cross-country skiing or swimming is your thing, introduce your children to this when they are young. Your enthusiasm is a good teacher. Families that exercise together seem happy both while they are doing it and during other times—almost as though exercise eliminates or "burns off" interpersonal or interfamily tensions.

Another thing parents can do is to encourage their children to learn a *variety* of sports. Expose your children to all you can think of and afford. You never know where your child is going to end up. Your child may love tennis but live in an area where there are no tennis courts or may love to swim but may end up in a climate where that's expensive or impossible. A variety of sport interests when the child is young provides more choices when the child becomes an adult.

When your child is older, say between six and twelve, structured games and sports are available in school and in organizations such as Little League. By about age six, children begin to compare themselves with other children in sports skills. By ten most are ready for contact sports. It is suggested that if you want to develop sports skills and love of exercise in your school-age child, you set aside regular times for sports and make it fun. Instruction in sports is important and can be quite cheap if done through neighborhood recreation facilities. Participation in organized athletics, provided they don't overemphasize competition, is fine, especially for the "natural" athlete or the child who truly wants to participate. Running laps or other conditioning exercises should not begin before school age although cardiovascular endurance can be strengthened with family fun runs.

Your role as a parent also includes being a role model. If you have a healthy attitude toward life and exercise, so will your children. You also will have to provide understanding and support for the slow child whose sports skills development is below that of his or her peers. Non-athletic girls may particularly need encouragement to get enough exercise, since peer pressure to do so may be less.

Exercise and Sports in Schools

School sports programs should provide proper conditioning, good coaching, good equipment facilities, good officiating, and competent medical care. Doctors and coaches need to know three things in the medical evaluation of a child as far as school athletics is concerned: 1) Is the growth and development equal to that of peers? 2) Is the boy or girl physically qualified for the sport? and 3) If there are restrictions, which sports would be appropriate?

In boys the stage of puberty helps predict the individual's capacity in strength, endurance, coordination, and agility. In girls, menarche is the time when these capacities increase.

Sports are divided into strenuous with contact (hockey, wrestling, football); strenuous with limited contact (basketball, soccer); strenuous with non-contact (gymnastics, swimming, track); moderately strenuous (baseball, badminton); non-strenuous (archery, bowling, riflery). It is felt that almost every child with reasonably normal mental and physical status can participate in *one* of these sports at school. And children whose mental or physical status is not normal still need exercise—but many need special planning to get it.

Competitive Sports

As children get older, there are both advantages and disadvantages to competitive sports. An overly competitive situation could cause excessive stress in the child. However, complete avoidance of competitive sports is a deprivation. Marilyn was against Little League because she felt children should play on their own and not be manipulated and managed by grown-ups. But her son adored Little League. Little League may foster excessive parental involvement in winning, but the concept of learning about team play and competition *is* important.

If your child is a natural athlete, competitive athletics in and outside school may be an important entry to a future career.

Both schools and the leagues for organized sports pay a good deal of attention to the possible dangers of competitive athletics on children. Pediatricians also have voiced concern. There are three possible physical hazards resulting from excessively competitive sports. One is that both physical and psychological stresses could adversely affect the child's development. The second is that repeated stress could hurt a body part, such as the knee or an elbow, and could actually impair growth of a limb. Three, there could be a forceful blow that could do serious or permanent damage.

There does not seem to be any evidence that physical growth of the young athlete is impaired. Young athletes of both sexes do have less body weight as fat and more as muscle. There have been eating and sleep disturbances reported after Little League games, but these were also found in children who were in a school play or concert. It seems to be related to being "on stage," rather than the sport itself.

It is especially important in children to prevent injuries to the epiphyses or growing plates of the bone. Approximately, 13 percent of athletic injuries which occurred in children fifteen and under were injuries of the growth plate but the likelihood of a growth disturbance following each injury was small. In our opinion, competitive football should not be played until puberty as injuries may occur before the child has sufficient muscle mass to protect against them. Also, boxing is dangerous at *any* age.

Socialization for Sports

Interestingly enough, sexual socialization plays a great part in sports in school and later life. An excellent review of sex differences showed most of our sexual stereotypes were unsubstantiated.[34] The ones that could be substantiated were that girls have greater verbal ability and peripheral vision while boys excel in visual and spatial ability and males demonstrate more aggressive behavior.

Sex differences in play behavior have been observed for a long time. A baby is usually handled differently by its parents, depending on whether it is a boy or a girl. Even in infancy girls show less exploratory behavior while boys play with toys that require gross motor activity and do more toy banging in nursery school. Girls at play use more fine motor manipulation while boys do more gross motor play. There are also differential toy preferences. It is hard to tell how much of these differences are innate, as opposed to coming from gender stereotyped parental treatment of the infant and different social expectations for boys and girls.

Parents also have differential expectations of their children in sports. Sports are much more likely to be encouraged for boys than for girls. Fathers encourage certain motor abilities in their sons, such as wrestling, and other gross motor skills. It is not surprising, therefore, that play behavior of children differs by sex. One study, for example, found that 40 percent of girls were outdoors for less than a quarter of their playing time, compared to 15 percent of boys.[35] Boys ages nine to eleven spend more time in free play, while girls the same age are more often in organized activities and chores.[36] Also, boys play farther away from home than girls do.[37] Obviously, if you play indoors, your body movement is more restricted than if you play out of doors. There is no question that by puberty, games and sports are more a male pursuit than a female one, although this may change as women become more interested in exercise and raise their daughters differently.

Parents are instrumental in whether their sons and daughters participate in organized sports or not. Most excellent athletes, male or female, had parents and coaches who encouraged them. Although schools also play a role, schools have in the past emphasized cooperative play for girls and competitive play for boys. Parents of a "natural" female athlete may want to work closely with the school to assure that their daughter is not getting cheated.

The Girl Athlete

There is no evidence that the young female is harmed by competitive sports. Indeed they may help her deal with our competitive society. Sports during menstruation is perfectly all right. Exercise does *not* damage reproductive organs. Indeed, the reproductive organs of women are internal and less likely to be damaged than those of men. Breasts could be injured in contact sports but this occurs very rarely. Former women athletes have normal pregnancy and childbirth with some indication of shorter labor and faster return to prepregnancy activities.

Occasionally, girls in vigorous training will not menstruate, which is related to the replacement of body fat by muscle. The mean age of menarche is significantly later in athletes and ballet dancers and menstrual irregularity and/or cessation of periods are both found more frequently in athletes than non-athletes.[38] Girl athletes, as well as boys, need proper conditioning, proper coaching and supervision, appropriate equipment, and safe facilities, as well as access to adequate medical care.

Interestingly enough, before the age of ten or twelve, girls and boys test about the same in specific motor skills and general athletic ability (except for softball throw).[39] After puberty, most boys become more active and most girls more sedentary. We know that sedentary lifestyles lead to deterioration of general fitness in the parameters of strength, muscular endurance, and cardiovascular endurance, and we also know that a sedentary existence leads to the accumulation of body fat. All of this can happen to girls at puberty but it also happens to men in mid-life when their activity patterns decrease.

When one measures the female and the male *trained* athlete there seems to be little difference in strength, endurance, and body composition. The male has greater upper body strength, although lower body strength is equal. Obviously, the key to this lack of difference is frequent exercise and good conditioning for the female athlete.

Scholastic sports have changed dramatically from the little one-room schoolhouse days, with a marked increase in girls' participation. Currently there are twenty-six officially recognized interscholastic competitive sports for boys in American schools and twenty-five for girls.

The Handicapped Child

What about handicapped children? Can they participate in sports? There is no question that physical activity should be encouraged in children with both chronic illness and with mental and motor retardation. A recent study of Down syndrome children showed that an exercise program enabled boys with Down syndrome to reach almost a normal strength and endurance level.[40] Studies have been done with retarded children and on those with cerebral palsy, showing that individualized exercise programs can be beneficial physically, psychologically, and socially to such children and should be encouraged whenever possible.

Children with asthma can also benefit by an exercise program. In a distance running program for fifteen children with severe chronic asthma, their clinical status and need for treatment did not worsen and their fitness definitely improved. Positive results of exercise were also found in overweight children and children with diabetes and cystic fibrosis.

STRESS MANAGEMENT

Stress is defined as physical, mental, or emotional strain or tension. These external or internal pressures trigger physiologic changes in the body. All humans experience and perceive stress, even babies. We agree with stress researchers that there is an optimal level of stress. Too much stress can hurt us, both physically and mentally. Perhaps too little stress leaves us bored and also less able to handle a later stress when it does occur.

Determining the optimal level of stress for each person or each child is difficult. Ideally, the environment should provide an amount of stimulation and stress which can be mastered—stress without "distress." Remember there are stressful households that accomplish a lot; calm households that acomplish lots; stressful households that accomplish nothing; and calm households that accomplish nothing. Somewhere in the middle of this matrix is probably the best place to be.

Some human events, such as the loss of a loved one, will always be stressful. To a child, change of schools, the birth of a sibling, parental divorce, or a move to a new neighborhood can be markedly stressful. The way children handle stress is very varied, based partially on their own genes, which in part determine whether they are anxious or calm children, and also based on the cultural and familial clues they have picked up from their environment. The degree to which an event is stressful is very much dependent on the age and developmental stage of the child. Psychiatrists feel that a single stressful event, unless extreme, is less harmful than repeated episodes of stress.

Reactions to Stress

Symptoms of stress reaction in children vary tremendously from emergence of previous patterns (regression) to exacerbation of existing maladaptive behaviors to the appearance of new ones. Certain symptoms are likely to occur in a given developmental stage. In infancy, stress is most apt to cause biological functional changes such as appetite and sleep disturbances or apathy and withdrawal. Older stressed children often become either hyperactive and restless or sad and dejected. Adolescents are like adults: some display depression while others have physical symptoms or complaints like headaches, bellyaches, loss of energy, loss of appetite, sleep disturbance, or the use of drugs or alcohol.

The family can influence how the child reacts to stress. As most life events will impose some degree of stress that is shared by the family, the way the family responds and supports the child may determine the outcome. There is no question that with severe emotional trauma, almost all children will become symptomatic as will almost all adults. Reassurance that this is normal can be very helpful.

A cluster of behaviors and attitudes found in stress-resistant children include optimism, adaptability, and a sense of control over their environment. As pointed out by Alayne Yates, we can foster these attitudes in our children through teaching them problem-solving skills.[41] Further, if a stressful life event has occurred, we can help the child develop a sense of power over external events by encouraging the child to talk about and play out the event. Helplessness to a degree is learned behavior; so is mastery. As youngsters find that they can achieve mastery and control over their environment even under conditions of stress, coping with stress gets easier. However, levels of stress tolerance vary with age, the individual, and the meaning of an event to an individual. One child may come unglued over something that a sibling can tolerate quite well.

One of the most important things we both have learned in our own lives is how to handle stress in ourselves. First, how to recognize stress, and second, what to do about it. The clue is to get in touch with your own feelings and find out what is *really* bothering you. With dramatic external stresses like earthquakes or the loss of a loved one, what's bothering us is easy to figure out, but it can be more difficult to figure out the reason we are feeling down sometimes is

because something happened—at work or at home—that we are not happy
with.

Relaxation Techniques

Mary Howell[42] notes that the message society gives children is that achieving is valued, daydreaming is almost shameful so you do it in private, and
relaxation must be paid for with work. In point of fact, children who learn how
to relax are promoting their health in a very positive way.

There are stress relaxation techniques that are useful for children as well as
for adults. Exercise or running when you are feeling down or anxious can be
helpful for both parents and children. Hot liquids like cocoa are soothing. Hot
baths can be very relaxing. Imagine the following scenario with a tired, cranky
toddler and a tired, cranky mother. The wise mother says, "We both feel pretty
bad, let's soak away all our meanness by taking a bubble bath together." This is
better than a confrontation or clash which only adds to both parties' crankiness.

Time spent rocking small children is great for *both* parent and child.
Massages and backrubs are wonderful tension-reducers and children can be
taught to reciprocate at a very early age. We also recommend music and dance.
You can also "symphony conduct" to music on TV, radio, or records. This is
great exercise. A good way to both exercise and get rid of tension is to put on a
record or the radio. You and your child can do any kind of dance steps you like
together in front of a mirror.

As the child gets older, there are ways of teaching children to get in touch
with their own feelings.[43,44] Try interpretive comments like, "I think you are
feeling cranky. Do you know why? Let's try and figure it out together." The
older child, as well as the parent, can be encouraged to keep a diary. Sometimes
when people write down feelings they understand them better and the feelings
lose their painfulness. You can also remember what brought those feelings on
when you reread the diary at a subsequent date.

You can teach your child how to deal with anger—a major cause of tension
and stress. The three cardinal rules about anger are: 1) Don't hurt people or
property. 2) Express your anger in ways that don't do that. 3) When you calm
down a bit, *use* your anger as a motivator to problem-solve (just like you use pain
as a motivator to find out and fix what is wrong).

Discharging anger by pounding pillows can sometimes help a young child,
especially if you make a game out of it while teaching that pounding cannot be
done on brother's head.

We are great believers in taking some action when angry. You yourself as
well as your child can pound a pillow and yell, or roll up a magazine and hit the
table. Hitting a ball is a good anger valve. As the child gets older teach the child
to scream in the shower (a good place to scream those words which would hurt

another person if they were heard) or to write angry thoughts on a piece of paper, then rip the paper up into tiny pieces and throw them away.

Indeed, many techniques can be as successfully used in children as in adults. Behavior modification, biofeedback, yoga, relaxation techniques with feedback, conditioning, relaxation, breathing exercises, and deep breathing have all been tried in children with good results.

You can also encourage children who can't yet write to draw or paint in order to express their feelings. Anne's cousin Mary remembers her daughter at age five got furious at Grandmother, drew a *very* angry caricature of her, and slid it under her door. Grandmother loved it because the picture expressed the child's anger in an acceptable and creative way.

There are specific relaxation exercises that you and your child can learn together. First, and easiest, is deep breathing. When you feel tense, sit or lie down and breathe deeply for a few minutes. Tell yourself and your child you are both breathing out all the bad feelings and breathing in good feelings.

One of the best ways to learn muscle relaxation is by tensing specific groups of muscles so you know when they are relaxing. You and your child lie on the floor together. First tense and relax face muscles; lift your head to tense neck muscles and then let your head fall back; press your shoulders down and then relax. Stretch arms out and relax; lift buttocks up and relax; stretch legs out and relax. By then you should feel limp and relaxed. Stay relaxed for a few moments.

Meditation is useful for some people and can be self-taught and also taught to older children. Sit quietly with your eyes closed in a quiet room. Repeat a word or a sound that has no meaning to you—or even your own first name, which becomes amusingly meaningless with repetition (children love this). Concentrate on that word or sound. The goal is to empty your mind of everything (especially stress) by filling it with only that sound. Doing this for even a few minutes a day actually has positive physiological effects. The alpha waves of your brain are activated, which promotes a beneficial state of relaxation—for your muscles as well as your mind.

Marilyn has a favorite three-part recipe for curing the blues: 1) No matter how bad you feel, go through the motions and do what you are supposed to do that day even though you would rather crawl into bed and pull a blanket over your head. 2) Get some vigorous physical exercise until you are exhausted. 3) Give yourself a present every day that you get through when you would really rather do nothing. The present can be anything from a candy bar (we think depression is worse than cavities), to a new scarf, record, book, or watching "Gilligan's Island" reruns on television. Anne adds: 1) *Talk* about your feelings with someone who cares and can empathize—even if it's by long distance phone. If your family is caught up in the same stress, they may be needy instead of supportive, but a relative or friend from out of town may be of help. 2) Look at all the things you are supposed to do, and decide which are both *do-able* and *essential.* Give yourself permission to cut back on non-essentials at a time of stress, while feeling pride at getting the essentials done. Let other people help you!

Children can be taught the same coping techniques, in an age-appropriate way: 1) some vigorous exercise or play; 2) emotional support; 3) a treat to oneself; 4) someone to talk about it with. Fortunately, stressed or depressed children can often enjoy a treat or distraction better than many depressed adults. Unfortunately, this fact leads some adults to think the child's depression isn't real.

YOUR CHILD'S ENVIRONMENT

Health maintenance includes paying attention to the environment of our children. The air that we breathe and the water that we drink may contain substances that are harmful to our health. Some of these contaminants can cause potential physical problems. On the other hand, we have to be concerned about the psychological effects of fear of the environment. Parents, however, have the responsibility of dealing with the political and social issues involved in keeping our environment healthy.

Air Pollution

Even on a clear, crisp day in the mountains, far from any cities, the air we breathe contains pollutants. Normal air contains oxygen, nitrogen, argon, carbon dioxide, and water vapor. What else is in our air? First of all, there are three kinds of "natural" substances that make up the particles in our air. The first kind comes from volcanic eruptions, meteoric dust, and natural radiation. Organic decay substances, which result from putrefaction of vegetable and animal materials, make up the second category of particles, and the third is a sea spray, which puts salt in our air.

Then there are all the pollutants that are a by-product of civilization. Ever since humans discovered fire, the effects of our ingenuity and inventiveness have spread into the air. In addition to creating smoke and other products of fuel combustion, we also invented the automobile. It is currently estimated that 60 percent of our total air pollutants comes from the automobile (exhausts and the pollution which results from making and scrapping cars). The petroleum industry further contributes to air pollution through refinery pollutants and jet airplanes. A textbook called *Health Effects of Environmental Pollutants* lists dozens of compounds that get into our air.[45] These are categorized into compounds from combustion (coal, wood, gas, fuel oil, refuse incineration); the metallurgical industry; the chemical industry; the construction industry (asphalt, cement); and the food, agriculture, and household industries (feed and grain mills, dry cleaning, cotton ginning, etc.). Virtually every industrial process invented leads to air pollution, although the worst industries are construction, mining and smelting, chemical production, and food processing. Obviously the closer one lives to where these products are being made, the higher the risk of breathing a high concentration of the toxic substances.

We are becoming increasingly aware of a new type of air pollution: internal pollution in our own households. Indoor air pollution results from cooking, heating, household sprays, formaldehyde and other materials used in construction, *and* cigarette smoke. There is no question that the interior of a household where there is a good deal of smoking is polluted. This may have an effect not only on the smoker's health but also on the health of others in the household— especially children.

Another risk to children comes from the occupations of their parents and other members of the household. Parents who work with asbestos or lead can carry home enough of these environmental contaminants from the workplace to adversely affect the child. Asbestos can cause a lung disease called interstitial fibrosis, and also a pleural malignancy called mesothelioma. Over a third of 378 family members of asbestos manufacturing workers had X-ray abnormalities of their lungs and five wives or daughters had mesothelioma.[46] Children of lead workers had higher blood lead levels than those of non-lead workers. Preventive measures to reduce the amount of workplace contaminants should be carried out. Showers and changing clothes help but the clothes must also be laundered outside the home. As the fetus may be even more susceptible to environmental hazards, the mother's occupational status during pregnancy is also of concern. Pregnant women who work in occupations known to be hazardous (such as an X-ray technician) should decide with their doctors whether the fetus is at risk. A specialist in occupational medicine can be consulted if occupational risk is unusual or unclear.

Parents have a responsibility to protect children from the adverse effects of air pollution. If there is an "air pollution alert" in your community, children should be kept indoors with windows closed. Conversely, homes should be well ventilated when sprays or solvents are being used.

There is now good evidence that infants exposed to parental smoking absorb nicotine[47] and that children exposed to smoking have more respiratory illnesses and poorer pulmonary function.[48,49,50]

The most important thing parents can do is not permit themselves or others to smoke in a home or car where children breathe. If you can't quit, at least have a well-ventilated "smoking room" which the children do not enter or go out of doors to smoke.

Water Pollution

Water pollution is also a long-standing problem. Humans always dumped wastes into water. Waters receive both sewage and the products of civilization from the factory and home: industrial wastes and detergents. The major water pollutants are inorganic phosphates and nitrates which are not removed from sewage when it is treated. Water polluted with sewage also contains water-borne viruses like hepatitis, and bacteria. Industrial pollutants as well as waste heat from factories affect the water and carcinogens such as asbestos may be found in water.

Another problem is sewage contamination of recreational water. The nitrates present in our water get there in part because we continually flush human fecal material into our waters. As noted before, you can ask your health department about the safety of your drinking water, but vigilance is in order. Children can also become infected from *swimming* in contaminated water. If you have any question about the pollution of a lake, the ocean, or a pool, your local health department should be able to advise you.

Food Pollution

We have already talked about bacterial contamination of food. Food can also contain other contaminants such as the pesticide DDT, which has saved many lives by getting rid of insects that either kill people (malaria) or starve them (by eating their food). Unfortunately the DDT itself remains in the environment for a very long period of time. It is stored in fat so that when humans, who are at the top of the food chain, eat DDT-contaminated food it is stored in human fat. When the St. Lawrence Seaway was opened and the fish population of alewives exploded, the coho salmon (a wonderful sport and eating fish) was introduced to eat the alewives. DDT washed from the farms into the lakes, the alewives developed high levels of DDT, the coho ate the alewives, and those coho became unfit for human consumption because of high DDT levels. By the way, DDT has also been found in breast milk, because it is concentrated in fat. Mercury has also been found in Great Lakes fish. A toxic fire retardant called PBB, thanks to an industrial accident, was eaten by Michigan cows and found its way into the Michigan hamburger and also into the breast milk of 90 percent of the mothers who lived in the lower peninsula of Michigan. Take notice of local warnings about foods that may have become contaminated.

Noise Pollution

Noise pollution is another problem. Once again human inventiveness and technology play a role. Today we have jet planes, supersonic planes, rock music, firecrackers, snowmobiles, bulldozers, jackhammers, road traffic, and industrial noise. There is good evidence that noise levels above the suggested maximum of fifty-five decibels can damage the ear permanently and irrevocably. The worst kind of noise is both loud and long-lasting and most people who are exposed to that kind of noise (for example, those who help jet airplanes leave the runway) wear ear protection.

Noise can affect the body as do other stresses like pain and vibration. Hormonal changes and a rise in blood pressure have been described with exposure to excessive noise.

Pediatricians are especially concerned about children and adolescents because of their propensity for listening to rock and other music at a loud level. Children also like to wear stereo headsets, which give the loud noises a direct conduit into the middle ear and cannot be monitored by the parents. We suggest parents pay attention to the noises their children are exposed to. Quality protective gear should be worn for noisy sports (trapshooting, for example) and every effort should be made to keep the stereos at safe rather than thundering levels.

Radiation

Radiation is another potential hazard. Naturally occurring radiation is present in our environment from the earth itself, the sun, and the stars. Our bodies contain small amounts of naturally occurring radioactive isotopes. We are exposed to radiation from these sources throughout our lives. We may also be exposed to human sources of radiation. For most of us the most important human source of exposure is from medical X-rays and radioactive isotopes used for diagnostic tests. Production and use of nuclear fuel in power plants, ships, and spacecraft can potentially cause exposure to radiation in the case of accidents. However, normally operating nuclear plants are of negligible health significance in terms of escaped radioactivity.

Atmospheric testing of nuclear weapons, in contrast, has caused a demonstrable increase in background radiation. "Fallout" from weapons testing refers to radioactive isotopes that are released by the explosion, fall to the ground, and then may enter our bodies in the air we breathe, the water we drink, or the food we eat. You probably have heard of a radioactive isotope called strontium 90 that may occur in fallout. Strontium 90 is taken up by growing plants, which are then eaten by cows, which pass the strontium 90 to humans through milk. Strontium 90 in the milk is taken up by the growing bones of infants and children, just like calcium, and exposes the blood-forming cells of the bone marrow to needless and potentially harmful radiation. In order to prevent environmental contamination with substances like strontium 90, nuclear weapons testing must be held to a minimum.

DIAGNOSTIC X-RAYS

Diagnostic X-rays can never be considered absolutely "safe" if one assumes that potential hazards are proportional to dose and that there is no threshold below which we can be absolutely certain that no hazard exists. Thus the decision to order any X-ray or radioactive isotope test must be based on a balance between benefit and potential risk. Some children definitely need X-ray or isotope tests to help the doctor make a diagnosis or follow the course of a disease. Parents have *every right* to ask *every doctor or dentist* whether *every X-ray* exposure is necessary and why.

The Council of the American College of Radiology recommends against "routine" X-rays, for example, a chest X-ray on every child admitted to the hospital.[51] When X-ray examinations of children are necessary, the sex organs should be shielded. Dental X-rays are considered safe provided the equipment is up-to-date and shielding is used. X-ray studies of pregnant women should not be done unless the information to be gained is absolutely necessary, because rapidly developing fetal tissues are very sensitive to X-rays, particularly early in pregnancy. It is reassuring to know that in a study of a large number of children with congenital heart disease who had many X-ray examinations of the heart, there was no greater rate of leukemia or other cancers over the following ten years than in the normal population.[52] However, this does not entirely rule out the possibility that disease could develop later in these children, since we know that high cumulative X-ray exposures in adults have been associated with an increased risk of developing certain cancers. For this reason, and because diagnostic X-rays carry a theoretical risk of genetic damage, there should always be a good medical reason for having any X-ray examination. When there is a good reason, however, X-ray and radioisotope examinations may provide information that cannot be obtained in any other way, and the benefit greatly outweighs the very small risk involved.

HOUSEHOLD RADIATION

Low level radiation also comes to us from color television receivers, luminous dials of clocks and watches, and other luminous signs and markers. But exposure from these sources is minimal, as is the exposure from smoke detectors, whose use we highly recommend.

Color TV sets manufactured today are safe; older models made before the early seventies have high levels of radiation so children should not sit close to the earlier models.

Microwave radiation is theoretically a problem. Microwaves are used in industry and medical diathermy and many homes have microwave ovens. Large doses of microwaves can affect the testicles and the eyes. It is suggested that children be not unduly exposed to microwaves in the home. In the absence of leakage (a damaged door, for example), home microwave ovens have not been shown to be a hazard because microwave radiation does not travel far and is easily shielded. Home microwaves can be tested for leakage either by service dealers or with home testing kits. The heat of food produced in a microwave oven is a *real* hazard.

There is another "wave" that is everywhere in our environment which can be hazardous. Sunlight—ultraviolet wavelength light—can be dangerous, especially in excess. As with most things in life, a little bit of sunshine is good. Sunshine is needed to make our food via photosynthesis and to make vitamin D in our bodies, but too much sun can cause skin cancer as well as skin wrinkles, because repeated exposure to the sun leads to a loss of skin elasticity. Doctors are now recommending that sunscreens (with a high protective rating of fifteen) be used on the exposed skin areas of people, including children, who are out in the sun a good deal. In Arizona where there are few clouds and children play out of doors virtually every day, the wise mother puts sunscreen on her children the way mothers in Minneapolis put on mittens—routinely when the weather warrants it. Some doctors in high sunlight areas advocate putting on sunscreen every morning right after washing your face and brushing your teeth.

Parents and Pollution

There is no question that environmental hazards may be most serious for the young and the unborn. The fetus seems to be more vulnerable to pollutants and drugs like thalidomide. We know the fetus is susceptible to anesthesia, sex hormones, DES, viruses like rubella, organic mercury poisoning, radiation, marijuana, heroin, alcohol, and cigarette smoke. Some pollutants or drugs can cause mutations in genetic material, and thus cause problems in future generations. It's a bit scary because it has been estimated that there are 2 billion synthetic or natural chemicals already and new chemicals are being synthesized at the rate of 4 million a year—many of which could affect fetuses, children, or their gonads (sex glands).

What can a parent do about the child's environment? We have talked about a great many potential hazards. Perhaps you are thinking that it seems hopeless. Is there any place on earth without hazards?

We do *not* want to scare you. It is healthy that the media keep us all aware of our environment—which is the only one we have. There are government agencies (OSHA and the EPA) that handle and monitor environmental problems.

The best advice we can give parents is to develop what we call *informed awareness.* Know what the potential dangers are in your own community, read your newspapers, be prepared for social or political action if necessary. Do not expose your child to unnecessary hazards such as unneeded X-rays. Be an informed, cautious person with appropriate fear and take appropriate action when necessary. Teach your children how to take the same stance, because they need to learn how to protect themselves in the future. Be your own environmental protection agency in your own household. If you or your partner are employed in a hazardous workplace, change your clothes before you come home and launder them outside of the home. Be sure all equipment, like a microwave, is in good working order. Know what is in your water.

One can hear parents asking, "What about unknown or unseen agents lurking out there, whose hazards to our children are not clear?" It's a problem—but actually things are no different now than they were in the past when parents worried about the unknown causes of infectious disease. Our society has conquered many infections. We can lick environmental problems as well and are beginning to do so.

In fact, we *are* cleaning up our air and water. Despite the billions of chemicals that we now have in our environment, never has our mortality rate been so low. Marilyn's father says, with a chuckle, that he can correlate the number of new chemicals synthesized with the decrease in the nation's mortality rate! It is very unlikely that these two things are causally related, but it is comforting to know that chemicals have not caused us, as a population, to die off earlier.

In Anne's opinion, there are so many potential hazards, most of them remote, that one can keep one's sanity best by worrying only selectively. Save your worry for things you can do something about!

Is There Such a Thing as Television Pollution?

Television is a potential pollutant. There is at least one television set in virtually every home in America. Just as the fetus is more susceptible to certain chemicals, Marilyn suspects that the child may be more susceptible than the adult to certain effects of television that could be potentially unhealthy.

In 1983 American TV viewing reached an all-time high with an average daily viewing per household of *seven hours.* Viewing has increased in each year since records were kept.[53]

The average child spends 11,000 hours in the classroom by graduation from high school—but will have watched 15,000 hours of TV! Our children are exposed to 350,000 TV commercials before they are eighteen! The average child will watch 18,000 murders and other acts of violence![54] Someone recently pointed out a person would have to read *all* of Shakespeare's thirty-seven plays to see the same number of violent acts as portrayed in three nights of prime time TV.[55] Even preschoolers watch TV an average of 54 hours per week.[56]

There are also positive effects of TV. Preschool children exposed to certain children's programs such as "Mr. Rogers' Neighborhood," "Sesame Street," or a controlled series of nature and animal films showed positive changes in imaginative play, emotion, concentration, and social interaction. A specific study looking at the correlation between sleep duration and television viewing has shown that TV viewing had little effect on the amount of sleep children get.

One concerned psychiatrist, Michael Rothenberg, has been worried about the effects of television violence on children. In 1975 he summarized a report of 146 articles in behavioral science journals representing 50 studies involving ten thousand children and adolescents from all backgrounds.[57] He found that all studies showed that viewing violence on TV is followed by an increase in aggressive behavior. Research has shown that aggressive behavior is learned by children exposed to TV violence, and they remember what they have learned. There is decreased emotional sensitivity to media violence because repeated viewing desensitizes the child—just as in desensitization behavioral modification therapy. There was no evidence that watching pain or suffering led to a catharsis which might dissipate aggression. Aggression can be inhibited by reminders that it is morally wrong, or by an awareness of the painful consequences to the victim of aggression, but it can also be facilitated by repeated stimuli and by the state of the aggressor. For example, people who are verbally attacked and then exposed to film violence later are more aggressive than those who weren't attacked before being exposed.

Two federal commissions have agreed that television is a contributing factor to violence in society and have asked for immediate action, which has still not taken place.

There is also evidence that television fosters imitative behavior in children, the so-called "Evel Knievel Syndrome."[58] After watching Evel Knievel perform in 1974, many injuries, some of which were serious, were reported in children who imitated his stunts. There is anecdotal evidence that television is also contributing to the marked increase in the number of young Americans who die in motor vehicle accidents, murder, or suicide.

Is TV increasing the violence in our culture? One could debate whether television is a mirror or a model, but it is a little scary to realize that three quarters of the evening prime time shows portray violence up to nearly once every seven minutes. Portrayal of violence goes back to the beginning of art. But there are two major differences between the earlier treatments of violence and the television treatment of violence. Before TV, violence was portrayed as high tragedy or slapstick. Unfortunately, today's TV violence looks very much like ordinary life. Also, television is available to every child, not just the ones who can afford to go to a matinee on Saturday afternoon.

Children who watch television are more sex-stereotypic. Explicit sex on television is also a problem, especially as we know many young children are watching when they are supposed to be asleep. More than 20 million children, between ages two and seventeen, will still be up watching television at 9 P.M., 13 million at 10 P.M., AND 5 MILLION AT 11 P.M.[59] Sixty percent of music videos portray sexual feelings or impulses and soap operas contain 1.5 mentions of intercourse per hour! Also 800,000 homes subscribe to the Playboy channel and "adult" video cassettes make up 15 to 25 percent of sales.[60] Yet while sexual activity is frequently shown, there is no mention of responsible contraception.

Another area of concern about TV is its advertising, which conveys a message to children that they should have every toy they wish, and that their kitchen cupboards should be filled with nothing but candy and sugared cereal. This encourges a materialistic mentality by implying possessions bring success and happiness. Children are very susceptible to TV advertising, which is designed to appeal to them. Television fosters faulty nutritional habits, including faulty dental health, and a sedentary life. TV also encourages a pill mentality because so many adults are seen taking medication in commercials. We suggest parents encourage their children to question slick commercials and to recognize how they are being "sold" to buy a product.

One study found that prime time and children's weekend and daytime programs are dreadful![61] Men outnumber women and almost all the people shown are professionals, law breakers, law enforcers, or entertainers. Crime is ten times more frequent on the screen than in the real world. There are an average of *five acts of violence per hour in prime time* and *eighteen acts per hour in children's weekend daytime programming.* Pain, suffering, or medical help do not seem to follow violence as very few of the victims are shown as requiring treatment. Lots of doctors and nurses and patients are portrayed, but the doctor is almost always male and he seems to have control not only of the health but the emotional and social life of his patient. Eating and drinking or talking about food occurs very frequently. Most of the beverages ingested are alcohol, followed by coffee and tea. Food commercials account for a quarter of the commercials during prime time and children's daytime, with sweet snacks and junk food making up half of the food commercials. Despite this, prime time characters look healthy, sober, and *slim.*

The author of a wonderful book called *The Read-Aloud Handbook,* Jim Trelease outlines the reasons TV impedes the personal growth of children. He sagely points out that TV differs from reading in that it fosters a short attention span (between commercials); TV is antisocial—even when others are in the room, everybody is likely to watch not talk; TV deprives children of their best learning tool, questions; TV cannot portray thinking; TV stimulates an antireading attitude (children will take TV over a book when offered the same story); TV stifles the imagination; TV discourages creative play; TV is addictive.

TV is inversely correlated with the presence of print media in the home. Newspapers, books, and magazines in the home are correlated with the social class of the family. Heavy TV viewing is also related to social class as better educated parents are more likely to have rules about TV and pay attention to the programs their children watch.[62]

Further study of reading and TV revealed that skilled readers could watch TV and read simultaneously while poor readers could not keep up with TV without total absorption.[63] By age twelve, the more TV students watched, the more their total knowledge decreased. High ability children get news from the print media and ask questions about it; low ability children get information from TV and accept what they see.

Marilyn worries about what a colossal waste of time TV is! Think of the hours children lose from those allotted to their learning years. Yes, TV enhances vocabulary acquisition in preschoolers but there is good evidence that it decreases reading grade levels and is probably responsible—in part—for the decline in SAT scores of students who are entering college.

When Marilyn's grandchildren visited recently, they watched TV while their parents and grandparents were having another cup of coffee. Marilyn happened to notice the faces of her two grandchildren, who were sitting close to the TV set with their eyes glued to the screen. Even their eyes did not move! The children were almost in a trance; they looked like zombies. Marilyn had a flashback to her own daughter reading a book when she was the same age: *her* eyes darted back and forth. Although both books and television can be considered sedentary, the enormous passivity of television suddenly struck Marilyn. She feels one of the mistakes she has made as a pediatrician was not to warn parents about the hazards of TV. Anne feels differently, remembering the "zombie" state she got into as a child while reading (which she still does).

Brazelton, one of America's foremost pediatricians, likens the passivity we note in children watching television to the "shutdown" mechanism of a new-born who is exposed to visual overstimulation.[64] Newborns are at first startled by a bright light but then tune it out, shutting down the gateway which admits the stimulus. Children who are what Dr. Brazelton calls "assaulted" and "over-whelmed" by television use this shutdown mechanism and become utterly pas-sive. The set is blasting away, all kinds of horrible things are happening, and the child is almost in a trance. We suggest that if you see your child in such a state, this is a symptom of "televisionitis"—the cure is to remove your child from the passive overstimulation and engage in some active conversation.

Television is also used as an "electronic baby-sitter." When parents are trying to cook a meal, write a paper, or do anything that requires concentration, being able to sit the children in front of something that will entertain them can truly be a godsend. No one will fault you for using this "sitter" on occasion. However, Marilyn remembers a woman she talked to in the Soviet Union, who ran an after-school program for children, saying quite pointedly, "In Russia we consider our children too important to be put in front of a television set after school."

If you have no television in the house at all, you are probably handicapping your child because there are certain programs that the child's peers will be watching, and some teachers assign programs as homework to prepare students for class discussion. Watching educational or public television can broaden chil-dren's horizons. They may hear discussions of issues that you might not think to discuss with the children. A child seeing an old movie can learn something about the real and/or fantasied past. A child whose parents are not highly educated can hear sophisticated discussions of public events. Conversely, a child whose parents are very bookish can learn something about mainstream culture such as sporting events. Everybody can learn geography and contemporary his-tory from watching the news.

We both agree that there is something wrong when children watch televi-sion from morning until night. Marilyn suggests *limiting* TV for preschoolers and children. One woman we know keeps the television in the closet. The children are allowed to view certain programs on Saturday evening when the parents are out and on Sunday morning. The rest of the time the television is in the closet. The children themselves unplug the set and wheel it away as some-one might put away the tennis rackets when the tennis game is over. Other parents have rules: no TV on school nights or no TV until homework is done or only one hour a night, etc.

Anne feels it is not just a matter of limiting TV, but rather a question of what alternative social or helpful or creative activities are available. One grandmother observed sagely that she had never seen a small child prefer TV over personally being read to or told a story.

Be a good role model. If you sit passively in front of the television set all the time or the TV set is always on, your children may pick up this habit. Viewing schedules can be planned with the children. Know the programs and don't watch offensive ones or else talk about why you find them offensive. Don't give in to commercials. Talk about violence when you see it. Remember public television. Talk about commercials and the unreal world they present. Teach your children sales resistance.

There is an organization called Action for Children's Television, which publishes a family guide to children's television. (See "Suggested Readings and Resources.") Parents' groups, teachers, and religious organizations also monitor television programs. There are several organizations you can write to get information about TV.

If your children do watch TV, ophthalmologists say it doesn't matter whether they watch in a dark room or not. But people who use screens a lot (word processor operators) say a lit room is best. A room that is lit is a more normal social environment.

In summary, Marilyn is personally convinced that television is a household environmental pollutant as well as a potential educational tool. She suggests that it be used with extreme caution, as it may be even more damaging to a child than to an adult, who can choose and decide and thus is less vulnerable to being bombarded by the effects of this pollution.

Anne feels Marilyn is overreacting here. Anne feels television, like food, can be harmful or helpful, and that children given a menu of choices can select programs good for them, as they select a diet good for them. Anne also observed that a video recorder, which enables her family to stop the tape to talk, makes TV active rather than passive. A video camera enables the children to make their own tapes, thus adding even more creativity and active control of the medium. She further feels that if children enjoy TV more than school, it might partly be because our society is currently paying much more to hire good talent for the screen than for the classroom.

We *both* feel violence on TV, materialism, and sex stereotyping are unhealthy for children and other living things and need to be counteracted by parental wisdom.

SUGGESTED READINGS AND RESOURCES

NUTRITION/DENTAL NUTRITION

American Academy of Pediatrics, Committee on Nutrition. *Pediatric Nutrition Handbook,* 2nd ed. Elk Grove Village, Ill. 1985.

Brief, technical, but informative.

Boston Children's Hospital with Baker, Susan, and Henry, Roberta R. *Parents' Guide to Nutrition.* Reading, Mass.: Addison-Wesley, 1986.

Useful information.

Cohen, Mindy, and Abramson, Louis. *Thin Kids: The Proven, Healthy, Sensible, Weight-Loss Program for Children.* New York: Beaufort, 1985.

Good recipes for overweight children.

Committee on Nutrition of the Mother and Preschool Child, Food and Nutrition Board, Commission on Life Sciences, National Research Council. *Alternative Dietary Practices and Nutritional Abuses in Pregnancy: Proceedings of a Workshop.* Washington, D.C.: National Academy Press, 1982.

Technical but comprehensive series of articles on alternate diets and nutritional abuses in pregnancy. Also includes review of the hazards of smoking and alcohol in pregnancy.

Howard, Rosanne B., and Winter, Harland S., eds. *Nutrition and Feeding of Infants and Toddlers.* Boston: Little, Brown, 1984.

A fairly comprehensive book on infant feeding written primarily for doctors. May be of interest to parents. Good tables and a long list of references.

Krieger, Ingeborg. *Pediatric Disorders of Feeding, Nutrition, and Metabolism.* New York: Wiley, 1982.

One of the most up-to-date of pediatric nutrition books.

Lansky, Vicki. *Feed Me! I'm Yours.* New York: Bantam, 1981.

Good recipes.

———. *The Taming of the C.A.N.D.Y. Monster.* New York: Bantam, 1978.

More good recipes.

Lappe, Frances Moore. *Diet for a Small Planet.* 10th anniversary ed. New York: Ballantine, 1982.

A thoughtful analysis of the American diet. Some good veggie recipes.

McGuire, Thomas. *The Tooth Trip: An Oral Experience.* New York: Random House–Bookworks, 1972.

Written over a decade ago by a California dentist. Very complete chapters on teeth and dental care both at home and in the dentist's office. Somewhat surprisingly, the author feels diet and hygiene surpass fluoride—a view not held by many.

McLaren, Donald S., and Burman, David, eds. *Textbook of Paediatric Nutrition.* Edinburgh, Scotland: Churchill Livingstone, 1976.

Informative, well-written book.

Robertson, Laurel; Flinders, Carol; and Godfrey, Bronwen. *Laurel's Kitchen.* New York: Bantam, 1978.

Excellent vegetarian recipes and clear explanation of the tasks of vegetarianism (i.e., how to provide good nutrition without meat).

Satter, Ellyn. *Child of Mine: Feeding with Love and Good Sense.* Palo Alto, Calif.: Bull, 1983.

Another easy-to-read book on nutrition for children. Good chapters on regulation of intake and obesity.

Suskind, Robert M., ed. *Textbook of Pediatric Nutrition.* New York: Raven, 1981.

Definitive text. Especially good in the area of infant nutrition, deficiencies and nutrition in diseases of childhood.

Winick, Myron. *Growing Up Healthy: A Parent's Guide to Good Nutrition.* New York: Berkley, 1983.

Renowned pediatric nutrition expert writes for the general public. Not much detail but good overview of infant kidney and gastrointestinal physiology as well as breast-feeding.

EXERCISE

Block, Susan Dimond. *"Me and I'm Great:" Physical Education for Children Three Through Eight.* Minneapolis, Minn.: Burgess, 1977.

Although designed for teachers, this book is also useful for parents. Children *do* have to be taught how to move and exercise. Chapters on movement exploration, rhythm activities, exercises, and games all have useful suggestions for ways parents can help their children enjoy using their bodies.

Lorin, Martin I. *The Parents' Book of Physical Fitness for Children from Infancy Through Adolescence.* New York: Atheneum, 1978.

Very practical, well written, informative. Covers general fitness, nutrition, and specific sports for various ages.

STRESS

Bramson, Robert M., and Bramson, Susan. *The Stressless Home: A Step-by-Step Guide to Turning Your Home into the Haven You Deserve.* Garden City, N.Y.: Doubleday, 1985.

An easy-to-read book providing suggestions for just what the title implies.

Freed, Alvyn M. *TA for Tots.* Vol. 11. Sacramento, Calif.: Jalmar, 1980.

A rather charming read-aloud-with-pictures book which attempts to help very young children understand feelings and interpersonal relationships.

Freed, Alvyn M., and Freed, Margaret. *TA for Kids.* Sacramento, Calif.: Jalmar, 1977.

Transactional analysis for kids—or for adults who want an easy explanation of how people do (and should) interact for themselves or their children.

Goldberger, Leo, and Breznitz, Shlomo, eds. *Handbook of Stress: Theortetical and Clinical Aspects.* New York: The Free Press, 1982.

Technical, very comprehensive.

Kuczen, Barbara. *Childhood Stress: Don't Let Your Child Be a Victim.* New York: Delacorte, 1982.

Somewhat technical but provides a very thorough review of sources of stress in children's and parents' lives—with sensible suggestions.

National Institute of Mental Health. Goldman, Howard, and Goldston, Stephen, eds. *Preventing Stress-Related Psychiatric Disorders*. DHHS Publication No. (ADM) 85-1366. Washington, D.C.: U.S. Government Printing Office, 1985.

Technical but readable. Covers research issues as well as prevention.

Saunders, Antoinette, and Remsberg, Bonnie. *The Stress-Proof Child: A Loving Parent's Guide*. New York: Holt, Rinehart & Winston, 1985.

A sensitive, loving, well-written book with helpful suggestions for parents' own stress as well as children's. Covers the essentials in about two hundred pages.

ENVIRONMENT

Waldbott, George L. *Health Effects of Environmental Pollutants*, 2nd ed. St. Louis, Mo.: C. V. Mosby, 1978.

Easy-to-read book on pollution.

TELEVISION

Action for Children's Television, 46 Austin Street, Newtonville, Md. 02160.

Sponsors "A Family Guide to Children's Television" by Evelyn Kaye (New York: Pantheon, 1977); produced the poster "Treat TV with T.L.C."

Ambulatory Pediatric Association, Office of the Executive Secretary, 1311A Dolley Madison Blvd., McLean, Va. 22101.

Send $1.00 check or money order for brochure "TV and Children."

Liebert, Robert M.; Sprafkin, Joyce N.; and Davidson, Emily S. *The Early Window: Effects of Television on Children and Youth*, 2nd ed. New York: Pergamon, 1982.

Well-written, up-to-date book on TV and children.

Media Action Research Center, 475 Riverside Drive, Suite 1370, New York, N.Y. 10115.

Offers television awareness training workshops open to the public.

Teachers' Guides to Television, 699 Madison Avenue, New York, N.Y. 10021.

Provides study guides to current programs for parents, teachers, and children.

19

CHOOSING HEALTH PROFESSIONALS
FOR YOUR CHILD'S CARE

Scope of Chapter

This chapter will deal with how to choose doctors and other health professionals for your children and will touch on strategies for best utilizing these professionals. We first discuss choosing and using a doctor for children and we will then discuss choosing dentists and mental health therapists. The goal of this chapter is to help parents become comfortable with the responsibility we all have for our children's health. We do this by giving parents information about health professionals, but also by stressing the autonomy parents can and should retain in the professional care of their children.

DOCTORS FOR YOUR CHILDREN

Today's Doctors

What is a doctor? We all know that the answer to that question is that doctors have completed medical school, in most cases have completed training in a specialty and are licensed to practice medicine, which means to prevent, diagnose, and treat disease.

Why are doctors today under fire for not providing what patients want at a time when our health as individuals and as a nation has never been better? There are two reasons: one from the past, one from the present.

Even today doctors inherit the legacy of the witch doctors or the medicine men and women of the past. People thought the witch doctor possessed special abilities to cure them and that the medicine the witch doctor practiced was a special magic. They both feared and revered healers. In the present day, technology with its myriad of superspecialists, diagnostic modalities, and heroic treatments results in distancing between the patient and the doctor. When we are sick we want someone close, someone to hold our hand. However, on reflection, most of us want more. We also want the bounties and blessings of scientific medicine.

Lewis Thomas says it clearly: "The mechanization of scientific medicine is here to stay. The new medicine works. It is a vastly more complicated profession, with more things to be done on short notice on which issues of life or death depend. The physician has the same obligations that he carried, overworked and often despairingly, fifty years ago, but now with any number of technological maneuvers to be undertaken quickly and with precision. It looks to the patient like a different experience from what his parents told him about, with something important left out. The doctor seems less like the close friend and confidant, less interested in him as a person, wholly concerned with treating the disease. And there is no changing this, no going back; nor, when you think about it, is there really any reason for wanting to go back. If I develop the signs and symptoms of malignant hypertension or cancer of the colon or subacute bacterial endocarditis, I want as much comfort and friendship as I can find at hand, but mostly I want to be treated quickly and effectively so as to survive, if that is possible. If I am in bed in a modern hospital, worrying about the cost of that bed as well, I want to get out as fast as possible, whole if possible."[1]

There has been a recent increase in the number of doctors available to provide health care to the American public. Currently, except for very rural areas, there are few towns without a physician.[2] This means we have a heretofore unprecedented availability of doctors to take care of our children and ourselves.

As parents we have a special responsibility to our children to provide them with good medical care, which means choosing a good doctor, using the doctor properly, and communicating with the doctor properly—all on behalf of our children's needs and our own.

Obviously, when you choose any professional, you should find one that is *competent*. It is also important to find one that you feel *comfortable* with and whose practice style is *compatible* with what you want. The old days, when doctors pontificated and patients were supposed to do exactly what the doctor said without question, are gone forever. In the medical care of a child there is a partnership—a three-way partnership—in which all three parties have to work together and be satisfied: the parent, the physician, and the child.

There are two kinds of doctors that take care of children, pediatricians and family practitioners. A *pediatrician* is a doctor who has had three years of specialty residency training in the care of infants, children, and adolescents. Most pediatricians care for children from birth through late adolescence.

About one third of all the children in America are cared for by pediatricians.[3] Over one half of children between ages eleven and eighteen use a pediatrician for medical care.[4] Poor children are likely to have no regular doctor and are less likely to receive care from a pediatrician.

Pediatric care includes checking the newborn; monitoring nutrition and physical growth, as well as all developmental parameters; providing immunizations and screening tests (TB, vision, hearing, urinary tract infection, etc.); care of common illnesses; diagnosis and treatment of the rare, serious illnesses in childhood; providing parental guidance in child rearing; and child and adolescent guidance and counseling.

A *family practitioner* is a doctor who has had at least three years of residency training in the care of families. This doctor is trained to take care of not only children but also adults. In some cases the family practitioner will deliver the child. Because family practice is the broadest of all medical specialties, recertification every six years is required to be sure that the doctor has kept up with advances in both adult and child medicine. *General practitioners* are not the same as family practitioners. They have not received any specialty training, but rather began to practice after one year of internship.

In some areas, care may be provided by *pediatric nurse practitioners*, who are registered nurses with additional training in pediatric nursing. Generally they work in association with a physician. If both the nurse practitioners and the physician are competent and work well together, this kind of team can provide excellent care. The physician will deal with those issues that really need a physician and the nurse generally has more time and ability to answer questions than busy doctors often do. Marilyn feels strongly that a physician should supervise the care of your child whenever possible.

There are other kinds of doctors you may come in contact with. In teaching hospitals, doctors called *"residents"* may care for your child. A resident is a doctor in training who has graduated from medical school and is licensed by the state where he or she is training but only to practice under supervision in the hospital. Some residents will have already passed the state licensing exam and be qualified to practice anywhere in that state. Residencies vary in length and residents may be called first- or second- or third-year residents. In pediatrics they are referred to as PL-1, 2, or 3 (Pediatric Level One, etc.). Senior resident is the term usually given to a resident who has had one or more years of training. The chief resident is just that: the one resident chosen to stay on after the three years of pediatric training are over, to work with the faculty as a teacher/administrator for the residency program.

A *fellow* is a doctor taking a post-residency fellowship, generally in a subspecialty like pediatric cardiology or neonatology. Fellowships may last from one to several years.

The term *intern* is still used to describe house officers (another term for residents) who are in their first year of training right after medical school. The old "internship" became the first year of residency over ten years ago when the internship per se was abolished in favor of three or more years of residency training for virtually all doctors. This coincided with the advent of specialization for everyone, even family practitioners.

An *attending* is a faculty member of a medical school whose role in a teaching hospital is to teach as well as take care of patients. The resident presents cases to the attending and asks the attending for advice on how to manage patients. Attendings come in at least three ranks: assistant, associate, and full professor, with the latter usually being the oldest and most experienced.

These doctors not only take care of patients and teach, but also do research. They are usually at the forefront of medicine in their area of specialization.

In some teaching hospitals your child may also come in contact with medical students. In the past most medical students were taught to introduce themselves to the patient as "Dr. So-and-so." The ethics of this practice has been questioned. At the medical school Marilyn works at, students are prohibited from doing this. They introduce themselves as follows: "I'm Fourth-Year Medical Student Smith. I will do a history and physical on Johnny. Then the resident and I will discuss his case before talking to you."

If you are ever unsure of who's who in the hospital taking care of your child —ASK! Ask both their name and rank. Further ask *what* they are doing. In a hospital very specialized doctors may be helping in the care of your child because of their special training. Generally, however, the overall care of your child's case remains in the charge of the pediatrician. To avoid confusion, write down who is who and what their job is so you can keep track. It's also helpful to know who is doing what so that you know where your questions go.

In non-teaching community hospitals, one does not have these confusions of rank. Your doctor is your own private doctor, or a member of an HMO affiliated with that hospital. The doctor will have met criteria for staff membership.

How do you find out if a physician or practitioner is competent? There are several attributes to look for. First of all, you must make certain the physician is licensed and certified.

"Licensed" means that the physician has graduated from an accredited medical school, has passed an examination acceptable to the state he or she wishes to be licensed in, and has demonstrated no moral or character defects. No physician can practice in any state without a license. A few physicians lose their licenses every year for gross incompetence, unethical behavior, drug addiction, or mental or physical illness thought to be incompatible with carrying out a doctor's responsibilities. In many states, licensure, which must be renewed periodically, is dependent on proof that the physician has attended a certain number of continuing medical education courses.

"Certification" in a specialty means that the doctor has taken the prescribed number of years of postgraduate training (also called residency) for a specialty. The training must take place in a hospital approved for that specific residency training by the Accreditation Council on Graduate Medical Education. Residency training can range in length from three years in pediatrics or family practice to five or six years in child psychiatry or seven years in cardiothoracic surgery. After the residency training, the doctor must also pass an examination in the specialty to be certified.

"Recertification" is a relatively new concept. Family practitioners must sit for a recertification examination every six years. Starting in 1988 certification for pediatricians will be time-limited as it is for family practitioners.

"Hospital Privileges" is another important term. Even though we all hope our children will never need hospital care, we want to know the doctor is able to

admit our child if such care is needed. Hospital privileges generally mean: 1) the doctor is qualified in his or her specialty; and 2) the doctor takes good care of his or her patients in the hospital as evidenced by periodic audits done by the hospitals' quality assurance committee.

"Specialty Societies." Both Marilyn and Anne belong to their respective specialty societies. Marilyn is a Fellow of the American Academy of Pediatrics, which means she is a board certified pediatrician who completed a pediatric residency in an approved hospital. Anne is a Fellow of the American Psychiatric Association. This means she completed residency training, board certification, and continuing medical education requirements, and was nominated by her local and national psychiatric associations for the fellowship, which is awarded for significant professional achievement. Some specialty societies require verification of a specified number of continuing medical education hours per year. Some, as we just mentioned, require reexamination for recertification. All provide courses and meetings to help their members keep up-to-date in their field. However, membership in a society does not always guarantee competence!

Marilyn is a pediatrician, which means she is one of more than twenty-nine thousand doctors who passed the examination given by the American Board of Pediatrics. As we said before, all of these pediatricians received specialty training as pediatric residents and were certified in that specialty by an external examination. Most are also members of the American Academy of Pediatrics. Acknowledging personal bias, Marilyn says that she took her own children to a pediatrician (so did Anne). Marilyn would recommend that others do so, because there is no other specialist trained solely in the care of children.

In addition to general pediatricians, there are pediatric subspecialists. Some of them have their own board certification, which attests to additional years of subspecialty training (called fellowships in some instances) and passage of an additional examination. Examples of pediatric subspecialties are pediatric allergy, pediatric cardiology, pediatric endocrinology, pediatric hematology-oncology (cancer), neonatal-perinatal medicine, pediatric nephrology and pediatric pulmonary medicine.

Other pediatricians are not board certified subspecialists but they "concentrate" in one area. Usually they have had additional training in that field.

There are many non-pediatric specialists who provide superb care for children. There is a special certification in pediatric surgery which requires two additional years of training in pediatric surgery and an examination. Some otolaryngologists (ear, nose, and throat, or E.N.T., specialists), orthopedists (bone and joint doctors), ophthalmologists (eye doctors), etc., have taken extra training in the care of children in their specialty. Some of these surgical specialists see only children but this is rare except in large cities or academic health centers. When a referral is needed to such a specialist, your pediatrician will generally make it for you.

If elective (non-emergency) surgery is recommended for your child, a second opinion is in order if you do not feel comfortable with the diagnosis or proposed treatment. Some say a second opinion should *always* be obtained when non-emergency surgery is recommended. In some instances, this is pretty silly. For example, your child may have been born with a cleft palate and your doctor and the surgeon work together and plan surgery when the baby is a year old. You like both doctors and respect their judgment. Why bother to get a second opinion? On the other hand, if your doctor refers you to an E.N.T. surgeon who recommends an elective tonsillectomy, a second opinion is in order.

If your child is healthy and develops no serious or chronic illness, your general pediatrician is superbly trained to monitor your child's growth and development, to administer all necessary immunizations, and to care for the child's minor and major illnesses, both those that do and do not require hospitalization.

If your child has a problem that needs care by another specialist or pediatric subspecialist, virtually every general pediatrician will make a referral. In some instances, the pediatrician will only consult with the subspecialist or surgeon on which laboratory tests to order or what the latest treatment is for a certain disease. Other times the pediatrician will want the child seen by the specialist. Often the subspecialist will refer the child back to the pediatrician for care after the diagnosis has been established and the treatment plan outlined. Sometimes the child will need constant medical attention from the subspecialist and he or she will become your child's doctor. In some instances this subspecialist will also provide routine pediatric care (immunizations, school physicals, etc.) but often will not. This means you will be seeing two doctors: one for the disease, one for routine stuff.

There are over thirty-five thousand family practitioners in the United States today. About half the children in America are cared for by family practitioners. It is possible that some of the readers of this book live in small towns in which there may not be a pediatrician. These parents can feel confident that most family practitioners are able to take good care of the vast majority of illnesses their children might have. If you are ever concerned that your child is *not* getting state-of-the-art pediatric care, get a consultation from a pediatric specialist even if it means traveling a long distance to a medical center.

Parents' Prerogatives

There are three things you have the right to do as your child's parent: (1) You can *choose* your child's doctor; (2) You can *challenge* what the doctor is doing or why; and (3) You can *change* doctors. Many people are convinced that it is very difficult to change doctors and impossible to challenge anything they say or do. However, we feel choosing, challenging, and changing is not only your right, but also your responsibility as a parent. In one sense your doctor is your employee (even when the insurance company pays the bill). When things are going smoothly it feels like a good partnership—when they aren't, you'll want to do something—like change.

CHOOSING A DOCTOR

Sources of Information

A good source of information about doctors in your community is other professionals—not just dentists or nurses but also ministers or lawyers. Try to ascertain what physician they take *their* children to. We like to check with doctors we know to find out which doctor *they* use. Generally, doctors' doctors (like lawyers' lawyers) are top quality because doctors have used their professional knowledge in making their choice.

Always try to check with friends or neighbors about physicians they go to. Though the county medical society can verify that a physician is licensed and certified, only a patient can tell you whether this doctor has a personality that you can comfortably relate to and has the attributes *you* want from a doctor such as accessibility and practice style. However, always check the credentials of a doctor recommended by a friend or neighbor. Your neighbor may really like a quack who hasn't read a medical journal in thirty years.

Your local library is also an excellent resource to use to find out more about doctors whose names you have obtained. Books you may find helpful include the *Directory of Medical Specialists,* which contains the doctor's age, medical school, hospital training, and specialty certification; and the *American Medical Directory,* which also lists the doctor's specialty societies; and state and local medical society directories, which contain addresses and phone numbers.[5,6]

Your county medical society will give you the names of pediatricians in your area—or of family practitioners if you want a doctor caring for yourself and the whole family as well as the child. Generally, you will be provided with the names of several physicians from whom you can choose. These physicians will be fully licensed in the state they are practicing in and will be certified in their specialties. They may be new to the community as the established doctors are often too busy to accept referrals.

One doctor suggests using the yellow pages to make a list of the doctors in your community.[7] Then check the *American Medical Directory* to get further information such as age, board certification, and what specialty societies the doctor belongs to. Next, ask lots of people *specific* questions about these doctors, like accessibility, waiting-room time, etc. At each step you weed out those doctors who do not suit your needs. Ideally, two or three doctors' names will remain on the list. The best procedure then is to make an appointment with each for a face-to-face interview where you can ask questions pertinent to *your* needs.

If you are about to have a baby, or you have moved to a new community and are deciding on a pediatrician, we suggest you ask lots of questions to find out what sort of a person the doctor is. Try to meet the pediatrician before the baby is born or before you decide to bring in your children. If you call to say you want to meet the pediatrician and would be happy to pay for an office visit or a consultation, this can usually be arranged. It is currently fashionable, especially in big cities, to meet the pediatrician before the child is born. This gives you an opportunity, while you are still pregnant, to find out about the doctor, to see the office, and to find out what sort of a person he or she is and how he or she practices.

WHAT TO LOOK FOR IN A PEDIATRICIAN

What should you look for in a pediatrician? Besides the competency we have already discussed, there are many other important things, including the way the office is run. You might want to ask the following questions: When are office hours? Do you have partners? Who can I see when you are out of town? Do you have telephone hours? When? Can I get through to you when I call? Do you call back promptly? Can you be reached at home? Which hospitals do you use? What are your fees? Will the office staff file insurance claims? How often do you see children for routine care? Will you see my child if brought in by my baby-sitter? Do you have a separate waiting room for children with infections? How long do I have to wait for an appointment? If my child gets sick, will you see the child that day? Not every doctor will provide all the "correct" answers you want, but you can pick the doctor who scores the best.

Less measurable, but perhaps more important qualities have to do with the kind of person the pediatrician is. Does the doctor like children? Seem happy with the work he or she is doing? Understand and tolerate maternal anxieties— especially with first babies? Try to minimize discomfort in your child when doing the physical examination or treatments? Employ a staff that is child-centered and kind? Provide a pleasant waiting area with appropriate toys for children? Provide *reasonably* current magazines for parents and children? Provide parents (and older children) with educational material?

There are also medical issues of importance. Does the doctor prescribe excessive medication? Does the doctor reach for a pen everytime the child is ill or does he or she first consider whether the child will be able to handle the illness without a prescription? Does the doctor always order laboratory tests and X-rays? We will discuss these issues further under *challenging*.

Parents have told us repeatedly that their major dissatisfaction with their child's pediatrician was the doctor's failure to communicate—in both directions: talking and listening. "My pediatrician always makes me feel that either I called with something I shouldn't have bothered him with or I should have called earlier." Or, "My doctor never explains things to me and seems amazed when I ask." Or, "My doctor doesn't listen to what I have to say about Jesse."

Marilyn has trained many "new" pediatricians who are sincerely interested in the partnership they have with the parent in the child's health care and she is convinced these sorts of complaints are less frequent today. Anne still hears too many stories about medical care that is not consumer-oriented.

It is even possible the pendulum toward medical care based on consumer wants has swung too far. Ellen Goodman noted in a recent column that the doctor who formerly was "Doctor-God-Sir, the professional keeper of the Temple of the Body," has been transformed into the doctor who introduces himself as your "Junior partner in health care."[8] The JP doctor has an aura of humility

("We really don't know"), and a passion for education (answers to all requests for advice start with a lecture on the topic). The new doctor never gives answers (just odds that you will get better or worse), always informs you—with or without your consent—about every possible side effect, and never tells you what to do (responsibility for your health is up to you, the senior partner).

Humor often points out to a society those areas in which it has gone too far. Seriously though, we feel a *balance* is needed between yesterday's doctor who prescribed exactly what you had to do and some doctors of today who might never tell you what to do, even if that was what you wanted.

There's more to this communication issue than your comfort. Measurements of compliance—carrying out the doctors' recommendations—are lower in patients of physicians who lack warmth and friendliness, do not explain, and do not meet the patients' expectations. Because your agreement with the doctor on a treatment plan which you will actually carry out has a tremendous impact on your child's health, find a doctor who is warm, does explain, and does meet your expectations. To make this point in an even stronger way, there is a connection between how well the physician is aware of maternal concerns early on and measures of mother-child adaptation at eleven months of age.[9]

One witty mother told Marilyn what she wants in a doctor is ability: avail*ability*, ami*ability*, and medical *ability!* Marilyn says she wants competence, conscientiousness, and compassion—in that order. Anne wants the same qualities but especially *honesty* about the limitations of knowledge which are always there.

WHEN OTHERS CHOOSE FOR YOU

Most hospitals will assign a pediatrician to see your baby when the baby is born. This pediatrician examines your baby to be sure he or she is healthy and prescribes the care your child will receive in the hospital. As this doctor's orders on the chart determine whether your baby will be brought to you for breastfeeding or be started on bottle-feeding, be sure to tell the nurses and your baby's doctor your wishes. Your baby's doctor must also write the baby's orders for discharge.

You can, of course, request a specific pediatrician if that doctor has staff privileges at the hospital where you give birth. This is handled by telling your obstetrician which pediatrician you want. If there is no pediatrician on the hospital's staff, the obstetrician or family practitioner who delivered your baby will check your baby and write the orders.

Ideally, the pediatrician who sees your child at birth will be the one you have already chosen. Then the partnership between you and the pediatrician can start at or before birth.

The pediatrician you choose may not be on the staff of the hospital where you deliver. Not to worry. The partnership can start six or eight weeks later when you bring your baby in for the first checkup. The doctor you have chosen can be sent the baby's birth record and hospital data. Just request this of your obstetrician and sign a release.

What if your family belongs to a Health Maintenance Organization (HMO) where you sign up for prepaid medical care and are usually assigned to a doctor? Almost every HMO has more than one pediatrician. Transfer to another doctor can usually be smoothly accomplished if you ask. HMO doctors want you to be satisfied as much as doctors in private practice do. If your child needs a subspecialist not on the HMO staff, a referral can generally be made although some HMO's may be reluctant to do so, or may refer to adult subspecialists in the HMO rather than to a pediatric subspecialist.

What if you have your baby at home? Then it is critical to know whether your doctor or midwife is a family practitioner who can care for the baby or, if not, whom you can call for baby care in case of an emergency. You need a newborn checkup within the first twenty-four hours, which would generally mean a house call, and not all pediatricians do this. A responsible home birth practitioner will either be qualified to provide routine newborn care or recommend a doctor who can. (Marilyn cannot, in good conscience, recommend a home delivery.)

PARENTAL TASKS

We talked about a three-way partnership between the physician, the parent, and the child. What is the role of the parent in this partnership? What are your responsibilities? What are the best ways to deal with your child's doctor?

The most important part of the relationship between you and the pediatrician is *communication*. You have the responsibility of reporting accurately to your doctor the symptoms your child has, the past medical history of the child, the family history, etc.

Both of us have good enough memories to have graduated from medical school but we would never trust ourselves to remember details of our own illness or our child's illness. Marilyn always writes things down and recommends this practice to you. Some parents keep a daily diary with details of what date Susie came down with chicken pox, etc. Others have a notebook for each child with records of immunizations, visits to the doctor, and dates of illnesses. Some use a blank sheet of paper or an index card for each illness. The method doesn't matter. But *keep a record*.

The record should not only include "charts" of your child's illness (see Table 54) but also a chronological record of all illnesses (not every one is called to the attention of the doctor), immunizations, development, etc. Your observations of your child will always be more frequent than your doctor's. Don't let the richness of these observations dissolve with memory loss.

If you and your child are seeing a new doctor, organize your thoughts and questions ahead of time. Be sure you can answer questions not only about current symptoms but also about your child's past illnesses, allergies, hospitalizations, operations, etc. It is also important to bring a list of the medicines your child may be taking, both prescription and non-prescription.

Another important aspect of parent-doctor communication is for the parent to *ask questions*. Here again, don't trust your memory. Before you go to the doctor write down the questions you want to ask about your child's health in general or about a specific illness. Always ask your doctor to explain anything you don't understand. If it is a complicated subject, ask for written material— either a brochure your doctor might have, or a book in the library. Always ask *why* a lab test is being ordered and what it will show or not show. Why is the drug being prescribed? What will it do? When? Are there any side effects? Always ask the *name* of things. What is the diagnosis? What is the drug?

Sometimes concerned parents really forget to ask about what is bothering them. They panic or get flustered when they are in the doctor's office. They sense that something is disturbing them but can't or won't verbalize it. You can look at your notes to remember to say, for example: "Dr. Lewis, I am concerned because the last time you gave Angie penicillin, she broke out in a rash three days later. Could she be allergic to penicillin?"

Become informed about child health. Don't expect your doctor to teach you everything. Get books and pamphlets from your library on child health. Become knowledgeable about *preventive* aspects of health care as well. This knowledge could actually save you money by reducing your visits to the doctor.[10] There were statistically fewer total medical visits and minor illness visits in patients who were provided with self-care educational intervention than those who were not. Armed with knowledge, especially when it helps your own decision-making about when and whether to call the doctor, you may be able to decrease your need for medical advice.

Another parental task is *cooperation*. Follow your child's doctor's instructions or discuss the instructions if you have any problem with them. Keep appointments, get prescriptions filled, give the medicine on schedule, follow the diet. If you have doubts that were not resolved by your questions, then challenge (see below) but don't ignore the doctor's advice. This is not only a waste of times and money but could be fatal.

WHAT DOES THE DOCTOR EXPECT OF THE PARENT?

Doctors expect the parent partner to work with them on behalf of the child. Making careful observations and recording them to inform the doctor are important. Health maintenance at home is also important. Doctors want to be called when it is important but not for trivial reasons (Marilyn remembers a doctor telling of the patient's mother who called him at 3 A.M. to ask if her son was up-to-date in his tetanus shots. When the doctor asked what happened she told him, "I dreamed Johnny stepped on a rusty nail and I got so worried about tetanus I couldn't fall back asleep!") Doctors want parents to follow instructions, which means telling them if they don't understand and, most important, telling them when they *don't* follow the instructions.

Your child needs to feel the doctor is a trusted friend. Doctors want your child to feel this way. Please don't threaten children with a visit to the doctor if they have done something wrong. Don't ever tell your children they will get a shot if they don't behave.

When you get to the office, remember to bring small toys or coloring books so your child can keep amused in case there is the wait often experienced in any professional office. Hold your child still if the doctor asks you to. Don't let your child fall off the examining table. Don't leave your child alone in the waiting room. Try to leave the other children home if you possibly can, as most doctors have limited space in their waiting rooms *and* a pediatrician's waiting room can be a hot bed of infection!

You can help both your child and the doctor by the way you handle the inevitable painful procedure. The infant requires only firm holding during the procedure and lots of comforting afterward. The older child should be encouraged to scream, cry, or at least say "Ouch!" If the child needs repeated painful procedures we advise a small, special treat from the parent after each one.

Be prepared to answer the doctor's questions. Don't feel embarrassed to read from your notes or your child's health diary. Try not to be late for an appointment and call if you have to break an appointment. Doctors want what you want: optimal health and happiness for your child. They want to work with you toward this goal.

In summary, parents are the guardians of their child's health maintenance, observers of any departure from health in their child, and observers of any health idiosyncrasies in their child (i.e., how does their particular child react to an illness). This is one of the big jobs of parenthood.

How to Call Your Doctor (Telephone Effectiveness)

The wise parent learns the following telephone protocol useful in communicating with physicians. 1) Identify yourself and your child by name and remind your doctor of the child's age. 2) State the *facts* or the problem (before you call write down what is happening that prompted the call so you will have your thoughts in order). For example, "Steve woke up from his nap crying, flushed, and pulling at his left ear. His temperature is 101.5°. He won't stop whimpering." 3) Be sure to tell your doctor what medicines you have already given your child. 4) Have the *questions* you want to ask written down: "Should you see Steve?" "When can you see him?" "What should I give him now for the pain?" 5) Be ready with the phone number of your pharmacy if the doctor wants to call in a prescription. 6) Write down the doctor's instructions.

If the doctor is not available, give the same information to the nurse or answering service. Add the question, "When will the doctor call back?" or "What other doctor is available?"

How Often Should Your Child See the Doctor?

The American Academy of Pediatrics recommends a minimum of five well-baby visits for the healthy infant between birth and age two.[11] Each of these visits should include a complete history and physical as well as the required immunizations.

Babies should be seen at two months, four months, and six months for DPT immunization (Diphtheria-Pertussis-Tetanus) and oral polio (the oral polio can be omitted at six months, unless your state borders on Mexico). Boosters for both of these immunizations are given at eighteen months. A tuberculin test is recommended at twelve months. Mumps, measles, and rubella (MMR) is administered at fifteen months (see Table 49). The baby should be seen again at two (which makes the fifth visit) to be immunized against Hemophilus influenzae type b (Hib), a new vaccine to prevent one form of meningitis and other serious infections,[12] and yearly thereafter for routine or well-child care. Yearly physical examinations are important to assess growth and development and to identify problems that might have developed. Even though your child may have screening at school (vision, hearing, blood pressure, etc.) the physical examination is needed. Physical examinations reveal eleven times more problems per contact than screening tests.[13] Obviously, some children will need to be seen by the pediatrician more often than outlined above because of illness.

In the past, more frequent visits were recommended. Indeed, babies were supposed to be seen every month. This is no longer considered necessary, unless there is a problem. A doctor caring for a premature might want to weigh the baby and assess development every month, for example. However, a study comparing babies seen ten times for well-baby visits in the first two years of life with those seen five times revealed no differences in health or development outcomes. It is perfectly safe to recommend five well-baby visits for low risk infants.[14]

You have probably heard that DPT vaccine could cause serious side effects in babies. This most recently came to the fore after a TV documentary entitled "DPT: Vaccine Roulette" dramatically reported cases of convulsions and brain damage after DPT injections.

Every vaccine carries some risk. In deciding what a child should have, doctors weigh benefits against risk. The actual number of cases of permanent brain damage occur in one out of 310,000 injections, much lower than the TV documentary implied.[15] In areas where DPT immunizations were *not* given, epidemics of whooping cough (pertussis) occurred with deaths which are tragic in a disease that is almost completely preventable. Pertussis, itself, can cause convulsions and encephalopathy (brain inflammation) in infants. DPT is about 80 percent effective in preventing the disease, which is highly contagious.[16]

Except in babies for whom DPT is contraindicated (those with histories of convulsions or those who have a convulsion or a severe reaction [high fever, collapse, persistent screaming] after an injection of DPT), we recommend your child be immunized according to the recommendations of the AAP.[17,18,19] If your child has one of the contraindications to pertussis, a vaccine containing tetanus and diphtheria vaccine should be given.

TABLE 49

RECOMMENDED SCHEDULE FOR ACTIVE IMMUNIZATION OF NORMAL INFANTS AND CHILDREN

	DTP	Polio	TB Test	Measles	Mumps	Rubella	Hib	Tetanus-Diphtheria
2 months	✓	✓						
4 months	✓	✓						
6 months	✓							
1 year			✓					
15 months				✓	✓	✓		
1½ years	✓*	✓*						
2 years							✓	
4-6 years	✓	✓						
14-16 years								✓

*May be given at 15 months.

Reprinted by permission from the American Academy of Pediatrics, "Protecting Your Child Against Diphtheria, Tetanus, Pertussis," November 1986.

WHEN SHOULD YOU TAKE YOUR CHILD TO THE DOCTOR?

You, as parent, will always spend more time with your child than will the doctor. This means that: 1) You will *always know more about your child than the doctor does;* and 2) You have a *responsibility to learn how to observe your child for signs of illness.*

One of the most difficult things parents have to learn is when to call the doctor. What symptoms are important? Which ones should be called to the attention of the doctor? What symptoms can be ignored or treated at home?

One way of determining when a child should be taken to the doctor (or when an adult should go to the doctor, for that matter) is to use the "Three P's." The first "P" stands for *Personal* or, rather, for *Personal Pattern.* You already know the personal pattern of *your* child. Does your daughter throw up every time she gets excited? If so, the vomiting may not be very significant. If, on the other hand, the child never vomits, such a symptom could be important.

The second "P" is *Persistence.* Many tummy aches go away, but if they persist, they should be called to the doctor's attention. What is a persistent tummy ache? One that doesn't go away all day or one that comes back every day for several days.

The third "P" is *Progression*. Are the symptoms getting worse? Are they getting more frequent? Are they lasting longer?

If your child's tummy ache is unusual (not the child's personal pattern), does not go away (persistent), and is getting worse (progression), your doctor should be called. If your son complains of a headache which he always seems to have after going to the movies, if it gets better after he rests for a while, and it is gone by the next morning, you don't have to call.

Parents tell us their biggest concern is "When is my child sick enough to be taken to the doctor?" There is no formula we can write to answer this concern. We can offer no pat answers. Thinking about *P*ersonal Pattern, *P*ersistence, and *P*rogression of symptoms may help you decide. Reading about specific symptoms in the next chapter may also help.

If you are in doubt, call your child's doctor. The doctor's responsibility in the partnership is to take care of the child and also to alleviate anxiety of the partner—you, the parent.

CHALLENGING THE DOCTOR

Everyone has heard the phrase "Ask your doctor." We want to emphasize a new concept: "*Tell* your doctor." Tell your doctor what kind of person you are and whether you want the doctor to tell you what to do, to explain every action, or both. Tell your doctor exactly what you have observed and be sure he or she pays attention.

Parents are beginning to question doctors about treatment. Not too long ago parents were expected to always follow the directions the doctor gave. Today nearly all the parents we know, even those who prefer a doctor who gives lots of advice, ask questions. They want to know *what* the doctor is recommending and *why*. They don't hesitate to get another opinion, or another doctor, if they don't like the answers.

What about challenging your child's doctor? Do you think that the care of your child is not optimal or do you disagree with what the doctor has done or recommends? Tell the doctor so!

We think you should trust your instincts. If there is something a doctor is doing or prescribing that you instinctively find wrong, or that you have a question about, it is vitally important that you verbalize this. (If a doctor says he or she is too busy to talk to you, this is one reason to *change*, which we will talk about below). Most doctors are pleased to answer your questions.

What are some things that parents should challenge?

First of all, as we said earlier, parents should always know *what* the doctor is prescribing and *why*. If the doctor does not answer your questions about your child's medications, or does not spend enough time with you to explain things, you should challenge this.

Parents should always ask for (and receive) *the exact name of the medication* they will be giving the child. They must also know what side effects there may be and how to store the medicine. (Does it need refrigeration? How long may it be safely kept?) Challenge the doctor to tell you these things if the information is not volunteered.

You should also challenge when the doctor will not see your child, if you *really* think the child should be seen. We recently heard about a mother whose teenage daughter ran a high fever for several days. It was flu season; the pediatrician said it was not necessary to see the girl and prescribed fluids and aspirin. After three days of frantic phone calls the mother said, "Doctor, she doesn't even *smell* the way she does when she has the flu. Something else is going on! You *must* see her!" The girl had toxic shock syndrome and was extremely ill by the time the doctor finally saw her—fortunately she recovered.

Be insistent if you have to be!

Although doctors have different practice styles and personalities, you have every right to challenge a doctor who doesn't seem to spend enough time with your child in the office, who makes telephone diagnoses without follow-up, or who always prescribes drugs for symptoms without finding out what is causing the symptom. A healthy index of suspicion is justified if the doctor always prescribes antibiotics for a fever, either over the phone or after a cursory examination. Challenge the doctor to find out why.

We get nervous when parents tell us about doctors who *always* order lab tests and X-rays at every visit or about those who *never* do anything except smile at the child.

We also get nervous when doctors refuse to seek necessary consultations or are angry when parents want help in getting a second opinion.

Another legitimate concern of parents is exorbitant fees, especially when the doctor's fees are compared with other doctors in the community.

CHANGING DOCTORS

You can also change doctors. It is possible that you will come to feel that your child's physician is unsatisfactory. You may want a more specialized, or a better-trained, doctor or one that you feel more comfortable with.

Why would a parent change doctors? The most common reason is a mismatch between your personality and the doctor's. You want to be told exactly what to do every hour of the day with your first baby and your doctor is a laissez-faire type who tells you to do whatever you feel like doing. Or you want to make your own decisions and your doctor tells you exactly what to do and makes you feel guilty if you don't do it. Because the partnership is so important, and because partners should be comfortable with each other, these are perfectly valid reasons for changing.

Marilyn, who lived in the Detroit area for twenty years, was often asked by friends or acquaintances to suggest another pediatrician because they did not like their own. She would try to ascertain what "type" of doctor the parents wanted and make a referral to such a person. By the time she left Detroit, she had "cross-referred" parents to almost every doctor in town with good results.

Dr. X, whom Mrs. A couldn't stand, was doing very well by Mrs. B., while Mrs. A was now perfectly happy with Dr. Y!

What are some other reasons for changing?

The doctor doesn't seem to like children, doesn't try to prevent or alleviate pain in procedures, or seems bored with practice.

The doctor seems so busy that there is not enough time for you.

The doctor does not seem to know your child apart from all the others.

The doctor makes a careless medical mistake (prescribes a medicine your child is allergic to).

The doctor doesn't seem to know much about your child's problem—especially if your child has a chronic or rare disease—and doesn't get help or make a referral.

The doctor doesn't seem to keep up with the latest medical information. You knew about the possible association between aspirin and Reye's syndrome before the doctor did.

The doctor doesn't seem concerned about other health needs of your child —can't or won't help you find a good dentist or eye doctor for example.

Pediatricians should also be sensitive to *parents'* needs. They should always respect you and support your sense of dignity. They should be patient with you when you need extra attention and sensitive to your problems when you share them.

How do you change doctors? Simple. First, tell your doctor you want to be referred to someone else or to a subspecialist. Most doctors will make the referral.

Don't worry that your doctor will refuse to cooperate. Even if they do not make a referral, doctors *will* transfer records to the new doctor you choose. Doctors do not wish to have a dissatisfied parent in their practice. Every parent can say to a doctor, "I'm simply not happy with you. I don't think you spend enough time with parents. I want to transfer to Dr. X. Can you help me arrange that?"

What if your doctor does not feel it's necessary to obtain a consultation, but you feel your child needs a specialist? Ask other people in town for the name of a specialist or call the county medical society. If you live in a rural area and can't find a subspecialist, one resource is the medical school in your state (forty-four states, the District of Columbia, and Puerto Rico have medical schools). Ask to speak to the chair of the Department of Pediatrics or to the Chief Resident in Pediatrics. It would be unusual for you to have to make such a call, because most of the time your own doctor will help refer you to such a medical center if your child has a special or unusual problem. But you *can* do it yourself.

In summary, the important thing for you to remember is that you are in *control,* which means you can *choose* your child's doctors, you can *challenge* the doctors, and you can *change* doctors.

You can complain about bad care. Most pediatricians give competent and kind care to children. However, among any large group of people there may be some who are atypical in a negative sense. If you feel your child has been given bad or brutal care, you do have recourse. County medical societies have a committee that receives and handles complaints from the public about physician performance. You can also complain to the chair of Pediatrics or chief of staff of the hospital(s) the doctor uses.

You may think it is not worth your trouble or you may have heard that doctors protect each other. Wrong, on both accounts! It is worth the trouble to protect another child from incompetent care. We have seen these medical society committees work effectively. Also medical malpractice is legally defined. Briefly, if your child is harmed in any way by the actions of a physician who is not practicing in accordance with the standards of medical practice in your community, you may have legal recourse.

A Word About Science, Statistics, and Uncertainty

We take science for granted; it is part of our lives. We can go to the moon, cure pestilence, and build missiles that can go halfway around the world to destroy a city.

"Science" as we know it is defined as the way we gain knowledge in empirical fields like physics and physiology. Science used to mean all knowledge from mathematics to theology. Plato and Aristotle's science was "mathematical" in that it held that all propositions not self-evident should be derived from self-evident propositions.

The word scientist was not used before 1840; before that chemists were called philosophers—and still get a doctor of philosophy degree after completing graduate training in chemistry.

The scientific method enables us to test and prove hypotheses. The dictionary defines a hypothesis as a proposition which is supposed to be taken for granted in order to draw a conclusion for proof of the point in question. Any assertion that can't be checked by thinking alone or observing alone has to be studied by the scientific method, which includes formulating and proving hypotheses.

Medicine wasn't always scientific. Medicine was magic and mystery—and to many still is. Books have been written describing the history of medicine's transition from the era of magic to the scientific era.[20] Currently, advocates of the holistic health movement believe some aspects of medicine, such as spiritual and psychological factors, should be "put back into medicine," as people need more than science. Few would disagree. On the other hand, alternative health care for children which consisted, for example, only of prayer, but left out penicillin, could be dangerous.

Because science is so precise—at least in the minds of many people—we often expect precise answers from physicians. Physicians who are highly committed to observational science are themselves often uncomfortable with uncertainty. But the fact that we are in a scientific era of medicine does not mean there is no uncertainty—on the contrary, far from it. In some respects, the more we learn about very complex disease states, diagnostic modalities, and therapeutic interventions, the more uncertainty there may be. The physician's task in making a clinical decision about the patient is often harder today than it was previously when there were fewer choices to be made.

What leads to uncertainty in clinical decision-making? First of all, let's acknowledge that every physician must make clinical decisions. What does the physical finding mean? What lab test is needed? Is therapy indicated at this time? Can the parents handle this sick child at home? Should the child be hospitalized? Are the risks of the treatment justifiable?

A doctor caring for patients makes such decisions every day for every patient. Why is this task difficult? Clinical decision-making, critical to the well-being and very life of the patient, not only must be made but must be made in the face of uncertainty.[21]

Uncertainty stalks the doctor at every turn. First of all, there can be errors in the clinical data. The patient may not have given an accurate history. There can be errors of observation or recording of data. There can be laboratory errors.

The good physician will repeatedly question a patient about an ambiguous history, and few errors are made in a good laboratory. But, unfortunately, the clinical data on which decisions must be made by their very nature may be ambiguous. Every patient is different. Not all will have exactly the same signs and symptoms even when afflicted with the same disease. Not every laboratory or X-ray finding will be the same in similarly diseased patients. Treatment will not affect all patients in the same way.

How do doctors make clinical decisions? Doctors go through a process called clinical problem-solving.[22] Clinical problem-solving starts with *collecting the data* which comes from the medical history and physical examination, the laboratory, and X-ray. After data is collected, the doctor sets *hypotheses*, which means the doctor looks at the possibilities and probabilities that the data could lead to. Data can lead to a single hypothesis or multiple hypotheses. Doctors use pattern recognition and their knowledge base about diseases to set these hypotheses.

The physician then *tests these hypotheses.* The doctor may order further laboratory or X-ray examinations and continue to observe the patient. The doctor may even do a therapeutic test, i.e., try a treatment to see if it has any effect on the disease. The next step is *action (or inaction),* with the goal of returning the patient to wellness.

Obviously, the experienced physician can do a better job of clinical problem-solving than the medical student—because of the wealth of information and the ability that experience has brought.

In order to do good clinical problem-solving your doctor must obtain the best and most accurate data, recognize the linkage between bits of data, form hypotheses to explain the data in a given patient, and be able to assign probabilities to the hypotheses.

The doctor uses a statistical approach to determine the probability that a given hypothesis is correct. It is beyond the scope of this book to discuss probability theory or practice. But you must realize, the doctor is almost never able to say, "If I do X, the patient will get better 100 percent of the time or if I do Y, the patient will die 100 percent of the time." Instead the statement is more likely to be, "If I prescribe X, there is a 60 percent chance that the patient will respond."

One concept sometimes hard to understand has to do with diagnostic tests. Not every test gives the doctor an absolute answer. Diagnostic tests vary in their sensitivity (how many people with the disease have positive tests?) and their specificity (is the test positive in some people who don't have the disease?). Sometimes doctors wish they could tell you the answer but need to order further tests because they could not get an answer from the earlier ones.

We all know enough probability to argue that if we flip a coin it is equally likely to come up heads or tails. In medicine, *commonness* enables us to do better than 50–50. Even though every patient is different, there are a finite number of responses to a finite number of possible insults to the homeostasis (balance) of the body.

Clinical problem-solving, properly done, looks at the *common possibilities first* while being aware of the unusual. Doctors remind themselves, for example, that an uncommon manifestation of a common disease is more common than a common manifestation of an uncommon disease. The old adage that if you hear hoofbeats it is more likely to be horses than zebras also applies to clinical medicine. The knowledge of which diseases are common and the various ways they can manifest themselves is the hallmark of the competent physician.

It sounds very complicated—and this is why in the scientific era, the competence of the physician is so important.

Some doctors, as we said earlier, are uncomfortable with uncertainty—so much so that they protect themselves with a facade of always being certain. This is understandable. However, in our opinion, the good doctor must not only be able to handle uncertainty and ambiguity but must also be able to explain his or her thought processes and actions to the patients even when these include uncertainty.

Parents should have a good deal of empathy with the doctor about the discomfort of uncertainty. (What am I seeing in my child? Does it mean my child is sick? When should I call the doctor? What should I do?) Parents want to err on the safe side—and so do doctors. However, both parents and doctors may be faced with uncertainty in their observations and in their interpretations of these observations. Making a decision in the face of uncertainty is never easy.

Parents have to realize that though they really want answers of *certainty*, these may not exist. Accept the frailties of clinical problem-solving and have sympathy with your doctor. Remember you both have the same goal (restoring your child to health without doing any harm) and the same problem (you are not always sure what to do) and both of you must make your best choice in the face of uncertainty.

A DENTIST FOR YOUR CHILD

Large communities usually have pedodontists, dentists who specialize in the dental care of children. Some dentists see both adults and children and they often have a special room equipped for children and use special techniques with children.

Because every child should be seen annually from age two, parents should look for a dentist who makes the first visit a fun experience. Unfortunately, there are still communities in which there is no dentist, or the dentist is too busy for routine prophylactic care.

The best way to find a dentist for your child is to ask your pediatrician. Most cities have local dental societies which provide referral services; most societies will be able to give you the names of dentists who specialize in childrens' dentistry or those who work well with children.

The American Dental Association has the following hints for finding a dentist: Ask friends and neighbors who want the same high standards of care you do; ask the faculty of dental schools in your area to suggest practitioners; check the ADA directory in your library; ask your child's doctor (we think this is probably the best source).

A MENTAL HEALTH PROFESSIONAL FOR YOUR CHILD

Although the same principles apply in choosing a mental health professional (often called a therapist) as apply to choosing a physician, the problem of finding the right one may be a bit more difficult. There are many varieties of mental health professionals, which adds to the confusion. The credentialing of some of these is not as rigidly controlled as is the credentialing of physicians. Also, many people have a distrust of, and aversion to, *any* psychotherapists, partly because they fear mental illness and partly because they are not sure therapy works.

General psychiatrists are physicians who specialize in emotional, behavioral, and mental disorders. They have had four years of residency training in general psychiatry and have had some exposure to child psychiatry, which may be quite limited. A board certified psychiatrist has passed the exams of the American Board of Psychiatry and Neurology.

Child psychiatrists have an additional two years of sub-specialty training in child psychiatry. Board certified child psychiatrists have passed both general and child psychiatry boards.

Psychologists have a Ph.D. or Psy.D. in psychology and are usually licensed or certified by the state. The American Board of Examiners in Professional Psychology (ABEPP) awards diplomate status to clinical psychologists who have had five years of post-doctoral experience and pass an examination. In a few states there is no licensure requirement and untrained persons can call themselves psychologists.

A *licensed school psychologist* is either a clinical or educational psychologist, additionally trained to diagnose school and learning problems. Many school systems provide evaluation by a licensed school psychologist. When there are severe school problems there is often a lengthy wait for an appointment, but the school may accept a private evaluation if done by a licensed school psychologist.

A *social worker* (or, depending on training, a *psychiatric social worker)* has a Master of Social Work (M.S.W.) degree and may be certified by the state and or by the Academy of Certified Social Workers (A.C.S.W.).

A *counselor* could be trained in education as a school counselor or could be a family or marriage counselor or therapist. Here training and certification should be checked, because in many areas such self-designated terms may be used by anyone whether trained or not.

If your child or anyone in the family needs a mental health professional for testing or treatment, your best bet is a specific referral or suggestion from your doctor, your child's school, or another knowledgeable professional such as a member of the psychiatry department of a medical school or the staff of a mental health center, a lawyer, or a member of the clergy.

If the school suggests treatment, the school or your child's doctor generally can make recommendations for therapists. Clergymen usually know the good therapists in the community because they often make referrals in the course of their pastoral counseling.

Parents should always want to know which *kind* of mental health professional the recommended therapist is. You should verify the certification or licensure of the therapist. It is also worthwhile to know the age of the therapist and length of time in practice as well as the type of therapy practiced. Some therapists do only group work, for example. Hospital privileges and teaching appointments may also be of interest to parents. Generally, hospital privileges mean the therapist has met standards of peer review, while teaching privileges mean the therapist is keeping up with the field.

It is also important to find out about fees and whether the therapist is eligible for insurance reimbursement. Health insurance often pays only for M.D.'s, or only for a certain number of visits, or only part of the fee.

Location of the therapist's office may be an important consideration, especially if you have to drive the child to the office. Telephone access and vacation coverage should be assessed as in the case of any health professional.

Confidentiality between your child and the therapist is vital if the child is to develop trust in the therapist. However, parents are often concerned if they do not know what is happening in therapy. Generally, it is best if there is a clear understanding before therapy starts as to *who* will tell *what* to *whom.* Many therapists will not breach a confidence with a child unless there is an emergency (potential suicide, for example) which necessitates immediate communication with the parent.

COSTS OF HEALTH CARE

A lengthy discussion of fees and health care costs is beyond the scope of this book. Obviously, wise parents check to see what their health insurance will cover. For example, some plans provide well-child care while others do not. Some plans offer total coverage, others cover only a portion of the bill, still others have a variable deductible, which you pay. Mental health benefits are often severely restricted in health plans.

We recommend adequate health insurance coverage for all families. If total coverage is too costly, you might consider catastrophic or major medical type insurance. Many families prefer to pay some of the costs of health care themselves but want coverage for major problems. With this type of policy a family can have coverage above a certain dollar level, which means they are insured for a medical disaster that might occur. Be sure you find out whether hospital care, lab tests, doctor's office visits, psychiatric care, nursery care, dental care, and drugs are covered—and for how long. Major medical policies sometimes have lifetime limits for each health problem so be sure you understand *your* policy and its limitations.

You should know whether your children are covered on your insurance and for how long. Some policies cover the newborn at birth, others start at thirty days, which eliminates coverage for expensive neonatal care. Some policies cover children until age twenty-five provided they are single, in college, and dependent on their parents; others cut off children's coverage at twenty-one or earlier.

If you decide to join a prepaid program like an HMO find out what care you will receive when you enroll. Drugs? Dental care? Psychiatric care? What choice will you have of primary doctors? Specialists? Hospitals? If both parents are working and have insurance options it may make sense for one to join an HMO—which provides complete coverage for primary care—and the other to join a major medical insurance plan, which gives more choice of specialty care and individual practitioners.

The American Academy of Pediatrics lists the following as health insurance priorities and suggests parents ask their insurance representative how their policy covers these items.

1. Medical care, including health supervision and preventive care, performed or supervised by a physician either in or out of a hospital.
2. Surgical care, performed in or out of a hospital including plastic or reconstructive procedures where medically indicated.
3. Pregnancy including:
   A. All complications.

B. Care of the unborn child.

C. Pregnancy of a single dependent of the policyholder.

4. Care of all newborn infants including health supervision from time of birth.
5. Laboratory and pathological services.
6. X-ray services in or out of the hospital.
7. Services for anesthesia performed in or out of a hospital.
8. Consultations in or out of the hospital.
9. Services rendered by more than one physician for the same illness or during the same hospitalization.
10. Mental health services.
11. The following services on an outpatient as well as inpatient basis under the direction of a physician:

    A. Physical therapy and other rehabilitative services.

    B. Chemotherapeutic services for malignancy.

    C. Inhalation therapy.

    D. Rental or purchases of medical equipment, eyeglasses.

12. Dental care.

About 10 percent of families will require psychiatric help, in most cases brief, in some cases extensive. The best plans today offer full coverage of hospital care and 50 percent coverage of outpatient visits. Some provide much less—no mental health benefits or only token ones. Check your policy carefully.

If you pay for your child's pediatric care yourself, though it may seem like small consolation, pediatricians are at the bottom of the list of specialists when it comes to average earnings—even below family practitioners. No one goes into pediatrics to get rich. Pediatricians, especially those who spend time with the child and family, have incomes considerably lower than other doctors, notably those in the surgical fields.

HEALTH CARE FOR PARENTS

Although this chapter deals with health care for children we want to point out to parents that health is important not only for your children but for you.

A higher percentage of women than men visit doctors, but this includes visits made with children. In point of fact, sometimes women take their children to the doctor but neglect their own health. We urge you to take care of yourself and to arrange for your own competent medical care.

Women should have an annual physical examination to include blood pressure, pelvic examination, Pap smear, and breast examination. Most women go to a gynecologist for this annual exam—Marilyn does. Anne prefers a good internist who is interested in primary care.

Current cost containment efforts have led to a new policy recommending a Pap smear only every three years for women under forty. Why did the American

Cancer Society shift from recommending a Pap smear every year to every three years? The decision was based on two factors. Cancer of the cervix, which is screened by the Pap smear, starts out as a detectable precancerous lesion which takes a period of years to become actual cancer. But the other factor is cost. This new recommendation is a compromise between costs and risks. With the every-three-year protocol, women end up with 97 percent of the theoretical 100 percent increase in life expectancy the annual Pap smear provides and there is a two-fold savings in cost.[23]

There is no way Marilyn would accept this 3 percent decrease, so she has her annual Pap smear and recommends all women do so. The American College of Obstetrics and Gynecologists agrees with her and still recommends an annual Pap smear.

Remember, the Pap smear is only *part* of the annual examination. A total of over fifty-eight thousand women die each year of cancer of the breast, uterus, ovary, or cervix. The annual visit to your gynecologist—along with self-examination of the breast—allows for early detection of *all* of these. Your doctor will show you how to self-examine your breasts or you can get a pamphlet explaining how to do this from the American Cancer Society.

Ideally, your spouse would be equally committed to his health care, but many men neglect it. The annual physical exam for patients without symptoms is less advised lately, but certainly all symptoms should be evaluated using the three P's—personal pattern, persistence, and progression.

Lifestyle factors are the biggest risk of making you a widow or your child an orphan. At every age up to thirty-nine the "violent death triad" of accidents, homicides, and suicides cause more deaths than any other cause. At later ages they are still as prevalent but get overtaken by cancer and heart disease. Smoking cessation and better diets are the apparent causes of recent decreases in early deaths from these causes. Men are also susceptible to testicular cancer, prostatic cancer, and, like women, lung and colon cancer. Men often need a push from their spouses to get medical evaluation of symptoms—even serious ones.

Take care of your mental health and your marital health as well. Women are more often diagnosed as depressed than are men. Sometimes fatigue or physical complaints are masked symptoms of depression. If you are feeling "down" and can't shake the feelings, get help. If you and your spouse are not relating in a comfortable, caring way, get help.

Remember, if you don't take care of yourself, it will be much harder, if indeed possible, to take care of your children.

Suggested Readings and Resources

Belsky, Marvin S., and Gross, Leonard. *How to Choose and Use Your Doctor.* New York: Arbor House, 1975.

Although this book does not deal with pediatrics, the authors present useful suggestions about how to best choose and use a doctor. Emphasis is placed on patient rights and responsibilities.

Danto, Bruce L., and Ancog, Romulo S. *So You Want to See a Psychiatrist?* New York: Arno, 1980.

A chatty book about choosing and seeing a psychiatrist. One of the chapters is on problems of childhood such as hyperactivity and autism.

Gilbert, Sara. *What Happens in Therapy.* New York: Lothrop, Lee & Shepard, 1982.

A book suitable for teenagers contemplating or needing psychotherapy or already started in therapy. The author uses cases in different kinds of therapy and touches on the results of therapy. A good bibliography of fiction and non-fiction is included.

Gots, Ronald, and Kaufman, Arthur. *The People's Hospital Book.* New York: Avon, 1981.

A thoughtful, reasonably informative book on hospitals, including types of hospitals, hospital personnel, procedures, insurance, etc.

Heck, Edward T.; Gomez, Angel G.; and Adams, George L. *A Guide to Mental Health Services.* Pittsburgh, Pa.: University of Pittsburgh Press, 1973.

Useful chapters on mental health professionals and sources of mental health information.

Huttmann, Barbara. *The Patient's Advocate.* New York: Viking, 1981.

A book written to educate patients about hospitals. Though it rarely deals with children, it is a useful book which describes how hospitals work and outlines the rights and responsibilities of patients. The author-nurse proposes that every hospitalized patient have an advocate. In the case of a hospitalized child, the parent will serve in this role and will gain useful ideas from reading this.

Lazarus, Herbert R. *How to Get Your Money's Worth Out of Psychiatry.* Los Angeles: Sherbourne, 1973.

Not much about children but a cleverly written book about kinds of psychiatrists and patients that offers useful information.

Mishara, Brian L., and Patterson, Robert D. *Consumer's Guide to Mental Health.* New York: Times, 1977.

A 1977 guide by a psychologist and a psychiatrist. The writing is clear. The advice is generally good. Very little specifically about children but the suggestions for finding and choosing a therapist are applicable to all age groups.

Sobel, David S., and Ferguson, Tom. *The People's Book of Medical Tests.* New York: Summit, 1985.

Worth reading if you have questions about a medical test.

20

SYMPTOMS OF ILLNESS IN CHILDREN—
AND WHEN TO CALL FOR HELP

Scope of Chapter

This chapter lists the common medical and psychological symptoms of illnesses that children may develop. Some of the symptoms, like a runny nose, will *definitely* occur in your household! Other symptoms, like jaundice, are uncommon and may never occur in any of your children.

Each listed symptom will be described. We will also tell parents what they can do to relieve the symptoms and what observations they should be making.

We have organized this chapter by systems. A system is a set of individual parts, like organs, that function in a common purpose. Examples are the respiratory system or the cardiovascular system.

This chapter is not a complete, conclusive, or exhaustive list of childhood symptoms. We have included only the most common symptoms and signs. We used medical terms (always defined) so that you can understand the terms if your doctor uses them.

This chapter will not make you into a pediatrician. However, it may help you make clearer observations, organize your observations, and understand and communicate better with your child's physician.

In addition to telling you what to do for these symptoms at home, we have tried to make it easier for you to decide when to call the doctor. When logical, we have included a section called "Call Your Child's Doctor If": for each symptom category.

Parents tell us they want to know two things when their child is sick: "What should we do for the child?" and "When should we call the doctor?" Both areas have been covered for each symptom.

Introduction

What is a symptom anyway? A *symptom* is any subjective evidence of a disease or a condition that is perceived by the patient. A *sign*, on the other hand, is an indication of the existence of a disease or condition provided by objective evidence. A symptom is "I feel nauseated." The doctor cannot objectively tell whether or not you feel nauseated—you must tell the doctor about it. A sign, which will be objectively obvious to the patient or the doctor, is vomiting. Some signs may not be obvious to the patient but are obvious to the doctor. An example is jaundice, or yellow discoloration of the skin and the whites of the eyes, which sometimes the patient has not noticed before going to the doctor. Putting together just this one symptom (nausea) and the two signs (vomiting and jaundice) might lead the doctor to suspect hepatitis (a liver infection).

Symptoms and signs are what your child is telling you about his or her illness. Obviously, it is easier to figure out what illness your child may have when he or she can say in words, "I have a headache," or "My throat is sore," or "I feel hot and ache all over." It's tougher to pick up signals from preverbal or nonverbal children but there *are* clues which we will point out to you. It is important that parents learn about those signs of illness that are likely to occur in young babies before they are old enough to tell you how they feel or where it hurts.

How to Use This Chapter

If you want to know about a symptom, we suggest that you use this chapter in the following way. If you know that a cough is a respiratory symptom, look under respiratory in this chapter to read what we say about coughs. Coughs are pretty simple; as most of us know coughs have to do with the lungs and lungs are part of the respiratory system. But if you don't know that a cough is a respiratory symptom, look up "cough" in the Index.

Let's take a harder example. Your child looks yellow to you. This is called jaundice but you might not know that jaundice would be listed under skin because it stands for yellow skin. Use the Index. Look up "jaundice" if you know that that means yellow skin, or look under "skin, yellow," if you don't. Hopefully, you will always find what you need.

Keeping Track of Symptoms

The goal of this chapter is to help you become a good observer of symptoms in children. The way one becomes a good observer is the same way one becomes a good bird-watcher. First you learn *what* to observe by using a good bird guide and finding out which features distinguish a warbler from a grosbeak. We discuss what features help distinguish a well child from a sick child, both in general and by specific systems. You already know, from seeing illness in others and being ill yourself, more than you may think you know about what distinguishes illness from wellness. Reading about symptoms in this chapter may help fine-tune your knowledge.

It is important to give doctors accurate information, if you must contact them. Also, your decision about contacting the doctor may depend on what happens to the symptom. So it is important for parents to learn how to keep track of symptoms. This means you should get in the habit of writing down your observations.

We have talked about charts before. They can be very simple and easy to construct and fill out. A chart need consist only of a piece of paper on which you rule off a column for the date and hour and a column for the symptom or sign that you are observing in your child. The sign should be documented specifically whenever possible. "He feels hot" is not as helpful to nudge your memory or give information to the doctor as "September 8, 4 P.M. Temperature 104°" (see sample charts on pages 695, 699).

GENERAL SYMPTOMS

Seven general symptoms of children, ranging in frequency from very common to somewhat common, will be discussed first before we list the symptoms by systems.

FEVER

In the earliest recorded medical books, fever was a dreaded sign. Fever, which often coincides with the child's first illness, is frightening to new parents. Indeed, fever is so frightening that pediatricians have described fever phobias in parents.[1] Such phobias may result in overtreatment of the child with aspirin and unnecessary visits to the pediatrician.

First of all, it is important to understand that fever is a *natural defense mechanism* as well as a signal of illness. There is evidence that a high body temperature kills certain disease-causing organisms at a faster rate than a normal body temperature does. Unfortunately for parents who are trying to determine whether or not there is a serious problem, fever may signal anything from the most trivial of diseases (such as a common cold) or even non-diseases (such as exercise or excessive clothing), to a potentially life-threatening disease (such as meningitis—an infection of the lining around the brain). But fever in itself is only a problem when it is extremely high (see below).

You ascertain if there is a fever by using a thermometer (see page 672). If the temperature is low or only moderately elevated (under 103° F. or 39.5° C.) or the fever is "new" (i.e., the child was previously well), we advise parents to use *nothing* but extra liquids and observation. We do not even recommend that parents give aspirin or acetaminophen because it may mask how high the fever is going to go.[2] Generally, in most children, temperatures up to 104° are not dangerous. However, if you know your child is subject to febrile convulsions (convulsions which occur in young children at the onset of an episode of fever) you should give a fever-reducing medicine at the first sign of a fever and at a relatively low temperature. However, fever reduction in children not subject to convulsions is neither necessary nor desirable unless the temperature is over 103°.

If there is a fever, parents should look for clues as to what may be causing it. Does the child have a stuffy nose? Perhaps the child is coming down with a cold. Is the baby pulling at the ears (otitis, see page 636)? Does there seem to be painful urination? Is there any sign of infection (swelling or redness) in the joints or on the skin? Is there a stiff neck, which could mean meningitis?

Call your child's doctor if:

1. Your child's temperature is over 103° (or over 100.4° in a child under two months).
2. Symptoms of infection develop anywhere.
3. The temperature persists for forty-eight hours *without* any other symptoms.
4. The temperature is progressing, i.e., getting higher.

CRYING

Excessive crying in a baby is more of an annoyance to the parents than a sign that the child is ill. The problem parents have is to determine what is excessive and to be sure there is no physical cause for this symptom. It is important that parents try to find out if the onset of crying was associated with something that might point you and the doctor in the right diagnostic direction.

Does the child start crying at the start of urination, which could mean a urinary tract infection? Does the child start crying when you move an arm or a leg? (This might indicate that the limb has been injured or has an infection in it.) Does the child start crying before passing gas? Does the child draw up the legs as though suffering from colic? Of course colic is a common cause of crying in young babies. (For a word about colic, see page 352.)

Crying is one of the few sources of relief from tension that a young baby has. In point of fact, the baby that is crying lustily probably is *not* sick. The young baby that is sick tends more to whimper and also to refuse to feed or to show fatigue on feeding. Such a baby can best be characterized by the word apathetic.

WEIGHT LOSS (OR NO WEIGHT GAIN)

Babies are supposed to gain about an ounce a day (six to eight ounces a week) in the early weeks of life. As a matter of fact, all young mammals put on weight rapidly in infancy.

If the baby is not gaining weight, if you feel the baby has lost weight (based either on scale measurements or your impressions of how clothes fit), or if there are wrinkles in the skin indicating weight loss in the baby, this should be called to the attention of the doctor. Some babies do not gain weight or lose weight because they are vomiting or having diarrhea; others because they are not taking in enough calories. Sometimes parents do not feed babies sufficient calories for growth.

During childhood and adolescence weight loss can also be a serious symptom. It is quite rare in childhood, however, and is usually accompanied by other signs, such as fever, malaise (see p. 633), or lack of energy. One type of weight loss that is becoming relatively common is anorexia nervosa, seen mostly in adolescent girls. Your previously chunky teenager will announce that she is going on a diet but she doesn't seem to stop dieting or stop losing weight. If her figure begins to approach that of a fashion model, be on the alert. If weight loss continues, the child must be taken to the doctor.

Call your child's doctor if:

1. Your baby or child has lost weight.
2. Your infant is not gaining weight.
3. Your teenager is already very thin but continues to diet and lose weight.

DROWSINESS, EXCESSIVE SLEEPINESS, "ACTING FUNNY"

Continued drowsiness or excessive sleepiness can indicate that there is something going on in the central nervous system (brain). This is a bit tricky because many babies will sleep more when coming down with a cold or any infection. Also, sometimes older children have just been playing so hard they will sleep longer than usual. If you are really concerned about the length of time your child is sleeping, the clue as to whether or not something is going on in the central nervous system is *arousability*. If you can arouse your child to a full state of consciousness, the brain is okay. If you cannot, call your doctor.

Call your child's doctor if:

1. You cannot arouse your child.

DELIRIUM

Delirium is defined as extreme mental excitement characterized by a rapid succession of confused and unconnected ideas, often with illusions and/or hallucinations. An illusion is a misperception: mistaking something that is there for something else. Hallucinations are defined as strongly experienced false perceptions. An auditory hallucination is hearing voices and a visual hallucination is seeing things that are not there.

Children who are delirious may be excessively drowsy with intermittent strange behavior in which they appear to be seeing or hearing things or otherwise talking "out of their head." There may also be the excited stage of delirium in which the child literally rants and raves. Things that can cause delirium include high fever, so the temperature should be checked, and certain drugs, including atropine or atropine-like drugs which might be in your home to treat daddy's stomach ache or grandpa's glaucoma. Recreational drugs can also be the culprit. Other causes are Reye's Syndrome (p. 684) or heat stroke (p. 745). Delirium is reasonably frequent with the very high fever seen in pneumonia.

Call your child's doctor if:

1. The child is delirious or "out of his or her head."

MALAISE

Malaise is defined as a bodily discomfort, in other words, a general feeling of not feeling good. You already know what malaise is: it is how you feel the day you are coming down with a cold or the flu. Everything seems wrong and nothing seems wrong. You may feel vague aches and pains but there is nothing specific; your head aches a little but it is not really a headache; your throat is a little scratchy but it is not really a sore throat; your energy levels are down, your irritability levels are up.

Your child may also feel this way when getting the flu. Generally what to do is watch and wait. Malaise is what doctors often call the prodrome (what comes before a disease). You will know soon enough whether your child is just feeling generally punk because of overtiredness or is really coming down with an illness.

On the other hand, we would never tell you to ignore malaise because if this feeling persists in your child, even if nothing else is demonstrated, you should share this information with the doctor.

FATIGUE

We debated whether even to include fatigue in the list of symptoms. In point of fact, fatigue is generally uncommon in children and very short-lived when it does occur. Of course, babies who are kept up too long and overstimulated will show irritability and fatigue. Of course, the toddler who has been playing hard at nursery school all day comes home tired. Of course, the high-schooler who stays up to do homework after too many school activities and doesn't get to bed on time is tired. For the most part children bounce back so quickly that fatigue is rarely a major symptom. If fatigue is progressive or persistent, however, this should be called to the attention of your doctor. It could be a sign of chronic medical illness or depression.

SYMPTOMS BY SYSTEMS

Nervous System

HEADACHE

Although probably 100 percent of adults have headaches at least once in a while, headaches are rare in children. Sinus headaches are infrequent and tension headaches are less common in children than in adults, although in our high pressure world many children are under pressure themselves or pick up tension from their families. Migraines may start in childhood and can be diagnosed by the typical symptoms of severe, throbbing headaches usually accompanied by nausea. If these occur, take your child to the doctor because today we can prevent most attacks.

Headaches accompanied by vomiting and/or blurred vision always should be called to the attention of your doctor, as should headaches following a head injury. Rarely, headaches may be associated with hypertension (high blood pressure), so that persistent headaches require that the child's blood pressure be checked.

One type of headache we want to call to your attention is the *morning headache* because it may signal a brain tumor, or anything else that is causing increased intracranial pressure (pressure inside the skull). If your child complains of a severe headache in the morning, especially if accompanied by vomiting without nausea, this should be called to the attention of your doctor. What about the child who seems to have a headache every morning and wants to stay home from school? If the headache does not occur immediately upon arising and there is no vomiting without nausea you can safely proceed to sort out what is really bothering the child about school.

In the preverbal child, the cause of a headache is almost always medical. The child has bumped the head or is coming down with an illness, usually respiratory. The kind of headache associated with emotional tension usually requires the capacity to anticipate future stress or remember past stresses. The ability to deal with past and future this way normally develops along with the capacity for language. So tension headaches do not usually occur until after school has started. The older child who always gets a headache before acting in a school play or taking part in some other emotionally charged task should be encouraged to talk about what is bothering him or her. Persistent or incapacitating headaches (such that the child stays home instead of performing), should be evaluated with your doctor.

Call your child's doctor if:

1. Headache is accompanied by blurred vision or vomiting.
2. Headaches occur immediately after arising from sleep.
3. Headache is persistent, progressive, or is interfering with the child's normal activities.

STIFF NECK

The most common cause of a stiff neck is muscular but because a stiff neck along with a fever can herald meningitis, a stiff neck is a serious symptom.

The head turns in several directions and people use the word "stiff neck" to describe aching movements in all directions. Thus, parents are sometimes unduly concerned about the wrong kind of stiff neck. The stiff neck you have to worry about is when the child cannot flex (bend) the head down to the chest. When the child attempts to do so, there is pain in the back of the neck and also sometimes in the back. This type of stiff neck is likely to be related to meningitis, either bacterial or viral.

Difficulty or stiffness in bending the head backward or turning it to the side is not associated with meningitis.

If your child has a high fever or drowsiness, you can do what the doctor will do when examining the child. Ask your child to bend the head down so that the chin touches the chest or move the head that way yourself. If the child can do that without any difficulty (provided the child is over about age two), you have virtually ruled out meningitis yourself. If you are not sure whether the child has a stiff neck or not by your examination, call the doctor.

Call your child's doctor if:

1. Your child cannot bend the neck toward the chest (especially when there is fever).

Special Senses

EYES

The most common eye symptom is, "I've got something in my eye" (see p. 763). Pink eye (conjunctivitis) is fairly common in children and may be becoming more frequent because it is an infection which can be passed around in nursery schools. Pink eye treatment requires antibiotic eye drops or ointment and the child should be seen by the doctor.

Sometimes children complain that their eyes hurt but there is no pus and the eyelids are not stuck together. There may be a little bit of redness, but it just doesn't seem like an infection. This can be an allergy, especially if it occurs in the hay fever season. Sometimes an antihistamine will help and in certain cases is all that is needed.

Cross-eyes always concern parents. Under the age of six months, intermittent crossing of the eyes *(squint)* is nothing to worry about. After six months, intermittent or persistently crossed eyes should be seen not only by a pediatrician but also by an ophthalmologist. The problem is more than a cosmetic one. An eye that is crossed may not be used properly and may cause what is called *amblyopia ex anopsia*, which means blindness due to not using one eye. The myth that a child six months or older will "grow out" of a squint is false and should be ignored.

What about suspicion of impaired vision? If ever an older child tells you he or she can't see or can't see properly, this should be immediately called to the attention of a doctor.

What about vision in a newborn baby? Although denial is often prominent, parents of a young child who is born blind usually know something is wrong. The child does not focus on the mother's face, the eyes wander back and forth,

or the child has what is called nystagmus (rapid side-to-side eye movements).
The young baby often has other "blindisms"; these babies turn their heads from
side to side or move their arms out to tap the sides of the bed almost as though
they are trying to define their world tactilely because they cannot define it
visually.

Call your child's doctor if:

1. There is pus or redness in the eye.
2. You suspect your child cannot see properly.
3. The child has crossed eyes after six months of age.

EARS

EARACHE

The verbal child complains in no uncertain terms about an earache because
the pain is severe and generally easy to localize. Complaints of an earache may
be accompanied by crying and often by fever. The preverbal baby may be fussy,
tug at the earlobe, or roll the head back and forth, and have fever.

An earache may come on very suddenly. Your child may have just a runny
nose when put to bed but wakes up screaming with earache pain. Pulling on the
earlobe does *not* make the pain worse.

Rarely, you may see a discharge of pus coming from the ear canal. Do not
confuse pus with liquid wax; the wax is a dark yellowish, clear, resinous material
which may melt when the child has a high fever and start running out. This is
not the same as pus coming from a boil, which is cloudy yellow or white.

Pain in the ear accompanied by fever almost always means *otitis media* (a
middle ear infection) and requires the attention of the doctor for antibiotic
therapy.

Please don't put anything in the ear. Many people of our generation, who
spent some of their childhood in the preantibiotic era, had enough warm olive
oil poured in their ear to make several good Greek salads, but this really doesn't
do any good. Over-the-counter medicines sold to relieve earaches don't do any
good either. But the most important reason we suggest you not put anything in
your child's ear unless it is recommended by a doctor is that the doctor simply
cannot see the eardrum through a coating of olive oil or other goo. If you are far
from medical attention and your child cries in pain from an earache, try a
decongestant and acetaminophen or aspirin (see p. 684) for the pain until you
can get the child to the doctor.

A child with a severe earache who suddenly says it is all better may have a
real problem. It could be that the eardrum has ruptured. Watch for pus coming
out of the ear. Even if you see nothing coming out of the ear, we suggest having
the child seen promptly by a doctor as rapidly as possible because a ruptured
eardrum should be treated promptly.

Sometimes a child may have a severe earache without fever. Moving the
earlobe in any way causes exquisite pain and sometimes you can actually see

swelling of the ear canal. This is *otitis externa* or inflammation of the outer ear, more frequently known as swimmer's ear. If otitis externa is the diagnosis, antibiotic eardrops, which your doctor will prescribe, are used. Some young children are prone to get ear infections with every respiratory infection.

DEAFNESS

Years ago Marilyn was taught that one of the most important questions a pediatrician can ask parents at the first well-baby visit is, "When were you sure your child could hear?" Parents of even very young babies can, if asked the question in that way, remember when they recognized their child could hear. The baby may have turned at the sound of their voice, for example, or jumped at loud noises.

If you are not sure your baby can hear or if an older child has delayed language development (see p. 279) or if the child says "What?" a lot, call this to the doctor's attention. There are critical periods for language acquisition, so prompt detection and treatment of poor hearing helps prevent language handicap.

Call your child's doctor if:

1. Your child has an earache with fever.
2. Your child has an earache with pain on moving the earlobe.
3. You suspect your child does not hear properly.

Respiratory System

RUNNY NOSE

We have no data on this but we suspect that the runny nose is probably *the* most common sign of illness that a child presents during childhood. The most common reason for a runny nose is an upper respiratory infection, which can be caused by many viruses that are found all over the world, such as rhinoviruses ("rhino" means nose, as in rhinocerous). They are tricky little viruses because immunity to them is not lifelong as, for example, is immunity to the measles virus. Therefore, all of us are susceptible to upper respiratory infections all of our lives.

Two things make the situation worse for children. 1) They are more likely to get respiratory infections than are adults. Indeed, during the nursery school years the toddler could have as many as eight to twelve respiratory infections a year, which amounts to one a month. 2) The second reason is the tiny nose. If mucus is running down half of the diameter of a tiny nose the baby can have lots of trouble breathing. Those of us with big noses, miserable as we may feel, are able to breathe a little easier.

Although bacteria are not a common cause of upper respiratory infections, there is one bacterium (the streptococcus) that does cause runny noses in infants. Though it usually causes sore throats in older children and adults, in young babies under six months or so, the only symptom of streptococcal infection may be a runny nose. A baby with a runny nose whose sibs have a sore throat should be checked by the doctor and a nasopharyngeal culture should be done to see if strep is causing the runny nose.

The other common cause for a runny nose is allergy. But interestingly enough, allergy does not always cause the nose to run, i.e., to have mucus drip or pour out of the nostrils. Instead, allergy may swell the membranes of the nose so that they are almost shut with pale, boggy mucosa (lining of the nose). This causes the child to sniffle a lot but the actual outpouring of liquid mucus may be less than with a respiratory infection.

If your child has a runny or stuffy nose all the time, statistically this is likely to be an allergy because the natural history of a cold is that it starts with a runny nose and dries up, and gets better. Another cold won't usually come along for several weeks. The natural history of an allergy is that the child has a runny nose constantly as long as he or she is exposed to the allergen, as, for example, house dust, cat dander, or an offending food.

Another imitator of a cold that can cause a discharge from the nose is a *foreign object*. As a matter of fact, parents often make this diagnosis by noticing that the child has a continuous discharge from *one* nostril. Remember to tell your doctor if *one* nostril runs, especially if you have a child old enough to poke something like a bean or pea into the nose, or if an older sibling may have done so.

What do you do for a runny nose in a child? First of all, this is certainly one of the things you can handle at home. In the absence of a high fever or a cough which is getting progressively worse, a respiratory infection is handled by the *parents* and does not usually need a doctor's attention.

Clearing the Nose of Mucus

In a baby, use a soft rubber bulb syringe with which you gently aspirate the mucus out of each nostril, as often as needed. Nose drops used to be very popular, but we have found that nose drops lead to "rebound" congestion. In addition, getting nose drops into a baby's nose is something we both found very difficult; and it was a task we dreaded, as did our children. Also, nose drops are unsafe in babies.

Oral decongestants can also be used. Marilyn feels these do not work as well in colds as in allergies, but some children do respond. As the medicines are safe when properly used (do not use in babies under six months) and reasonably inexpensive, they are worth a try.

Parents usually have to wipe the nose of toddlers as the child is too young to do it alone. As a child gets older, correct nose-blowing techniques should be taught. This means blowing *one nostril* at a time and *blowing out* rather than in, which is something very hard for even bright children to grasp at first.

When the nose stops running and gets crusty, a tiny bit of Vaseline or baby oil on the tip of your little finger may help remove the crust from the front part of the nostril. Don't get the Vaseline or oil anywhere near the inside of the child's nose because you don't want to get any in the lungs.

Humidification

Interestingly enough, even though there is a lot of moisture coming out of the nose, one treatment for a runny nose is to moisturize the home air or the air in the child's room, especially if the child is prone to lots of runny noses. Many houses are heated in such a way that the humidity is very low and dry air makes a cold worse. We recommend a cold mist vaporizer (see p. 676). Some parents may wish to put a humidifier on their furnace in order to keep the air in their house moist, especially if their children get frequent colds.

Emergency humidification is easy to do. You simply take the child into the bathroom, close the doors and windows, and turn on the hot water in the shower and in the sink. Soon the room will be filled with moist warm air. If you hold your baby in your arms for about ten minutes, often the baby will breathe easier as the crusts in the nose loosen up. You should gently remove the crusts with a tissue or your finger.

Liquids

In addition to humidifying the air that the child breathes (external humidification) you can also humidify the nose secretions by giving the child lots of liquids (internal humidification). For some strange reason, when milk and mucus are mixed they form an unpalatable curd which babies often vomit. One trick is to dilute the baby's milk with water. Marilyn used to give her own children diluted milk using equal parts of water and milk (or formula). Breast-fed babies seem to vomit less but they may not feed well because of the stuffiness. Water by bottle should be offered.

If your baby takes water, give lots of water. You can also try other liquids such as carbonated beverages from which the bubbles have been removed by allowing the drink to stand in a shallow dish for a couple of hours. (If you put fresh pop in a bottle, the baby gets a painful amount of gas via the nipple.) Colas contain caffeine so they should be avoided. Very weak tea with a little sugar or honey is good. However, honey should not be used for babies under one year because it may contain botulism spores which a young baby cannot handle. Because certain herb teas are dangerous we do not recommend their use.

What about calling the doctor when your child has a cold? There are probably not enough pediatricians in America to answer the hypothetical phone calls that would occur if every parent phoned about every runny nose. Well over 90 percent of colds are self-limited and will go away without any medical attention. However, children with prolonged colds (two weeks or more) should be called to the doctor's attention. Children with foul-smelling pus coming from their nose might have a foreign object or chronic sinusitis and should be seen. Babies under six months who may have been exposed to someone with strep, should be seen. Children who seem to be chronically (or seasonally) "stuffed up" may have an allergy and should be evaluated.

The overwhelming majority of children with a runny nose have one of the more than one hundred colds they will have between birth and eighteen. Even with a moderate fever the cold can be treated at home although the febrile child should be watched for signs of complications of respiratory infection.

When your child has a cold, call your child's doctor for:

1. A high fever over 103° F. (39.5° C.)
2. Refusal to take liquids.
3. Excessive irritability.
4. Excessive sleepiness.
5. Pulling at the ear.

SORE THROAT

It is a good idea to learn how to look down your child's throat. Place the child in front of a window or in a bright light, ask your child to open the mouth wide and say "Ahhh" at the same time. This is hard for the child to do, but with patience you should be able to teach this. When the child says "Ahhh" while holding the mouth wide open, the tongue will push forward and you will be able to see the back of the throat *without* using a tongue depressor or spoon or any other object which can frighten a child and cause gagging.

If your child's throat is beefy red (like raw meat) or if there are white spots on it, call this to your doctor's attention.

If the child has a high fever, or if there are lumps in the child's neck (lymph nodes), the child should be taken to the doctor because a diagnosis of strep throat can *be made only by means of a throat culture.* Some doctors provide mothers with materials and instructions for taking throat culture samples at home which must be taken to the doctor's office or a laboratory. If your child has a strep throat, ten days of antibiotics must be given in order to prevent such complications of strep as scarlet or rheumatic fever.

If the throat has little red lines in it that look almost like they have been drawn with a red pen, this is probably irritation of the back of the throat due to a cold or coughing. You may also see tiny blisters sometimes surrounded by a red circle. These are usually due to a virus but are painful and may keep your child from eating and drinking.

Treatment of a sore throat at home includes old remedies like honey and lemon juice (no honey for infants), lots of liquids, especially hot liquids, which are soothing, and humidifying the air.

Call your child's doctor if your child has:

1. Beefy red throat.
2. White spots on throat.
3. High fever with sore throat.
4. Lumps in the neck.

COUGH

A cough is a good symptom, as the cough is a protective reflex which clears the respiratory tree of stuff that shouldn't be there, such as mucus.

The cough reflex is present at birth. A cough occurs when there is some irritant present in the back of the throat, trachea, larynx, or lung that should be expelled. The irritant can be particulate matter like smoke or a chemical. It can be mucus or dryness caused by allergy or infection. It can even be actual particles of lung tissue coughed up during pneumonia.

There are many different reasons a child coughs. Your role as a parent is not necessarily to stop the cough but to observe why the child is coughing and, if desirable, try to modify the child's environment so the cough is less.

There are different kinds of coughs. The so-called *loose cough* sounds as though the child is bringing up lots of mucus (children rarely spit mucus out to the external world; they usually swallow it even if it does come up to the back of their throat). There is a tight cough, which doesn't seem to be producing anything, which is why doctors call it a *"non-productive cough."* There is the brassy, metallic or *croupy cough* which sounds like a barking seal. There is a *paroxysmal* (severe and recurring) *cough* with whooping that means whooping cough. There is a cough that accompanies severe asthma, which is kind of a *wheezing cough* (you can sometimes hear the wheezing by putting your ear to your child's chest).

Everyone with a cold coughs a little bit because mucus runs down the back of the throat. Chest coughs are usually deep, hoarse coughs that sound as though they are coming from the big tubes (bronchi) in the chest instead of from the back of the throat.

A prolonged cough along with a fever could be pneumonia. Here the *progression* and *persistence* concepts are important. The most important thing that observant parents can do when the child has a cough is to see whether or not "respiratory distress" accompanies it. Respiratory distress means the child is having trouble breathing air in or out; the respirations are rapid and/or labored. This plus a cough means you should call the doctor. If there is a cough without respiratory distress, generally you can wait and see what is happening. If the cough is getting a little better each night, you don't have to take the child to the doctor. If it is getting more frequent, or worse, the child should be taken to the doctor. Also, if it persists beyond ten days, the child should be taken to the doctor because this might be a chronic problem, such as an allergy which has masqueraded as a cold.

A cough suppressant is a medication that actually dulls the cough reflex so the child will cough less. This can have a positive effect, i.e., the child can sleep for the first time in three nights (and so, incidentally, can the parents). It also can have a negative effect because the cough is there for a reason, to clear the mucus from the child's respiratory tree. There are two things you can try first before using cough suppressants. One is to humidify the air around the child. The second is to try a home remedy that is soothing and may work. For older children a mixture of honey and lemon juice, or honey, lemon juice, and whiskey, often stops a cough.

Marilyn shares a story that a woman told her many years ago. The mother dutifully made up a little bottle of Marilyn's mixture of honey, lemon juice, and whiskey to give to her little girl, who had a cough. After a day or two, the twenty-month-old began to toddle over to the cabinet where the medicine was kept and *pretend* to cough! This is why many doctors no longer recommend giving *any* alcohol to children.

Incidentally, sometimes in older children, just taking a teaspoonful of honey before bedtime soothes the throat enough so that it seems to reduce the coughing. Dentists would prefer that teeth be brushed before bedtime, so that all sugar materials (including honey) are removed. But sometimes the child's cough seems more important than the child's teeth.

We rarely recommend bed rest, but sometimes a child who has a lingering cough after a respiratory infection is fine while quiet but starts coughing on exertion. We think this is a signal to the parents that perhaps another day or two of quiet play (lots of lap time and reading to the child) is a treatment that makes sense. By the way, a cough on exertion may indicate a form of asthma even if the child is not wheezing.

Call your child's doctor if:

1. Cough is accompanied by respiratory distress.
2. Cough persists more than ten days.

SWOLLEN GLANDS

Swollen glands or enlarged lymph nodes theoretically belong in the blood and immune system. However, most of the swollen glands you are going to see in your child will be in the neck. Also most of the ones you are going to see result from a respiratory infection with secondary infection of the lymph nodes of the neck. Therefore, we are including them here. Children have larger, more easily distensible lymph nodes until they are about age eight, so that many will have swelling of the lymph nodes with every respiratory infection. Some children are more prone to swollen glands with infections than others.

Sometimes lymph nodes on one side of the neck are swollen but the child does not seem to have a respiratory infection. Look at the child's throat to see if that is inflamed. Also check the teeth because an abscessed tooth (collection of pus under the tooth) can cause swollen neck glands. (Tap on each tooth with the eraser end of a pencil. The child will experience pain if the tooth is abscessed.) Enlarged lymph nodes in the neck are very rarely caused by tuberculosis. Nodes in the back of the neck below the hairline can be due to rubella (German measles) and sometimes these pop out before the rash does.

Lymph nodes you can feel or see above the collarbone, in the groin, or in the armpit may be somewhat more dangerous as they could be a sign of a malignancy. These should be called to the doctor's attention. Of course, a child with a cut on the knee which gets infected could have enlarged lymph nodes in the groin from the infection. Nodes due to a malignancy almost never hurt, whereas lymph nodes due to infection usually are generally tender or cause the child pain.

CROUP

Croup is a frightening symptom in childhood. Croup is actually a term for several diseases manifested by noises of respiration: hoarseness, stridor (harsh, rasping voice or breathing), and a "barking" cough (which sounds more like a seal than a schnauzer).

Croup occurs in young children and comes on at night. The noises of croup can be frightening but the important thing to determine is whether the child is in respiratory distress. Quiet, rapid breathing is more serious than noisy breathing at a normal rate. The child in respiratory distress may have retractions (when the child breathes you can see the flesh under the ribs get sucked inward), may be blue around the lips, or very restless pointing to oxygen lack. Usually there is no fever or only a slight elevation.

At home you should try humidifying the air your child breathes. You can place a washcloth wrung out in very warm (but not hot) water over the child's mouth and nose (take it off if your child cries) while you start running hot water in the tub, shower, and sink of your bathroom at full blast. Close the door and sit with your child in the steam-filled room. Make a game of this and give your child sips of a cold, clear liquid. Milk often makes croup worse, but if your child wants it, dilute it with water, add a little sugar, and cool it with ice cubes. Don't use commercial cough medicines as you don't want to suppress this kind of cough.

Call your child's doctor if:

1. Your child has retractions (you can see the ribs sucked in) when the child breathes.
2. The child is blue (look at the lips).
3. There is extreme restlessness or agitation.
4. There is a sudden onset of high fever and hoarseness with drooling.

WHEEZING

The clues that your child may be wheezing are that the child begins to cough and seems to be having difficulty breathing. Sometimes you can actually hear the wheezing sounds when the child breathes out (put your ear to the child's chest). Remember it is not the noise of the breathing that alerts you to call the doctor. It is the degree of *respiratory distress* your child has. Respiratory distress is manifested by a high *rate* of respiration, air hunger demonstrated by retractions (sucking in of the ribs), exhaustion, and cyanosis (blueness). If respiratory distress accompanies wheezing, the child should be taken to the doctor. Occasionally, if you remove the child from, for example, a smoke-filled room, the child will stop wheezing, but if not call your doctor or take the child to an emergency room.

Cardiovascular System

RAPID OR IRREGULAR HEARTBEAT (Arrhythmias)

Your child may complain that his or her heart is beating "funny" or beating fast or skipping beats. It is almost impossible to take the pulse of a child in the wrist when the child's heart is beating rapidly so we suggest that you put your hand on the pulse in the child's neck and try to count. If the heart is beating so fast you can't count, there is probably an arrhythmia (supraventricular tachycardia) and this should be called to the immediate attention of the doctor.

Skipped beats may be no problem at all. These are called premature ventricular contractions and most of us have had them at one time or another. However, skipped beats *can* be a more serious arrhythmia. If they are frequent or the child complains of them a lot, the child should be taken to the doctor for an electrocardiogram. Also if the heartbeat is very fast or very irregular, call the doctor or take the child to the emergency room.

Call your child's doctor if:

1. Your child's pulse is so fast you can't count it.
2. The heartbeat is very irregular.

CHEST PAIN

Chest pain as a symptom by itself is almost always *not* serious in a child. The child may complain of chest pain when there is wheezing or coughing, due to asthma or pneumonia. Chest pain can, of course, be due to a broken rib or injury. Most of the time when a child complains of chest pain, in the absence of respiratory problems, there is nothing wrong. Reassurance is all that is needed. Children are often quite concerned that they are having a heart attack, especially bright school-age, overachieving children, but this almost never occurs in the young.

Digestive System

MOUTH

TOOTHACHE

Toothaches should always be called to the attention of the dentist. Sometimes your child will say the mouth hurts and you can't quite tell whether the child means he or she has a toothache. One easy way of finding out is to use the eraser end of a pencil to tap firmly on each tooth. If there is an abscess under the tooth that you tap on, the child will complain of pain.

One home toothache remedy that worked once when Marilyn was in rural

Costa Rica with a toothache and no dentist, was the old-fashioned remedy of biting on a tea bag. Though it didn't taste very good, the tannic acid relieved the pain temporarily. Acetaminophen or aspirin can also be used for pain until the child can get to the dentist.

THRUSH (Moniliasis)

Thrush, which often occurs in young babies, is manifested by little white spots in the mouth that look like little cottage cheese curds. Thrush should be called to the attention of the doctor as it can interfere with the baby's eating. The doctor will prescribe something like Mycostatin. Thrush can be confused with Koplik's spots in measles, but not in the absence of fever.

CANKER SORES

The most common sore in the mouth is the so-called canker sore, which is actually an ulcer of the lining of the mouth. Children (and some grown-ups) get canker sores quite frequently. They may be caused by biting the side of the tongue or mouth, allergy, or minor infections. Generally, these do not have to be called to the attention of your doctor as they will heal, usually quite rapidly. The only problem is they may be painful enough that the child avoids eating or drinking and could get dehydrated. One trick that might help in canker sores is making a paste out of a Gelusil tablet, dissolved in a bit of water, to rub on the child's mouth. Another thing that helps is Gly-Oxide, which can be bought without a prescription. Sores in the mouth can also be due to a malignancy or a virus like Herpes Simplex or Coxsackie. Malignancies almost never begin with sores in the mouth, but if the sores persist or get any worse, call them to the attention of the doctor.

COLD SORES ("fever blisters")

Sores on the lips may be due to recurrent herpes (not sexual herpes) infections. They often occur in young children with fever or sunburn. Generally, they go away without any treatment.

Digestive System

"POOR APPETITE"

Poor appetite alone is almost never of significance in children. If poor appetite is seen in conjunction with other symptoms, such as fever and nausea, it can be explained by whatever illness the child is coming down with or has. What parents call poor appetite is often seen in the toddler age group but this is because the child's rate of growth has slowed down considerably and will never be the same again until adolescence. There are two common reasons for this "poor appetite." One is overfeeding or expectation that the child should eat more than the child is doing; the other is allowing the child to snack so often that the child is never really hungry.

STOMACHACHE

Most abdominal pain in children is of no consequence, especially when unaccompanied by other symptoms. When children say, "My belly hurts," they almost always point to the umbilicus (belly button). They may lie down for a minute or two, get up and go out and play. This is usually due to gas, or something they have eaten that caused a bit of indigestion. Sometimes this is associated with mild constipation.

Often when children complain of an abdominal pain they are really saying they are stressed for some reason or another. A bellyache, often with nausea and sometimes even with vomiting, can occur as a stress response. Stress-related abdominal pain is caused by a painful contraction of part of the gut and is a normal response to fear or anxiety. It occurs in lower animals as well as humans. Laboratory rats, for example, will defecate if exposed to a conditioned danger signal.

There are some bellyaches that are serious. Abdominal pain that causes a child to scream in agony every few minutes, especially when accompanied by bloody diarrhea or the passage of bloody mucus, is an emergency that should be immediately called to the doctor's attention. This might be an intussusception (part of the intestine slips into the next part and gets stuck). Immediate reduction of the intussusception by barium enema or surgery is necessary.

Abdominal pain of increasing intensity, along with nausea and vomiting and a low grade fever, may be *appendicitis*. In the older child these symptoms tend to localize in the right lower quarter of the abdomen. In the younger child the picture may be not as clear, so any abdominal pain with nausea, vomiting, and fever should be called to the attention of the doctor.

Abdominal pain with diarrhea, with or without fever, can be caused by *acute gastroenteritis* (infection of the gut, usually caused by a virus). If these same symptoms persist, *malabsorption* or *regional enteritis* might be the problem.

Another cluster of symptoms which can be serious is constipation, bloating of the abdomen, pain, and vomiting (especially with bile in the vomitus). This can be a sign of intestinal obstruction, which can occur anywhere in the gut. Such a child should be immediately taken to the doctor.

Children rarely have ulcers but symptoms of an ulcer include upper abdominal pain accompanied by vomiting, especially if the pain occurs after meals.

Abdominal pain, especially on the left side, accompanied by shoulder pain, may indicate a ruptured spleen. Please remember this if your child has had a recent injury like falling off of a swing.

Postpubertal girls who have abdominal pain can be suffering from mittelschmerz, which is painful ovulation that occurs in mid-cycle. Because of the irregularity of periods in teenagers, this is sometimes hard to diagnose.

Abdominal pain with a high fever and cough may be pneumonia. Abdominal pain with low grade fever and symptoms of a upper respiratory infection is usually mesenteric adenitis (inflamed lymph nodes around the intestine).

Call your child's doctor if there is:

1. Severe abdominal pain every few minutes when accompanied by bloody diarrhea.
2. Pain, nausea, vomiting, low grade fever.
3. Pain, constipation, vomiting, bloating of the abdomen.
4. Pain in the belly and left shoulder.
5. Persistent abdominal pain.

VOMITING

Vomiting is an extremely common symptom, although there are vomiters and non-vomiters. Marilyn's daughter is the former and Marilyn is the latter. She can actually remember all the times in her life that she vomited, which are very few. It is probably safe to say that vomiting is so common in childhood that none of you will get through parenting without cleaning up vomitus.

The most common cause of vomiting is to rid the stomach of contents it doesn't particularly like or want. The child may have eaten something that doesn't agree with the child or that the child is allergic to. The child may have overeaten, such as too many sweets at a birthday party, or eaten something spoiled.

Infection, either viral, bacterial, or the food poisoning variety, is a common cause of vomiting. Vomiting can also have a psychological basis. Indeed, many children vomit when they are upset. If they do this frequently enough, the wise parent will be sure the child knows how to head for the toilet bowl at the first sign of upset. We used to put a wastebasket, into which we placed a heavy-duty plastic bag, next to a sick child's bed, especially at night. The child who might not make it to the toilet bowl could usually make it to the wastebasket.

Most of the time vomiting in childhood is relatively minor and self-limited. The only treatment we recommend is ice chips, ginger ale, and not eating for a while. If a child seems to have indigestion along with vomiting, try a Tums.

There are two things parents have to watch out for. The first is vomiting as a symptom of intestinal obstruction. Obviously, if nothing can pass through the intestines you will know about it. All of the digestive juices, as well as the food the child has ingested, if blocked going downward will come upward (i.e., will be vomited). The child will vomit bile (green digestive juices). If vomiting is frequent, especially after the stomach contents are emptied, or if vomiting is accompanied by adominal pain and constipation, this is a medical emergency. Intestinal obstruction can be caused by many things, but all of them have to be seen by the doctor.

The only other thing parents have to worry about is that prolonged vomiting can cause dehydration. Obviously, when the child is vomiting, the child is not getting fluids in. It is a good idea to keep a chart so you have an idea of how often and how much the child is vomiting (see p. 699). Look for signs of dehydration like dry mouth and eyes and dry diapers.

Persistence and progression are very important concepts here. There is a real entity called the twenty-four-hour flu. These children (or adults) can be truly miserable with vomiting and diarrhea which may actually be almost continuous, but the symptoms usually turn off as rapidly as they begin. In the older child, in whom dehydration does not seem to be an immediate problem, waiting for twenty-four hours, especially if the vomiting is accompanied by diarrhea, is okay. If there are no stools so that you worry about intestinal obstruction, call a doctor. A young infant who vomits all feedings for twelve hours is an emergency.

Call your child's doctor if:

1. Vomiting is accompanied by abdominal pain, bloating, and constipation.
2. Vomiting persists for more than a day.
3. Vomiting in a baby persists for twelve hours.

DIARRHEA

Diarrhea, which is quite common in babies, can be caused by many things, including infection (bacterial, viral, or parasitic), allergy, overfeeding, food intolerance or malabsorption, bowel disease like colitis, malnutrition, and immune disorders, to name a few. It may also result from antibiotics or something as simple as introducing a new food to an infant.

Clinical manifestations of diarrhea are frequent, soft to watery stools. Sometimes the stools are green because they do not stay in the gut long enough to become their normal color, and there may be blood, pus, or mucus in the stool.

Diarrhea can be a very serious disease for young infants, (although the disease is usually 100 percent curable) because, during the course of diarrhea, the baby can get dehydrated. An adult can tolerate much more fluid loss than can a child. Parents may not realize how quickly—and with what grave results— dehydration can occur. One young couple we know were traveling when their baby got diarrhea. They were due to go home the next day and decided to go ahead with their plans. The baby died on the airplane.

Many cases of diarrhea in young infants are self-limited and do not require medical attention. When Marilyn taught pediatric residents about diarrhea, she divided the disease into "Inpatient Diarrhea," meaning diarrhea so severe that the child is dehydrated and needs to be hospitalized for intravenous fluids, and "Outpatient Diarrhea," which does not require admission to the hospital. Residents were taught to tell the parents how to keep track of what was happening to the child so that the distinction could be made between these two types of diarrhea.

It is easy to keep a chart of what is happening to your baby with diarrhea (see p. 699). You need a piece of paper with five columns headed Stools, Vomiting, Temperature, Ounces Liquid Taken, Urine (see Table 57). Put the date on it. In the first column every time the baby has a bowel movement record the time and write down whether it is watery, a large or small amount, and the color. If your child vomits, record the approximate amount (e.g., a cupful) and the contents (e.g., particles of carrots). The child's temperature should be taken and recorded. The number of ounces of liquids that the child takes should also be listed. In the last column you should keep track of when your child urinates and whether it is a normal or less than normal amount. It can be difficult to tell this when the stools are liquid.

If you keep such a chart, when you call your doctor you can say, "The diarrhea was bad yesterday evening when it started, Doctor, but today the child has had only three loose stools and they are no longer watery. Johnny hasn't vomited; he took forty-two ounces of clear liquids and kept it all down. His temperature is 99°, and he seems to be urinating a lot." The doctor can tell that this child is not dehydrated and does not have to be admitted to the hospital. On the other hand, if the child has had ten stools, only took fifteen ounces of liquids and vomited most of it, the temperature is up to 102°, and the child apparently has not voided for several hours, this means the child needs immediate medical attention so that the doctor can assess the degree of dehydration.

Clear liquids, the time-honored home treatment of diarrhea, include water, weak tea with a little sugar (don't use herb teas as some of these can be quite hazardous to children), flat soda pop. The simplest thing to do for a young baby, however, is to use the child's formula or milk. Pour out one half of the milk and replace it with water. Then offer the child this diluted mixture. Your child is used to the taste of milk and generally takes it quite well—better than clear liquids, in some cases. Do not use Jell-O water or Kool-Aid as the sugar content is so high that diarrhea can be made worse. Do not use boiled skimmed milk, which used to be prescribed for diarrhea (see p. 532).

You can also use Pedialyte, a solution of electrolytes (dissolved salts) which can be depleted because of diarrhea. This can be purchased without a prescription. The directions say to consult your doctor before using in children under two, and we agree. For children over two, offer some to the child every one or two hours to a total of one quart a day or what the doctor recommends.

In most children, diarrhea lasts only a day or two and regular feedings can gradually be resumed starting with starches first like crackers and toast.

A breast-feeding mother can let the baby take what he or she wants from the breast and also offer water by bottle.

In the young baby, following a case of ordinary viral diarrhea, the child may continue to have diarrhea because of temporary lactose intolerance, which means that the infection has somewhat damaged the border of the lining of the intestine and the enzyme lactase is not working properly, so milk is not absorbed well. In older children with persistent diarrhea, things like ulcerative colitis come to mind. What is persistent? Diarrhea that goes on longer than a week or that recurs every few days should be called to the attention of the doctor.

Call your child's doctor if:

1. Signs of dehydration are present (dry mouth and eyes and no urination).
2. The child is vomiting and/or refusing liquids.
3. The child has a high fever (over 103° F. or 39.5 C.).

CONSTIPATION

Constipation is the difficult passage of a hard stool. A breast-fed baby who has a normal stool, even if passed only every couple of days, is not constipated. The older child who just happens to be on a "schedule" where he or she defecates every two to three days without pain or any other symptom is not constipated. Nowhere is it written that human beings must defecate daily. Perfectly normal health can be enjoyed by those who don't.

The most common cause of constipation in a young baby is not giving the baby enough fluid. Constipation in the older child is generally caused by not eating enough dietary fiber. The best treatment of constipation is adding liquid or fiber as the case may be.

There are some children who have a tendency toward constipation which may be troublesome to the children and their parents. We do not ordinarily recommend laxatives or the use of suppositories. However, if a person defecates infrequently, the stool gets harder because water is absorbed in the lower intestine, so the passage of a stool every three or four days could mean the stool gets so hard that it is painful to pass or it causes bleeding. Thus we do recommend increasing the fiber in your child's diet. Enemas should never be given unless prescribed by your doctor, as these may be dangerous in infants and children.

You should take the child with constipation to the doctor if vomiting accompanies the constipation, as we discussed above (see p. 647). If the child goes for more than six or seven days without a bowel movement, even if there are no other symptoms, tell the doctor. *Encopresis*, or leakage of stool, should also be called to the doctor's attention. Leakage of liquid stool around the hard stool can occur because the child withholds stool.

Call your child's doctor if:

1. Constipation is accompanied by vomiting.
2. Constipation is accompanied by leakage of stool.
3. The child does not have a bowel movement for a week.

STOOLS: BLACK, RED, WHITE, OR WORMY

Black stools signify bleeding high in the upper intestinal tract. This should always be called to the doctor's attention. If your child is taking iron for anemia this also can cause black stools but a simple test done in the doctor's office can determine whether blood is present or not. Red stools may be due to beet ingestion. Blood streaks on the stool are usually due to a fissure (crack) in the anus (if the bleeding were higher up, the stool would have turned black). Blood with mucus in the stools may indicate bacterial diarrhea. White stools usually signify that the liver is having problems getting bile into the stool. This is an early sign of hepatitis or a sign of blockage of the bile ducts and should always be called to your doctor's attention. Do not confuse white or light stools with the stools of breast-fed babies, which are often pale in color. Wormy stools are almost never seen but occasionally a child will pass a worm segment. Retrieve it and take it to the doctor for identification as it is very difficult to diagnose worms over the phone.

Urinary System

INFREQUENT URINATION

The most common cause of not putting out as much urine as usual is that the child is not drinking the amount of fluid needed, especially if the weather is hot and the child has been exercising. Most children who have access to water and normal thirst mechanisms will drink enough to meet needs. The child will be thirsty, will drink more, and the urine output will become normal.

In a young baby who does not have access to water, nor the means to ask for it, anything that causes dehydration like diarrhea can reduce the urine output. It is important to check the baby's diapers frequently when there is dehydration or high fever, both of which can cause decreased urinary output.

Call your child's doctor if:

1. Your baby has totally dry diapers for more than twelve hours.

EXCESSIVE URINATION

The most common cause of excessive urination is excessive drinking. At parties some children drink a lot of soda pop. Sometimes when children play they get so thirsty that they drink lots of liquid and then have to urinate more than usual. Again this is normal; the homeostatic (balancing) mechanisms of the body regulate fluid intake and output. If the child has been drinking more than usual, the extra water will be urinated out.

Some children, however, seem to have to go to the bathroom every half-hour or so and also complain of excessive thirst. As you probably know, *diabetes* can cause this. A friend told Marilyn that her daughter stopped at every bathroom and drinking fountain at Disney World on their spring vacation. The friend thought it was excitement and the heat of Florida. Because the symptoms persisted when they got home the child was checked by the doctor and turned out to have diabetes.

Knowing your child's pattern and noting whether the excessive urination is progressive or persistent helps you decide whether or not to call your doctor.

PAIN ON URINATION

Pain on urination almost always signifies a urinary tract infection. Sometimes children complain of pain on urination because the perineum (the area around the urethra) is irritated due to poor hygiene, irritation from bubble bath, or scratching because of pinworms. Marilyn remembers a child who complained of pain on urination because she had some chicken pox on the inside of her thigh, so when she urinated, urine got on the pox and caused pain.

A urinary tract infection itself can cause some irritation of the perineum but it doesn't usually work this way. If your child complains of pain or burning on urination, inspect the area. If there is no rash that could account for it, take the child to the doctor so that a urinalysis can be done.

Call your child's doctor if:

1. Your child complains of pain on urination.

URINE: RED, BROWN, CLOUDY, OR SMELLY

Red urine can contain blood or can be due to beet ingestion. Some children may lack an enzyme which means that their urine will be colored red after they have eaten beets. It is of absolutely no consequence, but some mothers don't like red diapers so they do not give their child beets. This is fine because there are lots of other vegetables. Rifampin, an antibiotic used to prevent Hemophilus influenzae infections after exposure, can also cause red urine.

If the urine is clear to start with, but then blood appears at the end of urination, this might be a urinary tract infection, such as cystitis or urethritis. A dark yellow urine is often due to dehydration. Brown or very dark urine can be due to hepatitis and should be called to the attention of your doctor.

Odiferous urine may follow the ingestion of certain vegetables such as asparagus. An odor of ammonia usually means that the diapers need more frequent changing. There is ammonia in all urine and when the water evaporates, the ammonia is left. The odor of rancid butter may result from a lack of cleanliness as butyric acid (the same acid found in rancid butter) accumulates. More frequent baths will clean this up.

ENURESIS (Bedwetting)

If a child has been completely dry and then starts wetting the bed more than once or twice, you have to consider either a physical problem, such as diabetes or diabetes insipidus, or a potentially serious emotional problem. Most children with typical familial bed-wetting have never been dry at night, and most eventually do become dry. Neither of us worries about bedwetting until about age five.

There are two types of enuresis. *Diurnal enuresis* is frequent dribbling during the day, sometimes seen in anxious children who are afraid to ask to go to the bathroom. Wetting periodically during the day or being constantly wet are different symptoms, however. If the child is constantly wet this may be an indication of neurological or renal damage.

Nocturnal enuresis is the term for bedwetting. This is a familial problem and the chance of a child whose parents were not enuretic having enuresis is small. Studies of children who wet the bed at night reveal that their bladder capacity is not particularly smaller than other children, nor do they sleep deeper. However, they do seem to have reduced external sphincter control. The problem is much more common in boys than girls.

Time-honored fluid restriction after a certain hour works in some children. Behavioral modification has been successful. Paradoxically, this includes forcing fluids and teaching children to "wait and hold it" in order that they may develop increased control and increased bladder capacity. Gold star charts for dry nights with incremental rewards work in many cases. Drug therapy with imipramine (Tofranil) has been effective in some but is not without risk. There is a conditioning apparatus on the market which wakes the child by a bell when the child begins to urinate and the bed first becomes wet. We personally do not recommend these except in very specific instances, but some parents feel they have been very effective.

We favor making it very easy for the child to get to the bathroom alone at night. This means no diapers, no tight pajamas with tough buttons, a night-light on in the hall, etc. Waking up the child after the Johnny Carson show is not a bad idea, either.

Anne suggests that the child place a large heavy cotton bath towel over the sheet before sleeping (with parental help if needed). Then the child who wakes up wet can easily put the towel and wet clothing in the regular hamper.

Waiting until the child is able to get through the night without wetting is probably the best treatment. If a child wets the bed at age five, the child has about a 15 percent chance of ceasing bedwetting each year if nothing is done, which means almost all children will be dry by the teen years.

By the way, do not restrict the bedwetter from overnights or camp. The child can pack a rubber sheet if need be. Bedwetting should not isolate a child; rather, the child should appreciate that the problem is a developmental one which means the child will grow out of it.

Musculoskeletal System

THE CHILD WHO LIMPS

If you notice your child is limping, the first thing you should do is look at the child's feet and shoes. The most common cause of a limp is either a lesion at the bottom of the foot, such as a blister, thorn, or a bite, or something in the shoe itself, like a nail (or in the case of some children who dress carelessly, a wadded-up sock in the sneaker!). If treating the bottom of the foot or the inside of the shoe does not help, the child should be taken to the doctor as a limp can be caused by something wrong with the foot, knee, hip, or back.

GROWING PAINS

There is no such thing as growing pains, but something does happen in some preschool and early school-age children that causes them to be awakened at night by pains in the thighs or calves. No treatment is necessary except soothing and rubbing. No one quite knows what these pains are but they are of no consequence. You can tell this is not rheumatic fever because the pain is not in the joint and the joint is not warm or red.

THE CLUMSY CHILD

All babies are clumsy when they are beginning to walk. A child cannot really run like an adult until he or she is in school. Children who remain clumsy may do so because of developmental delay. Some of these children don't have as good coordination as others and sometimes profit by exercise programs. The only clumsiness parents have to be concerned about is in those children who seem to have a really large deficit or those children who were previously coordinated and then develop clumsiness, as this could signal muscular dystrophy or another problem. If a child, when compared to peers in nursery school or school, is definitely more clumsy, you should call this to the doctor's attention.

Skin

SKIN COLOR: YELLOW, BLUE, RED, OR PALE

Jaundice means yellow color of the skin and whites of the eyes. It is easier to notice in the whites of the eyes. Because of the blood flowing through the skin, it may be hard to see the jaundice there especially in a young baby. Gentle pressure on the skin (the doctor uses the stethoscope but you can use a jar lid provided it is not sharp), will show you, when blood is pushed out of the skin by the pressure, whether there is yellow underneath or not.

Jaundice is due to either a liver problem such as hepatitis, blockage of the bile ducts, or hemolysis, which is the breaking down of red cells. If you notice jaundice in your child, tell your doctor right away. Jaundice which occurs in very young babies may be so-called physiologic jaundice. It should be reported to your doctor, even though the doctor may tell you to do nothing about it. The doctor may want a blood test to determine the level of the jaundice.

Yellow skin can also be due to carotenemia which is caused by eating too many yellow vegetables like carrots and will go away when fewer are eaten. Carotenemia does *not* cause the eyes to turn yellow.

Blueness (cyanosis) can be seen in the nails and lips of children with certain congenital heart diseases or respiratory problems which prevent them from getting enough oxygen to the skin. Some poisons can also cause cyanosis. Nitrites convert hemoglobin into methemoglobin, which is darker and therefore makes the child look blue. Although cyanosis of the nails may be common in newborn babies, by the time they are several days old they should have pink nails so cyanosis is a sign that should always be called to the attention of the doctor.

Perhaps the most common cause of red skin is sunburn. Babies do not have much melanin (tanning pigment) in their skin and should be protected from the sun, especially in hot climates. The best way to protect a baby from the sun is to keep the baby in the shade. When the child gets older and plays outdoors, sunscreens should be used. This prevents sunburn today and skin cancer tomorrow.

A child who looks pale may look so because he or she inherited the pale complexion of Nordic ancestors. If you want to determine real paleness, or pallor, look at the lips and nail beds or tongue and compare them with your own. Another trick is to look at the palm of the hand. When you push the fingers back from the palm of the hand, the lines in the hand should still have red in them. If the child is anemic, the lines will be pale.

A child can get pale suddenly if the child is about to faint or is in shock (see p. 738). If your child is not thriving very well and you notice that the lips and fingernails or the mucous membranes of the mouth (inside of the mouth) are pale instead of pink, this should be called to the attention of the doctor. Your pale child can be suffering from anemia (low red blood cell count).

RASHES

Pediatricians get a large number of calls about rashes. Rashes are visible and they are evidence that something is amiss with a child. Parents would much rather have a child with clear skin than a rash but rashes that don't bother the child are generally benign. Rashes also cause itching and general miserableness. Call the doctor if the rash looks like *purple blood blisters*, especially if the child has a *fever* and looks sick. This could be a very serious infection called meningococcemia.

BLISTERS

A bumpy rash can be either blisters, which have fluid in them, or what the doctors call maculopapular lesions, which are raised lesions without fluid. Blisters may be due to chicken pox or rubbing, such as from an ill-fitting shoe. It is useful to be able to diagnose chicken pox at home—perhaps with the help of your doctor on the telephone—as it is wise not to bring a child with chicken pox to the doctor's office because it is so contagious. If you are a good observer, you can notice the red base and the clear fluid of the blister of chicken pox. You will also be able to see crops of blisters at different stages—some clear, some crusted.

WEEPY RASHES

Weepy rashes are open rashes which are oozing (they later become crusted) such as *eczema*. Usually eczema occurs in the folds of the arms at the elbow and in the creases of the neck and face.

SCALY RASHES

Scaly rashes or crusted rashes can occur on the scalp as in seborrheic dermatitis or on the face and arms as a result of chronic eczema.

ACNE

Most people know what acne looks like. A few zits can be handled at home but even mild acne should be seen and treated by the doctor as teenagers suffer greatly if they have an appearance problem.

RINGWORM

Ringworm of the scalp or skin is a circular lesion and requires attention by the doctor.

DIAPER RASH

Interestingly enough, there are several varieties. The diaper rash caused by candida (monilia) a fungus that thrives in warm, wet places, is deep red and has a sharp line of demarcation between the rash and the normal skin—almost like a line drawn by a pencil. Ordinary diaper rash, caused by ammonia in the urine, is not as red. There are patches of little bumps and the rash has an irregular border. Candida needs treatment from the doctor but ordinary diaper rash can be handled at home with zinc oxide ointment and frequent changes—or no diapers at all.

RASHES IN GENERAL

In general, if a child has a rash with a fever, if the rash is causing the child to feel miserable or itch, or if the rash appears while the child is taking medication, the doctor should see it.

Treatment of a rash at home is relatively simple. The rules are as follows:

1. Keep the skin clean. You can safely use soap and water on nearly all rashes. Rinse completely.
2. If the rash is open and weepy, keep the skin clean and use wet compresses with Burow's solution.
3. For crusted and scaly rashes, use an ointment that will get under the scales and help get rid of the crust.
4. If there is a lot of itching you can try Benadryl.

If the rash covers a lot of your child, do not put anything on it before you take the child to the doctor. Many of the lotions and ointments you may have will modify the rash so the doctor will have trouble diagnosing it.

Psychosocial Symptoms

There isn't a family today in which some of the complaints in this section won't arise. Some of the symptoms truly represent the "common colds" of psychiatric practice, usually benign but occasionally more serious. With emotional or behavioral problems it is usually even harder than with physical illnesses for parents to know when they are overreacting and when they are underreacting.

If you find yourself getting very upset about a problem that we suggest is common and self-limiting, feel free to get some consultation anyhow. It could be that the child's problem is mild, but is a trigger for you. Even though the symptom might not bother another parent, it may send you "up the wall."

ANGER, AGGRESSION, CRUELTY

Every normal person, child and adult, gets angry. In one sense, people would be defenseless if they couldn't get angry because anger gets you physiologically ready to protect your interests. Sometimes anger is so unpleasant people want to avoid it. Yet, it is healthier to learn to express and use anger constructively than to repress angry feelings.

Parents want to know: When is anger "normal"? When is it "excessive"? When might anger be a symptom of a possible emotional disturbance or illness in a child?

Some children are "angry all the time"—not alternating with sunnier moods—or have frequent temper tantrums or chronic inability to handle frustration and control temper. Angry children may demonstrate persistent irritability, a "short fuse," excessive fighting, bullying and picking on pets or younger children.

Anger could be a symptom if:

1. It is causing a problem for someone—the child, parent, siblings, playmates, or the school.

2. It doesn't seem to be working, i.e., it isn't helping the child get what he or she wants, defend legitimate interests, get heard rather than ignored.

3. It is working *too well*. The child is getting what he or she wants, but at too much cost to others. Parents are caving in to the child's demands or not standing up for their own interests. The child gets what is wanted from a playmate but the playmate doesn't want to play with the child again.

4. Your child's degree of anger and means of expressing it are getting *you* so angry that you are afraid of losing control yourself.

5. Your child's inability to use anger (the child never gets mad enough to fight back even when he or she should) is seriously interfering with the child's ability to stand up for himself or herself.

In other words, for anger to be considered a symptom, it has to be *dysfunc-*

tional in some way. Also, it has to *persist* in a dysfunctional way for some period of time. Anger is serious and urgent if the child is acting destructively to people or property or getting *you* so angry that you are out of control.

Causes of anger and aggression include:

1. Normal development. Somewhere between one and a half and three or four years old ("terrible twos"), most children go through a stage in which they have strong or seemingly exaggerated differences of opinion with parents. This is part of the child's normal development of a sense of self.

2. Benign developmental delay. Most children enjoy playing with this new skill of anger and then move on to other things. Some children take longer to move out of it, just like some take longer to cut their teeth or learn to read.

3. Depression. Depressed children, like depressed adults, get irritable. Things make them angry that wouldn't if they were not depressed.

4. "Undersocialization." Some children don't learn to handle anger very well because they need more teaching in how to do it. Just like children won't learn language if they don't have a chance to speak with someone, children don't learn to handle anger easily if they don't have a chance to "play" at anger with family and peers.

5. Temperament. Some children are more aggressive and/or dominant than others. If your child acts like someone who expects to be the boss, it might be more effective to teach him or her how to be an *effective* boss than to be a subordinate. That doesn't mean your authority has to be undermined. After all, even bosses have bosses!

6. Mild brain damage. This can cause difficulty in handling anger.

7. Parental handling. Inappropriate responses to children's anger and aggression can actually reinforce the child's angry or aggressive behavior.

Parents can try to:

1. Avoid power struggles with a child who is having problems with anger or aggression (see Chapter 3 on Socialization).

2. Consider whether your child is getting enough sleep. Almost all children have more trouble handling anger and aggression when they are fatigued. Fatigued adults tend to get wiped out, fatigued children tend to get "hyped up."

3. Consider whether your child might be depressed.

4. See whether your child is sick. Many illnesses begin with a phase of irritability and poor control of anger.

5. Consider whether you yourself are overstressed so that you are getting into a vicious circle of anger with your child. Maybe you are the one who needs some additional support.

6. Notice whether the problem seems to exist in all areas or just at home, just at school, just with certain playmates, etc. If it is just at home, maybe you and your child need some vacation from each other. Can playmates, grandparents, other settings provide some more neutral relief for the child? Can you find some avenues for more neutral relief for yourself?

If the problem is progressive and persistent, seek help. Start with a good pediatric evaluation to rule out medical problems. If no medical problem is found, a child psychiatrist, child psychologist, or counselor should be consulted.

"BAD BEHAVIOR"

Children are usually described as "bad" when they are in conflict in some way with authorities—either with their parents, their school, or the law. They may disobey openly or sneakily. They may break rules, refuse to do chores or homework, or never take any responsibility. They may take excessive risks or be destructive to property, people, or animals. They may seem oblivious to the feelings and expectations of others. Sometimes they behave "bad" everywhere, sometimes just in one setting. Sometimes it is only with a younger sibling that they are "bad."

Since virtually all children show some of these behaviors some of the time, we have to decide when "badness" is normal and when it is a symptom.

"Badness" is a serious symptom if:

1. The behavior in question poses real risks to the child or others.

2. The behavior persists for some significant period of time. Almost all children have days when they misbehave in a way unlike their usual pattern due to fatigue, illness, or overstimulation.

3. The "bad behavior" occurs in several areas of the child's life.

Causes of "bad behavior" include:

1. Normal development. Children are not born knowing all the rules. They gradually develop the capacity to understand what is expected and behave accordingly, just like they gradually develop their ability to speak in clear, grammatical language. Some "bad behavior" in young children is the behavioral equivalent of "baby talk."

2. Benign developmental delay. Some children take longer to learn to adjust their behavior to other people's expectations, just as some take longer to learn to talk.

3. Minimal brain damage, hyperactivity, or attention deficit disorder can all cause these behaviors.

4. Temperament. Some children are just more docile than others (one of Marilyn's children loved to please; the other questioned every rule).

5. Parental expectations. If parents expect more than a young child can deliver, they won't get it. If parents start calling the child bad, the child may get the idea that he or she is bad and give up trying to be good.

6. Parental temperament. Some parents have a short fuse themselves and have trouble tolerating the normal behaviors of early childhood. Such parents may think their children are being "bad" when they really are just being children.

7. "Undersocialization." Some children don't behave very well because they haven't been taught or expected to do so. Some parents who love little babies may convey—perhaps unconsciously—that they like babyish behaviors. Some parents let children walk all over them because they lack enough self-confidence to stand up for their own rights. When parents are overworked or

overtired, it may take less energy to give in to the child than to deal with or chastise the bad behavior.

8. Relying on "punishment" instead of "discipline" (see Chapter 3 on Socialization). Punishment may make a child stop doing a particular act at a particular time, but it may look like revenge to the child, who finds ways to get revenge on us.

9. Children may want or need more attention than they are getting. Children may act "bad"—consciously or unconsciously—because it is a sure way of getting the parent's or teacher's attention. The child may not be getting enough attention.

10. Some children who are seriously depressed do not know what's the matter, but have a deep sense that something is terribly wrong. They may act "bad" as a rather desperate way of crying for help—the equivalent of saying, "Won't somebody notice that something is terribly wrong?"

Parents might try to:

1. Consider whether the problem is anger, depression, or anxiety, since any of these can be major causes of "badness."

2. Talk to teachers, parents of your child's playmates, and others in order to get a clear picture of where the bad behavior occurs. If your child is "good" in school, but "bad" at home, maybe it is because the rules are clearer and easier to follow at school than at home.

3. Take a good look at your own "rules." Are you demanding too much? Making mountains out of molehills? Or demanding too little and letting your child walk all over you? Does your child really know what to expect, why, and how you feel about it when it does not happen?

4. Talk frankly with your child and get his or her point of view. Does the child understand what is expected? Does the child think what is expected is reasonable? If not, why not? Maybe the child is right.

5. Does your child think *you* are acting bad? One girl began acting up out of resentment because her mother was paying much more attention to her brother. The brother had a complex illness that was potentially fatal. The mother was terribly worried about the boy, but didn't want to worry either child about something that might not even happen. All the girl could see was that her mother was neglecting her.

6. Specific disobedience often has a hidden reason. One generally well-behaved girl refused to practice her music lessons and tried to avoid going to the lessons. The parents found out years later that the girl was being sexually abused by her music teacher and had been threatened not to tell.

If you have tried all of the above suggestions, and the problem is progressive and persistent, get professional help.

BEHAVIOR THAT IS "TOO GOOD"

Most children get along with their parents, comply with their requests, and, in general, act pretty "good"—much of the time. Parents are glad when that happens and wish it would happen more often. Parents rarely complain that their children are too good, but this does happen occasionally. Sometimes teachers and parents of a child's playmates notice "excessive goodness" before the child's own parents do.

When is compliance normal or healthy and when is it a possible symptom of emotional disturbance in a child?

Overcompliance is a problem if your child:

1. Never seems to have any strong preferences of his or her own. A child who eats exactly what you dish up, puts on whatever clothes you lay out, goes to bed exactly when you tell the child to, or hardly ever comes crying to you for support can be called overcompliant.

2. Doesn't ever make any noise or messes.

3. Doesn't exhibit strong feelings about anything—i.e., doesn't show anger or sadness or fearfulness in situations that should evoke such feelings.

4. Doesn't ever question any of your rules or directives.

5. Gets along much better with adults than with children his or her own age.

Causes of overcompliance include:

1. Normal development. Some children around four are so very interested in learning how to do things "right" that they may appear overcompliant.

2. Benign developmental delays. Just as with other behavior problems, children may stay in this stage a little longer than others.

3. Lack of opportunity for rough and tumble play with other children in the two- to four-year-old age range. Children need opportunities to interact with children. Those who don't may spend their time pleasing grown-ups instead.

4. Younger siblings. When parents are busy with the needs of new babies, they often reward the older child's "goodness" and "mature" behavior, which overly reinforces such behavior.

5. Some children respond to any frightening event such as a death, serious illness, accident, or divorce with overcompliance which in their minds will prevent a recurrence or remedy the situation.

6. Guilt. Some children who have done something they feel very guilty about may try to make up by being overly good. Usually the guilt is way out of proportion to the offense. Sometimes children who have been sexually abused feel extremely guilty.

7. Depression, anxiety, and obsessive-compulsiveness. Often adults who are diagnosed with these psychiatric problems report that they were extremely compliant children. The overcompliance could have been an early manifestation of the illness or it may be that the childhood problem contributed to the development of the adult disorder. These illnesses tend to run in families and there may be a strong hereditary component.

8. More serious mental disorders. Some adults who develop schizophrenia, multiple personalities, or extreme violence are described as having been "perfect" children.

9. Mild mental retardation. Children who are mildly retarded have to work

harder at learning to comply with basic parental and societal expectations. Sometimes extreme "eagerness to please" becomes a basic way of life.

10. Adoption and foster-rearing. Some adopted children get the idea that it must have been their fault that their birth mother gave them up. They figure out they had better be super good to prevent this happening again (the opposite strategy occurs also, of course) (see Chapter 25 on Non-Biological Children).

Parents might try to:

1. Find ways to give the child attention based on age-appropriate play, not just on pleasing you.

2. Try to find another adult who can spend time with the child (a friend, relative, or the Big Brothers and Sisters organizations).

3. Get someone else to help care for a new baby or sick sibling while you spend more time with the child who feels neglected.

4. Encourage those personal preferences which the child does have.

5. Talk about feelings with the child, if the child doesn't spontaneously do it with you. "That would make me mad if it happened to me" gives the child permission to name the feeling and consider experiencing it.

6. Take a good look at your "rules." Are they really a little too demanding? Can you tolerate some imperfection in your child and in yourself?

7. Help the child set up play situations with other children. Some overcompliant children can enjoy play relationships but can't initiate them. Some can't play comfortably with children their own age, but can play with much younger or older children. You can hire a somewhat older child as a "play-sitter" or bring in a younger child whose mother needs a sitter for a few hours (under your supervision). Gradually you can bring in other children who are closer and closer to your child's age.

8. Some children who have trouble with other children can play more easily with pets (the size and temperament of the pet must be chosen carefully, for the protection of both the child and the pet!).

If the home approaches are not working and the situation has persisted for many months, get professional help. Psychological testing might be helpful as some overcompliant children will not reveal their anxieties or guilt directly to anyone but will communicate it when they talk about picture stories in the course of psychological testing.

The main complication of overcompliance is its interference with the child's sense of self as an active evaluator of both self and the world. This can lead to depression and ineffectiveness in later adolescent and adult life where the rules are not as clear cut as in childhood. The compliance habit may continue, but the people that the child chooses to comply with change. Compliant children may fall in with the wrong crowd in adolescence or make an unfortunate choice of sexual partners, situations in which compliance becomes very dangerous.

SEXUAL BEHAVIOR

Some sexual behavior in children may be of considerable concern to parents. Parents are usually upset about masturbation in public, obsessive concern with sexual matters, exploitative sex play with other children, exhibitionism, sexual victimization by adults, or early adolescent sexuality.

MASTURBATION

Virtually all young children masturbate. This is something they discover on their own. It feels good to rub "down there" just like it feels good to scratch an itch. By the way, not all genital handling is sexual—the child may have an itch. Young children have no way of knowing that touching their genitals embarrasses grown-ups. As parents encourage children to pick their noses privately rather than publicly, they can tell them to pet themselves privately rather than publicly —for the same general reasons.

Masturbation is not only acceptable but may be desirable. For example, adolescents with strong sexual urges are not usually in a social position to find a partner. Masturbation helps people adjust their sexual needs to their situation and to experience their sexuality as their own.

If your child cannot accept your commonsense advice that masturbation is private, either your child is in conflict with you about other matters, needs more attention, or is trying to get your goat in some fashion. Sometimes excessive masturbation is found in retarded children.

Lots of people were brought up to believe that masturbation was always bad. Today they enjoy their children's freedom so much that they encourage them (perhaps unconsciously) to be uninhibited about genital touching.

EXHIBITIONISM

Some sexual exhibitionism in young children is perfectly normal. Running nude around the home, giggling and getting you to chase him or her, can be a fun game for a two-year-old. Situationally appropriate nudity such as "skinny-dipping" can be perfectly normal.

More conspicuous sexual exhibitionism at any age probably indicates a problem. If the child is publicly exposing his or her genitals or undressing in a way that calls attention to himself or herself, the child is almost certainly communicating some sexual or other anxiety which should be addressed.

SEX PLAY

Sex play with children of about the same age is normal in the preschool and early school years. Most children manage to see their parents' nude bodies but unless they have sibs of both sexes at close to the same age, they don't get to satisfy their natural curiosity about differences between boys and girls. "Playing doctor" and "playing house" are common childhood games in which children may undress each other and even play out their ideas of adult sexual intercourse.

Sex play may be a symptom requiring further attention if the children involved are very different in age, size, or temperament so that one is coercing the other, or if this is the only game that children want to play to the exclusion of other play activities.

It may also be a symptom if the children are playing sex games in front of you instead of off by themselves. That could mean that they are trying to get your attention to talk about sexual matters more, and/or to limit the play.

A few parents who understand that this kind of play is healthy and normal get worried if their children *don't* engage in it. That shouldn't be a concern because children satisfy their curiosities about other children's bodies and their own sexual feelings at different times and in different ways. Some prefer books.

It is definitely a problem if an older child or adolescent engages in sex games with much younger children. This does happen in families (and sometimes between baby-sitters and their charges) and should not be permitted to continue. Get help if you can't handle this yourself!

Needless to say, there is a definite and severe problem if adults engage in sex play with children. Again, this happens in families much more often than most people realize. One recent study revealed that 28 percent of women had experienced unwanted sexual touching in childhood; another study found that 6 percent of males and 15 percent of females had experienced sexual abuse.[3] The vast majority of the children involved were deeply shaken by the experience but did not feel that they could tell their parents. If you do have reason to believe a child is being sexually abused, get help!

Parents might:

1. Do nothing if you happen to come in on your child in the middle of age-appropriate sex play. Just say "Excuse me" and leave.

2. Talk with the child if you have the impression that your child is using sex play to communicate something to you.

3. Avoid letting children do anything that is upsetting to them or you. You can certainly say: "I don't like those kinds of games—why don't you play something else instead."

4. Convey from infancy on that your child's body belongs to him or her and that nobody, but nobody, has a right to intrude on it against the child's will.

5. *Believe* the child if a child ever tells you a family member or friend or stranger has been sexually abusing him or her. Get some appropriate outside help. Commonly in these situations, the adult involved will deny it and insist that the child is making it up. Children almost never make up such stories.

SEXUAL ACTIVITY

From age seventeen in males and age eighteen in females, the majority of teenagers are sexually active and many start much earlier.[4] Parents may be concerned that their sexually active adolescents are violating their moral norms, getting into situations that they cannot handle emotionally, or getting hurt by sexual experiences. Parents may also be concerned if their teenagers are *not* dating when others their age are.

Sometimes we cannot talk to our teenagers about sexual activity because of our own embarrassment; sometimes because the adolescent doesn't want to talk. Some adolescents want a healthy degree of privacy about their sexual feelings and behaviors, just as most adults do. Others are not talking because of overwhelming guilt, depression, or anxiety about these matters. It can be hard for a parent to know the difference.

Society as a whole is certainly in conflict in the area of teenage sex. Sexual activity which is biologically normal at this age may nevertheless be illegal, socially unacceptable, contrary to parents' moral standards, and not even very pleasurable to the adolescents involved. The risks of unwanted pregnancy and sexually transmitted diseases including AIDS are obvious. For many of us, this is a topic that is hard to discuss with our adolescents.

Many adolescents feel pressured to engage in sexual activity and may be subject to a certain amount of sexist stereotyping. Boys may feel that they have to prove their masculinity by sexual conquests or that masturbation is an indication of defeat—the inability to find a partner. Girls may feel that they have to have sex whether they want to or not, in order to participate in the dating world which is their social milieu.

We have the highest teen pregnancy (and abortion) rates in the world. Comparisons with other countries show that intercourse is as common but there is less pregnancy because in those countries the clear message is, "Don't get pregnant!" Here the message is mixed. Parents: "Don't have sex!" Media: "Everybody does!"[5]

It seems a shame for young people to be pressured into participation in risky activities which may not even be enjoyable. Parents often cannot help as much as they would like because of the barriers to communication in this area. At the very least parents can avoid adding to the adolescent child's pressures. For example, some parents who weren't very popular in high school want very much to have their children be more successful and try to push them into popularity. Don't consciously or unconsciously push your child into dating.

About 10 percent of the population as a whole becomes exclusively or predominantly homosexual. Many of these people suffer terribly during adolescence, sensing that their interests are different from those of their peers. Many other adolescents who are a little slower than their peers in getting interested in the adolescent social scene suffer needlessly from fears that maybe they really are gay. We recommend counseling help for families troubled by these issues.

Adolescent sexuality which is associated with a risky lifestyle, such as promiscuity, prostitution (hetero- or homosexual), serious substance abuse, neglect of schoolwork, truancy, running away, etc., clearly needs intervention. The problem may be an overcompliant child who has begun to comply with a dangerous crowd, a serious underlying depression, or a personality disorder. Parents feel, often justifiably, victimized by such youngsters and need help for the family even if the child refuses to cooperate.

SCHOOL PROBLEMS

Some children dislike school, mildly or strongly. Some refuse outright to go. Others do not achieve as well as the parents or the school expects them to, either generally or in certain specific areas. Some children become overinvolved in school achievement and either worry excessively about their grades or neglect other important areas of life like play and friendships. Still others seem to have specific behavior problems related to school, such as getting to school on time or completing their assignments.

Some children are not as bright as others; some are bright but not academically inclined; some are slow starters and will catch up later. Some children, particularly younger siblings of high achievers, are afraid of the competition and opt out of the contest. Some children have mild hearing impairment or poor eyesight that affects their learning, although today most schools test for that. A variety of emotional and social problems in the family or within the child can interfere with the child's learning ability.

A child who likes school and generally does well but has trouble in a particular subject may require some assessment. There could be a personality clash with the teacher rather than a problem with the subject matter. If your child is having behavior problems in school, find out whether the problems are similar to, or opposite from, the child's behavior at home and in other group settings. Remember your child is not going to hit it off with all teachers, anymore than you are going to hit it off with all bosses.

Children who just cannot sit still in the classroom and learn may have attention deficit disorder with or without hyperactivity. Children who cannot learn to read will face serious problems in school, so if your child is not reading at the end of first grade, a thorough evaluation is a good idea. There are also a variety of medical problems which can interfere with school performance, such as petit mal epilepsy or minimal brain dysfunction.

SUBSTANCE ABUSE

Most children do not become involved in abuse of alcohol, marijuana, or other drugs before adolescence, though a few do. Giving young children a sip of wine or beer does not seem to cause alcohol abuse.

Social and recreational use of drugs in preadolescence and adolescence is a matter that most parents worry about a great deal. Sudden personality change, irritability, lethargy, loss of interest in schoolwork and usual pursuits all could be symptoms of drug use, typically alcohol or marijuana. Hallucinations or very bizarre behavior, particularly in a previously normal adolescent, could be due to ingestion of hallucinogens or phencyclidine (PCP). Alcohol is still the most serious drug of abuse among the adolescent population, just as among adults. The interaction of alcohol use with driving is the most serious risk to life associated with drugs and kills many adolescents each year.

Some casual use of alcohol and marijuana is so common in adolescence that it is not always necessary to do anything about it other than keep the lines of communication open and warn your child about the dangers of driving and drugs. However, all parents will want to take action under the following circumstances: if preadolescents are being seduced into drug use by older kids; if drug use is repetitive or causing any adverse consequences in school or social life; if community standards of law enforcement are so rigid that there is a real risk of criminal charges; if the child is getting involved directly with theft or criminal pushers. Many parents feel strongly enough about the use of unhealthy substances that they are in real conflict with their children about *any* drug use and they should not be afraid to say so.

The first approach is to try to talk with the child about it. This subject requires a tactful approach and setting up favorable circumstances for what could be a tense discussion.

If parents are worried about their child's use of substances, they will probably need some outside help. Make an appointment with a knowledgeable pediatrician, mental health professional, or substance-abuse counselor to work on your own concerns even if your child will not cooperate.

IDENTITY PROBLEMS

Sometimes parents drift into only making comments about a particular child's negative aspects. "You are clumsy!" "Your room is always a mess!" "Stop being mean to the baby!" are familiar examples. Middle children in families of three or more often get a lot of this.

Sometimes another parent, relative, or friend will be the first to notice if parents have unconsciously drifted into this pattern. If they call it to your attention, thank them heartily! If you catch yourself giving one of your children all negatives, make a conscious effort to comment on some positives. Also take a good look at the negatives. If you say the same negative thing about your child often, this is ineffective nagging which really doesn't work. (See Chapter 3, p. 68.)

Sometimes a parent has problems with a particular child because the child or the child's behavior reminds the parent of someone they cannot stand. Just realizing this can help the parent back off and see the child for who she or he is personally.

Gender identity can sometimes be a problem. Transexualism, where the young boy becomes convinced that he is *really* female and only trapped in a male body (or, more rarely, the reverse with young girls) is very rare. If your son is caught up in the belief that he is really a girl, this is a potential problem which is very different from casual play with fancy clothes or fancy makeup.

Some children have problems with family identity, feel different from the other children, or develop a persistent fantasy that they were not really born into the family. Most children flirt with the idea that they might have been adopted, maybe they are really the child of royalty. However, a child who continues to feel very different from the rest of the family or to have conflicts about ethnic identity has a serious problem.

Children, as soon as they can talk, begin to project themselves into the adult occupational world. Children talk about occupations they are familiar with: parents' occupations, teachers, doctors, nurses, police officers, etc. In early childhood, the idea of future adult roles is both fantastic and unrealistic. Normally, as childhood progresses, there is continued revision of what the child wants to do as adult work. A child whose identity does not include projection into the adult occupational world may have a problem.

Problems with vocational identity in late adolescence seem to be common these days. There was a time in history when people expected to grow up and do what their parents did. Even their names reflected this: Smith or Farmer. This is no longer true.

There may be a need for professional consultation, if:

1. A child continues over a period of some months to have a sense of negative identity and persists in not feeling good about himself or herself.

2. A child demonstrates gender identity conflicts.

3. A child persists in not feeling like part of the family over a period of some months, regardless of biological parentage.

4. An older adolescent or young adult has no idea of what he or she wants to do as an adult vocation and is not even willing to discuss the subject. In a few rare cases, this could be an early symptom of serious psychiatric illness, such as major depression or even schizophrenia. It could also be a part of the "amotivational syndrome" sometimes seen with substance abuse.

WHEN TO CALL THE DOCTOR

General Advice

This matter is discussed in detail in Chapter 19, Choosing Health Professionals for Your Child's Care, but before we finish this chapter on symptoms, we want to point out something about parents and doctors. You, as parent, will always spend more time with your child than will the doctor. This means that: 1) You know more about your child than the doctor does; 2) You have a responsibility to learn how to observe your child for signs of illness; and 3) You have a responsibility to notify your doctor about serious signs of illness.

Specific Reasons to Call the Doctor

1. Emergencies—see Chapter 23.
2. Difficulty breathing (see p. 643 for differentiation between noisy and difficult breathing).
3. Unexplained fever lasting more than forty-eight hours.
4. High fever (greater than 103°).

5. Persistent abdominal pain.
6. Earache.
7. Persistent vomiting (more than twelve hours in an infant or twenty-four hours in an older child).
8. Diarrhea with signs of dehydrating. (See p. 648.)
9. Refusal of all food and drink.
10. Stiff neck (can't bend head toward chest).
11. Excessive drowsiness, sleepiness, or delirium.
12. Pain on urination.
13. Blood in urine.
14. No urine for twelve hours.
15. Increasing pallor.
16. Bleeding into the skin (petechiae).

Marilyn has always tried very hard to get two points across to the residents and medical students she has been responsible for teaching: 1) A parent spends more time with a child than the doctor does and often more time than the nurse does in the hospital. Listen to parents: their observations are valuable. It may take patient listening because the parent may not know what words doctors use. If the parent instinctively feels there is something wrong with the baby, listen! The parent is right in most cases. 2) It is dangerous to assume that you can explain away a baby's symptoms by saying the parent is overanxious. Always check the symptoms very carefully. First of all, be sure there is nothing wrong with the baby. Second, find out why the parent is overanxious. Overly worried parents *can* have babies with meningitis. The moral of the story is for residents to *listen to parents.*

The message to parents is: *Be sure your child's doctor listens to you.*

SUGGESTED READINGS AND RESOURCES

Brace, Edward R., and Pacanowski, John P. *Childhood Symptoms: Every Parent's Guide to Childhood Illnesses.* New York: Harper & Row, 1985.

Alphabetically arranged. More for background information than a guide to when to call the doctor.

Brown, Jeffrey L. *The Complete Parents' Guide to Telephone Medicine.* New York: Berkley, 1983.

A guide to children's illnesses specifying when to call the doctor. Rather superficial but it may be useful to some parents because of its cookbook-like directions which are easy to follow.

Chapman, Charles F. *Medical Dictionary for the Nonprofessional.* Woodbury, N.Y.: Barron's, 1984.

An excellent medical dictionary for those who have not gone to medical school or majored in biology. Definitions and explanations are clearly written in easy-to-understand language. Worth buying if you plan to read medical textbooks or articles.

Clayman, Charles B., and Kunz, Jeffrey R. M. *The American Medical Association, Children: How to Understand Their Symptoms.* New York: Random House, 1986.

A well-illustrated book put out by the American Medical Association.

Illingworth, R. S. *Common Symptoms of Disease in Children*, 7th ed. Oxford, England: Blackwell, 1982.

Written for medical students and doctors but it contains a good deal of information about what causes common (and unusual) symptoms in childhood.

Martin, Richard. *A Parent's Guide to Childhood Symptoms.* New York: St. Martin's, 1982.

Lists common symptoms, probable causes, and treatment.

Kunz, Jeffrey R. M., ed. *The American Medical Association Family Medical Guide.* New York: Random House, 1982.

Decision trees; good picture section.

Meadowbrook Medical Reference Group. Hart, Terril H., ed. *The Parents' Guide to Baby and Child Medical Care.* Deephaven, Minn.: Meadowbrook, 1982.

Another book which tells parents what to do for certain symptoms and health problems. The format will be useful for some parents.

Pantell, Robert H.; Fries, James F.; and Vickery, Donald M. *Taking Care of Your Child: A Parents' Guide to Medical Care.* Reading, Mass.: Addison-Wesley, 1977.

The use of decision trees may appeal to some parents.

Schmitt, Barton D. *Pediatric Telephone Advice.* Boston: Little, Brown, 1980.

Designed to teach nurses and doctors what to say on the telephone in response to parents' questions about childhood illness. Parents may find the outline approach useful.

Shiller, Jack G. *Childhood Illness and Childhood Injury.* New York: Stein & Day, 1979.

Talks in depth about some areas of childhood illness. Somewhat dated.

Vaughan, Gerard. *Mummy, I Don't Feel Well.* London: Heinemann; North Pomfret, Vt.: David & Charles, 1980.

A British book (diapers = napkins) which teaches how to do a complete visual physical examination of a child. Could be used to teach medical students so that it is more comprehensive than most parents want or need, but it's worth looking at just for the color photographs of childhood rashes.

Werner, David. *Where There Is No Doctor.* Palo Alto, Calif.: The Hesperian Foundation, 1977.

King, Maurice; King, Felicity; and Martodipoero, Soebagio. *Primary Child Care: A Manual for Health Workers.* Oxford: Oxford University Press, 1978.

Parents who have to provide much of the medical care of their children because they live where there are no doctors may find these two books useful. *Primary Child Care* is published in Britain and has an African/Asian orientation while *Where There Is No Doctor* deals with rural care in Central and South America.

21

CARE OF THE SICK CHILD AT HOME

Scope of Chapter

This chapter focuses on how to care for a sick child. First there is a section on equipment and medicines that we believe should be in every home. We discuss over-the-counter drugs, prescription drugs, and home remedies and also talk about drug dosages and the philosophy of giving medicine to children. Next is a section on making the child comfortable when sick. We then discuss food and activity for sick children.

Introduction

Most of the care for most of the children who are sick is provided by parents at home, not by doctors or nurses in hospitals. Parents take care of minor illnesses which do not require the attention of a physician. Parents act on their own initiative, doing what they think is needed for the child. Other times parents will care for a child with a more serious illness for which the physician was contacted, and then will follow the directions or suggestions of the physician. Less frequently parents will care for a severely ill child, or even a child who is dying, after the child has been discharged from the hospital or instead of hospitalization.

Why do parents need such a chapter? Because most illness in children is self-limited. Most sick children can be well and safely cared for at home. Many times you will not even need to call your doctor, but will care for the child yourself with the knowledge you already have about illness in childhood. When your child is seriously ill, it is important to know what to do *before* you can get your doctor, or *if you cannot get your doctor.* And, as hospitalization should be avoided whenever possible for all children—especially young children—sometimes your doctor will suggest you care for a seriously ill child at home.

Despite your good child care and despite the best of nutrition, rest, and exercise, your child *will get sick.* The incidence of respiratory infections, for example, in the temperate climate zone is about six to nine per year for school children. This could mean up to one cold per month during the winter. Colds may be even more frequent among children in day care or nursery schools where they come in contact with some of the respiratory viruses earlier in life. Young children who have older brothers or sisters also may have more frequent infections brought home to them.

WHAT YOU NEED TO HAVE

Your home is not a hospital nor should you attempt to make it one (except in specific instances when you are caring for a chronically or seriously ill child with help from your doctor and perhaps a visiting nurse). But everybody needs certain things in the home for the care of illness.

Equipment

THERMOMETER

Every home needs a thermometer. Because thermometers are both important and inexpensive, we describe them as a vital parenting tool that every household should have.

WHY DO PARENTS AVOID THERMOMETERS?

Marilyn has observed that there are four reasons parents don't have—or use —thermometers. They may not think it is important to know what the child's temperature is. They may feel they can tell whether there is a fever by touch. They may be *afraid to use* a thermometer. They may be ashamed to admit they *can't read* a thermometer. None of the four reasons holds up to scrutiny.

Let's take all four antithermometer attitudes in turn.

It is *extremely* important to know what your child's temperature is when he or she becomes ill. The level of fever is often an important diagnostic clue for your doctor and an extremely high temperature may require emergency measures. It is also important to see whether and when the temperature goes down when an illness is being treated. Both diagnosis and efficacy of treatment are determined, in part, by knowing the temperature reading.

You *cannot* be sure what your child's temperature is by feeling the forehead. Many mothers have told us (and we believe them because we have said the same thing) that they can tell whether their child is feverish or not by touch. In many instances, the mothers were right, but all of us have been fooled. A child who has been exercising or out in the sun may feel warm and not be feverish. In the early stage of a fever the child's body temperature may be going up at a fast rate, but the skin does not yet feel hot. A recent study showed that parents who said their child had a fever by touch were right only 55 percent of the time[1] although mothers were pretty accurate in judging the presence of a *high* fever.[2]

Why are parents afraid to use a thermometer? Because thermometers are made of glass, which breaks, and contain mercury, which everyone knows is poisonous. "What will I do if the thermometer breaks? My baby can get glass in the rectum!" "My child may swallow glass or mercury!" Not to worry. Thermometers, properly used, almost never break in the mouth or rectum. Most thermometers break when we are shaking them down and we accidentally hit the thermometer on the edge of the sink. This brings us to our next point. Mercury, in the metallic form used in thermometers, will not harm your child either in the mouth or in the rectum. The biggest danger in cleaning up a broken thermometer is in cutting yourself on the glass. The mercury on your hands will not hurt you. If you are not convinced of the safety of glass thermometers in the mouth or rectum, you can use the armpit method or invest in an electronic thermometer (see below).

Many parents confessed to Marilyn, when they got to know and trust her, that although they hated to admit it, they couldn't figure out how to read a thermometer. There is only one trick to reading a thermometer: you must *slowly* rotate the thermometer until you can see the highest number to which the column of mercury—either red or silver—has risen.

So, because thermometers are inexpensive and safe and because they will be needed so often throughout childhood, we consider thermometers indispensible. Get a spare one since they are easy to drop.

For those parents who need a course in temperature taking, read on.

KINDS OF THERMOMETERS

There are two kinds of glass thermometers: oral and rectal. They are identical instruments except that the rectal thermometer is thicker and has a thicker bulb (the reservoir where the mercury stays when it is not in the column). You *can* use an oral thermometer in the rectum but, because it is thinner, there is slightly more danger of breaking, so we don't recommend this. A rectal thermometer can be used orally, but should be carefully cleaned before being inserted in the mouth. Both can be used in the armpit.

There are tapes on the market which change color when applied to the forehead of a child with a fever and also electronic thermometers which read out the temperature directly the way a digital clock reads out the time. The tapes may be quite inaccurate when compared with a glass thermometer, which is always accurate because mercury expands in a very predictable way.[3] Once calibration is done at the time of manufacture, the mercury thermometer will stay accurate. Because of the additional cost of electronic thermometers over the old-fashioned and more accurate kind, we recommend that you save your money.

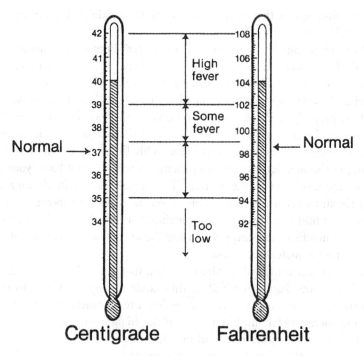

Thermometers.

THE SHAKE DOWN

A thermometer works on the principle that the liquid metal mercury expands when it gets heated and rises in the column. It stays at the level your child's temperature is, which is fortunate, because then you can read it. If the mercury went down the tube as it cooled, the moment you took the thermometer out, the mercury would start falling so you couldn't get an accurate reading. How do you get the mercury down below where your child's temperature is likely to be, i.e., below the normal mark? Hold the upper end of the thermometer (the opposite end from the bulb) and shake hard with a snap of your wrist. Be sure the mercury goes down a degree or two below normal before inserting the thermometer.

INSERTING THE THERMOMETER

The rectal thermometer is first greased with Vaseline. The easiest way to insert a rectal thermometer in a young baby is to place the baby on the *back* and lift up the legs like you do when changing the diaper. Gently spread the buttocks and insert the bulb of the thermometer in the rectum. Hold the thermometer between two fingers like a cigarette. The thermometer only has to be inserted about an inch, no more. Keep the thermometer in for one minute or until the mercury stops rising. Children older than a year who need a rectal temperature should be placed on their stomach. You spread the buttocks with one hand and insert the greased thermometer with the other. Keep the child flat by pressing the child down with the hand not holding the thermometer.

Oral thermometers need no grease. They are inserted under the tongue, after which the child is instructed to close the mouth without biting the thermometer and to keep the thermometer in the mouth for two minutes. Children under eight or ten can't follow these directions very well and even older children with stuffed noses—the very ones whose temperature you may want to check—can't do this because they are obliged to breathe through their mouth.

Either an oral or rectal thermometer can be placed in the armpit (axilla). The bulb is placed deep in the armpit and the arm is held against the body holding the thermometer in place. An axillary (armpit) reading takes four to five minutes.

WHAT DOES THE THERMOMETER SAY (HOW HIGH IS THE MERCURY)?

Thermometers are calibrated in Celsius (Centigrade) or Fahrenheit. They generally read from 92° F (34° C) to 108° F (42° C). Usually 98.6° F or 37° C is marked "normal" with an arrow. The reading is the highest number the column of mercury has reached. (See illustration.)

Usually each degree of temperature is subdivided into tenths. In order to read a thermometer you must grasp it by the end that does not go in the child and rotate it until you can read the column of mercury. Rotate *slowly* until you can read the numbers; then turn a bit more and you will see the mercury column. Hold the thermometer still until you are sure what it says.

WHAT IS NORMAL?

Although the arrow in your thermometer will point to 98.6°, the body temperature of your child will vary—as it is supposed to. Body temperatures are lowest in the morning and highest in late afternoon. Other bodily functions have similar peaks and valleys. These peaks and valleys are the result of our so-called circadian rhythms—those biorhythms with which jet lag interferes. The word circadian refers to our daily—or twenty-four-hour—cycle or circle.

Rectal temperatures are slightly higher than oral temperatures because the mouth is cooler than the rectum (the air we breathe through our nose cools the mouth cavity).

AFTER YOU USE THE THERMOMETER

There are only three things to remember after using a thermometer. First, write down what your child's temperature was. If your child is sick, start a sheet of paper on which you write down the date, time, temperature, and symptoms. Second, clean the thermometer with soap and cool water (hot water will shoot the mercury up) or alcohol. Third, store the thermometer in its case so it doesn't break. Store the thermometer case in a safe place where your baby can't reach it, but where you can find it when you need it.

VAPORIZER

Because respiratory infections are so common in children and because breathing moist air offers symptomatic relief, we recommend a vaporizer when your children are small. This is especially true if you live in a house heated by forced hot air, which delivers dry hot air to your respiratory tree though the tree prefers moist air.

Hot steam vaporizers are cheap but not as safe or as effective as cold mist humidifiers, which we recommend. In the discount drugstore at which Marilyn shops, a good cold mist vaporizer costs $20.99 compared with the hot steam version, which costs $9.99. We feel the price of the cold one, though double that of the hot, buys you a much more effective and safer product.

Even in a camp tent, you can improvise vaporizing. Boiling water in a kettle in a closed space provides moist air. You can quickly humidify your child's air at home by turning on the hot water in the bathtub and sink and cloistering both you and the baby in the bathroom to breathe the steam. We don't recommend putting anything in a vaporizer but water. The oils do no good.

BULB SYRINGE (nasal aspirator)

This inexpensive gadget should be in your home from birth on. The soft rubber enables you to aspirate mucus from your baby's nose—safely and easily. The nasal syringe available in drugstores has a hard plastic tip to prevent mucus from running out. What is called an "ear syringe" is all rubber with a soft tip. This is better than the nasal syringe because it is easier to use in babies so we recommend it. (However, we do *not* recommend using it in your baby's ear.)

Because the young infant can't mouth-breathe, even a little mucus goes a long way toward discomfort. The bulb syringe is easy to use—just insert in each nostril while the bulb is compressed and gently release your fingers so the bulb opens and creates the suction needed to pull the mucus out. Clean the syringe with soapy water, let it dry, and keep it handy.

OTHER SICKROOM EQUIPMENT

Chapter 23 has a section on first-aid supplies every home should have (see p. 724) and suggestions for improvising equipment in an emergency. Very little else is needed for home care of the "normally" sick child. If you have a child with a problem that requires special equipment (for example, a suction machine for a child with cystic fibrosis), your doctor, hospital, or visiting nurse will help you select the right equipment and teach you how to use it.

In the case of our own sick children at home, we just used ordinary household stuff. Anne found a bed tray handy; Marilyn didn't bother.

We both keep "comfort" supplies handy. Sick children like straws so we always have a package of flexible ones. We bought tissues by the case so we would never run out. However, for really drippy noses, we keep on hand a dozen cheap white men's hankies. For some reason, despite the softness battles waged by tissue commercials, our children preferred a hankie like Dad's when they were in a cold's maximum pouring stage.

One trick we both used was a "sick box." We kept on hand a few small new toys, new coloring books, books, etc., to amuse a cranky child. Sometimes there are "special" toys in a household which are brought out only when a child is sick. The rationale is not to reward sickness but to acknowledge that the sick child feels bad and that we want to do something special to help that child feel better. Special toys may be those that shouldn't be mixed in with all the others for one reason or another. Marilyn has a Russian grandmother doll, which opens up to reveal thirteen smaller dolls within it. This was a special toy because 1) she bought it on a trip to the Soviet Union; and 2) it was easier to retrieve all the pieces from the bed than from the playroom floor.

Special privileges can help the sick child feel better—like unlimited TV. TV passivity which parents worry about in well children may be just what a sick child needs. Anne's brother, who chooses not to own a TV, rents one when anyone is sick. Renting a video cassette machine and movies to use when a child (or adult) is bedridden is reasonably inexpensive these days and quite effective in alleviating boredom.

Remember you'll need lots of plastic bags for used tissues and other debris. Several plastic trays come in handy for taking dishes to and from the kitchen and keeping medicines in one place. Don't forget pencil and paper for charts.

You don't need a "sickroom." Years ago in the preantibiotic and pre-immunization era, when contagion was more of a problem than it is today, a room *was* set aside in the house for use of the sick person. The room was off-limits to everyone except the mother, who served as nurse. Today we suggest keeping your sick child wherever it is most convenient: in the child's room, your bedroom, or the living room. Wherever you decide to set up your "nursing station," keep all the things you need in one place to save steps—just as nurses do.

The Home Medicine Chest

There are basically two kinds of medicines: 1) prescription drugs, which are specified by a doctor for a particular patient with a particular problem and which come with specific instructions for administration, and 2) over-the-counter (OTC) drugs, which anyone can buy in the drugstore or grocery store without a prescription. Because these are available to everybody, over-the-counter drugs tend to be less "powerful." However, because of their wide variety and availability, these often cause problems for children. In the first place, sometimes parents store prescription drugs safely but figure that OTC drugs are not harmful. Not true! Until child-proof bottle legislation was enacted, ingestions of ordinary aspirin caused one of the highest mortality rates of all childhood poisonings. Almost any drug that is powerful enough to have a beneficial effect is toxic in overdoses. Another hazard for children is that parents may not recognize that several different OTC products may contain similar drugs. If both preparations are given, this can lead to an overdose of that ingredient for the child. Also, parents may not always be aware of the dangers and side effects of ingredients in the OTC drug.

We would never say to parents that the only medicine you should permit to cross your child's lips be sanctioned by your child's doctor or prescription. We believe you have the intelligence to recognize that your child has a runny nose, to figure out whether medicine is indicated, and to pick the proper one from the drugstore shelf. The pharmacist is generally quite helpful if you have a question. Self (non-physician) health care is perfectly fine for children provided parents learn a few basic guidelines.

OTC MEDICATIONS

As with everything else, parents need *information* about OTC medicines. Several books available in most libraries contain valuable information. Such books can teach you indications for the product and warning about possible hazards. Examples are the *Physicians' Desk Reference for Nonprescription Drugs*[4] and the *Handbook of Nonprescription Drugs.*[5]

By law, all OTC medicines must have a label which lists directions and ingredients. A good deal of information is contained on labels so we advise parents to *read labels carefully.* Of course, you should pay attention to manufacturers' recommended dosages but *always read what the ingredients are as well.*

Some labels have awfully small print. Unless you have great vision, you might want to carry a small magnifying glass to the drugstore. Pharmacists are trained to advise about non-prescription drugs as well as the prescription ones they dispense—and they love to do so, especially in small neighborhood drugstores which are not too busy.

Table 50 lists active ingredients in common OTC preparations. When you are reading labels you can refer to this to find ingredients whose action or use are unfamiliar to you. You can also use the books we just suggested.

It is important that you *not* give your child multiple OTC drugs. A good rule of thumb: only one drug at a time. If you have to give more than one medicine, be sure you know the active ingredients of each. Then you can figure out if you would be giving an excess of something or if the two medicines are incompatible.

This scenario can take place if you don't read labels. Your two-year-old develops a cold and a temperature of 102°. Everyone else in the home is sick although a throat culture on your four-year-old two days ago was negative for strep. You want to start treatment now because you know your child would feel better with a decongestant and some Tylenol to reduce the fever if it goes higher late in the day. You get a child's "cold medicine" at the local pharmacy. You give your child the correct dose of this preparation and the correct dose of baby Tylenol. However, because you didn't read the label, you don't know the child's cold medicine contains acetaminophen—the same ingredient as Tylenol. You are overdosing your baby with a potentially dangerous drug!

Another common scenario: Your four-year-old has a cold for which you are using an OTC cold preparation. After three days the child is no better and begins to complain of an earache. You take your child to the doctor, who notices an otitis and prescribes an antibiotic along with a prescription decongestant. You give the decongestant along with the OTC cold medicine, not realizing the ingredients are similar. Your child gets an overdose of both antihistamines and decongestants.

The table should also be referred to any time you are giving OTC medicine along with a prescription drug. You should always ask your doctor what is in every preparation prescribed. Obviously, if the doctor prescribes a bronchodilator for your six-year-old wheezer you should stop giving the OTC bronchodilator you have tried for two days.

With a little help from Table 50, which lists active ingredients of common OTC medications, and after you've developed the habit of careful label reading, you can figure out whether each ingredient is likely to help your child's symptoms, whether the medicine is similar to other medicines you or the doctor are giving the child, and what hazards to watch for.

Parents must be careful about *any* medication given to a young baby. Young babies may have adverse reactions to some antibiotics. Even simple preparations ordinarily quite safe for older children can be hazardous for babies if they contain aspirin or antihistamines. We repeat: to be on the safe side, do not give *anything* to a baby under six months of age without checking with the baby's doctor.

If your child seems to have an adverse reaction to an OTC drug, stop it immediately and call your child's doctor.

TABLE 50

ACTIVE INGREDIENTS IN COMMON OTC PREPARATIONS

Name	Action/Use	Similar To	Warnings
Acetaminophen	Decreases fever	Aspirin	
Aspirin	Decreases fever	Acetaminophen	Do not use when influenza or chicken pox is suspected.
Belladonna	Antispasmodic	Atropine	
Benzocaine	Local anesthetic	Novocaine, Lidocaine	May cause allergic reaction.
Brompheniramine Maleate	Antihistamine*		
Calcium Carbonate	Antacid		
Chlorpheniramine Maleate	Antihistamine*		
Dextromethorphan Hydrobromide	Cough suppressant	Codeine	
Dibucaine	Local anesthetic	Lidocaine, Benzocaine	May cause allergic reaction.
Dimenhydrinate (Dramamine)	Antinausea		
Diphenhydramine Hydrochloride (Benadryl)	Antihistamine*		
Doxylamine Succinate	Antihistamine*		
Ephedrine	Bronchodilator (for wheezing)	Epinephrine	
Epinephrine	Bronchodilator (for wheezing)	Ephedrine	
Guaifenesin	Expectorant (for cough)		
Hydrocortisone	Anti-itch steroid		
Lidocaine	Local anesthetic	Benzocaine	May cause allergic reaction.

TABLE 50 (Continued)

ACTIVE INGREDIENTS IN COMMON OTC PREPARATIONS

Name	Action/Use	Similar To	Warnings
Magnesium Hydroxide (or trisilicate)	Antacid		
Meclizine Hydrochloride	Antinausea	Dramamine	
Pheniramine Maleate	Antihistamine*		
Phenylephrine Hydrochloride	Decongestant		
Phenylpropanolamine Hydrochloride	Decongestant		
Phenyltoloxamine Citrate	Antihistamine*		
Pseudoephedrine Hydrochloride (or sulfate)	Decongestant		
Pyrilamine Maleate	Antihistamine*		
Simethicone	Antigas		
Sodium Bicarbonate	Antacid		
Terpin Hydrate	Expectorant (for cough)		
Theophylline	Bronchodilator (for wheezing)	Aminophylline	Overdose is dangerous.
Triprolidine	Antihistamine*		
Xylometazoline Hydrochloride	Decongestant		

*All antihistamines can cause drowsiness but in some children can cause excitement.

Before we leave this section on OTC drugs, we urge you to be vigilant against drug tampering—a recent "epidemic." Inspect *all* OTC medicines to be sure the package has not been tampered with. Return any package you are suspicious about and *do not use.*

PRESCRIPTION DRUGS

Though your doctor prescribes specifically for your child, you as a parent still have a responsibility. Doctors *can* make mistakes. One common mistake is not to realize what other medicines (perhaps prescribed by another doctor) the child is taking that may interfere with the prescription or be equivalent to an overdose when both drugs are taken. You can help by taking responsibility for telling your child's doctor what other medicine your child is taking.

Always know the *name* of any medicine you are giving your child (Johnny isn't taking any old antibiotic for his earache, but Amoxicillin). If your doctor doesn't tell you what is prescribed, ask. If you are not sure how to pronounce it, ask the doctor. If you forget how to pronounce it, ask the pharmacist when you have the prescription filled.

Always know *why* the drug is being prescribed. Be sure to ask about *side effects* or dangers of the drug. Be sure to ask whether the drug can be safely given with other medicines the child may be taking (always have a list of everything your child is taking).

It is also important to know the *dosage, times of administration,* whether the drug should be given *before or after meals,* how the medicine should be *stored* (i.e., does it need refrigeration?), how *long* (how many days) your child should take the medicine, and whether the medicine can safely be used again for the same symptoms or whether the bottle should be discarded after the last prescribed dose is taken.

If the medicine your child's doctor prescribed seems to cause an adverse effect, call your child's doctor immediately. Also, if the medicine is not working, be sure to call the doctor. Never give your child a prescription written for another without asking the doctor. Always read labels to be sure you are giving the right child the right prescription medicine in the right dosage.

Table 51 puts in tabular form what you should *tell* your doctor and *ask* your doctor when a medication is prescribed for your child.

TABLE 51

WHEN YOUR DOCTOR PRESCRIBES MEDICINE FOR YOUR CHILD

Tell Your Doctor About—
- drugs your child is taking now or in the past few weeks by *name*
- any *allergic reactions* your child has had to any medication
- any special *diet* your child is on

Ask Your Doctor—
- what is the *brand/generic name* of any drug prescribed for your child
- *how much* your child is to take and how often: before? with? after *meals?* at

bedtime? will your child have any *side effects?* any *allergic reaction?* should your child avoid any foods or any other medication?
- how long should your child take the medicine?
- what if you forget a dose?

Check with Your Doctor—
- if the medicine is not working
- if your child has any reaction
- if you don't understand the instructions

Remember—
- don't give the medicine to another
- be sure the medicine is safely kept where no child can get it
- keep in original container and do not remove label
- do not mix with another medicine
- always have the number of the Poison Control Center available

GENERIC DRUGS

Many parents ask us if generic drugs are safe. They are subject to the same Food and Drug Administration regulations as brand-name drugs. They are cheaper because they do not bear a trade name so you do not have to pay for the advertising that adds to the cost of brand-name prescription drugs. Some brand-name drugs have better bioavailability than generic drugs and therefore are more effective. Some brand-name drugs, especially the antibiotics, taste better than the generic ones do. A drug that your child spits out does not cure the strep throat. It is possible you may have to get one of the more expensive drugs if that is the only one your child will take. Some brand-name medicines are combinations that really do work. Some purists have argued that combinations add to cost and are not effective but there *are* effective combinations. Use your doctor's advice coupled with your own judgment.

DRUG DOSAGES

Medicine must be administered in precise amounts. Therefore, you must know something about how medicines are measured in order to safely administer them to your children.

The measurement for liquid medicine is the milliliter (ml) or $1/1000$ of a liter. 1 teaspoon equals 5 ml; 1 tablespoon equals 15 ml; 2 tablespoons or 6 teaspoons equals 1 ounce. One other fact: ml equals cc (cubic centimeter).

Some medicines (certain antibiotics, digitalis) are given to infants by the *drop*. Only a calibrated dropper should be used for these, and directions should be followed very carefully.

Solid medicines are measured in milligrams (mg): 1,000 mg equals 1 gram. An adult aspirin contains 325 mg of aspirin (0.3 gram). Just to confuse things, all medicines used to be weighed in grains and sometimes are still designated that way. Don't panic! One grain equals 65 mg. A 5-grain adult aspirin contains 5×65 mg or 325 mg. Adult aspirin can range from 300 to 325 mg; Extra Strength Tylenol has 500 mg acetaminophen; Anacin contains 400 mg aspirin.

Solid medicines may also come in capsules. Generally, it is not advisable to try to create a pediatric dose of medicine from an adult capsule for two reasons. First, it is difficult to divide the powder in the capsule accurately. Second, such powder often tastes terrible, which is one reason capsules are used in the first place (by the time they dissolve in the intestine, you won't be able to burp up the bad flavor). If you must give your child the contents of a capsule, calculate the dose carefully, measure accurately, and dissolve in sweetened water.

In an emergency when there is no medical advice available, children ages eight to thirteen (66 pounds or 30 kg) can generally be given half an adult dose; ages four to seven (33 pounds or 15 kg) one quarter dose; ages one to three (17 pounds or 8 kg) one eighth the adult dose. This is reasonably safe because an adult weighs about 132 pounds or 60 kg, and the rules of arithmetic hold. This means that if all you have at home is Excedrin for which the adult dose is one tablet, you can give half a tablet to an eight-to-thirteen-year-old; one quarter of a tablet to a four-to-seven-year-old; and one eighth of a tablet to a one-to-three-year-old.

WHAT MEDICINES EVERY HOUSEHOLD SHOULD HAVE

SOMETHING TO RELIEVE FEVER, SUCH AS ASPIRIN OR ACETAMINOPHEN (TYLENOL)

Marilyn always used baby aspirin for her children. The dosage schedule is easy to calculate and the tablet is easy to crush in liquid or can be chewed by an older child. Many doctors prefer liquid preparations like Liquiprin or Tylenol, which are both acetaminophen.

Today, because of the association between aspirin and Reye's syndrome (pronounced "rye" as in bread)—a serious complication of viral diseases which involves the brain and has a high mortality rate—following influenza or chicken pox, current recommendations are *not* to give aspirin to children with flu or chicken pox. Do *not* give aspirin to a child you think (because of exposure or cases in the neighborhood) may be coming down with chicken pox or to any child who has chicken pox. Do *not* give aspirin to a child when there is influenza going around your town (this information is often in the news media). Many doctors and parents prefer to use acetaminophen in *all* instances when an anti-pyretic (antifever) medicine is needed. Great Britain no longer sells children's aspirin products.

A regular adult-size aspirin or Bufferin *(not* Extra-Strength Excedrin or other arthritis medicines which contain more) contains five grains of aspirin or its equivalent (300 or 325 mg). A regular adult-size Tylenol contains 325 mg (see Table 52). Baby aspirin or children's Tylenol tablets each contain one and a quarter grains (75 or 80 mg) of the medicine, which means that four baby aspirin or children's Tylenol equal one adult aspirin or Tylenol. It also means if you are caught without baby fever medicine you can cut an adult aspirin or Tylenol in half and cut that half in half with a sharp knife on a cutting board (some may crumble but generally you can get a pretty good quarter of a tablet after one or two tries). Dissolve in a little water, add some sugar or applesauce, and give it to the baby in a teaspoon. *Write down* what the baby's temperature was and what time you administered the medicine.

Tylenol also comes in Children's Elixir (160 mg per teaspoon), which equals 80 mg per one-half teaspoon, and Infant Drops, which come 80 mg per dropper. Even though the dosages on the table can be given as often as every four hours, do not give aspirin or its equivalent around the clock (which amounts to six doses in twenty-four hours) unless your doctor specifically prescribes it. Instead, we recommend acetaminophen or aspirin no more than four or five times in twenty-four hours, never more often than every four hours. In babies under six months, give acetaminophen or aspirin *one time only.* Do not repeat unless the baby is drinking well and your doctor tells you to repeat the medication.

Some doctors say you shouldn't give any antifever medicine, as fever is a protective mechanism of the body which has been shown to kill or prevent multiplication of certain microorganisms. Marilyn feels a fever of 103° or more can make the child so miserable that an aspirin equivalent (and/or sponging) is indicated.

If the temperature does not immediately respond to aspirin (or any time it is over 105°), we suggest sponging the baby with cool, but not cold, or warm water. Put the baby on a towel, wring out washcloths in cool water, and cover the baby with the wet washcloths. When the washcloths get warm from the baby's skin, replace with fresh wet washcloths. If the child's temperature is over 104°, an alternative route to sponging is to put the child in a tub of water that is between body temperature and cool.

For any temperature over 106°, the child should be immediately immersed in cool water and then wrapped in a towel and transported to a hospital.

TABLE 52

ANTIFEVER (ANTIPYRETIC) MEDICINE

Age	Infant Tylenol* Drops (80 mg/0.8 ml)	Children Tylenol* Elixir (160 mg/5 ml)	Children Tylenol* Tabs (80 mg)	Adult Tylenol* Tabs (325 mg)	Baby Aspirin 1¼ gr (81 mg)	Adult Aspirin 5 grs (325 mg)
†0–3 months	0.4 ml					
†4–11 months	0.8 ml	½ tsp				
12–23 months	1.2 ml	¾ tsp	1½ tabs		1½ tabs	⅓ tab
2–3 years	1.6 ml	1 tsp	2 tabs		2 tabs	½ tab
4–5 years	2.4 ml	1½ tsp	3 tabs		3 tabs	¾ tab
6–8 years		2 tsp	4 tabs	1 tab	4 tabs	1 tab
9–10 years		2½ tsp	4–5 tabs	1 tab	4–5 tabs	1–1¼ tabs
11–12 years		3 tsp	4–6 tabs	1–1½ tabs	4–6 tabs	1–1½ tabs
12+ (adult)			4–8 tabs	1–2 tabs	4–8 tabs	1–2 tabs

ALL DOSES CAN BE GIVEN EVERY FOUR HOURS UP TO FOUR OR FIVE TIMES IN TWENTY-FOUR HOURS.

* Acetaminophen

† Infants under 6 months should receive anti-fever medicine only once unless the doctor tells you to repeat it.

Something to Relieve Pain

Aspirin in the same dosage recommended for fever is a good painkiller for sprains, headaches, etc. Generally, children need nothing stronger as they are resilient when it comes to pain and they heal quickly. Acetaminophen also can be used but may not work as well. For severe or chronic pain, you must work with your child's doctor.

Syrup of Ipecac

Syrup of ipecac (a measured dose to induce vomiting if your child has ingested a poisonous substance) should be in every household (see p. 742). Syrup of ipecac is available over the counter in one- or two-dose vials. A young child (under eight) would get one tablespoon as a single dose; a child eight to twelve, depending on body weight, one to two tablespoons; a child over twelve, two tablespoons. *Always call the Poison Control Center prior to using syrup of ipecac.* Pharmacies often give a free one-dose bottle to mothers with young children. Never be without it!

Antihistamines

It's a good idea to have an antihistamine syrup or tablets for nasal allergies. Chlortrimeton is available without a prescription. The syrup contains 2 mg of chlortrimeton per teaspoon. Young babies should *not* be given an antihistamine as it may cause side effects like nervous system irritability. Children two to five can get 1/2 teaspoon every four to six hours. Children five to twelve can take one teaspoonful every four to six hours. Over age twelve, the adult dose (two teaspoons every four to six hours) is fine. Never exceed six doses in a day.

Some doctors prescribe antihistamines for colds. Marilyn feels it doesn't do much good but she does use these preparations for hay fever and nasal allergy. Antihistamines should *not* be used when there is wheezing or asthma, because they can make the asthma worse.

Oral Decongestants (Sudafed, et al.)

These products cause the mucus membranes of the nose to shrink somewhat, giving relief from colds or allergy. They work by causing the blood vessels in the lining of the nose to constrict. This cause an increase in blood pressure and should not be used by anyone with hypertension. Also, decongestant use results in *rebound congestion,* which means the membranes can get even more swollen after the medicine has worn off than before it was given. Thus, these should be used sparingly and *not* continuously.

Controlled studies show that generally decongestants don't prevent ear infections, though one would expect they might help keep the Eustachian tubes open. Anne found that with two of her children, who tended to get ear infections with every cold, the quick use of decongestants seemed to head off the ear infection. With the other child, who was not so vulnerable, a decongestant made no obvious difference.

There are many OTC preparations which contain both a decongestant (usually an ingredient ending with "ephrine") plus an antihistamine. Do not give any of these preparations to young babies without asking your child's doctor. Generally, by the time a child is three, it is safe to give half of the recommended dose for six- to twelve-year-olds.

BENADRYL

Benadryl is useful for skin allergies, hives, itching, and insect stings. This is an antihistamine which we feel has superior effectiveness for hives and other allergic itchy skin problems like multiple insect bites. Benadryl Elixir is available over the counter and should be kept on your medicine shelf. It makes kids sleepy but sleep is good for the itches. Do not give to babies under one year without checking with your doctor. Generally, the dose is one teaspoonful three or four times a day for children over twenty pounds.

COUGH SYRUPS

There are two types of prescription and OTC cough medicines. Expectorants are supposed to loosen the mucus by liquefying it, which theoretically makes it easier to "bring it up" and expectorate it. Children almost always swallow mucus so all you can hope for is that the mucus gets easier to cough out of the throat and bronchi. In point of fact, there is precious little evidence that any of these expectorants do what they are supposed to do.

The second type of cough medicine has ingredients that suppress the cough reflex so there is less coughing. This is useful, especially when there is no lower respiratory disease that has filled the bronchi with mucus and when the cough (usually due to irritation of the back of the throat) is keeping the child—or the parents—awake. Some cough preparations combine both an expectorant and a cough suppressant. Many combine an antihistamine and decongestant with the cough ingredients.

It is important to know whether the prescription medicine is for cough suppression or mucus-dissolving. Following directions on the label goes without saying. Also, follow the "Rule of Thumb": Unless specifically prescribed by your doctor, give only one preparation for one reason at one time. In other words, don't give your child the OTC and prescription cough syrup at the same time because the ingredients are likely to be similar and overdose could occur.

You can make a cough preparation at home. A lemon/honey/whiskey preparation (equal parts of each ingredient) is easy to make, cheap, available, and effective. Because whiskey is a sedative, and honey cannot be used for babies, use only in children over one year. Try 1/2 to 1 teaspoon at bedtime. Repeat once if needed. This preparation must be used cautiously when giving a cough suppressant like codeine. No codeine to children under six unless prescribed.

ANTIBIOTIC OINTMENT

An antibiotic ointment like Bacitracin is used for infected insect bites or any mild skin infection. Those preparations containing neomycin (Neosporin) may cause allergic reactions, so we recommend Bacitracin instead.

STEROID CREAM OR OINTMENT

Steroids are preparations of adrenal gland hormones which have remarkable anti-inflammatory properties. Steriods can be taken internally only under strict medical supervision. Even the external use of topical cream (placed on the skin) needs some caution as these compounds are absorbed through the skin. In young babies who require treatment over large areas of skin, absorption of the steriods might cause difficulties. However, steroids are wonderful drugs when rubbed into the skin and can effect rapid relief of itching.

OTC preparations containing 0.5 percent hydrocortisone are available and are *mildly* effective for *mild* problems. A child with eczema would probably need a higher strength preparation available only by prescription.

You can purchase these preparations over the counter in three forms: ointment, cream, or lotion, all with 0.5 percent hydrocortisone. Which to use? If the skin is weepy, use a lotion or cream; if the skin is dry or crusty, use an ointment because you want a greasy base to lift off the crusts. Creams may contain preservatives which can cause an allergic reaction.

EYE OINTMENT

Although you need a prescription, we recommend you have an antibiotic eye ointment on hand because eye infections are reasonably common and may be painful. Your doctor can give you a prescription for sulfacetamide ophthalmic ointment, which you can fill when needed. Throw the ointment out when the treatment is over. You want a fresh tube every time.

ANTACID (TUMS, PEPTO-BISMOL)

Antacids are sold by the ton in our country. There is no one alive who has not had heartburn or gas or acid indigestion. Children get this too—although not so frequently as grown-ups. Often a sip or two of club soda or ginger ale does the trick by causing burping, which seems to help. If the heartburn still is troublesome, your child can have the appropriate dose of Pepto-Bismol or one or two Tums. This should do the trick. Persistent or recurring indigestion requiring antacids needs to be evaluated by a doctor.

SPECIFIC MEDICINES FOR YOUR CHILD

Children are different—and react to the insult of illness differently. If you have a vomiter (in the car or out), you will need a dramamine-type medicine on hand. If you have a wheezer, you need bronchodilators.

Always ask your doctor how long a prescription drug prescribed for a specific child is safe and effective. Some medicines become toxic with age, others lose potency. Keep track of amounts left so *before* you run out you can ask your doctor for a prescription or stock up at the drugstore.

MEDICINE SAFETY

All medicines are potentially poisonous if given to the wrong person or in the wrong amounts. This means every home medicine cabinet is a potential hazard. *All* medicines—even OTC ones—must be kept where crawlers and toddlers cannot get into them. Never tell children medicine is candy—between imitation and sweet-seeking behavior you are setting them up for "accidental" ingestions.

Any medicine whose label is unreadable or missing should be flushed down the toilet. Do not give your child—or yourself—any medicine reached for in the dark when you are sleepy. Turn on the light and force yourself to read the label. If you feel too sleepy to understand it, copy the label and directions on a piece of paper. By the time you have finished copying, you will be awake enough to comprehend.

Throw out any pills that are crumbly, any capsules that are wrinkled or open, and any liquid that is discolored or a different consistency (thicker or thinner) than you remember it was. Never give medicine after the expiration date. Never give your child a prescription written for yourself or someone else.

MEDICINES YOU DON'T NEED—AND WHY

There are several medicines you *don't* need because they don't work. Marilyn has never found kaopectate preparations effective in children. She almost never prescribes the antispasmodic medicines containing belladonna and a barbiturate (like Donnatal) as she treats diarrhea with diet. However, if your child has cramping, abdominal pain, or fever with diarrhea, the doctor should be called. Paregoric (camphorated tincture of opium) is sometimes used for cramps. You need a prescription to buy this, so your doctor will tell you the dosage for your child.

Laxatives for children are almost never needed. Natural substitutes such as adequate water intake, dried fruit, bran sprinkled on cereal, or a high fiber diet work better and are cheaper. (If your child has a problem with constipation that natural methods don't help, tell the doctor.) Do *not* give mineral oil or a laxative containing oil to young babies: the baby could inhale the oil into the lungs (aspiration).

Cough drops have little value. If your child complains of a dry throat or has a "dry throat" cough, a lemon drop or lollipop works as well. "Tonics" to pep a child up are worthless. They usually contain vitamins and alcohol: vitamins are best given in food and kids don't need alcohol. Teething medicines to rub on the gums are equally worthless; a hard teething biscuit or a parent's finger does the trick.

Although some doctors recommend nose drops for children, Marilyn did not use them for her patients or her children.

There is never a need for aspirin compounds with caffeine and phenacetin for children. Plain acetaminophen or plain aspirin will do.

HOME REMEDIES

There may be danger in some home remedies. Certain herbs are toxic and have caused illness or even fatalities in young children (example: oil of wintergreen in tea). Salt and salt substitutes are not without hazard. A colic remedy, consisting of one quarter to one half teaspoon salt substitute in four ounces of water after each feeding was recommended in a popular health food book. This becomes a solution with five to eight times the recommended daily intake of potassium, which could be fatal. Never give your child a home remedy if you don't know what the ingredients are and that they are safe for children.

Some home remedies *are* useful. We have already talked about honey and lemon juice for sore throats. A paste of baking soda or cornstarch is good for insect bites. A paste of meat tenderizer also works. Peppermint tea is soothing for upset tummies. You can make a remedy for colic that some swear by which is nothing more than a peppermint Necco wafer dissolved in four ounces of warm water. Rubbing an aloe leaf on a skin lesion like a sunburn is soothing (don't let your child eat the leaf or sap). Howell's book *Healing at Home* also suggests applying a freshly peeled banana skin to a bruise and covering the area with a cool wet cloth.[6] She says a flat soft cabbage leaf applied to an insect bite and covered with a cool damp cloth relieves the itch and sting.

One home remedy that is time-tested and really works is chicken soup. We now know that hot liquids, especially chicken soup, actually help dissolve the mucus of a cold and provide water and salt to prevent dehydration.

Marilyn is delighted to include her recipe for chicken soup made with the types of chicken easily found at the supermarket (she has given up trying to find old stewing hens like her grandmother used!).

2 whole fryers with gizzards and neck, skin removed
2 carrots, scraped and quartered
1 onion, quartered
2 stalks of celery, with tops
1/4 of a Spice Island bay leaf
1/4 teaspoon (or more to taste) pepper
4 cups water (measure)
(Marilyn makes the soup without any salt, which can be added to taste)

1. Place all ingredients except chicken liver in large pot.
2. Bring to boil.
3. *Simmer* 1 hour, or until chicken is tender (add liver for last 15 minutes).
4. Strain broth into jar and *refrigerate*. Remove bay leaf.
5. Refrigerate chicken and vegetables separately.
6. The next day remove all fat, which will be a solid layer on top of the jellied broth.

7. Put chicken and vegetables back (you can serve chicken in pieces or cut into bite sizes to put in the bowl with the soup) in broth and reheat.
8. Serve soup with cooked thin noodles or rice.

This recipe serves four. You'll have lots of chicken left over for sandwiches, casseroles, etc. The soup freezes well so you can always have homemade chicken broth on hand as you never know when your child will come down with a cold.

Canned chicken soup is also good for the mother who hasn't time to cook or the child who can't wait a day.

NO MEDICINE AT ALL

Remember fever is not always bad and does not always need treatment. It may play a useful role in helping the baby kill viruses. Vomiting has a purpose: to rid the stomach of contents which it doesn't want for some reason. Treat vomiting only if it is prolonged. Diarrhea rids the intestine of contents which may be infectious or irritating. We treat it only if it is prolonged or the child has severe cramps.

HOW TO ADMINISTER MEDICINES

Liquid medicine can be given using a nipple, dropper, spoon, medicine cup, or syringe. The important thing is to understand the unit of measurement recommended and to be sure you are accurately providing that dosage. Young babies will often take medicine right from a rubber nipple not even attached to a bottle. If you do use a nipple with a bottle attached, only put a half ounce or so of water in the bottle along with the medicine so you will be sure that the baby took it all.

Many liquid medicines for children come with their own premeasured droppers, which are very convenient. Drugstores now have special medication spoons with a hollow measuring handle and a spoon bowl on the end: if the child tries to spit the medicine out, it goes into the handle so you can try again. Syringes (which can be purchased for oral medication at the drugstore without a prescription in many states) are usually graded in milliliters for accurate administration (just squirt gently into the baby's mouth). Plastic or glass medicine cups also make measuring easy.

One problem in accurate measuring is the spoon because different spoons hold different amounts of liquid, depending on the shape and depth of the bowl —even when all are called teaspoons. However, every household has kitchen measuring spoons, which are usually accurate, and the half-teaspoon size is small enough to fit in a baby's mouth. For convenience, Marilyn kept ordinary teaspoons and tablespoons handy in her medicine cabinet but she measured their exact capacity by pouring water out of the spoon into a calibrated medicine cup, so she knew that the teaspoon held exactly 5 ml.

Because it is hard to give medicine to a squirming toddler who would prefer not to take it, we suggest dividing a teaspoon dose. A full teaspoon usually loses something in the transition between bottle and baby. Two half-teaspoons are easier to manage.

Pills can be buttered to slip down easier but some children have trouble swallowing *any* pill. Almost all pills can be crushed between two spoons or between waxed paper with a rolling pin. Then mix with sugar and a few drops of water or stir into a spoonful of applesauce. A capsule should only be swallowed whole, which means they are useful only for older children.

Don't say medicine tastes good if it doesn't, although you can indicate to your child that it tastes okay if it does. We advocate disguising poor-tasting medicines when it can be done. Sometimes a modicum of force is necessary and this will take four hands: two to hold the child's head and arms still, and two to open the mouth and pour.

What about spitters, sputterers, and vomiters? You have our sympathy. All we can say is try again after estimating how much was spit out. Sometimes using a syringe to direct medicine to the back of the mouth will work. If it is absolutely impossible to get the medicine into your child, and the medicine is absolutely necessary, tell your doctor. Sometimes, for example, an injection must be given.

TIMING OF MEDICINE ADMINISTRATION

Medicines are prescribed to be given at certain intervals for a good reason. Doctors know from pharmacological studies on the absorption rate and excretion of the medicine how often it must be given to ensure that the level of medicine in the bloodstream remains in the therapeutic range. Medicine must be given at a certain interval in order to maintain the proper or effective level needed.

Some medicines must be given *exactly* as directed. For example, a drug used to treat hyperthyroidism must be given at precise eight-hour intervals around the clock. When a prescription reads "every eight hours" or "every six hours," follow these directions exactly even if it means waking the child.

Many times the directions on prescriptions will say "4 times a day," or "3 times a day." All you have to do in that case is divide your child's waking day into 4 or 3 and give the medicine at those times.

However, you must ascertain whether the medicine should be taken on a full or empty stomach, and if necessary build mealtimes into the schedule, keeping the time interval as close to what was recommended as possible. For example, some penicillin is inactivated by food in the stomach and should be taken one hour before meals. If the prescription reads "1 teaspoon 3 times a day before meals" and your child's waking day is usually from 7 A.M. to 7:30 P.M., give your child the first dose at 6:30 A.M. and hold breakfast until 7:30 A.M. The second dose should be given at 12:30 P.M. Hold lunch until 1:30 P.M. The third dose should be given at bedtime, after an early supper, at 5 P.M.

Other medicines, like aspirin or iron, should be taken after meals, as they may upset the stomach. If the child needs aspirin and has not eaten for a while, you can give a swallow or two of milk or a few crackers before giving the aspirin.

Generally, one or two doses of aspirin do not upset the stomach but, if the child is on prolonged aspirin because of arthritis, for example, giving it after meals can make a real difference in the incidence of stomach upsets.

Some medicines are prescribed to be given p.r.n. (this stands for *pro re nata* or "according to circumstances"). This means the drug needs to be given only as wanted or needed for specific symptoms. An antihistamine, for example, might be prescribed as follows: "1 teaspoon every 6 hours as needed for nasal congestion." Other examples for other drugs might be "1 teaspoon as needed at bedtime" or "1 teaspoon every 4 hours if needed for nausea."

DOSAGE CHARTS

We strongly recommend keeping a dosage chart. Marilyn regularly did this; Anne didn't, and often found herself forgetting. A dosage chart is especially important if you have multiple medicines to administer to one child or multiple children who need different doses of medicine, or if you are giving some doses and your spouse or a baby-sitter is giving others. It also helps to remember to give the medicine—if an antibiotic is needed for ten days, and the child is well in four days, it's very easy to forget. The chart, magnetized to the refrigerator door, helps remind you.

All you have to do to create a dosage chart is write down the date, hour, and amount of medicine administered. You can add remarks like "still coughing" or "slept well." You can keep track of multiple medicines either on separate pieces of paper or make one multiple medicine chart. See Table 53, for example.

TABLE 53

SAMPLE DOSAGE CHART

Penicillin—One teaspoon three times a day before meals for ten days.

Monday 1-6

	7 P.M.	1 tsp.	Temp. 103°
Tuesday 1-7	6 A.M.	1 tsp.	
	12 noon	1 tsp.	
	6 P.M.	1 tsp.	
Wednesday 1-8	6 A.M.	1 tsp.	Temp. normal
	12 noon	1 tsp.	
	6 P.M.	1 tsp.	
Thursday 1-9	6 A.M.	1 tsp.	
	12 noon	1 tsp.	
	6 P.M.	1 tsp.	Still coughing
Friday 1-10	6 A.M.	1 tsp.	
	12 noon	1 tsp.	
	6 P.M.	1 tsp.	

Saturday 1-11	6 A.M.	1 tsp.	Much better
	12 noon	1 tsp.	
	6 P.M.	1 tsp.	
Sunday 1-12	6 A.M.	1 tsp.	
	12 noon	1 tsp.	
	6 P.M.	1 tsp.	
Monday 1-13	6 A.M.	1 tsp.	
	12 noon	1 tsp.	
	6 P.M.	1 tsp.	
Tuesday 1-14	6 A.M.	1 tsp.	
	12 noon	1 tsp.	
	6 P.M.	1 tsp.	
Wednesday 1-15	6 A.M.	1 tsp.	
	12 noon	1 tsp.	
	6 P.M.	1 tsp.	
Thursday 1-16	6 A.M.	1 tsp.	
	12 noon	1 tsp.	

Note that ten full days' worth of medicine are given. Because the penicillin wasn't started until nighttime, the two daytime doses were given on the eleventh day.

PHILOSOPHY OF MEDICATION

You do *not* have to run for a pill every time your child has the sniffles. We all know that tons of drugs, both prescription and over-the-counter, are consumed by Americans annually. We are truly a nation of pill poppers. We get upset when our teenagers take recreational drugs but, remember, all their lives they have seen us seek relief from pain or tension out of a medicine bottle. Don't be a pusher to your child.

Stop and think a moment. Does your child really need this medicine? What, besides medicine, will soothe or help your child? Sometimes a rocking chair is better than a pill. Will tincture of time relieve the symptoms shortly? If so, isn't this a good time to teach patience and self-reliance on the curative powers of one's own body? Sometimes the soothing voice of a parent applied to the ears and the lulling motion of a rocking chair applied to the child's body work wonders. Many young children complain of a stomach or headache when the real problem is fatigue or stress. We always suggested our children lie down for a half hour to see if such symptoms went away. Sometimes it helps if you lie down with the child and concentrate on relaxation together.

On the other hand, the relief of annoying symptoms, like those of a cold, can be a blessing. We should *not* deprive our children of safe, effective relief when such relief is available. We have seen parents who are ideologically opposed to any medication for their children as they wish to use only "natural" remedies or methods of healing. In some cases, the parents' ideology has bordered on cruelty and even caused fatalities.

With medication, as with everything else, common sense must prevail.

GENERAL ADVICE ABOUT SICK CHILDREN

Children who feel sick need more mothering and more attention. (So do you when you feel sick, but you may not have a mother's lap handy!) It's important to recognize that the clinging or whining is normal, that the regression is not permanent, and that your child cannot help it. (See Chapter 22.)

But try not to overdo it beyond your *own* limits. One of the most important principles about caring for a sick child is that the parents must take care of themselves. If you become sick, your care of the child may become less than optimal.

Soothing, which parents can do so well, such as cuddling or holding the child in a rocking chair, actually can help healing. If you are becoming exhausted with the care of a sick child, lying down together for a cuddle gives needed rest to both of you. Attitudes are important in recovery and there is evidence that laughing helps healing. Encouraging the child by saying that the illness will be over soon also may help healing and relieve fears.

The working mother has a particular plight when her child is sick, although today some fathers are sharing the burden. Some mothers have to stay home from work if the child is too ill to take to the place of substitute child care. In some enlightened communities, sick child care is available. In Tucson, for example, a mother whose child is ill can call the Tucson Association for Child Care in the morning to request that a child care worker be sent to the home. This costs money, but it can be worth it.

Another problem is that the child of the working mother sometimes uses illness to gain attention and keep Mother home. It is important that the working mother avoid having her child think illness is the only prolonged time the child has with Mother.

FOOD

In general, when children are sick, they will not, and need not, eat a normal diet. Usually they feel better if they eat lightly, and often have a sound "gut instinct" about what will taste good to them.

The trick is to ensure that the child is taking enough liquids. We have learned several techniques over the years for getting liquids into children. When liquids are needed, it's a good time to forget about the nutritional avoidance of soda pop. Carbonated beverages can be given, even to young babies (provided they have been opened for a while to let the bubbles out), and they can be a special treat to most children whose parents limit the daily use of pop. Popsicles, store bought or homemade, are soothing when the child has a sore throat. Jell-O, ice cream, sherbet, and pudding all "count" as liquids. In other words, four ounces of Jell-O is equivalent to four ounces of water. Some children love tea with sugar or honey. Soups are liquid and the salty, processed ones encourage further drinking. You might offer salty crackers as snacks to promote thirst, which helps encourage more drinking.

Offer small amounts of varied liquids frequently. Try a straw (especially effective if straw usage is saved for sick times). Consider a special "sick" cup or glass used only when the child is sick. Ask older children to keep their own chart of liquids ingested.

Usual meals generally won't be eaten, so don't bother to prepare them for sick children—unless the child requests it. Bland, simple foods are usually preferred. Often several small meals are appreciated by a sick child who really doesn't want the spaghetti dinner the rest of the family is having that night. Poached eggs on toast, soup and crackers, cereal, crackers with jelly, french toast, simple sandwiches like jelly or chicken are examples of foods our children asked for when they were sick. Some children want the same thing over and over again; others want to be tempted with a new offering every two hours.

ACTIVITY

In the old days bed rest was considered vitally important. Marilyn can remember not being allowed to let her feet touch the floor when she was sick. However, she probably expended more energy crawling around in the bed than she would have if she had been allowed out of bed. So, if keeping her quiet was the goal, it was not met.

Nowadays, bed rest is usually considered unnecessary except perhaps when the child has a broken leg—and not even all broken legs need bed rest.

Avoiding exhaustion which lowers resistance is the key. Keeping a young child quiet does require some ingenuity. Rocking, reading to the child, quiet games or play like coloring, all can be tried. This is one time that television is useful, especially if the child is ordinarily limited in watching TV, in which case it becomes a special treat.

Bring out the special activity box you keep for when the children are sick. There are lots of things kids can do to keep both quiet and interested: embroidery, puzzles, coloring, stringing beads, etc. Marilyn's mother had a button box filled with hundreds of discarded buttons which Marilyn remembers loving to sort. Save your picture postcards in a shoe box—an older child can sort them geographically. The older child might also love a new crossword puzzle or new library books.

SPECIAL TASKS FOR YOU

If your child is seriously ill, you must learn how to keep a chart of important items such as your child's temperature, intake and output (i.e., what your child has swallowed and what is excreted in the urine, stool, or vomit), and all medicines administered (see Table 54). Be sure you know how to get medical help including the doctor, the emergency room, fire department, sheriff, etc. (see Chapter 23). Every home with a sick child needs the number of an all-night drugstore. In a small town you can sometimes call the pharmacist at home.

By the way, if no doctor is available (maybe you live in the African bush where you are doing research on elephants *and* raising children), there are two books you might want to know about, *Primary Child Care*[7] and *Where There Is No Doctor.*[8] The former is published in Britain and has an African/Asian orientation, while the latter deals with rural health care in Central and South America. These books teach you how to do special things like give an injection. Obviously, if you *do* take your children into the wilderness, you should take medical supplies and drugs and the knowledge with which to use them, based on your doctor's specific suggestions. If your child's illness requires you to perform tasks like injections, you need to work with your child's doctor.

TABLE 54

SAMPLE SICKNESS CHART

Date/Time	Temperature	Ounces In	Urinating	Stools	Vomiting	Activity	New Symptoms	Remarks	Medicine
5-4/4 P.M.	103°	4 water							Tylenol
/5 P.M.			Yes	Loose		Fretful			
/8 P.M.	104°	6 ginger ale							
/10 P.M.	103°	4 water	Yes		All water	Fretful			
5-5/6 A.M.	101°	Refused		Watery			Not sleeping	Cramps	

RETURN TO WELLNESS

As a general rule, children should not go outdoors or to school when they have a fever. Although we would not keep a child home because the temperature was 98.8° instead of 98.6°, a morning temperature over 99.5° would lead us to keep the child home, because it may well get higher over the day.

To determine when your child is ready for normal activity, you have to ask two questions: 1) Will going out make the child sicker or cause a relapse? Generally, when fever has been down for twenty-four hours and the child asks to or seems able to resume ordinary activity, the child can go back to school. Almost never, except in rare chronic illnesses, does prolonged inactivity have a beneficial effect. 2) Can the child hurt the other children—i.e., is he or she still contagious? Unfortunately, your child is most likely to give a cold to another child during the first few hours of sneezing, even before you *thought* your child was sick enough to keep away from other children. When the nose starts crusting after a cold, children can go back to school without spreading too many viruses. After forty-eight hours of treatment with antibiotics for a bacterial infection, children are usually no longer infectious. Children with a contagious rash like measles should stay out of school until they have had no fever for three days. Chicken pox is contagious for seven days after the rash breaks out, but after that, even if there are some pox still around, the child can go to school.

Some children play illness to the hilt. They exaggerate or magnify minor symptoms so they can stay home an extra day. They want to "goof off," relax, not be pressured. This is okay once in a while. We all need a respite every now and then. Other children are so conscientious about school that they conceal symptoms—a bit more ominous. Most children will be ready to go back to school at the appropriate time.

SPECIALIZED HOME CARE

Home Care for the Seriously Ill Child

Some parents have the burden of a seriously ill child who requires very specialized care at home. You may have a diabetic child who requires injections of insulin, urine testing, diet restrictions, charting of urine or blood sugar, etc. Your doctor is your major resource, especially during your "learning" period. However, don't overlook community resources such as visiting nurses. Often the confidence you need is brought about by the nurse in your home telling you, "You do that just right!"

Sometimes special equipment is needed. A premature infant might need an apnea monitor (a device that warns you if the baby stops breathing) or a child with brain damage might need a suction machine so that you can remove secretions from the throat. Generally, you will be taught how to use this special equipment when the child is still in the hospital. Often hospital personnel will come to your home to help teach you what to do in that setting.

Two words of advice. First, become competent in the use of the equipment. One measure of competence is when you can explain how you use the equipment to someone else. Be sure you know the principle behind what you are doing, don't just learn about it mechanically. Second, if your child requires specialized care for a long period of time, find a community resource to provide respite care. Sometimes a nurse from the hospital will be available for hire so you can get out of the house for a while.

Special—But Not Serious—Home Care

Sometimes you have to do things for a child at home that fall into the category of time-consuming—or even annoying—but not unduly burdensome. Generally, the problem in the child is not terribly severe.

An example is heel stretching—a form of physical therapy that might be prescribed for a baby with a mild neurological deficit. Another example is keeping track of every bite your child with hives eats so you can try to track down which food is causing the allergy.

We appreciate that a time-consuming task added to a busy parent's schedule is sometimes hard to accept gracefully. Also, it's annoying to have to explain or show the task to care givers *or* be told by them that they don't wish to do the task. Hopefully, these mild burdens cease when the child gets over the problem.

SUGGESTED READINGS AND RESOURCES

American Medical Association. *AMA Drug Evaluations,* 5th ed. Chicago: American Medical Association, 1984.

Useful book with a good chapter on drug interactions and drugs in breast milk.

Bressler, Rubin; Bogdonoff, Morton D.; and Subak-Sharpe, Genell J., eds. *The Physicians' Drug Manual, Prescription and Nonprescription Drugs.* Garden City, N.Y.: Doubleday, 1981.

An encyclopedia of drugs organized by disease categories. Charts of drugs used for each disease include dosage, side effects, contraindications to use, drug interactions, and use in children or pregnant/lactating women. A useful home health reference.

Carey, Anne. *The Children's Pharmacy.* New York: Warner, 1984.

A listing of drugs which can be prescribed or purchased for children. To us, the organization is confusing but some parents may find the book useful. Nothing here that cannot be found in the *Physicans' Desk Reference for Prescription or Over-the-Counter Drugs.*

Cohen, Matthew M. *Instructions for Parents.* New York: Appleton-Century-Crofts, 1979.

Not very profound but gives brief outlines of what parents should do about illness in their children. May be useful for those parents who want just a few words of advice when a child is sick.

Haessler, Herbert A. *How to Make Sure Your Baby Is Well—and Stays That Way.* New York: Rawson Associates, 1984.

Another medical guide for parents. Detailed information on the physical examination in a child including how to use a stethoscope, take blood pressure, etc. The problem is it is hard to tell what you are looking at without medical training.

Handbook of Nonprescription Drugs, 8th ed. Washington, D.C.: American Pharmaceutical Association, 1986.

Written for pharmacists but could be useful for parents. Chapters on categories of products like antacids, diaper rash products, etc.

Howell, Mary. *Healing at Home: A Guide to Health Care for Children.* Boston: Beacon Press, 1978.

An interesting book that concentrates on health rather than illness. Dr. Howell suggests home remedies and also outlines how you can examine your own child for signs of illness.

Jones, Monica Loose. *Home Care for the Chronically Ill or Disabled Child.* New York: Harper, 1985.

All parents with a chronically ill child should read this book. Very good sections on feeding, medication, respiratory therapy, and orthopedic devices as well as meeting the child's educational and social needs and meeting the whole family's needs.

Pantell, Robert H., and Bergman, David A. *The Parent's Pharmacy.* Reading, Mass.: Addison-Wesley, 1982.

This book is from the doctors who brought you *Taking Care of Your Child.* Briefly discusses drugs and diseases that parents must be familiar with to keep their children healthy. A section on treating common diseases in children and one with an alphabetical listing of commonly used drugs.

Pantell, Robert H.; Fries, James F.; and Vickery, Donald M. *Taking Care of Your Child. A Parents' Guide to Medical Care.* Reading, Mass.: Addison-Wesley, 1977.

Decision trees are used for childhood illnesses and symptoms.

Physicians' Desk Reference, 41st ed. Oradell, N.J.: Medical Economics, 1987 (updated annually).

The book doctors use for drug information. After naming and describing the drug, each section lists the action, pharmacology, contraindications, warnings, precautions, adverse reactions, dosage and administration, overdosage, and how the product is applied. Each product is listed several ways (by manufacturer, product brand name, product category, generic and chemical name). There is a colored photograph section for rapid identification of products. Available at libraries and book stores.

Physicians' Desk Reference for Nonprescription Drugs, 8th ed. Oradell, N.J.: Medical Economics Company, 1987 (updated anually).

Lists over-the-counter products by manufacturer, product name, product category and active ingredients. The product information section contains name, action, uses, administration and dosage, and precautions. There is also a color section of packaging and products for rapid identification.

Schmitt, Barton D. *Pediatric Telephone Advice.* Boston: Little, Brown, 1980.

Designed to teach nurses and doctors what to say on the telephone in response to parents' questions about childhood illness. Parents may find the outline approach useful.

Spock, Benjamin, and Rothenberg, Michael B. *Dr. Spock's Baby and Child Care.* New York: Pocket Books, 1985.

The classic. We both referred to Spock frequently but it contains only a short section on health care and illness.

Werner, David. *Where There Is No Doctor.* Palo Alto, Calif.: The Hesperian Foundation, 1977.

King, Maurice; King, Felicity; and Martodipoero, Soebagio. *Primary Child Care, A Manual For Health Workers.* Oxford, England: Oxford University Press, 1978.

Parents who have to provide much of the medical care of their children because they live where there are no doctors may find these two books useful. *Primary Child Care* is published in Britain and has an African/Asian orientation while *Where There is No Doctor* deals with rural care and Central and South America.

22

HOW ILLNESS AFFECTS
CHILDREN AND PARENTS

Scope of Chapter

This brief chapter will deal with the impact of illness on children. We address the psychological impact of illness looking at the practical and emotional costs and consequences of illness on children, their parents, and their siblings.

Introduction

In the book *Healing at Home*, Mary Howell eloquently discusses what she terms "dis-ease," making a distinction between "*dis*-ease" and the "diseases" that doctors work to discover, understand, and cure.[1] She talks about the four elements of "dis-ease." 1) Distress is pain or discomfort that can arise anywhere from cramping in the intestinal tract to anxiety in the brain. 2) Dysfunction is something gone wrong in the way the body functions so that there is vomiting or fever or croup or wheezing. 3) Disability is defined as weakness or lack of agility or endurance, and 4) Disfigurement is an interruption of integrity or wholeness which can range from simple cuts or bruises to loss of hair, severe weight loss, amputation, tumor, or anything that affects self-image. Dr. Howell defines health as having four aspects: serenity, function, capability, and beauty and wisely points out that each child is a unique individual with his or her own characteristics in these four areas.

What happens in a child when "dis-ease" develops so that distress, dysfunction, disability, or disfigurement occurs?

First, let's recognize that all of us, by definition, do not feel *well* when we are ill. Feeling well is important to us. The absence of feeling well affects the way we feel about ourselves, our relationships, and our work, which is just about everything. Even an ordinary cold, in addition to the physical symptoms like a scratchy throat, a pouring nose, and an aching head, makes us feel down, irritable, and less energetic and productive than usual. A cold can even hurt our self-esteem. If we stay at home we may feel guilty that we are pampering ourselves. If we carry on our usual work or activities we feel guilty that we are spraying our colleagues or friends with virus, and we feel depressed because we *know* we are not functioning the way we should.

As adults we know that in a few days we will feel better. We understand that we have a respiratory infection caused by a virus. We know we are not being punished for doing something bad (although most of us at our "downest" find ourselves thinking we should have avoided getting our feet wet, or used some talisman to ward off the infection). We know our spouse and children still value us—red nose and all—and that our boss will not fire us for catching a cold.

Children who do not feel *"well"* don't have the luxury of our knowledge. They don't know they will feel better soon. They don't know that the medicine their mother is trying to administer will alleviate their symptoms. They often can't even talk about how bad they feel because they are preverbal or don't yet have the vocabulary.

The way a child responds to an illness or injury will depend on what sickness the child has, what part of the body it affects, and the age of the child. In addition, the way the family handles illness in general, and specifically in the child, also plays a role.

Interestingly enough, children (like adults) are more likely to get sick after cumulative social-psychological crises in their lives. One study looked at children with a chronic disease or those admitted to a hospital with an acute pediatric or surgical problem.[2] More of these children than would be expected had experienced either more frequent or more severe life events prior to the onset of their illness. Life events were scored by age and included such stresses as death of a parent, divorce, birth of a sibling, starting school, etc.

IMPACT OF ILLNESS ON CHILDREN

Ways in Which Children React to Illness

1. *Fear* is especially common in young children who don't understand the natural causes for illness. They only know they don't feel like themselves and they don't understand why. Older children who are smart enough to know when they have a serious illness can be very frightened. They may be old enough to figure out that they don't have a simple cold or earache but instead have more serious symptoms which don't go away. Such children may be terribly concerned about their increasing disability as well as the possibility of their death, especially before the diagnosis is made and explained.

2. Children are often quite *irritable* when they are sick—as are adults. They are fretful and impossible to comfort. Whining and crying are common.

3. Almost all sick children exhibit *regression* of their behavior, which can be manifested in various ways. The baby may refuse solids and only want the breast or bottle; the previously trained toddler may wet or soil again; the older

child may demonstrate clinging or whining—behavior that you thought was outgrown.

4. Sleep disturbances—*insomnia* or *hypersomnia* are often found in children who are sick.

5. Some children who feel sick are *restless* and even *hyperactive*.

6. Older children are often *angry* with themselves for being sick, especially if it interferes with something they had wanted to do—a school play, for example.

7. *Poor appetite* is fairly common in both children and adults when illness prevails.

8. Children may *blame themselves* for illness and therefore feel guilty. They may think they did something wrong and are being punished. Indeed, parents often reinforce this. How many times have we heard, "If you get your feet wet, Johnny, you are going to get a cold!" Obviously, if he gets his feet wet and if he does get sick, he is going to think that he brought the cold on himself. Then, in addition to the cold, Johnny has that old guilt-and-blame syndrome, which can lead to depression.

9. Children who are chronically or recurrently ill often have *impaired self-esteem*. They feel they are not as good or attractive or lovable as their healthy siblings or playmates. They begin to expect to be rejected by others because they are sick.

10. Frank *depression* can occur in children who are chronically ill. This may be manifested in sadness, lack of interest, and a feeling of hopelessness.

How Illness Affects Children of Different Ages

1. Infants who are sick usually demonstrate marked behavior changes in those areas in which an infant functions: feeding, sleeping, and reacting to the environment. Parents may expect the sick baby to feed poorly and sleep restlessly but may not be prepared for the withdrawal the baby shows. This may range from no interest in reaching for a toy to turning away from the parent. Babies may also *protest* their illness by doing lots of crying. A usual sunny disposition may change to one of fretfulness; the baby may refuse to be comforted. Even a young baby who had not developed very far may show *regression* when ill. The baby may refuse to drink from a cup, for example, and only take liquids from a nipple. It can be frightening to parents when they see their baby has lost developmental ground. But adults who feel sick often regress as well. Previously capable of fixing their own meals, sick adults may insist on being catered to. Childish behavior and demands to be cared for are normal adaptive responses to illness in both children and adults.

2. Regression is probably the most common reaction to illness in the toddler. This includes wetting in the previously trained child, refusing adult-type

food, irritability, whining, clinging, etc. In addition, illness can cause toddlers to act depressed and disinterested in their surroundings.

3. Preschoolers and school-age children believe that illness is caused by magic or some transgression of theirs. Thus, they think the illness they have is punishment for their misbehavior. They have already internalized many of our rules and guidelines about behavior. They have learned that if they are bad they may be punished. It is very logical to suppose if they have something painful or uncomfortable it is punishment for a "badness" they have done or thought. They may also blame others. One child with diabetes felt her illness was caused by her stepbrother feeding her candy.

4. By fourth grade, children think all illness is caused by germs, although by eighth grade multiple causation is understood.[3] Older school-age children worry a lot about their appearance. Fears of body mutilation are paramount. Not being able to keep up with classmates or playmates because of illness is particularly distressful. Illness makes the child feel, and appear, different, which is devastating to a child whose goal at this age is to conform and to be accepted.

5. Adolescents are also concerned about body images and looking or acting different. In addition, teenagers worry about illness leading to loss of self-control, autonomy, and independence. Adolescents also understand the principle of permanence and may despair that they will never get better, and thus worry about their future. These young adults often deny symptoms and illnesses or may vacillate between clinging behavior and outrageous disobedience of the rules.

The Impact of Treatment on Children

Being sick and not feeling well are bad enough but contact with health professionals can make a child feel even worse before—hopefully—the child will feel better. The physical examination, laboratory diagnostic procedures, and treatment procedures can all be traumatic for children. First of all, the child is confronted with a *stranger* handling the child's body in an intimate way. The stethoscope may be cold; it hurts to have your ears examined when you have an ear infection; inspection of the genitals may embarrass children (a pubertal boy might get an erection when the doctor feels his groin for lymph nodes).

Diagnostic procedures can be painful or unpleasant. To get a proper throat culture, the back of the throat must be touched. This is not painful but most children will gag, which is not a pleasant sensation. Some children who have an active gag reflex might vomit. Drawing blood is an *invasion* of the child's body with a painful instrument—the needle—that violates the integrity of the child's protection from the world—the skin.

No matter how good a relationship the parents and child have with the doctor, it may become strained when the child is ill. The doctor may have to do painful diagnostic or therapeutic procedures on an already irritable and cranky child. If just one throat culture has to be done, things aren't so bad. However, when there are repeated procedures, such as may be needed in seriously ill children, going to the doctor can become very distressing to the child. Children may do all sorts of things to avoid the treatment, from running away on the day they are supposed to go, to denying symptoms, to faking the results of their urine tests if they are diabetic.

Medical professionals who know children and deal with them in a caring way can be helpful here. If your child is fortunate enough to consider the pediatrician a friend, an individual who can be trusted, this helps. Parents can help, also, by explaining to the best of their ability what the child can expect. Parents can use helpful devices to focus attention away from worry. Marilyn tells children to count; by the time they get to three the needle stick will be over.

It is important for the child's doctor or the nurse to explain what is going to be done. Even young children, who may need gentle restraint to keep them still, should be told what will happen. Even the restraining itself should be explained ("I'm wrapping you in this blanket so you will be able to stay still to help the doctor"). Older children should be encouraged to ask questions about what will be done, to see the instruments ahead of time, to ask very specifically about what will hurt, how much, and for how long. Parents are urged to minimize their tendency to say it won't hurt (much as they wish it wouldn't.) Instead tell your child, "This will hurt; you can manage it; I'll help you manage."

Remember that the "good" or overly compliant child may actually be in a less healthy psychological state. It is often useful for the parent, as well as the health professional, to encourage the child to scream or shout or swear when the needle punctures the skin even though the child's cooperation is needed. Children *must* be able to express their dislike of the procedure, even though they must endure it. A tangible reward for cooperation is well earned. This can mean a restaurant treat, going to a movie that the child especially wants to see, buying a book or a small toy, etc., after the procedure.

What If the Child Must Be Hospitalized

Some children *will* be hospitalized. Almost 3.7 million children under age fifteen are hospitalized each year.

Hospitalization means separation from parents and home at a time in the life cycle when such separation is dreaded. In addition, the hospitalized child is subjected to procedures which are always unfamiliar and often painful.

Whenever possible, hospitalization should be avoided for children. If your doctor recommends the hospital for a diagnostic or therapeutic reason, it is *always* worth asking, "Is the hospital necessary or is there an alternative?" Sometimes simple surgery can be done in an ambulatory setting. This means the child is brought to the facility the same day of the operation by the parents, who can stay with the child until he or she is anesthetized. The parents are present when the child awakens from the anesthetic and take the child home the same day. Some medical centers have nearby motels where the child and family can stay during a lengthy diagnostic work-up or prolonged course of treatment. Sometimes parents can be taught to provide medical care and treatments at home with the assistance of visiting nurses or home care helpers.

If hospitalization *is* required, we have several suggestions. First of all, recognize the impact the hospitalization of your child will have on *you.* You are already worried about your child's illness; hospitalization will increase your apprehensiveness. You may feel guilty that you have somehow failed as a parent. Else why would your child be so sick as to have to go to the hospital? You may worry that the hospital personnel will criticize your care of your child.

Having a child in the hospital will greatly impact on your life. Visiting or staying with the child can interfere with your job. Who will care for the other children? How will you deal with your fears for your child?

Upset as you may be, your first task should be to recognize and *deal with your feelings.* Next you should *call for help*—a relative or neighbor may be able to care for your other children. You may be able to get a short leave of absence from work. Some companies permit parents to use sick leave for illness in a child. It's worth asking your boss about. Besides *practical help,* you will need *emotional support*—someone to hear your worries. Your usual supports like spouse and family may not be helpful because they are worried too. You may hesitate to share your worst worries for fear of worrying them. (Chances are they already have the same worries and are afraid of worrying *you.)* But if you need someone outside the family to talk to, most good hospitals have social workers who are there for your support.

Next, your child needs help and support. Every child old enough to understand (this is as young as eighteen months) should be told: 1) they are going to a hospital; 2) what a hospital is like; 3) who will take care of them there; 4) what will happen to them; and 5) most important of all that *you* will be there—all the time, or every day.

Preparation is age-specific. Preschoolers should be told about the hospital but not more than a day or two before they are to be admitted. Your library has many books available such as *Curious George Goes to the Hospital* and *The Hospital Book* that you can read to children before they have to be hospitalized to help them visualize the process.

Whenever possible, children should visit the hospital before they become patients there. Seeing what the anesthesia machine is going to be like and being told in advance what is going to happen is beneficial. Often a procedure can be "played out" with toys or stuffed animals.

Many children's hospitals have their own booklets describing what it will be like there. This may be the time to invest in a doctor or nurse kit so that you and your child can "act out" scenes that are likely to happen. Obviously, before you can do this, *you* must have a good idea yourself. Ask your doctor or the admitting clerk at the hospital what to expect.

Older children and adolescents who ask for information should be told but generalities are better than gory details for younger children. It is not necessary that a young child know how many layers the surgeon will cut through, only that "The appendix that's making you sick will be taken out. You won't feel the operation and people don't need their appendix."

Be careful what words you choose. Marilyn remembers a young boy who became hysterical when an experienced anesthesiologist came to the ward with the plastic hood she was planning to use "—when I put you to sleep." It seems the child's pet beagle had been "put to sleep" the week before. Words like, "when you breathe the special air in the mask, you will fall asleep for a while" are better, followed by "When you wake up, Mommy and Daddy will be right there by your bed." One can even say honestly, "The operation would hurt if you were awake, so it's better to be asleep while it's going on."

In addition to making every effort to prepare your child for what will happen, we also suggest you give your child *permission to regress*. It's perfectly all right for a scared, lonely child who's feeling sick to cry or want Mommy. Tell your child you understand how he or she feels and that you would feel the same way if you were hospitalized. Also, to avoid feeling very separated from family and familiar surroundings, your child should take clothes, toys, and photographs to the hospital. Most children's hospitals allow this. If your young child has a favorite blanket or teddy bear, you have a dilemma about whether to take it. If it gets lost at a time of illness or surgery, your child might be inconsolable. Sometimes it's better to say, "I'm keeping Teddy with me to be sure he's safe, but I'll bring him to visit."

Children are particularly susceptible to emotional trauma during hospitalization. Painful procedures and separation from home and family cannot be avoided, but the caring physician can do a great deal to diminish fear in the child and gain the trust of parents.

Useful hints for parents of hospitalized children include: be present at hospital mealtimes so you can help and encourage your child to eat; talk to the dietician about your child's likes and dislikes; bring food to your children, unless they are on a restricted diet; bring a little toy or other remembrance from home each day; if your child is in a room with another child undergoing a procedure, explain to your child that he or she will not be involved in it; be sure your child's doctor explains procedures ahead of time; ask your doctor to write special orders for unlimited visiting hours if hospital rules limit visiting; encourage your child to talk about the hospital and procedures.[4] Stay with your child if you possibly can—most hospitals now encourage this.

Children react to hospitalization in age-specific ways which require age-specific remedies to minimize "hospitalitis."

1. Infants under six months of age may react to different handling and surroundings by global changes in eating, sleeping, and elimination patterns. When you stop to think about it, these are the *only* ways a young baby has to react to any stress. We recommend frequent visiting and handling by the parents to help prevent these reactions.

2. Older infants who have developed to the point of knowing they don't

like separation from their parents show true anxiety on separation, and also suffer from exposure to multiple strangers in a hospital. They respond with crying, depression (avoidance or withdrawal), as well as regression (refusing a cup, for example). The more time parents can spend with the child, the better.

3. Children from one to three react to hospitalization and separation from the parents with anxiety, which probably reflects the fact that they associate the "loss" of the parents with punishment for being bad. The typical pattern is screaming protest when the parents leave, followed by despair and detachment, then regression (loss of bowel and bladder control is common). Parents can cope better with protest and despair if they understand how their child feels. Detachment is hard for parents to deal with because children avoid eye contact, turn away, and generally act as though they don't care about the parents anymore. Some children will even refuse food and toys from parents.

Marilyn prescribes a very specific therapy when this happens: the rocking chair. Pick the child up (most children even with intravenous lines can be picked up) and rock the child in your arms as often and as long as possible. If the child can't be picked up, you can still stroke the child and talk to the child even when the head is turned away. Don't *you* despair. When the child comes home from the hospital, he or she will not only stop avoiding you but will most likely cling very closely for a while.

4. Older children worry about mutilation as well as separation and need a good deal of verbal reassurance. Older children also have concerns about body functioning and loss of body control or helplessness under anesthesia. In addition, these children also unconsciously feel treatments are punishment for past bad behavior. To complicate things further, school-age children feel embarrassed about regression to dependency, and want to keep up with their peers at school.

5. The adolescent struggles with the forced dependency of hospitalization at the very time independence is becoming so important. Concerns over body image and function are paramount especially as related to the developing interest in the opposite sex.

After hospitalization, children (like adults) may exhibit certain behaviors. Even children who appeared to have made a good adjustment to the hospital often regress at home, exhibit anxiety or fears, avoid bed or have difficulty falling asleep (some children and adults experience prolonged insomnia after anesthesia). Reassurance, acceptance of the regression, and lots of attention all help the child return to a prehospitalization state. Posthospitalization reactions are self-limited in most children. They are part of our usual useful capacity to delay emotional response—like the parent who heroically ignores anxiety in a fire, saves the children, and *then* collapses emotionally.

We recommend reminding children of their mastery. "Remember when you were scared of needles in the hospital, you figured out how to help the nurse do it quick. What a big girl you are getting to be!" Also, encourage the child to talk about the hospital and to read the books about hospitals again ("Look, Curious George had the same kind of crib you did when *he* was in the hospital!") It's also wise to encourage the child to express negative feelings about the hospital by prompting ("It felt bad to be in the hospital bed, didn't it?") and asking ("How did you feel when you got a needle?").

If at all possible, hospitalization should be avoided until the child is over five so that procedures can be explained to the child. This means that any elective surgical procedure which requires hospitalization should be put off until then.

If hospitalization cannot be avoided, it is preferable that a parent stay in the hospital with the child. Most good pediatric hospitals will either have rooming-in where parent and child share a room or will have a chair that turns into a bed (or at the very least will permit a parent to stay even if sleeping is only possible on a chair). The days of very restricted visiting hours (one or two hours a day), which were common some years ago, have now given way to unlimited (or very close to unlimited) visiting hours in most hospitals. Most health professionals recognize the importance of not disrupting parent and child bonds at a time of stress in the child.

Children's hospitals or general hospitals with large pediatric wards which have well-trained pediatric nurses and play therapists are better places for children than adult hospitals. It is often worth transporting the child—and family— a long distance to reach such a hospital. Some hospitals or communities have Ronald McDonald houses, where children and their families live together while the child goes to the hospital as often as daily for prolonged treatment. This is especially helpful in the case of childhood cancer.

Chronic Illness

Chronic illness has its own set of problems. Most parents can cope with a few weeks of chicken pox bouncing from child to child but all will experience difficulty when facing months of illness and dread the implications of a lifetime of illness for the child. Chronic illness brings all the problems of acute illness for the child, parents, and siblings—only more so. There is greater depletion of parental resources—both emotional and financial. Sometimes parents, usually mothers, have to leave outside jobs to care for the child. Sometimes the household is moved to a possibly more favorable climate. Siblings and spouses resent the time and attention the mother devotes to the ill child. The mother resents her unexpected new tasks. Guilt pervades along with grief—the two emotions most difficult for humans to cope with.

There are two kinds of chronic illness in childhood, one with hope of eventual recovery, the other with no recovery possible.

An example of a chronic illness that gets better might be a child with congenital heart disease which restricts activity, but provides hope of a curative operation when the child is older. Another is rheumatoid arthritis or asthma, which a child may "grow out of." Unfortunately, there are many children who will never grow out of their diseases. They will either die, as some children with leukemia will do, or will live a close to normal life span in a handicapped condition, as in the case of severe cerebral palsy.

The ways in which chronic illness affects children, and our special suggestions for parents who want to make life as easy as possible for the child under these difficult conditions, are also age-specific.

1. All babies need food and cuddling whether they are sick or well. They also need to move. A chronically ill baby may need special help with feeding which can take longer because the baby's ability to suck may be impaired. Parents should try to move an inactive baby as much as possible by carrying, active cuddling, massaging, and exercising the limbs. Whenever possible, these babies should be talked to and encouraged to play. The more a baby is immobilized (a lengthy time in a cast, for example) the more important it is to encourage the baby's assertiveness and even the negativism. A child Marilyn knew was hospitalized repeatedly in a body cast for a hip problem. One wise doctor told her mother to bring rubber and cloth toys and teach her daughter how to throw them on the floor or at her family!

2. The young child afflicted with a chronic illness needs help in dealing with worries and possibly mistaken ideas about illness. Children can be encouraged to talk about their illness and its meaning. One technique is to ask, using the child's teddy bear, "Where does Teddy hurt?" or "What does Teddy think about his legs that don't work?"

Parents can help by giving correct information to the child about the illness and by helping interpret what the doctor has said. In addition, parents can offer corrective information. "Teddy didn't get sick because he was bad." You can add that the bear, like some children, was born with part of him not right and can then explain that the same thing happened to your child. Every effort should be made to enable the child to engage in age-appropriate play and to interact with other children if possible.

3. The older child who is chronically ill needs a good deal of help from parents. Explaining the illness, answering the "Why me?" questions, and helping the child understand and cope with the treatment are all important and take a good deal of parental energy and effort. Even a bright child may need interpretive and corrective help with understanding the illness. A friend of Marilyn's, whose seven-year-old daughter was recently diagnosed as a diabetic, was astounded to hear her daughter say a week later, "Why do they call it di-abetes. Am I going to die?"

Parents should begin working with the child to take responsibility for the self-management of the illness (testing one's own urine and administering one's own insulin for diabetes or taking aspirin for arthritis, for example). Most children will be ready to do this somewhere between age seven and eleven. There are wonderful books that teach children about diabetes and asthma. (See Suggested Readings and Resources.)

4. Chronically ill adolescents pose special problems which often are best handled in a group setting with other afflicted adolescents. One hard task for

parents is finding ways to foster age-appropriate independence in an ill teenager, and to help in formulating realistic goals for school, career, and relationships.

The adolescent with chronic illness has to be helped to develop autonomy in the face of an illness which increases dependency. This task is difficult for both teenagers and their parents. Yet parents want to see their children able to care for the chronic illness by themselves. Compliance with medical treatment was correlated with high self-esteem and autonomy in adolescents.[5]

One adolescent girl Marilyn knows was afflicted with ulcerative colitis at a young age, requiring lifelong medication, frequent hospitalizations, and occasional interference with the normal activities of a teenager. She pointed out that because she felt hopeless when ill, regulating her own treatment was important to her. She always thinks of herself as a teenager with long-term life goals like college and a career—but who has a disease. However, she leads as normal a life as possible. She says, "I put my disease out of myself and only think about it when I have to. I am *me*, I'm not my disease. My disease is something I take care of with my doctor, but it is *not* me."

Anne had polio as a teenager and handled the slow and uncertain convalescence by thinking about recovery as a long-term process—"when I get well" is like "when I grow up." In the meantime her parents actively sought to make the most of the positive aspects of the situation. For example, not having school in the morning freed Anne from schedules so she could read as late as she wanted at night.

The most serious impact of chronic illness is when it causes children to feel that they *are* different and *look* different from other children. Chronically ill children may be unable to be active with, or even to *be* with, other children. One of the most important things parents can do is to keep the child functioning at a level as close to normal as possible. If the child is bedridden or wheelchair bound, it is important that the parents find ingenious ways of having other children spend as much time with this child as possible. The child's education should be kept up, preferably at school or using home teachers, or self-directed work on school assignments with parental help if needed.

Marilyn read a story in the Tucson newspapers about a three-year-old boy with spina bifida who had some impairment in walking as well as problems with bladder and bowel control. His mother invited twenty-five neighborhood children over for his birthday party at which point she explained his problems and suggested ways the children could understand his illness and play with him. What a good idea! Other children need explanation of such a problem. They are frightened by a child who is "different." They may wonder if it's contagious or not know how to respond.

THE IMPACT OF CHILDREN'S ILLNESS ON PARENTS

Ordinary Illnesses

A well child can be demanding to a parent. A sick child is even more so. The demands, in terms of time and energy, may be especially hard on parents who are both employed. A sick child needs care, even when it is a relatively minor illness. The parent must figure out how often to give the medicine, keep records, try to encourage fluids, change the diaper more often if it is diarrhea, etc. All this takes more time in what is usually an already busy day for the parent.

In addition, children's regression during illness means they may become irritable and clinging and more demanding of parents than usual. Parents are often exhausted by these demands and may even feel sick themselves at the very time they are most needed by their children. Sometimes everybody comes down with the same virus at the same time.

Parents can also get *angry* at the fact that their child got sick. Sometimes they are angry at the neighbor who brought over the child who got chicken pox the next day. Sometimes they blame their spouse, who may have left the window open in the car. In addition, they feel quite *guilty* about the fact that they let their child get sick, i.e., they *let* the neighbor bring the chicken pox-ridden child over and they didn't tell their spouse to close the window in the car. You can already see that the combination of exhaustion, anger, and guilt causes unhappiness in the parents. This can be true for minor illness as well as chronic or serious illness.

We have some suggestions for parents of sick children here based on what we have learned from having sick children ourselves and from listening to other mothers. In the first place, the mother (the one who is usually at home with the child) and also the father or other care giver must guard against getting sick themselves. This is one of those times when you should forget about many of the other household tasks you ordinarily do. Don't cook dinner if you have already been at the stove all day trying to tempt a sick child with just the right liquids. This is a perfect time for the TV dinner or sending out to the local fast-food establishment.

Ditto with big laundry or housecleaning jobs. Somehow they always get done afterward. Spend most of the day resting with the child, perhaps watching television or reading. This way you won't be exhausted if you have to be up that night with a cranky child.

This is also a good time to find someone who can relieve you so that you can get out of the house. Ask a neighbor, a relative, or your spouse for "relief time." There is nothing worse than being cooped up twenty-four hours a day with a sick child. Even nurses at hospitals only work eight-hour shifts. If you are a single parent, this is *really* the time to call on your friends. If a baby is too sick or irritable for you to be gone a long time, perhaps a friend can come over when the child drops off to sleep so you can at least take a walk, go to the library, do an errand, or sleep yourself.

There is one suggestion about illness which may sound as though it adds to your workload, but it really doesn't. Keep a diary of what is happening. In the first place this enables you to give your doctor accurate information. In the second place, once we have written something down we often find it is not as bad as it seemed. In the third place, you may be too tired to notice, but rereading your diary notes can remind you that the child's temperature has indeed gone up and then you remember the doctor asked you to call if that happened. Last but far from least, you can use your diary to express your feelings.

Chronic Illness

Chronic illness in a child takes an enormous amount of parental understanding, knowledge, and courage in order to cope. All parents want healthy children. There is no question parents are disturbed when they are told, or finally realize, that they have a not-so-healthy child instead. The chronically ill child will require more care and more understanding, perhaps forever.

When a chronic illness such as diabetes, which is known to have a genetic origin, occurs, this can put a stress on parents and a strain on the marital relationship. The bit about "Nobody had diabetes in my side of the family!" doesn't help and yet it is an understandable exclamation. In point of fact, many chronic diseases that children get are genetic, even if they come on in later childhood. Usually, it is the *combination* of genes in the parents that leads to the disease (except in the case of a disease like hemophilia, which is carried through the mother).

Some very common first reactions are, "I have done something wrong"; "I have not taken good enough care of my child"; or, "My genes were wrong"; all of which lead to guilt which can lead to depression. As a matter of fact, the diagnosis of a chronic or fatal illness in a child almost always leads to depression in parents. Some parents get over it by themselves, but most can benefit from counseling or professional help.

A recent study of children with chronic illness and their families[6] noted that parents reported the following areas of impact on the family: worry, finances, fatigue of parent, changes in household routine (sleep arrangements, furnishings), social life, travel restrictions, parental friction, sibling neglect or resentment, and embarrassment. Children who were chronically ill, when compared with control children who were not ill, had more school and adjustment problems.

Marilyn's friend said the hardest thing to cope with was the realization that her daughter would *always* have diabetes. "One day you have a perfectly healthy child and the next day everything has changed. Even though Sarah is doing well and has accepted her disease and its treatment, she will never be well. We will never be the parents of a perfectly well child." Every aspect of the child's life is affected: school, camp, vacations, dealings with relatives, etc. "It sure doesn't help when well-meaning friends say it could have been worse!"

How is this family coping? They are learning all they can about juvenile diabetes and its treatment. They are teaching their children the principles of self-care. They are making every effort to treat their daughter as a normal girl who happens to have diabetes, rather than as a diabetic child. Both parents recognize that coping presupposes that they are able to get in touch with *their own feelings;* they plan to get counseling help when and if needed.

When chronic illness strikes there are three challenges for the parent, the family, and the sick child.[7] There is a cognitive challenge: parents must learn about a disease, its treatment, and its impact on the child. The emotional challenge centers around the fact that the parents lose a healthy child who is replaced by one not only physically ill but unnaturally dependent. The behavioral challenge may be the hardest: they must take care of a sick child while maintaining, to the best of their ability, normal family functions of work and nurturance of the siblings.

Parents who are successful at coping with chronic illness in a child share certain similarities. The family is supportive of its members, the family can communicate with each other, the parents can shift roles, and the parents make joint decisions.

THE IMPACT OF YOUR CHILD'S ILLNESS ON SIBLINGS

Children are afraid of getting sick or of catching a disease. In one sense this is good, as it may help your child stay away from someone contagious and avoid bad health habits. But people get sick anyway, even if they are careful. Illness is one of the things most of us have to expect in life. It may not be fair, but it is a part of the real world.

Siblings of chronically ill children are never uninvolved. Indeed, they are a population at risk.[8] Sibling illness ranks as a high stress factor. Healthy siblings are caught up in the family isolation caused by the illness; parenting skills are often adversely affected by parental stress; marital problems often occur; and role shifts may lead to the healthy sibling serving as the parents' comforter and keeper. In addition, family resources may be strained by medical expenses so that the sibling may be deprived of not only luxuries but even basic needs.

Children react two ways when they have a sick sibling. One feeling is guilt that they caused the serious illness by doing one of the bad things they might have done to their siblings. All children remember, or imagine, a bad thing they did that may have caused the sib's sickness.

The other feeling is jealousy. The sibling can be quite jealous of the sick child, who is getting all the attention in the household. Jealousy often manifests itself by the sibling wanting increased attention from the parent just, of course, at a time when the parent is most exhausted with care and worry over the sick child. Here again, this is the time to call on your spouse or friends or grandparents or other relatives. The well, but angry, jealous, or guilty child can be taken to the movies or the zoo. You can also offer a reward for especially good behavior. We always encourage the use of earned rewards to encourage mature behavior until the child can manage the good behavior on his or her own. We do not mean you have to buy out F.A.O. Schwarz. We just mean a small but tangible and well-earned recognition, like a special present you know the child will like. Parents generally know which special presents will mean the most to their children. We don't suggest giving such a present when the child whines or cries for it, but when the child *deserves* it. (The same principle applies to ourselves— dinner out at a good restaurant might be a respite we have earned.)

How much parents tell a sibling obviously depends on the child's age. It is important not only to answer questions truthfully but also to point out that the illness was not caused by any deeds or thoughts of the sibling. Another concern of a sibling is, "Will I get sick too?" which also has to be addressed. Most of the time the answer is "No!" but in the case of an infection which the sibling could be incubating or a genetic disease that could be also present in the sibling, the answer is "Maybe." Perhaps before worrying a child with such an answer it would be wise to ask your doctor or even a specialized genetic counselor about the risks of the siblings getting the illness.

If hospital rules and your child's condition permit, siblings of a hospitalized child should visit. Being able to see, rather than imagine, what the sick child looks like can alleviate anxiety. A study of siblings assigned randomly to visiting their sibling in a neonatal intensive care unit showed that the non-visiting sibling described the hospital as negative while the visiting siblings were positive.[9] The visiting sibling did not show fear or anxiety during the visit and parents had favorable comments about the visits. Every visiting sibling asked to come see the baby again.

If you are limited to a hospital whose rules archaically forbid sibling visitation, do your bit, when you can, to try to change those rules. But in the meantime, Polaroid photographs and phone calls can help maintain sibling communication.

*   *   *

Times of illness are stressful for everyone involved. With an understanding of how illness affects children and their families and a knowledge of what support is available, you can better weather the stress.

SUGGESTED READINGS AND RESOURCES

Elder, Barbara Schuyler-Haas. *The Hospital Book.* Baltimore: John Street Press, 1975.
Very good.

Howe, James. *The Hospital Book.* New York: Crown, 1981.
An up-to-date book, well illustrated with actual photos of children in hospitals. This book is useful for parents to read with children before they must be hospitalized.

Howell, Mary. *Healing at Home: A Guide to Health Care for Children.* Boston: Beacon Press, 1978.
A very interesting book that concentrates on health rather than illness. Dr. Howell suggests home remedies and also outlines how you can examine your own child for signs of illness.

Isler, Charlotte. *Pocket Dictionary of Diagnostic Tests, Procedures and Terms.* Oradell, N.J.: Medical Economics, 1981.
Lists and explains common medical terms in the area of diagnostic tests and procedures. More complete, though brief, explanations than are found in a medical dictionary.

Jones, Monica Loose. *Home Care for the Chronically Ill or Disabled Child.* New York: Harper, 1985.
All parents with a chronically ill child should read this book. Very good sections on feeding, medication, respiratory therapy, and orthopedic devices. Good sections on meeting the child's educational and social needs and on meeting the whole family's needs.

Kersey, Katharine C. *Helping Your Child Handle Stress: The Parent's Guide to Recognizing and Solving Childhood Problems.* Washington, D.C.: Acropolis Books, 1986.
Some useful suggestions on helping your children with possible problems.

McCollum, Audrey T. *The Chronically Ill Child: A Guide for Parents and Professionals.* New Haven: Yale University Press, 1981.
A useful reference for parents of chronically ill children, from infancy to adulthood.

Miller, Jonathan. *The Human Body.* New York: Viking, 1983.
A clever three-dimensional and movable-parts book about how the body looks and works. A bright ten-year-old will love it.

Parcel, Guy S.; Tiernan, Kathy; Nader, Philip R.; and Weiner, Larry. *Teaching Myself About Asthma.* St. Louis, Mo.: Mosby, 1979.
An excellent book for asthmatic children between ages 7 and 12 who are good readers. Actually the first pages of the book are useful for helping *any* child learn what illness means and how to cope with it.

Rey, Hans Augusto, and Rey, Margret. *Curious George Goes to the Hospital.* New York: Scholastic Book Services, 1974.
A charmingly illustrated book about a monkey who goes to the hospital. Marilyn's son loved it even though he did not particularly like going to the hospital!

Schneider, Herman, and Schneider, Nina. *How Your Body Works*. London: Heinemann, 1960.

It's a bit dated, but a very good book nonetheless. It teaches school-age children how their bodies work by means of clever experiments that can be done at home.

Singer, Marilyn. *It Can't Hurt Forever*. New York: Harper, 1981.

A good book to read to the younger child (four to eight) or for older children to read by themselves prior to heart surgery. Fictionalized account of a little girl who has a congenital heart lesion and needs cardiac catheterization and surgery.

Stein, Sara Bonnett. *A Hospital Story*. New York: Walker, 1974.

Excellent.

Travis, Luther B. *An Instructional Aid on Juvenile Diabetes Mellitus*, 5th ed. Galveston, Tex.: University of Texas Medical Branch, 1978.

A must for any child with diabetes and for the parents.

Weber, Alfons. *Elizabeth Gets Well*. New York: Crowell, 1970.

Excellent.

Winn, Marie. *The Sick Book: Questions and Answers About Hiccups and Mumps, Sneezes and Bumps, and Other Things That Go Wrong with Us*. New York: Four Winds, 1976.

A book for children about how the body works in sickness and in health. A question-and-answer format with superb illustrations. The book would delight a bright eight-year-old who wanted to be a doctor.

23

EMERGENCIES

Scope of Chapter

This chapter will cover emergency situations that can happen to *any* child in *any* family, stressing the role of the parent or care giver in both first aid and getting help.

We will first discuss being prepared for emergencies. Next we list the common emergencies in childhood and discuss what the parent should *do*—and *not do*. We then cover first aid for minor emergencies. The last section of the chapter offers suggestions for teaching your children how to prevent and react to emergencies themselves.

BE PREPARED!

Prevention and Preparation

Many emergencies are preventable, especially injuries. As parents and as doctors we know that it is easier and far better to prevent an emergency than to handle one.

More than half the children who die each year in our country die as a result of serious injuries. Many more suffer permanent or crippling disabilities. Trauma is a killer; everything we can do to prevent it, and to provide prompt medical care for injuries, helps fight this scourge.

Prevention will not eliminate all emergencies, but you can definitely reduce the odds. Child-proofing your home and yard, safety rules, and safety pointers for each age and stage are discussed in Chapter 5, page 123. Let us just remind you here that there are certain hazardous times when childhood accidents are most apt to occur. First, there is a "fatigue factor." When the child—or parent —is tired, accidents are more likely to happen. Hunger also plays a role; late afternoon, or before meals, is a dangerous time. Accidents are more frequent when you or your child is ill or when the household routine is broken because of moving, vacation, or a family crisis.

As parents—and as doctors who see firsthand the results of childhood accidents in hospital emergency rooms—we believe in prevention and preparedness. But we must point out that *every* child will have an accident serious enough to *scare* the parents even if the injury which results is minor. We are saying this for two reasons: to convince you of the importance of being prepared, and to prevent you from feeling guilty when an accident occurs even though you have tried to prevent them all.

Because *every* child will have an emergency, *every* parent must prepare for such an event. We never know ahead of time what will happen but we can make ourselves ready to help our children.

Be ready *in advance.* You can save precious seconds if every phone in your home has the following numbers pasted on the phone itself, the wall, or the table.

> Fire Department
> Police or Sheriff
> Paramedics
> Your child's doctor
> Poison Control Center
> Ambulance
> Taxi
> Hospital (closest hospital with an emergency room)
> Father's phone at work
> Mother's phone at work
> Gas Company
> Electric Company
> Pharmacy (a twenty-four-hour pharmacy)
> Neighbor (you may have to leave your other children there)
> Relative

These numbers should also be in your purse or wallet (accidents can happen *away* from home). Everyone in the house must know where these numbers are and baby-sitters must be informed of the location of emergency numbers.

Study Ahead

Every parent should be certified in Cardiopulmonary Resuscitation (CPR). Marilyn would love to make this a required part of prenatal classes or a prerequisite to getting a driver's license or a marriage license. Not only can CPR teach you how to save a life, but it can give you the confidence that *you* can function in any emergency that befalls your child.

You may also want to take a first-aid course to increase that confidence.

These are usually given in schools or community centers and include practice in putting on splints, maintaining an airway, bandages and tourniquets, transportation of the injured, and information about specific emergencies.

Rehearse Ahead

Parents should *rehearse* to give themselves confidence. Just as families are advised to rehearse how to get out of the house in case of a fire at night, we suggest you rehearse what you would do if your child was found floating face down in your pool or if your child fell from a tree in the backyard and was unconscious.

What do we mean by "rehearse"? First identify the emergency facilities closest to your home. Ideally, the facility is in a *hospital,* is staffed by *board certified emergency physicians.* The hospital you decide on should have pediatric beds and an intensive care unit, just in case. Remember, not all facilities with signs that read "Emergency-Doctor on Duty" have either physicians who are trained to handle emergencies or the equipment needed in emergencies.

The next step in this rehearsal is to *drive the route to the emergency facility.* Find the shortest route. Drive it in heavy traffic so you have some idea of how long it may take to get there.

Speaking of confidence, don't say you will fall apart when it is your own child, though you would be able to help a neighbor's child—even if you think you might fall apart. Confidence is developed by *knowledge,* which you can obtain from the courses and rehearsals we suggest. Also, when we realize in an emergency that we are the only one around and we *must* perform, usually we can.

It is hard for any parent not to panic. Marilyn remembers the time her son ran into the house with blood pouring from his mouth. He had been running with a stick in his mouth and it went through his lip as he fell. Marilyn quickly put pressure on the wound but her impulse was to take the child to the hospital immediately because the bleeding seemed massive. Her husband suggested waiting for a moment. He put their son on the floor while keeping pressure on the bleeding, which stopped within a minute or two.

We know—from our own heart-thumping experiences and those of others —that everyone can hold panic in check when they have to. We also know the best insurance that you will be able to do so is the studying and rehearsal we advocate.

Sometimes the very people who most need to rehearse don't like to think about disaster. Their defense is to put it out of their mind and therefore they never get prepared. Sometimes such people manage in a crisis but they may panic and be useless to their child.

If you are one of those people, stop reading right at the end of this paragraph and ask yourself what you would do if your baby stopped breathing. Force yourself to deal with the unpleasant possibility that no one is around to help your baby but you. Rehearse in your mind what you would do. Write down the steps you would take. Look at that list. Are there any tasks you don't know how to perform? Are there any things you should do (make a telephone list, practice the drive to the hospital)? If there are any gaps in your knowledge or abilities, fill them in. You may never have to use the knowledge, but just in case . . . .

Incidentally, the responsibility in an emergency does not end with you. Teach your baby-sitter or other care givers to be prepared. Every baby-sitter needs three tiers of phone numbers and needs to understand when to use them.

A diagram to illustrate our point is shown in Table 55. The bottom tier is the number where you can be reached. This number is used for minor problems: the baby won't eat or the sink is plugged up. The middle tier is for sickness: most parents want to be called if the baby has a fever or is throwing up. Parents should be called first but some parents also want the sitter to call the doctor. The top tier is for a disaster. This includes a major emergency (like a house fire) or a major injury or illness (an unconscious child or a child that isn't breathing). The sitter should call 911 or Fire or Police *first* before calling the doctor and before calling you.

Your job is to make sure your sitter understands the three-tier system and how to decide (quickly) which tier to use. Instructions should include: "When in doubt use the highest tier and always go from left to right."

TABLE 55

PRIORITY PHONE NUMBERS

Disaster	(1) Fire and/or Police	(2) Doctor	(3) Parents
Sickness		(1) Parents	(2) Doctor
Problem		Parents	

First-Aid Supplies

You don't have to buy an expensive first-aid kit, but every household needs some basic supplies to be ready for an emergency.

First of all, set aside a place where emergency supplies are kept. A drawer, medicine cabinet, or labeled box is fine. This place should *not* be accessible to young children. If you have a summer cottage or boat or camper have a duplicate set of supplies—and be sure everyone knows where it is. Automobiles also need a few emergency supplies. A small labeled box can hold Band-Aids, sterile gauze pads, adhesive tape, and a small bandage roll.

BANDAGING MATERIAL

In addition to Band-Aids, keep on hand sterile gauze pads (2 × 2 and 4 × 4 are good sizes) and gauze bandage rolls (2 inches). Don't forget adhesive tape and scissors. An elastic bandage is handy for sprains. Butterfly Band-Aids (see p. 758) are useful for a clean cut that is gaping apart but no longer bleeding.

Cotton application sticks and cotton balls can be used to clean wounds. These come sterile but once the package is opened are merely clean so you can save money by purchasing the non-sterile type. Sterile wads of cotton batting are also useful for padding. Again, once opened, this cotton is no longer sterile but if kept covered (Marilyn uses a plastic food bag and closes it with a twist) is clean enough.

An elastic bandage is also useful to make a pressure dressing in the case of severe bleeding.

DISINFECTANT

Yes, soap and water, used very liberally, is one of the best disinfectants and, furthermore, is readily available. Benzalkonium chloride (Zephiran), Hibiclens, hydrogen peroxide, and alcohol all can be used. Alcohol stings so Marilyn used Zephiran in her house. She (and her children) called it "Magic Medicine"— magic because it killed the bad bacteria but never stung. Tincture of iodine both stings and burns tissue; Mercurochrome stains, and neither offers any advantage. First-aid sprays (most contain benzalkonium chloride) are fine for little scrapes but for deep wounds, soap and water followed by Zephiran on clean cotton or gauze is better because of the cleansing action created by washing.

You may also wish to have on hand an antibiotic ointment. The best is Bacitracin. Ointments with neomycin are *not* recommended because sensitization (allergy) is more likely to occur with this than with any other topical antibiotic.

HANDY GADGETS

Tweezers are handy for big splinters but fresh needles (not blunted by sewing) can be used to lift the skin to get out little slivers. (You sterilize the needle with alcohol or flame it with a match.) Safety pins are useful for slings.

SYRUP OF IPECAC

In a house with small children, syrup of ipecac is a must (see p. 742). Because we never know what or when a toddler will swallow, syrup of ipecac, which will make the child vomit, should always be on hand.

You do not need a prescription to purchase one ounce, which costs less than two dollars. Syrup of ipecac has a shelf life of at least five years.[1]

BOOKS, CHARTS

Every home should have a book on emergency first aid. Check your library to see which one suits you and purchase it. Charts published by the AMA and the American Academy of Pediatrics are available. Some doctors provide handbooks or handouts about what to do for your child in an emergency. The telephone book has a good section on emergencies.

WHY THE LIST IS SHORT

This list is quite short for two reasons. First, we are talking only about first-aid supplies and equipment. (Items for home health care in general are discussed in Chapter 21, p. 672.) We feel the first-aid box should be small so you can easily carry it to the yard, sidewalk, etc., if necessary. Also, you can improvise.

HOW TO IMPROVISE SUPPLIES

Diapers, sanitary napkins, clean towels, and sheets all can be used as bandages, compresses, or padding for splints. Rolled up, a towel or sheet can wedge a sprained arm or leg next to the body to keep it comfortable. A pillow can be wrapped around an arm or leg as a splint. Boards, sticks, straight sections of metal vacuum cleaner attachment tubing, broom handles, etc., can be used as splints. The inside of a tampon is clean cotton.

As you are reading through the emergencies listed below, think of what you have in your house that might be used if you needed equipment or supplies in a hurry.

Emergency Attitude

The first rule is DON'T PANIC. Keep cool so you can *think* and *remember* what you have learned about emergencies or what you know from past experience and common sense.

Keep cool for your sake and for your child's sake. Children get upset when their parents are. Even if you are shaking inside, keep the outside of you calm and collected. Later, when the emergency is taken care of, you can fall apart.

SPECIFIC EMERGENCIES

Each of the emergencies we include will be covered under three headings. First, the *Scenario*—what is likely to have happened or be happening to cause the emergency. Second, the *Symptoms* your child will likely show. Third, the *Steps to Take* to handle the emergency.

When you take a CPR course, you will learn your ABC's for Airway, Breathing, Circulation (see p. 728). Parents might be helped in handling emergencies by another memory aid: *ACT* for *Assess*—find out what is wrong as quickly as possible. *Call*—get help by screaming for a neighbor or calling for emergency help on your telephone. T stands for *Think*—think what can you do to help your child until a professional arrives or takes over?

T also stands for *Try, Take Over,* and *Trust Yourself.* If you have taken a CPR or first-aid course—or even read this chapter—you know a great deal. No matter how frightened you are or how panic-stricken you feel, you can *ACT.*

ACT also encompasses knowing what *not* to do, which will be covered below.

A CHILD IS NOT BREATHING

This is the most critical emergency of all—because you must act *fast.* You have four minutes in which to resuscitate. If a person does not get air within four to six minutes, that person will die or suffer irreversible brain damage.

SCENARIO

There are several reasons a child may stop breathing. Food can be stuck in the throat, or the tongue or vomitus could be blocking the throat of an unconscious child. Other causes are drowning, smoke inhalation, severe trauma to the head or chest, a heart stoppage due to a heart attack or arrhythmia, or poisoning. (Breath-holding spells which follow a tantrum need no treatment.)

SYMPTOMS

You must learn how to recognize whether your child is not breathing. Rehearse! We suggest you check your child's breathing right now. Put your cheek and ear over your child's mouth so you know what the breathing feels and sounds like. Watch your child breathe. In a baby, breathing may be irregular, but both the chest and abdomen move in and out.

When a child stops breathing, these movements cease, and when you put your cheek or ear to the mouth, you don't feel the exhaled breath. Children who have stopped breathing usually become bluish gray in color.

When you rehearse, also check your child's pulse. In an emergency situation when shock might be present, the pulse at the wrist will be difficult to feel. Feel under the left nipple for a heartbeat so you know what the heartbeat feels like in a normal baby.

STEPS TO TAKE

Rescue Breathing

1. Scream for help!
2. Check the pulse. If you do not feel a heartbeat under the left nipple, start CPR (see p. 729).
3. To start rescue breathing, quickly remove anything stuck in the mouth or throat by pulling the tongue forward and putting your finger in the mouth to clear out mucus or vomit.
4. Put the child face up. Put your hand beneath the child's neck and lift. This extends the neck and brings the chin up.

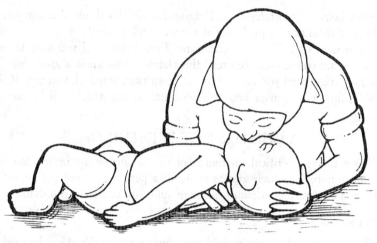

Rescue breathing.

5. Cover the baby's or child's nose and mouth with your mouth, forming a seal (see illustration). Blow four quick breaths of air into the lungs. Look to see that the chest rises and falls. Then breathe into the child's nose and mouth at the rate of one breath every two to three seconds, which comes out to twenty to thirty breaths per minute for babies. With children or adults, give one breath about every five seconds or twelve breaths a minute. For purposes of rescue breathing and CPR a *baby is one year or younger*, a *child is between one and eight*, and an *adult is over eight*.

6. Remove your mouth after each breath to listen for air coming out and stop to watch the child's chest move with the air. If the chest does not move or no air is getting in or out, there may be a foreign object in the child's airway (see Choking, p. 731).

7. Transport to hospital. *Continue rescue breathing on the way* if the child is not breathing spontaneously.

ABC's

You must remember your "ABC's." First: *Airway;* second: *Breathing;* third: *Circulation*. The heart often stops when breathing ceases.

1. How do you tell whether the heart has stopped while you are rescue-breathing?

Feel for the heartbeat under the left nipple or feel the pulse in the side of the neck. (Try it now. While your baby is lying on the stomach and on the back and while sitting up, feel for the baby's pulse in the neck so you know what it feels like. Note the pulse is more rapid in the baby than in yourself.)

2. After you have established the airway by clearing the mouth and throat, if the child is not breathing, start CPR to restore breathing and circulation. In the case of drowning, do not lose time trying to empty water from the child's lungs. You can press on the stomach with the child's head down to get the water that was swallowed out of the stomach.

CPR

We feel that CPR should be administered by trained people and we strongly recommend all parents get training in CPR. However, we are printing instructions for CPR below in case you are not trained or were trained a long time ago and need a refresher course.

If your child is not breathing and there is no pulse below the left nipple, the first thing you should do is:

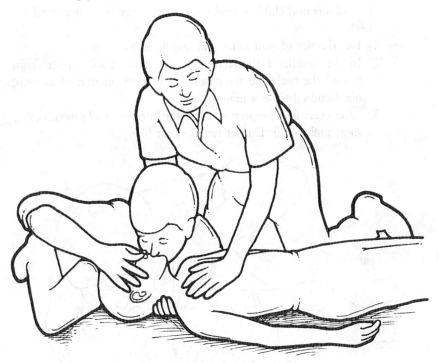

Cardiopulmonary resuscitation.

1. Yell for help as the child will need oxygen and an ambulance.

2. Call the child's name loudly and quickly. Pinch the child to see whether or not there is any response. If the child is unconscious, is not breathing, and has no pulse, the child's heart and lungs have stopped. The child will not survive unless both heartbeat and breathing are rapidly established.

3. Place the child face up on a firm surface. Put a hand behind the neck and lift the neck with your hand to extend the neck and to bring the chin up. Cover the child's mouth and nose with your mouth to make a seal, and give four quick breaths.

4. If the pulse starts, continue rescue breathing (see p. 727).

5. If the pulse has not started, then start the cardiac part of cardiopulmonary resuscitation (see illustration opposite).

A. For children *over* one year of age:
  1) Place the heel of one hand about two fingers above the bottom of the sternum. (See illustration p. 729.)
  2) Make quick, hard thrusts down toward the backbone. Press in about three-quarters to one and one-half inches, eighty times a minute.
  3) After every five compressions, breathe into the child's mouth but do not remove your hand between compressions.
B. For infants and children *under* one year of age (see illustration below):
  1) Use the tips of your index and middle finger.
  2) In the middle of the sternum make short, quick thrusts down toward the backbone about one-half to three-quarters of an inch, one hundred times a minute.
  3) After every five compressions, breathe into the child's mouth using short puffs of air. Do not remove your fingers.

Chest compressions on infant.

In both infants and older children you can stop pushing when the heartbeat is restored (feel for pulse under the left nipple), but you should continue rescue breathing until the child breathes spontaneously.

Ideally, two people perform CPR; one does rescue breathing and the other does cardiac compression. However, if no one else is around, one person *can* do both procedures.

In summary, if a child stops breathing:

1. *Scream for help.*
2. *Airway* ("A")—clean out mouth.
3. *Breathing* ("B")—four quick breaths, then one breath every two to five seconds.
4. *Circulation* ("C")—compress heart eighty to one hundred times per minute.
5. *Continue CPR until breathing and heartbeat are restored* or until a doctor pronounces the child dead. Never give up!
6. *Transport to hospital.* An emergency rescue vehicle is best but if unavailable, CPR can be continued on the floor of a station wagon or truck.

A CHILD IS CHOKING

SCENARIO

You hear a choking or strangling noise from the crib—or—while eating your child suddenly stops making normal noises, turns blue, and collapses.

SYMPTOMS

Strangling noise, can't cry or talk, pointing to throat, blue, not breathing, unconscious.

STEPS TO TAKE IN THE OLDER CHILD

1. *Do nothing if your child can breathe, speak, or cough.*
2. If your child cannot breathe, speak, or cough, put your arms around the child and place the *thumb side of your fist* against the stomach between the navel and rib cage (see illustration p. 732). Grasp your fist with the other hand and make *four quick upward thrusts* just under the rib cage. Repeat if necessary. Usually the object that is obstructing the throat will be expelled and the child will start breathing. If not, start rescue breathing as above.

The abdominal thrusts we have recommended are called the "Heimlich Maneuver," named after the surgeon who first described this life-saving act in the medical literature. There has been controversy about whether these abdominal thrusts should be used in small children.

Here are the American Academy of Pediatrics' recommended *Steps to Take* for a *small* child who is choking and cannot cough, speak, or breathe:[2]

1. Place child on back with rescuer kneeling next to victim.
2. Place one hand on the child's abdomen in the midline between the umbilicus and the ribs and apply up to six to ten abdominal thrusts (Heimlich maneuver) which are rapid inward and upward thrusts.
3. If obstruction is not relieved, open victim's mouth using tongue-jaw lift. If you can see the object, remove with finger sweep. (Do not use your finger if you cannot see a foreign object.)

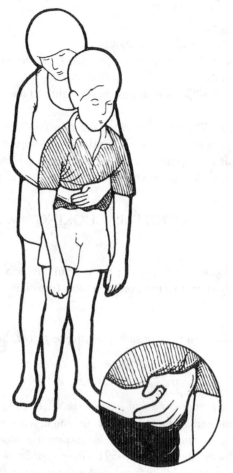

Heimlich maneuver.

In the case of an older child, the abdominal thrusts can be delivered as for an adult in the standing or sitting position.

In the case of an *infant* who is choking and cannot breathe or make any sounds:

1. Place the infant face down on your forearm with the head down at a 60-degree angle and with your arm against your body for support.
2. Administer four back blows rapidly with heel of your hand high between the shoulder blades.
3. If obstruction is not relieved, turn infant over, place on firm surface, and deliver four chest thrusts over the breastbone using two fingers as in CPR cardiac compressions (see p. 730).
4. If there is no relief, open the mouth to look for the foreign body, but do not use blind finger sweeps.
5. If no breathing occurs try four mouth-to-mouth breaths.

Some recent articles present evidence that back blows may actually make things worse by displacing the foreign object farther down the respiratory tree.[3,4]

The *Journal of the American Medical Association* recommends abdominal thrusts in a child but back blows and chest thrusts for babies under a year.[5] When there is controversy, as in this case, parents want to know what to do. After reviewing the literature, we came to the conclusion that on our own children we would first consider *abdominal thrusts*—regardless of the age of the child. Obviously if one method fails, try the other.

SEVERE BLEEDING

SCENARIO

You hear the sound of breaking glass as your child falls through the patio door—or—your child is carving a pumpkin and the knife slips.

SYMPTOMS

Blood spurts or flows rapidly.

STEPS TO TAKE

In severe bleeding the important thing to remember is *pressure*. First, *direct pressure;* second, *pressure points.*

Direct Pressure

Direct pressure is the easiest and everyone knows instinctively how to do it. However some people are afraid to touch a wound lest they make it worse.

Take any *thick clean compress* (you can make one out of virtually anything: a handkerchief, towel, your clothes, bedsheet), and *press this directly over the entire wound.* Press firmly with the palm of your hand. If you don't have a cloth, use your *bare hand.* Press hard enough to stop the bleeding.

Try to *elevate the limb above the heart* while continuing direct pressure but don't elevate the limb if you suspect a fracture. The important thing to remember is that you should not move any clots; therefore, if blood soaks through, don't remove your compress but place another one over it. When the bleeding slows you can apply a presure bandage to hold the compress in place, but don't put the bandage on too tight. Transport to hospital.

Pressure Points

Pressure points are where the artery can be pressed against the underlying bone. Pressure on one of these points cuts off all arterial blood to the area below it. If direct pressure is not working, go to pressure points (see illustrations pp. 734, 735).

1. Severe bleeding from the arm: Grasp the arm midway between the

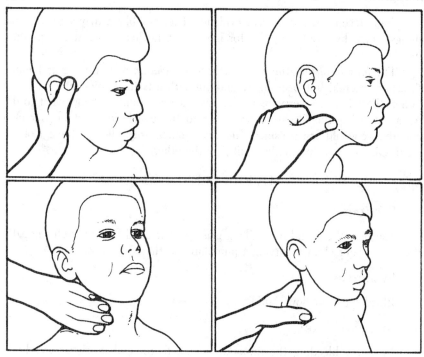

Pressure points.

armpit and the elbow, with your thumb on the outside and the flat surface of
your fingers on the inside. Squeeze until the bleeding stops.

2. Severe bleeding from a leg: Put the victim on the back, place the heel of
your hand on the front center part of the thigh at the crease of the groin (see
illustration p. 735, center).

Tourniquets

We do not recommend the use of tourniquets, except in life-threatening
situations such as partial or complete amputation where the greatest danger is
bleeding to death. Tourniquets should be two inches wide and should be
wrapped around the limb twice. A tourniquet should be above the wound but not
touch it. A half-knot should be tied, then a stick or strong object should be
placed on top of the half-knot and two full knots should be tied over the stick.
The stick can then be twisted to tighten the tourniquet, which will totally stop
bleeding. Because a tourniquet can lead to death of the limb below it, only do
this if there is partial or complete amputation of an arm or leg. Transport to
hospital.

Amputation

Speaking of amputations, though this is a gruesome subject, you should try
to save the part. Doctors are doing miraculous reattaching of severed limbs

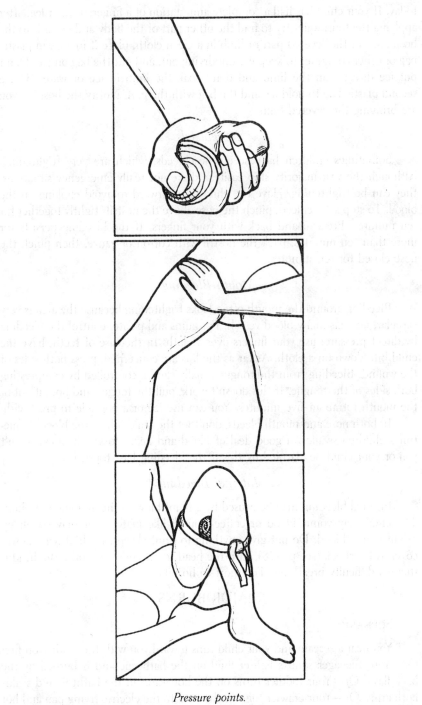

Pressure points.

today. If your child has had a complete amputation of a finger, arm, or leg, after applying the tourniquet try to find the other part of the body and bring it to the hospital. Put the severed part or limb in a clean cloth, place it in a clean plastic bag or other container to keep it from drying out, and put the bag on ice. Don't put ice directly on the limb and don't soak the limb in ice or water. Use a second plastic bag to hold ice and the bag with the part. Notify the hospital you are bringing the severed limb.

Nosebleeds

Sometimes children have severe nosebleeds, which are very frightening. Although the vast majority stop easily and are not really emergency situations, they can be frightening. Have the child lean forward to avoid choking on the blood. To stop a nosebleed, pinch the nose above the nostrils tightly together for ten minutes. Press in and back with your fingers. If the bleeding persists for more than ten minutes, pack the nostril with cotton or gauze, then pinch the nose closed for ten minutes.

Mouth Bleeding

Bleeding around the mouth often looks frightening because the area is very vascular, i.e., has many blood vessels. For gums and palate, control the bleeding by direct pressure; use your fingers over a cloth. In the case of teeth, have the child bite down on a cloth. As far as the lips are concerned, press both sides of the wound. Bleeding from the tongue usually can be controlled by compressing both sides of the tongue. If this doesn't work, pull the tongue and hold it out of the mouth for about five minutes. You can use ice or a popsicle to press with.

In both nose and mouth bleeds, don't let the child inhale the blood. Sometimes children swallow a good deal of blood and begin to vomit blood. Don't you or your child be alarmed by this if the bleeding has stopped.

Internal Bleeding

Internal bleeding may be caused by a blunt blow to the abdomen or chest. The child may vomit blood or coffee-grounds-like material or may cough up bright foamy blood. Do not give anything to drink, keep the child lying down, cover as for shock (see p. 738), turn the head to one side, and raise the head if there is difficulty breathing. Transport to hospital.

MAJOR BURNS

SCENARIO

You hear a scream and your child runs toward you with the clothes on fire! Or—Your teenager squirts lighter fluid on the barbecue and is burned by the back flash. Or—Your toddler turns on the hot water in the bathtub and scalds both arms. Or—Your crawler tugs on the cord to the electric frying pan and hot grease spills on the head and chest.

SYMPTOMS

Severe pain, reddening, blisters, or charring of the skin.

The word burn is used to describe any injury to the skin that results from extreme heat such as fire and includes scalding with a hot liquid or steam. Burns can also result from chemicals or electricity or friction, such as in a fall from a speeding motorcycle.

A first-degree burn causes just redness of the skin. In second-degree burns, the skin is blistered. A third-degree burn, which is the most severe, destroys all the skin. The area may not be painful because the nerves are dead; the skin looks either white or charred. This is the worst possible burn and will result in severe scarring.

STEPS TO TAKE

1. If your child is on fire, throw the child to the ground with the burning side uppermost and roll the child to smother the flames or cover the flames with whatever you have. Flames should be directed away from the child's head.
2. Don't burst blisters, but quickly remove anything like shoes or rings or bracelets because you won't be able to get them off later after swelling or oozing has started.
3. Do not put anything on a first- or second-degree burn except cool water. If clothing has been heated by boiling fat or water, remove the clothes immediately but don't try to remove any dry or burned clothing or anything that is stuck to the skin. Use cool water for at least ten minutes. Then lightly bandage the whole area until you get help. A clean cloth or sheet can be used to cover the burn, or a burned limb can be covered with a clean plastic bag. Limbs should be elevated. Ice in a towel is good for pain.
4. For chemical burns, put the child under a heavy cool shower and remove all clothing. Use a hose if there is no shower or keep pouring cool water over the burn for twenty to thirty minutes.
5. If there are burns around the face or mouth, a doctor should always be called. If the child has breathed superheated air as in a house fire, take the child to a hospital even if the burns are minor.
6. For third-degree burns, call an ambulance immediately. Do not apply water—or anything—to the burn. Do not try to remove clothing. Lightly cover the burned area with something like a sheet, elevate arms or legs higher than the heart, treat for shock (see p. 738) if necessary. Call the Emergency Room; they may recommend a hospital with a specialized burn unit.

7. Do not use *any* antiseptic spray, ointment, butter, or any other home remedy on *any* burn. Pressure should *not* be applied to burned areas. Do *not* try to remove shreds of tissue. Do *not* break blisters.
8. If there is a burn on any area larger than the front of the child's forearm, the doctor should *always be called.*
9. For minor burns, apply an ice cube on, for example, a blistered finger. But for any burn bigger than that, follow the directions above.

Infection can complicate even minor burns so try to keep the area as clean as possible.

SHOCK

Shock is defined as circulatory collapse due to loss of blood or a severe disturbance in circulatory control.

SCENARIO

You hear the squeal of brakes and a crash. A car has hit your bike-riding child!

SYMPTOMS

Your child is on the ground; the skin is pale, cold, and mottled; your child is barely conscious and breathing shallowly. Other symptoms will depend on the injury; there may be fractures, head injury, internal injuries, etc. With severe trauma, multiple injuries are the rule.

STEPS TO TAKE

Shock should be suspected in *every* seriously injured child. If you see the symptoms of shock there are three cardinal rules: Don't give the child anything to drink, prevent loss of body heat, and get help.

1. Lay the child down on the ground. Be sure to *immobilize the neck* in case of spine injuries (see p. 740). If the child has trouble breathing, elevate the neck and shoulders. If not, elevate the legs about twelve inches.
2. Cover the child lightly with a blanket.
3. Begin first aid for the injuries—i.e., bleeding, fractures.
4. Get the child to the hospital!

HEAD INJURY

SCENARIO

You hear a crack and a thud in the backyard. Your child, though forbidden to climb the tree, has done so and fallen eight feet to the ground. Or—Your child runs out into the street and is struck by a car; the bumper hits the child's leg and the child's head strikes the curb.

SYMPTOMS

Unconsciousness or drowsiness, vomiting, difficulty breathing, fluid (clear or bloody) running from the ears or nose, deformity of the skull, paralysis, possible loss of bladder or bowel control, amnesia (or loss of memory) from the accident.

Head injuries can range from relatively simple concussions to bleeding into the brain that can cause death. Every child will at one time or another fall forward and hit the head. Though the child can get a big lump on the forehead, this is generally nothing to worry about. The child that falls *back* on the head, especially on a hard surface and especially from a height (falling off a tree or a playground swing), could be seriously injured. A child struck on the *side* of the head (as by a baseball or bat) may briefly lose consciousness, and then appear fine (the so-called "lucid interval"). But slow bleeding inside the head can occur. If the child is unconscious over five minutes, has prolonged headaches, vomits, or is difficult to arouse, seek medical attention immediately.

The most important thing you should note is whether there is *unconsciousness* and how *long it lasts*. A child who fell on the head may be stunned, or even unconscious for a few seconds, but if it lasts longer than that, the child should always be taken to the doctor.

STEPS TO TAKE

1. If the child is not breathing, start resuscitation (see pp. 727–31).
2. If the child has to be moved (it is preferable not to move a head injury case until an ambulance arrives), you must assume there is an associated *neck injury*. Therefore, you cannot move the head without moving the shoulders. Make a stretcher out of a board or an ironing board or a door. The child should be moved as a single unit with the head in line with the spine because of the danger of paralysis. The head should be *immobilized* with sandbags or pillows or rolls of blankets and the forehead taped to the board. The child should be *tied to the stretcher*.
3. As it is preferable not to try to move the child alone, the child should be kept quiet while waiting for help. If there is an open wound, treat for bleeding as above (see p. 733).
4. Get help—a head injured child can have rapid swelling of the brain, which is extremely serious. Such a child belongs in a hospital.

UNCONSCIOUSNESS

SCENARIO

You find your child in the backyard—unconscious. You heard no noise and there did not appear to be an accident. Your unconscious child could have had a seizure, or the cause might be heatstroke, simple fainting, cardiac arrhythmia, poisoning, smoke inhalation, electric shock, or allergic reaction to an insect bite.

Or there could also have been an obvious accident: Your child fell off the slide, hitting the head.

SYMPTOMS

The symptoms of unconsciousness are simple. The child is unresponsive and is not aware of anything going on. The difference between an unconscious child and one that is asleep (remember you may find your child lying in the backyard and won't know what happened) can be quickly ascertained by the child's responsiveness. *Call the child's name*—loudly. If there is no response, *pinch* the child hard on the cheek. These maneuvers will awaken a sleeping child, but not an unconscious one.

STEPS TO TAKE

1. Check to see if the victim is breathing. If not, start rescue breathing (see p. 727).
2. Call for help.
3. Because there might have been an injury that could have hurt both the head and neck, do not move the child without supporting the back, neck, and head in the same plane (see above).
4. Try to keep track of the time. It is very important for your doctor to know how long your child has been unconscious after a head injury. Whether the child is "out" for seconds or minutes makes a difference in the diagnosis.
5. If you come across an unconscious child in a situation where you suspect poisoning or drugs, look around for the bottle or paraphernalia.
6. If you come across your child in a smoked-filled or tightly closed room in which you smell gas, be sure to immediately remove the child from the room and start rescue breathing if necessary.

Note: Fainting is a brief loss of consciousness, because not enough blood is going to the brain. Children who have fainted usually are pale and have a cool, clammy skin. Before they faint, they may complain of dizziness or nausea, or when they wake up they may feel this way. If your child has fainted, elevate the feet eight to twelve inches from the floor unless you suspect a head injury. Place the head to the side in case the child vomits. Water on the face generally revives the child.

NECK AND SPINE INJURIES

SCENARIO

Your child fell from the roof while helping make repairs. Or—Your child's friend dove into your swimming pool at the shallow end. Or—Your child was thrown from your car, which was involved in a collision.

SYMPTOMS

There may or may not be loss of consciousness. If the child has a broken neck or spine, there may be numbness of the legs or the legs and arms or there may be no symptoms. The child may not be able to move or feel anything below a certain level of the body. The child may be in shock (see p. 738).

STEPS TO TAKE

1. The most important thing with a neck or spine injury is what you *don't* do. Do not move the child or lift any part of the body until you are ready to transport the child on a stretcher to medical help.
2. Call for help.
3. Find a board, door, or ironing board if you have to move the child. When the child is lifted onto the board, several people should lift at once to support the head and shoulders, the hips and the legs. One person should put longitudinal (lengthwise) traction on the head by gently pulling the head straight away from the body without changing the plane of the head. (It's as though you were pulling the head straight out of the body.) Sandbags or folded clothing should be placed on either side of the head to keep it in place and the forehead should be taped to the board to prevent any moving. If you cannot find a board, support the head and neck in the same plane. You do this to prevent paralysis which could result from a piece of broken bone cutting through the spinal cord.
4. Transport to hospital.

POISONINGS

SCENARIO

You hear a gagging sound and find your crawler with a bottle of furniture polish. Or—You see your toddler chewing pills next to your mother-in-law's open purse.

SYMPTOMS

The symptoms will depend on what poison your child has taken.

Poisons may be *inhaled,* so the child may have difficulty breathing, or the child may be gagging or choking. The child may complain that the eyes or mouth or throat are burning. There may be unconsciousness.

Most poisons are *swallowed.* Acids or alcohols cause burns around the mouth or tongue; the child complains of burning in the mouth, throat, and stomach. Petroleum distillates like furniture polish cause coughing and gagging, a burning sensation, and possibly unconsciousness. Other symptoms of poisonings include: nausea, thirst, cramps or bloody diarrhea, dizziness, drowsiness, difficulty speaking, difficulty in coordination, convulsions, coma, and shock.

STEPS TO TAKE

1. Be prepared ahead of time.
   Every household should have *syrup of ipecac* on hand (see
   p. 687). Syrup of ipecac should *not* be given if the child:

   is not breathing
   is having trouble swallowing
   is drowsy or convulsing
   has swallowed something *oily* (kerosene, gasoline, furniture polish or lighter fluid) or something *caustic* (lye or drain cleaner)

2. Call the local Poison Control Center or your physician immediately.
   When you call the Poison Control Center, be sure to give the child's
   age, the *name of the poison, how much* and *when* it was taken,
   whether or not there was vomiting, and how long it will take to get
   the patient to a hospital. Follow the advice of the PCC or physician
   about ipecac.

3. If the Poison Control Center advises that ipecac is safe to use, induce
   vomiting by giving a child under eight one tablespoon (one-half
   ounce) of syrup of ipecac followed by six to eight ounces of water, or
   other clear liquid if your child won't take water. If a child is over
   eight, give one to two tablespoons (one ounce) depending on body
   weight, and if the child is over twelve, give 2 tablespoons followed by
   six to eight ounces of water. Some say that if children walk around
   they are more likely to vomit. You may wish to keep the child in the
   bathroom or outdoors, as 98 percent will vomit after one dose of
   syrup of ipecac. Have the child vomit into a plastic bag; be sure the
   head is down when the child is vomiting. If the child doesn't vomit
   within twenty to thirty minutes, encourage more clear fluids. If there
   is still no vomiting, repeat the dose *once only*. If within fifteen minutes there is still no vomiting, call the Poison Control Center or take
   the child to the hospital.
       After the child vomits, give water again. The child will often
   vomit again. Repeat the water until the vomit is clear, which may
   take four or five vomits, depending on what was in the child's stomach. After the last vomit do *not* give any liquid or fluid for one and
   one-half hours. The child may be sleepy from the syrup of ipecac *or*
   from vomiting. If the child wants to nap, place the child on the
   stomach or side, in case of further vomiting.

4. Save the poison and the vomit. If you are told to bring the child to
   the hospital, you will need to bring the poison, the package or container, and some of the vomit to the hospital.

5. Do not give anything to drink if the child is unconscious.

PLANTS

If the child ingests any part of a plant, call the Poison Control Center and seek medical aid as some plants are quite toxic. If you can't reach the Poison Control Center, induce vomiting (see Table 11, p. 157).

ANTIDOTES

Specific antidotes are usually not recommended as it is preferable to get your child to medical help at once. Call the Poison Control Center.

NON-TOXIC INGESTIONS

Note there are many things your child may ingest that are *non-toxic* (see Table 10, p. 156). Ordinarily nothing has to be done (except to try to clean up the child whose mouth is filled with Magic Marker)! However, we feel very strongly that you should *always* call your local Poison Control Center. In the first place not everything is clearly labeled. In the second place, we believe in being safe rather than sorry. So, with *every* ingestion, call!

BROKEN BONES

SCENARIO

Your child has fallen from the top of the slide and now complains that the arm hurts and the child can't move it. Or—Your child was hit by a car and the leg is at a strange angle.

SYMPTOMS

There are three types of broken bones or fractures:

1. In *compound fractures,* the skin is broken and a piece of bone is sticking out, which makes the diagnosis quite easy.
2. The second kind of fracture is when the *bone is twisted or obviously out of place* but the skin is not broken.
3. The third fracture is when the child complains of a great deal of pain, but the *limb is still straight* and there is no apparent swelling when you inspect it. However, when you press on where the child says it hurts there may be a great deal of pain. The third variety may be hard to diagnose for the doctor as well as the parent. X-rays are needed (X-rays are needed in the other fractures as well to see how far the bone is out of alignment).

As nobody has an X-ray machine on the playground and as it is impossible to tell by inspection alone whether bones are broken after an injury, all bone injuries should be treated as though they were fractures.

The child may also have a *dislocation.* This is defined by the dictionary as a displacement of any part, especially of a bone. Dislocation of the arm is fairly common. A *fracture dislocation* is a dislocation complicated by a fracture located next to a joint.

If the child tells you he or she felt or heard the bone snap, pay attention, as this is a good sign of a broken bone. Difficulty in moving is not always diagnostic because a child may be able to move a leg or arm even if the bone is broken. When a fracture is present, there is usually pain or tenderness at the site of the injury. There may be movement between two parts of the bone or the victim can feel the bones grating together. There may also be swelling, deformity, or discoloration. But once again, if none of these signs are present, the bone can still be broken.

It can be especially hard to diagnose what is called a greenstick fracture in children. This occurs in young bones which do not break through because they bend under the trauma like a green stick. One side of the bone is broken and the other is bent, as a green stick or a willow stick would bend. (See illustration below.)

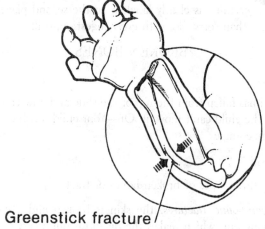

Greenstick fracture

STEPS TO TAKE

1. When you suspect a fracture, do not have the child put weight on the part or move it.
2. Ascertain how serious the injury is. If there is a head injury, potential spine injury, or unconsciousness, or if the child is not breathing, immediately treat for any of the above.

    In the case of neck or spine or skull fractures, do not move the child unless there is danger of fire. Instead, seek immediate medical aid. If you do have to move the child, follow directions for neck and spine injuries (see p. 740).

    Sometimes a broken rib punctures the lung and the child may cough up blood or have difficulty in breathing. If so, medical attention is also needed immediately.

    If the bone is sticking through the skin, cover it with a clean cloth and stop the bleeding. Do not try to put the bone in. Treat for shock (see p. 738).

3. For an obviously broken bone, the important thing is to keep the bone in a fixed position to allow it to mend properly. Do not move or carry the child without first *splinting the bone* to prevent the bone getting out of place. Splint the limb where it lies unless the limb is blue or has no pulse in which case the limb should be gently moved to see if a change of position will cause a pulse to return. Always splint to prevent a joint from moving. For example, put the splint behind or on the side of the leg so the knee can't move.

4. *Specific Hints.*

For a broken collarbone or shoulder, use a sling to keep the arm supported and a bandage to fold the arm tight against the body. This helps the pain.

An arm can be splinted with a stick that you pad with bandages, magazines, or cloth. Support the arm, splint and all, with a sling that keeps the injury above the level of the elbow. If the elbow is straight, splint it in that position with a splint from the armpit to the wrist.

A finger can be splinted with a tongue depressor or a popsicle stick and taped to the next finger.

The best way to splint a leg if you don't have anything large enough handy is to tie one leg to the other and transport the child on a board or a door. You should also transport a child in that manner if there is a suspected broken pelvis (hip bone). A broken or dislocated knee should be splinted and transported in the position found.

If you suspect a broken foot or toes, take off (or cut off) the shoe before splinting. You can use a blanket or pillow tied around the whole foot for a splint.

Remember, we have pointed out that all bone injuries should be treated as fractures. This means you will splint children who do not have a fracture but rather a sprain or bruise. That is okay. It is better to be safe than sorry because the risk of not splinting a break and worsening the fracture is too great to take. Besides it gives you a chance to practice your first-aid skills!

HEATSTROKE AND HEAT EXHAUSTION

Scenario

It is a very hot day and your child who has been playing vigorously outdoors, falls to the ground. Or—Your high-schooler who has been training for a marathon on a very hot, humid day, collapses.

Symptoms

In the case of *heatstroke*, the body temperature is extremely high, the skin is flushed and dry, the child is usually not sweating. In the case of *heat exhaustion*, the child may feel faint from the heat but the skin is moist and cool. There may be cramps and muscle spasms, but the body temperature is normal or subnormal.

STEPS TO TAKE

Heatstroke

The important thing to remember is that the body temperature must be lowered immediately. If the child feels very hot and dry, cool the child off using fans, cold water, cold or ice water on sheets, anything. You can even spray the victim with a hose. Ice can be applied to groin, armpit, and neck.

The best thing is to place the child in a tub of cool water and sponge the entire body until the temperature is down or alternatively wrap the child in wet, cold sheets until the temperature is reduced. Take to hospital if temperature remains elevated after home treatment.

Heat Exhaustion

Take the child to a cool, shady spot, remove the clothing or wet the clothing to encourage evaporation, place the child on the ground, cool off with fans or cold moist cloths, give sips of salt water (one-half teaspoon in a glass) every few minutes for one hour. Then give sweetened liquids.

HYPOTHERMIA (Abnormally low body temperature)

SCENARIO

Your child has fallen through the ice in the pond and the clothes are frozen to the body. Remember, hypothermia can occur very quickly in cold weather, especially when there is high wind, immersion in water, or wet clothing.

SYMPTOMS

Persistent shivering, slurred speech, no control of the hands, exhaustion, drowsiness. The child may also say, "I feel fine," even though the shivering does not stop. The child may lose consciousness or seem very ill.

STEPS TO TAKE

1. Get the child out of the wind and cold and into a warm place.
2. Do not let the child fall asleep.
3. Remove wet clothing. Wrap the child in blankets in the bed or sleeping bag. Get in bed with the child if necessary, to warm the body.
4. Do not rub the skin.
5. If the child is conscious, give sweetened warm drinks or soup.

Do *not* give anything to drink to an unconscious or drowsy child. Take to hospital if the body temperature remains below normal.

FROSTBITE

SCENARIO

This can occur when the child is out of doors in very cold weather without adequate covering (no mittens or an exposed face on a day with a very high windchill factor).

SYMPTOMS

Cold, pale parts of the face, nose, ears, or fingers or toes.

STEPS TO TAKE

1. Warm the frozen parts against your body.
2. Take the child inside.
3. Remove clothing.
4. Do not rub the skin.
5. Immerse the frozen parts in warm (but not hot) water. Stop warming when the frozen parts flush with color.
6. Raise and lower the part to stimulate circulation.
7. Give the child warm drinks.
8. Get to medical help.

Note: Keep toes or fingers separated with clean cloth until you get to medical aid. If the hands are frostbitten, you can tuck them into the child's armpits under the coat until you get the child indoors. The face can be covered with dry gloved hands until normal color returns. If the feet or toes are affected, keep them elevated and do not let the child walk.

CONVULSIONS (Seizures)

SCENARIO

Your child is playing in the next room. You hear a strange, almost strangling, cry and a crash. When you rush in your child is on the floor—convulsing.

SYMPTOMS

A *grand mal* or major motor convulsion consists of jerking, uncontrollable movements of the body. The eyes roll upward. The child is unconscious and may froth at the mouth. The body may be stiff. The child may wet and/or soil the pants. The child may make choking sounds because the child's tongue has fallen back in the throat. The child may be blue.

After the convulsion there is sleepiness and confusion.

Convulsions look frightening, but they rarely cause problems by themselves. Injuries can be caused by falling during the seizure or from surrounding objects the child hits while convulsing.

Steps to Take

1. Do not give the child anything to drink.
2. Loosen tight clothing. Turn the child on the left side when the convulsion has stopped. Watch breathing closely. It's normal not to breathe effectively during a seizure but seizures usually last only a short time.
3. Do *not* force an object between the teeth. Check and make sure the tongue is not blocking the throat. If necessary, roll the tongue out with your own fingers but be careful not to get bitten.
4. Get medical help. Remember to tell your doctor about all convulsions, even if they last just a few seconds.

If a young child has a febrile convulsion, which is a brief convulsion that occurs with a high fever, take the child's clothes off and sponge the child with cool water. Do not throw water in the child's face, as the child could inhale it.

DRUG OVERDOSE OR WITHDRAWAL

Scenario

You suspect your teenager is using drugs but have not been able to prove it. One day you find your child unconscious. You find a syringe or pills or packets on the floor.

Symptoms

The symptoms of drug overdose or withdrawal depend on the drug (or combination of drugs) taken.

Alcohol and depressants (sedatives, downers, sleeping pills)

Drunken behavior, slurred speech, a staggering walk, and unconsciousness. There may be an alcohol odor on the breath. Withdrawal from chronic use can cause hallucinations or convulsions.

Narcotics (heroin, morphine, codeine)

Deep sleep or coma, slow breathing, very relaxed muscles, sweating, and very small pupils. Withdrawal can cause nervousness, sweating, runny nose, cramps, tearing.

Hallucinogens (LSD, mescaline, psilocybin)

Bizarre behavior, delusions (misinterprets sounds or objects), hallucinations (sees or hears things), flushed face, enlarged pupils.

Inhalants (glue, paint thinner, gasoline, etc.)

Drunken behavior, dizziness, double vision, chemical odor to breath.

Stimulants (uppers, benzedrine, pep pills, speed, cocaine, PCP)

Overactivity, confusion, disorganization, repeats particular acts over and over, fear, immobility, suspicious, aggressive and even dangerously violent behavior, especially with PCP ("angel dust"). Withdrawal can cause depression, hunger, hallucinations, or extreme lack of energy.

STEPS TO TAKE

1. Restore breathing if necessary.
2. Turn head to side if child is unconscious.
3. Try to keep child awake if drowsy (walk child, use wet cloth on face).
4. Keep warm.
5. Prevent from hurting self or others.
6. Reassure if in a state of panic. Keep the room quiet and peaceful.
7. Transport to emergency room for medical and psychiatric evaluation.

Note: Ignorance of the drug's effects, miscalculation of dose, or misinformation about the potency of a street drug all can lead to overdose. Sometimes a teenager suffers from drug overdose in the course of casual experimentation. However, statistically, if your child has demonstrated overdose, it is likely you have a chronic drug abuser to worry about. We suggest prompt evaluation and counseling for the child *and* family; inpatient treatment for the child may be essential.

Chronic drug use symptoms depend on the drug (or combinations) taken.

Chronic use of depressants can cause intermittent or continuous sleepiness, slurred speech, lack of coordination, dulled reactions, confusion, and poor memory.

Stimulants may cause incessant talking, insomnia, irritability, restlessness, weight loss, and paranoia.

Chronic use of narcotics gives the person a tranquil feeling, dizziness, nausea, vomiting, sweating, constipation, loss of appetite, loss of energy, small pupils, slurred speech, and weight loss.

Cannabis drugs such as marijuana and hashish can cause reddened eyes, intensification of mood and feeling, lessening of anxieties, increased appetite for sweets, distortion of time and space, euphoria, irritability, nervousness, fear, and paranoia.

Chronic alcohol abusers may show drowsiness, slurred speech, dizziness, nausea or vomiting, uninhibited behavior, and impaired reaction and judgment.

ANAPHYLAXIS—SERIOUS ALLERGIC REACTION

SCENARIO

Your child is out of doors and gets stung by a bee. Or—Your child is exquisitely sensitive to a certain food or medicine and inadvertently is given some of that food.

SYMPTOMS

Anaphylaxis is a total body reaction to an allergen. Swelling of the eyes, lips, or tongue as well as the bite site may be the first sign. There may be rapid onset of weakness, wheezing or coughing, itching, stomach cramps, nausea or vomiting, anxiety, difficulty in breathing, dizziness, and collapse.

STEPS TO TAKE

1. Restore breathing if necessary.
2. Get medical help.
3. Remove the stinger if it is a honey bee by gently scraping with a knife, blade, or fingernail. Do not squeeze the stinger with tweezers.
4. Place cold compresses or ice on the sting area.
5. Keep the victim lying down.
6. If there are multiple stings, the child should be wrapped in a cold sheet and taken to the hospital.
7. If you know your child is subject to severe reactions when stung by a bee, get an emergency insect sting kit that enables you to administer adrenalin.

BITES

SCENARIO

Your child may be bitten by an insect, a spider, a snake, or a mammal ranging from a bat or skunk to a dog or cat, or even a human.

The child is playing out of doors; the parent hears a cry. On investigation, the child complains of being bitten. Alternatively, in a preverbal child, the parent may notice redness, swelling, or a spider in the child's clothing. Look for what may have done the biting but don't get so close that there are two victims.

SYMPTOMS AND STEPS TO TAKE

Multiple Insect Bites

Multiple stings from bees or wasps can cause shock. See above under anaphylaxis.

Spiders

Because young children can have severe adverse reactions to poisonous spider bites, parents have to know something about these.

There are three spiders that cause trouble: black widow, brown recluse, and tarantula.

In the case of a *black widow spider* bite, there is a good deal of pain at the site of the bite but only slight redness and swelling. There may be sweating, muscle cramps, difficulty in breathing, and nausea. With a *brown recluse spider* bite, the sting may or may not be felt at the time of the bite, but redness appears. The redness disappears and then a blister forms. Pain is not severe in the beginning but it becomes worse over the next two days. Chills, fever, nausea, vomiting, joint pains, and rash may occur and there is destruction of the tissue at the site of the bite which forms an open ulcer. A *tarantula* bite is not as serious although the tarantula, which is big and hairy, looks frightening. There is not much pain when the bite occurs but a painful wound may develop.

Treatment of a black widow or brown recluse spider bite includes keeping the airway open, keeping the bitten area lower than the victim's heart, placing ice or cold compresses on the bitten area, taking the child to the emergency room along with the spider, if possible. In the case of a tarantula bite, usually just ice and a soothing lotion like calamine is all that is needed.

Scorpions

Scorpions, commonly found in the South and Southwest, can inflict a mean bite. With *scorpion stings*, there may be severe burning and pain at the site along with nausea, vomiting, stomach pain, numbness, and tingling in the affected area. There may be jaw muscle spasms, shock, convulsions, or coma. Although these serious symptoms rarely occur, you must be on the lookout for them. The treatment is the same as for the black widow spiders. Most scorpion bites are not serious and result in few of these serious symptoms.

Marilyn's teenage neighbor was bitten by a scorpion in her shoe (a common place for them to hide). She told Marilyn that, though it was painful, it was no worse than a bee sting and there were no symptoms other than pain.

Marine Life Stings

Marine life stings (Portuguese man-of-war or other jellyfish, sea urchin, coral scrapes, etc.) can cause intense, burning pain and spreading redness of the skin, muscle cramps, nausea and vomiting, even difficulty in breathing, and shock. Wrap a cloth around your hands and remove the tentacles, *or* cover with dry sand, *or* wash the area with rubbing alcohol or ammonia diluted with water (both of which will sting). Use ice if you have any. Treat for shock if present (see p. 738).

Snakebite

Even in Tucson, which is the rattlesnake capital of the world, snakebites in childhood are rare. While poisonous snakes may be found throughout the U.S., snakebites are uncommon in most parts of the country. If you are in a snake area, however, you must learn to recognize which snakes are poisonous.

Most poisonous snakes in this country are pit vipers (rattlesnakes, cottonmouth or water moccasins, and copperheads), which have a large triangular head and pits on each side of the head. The coral snake, found in southern states, is also poisonous. These are small brightly colored striped snakes. The coral snake, unlike its imitators, is "red next to yellow, kill a fellow" while the harmless snake is "red against black, venom lack." (Marilyn had to remember this when she found her dog playing with a snake which *was* "red next to yellow".)

Not every snakebite is inflicted by a poisonous snake and not every bite from a poisonous snake results in envenomization. If envenomization occurred there will be two "P's" *(pain* and *puncture)* and two "E's" *(erythema,* or redness, and *edema,* or swelling). Symptoms include pain, rapid swelling, discoloration, weakness, nausea, vomiting, difficulty in breathing, blurring vision, and convulsions and shock.

To treat, wipe the area clean first, then wash with soap and water. Do *not* pack in ice, although you can use a cool compress for comfort. *Do not cut* or suck the wound. Remove any jewelry on affected limb. Put a band above the bite two to four inches above the puncture but *do not bind it tightly.* (Leave enough room between band and skin to insert one finger. You should be able to feel the pulse below the wound and the wound should ooze.) If the band is surrounded by the swelling, remove the band and place it higher than before. Keep the infected part below the level of the heart. *Immobilize the limb.* Seek medical attention promptly. Do not let the victim walk. Do not give alcohol. Reassure and calm the victim.

Marilyn has been told the best thing to use in the case of snakebite is your car keys, to get the victim to the hospital quickly. Call ahead to describe the snake, if you can, so the right antivenin will be ready. Do *not* risk getting bitten yourself, but if the snake is *really* dead (rattlers can fool you; use a stick to see if the snake moves), bring it to the hospital.

Mammals

With bites of mammals like bats, skunks, and foxes, you have to worry about rabies. Treat the wound exactly the way you treat any other puncture wound. Try to clean it out with vigorous use of soap and water and pour hydrogen peroxide over it. Promptly take the child for medical attention. Try to take the creature with you to test for rabies but do not get bitten yourself.

With dog and cat bites, there is less worry about rabies. Cats almost never transmit rabies (not because cats don't get rabies, but because they go away from people when they are sick). If your child is bitten by a known dog, identify the dog. Almost every town has a rabies control officer who will investigate the animal bite incident. Find out whether the dog is currently immunized against rabies, in which case nothing has to be done. If it is an unknown dog, a decision has to be made with your doctor as to whether or not rabies treatment should be given. This decision will depend on the circumstances of the bite and whether there is rabies in the community. This decision is not something that you make from a book, you have to talk with a doctor.

Gerbils and rodents do not get rabies. Just treat as any other bite.

Human bites can be particularly dangerous because they are more apt to get infected. Bleeding should be controlled, and the wound should be washed with soap and water. Human bites should be brought to medical attention so that antibiotics can be given if necessary. In all puncture wounds, tetanus toxoid must be considered.

EYE INJURY

Scenario

Your child is playing with the chemistry set when an explosion occurs and chemicals get in the eye. Or—Your child is running with a pop bottle and falls —the glass shatters into the eye.

Serious eye injuries can result from chemicals, especially alkali, foreign objects, or a laceration of the eyeball or the cornea. (For a speck in the eye, see p. 763.)

Steps to Take

1. If chemicals get in your child's eye, hold the eyelids open, flush the eye immediately in running water (hold the child under a faucet, use a hose on which you can control the pressure, or gently—but continuously—pour water in the eye from a container. Flush for at least ten minutes. Don't let the water run into the other eye.

    Speed is important because eye damage can occur in one to five minutes. So even *before* you call the doctor, start flushing with water. You can use milk if water is not available. You can also place the top of the victim's face in a bowl of water and have the victim move the eyelids up and down. If both eyes are affected let water flow over both or quickly alternate from one to the other, but you have to keep both eyelids open.

    Cover the eye with gauze and hold the gauze in place with a bandage. Get the child to the hospital fast.

2. If there is a lacerated eyeball or impaled object, do not wash out the eye. Cover both eyes loosely with gauze. Do not apply pressure. Don't let the child touch the eyes. Get the child to the hospital fast.

3. If there is an impaled object, do not remove it. Cut a hole in the center of a gauze pad. Put this dressing on over the object carefully so the dressing doesn't touch the eye or the object. Put a paper cup or cone over the eye. Bandage both eyes to prevent movement in the injured eye and transport the child to the hospital.

    A corneal abrasion may result from a speck getting in the eye, but will be discussed here because such abrasions can be serious and they are quite painful. The way you tell the difference between a speck in the eye (which is not going to cause a problem) and a corneal abrasion is usually simple. With an abrasion the child has persistent pain and photophobia (light hurts). The pain and photophobia become marked and do not go away after the speck is removed. If your child complains of pain and photophobia, the child should be taken to the hospital because doctors will have to ascertain whether the cornea is damaged or not. If the cornea is abraded, your child needs an antibiotic ointment and bandaging for twenty-four hours.

ELECTRIC SHOCK

SCENARIO

Your toddler has received a shock by placing a metal object inside an electric plug. Or—Your child touched a downed power line.

SYMPTOMS

Unconsciousness, not breathing, sometimes burns where the electrical contact was made.

STEPS TO TAKE

1. Do *not* touch the child if the child is still in contact with the current. *Turn off the current* by removing the fuse or unplugging the electrical cord or turning off master switches. If the child is against a live wire, stand on something dry (like newspapers) and push the child away with a dry board or pole or wooden chair or pull the child away with a dry rope looped over the arms. Do not use anything metallic or wet. If there is a downed power line over a car, all the car's occupants must remain inside the car until the line is removed. Victims struck by lightning can be touched immediately.
2. Immediately start rescue breathing (see p. 727).
3. Treat for shock (see p. 738) and burns (see p. 736).
4. Transport for immediate medical help.

CHEST INJURIES

There are two serious kinds of chest injuries: a crushed chest and an open wound in the chest. Both are true emergencies.

SCENARIO

Usually this injury results from a car accident, a serious fall, or a penetrating wound.

SYMPTOMS

There may be many broken ribs and the child may be having trouble breathing. You may actually see that the chest is crushed in. You also might see a gaping open wound in the chest from a gunshot or knife wound or from a fall on a sharp object.

Steps to Take

1. Seek medical help immediately.
2. Treat for shock (see p. 738).
3. Open the child's air passages by placing the child face up on a firm surface. Put a hand behind the neck and lift the neck with your hand to extend the neck and to bring the chin up.
4. If the injury is on one side only, turn the injured side down if possible. If the injury is in the center of the chest or on both sides or there is trouble breathing, prop the child up in a comfortable position.
5. If there is an open wound, seal it immediately during exhalation (breathing out) with any kind of non-porous dressing (plastic, tape, aluminum foil.) The dressing must be large enough to cover the wound and be airtight. Tape it into place.

   If the child worsens after the wound is sealed, the lung may have collapsed, in which case remove the seal immediately and listen for the escape of air. Replace the seal quickly during exhalation before air is sucked into the wound.

   If there is no material to make a pad, place a hand on each side of the wound and push the skin together to close the wound, then apply a bandage.

DROWNING

Scenario

You find your toddler face down in the family swimming pool. Or—Your fourteen-year-old, who tries to swim across the lake and fails, is pulled unconscious to shore by a friend.

Steps to Take

1. In the case of a water rescue, try to reach the child from land or with your hand, clothing, rope, etc. Throw anything that floats to where the child was seen last.
2. If the child is found in a swimming pool, rescue breathing can be started even before exiting the water (see p. 727).
3. If a drowning victim is unconscious or neck or back injury is suspected, place a board under the victim's head and back while the victim is still in the water. Lift the victim out of the water on the board.
4. If the victim is not breathing, begin CPR at once before the victim is out of the water as soon as the child's body can be supported. Once out of the water, lay the victim on the back on a firm surface and continue mouth-to-mouth breathing. Do not waste time trying to drain water from the lungs at this point.
5. Get medical help fast.

6. Keep on doing CPR until the ambulance comes. Occasionally a child has been successfully resuscitated even after some time has elapsed before CPR was started. This is especially true in cold water because hypothermia (low body temperature) somewhat protects against lack of oxygen. Even in warm climates immersion in water causes lowering of body temperature, so don't stop CPR.

SUICIDE ATTEMPTS

It may seem unbelievable, but suicide can occur in *young* children, although it is more common in teenagers and is one of the leading causes of death in that age group.

SCENARIO

You find your child unconscious next to a bottle of pills. Or—Your child has attached the hose to the exhaust pipe of a car and turned on the motor.

STEPS TO TAKE

1. Restore breathing (see p. 727).
2. Get *medical help.*
3. Get *psychiatric help.*

Any suicide attempt is serious. In addition to the emergency care that follows there must be an *assessment of the seriousness* of the attempt and a *follow-up* by competent psychiatric personnel.

If the child tried to prevent rescue, had a previous suicide attempt, or there is a family history of suicide, the child needs immediate psychiatric treatment, often including hospitalization. Even without these risk factors, an apparent "suicidal gesture" which could not be fatal should be interpreted as a cry for help in the form of competent treatment. Those who make gestures first are at risk of making successful suicides later. Evaluation by a skilled mental health professional is essential.

Males are more likely to be successful at suicide, although females are more likely to make attempts. The typical "successful" suicide is a resolute, calm, isolated, hard-working, obsessive teenager. Usually these are described as "good kids." Depression symptoms are common, with fatigue, insomnia, apathy, hopelessness, and a feeling that life is miserable. Often such a child does not communicate the extent of his or her depression before making an attempt. Suicide attempts by young children can also occur and may be disguised as accidents.

There are several psychiatric emergencies which can occur in children including *attempted suicide, severe* or *incapacitating depression, drug overdose,* and *psychotic behavior.* In a psychiatric emergency, you must keep cool. Most communities have a Community Mental Health Center that can advise you. If your child or you seem to be in danger, call the emergency room of your hospital and ask for a psychiatrist on call. The police can also help in a crisis by transporting the patient to the hospital.

LIFE-THREATENING CONSEQUENCES OF INFECTION

Reye's syndrome, meningococcemia, etc.

SCENARIO AND SYMPTOMS

Your child is sick with a viral infection or chicken pox. The child seems to be no sicker than any other child with the flu in the beginning but then begins to vomit, becomes irrational, becomes drowsy, and lapses into coma.

STEPS TO TAKE

Get the child to the hospital immediately when irrational behavior or drowsiness begins.

If the child vomits frequently—especially a child who usually does not throw up with a viral infection—call your doctor at once.

Note the children may start out with what seems to be an "ordinary" infection which is really meningitis, sepsis, or toxic shock syndrome. Remember your child's *pattern* is important. If your child is one that can play happily with a temperature of 102° but this time, with the same temperature, is sleeping all day, report this to your doctor. If your teenage daughter who is menstruating develops a rash along with a high fever, think of toxic shock syndrome. Most infections in children are self-limited and not serious but parents must always be alert to possible complications.

FIRST AID FOR MINOR "EMERGENCIES"

Bruises

A bruise is the most common injury a child will receive. When there is any injury to the body which causes small blood vessels underneath the skin to break, a bruise will result. What turns a bruise, also known as a black and blue mark, into those colors is blood escaping to the tissues because the blood vessels were broken by the injury. If there is a lot of blood under the tissues, a *hematoma* or lump of blood can form, which is not only colorful, but painful. It may take ten to fourteen days or longer for a bruise to fade and it often turns yellow or green before it goes back to the normal skin color.

For small bruises, apply an ice cube. For bigger ones, use an ice pack and elevate the arm or leg to decrease blood flow.

If your child has a black eye, cover the eye with a cold cloth. Don't put too much pressure on it, however. If there are any visual problems, take the child to a doctor immediately.

Many bruises, of course, may never come to your attention when they happen. The child falls but is playing so hard that he or she is not even aware of the injury. Parents often ask us, "What is easy bruisability?" Sometimes it is difficult for parents or doctors to sort out whether the ten or twenty bruises on a child's legs are present because there is a clotting problem (or even a child abuse problem) or just because the child was playing hard. If bruising seems excessive or occurs all over the body, tests for clotting disorders can be done.

Scrapes (Abrasions)

A scrape is a shallow break in the skin with a depth less than the full thickness of the skin. Though a scrape doesn't go through all of the layers of the skin as a cut may do, nonetheless it's painful. Scrapes are most often caused by falls onto hands or elbows or knees.

The treatment is to remove all the dirt and debris by gently but firmly scrubbing the wound out with soap and warm water. This is going to hurt a bit but it is important to do. You can follow the scrub by a disinfectant of the non-sting variety. Most scrapes will scab quickly. Keeping these wounds open to the air is a good idea, although you may need a bandage if the wound oozes continuously.

If there is a lot of sand or gravel embedded into the wound, take the child to a doctor. Watch for signs of infection.

Cuts

Obviously if blood is spurting from a cut, this is an emergency: refer to page 733. Most of the time your child's cuts will not spurt, though they may bleed heavily. Put pressure on the wound with a clean gauze pad.

Your next decision is to decide whether or not the child needs stitches. If the cut is on the face, is deep or jagged, or gapes so the edges can't be drawn together easily, go to the doctor for stitching.

Unlike a scrape, bleeding will carry the dirt out of a cut so that you only have to clean around it. You may make your own butterfly bandage (this is used for a clean cut that is gaping but no longer bleeding), or you may just use a Band-Aid, depending on whether the wound is gaping. Butterfly bandages must be put on carefully to allow the cut to heal properly and are often put on by the doctor who decides stitches aren't needed. But if you are far from help you can clean the wound yourself and, after it is dry, carefully pull the edges together and place the butterfly to hold the edges together. You can make a butterfly bandage by cutting a Band-Aid with scissors you have dipped in alcohol to clean. (See illustration p. 759.)

If there is a puncture wound from a nail or an animal's tooth, you should go to the doctor, as your child may need antibiotics and a tetanus immunization. A puncture wound of the hand is always treated with antibiotics. The doctor must

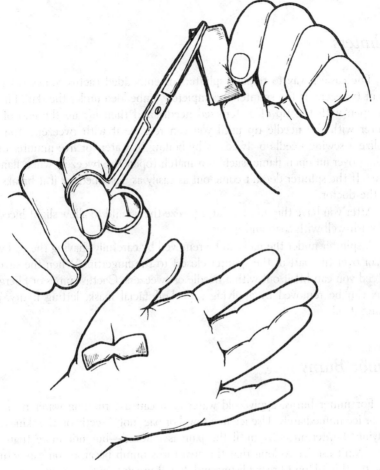

Butterfly bandage.

also check to be sure there is nothing left in a puncture wound like a piece of a broken needle.

Blisters

A blister occurs because of an allergic reaction or when the skin gets damaged by friction or a burn. New skin will form under the blister and the fluid will be absorbed. Do not break the blister or try to remove it. Keep the area clean. If the blister breaks by itself, wash the area and cover with a bandage—remove the dead skin as it dries.

Splinters

The easiest way to remove splinters or embedded cactus spines is with a pair of tweezers. If the splinter is completely embedded under the skin, flip the skin open with the tip of a sterilized needle and then lift up the end of the splinter with the needle tip until you can remove it with tweezers. You can sterilize a sewing needle or tweezers by boiling in water for five minutes or by holding over an open flame, such as a match (open the tweezers when flaming them). If the splinter doesn't come out as easily as described, or if it breaks off, call the doctor.

After you have the splinter out, squeeze the wound to allow slight bleeding and wash well with soap and water.

A splinter under the nail can be removed by carefully shaving the nail with a razor over the part of the splinter closest to the fingertip. When the sliver is exposed you can lift it out with a needle or tweezers. Cactus spines or fiberglass fibers can be removed by applying a peel-off facial mask, letting it dry, and peeling it off.

Minor Burns

For minor burns, apply cold water (you can use running water from the tap) or ice immediately. Use ice in a towel or bag, not directly on the skin. Keep applying it intermittently until the pain is relieved—but not more than one hour. Don't use ice so long that the area turns numb because you can actually cause frostbite. Don't break blisters and do not use antiseptic creams or sprays or butter or grease. If a blister bursts by itself, do not remove the skin edges. It's best to leave a small burn alone, but if your child wants a bandage, apply an antibiotic ointment covered by a sterile gauze pad. If your child has any burn that hurts for more than forty-eight hours, take the child to the doctor.

Foreign Objects in Strange Places

If the child has put something in the ear or nose like a pea or a bean or a bead, the child will probably need medical attention. Food tends to swell with moisture and becomes difficult to remove. If you see paper or cotton you can try to remove it with tweezers. Do not put water or oil into the ears. Little girls sometimes put foreign objects such as cotton, toilet paper, or a small bead in the vagina. This usually causes a vaginitis, which needs treatment.

Insect Bites

Most insects love the taste of children, who are both low to the ground and not skilled at swatting. Scratching of multiple bites can lead to skin infections like impetigo.

We discussed serious bites under emergencies. The best treatment for a *mosquito bite* is to wash with soap and water and use cold compresses or calamine lotion. Hot water on a mosquito bite for a minute will also stop itching. (Be careful not to burn your child.) Insect bites can become infected if the child scratches a lot, so children should be kept clean in the mosquito season.

The same treatment is used for *bee stings*, although the pain usually requires ice. If you mix meat tenderizer and a drop or two of water together and massage the bee sting with this mixture for five minutes, the pain goes away.

If you see a *tick*, do not pull it from a child's skin. Apply heavy oil, like mineral oil, to the area and then after thirty minutes remove the parts carefully with tweezers (do not touch the tick with bare hands) and wash carefully with soap and water. If this treatment doesn't work, go to a doctor.

Chigger bites are treated like mosquito bites. If the chigger is still there, paint the bite with clear nail polish. The chigger will smother and the itch will stop.

If a live insect gets in the *ear*, try shining a flashlight in the ear to entice the bug out. If this doesn't work, tilt the head so that the affected ear is up and float out the insect by pouring a few drops of mineral oil in the ear. This is the *only* time you should put any liquid in the ear unless instructed to do so by your doctor. You have to pull the earlobe backward and upward to straighten the ear canal while you do this.

If your child gets *lice*, don't panic. Head lice are usually diagnosed when the parent notices the nits (white eggs which adhere to the hair shaft). Often the parent is tipped off to look at the hair because the child is scratching the head repeatedly. Kwell shampoo is the treatment of choice. Your doctor will give you a prescription. Kwell is toxic to infants so use only for the child prescribed and store safely.

Sprains

Most sprains, which are defined as an injury to ligaments which were stretched or torn, will respond quickly to therapy. A sprain results when you overextend or twist a limb. There is pain when you move the part, pain in the joint, swelling of the joint, black and blue discoloration, and tenderness.

Doctors sometimes use the phrase "ICE" to remind them what to do for bruises or sprains: "I" for ice, "C" for compression (pressure bandage), and "E" for elevation.

It is important to be sure there are no broken bones. Of course, if you can't tell, get an X-ray *promptly*. Don't let the child walk. Do not use heat within twenty-four hours of the injury. For an arm sprain, a sling is a good idea.

Embedded Fish Hook

The treatment is to push the hook on through the skin until the barb protrudes. Cut off the barb close to the skin with pliers or clippers and draw the unbarbed portion gently through the skin. Then clean the wound and cover it with a dressing. If the barb is already embedded in the skin, usually a doctor has to remove it. Never try to remove a fish hook caught in the eye or in the face. If only the point of the hook (and not the barb) has entered the skin, remove the hook by backing it out. Watch for infection. The child may need a tetanus booster.

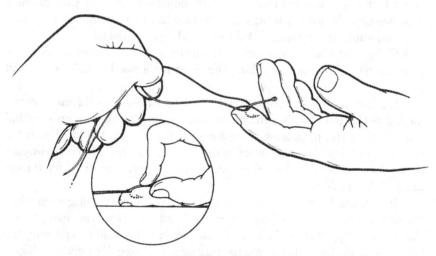

Fish hook removal.

Another method for removing an embedded fish hook in a finger is to loop fishing line around the curved part of the hook. Wrap the ends of the line around your finger a foot away from the hook. Hold the child's finger with your other hand against a table or the ground. Press the shank against the finger until the barb is disengaged. Then yank hard on the string, as shown above.

Injured Fingertip

This is fairly common in young children thanks to a hammer or a slammed car door. An injured fingertip can be very painful, because blood vessels under the fingernail break and a clot forms under the nail. It is recommended that a doctor remove the clot. However, you can alleviate pain yourself if you are far away from medical attention. Sterilize a paper clip (straightened out) by holding over an open flame until red hot. Use a large clip or a clot will form again. Hold the paper clip with a pair of pliers and place the hot tip against the nail. As it melts its way through the fingernail, be sure to steady your hand so that the paper clip doesn't go into the flesh below. If the hole closes, you can repeat the treatment. The nail will melt and the blood will come out. Cover with a sterile bandage.

Don't pull off the fingernail. Rather, keep it in place with a Band-Aid to allow a new one to push through. If the injury is severe, there may be a broken bone so take the child to a doctor.

"There's Something in My Eye!"

The first thing you do when your child says, "There's something in my eye!" is to wash your hands with soap and water. Then pull the upper eyelid down over the lower eyelid and hold for a moment. This causes tearing, which, hopefully, will wash out the particle.

If it doesn't work, you can fill a medicine dropper up with warm water and squeeze the water over the eye to flush out the particle, or hold the head under a gentle stream of running water to flush out the particle in the eye.

If this doesn't work either, gently pull the lower eyelid down. If you can see the foreign object in the inside of the lower lid, lift out the particle with a moistened corner of a clean handkerchief or Kleenex. A wet Q-tip works well. The Q-tip is rolled over the speck, which sticks to the Q-tip. Eyelashes often get stuck in the gutter of the lower lid but can be removed with a clean cloth or Q-tip.

The Whole Pediatrician Catalogue suggests a simple new way for doctors to remove foreign objects from the eye.[6] Use a clean Band-Aid and touch the object with the adhesive part of the Band-Aid. We haven't tried it, but it is said one can take out a speck from one's own eye using a Band-Aid and a mirror.

If the speck is not visible on the lower lid, you have to check the inside of the upper lid by holding the lashes of the upper eyelid and pulling down as the victim looks downward. While holding the eyelid down, place a kitchen match or Q-tip horizontally on the lid. Grasp the eyelid and flip the eyelid backward over the stick. Remove the particle as above.

If the speck still remains, cover the eye with a compress and go to the doctor.

Remember, don't attempt to remove anything stuck in the eye. Don't allow the child to rub the eyes.

A Knocked-out Tooth

If a child's tooth is knocked out, stop the bleeding by compressing the hole with a clean cloth. Rinse the tooth but do *not* scrub it. Place in the socket and have the child hold in place while transporting the child to the dentist. If you can't get the tooth back in place, have the child transport the tooth between the cheek and gums (provided the child is old enough not to swallow it). If you can get to a dentist in thirty minutes, there is a good chance the tooth can be saved. You can also transport the tooth in milk or in a moist tissue or cloth.

Toothache

If the child is in a lot of pain from a toothache, place a tea bag in boiling water for five to ten minutes. Allow it to cool and then rinse the mouth with salt water and place the tea bag on the tooth. Have the child gently bite the tea bag. Get the child to the dentist.

Penis Caught in Zipper

Cut the U-shaped bar at the bottom of the zipper with wire cutters. The zipper will then come apart. If the skin remains attached to the zipper teeth, grasp them on the side and rotate the sides away from each other.[7]

Tar and Gum Removal

Tar can be removed from the skin by rubbing with ice until the tar gets hard so it can be pulled away easily. Gum in the hair can be removed by rubbing the gum with peanut butter until the gum and hair are separated. Then shampoo!

Hiccups

Most of the time in young babies you don't have to do anything about hiccups—they go away by themselves. In older children you don't have to do anything, either. But if the hiccups have gone on for a while you can try some of the old tricks. Have the child sip very, very slowly from a glass of water. Feed the child a spoonful of sugar. Have the child breathe into a paper bag. Very, very rarely hiccups persist pathologically, usually due to a neurological irritation. After two hours call your doctor.

TEACHING YOUR CHILD HOW TO REACT IN AN EMERGENCY

The best thing you can do to teach your child how to function in an emergency is to be a good role model. If your child sees you acting cool in an emergency (even if you don't feel that way), chances are your child will imitate your behavior.

As soon as possible, children should be taught the knowledge you have learned. By high school age, or even earlier, every child should have training in how to deal with emergencies. Teenagers can and should take CPR, first-aid, and water safety courses. These courses also are a good way to make children conscious of safety rules and principles. In addition, the sooner a child learns competency skills and ability in every area, the better off the child will be.

Children should also be taught first aid at home. Even while you are soothing a young child, you can teach the principles of washing a cut, putting ice on bruises, etc. Older children will enjoy reading *What to Do When There's No One But You.* [8] One of the early things to teach your child is how to *get help* in emergencies. A parent will not always be there. In public places, or if lost, the child should know how to call the police. This lesson should be taught *before* the child walks to school alone. The child should also know the home telephone number.

At as young an age as possible, a child should know whom to call for help if the child is injured when no one is home or if the child is away from home. It used to be pretty simple: we could tell our child to ask any adult for help. Unfortunately, this is not wise today.

You are going to have to judge for yourself what to tell your child about your community. Generally, police and other uniformed people (like mail carriers and bus drivers) are safe to approach, as are teachers in school and familiar people like neighbors and proprietors of frequently used stores.

Children should also be taught how to get help if a friend is injured. You should make it clear that if someone is injured, an adult must be called right away even if the injury resulted from forbidden play. Children need to know that if there is an injury, they must break the children's code of secrecy to protect other children.

SUGGESTED READINGS AND RESOURCES

American Academy of Pediatrics. *First Aid and First Aid for Poisoning Chart.* Elk Grove Village, Ill., 1986.

Your pediatrician may order these in bulk for parents; you can also write to the American Academy of Pediatrics, Publication Department, P.O. Box 927, Elk Grove Village, Ill. 60007, and request a single copy for $2.50. A useful hanging for your wall; one side is devoted to emergency first aid, the other to poisoning.

American Medical Association. *Handbook of First Aid and Emergency Care.* New York: Random House, 1980.

Comprehensive handbook of first aid and emergencies in adults as well as children.

American National Red Cross. *Advanced First Aid and Emergency Care*, 2nd ed. Garden City, N.Y.: Doubleday, 1979.

American National Red Cross. *Standard First Aid and Personal Safety*, 2nd ed. Garden City, N.Y.: Doubleday, 1979.

Both are still useful books, though there has not been a recent revision. Both books are well illustrated; the "advanced" book is more comprehensive.

Chewning, Emily Blair. *Emergency First Aid for Children.* Reading, Mass.: Addison-Wesley, 1984.

A handy book to have. Clear directions and good illustrations.

Gore, Harriet Margolis. *What to Do When There's No One But You.* Englewood Cliffs, N.J.: Prentice-Hall, 1974.

A clever book, charmingly illustrated, to teach children first aid when there are no grown-ups around. Good suggestions like using frozen food packages for bruises if you have no ice handy.

Green, Martin I. *A Sigh of Relief.* New York: Bantam Books, 1984.

This handbook covers emergencies in children. It is a well-constructed and illustrated book that is very easy to use. Many parents will want a copy.

Kunz, Jeffrey R. M., ed. *The American Medical Association Family Medical Guide.* New York: Random House, 1982.

How to make medical decisions; good picture section.

Pantell, Robert H.; Fries, James F.; and Vickery, Donald M. *Taking Care of Your Child: A Parents' Guide to Medical Care.* Reading, Mass.: Addison-Wesley, 1977.

Only a short section on emergencies, but the use of decision trees may appeal to some parents.

Part Six

THINGS
THAT COULD BE
DIFFERENT

DIFFERENT KINDS OF PARENTS

Scope of Chapter

This chapter will deal with different kinds of parents. We cover the older parent, the single parent, and the increasingly common employed mother.

Introduction

Many books on child rearing make it seem as though all parents are alike. And not only are all parents alike but they are all concentrating on only one task —that of raising the child. Of course, lip service is given to the fact that some parents work, some stay at home, some have one child, some have several. But the implication is that parents are alike *because* they are parents.

It goes without saying that there are some similarities in parents, especially those of us who read child-rearing books. We have, or are about to have, a child and want to increase our knowledge so we can feel comfortable in our multiple roles. We are generally spending part or most of our energies concentrating on the child or the child to be. We also want to do the very best job we can as a parent.

However, there can be major basic differences among parents. Parents come in all ages—mothers from early teens to the late forties and fathers throughout the life cycle. Parents come from different races and cultures, all of which play different variations on the parenting theme. Each of us comes to parenthood with differing levels of education, confidence, and insight as well as differing commitments and expectations.

OLDER PARENTS

At this point in time, the greatest increase in birth rate is among women thirty-five to forty. First pregnancies in the late thirties are quite common today and we even see some first pregnancies in the early to middle forties. This phenomenon in part came from the feminist movement, which legitimized women's quest for a career. Currently, many women wish to enter and become established in a career before they decide to become mothers. Some women, though not committed to a career, want financial security so they work for a good many years before having a child. Some women may have decided not to have children but then change their mind when they realize their biological clock is running down and they are in a "now or never" time frame.

It is well known that maternal age is associated with an increased risk of chromosomal disorders such as Down syndrome and is also associated with slightly greater difficulty in labor and delivery. There are also non-medical concerns. Older couples often wonder whether or not they will be able to stay in good enough health, or indeed stay alive and working, long enough to raise the child. Older parents may not have young, vigorous grandparents to help them. Also they may have been working so hard at their careers that they lack nonfamily support systems, which understandably makes them feel even less secure in parenting.

Although many older parents are very happy in this new role, there are definitely psychological adjustments to make. Your energy levels and health may be decreasing. You may worry about how you will be able to stand the long hours, the clutter, and the noise levels which are present whenever there are children around.

However, we both know many women in their late thirties and early forties who had a first child. Generally, these have been career women who managed to combine their very much wanted baby and their career, achieving fulfillment from both.

The man who fathers a child in his fifties or later is sometimes overwhelmed by fatherhood. Often such men are in a second marriage and have grown children or even grandchildren. They may worry about what their children or contemporaries will think. Starting all over again can cause them to become depressed or anxious. They often worry about continuing to work long enough to raise the child, especially if they are approaching retirement age. Buying a house again, thinking about baby-sitters and schools again, curtailing vacations again, etc., all can add to the mid-life crisis.

On the positive side, older fathers are generally more secure financially. They also have maturity and a lifetime of experiences to draw on. They usually are more secure in the fathering role than they were when younger. Marilyn's husband told her he never had enough time for his two older children when they were young and valued the time he spent with the two younger ones. In addition, our culture formerly devalued things men did unless they were related to getting ahead in the world of work. Children born when their fathers are older are said to keep their fathers "young" and this is probably true.

Though Marilyn's husband adored his two younger children, born when his older boys were in their teens, he verbalized that starting all over again is not easy. He worried a good deal about providing for *all* his children both financially and emotionally. He sometimes envied his friends whose children were grown because they had greater mobility than he did.

We have each seen a "postpartum depression" in a *father* related to starting a second family in his fifties. A word of advice: if you are contemplating starting a second family when the father is in his late forties or fifties, think about the pros and cons carefully; sometimes counseling is in order.

SINGLE PARENTS

The single parent household is another modern phenomenon, increasing from 13 percent of households in 1970 to 26 percent in 1984.[1] It is estimated that 1 in 5 children in the United States spends at least a portion of childhood in a single parent family[2] and projected that by 1990, over 50 percent of children born today will spend part of their childhood in a single parent family.[3]

The first written description of a non-attached family is provided rather bleakly in Genesis. Hagar and Ishmael were thrown out of Abraham's home because of Sarah's jealousy. Ishmael grew into a "wild ass of a man with his hand against everyone and everyone's hand against him."

The single parent family today has a special set of problems. Family interaction is different. There is only one parent around to socialize the child. Numerically there will probably be fewer positive characteristics in that one parent than in a two-partner family. The single parent becomes more important to the child and the child's development, as there is no spouse around to buffer.

There is strain in a single parent family where the parent has to both work and socialize the child. A single parent must provide all the love plus financial support, fill both parents' roles, and handle anger or depression in the child as well as self. Such a parent suffers from social isolation in a coupled world. All of this makes single parenthood a hard task.

Single mother parenting can occur after the death of the husband or after divorce and, of course, some mothers have never been married, including those who chose single motherhood. Today the most common way to become a single parent is through divorce. Divorced mothers have more difficulty with authority and discipline and some describe this task as overwhelming. These women may be forced to enter the job market for the first time to support their family on a beginner's salary and many cannot count on their ex-husband for either financial or emotional support. We know that less than 50 percent of fathers ordered to pay child support do so.[4]

There is an additional recent change, in that widowed, divorced, or abandoned mothers usually went back to their parental home. Today's ethos of independence pushes them to go it alone. Yet there is a lot of evidence that children do better in a home with at least two adults rather than just one, regardless of whether the other adult is a mother's own mother, sister, spouse, or even a female friend.[5]

Men who become single parents may be very unfamiliar with housework but thanks to modern household technology they can learn women's traditional tasks rather quickly, and single fathers often say that housekeeping is easy and not too important. Labor-saving household devices are easy to operate. By contrast most women have to struggle with learning how to unclog a gutter or nail a shingle. These tasks, which don't come with directions, must be done the way they have always been done, which most women have never learned.

Divorced mothers are often overwhelmed, too broke to enjoy life, and too burdened with child care to have personal growth. No wonder they get depressed!

If you find yourself a single parent, we suggest you try to find new options, including friends and/or a professional counselor in your own life.[6] Find activities for your child that include other children as well as support people for both of you. Find models of the missing parent for your child and also arrange for visits to your favorite intact families so your child can see what such a family is like. Join Parents Without Partners to get peer support as well as tips on single parenting. Look into groups at church and school. Remember there are so many single parents in our culture today that any group which comes together for any purpose, such as a hiking club or church choir, is likely to include single parents.

We also suggest you keep a diary to clarify your thoughts and progress, to pay attention to your *own* needs so that you are healthy enough to parent, and to consider sharing living quarters and lives for a while with other single parents. You not only can pool your money, resources, and child care duties but can also avoid being a lonely mother trapped in the only size apartment you can afford. Since isolation can be your biggest problem, we are convinced that creating an extended family by sharing is a good answer for many single parents.

Single father families have definitely come on the scene, probably as a result of men's changing lifestyles and roles, the father's desire to continue his parenting role after a divorce, knowledge that fathers can function well as single parents, and the greater economic resources of men.[7] More than a million children are being raised by fathers alone—a number which has increased 65 percent since 1970.[8]

In single parent households, children's roles change and they have both more responsibility and more decision-making power. The "family" itself changes. There is no longer a self-contained predivorce household but rather a network of neighbors, dating people, friends at church, therapists, Parents Without Partners, Big Brothers, etc.

EMPLOYMENT PATTERNS IN PARENTS

Parenting doesn't take all of the parent's time and it never did. In tribal times there were always others to hold the baby while the mother was gathering food or the baby swung along with her. Virtually all parents work at something else while parenting, such as housework. There is a good deal of "work" around the house that is *not* parenting and, in addition, there is "work" that is but tangentially part of parenting (chauffeuring a child to school, for example).

There are many patterns of parental employment. First of all, there is the nuclear family with an employed father and a stay-home mother, the traditional pattern. A mother can be employed outside the home full-time, or part-time, or can do work, like writing plays, inside the home. Another pattern becoming more common today is that of both parents working at home.

We get the most questions about mothers employed outside the home, so we are going to discuss this pattern in some detail.

Mothers have always "worked," caring for their children *and* households, which once included the family farm and animals. Mothers working for money outside of the home is a relatively new phenomenon, resulting from the industrial revolution. As long ago as 1791, Alexander Hamilton encouraged industrialization and 50 percent of America's mills employed women and children. As industrialization increased after the Civil War, many poor and immigrant mothers worked outside the home. During World War I and, to a much greater degree during World War II, women worked in factories and some stayed in the work force when the war ended. The sixties brought both job antidiscrimination legislation and the impetus of the feminist movement, resulting in women aspiring to, and achieving, success in professions and careers.

Marilyn's mother worked as a commercial artist but was able to spend many of her working hours at home where she could keep an eye on the household from her studio (a converted closet). Marilyn and Anne have both worked outside the home at a demanding profession throughout their marriages. The major difference between these three women and the women working outside the home today is one of degree. Marilyn's mother was an oddity while Anne and Marilyn were rarities at the beginning. Today the *majority* of married women with children are employed outside the home.

The model "Dick and Jane" family—a unit consisting of a Dad who goes to work, a Mom who stays home in an apron, a Dick and a Jane (and a Spot and a Puff)—was very real in the fifties and made up 70 percent of American households. Today about 10% of American households consist of a two child family with a working father and a stay-at-home mother. The rest of the households are single parent families, stepfamilies, and families with only one child or more than two. But the most common variation on the Dick and Jane theme is a family in which the mother works outside the home. Mom, too, goes off with her briefcase in the morning, not just Dad.

About half of all working-age American women worked outside the home in 1980 compared with one third in 1950. The number of women in the work force grew by more than 173 percent from 16.7 million in 1947 to 45.6 million in 1980, while the number of working men increased by only 43 percent during the same three-decade period.[9] In 1985, 33.5 million youngsters below the age of eighteen—nearly 60 percent of all our nation's children—have employed mothers.[10] Probably no other change in American society has had a more profound effect than the extraordinarily rapid growth of the female labor force, particularly over the last three decades.

Why Women Work

Most mothers work because of economic necessity. Employment outside the home may be the only way that single or divorced mothers can support themselves and their families, even at the impoverished level which characterizes many single parent households.

Many married women with children enter the job market temporarily to assist the family through an economic squeeze, or more permanently to help the family achieve the lifestyle to which they would like to become accustomed.

Many women work for reasons which can be considered primarily personal, although the distinction between economic and personal reasons is neither rigid nor mutually exclusive. Women today no longer feel limited to the homemaker/mother role and housewifery and mothering do not fulfill everyone.

Some career mothers work for satisfaction and fulfillment, while others fear that taking time out from their job or career to raise a family will leave them stuck at the lower rungs of the career ladder. For many women today, as for men, a sense of self-worth is tied to the rewards of employment. Some mothers decide to join the work force as the "empty nest" time approaches.

So, for reasons ranging from discontent with exclusive mothering to the need for two paychecks to support a family, from a demanding career to a vague need to "get back to the office," millions of women with children are in the work force. In fact, so many women are doing it that one would assume it's easy! We know better—from personal experience and from talking to many employed mothers.

The Dual-Worker Family

Take it from two women who know, trying to combine the joys and responsibilities of motherhood with the joys and responsibilities of a job is a difficult juggling act. Although some women can command control over their work schedules and afford household help, most are at the mercy of employer demands ranging from inflexible hours to required overtime. *Just about all working mothers feel torn between job and family—at least part of the time.*

We working mothers, no matter what our circumstances, face a multitude of conflicting messages from our families, our professional worlds, society in general, and even from *ourselves*. Should we consider ourselves primarily nurturers or providers? Can we combine the two roles successfully, and if so, at what cost to each? Can we stay in touch with our children and spouses when we are already working ten hours a day and may have to work overtime to meet a project deadline? What happens when fathers mother? When mothers are absorbed in careers? When families share responsibilities?

Dual-worker families are far from a single homogeneous group. However, many of the problems faced by dual-worker families, such as sharing child care and household responsibilities, are universal. Managing two jobs is arduous and often a source of stress. Old values are questioned; new lifestyles emerge. Many determined and inventive families are hammering out new solutions even as we write.

Sharing Household Responsibilities

Both of us have been employed mothers virtually all of the time since our first child was born. Marilyn worked slightly less than full time until her youngest was about two but worked all during her pregnancies and went back to her job when her children were only a few weeks old. Similarly, Anne worked continuously through all three pregnancies and resumed work shortly thereafter—half-time for three months with the third child. We would like to share some ideas and strategies with you—from our reading and from our own experiences.

A major decision of a dual-worker family is dividing the business of daily life: Who will wash the dishes? Who will pay the bills? Who will repair the car? Who will feed and dress the children? Who will plan social activities with family and friends? Who will take the dog to the veterinarian?

Most women and men were raised traditionally so that both feel domestic duties are the woman's responsibility. However, sharing in household chores can increase pleasures of parenthood for the father, give each parent the opportunity to "break out" of traditional gender roles, decrease stress and overwork for the woman, and decrease resentment and conflict in the relationship.[11] But role-sharing is difficult. Of all possible areas of role-sharing (breadwinner, handyman, kinship, child care, and decision-maker), couples most often reported problems dividing domestic chores. Spouses reported a disinclination to perform non-traditional tasks, even those that required little or no skill.

Successful sharing doesn't always happen. A recent study showed that most working wives remain responsible for the housework and that only 30 percent of husbands believe both spouses should work although 60 percent of the women in the study had jobs![12] In addition, nearly every family had a "caretaker" of the relationship; those families in which both spouses were "work-centered" often fell apart. An AT&T study, which could be considered troublesome to those advocating shared-role marriage, found younger male managers had the same abilities as older managers but less motivation and less interest in getting ahead in the company. This was felt to be directly related to greater involvement in family and fatherhood.[13]

How should responsibilities be shared? Here are some basic "do's" and "don'ts" taken from *The Working Mother's Complete Handbook* and our own fifty-two collective years of sharing in our own households.[14]

1. Make a list of all household tasks and decide which ones you can omit or delegate (as to a cleaning woman, for example). Really concentrate on what can be omitted. If you purchase the right kind of clothes and sheets you can throw away your iron. Down quilts turn bedmaking into quilt shaking. Every working woman has to create her own list of what she can comfortably not do or ignore in her own house.

Alas, you will be left with a list of chores to be done. Write down *when* they should be done (daily, seasonally, as needed), the *time it takes* to do them, and *who wants to do them*. If all chores are not spoken for, negotiate who does the bummers that everyone hates to do. Preferences for or against tasks can be written down on a scale from 1 to 10. If everybody hates a chore it can be rotated. Don't forget you can always rotate or trade tasks by mutual negotiation to prevent boredom or learn a new skill.

2. Both spouses should take the list and make objective, realistic evaluations about what *really* needs to be done and how often. Try to get a clear fix on what is really important to each of you and to your family right now . . . and close your eyes to everything else.

3. Try to run your household as efficiently as possible—neatness does not count! Own as many useful appliances as you can afford, streamline your house to cut down on housekeeping chores, part with possessions you really don't need, and clean the house as you go along rather than letting dirt and clutter accumulate for a major overhaul.

4. To manage a kitchen in your spare time make certain your kitchen equipment is in good order, plan your shopping and meals in advance, simplify your cooking and meal preparation, keep your cupboard stocked with basics so that a last-minute meal is only a can opener away, share the work of meal preparation, and encourage your spouse and children to develop cooking expertise. A child can be taught to prepare a simple meal not only when alone but also for the whole family.

Conserve your time and energy by using the telephone to order groceries or a pizza on a night you both work late. We both have blank grocery lists on the refrigerator door so everyone can jot down what we are running out of. Anne's husband usually does the shopping, so he devised and Xeroxed a check-off grocery list, with items corresponding to the aisles of their usual grocery store. This cut the shopping time in half. We also both buy in quantity and stock up when we *open* the last package of aluminum foil, not when we run out. Use your freezer to stockpile staples and extra batches of stews, casseroles, and soups you have prepared.

Neither of us would be without a microwave oven or a food processor. However, beware of too many kitchen appliances. If you don't use them often they are not worth it as they get in the way either in the cupboard or on the counter; to cook fast, or to cook with spouse or children, you need uncluttered space.

The toughest meal is dinner. In most families, especially those with employed mothers, breakfast is fixed and eaten by individual family members. Lunch is eaten at school or in the workplace or is a light meal served at home. The huge noontime "dinners" farmhands expected are a meal of the past (except maybe at Thanksgiving). The working mother worries about the evening meal. She wants it to be nutritious, easy to prepare and clean up after, varied, pleasing—or at least acceptable—to most family members. Doing all this when you're tired after a hard day's work and hungry yourself is no small task.

If you can possibly afford it, household help for meal preparation is great. Even having someone start the meal or partially prepare it is a big help. Some working mothers find help who work in the afternoon—say from three to seven, to be in the house when the children come home and prepare dinner. The next best thing is buying prepared food. Some communities have "Gourmet to Go" shops. Chicken, Chinese food, and pizza as well as the usual fast-food hamburgers can all be used in a pinch. Some families elect to use prepared food in tight moments. Others schedule a meal or two each week using prepared food. This may be the better way to go as you eliminate grocery shopping for those meals— or avoid throwing out spoiled food you bought and don't have time to cook. We also recommend eating out on set evenings for the same reasons. In our experience the happiest households at the dinner hour are those in which the responsibility and task for the evening meal are rotated.

As Eisen said, you can have two out of the three "E's"—ease, economy, or elegance—but you can't have all three![15] Choices will have to be made. For example, the microwave oven, food processor, and freezer all add to ease in such a major way that they should have high priority when economics permit.

5. Both of us find shopping very time-consuming and use the telephone and catalogues frequently. We both buy clothes, shoes, and gifts from catalogues and have learned which companies are reliable, which stock quality merchandise, and how to order clothes which will fit without trying them on.

6. Don't make assumptions about "man's work" and "woman's work." If your husband likes to cook meals and you like to unclog stuffed drains, do it! When your husband takes over traditional womanly responsibilities, let him handle them his way—without your advice. Don't let your husband fall into the I'll-help-you-when-it-is-convenient-for-me trap. Men who view their domestic contributions as gifts are giving nothing to anyone.

7. Involve your children in regular family meetings at which household routines are discussed and negotiated. Children as young as three can learn how to do and be responsible for simple tasks. Older children as well as adults should choose the jobs they would like to tackle and learn to rotate the jobs no one wants. Consider each child's abilities when tasks are being distributed and be realistic in your expectations.

8. Accept help from whomever you can. A friend may be willing to carpool your children to Little League practice in exchange for your driving her children to the movies on Saturday. Line up local teenagers to help with cleaning the house, doing yard work, or changing the oil in the car. Remember you

can pay or trade off with relatives for baby-sitting. Many women give up "luxuries" to pay for help so they can spend more time with their children.

9. Expect the unexpected and try to be flexible. Children get sick, school and work schedules change, cars break down. Some of the worst crises are service calls on sick appliances when no one is home to let the repair person in. Holidays, with extra shopping, and impending vacations all add to the mother's workload. Employed mothers must learn how to adapt, often instantaneously! It is frustrating to have to depend on other people in order to even get to work but the best of planning and high-level organization won't prevent all of the unpredictable upheavals in the life of a working mother.

Marilyn always had backup child care help when her children were small. In the summers she paid a high school student a retainer to be available to drive the children as needed. Often you can find a neighbor woman or a retired man who is willing to help in an emergency, even though they do not wish to work full-time.

We have a few practical suggestions for the busy employed mother. Call the children frequently, especially when you're traveling out of town. A daily, or twice daily, call helps maintain loving contact. Also carry a beeper if you can. A child who knows mother is only a seven-digit dial away has less concern about being left.

Be prepared ahead of time for birthdays and holidays. Marilyn had a big box with cards, wrapping paper, and emergency gifts. As early as possible, involve children in shopping for gifts themselves or making them when a friend has a birthday party.

10. Know your limitations and learn to say *no* (not a difficult word to pronounce) when you just can't do another thing. It is *not* selfish to protect your time, energy, and physical and emotional well-being.

11. If you are new to the workforce, find the patience to stick it out while everyone in the family adjusts to the new chores and demands. Don't fall in the trap of doing your child's chores because it's easier to do things right.

12. The biggest problem area may be deciding who has *responsibility* for the chore in emergencies—not just who does it. This is tough to do. One very egalitarian man Marilyn knows realized that, though he shared the chores, his wife remained the one with the *responsibility* for the chores. If the housekeeper was ill or the child got sick at school, the wife was called. The couple tried several methods, including dividing responsibilities, alternating responsibilities, and co-responsibility. No arrangement was completely satisfactory but when last heard from they were alternating the "household boss role" every month. The person who was boss literally took responsibility for everything, including planning the social life and even giving dinner parties.

13. Find or make time for *yourself.* We really have concerns about the overcommitted working mother. We worry about the ones who are in a relatively low-paying job who do not have the money to purchase services or even buy things in bulk.

We also have sympathy and empathy for professional women, like ourselves. We know sometimes days and weeks go by when we are doctor, mother, wife, but almost never do we have the time to be ourselves and ourselves only. Try to build in self-time from the very beginning. If you learn to use this time properly it doesn't have to be much. A fifteen-minute jog or dance exercise or walk can go a long way. Try listening to your favorite music, not while you are working but while you are just sitting there listening.

SHARING CHILD CARE

Most children of employed mothers are taken to day care centers or baby-sitters (see Helpers in Child Care). However, there remains a good deal of child care left to do before the parents go to work and after they return.

Some parents alternate getting the children ready for school and for bed. Some parents divide staying home with an ill child—one misses work in the morning, the other in the afternoon. Some alternate taking time off from work for pediatrician appointments, etc. Both of our husbands' offices were closest to the children's school so they were the ones whose phone numbers were listed first with the school for emergencies.

Women should be careful not to fall into the trap that only *they* can perform certain child care functions, or that their presence is invariably essential. A prominent woman psychiatrist tells the story of her child asking her to be at school for a school play because *every* mother would be there. She carefully explained to her child it was impossible for her to be there because she had a meeting in another city that day. On the way to the airport, her concerns for her child were so overwhelming, she canceled her meeting to go to the child's school and found she was the *only* mother there!

Edith Seashore, Director of the National Training Labs, tells a similar story. She was asked to appear at her child's kindergarten class on the child's birthday, to celebrate the tradition of Mother bringing in cupcakes for the entire class. All the children looked forward to celebrating every birthday on the list. When Dr. Seashore realized that she had a conflict because she was scheduled to do an important consultation out of town, her first thought was to change the child's birthday! Her second thought was to try to change the date of the consultation, which was impossible. Finally, she thought of her husband, who took store-bought cupcakes to school on the appropriate day. The children *loved* having a father preside at the party though the teacher assumed the father was unemployed!

This anecdote highlights one of the biggest problems of working mothers: travel schedules. In a two-profession household where both parents have travel obligations, the logistics can get incredibly difficult. With exquisitely careful planning, usually one parent can be in the home city at all times but this busy parent can be burdened with the child care tasks of both parents while the other is on a trip. Extra help or retired relatives can be a backup. They may love being needed occasionally.

A word to mothers who work or are contemplating work: Families are resilient and children far more adaptable than you might imagine. Children do not require your constant attention to grow into self-reliant and self-respecting adults. In fact, they may do better without constant hovering. Further, as working mothers, we can provide our children with models of men and women breaking away from traditional patterns to enrich their own lives and those of others.

If you are, as we are, career women with a demanding job as well as children, we feel it's very important that you get in touch with your feelings about women, work, and child care. Some of us get frazzled because we are being driven to do things by voices from a distant past or by ideological pressures. For example, we feel mothers *must* do the cooking because that's the way it was when we were little girls. Or we may feel we cannot employ household help because having a "servant" is not in our liberal thinking schema.

We are all products of our background and our beliefs. However, we suggest you closely examine those precepts—conscious or unconscious—from your background and your current beliefs when you take on the dual burden of career and child rearing. What is *really* important is that you spend time with your child. Most other traditionally female chores can be delegated.

As Marilyn looks back she knows now she "wanted it all." She *wanted* to cook a big holiday dinner as well as spend time with the children *and* be a doctor. In retrospect she wishes she had employed *more* help. If she were to do it over again, she would have household help every day including weekends. She would have delegated even more than she did with help five days a week. What Marilyn has learned is that you don't have to pay the price of playing superwoman to justify your love of career *and* children. She didn't know this twenty-five years ago because she was not aware of the reasons she felt she had to play superwoman. If any of you women readers can profit by this revelation, this book is well worth the writing!

A recent survey of women not only showed that three out of four women work, two thirds of them full-time, but that they enjoy their dual lives![16] Almost half of the women surveyed would not trade places with anyone and 80 percent would not choose to be full-time homemakers. Thus, despite the possible and likely stresses of maternal employment, most women are thriving and enjoying. A more scientific survey corroborates this in that employed women with children rank high in measurements of both mastery and pleasure.[17]

It *is* possible to combine careers and families in ways that are rewarding and healthy. The task is not easy. However, shared goals, mutual respect for your spouse and children, and a commitment to the family all underscore relationships in which both husbands and wives work together to provide for home and family needs, job satisfaction, and personal growth. You *can* have it all! We know from our own experience that you can!

The Effects of Maternal Employment on Children

One of the questions we are asked most often is "What effect will the mother working outside the home have on the child?" Since the 1930s, there have been numerous studies of the effects of maternal employment on children, measuring (or attempting to measure) infant behavior, school achievement and adjustment, attitudes of children, adolescents, and delinquency. In 1960 a reviewer of the literature to that date concluded, "After reading these studies, it looks as if the fact of the mother being employed or staying at home is not such an important factor in determining the behavior of the child as we have been led to think."[18] Similar conclusions were reached in 1974 by Mary Howell, who wrote: "—no uniformly harmful effects on family life or on the growth and development of children have been demonstrated."[19,20] Dr. Howell warned that work conditions or attitudes of the family, by lowering the mother's self-esteem and energy levels, can affect the employed mother's relationship to her children. On the other side of the coin, she cited advantages to children which can result from increased self-esteem of the mother and from the fact that children of employed mothers are less likely to develop a stereotyped view of males and females. A 1981 review entitled "Determinants and Consequences of Maternal Employment" again found little evidence that maternal employment affects the child, but a good deal of evidence that the mother's sense of role satisfaction does affect both the mother and child.[21]

There are several flaws that one can demonstrate in past studies of maternal employment. Many of the research studies relied on mothers' descriptions or recall or were observations of children that took place over too short a period to be necessarily valid. Also the presence of the mother in the home does not guarantee quality motherhood, and mothering may not always have a positive relation to the child's behavior. In addition, working mothers encompass a large group of women with different reasons for working and different attitudes toward child rearing.

However, despite the fact that much of the literature on the effects of having two parents work is dated and based on maternal employment at a time when it was far less commonplace than today, proof of harmful effects of maternal employment on children just hasn't emerged.

The American Academy of Pediatrics Committee on Psychosocial Aspects of Child and Family Health advises pediatricians how to answer the questions mothers ask about working outside the home.[22] To the question "Is working harmful to my child?" the answers depend on a safe and caring substitute child care environment and the mother's satisfaction in her work, the support she has, and her vitality at the end of the day. "Are there possible negative effects on my child?" Inadequate child care, maternal fatigue, and lack of after-school supervision are possible answers. "What kind of reactions in self, child, and family can

I expect if I return to work?" Guilt on the part of the mother is the major problem along with maternal feelings of loss and inadequacy. The Academy is correct in its answers but perhaps a bit negative in its implications. In point of fact, most pediatricians surveyed are supportive of maternal employment.[23]

One of our favorite pediatricians, T. Berry Brazelton, told an interviewer that the full-time at-home mother is a thing of the past.[24] Brazelton feels that today's women are more prepared, confident, and responsible about child rearing than in the past. He also knows that within a few months after birth the baby is able to handle separation. Who does Brazelton worry about? The mother! He feels the mother needs the first four months of close interaction with the baby and he favors a mandatory four-month maternity leave and one-month paternity leave.

What do we personally think about mothers who work outside the home? We can be accused of bias as both of us are employed mothers. However, we agree objectively with the literature which finds no proof of harmful effects of maternal employment on the child. Though the data is sparse, we also tend to believe that the mother's employment outside the home can be helpful to children, who develop an early self-reliance and a sense of the real world of work today. Also, in many instances, children have the advantage of being raised by two happy and fulfilled parents.

We feel, however, that there may be problems for employed mothers, especially those with young children. Our concern is for the mothers of young children who work and also have the majority of child care responsibilities and household work. We worry about the working mother who may have a feeling of overcommitment and too many drains on her time and energy—at least part of the time.

Married mothers work 85 hours per week on combined job and family duties while married fathers work 66 hours.[25] No wonder mothers are tired and stressed. We both remember these harassed days and sleepless nights well and realize a woman needs a high energy level, good health and stamina, and a sense of humor to survive such hours for long.

Do We Have Any Guilt As We Look Back?

Marilyn remembers when every time she left the house in the morning she felt guilty about leaving her two preschoolers, and every time she left the hospital at night she felt guilty about leaving the sick children! She refers to this as her "bilateral highway guilt" period. One day she realized that this was not productive and refused to let herself feel that way anymore. In other words, she accepted her dual role. This required a good deal of soul searching and some help from a therapist.

Several years ago at one of the first meetings between Anne and Marilyn, Marilyn's daughter, who was just entering medical school, joined them at a restaurant, where they were discussing this book. Anne called home and found out that her baby-sitter was indisposed and told us not to order dinner as she would probably have to take us to her house and pick up some fast food on the way. However, when she called home a few minutes later, one of their student roomers had taken over Sam's care and all was well so that the dinner meeting proceeded. Marilyn commiserated with Anne and related a time when she and her husband had to fly back from an out-of-town meeting because her house-keeper was inebriated.

As we chatted about the problems of finding and keeping housekeepers and other problems of working mothers, Marilyn's daughter said, "Do you know what the worst thing was about having a working mother?" Marilyn's heart thumped; she thought, Now I am *really* going to find out all that I did wrong! Rachel said, "The worst thing was having to go to the orthodontist alone. First of all I had to take the bus alone, and that was scary. Second, I was the *only* child without a mother in the waiting room and that was no fun." Marilyn sighed with relief. She had great empathy for the eleven-year-old child who had to board a bus and wait in a waiting room without a mother, but she was (and continues to be) very relieved that this was "the worst thing!"

A Word About Fathers at Home

Today we are seeing a new phenomenon in reasonably large numbers: the house husband. Men achieve this role in one of two ways. They gain custody after a divorce and are in the same spot as the working single mother with a job to do at work *and* at home. Other men today, who are egalitarian in philosophy, decide to stay at home with the children so their wife can work. Some men actually prefer staying at home. Marilyn has a friend whose husband writes and is content to work at home while his wife is employed outside the home in her profession.

The problems of a working housewife and house husband do not differ much. If you are burdened with two jobs and no sources of help, it doesn't matter what sex you are. Fathers at home should read the section on maternal employment for helpful hints.

The house husband whose wife goes off to work each day can suffer from the bored housewife syndrome despite his sex. For a while the novelty keeps them going but many men cannot wait to get back to work. We recommend work at home or hobbies for house husbands—as we do for housewives who love being at home but are becoming bored.

SUGGESTED READINGS AND RESOURCES

Atlas, Stephen L. *The Parents Without Partners Handbook.* Philadelphia: Running Press, 1984.

Just what the title implies. Empathic, practical advice.

Berg, Barbara J. *The Crisis of the Working Mother: Resolving the Conflict Between Family and Work.* New York: Summit, 1986.

How guilt stresses the working mother.

Berman, Eleanor. *The New-Fashioned Parent: How to Make Your Family Style Work.* Englewood Cliffs, N.J.: Prentice-Hall, 1980.

Brief, thoughtful discussion of basic child-rearing issues in differently structured families.

Bodin, Jeanne, and Mitelman, Bonnie. *Mothers Who Work: Strategies for Coping.* New York: Ballantine, 1983.

A book based on a survey of employed mothers. Well written and organized. If you don't find solutions to your stress as a working mother, you sure will learn how many working women share your stress.

Brazelton, T. Berry. *Working and Caring.* Reading, Mass.: Addison-Wesley, 1985.

The latest Brazelton book on working mothers and their babies. Well worth reading.

Gardner, Richard A. *The Boys and Girls Book About One Parent Families.* New York: Bantam, 1978.

Written for children in single parent homes but also useful to their parents.

Gerson, Kathleen. *Hard Choices: How Women Decide About Work, Career, and Mother-hood.* Berkeley, Calif.: University of California Press, 1985.

How mothers choose.

Goldstein, Sonja, and Solnit, Albert J. *Divorce and Your Child: Practical Suggestions for Parents.* New Haven: Yale University Press, 1985.

A lawyer and child psychiatrist attempt to integrate the legal and psychiatric ramifications of divorce with highly practical suggestions.

Hall, Francine S., and Hall, Douglas T. *The Two Career Couple.* Reading, Mass.: Addison-Wesley, 1979.

A learned book worth reading.

Hirsch, Roseann C. *Super Working Mom's Handbook.* New York: Warner, 1986.

Lots of useful hints for the working—or stay-at-home—mother.

Ives, Sally Blakeslee; Fassler, David; and Lash, Michele. *The Divorce Workbook: A Guide for Kids and Families.* Burlington, Vt.: Waterfront Books, 1985.

A workbook format to help children sort out and handle their feelings about divorce. Can be read aloud to young children who can draw pictures to express their feelings, but be prepared to answer many questions that this book may evoke.

Kimball, Gayle. *The 50-50 Marriage.* Boston: Beacon Press, 1983.

Based on interviews with egalitarian couples. This book offers suggestions that some will find valuable.

Scarr, Sandra. *Mother Care/Other Care.* New York: Basic Books, 1984.

A readable account of the mother's dilemma: my care or other care. Well worth reading.

Sullivan, S. Adams. *The Father's Almanac.* Garden City, N.Y.: Doubleday, 1980.

Written by fathers for fathers. Lists of good practical hints, especially about playing with children, working with children, and learning with children. For mothers as well as fathers.

*　　*　　*

Parents Without Partners, 7910 Woodmont Ave., Suite 1000, Bethesda, Md., 20814, Phone 301-654-8850.

25

PARENTING NON-BIOLOGICAL CHILDREN

Scope of Chapter

This chapter will deal with parenting of non-biological children. First we discuss adoption. We then cover stepparenting, spending a good deal of time on how most children become stepchildren: through divorce.

Introduction

Parenting encompasses two concepts. Parents are responsible for the birth of the child. Parents are also responsible for the care of the child until the child can care for himself or herself. Most people recognize that, in reality, the most important part of parenting is *raising* the child. Our working definition of parenting is protecting and guarding the children from the time you are introduced until the time the children have grown into young adults.

The two concepts of parenting don't always go together. Today, there are several ways people parent without giving birth. Adoption, stepparenting, temporary care or custody of relatives' children, and foster parenting are all common.

There is probably more chance that you will be a parent of a non-biological child today than ever before, because of the rapid changes we are seeing in the nuclear family, in the concepts of both marriage and divorce, and perhaps more basically, in the way people relate to each other.

The focus of the chapter will be on the *differences*, when there are any, between parenting a biological and non-biological child. Obviously, if you have any question about a child at a specific age or stage or about an illness in a child, it does not matter whether the child is biologically or non-biologically yours. You will turn to the chapter that covers the age/stage or the illness. For this chapter, then, it makes sense to concentrate on those aspects where differences do matter.

Areas in which things may be different are your feelings toward the child, other people's feelings toward that child, the child's feelings toward you, and the "results" of parenting a non-biological child.

PARENTING ADOPTED CHILDREN

A woman with two children adopted in infancy told Marilyn that this chapter wasn't needed. She felt a special section for adopted children is unnecessary because there is *absolutely* no difference in the way you parent. The only two things which she acknowledged are different for an adoptive parent is that you may not know the family history of the child and that *other* people may say these aren't your *real* children. Another adoptive mother told us that there was absolutely no difference in the way *she* felt. She bonded to her children and very quickly. However, she told us that adopted *children* feel different because adoption means you were rejected by someone. Her children were "always" told they were adopted and they were also told, when they got older, that their adoptive parents would help them find their biological parents if they wanted to do so. She remembers only one incident when her son who was about eight said in anger, "You can't do that—you're not my real mother!"

Getting Started

Adoptive parents who are lucky enough to get an infant may not have time to prepare for the infant's "arrival." There may not be a crib or clothing ready. The prospective mother is likely to be employed and may not have enough time even to give notice or get a replacement on the job. In some respects preparation for the adoptee takes longer (getting a baby can take years) but quite often there is precious little time between notification that a baby is available and taking that baby home. Thus preparation for an adopted baby differs greatly from preparation for a birth. There are all sorts of things to do in a hurry from buying clothes and equipment to remembering to include your new child on your health insurance policy.

Pregnant women generally have a friendly, loving support system consisting of family, friends, counselors, and health professionals. Everyone is happy about the forthcoming birth. There are showers, childbirth classes, and lots of conversation about pregnancy: ("When I was pregnant with Johnny . . ."). Adoptive mothers, worrying that the adoption might not come to pass, often do not tell others that they are "expecting." They don't tell co-workers they are going on maternity leave at a certain time, and there may be no showers. Perhaps most important, family members are sometimes *not* supportive because they are negative or ambivalent toward adoption.

Although delivery and "arrival" are different, once the baby is with the parents, bonding generally begins. Some adoptive mothers, in their quest for a bonding experience as close as possible to that of a natural child, attempt adoptive nursing or induced lactation. These terms are used to describe breast-feeding without prior pregnancy. With very young and vigorous infants and with very determined mothers, lactation can indeed be induced. Those that wish to do this need dietary supplementation, nipple stimulation for weeks prior to the baby's arrival, very frequent nursing and, often, hormones. Most babies will need a supplementation to the breast-feeding. Mothers who have chosen to go through this arduous regimen did so because they felt the maternal infant relationship would be enhanced, there would be great emotional and nutritional benefits for the baby, and great fulfillment for the mother.[1] Most adoptive mothers do not choose to attempt induced lactation, however.

Mothers who were asked to describe their first encounter with their adopted child reacted positively to the child's appearance, in most instances with joy.[2] The feeling of closeness they rapidly developed was related to physical touch and, later, to doing things together. Those who had both biological and adopted children said, "It's the same," so we can infer that maternal attachment *does* occur.

All parents have to adjust to being *parents* whether the child is biological or adopted. Adoption brings still another adjustment period. Mothers who instantly bonded to their infant adoptee tell us they worried until the adoption papers were final, so that they never felt the baby was really theirs for quite a while. In the case of fathers adopting infants, the feeling of closeness may not be instant as the affection bond takes time to develop. With an older child, the feeling of closeness and attraction on the part of both parents may not occur instantly. As a matter of fact, the affection bond can take quite a while to develop. Both the parent *and* the child have to adjust to each other. Though this should go without saying, we have to say it anyway.

Even from the very beginning adoptive parents should know certain vital things about their adopted child: the child's birthdate, the biological family's background and medical and genetic history, and the history of the pregnancy and birth. In the excitement of getting your baby, don't forget to write things down and to stash documents like the birth certificate in a safe and retrievable place.

There was an old belief which held that after a couple adopted a baby they were more likely to have one of their own. We all know families in which this has happened. However, the facts are that pregnancy rates for adopting and non-adopting couples being seen in an infertility clinic were about the same. It happens, but it is far from a common occurrence.[3]

Going On

Adoptive and biological families are more *alike* than they are different because parenting a toddler is the same, whether the toddler is yours by birth or adoption. This does not diminish the importance of two special concerns in every adopting family: telling the child and shaping the identity of the child.

Adoptive families *are* different from other families in certain respects. All adoptive parents have doubts when the child misbehaves or becomes ill and feel that perhaps they are not good enough parents or the problem would not occur. All adopted children fantasize about real birth parents. (And most children, including natural ones, have fantasies about being adopted.)

Stresses inherent in the adjustment to adoption include the fact that the adopted child is a reminder of the parents' infertility. Also, adoptive parents have differing obligations to the child because adoptive parents may, indeed, return a child. One adoptive mother told us she resents books about the "chosen" child because something you choose, like a dress off a rack, can be returned to the store! Very few children are returned but the very fact that this could happen *does* sometimes delay the attachment. Adoptive parents also have two social handicaps: they are members of a minority group because they achieved parenthood in a special way and generally they have had no role models of adoptive parents.[4]

As one would expect, the qualities found in a good parent are the *same* whether the child is adopted or biological: a good marriage and/or support system, love for the child, acceptance by the child, and the ability to give freedom to the child.[5] Adoptive parents have told us they knew they were successful at adoptive parenting when they could feel both love and hate for the child, just as parents do with a biological child.

Adopted children must face not only the feeling that they were abandoned once but they must also deal with the knowledge of two sets of parents—one giving up or rejecting, the other seeking out and caring for. Both sets of parents could be expressing love by seeking the best home for the child, but this is hard for the child to grasp. At any rate, it is difficult for a child to fuse these two parental images. Children often deal with this by idealizing the birth parents, which then leads the children to the conclusion that they were no good or their birth parents wouldn't have given them up.

Most adopted children go through a stage in which their birth parents are fantasied to be of great wealth and power. As adoptees get older they have concern about falling prey to hereditary illnesses and committing incest unwittingly. There is no question that there are special stresses on an adopted child not only because of multiple parent figures but also because of the heightened anxieties of adoptive parents and the very real issues of identity and uncertainty of biological origins.

Adoptive parents often consult the pediatrician about behavioral and parenting problems that are normal but, because of parental anxiety, loom larger than life. Difficult moments occur in the lives of *all* parents. Two-year-olds can have negative behavior, four-year-olds can get night terrors, adolescents can act out in *all* families, but these things may be more troublesome to the adoptive family. Adoptive parents are very apt to think their parenting or the child's genetic heritage caused the problem. We suggest adoptive parents read the pertinent age/stage chapters as well as the chapters on Development and Socialization to provide perspective on children's behavior. We also suggest repeated counseling, if needed, because as life with an adopted child progresses—as with any child—new problems may arise.[6] Group meetings with other adoptive parents are often helpful.

WHEN TO TELL

There is a bit of controversy in the literature about when to tell a child that he or she is adopted. Some have said, including those who were adopted children, that until age five it is confusing to deal with the knowledge that you have two sets of parents. However, there is no real data about what age is best to tell the child nor is there any evidence that telling them early is harmful. It *is* harmful to children to be told by outsiders that they were adopted, so it is recommended that parents *not* plan to keep the adoption a secret or delay the telling beyond school age. Children *don't* want to talk about adoption all the time or have it pointed out all the time. They *do* want always to be treated as though they were the biological sons or daughters of the adopted parents.

"Telling" implies sharing facts that may be difficult for some parents: their own infertility and how babies are born. The adoptive parents also lose their exclusive parent status. Some parents will need help in finding the right words to tell their adopted child about the adoption. Others may need counseling to deal with their own feelings.

We both feel that adoption should *not* be kept a secret from the child or the community. We also both feel that adopted children should be familiar with the word adoption and, by the age of four or five, be told that their mothers and fathers got them through what is called adoption. Parents should explain, "You did not grow inside *this* mother." Casual explanation about the adoption should accompany early sex education from the parents. Also, parents should read books about adoption to their young adopted children. (See Suggested Readings and Resources.)

Ultimately, adopted children need to "be helped to understand and accept their dual identity, inherited from both their psychological (adoptive) parents and their genetic (natural) parents."[7] This process takes a long time so that it is important to realize telling is *not* a one-time event.

As adopted children get older they will need skills in how to explain to their friends that they are adopted. Most children handle this without much difficulty. Often their schoolmates, because their own fears are provoked by learning about adoption, wonder if *they* were adopted. If your natural child is in school with an adopted child who talks about it, you may get some questions about what adoption is or whether your child was or wasn't. Older siblings in the course of normal fighting sometimes tease the younger sibling by saying, "You don't even look like us—you were adopted!" Very rarely adopted children are teased by their schoolmates about the fact they are adopted. One mother we know asked her son's first-grade teacher to read the class a book about adoption and the teasing stopped.

Occasionally in a home where there are both natural and adopted children, normal sibling rivalry leads to "She's my *real* mommy—not yours!" kinds of remarks. Generally, parents shouldn't have to make too much of this sort of thing. Occasionally, real and morbid jealousy between siblings exists which needs treatment in any family.

Today the "search" is a new term that concerns those involved in adoption. The search is predicated on the individual's right to know about his or her own birth parents. Though previously adoption records were sealed to symbolize how completely the relationship between the child and the birth parents was severed, in some states under some conditions adopted children can look at the records when they become adults. Based on the identifying data about the birth parents, the adoptee can then try to find them. However, most states still permanently deny the adoptee access to records.

Sorich and Siebert, in an article called "Toward Humanizing Adoption," discuss "sharing," "semi-open," and "open adoption."[8] Sharing adoption includes sharing pictures and developmental information with the birth parents through an intermediary organization. In semi-open adoption, the birth parents meet the parents who will be adopting the child without identifying information being shared. Open adoption means both adoptive and birth parents meet and share identifying information. Open adoption, of course, has always occurred in placement of children within extended families, when children were adopted by foster parents whom the birth parents already knew, and also in some private placements. The acknowledged need for adopted children to know about their birth parents may encourage such alternatives to become more common in the future.

It is now recognized that every adoption is a lifelong process for *everyone* involved. Ideally everyone's needs will be met in the adoption process: adoptee, birth parents, and adoptive parents.

Do Adopted Children Have More Problems?

Adjustment and development problems are seen in adopted children at a slightly greater rate than in biological children. Some authors have suggested that biological children are less likely to develop psychiatric and social problems than are adopted children because of the identity problems in the latter.[9] Adopted children may also have "congenital" problems resulting from what was probably a stressful pregnancy of a teenage mother with less than optimal nutrition and medical care. Such pregnancies result in lower birth weight and its complications.

Carol Nadelson[10] points out that adopted children *are* emotionally vulnerable. Their emotional problems center around the difficulty they have in developing a sense of identity and self-concept. When you realize that you are adopted, it means *de facto* you were given up or rejected. This sense of abandonment can result in adopted children feeling they must have been very bad to deserve this rejection. Alternatively, they may feel guilty about thinking their birth parents were very bad to have rejected them. Worst of all, adopted children may worry about whether they will be abandoned *again*.

Adopted children seem to be more vulnerable than the population at large to identity problems in late adolescence.[11] They may be preoccupied with a feeling of isolation and alienation, not only in the teen years but also at the time of marriage, the birth of their own child, or the death of the adoptive parent. They may worry about committing inadvertent incest. Some adoptees become obsessive about finding their birth parents. Sometimes adolescents are only acting out when they threaten to be a searcher—in order to "test" their adoptive parents. For some the search for their birth parents is a positive experience.

Although many agree that adopted children may have more problems than natural children—and for good reasons—most adopted children do well and many do beautifully.

Space does not permit complete coverage of the topic of adoption. However, information about agencies arranging private adoption and legal rights of birth parents, adoptive parents, and adoptees can be found in several good books on adoption including *Adoption: The Grafted Tree* and *The Adoption Adviser* (See Suggested Readings and Resources.) These books include information on finances and law; a directory of adoption resources such as state agencies; state laws; and information about international adoption. In addition, there are many books written for adopted children of differing ages which can be used as you are going through each period of helping your child understand and adjust to adoption.

*   *   *

In summary, adoption is bittersweet—on the whole more sweet than bitter. By understanding the basis of the differences between natural and adoptive families, adoptive parents can learn to minimize problems and maximize success.

STEPPARENTING

Marilyn became a stepparent when she married her husband. His two preadolescent boys spent summers and holidays with their father and, after the marriage, with Marilyn and their father. Marilyn knows both the problems of stepparenting and its rewards, which for her has culminated in the joy of stepgrandchildren.

Stepparenting is a very common occurrence today. There are many more stepparents than there are parents who adopt or who become foster parents. The statistics are truly amazing. Over 15 million children under eighteen live in stepfamilies in the United States, representing 13 percent of the total child population.[12] Because (to date, at any rate) mothers tend to keep the children after a divorce, the majority of stepparenting is done by stepfathers. However,

there are many blended families in which the father with permanent or temporary custody of the children remarries, so stepmothering is far from uncommon.

How Children Become Stepchildren

DEATH

How does a child become a stepchild? A child becomes a stepchild because
of two possible disasters in the child's life: the death of a parent or divorce. The
word "step" comes from the old English word "stoep," which means a bereaved
child or orphan. The death of a parent always causes difficulties for a child,
much of which is age-specific. Children who have lost a parent will grieve, will
feel abandoned, and may feel guilty because children, in their preoperational
thinking, often are convinced that they have caused the bad thing which happened to them. Children invest a great deal in their remaining parent. With a
stepparent on the horizon children experience double abandonment when they
perceive or fear the loss of the surviving parent's attention.

DIVORCE

Most children today become stepchildren because there has been a *divorce*.
What do we know about divorce and its effect on children? Recent data show
that 1 million *new* children and adolescents are involved in divorce yearly. The
startling figure is that between 32 and 46 percent of all children who grew up in
the seventies will experience separation or divorce of their parents.[13] The rate of
divorce in America has definitely increased, jumping 125 percent between 1960
and 1976, although the rate is leveling off.[14] Most divorced persons remarry
within three years, which means that when there are children involved, there
will be stepparenting.[15]

From the child's point of view, divorce occurs with the physical separation
of a parent, usually the father.[16] This is the crisis from the child's point of view
and this is when the family breaks apart, not when the final papers are signed.
All children are greatly disturbed by the rupture of their family. They feel
abandoned and may exhibit anger, grief, anxiety, and guilt. Children are generally quite unhappy even though the separation may result in a more tranquil
household because the fighting and violence have stopped. Schoolchildren may
show regression, increased fears, and sleep disturbances. Often they are ashamed
to tell their friends that the parent has left the home, and they may begin to do
poorly in school. Older children generally exhibit anger, especially directed at
the parent who has left the home. Adolescents are often extremely judgmental
about their parents and they also worry about their own future marriage. Acting
out, especially sexual activity, often occurs.

It's easy to see why such children are upset. Not only is their home ruptured so that they are now different from children who have both parents, but

the parents they do have are often very troubled. Almost never is a divorce completely mutual; one parent wants it more than the other. In some cases there was lots of anger and fighting before the divorce, which may persist even after the divorce—for a lifetime in some instances.

One partner may have left the household to go to something else: a new spouse or relationship or lifestyle. The other partner is left behind with feelings of anger, jealousy, depression, and helplessness. The parent left at home with the children, especially when it's a woman struggling with her own needs for a career and a new life, is left at best with the same old lifestyle, usually with *much* less money. The left-behind parent has a great need for adult companionship, affection, and a great need to build a new life at the very time when the children are making increasing demands on the single parent.

The non-custodial parent may feel guilt, deprivation of the children, or depression, which also affects the relationship with the children. It has been shown that it takes two and a half to three and a half years for adults involved in a divorce to restabilize their lives. That's a long time in the life of a child during which he or she must relate to a troubled parent.

THE EFFECT OF DIVORCE ON CHILDREN

Wallerstein, who studied children of divorce up to five years later, clearly showed that divorce is only the *beginning* of a period of stress for the children. Wallerstein notes that the initial period, starting with the decision to divorce and followed by parental separation, was stressful for almost everyone involved.[17] Separation paradoxically can cause escalation of conflict and unhappiness in the parents. Boys and girls experience pretty much the same initial reaction to divorce. About a year following the separation, the acute responses of the children were subsiding or gone. Children actually recovered from their acute response reactions faster than their parents, and girls recovered faster than boys.

The "transitional" period which follows the acute phase lasts two to three years and is marked by changes in the social-economic structure of the family as well as its relationships. At five years most parents and children are in the "restabilized" postdivorce family or the new marriage. Some families re-created a stable home. Other families were as unhappy as before the divorce, or in some cases, more unhappy because of both the massive life changes and the realization that expectations of postdivorce happiness were not met.

Interestingly enough, children can be very happy in a home in which parents are so unhappy divorce results. Half of the children five years later felt that divorce was *not* an improvement over the predivorced family. Many of the adults, especially the women, were feeling better, even though they had greater economic pressures and stress, because they had higher self-esteem.

At the five-year follow-up, one third of the youngsters were not in difficulty; they were both well adjusted and content. Successful outcome was correlated with a stable close relationship with *both* parents, who were not feuding any longer. There was regular, dependable visiting with the non-custodial parent.

About one third were in the middle adjustment range, characterized by Waller-stein as "adequate but uneven function." Another third were still unhappy and angry at one or both parents and still yearning for the family of yore. Almost all children, even those who were functioning well, had the sense of having gone through a difficult period. *All* of the children said the divorce caused them to have a sad or frightening time or both. Alas, divorce was *not* better for the children than an unhappy marriage. Neither is good for children (though it should go without saying that mothers should not stay in an abusive situation "for the sake of the children").

At the ten-year follow-up of children who were between two and a half and six at the time of divorce, few had conscious memories of either the infant family or the divorce and most were performing adequately in school although all of these children had been troubled at the time of divorce.[18] However, they spoke of both emotional and economic deprivation and half still had reconcilia-tion fantasies. They expressed closeness to and appreciation for the custodial mother but also anger at her emotional and physical unavailability. The impor-tance of the father was paramount whether he visited often or not, including anger at those fathers who did not provide economic support when they could do so. Most of the children looked forward to marriage and a family although a few worried about repeating their parents' mistake. It is interesting to note that these children seemed to do better than children who were older at the time of the marital crisis and who retained bitter memories.

It is very important to recognize that the child's need for both parents does not diminish with time. Even with an early remarriage and a prominent stepfa-ther in the child's life, the biological father's emotional significance remains, and will remain forever. Wallerstein claims that there is no such thing as a one-parent family. Children, even though they are very aware of their parents' shortcomings, still long for them.

There is no question that the developmental and parenting needs of chil-dren do not diminish in a divorce. Also, the divorced family is less adaptive—economically, psychologically, and socially—to the raising of children. There is always more stress in a family when the burden of parenting falls on one parent. Usually both less money and fewer emotional reserves accompany the lack of buffering and support of another adult in the home. This is true even with shared custody. There is nothing two people ever share perfectly; one parent usually has more burden than the other.

How to Parent in a Divorce

From the child's point of view, how should the breakup be handled? We recommend that parents tell their children—together if possible—about the divorce in order to prepare them for the rupture in the household which will occur when one parent moves out. It would be unwise to say something to your children every time the thought of divorce creeps into your heads after a family spat. However, when the decision is made, the *process* of telling should begin. We say "process" because it is not one announcement such as you might make to your mother or employer at work. The process of explanation starts when you tell your child that his or her parents are not going to live together anymore. A further explanation that both parents will always love the child is needed. Still further explanations must follow. The children will always have a home, will be taken care of, and (hopefully) will not be deprived of seeing the non-custodial parent.

Children have very concrete questions about what is going to happen to the family. Where are they going to live? Where are their bed and toys going to be? What school they are going to go to? What is going to happen to their everyday routine? All these questions should be answered truthfully by parents. This means you have to work out details about visiting with the non-custodial parent. The children have to know that the parent not living in the house also has a roof over his or her head and a place to eat—children worry a lot about things like that.

Also important, although many parents wish to avoid this, the children should understand *why* the divorce is taking place. Young children can tolerate the explanation that the parents were unhappy together, perhaps always fighting, and that the divorce will end the fighting and the unhappiness. It is important to outline to the child the attempts that have been made to save the marriage and to emphasize that both parents are sorry that the marriage has failed. Even in the case of an extramarital relationship, many feel that this should be told to the children, not in great detail but as a symptom of the problem with the marriage.

It is not enough to stop there. Children must be told *explicitly* and *repeatedly* that they did not cause the divorce, that they were not, and are not, responsible for the unhappiness. Children often get involved in marital fighting and sometimes fighting spills over. For example, the mother may have been so furious with her husband that she lashed out at the children. The children then assume that *they* have done something wrong. They feel that whatever they did wrong must be tied up with the marital rupture so they feel guilty. One of the hardest things for parents to do is to assure their children that they don't have to take sides—and mean it. Sometimes it may be really difficult for an angry parent to do this. If you're a mother who was left with the children, you may feel great anger at the spouse who walked out, as well as deep feelings of abandonment. The same is true for the father who's left with the children when the mother walks out.

Nonetheless, it is important—though very difficult—to be able to say to your children that: 1) It is all right for them to love both their mother and father; 2) It is all right to feel sad and angry that the family is broken up; and, 3) Life will continue with the new routine that you and the child develop together.

How to Care for Yourself as Parents

Our advice to a single parent, a parent contemplating divorce, or undergoing divorce, is to take care of *yourself* and concentrate on *your needs* and *your support systems* in order that you may parent. It is very easy to fall into the trap of saying, "I will be a sacrificing parent and I will concentrate on my children." We know from the problems we have had in our own lives as well as from listening to our patients, that when there is parental depression or stress (for whatever reason), counseling for yourself is probably the best thing you can do for your child. Just as you should put your oxygen mask on *first* if your plane loses cabin pressure so you can then provide oxygen to your child, in severe stress you should care for *yourself* first so you can parent your child. Knowing your breaking point, knowing what is disturbing you, and knowing your sources of strength enable you to be a better parent. There is probably no area in which we recommend counseling more than in the area of predivorce counseling, marriage counseling if the marriage can be saved, divorce mediation, and postdivorce counseling.

Divorce or No Divorce

No one can really answer the question, "Should we stay together because of the children?" This question cannot be answered globally or generally. It is an *individual* decision.

Years ago, staying together because of the children was the norm and this resulted in lots of children growing up in unhappy homes. Today it seems as though divorce, rather than any attempt at reconciliation, is the norm whether or not there are children. We know, as we said above, that neither divorce nor living in an unhappy home is good for children. Remember, divorce does not usually bring relief to marital stress because the parents still carry the baggage of residual anger and humiliation.

In the case of divorce *or* marital stress, we feel parents—as well as children —should get help in dealing with the problem. Counseling often helps parents make the decision about divorce when they are agonizing over it. Marriage counseling, even when it does not save the marriage, often helps the partners get in touch with, and sort out, their feelings so that decision-making can follow.

When to divorce is still a difficult question. *All children, at all ages,* will be affected by divorce. Knowing the age-specific responses of children to divorce may be of help to parents in making the decision. Thoughtful parents will try to provide what support the children need at their age-specific level and will try to ensure good parenting whatever the decision.

Custody

Before the turn of the century the father *always* had custody because women had very few legal rights. However, the courts began to award custody to women because the father was in the work world and it came to be felt that nurturance was the major need of the child. This was the so-called "tender years" doctrine, which held that the child belongs with the mother during the early years. In 1925, the phrase "best interest of the child," crept into the law and is included in the statutes of all but two states. Maternal custody was considered "best interest" from the twenties until recently. In the late sixties, fathers began to be named as custodial parents more often, ending the presumption that mothers are always best.[19]

A study of men who sought custody revealed that they reported they were closer to their mothers[20] and usually had an older brother and sister, so perhaps were less bound by gender stereotypes. They felt their fathering led to personal growth, increased empathy and emotional responsiveness, and to less compulsion about their careers. A study of children living with the same-sex parent showed they were more socially competent than those living with cross-sex parents, perhaps because it is easier to identify, but also because the cross-sex child may remind the custodial parent of the ex-spouse, leading to hostility.[21]

Joint custody, also known as shared custody, co-custody, and co-parenting, has different variations, but always implies *both* parents will share the responsibility for all vital decisions about the child. Twenty-three states have laws authorizing joint custody and ten others are considering them. Two factors associated with a positive outcome in joint custody cases are easy access to both parents and a good postdivorce relationship between mother and father. Some argue that joint custody can hurt a child because the child without an intact family needs one stable relationship with an adult. Others argue that joint custody is the only way to go. There are no clear-cut answers.

Joint custody, at its best, is superior to single parent custody.[22] Joint custody fathers and mothers both reported several advantages, including fewer court battles over money and less discrimination in housing and credit. Joint parents are not as overwhelmed as single parents because they have some time off from the parenting role. They have the benefit of another parent's perspective to help them see themselves as a parent, not as a visiting uncle who takes the children to the museum and buys them ice cream. The disadvantages include the closeness forced on the divorced couple (they can't leave town) and the hassles children may experience moving from house to house at frequent intervals—although children apparently experience no *great* disruption from living in two houses. Joint custody children are sometimes caught in the middle of a very differing parental lifestyles and roles, but they usually handle this pretty well.

There was no difference by custody type (joint custody, father custody, or mother custody) in a small sample of divorced parents and children studied at least two years after the separation. Regardless of custody type, if there was high parental conflict, the children studied had more behavior problems, more psychosomatic problems, and lower self-esteem.

One problem in making the custody decision is that, although children should be consulted, young children *cannot* always make good judgments about their best interest. Children must always be assured that the final choice rests with the *adults* because children are so concerned about hurting the other parent.

WHAT DO WE KNOW ABOUT STEPFAMILIES?

Stepfamilies have always existed when a widowed parent remarried. However the "new" stepfamily resulting from remarriage after divorce is a relatively recent phenomenon. There are several variations: one stepfamily out of three is the kind where children live with a remarried parent and stepparent; children also visit the remarried parent making a stepfamily; and there are also families in which the couple is not married.

Our language has not caught up with our culture. We don't have the words yet to describe the family unit which encompasses everybody involved—remarried parent, stepparent, and all of the "Yours, Mine, and Ours" children. We don't have names for extended relatives. What do you call your stepmother's sister, for example, your step-aunt? Ellen Goodman points out that divorce creates complicated and new kinship ties which, by the way, when they work are great supports for children.[23]

When it is hard to define something precisely, that something often has many names. Blended and reconstituted family are hot words today, but other terms used to describe this recent and profoundly important type of family in our culture include remarried family, instant family, amalgamated family, synergistic family, and binuclear family. We like the definition Visher and Visher[24] use. "Stepfamily" refers to *any* family in which there is a *stepparent* whether or not children live in that household.

There are six subsystems which exist in a stepfamily: the *divorced spouses* who may be held together by history or anger; the *single-parent subsystem*, which consists of the single parent and his or her children; the *children and their out-of-home system*, which includes the children and their biological parent either single or remarried, with or without children, either biological or step; the *biological siblings*, who often cling together more than they might have in their original family; the *step-sibling subsystem;* and the *new couple*, whose ties to each other are much less strong than all of the others. Bonds which were as deep as the ones which parents hope to develop in the new marriage preceded the new relationship by definition. In addition, there are all the combinations and permutations of relatives—old and new—including new grandparents.[25]

Now that we have defined a stepfamily and briefly outlined the dynamics of interaction within such a family, we can ask, "Are stepfamilies different from other families?" The answer is yes. The best analysis of these differences we've seen was done by O'Hern and Williams, who thoughtfully call our attention to six important differences based on the work of Emily and John Visher.[26]

1) First of all, every stepfamily came about because of *loss*. Both divorce and death bring with them loss of relationships and dreams. 2) Everybody involved comes to a stepfamily with *previous histories*. This means they bring to the stepfamily their own lifestyle, values, and traditions. 3) The *relationship between the parent and child predates the relationship between the couple.* Often, especially after a period of single parenting, the parent and child isolate the new spouse, consciously or unconsciously. 4) The *biological parent is always*

present—even if that parent has died or does not visit the child. 5) Stepchildren are often *part of two households*, not one as most of us are. 6) As there is *no legal relationship between stepparents and stepchildren* (unless legal adoption takes place), if the marriage ends so does the relationship. Incidentally, second divorces are reasonably common, especially if the remarriage occurred within a year of the divorce.

There are also five tasks for stepfamilies which must be accomplished before the family can integrate. O'Hern and Williams say the tasks should begin immediately when the stepfamily is founded and must be ongoing. The first task is for everybody in the stepfamily to *mourn* their respective losses. The second task is to establish *new traditions* and family rituals. This is more than deciding how to celebrate Thanksgiving. It includes everything from family words used to express things to ways of handling conflict to everyday lifestyles. The third task is to *establish new alliances with each other* while maintaining the old alliances. The fourth task is that of *integrating and restructuring* a new family to which everyone has a commitment. The fifth task sounds almost paradoxical but it is the task of every stepfamily member to *develop individualization and autonomy* within the new family.

Most studies of stepchildren and stepfamilies have no controls, do not cover a large enough series, and have resulted from recalled rather than prospective data. We have been able to learn a few things about stepfamilies, however. For example, there is a positive correlation between the socioeconomic status and the stepfamily's success. Stepmother relationships are generally more difficult than stepfather relationships. Sibling relationships can be surprisingly good, especially with a half-sibling who joins the two families together.

Mothers without children of their own often have a more difficult time than stepmothers with children of their own or than stepfathers. They may not know what to expect or how to parent. However, when they have a loving relationship with a man who has children, it means taking the children. (A friend of Marilyn's who has three stepchildren once used an interesting phrase: "When I married my children, I knew it would be difficult.")

Men in remarried relationships also have to join a functioning group with existing rules of family behavior and learn to handle their own sometimes unrealistic expectations. If the man is already a father and has, in a sense, abandoned his previous children who live with their mother, he may have profound guilt about parenting someone else's children. Sexuality issues in the stepfamily can cause turmoil, especially when the man becomes stepfather to teenage daughters. Money worries may abound as supporting two households is always difficult and guilt may occur if the stepfamily has more material goods than the original family or a father spends all week with his stepchildren and only weekends with his own.

Blended stepfamilies have what Messinger called "permeability" of the stepfamily boundaries.[27] There are still ties to the former spouses so that the boundaries of the new family are less distinct. Two sets of grandparents and other relatives may be involved, adding to the indistinct boundaries. Friends and neighbors don't seem to know how to relate to such new families and institutions like schools don't know what to do with more than one set of parents.

One of the big differences between an original family and a stepfamily is *time*. A couple generally has time as husband and wife before they have children and also have time to get used to being parents. But the stepfamily is an *instant* family so that roles must be defined as you go along.

A stepfamily differs from a natural family in other characteristics. There are usually two last names. The birth order is no longer constant if a stepchild falls in between. Non-custody children may come to visit so that organization of holidays and vacations are a problem. In the case of a dead parent, there is the taboo of talking about the dead person who, in a sense, is part of the new family. More people are involved who can intrude on the family. There may be lots of both old and new relatives and friends, including up to four sets of grandparents.

When stepparents have a child of their own, older stepchildren may be upset. There is no question that when the baby arrives the older children know two things: the new marriage is likely to last and the new parent is not going to vanish. Sibling rivalry may, of course, occur but often there is such an age difference that there is a great deal of love for the little one. Marilyn's two children were born when their stepbrothers were entering their teens. The four have a very good relationship. Marilyn's daughter may be the only six-year-old in the world who was taken to a Beatles' concert by her big stepbrother! There was sibling rivalry between the two older boys and between the two younger children, but almost none between the two cohorts.

HOW TO STEPPARENT

Can we provide cookbook rules for you as a stepparent? No, because such a task is impossible, although several books on the market try to do this. We have pointed out some of the differences between parenting and stepparenting. It *is* different. If stepparenting is on your horizon (or it is your current role and you need some help) we suggest you read at least some of the books referred to at the end of this chapter. A newsletter entitled *Stepfamily Bulletin*, from the Stepfamily Association of America, Inc., is published quarterly and stepparents tell us it is helpful. Counseling—individual, marital, family, or group—is reported by many to be very helpful, especially in the beginning or at time of crisis.

We know that prospective stepparents have to look at their lifestyles, parenting philosophies, each parent's individual needs, and each parent's career. Hopefully, this is done before the marriage which creates the stepparent. Also, each child should be looked at separately in terms of physical maturation, emotional maturation, relationships with others, recurring problems, reactions to authority, and the way he or she communicates.[28] In the case of older children you should learn about school adjustment, hobbies, self-discipline, planning for the future, dating, etc. By the time you have talked all these things through, you are in better shape to start stepparenting.

The specific suggestions which follow are based on those offered to *counsel-*

ors of stepparents[29] but are useful for parents as well. They are related to the tasks of stepfamily members we have already listed. To facilitate mourning for personal loss, parents should strive for honest and open expression of feelings. Children can be helped to express their feelings about *both* families through drawings or writing stories. Parents should encourage mutual acceptance of feelings and understand that anger can be a result of grieving for a personal loss rather than an attack. Individual time with each child is important. One good suggestion is that the biological parent spend some time away, giving the stepparent full responsibility.

The name issue should be settled early on. Does the stepmother want to be called Mom? Can the child accept two Moms? How does the stepmother want to be introduced? Every child, in addition to being asked about what names he or she feels comfortable with, should be given a present when the stepfamily begins: personal and inviolable space in the new home. Whether this is a room, a bunk, a desk, or a drawer, it is very important. Everybody needs his or her own place.

Visher and Visher, who are stepparents themselves, bravely set out guidelines for stepfamilies.[30] They suggest that, if possible, start out with a *new house* or apartment so the living space is different for everybody—not the old space with fixed living patterns. (One stepmother, in showing off the new house in which five children from two marriages are "blended" together, said that without the new house the marriage would not have survived.) Develop a relationship with the children *before* you remarry if possible. Recognize that children are going to have ties to their natural parents and nurture this. Try to keep good relationships with ex-spouses, if possible, not only for the children but for the family. Learn to have family negotiation sessions to work out new family traditions and patterns and to set up different rules. Don't fall into the myth of the wicked stepparent yourself—you're not wicked. Recognize the special problems of teenagers and of visiting stepchildren (include them in everything that you can). Recognize, and deal with, the potential problems with sexuality. The usual incest taboos between stepsiblings may not exist and the sexuality of a teenager can be a problem for both fathers and mothers. Recognize that *all* families will have stress but remember, time and maturation of the children are in your favor.

Perhaps the most important task in the stepfamily is for each person in the new couple to prioritize time to be able to spend with self and spouse. If you really want to be a good stepparent, your new marriage has to last, so give it your priority attention. Stepparents must know themselves and be themselves. When you feel good about yourself and the marriage, you will find it easier to parent, to assert your own needs and to set limits on the children.

One article[31] listed strategies which successful stepparents used: 1) Spend time with the child, using good timing so you don't intrude on the child at an inconvenient time; 2) Say the right thing at the right time (which means having the courage to tell the child something displeases you as well as having the courage to tell the child you love him or her); 3) Boost self-esteem in the child whenever you can; 4) Spend money on the child (Don't try to buy the children's love but do try to recognize their own needs for little, but appropriate, gifts as a symbol of love); 5) Be a good role model; 6) Use teaching skills when you can to show your stepchild something useful; 7) Be reliable in a family or personal crisis so the children learn they can count on you; 8) Speak the truth about what you want; don't conceal feelings but rather level with the children; 9) Develop trust, recognizing the children will not trust you on sight; 10) Be accepting rather than rejecting. To this we add: Be *patient*—all of these things take time to learn and time for results.

One of the biggest problems in stepparenting is the legal status of the stepparent, which is zilch. To put it more elegantly, a stepparent has no legal rights. You cannot legally sign for a child at school or give permission for medical treatment in a hospital. You can't even legally look at your stepchild's school records. Today there are so many stepparents around that some schools are beginning to accept a stepparent's signature but to be on the safe side you should have notarized authority to sign for your stepchild.

One of the most important areas to deal with in a stepfamily is *discipline*. It is inevitable that children will test new limits. This may set up a vicious circle in which the child misbehaves, often provocatively, but sometimes just normal misbehavior. The stepparent then tries to discipline. The child is unhappy with the discipline and goes to the natural parent. The natural parent sides with the child and the stepparent is overruled but, more important, is forced out of the circle. The parent-natural child dyad is deciding on discipline rather than the parent-stepparent dyad. It's apparent how this can lead to serious problems in the stepfamily.

Before troubles can even start, we suggest both parents talk together about discipline. Each parent should share how he or she was disciplined as a child, what kind of discipline was used in the first marriage, what type of discipline the absentee parent used, and the roles each wishes to play in disciplining the children. Can each of them back the other up 100 percent? What should be disciplined? What should be considered serious infractions in this new home? What is important and what can be overlooked? What are you going to do when the child is deliberately provocative? Obviously, there will be differences which should be resolved. If there is difficulty in resolving the differences, counseling can help. This is also an area in which Parent Effectiveness Training can be very useful, downplaying power struggles and emphasizing communication, negotiation, and mutual assertiveness.

There must be a *way*, and a *place*, for the parents to come together in private if they don't agree, so they neither undermine each other nor take sides with the child. Messages to the children should be clear. The usual rules of discipline, like being specific and following through, should be carried out.

The last and best advice we can give you is get counseling help—preferably before, but also during, a crisis or rough spot. The pitfalls of stepparenting are so deep, the interpersonal dynamics so fraught with potential difficulties, that it is the rare person or couple that can make things work without help. How do you tell if you need help? Parents may need help if there is frequent fighting and tension, loss of sexual desire, and depression. Children could profit from help if they are having difficulty with school, peer relationships, or home relationships, with behavior at school perhaps the best barometer.[32]

One of the great advantages in living today when divorce and subsequent stepparenting are so common is that there are lots of other couples (and children) in the same boat. Support groups are often available in churches or agencies. Take advantage of them. Some communities have a crisis hot line for frazzled stepfamilies, which is a great idea. Utilize every bit of support you can get.

Good luck!

ADOPTING STEPCHILDREN

We have already said that stepparents have absolutely no legal rights. The one way stepparents can achieve legal rights and stepchildren can acquire rights of inheritance is through adoption. Adoption means the natural parent must legally surrender all rights to the child. While some parents are angry enough with the ex-spouse to cut all ties, including those with children, most parents are reluctant to do so.

What does adoption accomplish? The legal issues are clear. The child who is adopted has full legal rights and status. After adoption there is absolutely no legal difference between the adopted child and any other child born to that marriage. Even the birth certificate is changed legally to reflect the stepparent's name. One friend who adopted her husband's three small children is amused by the fact that her children's birth certificates say they were born in Texas at the time the adoptive mother now listed on the certificate lived in a college dormitory in Arizona!

When we asked stepparents why they adopted, we found in most cases the adoption followed death, not divorce. The instances of adoption following divorce usually occurred in families where the divorce occurred very early—in one case before the baby was born and his natural father had no ties to the baby. Adoption is reasonably common after a single parent birth where the natural father is unknown or has never seen or supported the baby.

One friend told us she decided to adopt her stepchildren (whose mother had died) for three reasons: she wanted to be a real parent both legally and emotionally; she could tell her relatives who asked about children of her "own" that she *had* children of her own; and, there would never be any question about inheritance.

*   *   *

In summary, stepparenting—like natural parenting—brings problems and joys. It *can* work!

SUGGESTED READINGS AND RESOURCES

ADOPTION

Berman, Claire. *We Take This Child.* Garden City, N.Y.: Doubleday, 1974.

A case study book on all kinds of adoptions: classic, interracial, older children, handicapped children, single parent, foster children, intercountry, and independent adoption. Even a chapter on failed adoption.

Caines, Jeanette. *Abby.* New York: Harper, 1984.

Story from a three-year-old adopted child's point of view about family acceptance (particularly with non-adopted older brother) and about the curiosity of the adopted child to hear her "baby story."

De Hartog, Jan. *The Children: A Personal Record for the Use of Adoptive Parents.* New York: Atheneum, 1969.

A moving and practical book based on the adoption of two older Oriental children.

Forrai, Maria S. *A Look at Adoption.* Minneapolis: Lerner Publications, 1978.

Factual, photographic essay about adoption. Discusses reasons why a child may become available for adoption.

Krementz, Jill. *How It Feels to Be Adopted.* New York: Knopf, 1982.

A useful book which may help young adopted children identify with peers who have also been adopted.

Livingston, Carole. *"Why Was I Adopted?"* Secaucus, N.J.: Lyle Stuart, 1978.

In a cute cartoon format highlighting the uniqueness/sameness of the adopted child, this book addresses emotional issues of why both parents would give up a child. Emphasizes specialness of adoptive parents and explores issues of love, anger, and discipline.

McNamara, Joan. *The Adoption Adviser.* New York: Hawthorn, 1975.

A handbook on adoption including information on finance and law and a directory of adoption resources—state agencies, adoption exchanges, state laws, counseling, international information.

Meredith, Judith C. *And Now We Are a Family.* Boston: Beacon Press, 1972.

A wonderful book for parents and kids, covering the bases about the adopted child's concerns about his or her adoption, birth parents, and belongingness.

Raymond, Louise. *Adoption and After.* New York: Harper, 1974.

Originally published in 1955 and revised in 1974. Thoughtfully written. The last chapter suggests a talisman for adoptive parents: "Always remember he's your own—and never forget he's adopted."

Smith, Dorothy W., and Sherwen, Laurie Nehls. *Mothers and Their Adopted Children—the Bonding Process.* New York: Tiresias Press, 1983.

Data based on interviews or written responses from 117 adoptive mothers and 33 adopted children over the age of ten. The majority of mothers felt strongly positive toward the adopted children at "entry." Most of the mothers were at least partly supportive of open adoption records.

Wishard, Laurie, and Wishard, William R. *Adoption: The Grafted Tree.* San Francisco: Cragmont Publications, 1979.

This is a well-written, easy to understand handbook on adoption. It covers the decisions for birth parents and adoptive parents and outlines the legal and practical aspects of adoption. There is a section on the adjustment period and "the search."

STEPPARENTING

Berger, Terry. *Stepchild.* New York: Julian Messner, 1980.

Photographs and text tell the story of a boy who adjusts to a stepfather and step-siblings, for ages five to ten.

Berman, Claire. *Making It As a Stepparent: New Roles, New Rules.* Garden City, N.Y.: Doubleday, 1986.

A readable, short, and to-the-point book. Although not a how-to-stepparent book, readers will find many good hints. Well organized and thoughtful.

Berman, Claire. *What Am I Doing in a Stepfamily?* Secaucus, N.J.: Lyle Stuart, 1982.

A good read-aloud book for children from the age of four to ten. It stresses that being in a stepfamily has some advantages and tells how to capitalize on them. Also helps the biological parent to accept that another adult will care for the child.

Burt, Mala Schuster, and Burt, Roger B. *What's Special About Our Stepfamily?* Garden City, N.Y.: Doubleday, 1983.

A participation book for stepchildren. After reading a brief vignette about subjects like the divorce, getting used to the new family, how to live in two homes, etc., the child fills in blanks about his or her own life as a stepchild. There are suggestions for parents about how to discuss each subject with their children. A young child can also color the pictures. A useful book; we highly recommend it.

Bustanoby, André. *The Readymade Family: How to be a Stepparent and Survive.* Grand Rapids, Mich.: Zondervan, 1982.

An easy-to-read book on stepparenting. Has a good self-evaluation test on how good a stepparent you are, and a good chapter on the importance of the primary marriage relationship.

Capaldi, Fredrick, and McRae, Barbara. *Step-families: A Cooperative Responsibility.* New York: New Viewpoints/Vision Books, 1979.

This book uses diagrams to help define roles in different kinds of families: original family, single-parent family, and stepfamily. There is a good chapter on communication, including some practice exercises.

Getzoff, Ann, and McClenahan, Carolyn. *Stepkids: A Survival Guide for Teenagers in Stepfamilies.* New York: Walker, 1984.

Good bits of advice.

Juroe, David J., and Juroe, Bonnie B. *Successful Stepparenting—Loving and Understanding Stepchildren.* Old Tappan, N.J.: Fleming H. Revell Co., 1983.

A commonsense and practical way to deal with the problematic behavior of stepchildren in their strive to adjust to a new stepfamily. Emphasis is placed on the role of the church in handling this type of family structure. The authors feel that for too long the stepfamily has been alienated and that the time has come to accept the instability of the American family and address this real-life situation realistically.

Kalter, Suzy. *Instant Parent: A Guide for Stepparents, Part-Time Parents and Grandparents.* New York: A & W Publishers, 1979.

A useful book about becoming an instant parent. Chapters on part-time parenting and how to talk and think like a parent. One chapter gives hints about parenting—from how to shampoo a child's hair to how to make cinnamon toast.

Maddox, Brenda. *The Half-Parent.* New York: M. Evans, 1975.

A painfully truthful personal sharing of what it is like to be a stepparent, interwoven with thoughtful analyses of the myths, roles, and realities of stepparents from literature and interviews.

Roosevelt, Ruth, and Lofas, Jeannette. *Living in Step.* New York: McGraw-Hill, 1977.

Written by two women who have been "in step." Well organized, easy reading.

Rosenbaum, Jean, and Rosenbaum, Veryl. *Stepparenting.* Corte Madera, Calif.: Chandler & Sharp, 1977.

Easy-to-read book about parents and children involved in a stepparent family. Centers on children of different ages, outlining the special aspects of those ages to help the stepparent understand.

Sobol, Harriet Langsam. *My Other-Mother, My Other-Father.* New York: Macmillan, 1979.

Nicely photographed, well-written, realistic book about an eleven-year-old girl in a stepfamily. Deals openly with guilt, sadness, anger, confusion, and wishful thinking of such children.

Stenson, Janet Sinberg. *Now I Have a Stepparent and It's Kind of Confusing.* New York: Avon, 1979.

A helpful book for the young child.

Visher, Emily B., and Visher, John S. *Stepfamilies: A Guide to Working with Stepparents and Stepchildren.* New York: Brunner/Mazel, 1979.

A very good book written for therapists and counselors by two professionals who had "blended" a family. Because of its thoughtful approach and excellent organization, this book is also useful for stepparents, or those teaching about stepparenting.

DIVORCE

Gardner, Richard A. *The Boys and Girls Book About Divorce.* New York: Jason Aronson, 1970.

A useful book to answer children's questions about divorce. The author tells it "like it is" (sometimes divorce is better, sometimes a parent doesn't love a child) and tells the child what to do about it.

Newman, George. *101 Ways to Be a Long Distance Super-Dad.* Mountain View, Calif.: Blossom Valley Press, 1981.

Lots of suggestions for parenting from afar. Useful for non-custodial fathers, but also fathers and mothers who travel a lot might learn some tips like using distinctive-color stationery so your child always knows it's a letter from you.

Rowlands, Peter. *Saturday Parent: A Book for Separated Families.* New York: Continuum, 1980.

A short book that concentrates on the absentee parent.

Wallerstein, Judith S., and Kelly, Joan Berlin. *Surviving the Breakup: How Children and Parents Cope with Divorce.* New York: Basic Books, 1980.

A report of the California Divorce Study, which followed 131 children for five years. Points out that divorce is the start of a long period of stress for children.

Weitzman, Lenore J. *The Divorce Revolution: The Unexpected Social and Economic Consequences for Women and Children in America.* New York: Free Press, 1985.

Divorced women and their children have not fared well in the "legal revolution" resulting from the no-fault divorce laws. Read all about it!

Part Seven

THE FUTURE
OF
PARENTING

26

PARENTING AND SOCIETY

There is another aspect of parenting in addition to the "individual" parenting this book has so far addressed. A nation needs a public parenting philosophy and policy in order to make parenting work—and indeed to make society work.

In parenting today, many difficulties that cause pain in children and parents, and guilt in parents (and sometimes children) are not the fault of the individuals. Difficulties in the parenting process are common and some of these are beyond the control of individual parents.

Public policy recommendations that help the family are important to the nation, not just to parents. Crime on the streets or unemployable citizens supported at public expense are of concern to all. This means that the kinds of environments and educational experiences which help children become successfully integrated into the mainstream of society are important to all of us, not just to parents. Parents may be the first to be concerned, because our children's problems affect us before they impact on the larger society. But in the long run *everything* that affects the overall success of the parenting enterprise is essential to the quality of life for all Americans.

The quality of parenting that parents can provide depends on the social, psychological, and economic climate in which we live. Parents alone cannot raise a healthy, social child as a solo enterprise.

Parenting requires learning, because unlike other mammals, we cannot rely on instinct. Parents need education about children and knowledge about how to help children thrive, prosper, and mature into functioning adults. High schools should have required courses in parenting which encompass not only specifics of child development and child care, but also deal with *feelings* of children and parents. Such courses must stress the responsibilities of parenthood in terms of demands on the parents as well as the economics of parenthood in terms of dollars. How wonderful it would be if every high school had a day care center staffed, in part, by students of both sexes who would care for young children under supervision and get credit for this work!

Parenting requires investment of resources: time, money, and energy. We parents need help in making these investments at times in our lives when there may be conflicts with other investments we need to make: to ourselves, our own education, our social life, other children, and other responsibilities.

To this end, family policy should strongly support the concept that parenting always be voluntary, that quality child care services should be available, and that social services and supports be part of every community.

The *basic* needs of children have, of course, not changed throughout history despite the social changes occurring around them. But *some* needs of children have changed. The world into which they are being socialized makes far greater demands on them in terms of education and the ability to fit into a complex society than ever before. There are many choices, as well as more value conflicts, than ever before. Our commercially oriented society teaches children to value themselves in terms of the material possessions they have. The crowded world into which they are born makes them compete harder for resources and success.

We must bring children back into the mainstream of American life. Why should the workplace in which the majority of adults (who are also parents) spend their days be a place where children are not welcome, and a place geographically removed from where the children are?

Ecologists have convinced us that every policy matter likely to affect the physical environment should be accompanied by a well-thought-out "environmental impact statement" showing what is the anticipated effect of, e.g., a new road or a new dam on the wildlife in the region. We suggest a *"child impact statement"* for all matters of public policy which can affect children or families.

Society must protect those children whose parents are absent or whose parents cannot or will not care for them. This societal responsibility is what Bronfenbrenner called "the concern of one generation for the next." He proposed this as a criterion for judging the worth of a society, along with the Gross National Product, to predict how well a nation will prosper. "If the children and youth of a nation are afforded opportunity to develop their capacities to the fullest, if they are given the knowledge to understand the world and the wisdom to change it, then the prospects for the future are bright. In contrast, a society which neglects its children, however well it may function in other respects, risks eventual disorganization and demise."[1]

Parents have considerable potential power to achieve societal changes. In our society, the overwhelming majority of voting citizens are parents. For those issues which require collective action, we have the votes to bring about that action.

In a heterogeneous society such as ours, where parents come from many religions, many ethnic groups, and have many different values, we cannot expect agreement about all parenting issues. Some people will feel adamant about supporting the authority of parents; others about encouraging the autonomy and decision-making capacity of the young. Some will make great sacrifices to support the right to life of the unborn; others will make equally great sacrifices to support the right of a woman to determine when and whether to bear children.

We cannot expect these value differences to disappear. But we can insist that our society give high priority to the parenting enterprise. We can insist on government support of child-related research and child-related services. Fostering more rewarding and more effective parenting could become one of the most challenging and interesting issues of our future.

To that end, this book is dedicated—to you as a parent, as a citizen, and as an involved and thinking human being concerned about all children and the future of society.

SUGGESTED READINGS AND RESOURCES

Bronfenbrenner, Urie. *Two Worlds of Childhood: U.S. and U.S.S.R.* New York: Russell Sage Foundation, 1970.

Although published in 1970, this study of children in two cultures makes for fascinating reading.

Packard, Vance Oakley. *Our Endangered Children: Growing Up in A Changing World.* Boston: Little, Brown, 1983.

A look at how our changing world affects children.

Pizzo, Peggy. *Parent to Parent: Working Together for Ourselves and Our Children.* Boston: Beacon Press, 1983.

An important book that points out the "power" of parents who join together in parent groups. There is a history of parent activism, an analysis of the resourceful parent, and an outline of what parent groups provide and can accomplish. There are excellent chapters on how parents can change institutions and law.

AN AFTERWORD

All parents who are concerned about children—their own or the children of others—are, by definition, thinking of the future. No one can talk or think about children without implicitly or explicitly talking or thinking about a *future*.

However, we can no longer assume there will be a future. Since the beginning of the nuclear age, the future of all living beings has been in jeopardy. The most important reason to ensure that we do not destroy ourselves is to ensure that our children will have a future.

This book is not a political work. We are physicians who do not profess to know much about war or defense or arms control. However, we feel strongly that *every parent* must come to terms with whether increasing the number of nuclear armaments is the way to prevent nuclear war. We think not.

It has been pointed out that nuclear war will cause the "last epidemic," which will occur in a world that no longer has hospitals or doctors. Thinking beyond the horrors of a nuclear attack itself, there will be long-term, permanent damage to the ecology of the earth and genetic damage to the offspring of survivors, if any.

The psychological impact of the nuclear arms race on children and adolescents is very real. Our children are growing up with the ever-present threat of nuclear holocaust—and it worries many of them who feel helpless to do anything about it.

Parents also feel helpless. We want to be honest with our children, but do not want to frighten them. People must live as though there *will* be a future, because all meaningful work and relationships, as well as morality, are based on this premise.

It is difficult to give advice on specific action. However, we urge that you (1) become aware of the dangers of the nuclear arms race, (2) do all you can locally and nationally to promote peace and prevent the kind of paranoia that will lead to a nuclear holocaust, and (3) recognize, with us, that parenting deals with children and children must have a future. This planet must survive; humankind must survive.

The late Peter Farb, in his superb book *Humankind*, said: "Our species has always been beset by problems. The uniquely human capacity to solve problems has always produced innovations—biological, cultural, and technological—

which in turn have brought our species to new levels of adaptations. No reason whatever exists for doubting that such will continue to be the case in the future. I have therefore written this book not as an obituary for our species, but as a celebration of it."[1] We agree with Farb that we should celebrate humankind but know we cannot afford complacence. We must adapt, we must replace violence with alternative ways of resolving conflicts, and we must use science in a positive, not negative, way.

Parents: Together we can make a difference by working now to ensure a future for our children and our children's children.

CHAPTER REFERENCES AND SOURCE MATERIAL

CHAPTER 1
BASIC REALITIES OF PARENTING

REFERENCES

1. Packard, Vance Oakley. *Our Endangered Children: Growing Up in a Changing World.* Boston: Little, Brown, 1983.
2. Ariès, Philippe. *Centuries of Childhood: A Social History of Family Life.* (Robert Baldick, tr.) New York: Knopf, 1965.
3. deMause, Lloyd (ed.). *The History of Childhood.* New York: Psychohistory Press, 1974.
4. Goodall, Jane. *In the Shadow of Man.* Boston: Houghton Mifflin, 1971.
5. Friedan, Betty. *The Feminine Mystique.* New York: Dell, 1977.
6. French, Marilyn. *The Women's Room.* New York: Jove Publications, 1978.
7. Heins, Marilyn; Stillman, Paula; Sabers, Darrell; and Mazzeo, John. "Attitudes of Pediatricians Toward Maternal Employment." *Pediatrics,* Sept. 1983, 72(3), 283–90.
8. Grohman, Joann S. *Born to Love: Instinct and Natural Mothering.* Dixfield, Maine: Coburn Farm Press, 1976.
9. Bricklin, Alice G. *Mother Love: The Book of Natural Childrearing.* Philadelphia: Running Press, 1979.
10. Morgan, Marabel. *The Total Woman.* New York: Pocket Books, 1983.
11. Bernard, Jessie. *The Future of Marriage.* New Haven, Conn.: Yale University Press, 1982.
12. Pleck, Joseph H. *The Myth of Masculinity.* Cambridge, Mass.: MIT Press, 1981.
13. Campbell, Angus. *The Sense of Well-being in America.* New York: McGraw-Hill, 1981.
14. Baruch, Grace, Barnett, Rosalind, and Rivers, Caryl. *Lifeprints: New Patterns of Love and Work for Today's Women.* New York: McGraw-Hill, 1983.
15. Heins, Marilyn; Smock, Sue; Martindale, Lois; Stein, Margaret; and Jacobs, Jennifer. "A Profile of the Woman Physician." *Journal of the American Medical Women's Association,* Nov. 1977, 32(11), 421–27.
16. Packard, op. cit., p. 357.
17. Harlow, Harry F. "The Affectional System." In Schrier, Allan Martin; Harlow, Harry F.; and Stollnitz, Fred, eds. *Behavior of Non-Human Primates: Modern Research Trends.* New York: Academic Press, 1965, pp. 187–334.
18. Kerr, Jean. *Please Don't Eat the Daisies.* Garden City, N.Y.: Doubleday, 1953.
19. Skolnick, Arlene. "The Myth of the Vulnerable Child." *Psychology Today,* Feb. 1978, 11(9), 56–65.

SOURCE MATERIAL

Anthony, E. James, and Benedek, Therese, eds. *Parenthood: Its Psychology and Psychopathology*. Boston: Little, Brown, 1970.

Anthony, E. James, and Pollock, George H., eds. *Parental Influences in Health and Disease*. Boston: Little, Brown, 1985.

Austin, C. R., and Short, R. V., eds. *Reproduction in Mammals*, Vols. 1–5. London: Oxford University Press, 1982.

Bombeck, Erma. *Motherhood, The Second Oldest Profession*. New York: McGraw-Hill, 1983.

Bowen, Murray. *Family Therapy in Clinical Practice*. New York: Aronson, 1978.

Cable, Mary. *The Little Darlings: A History of Child Rearing in America*. New York: Scribner's, 1975.

Corfman, Eunice, ed. U.S. Department of Health, Education, and Welfare Science Monographs. *Families Today: A Research Sampler on Families and Children* (Vol. 1). National Institute of Mental Health, Rockville, Md., 1979.

Corfman, Eunice, ed. U.S. Department of Health, Education, and Welfare Science Monographs. *Families Today: A Research Sampler on Families and Children* (Vol. 2). National Institute of Mental Health, Rockville, Md., 1979.

Demos, John. *A Little Commonwealth: Family Life in Plymouth Colony*. New York: Oxford University Press, 1970.

Eisen, Carol G. *Nobody Said You Had to Eat off the Floor: The Psychiatrist's Wife's Guide to Housekeeping*. New York: McKay, 1971.

Elias, Norbert. *The Civilizing Process: The Development of Manners*. New York: Urizen, 1978.

Friedan, Betty. *It Changed My Life: Writings on the Women's Movement*. New York: Norton, 1976.

———. *The Second Stage*. New York: Summit Books, 1982.

Fuchs, Victor R. *How We Live: An Economic Perspective on Americans From Birth to Death*. Cambridge, Mass.: Harvard University Press, 1983.

Gordon, Sol; Wollin, Mina McD. *Parenting: A Guide for Young People*, rev. ed. New York: Sadlier-Oxford, 1980.

Greer, Germaine. *The Female Eunuch*. London: Grafton, 1986.

Greven, Philip. *The Protestant Temperament: Patterns of Child-Rearing, Religious Experience, and the Self in Early America*. New York: Knopf, 1977.

Hobsbawm, Eric, and Ranger, Terence, eds. *The Invention of Tradition*. New York: Cambridge University Press, 1983.

Hunt, David. *Parents and Children in History: The Psychology of Family Life in Early Modern France*. New York: Harper, 1972.

Keniston, Kenneth, and the Carnegie Council on Children. *All Our Children: The American Family Under Pressure*. New York: Harcourt, Brace, 1978.

Lane, Mary B. *Education for Parenting*. Washington, D.C.: National Association for The Education of Young Children, 1975.

Masnick, George, and Bane, Mary Jo. *The Nation's Families: 1960–1990*. Boston: Auburn House, 1980.

Mead, Margaret, and Metraux, Rhoda. *A Way of Seeing*. New York: Morrow, 1974.

Morgan, Elaine. *The Descent of Woman*. New York: Stein & Day, 1980.

Parke, Ross D. *Fathers*. Cambridge, Mass.: Harvard University Press, 1981.

Pleck, Elizabeth H., and Pleck, Joseph H. *The American Man*. Englewood Cliffs, N.J.: Prentice-Hall, 1980.

Rapoport, Rhona; Rapoport, Robert N.; and Strelitz, Ziona. *Fathers, Mothers, and Society: Towards New Alliances*. New York: Basic Books, 1977.

Schorsch, Anita. *Images of Childhood: An Illustrated Social History.* New York: Mayflower, 1979.

Stone, Lawrence. "Family History in the 1980s: Past Achievements and Future Trends." *Journal of Interdisciplinary History,* Summer 1981 (XII)I, 51–87.

The National Research Council. *Toward a National Policy for Children and Families.* National Academy of Sciences, Washington, D.C., 1976.

Winn, Marie. *Children Without Childhood.* New York: Pantheon, 1983.

Wishy, Bernard. *The Child and the Republic: The Dawn of Modern American Child Nurture.* Philadelphia: University of Pennsylvania Press, 1968.

CHAPTER 2
BIOSOCIAL RHYTHMS

REFERENCES

1. Mead, Margaret, and Newton, Niles. "Cultural Patterning of Perinatal Behavior." In Richardson, Stephen A., and Guttmacher, Alan F., eds. *Childbearing: Its Social and Psychological Aspects.* Baltimore, Md.: Williams & Wilkins, 1967, p. 177.
2. "Nighttime Sleeplessness Often Learned Behavior in Children. Parental Reinforcement." *Pediatric News,* Feb. 1986, 20(2), 1;82.

SOURCE MATERIAL

Anthony, E. James, and Benedek, Therese, eds. *Parenthood: Its Psychology and Psychopathology.* Boston: Little, Brown, 1970.

Kay, Margarita Artschwager. *Anthropology of Human Birth.* Philadelphia: F. A. Davis, 1982.

Levine, Melvin D.; Carey, William B.; Crocker, Allen C.; and Gross, Ruth T. *Developmental-Behavioral Pediatrics.* Philadelphia: Saunders, 1983.

Lidz, Theodore. *The Person.* New York: Basic Books, 1976.

Schuster, Clara Shaw, and Ashburn, Shirley Smith. *The Process of Human Development: A Holistic Approach.* Boston: Little, Brown, 1980.

Vaughn, Brian; Deinard, Amos; and Egeland, Byron. "Measuring Temperament in Pediatric Practice." *The Journal of Pediatrics,* March 1980, 96(3), Part I, 510–14.

CHAPTER 3
SOCIALIZATION

REFERENCES

1. Wilson, Ann L.; Witzke, Donald B.; and Volin, Ann. "What It Means to 'Spoil' a Baby." *Clinical Pediatrics,* Dec. 1981, 20(12), 798–802.
2. Gordon, Thomas. *P.E.T. In Action.* New York: Bantam, 1976.
3. ———. *P.E.T. Parent Effectiveness Training.* New York: Plume Book/N.A.L., 1970, p. 151.
4. Briggs, Dorothy Corkille. *Your Child's Self-Esteem: The Key to Life.* Garden City, N.Y.: Doubleday/Dolphin, 1975.
5. Nelson, Gerald E. *The One-Minute Scolding.* Boulder, Colo.: Shambhala Publications, 1984.
6. Bach, George Robert, and Wyden, Peter. *The Intimate Enemy: How to Fight Fair in Love and Marriage.* New York: Morrow, 1969.

7. Fisher, Roger, and Ury, William. *Getting to Yes: Negotiating Agreement Without Giving In.* New York: Penguin, 1983.
8. Gordon (1976), op. cit., p. 25.
9. Nelson, op. cit., pp. 15, 30.
10. Johnson, Spencer. *The One-Minute Father.* New York: Morrow, 1983.
11. ———. *The One-Minute Mother.* New York: Morrow, 1983.
12. Gordon (1976), op. cit., pp. 244–47.
13. Nelson, op. cit., pp. 10–11.
14. Krueckeberg, Karin. Personal communication.
15. Forehand, Rex L., and McMahon, Robert J. *Helping the Noncompliant Child: A Clinician's Guide to Parent Training.* New York: Guilford, 1981.
16. Sahler, Olle Jane Z., and Oosting, Rose S. "Discipline and Rage in Childrearing." In *Ambulatory Pediatric Association: Program and Abstracts*, 1981.
17. York, Phyllis; York, David; and Wachtel, Ted. *Toughlove.* New York: Bantam, 1983.
18. Potter, Jessie. Personal communication.
19. Kinsey, Alfred Charles, et al. *Sexual Behavior in the Human Female.* Philadelphia: Saunders, 1953.
20. Kinsey, Alfred Charles; Pomeroy, Wardell B.; and Martin, Clyde E. *Sexual Behavior in the Human Male.* Philadelphia: Saunders, 1948.
21. Lerner, Harriet. Personal communication.
22. Hill, Langdon. "Romance! 7th-Grade Message: Live Love, Don't Hide It." *Arizona Daily Star*, April 25, 1984.
23. Yates, Alayne. *Sex Without Shame: Encouraging the Child's Healthy Sexual Development.* New York: Morrow, 1978.
24. Pogrebin, Letty Cottin. *Growing Up Free: Raising Your Kids in the 80's.* New York: McGraw-Hill, 1980.
25. Bach and Wyden, op. cit., p. 288.
26. Schuster, Clara Shaw, and Ashburn, Shirley Smith. *The Process of Human Development: A Holistic Approach.* Boston: Little, Brown, 1980, p. 519.
27. Winston, Stephanie. *Getting Organized.* New York: Warner, 1978.
28. Eisen, Carol G. *Nobody Said You Had to Eat off the Floor: The Psychiatrist's Wife's Guide to Housekeeping.* New York: McKay, 1971.
29. Kagan, Jerome. *The Nature of the Child.* New York: Basic Books, 1984.
30. Chess, Stella, and Thomas, Alexander. *Origins and Evolution of Behavioral Disorders.* New York: Brunner/Mazel, 1984, p. 293.

SOURCE MATERIAL

Arnold, Eugene L. *Helping Parents Help Their Children.* New York: Brunner/Mazel, 1978.
Azrin, Nathan, and Besalel, Victoria A. *A Parent's Guide to Bedwetting Control: A Step-by-Step Method.* New York: Pocket Books, 1981.
Babcock, Dorothy E., and Keepers, Terry D. *Raising Kids O.K.: Transactional Analysis in Human Growth and Development.* New York: Avon, 1976.
Bergling, Kurt. *Moral Development: The Validity of Kohlberg's Theory.* Stockholm: Almqvist & Wiksell International, 1981.
Bettelheim, Bruno. "Punishment vs. Discipline." *The Atlantic*, Nov. 1985, 256(5), 51–59.
———. *The Uses of Enchantment: The Meaning and Importance of Fairy Tales.* New York: Knopf, 1976.
Greenberg, Bradley. "Child Nurturing and Television in the 1980s." In Boger, R. P., Blom, G. E., Lezotte, L. E., eds. *Child Nurturing in the 1980s*, Vol. 4 of *Child Nurturance.* New York: Plenum Press, 1984.

Bricklin, Alice G. *Mother Love: Natural Mothering, Birth to Three Years*. Philadelphia: Running Press, 1979.

Carton, Lonnie. *Raise Your Kids Right*. New York: Pocket Books, 1984.

Chamberlin, Robert W. "Behavioral Problems and Their Prevention." *Pediatrics in Review*, July 1980, 2(1), 13–18.

———. "Parenting Styles: Child Behavior and the Pediatrician." *Pediatric Annals*, Sept. 1977, 6(9), 50–63.

Chess, Stella; Thomas, Alexander; and Birch, Herbert G. *Your Child Is a Person: A Psychological Approach to Parenthood Without Guilt*. New York: Parallax, 1965.

Dinkmeyer, Don, and McKay, Gary D. *The Parent's Handbook: Systematic Training for Effective Parenting (STEP)*. Circle Pines, Minn., American Guidance Service, 1982.

Dodson, Fitzhugh. *How to Father*. Los Angeles: Nash Publications, 1974.

Dreikurs, Rudolf, and Grey, Loren. *A Parent's Guide to Child Discipline*. New York: Dutton, 1970.

Dunn, Judy. *Distress and Comfort*. Cambridge, Mass.: Harvard University Press, 1977.

Erlanger, Howard S. "Social Class and Corporal Punishment in Childrearing: A Reassessment." *American Sociological Review*, Feb. 1974, 39:68–85.

Ernst, Cecile, and Angst, Jules. *Birth Order: Its Influence on Personality*. New York: Springer-Verlag, 1983.

Gattozzi, Ruth. *What's Wrong with My Child?: How to Understand and Raise a Behaviorally Difficult Child*. New York: McGraw-Hill, 1986.

Giffin, Mary, and Felsenthal, Carol. *A Cry for Help*. Garden City, N.Y.: Doubleday, 1983.

Gilbreth, Frank B., and Carey, Ernestine G. *Cheaper by the Dozen*. New York: Crowell, 1963.

Gilligan, Carol. *In a Different Voice: Psychological Theory and Women's Development*. Cambridge, Mass.: Harvard University Press, 1982.

Goodall, Jane. *In the Shadow of Man*. Boston: Houghton Mifflin, 1971.

Gordon, Sol, and Gordon, Judith. *Raising a Child Conservatively in a Sexually Permissive World*. New York: Simon & Schuster, 1983.

Gordon, Thomas, with Burch, Noel. *T.E.T.: Teacher Effectiveness Training*. New York: McKay, 1978.

Judson, Stephanie, ed. *A Manual on Non Violence and Children*. Philadelphia: New Society, 1984.

Kaplan, Louise J. *Oneness and Separateness*. London: J. Cape, 1979.

Kaufman, Charles. "Biologic Considerations of Parenthood" (Chapter 1). In Anthony, E. James, and Benedek, Therese, eds. *Parenthood, Its Psychology and Psychopathology*. Boston: Little, Brown, 1970.

Keeton, Kathy, with Borskin, Yvonne. *Woman of Tomorrow*. New York: St. Martin's/Marek, 1985.

Kelley, Michael R. *A Parent's Guide to Television: Making the Most of It*. New York: Wiley, 1983.

Kersey, Katharine C. *Sensitive Parenting: From Infancy to Adulthood*. Washington, D.C.: Acropolis, 1983.

Lickona, Thomas. *Raising Good Children: Helping Your Child Through the Stages of Moral Development*. New York: Bantam, 1983.

Miller, Alice. *The Drama of the Gifted Child*. New York: Basic Books, 1983.

Miller, Alice. *For Your Own Good: Hidden Cruelty in Child-rearing and the Roots of Violence*. (Hildegarde Hannum and Hunter Hannum, tr.) New York: Farrar, Straus, 1983.

Minshull, Ruth. *Miracles for Breakfast*. Ann Arbor, Mich.: Scientology, 1968.

Munnion, Catherine, and Grender, Iris, eds. *The Open Home*. New York: St. Martin's, 1976.

Mussen, Paul; Eisenberg-Berg, Nancy. *Roots of Caring, Sharing, and Helping.* San Francisco: Freeman, 1977.

Mead, Margaret, and Newton, Niles. "Cultural Patterning of Perinatal Behavior." In Richardson, Stephen A., and Guttmacher, Alan F., eds. *Childbearing: Its Social and Psychological Aspects.* Baltimore: Williams & Wilkins, 1967.

Parke, Ross D. *Fathers.* Cambridge, Mass.: Harvard University Press, 1981.

Parkes, Colin Murray, and Stevenson-Hinde, Joan, eds. *The Place of Attachment in Human Behavior.* New York: Tavistock, 1982.

Patterson, Gerald R. *Living With Children: New Methods for Parents and Teachers.* Champaign, Ill.: Research Press, 1976.

Pryor, Karen. *Don't Shoot the Dog.* New York: Simon & Schuster, 1984.

Rice, Elizabeth Prince; Ekdahl, Miriam C.; and Miller, Leo. *Children of Mentally Ill Parents: Problems in Child Care.* New York: Behavioral Publications, 1971.

Safran, Claire. "Speaking of Sex." *Parents,* Feb. 1984, 59(2), 65–70; 149.

Schaffer, Rudolph. *Mothering.* Cambridge, Mass.: Harvard University Press, 1977.

Schwartz, Arthur; Goldiamond, Israel; and Howe, Michael W. *Social Casework: A Behavioral Approach.* New York: Columbia University Press, 1975.

Shure, Myrna B., and Spivack, George. *Problem-Solving Techniques in Child-rearing.* San Francisco: Jossey-Bass, 1978.

Simon, Sidney B.; Howe, Leland W.; and Kirschenbaum, Howard. *Values Clarification: A Handbook of Practical Strategies for Teachers and Students.* New York: Dodd, 1985.

Skolnick, Arlene. "The Myth of the Vulnerable Child." *Psychology Today,* Feb. 1978, 11(9), 56–65.

Steinmetz, Suzanne K., and Strauss, Murray A., eds. *Violence in the Family.* New York: Harper, 1974.

Stern, Daniel. *The First Relationship: Mother and Infant.* Cambridge, Mass.: Harvard University Press, 1977.

Stern, Daniel. *The Interpersonal World of the Infant: A View From Psychoanalysis and Developmental Psychology.* New York: Basic Books, 1985.

Weiss, Joan S. *Your Second Child.* New York: Summit, 1981.

Windmiller, Myra; Lambert, Nadine; and Turiel, Elliot. *Moral Development and Socialization.* Boston: Allyn & Bacon, 1980.

CHAPTER 4
SPECIAL EVENTS AND STRESSES

REFERENCES

1. U.S. Department of Health and Human Services, Centers for Disease Control. *Health Information for International Travel,* June 1986. Atlanta, Ga., (HHS Pub. #(CDC) 86-8280).

2. Coddington, R. Dean. "The Significance of Life Events as Etiologic Factors in the Diseases of Children." *Journal of Psychosomatic Research,* 1972, 16:7–18.

3. Holmes, Thomas H., and Rahe, Richard H. "The Social Readjustment Rating Scale." *Journal of Psychosomatic Research,* 1967, 11:213–18.

4. Coddington, op. cit., p. 12.

5. Lazarus, Richard S. "Little Hassles Can Be Hazardous to Health." *Psychology Today,* July 1981, 15:58–62.

6. Lazarus, op. cit., p. 60.

7. Ardrey, Robert. *The Territorial Imperative.* New York: Atheneum, 1968.

8. Finkelhor, David. *Child Sexual Abuse: New Theory and Research.* New York: Free Press, 1984.

9. Kempe, C. Henry. "Sexual Abuse, Another Hidden Pediatric Problem: The 1977 C. Anderson Aldrich Lecture." *Pediatrics*, Sept. 1978, 62(3), 382–89.
10. Rimsza, Mary Ellen, and Niggemann, Elaine H. "Medical Evaluation of Sexually Abused Children: A Review of 311 Cases." *Pediatrics*, Jan. 1982, 69(1), 8–14.
11. Sarles, Richard M. "Incest." *Pediatrics in Review*, Aug. 1980, 2(2), 51–54.
12. Greenberg, Nikki Finke. "The Simple Rules of Safety." *Newsweek*, March 19, 1984, pp. 80–81.
13. Bergman, Abraham B. "The Business of Missing Children." *Pediatrics*, Jan. 1986, 77(1), 119–21.
14. Black, B.L. "The Frightening Epidemic of Child Snatching." *Medical News Magazine*, 1982, 26:162.
15. Terr, Lenore C. "Child Snatching: A New Epidemic of an Ancient Malady." *The Journal of Pediatrics*, July 1983, 103(1), 151–56.
16. Straus, Murray A.; Gelles, Richard J.; and Steinmetz, Suzanne K. *Behind Closed Doors: Violence in the American Family*. Garden City, N.Y.: Anchor Press/Doubleday, 1980.
17. Straus, op. cit., p. 32.
18. Roy, Maria, ed. *Battered Women: A Psychosociological Study of Domestic Violence*. New York: Van Nostrand, 1977.
19. Gil, David G. *Violence Against Children*. Cambridge, Mass.: Harvard University Press, 1970.
20. Kempe, C. Henry; Silverman, Frederic N.; Steele, Brandt F.; Droegemueller, William; and Silver, Henry K. "The Battered-Child Syndrome." *Journal of the American Medical Association*, July 7, 1962, 181:17–24.
21. Heins, Marilyn. "The 'Battered Child' Revisited." *Journal of the American Medical Association*, June 22/29, 1984, 251(24), 3295–330.
22. Helfer, Ray M. "The Etiology of Child Abuse." *Pediatrics*, April 1973, 51(4), Part II, 777–79.
23. Dietrich, Kim N.; Starr, Raymond H., Jr.; and Weisfeld, Glenn E. "Infant Maltreatment: Caretaker-Infant Interaction and Developmental Consequences at Different Levels of Parenting Failure." *Pediatrics*, Oct. 1983, 72(4), 532–40.
24. *Morbidity and Mortality Weekly Report*. "Blood Alcohol Concentrations Among Young Drivers—United States, 1982." *Journal of the American Medical Association*. Jan. 6, 1984, 251(1), 23.
25. Vaillant, George E. *Adaptation to Life*. Boston: Little, Brown, 1977.

SOURCE MATERIAL

Bandler, Richard; Grinder, John; and Satir, Virginia. *Changing with Families: A Book About Further Education for Being Human*. Palo Alto, Calif.: Science and Behavior Books, 1976.
Barrett, Michele, and McIntosh, Mary. *The Anti-Social Family*. London: Verso, 1982.
Berger, Brigitte, and Berger, Peter L. *The War Over the Family: Capturing the Middle Ground*. Garden City, N.Y.: Anchor Press/Doubleday, 1983.
Boyd, Jeffrey H., and Weissman, Myrna M. "Epidemiology of Affective Disorders." *Archives of General Psychiatry*. Sept. 1981, 38:1039–46.
Brazelton, T. Berry. *On Becoming a Family: The Growth of Attachment*. New York: Delacorte, 1981.
Brim, Orville G., Jr., and Kagan, Jerome, eds. *Constancy and Change in Human Development*. Cambridge, Mass.: Harvard University Press, 1980.
de Young, Mary. *The Sexual Victimization of Children*. Jefferson, N.C.: McFarland, 1982.
Gurman, Alan S., ed. *Questions and Answers in the Practice of Family Therapy*, Vol. 1. New York: Brunner/Mazel, 1981.

Gurman, Alan S. *Questions and Answers in the Practice of Family Therapy,* Vol. 2. New York: Brunner/Mazel, 1982.

Gurman, Alan S., and Kniskern, David P. *Handbook of Family Therapy.* New York: Brunner/Mazel, 1981.

Herman, Judith. *Father-Daughter Incest.* Cambridge, Mass.: Harvard University Press, 1982.

Kramer, Rita. *In Defense of the Family: Raising Children in America Today.* New York: Basic Books, 1983.

Lansky, Vicki. *Traveling With Your Baby.* New York: Bantam, 1985.

McGoldrick, Monica, and Carter, Elizabeth A. "The Family Cycle." In Walsh, Froma, ed. *Normal Family Processes.* New York: Guilford, 1982.

McGoldrick, Monica; Pearce, John K.; and Giordano, Joseph, eds. *Ethnicity and Family Therapy.* New York: Guilford, 1982.

Oakley, Ann. *The Sociology of Housework.* New York: Pantheon, 1975.

Patterson, Gerald R. *Families: Applications of Social Learning to Family Life.* Champaign, Ill.: Research Press, 1975.

Pogrebin, Letty Cottin. *Family Politics: Love and Power on an Intimate Frontier.* New York: McGraw-Hill, 1983.

Poster, Mark. *Critical Theory of the Family.* New York: Continuum, 1978.

Procaccini, Joseph, and Kiefaber, Mark W. *Parent Burnout.* New York: New American Library, 1983.

Rapoport, Rhona; Rapoport, Robert N.; and Strelitz, Ziona. *Fathers, Mothers and Society: Perspectives on Parenting.* New York: Random House, 1980.

Rubin, Theodore Isaac, and Rubin, Eleanor. *Not to Worry: The American Family Book of Mental Health.* New York: Viking, 1984.

Simonton, Stephanie Matthews, and Shook, Robert L. *The Healing Family: The Simonton Approach for Families Facing Illness.* New York: Bantam, 1984.

Vine, Phyllis. *Families in Pain.* New York: Pantheon, 1982.

Yates, Alayne. "Book Review: *It's OK to Say No!*" by Smith, Frank, and Lurie, Susan. New York: Playmore, Inc., Publishers, and Waldman Publishing Corp., 1984. In *American Journal of Diseases of Children,* June 1985, 139:613.

CHAPTER 5
SAFETY FIRST, SAFETY ALWAYS

REFERENCES

1. Haller, J. Alex, Jr. "Pediatric Trauma, The No. 1 Killer of Children." *Journal of the American Medical Association,* Jan. 7, 1983, 249(1), 47.

2. Margolis, Lewis H., and Runyan, Carol W. "Accidental Policy: An Analysis of the Problem of Unintended Injuries of Childhood." *American Journal of Orthopsychiatry,* Oct. 1983, 53(4), 629–44.

3. Ibid.

4. Klein, David. "Societal Influences on Childhood Accidents." *Accidental Analysis and Prevention,* 1980, 12:275–81.

5. U.S. Department of Health and Human Services, Centers for Disease Control, Atlanta, Ga. "Unintentional and Intentional Injuries—United States." *Morbidity and Mortality Weekly Report,* May 14, 1982, 31(18), 240–48.

6. Margolis, op. cit., p. 629.

7. Stover, Samuel, and Fine, Philip R., eds. *Spinal Cord Injury, The Facts and Figures.* Birmingham, Ala.: University of Alabama, 1986.

8. Harmon, Murl. *A New Vaccine for Child Safety.* Jenkintown, Pa.: Safety Now Co., 1976.

9. Kalt, Bryson R., and Bass, Ralph. *The Mother's Guide to Child Safety*. New York: Grosset & Dunlap, 1971.
10. Bass, Joel L., and Mehta, Kishor A. "Developmentally-Oriented Safety Surveys." *Clinical Pediatrics*, May 1980, 19(5), 350–56.
11. Reisinger, Keith S., and William, Allan F. "Evaluation of Programs Designed to Increase the Protection of Infants in Cars." *Pediatrics*, Sept. 1978, 62(3), 280–87.
12. American Academy of Pediatrics, Committee on Accident Prevention. *"Responsibility Means Safety for Your Child."* Elk Grove Village, Ill., 1964.
13. Lovejoy, Frederick H., and Chafee-Bahamon, Claire. "The Physician's Role in Accident Prevention." *Pediatrics in Review*, Aug. 1982, 4(2), 53–60.
14. O'Shea, John S.; Collins, Edward W.; and Butler, Christine B. "Pediatric Accident Prevention." *Clinical Pediatrics*, May 1982, 21(5), 290–97.
15. Wheatley, George M. "Childhood Accidents 1952–72, An Overview." *Pediatric Annals*, Jan. 1973, 2(1), 10–28.
16. Langley, John; Silva, Phil A.; and Williams, Sheila. "A Study of the Relationship of 90 Background, Developmental, Behavioral, and Medical Factors to Childhood Accidents. A Report From the Dunedin Multidisciplinary Child Development Study." *Australian Paediatrics Journal*, Dec. 1980, 16:244–47.
17. Spiegel, Charlotte N., and Lindaman, Francis C. "Children Can't Fly: A Program to Prevent Childhood Morbidity and Mortality from Window Falls." *American Journal of Public Health*, Dec. 1977, 67(12), 1143–53.
18. O'Shea, op. cit., p. 294.
19. Christoffel, Katherine K., and Tanz, Robert. "Motor Vehicle Injury in Childhood." *Pediatrics in Review*, Feb. 1983, 4(8), 247-54.
20. Ibid.
21. Robertson, Leon S. "Crash Involvement of Teenaged Drivers When Driver Education Is Eliminated from High School." *American Journal of Public Health*, June 1980, 70(6), 599–603.
22. Christoffel, op. cit., p. 250.
23. Scherz, Robert G. "Fatal Motor Vehicle Accidents of Child Passengers from Birth Through 4 Years of Age in Washington State." *Pediatrics*, Oct. 1981, 68(4), 572–78.
24. Karwacki, Jerome J., Jr., and Baker, Susan P. "Children in Motor Vehicles." *Pediatric Alert*, Jan. 17, 1980, 5(2), 5–7.
25. Hletko, Paul J.; Hletko, Jana D.; Shelness, Annemarie M.; and Robin, Stanley S. "Demographic Predictors of Infant Car Seat Use." *American Journal of Diseases of Children*, Nov. 1983, 137:1061–63.
26. American Academy of Pediatrics. "AAP Schedules Launching of 'First Ride' Successor." *News and Comment*, Sept. 1983, 34(8), 1; 3.
27. Colletti, Richard B. "Hospital-Based Rental Programs to Increase Car Seat Usage." *Pediatrics*, May 1983, 71(5), 771–73.
28. U.S. Department of Health and Human Services, Centers for Disease Control, Atlanta, Ga. "State Action to Prevent Motor Vehicle Deaths and Injuries Among Children and Adolescents." *Morbidity and Mortality Weekly Report*, Sept. 10, 1982, 31(35), 488–90.
29. Christophersen, Edward R. "Automobile Accidents: Potential Years of Life Lost." *Pediatrics*, May 1983, 71(5), 855–56.
30. ———. "Children's Behavior During Automobile Rides: Do Car Seats Make a Difference?" *Pediatrics*, July 1977, 60(1), 69–74.
31. King, K.; Negus, K.; and Vance, J. C. "Heat Stress in Motor Vehicles: A Problem in Infancy." *Pediatrics*, Oct. 1981, 68(4), 579–82.
32. Rivara, Frederick P., and Barber, Melvin. "Demographic Analysis of Childhood Pedestrian Injuries." *Pediatrics*, Sept. 1985, 76(3), 375–81.
33. O'Shea, op. cit., p. 294.
34. Watson, Geoffrey S.; Zador, Paul L.; and Wilks, Alan. "The Repeal of Helmet Use

Laws and Increased Motorcyclist Mortality in the United States, 1975–1978." *American Journal of Public Health,* June 1980, 70:579–85.

35. McCormick, Mary A.; Lacouture, Peter G.; Gaudreault, Pierre; and Lovejoy, Frederick H. "Hazards Associated with Diaper Changing." *Journal of the American Medical Association.* Nov. 5, 1982, 248(17), 2159–60.

36. Mofenson, Howard C.; Greensher, Joseph; DiTomasso, Anthony; and Okun, Sharon. "Baby Powder—A Hazard!" *Pediatrics,* Aug. 1981, 68(2), 265–66.

37. Thompson, Janet C., and Ashwal, Stephen. "Electrical Injuries in Children." *American Journal of Diseases of Children,* March 1983, 137:231–35.

38. O'Shea, op. cit., p. 295.

39. U.S. Department of Health and Human Services, Centers for Disease Control, Atlanta, Ga. "Aquatic Deaths and Injuries—United States." *Morbidity and Mortality Weekly Report,* Aug. 13, 1982, 31(31), 417–19.

40. Sokol, Anthony B., and Houser, Robert G. "Dog Bites: Prevention and Treatment, Comments from the Surgeon's Viewpoint." *Clinical Pediatrics,* June 1971, 10(6), 336–38.

41. Klein, Daniel. "Friendly Dog Syndrome." *New York State Journal of Medicine,* Sept. 1, 1966, 66:2306–9.

42. Lauer, Eleanor A.; White, Wallace C.; and Lauer, Brian A. "Dog Bites: A Neglected Problem in Accident Prevention." *American Journal of Diseases of Children,* March 1982, 136:202–4.

43. Chun, Yoon-Taek; Berkelhamer, Jay E.; and Herold, Terry E. "Dog Bites in Children Less Than 4 Years Old." *Pediatrics,* Jan. 1982, 69(1), 119–20.

44. McMillan, Julia A.; Stockman, James A. III; and Oski, Frank A. *The Whole Pediatrician Catalog,* Vol. 3. Philadelphia: Saunders Co., 1982.

45. Pinckney, Lee E., and Kennedy, Leslie A. "Traumatic Deaths From Dog Attacks in the United States." *Pediatrics,* Feb. 1982, 69(2), 193–96.

46. Klein, op. cit., p. 2308.

47. Macknin, Michael L. "Dog and Cat Bites." *Pediatric Basics,* June 1983, 35:7–11. Fremont, Mich.: Medical Marketing Services, Gerber Products.

48. Copperman, Stuart M. "Cherchez le Chien: Household Pets as Reservoirs of Persistent or Recurrent Streptococcal Sore Throats in Children." *New York State Journal of Medicine,* Nov. 1982, pp. 1685–87.

49. Elliot, Diane L.; Tolle, Susan W.; Goldberg, Linn; and Miller, James B. "Pet-Associated Illness." *The New England Journal of Medicine,* October 17, 1985, 313(16), 985–95.

50. Diesch, Stanley L. "Reported Human Injuries or Health Threats Attributed to Wild or Exotic Animals Kept as Pets (1971–1981)." *Journal of the American Veterinary Medicine Association,* Feb. 15, 1982, 180(4), 382–83.

51. Heins, Marilyn; Kahn, Roger; and Bjordnal, Judy. "Gunshot Wounds in Children." *American Journal of Public Health,* April 1974, 64(4), 326–30.

52. Christoffel, Katherine K.; Tanz, Robert; Sagerman, Scott; and Hahn, Yoon. "Childhood Injuries Caused by Nonpowder Firearms." *American Journal of Diseases of Children,* June 1984, 138:557–61.

53. Blocker, Sterling; Coln, Dale; and Chang, Jack H. T. "Serious Air Rifle Injuries in Children." *Pediatrics,* June 1982, 69(6), 751–54.

54. Klein, F. C. "On Sports." *The Wall Street Journal,* Sept. 7, 1983.

55. Selbst, S.; Ruddy, R.; and Alexander, D. "Bicycle Related Injuries." *Ambulatory Pediatric Association Program and Abstracts,* 24th Annual Meeting, 1984.

56. Weiss, Barry D. "Bicycle Helmet Use by Children." *Pediatrics,* May 1986, 77(5), 677–79.

57. Sneed, R. C.; Stover, Samuel L.; and Fine, Philip R. "Spinal Cord Injury Associated With All-Terrain Vehicle Accidents." *Pediatrics,* March 1986, 77(3), 271–74.

58. American Academy of Pediatrics. "AAP Hits Three-Wheel ATVs." *Government Activities Report*, Washington, D.C., June 1985.
59. Beautrais, A. L.; Fergusson, D. M.; and Shannon, F. T. "Life Events and Childhood Morbidity: A Prospective Study." *Pediatrics*, Dec. 1982, 70(6), 935–40.
60. Graves, C. "A Case for Prevention: Childhood Power Lawnmower Injuries." *Ambulatory Pediatric Association Program and Abstracts*, 25th Annual Meeting, 1985.
61. Rivara, Frederick P.; Bergman, Abraham B.; LoGerfo, James P.; and Weiss, Noel S. "Epidemiology of Childhood Injuries, II. Sex Differences in Injury Rates." *American Journal of Diseases of Children*, June 1982, 136:502–6.
62. Harris, Carole Stallings; Baker, Susan P.; Smith, Gary A.; and Harris, Richard M. "Childhood Asphyxiation by Food: A National Analysis and Overview." *Journal of the American Medical Association*, May 4, 1984, 251(17), 2231–35.
63. Budnick, Lawrence D. "Toothpick Related Injuries in the United States, 1979 Through 1982." *Journal of the American Medical Association*, Aug. 10, 1984, 252(6), 796–97.
64. Siegel, Leighton G.; Mendenhall, H. V.; and Liston, Stephen L. "Christmas Bow Pins: Potential Inhaled Foreign Body Made Safer by Industrial Modifications." *Southern Medical Journal*, Jan. 1981, 74:17–20.
65. Kravath, Richard E.; Kleinhaus, Sylvain; and Goldfarb, Joseph D. "Prevention of Childhood Accidents by Eliminating the Agent of Injury." *The Journal of Pediatrics*, Oct. 1981, 99(4), 575–76.
66. U.S. Consumer Product Safety Commission. " 'Questor' Crib Brackets and Mattress Support Hangers to be Replaced." *Consumer Product Safety Alert*, Washington, D.C., July 1985.
67. Fazen, Louis E. III, and Felizberto, Pamela I. "Baby Walker Injuries." *Pediatrics*, July 1982, 70(1), 106–9.
68. U.S. Consumer Product Safety Commission. "CPSC Warns Consumers of Dangers With Mesh Drop-Side Playpens and Portable Cribs." *Consumer Product Safety Alert*, Washington, D.C., July 1985.
69. Millunchick, E. W., and McArtor, R. D. "Fatal Aspiration of a Makeshift Pacifier." *Pediatrics*, March 1986, 77(3), 369–70.
70. U.S. Department of Health and Human Services, Centers for Disease Control, Atlanta, Ga. "588,000 Children in ER with Toy-Related Injuries During '84." *Pediatric News*, March 1986, 20(3), 37.
71. "Toy Safety—United States, 1984." Leads from the MMWR. *Journal of the American Medical Association*. Jan. 17, 1986, 255(3), 312–13.
72. U.S. Consumer Product Safety Commission. "CPSC Warns Consumers of Suffocation Danger Associated with Children's Balloons." *Consumer Product Safety Alert*, Washington, D.C., March 1985.
73. Axelsson, Alf, and Jerson, Thomas. "Noisy Toys: A Possible Source of Sensorineural Hearing Loss." *Pediatrics*, Oct. 1985, 76(4), 574–78.
74. U.S. Consumer Product Safety Commission. "CPSC Issues Complaint Seeking Recall of Johnson & Johnson Crib Toys." *Consumer Product Safety Alert*, Washington, D.C., June 1986.
75. Harmon, op. cit., pp. 153–63.
76. The Editors of *Consumer Guide. The Complete Baby Book*. New York: Simon & Schuster, 1979.
77. U.S. Consumer Product Safety Commission. "CPSC Warns Parents About Child Accidents in Recliner Chairs." *Consumer Product Safety Alert*, Washington, D.C., July 1985.
78. U.S. Consumer Product Safety Commission. "CPSC Warns Consumers of Bunk Bed Hazards." *Consumer Product Safety Alert*, Washington, D.C., March 1985.
79. Kavanagh, Kevin T., and Litovitz, Toby. "Miniature Battery Foreign Bodies in Audi-

tory and Nasal Cavities." *Journal of the American Medical Association*, March 21, 1986, 255(11), 1470–72.

SOURCE MATERIAL

Agran, Phyllis F.; Dunkle, Debora E.; and Winn, Diane G. "Motor Vehicle Accident Trauma and Restraint Usage Patterns in Children Less Than 4 Years of Age." *Pediatrics*, Sept. 1985, 76(3), 382–86.

Agran, Phyllis F., and Dunkle, Debora E. "Motor Vehicle Occupant Injuries to Children in Crash and Noncrash Events." *Pediatrics*, Dec. 1982, 70(6), 993–96.

American Academy of Pediatrics, Michigan Chapter. *Pointed Facts About Glass Safety.* Ann Arbor, Mich.

Arizona Poison Control System, University of Arizona Health Sciences Center. *Safety Guide for Poisoning.* (Toll-free statewide: 1-800-362-0101, 24-hour poison and drug information.)

Awan, Khalid J. "Smoking and Eye Injuries to Toddlers." *Journal of American Medical Association*, June 15, 1984, 251(23), 3080.

Bijur, Polly E.; Stewart-Brown, Sarah; and Butler, Neville. "Child Behavior and Accidental Injury in 11,966 Preschool Children." *American Journal of Diseases of Children*, May 1986, 140:487–92.

Budnick, Lawrence D. "Bathtub-Related Electrocutions in the United States, 1979 to 1982." *Journal of American Medical Association*, Aug. 17, 1984, 252(7), 918–20.

Chang, Albert; Dillman, Arline S.; Leonard, Elaine; and English, Patricia. "Teaching Car Passenger Safety to Preschool Children." *Pediatrics*, Sept. 1985, 76(3), 425–28.

Dershewitz, Robert A. "Insect Bites." *Pediatric Basics*, June 1983, 35:12–15. Fremont, Mich.: Medical Marketing Services, Gerber Products.

Kavanagh, Carol A., and Banco, Leonard. "The Infant Walker." *American Journal of Diseases of Children.* March 1982, 136:205–6.

Litovitz, Toby L. "Button Battery Ingestions: A Review of 56 Cases." *The Journal of the American Medical Association*, May 13, 1983, 249(18), 2495–500.

Miller, Robert E.; Reisinger, Keith S.; Blatter, Mark M.; and Wucher, Frederick. "Pediatric Counseling and Subsequent Use of Smoke Detectors." *American Journal of Public Health*, April 1982, 72(4), 392–93.

National Safety Council. "School Bus Accidents, 1982." *Accident Facts*, 1983, pp. 92–93.

Osborne, Sheri C., and Garrettson, Lorne K. "Perception of Toxicity and Dose by 3- and 4-Year-Old Children." *American Journal of Diseases of Children*, Aug. 1985, 139:790–92.

Pless, I. Barry, and Stulginskas, Joan. "Accidents and Violence As a Cause of Morbidity and Mortality in Childhood." *Advances in Pediatrics.* 1982, 29:471–95.

Shaffer, T. E. "Accident Prevention at Various Age Levels." *Pediatric Clinics of North America*, 1954, 1:426, 427.

U.S. Department of Health and Human Services. Centers for Disease Control, Atlanta, Ga.: "Update: Childhood Poisoning—United States." *Morbidity and Mortality Weekly Report*, March 8, 1985, 34(9), 117–18.

CHAPTER 6
HELPERS IN CHILD CARE

REFERENCES

1. Siegel-Gorelick, Bryna. *The Working Parents' Guide to Child Care*. Boston: Little, Brown, 1983.

2. Alston, Frances Kemper. *Caring for Other People's Children: A Complete Guide to Family Day Care.* Baltimore: University Park Press, 1984.
3. Department of the Treasury, Internal Revenue Service, *Child and Disabled Dependent Care.* Washington, D.C.: Publication 503, Nov. 1982.
4. Clarke-Stewart, Alison. *Daycare.* Cambridge, Mass.: Harvard University Press, 1982.
5. Watson, Russell. "What Price Day Care?" *Newsweek,* Sept. 10, 1984, pp. 14–21.
6. DeConcini, Susan. "Need for Day Care Grows as More Moms Go to Work." *Arizona Daily Star,* Dec. 4, 1983.
7. Langway, Lynn. "Schools for Modern Nannies." *Newsweek,* May 21, 1984, pp. 63–64.
8. Clarke-Stewart, op. cit., p. 139.
9. Goodman, Richard A.; Osterholm, Michael T.; Granoff, Dan M.; and Pickering, Larry K. "Infectious Diseases and Child Day Care." *Pediatrics,* July 1984, 74(1), 134–39.
10. Pickering, Larry K.; Woodward, William E.; DuPont, Herbert L.; and Sullivan, Peggy. "Occurrence of Giardia Lamblia in Children in Day Care Centers." *The Journal of Pediatrics,* April 1984, 104(4), 522–26.
11. Sullivan, Peggy; Woodward, William E.; Pickering, Larry K.; and DuPont, Herbert L. "Longitudinal Study of Occurrence of Diarrheal Disease in Day Care Centers." *American Journal of Public Health,* Sept. 1984, 74(9), 987–91.
12. Marwick, Charles. "Changing Childhood Disease Pattern Linked with Day-Care Boom." *Journal of the American Medical Association,* March 9, 1984, 251(10), 1245–47, 1250–52.
13. Aronson, Susan S., and Gilsdorf, Janet R. "Prevention and Management of Infectious Diseases in Day Care." *Pediatrics in Review,* March 1986, 7(9), 259–68.
14. Redmond, Stephen R., and Pichichero, Michael E. "Hemophilus Influenzae Type b Disease: An Epidemiologic Study with Special Reference to Day-Care Centers." *Journal of the American Medical Association,* Nov. 9, 1984, 252(18), 2581–84.
15. Phillips, Carol F. "New Immunizations for Children." *Pediatrics in Review,* April 1986, 7(10), 291–95.
16. U.S. Department of Health and Human Services, Centers for Disease Control, Atlanta, Ga. "Education and Foster Care of Children Infected with Human T-Lymphotropic Virus Type III/Lymphadenopathy-Associated Virus." *Morbidity and Mortality Weekly Report,* Aug. 30, 1985, 34(34), 517–21.
17. "Pediatricians Need to Be Able to Counsel Parents About Day Care, Including Pitfalls." *Pediatric News,* Jan. 1986, 20(1), 1; 54.
18. Brazelton, T. Berry. *Working and Caring.* Reading, Mass.: Addison-Wesley, 1985.
19. Siegel-Gorelick, op. cit., pp. 116–19.

SOURCE MATERIAL

American Public Health Association. "Policy Statement 7916: Provisions for Childcare." *American Journal of Public Health,* March 1980, 70(3), 308.
Aronson, Susan S., and Aiken, Leona S. "Compliance of Child Care Programs with Health and Safety Standards: Impact of Program Evaluation and Advocate Training." *Pediatrics,* Feb. 1980, 65(2), 318–25.
Bartlett, Alfred V.; Moore, Melinda; Gary, G. William; Starko, Karen M.; Erben, John J.; and Meredith, Betty A. "Diarrheal Illness Among Infants and Toddlers in Day Care Centers. I. Epidemiology and Pathogens." *The Journal of Pediatrics,* Oct. 1985, 107(4), 495–502.
———. "Diarrheal Illness Among Infants and Toddlers in Day Care Centers. II. Comparison with Day Care Homes and Households." *The Journal of Pediatrics,* Oct. 1985, 107(4), 503–9.

Belsky, Jay, and Steinberg, Laurence D. "The Effects of Day Care: A Critical Review." *Child Development*, Dec. 1978, 49(4), 929–49.

Chang, Albert; Zukerman, Steven; and Wallace, Helen M. "Health Service Needs of Children in Day Care Centers." *American Journal of Public Health*, April 1978, 68(4), 373–77.

Chang, Albert. "Health Services in Licensed Family Day Care Homes." *American Journal of Public Health*, June 1979, 69(6), 603–4.

Child Development Associate Credential. CDA National Credentialing Program, Bank Street College of Education, Washington, D.C.

David, Miriam E. "Day Care Policies and Parenting." *Journal of Social Policy*, 1982, 11(1), 81–91.

Dittman, Laura L. "Finding the Best Care for Your Infant or Toddler." *Young Children*, March 1986, pp. 43–46.

Endsley, Richard C.; Bradbard, Marilyn R.; and Readdick, Christine A. "High-Quality Proprietary Day Care: Predictors of Parents' Choices." *Journal of Family Issues*, March 1984, 5(1), 131–52.

Etaugh, Claire. "Effects of Nonmaternal Care on Children: Research Evidence and Popular Views." *American Psychologist*, April 1980, 35(4), 309–19.

Fenn, Donna. "Day Care Chains." *Working Woman*, Aug. 1983, pp. 104, 106, 108.

Galinski, Ellen, and Hooks, William A. *The New Extended Family: Day Care Programs That Work.* Boston: Houghton Mifflin, 1977.

Greenleaf, Barbara Kaye, with Schaffer, Lewis A. *Help: A Handbook for Working Mothers.* New York: Berkley, 1979.

Haskins, Ron, and Kotch, Jonathan. "Day Care and Illness: Evidence, Costs, and Public Policy." *Pediatrics* (Supplement), June 1986, 77(6), Part II, 951–82.

Hoang, Thu. "Community Family Day Care: An Intermediate Solution Between Family Care and Institutional Care." *Pediatrics*, Nov. 1981, 68(5), 748–49.

Istre, Gregory R.; Conner, Judy S.; Broome, Claire V.; Hightower, Allen; and Hopkins, Richard S. "Risk Factors for Primary Invasive Hemophilus Influenzae Disease: Increased Risk From Day-Care Attendance and School-Aged Household Members." *The Journal of Pediatrics*, Feb. 1985, 106:190–95.

Lamb, Michael E., ed. *Nontraditional Families: Parenting and Child Development.* Hillsdale, N.J.: Lawrence Erlbaum Associates, 1982.

Lansky, Vicki. *Dear Babysitter: Sitter's Handbook and Notepad.* Deephaven, Minn.: Meadowbrook Press, 1982.

Meredith, Dennis. "Day Care: The Nine-to-Five Dilemma." *Psychology Today*, Feb. 1986, 20(2), 36–39, 42–44.

Mitchell, Grace. *The Day Care Book.* New York: Stein & Day, 1979.

Nelton, Sharon. "Today's Compact Living: How to Choose a Day Care Center." Dec. 18, 1983.

Pass, Robert F.; Hutto, Cecelia; Ricks, Rebecca; and Cloud, Gretchen A. "Increased Rate of Cytomegalovirus Infection Among Parents of Children Attending Day Care Centers." *The New England Journal of Medicine*, May 29 1986, 314(22), 1414–18.

Pickering, Larry K. "The Day Care Center Diarrhea Dilemma." *American Journal of Public Health*, June 1986, 76(6), 623–24.

Provence, Sally; Naylor, Audrey; and Patterson, June. *The Challenge of Daycare.* New Haven: Yale University Press, 1977.

Provence, Sally. "Infant Day Care: Relationships Between Theory and Practice." In Zigler, Edward F., and Gordon, Edmund W., eds., *Day Care: Scientific and Social Policy Issues*, Boston: Auburn House, 1982.

Redmond, Stephen R., and Pichichero, Michael E. "Hemophilus Influenzae Type b Disease: Epidemiologic Study with Special Reference to Day-Care Centers." *Journal of the American Medical Association*, Nov. 9, 1984, 252:2581–83.

Rice, F. Philip. *The Working Mother's Guide to Child Development.* Englewood Cliffs, N.J.: Prentice-Hall, 1979.

Ross Laboratories. *Daycare.* Report of the Sixteenth Ross Roundtable on Critical Approaches to Common Pediatric Problems in Collaboration with the Ambulatory Pediatric Association. Columbus, Ohio: Ross Laboratories, July 1985.

Scott, Niki. *The Working Woman: A Handbook.* Fairway, Kans.: Andrews, McMeel & Parker, 1977.

Sealy, David P., and Schuman, Stanley H. "Endemic Giardiasis and Day Care." *Pediatrics,* August 1983, 72(2), 154–58.

Steinfels, Margaret O'Brien. *Who's Minding the Children? The History and Politics of Day Care in America.* New York: Simon & Schuster, 1973.

Weisner, Thomas S., and Gallimore, Ronald. "My Brother's Keeper: Child and Sibling Caretaking." *Current Anthropology,* June 1977, 18(2), 169–90.

Werner, Emmy E. *Child Care: Kith, Kin, and Hired Hands.* Austin, Tex.: Pro Ed, 1984.

Zambrana, Ruth E.; Hurst, Marsha; and Hite, Rodney L. "The Working Mother in Contemporary Perspective: A Review of the Literature." *Pediatrics,* Dec. 1979, 64(6), 862–70.

Zigler, Edward F., and Gordon, Edmund W. *Day Care: Scientific and Social Policy Issues.* Boston: Auburn House, 1982.

CHAPTER 7
CHILDREN'S GROWTH AND DEVELOPMENT

REFERENCES

1. Darwin, Charles R. "A Biographical Sketch of an Infant." *Mind,* July 1877, 2:286.
2. Menaker, Daniel. "Bringing Up Baby, or Vice Versa." New York *Times Magazine,* Nov. 27, 1983.
3. Will, George F. "Don't Look to Einstein for Child-Raising Theory." *Arizona Daily Star,* June 11, 1984.
4. Caldwell, Bettye M., and Richmond, Julius B. "The Impact of Theories of Child Development." *Children,* March–April 1962, 9(2), 73–78.
5. Kessen, William, and Scott, David. "The Development of Behavior: Problems, Theories, and Findings." In Levine, Melvin D.; Carey, William B.; Crocker, Allen C.; and Gross, Ruth T., eds. *Developmental-Behavioral Pediatrics.* Philadelphia: Saunders, 1983, p. 32.
6. Holt, L. Emmett, Jr. *Care and Feeding of Children.* 14th ed. D. Appleton and Co., New York, 1929.
7. Freud, Sigmund. *Civilization and Its Discontents.* (1930) In *The Standard Edition of the Complete Psychological Works of Sigmund Freud.* 21:59–145, London: Hogarth Press, 1955.
8. Freud, Sigmund. *New Introduction Lectures on Psycho-Analyses.* (1933) In *The Standard Edition of the Complete Psychological Works of Sigmund Freud.* 22:3–182, New York: Norton, 1933.
9. Mussen, Paul H., ed. *Handbook of Child Psychology: History, Theories and Methods.* Vol. 1, 4 ed. New York: Wiley, 1983.
10. Kohut, Heinz. *The Analysis of the Self: A Systematic Approach to the Psychoanalytic Treatment of Narcissistic Personality Disorders.* New York: International Universities Press, 1971.
11. Kohut, Heinz. *The Restoration of the Self.* New York: International Universities Press, 1977.
12. Ornstein, Paul H. "Self-Psychology and the Concept of Health." In Goldberg, Ar-

nold, ed. *Advances in Self-Psychology*, Vols. 1 and 2. New York: International Universities Press, 1978.

13. Gesell, Arnold. *The First Five Years of Life: The Preschool Years.* New York: Harper, 1940, p. 22.
14. Caldwell, op. cit., p. 75.
15. Maslow, Abraham H., ed. *Motivation and Personality*, 2nd ed. New York: Harper, 1970.
16. ———. *Toward a Psychology of Being*, 2nd ed. Princeton: Van Nostrand, 1968.
17. Havighurst, Robert J. *Developmental Tasks and Education*, 3rd ed. New York: Longman, 1979.
18. Chess, Stella, and Thomas, Alexander. "Individuality" (Chapter 10) in Levine, Melvin D.; Carey, William B.; Crocker, Allen C.; and Gross, Ruth T., eds. *Developmental-Behavioral Pediatrics.* Philadelphia: Saunders, 1983.
19. Lewis, Melvin. *Clinical Aspects of Child Development*, 2nd ed. Philadelphia: Lea & Febiger, 1982.
20. Ibid., p. 4.
21. Ibid., p. 7.
22. Hofer, Myron A. *The Roots of Human Behavior: An Introduction to the Psychobiology of Early Development.* San Francisco: W. H. Freeman, 1981, p. 73.
23. Kolata, Gina. "Studying Learning in the Womb." *Science*, July 20, 1984, 225:302–3.
24. Thoman, Evelyn B., and Trotter, Sharland, eds. *Social Responsiveness of Infants.* Piscataway, N.J.: Johnson & Johnson Baby Products Co., 1978.
25. Bower, T.G.R. *The Perceptual World of the Child.* Cambridge, Mass.: Harvard University Press, 1977.
26. WGBH Educational Foundation. *Baby Talk.* NOVA #1207, February 26, 1985, Boston, Massachusetts.
27. de Villiers, Peter A., and de Villiers, Jill G. *Early Language.* Cambridge, Mass.: Harvard University Press, 1979.
28. Mindel, Eugene. Personal communication.
29. de Villiers, op. cit., p. 59.
30. Lewis, op. cit., p. 92.
31. Lewis, op. cit., p. 95.
32. Ausubel, David P.; Sullivan, Edmund V.; and Ives, S. William. *Theory and Problems of Child Development*, 3rd ed. New York: Grune & Stratton, 1980.
33. Schuster, Clara Shaw, and Ashburn, Shirley Smith. *The Process of Human Development: A Holistic Approach.* Boston: Little, Brown, 1980, p. 545.
34. Sullivan, Edmund V. "Can Values Be Taught?" In Windmiller, Myra; Lambert, Nadine; and Turiel, Elliott, eds. *Moral Development and Socialization.* Boston: Allyn & Bacon, 1980, pp. 219–43.
35. Gilligan, Carol. "In a Different Voice: Women's Conceptions of Self and of Morality." *Harvard Educational Review*, Nov. 1977, 47(4), 481–517.
36. Haan, Norma; Aerts, Eliane; and Cooper, Bruce A. B. *On Moral Grounds: The Search for Practical Morality.* New York: New York University Press, 1985.
37. Coles, Robert. *Moral Life of Children.* Boston: Atlantic Monthly Press, 1986.
38. Lewis, op. cit., p. 19.
39. Stern, Daniel. *The First Relationship, Infant and Mother.* Cambridge, Mass.: Harvard University Press, 1977, p. 18.
40. Ibid., p. 27.
41. Brazelton, T. Berry. *Infants and Mothers: Differences in Development.* New York: Dell, 1983.
42. Schuster, op. cit., p. 188.
43. Ibid., p. 190.
44. Ibid., p. 282.
45. Ibid., p. 504.

46. Holden, Constance. "Identical Twins Reared Apart." *Science,* March 1980, 207(21), 1323–25; 1327–28.
47. Kaye, Kenneth. *The Mental and Social Life of Babies: How Parents Create Persons.* Chicago: University of Chicago Press, 1979.
48. Spitz, R. A., and Wolf, K. M. "Anaclitic Depression: An Inquiry into the Genesis of Psychiatric Conditions in Early Childhood." *The Psychoanalytic Study of the Child,* Vol. II. New York: International Universities Press, 1946, p. 313.
49. Bowlby, J. M. *Maternal Care and Mental Health,* 2nd ed. Geneva: World Health Organization, Monograph Series No. 2, 1952.
50. Schuster, op. cit., p. 199.
51. Trelease, Jim. *The Read-Aloud Handbook.* Wheaton, Ill.: Tyndale, 1983.
52. "Impact of Infancy on Later Life Called 'Complex'." *News Bulletin,* American Academy of Pediatrics, 1985, 22(1), 2.
53. Garvey, Catherine. *Play.* Cambridge, Mass.: Harvard University Press, 1977.
54. Chance, Paul. *Learning Through Play.* New York: Gardner Press, 1979.
55. Garvey, op. cit., p. 7.
56. Ibid., p. 35.
57. Ibid., p. 39.
58. Ford, Barbara. "Learning to Play. Playing to Learn." *National Wildlife,* June/July, 1983, 21:13.
59. Chance, op. cit., p. 35.
60. Yahraes, Herbert. "Developing a Sense of Competence in Young Children." In Corfman, Eunice, ed. *Families Today,* Vol. II. Rockville, Md.: NIMH Science Monographs 1. U.S. Department of Health, Education, and Welfare, National Institute of Mental Health, 1979.
61. White, Burton L. *The First Three Years of Life:* revised ed. New York: Prentice-Hall, 1985.
62. Marshall, Loretta Slota, and Marshall, W. E. "Your Artist-in-Residence." *Sesame Street Parents' Newsletter,* June 1982, 2(4), 1; 4–5.
63. Field, Tiffany M.; Woodson, Robert; Greenberg, Reena; and Cohen, Debra. "Discrimination and Imitation of Facial Expression by Neonates." *Science,* Oct. 1982, 218:179–81.
64. Rubin, Zick. *Children's Friendships.* Cambridge, Mass.: Harvard University Press, 1980, p. 28.
65. Selman, Robert. Cited in Rubin, Zick, *Children's Friendships.* Cambridge, Mass.: Harvard University Press, 1980, p. 37.
66. Rubin, op. cit., p. 52.
67. Ibid., p. 122.
68. Schuster, op. cit., p. 541.
69. Ibid., p. 548.
70. Cucinatto, John. "A Public School Teacher's Lament." Boston *Globe,* Aug. 8, 1983.
71. Coplan, James. "Parental Estimate of Child's Developmental Level in a High-Risk Population." *American Journal of Diseases of Children,* Feb. 1982, 136(2), 101–4.
72. Kupfer, Fern. *Before and After Zachariah.* New York: Delacorte, 1982.
73. Korsch, Barbara; Cobb, Katharine; and Ashe, Barbara. "Pediatricians' Appraisals of Patients' Intelligence." *Pediatrics.* June 1961, 27(6), 990–1003.
74. Opitz, John M. "Mental Retardation: Biologic Aspects of Concern to Pediatricians." *Pediatrics in Review,* Aug. 1980, 2(2), 41–50.
75. Oberklaid, Frank, and Levine, Melvin D. "Precursors of School Failure." *Pediatrics in Review,* July 1980, 2(1), 5–11.
76. Rappaport, Leonard; Levine, Melvin D.; Aufseeser, Cary; and Incerto, Richard A. "Children's Descriptions of Their Developmental Dysfunctions." *American Journal of Diseases of Children,* April 1983, 137:369–74.
77. Schuster, op. cit., p. 4.

SOURCE MATERIAL

Behrman, Richard E., and Vaughan, Victor C. III, eds. *Nelson Textbook of Pediatrics*, 12th ed. Philadelphia: Saunders, 1983.

Birren, James E.; Kinney, Dennis K.; Schaie, K. Warner; and Woodruff, Diana S. *Developmental Psychology, a Life-Span Approach*. Boston: Houghton Mifflin, 1981.

Brown, Catherine Caldwell, and Gottfried, Allen W., eds. *Play Interactions: The Role of Toys and Parental Involvement in Children's Development*. Pediatric Round Table: 11, Sponsored by Johnson & Johnson Baby Products Company, Piscataway, N.J.: 1985.

Cadden, Vivian. " 'Yes' to Love and Joyful Faces." *Life*, Dec. 17, 1971.

Capute, Arnold J., and Shapiro, Bruce K. "The Motor Quotient: A Method for the Early Detection of Motor Delay." *American Journal of Diseases of Children*, Sept. 1985, 139:940–42.

Carey, William B. "Validity of Parental Assessments of Development and Behavior." *American Journal of Diseases of Children*, Feb. 1982, 136:97–99.

Chess, Stella, and Thomas, Alexander, eds. *Annual Progress in Child Psychiatry and Child Development*. New York: Brunner/Mazel, 1980.

Chess, Stella, and Thomas, Alexander. "Individuality" in Levine, Melvin D.; Carey, William B.; Crocker, Allen C.; and Gross, Ruth T. *Developmental-Behavioral Pediatrics*. Philadelphia: Saunders, 1983.

Chugani, Harry T., and Phelps, Michael E. "Maturational Changes in Cerebral Function in Infants Determined by [18]FDG Positron Emission Tomography." *Science*, Feb. 21, 1986, 231:840–43.

Ernst, Cecile, and Angst, Jules. *Birth Order: Its Influence on Personality*. New York: Springer-Verlag, 1983.

Frankenburg, William K. Denver Prescreening Developmental Questionnaires. Ages 3–4 Months; 5–8 Months; 9–10 Months; 11–15 Months; 16–23 Months; 2 Years–2 Years, 9 Months; 3 Years–3 Years, 9 Months; 4 Years–4 Years, 9 Months; 5 Years–5 Years, 9 Months; 6 Years. University of Colorado Medical Center, 1975.

Frankenburg, William K. "Routine, Periodic Developmental Screening: Practical Approaches for Primary Health Care Providers." *Public Health Currents, Ross Timesaver*. Ross Laboratories, Columbus, Ohio, July–Sept. 1984, 24(4), 15–18.

Frankenburg, William K.; Fandal, Alma W.; Sciarillo, William; and Burgess, David. "The Newly Abbreviated and Revised Denver Developmental Screening Test." *The Journal of Pediatrics*, Dec. 1981, 99(6), 995–99.

Frankenburg, William, K.; van Doorninck, William J.; Liddell, Theresa N.; and Dick, Nathan P. "The Denver Prescreening Developmental Questionnaire (PDQ)." *Pediatrics*, 1976, 57:744–53.

Galenson, Eleanor, and Call, Justin D., eds. *Frontiers of Infant Psychiatry*, New York: Basic Books, 1983.

Gilligan, Carol. *In a Different Voice: Psychological Theory and Women's Development*. Cambridge, Mass.: Harvard University Press, 1982.

Goodnow, Jacqueline. *Children Drawing*. Cambridge, Mass.: Harvard University Press, 1977.

Kidwell, Jeannie S. "The Neglected Birth Order: Middle Borns." *Journal of Marriage and the Family*, Feb. 1982, 44:225–35.

Lidz, Theodore. *The Person, His and Her Development Throughout the Life Cycle*. New York: Basic Books, 1976.

Mayman, Martin, with Applebaum, Ann, and Basch, Michael, eds. "Infant Research: The Dawn of Awareness." Special issue of *Psychoanalytic Inquiry*, 1982, 1(4), 499–738.

Mussen, Paul. *Handbook of Child Psychology: Cognitive Development*. Vol. 3. Flavell, John H., and Markman, Ellen M., eds. New York: Wiley, 1983.

Mussen, Paul, ed. *Handbook of Child Psychology: History, Theories and Methods.* Vol. 1, 4th ed. New York: Wiley, 1983.

Mussen, Paul, and Haith, M. *Handbook of Child Psychology: Infancy and Developmental Psychobiology.* Vol. 2, 4th ed. New York: Wiley, 1983.

Mussen, Paul, and Hetherington, E. Mavis, eds. *Handbook of Child Psychology: Socialization, Personality and Social Development.* Vol. 4, 4th ed. New York: Wiley, 1983.

Pulaski, Mary Ann Spencer. *Understanding Piaget: An Introduction to Children's Cognitive Development.* New York: Harper, 1980.

Reilly, Abigail Peterson. *The Communication Game: Perspectives on the Development of Speech, Language and Non-Verbal Communication Skills.* Piscataway, N.J.: Johnson & Johnson Baby Products Co., 1980.

Rosenberger, Peter B. "The Pediatrician and Psychometric Testing." *Pediatrics in Review.* April 1981, 2(10), 301–10.

Rudolph, Abraham. *Pediatrics,* 17th ed. Norwalk, Conn.: Appleton-Century-Crofts, 1982.

Sturner, Raymond A.; Green, James A.; and Funk, Sandra G. "Preschool Denver Developmental Screening Test As a Predictor of Later School Problems." *The Journal of Pediatrics,* Oct. 1985, 107:615–21.

CHAPTER 8
PARENTS' GROWTH AND DEVELOPMENT

REFERENCES

1. Levinson, Daniel J. *The Seasons of a Man's Life.* New York: Knopf, 1978.
2. Sheehy, Gail. *Passages: Predictable Crises of Adult Life.* New York: Dutton, 1976.
3. Galinsky, Ellen. *Between Generations: The Stages of Parenthood.* New York: Berkley, 1981.
4. Erikson, Erik H. *Childhood and Society,* 2nd ed. New York: Norton, 1963.
5. Kaye, Kenneth. *The Mental and Social Life of Babies: How Parents Create Persons.* Chicago: University of Chicago Press, 1982.
6. Parsons, Talcott, and Bales, Robert F. *Family Socialization and Interaction Process.* Glencoe, Ill.: Free Press, 1955.
7. Haley, Jay, cited on p. 179 in McGoldrick, Monica, and Carter, Elizabeth A. "The Family Life Cycle." In Walsh, Froma, ed., *Normal Family Processes.* New York: Guilford, 1982.
8. McGoldrick, Monica, and Carter, Elizabeth A. "The Family Life Cycle." In Walsh, Froma, ed., *Normal Family Processes.* New York: Guilford, 1982.
9. Sidel, Victor W., and Sidel, Ruth. *Serve the People: Observations on Medicine in the People's Republic of China.* New York: Josiah Macy, Jr., Foundation, 1973.
10. French, Marilyn. *The Women's Room.* New York: Jove Publications, 1978.
11. McBride, Angela Barron. *The Growth and Development of Mothers.* New York: Harper, 1973, p. xiv.
12. Brazelton, T. Berry. "Developmental Framework of Infants and Children: A Future for Pediatric Responsibility." *Pediatrics,* June 1983, 102(6), 967–72.
13. Boyle, M. Patricia. "Evolving Parenthood: A Developmental Perspective." In Levine, Melvin D.; Carey, William B.; Crocker, Allen C.; and Gross, Ruth T., eds. *Developmental-Behavioral Pediatrics.* Philadelphia: Saunders, 1983, pp. 50–63.
14. Schwebel, Robert. "Decision-Making Requires Cooperation for the Needs of Both People to be Met." *Arizona Daily Star,* May 13, 1984.
15. Anthony, E. James, and Benedek, Therese, eds. *Parenthood: Its Psychology and Psychopathology.* Boston: Little, Brown, 1970.
16. Langway, Lynn. "A New Kind of Life with Father." *Newsweek,* Nov. 30, 1981.

17. Coleman, Robert. "The Nurturing Father—Saving the American Family." In *Child and Family.* Vol. 1 of *Current Research on Children: Birth Through Adolescence.* New York: Atcom, 1983, p. 30.
18. Henderson, James. "On Fathering (The Nature and Functions of the Father Role)," Pts. I, II *Canadian Journal of Psychiatry,* Aug. 1980, 25(5), 403–31.
19. Appleton, William S. *Fathers and Daughters.* Garden City, N.Y.: Doubleday, 1981.

SOURCE MATERIAL

Bernard, Jessie. *Women, Wives, Mothers: Values and Options.* Hawthorne, N.Y.: Aldine, 1975.
Bronfenbrenner, Urie. *The Ecology of Human Development: Experiments by Nature and Design.* Cambridge, Mass.: Harvard University Press, 1981.
Cahill, Susan. *Motherhood: A Reader for Men and Women.* New York: Discus/Avon, 1982.
Campbell, Angus. *The Sense of Well-Being in America: Recent Patterns and Trends.* New York: McGraw-Hill, 1981.
Chodorow, Nancy. *The Reproduction of Mothering: Psychoanalysis and the Sociology of Gender.* Berkeley: University of California Press, 1978.
Cobb, John. *Babyshock: A Survival Guide for the New Mother.* Englewood Cliffs, N.J.: Prentice-Hall, 1983.
Erikson, Erik H. *The Life Cycle Completed.* New York: Norton, 1985.
Greenspan, Stanley I. *Psychopathology and Adaptation in Infancy and Early Childhood: Principles of Clinical Diagnosis and Preventive Intervention.* New York: International Universities Press, 1981.
Kiley, Dan. *The Peter Pan Syndrome: Men Who Have Never Grown Up.* New York: Dodd, Mead, 1983.
Lamb, Michael E., ed. *The Role of the Father in Child Development.* New York: Wiley, 1976.
LeMasters, E. E., and Defrain, John. *Parents in Modern America,* 4th edition, Homewood, Ill.: Dorsey Press, 1983.
Mead, Margaret, and Metraux, Rhoda. *A Way of Seeing.* New York: Morrow, 1970.
Pleck, Joseph. Personal communication.
Reynolds, William. *The American Father.* New York: Paddington Press, 1980.
Schwartzman, Helen B., ed. *Transformations: The Anthropology of Children's Play.* New York: Plenum, 1978.
Selye, Hans. *Stress Without Distress.* New York: Harper, 1974.
Vaillant, George E. *Adaptation to Life.* Boston: Little, Brown, 1977.
———. *The Natural History of Alcoholism.* Cambridge, Mass.: Harvard University Press, 1983.

CHAPTER 9
GETTING STARTED

REFERENCES

1. Kay, Margarita Artschwager. *Anthropology of Human Birth.* Philadelphia: F. A. Davis, 1982.
2. Kolata, Gina. "Studying Learning in the Womb." *Science,* July 20, 1984, 225:302–3.
3. Hofer, Myron A. *The Roots of Human Behavior: An Introduction to the Psychobiology of Early Development.* San Francisco: W. H. Freeman, 1981.
4. De Carvalho, Manoel; Klaus, Marshall H.; and Merkatz, Ruth B. "Frequency of

Breast-feeding and Serum Bilirubin Concentration." *American Journal of Diseases of Children*, Aug. 1982, 136:737–38.
5. Leventhal, J. M.; Aten, C. A.; Egerter, S. A. "Does Breast-feeding Protect Against Infections in Infants Younger Than Three Months of Age?" *American Journal of Diseases of Children*, June 1983, 137:534.
6. Lawrence, Ruth A. *Breast-feeding: A Guide for the Medical Profession.* St. Louis, Mo.: C. V. Mosby, 1985, p. 195.
7. Auerbach, Kathleen G., and Guss, Elizabeth. "Maternal Employment and Breastfeeding: Study of 567 Women's Experiences." *American Journal of Diseases of Children*, Oct. 1984, 138:958–60.
8. Lawrence, op. cit., pp. 194–95.
9. Riordan, Jan. *A Practical Guide to Breastfeeding.* C. V. Mosby, St. Louis, Mo.: 1983.
10. Dusdieker, Lois B.; Booth, Brenda M.; Stumbo, Phyllis J.; and Eichenberger, Julie M. "Effect of Supplemental Fluids on Human Milk Production." *The Journal of Pediatrics*, Feb. 1985, 106(2), 207–11.
11. Henningsson, Annelie; Nyström, Bertil; and Tunnell, Ragnar. "Bathing or Washing Babies After Birth?" *The Lancet*, Dec. 19/26, 1981, 2:1401–3.
12. Stotland, Nada. Personal communication.
13. Hofer, op. cit., p. 197.
14. Klaus, Marshall H., and Kennell, John H. *Parent-Infant Bonding*, 2nd ed. St. Louis, Mo.: Mosby, 1982.
15. Kaye, Kenneth. *The Mental and Social Life of Babies: How Parents Create Persons.* Chicago: University of Chicago Press, 1979.
16. Brazelton, T. Berry. *Neonatal Behavior Assessment Scale.* Clinics in Developmental Medicine. No. 50. Spastics International Medical Publications, Philadelphia: Lippincott, 1973.
17. De Carvalho, op. cit., p. 737.
18. Pedreira, Frank A.; Guandolo, Vincent L.; Feroli, Edward J.; Mella, Gordon W.; and Weiss, Ira P. "Involuntary Smoking and Incidence of Respiratory Illness During the First Year of Life." *Pediatrics*, March 1985, 75(3), 594–97.

SOURCE MATERIAL

Adams, Joyce A.; Hey, Dennis J.; Hall, Robert T. "Incidence of Hyperbilirubinemia in Breast-Versus Formula-Fed Infants." *Clinical Pediatrics*, Feb. 1985, 24:69–73.
American Academy of Pediatrics. *Care of the Uncircumcized Penis.* (1984) Publications Department, P.O. Box 927, Elk Grove Village, Ill. 60007.
American Academy of Pediatrics. *Diaper Rash.* (1986) Publications Department, P.O. Box 927, Elk Grove Village, Ill. 60007.
Behrman, Richard E., and Vaughan, Victor C., III, eds. *Nelson Textbook of Pediatrics.* 12th ed. Philadelphia: Saunders, 1983.
Brown, Kenneth H.; de Kanashiro, Hilary Creed; del Aguila, Roberto; de Romana, Guillermo Lopez; and Black, Robert E. "Milk Consumption and Hydration Status of Exclusively Breast-fed Infants in a Warm Climate." *The Journal of Pediatrics*, May 1986, 108(5), Part I, 667–80.
Caplan, Frank. *The First Twelve Months of Life.* Edcom Systems, N.J.: Princeton, 1973.
Chess, Stella, and Thomas, Alexander. "Infant Bonding: Mystique and Reality." *American Journal of Orthopsychiatry*, April 1982, 52(2), 213–22.
Eden, Alvin N. *Handbook for New Parents.* New York: Berkley, 1978.
Fox, Gary N. "Care of Uncircumcised Children." *The Western Journal of Medicine*, Feb. 1985. (142)2, 270–72.
Inwood, David G. *Recent Advances in Postpartum Psychiatric Disorders.* American Psychiatric Press, Washington, D.C., 1985.

Kivlahan, Coleen, and James, Elizabeth J. P. "Natural History of Neonatal Jaundice." *Pediatrics*, Sept. 1984, 74(3), 364–70.

Klaus, Marshall. "Parent to Infant Bonding: Setting the Record Straight." *Pediatrics*, April 1983, 102(4), 575–76.

Klaus, Marshall H., and Robertson, Martha Oschrin. *Birth, Interaction and Attachment: Exploring the Foundations for Modern Perinatal Care.* Skillman, N.J.: Johnson & Johnson Baby Products, 1982.

Korsch, Barbara M. "More on Parent-Infant Bonding." *The Journal of Pediatrics*, Feb. 1983, 102(2), 249–50.

La Leche League International. *The Womanly Art of Breastfeeding*, 3rd ed. New York: New American Library, 1983.

Lamb, Michael E. "The Bonding Phenomenon: Misinterpretations and Their Implications." *The Journal of Pediatrics*, Oct. 1982, 101(4), 555–57.

———. "Early Contact and Maternal-Infant Bonding: One Decade Later." *Pediatrics*, Nov. 1982, 70(5), 763–68.

Lascari, André D. " 'Early' Breast Feeding Jaundice: Clinical Significance." *The Journal of Pediatrics*, Jan. 1986, 108(1), 156–58.

Leach, Penelope. *The Child Care Encyclopedia: A Parents' Guide to the Physical and Emotional Well-Being of Children From Birth Through Adolescence.* New York: Knopf, 1984.

Lowrey, George. *Growth and Development of Children*, 8th ed. Chicago: Year Book Medical Publishers, 1986.

McCall, Robert B. "A Hard Look at Stimulating and Predicting Development: The Cases of Bonding and Screening." *Pediatrics in Review*, Jan. 1982, 3(7), 205–12.

McCall, Robert B. *Infants: The New Knowledge.* Cambridge, Mass.: Harvard University Press, 1979.

Novy, Miles J. "The Puerperium." In Benson, Ralph C., ed. *Current Obstetric and Gynecologic Diagnosis and Treatment.* Los Angeles: Lange Medical Publications, 1976, pp. 697–721.

Raphael, Dana. *The Tender Gift: Breastfeeding.* New York: Schocken, 1976.

Salmenperä, Leena, Perheentupa, Jaakko, and Siimes, Martti A. "Exclusively Breast-Fed Healthy Infants Grow Slower Than Reference Infants." *Pediatric Research*, March 1985, 19(3), 307–12.

Samuels, Mike, and Samuels, Nancy. *The Well Baby Book.* New York: Summit, 1979.

Stone, L. Joseph; Smith, Henrietta T.; and Murphy, Lois B., eds. *The Infant's First Year: Learning and Development.* New York: Basic Books, 1973.

Winikoff, Beverly; Laukaran, Virginia Hight; Myers, Deborah; and Stone, Richard. "Dynamics of Infant Feeding: Mothers, Professionals, and the Institutional Context in a Large Urban Hospital." *Pediatrics*, March 1986, 77(3), 357–65.

CHAPTER 10
GETTING SETTLED

REFERENCES

1. Prechtl, H.F.B. "Problems of Behavioral Studies in the Newborn Infant." In Lehman, D. S., and Hinde, R. A., eds. *Advances in the Study of Behavior*, Vol. 1. New York: Academic Press, 1965.

2. White, Burton L. *The First Three Years of Life.* Revised ed. New York: Prentice-Hall, 1985.

3. Mahler, Margaret S.; Pine, Fred; and Bergman, Anni. *The Psychological Birth of the Human Infant: Symbiosis and Individuation.* New York: Basic Books, 1975.

4. Foye, H. R.; Keller, B.; and Berko, J. K. "Prospective Study of Crying in Early

Infancy." *Ambulatory Pediatric Association Program and Abstracts*, 24th Annual Meeting, 1984.
5. Chess, Stella, and Thomas, Alexander. "Temperamental Traits and Parent Guidance." In Arnold, L. Eugene, ed. *Helping Parents Help Their Children.* New York: Brunner-Mazel, 1978, pp. 135–44.
6. Leach, Penelope. *Your Baby and Child: From Birth to Age Five.* New York: Knopf, 1978.
7. Jakobsson, Irene, and Lindberg, Tor. "Cow's Milk as a Cause of Infantile Colic in Breast-Fed Infants." *Lancet*, Aug. 26, 1978, 2:437–39.
8. ———. "Cow's Milk Proteins Cause Infantile Colic in Breast-Fed Infants: A Double-Blind Crossover Study." *Pediatrics*, Feb. 1983, 71(2), 268–71.
9. Said, Gilles; Patois, Elisabeth; and Lellouch, Joseph. "Infantile Colic and Parental Smoking." *British Medical Journal*, Sept. 15, 1984, 289:660.
10. Waldman, William H., and Sarsgard, Deborah. "Helping Parents to Cope with Colic." Freemont, Mich.: Gerber Products Co., 1983, 33:12–14.
11. Taubman, Bruce. "Clinical Trial of the Treatment of Colic by Modification of Parent-Infant Interaction." *Pediatrics*, Dec. 1984, 74(6), 998–1003.
12. McMillan, Julia A.; Stockman, James A., III; and Oski, Frank A. *The Whole Pediatrician Catalog*, Vol. 2. Philadelphia: Saunders, 1979.
13. Brewster, Dorothy Patricia, *You Can Breastfeed Your Baby . . . Even in Special Situations.* Emmaus, Pa.: Rodale Press, 1979.
14. Pryor, Karen. *Nursing Your Baby.* New York: Harper, 1973.
15. Duncan, Burris; Schaefer, Catherine; Sibley, Barbara; and Fonseca, Ney Marques. "Reduced Growth Velocity in Exclusively Breast-fed Infants." *American Journal of Diseases of Children*, March 1984, 138:309–13.
16. American Academy of Pediatrics Committee on Nutrition. *Pediatric Nutrition Handbook*, 2nd ed. Elk Grove Village, Ill., 1985.
17. Ibid., p. 172.
18. Leach, op. cit., p. 151.
19. Beck, Joan Wagner. *How to Raise a Brighter Child: The Case for Early Learning.* New York: Trident Press, 1967.
20. Hunziker, Urs A., and Barr, Ronald G. "Increased Carrying Reduces Infant Crying: A Randomized Controlled Trial." *Pediatrics*, May 1986, 77(5), 641–48.
21. Kitzinger, Sheila. *Education and Counseling for Childbirth.* New York: Schocken Books, 1979.
22. Brazelton, T. Berry. *Working and Caring.* Reading, Mass.: Addison-Wesley, 1985.
23. Galinsky, Ellen. *Between Generations: The Stages of Parenthood.* New York: Berkley, 1981.
24. Greenspan, Stanley, and Greenspan, Nancy T. *First Feelings: Milestones in the Emotional Development of Your Baby and Child from Birth to Age 4.* New York: Viking, 1985.
25. Stern, Daniel. *The Interpersonal World of the Infant: A View From Psychoanalysis and Developmental Psychology.* New York: Basic Books, 1985.
26. American Academy of Pediatrics, *Report of the Committee on Infectious Diseases*, 20th ed. Elk Grove Village, Ill., 1985.
27. Fulginiti, Vincent A. "Immunizations: Current Controversies." *Journal of Pediatrics*, Oct. 1982, 101(4), 487–94.

SOURCE MATERIAL

Aronoff, Stephen C., ed. *Advances in Pediatric Infectious Disease*, Vol. 1. Chicago: Year Book Medical Publishers, 1986.
Behrman, Richard E., and Vaughan, Victor C., III, eds. *Nelson Textbook of Pediatrics*, 12th ed. Philadelphia: Saunders, 1983.

840   CHAPTER REFERENCES AND SOURCE MATERIAL

Bernath, Maja. *Parent's Book for Your Baby's First Year.* New York: Ballantine, 1983.

Brazelton, T. Berry. *On Becoming a Family: The Growth of Attachment.* New York: Delacorte, 1981.

Caplan, Frank. *The First Twelve Months of Life: Your Baby's Growth Month by Month.* Princeton, N.J.: Edcom Systems, 1973.

DelliQuadri, Lyn, and Breckenridge, Kati. *The New Mother Care: Helping Yourself Through the Emotional and Physical Transitions of Motherhood.* Boston: Houghton Mifflin, 1984.

Eden, Alvin N. *Handbook for New Parents.* New York: Berkley, 1978.

Elias, Marjorie F.; Nicholson, Nancy A.; Bora, Carolyn; and Johnston, Johanna. "Sleep/Wake Patterns of Breast-Fed Infants in the First 2 Years of Life." *Pediatrics,* March 1986, 77(3), 322–29.

Fraiberg, Selma. *Clinical Studies in Infant Mental Health: The First Year of Life.* New York: Basic Books, 1980.

Fraiberg, Selma, ed. *Clinical and Infant Studies in Infant Mental Health.* New York: Basic Books, 1980.

Galenson, Eleanor, and Call, Justin D., eds. *Frontiers of Infant Psychiatry,* New York: Basic Books, 1983.

Gerber, Michael A.; Berliner, Benjamin C.; and Karolus, John J. "Sterilization of Infant Formula." *Clinical Pediatrics,* May 1983, 22(5), 344–49.

Gesell, Arnold. *The First Five Years of Life: The Preschool Years.* New York: Harper, 1940.

Gesell, Arnold; Ilg, Frances L.; and Ames, Louis Bates. *Infant and Child in the Culture of Today.* New York: Harper, 1974.

Grant, Wilson W.; Street, Luther; and Fearnow, Ronald G. "Diaper Rashes in Infancy: Studies on the Effects of Various Methods of Laundering." *Clinical Pediatrics,* Dec. 1973, 12(12), 714–16.

Greenspan, Stanley I., and Pollock, George H., eds. *The Course of Life: Psychoanalytic Contributions Toward Understanding Personality Development,* Vol. I. Adelphi, Md.: Mental Health Study Center, 1980.

Greenspan, Stanley I. *Psychopathology and Adaptation in Infancy and Early Childhood: Principles of Clinical Diagnosis and Preventive Intervention.* Clinical Infant Reports, Series of the National Center for Clinical Infant Programs, Number One, 1981.

Grohman, Joann S. *Born to Love: Instinct and Natural Mothering.* Dixfield, Maine: Coburn Farm Press, 1976.

Jones, Sandy. *Crying Baby, Sleepless Nights: How to Overcome Baby's Sleep Problems—and Get Some Sleep Yourself.* New York: Warner, 1983.

Kagan, Jerome, and Moss, Howard A. *Birth to Maturity.* New Haven: Yale University Press, 1983.

Kahn, A.; Mozin, M. J.; Casimir, G.; Montauk, L.; and Blum, D. "Insomnia and Cow's Milk Allergy in Infants." *Pediatrics,* Dec. 1985, 76(6), 880–84.

Kaplan, Louise J. *Oneness and Separateness.* London: J. Cape, 1979.

Kaye, Kenneth. *The Mental and Social Life of Babies: How Parents Create Persons.* Chicago: University of Chicago Press, 1979.

Kelly, Paula, ed. *First-Year Baby Care.* Deephaven, Minn.: Meadowbrook Press, 1983.

Klaus, Marshall H., and Kennell, John H. *Bonding: The Beginnings of Parent-Infant Attachment.* New York: Plume, New American Library, 1983.

LaCerva, Victor. *Breastfeeding: A Manual for Health Professionals.* Garden City, N.Y.: Medical Examination Publishing Co., 1981.

Leboyer, Frederick. *Loving Hands.* New York: Knopf, 1976.

Lichtenberg, Philip, and Norton, Dolores G. *Cognitive and Mental Development in the First Five Years of Life: A Review of Recent Research.* Rockville, Md., National Institute of Mental Health, 1972. DHEW Publication No. (HSM) 72-9102.

Lowrey, George H. *Growth and Development of Children*, 8th ed. Chicago: Year Book Medical Publishers, 1986.

Madden, Chris Casson. *Baby Hints Handbook*. Mary Ellen Enterprises, St. Louis Park, Minn., 1982.

Mahler, Margaret S.; Pine, Fred; and Bergman, Anni. *The Psychological Birth of the Human Infant: Symbiosis and Individuation*. New York: Basic Books, 1975.

Marzollo, Jean (comp.). *Nine Months, One Day, One Year: A Guide to Pregnancy, Birth, and Babycare*. New York: Harper, 1976.

McCall, Robert B. *Infants: The New Knowledge*. New York: Random House, 1980.

McMillan, Julia A.; Nieburg, Phillip I.; and Oski, Frank A., III. *The Whole Pediatrician Catalog*, Vol. 1. Philadelphia: Saunders, 1979.

Meyers, Carole T. *How to Organize a Babysitting Cooperative and Get Some Free Time Away from the Kids*. Albany, Calif.: Carousel Press, 1976.

Newton, Niles. *The Family Book of Child Care*. New York: Harper, 1957.

Parkes, Colin Murray, and Stevenson-Hinde, Joan, eds. *The Place of Attachment in Human Behavior*. New York: Basic Books, 1982.

Rasmussen, James E. "Diaper Dermatitis." *Pediatrics in Review*, Sept. 3, 1984, 6(3), 77–82.

Rexford, Eveoleen N.; Sander, Louis W.; and Shapiro, Theodore, eds. *Infant Psychiatry: A New Synthesis*. New Haven: Yale University Press, 1976.

Ribble, Margaretha A. *The Rights of Infants: Early Psychological Needs and Their Satisfaction*, 2nd ed. New York: Columbia University Press, 1965.

Rothenberg, B. Annye; Hitchcock, Sandra; Harrison, Mary Lou; and Graham, Melinda. *Parentmaking: A Practical Handbook for Teaching Parent Classes About Babies and Toddlers*. Menlo Park, Calif.: Banster Press, 1981.

Rozdilsky, Mary Lou, and Banet, Barbara. *What Now? A Handbook for New Parents*. New York: Scribner, 1975.

Samuels, Mike, and Samuels, Nancy. *The Well Baby Book*. New York: Summit Books, 1979.

Schneider, Vimala. *Infant Massage: A Handbook for Loving Parents*. New York: Bantam, 1982.

Stein, Howard. "Incidence of Diaper Rash When Using Cloth and Disposable Diapers." *The Journal of Pediatrics*, Nov. 1982, 101(5), 721–23.

Stone, L. Joseph; Smith, Henrietta T.; and Murphy, Lois B., eds. *The Infant's First Year: Learning and Development*. New York: Basic Books, 1973.

Stoutt, Glenn R. *The First Month of Life: A Parent's Guide to Care of the Newborn*. Oradell, N.J.: Medical Economics, 1977.

Thomas, Alexander, and Chess, Stella. *Temperament and Development*. New York: Brunner/Mazel, 1977.

Wiener, Fred. "The Relationship of Diapers to Diaper Rashes in the One-Month-Old Infant." *The Journal of Pediatrics*, Sept. 1979, 95(3), 422–24.

Winnicott, Donald Woods. *The Maturational Processes and the Facilitating Environment*. London: Hogarth, 1965.

Wolff, Peter H. "The Development of Attention in Young Infants." *Annals of New York Academy of Sciences*, 1965, 118(21), 815–30.

CHAPTER 11
GETTING GOING

REFERENCES

1. Leach, Penelope. *Babyhood*, 2nd ed. New York: Knopf, 1983, p. 189.
2. McMillan, Julia A.; Stockman, James A., III; and Oski, Frank A. *The Whole Pediatrician Catalog*, Vol. 2. Philadelphia: Saunders, 1979.
3. Mindel, Eugene. Personal communication.
4. Mahler, Margaret S.; Pine, Fred; and Bergman, Anni. *The Psychological Birth of the Human Infant: Symbiosis and Individuation*. New York: Basic Books, 1975.
5. Leach, op. cit., p. xii.
6. Chess, Stella, and Thomas, Alexander. "Temperamental Traits and Parent Guidance." In Arnold, L. Eugene, ed. *Helping Parents Help Their Children*. New York: Brunner-Mazel, 1978, pp. 135–44.
7. McMillan, op. cit., p. 66.
8. Dusdieker, L. B., and Brooks, B. M. "Breastfeeding and Returning to Work." *Ambulatory Pediatric Association Program and Abstracts*, May 7–10, 1985.

SOURCE MATERIAL

Beck, Joan. *How to Raise a Brighter Child: The Case for Early Learning*. New York: Trident Press, 1967.
Behrman, Richard E., and Vaughan, Victor C., III, eds. *Nelson Textbook of Pediatrics*, 12th ed. Philadelphia: Saunders, 1983.
Bernath, Maja. *Parents' Book for Your Baby's First Year*. New York: Ballantine, 1983.
Brazelton, T. Berry. *On Becoming a Family: The Growth of Attachment*. New York: Delacorte, 1981.
Caplan, Frank. *The First Twelve Months of Life*. New York: Bantam Books, 1978.
Fraiberg, Selma, ed. *Clinical Studies in Infant Mental Health: The First Year of Life*. New York: Basic Books, 1980.
Galenson, Eleanor, and Call, Justin D., eds. *Frontiers of Infant Psychiatry*, New York: Basic Books, 1983.
Galinsky, Ellen. *Between Generations: The Stages of Parenting*. New York: Berkley, 1981.
Gesell, Arnold. *The First Five Years of Life: The Preschool Years*. New York: Harper, 1940.
Gesell, Arnold; Ilg, Frances L.; and Ames, Louise Bates. *Infant and Child in the Culture of Today*. New York: Harper, 1974.
Greenspan, Stanley I., and Pollock, George H., eds. *The Course of Life: Psychoanalytic Contributions Toward Understanding Personality Development*, Vol. 1. Adelphi, Md.: Mental Health Study Center, 1980.
Greenspan, Stanley I. *Psychopathology and Adaptation in Infancy and Early Childhood: Principles of Clinical Diagnosis and Preventive Intervention*. Clinical Infant Reports. Series of the National Center for Clinical Infant Programs, Number One, 1981.
Grohman, Joann S. *Born to Love: Instinct and Natural Mothering*. Dixfield, Maine: Coburn Farm Press, 1976.
Kagan, Jerome, and Moss, Howard A. *Birth to Maturity: A Study in Psychological Development*. New Haven: Yale University Press, 1983.
Kaplan, Louise J. *Oneness and Separateness*. London: J. Cape, 1979.
Kaye, Kenneth. *The Mental and Social Life of Babies: How Parents Create Persons*. Chicago: University of Chicago Press, 1979.
Kelly, Paula, ed. *First-Year Baby Care: An Illustrated Step-by-Step Guide for New Parents*. Deephaven, Minn.: Meadowbrook Press, 1983.
Leach, Penelope. *Your Baby and Child: From Birth to Age Five*. New York: Knopf, 1978.

Leach, Penelope. *Babyhood*, 2nd ed. New York: Knopf, 1983.

Leboyer, Frederick. *Loving Hands*. New York: Knopf, 1976.

Lichtenberg, Philip, and Norton, Dolores G. *Cognitive and Mental Development in the First Five Years of Life: A Review of Recent Research*. Rockville, Md.: National Institute of Mental Health, 1972. (DHEW Publications No. (HSM) 72–9102.)

Lowrey, George H. *Growth and Development of Children*, 8th ed. Chicago: Year Book Medical Publishers, Inc., 1986.

Madden, Chris Casson. *Baby Hints Handbook*. St. Louis Park, Minn.: Mary Ellen Enterprises, 1982.

Marzollo, Jean, comp. *Nine Months, One Day, One Year: A Guide to Pregnancy, Birth, and Baby Care*. New York: Harper, 1976.

McCall, Robert B. *Infants: The New Knowledge*. New York: Random House, 1980.

Meyers, Carole T. *How to Organize a Babysitting Cooperative and Get Some Free Time Away from the Kids*. Albany, Calif.: Carousel Press, 1976.

Newton, Niles. *The Family Book of Child Care*. New York: Harper, 1957.

Parkes, Colin Murray, and Stevenson-Hinde, Joan, eds. *The Place of Attachment in Human Behavior*. New York: Basic Books, 1982.

Rexford, Eveoleen J.; Sander, Louis W.; and Shapiro, Theodore, eds. *Infant Psychiatry: A New Synthesis*. New Haven: Yale University Press, 1976.

Ribble, Margaretha A. *The Rights of Infants: Early Psychological Needs and Their Satisfaction*, 2nd ed. New York: Columbia University Press, 1965.

Rothenberg, B. Annye; Hitchcock, Sandra; Harrison, Mary Lou; and Graham, Melinda. *Parentmaking: A Practical Handbook for Teaching Parent Classes About Babies and Toddlers*. Menlo Park, Calif.: Banster Press, 1982.

Samuels, Mike, and Samuels, Nancy. *The Well Baby Book*. New York: Summit Books, 1979.

Schneider, Vimala. *Infant Massage: A Handbook for Loving Parents*. New York: Bantam, 1982.

Stone, L. Joseph; Smith, Henrietta T.; and Murphy, Lois B., eds. *The Infant's First Year*. New York: Basic Books, 1973.

Thomas, Alexander, and Chess, Stella. *Temperament and Development*. New York: Brunner/Mazel, 1977.

Thomas, Alexander; Chess, Stella; Birch, Herbert G.; Hertzig, Margaret E.; and Korn, Sam. *Behavioral Individuality in Early Childhood*. New York: New York University Press, 1963.

Timmermans, Claire. *How to Teach Your Baby to Swim*. New York: Stein & Day, 1976.

Weissbluth, Marc. *Crybabies, Coping with Colic: What to Do When Baby Won't Stop Crying*. New York: Arbor House, 1984.

Winnicott, Donald Woods. *The Maturational Processes and the Facilitating Environment*. London: Hogarth, 1963.

CHAPTER 12
GETTING CAREFUL

REFERENCES

1. White, Burton L. *The First Three Years of Life*. Revised ed. New York: Prentice-Hall, 1985.
2. Stern, Daniel. *The Interpersonal World of the Infant: A View from Psychoanalysis and Developmental Psychology*. New York: Basic Books, 1985.
3. Lunde, Donald T., and Lunde, Marilynn K. *The Next Generation: A Book on Parenting*. New York: Holt, 1980.

4. McMillan, Julia A.; Stockman, James A., III; and Oski, Frank A. *The Whole Pediatrician Catalog*, Vol. 2. Philadelphia: Saunders, 1979.
5. Weissbluth, Marc; Davis, A. Todd; and Poncher, John. "Night Waking in 4- to 8-month-old Infants." *The Journal of Pediatrics*, March 1984, 104(3), 477–80.
6. Parke, Ross D. *Fathers*. Cambridge, Mass: Harvard University Press, 1981.

SOURCE MATERIAL

Behrman, Richard E., and Vaughan, Victor C., III, eds. *Nelson Textbook of Pediatrics*, 12th ed. Philadelphia: Saunders, 1983.
Caplan, Frank, ed. *The First Twelve Months of Life*. New York: Bantam Books, 1978.
Kaye, Kenneth. *The Mental and Social Life of Babies: How Parents Create Persons*. Chicago: University of Chicago Press, 1979.
Kelly, Paula, ed. *First-Year Baby Care: An Illustrated Step-by-Step Guide for New Parents*. Deephaven, Minn.: Meadowbrook Press, 1983.
Leach, Penelope. *Your Baby and Child: From Birth to Age Five*. New York: Knopf, 1978.
Oski, Frank A. "Is Bovine Milk a Health Hazard?" *Pediatrics* (Current Issues in Feeding the Normal Infant, Part 2), Jan. 1985, 75(1), 182–86.
Pomerance, Herbert H. *Growth Standards in Children*. New York: Harper, 1979.
Rothenberg, B. Annye; Hitchcock, Sandra; Harrison, Mary Lou; and Graham, Melinda. *Parentmaking: A Practical Handbook for Teaching Parent Classes About Babies and Toddlers*. Menlo Park, Calif.: Banster Press, 1982.
Samuels, Mike, and Samuels, Nancy. *The Well Baby Book*. New York: Summit Books, 1979.
Scott, Roland B.; Ferguson, Angella D.; Jenkins, Melvin E.; and Cutter, Fred F. "Growth and Development of Negro Infants. Neuromuscular Patterns of Behavior During the First Year of Life." *Pediatrics*, July 1955, 16:1, 24–29.
Stone, L. Joseph; Smith, Henrietta T.; and Murphy, Lois B., eds. *The Infant's First Year*. New York: Basic Books, 1973.

CHAPTER 13
GETTING ON

REFERENCES

1. Stern, Daniel. *The Interpersonal World of the Infant: A View from Psychoanalysis and Developmental Psychology*. New York: Basic Books, 1985.
2. Brooks, Jane B. *The Process of Parenting*. Palo Alto, Calif.: Mayfield Publishing, 1981.
3. McMillan, Julia A.; Stockman, James A., III; and Oski, Frank A. *The Whole Pediatrician Catalog*, Vol. 2. Philadelphia: Saunders, 1979.
4. Spock, Benjamin, and Rothenberg, Michael B. *Dr. Spock's Baby and Child Care*. New York: Pocket Books, 1985, p. 341.
5. Rosenfeld, Alvin A.; Wenegrat, Anne O'Reilly; Haavik, Diane K.; Wenegrat, Brant G.; and Smith, Carole R. "Sleeping Patterns in Upper-Middle-Class Families When the Child Awakens Ill or Frightened." *Archives of General Psychiatry*, Aug. 1982, 39:943–47.
6. Litt, Carole J. "Children's Attachment to Transitional Objects: A Study of Two Pediatric Populations." *American Journal of Orthopsychiatry*, Jan. 1981, 51:131–39.
7. Rubin, Richard R.; Fisher, John J., III; Doering, Susan G. *Your Toddler*. New York: Macmillan, 1980.
8. Brazelton, T. Berry. *Toddlers and Parents*. New York: Dell, 1976.

9. Azrin, Nathan H., and Fox, Richard M. *Toilet Training in Less Than a Day.* New York: Pocket Books, Inc., 1981.
10. "Leather Shoes Found Superior to Sneakers for Learning to Walk." *Pediatric News,* March 1986, 20(3), 11.

SOURCE MATERIAL

Behrman, Richard E., and Vaughan, Victor C., III. *Nelson Textbook of Pediatrics,* 12th ed. Philadelphia: Saunders, 1983.
Caplan, Theresa, and Caplan, Frank. *The Early Childhood Years: The 2 to 6 Year Old.* New York: Putnam, 1983.
Caplan, Frank, and Caplan, Theresa. *The Second Twelve Months of Life: Your Baby's Growth Month by Month.* New York: Bantam, 1977.
Fraiberg, Selma H. *The Magic Years: Understanding and Handling the Problems of Early Childhood.* New York: Scribner's, 1959.
Lansky, Vicki. *Getting Your Baby to Sleep (and Back to Sleep).* New York: Bantam, 1985.
Lansky, Vicki. *Toilet Training.* New York: Bantam, 1984.
Leach, Penelope. *Babyhood,* 2nd ed. New York: Knopf, 1983.
Pomerance, Herbert H. *Growth Standards in Children.* New York: Harper, 1979.
Rothenberg, B. Annye; Hitchcock, Sandra; Harrison, Mary Lou; and Graham, Melinda. *Parentmaking: A Practical Handbook for Teaching Parent Classes About Babies and Toddlers.* Menlo Park, Calif.: Banster, 1981.

CHAPTER 14
MOVING OUTWARD

REFERENCES

1. Erikson, Erik H., cited in Schuster, Clara Shaw, and Ashburn, Shirley Smith. *The Process of Human Development: A Holistic Approach.* Boston: Little, Brown, 1980.
2. McMillan, Julia A.; Stockman, James A., III; and Oski, Frank A. *The Whole Pediatrician Catalog,* Vol. 2. Philadelphia: Saunders, 1979.
3. Beal, Virginia A. "The Finicky Eater." *Family Health Magazine,* June 1971.
4. Gates, Dorothy. Seminar on Spectra Dynamics, Tucson, Arizona, 1980.

SOURCE MATERIAL

Ames, Louise Bates, and Chase, Joan A. *Don't Push Your Preschooler.* New York: Harper, 1981.
Beal, Virginia A. "On the Acceptance of Solid Foods, and Other Food Patterns, of Infants and Children." *Pediatrics,* Sept. 1957, 20:448–56.
Behrman, Richard E., and Vaughan, Victor C., III, eds. *Nelson Textbook of Pediatrics,* 12th ed. Philadelphia: Saunders, 1983.
de Villiers, Peter A., and de Villiers, Jill G. *Early Language.* Cambridge, Mass.: Harvard University Press, 1979.
Forman, George E., and Kuschner, David S. *The Child's Construction of Knowledge, Piaget for Teaching Children.* Washington, D.C.: National Association for the Education of Young Children, 1983.
Gordon, Ira J.; Guinaugh, Barry; and Jester, R. E. *Child Learning Through Child Play: Learning Activities for Two- and Three-Year-Olds.* New York: St. Martin, 1972.
Hymes, James L., Jr. *The Child Under Six.* Englewood Cliffs, N.J.: Prentice-Hall, 1983.
Lowrey, George H. *Growth and Development of Children,* 8th ed. Chicago: Year Book Medical Publishers, 1986.

Riley, Sue Spayth. *How to Generate Values in Young Children*. Washington, D.C.: National Association for the Education of Young Children, 1984.

Rosenfeld, Alvin A.; Wenegrat, Anne O'Reilly; Haavik, Diane K.; Wenegrat, Brant G.; and Smith, Carole R. "Sleeping Patterns in Upper-Middle-Class Families When the Child Awakens Ill or Frightened." *Archives of General Psychiatry*, Aug. 1982, 39:943–47.

Spock, Benjamin, and Rothenberg, Michael. *Dr. Spock's Baby and Child Care*. New York: Pocket Books, 1985.

Watrin, Rita, and Furfey, Paul Hanly. *Learning Activities for the Young Preschool Child*. New York: Van Nostrand, 1978.

CHAPTER 15
THE THREE-YEAR-OLD

REFERENCES

1. McMillan, Julia A.; Stockman, James A., III; and Oski, Frank A. *The Whole Pediatrician Catalog*, Vol. 2. Philadelphia: Saunders, 1979.
2. Ilg, Frances L., and Ames, Louise Bates. *The Gesell Institute's Child Behavior*. New York: Dell, 1955, p. 37.
3. Muellner, S. Richard. "Development of Urinary Control in Children: Some Aspects of the Cause and Treatment of Primary Enuresis." *Journal of the American Medical Association*. March 19, 1960, 172(12), 1256–61.
4. Rubin, Richard R., and Fisher, John J., III. *Your Preschooler: Ages Three and Four*. New York: Collier Books, 1982.
5. Lewis, Melvin. *Clinical Aspects of Child Development*, 2nd ed. Philadelphia: Lea & Febiger, 1982.
6. Ilg, op. cit., pp. 138–71.
7. Garrison, William, and Earls, Felton. "Attachment to a Special Object at the Age of Three Years: Behavior and Temperament Characteristics." *Child Psychiatry and Human Development*. Spring 1982, 12(3), 131–41.
8. Earls, Felton. "Prevalence of Behavior Problems in 3-Year-Old Children: A Cross-National Replication." *Archives of General Psychiatry*. Oct. 1980, 37:1153–57.
9. McMillan, op. cit., p. 67.
10. Leach, Penelope. *Your Baby and Child: From Birth to Age Five*. New York: Knopf, 1978.
11. Stoppard, Miriam. *Day-by-Day Baby Care: An Owner's Manual for the First Three Years*. New York: Random House, 1983.
12. Rubin, op. cit., pp. 176–80.
13. Spock, Benjamin, and Rothenberg, Michael. *Dr. Spock's Baby and Child Care*. New York: Pocket Books, 1985.
14. Ames, Louise Bates, and Ilg, Frances L. *Your Three-Year-Old: Friend or Enemy*. New York: Delacorte, 1976.
15. Rubin, op. cit., pp. 174–75.

SOURCE MATERIAL

Behrman, Richard E., and Vaughan, Victor C., III, eds. *Nelson Textbook of Pediatrics*, 12th ed. Philadelphia: Saunders, 1983.

DeLorenzo, Lorisa, and DeLorenzo, Robert. *Total Child Care*. Garden City, N.Y.: Doubleday, 1982.

Lowrey, George H. *Growth and Development of Children*, 8th ed. Chicago, Ill.: Year Book Medical Publishers, 1986.

CHAPTER 16
FOUR-YEAR-OLD

REFERENCES

1. Lewis, Melvin. *Clinical Aspects of Child Development.* Philadelphia: Lea & Febiger, 1982.
2. McMillan, Julia A.; Stockman, James A., III; and Oski, Frank A. *The Whole Pediatrician Catalog,* Vol. 2. Philadelphia: Saunders, 1979.
3. Dreikurs, Rudolf, and Soltz, Vicki. *Children: The Challenge.* New York: Hawthorn Books, 1964.
4. Ames, Louise Bates, and Ilg, Frances L. *Your Four-Year-Old.* New York: Delacorte, 1976.

SOURCE MATERIAL

Abraham, Willard. *Living with Preschoolers.* Pheonix, Ariz.: O'Sullivan, Woodside, 1976.
Behrman, Richard E., and Vaughan, Victor C., III, eds. *Nelson Textbook of Pediatrics,* 12th ed. Philadelphia: Saunders, 1983.
Dinkmeyer, Don, and McKay, Gary. *Raising a Responsible Child: Practical Steps to a Successful Family Relationship.* New York: Simon & Schuster, 1982.
Elkind, David. *The Hurried Child: Growing Up Too Fast Too Soon.* Reading, Mass.: Addison-Wesley, 1981.
Gordon, Thomas, and Sands, Judith S. *P.E.T. in Action.* New York: Bantam, 1978.
Lowrey, George H. *Growth and Development of Children,* 8th ed. Chicago: Year Book Medical Publishers, 1986.
Maslow, Abraham H. *Toward a Psychology of Being.* New York: Van Nostrand, 1968.
Mayesky, Mary; Neuman, Donald; and Wlodkowski, Raymond. *Creative Activities for Young Children.* Albany, N.Y.: Delmar, 1980.
Rubin, Richard R., and Fisher, John J., III. *Your Preschooler.* New York: Collier Macmillan, 1982.
Safran, Claire. "Speaking of Sex." *Parents* magazine, Feb. 1984, 59(2), 65–70.

CHAPTER 17
KINDERGARTEN

REFERENCES

1. McMillan, Julia A.; Stockman, James A., III; and Oski, Frank A. *The Whole Pediatrician Catalog,* Vol. 2. Philadelphia: Saunders, 1979.
2. Ibid., p. 84.
3. Hoder, E. Lawrence, and Cohen, Donald J. *Repetitive Behavior Patterns of Childhood,* Chapter 33 in Levine, Melvin D.; Carey, William B.; Crocker, Allen C.; and Gross, Ruth T., eds. *Developmental-Behavioral Pediatrics.* Philadelphia: Saunders, 1983.
4. Dodson, Fitzhugh. *How to Discipline with Love.* New York: Signet, 1978.
5. Rudolph, Marguerita, and Cohen, Dorothy H. *Kindergarten and Early Schooling,* 2nd ed. Englewood Cliffs, N.J.: Prentice-Hall, 1984.

SOURCE MATERIAL

Ames, Louise Bates, and Ilg, Frances L. *Your Five-Year-Old: Sunny and Serene.* New York: Delacorte, 1979.

Behrman, Richard E., and Vaughan, Victor C., III, eds. *Nelson Textbook of Pediatrics*, 12th ed. Philadelphia: Saunders, 1983.

Lorton, J., and Walley, B. *Introduction to Early Childhood Education*. New York: Van Nostrand, 1979.

Lowrey, George H. *Growth and Development of Children*, 8th ed. Chicago: Year Book Medical Publishers, 1986.

Margolin, Edythe. *Teaching Young Children at School and Home*. New York: Macmillan, 1982.

Rudolph, Marguerita, and Cohen, Dorothy H. *Kindergarten—A Year of Learning*. New York: Appleton-Century-Crofts, 1964.

Williams, J., and Smith, M. *Middle Childhood: Behavior and Development*. New York: Macmillan, 1974.

CHAPTER 18
HEALTH MAINTENANCE

REFERENCES

1. American Academy of Pediatrics, Committee on Nutrition. *Pediatric Nutrition Handbook*, 2nd ed. Elk Grove Village, Ill., 1985.
2. Yeung, David L.; Leung, Marie; and Pennell, Murray D. "Relationship Between Sodium Intake in Infancy and at Four Years of Age." *Nutrition Research*, 1984, 4:533–60.
3. Fomon, Samuel J.; Filer, Lloyd J.; Anderson, Thomas A.; and Ziegler, Ekhard E. "Recommendations for Feeding Normal Infants." *Pediatrics*, January 1979, 63(1), 52–59.
4. Duncan, Burris. "Breast-Fed Infants Grow More Slowly Than Formula-Fed." *American Academy of Pediatrics*, Spring Session, 1984, p. 4.
5. Siimes, Martti A.; Salmenperä, Leena; and Perheentupa, Jaakko. "Exclusive Breast-Feeding for 9 Months: Risk of Iron Deficiency." *The Journal of Pediatrics*, February 1984, 104:196–99.
6. Committee on Drugs. "The Transfer of Drugs and Other Chemicals into Human Breast Milk." *Pediatrics*, September 1983, 72(3), 375–83.
7. Ekstrand, J.; Boreus, L. O.; and de Chateau, P. "No Evidence of Transfer of Fluoride from Plasma to Breast Milk." *British Medical Journal*, September 19, 1981, 283:761–62.
8. American Academy of Pediatrics, Committee on Nutrition. *Pediatric Nutrition Handbook*, 2nd ed. Elk Grove Village, Ill., 1985.
9. Brams, Michael, and Maloney, Joseph. "Nursing Bottle Caries in Breast-Fed Children." *The Journal of Pediatrics*, September 1983, 103(3), 415–16.
10. Martinez, Gilbert A., and Dodd, David A. "1981 Milk Feeding Patterns in the United States During the First 12 Months of Life." *Pediatrics*, February 1983, 71(2), 166–70.
11. Oski, Frank A. "Iron-Fortified Formulas and Gastrointestinal Symptoms in Infants: A Controlled Study." *Pediatrics*, August 1980, 66(2), 168–70.
12. American Academy of Pediatrics, Committee on Nutrition. "On the Feeding of Supplemental Foods to Infants." *Pediatrics*, June 1980, 65(6), 1178–81.
13. Dallman, Peter R. In Oski, Frank A., and Stockman, James A., III. *The Yearbook of Pediatrics*. Chicago: Year Book Medical Publishers, 1982.
14. Puczynski, Mark; Rademaker, Dennis; and Gatson, Robert L. "Burn Injury Related to the Improper Use of a Microwave Oven." *Pediatrics*, November 1983, 72(5), 714–15.
15. Wurtman, Judith J. "What Do Children Eat? Eating Styles of the Preschool, Ele-

mentary School and Adolescent Child." In Suskind, Robert M., ed. *Textbook of Pediatric Nutrition*. New York: Raven, 1981, pp. 597–607.

16. Weiss, Robert L., and Trithart, Albert H. "Between-Meal Eating Habits and Dental Caries Experience in Preschool Children." *American Journal of Public Health*, August 1960, 50(8), 1097–1104.

17. Spock, Benjamin, and Rothenberg, Michael B. *Dr. Spock's Baby and Child Care.* New York: Pocket Books, 1985.

18. Fulginiti, Vincent A. "The Infectious Disease Consequences of the 'Back to Nature' Health Fad or Mother Nature Is Cruel." *Infectious Diseases Newsletter*, November 1981, 1(2), 9–10.

19. Christoffel, Katherine. "A Pediatric Perspective on Vegetarian Nutrition." *Clinical Pediatrics*, October 1981, 20(10), 632–43.

20. Robertson, Laurel; Flinders, Carol; and Godfrey, Bronwen. *Laurel's Kitchen.* New York: Bantam, 1978.

21. Christoffel, op. cit., p. 639.

22. Forbes, Gilbert B. "Food Fads: Safe Feeding of Children." *Pediatrics in Review*, January 1980, 1(7), 207–10.

23. Klein, Daniel. "Friendly Dog Syndrome." *New York State Journal of Medicine*, September 1, 1966, 66(17), 2306–9.

24. Voith, Victoria L. "Procedures for Introducing a Baby to a Dog." *Modern Veterinary Practice*, July 1984, 65(7), 539–41.

25. Strasser, Susan. *Never Done: A History of American Housework.* New York: Pantheon, 1982.

26. McDonald, Simon P.; Cowell, Colin R.; and Sheiham, Aubrey. "Methods of Preventing Dental Caries Used by Dentists for Their Own Children." *British Dental Journal*, August 18, 1981, 151:118–21.

27. Anders, Thomas F., and Weinstein, Pearl. "Sleep and Its Disorders in Infants and Children: A Review." *Pediatrics*, August 1972, 50(2), 312–24.

28. Lozoff, Betsy; Wolf, Abraham W.; and Davis, Nancy S. "Cosleeping in Urban Families with Young Children in the United States." *Pediatrics*, August 1984, 74(2), 171–82.

29. Thevenin, Tine. *The Family Bed: An Age-Old Concept in Child Rearing.* Franklin Park, Ill.: La Leche League International, 1983.

30. Simonds, John F., and Parraga, Humberto. "Prevalence of Sleep Disorders and Sleep Behaviors in Children and Adolescents." *Journal of the American Academy of Child Psychiatry*, July 1982, 21(4), 383–88.

31. Weissbluth, Marc. "Sleep Duration and Infant Temperament." *The Journal of Pediatrics*, November 1981, 99(5), 817–19.

32. Beltramini, Antonio U., and Hertzig, Margaret E. "Sleep and Bedtime Behavior in Preschool-Aged Children." *Pediatrics*, February 1983, 71(2), 153–58.

33. Lévy, Janine. *The Baby Exercise Book for the First Fifteen Months.* New York: Pantheon, 1975.

34. Maccoby, Eleanor E., and Jacklin, Carol N. *Psychology of Sex Differences.* Stanford, Calif.: Stanford University Press, 1974.

35. Lever, Janet. "Sex Differences in the Games Children Play." *Social Problems*, 1976, 23:478–87.

36. Long, Barbara H., and Henderson, Edmund H. "Children's Use of Time: Some Personal and Social Correlates." *The Elementary School Journal*, January 1973, 73:193–99.

37. Saegert, S., and Hart, R. "The Development of Environmental Competence in Girls and Boys." *The Association for the Anthropological Study of Play Newsletter*, Spring 1977, 3:8–13.

38. Smith, Nathan J., ed. Committee on Sports Medicine, American Academy of Pedi-

atrics. *Sports Medicine: Health Care for Young Athletes.* Elk Grove Village, Ill., 1983.

39. Wilmore, Jack H. "The Female Athlete." In Magill, Richard A.; Ash, Michael J.; and Smoll, Frank L., eds., *Children in Sport.* Champaign, Ill.: Human Kinetics, 1978.

40. Skroabak-Kaczynski, J., and Vavik, T., eds. *Physical Fitness and Trainability of Young Male Patients with Down Syndrome.* In Berg, Kristina, and Eriksson, Bengt O., eds. *Children and Exercise IX.* Baltimore, Md.: University Park Press, 1980, pp. 300–16.

41. Yates, Alayne. "Stress Management in Childhood." *Clinical Pediatrics,* February 1983, 22(2), 131–35.

42. Howell, Mary. *Healing at Home: A Guide to Health Care for Children.* Boston: Beacon, 1978.

43. Freed, Alvyn M. *TA for Tots.* Vol. 11. Sacramento, Calif.: Jalmar, 1980.

44. Freed, Alvyn, and Freed, Margaret. *TA for Kids.* Sacramento, Calif.: Jalmar, 1977.

45. Waldbott, George L. *Health Effects of Environmental Pollutants,* 2nd ed. St. Louis, Mo.: C. V. Mosby, 1978.

46. Fischbein, Alf; Cohn, Jessica; and Ackerman, Gary. "Asbestos, Lead, and the Family: Household Risks." *The Journal of Family Practice,* June 1980, 10(6), 989–92.

47. Greenberg, Robert A.; Haley, Nancy J.; Etzel, Ruth A.; and Loda, Frank A. "Measuring the Exposure of Infants to Tobacco Smoke: Nicotine and Cotinine in Urine and Saliva." *The New England Journal of Medicine,* April 26, 1984, 310(17), 1075–78.

48. Bonham, Gordon Scott, and Wilson, Ronald W. "Children's Health in Families with Cigarette Smokers." *American Journal of Public Health,* March 1981, 71(3), 290–93.

49. Tager, I. B.; Weiss, S. T.; Rosner, B.; and Speizer, F. E. "Effect of Parental Cigarette Smoking on the Pulmonary Function of Children." *American Journal of Epidemiology,* July 1979, 110:15–26.

50. Ekwo, Edem E.; Weinberger, Miles M.; Lachenbruch, Peter A.; and Huntley, William H. "Relationship of Parental Smoking and Gas Cooking to Respiratory Disease in Children." *Chest,* December 1983, 84:662–68.

51. The Council of the American College of Radiology. *Policy Statement: Referral Criteria for Chest X-ray Examinations.* September 22, 1982, Reston, Va.

52. Spengler, Robert F.; Cook, David H.; Clarke, E. Aileen; Olley, Peter M.; and Newman, Alice M. "Cancer Mortality Following Cardiac Catheterization: A Preliminary Follow-up Study on 4,891 Irradiated Children." *Pediatrics,* February 1983, 71(2), 235–39.

53. "Americans Watching Television About Seven Hours Daily, Poll Shows." *Arizona Daily Wildcat,* Wednesday, January 25, 1984.

54. Rothenberg, Michael B. "Effect of Television Violence on Children and Youth." *Journal of the American Medical Association,* December 8, 1975, 234(10), 1043–46.

55. Trelease, Jim. *The Read-Aloud Handbook.* New York: Penguin, 1982.

56. Somers, Anne R. "Violence, Television and the Health of American Youth." *The New England Journal of Medicine,* April 8, 1976, 294(15), 811–17.

57. Rothenberg, Michael B., op. cit., p. 1043.

58. Daven, Joel; O'Connor, J. F.; and Briggs, Roy. "The Consequences of Imitative Behavior in Children: The 'Evel Knievel Syndrome.'" *Pediatrics,* March 1976, 57(3), 418–19.

59. Hickey, N. "Does America Want Family Viewing Time?" *TV Guide,* December 6–12, 1975.

60. Brown, Jane D. "Sex in the Media." *Planned Parenthood Review,* Winter 1986, 6(1), 4–19.

61. Gerbner, George; Gross, Larry; Morgan, Michael; and Signorielli, Nancy. "Health

and Medicine on Television." *The New England Journal of Medicine*, October 8, 1981, 305(15), 901–4.
62. Gollin, Albert E. "Mass Media in the Family Setting." In *Current Research on Children: Birth Through Adolescence*, Vol. 1. New York: ATCOM, 1983, p. 44.
63. Busch, Jackie S. "Television's Effects on Reading: A Case Study." *Phi Delta Kappan*, June 1978, pp. 668–71.
64. Brazelton, T. Berry. "How to Tame the TV Monster." *Redbook*, April 1972, pp. 47, 49, 51.

SOURCE MATERIAL

Nutrition/Dental Nutrition

American Academy of Pediatrics, Committee on Nutrition. "Vitamin and Mineral Supplement Needs in Normal Children in the United States." *Pediatrics*, December 1980, 66(6), 1015–21.

American Dental Association, Council on American Dental Therapeutics Fluoride Compounds. In *Accepted Dental Therapeutics*, 40th ed., Chicago: American Dental Association, 1984.

Behrman, Richard E., and Vaughan, Victor C., III, eds. *Nelson Textbook of Pediatrics*, 12th ed. Philadelphia: W. B. Saunders, 1983.

Berenson, G. S., et al. "Cardiovascular Risk Factors in Children: Should They Concern the Pediatrician?" *American Journal of Diseases of Children*, September 1982, 136:855.

Bowes, Anna DePlanter; Church, Charles Frederick; and Church, Helen Nichols. *Food Values of Portions Commonly Used*, 12th ed. Philadelphia: Lippincott, 1975.

Burton, Benjamin T. *Human Nutrition*. New York: McGraw-Hill, 1976.

Butte, Nancy F.; Garza, Cutbeto; Smith, E. O'Brian; and Nichols, Burford L. "Human Milk Intake and Growth in Exclusively Breast-fed Infants." *The Journal of Pediatrics*, February 1984, 104:187–94.

Committee on Dietary Allowances, Food and Nutrition Board. *Recommended Dietary Allowances*, 9th ed. Washington, D.C.: National Academy of Sciences, 1980.

Committee on Nutrition. "Fluoride Supplementation." *Pediatrics*, May 1986, 77(5), 758–61.

Committee on Nutrition of the Mother and Preschool Child, Food and Nutrition Board, Assembly of Life Sciences, National Research Council. *Nutrition Services in Perinatal Care*. Washington, D.C.: National Academy, 1981.

Committee on Nutrition, 1982–83. "Toward a Prudent Diet for Children." *Pediatrics*, January 1983, 71(1), 78–80.

Eastham, Edmund J., and Walker, W. Allan. "Adverse Effects of Milk Formula Ingestion on the Gastrointestinal Tract, an Update." *Gastroenterology*, February 1979, 76(2), 365–74.

Glueck, Charles J. "Pediatric Primary Prevention of Atherosclerosis." *The New England Journal of Medicine*, January 16, 1986, 314(3), 175–77.

Hayden, Dolores. *The Grand Domestic Revolution: A History of Feminist Designs for American Homes, Neighborhoods and Cities*. Cambridge, Mass.: MIT Press, 1981.

McMillan, Julia; Stockman, James A., III; and Oski, Frank A. *The Whole Pediatrician Catalog*, Vol. 3. Philadelphia: W. B. Saunders, 1982.

Newman, W. P., III; Freedman, D. S.; Voors, A. W.; et al. "Relation of Serum Lipoprotein Levels and Systolic Blood Pressure to Early Atherosclerosis: The Bogalusa Heart Study." *New England Journal of Medicine*, Jan. 1986, 314(3), 138–44.

Ogra, Pearay L., and Greene, Harry L. "Human Milk and Breast Feeding: An Update on the State of the Art." *Pediatric Research*, April 1982, 16:266–71.

Roper, Nancy. "Man, His Health and Environment: Nutrition in Relation to Health,

Food Poisoning, Milk, Water." In *Man's Anatomy, Physiology, Health and Environment.* Edinburgh, Scotland: Churchill Livingstone, 1976, pp. 217–64.

Sarett, Herbert P.; Bain, Kevin R.; and O'Leary, John C. "Decisions on Breast-feeding or Formula Feeding and Trends in Infant-Feeding Practices." *American Journal of Diseases of Children,* August 1983, 137:719–25.

Stare, Fredrick J.; Whelan, Elizabeth M.; and Sheridan, Margaret. "Diet and Hyperactivity: Is There a Relationship?" *Pediatrics,* October 1980, 66(4), 521–25.

Sturtevant, F. M. "Use of Aspartame in Pregnancy." *International Journal of Fertility,* August 1985, 30(1), 85–87.

Webber, L. S., et al. "Occurrence in Children of Multiple Risk Factors for Coronary Artery Disease: The Bogalusa Heart Study." *Preventive Medicine,* May 1979, 8(3), 407–18.

Sleep

Anders, Thomas F., and Keener, Marcia A. "Sleep-Wake State Development and Disorders of Sleep in Infants, Children, and Adolescents." In Levine, Melvin D.; Carey, William B.; Crocker, Allen C.; and Gross, Ruth T. *Developmental-Behavioral Pediatrics.* Philadelphia: W. B. Saunders, 1983.

Behrman, Richard E., and Vaughan, Victor C., III, eds. *Nelson Textbook of Pediatrics,* 12th ed. Philadelphia: W. B. Saunders, 1983.

Beltramini, Antonio U., and Hertzig, Margaret E. "Sleep and Bedtime Behavior in Preschool-Aged Children." *Pediatrics,* February 1983, 71(2), 153–58.

Jovanovic, Uros J. *Normal Sleep in Man.* Stuttgart, Germany: Hippokrates Verlag, 1971.

Lansky, Vicki. *Getting Your Baby to Sleep (and Back to Sleep).* New York: Bantam, 1985.

Rudolph, Abraham M., ed. *Pediatrics,* 17th ed. East Norwalk, Conn.: Appleton-Century-Crofts, 1982.

Schuster, Clara Shaw, and Ashburn, Shirley Smith. *The Process of Human Development: A Holistic Approach.* Boston: Little, Brown, 1980.

Exercise

Albinson, J. G., and Andrew, G. M., eds. *Child in Sport and Physical Activity.* Baltimore, Md.: University Park Press, 1976.

Fahey, Thomas D. *Good-Time Fitness for Kids.* New York: Butterick, 1979.

Garvey, Catherine. *Play.* Cambridge, Mass.: Harvard University Press, 1977.

Nickerson, Bruce G.; Bautista, Daisy B.; Namey, Marla A.; Richards, Warren; and Keens, Thomas G. "Distance Running Improves Fitness in Asthmatic Children Without Pulmonary Complications or Changes in Exercise-Induced Bronchospasm." *Pediatrics,* February 1983, 71(2), 147–52.

Rarick, G. Lawrence, ed. *Physical Activity: Human Growth and Development.* New York: Academic, 1973.

Smith, Nathan J. "Medical Issues in Sports Medicine." *Pediatrics in Review,* February 1981, 2(8), 229–37.

———. "The Prevention of Heat Disorders in Sports." *American Journal of Diseases of Children,* August 1984, 138:786–90.

Stress

Benson, Herbert. *The Relaxation Response.* Boston: G. K. Hall, 1975.

Kersey, Katharine. *Helping Your Child Handle Stress: The Parent's Guide to Recognizing and Solving Childhood Problems.* Washington, D.C.: Acropolis, 1986.

Schaefer, Charles E.; Millman, Howard L.; and Levine, Gary F., eds. *Therapies for Psychosomatic Disorders in Children.* San Francisco: Jossey-Bass, 1979.

Environment

Brent, Robert L. "Cancer Risks Following Diagnostic Radiation Exposure." *Pediatrics*, February 1983, 71(2), 288–89.

Brent, Robert L. "X-ray, Microwave and Ultrasound: The Real and Unreal Hazards." *Pediatric Annals*, December 1980, 9(12), 469–73.

Brent, Robert L., and Gorson, Robert O. "Radiation Exposure in Pregnancy." *Current Problems in Radiology*, September–October 1972, 2(5), 2–48.

Bryan, John A.; Lehmann, James D.; Setiady, Ignatius F.; and Hatch, Milford H. "An Outbreak of Hepatitis-A Associated with Recreational Lake Water." *American Journal of Epidemiology*, 1974, 99(2), 145–54.

Committee on Environmental Hazards. "Involuntary Smoking: A Hazard to Children." *Pediatrics*, May 1986, 77(5), 755–57.

Committee on Radiology. "Radiation of Pregnant Women." *Pediatrics*, January 1978, 61(1), 117–18.

Cooke, Robert E., ed. *The Biologic Basis of Pediatric Practice*. New York: McGraw-Hill, 1968.

Decoufle, Pierre. "Hazards of Radiation at Work and in the Environment." *Project Module*, Arizona Center for Occupational Safety and Health, Tucson, Arizona, September 1980.

Executive Office of the President, Council on Environmental Quality. *Environmental Quality-1980*, the Eleventh Annual Report of the Council on Environmental Quality, Washington, D.C., December 1980.

Guidotti, Tee L., and Goldsmith, John R. "Air Pollution and Family Health." *American Family Physician*, April 1983, 27(4), 165–72.

Gustafsson, M., and Mortensson, W. "Radiation Exposure and Estimate of Late Effects of Chest Roentgen Examination in Children." *Acta Radiologica Diagnosis*, 1983, 24(4), 309–14.

Hunt, Vilma R.; Smith, M. Kate; and Worth, Dorothy, eds. *Banbury Report 11, Environmental Factors in Human Growth and Development*. Cold Spring Harbor, N.Y.: Cold Spring Harbor Laboratory, 1982.

Karsh, Robert S. "Environment, Clinical Conference from the St. Louis Children's Hospital." *Clinical Pediatrics*, October 1971, 10(10), 590–96.

Legator, Marvin S.; Harper, Barbara L.; and Scott, Michael J., eds. *The Health Detective's Handbook: A Guide to the Investigation of Environmental Health Hazards by Nonprofessionals*. Baltimore, Md.: Johns Hopkins University Press, 1985.

Miller, Robert W. "Carcinogens in Drinking Water." *Pediatrics*, April 1976, 57(4), 462–64.

Norwood, Christopher. *At Highest Risk: Environmental Hazards to Young and Unborn Children*. New York: McGraw-Hill, 1980.

Pattishall, Edward N.; Strope, Gerlad L.; Etzel, Ruth A.; Helms, Ronald W.; Haley, Nancy J.; and Denny, Floyd W. "Serum Cotinine as a Measure of Tobacco Smoke Exposure in Children." *American Journal of Diseases of Children*, November 1985, 139:1101–4.

Poznanski, Andrew K. *Practical Approaches to Pediatric Radiology*. Boston: Little, Brown, 1976.

Roper, Nancy. "Man, His Health and Environment: Sanitation and Disposal of Refuse, Air or Atmosphere." In *Man's Anatomy, Physiology, Health and Environment*. Edinburgh, Scotland: Churchill Livingstone, 1976, pp. 303–46.

Sandler, Dale P.; Wilcox, Allen J.; and Everson, Richard B. "Cumulative Effects of Lifetime Passive Smoking on Cancer Risk." *The Lancet*, February 9, 1985, 1(8424), 312–15.

Vogt, Thomas M. "Effects of Parental Smoking on Medical Care Utilization by Children." *American Journal of Public Health*, January 1984, 74(1), 30–34.

Weiss, Scott T.; Tager, Ira B.; Speizer, Frank E.; and Rosner, Bernard. "Persistent Wheeze: Its Relation to Respiratory Illness, Cigarette Smoking, and Level of Pulmonary Function in a Population Sample of Children." *American Review of Respiratory Disease*, November 1980, 122:697–707.

Zamm, Alfred V., with Gannon, Robert. *Why Your House May Endanger Your Health*. New York: Simon & Schuster, 1980.

Television

Feinbloom, Richard I. "Television and Children." *Ambulatory Pediatric Association Newsletter*, November 1977, 13(1), 12–14.

Feinbloom, Richard I. "TV Update." *Pediatrics*, September 1978, 62(3), 428–31.

Greenberg, Bradley. "Child Nurturing and Television in the 1980s." In Boger, R. P.; Blom, G. E.; Lezotte, L. E., eds. *Child Nurturing in the 1980s*, Vol. 4. of *Child Nurturance*. New York: Plenum Press, 1984.

Rothenberg, Michael B. "Effect of Television Violence on Children and Youth." *Journal of the American Medical Association*, December 8, 1975, 234(10), 1043–46.

Rothenberg, Michael B. "Television and Children." *Pediatrics in Review*, April 1980, 1(10), 329–32.

Rubinstein, Eli A. "Television and the Young Viewer." *American Scientist*, November–December 1978, 66:685–93.

Tower, Roni Beth; Singer, Dorothy G.; Singer, Jerome L.; and Biggs, Ann. "Differential Effects of Television Programming on Preschoolers' Cognition, Imagination and Social Play." *American Orthopsychiatric Association, Inc.*, April 1979, 49(2), 265–81.

Weissbluth, M.; Poncher, J.; Given, G.; Schwab, J.; Mervis, R.; and Rosenberg, M. "Sleep Duration and Television Viewing." *The Journal of Pediatrics*, September 1981, 99(3), 486–88.

Zuckerman, Diana M., and Zuckerman, Barry S. "Television's Impact on Children." *Pediatrics*, February 1985, 75(2), 233–40.

CHAPTER 19
CHOOSING HEALTH PROFESSIONALS FOR YOUR CHILD'S CARE

REFERENCES

1. Thomas, Lewis. *The Youngest Science: Notes of a Medicine Watcher*. New York: Viking, 1983, pp. 58–59.
2. Ernst, Richard L., and Yett, Donald E. *Physician Location and Specialty Choice*. Ann Arbor, Mich.: Health Administration Press, 1985.
3. Starfield, Barbara. "Special Responsibilities: The Role of the Pediatrician and the Goals of Pediatric Education." *Pediatrics*, March 1983, 71(3), 433–40.
4. American Academy of Pediatrics. "Survey Shows Parents See Pediatricians as 'Baby Specialists.'" *News and Comment*, January 1983, pp. 1–2.
5. *Directory of Medical Specialists*, 20th ed. American Board of Medical Specialties. Chicago: Marquis Who's Who, 1981.
6. *American Medical Directory*, 29th ed. Chicago: American Medical Association, 1985.
7. LeMaitre, George D. *How to Choose a Good Doctor*. Andover, Mass.: Andover Publishing Group, 1979.
8. Goodman, Ellen. "Health Care's Junior Partner." *Arizona Daily Star*, July 15, 1984.
9. Liptak, Gregory S.; Hulka, Barbara S.; and Cassel, John C. "Effectiveness of Physician-Mother Interactions During Infancy." *Pediatrics*, August 1977, 60(2), 186–92.

10. Vickery, Donald M.; Kalmer, Howard; Lowry, Debra; Constantine, Muriel; Wright, Elizabeth; and Loren, Wendy. "Effect of a Self-care Education Program on Medical Visits." *Journal of the American Medical Association*, December 2, 1983, 250(21), 2952–56.
11. American Academy of Pediatrics. *Report of the Committee on Infectious Diseases*, 20th ed. Elk Grove Village, Ill., 1986.
12. American Academy of Pediatrics (1986), op. cit., p. 173.
13. DeAngelis, Catherine; Berman, Barbara; Oda, Dorothy; and Meeker, Robert. "Comparative Values of School Physical Examinations and Mass Screening Tests." *The Journal of Pediatrics*, March 1983, 102(3), 477–81.
14. Feldman, W.; Gilbert, J. R.; Mills, D. A.; Siegel, L. S.; Dunnett, C.; and Stoddart, G. "Parent-Initiated Utilization for Low-Risk Infants Randomly Allocated at Birth to Five v. Ten Well-Baby Visits in the First Two Years of Life." *American Journal of Diseases of Children*, June 1983, 137:528.
15. U.S. Department of Health and Human Services. Centers for Disease Control, Atlanta, Ga. "Pertussis Surveillance, 1979–1981." *Morbidity and Mortality Weekly Report*, July 2, 1982, (31)25, 333–36.
16. Harrison, H. Robert, and Fulginiti, Vincent A. "Bacterial Immunizations." *American Journal of Diseases of Children*, February 1980, 134:184–93.
17. Committee on Infectious Diseases. "Pertussis Vaccine." *Pediatrics*, August 1984, 74(2), 303–5.
18. U.S. Department of Health and Human Services. Centers for Disease Control, Atlanta, Ga. "Diphtheria, Tetanus, and Pertussis: Guidelines for Vaccine Prophylaxis and Other Preventive Measures." *Morbidity and Mortality Weekly Report*, July 12, 1985, 34(27), 405–28.
19. American Academy of Pediatrics (1986), op. cit., p. 9.
20. Haggard, Howard W. *Mystery, Magic, and Medicine*. Garden City, N.Y.: Doubleday, 1933.
21. Weinstein, Milton C., and Fineberg, Harvey V. *Clinical Decision Analysis*. Philadelphia: W. B. Saunders, 1980.
22. Fulginiti, Vincent A. *Pediatric Clinical Problem Solving*. Baltimore, Md.: Williams & Wilkins, 1981.
23. Shephard, Bruce D., and Shephard, Carroll A. *The Complete Guide to Women's Health*. Tampa, Fla.: Mariner, 1982.

SOURCE MATERIAL

American Dental Association. *How to Become a Wise Dental Consumer*. Chicago: Bureau of Public Information, 1978.
Arizona State Medical Directory. Board of Medical Examiners of the State of Arizona, Phoenix, Ariz., 1985.
Baraff, Larry J.; Cody, Christopher L.; Cherry, James D. "DTP-Associated Reactions: Analysis by Injection Site." *Pediatrics*, January 1984, 73:31–36.
Brazelton, T. Berry. *Doctor and Child*. New York: Delacorte/Seymour Lawrence, 1976.
Cherry, James D. "The Pertussis Epidemic in Oklahoma: A Warning for the Future." *American Journal of Diseases of Children*, May 1986, 140:417–18.
Cody, Christopher L.; Baraff, Larry J.; Cherry, James D.; Marcy, S. Michael; and Manclark, Charles R. "Nature and Rates of Adverse Reactions Associated with DTP and DT Immunizations in Infants and Children." *Pediatrics*, November 1981, 68(5), 650–60.
Golde, Roger A. *Can You Be Sure of Your Experts?* New York: Macmillan, 1969.
Hillman, Sheilah. *The Baby Checkup Book: A Parent's Guide to Well Babycare in the First Two Years*. New York: Bantam, 1982.
Hinman, Alan R., and Koplan, Jeffrey P. "Pertussis and Pertussis Vaccine: Reanalysis of

Benefits, Risks, and Costs." *Journal of the American Medical Association*, June 15, 1984, 251:3109–13.

Hoekelman, Robert A.; Klein, Michael; Strain, James E. "Who Should Provide Primary Health Care to Children: Pediatricians or Family Medicine Physicians?" *Pediatrics*, October 1984, 74(4), 460–77.

Horwitz, S. M.; Horwitz, R. I.; and Morgenstern, H. "Self-Care Prior to Pediatrician Contact: Reported vs. Actual Maternal Practices." *Ambulatory Pediatric Association Newsletter*, Spring 1986, 21(3), 23.

Kirchner, M. "Non-surgical Practice: What's the Key to Higher Earnings?" *Medical Economics*, Feb. 16, 1981, pp. 183–97.

Linde, Shirley M. *The Whole Health Catalogue: How to Stay Well Cheaper.* New York: Rawson, 1977.

Miller, Lewis. *The Life You Save.* New York: Morrow, 1979.

National Ambulatory Medical Care Survey. *Vital and Health Statistics.* Series 13, Number 66. Washington, D.C.: U.S. Department of Health and Human Services, 1979.

Phillips, Carol F. "New Immunizations for Children." *Pediatrics in Review*, April 1986, 7(10), 291–95.

Starfield, Barbara; Hoekelman, Robert A.; McCormick, Marie; Benson, Paul; Mendenhall, Robert C.; Moynihan, Christy; and Radecki, Stephen. "Who Provides Health Care to Children and Adolescents in the United States?" *Pediatrics*, December 1984, 74:991–97.

Thompson, Hugh C.; Bornstein, Suzanne L.; and Connelly, John P. *Demographic and Socioeconomic Fact Book on Child Health Care: A Survey of Trends in the United States.* Elk Grove Village, Ill.: American Academy of Pediatrics, 1980.

Welch, Nancy M.; Saulsbury, Frank T.; and Kesler, Richard W. "The Value of the Preschool Examination in Screening for Health Problems." *The Journal of Pediatrics*, February 1982, *100*(2), 232–34.

Young, Paul C.; Wasserman, Richard C.; McAullife, Tim; Long, John; Hagan, Joseph F.; Heath, Barry. "Why Families Change Pediatricians: Factors Causing Dissatisfaction with Pediatric Care." *American Journal of Diseases of Children*, July 1985, 139:683–86.

CHAPTER 20
SYMPTOMS

REFERENCES

1. Schmitt, Barton D. "Fever Phobia. Misconceptions of Parents About Fevers." *American Journal of Diseases of Children*, February 1980, 134:176–81.
2. Done, Alan K. "Treatment of Fever in 1982: A Review." *The American Journal of Medicine* (Supplement), June 14, 1983, 74:27–35.
3. Finkelhor, David. *Child Sexual Abuse: New Theory and Research.* New York: The Free Press, 1984.
4. The Alan Guttmacher Institute. *Teenage Pregnancy: The Problem That Hasn't Gone Away.* New York, 1981.
5. "U.S. Teens: Mixed Signals?" *Medical World News for Obstetricians, Gynecologists, Urologists*, April 11, 1985.

SOURCE MATERIAL

Behrman, Richard E., and Vaughan, Victor C., III., eds. *Nelson Textbook of Pediatrics*, 12th ed. Philadelphia: W. B. Saunders, 1983.

Book, Linda S. "Vomiting and Diarrhea." *Pediatrics*, November 1984, 74(5), 950–54.

Foxman, Betsy; Valdez, R. Burciaga; and Brook, Robert H. "Childhood Enuresis: Prevalence, Perceived Impact, and Prescribed Treatments." *Pediatrics*, April 1986, 77(4), 482–87.

Kempe, Henry G.; Silver, Henry K.; and O'Brien, Donough. *Current Pediatric Diagnosis and Treatment*, 8th ed. Los Altos, Calif.: Lange Medical Publications, 1984.

Kramer, Michael S.; Naimark, Lenora; and Leduc, Denis G. "Parental Fever Phobia and Its Correlates." *Pediatrics*, June 1985, 75(6), 1110–13.

Levine, Melvin D.; Carey, William B.; Crocker, Allen C.; and Gross, Ruth T., eds. *Developmental-Behavioral Pediatrics*. Philadelphia: W. B. Saunders, 1983.

Peter, Georges. "The Child with Group A Steptococcal Pharyngitis." In Aronoff, Stephen C., ed. *Advances in Pediatric Infectious Diseases*, Vol. 1. Chicago: Year Book Medical Publishers, 1986.

Rudolph, Abraham M., ed. *Pediatrics*, 17th ed. East Norwalk, Conn.: Appleton-Century-Crofts, 1982.

Schmitt, Barton D. "Fever in Childhood." *Pediatrics*, November 1984, 74(5), 929–36.

Tunnessen, Walter W. *Signs and Symptoms in Pediatrics*. Philadelphia: Lippincott, 1983.

Walson, Philip D. "Coughs and Colds." *Pediatrics*, November 1984, 74(5), 937–40.

CHAPTER 21
CARE OF THE SICK CHILD AT HOME

REFERENCES

1. Banco, Leonard, and Veltri, Daniel. "The Ability of Mothers to Subjectively Assess the Presence of Fever in Their Children." *Ambulatory Pediatric Association Program and Abstracts*, 1983.
2. ———. "Ability of Mothers to Subjectively Assess the Presence of Fever in Their Children." *American Journal of Diseases of Children*, Oct. 1984, 138:976–78.
3. Reisinger, Keith S.; Kao, Joan; and Grant, Deborah M. "Inaccuracy of the Clinitemp Skin Thermometer." *Ambulatory Pediatric Association Program and Abstracts*, 1979.
4. *Physicians' Desk Reference*, 41st ed. Oradell, N.J.: Medical Economics Co., 1987.
5. *Handbook of Nonprescription Drugs*, 7th ed. Washington, D.C.: American Pharmaceutical Association, 1982.
6. Howell, Mary. *Healing at Home: A Guide to Health Care for Children*. Boston: Beacon Press, 1978.
7. King, Maurice; King, Felicity; and Mortodipoero, Soebagio. *Primary Child Care: A Manual for Health Workers*. Oxford: Oxford University Press, 1978.
8. Werner, David. *Where There Is No Doctor*. Palo Alto, Calif.: The Hesperian Foundation, 1977.

SOURCE MATERIAL

Behrman, Richard E., and Vaughan, Victor C., III., eds. *Nelson Textbook of Pediatrics*, 12th ed. Philadelphia: Saunders, 1983.

Done, Alan K. "Treatment of Fever in 1982: A Review." *The American Journal of Medicine* (Supplement), June 14, 1983, 74:27–35.

Griffith, H. Winter; Mofenson, Howard C.; Greensher, Joseph; and Greensher, Arnold. *Information and Instructions for Pediatric Parents*. Tucson, Ariz.: Winter Publishing Co., 1980.

Kempe, Henry C.; Silver, Henry K.; and O'Brien, Donough. *Current Pediatric Diagnosis and Treatment*, 8th ed. Los Altos, Calif: Lange Medical Publications, 1984.

Remington, Patrick L.; Rowley, Diane; McGee, Harry; Hall, William N.; and Monto, Arnold S. "Decreasing Trends in Reye's Syndrome and Aspirin Use in Michigan, 1979 to 1984." *Pediatrics,* Jan. 1986, 77(1), 93–98.

CHAPTER 22
HOW ILLNESS AFFECTS CHILDREN AND PARENTS

REFERENCES

1. Howell, Mary. *Healing at Home: A Guide to Health Care for Children.* Boston: Beacon Press, 1978.
2. Heisel, J. Stephen; Ream, Scott; Raitz, Raymond; Rappaport, Michael; and Coddington, R. Dean. "The Significance of Life Events as Contributing Factors in the Diseases of Children." *The Journal of Pediatrics,* July 1973, 83(1), 119–23.
3. Perrin, Ellen C., and Gerrity, Susan P. "There's a Demon in Your Belly: Children's Understanding of Illness." *Pediatrics,* June 1981, 67(6), 841–49.
4. McMillan, Julia A.; Nieburg, Phillip I.; and Oski, Frank A. *The Whole Pediatrician Catalog,* Vol. I. Philadelphia: Saunders, 1977.
5. Litt, Iris F.; Cuskey, Walter R.; and Rosenberg, Anne. "Role of Self-Esteem and Autonomy in Determining Medication Compliance Among Adolescents with Juvenile Rheumatoid Arthritis." *Pediatrics,* Jan. 1982, 69(1), 15–17.
6. Satterwhite, Betty B. "Impact of Chronic Illness on Child and Family: An Overview Based on Five Surveys with Implications for Management." *International Journal of Rehabilitation Research,* Jan. 1978, 1(1), 7–17.
7. Sargent, A. John, III. "The Sick Child and the Family." *The Journal of Pediatrics,* June 1983, 102(6), 982–87.
8. McKeever, Patricia. "Siblings of Chronically Ill Children: A Literature Review with Implications for Research and Practice." *American Journal of Orthopsychiatry,* April 1983, 53(2), 209–18.
9. Schwab, Fred; Tolbert, Brenda; Bagnato, Stephen; and Maisels, M. Jeffrey. "Sibling Visiting in a Neonatal Intensive Care Unit." *Pediatrics,* May 1983, 71(5), 835–38.

SOURCE MATERIAL

Batshaw, Mark L., and Perret, Yvonne M. *Children with Handicaps.* Baltimore: Paul H. Brookes, 1981.
Forman, Marc A.; Hetznecker, William H.; and Dunn, John M. "Prevention of Psychologic Disorders in the Sick Child." In Behrman, Richard E., and Vaughan, Victor C., III, eds. *Nelson Textbook of Pediatrics,* 12th ed. Philadelphia: Saunders, 1983.
Freud, Anna. "The Role of Bodily Illness in the Mental Life of Children." *Psychoanalytic Study of the Child,* 1952, 7:69–81.
Mishara, Brian L., and Patterson, Robert D. *Consumer's Guide to Mental Health.* New York: Times Book Co., 1977.
Prugh, Dane G., and Eckhardt, Lloyd O. "Children's Reactions to Illness, Hospitalization, and Surgery." In Kaplan, Harold I.; Freedman, Alfred M.; and Sadock, Benjamin J., eds. *Textbook of Psychiatry III.* Baltimore: Williams & Wilkins, 1980, pp. 2766–74.
Shannon, F. T.; Fergusson, D. M.; and Dimond, M. E. "Early Hospital Admissions and Subsequent Behavior Problems in 6-Year-Olds." *Archives of Diseases of Children,* Sept. 1984, 59:815–19.
Statistical Abstract of the United States: 1986. U.S. Bureau of the Census, 106th ed., 1985.

CHAPTER 23
EMERGENCIES

REFERENCES

1. Mofenson, Howard C., and Caraceio, Thomas R. "Benefits/Risks of Syrup of Ipe-cac." *Pediatrics*, April 1986, 77(4), 551–52.
2. American Academy of Pediatrics, Committee on Accident and Poison Prevention. "Revised First Aid for the Choking Child." *Pediatrics*, July 1986, 78(1), 177–78.
3. Heimlich, Henry J. "First Aid for Choking Children: Back Blows and Chest Thrusts Cause Complications and Death." *Pediatrics*, July 1982, 70(1), 120–24.
4. Day, Richard L. "Differing Opinions on the Emergency Treatment of Choking." *Pediatrics*, June 1983, 71(6), 976–77.
5. "Pediatric Basic Life Support." *Journal of the American Medical Association*, June 6, 1986, 255(21), 2954–60.
6. McMillan, Julia A.; Stockman, James A., III; and Oski, Frank A. *The Whole Pediatrician Catalog*, Vol. 2. Philadelphia: Saunders, 1979.
7. Kempe, C. Henry; Silver, Henry K.; and O'Brien, Donough. *Current Pediatric Diagnosis and Treatment*, 8th ed. Los Altos, Calif.: Lange Medical Publications, 1984.
8. Gore, Harriet Margolis. *What to Do When There's No One But You*. Englewood Cliffs, N.J.: Prentice-Hall, 1974.

SOURCE MATERIAL

Banner, William, Jr. "Toxic Polypharmaceutical Problems from South of the Border." *Arizona Poison Control System*, Vol. 2. Tucson, Ariz.: College of Pharmacy, Arizona Health Sciences Center. March 1983.

Behrman, Richard E., and Vaughan, Victor C., III. *Nelson Textbook of Pediatrics*, 12th ed. Philadelphia: Saunders, 1983.

Day, Richard L.; Crelin, Edmund S.; and DuBois, Arthur B. "Choking: The Heimlich Abdominal Thrust vs Back Blows: An Approach to Measurement of Inertial and Aerodynamic Forces." *Pediatrics*, July 1982, 70(1), 113–19.

Greensher, Joseph, and Mofenson, Howard C. "Emergency Treatment of the Choking Child." *Pediatrics*, July 1982, 70(1), 110–12.

Harmon, Murl. *A New Vaccine for Child Safety*. Jenkintown, Pa.: Safety Now Co., 1976.

Heimlich, Henry J. "A Life-Saving Maneuver to Prevent Food-Choking." *Journal of the American Medical Association*, Oct. 27, 1975, 234(4), 398–401.

Linde, Shirley M. *The Whole Health Catalogue: How to Stay Well—Cheaper*. New York: Rawson Associates, 1977.

Lisman, C. "Tooth Reimplantation." *Pediatrics in Review*, Oct. 1983, 5(4), 105.

Litovitz, Toby L.; Klein-Schwartz, Wendy; Oderda, Gary M.; Matyunas, Nancy J.; Wiley, Scott; and Gorman, Richard L. "Ipecac Administration in Children Younger Than 1 Year of Age." *Pediatrics*, Nov. 1985, 76(5), 761–64.

Needham, Glen R. "Evaluation of Five Popular Methods for Tick Removal." *Pediatrics*, June 1985, 75(6), 997–1002.

Rohn, Reuben D.; Sarles, Richard M.; Kenny, Thomas J.; Reynolds, Brenda J.; and Heald, Felix P. "Adolescents Who Attempt Suicide." *The Journal of Pediatrics*, April 1977, 90(4), 636–38.

Schmitt, Barton D. *Pediatric Telephone Advice*. Boston: Little, Brown, 1980.

CHAPTER 24
DIFFERENT KINDS OF PARENTS

REFERENCES

1. Hanson, Shirley M. H., and Sporakowski, Michael J. "Single Parent Families." *Family Relations*, Jan. 1986, 35:3–8.
2. Glick, P. C. "Children of Divorced Parents in Demographic Perspective." *Journal of Social Issues*, 1979, 35(4), 170–82.
3. Norton, Arthur J., and Glick, Paul C. "One Parent Families: A Social and Economic Profile." *Family Relations*, Jan. 1986, 35:9–17.
4. Weitzman, Lenore J. *The Divorce Revolution: The Unexpected Social and Economic Consequences for Women and Children in America*. New York: Free Press, 1985.
5. Kellam, Sheppard G., et al. *Mental Health and Going to School: The Woodlawn Program of Assessment, Early Intervention and Evaluation*. Chicago: University of Chicago Press, 1979.
6. Kappelman, Murray M., and Ackerman, Paul R. *Parents After Thirty*. New York: Rawson, Wade, 1980.
7. Macklin, Eleanor D., and Rubin, Roger H., eds. *Contemporary Families and Alternative Lifestyles: Handbook on Research and Theory*. Beverly Hills: Sage Publications, 1982.
8. Langway, Lynn. "A New Kind of Life with Father." *Newsweek*, Nov. 30, 1981, pp. 93–94; 96–98.
9. "Three Decades See Sharp Rise in Female Work Force." *Arizona Daily Star*, Oct. 11, 1983.
10. U.S. Department of Labor, Bureau of Labor Statistics, *News*, Sept. 19, 1985, Washington, D.C.
11. Haas, Linda. "Role-Sharing Couples: A Study of Egalitarian Marriages." *Family Relations*, July 1980, 29:289–96.
12. Blumstein, Philip, and Schwartz, Pepper. *The American Couples: Money, Work and Sex*. New York: Morrow, 1983.
13. Dietz, Jean. "Fatherhood May Be Bad for Business." Los Angeles *Times*, Sept. 11, 1983.
14. Norris, Gloria, and Miller, Jo Ann. *The Working Mother's Complete Handbook*. New York: Dutton, 1979.
15. Eisen, Carol G. *Nobody Said You Had to Eat Off the Floor: The Psychiatrist's Wife's Guide to Housekeeping*. New York: David McKay, 1971.
16. Enos, Clive, and Enos, Sondra Forsyth. "Portrait of the American Woman Today." *Ladies' Home Journal*, Jan. 1984.
17. Baruch, Grace; Barnett, Rosalind; and Rivers, Caryl. *Lifeprints: New Patterns of Love and Work for Today's Women*. New York: McGraw-Hill, 1983.
18. Stolz, Lois Meek. "Effects of Maternal Employment on Children: Evidence from Research." *Child Development*, 1960, 31:779.
19. Howell, Mary C. "Employed Mothers and Their Families (I)." *Pediatrics*, Aug. 1973, 52(2), 252.
20. ———. "Effects of Maternal Employment on the Child (II)." *Pediatrics*, Sept. 1973, 52(3), 327–43.
21. Hurst, Marsha, and Zambrana, Ruth E. *Determinants and Consequences of Maternal Employment: An Annotated Bibliography 1968–1980*. Washington, D.C.: Business and Professional Women's Foundation, 1981.
22. American Academy of Pediatrics, Committee on Psychosocial Aspects of Child and Family Health, 1982–1984. "The Mother Working Outside the Home." *Pediatrics*, June 1984, 73(6), 874–75.

23. Heins, Marilyn; Stillman, Paula; Sabers, Darrell; and Mazzeo, John. "Attitudes of Pediatricians Toward Maternal Employment." *Pediatrics,* Sept. 1983, 72(3), 283–90.
24. Minsky, Terri. "Advice and Comfort for the Working Mother." *Esquire,* June 1984.
25. Burden, Dianne S. "Single Parents and the Work Setting: The Impact of Multiple Job and Homelife Responsibilities." *Family Relations,* Jan. 1986, 35:37–43.

SOURCE MATERIAL

Bolsen, Barbara. "How Mothers with Careers Affect Children, Selves." *American Medical News,* June 1, 1984, pp. 3; 15–16.
Grollman, Earl A., and Sweder, Gerri L. *The Working Parent Dilemma: How to Balance the Responsibilities of Children and Careers.* Boston: Beacon Press, 1986.
Klein, Carole. *The Single Parent Experience.* New York: Avon, 1978.
Lamb, Michael E., ed. *Nontraditional Families: Parenting and Child Development.* Hillsdale, N.J.: Lawrence Erlbaum Associates, 1982.
Masnick, George, and Bane, Mary Jo. *The Nation's Families: 1960–1990.* Boston: Auburn House, 1980.
Sasserath, Valerie J., ed. *Minimizing High-Risk Parenting: A Review of What Is Known and Consideration of Appropriate Preventive Intervention.* (Pediatric Roundtable: 7) Skillman, N.J.: Johnson & Johnson Baby Products, 1983.
Schlesinger, Benjamin. *The One-Parent Family: Perspectives and Annotated Bibliography.* Toronto: University of Toronto Press, 1978.

CHAPTER 25
PARENTING NON-BIOLOGICAL CHILDREN

REFERENCES

1. Auerbach, Kathleen G., and Avery, Jimmie Lynne. "Induced Lactation. A Study of Adoptive Nursing by 240 Women." *American Journal of Diseases of Children,* April 1981, 135:340–43.
2. Smith, Dorothy W., and Sherwen, Laurie Nehls. *"Mothers and Their Adopted Children—the Bonding Process."* New York: Tiresias Press, 1983.
3. Mishell, Daniel R., and Davajan, Val, eds. *Infertility, Contraception and Reproductive Endocrinology,* 2nd ed. Oradell, N.J.: Medical Economics Books, 1986.
4. Kadushin, Alfred. *Child Welfare Services,* 3rd ed. New York: Macmillan, 1980.
5. Hammons, Chloe. "The Adoptive Family." *American Journal of Nursing,* Feb. 1976, 76(2), 251–57.
6. Sokoloff, Burton. "Adoptive Families: Needs for Counseling." *Clinical Pediatrics,* March 1979, 18(3), 184–85; 188–90.
7. Sorosky, Arthur D. Letters to the Editor: Dr. Sorosky Replies on "Unsealing the Records in Adoption." *American Journal of Psychiatry,* Jan. 1977, 134(1), 95.
8. Sorich, Carol J., and Siebert, Roberta. "Toward Humanizing Adoption." *Child Welfare,* April 1982, LXI(4), 207–16.
9. Schwartz, Edward M. "Problems After Adoption: Some Guidelines for Pediatrician Involvement." *The Journal of Pediatrics,* Dec. 1975, 87(6) Part 1, 991–94.
10. Nadelson, Carol C. "The Emotional Aftermath of Adoption." *American Family Physician,* Sept. 1976, 14(3), 124–27.
11. Sorosky, Arthur D.; Baran, Annette; and Pannor, Reuben. "Identity Conflicts in Adoptees." *American Journal of Orthopsychiatry,* Jan. 1975, 45(1), 18–27.
12. Roosevelt, Ruth, and Lofas, Jeannette. *Living in Step.* New York: McGraw-Hill, 1976.

13. Wallerstein, Judith S. "Children and Divorce." *Pediatrics in Review,* Jan. 1980, 1(7), 211–17.
14. Luepnitz, Deborah Anna. *Child Custody: A Study of Families After Divorce.* Lexington, Mass.: Heath, 1982.
15. Roosevelt, op. cit., p. 16.
16. Wallerstein, op. cit., p. 211.
17. Wallerstein, Judith S., and Kelly, Joan Berlin. *Surviving the Breakup: How Children and Parents Cope with Divorce.* New York: Basic Books, 1980.
18. Wallerstein, Judith S. "Children of Divorce: Preliminary Report of a Ten-Year Follow-up of Young Children. *American Journal of Orthopsychiatry,* July 1984, 54(3), 444–59.
19. Luepnitz, op. cit., p. 3.
20. Ibid., p. 10.
21. Santrock, John W.; Warshak, Richard; Lindbergh, Cheryl; and Meadows, Larry. "Children's and Parents' Observed Social Behavior in Stepfather Families." *Child Development,* 1982, 53:472–80.
22. Luepnitz, op. cit., pp. 149–51.
23. Goodman, Ellen. "No Names for the Extended Family." *Arizona Daily Star,* Aug. 19, 1983.
24. Visher, Emily B., and Visher, John S. *Stepfamilies: A Guide to Working with Stepparents and Stepchildren.* New York: Brunner/Mazel, 1979.
25. O'Hern, Lynn, and Williams, Frank. "Stepfamilies." In Christensen, Oscar C., and Schramski, Thomas G. *Adlerian Family Counseling.* Minneapolis: Educational Media Corporation, 1983.
26. O'Hern, op. cit., pp. 222–33.
27. Messinger, Lillian; Walker, Kenneth N.; and Freeman, Stanley J. "Preparation for Remarriage Following Divorce: The Use of Group Techniques." *American Journal of Orthopsychiatry,* April 1978, 48(2), 263–72.
28. Kappelman, Murray M., and Ackerman, Paul R. *Parents After Thirty.* New York: Rawson, Wade, 1980.
29. O'Hern, op. cit., pp. 229–33.
30. Visher and Visher, op. cit., pp. 261–65.
31. Stern, Phyllis Noerager. "Affiliating in Stepfather Families: Teachable Strategies Leading to Stepfather-Child Friendship." *Western Journal of Nursing Research,* 1982, 4(1), 75–89.
32. Berman, Claire. *Making It As a Stepparent.* Garden City, N.Y.: Doubleday, 1980.

SOURCE MATERIAL

Adoption

American Academy of Pediatrics, Committee on Adoptions. "Identity Development in Adopted Children." *Pediatrics,* May 1971, 47(5), 948–49.
American Academy of Pediatrics, Committee on Adoption and Dependent Care. "The Role of the Pediatrician in Adoption with Reference to 'The Right to Know.'" *Pediatrics,* Sept. 1977, 60(3), 378–79.
Bohman, Michael. "A Study of Adopted Children, Their Background, Environment and Adjustment." *Acta Paediat Scand.,* 1972, 61:90–97.
Children's Home Society of California. *The Changing Picture of Adoption.* Los Angeles, 1984.
Christensen, Oscar C., and Schramski, Thomas G., eds. *Adlerian Family Counseling.* Minneapolis: Educational Media Corporation, 1983.
Schwartz, Edward M. "Problems After Adoption: Some Guidelines for Pediatrician Involvement." *The Journal of Pediatrics,* December 1975, 87(6), Part 1, 991–94.

Seglow, Jean; Pringle, Mia Kellmer; and Wedge, Peter. *Growing Up Adopted.* London: National Foundation for Educational Research, 1972.

Stepparenting

"20% of Children in U.S. Live with One Parent, Census Reports." *Arizona Daily Star,* Aug. 9, 1982.

Engebretson, Joan C. "Stepmothers as First-Time Parents: Their Needs and Problems." *Pediatric Nursing,* Nov./Dec. 1982, 8(6), 387–90.

Horn, Yvonne Michie, ed. *Stepfamily Bulletin.* Fall 1983. Stepfamily Association of America, Inc., 900 Welch Rd., Suite 400, Palo Alto, Calif. 94304.

Stern, Phyllis Noerager. "Conflicting Family Cultures: An Impediment to Integration in Stepfather Families." *Journal of Psychosocial Nursing and Mental Health Services,* Oct. 1982, 20(10), 27–33.

Divorce

Garmezy, Norman, and Rutter, Michael, eds. *Stress, Coping, and Development in Children.* New York: McGraw-Hill, 1983.

Hanson, Shirley May Harmon. "Single Custodial Fathers." Annual Meeting of the National Council on Family Relations, Milwaukee, Oct. 13–17, 1981.

Kalter, Neil, and Plunkett, James W. "Children's Perceptions of the Causes and Consequences of Divorce." *Journal of the American Academy of Child Psychiatry,* May 1984, 23:326–34.

Lebowitz, Marcia Lipman. "Divorce and the American Teenager." *Pediatrics* Supplement, Part 2, Oct. 1985, 76(4):695–98.

Rosenthal, Kristine M., and Keshet, Harry F. *Fathers Without Partners.* Totowa, N.J.: Rowman & Littlefield, 1981.

Wallerstein, Judith S. "Children of Divorce: The Psychological Tasks of the Child." *American Journal of Orthopsychiatry,* April 1983, 53(2), 230–43.

Wallerstein, Judith S., and Kelly, Joan Berlin. *Surviving the Breakup: How Children and Parents Cope with Divorce.* New York: Basic Books, 1980.

Wegman, Myron E. "Annual Summary of Vital Statistics—1982." *Pediatrics,* Dec. 1983, 72(6), 755–65.

CHAPTER 26
PARENTING AND SOCIETY

REFERENCE

1. Bronfenbrenner, Urie. *Two Worlds of Childhood: U.S. and U.S.S.R.* New York: Russell Sage Foundation, 1970, page 1.

AN AFTERWORD

REFERENCE

1. Farb, Peter. *Humankind.* New York: Bantam, 1978, pages 443–44.

SOURCE MATERIAL

Abrams, Herbert L. "Medical Resources After Nuclear War: Availability v. Need." *Journal of the American Medical Association*, Aug. 3, 1984, 252(5), 653–58.

Abrahms, Herbert L., and Von Kaenel, William E. "Medical Problems of Survivors of Nuclear War. Infection and the Spread of Communicable Disease." *New England Journal of Medicine*, Nov. 12, 1981, 305(20), 1226–32.

Cloud, Kate; Deegan, Ellie; Evans, Alice; Imam, Hayat; and Signer, Barbara. *Watermelons Not Wars!: A Support Book for Parenting in the Nuclear Age*. Philadelphia: New Society Publishers, 1984.

Coles, Robert. "Children and the Nuclear Bomb," Chapter 7 in Coles, Robert. *Moral Life of Children*. Boston: Atlantic Monthly Press, 1986.

Goldberg, Susan; LaCombe, Suzanne; Levinson, Dvora; Parker, K. Ross; Ross, Christopher; and Sommers, Frank. "Thinking About the Threat of Nuclear War: Relevance to Mental Health." *American Journal of Orthopsychiatry*, Oct. 1985, 55(4), 503–12.

Hiatt, Howard H. "The Final Epidemic: Prescriptions for Prevention." *Journal of the American Medical Association*, Aug. 3, 1984, 252(5), 635–38.

———. "Preventing the Last Epidemic." *Journal of the American Medical Association*, Nov. 21, 1980, 244(20), 2314–15.

———. "Preventing the Last Epidemic: II." *Journal of the American Medical Association*, Nov. 6, 1981, 246(18), 2035–36.

Judson, Stephanie, ed. *A Manual on Nonviolence and Children*. Philadelphia: New Society Publishers, 1984.

Kappy, Michael S. "The Longest Illness: Effects of Nuclear War in Children." *American Journal of Diseases of Children*, March 1984, 138:293–98.

Lown, Bernard. "Nobel Peace Prize Lecture: A Prescription for Hope." *The New England Journal of Medicine*. April 10, 1986, 314(15), 985–87.

Mack, John E. "The Perception of U.S.–Soviet Intentions and Other Psychological Dimensions of the Nuclear Arms Race." *American Journal of Orthopsychiatry*, Oct. 1982, 52(4), 590–99.

Schwebel, Milton. "Effects of the Nuclear War Threat on Children and Teenagers: Implications for Professionals." *American Journal of Orthopsychiatry*, Oct. 1982, 52(4), 608–18.

Schwebel, Robert. "Only One Way to Deal with N-War Fears." *Arizona Daily Star*, Oct. 30, 1983.

Seuss, Dr. *The Butter Battle Book*. New York: Random House, 1984.

Smith, M. Brewster. "Hope and Despair: Keys to the Socio-Psychodynamics of Youth." *American Journal of Orthopsychiatry*, July 1983, 53(3), 388–99.

Tobias, Sheila; Goudinoff, Peter; Leader, Stefan; and Leader, Shelah. *What Kinds of Guns Are They Buying for Your Butter?* New York: Morrow, 1982.

Van Ornum, William, and Van Ornum, Mary. *Talking to Children About Nuclear War*. New York: Continuum, 1984.

Index

ABC's (Airway, Breathing, Circulation), 726, 728
Abdomen
  in mothers of one-week- to twelve-week-old infants, 365
  of newborns, 318
Abdominal pain, as symptom of illness, 646–47
Abduction of children, 112–13
  Abnormal development, 276–81
  assessment of, 276–77, 280–81
  pediatricians and, 276–77
  "red flags" of, 277, 279, 277–80 (tables)
  school problems and, 280–81
  See also Delays in development
Abortion, 9, 10
Abrasions (scrapes), first aid for, 758
Abstinence, 9
Accident prevention. *See* Safety
Accidents
  definition of, 125
  magnitude of the problem, 126
  See also Safety
Acetaminophen (Tylenol), 678, 683–87
Achievement tests, 277
Acne, 656
Activity *See* Exercise(s)
Additives, food, 561–62
Adolescence (teenagers)
  as baby-sitters, 193
  calorie requirements of, 529
  chronically ill, 713–14
  driving cars, 144, 151
  moral development in, 236, 255 (table)
  motor development in, 254 (table)

parental development and, 296
  transition to parenthood of adolescents, 304–5
  parenting as seen by, 287–88
  play of, 254 (table)
  psychosocial development of, 254–55 (table)
  safety and, 141
  sexual activity in, 664–65
  teen pregnancy, 665
Adopted children, 662
  parenting, 787–92
  adjustment and development problems, 791–92
  getting started, 787–88
  special concerns, 788–90
  when to tell children, 790–91
  stepchildren as, 804
Adult children, transition to parenting, 305
Advertising
  for housekeepers, 202
  television, 595, 596
Advice
  on child care, 12, 183–86
  See also Experts
Affection
  of infants seven to fourteen months old, 401
  of toddlers, 416
  See also Love
Aggression (aggressiveness)
  in five-year-olds, 512
  in four-year-olds, 486
  inhibition of, 49–50
  Kohut's view of, 226

playful, 80–81
sibling rivalry and, 401
socialization and, 80–81
stressful, 113–17
child abuse, 115–17
wife abuse, 114
in toddlers, 240, 417
See also Anger
AIDS (acquired immune deficiency
syndrome), day care centers and,
211
Airplane travel, 102
Air pollution, 588–89
Air rifle, 162
Airway, 726
clearing the, 728
Alcoholic beverages
for babies during air travel, 103
overdose or withdrawal from,
emergency procedures for, 748–49
See also Drunk drivers
Alcoholics Anonymous, 117
Alcoholism, 117–18
of housekeepers, 204, 205
Alert periods
in one-week- to twelve-week-old
infants, 361, 362
See also Quiet-alert periods
Allergies
anaphylaxis (serious allergic reaction),
emergency procedures for, 750
Benadryl for, 688
to cow's milk, 558
colic and, 352, 353
eyes and, 635
food, infants three to six months old
and, 379
food additives and, 562
to pets, 568
runny nose and, 638
Alston, Frances, 191
Altricial animals, 4–5
American Academy of Pediatrics, 181,
358, 533, 535, 541–42, 606, 624–
25
American Automobile Association, 181
American Camping Association, 182
American Dental Association, 571, 572,
622
American Medical Association, 182
Ames, Louise Bates, 475, 500
Amino acids, 531
Amputation, emergency procedures for,
734, 736

Anal fixations, 225
Anal stage, 241
parental development and, 291
Anaphylaxis (serious allergic reaction),
emergency procedures for, 750
Anger
adult temper tantrum, 69–70
expressing, 586–87
guidance by modeling and, 60
in infants seven to fourteen months
old, 396
in parents, 69–70, 468
as symptom, 657–58
in three-year-olds, 467–68
See also Aggression
Animals
children's books about, 72
housebreaking, 32
play and, 261–63
See also Pets
Animism, 509
Antacids, 689
Antibiotic ointment, 689
Antibiotics, for traveler's diarrhea
(turista), 104
Antichild sentiments, 11
Antihistamines, 687
Antiparenting sentiments, 11
Anxiety
separation, 400
stranger, 385, 395, 405, 429
in three-year-olds, 461, 462
See also Fears
Appendicitis, 646
Appetite
poor, as symptom of illness, 645–46
See also Eating
Appliances, safety and, 168, 170, 173
Appreciation, parents' need for, 19
Aptitude tests, 277
Ariès, Philippe, 6
Arousability, 632
Art
encouraging enjoyment of, 266–67
of three-year-olds, 469
See also Drawings
Artificial sweeteners, 554
Ashburn, Shirley Smith, 45
Asians, 50
Aspiration
of food, 166–67
of toys, 178
Aspirin, 683–87
poisonings with, 153

Assertiveness
  aggression and, 80
  mutual, 52, 54, 58, 62–63
  of toddlers, 415, 416
  unilateral, as guidance method, 63–64
Athletic events, at school, 99
Athletics. *See* Sports
Attachments, 237
  of infants seven to fourteen months
    old, 401–2
  of infants three to six months old, 376
  to newborns, 341
  to objects, 383, 403
    transitional objects, 420, 462
  socialization and, 55–57
  stimulation and, 56
  See also Affection; Bonding; Love
Attending physicians, 604–5
Attention
  need for, of infants three to six
    months old, 376
  toddlers' ability to get and hold adults',
    415–16
Attention-deficit disorders, 281
ATV (all-terrain vehicles), 163
Au pair girls, 203
Authoritarian child rearing, 51–52
Automatic methods of guidance, 60–62
Automobiles. *See* Car restraints; Car
    safety; Car travel
Autonomy (independence)
  of four-year-olds, 490
  milestones of, 270 (table)
  of three-year-olds, 460–61
  in toddlers (15 to 23 months), 239–41
  in two-year-olds, 439, 440
Azrin, Nathan H., 427

Babbling, 234, 255 (table), 351, 368, 376
"Baby blues," 337–38, 364
Baby foods
  commercial, 380
  homemade, 380, 549
Baby honeymoon, 338–40, 365
Baby lotion, 334
Baby oil, 334
Baby powder, 334
  not recommended, 360
  poisonings with, 155
Baby-sitters
  emergency, 195
  occasional, as child-care option, 189,
    193–94
  older siblings as, 82

  overnight and vacation, 194
  teenagers as, 193
  traveling and leaving children with,
    104
  See also Care givers
Baby shots. *See* Immunizations
Baby wipes, 334
Bach, George Robert, 81
Backyards. *See* Yards
"Bad behavior," as symptom, 659–60
Balancing, 580
Balconies, safety and, 143
Balloons, safety and, 167, 178
Balls, playing with, 402–3, 412–13
Bandaging material, 725, 726
Barbecue, safety and, 174
Bar or Bat Mitzvah, 97
Bars, safety and, 169
Basement, safety in, 171
Basic trust, 340
Bathing
  five-year-olds, 514
  four-year-olds, 490
  newborns, 333, 334
  one-week- to twelve-week-old infants,
    359–61
  seven- to fourteen-month-old infants,
    399
  sponge, 360
  three-year-olds, 465
  toddlers, 418
  two-year-olds, 443
Bathroom, safety in, 132, 169–70
  poisoning-proofing and, 153, 154
Bathtub
  infants seven to fourteen months old
    and, 399
  safety and, 170
Batteries, button, 180
BB guns, 162
Bedroom
  of four-year-olds, 491
  safety in, 155, 170–71
Bedtime (bedtime routines or rituals), 42
  bottle-feeding at, 364, 381, 556
  for four-year-olds, 491
  for infants three to six months old,
    381–82
  sleep disturbances and, 576, 577
  for three-year-olds, 466
  for toddlers (15 to 23 months), 419
  for two-year-olds, 444
Bedwetting (enuresis), 500–1, 577, 652–
    53

Bee stings, first aid for, 761
Behavior analysis, guidance and, 65–66
Behaviorist theory of development, 224
Behavior modification, as guidance
    method, 65–66
Benadryl, 688
Bernard, Jessie, 14
Bicycles, safety and, 139, 140, 150–51,
    163
Bilirubin, 324
    in newborns, 343–44
Biological development, 232
    See also Motor development
Biological rhythms, 31–44
    elimination, 42–44
    feeding and, 33–36
    sleep and, 36–42, 575
    socialization and, 52
Biotin, 536 (table)
Birds, 4, 5
Birthdays, 93–95
Birthmarks, 343
Birth weight, 317
Bites
    emergency procedures for, 750–53
    insect, first aid for, 761
Biting, 439
Black children, motor development in,
    392
Bladder control, 435, 456
    elimination patterns and, 42
Blankets, receiving, 333
Blank slate concept of development, 223
Bleeding
    emergency procedures for severe, 733–
    36
    in mothers of newborns, 337
Blindness, 635–36
Blisters
    blood, 655
    first aid for, 759
    as symptom of illness, 655
Blocks, 515–16
    stacking, 392
Blow-dryers, 570
Blueness (cyanosis), 654–55
Boarding schools, 214–15
Boating, safety and, 160, 175–76
Body control, in infants one to twelve
    weeks old, 350
Body language, of infants one to twelve
    weeks old, 350, 351
Bonding, 55–56, 237
    in adoption, 787–88

failure of, 259–60
Books
    child-care, 185
    children's
        making your own, 73, 494–95
        for seven- to fourteen-month-old
            infants, 403
        socialization and, 72–73
    emergency first aid, 725
Bosses, parents as, 51
Bottle-feeding
    at bedtime, 364, 381, 556
    bottles for, 357
    of breast-fed newborns, 331
    early introduction of solid foods and,
        34
    formula for, 355–57
    health maintenance and, 541–43
    infants (to 14 months)
        from one to twelve weeks old, 355–
        56
        from three to six months old, 378
    nipples for, 356, 357
    sleep and, 39–40
    warming of bottles for, 357
    See also Formula, infant
Botulism, honey on pacifiers as cause of,
    363
Bouncer chairs, 384
Bowel, contractions of, 42
Bowel movements
    blood in, 647, 650–51
    constipation, 650
    diarrhea, 648–50
    frequency of, 43
    in infants (to 14 months), 247–50
        (table)
        from seven to fourteen months old,
        391
        from three to six months old, 374
    in preschoolers, 253 (table)
    in toddlers, 251 (table)
    See also Defecation; Elimination;
        Stools; Toilet training
Bowlby, J. M., 258
Brain
    development of, 232
    at one year of age, 391
Bras, nursing, 329
Brazelton, T. Berry, 45, 212, 239, 308,
    366, 424, 425, 597
Brazelton Neonatal Assessment Scale,
    342
Breakfast, 441, 552–53

Breast-feeding
   drugs contraindicated during, 541
   fluoride supplementation and, 541
   foods to avoid, 331
   health maintenance and, 541–43
   infants (to 14 months)
      colic and, 352–53
      from one to twelve weeks old, 352–
         55
      from seven to fourteen months old,
         397–98
      from three to six months old, 378–
         79
   is baby getting enough?, 354–55
   manual expression, 330
   newborns, 33, 34, 321, 323–31, 331–
      32
      bilirubin levels and jaundice, 344
      bottle-feeding of breast-fed babies,
         331
      breast engorgement, 325
      colostrum, 323–24
      duration of feedings, 325
      jiggling of babies, 341
      let-down problems, 328–29
      medical intervention which delays
         breast-feeding, 330–31
      mother's diet, 331
      mothers' nursing styles, 326–28
      nipple problems, 329–30
      position for, 324, 325 (illus.)
      sedated infants, 325
      starting, 324–25, 354
      storage of breast milk, 331
      styles of babies, 325–26
      weight loss, 343
   rooting reflex and, 318
   sleep and, 37–38, 40
   vitamin and mineral supplements and,
      357, 358
   water requirements and, 527–28
   weaning from, 397–98
      early, 355
   See also Lactation
Breast pumps, 330
Breasts
   engorgement of, breast-feeding and,
      325
      if not breast-feeding, 337
   if not breast-feeding, 332, 337
Breathing
   cessation of, emergency procedures for,
      727–31
   in newborns, 320

   rescue, 727–28
   See also Respiratory system
Brewster, Dorothy Patricia, 354
Bricklin, Alice, 13
Bronfenbrenner, Urie, 812
Bruises, first aid for, 757–58
Bubble gum, 167
"Bubble sounds," 351
Bulb syringe (nasal aspirator), 676
Burns
   infants (to 14 months) and, 132
   major, emergency procedures for, 736–
      38
   minor, first aid for, 760
   preschoolers and, 138
   school-age children and, 139
   toddlers and, 136
   See also Scalds
Burping, 332–33
Buses, school, 151
Butterfly bandages, 758, 759

Cabinets, safety and, 168
Calcium, 557–58
Calories, 528–31, 530 (table)
Camping, safety and, 175
Camps, summer, 215–16
Cancer
   detection of, 626
   food additives and, 562
Canker sores, 645
Can opener, electric, safety and, 168
Carbohydrates, 531, 533
Carbon monoxide, 154
Cardiopulmonary resuscitation (CPR),
      722, 726–31
Cardiovascular system, symptoms of
      illness in, 644
Care givers, 402
   care of
      of five-year-olds, 515
      of infants (to 14 months), 364–66,
         383–84
      of toddlers (15 to 23 months), 420–
         21
      of two-year-olds, 446
   of infants (to 14 months)
      care of, 364–66, 383–84
      obstetrical recuperation, 365–66
      outside world, 366
      myth of the ideal, 188
   of newborns, 323, 336–40
      baby honeymoon, 338–40
      emotional recovery, 337–38

fathers, 340
fatigue, 336
obstetric recovery, 337
recuperation from labor and birth,
336–38
See also Fathers; Helpers in child care
Caring for Other People's Children
(Alston), 191
Car restraints, 145–50, 345
brands of, 147–49
legislation on, 145
types of, 146–47
See also Seat belts
Car safety, 144–51
automatic windows and, 179
five-year-olds and, 520
four-year-olds and, 503
in garage, 172
heat and, 150
infants one to twelve weeks old and,
370–71
infants three to six months old and,
387
intoxicated drivers and, 144–45, 151
number of accidents, 144
pedestrian-car accidents, 150
preschoolers and, 138
school-age children and, 139, 140
teenage drivers and, 144, 151
toddlers and, 137
See also Car restraints
Carter, Elizabeth, 300, 301
Car travel, 101–2
with newborns, 333–34
Castration anxiety, 241
Catastrophes, 105
Catholic Church, 9–10
Cats, 567, 568
bites of, emergency procedures for,
752
safety and, 161–62
Cavernous hemangioma, 343
Cavities, 572
See also Dental care; Teeth
Centration, 458, 483
Cephalohematomas, 342
Ceremonies, milestone, 97–99
Cervix, after childbirth, 337
Chairs
bouncer, 384
high, 142–43, 177
recliner, 179
Checkups
one-year, 406

well-baby, 341–42, 369, 386, 406, 428,
451–52, 476, 502, 519
See also Medical care
Chess, Stella, 87
Chest
of infants (to 14 months), 349
of newborns, 318
Chest injuries, emergency procedures for,
754–55
Chest pain, as symptom of illness, 644
Chewing gum, 464
Chicken soup, 691–92
Chigger bites, first aid for, 761
Child abuse, 31
"end of your rope" with baby, 353
neglect as form of, 259
physical, 115–17
adult temper tantrum, 69–70
in day care centers or house day
care, 211
two-year-olds, 445
sexual, 111–13, 664
in day care centers or home day
care, 211
Childbirth, recuperation from, 336–38
Child care
advice on, 183–86
children's needs and, 187
in day care centers, 190
evaluation of, 208–12
in day care homes (informal day care),
190–91, 212–13
for four-year-olds, 501
helpers in. *See* Helpers in child care
models of, 6–9
for older children, 213–14
options for, 189–93
day care centers, 190
day care homes, 190–91
deciding about, 192–93
family care, 189–90
"house-husbands" option, 192
in-home child care, 190
you and/or spouse plus occasional
sitters, 189
yourself and spouse only, 189
yourself only, 189
parents' needs and, 187–88
sharing, 779–80
summer, 215–16
See also Care givers
Child Development Associate Credential
(CDA), 209
Childhood, history of, 6

Child-orienting the home, 83–85
Child-proofing, 23, 385, 429
  crawling and, 151–52
  infants seven to fourteen months old
      and, 406–7
  three-year-olds and, 477–78
  See also Safety
Child Protection and Safety Act, 178
Child Protective Service, 116
Child snatching, 113
Child-spacing, 34
Chimpanzees, 7, 13
China, 10
Choices, giving, 498–99
Choking, 442
  on balloons, 178
  emergency procedures for, 731–33
  on food, 166–67, 397
  See also Aspiration; Swallowing, of
      foreign objects
Chomsky, Noam, 234
Christianity, food and, 35
Christmas, 75
  celebrating, 95–96
  safety and, 164
Christmas bow pins, 167
Christmas tree, safety and, 169
Cigarette lighters, disposable, 179
Cigarette smoking. See Smoking
Circadian rhythm, 37
Circulation, in newborns, 320, 342
Circumcision, 334
Civic life, parental development and,
      306–7
Clarke-Stewart, Alison, 192
Classification, 459, 510
Cleaning
  newborns, 333–35
  one-week- to twelve-week-old infants,
      358–61
  toddlers, 418
  See also Bathing; Hygiene
Cleaning supplies, poisonings with, 152–
      53
Climbing, 580
  development of, 391
  trees, 143
  two-year-olds, 435
Closets, safety and, 170
Clothing
  flame-resistant, 158
  for infants (to 14 months)
    from one to twelve weeks old, 361
    from three to six months old, 380

  for newborns, 333–34
  for toddlers (15 to 23 months), 418
  See also Dressing
Clumsiness, as symptom of illness, 654
Coats, storage of, 84
Coercion, unilateral assertiveness as, 63–
      64
Cognition, definition of, 232
Cognitive development (cognitive skills),
      232–33
  in five-year-olds, 509–10, 515–16
  in four-year-olds, 493–98
  in infants (to 14 months)
    from one to twelve weeks old, 350–
      51
    from seven to fourteen months old,
      393, 402
    from three to six months old, 375–
      76
  in newborns, 322
  stages of (Piaget), 228–31 (table)
    concrete operations stage, 230
    formal operations stage, 230–31
    parental development and, 289–90
    preoperational stage, 229–30
    sensorimotor stage, 228–29
  in three-year-olds, 457–59
  in toddlers (15 to 23 months), 412–13
  in two-year-olds, 437–38, 447
Colds, common, 435, 456, 639, 640,
      671–72
Cold sores (fever blisters), 645
Cold weather, newborns and, 333–34
Coles, Robert, 237
Colic, 352–53
Colostrum, 37, 323–24
Combing, 399
Communication
  about problems, 86
  with doctors, 611–12
  P.E.T. approach to, 52
  socialization and, 55
  See also Conversation
Community responsibility for children, 9
Competent children, parents of, 264–65
Concrete operations stage, 228, 230
  parental development and, 290
Concussion, 739
Confirmation, 97
Congenital abnormalities, 344
Conjunctivitis (pink eye), 635
Conscience. See Moral development
Consciousness, 233

Consequences
  ability to anticipate, 413
  concept of, 498, 499
Conservation, 438
Consistency
  care givers and, 188
  myth of, 58–60
Consonant sounds, 351
Constipation, as symptom of illness, 650
Consumer products, safety of, 176–80
Consumer Product Safety Commission,
      United States (USCPSC), 177,
      178, 181, 182
Contexts of parenting, 15
Contraceptives, 10
Conversation, 20, 394
  at mealtime, four-year-olds and, 490
Convulsions (seizures), emergency
      procedures for, 747–48
Cooing, 234, 255 (table)
Cooking
  safety and, 165
  See also Food preparation
Cooperation, development of, 240
Cooperative play, 459–60, 511
Core gender identity, 242
Corneal abrasion, emergency procedures
      for, 753–54
Corporal punishment
  guidance by, 67–68
  See also Child abuse; Hitting children
Cosleeping, 574
Cough, as symptom of illness, 641–42
Cough drops, 690
Cough suppressants, 641–43, 688
Counseling
  help for children, 85–86
  help for parents, 70, 114, 116, 118,
      119–20
Counselors, 623
Counting, 437, 457, 459, 495, 509
Courtesy, 49–50
CPR (cardiopulmonary resuscitation),
      722, 726–31
Cradle cap, 361
Crawling, 579
  development of, 391
    social interaction and, 395
  safety and, 143, 151–52
Creative empathy, 267
Creativity
  four-year-olds and, 496–97
  parents' role in encouraging or helping
      develop, 265–67

Creeping, 391
Cribs, safety and, 165, 177
Crossed eyes, 349, 635
Croup, 643
Crowds, infants one to twelve weeks old
      and, 370
Cruising, 392
Crying, 11
  of infants (to 14 months), 259
    colic and, 352–53
    Holt's view of, 224
    hunger and, 34, 38
    as "language," 234
    leaving baby with a sitter and, 405
    from one to twelve weeks old, 351–
        53, 361–62
    from seven to fourteen months old,
        395
    sleep and, 38
  of mothers of newborns, 337–38
  of newborns, 322, 335
  as symptom of illness, 631
Culture, play and, 263
Cups, toddlers' use of, 412
Curiosity, 21, 350
Custody, divorce and, 797–98
Cuts
  first aid for, 758–59
  school-age children and, 139
Cyanosis (blueness), 654–55

Dark, fear of the, 417
Darwin, Charles, 222
Day care
  for toddlers (15 to 23 months), 427–28
  for two-year-olds, 450–51
  See also Child care
Day care centers
  as child-care option, 190–91
  evaluation of, 208–12
  See also Day care
Day care homes (informal day care),
      212–13
DDT, 590
Deadbolt locks, 159
Deafness, 637
Deaf parents, 375
Death, 510
  of family member, 105
  fear of, 487–88
  stepchildren and, 793
Decongestants, oral, 687–88
Defecation, 42–44

See also Bowel movements;
    Elimination; Toilet training
Dehydration
  diarrhea and, 648, 649
  in newborns, 343
  vomiting and, 647, 648
Delaney Clause, 562
Delays in development, 314
  in five-year-olds, 513
  in four-year-olds, 488
  in infants (to 14 months)
    from one to twelve weeks old, 354
    from seven to fourteen months old,
      397
    from three to six months old, 378,
      488
  psychosocial symptoms and, 658, 659,
    661
  in three-year-olds, 463
  in toddlers (15 to 23 months), 417
  in two-year-olds, 440
Delirium, as symptom of illness, 632–33
Denial, of abnormal development, 276
Dental care, 570–72
  for five-year-olds, 519–20
  for four-year-olds, 502
  for infants (to 14 months)
    from one to twelve weeks old, 370
    from seven to fourteen months old,
      406
    from three to six months old, 386
  nutrition and, 554–56
  for three-year-olds, 477
  for toddlers, 429
  for two-year-olds, 452
Dentist
  finding a, 622
  visits to, 502, 571–72
Dependency, 17
  of adolescents, 254 (table)
  of infants (to 14 months), 247–50
    (table)
  of newborns, 247 (table)
  of preschoolers, 252 (table)
  of school-age children, 253 (table)
  of three-year-olds, 462
  of toddlers, 251 (table)
  willingness and ability of a child to
    give up, 270. *See also* Autonomy
Depressants, overdose or withdrawal
    from, emergency procedures for,
    748–49
Depression, 706
  in children, 658, 661–62

postpartum, 338
psychosocial symptoms and, 658, 661
as stressor, 118
Deprivation, psychosocial, 259
Depth perception, 411
Development, children's, 221–84
  abnormal, 276–81. *See also* Delays in
    development
    assessment of, 276–77, 280–81
    pediatricians and, 276–77
    "red flags" of, 277, 279, 277–80
    (tables)
    school problems and, 280–81
  attitude parents need to develop
    toward, 222
  biological, 232. *See also* Motor
    development
  cognitive. *See* Cognitive development
  definition of, 221
  delays in. *See* Delays in development
  kinds of, 231–44
  language. *See* Language development
  moral. *See* Moral development
  motor. *See* Motor development
  parents' growth in response to, 289–98
    adolescence, 296
    anal stage, 291
    concrete operations stage, 290
    Eriksonian (psychosocial) stages,
      293–98
    formal operations stage, 290
    Freudian stages of development,
      291–93
    infancy, 294
    latency stage, 293
    middlescence, 297–98
    Oedipal stage, 292
    older adulthood, 298
    oral stage, 291
    phallic stage, 291–92
    Piagetian stages of development,
      289–90
    preoperational stage, 290
    preschoolhood, 295
    schoolhood, 296
    sensorimotor stage, 289–90
    toddlerhood, 294–95
    young adulthood, 297
  parents' role in, 256–67
    creativity, 265–67
    effective parenting, 264–65
    friendships and social interactions,
      269–71
    knowing factual information, 256–57

play, 261–63
school-age children, 272–76
stimulation, 258–61
toys, 263–64
twin studies, 257
values, 271
psychosocial. *See* Psychosocial
    development
safety and stages of, 130–41
    adolescents, 141
    early school years (ages 5 to 9), 139
    first year, 131–33
    preadolescents (ages 10 to 13), 140
    preschoolers (ages 2 to 4), 138
    toddlers (ages 1 and 2), 134–37
in school-age children, 272–76
    moral development, 236, 254 (table)
    motor development, 253 (table)
    parental development, 296
    psychosexual development, 241
    psychosocial development, 240, 253–
        54 (table)
stresses that come from, 109
theories of, 223–31
    behaviorist, 224
    Erikson's, 227
    Freudian, 223–26
    Gesell's, 226–27
    Havighurst's, 227–28
    Holt's, 224
    Kohut's, 225–26
    Locke's, 223, 224
    Maslow's, 227
    Piaget's, 228–31
    Rousseau's, 223–24
Development, parents', 285–310
civic life and, 306–7
enhancement of, 308–9
family and friendship roles and, 307–8
family life cycle and, 300–5, 301–3
    (table)
    adolescents, transition to parenthood
        of, 304–5
    adult children, transition to
        parenting, 305
    "between families" stage, 303
    marriage, transition to, 303
    old age, family transitions to, 305
    parenthood, transition to, 303–4
marital relationship and, 298–300
overall growth as people, 287–89
in response to children's stages of
    growth, 289–98
    adolescence, 296

anal stage, 291
concrete operations stage, 290
Eriksonian (psychosocial) stages,
    293–98
formal operations stage, 290
Freudian stages of development,
    291–93
infancy, 294
latency stage, 293
middlescence, 297–98
Oedipal stage, 292
older adulthood, 298
oral stage, 291
phallic stage, 291–92
Piagetian stages of development,
    289–90
preoperational stage, 290
preschoolhood, 295
schoolhood, 296
sensorimotor stage, 289–90
toddlerhood, 294–95
young adulthood, 297
work and, 306
Developmental delays. *See* Delays in
    development
De Villiers, Peter A., 234, 235
Diaper area, cleaning of, 359, 380
Diaper pins, 334
Diaper rash, 335, 359, 380, 656
Diapers (diapering)
    diaper service (cotton), 334, 335
    disposable, 334
        safety and, 178
    for newborns, 333–35
    one-week- to twelve-week-old infants,
        359
    poisonings during, 153
Diarrhea, 42–43, 692
    blood in, 647–48
    day care centers and, 210
    as symptom of illness, 648–50
    traveler's (turista), 104
    treatment of, 649
Diet
    balanced (happy, healthy), 549–50
    Feingold, 562–63
    macrobiotic, 565
    mother's breast-feeding newborns and,
        331
        colicky babies and, 352–53
        vegetarian, 563–65
    See also Nutrition
Difficult babies, 352–53

Digestive system, symptoms of illness in, 644–51
Directions, following, 437
Direct pressure, on bleeding wounds, 733
Dirt
definitions and types of, 566–69
eating, 566–67
Discipline, 21, 385–86
authoritarian vs. permissive approaches to, 51–52
consistency and, 59
controversies about, 48–50
infants (to 14 months) and, 259
from seven to fourteen months old, 404
Parent Effectiveness Training (P.E.T.) approach to, 51–52
for three-year-olds, 470–71
toddlers and, 422, 428
two-year-olds and, 448–49
See also Guidance; Self-discipline
"Dis-ease," 704
Dishes, storage of, 83
Dishwasher, safety and, 168
Disinfectants, 725
Dislocation, 743–44
Diving, 160
Divorce, 492–93
effects on children, 794–95
stepchildren and, 793–98
stepparenting and, 803
Doctors (pediatricians), 602–21
certification of, 605
challenging, 607, 616–17
changing, 607, 617–19
choosing, 603, 607–11
communication with, 611–12
cooperation with, 612
expectations of, 612–13
frequency of visits to, 613–14
hospital privileges of, 605–6
licensed, 605
recertification of, 605
science and, 619–20
telephoning, 613
types of, 603–6
when to call, 668–69
when to take children to, 615–16
See also Medical care
Dogs
bites of, emergency procedures for, 752
housebreaking, 32
safety and, 161–62, 567–68

Domestic help. See Housekeepers
Doors
garage, 172, 179
patio, 143, 160–61
Dosage charts, 694–95
DPT injection, 369, 386, 451, 502, 519, 613–15
Dramamine, 101–2
Dramatic play, 484
Drawings, 265, 457
Dreams, 41
See also Nightmares
Dreikurs, Rudolf, 498
Dressing
adolescents, 255 (table)
of infants (to 14 months), 247–50 (table)
from seven to fourteen months old, 399
preschoolers, 253 (table)
school-age children, 254 (table)
three-year-olds, 465–66
toddlers, 251 (table), 415, 418
two-year-olds, 439, 443–44
See also Clothing
Driver education courses, 144
Driveways
safety and, 173
toddlers in, 137
Driving
while intoxicated, 117–18
See also Car safety
Drowning, 159–60, 728
emergency procedures for, 755–56
infants (to 14 months) and, 132
preschoolers and, 138
school-age children and, 139, 140
toddlers and, 137
Drown-proofing, 159–60
Drowsiness, as symptom of illness, 632
Drug abuse, as symptom, 666–67
Drug overdose or withdrawal
emergency procedures for, 748–49
Drugs
recreational, driving and, 151
See also Drug abuse; Medicines
Drunk drivers, 144–45, 151
Ductus arteriosus, 320

Earaches, as symptom of illness, 636–37
airplane travel and, 102
Ears
foreign objects in, first aid for, 760
insects in, first aid for, 761

See also Hearing; Hearing loss
Easter, 75, 96
Eating (eating habits), 550–52
   of adolescents, 255 (table)
   in cars, 102
   conflicts over, 35–36
   dirt, 566–67
   feces, 405
   of infants (to 14 months), 247–50
      (table)
   manners and, 35, 464–65
   mealtime atmosphere and, 559–60
   parent-centered rule of, 36
   of preschoolers, 252–53 (table)
   in restaurants, 100–1, 490
   safety and, 167
   of school-age children, 254 (table)
   of toddlers, 251 (table)
   of two-year-olds, 441–43
   See also Diet; Feeding; Food(s);
      Nutrition
Ebstein's Pearls, 343
Education
   safety, 128
   sex, 78–79
   See also Learning; School
Egocentrism, 438, 458, 483, 484, 509
Einstein, Albert, 222
Eisen, Carol, 85
Electra complex, 241
Electrical injuries, 159
   emergency procedures for, 754
   in toddlers, 136
Electroencephalogram (EEG), 232
Elimination, 32–33, 42–44
   in newborns, 320–21, 342
   in toddlers (15 to 23 months), 410–11
   See also Bowel movements;
      Defecation; Stools; Toilet training
Emergencies, 721–66
   anaphylaxis (serious allergic reaction),
      750
   bites, 750–53
   bleeding, severe, 733–36
   blisters, 759
   bruises, 757–58
   burns
      major, 736–38
      minor, 760
   chest injuries, 754–55
   choking, 731–33
   convulsions (seizures), 747–48
   croup, 643
   cuts, 758–59

   delirium, 632–33
   dislocation, 743–44
   drowning, 755–56
   drug overdose or withdrawal, 748–49
   electric shock, 754
   embedded fish hook, 762
   eye injuries, 753–54
   fainting, 740
   fever, high, 630
   fingertip injuries, 763
   foreign objects
      in eyes, 763–64
      strange places, 760
   fractures, 743–45
   frostbite, 747
   head injury, 738–39
   heartbeat, fast or irregular, 644
   heatstroke and heat exhaustion, 745–
      46
   hiccups, 765
   hypothermia (abnormally low body
      temperature), 746
   infections, life-threatening
      consequences of, 757
   insect bites, 761
   neck and spine injuries, 740–41, 744
   nosebleeds, 736
   not breathing, 727–31
   penis caught in zipper, 764
   poisonings, 741–43
   preparation for, 721–26
      attitude, 726
      first-aid supplies, 724–26
      phone numbers, 724
      rehearsing, 723–24
      studying ahead, 722–23
   prevention of, 721–22
   scrapes (abrasions), 758
   shock, 738
   splinters, 760
   sprains, 761–62
   suicide attempts, 756
   tar and gum removal, 764
   teaching your child how to react in,
      765–66
   tooth, knocked-out, 764
   toothache, 764
   unconsciousness, 739–40
   vomits all feedings, 647–48
Emergency child agencies, 214
Emotional nutrition
   of five-year-olds, 515
   of four-year-olds, 493

of infants seven to fourteen months old, 401–2
of infants three to six months old, 383
of one-week- to twelve-week-old infants, 364
of three-year-olds, 468–69
of toddlers, 420
of two-year-olds, 445–46
Emotions (feelings)
expressing, 446, 586–87
in five-year-olds, 512–13
in four-year-olds, 486–88, 492–93
in infants (to 14 months)
from one to twelve weeks old, 351
from seven to fourteen months old, 396
from three to seven months old, 377
play and, 263
postpartum, 337–38
in three-year-olds, 460–62
in toddlers (15 to 23 months), 416–17
in two-year-olds, 439–40
See also specific emotions or feelings;
Emotional nutrition;
Temperaments
Empathy, 58
creative, 267
definition of, 56
in five-year-olds, 517
socialization and, 53, 56
in toddlers, 416–17
Employment agencies, for housekeepers, 202
Employment patterns in parents. See Work
Encopresis, 650
Enculturation, play and, 263
En face position, 238, 259
Enjoying, as guidance method, 62
Enuresis (bedwetting), 500–1, 577, 652–53
Environment
five-year-olds and, 520
four-year-olds and, 502–3
health maintenance and, 588–98
air pollution, 588–89
food pollution, 590
noise pollution, 590
parents and pollution, 593–94
radiation, 591–93
television pollution, 594–98
water pollution, 589–90
infants one to twelve weeks old and, 370

infants three to six months old and, 387
infants seven to fourteen months old and, 406–7
three-year-olds and, 477
toddlers and, 420, 429–30
two-year-olds and, 452–53
See also Child-proofing
Environmental control, as guidance method, 61
Erikson, Erik H., 45, 227, 239–41, 293, 439
Excretions. See Elimination
Exercise(s)
for five-year-olds, 514
for four-year-olds, 492
health maintenance and, 578–84
handicapped children, 584
infants (to 14 months), 578–79
older children, 580–81
sports, 580–84
toddlers and preschoolers, 579–80
for infants (to 14 months), 578–79
from one to twelve weeks old, 363
from seven to fourteen months old, 400
from three to six months old, 382–83
for mothers of newborns, 337
newborns and, 336
relaxation, 587
for three-year-olds, 467
for toddlers, 419
for two-year-olds, 444
See also Sports
Exhibitionism, as symptom, 663
Expectations, self-discipline triangle and, 57
Experts
on child care, 184–85
on parenting, 12, 22
See also Advice
Exploration, 350, 389
by infants seven to fourteen months old, 402–5
by infants three to six months old, 377
by toddlers, 412, 413, 429–30
Extended family, 5–7
Extrusion reflex, 544 (table)
Eye color, 318
Eye contact, 259
with newborns, 319, 321, 341

Eye-hand coordination
  in one-week- to twelve-week-old
    infants, 363
  in toddlers (15 to 23 months), 411
Eyelids, puffiness of, in newborns, 343
Eye ointment, 689
Eyes
  convergence of, 411
  crossed, 349, 635
  foreign objects in, first aid for, 763–64
  of infants from one to twelve weeks
    old, 349
  injuries to, emergency procedures for,
    753–54
  of newborns, 343
    focusing, 319
  symptoms of illness, 635–36
  See also Vision

Facial expressions, imitation of
  by infants one to twelve weeks old,
    368
  by newborns, 237–38, 267, 322
Failure to thrive, 258–59
Fainting, emergency procedures for, 740
Falls, 142–44
  infants (to 14 months) and, 131, 142–
    43
    from seven to fourteen months old,
      400
  newborns and, 142
  preschoolers and, 138
  toddlers and, 134
Family, 5
  extended, 5–7
  life cycle of, parenting and, 300–5,
    301–3 (tables)
    adolescents, transition to parenthood
      of, 304–5
    adult children, transition to
      parenting, 305
    "between families" stage, 303
    marriage, transition to, 303
    old age, family transitions to, 305
    parenthood, transition to, 303–4
  nuclear, 8–9
  parental development and, 307–8
Family care, as child-care option, 189
Family community models of child care,
    7–8
Family meetings, 499
Family practitioners, 604
Family solidarity, 21
Fans, electric, safety and, 171

Fantasy play, 262–63, 287, 460, 484
Farb, Peter, 815, 816
Farms, safety in, 176
Fathers
  development of, 309–10
  of four-year-olds, 497–98
  household chores and, 775–79
  as house husbands, 783
  of newborns, 340
  Oedipal stage and, 292
  older, 770–71
  of one-week- to twelve-week-old
    infants, 364–67
  of seven- to fourteen-month-old
    infants, play and, 403–4
  as single parents, 771–72
  of three- to six-month-old infants, 383
    bedtime, 381–82
Fatigue
  in mothers of infants (to 14 months),
    364–65
  in mothers of newborns, 336
  in one-week- to twelve-week-old
    infants, 361, 362
  sleep and, 39, 40
  as symptom of illness, 633
  in three-year-olds, 467
Fats, dietary, 531, 533–34
Favors, birthday party, 94
Fears
  of adolescents, 254 (table)
  of the dark, 41, 466–67
  of five-year-olds, 512
  of four-year-olds, 486–88
  illness and, 705
  of infants (to 14 months), 247–50
    (table)
  of newborns, 246 (table)
  of preschoolers, 252 (table)
  safety and, 180–81
  of school-age children, 253 (table)
  of sleeping alone, 41
  of three-year-olds, 461, 466–67
  of toddlers, 251 (table), 417
  of two-year-olds, 440
Feast days, 96–97
Feeding
  biological rhythms and, 33–36
  in day care centers, 210
  development of skills for, 544–45
    (table)
  infants (to 14 months)
    health maintenance and, 541–43
    stages of, 543–45, 548

from three to six months old, 378–80
scheduled, 34
self. *See* Self-feeding
temperament and, 352
during transition period, 33–34
See also Bottle-feeding; Breast-feeding;
    Eating; Food(s); Nutrition
Feelings. *See* Emotions
Feingold diet, 562–63
Fellows, 604
Feminine Mystique, The (Friedan), 8, 14
Feminism, 243
Fencing reflex (tonic neck reflex), 349
Fetus, cognitive development of, 233
Fever
    medicines to relieve, 684–85
    as symptom of illness, 630–31
Fever blisters (cold sores), 645
Fiber, dietary, 532
    constipation and, 650
Fights between parents, 81
    as stresses, 109–10
Fingernails, clipping, 361
Finger sucking, 405
    See also Thumb sucking
Fingertip injuries, first aid for, 763
Fire, 478
Firearms
    safety and, 162, 172
    school-age children and, 139, 140
Firecrackers, 139, 162
Fireplace, 169
Fires, 158–59
First-aid supplies, 724–26
First Communion, 97
Fisher, John J., III, 473
Fish hook, first aid for embedded, 762
Fissure sealing, 572
Five-year-olds, 506–21
    biophysical information, 507–8
    body functions of, 507
    care of care givers of, 515
    cleaning and grooming, 514
    cognitive development in, 509–10,
        515–16
    developmental warning signals, 513
    discipline and guidance of, 516–17
    emotional nutrition of, 515
    emotions and feelings of, 512–13
    exercise for, 514
    health care for, 519–20
    in kindergarten, 517–19
    language development in, 508–9

motor skills of, 508
nutrition and, 513–14
play of, 515–16
safety and, 520–21
size and shape of, 507
sleep in, 514
socialization tasks of, 515–17
social skills of, 511–12
Flame-resistant clothing, 158
Flea collar, 162
Floors, safety and, 134, 143, 168–70
Flossing, 520, 571
Flotation devices, 160
Fluoride, supplemental, 358, 370, 541,
    555
    in toothpaste and fluoride rinses, 571
Folacin, 536 (table)
Folk wisdom, xxiv–xxv
Fontanelles, 318
    in three- to six-month-old infants, 374
Food(s)
    allergies to, 379
    amounts of, 558–59
    aspiration of, 166–67
    baby
        commercial, 380
        homemade, 380
        making your own, 549
    choking on, 166–67, 397
    clean, 569
    foreign travel and, 103
    fresh vs. frozen vs. canned, 561
    learning activities for four-year-olds
        involving, 489–90
    moral and religious feelings about, 35
    "natural," 560–63
    playing with, 379–80, 397
    pollutants in, 590
    safety and, 166–68
    for sick children, 696–97
    solid
        early introduction of, 34, 357
        for three- to six-month-old infants,
            374, 379–80
        why, when, and how to introduce,
            543–45, 546–47 (table), 548
    for toddlers (15 to 23 months), 417–18
    See also Diet; Eating; Feeding;
        Nutrition
Food additives, 561–62
Food and Drug Administration (FDA),
    182, 562
Food dyes, hyperactivity and, 562–63
Food preparation

four-year-olds and, 489–90
  helping with, 441, 443
  See also Cooking
Foodstuffs, basic, 531–34
Foramen ovale, 320
Forehand, Rex L., 68
Foreign countries, travel to, 103
Foreign objects
  in eyes, first aid for, 763–64
  in nose, 638
  in strange places, first aid for, 760
Foreskin, 334
Formal operations stage, 228, 230–31
  parental development and, 290
Formula, infant, 34, 355–56, 543
  See also Bottle-feeding
Four-letter words, 500
Fourth of July, 75
Four-year-olds, 480–504
  biophysical information, 481–82
  body functions of, 481
  cleaning and grooming, 490–91
  cognitive development in, 483–84,
    493–98
  creativity and, 496–97
  developmental warning signals in, 488
  discipline and guidance for, 498–501
  emotional nutrition of, 493
  emotions and feelings of, 486–88, 492–
    93
  exercise for, 492
  health care for, 502
  height and weight of, 481
  language development in, 482–83,
    494–95
  motor skills of, 481–82
  nutrition and, 489–90
  play of, 484, 497
  preschool programs for, 501
  safety and, 503
  sleep in, 491
  socialization tasks of, 493–98
  social skills of, 485
  stress management and, 492–93
  values and, 501
Fractures, emergency procedures for,
  743–45
French, Marilyn, 8, 307
Freud, Anna, 227
Freud, Sigmund, 77
Freudian theory of psychosexual
  development, 25, 223–26, 241
Friedan, Betty, 8, 14
Friends (friendships), 267–71

with adults, 270–71
  cross-age, 268
  parental development and, 307
  parents' finding time for, 24
  parents' role in children's, 269–71
  between siblings, 268–69
Frostbite, 747
Frustrations
  of infants seven to fourteen months
    old, 400
  See also Stress(es)
Furnaces, safety and, 171
Furniture, 83
  safety and, 169, 170
Fussiness
  in one-week- to twelve-week-old
    infants, 362
  See also Irritability
Future, parents', 24

Gag reflex, 318
Galactosemia, 344
Galinsky, Ellen, 288, 367
Games
  for one-week- to twelve-week-old
    infants, 368
  with rules, 261–63
  three-year-olds and, 460
  word, 101
Garage, safety in, 155, 172
Garage doors, 172, 179
Garbage disposal, safety and, 168
Gardening supplies, safety and, 173
Gasoline, 172
Gastrocolic reflex, 43, 318
Gates, 83
Gaze aversion, 341
Gender identity, 242–44
  problems with, as symptom, 667
  in three-year-olds, 461
Gender roles, 242, 243
Gender role stereotypes, 242–44
General practitioners, 604
Generativity, 293, 297
Generic drugs, 683
Genitals, 461
  two-year-olds and, 440
Gesell, Arnold, 226–27, 455, 457
Gesell Institute, 462
Gestures
  in infants three to six months old, 375
  See also Body language
Gifts
  Christmas, 96

thank-you notes for, 97
Gilligan, Carol, 237
Girls
language development in, 414
See also Gender identity; Sex
differences
Giving instruction, as guidance method,
61
Godparenting, 9
Golden Rule guidance, 60
Goodall, Jane, 7, 13
Goodman, Ellen, 609, 799
Gordon, Thomas, 51, 60, 61, 92
Graduations, 99
Grand mal convulsion, emergency
procedures for, 747–48
Grandparents, 185
leaving children with, 104
parental development and, 307–8
Granuloma of navel, 359
Grasp(ing)
in infants one to twelve weeks old, 350
in infants three to six months old, 375
pincer, 392
Grasping reflex, 319
in infants one to twelve weeks old, 349
Grohman, Joann, 13
Growing pains, 654
Growing Up Free (Pogrebin), 79
Growth. *See* Development, children's;
Development, parents'
Guidance, 54
about manners, 86–87
consistency and, 58–60
definition of, 56
of five-year-olds, 516–17
of four-year-olds, 498–501
general principles of, 57–58
of infants (to 14 months)
from seven to fourteen months old,
404
from three to six months old, 385
methods of, 60–71
automatic methods, 60–62
behavior analysis and behavior
modification, 65–66
environmental control, 61
giving instruction, 61
isolation, 66–67
modeling, 60–61
mutual assertiveness methods, 62–63
one-minute scolding, 64–65
outside control, 70–71
persuasion, 64

physical power methods, 67–68
power methods, 63–67
simple enjoying, 62
simple ignoring, 61
strong power methods, 67–68
time-outs, 66
unilateral assertiveness, 63–64
verbal power methods, 68–71
for three-year-olds, 470–71
toddlers and, 422
two-year-olds and, 448–49
Guilt, 661
accepting, 25
of authors, 782–83
biological rhythms and, 31, 32
about employing housekeepers, 196–97
illness and, 706, 717–18
Gum removal, 764
Guns. *See* Firearms
Gurgling sounds, 351

Haan, Norma, 237
Hair
blow-drying, 570
combing, 399
of newborns, 318
shampooing
four-year-olds, 490
one- to twelve-week-old infants,
360–61
seven- to fourteen-month-old infants,
399
two-year-olds, 443
Haley, Jay, 300
Halloween, 97
safety and, 164
Hallucinations, as symptom of illness,
632
Hallucinogens, overdose or withdrawal
from, emergency procedures for,
748–49
Hand control
in infants one to twelve weeks old, 350
See also Eye-hand coordination
Handedness, 392–93, 412, 508
Handicapped children, sports and, 584
Hands
dominant (handedness), 392–93, 412,
508
of infants seven to fourteen months
old, 392–93
washing, 418
Happiness, presence of children and, 14
Harlow, Harry F., 21

Hassle Scale, 108
Hatching, 376
Havighurst, Robert J., 227–28, 240
Head
  circumference of
    infants one to twelve weeks old,
      348–49
    infants seven to fourteen months
      old, 391
    infants three to six months old, 374
    newborns, 318
    two-year-olds, 435
  shape of, in newborns, 342
  See also Skull
Headache, as symptom of illness, 633–34
Head control, in infants one to twelve
    weeks old, 350
Head injuries, emergency procedures for,
    738–39
Health, of parents, 24
Health care
  costs of, 624–25
  for five-year-olds, 519–20
  for four-year-olds, 502
  for infants (to 14 months)
    from seven to fourteen months old,
      406
  for infants one to twelve weeks old,
    369–70
  for newborns, 341–44
  for parents, 625–26
  for three-year-olds, 476–77
  for toddlers, 428–29
  for two-year-olds, 451–52
  See also Health maintenance; Illness;
    Symptoms of illness
Health insurance, 623–25
Health maintenance, 525–98
  environment and, 588–98
    air pollution, 588–89
    food pollution, 590
    noise pollution, 590
    parents and pollution, 593–94
    radiation, 591–93
    television pollution, 594–98
    water pollution, 589–90
  exercise and, 578–84
    handicapped children and, 584
    infants (to fourteen months), 578–
      79
    older children, 580–81
    sports, 580–84
    toddlers and preschoolers, 579–80
  hygiene and, 565–72

body care, 569–72
  dirt, 566–69
nutrition and, 526–65
  amounts of food, 558–59
  artificial sweeteners, 554
  balanced diet, 549–50
  basic foodstuffs, 531–34
  calories, 528–31, 530 (table)
  eating habits, 550–52
  feeding infants, 541–49
  mealtime atmosphere, 559–60
  milk, 557–58
  "natural" foods, 560–63
  nontraditional diets, 563–65
  snacks, 551–53
  sugar, 553–54
  teeth, 554–56
  vitamins and minerals, 534–40, 536–
    39 (table)
  water, 527–28
rest and sleep and, 572–77
stress management and, 584–88
Health Maintenance Organization
    (HMO), 611
Hearing
  in infants (to 14 months)
    from one to twelve weeks old, 349
  in newborns, 319
Hearing loss (deafness), 637
  from noise, 178, 590–91
  in two-year-olds, 435, 437
Heart. See Cardiovascular system
Heart rate, of infants seven to fourteen
    months old, 391
Heat exhaustion, emergency procedures
    for, 745–46
Heatstroke
  in cars, 150
  emergency procedures for, 745–46
Height
  of five-year-olds, 507
  of four-year-olds, 481
  of infants (to 14 months)
    from one to twelve weeks old, 348
    from seven to fourteen months old,
      390
    from three to six months old, 374
  of three-year-olds, 456
  of toddlers (15 to 23 months), 410
  of two-year-olds, 434
Heimlich maneuver, 731, 732
Helfer, Ray, 115
Helmets, motorcycle, 151
Helpers in child care, 183–218

au pair girls, 203
basic characteristics to look for in, 186–87
emergency and institutional, 214–15
housekeepers. *See* Housekeepers
See also Care givers; Child care
Helplessness, infants' feelings of, 400–1
Hemangioma, cavernous, 343
Hemophilus influenzae, type b, day care centers and, 210–11
Hib immunization, 210–11, 451, 614
Hiccups, first aid for, 765
High chairs, safety and, 142–43, 177
Hiking, safety and, 176
History of childhood, 6
Hitting
by infants seven to fourteen months old, 405
See also Aggression
Hitting children
as child abuse, 115–17
guidance by, 67–68
See also Child abuse
Hobby room, safety in, 172–73
Holding technique, guidance and, 67
Holidays, 95–97
Christmas, 75, 95–96
safety and, 164
feast days, 96–97
minor, 97
socialization and, 75
Holmes, Thomas H., 107
Holt, Emmett, 224
Homemaker services, 214
Homeostatic mechanisms, 525
Homosexuality, 665
Honey
botulism and, 363
for coughs, 642
Honeymoon, baby, 338–40, 365
Hookworm, 162
Hormones, in newborns, 321
Hospitalization, 708–12
Hot water heaters, safety and, 171
Household chores
safety and, 165
sharing, 775–80
three-year-olds and, 470–71
"Household Procedure Manual," 206
House husbands, 783
Housekeepers, 195–208
checking references of, 204–5
as child-care option, 190
children's complaints about, 207

defining the job of, 200–1
employer difficulties with, 196–97
ending relationships with, 200
finding and keeping, 199
interviewing and selecting, 203–4
live-in versus day, 197–98
perfect, 195–96
relatives as, 207–8
search for, 199, 202–3
starting the job, 205–7
wages and benefits for, 201
Howell, Mary, 586, 704
Hugging, infants seven to fourteen months old and, 395, 396
Humidification, 639, 643
Humor, sense of, in infants seven to fourteen months old, 396
Hydrocephalus, 348–49
Hygiene, 565–72
body care and, 569–72
in day care centers, 210, 211
dirt and, 566–69
See also Bathing; Cleaning; Washing
Hyperactivity
fatigue and, 40
food dyes and, 562–63
Hypertension, sodium intake and, 535, 540
Hyperventilation, swimming and, 160
Hypothermia (abnormally low body temperature), emergency procedures for, 746
Hypothyroidism, 344

Ideal images of parenting and children, 288
Identification, of three-year-olds, 461
Identity
moral development and, 237
parenting and, 299–300
problems with, as symptom, 667–68
sexual (gender), 242–44, 461, 667
Ilg, Frances L., 240, 475, 500
Illness, 523–24
care of the sick child at home, 671–701
activity, 697–98
equipment needed, 672–77
food, 696–97
general advice, 696
medicines. *See* Medicines
return to wellness, 700
sickness chart, 698, 699
specialized home care, 700–1

special tasks, 698
thermometers, 672–75
effect on children, 704–14
  chronic illness, 712–14
  at different ages, 706–7
  hospitalization, 708–12
  treatment, impact of, 707–8
effect on parents, 715–17
effect on siblings, 717–18
signs of, 628–29
symptoms of, 628–69
  appetite, poor, 645–46
  blisters, 655
  cardiovascular system, 644
  clumsiness, 654
  constipation, 650
  cough, 641–42
  croup, 643
  crying, 631
  definition of, 628–29
  delirium, 632–33
  diarrhea, 648–50
  digestive system, 644–51
  drowsiness, 632
  ears, 636–37
  eyes, 635–36
  fatigue, 633
  fever, 630–31
  general, 630–31
  growing pains, 654
  headache, 633–34
  heartbeat, rapid or irregular
    (arrhythmia), 644
  how to use chapter on, 629
  keeping track of, 629–30
  limping, 653–54
  malaise, 633
  in mouth, 644–45
  musculoskeletal system, 653–54
  nervous system, 633–35
  psychosocial. See Psychosocial
    symptoms
  rashes, 655–56
  respiratory system, 637–43
  runny nose, 637–40
  skin, 654–56
  sleepiness, excessive, 632
  sore throat, 640
  stiff neck, 634–35
  stomachache, 646–47
  stools: black, red, white, or wormy,
    650–51
  swollen glands, 642–43
  toothache, 644–45

urinary system, 651–52
vomiting, 647–48
weight loss (or no weight gain),
  631–32
wheezing, 643
See also Health care; Infections
Imaginary playmate, 265, 459, 470, 484
Imitation
  of facial expressions, by newborns, 322
  learning by, 394
  by toddlers, 413
  by two-year-olds, 439–40
Immigration and Naturalization Service
  (INS), 202–3
Immune system, in infants from one to
  twelve weeks old, 350
Immunizations
  DPT, 613–14
  for foreign travel, 103
  for four-year-olds, 502
  Hib, 210–11, 451, 614
  for infants (to 14 months)
    from one to twelve weeks old, 369
    from three to six months old, 386
  measles, mumps, and rubella (MMR),
    429
  polio, 369, 452, 613–15
Immunologic factors, in colostrum, 324
Incest, 111–12
Incisors, 391
Inconsistency, guidance and, 58–60
Independence (autonomy)
  of four-year-olds, 490
  milestones of, 270 (table)
  of three-year-olds, 460–61
  in toddlers (15 to 23 months), 239–41
  in two-year-olds, 439, 440
Independency-dependency crisis, in
  toddlers, 415
India, 10
Individualism, 287
Infanticide, 9
Infantile grandiosity, 225–26
Infantile symbiosis, stage of, 350
Infants (to 14 months)
  child care for. See Child care
  development in, 277–78 (tables)
    highlights, 246 (table)
  language development in, 255–56
    (tables)
    babbling, 234
    first words learned, 234–35
    sentences, 235
    before speech, 234

moral development in, 247–50 (tables)
motor development in, 246–49 (tables)
    from one to twelve weeks old, 350
    from seven to fourteen months old,
        391–93, 403
    from three to six months old, 375
at one to twelve weeks, 347–70
    biophysical information, 348–50
    body functions, 349–50
    care of the care giver, 364–66
    developmental warning signals, 354
    emotional nutrition, 364
    emotions, 351
    exercise, 363
    father's needs, 366–67
    feeding/nutrition, 354–58
    guidance, 369
    health care, 369–70
    language/cognitive skills, 350–51
    motor skills, 350
    play/stimulation, 367–68
    safety, 370–71
    siblings' needs, 367
    size and shape, 348–49
    sleep/activity, 361–63
    socialization tasks, 367–69
    social skills, 351
    stress management, 363–64
    temperaments, 352–53
parental development and, 294
parents' role in development of, 257–
    63, 294
    overstimulation, 260
    understimulation, 258–60
psychosocial development in, 237–39,
    246–50 (table)
reflexes in, 318–19, 342, 349. See also
    specific reflexes
safety and
    automobiles, 133
    burns, 132
    car seats, 146, 147
    crawling, 151–52
    cribs, 177
    drowning, 132
    falls, 131, 142–43
    high chairs, 142–43, 177
    playpens, 178
    poisonings and swallowings of small,
        indigestible objects, 133
    See also Safety
    suffocation, 131
    from three to six months old, 385–
        86

    toys, 178–79
    walkers, 177
at seven to fourteen months, 389–407
    biophysical information, 390–93
    body functions, 391
    care of the care giver, 402
    cleaning/grooming, 399
    cognitive development, 393–94
    developmental warning signals, 397
    discipline and guidance, 404–5
    emotional development, 396
    emotional nutrition, 401–2
    emotions, 396
    exercise, 400
    health care, 406
    language development, 394–95
    motor skills, 391–93
    nutrition, 397–98
    play/stimulation, 402–4
    safety, 404, 406–7
    size and shape, 390–91
    sleep/activity, 400
    socialization tasks, 402–5
    social skills, 395–96, 403
    stress management, 400–1
at three to six months, 373–87
    biophysical information, 373–75
    body functions, 374–75
    care of the care giver, 383–84
    cleaning/grooming, 380
    developmental warning signals, 378
    emotional nutrition, 383
    emotions, 376, 377
    environmental health, 387
    exercise, 382–83
    feeding/nutrition, 378–80
    guidance and discipline, 385–86
    health care, 386–87
    language/cognitive skills, 375–76
    motor skills, 375
    play/stimulation, 384–85
    safety, 387
    size and shape, 373–74
    sleep/activity, 381–82
    socialization tasks, 384–86
    social skills, 376–77
    stress management, 383
    temperaments, 377
    travel and trips, 386
    See also specific topics
Infections (infectious diseases)
    in day care centers and home care
        facilities, 210–12

in infants seven to fourteen months
old, 406
life-threatening consequences of,
emergency procedures for, 757
in newborns, 344
respiratory, 406
upper respiratory, 637–38
urinary tract, in toddler girls, 418
Informal home care (day care homes),
212–13
Ingestions
nontoxic, 743
See also Poisonings; Swallowing
Inhalants, overdose or withdrawal from,
emergency procedures for, 748–49
Injuries. See Emergencies; Safety
Inoculations. See Immunizations
Insect bites
emergency procedures for, 750
first aid for, 761
Instinctive view of parenting, 13
Instruction, giving, as guidance method,
61
Insurance, health, 623–25
Intelligence. See Cognitive development
Internal bleeding, 736
Internal ideas of objects, development of,
412–13
Interns, 604
Interviews with housekeepers, 203–4
Intestinal obstruction, vomiting as a
symptom of, 647, 648
Intimacy, dilution of parents', 299
Intussusception, 646
Ipecac, syrup of, 687, 725, 742
Iron
absorption of, 548
bottle-feeding and, 34
formulas fortified with, 356
Iron deficiency, 557
Ironing boards, safety and, 171
Iron supplements, 358, 540
Irritability
fatigue and, 40
in one-week- to twelve-week-old
infants, 368
See also Fussiness
"I sentences," 52
Isolation, as guidance technique, 66–67

"Jargon," 394
Jaundice, 324, 654
in newborns, 343–44
Jiggling of newborns, 341

Jobs
after-school, 214
See also Work
Jolting events, 105–7
Judaism, food and, 35
Jumping, 579
development of, 250 (table), 252
(table), 253 (table), 411
rope, 580

Kagan, Jerome, 87
Kaye, Kenneth, 257–58, 294
Kempe, C. Henry, 115
Kennell, John H., 341
Kerr, Jean, 25
Kindergarten, 517–19
Kisses
forcing children to accept unwanted,
112
infants seven to fourteen months old
and, 395, 396
Kitchen, safety in, 152–54, 167–68
Kitzinger, Sheila, 366
Klaus, Marshall H., 341
Knives, safety and, 168
Knowledge, parents' need for, 21
Kohlberg, 236, 237
Kohut, Heinz, 225, 226

Labor, Department of, 202–3
Lactation
caloric requirements and, 529
medications for suppressing, 328
phases of, 323, 324 (illus.)
stopping, 337
See also Breast-feeding
Lactose intolerance, 558
Ladders, safety and, 143
La Leche League, 326, 327, 331, 354,
528
Landers, Ann, 11
Language, body, 350, 351
Language acquisition system, 233–34
Language and cognitive skills of care
givers, 187
Language development (language
acquisition), 233–36
abnormal, 279 (table), 280 (table)
in five-year-olds, 508–9
in four-year-olds, 482–83, 494–95
in infants (to 14 months), 246–49
(tables), 255–56 (tables)
babbling, 234
first words learned, 234–35

from one to twelve weeks old, 351
sentences, 235
from seven to fourteen months old,
394–95, 403
before speech, 234
from three to six months old, 375–
76
parents' role in, 235
in three-year-olds, 457–58
in toddlers (15 to 23 months), 240,
250 (table), 413–14, 421–22
in two-year-olds, 436–37, 443
Lanugo, 318
Latency stage, 225, 241
parental development and, 293
Laughing, in infants one to twelve weeks
old, 351
Laundry, dirty, 84
Laundry area, safety in, 155
Lawrence, Ruth A., 325, 329, 330
Laxatives, 690
Lazarus, Richard S., 107, 108
Leach, Penelope, 352, 359, 373, 376, 464
Lead poisoning, 154
Learning
as fun, 272
by imitation, 394
outside of school, 273, 275–76
play and, 263
by two-year-olds, 446–47
See also Cognitive development
LeMasters, E. E., 26
Lerner, Harriet, 76
Let-down, 323
problems with, 328–29
Lewis, Melvin, 232
Libidinal development. See Psychosexual
development
Libido, Freudian theory of, 224–25, 241
Lice, 761
Life Events Scale, 107, 108
Life satisfaction, presence of children
and, 14
Lighting, safety and, 169
Limping, 653–54
Linoleic acid, 533
Liquids
runny nose and, 639–40
for sick children, 696–97
Little League, 581, 582
Lochia, 337, 365
Locke, John, 223, 224
Locks, deadbolt, 159

Logical consequences, concept of, 498,
499
Lordosis, 390
Loss of control
parental, 70
See also Temper tantrums
Love
development of, 246–49 (table), 251–
54 (table)
of mother for newborn, 341
for opposite-sex parent, 487
parents' need for, 18
See also Affection; Attachments
Lungs, in newborns, 320
Lying, 470
"white lies," 501
Lymph nodes, enlarged, 642–43

McBride, Angela Barron, 308
McGoldrick, Monica, 300, 301
McMahon, Robert J., 68
Macrobiotic diet, 565
Magazines
child-care advice in, 185
socialization and, 72
Mahler, Margaret, 239, 350, 376, 377
Make-believe play, 262–63, 287, 460, 484
Malaise, 633
Manipulation of objects
by infants seven to fourteen months
old, 392
mental, 413
See also Eye-hand coordination;
Grasp(ing)
Manners, 86–87
eating, 35
milestone ceremonies and, 97
table, 464–65
Manual expression of breast milk, 330–31
Marasmus, 532
Marine life stings, emergency procedures
for, 751
Marriage
transition to, 303
See also Relationship between parents
Marshmallows, 167
Maslow, Albert H., 227
Massage, 491, 579
breast, for manual expression, 330
Masturbation, 241, 440, 461
parental development and, 291–92
socialization and, 76–77
as symptom, 663
Maternity leave, 366

Math, 495
  See also Counting
Matrilineal societies, 7
Matrilocal societies, 7
Mattress, bunk bed, 179
Mead, Margaret, 575
Meals
  atmosphere during, 559–60
  See also Eating
Measles, mumps, and rubella (MMR)
      immunization, 429
Meconium, 324
Meconium stools, 320–21
Media
  sexual information from, 79
  socialization and, 72–74
  See also Television
Medical care
  for five-year-olds, 519
  for four-year-olds, 502
  for infants (to 14 months)
    from one to twelve weeks old, 369–
        70
    from seven to fourteen months old,
        406
    from three to six months old, 386
  for three-year-olds, 476
  for toddlers, 428–29
  for two-year-olds, 451–52
  See also Checkups; Doctors
      (pediatricians); Health care
Medical students, 605
Medicine, as science, 619–21
Medicine cabinets, 153, 169–70
Medicines
  administering, 692–95
  antacids, 689
  antibiotic ointment, 689
  antifever, 684–85, 686 (table)
  antihistamines, 687
  Benadryl, 688
  cough syrups, 688
  dosage charts, 694–95
  dosages of, 683–84
  that every household should have,
      684–90
  eye ointment, 689
  foreign travel and, 103–4
  generic, 683
  home remedies, 691–92
    cough preparation, 688
  oral decongestants, 687–88
  over-the-counter (OTC), 677–82
  pain relievers, 687
  philosophy of medication, 695
  poisonings with, 153–55
  prescription, 682–84
  safety and, 135, 690
  steroid cream or ointment, 689
  syrup of ipecac, 687
  unnecessary, 690
Meditation, 587
Meetings, family, 499
Men
  changing parenting realities for, 22
  See also Fathers
Mental health professionals (therapists),
      622–24
Mental retardation, psychosocial
      symptoms and, 661–62
Menu planning, 489
Messinger, Lillian, 800
Metabolic diseases, congenital, 344
Method 3, 52, 58
Mexico, travel to, 103
Microwave cooking
  radiation and, 592
  safety and, 165, 168, 180
Middlescence, parental development and,
      297–98
Milestone ceremonies, 97–99
Milia, in newborns, 343
Milk, breast
  infants' ability to discriminate smell
      and taste of, 349
  nicotine in, 345
  See also Breast-feeding; Lactation
Milk, cow's
  allergy to, 558
    colic and, 352, 353
  formula based on, 356
  for infants (to 14 months), 398, 542
  lactose intolerance and, 558
  low fat, 533
  minimum requirements for, 557–58
  in mother's diet, colic and, 352
  newborns should not be given, 332
  raw vs. pasteurized, 560–61
  skimmed or low fat, 558
  two-year-olds' consumption of, 442
  See also Bottle-feeding
Minerals, 535, 540
Mirrors, 377
Missing children, 113
MMR (measles, mumps, and rubella)
      immunization, 429
Modeling by adults, 447, 449
  aggressive behavior and, 80

as guidance method, 60–61
Modesty, 487, 513
Molars, 391
Molestation of children. *See* Sexual abuse
    of children
Mongolian spot, 343
Moniliasis (thrush), 645
Monsters, fear of, 417
Moral development, 236–37
    in adolescents, 255 (table)
    in five-year-olds, 511
    in four-year-olds, 484–85
    in infants (to 14 months), 247–50
        (table)
    in preschoolers, 252 (table)
    in school-age children, 236, 254 (table)
    in three-year-olds, 459
    in toddlers, 251 (table)
    See also Values
Moral values. *See* Values
Moro (startle) reflex, 142, 319, 349
Mosquito bites, first aid for, 761
Mother-alone model of child care, 6–7
Mothers. *See* Care givers
Motion sickness, Dramamine for, 101–2
Motorcycles, 151
Motor development (motor skills)
    in adolescents, 254 (table)
    in five-year-olds, 508
    in four-year-olds, 481–82
    in infants (to fourteen months), 246–
        49 (table)
        from one to twelve weeks old, 350
        from seven to fourteen months old,
            391–93, 403
        from three to six months old, 375
    in preschoolers, 251–52 (table)
    in school-age children, 253 (table)
    in three-year-olds, 457
    in toddlers (15 to 23 months), 250
        (table), 411–12
    in two-year-olds, 435–36
Motor vehicles. *See* Car restraints; Car
    safety; Car travel; Motorcycles
Mouth
    bleeding around, 736
    symptoms of illness in, 644–45
Moving, 105–7
Muscle tone, in newborns, 342
Musculoskeletal system, symptoms of
    illness, 653–54
Museums, visits to, 99
Music lessons, 265–66

Mutual assertiveness, as guidance
    method, 62–63
Myelinization, 232

Nadelson, Carol, 791
Nail biting, 514–15
Naps
    four-year-olds and, 491
    hints on, 574–76
    for infants three to six months old,
        382
    for toddlers, 419
    for two-year-olds, 444
Narcotics, overdose or withdrawal from,
    emergency procedures for, 748–49
Nasal aspirator (bulb syringe), 676
National Academy of Nannies, 209
National Association for the Education
    of Young Children, 209
National Center for Child Abuse and
    Neglect, 115
National Fire Protection Association, 182
Natural disasters, 105
"Natural" foods, 560–63
Navels, cleaning of, 359
Neck, stiff, as symptom of illness, 634–35
Neck injuries, emergency procedures for,
    740–41, 744
Needs
    children's, 16–17
        child care and, 187
    Maslow's theory of, 227
    parents', 18–19
        child care and, 187–88
    parents' awareness of their own, 58
    reciprocal, 19–21
    self-discipline and, 57, 58
    socialization and, 53
Negatives
    language acquisition and, 235
    See also "No"
Negativism
    of toddlers (15 to 23 months), 240,
        415, 422, 427
    in two-year-olds, 442
Neglect, as child abuse, 259
Nelson, Gerald, 59, 60, 61, 64–65
Nervous system
    symptoms of illness in, 633–35
    toilet training and, 43
Neurological development, 232
Newborns
    bathing, 333, 334

Brazelton developmental evaluation of, 342
breast-feeding, 321, 323–31, 331–32
  bilirubin levels and jaundice, 344
  bottle-feeding of breast-fed babies, 331
  breast engorgement, 325
  colostrum, 323–24
  duration of feedings, 325
  jiggling of babies, 341
  let-down problems, 328–29
  medical intervention which delays breast feeding, 330–31
  mother's diet, 331
  mothers' nursing styles, 326–28
  nipple problems, 329–30
  position for, 324, 325 (illus.)
  sedated infants, 325
  starting, 324–25
  storage of breast milk, 331
  styles of babies, 325–26
  weight loss, 343
  burping, 332–33
  care givers of, 323, 336–40
    baby honeymoon, 338–40
    emotional recovery, 337–38
    fathers, 340
    fatigue, 336
    obstetric recovery, 337
    recuperation from labor and birth, 336–38
  cleaning, 333–35
  clothing for, 333–34
  cognitive development of, 233
  diapering, 333–35
  elimination in, 42, 43, 320–21, 342
  emotional nutrition of, 336
  exercise and, 336
  falls and, 142
  fathers of, 340
  feeding, 33, 34
  health care of, 341–44
  hormones in, 321
  motor development in, 246 (table)
  play of, 340
  psychosocial development in, 246–47 (table)
  quiet-alert state of, 340–41
  reflexes in, 318–19, 342
  safety and, 164–65, 344–45
  sensory function in, 319
  sibling rivalry with, 81–82
  size and shape of, 317–18
  sleep patterns of, 36–38

sleep/wakefulness cycles in, 321, 335
socialization of, 340
special changes in adjusting to life outside the womb, 319–21
stress management and, 336
temperature regulation in, 345
See also Infants (to 14 months)
Newton, Niles, 33
Niacin (vitamin B3), 537 (table)
Night lights, 382
Nightmares, 444, 462, 466, 512–13, 576
  talking about, 488
Night terrors, 577
Nipples
  bottle, 332, 356, 357
  breast-feeding and problems with, 329–30
Nipple shields, 329
Nitrates and nitrites, 562
"No"
  saying, to seven- to fourteen-month-old infants, 404
  understanding the word, 375, 376, 386
  See also Negatives; Negativism
Noise
  hearing loss from, 178
  infants one to twelve weeks old and, 370
  keeping down, 84–85
  sleeping and, 382
Noise pollution, 590–91
Non-industrial societies ("primitive" cultures)
  rituals and customs of child care in, 33
  sleep in, 38, 39
  transition period in, 33–34
Nose
  blowing of, 411
  clearing mucus from, 638–39
  runny, 637–40
Nosebleeds, emergency procedures for, 736
Nostalgic view of parenting, 13–14
Notebook, household, 206
Nuclear arms race, 815–16
Nuclear family
  isolated, as model of child care, 8–9
  life cycle of, parenting and, 300–5, 301–3 (tables)
    adolescents, transition to parenthood of, 304–5
    adult children, transition to parenting, 305
    "between families" stage, 303

marriage, transition to, 303
old age, family transitions to, 305
parenthood, transition to, 303–4
Nudity, parental, 78
Nursery rhymes, 403
Nursery school, 269–70, 471–76
  choosing, 473–74
  crying of child when left at, 474–75
  preparing a child for, 474
  reaction of children to, 475–76
  who should go to, 471–73
Nurses, 604
Nursing. *See* Breast-feeding
Nursing bras, 329
Nutrition, 526–65
  basic foodstuffs, 531–34
  caloric requirements, 528–31, 530
    (table)
  five-year-olds and, 513–14
  four-year-olds and, 489–90
  health maintenance and, 526–65
    amounts of food, 558–59
    artificial sweeteners, 554
    balanced diet, 549–50
    basic foodstuffs, 531–34
    calories, 528–31, 530 (table)
    eating habits, 550–52
    feeding infants, 541–49
    mealtime atmosphere, 559–60
    milk, 557–58
    "natural" foods, 560–63
    nontraditional diets, 563–65
    snacks, 551–53
    sugar, 553–54
    teeth, 554–56
    vitamins and minerals, 534–40, 536–
      39 (table)
    water, 527–28
  infants from seven to fourteen months
    old, 397–98
  snacks and, 34–35
  of three-year-olds, 463–65
  of toddlers (15 to 23 months), 417–18
  of two-year-olds, 441–43
  vitamins and minerals, 534–40, 536–39
    (table)
  water requirements, 527–28
  See also Diet; Feeding; Food(s)

Obesity, 530–31, 558–59
Object permanence, 262, 394, 395, 400
Obstetrical recuperation, 365–66
Occupational hazards, 166
Oedipal complex, 226, 241

Oedipal stage, 110, 226
  parental development and, 292
Old age, family transitions to, 305
Older adulthood, parental development
  and, 298
Older parents, 769–71
One-Minute Father, The, 61
One-Minute Mother, The, 61
One-minute scolding, 64–65
One-Minute Scolding, The (Nelson), 60
Only children, socialization of, 82–83
Oppositional parenting, 288
Oral fixations, 225
Oral stage, 224, 241
  parental development and, 291
Organization, child-orienting and, 84
Original sin, doctrine of, 223
  discipline and, 48
O'Hern, Lynn, 799, 800
Overcompliance, as symptom, 660–62
Overstimulation, 260

Pacifiers, 363
  safety and, 178
Packard, Vance, 20–21
Pain relievers, 687
Painting, 265
Paleness, as symptom of illness, 655
Pantothenic acid, 537 (table)
Pap smear, 625, 626
Parallel play, 71, 267, 268
Parental development. *See* Development,
  parents'
Parent effectiveness courses, 92
Parent Effectiveness Training (P.E.T.),
  51–52, 62, 63, 92
Parenting
  adopted children, 787–92
    adjustment and development
      problems, 791–92
    getting started, 787–88
    special concerns, 788–90
    when to tell children, 790–91
  animal vs. human, 4–5
  authors' philosophy of, 23–25
  bottom-line realities of, 21–23
  in a changing society, 16
  contexts of, 15
  criticism of their parents', by children
    and adolescents, 287–88
  definition of, 786
  effective, 264–65
  fantasy (play), 287, 288
  ideal images of, 288

instinctive view of, 13
learning about, 21–22
needs of parents and, 18–19
nostalgic view of, 13–14
oppositional, 288
pessimistic view of, 14
present difficulties of, 3
realistic-eclectic view of, 15
restitutional, 288
romantic "traditional" view of, 14
self-acceptance and, 289
society and, 811–13
stepparenting, 792–804
transition to, 303–4
See also Development, parents'
Parent-proofing your life, 23–25
Parents
deaf, 375
older, 769–71
single, 771–72
working. *See* Work
See also Parenting
Parent substitutes. *See* Care givers
Parents Anonymous (PA), 116
Parsons, Talcott, 300
Parties, birthday, 93–95
Passover, 96
Paternity leave, 366–67
Patio doors, 143, 160–61
Peanut butter, babies not to be given, 167
Peanuts, safety and, 166, 167
Pedestrian safety, 150
preschoolers and, 138
Pediatricians, 603–4
abnormal development and, 276–77
breast-feeding and, 184
types of, 606
See also Doctors
Pediatric nurse practitioners, 604
Peek-a-boo games, 394
Penis
caught in zipper, 764
circumcised, 334, 359
uncircumcised, 334
Penis envy, 241
Permissiveness, discipline and, 51–52
Perspiration, in infants (to 14 months), 380
Persuasion, as guidance method, 64
Pessimistic view of parenting, 14
Pets, 567–68
safety and, 161–62
Phallic fixations, 225

Phallic stage, 224–25, 241
parental development and, 291–92
Phenylketonuria, 344
Physical contact, with newborns, 319
Physical overstimulation, 260
Physical power methods of guidance, 67–68
Physical punishment, 115
See also Child abuse, physical
Physicians. *See* Doctors (pediatricians)
Physicians for Automotive Safety, 182
Piaget, Jean, 228–31, 236, 261, 393, 458, 483, 509
cognitive development stages of, 228–31 (table)
concrete operations stage, 230
formal operations stage, 230–31
parental development and, 289–90
preoperational stage, 229–30
sensorimotor stage, 228–29
Picnics, 102
Pincer grasp, 392
Pink eye (conjunctivitis), 635
Plants, poisonous, 155, 157–58, 174, 743
Play(ing)
of adolescents, 254 (table)
of animals, 261–63
cooperative, 459–60
of five-year-olds, 511–12, 515–16
of four-year-olds, 484, 497
functions of, 263
of infants (to 14 months), 247–50 (table)
with food, 379–80
food play, 397
from one to twelve weeks old, 367–68
from seven to fourteen months old, 402–4
from three to six months old, 384–85
of newborns, 246 (table), 340
outdoors, safety and, 150
parallel, 71, 267, 268
parents' role in development and, 261–63
of preschoolers, 252 (table)
pretend (make-believe or fantasy), 262–63, 460, 484
parenting, 287
rough-and-tumble, 71, 72, 262, 579–80
with rules, 261–63
of school-age children, 253 (table)
sensorimotor, 261

sex, 77
  as symptom, 663–64
  socialization and, 71–72
  symbolic (representational), 261
  of three-year-olds, 459–60, 469
  of toddlers (15 to 23 months), 251
    (table), 416, 421
  of two-year-olds, 446–47
  See also Toys
Playground, safety in, 174
Playground equipment, safety and, 143–
    44, 174
Playpens
  for infants seven to fourteen months
    old, 405
  safety and, 178
  three- to six-month-old infants and,
    384–85
Playroom, 405
Please Don't Eat the Daisies (Kerr), 25
Pleasure, in infants seven to fourteen
    months old, 396
Pleck, Joseph, 14
Pneumonia, 641
Poison Control Centers, 158, 742, 743
Poisonings, 152–58
  carbon monoxide, 154
  with cleaning supplies, 152–53
  emergency procedures for, 741–43
  infants (to 14 months) and, 133
  lead, 154
  with medicines, 153–55
  places where children might be
    exposed to, 167–75
  with plants, 155, 157–58
  toddlers and, 135, 430
Poison-proofing your house, 154–55
Police, 70
Polio immunization, 369, 452, 613–15
Pollution
  air, 588–89
  food, 590
  noise, 590–91
  parents and, 593–94
  water, 589–90
Pools. See Swimming pools
Positive comments, discipline and, 448–
    49
Possessiveness, 438–39
Postpartum depression, 338
Potter, Jessie, 76
Potty chair, 424
Power struggle, discipline and, 51–52
Practical Parenting (newsletter), 27

Preadolescents (ages 10–13), safety and,
    140
Precocial animals, 4–5
Pregnancy
  anticipation of parenting during, 288
  caloric requirements during, 529
Premature babies
  breast-feeding, 541
  sleep patterns of, 36
  temperature regulation in, 320
Preoperational stage, 228–30, 483
  parental development and, 290
Preoperational thinking, 458, 509–10
Preschoolers (ages 2 to 4)
  abnormal development in, 278 (table)
  day care centers for, 208–12
  language development in, 256 (table)
  moral development in, 252 (table)
  motor development in, 251–52 (table)
  parental development and, 295
  play of, 252 (table)
  psychosexual development in, 241
  psychosocial development in, 252–53
    (table)
  safety and, 128
    burns, 138
    car safety, 138
    drowning, 138
    falls, 138
    ingestions, 138
  See also Four-year-olds; Three-year-
    olds; Two-year-olds
Presents
  birthday, 94
  See also Gifts
Preservatives, 561–62
Pressure points, 733–35
Pretend play, 262–63, 287, 460, 484
"Preventive I-message," 61
Pride, parents' need for, 18–19
Primitive societies, 9
Problems, helping children deal with
    their, 85–86
Problem solving
  P.E.T. approach to, 52
  by toddlers (15 to 23 months), 413
Promiscuity, 79
Proprioception, 578–79
Proteins, 441–42, 531–32
Pryor, Karen, 354
Psychiatrists, 622
Psychological stress. See Stress(es)
Psychologists, 622–23
Psychosexual development, 241–44

Freudian theory of, 223–26, 241
  parental development and, 291–93
parental development and, 291–93
sexual identity and, 242–44
Psychosocial deprivation, 259
Psychosocial development, 237–40
  in adolescents, 254–55 (table)
  care-giver behaviors and, 238–39
  friendships and, 267–71
  in infants (to 14 months), 237–39,
    246–50 (tables)
  in newborns, 246–47 (table)
  parental development and, 293–98
  in preschoolers, 252–53 (table)
  in school-age children, 240, 253–54
    (table)
  in toddlers, 239–40, 251 (table)
  See also Socialization; Social skills
Psychosocial separation, 259
Psychosocial symptoms, 657–68
  anger, 657–58
  "bad behavior," 659–60
  goodness, excessive (overcompliance),
    660–62
  identity problems, 667–68
  school problems, 666
  sexual behavior, 663–65
  substance abuse, 666–67
Psychotherapists, 622–24
Puncture wounds, 758–59
Punishment, physical, 115
  See also Child abuse, physical
Purses, as hazard, 154
"Put down" words, 68
Putting things away, 83–84, 460, 490
Puzzles, 413

"Quality time," meaning of, 216
Questions
  of five-year-olds, 509
  learning to ask, 235
  "why," 482
Quiet-alert periods
  in infants one to twelve weeks old, 350
  in newborns, 340–41
  in one-week- to twelve-week-old
    infants, 361, 368
  See also Alert periods
Quiet time, 467

Rabies, 752
Radiation, 591–93
Rahe, Richard H., 107
Rapprochement, 239

Rashes
  diaper, 335, 380
    cleaning and, 359
  in newborns, 343
  as symptom of illness, 655–56
Rattles, safety and, 178
Reading
  by five-year-olds, 509
  modeling, 274
  television and, 596–97
Reading aloud, 73, 495
  before birth, 322
  to infants seven to fourteen months
    old, 403
Realistic-eclectic view of parenting, 15
Reasoning
  as guidance method, 64
  socialization and, 54
Receiving blankets, 333
Reciprocal needs, 19–21
Recliner chairs, 179
Reflexes
  in infants from one to twelve weeks
    old, 349
  in newborns, 318–19, 342
  See also specific reflexes
Refrigerators, safety and, 171
Regression, illness and, 705, 707, 710
Relationship between parents
  creating an environment for, 24
  effects of parenting on, 298–300
  holidays and, 96
  Oedipal stage and, 292
  parental development and, 308–9
  sexual relationship, 110–11
  sleep patterns of children and, 40
  stresses in, 118
  three- to six-month-old infants and,
    384
  vacations or travel without children
    and, 104
Relationships
  parents' need for, 18
  See also Attachments; Friends
Relatives
  as care givers, 189–90
  Christmas and, 96
  as housekeepers, 207–8
  See also Grandparents; Siblings
Relaxation techniques, 586–88
Religion, 271
  biological rhythms and, 32
  food and, 35
  socialization and, 74–75

REM (rapid eye movement) sleep, 36,
     321, 572–73
Representational play (symbolic play),
     261
Rescue breathing, 727–28
Residents, 604
Resiliency, 87
Respiratory distress, 641, 643
Respiratory infections, 406
Respiratory system, symptoms of illness
     in, 637–43
Responsibility, 21
Restaurants
   birthday parties at, 95
   eating in, 100–1
   manners in, 465
Restitutional parenting, 288
Retardation, 277
   See also Delays in development
Reverse thinking, ability to, 510
Reye's syndrome, 684
Riboflavin (vitamin B2), 538 (table)
Ribs, broken, 744
Ringworm, 656
Riordan, Jan, 331
Rivalry
   sibling, 401, 468, 493
   as stressful, 110
Rolling over, by infants one to twelve
     weeks old, 350
Roman law, 9
Romantic naturalism, discipline and
     doctrine of, 48–49
Romantic view of parenting, 14
Rooting reflex, 318, 324, 349, 544 (table)
Rothenberg, Michael, 594
Rough-and-tumble play, 71, 72, 262
Roundworm, 162
Rousseau, Jean-Jacques, 223–24
Routines, 263
Roy, Maria, 114
Rubin, Richard R., 473
Rubin, Zick, 269
Rugs, oriental, 83
Rules, 54
   for four-year-olds, 499–500
   games with, 261–63
   self-discipline triangle and, 57
Running, 579, 580
   development of, 250 (table), 252
     (table), 253 (table), 411
   two-year-olds, 435
Runny nose, 637–40

Safety (accident prevention), 123–81
   in bathroom, 169–70
   in bedroom, 170–71
   bicycles and, 139, 140, 163
   boys and, 166
   car, 144–51. *See also* Car restraints
     automatic windows and, 179
     five-year-olds and, 520
     four-year-olds and, 503
     in garage, 172
     heat and, 150
     infants one to twelve weeks old and,
        370–71
     infants three to six months old and,
        387
     intoxicated drivers and, 144–45, 151
     number of accidents, 144
     pedestrian-car accidents, 150
     preschoolers and, 138
     school-age children and, 139, 140
     teenage drivers and, 144, 151
     toddlers and, 137
   consumer products, 176–80
   crawling and, 151–52
   efficiency of, 125
   equity and, 126
   falls, 142–44
     infants (to 14 months) and, 131,
        142–43, 400
     newborns and, 142
     preschoolers and, 138
     toddlers and, 134
   fear and, 180–81
   fire, 158–59
   firearms and, 162
   five-year-olds and, 520–21
   four-year-olds and, 503
   freedom of choice and, 125–26
   in garage, 172
   glass patio doors and, 160–61
   in hobby room, 172–73
   household chores and, 165
   infants (to 14 months) and
     from one to twelve weeks old, 370–
        71
     from seven to fourteen months old,
        404, 406–7
     from three to six months old, 387
   in kitchen, 167–68
   in living areas, 169
   medicines and, 690
   newborns and, 164–65, 344–45
   occupational hazards and, 166
   outdoors, 175–76

parents' role in, 127–30
pets and, 161–62
in playground, 174
poisonings, 152–58
    carbon monoxide, 154
    with cleaning supplies, 152–53
    emergency procedures for, 741–43
    infants (to 14 months) and, 133
    lead, 154
    with medicines, 153–55
    places where children might be
        exposed to, 167–75
    with plants, 155, 157–58
    toddlers and, 135, 430
in shopping sites, 175
socialization and, 52–53
sources of information on, 181–82
sports, 163
stages of development and, 130–41
    adolescence, 141
    early school years (ages 5 to 9), 139
    first year, 131–33
    preadolescents (ages 10 to 13), 140
    preschoolers (ages 2 to 4), 138
    toddlers (ages 1 and 2), 134–37
swimming and water, 159–60
three-year-olds and, 477–78
toddlers and, 429–30
toys, 178–79, 368
two-year-olds and, 452–53
in utility room and basement, 171–72
in yards, 173–74
Safety belts. See Seat belts
St. Valentine's Day, 97
Salt, 535, 540
Sandboxes, hygiene and, 567
Scalds, 159
Scaly rashes, 656
Schemata, cognitive development and,
    393–94
School
    abnormal development and problems
        in, 280–81
    athletic events at, 99
    boarding, 214–15
    exercise and sports in, 581
    graduation ceremonies at, 99
    kindergarten, 517–19
    moving and, 106
    nursery, 269–70, 471–76
        choosing, 473–74
        crying of child when left at, 474–75
        preparing a child for, 474
        reaction of children to, 475–76

who should go to, 471–73
    parents' relationship with, 273–74
    problems in, as symptom, 666
    socialization and, 75
    Sunday, 271
    walking to, 150, 516
    See also Teachers
School-age children
    child care for, 213–14
    development in, 272–76
    moral development in, 236, 254 (table)
    motor development in, 253 (table)
    parental development and, 296
    play of, 253 (table)
    psychosexual development in, 241
    psychosocial development in, 240,
        253–54 (table)
    safety and, 139–40
School buses, 151
School plays, 99
Schuster, Clara Shaw, 45
Science, 495–96
    medicine as, 619–21
Scolding, one-minute, 60, 64–65
Scooting, 344, 382–83, 391
Scorpions, emergency procedures for
    bites of, 751
Scrapes (abrasions), first aid for, 758
Scratching by one-week- to twelve-week-
    old infants, with their own nails,
    361
Seat belts, 145, 149, 520
Seeing. See Vision
Seizures, emergency procedures for, 747–
    48
Self
    development of awareness of, 239
    parents' sense of, 24
    verbal, sense of a, 413
Self-acceptance, parental, 289
Self-control
    development of sense of, 239–40
    See also Autonomy (independence);
        Self-discipline
Self-discipline, 21, 54
    growth and development required for,
        56–57
    sexual, 76
Self-discipline triangle, 57
Self-esteem, 20
    in five-year-olds, 516
    parents' need for, 19
    in three-year-olds, 468
    in two-year-olds, 439

Self-feeding, 397, 411–12
  development of, 544–45 (table)
  five-year-olds, 513–14
  by toddlers (15 to 23 months), 415
  two-year-olds, 442
Self-image
  of adolescents, 255 (table)
  of infants (to 14 months), 247–50
    (table)
  of newborns, 247 (table)
  of preschoolers, 252 (table)
  of school-age children, 254 (table)
  of toddlers, 251 (table)
Self-theory, 225, 257
Selman, Robert, 268
Sensorimotor play, 261
Sensorimotor stage, 228–29, 376
  early, 363
  parental development and, 289–90
Sensory functions
  in newborns, 319
  See also specific senses
Sentences
  learning to make, 235
  two-word (telegraphic), 414
Separation
  from newborns, 341
  psychosocial, 259
Separation anxiety, 400
Sewage, 566, 589, 590
Sewing corner, safety and, 171
Sewing supplies, safety and, 171, 172
Sex (sexuality)
  adolescents and, 664–65
  four-year-olds and, 486–87
  mothers of one-week- to twelve-week-
    old infants and, 365–66
  parental, 77–78
  promiscuous, 79
  socialization and, 76–80
  as stress source, 110–13
  symptoms related to, 663–65
  three-year-olds and, 461, 470
  See also Masturbation; Psychosexual
    development
Sex differences, 243
  in play and toy preferences of toddlers,
    421
  sports and, 582–84
  See also Gender identity
Sex education, 78–79
Sexism, 242–44, 461
Sex play, 77
  as symptom, 663–64

Sex role stereotypes. See Gender role
    stereotypes
  socialization and, 79–80
  television and, 595
Sexual abuse of children, 111–13, 664
  in day care centers or house day care,
    211
Sexual exhibitionism, as symptom, 663
Sexual identity. See Gender identity
Shaking children, 67, 68, 115
  See also Child abuse, physical
Shampooing, 570
  four-year-olds, 490
  one-week- to twelve-week-old infants,
    360–61
  seven- to fourteen-month-old infants,
    399
  two-year-olds, 443
Sharing, toddlers and, 416
Shock
  emergency procedures for, 738
  See also Electrical injuries
Shoes
  safety and, 143
  for toddlers, 430
Shopping, safety and, 175
Shyness, 462
Siblings
  friendships between, 268–69
  of infants seven to fourteen months
    old, 401
  of one-week- to twelve-week-old
    infants, 367, 371
  rivalry between, 401, 468, 493
  socialization and, 81–83
Sick children. See Illness
Siebert, Roberta, 791
Silverware, storage of, 83
Simple enjoying, as guidance method, 62
Simple ignoring, as guidance method, 61
Sims, Pamela, 281–82
Single parents, 771–72
Skating, safety and, 176
Skin
  blue, 654–55
  in infants (to 14 months), cleaning and
    bathing, 358–61
  in newborns, 318, 343
  pale, 655
  symptoms of illness, 654–56
  yellow, 654
Skolnick, Arlene, 25
Skull
  fractures of, 744

of newborns, 318
Slapping children, 117
  See also Hitting children
Sledding, safety and, 176
Sleep, 36–42, 572–76
  in adolescents, 255 (table)
  bottle-feeding and, 39–40
  breast-feeding and, 37–38, 40
  circadian rhythms of, 37
  conflict between parents and children
    about, 40–41
  crying and, 38
  entrainment of, 36–37
  fatigue and, 39, 40
  feeding and, 34
  in five-year-olds, 514
  in four-year-olds, 491
  hints on, 574–76
  in infants (to 14 months), 247–50
    (table)
    inducing sleep, 362
    from one to twelve weeks old, 350,
      361–63
    from seven to fourteen months old,
      400
    from three to six months old, 381–
      82
  in newborns, 36–38, 321, 335
  in non-industrial societies, 38, 39
  in preschoolers, 253 (table)
  REM (rapid eye movement), 36, 321,
    572–73
  stages of, 36
  in three-year-olds, 466–67
  in toddlers, 251 (table), 419
  in two-year-olds, 444
  waking at night, 361–63, 381–82, 400,
    419, 444, 512–13, 576–77
  See also Naps; Nightmares
Sleep disorders, 574, 576–77
Sleepiness, excessive, as symptom of
  illness, 632
Sleeplessness, 41
Sleepwalking, 577
Slipping, 143
  toddlers and, 143
Smallpox vaccination, for foreign travel,
  103
Smegma, infant, 334
Smell, sense of
  in infants from one to twelve weeks
    old, 349
  in newborns, 319
Smiling, 350, 396

in infants one to twelve weeks old, 351
in infants three to six months old, 376,
  377
Smoke detectors, 158
Smoking, 589
  car safety and, 145
  infants one to twelve weeks old and,
    370
  infants three to six months old and,
    387
  newborns and, 345
  toddlers and, 135, 136
Snacks, 442
  feeding rhythms and, 34–35
  health maintenance and, 551–53
  for three-year-olds, 463–64
  for toddlers, 418
Snakebites, emergency procedures for,
  751–52
Soap
  for newborns, 334
  safety and, 132
Social development. *See* Psychosocial
  development
Socialization, 46–92
  aggression and, 80–81
  attachments and, 55–57
  basic goals of, 52–53
  child-orienting the home and, 83–85
  communication and, 55
  definition of, 46
  desirable outcomes of, 47
  do's and don'ts of, 71
  empathy and, 53, 56
  families and, 53–54
  of five-year-olds, 515–17
  of four-year-olds, 493–98
  guidance and, 56
  of infants (to 14 months)
    from seven to fourteen months old,
      402–5
    from three to six months old, 384–
      86
  manners and, 86–87
  the media and, 72–74
  of newborns, 322, 340
  organized groups and, 75
  through play and friendship, 71–72
  problems of children and, 85–86
  reasoning and, 54
  religious groups and, 74–75
  rules and, 54
  self-discipline and, 54, 56–57
  sex and, 76–80

sibling relationships and, 81–83
by spontaneous learning vs. planned
    teaching, 50–51
for sports, 582–83
stimulation and, 56
of toddlers, 421–27
    discipline, guidance, and values, 422
    play, 421
    toilet training, 422–27
of two-year-olds, 446–50
values and, 74–75
See also Discipline; Guidance;
    Psychosocial development; Social
    skills
Social Security tax, 201
Social skills
of five-year-olds, 511–12
of four-year-olds, 485
of infants (to 14 months)
    from one to twelve weeks old, 351
    from seven to fourteen months old,
        395–96, 403
    from three to six months old, 376
of newborns, 322
of three-year-olds, 459–60
of toddlers (15 to 23 months), 415–16
of two-year-olds, 438–39
See also Psychosocial development;
    Socialization; specific skills
Social workers, 623
Soda pop bottles, 166
Soft spot. See Fontanelle
Soil, 566
See also Dirt
Soiling. See Encopresis
Solid foods. See Food(s), solid
Soltz, Vicki, 498
Songs, for infants seven to fourteen
    months old, 403
Sorich, Carol J., 791
Sound insulation, 84–85
Spanking, 49, 115
    guidance by, 67–68
    See also Child abuse, physical
Special events, 93–107
    jolting, 105–7
        catastrophes, 105
        moving, 105–7
    joyful, 93–104
        birthdays, 93–95
        holidays, 95–97
        leaving the children home, 104
        milestone ceremonies, 97–99
        outings and vacations, 99–101

special achievements, 99
    travel with children, 101–4
Speech
    in four-year-olds, 482–83
    in infants (to 14 months)
        from one to twelve weeks old, 351
    "jargon," 394
    language development before, 234
    of three-year-olds, 457–58
    truncated, 513
    See also Language development
        (language acquisition); Stuttering;
        Vocalizations
Spider bites, emergency procedures for,
    750–51
Spine injuries, emergency procedures for,
    740–41, 744
Spitting up, in newborns, 332–33
Spitz, R. A., 240, 258
Splinters, first aid for, 760
Splinting, 745
Spock, Benjamin, 419
Spoiling babies, 259, 362
Sponge bath, 360
Spontaneous learning, 50
Sports, 467, 580–84
    competitive, 581–82
    safety and, 163
    school programs, 581
    socialization for, 582–83
Sprains, first aid for, 761–62
Stairs, walking up, 411
Standing, by infants seven to fourteen
    months old, 391
Startle reflex (Moro reflex), 142, 319, 349
State, the, 9, 10
STEP (Systematic Training for Effective
    Parenting), 92
Stepparenting, 792–804
    adopting stepchildren, 804
    death and, 793
    divorce and, 793–98
Stepping, development of, 249–51
    (table), 253 (table)
Stepping reflex, 319, 349, 363
Stern, Daniel, 390, 413
Steroid cream or ointment, 689
Stimulants, overdose or withdrawal from,
    emergency procedures for, 748–49
Stimulation
    definition of, 56
    development and, 258–61
    of newborns, 341
    socialization and, 56

Stimulus barrier, 370
Stinnett, Nick, 27
Stools
  black, 650
  blood in, 650–51
  eating one's own, 405
  meconium, 320–21
  of newborns, 320–21
  playing with, 44
  white, 651
  wormy, 651
  See also Elimination
Storage, child-orienting and, 83, 84
Stories
  making up, 484, 497
  reading. See Reading aloud
Stork bite birthmark, 343
Stotland, Nada, 337–38
Stoves, safety and, 165, 167–68
Straddling, 411
Stranger anxiety, 385, 395, 405, 429
Strasser, Susan, 568–69
Strawberry birthmarks, 343
Straws, learning to use, 412
Stress(es) (stress management), 107–22
  aggression as, 113–17
    child abuse, 115–17
    wife abuse, 114
  alcoholism, 117–18
  common, 109–10
  depression, 118
  four-year-olds and, 492–93
  health maintenance and, 584–88
  infants (to 14 months) and
    from one to twelve weeks old, 363–64
    from seven to fourteen months old, 400
    from three to six months old, 383
  marital, 118
  mastery of, 299
  newborns and, 336
  as part of everyone's life, 107–22
  preparation of children for, 85
  problems with a child, 118–19
  reactions to, 585–86
  relaxation techniques and, 586–88
  sexuality as source of, 110–13
  three-year-olds and, 467–68
  toddlers and, 419–20
  two-year-olds and, 445
Strollers, safety and, 178
Strong power methods of guidance, 67–68

Strontium 90, 591
Stuttering, 436, 457–58
Substance abuse, as symptom, 666–67
Suburbia, 8
Sucking, 543
  finger, 405
  prenatal, 318
  rooting reflex and, 318
  thumb, 363–64, 405, 462
Sucking reflex, 318, 349, 544 (table)
Suffocation, infants (to 14 months) and, 131
Sugar, 463, 464, 553–54
  dental health and, 555–56
Sugar water, as substitute for formula, 332
Suicide attempts, emergency procedures for, 756
Sullivan, Edmund V., 236
Summer, learning opportunities during, 275–76
Summer camps, 215–16
Summer child-care, 215–16
Summer programs, 275
Sunburn, 655
Sunday schools, 74, 271
Sunlight, dangers of, 592–93
Surgery, 606–7
Swaddling, 319, 336
Swallowing
  of food, safety and, 166–67
  of foreign objects
    by infants (to 14 months), 133
    by preschoolers, 138
  of poisons. See Poisonings
Swallowing reflex, 318, 544 (table)
Sweeteners, artificial, 554
Swimming
  in contaminated water, 590
  safety and, 159–60, 176
Swimming pools
  preschoolers and, 138
  safety and, 160, 173, 174
  toddlers and, 137
Swollen glands, 642–43
Symbolic play (representational play), 261
Sympathy, empathy and, 56
Symptoms of illness, 628–69
  appetite, poor, 645–46
  blisters, 655
  cardiovascular system, 644
  clumsiness, 654
  constipation, 650
  cough, 641–42

croup, 643
crying, 631
definition of, 628–29
delirium, 632–33
diarrhea, 648–50
digestive system, 644–51
drowsiness, 632
ears, 636–37
eyes, 635–36
fatigue, 633
fever, 630–31
general, 630–31
growing pains, 654
headache, 633–34
heartbeat, rapid or irregular
    (arrhythmias), 644
how to use chapter on, 629
keeping track of, 629–30
limping, 653–54
malaise, 633
in mouth, 644–45
musculoskeletal system, 653–54
nervous system, 633–35
psychosocial, 657–68
    anger, 657–58
    "bad behavior," 659–60
    goodness, excessive
        (overcompliance), 660–62
    identity problems, 667–68
    school problems, 666
    sexual behavior, 663–65
    substance abuse, 666–67
rashes, 655–56
respiratory system, 637–43
runny nose, 637–40
skin, 654–56
sleepiness, excessive, 632
sore throat, 640
stiff neck, 634–35
stomachache, 646–47
stools: black, red, white, or wormy,
    650–51
swollen glands, 642–43
toothache, 644–45
urinary system, 651–52
vomiting, 647–48
weight loss (or no weight gain), 631–
    32
wheezing, 643
Synapses, 232
Syrup of ipecac, 154, 687, 725, 742

Taking turns, 460
Talking

to babies, 259
    See also Communication;
        Conversation; Speech
Tall tales, 484
Tantrums. See Temper tantrums
Tar removal, 764
Taste, sense of
    in infants from one to twelve weeks
        old, 349
    in newborns, 319
Teachers, 185
    expectations of, 275
    kindergarten, 519
    parents' relationship with, 274
Teeth
    abscessed, swollen neck glands and,
        642
    bedtime bottle and, 364, 381, 556
    of infants seven to fourteen months
        old, 391
    knocked-out, first aid for, 764
    normal development of, 245 (table)
    nutrition and, 554–56
    of toddlers (15 to 23 months), 410
    See also Dental care; Toothbrushing;
        Tooth decay
Teething, 374
Telegraphic sentences, 414
Television
    as pollutant, 594–98
    for sick children, 677
    socialization and, 72–74
    three-year-olds and, 477
    toddlers and, 429
    as two-dimensional experience, 520
Television receivers, color, radiation from,
    592
Temper, losing one's, 67
Temperaments
    of infants (to 14 months)
        from one to twelve weeks old, 352–
            53
        from three to six months old, 377
    psychosocial symptoms and, 658, 659
    self-discipline and, 57
Temperature, body
    abnormally low (hypothermia),
        emergency procedures for, 746
    regulation of, in newborns, 320, 345
    See also Fever
Temper tantrums, 50, 420, 445, 446
    by adults, 69–70
    in infants seven to fourteen months
        old, 396, 400–1

psychosocial development and, 240
in toddlers, 416
Temporal-sequential disorganization, 281
Tensional outlets, 462, 512, 514–15
"Terrible twos," as erroneous expression, 240
Territorial rivalries, 110
Thanksgiving, 96
Thank-you notes for gifts, 97
Therapists (mental health professionals), 622–24
Thermometers, 672–75
Thevenin, Tine, 574
Thinking. *See* Cognitive development
Third World countries, living in, 103
Thomas, Lewis, 603
Three-year-olds, 455–78
 biophysical information, 456–57
 body functions of, 456
 cleaning and grooming, 465–66
 cognitive development in, 457–59
 developmental warning signals in, 463
 discipline and guidance for, 470–71
 emotional nutrition of, 468–69
 emotions and feelings of, 460–62
 exercise for, 467
 health care for, 476–77
 height and weight of, 456
 language development in, 457–58
 moral development in, 459
 motor skills of, 457
 nursery school and, 471–76
 nutrition of, 463–65
 play of, 459–60, 469
 sleep in, 466
 social skills of, 459–60
 stress management and, 467–68
 values and, 471
Throat, sore, 640
Throwing, 579, 580
 development of, 249–53 (table), 411
Thrush (moniliasis), 645
Thumb sucking, 363–64, 405, 462
Tickling
 excessive, 385
 infants one to twelve weeks old, 351
Ticks, first aid for, 761
Time
 concept of, 438, 459, 484
 telling, 510
Time-outs, 517
 as guidance technique, 66, 68
 spanking as a backup to, 68
Tiredness. *See* Fatigue

Toddlers (15 to 23 months), 409–30
 abnormal development in, 278 (table)
 autonomy of, 239–41
 body functions of, 410–11
 care of care givers of, 420–21
 cleaning and grooming, 418
 day care for, 427–28
 developmental warning signals in, 417
 discipline, guidance, and values and, 422
 emotional nutrition for, 420
 emotions of, 416–17
 environmental care for, 429–30
 exercise for, 419, 579–80
 friendships among, 267–68
 health care for, 428–29
 language and cognitive skills of, 412–14
 language development in, 240, 250 (table), 256 (table), 413–14, 421–22
 moral development in, 236, 251 (table)
 motor development in, 250 (table)
 motor skills of, 411–12
 nutrition of, 417–18
 parental development and, 294–95
 play of, 251 (table), 416, 421
 psychosexual development in, 241
 psychosocial development in, 239–40, 251 (table)
 safety and, 128, 429–30
  burns, 136
  car restraints, 146–48
  car safety, 137
  cribs, 177
  drowning, 137
  falls, 134
  poisonings, 135, 430
 size and shape of, 410
 sleep in, 419
 socialization tasks of, 421–27
 social skills of, 415–16
 stress management for, 419–20
 toilet training of. *See* Toilet training
 See also Preschoolers (ages 2 to 4)
Toenails, clipping, 361
Toilet
 safety and, 170
 See also Bathroom
Toilet training, 43–44, 241, 422–27, 449–50
 checklist for readiness for, 423–24
 parental development and, 291
 process of, 424–27

Tone of voice, in talking to babies, 319, 351
Tonic neck reflex (fencing reflex), 349
Tools, safety and, 171–73
Toothache, 644–45
  first aid for, 764
Toothbrushes, 571
Toothbrushing, 406, 465, 502, 520, 570–71
  introduction of, 386–87
Tooth decay, nutrition and, 554–56
Toothpaste, 571
  for infants three to six months old, 387
Touch, sense of, in newborns, 319
"Toughlove" approach, 71
Tourniquets, 734
Toxocariasis, 162
Toxoplasmosis, 162
Toy chests, 179
Toy Manufacturers of America, Inc., 182
Toys
  for infants (to 14 months)
    from one to twelve weeks old, 368
    from seven to fourteen months old, 402–3
    from three to six months old, 384
  parents' role in development and, 263–64
  putting away, 83–84, 460, 490
  safety and, 178–79
    infants one to twelve weeks old, 368
  for sick children, 677
  for three-year-olds, 469
Trace minerals, 540
Traditional societies
  parental development in, 286, 288
  socialization in, 48
  See also Non-industrial societies
Traditional view of parenting, 14
Trampoline, safety and, 174
Transexualism, 667
Transformation, inability to follow, 483
Transitional objects, 420, 462
Transition period, 33–34
Trash cans, safety and, 168, 171, 172
Trash compactor, safety and, 168
Travel
  with children, 101–4
    three- to six-month-old infants, 386
  without children, 104
  See also Car safety; Vacations
Trees, climbing, 143
Trelease, Jim, 596

Tribal models of child care, 7
Tricycles, 411
Trust, basic, 340
Tuberculin test, 406, 476, 615 (table)
"Turf issues," rivalries over, 110
Turns, taking, 460
Twin studies, on development, 257
Two-year-olds, 433–53
  biophysical information, 434–36
  body functions of, 435
  care of care givers of, 446
  cleaning and grooming, 443–44
  cognitive development in, 437–38, 447
  day care for, 450–51
  developmental warning signals, 440
  discipline and guidance, 448–49
  emotions and feelings in, 439–40
  exercise for, 444
  health care for, 451–52
  height and weight of, 434
  language development in, 436–38, 443
  motor skills of, 435–36
  nutrition of, 441–43
  play and stimulation of, 446–47
  safety and, 452–53
  sleep in, 444
  socialization tasks of, 446–50
  social skills of, 438–39
  stress management and, 445
  toilet training, 449–50
  values and, 449
  See also Preschoolers
Tylenol (acetaminophen), 678, 683–87

Umbilical stump, 359
Unconsciousness, emergency procedures for, 739–40
Undersocialization, psychosocial symptoms and, 658–60
Understimulation, 258–60
Urinary system, symptoms of illness, 651–53
Urinary tract infections, in toddler girls, 418
Urination, 42, 43
  excessive, as symptom of illness, 651
  infrequent, as symptom of illness, 651
  pain on, as symptom of illness, 652
Urine
  of newborns, 320
  red, brown, cloudy, or smelly, 652
Uterus, after childbirth, 337
Utility room, safety in, 171–72

Vacations
  baby-sitters during, 194
  See also Travel
Vaillant, George, 120
Values, 21
  about food, 35
  four-year-olds and, 501
  parents' role in development of, 271
  socialization and, 74–75
  three-year-olds and, 471
  two-year-olds and, 449
Vaporizers, 132, 676
Vedder, Katherine, 116
Vegetarianism, 563–65
Verbal interacting, 20
Verbal power methods of guidance, 68–71
Verbal relatedness, 413
Verbal skills. *See* Language development (language acquisition); Speech
Vernix caseosa, 318
Vertebral column, of newborns, 318
Violence
  domestic
    child abuse, 115–17
    wife abuse, 114
  television, 594–95
Visher, Emily B., 799, 802
Visher, John S., 799, 802
Vision (seeing)
  in infants (to 14 months)
    from one to twelve weeks old, 349, 368
    from three to six months old, 374–75
  in newborns, 635–36
  in toddlers (15 to 23 months), 411
Visual acuity, of infants seven to fourteen months old, 391
Vitamin A (retinol), 534, 536 (table)
Vitamin and mineral supplements, 356, 397, 535
  for one-week- to twelve-week-old infants, 357–58
Vitamin B complex, 534
Vitamin B1 (thiamine), 538 (table)
Vitamin B6 (pyridoxine), 537 (table)
Vitamin B12 (cobalamin), 536 (table), 564
Vitamin C (ascorbic acid), 534, 535, 538 (table)
Vitamin D, 534–35, 538 (table)
  supplemental, 358
Vitamin E, 534, 539 (table)

Vitamin K, 534, 539 (table)
Vitamins, 534–35, 536–39 (table)
  formulas fortified with, 356
Vocabulary (vocabulary acquisition)
  four-letter words, 500
  of four-year-olds, 482, 483, 486
  of infants seven to fourteen months old, 394–95
  of toddlers (15 to 23 months), 414
  of two-year-olds, 436
  See also Language development
Vocalizations, in infants three to six months old, 376
Vomiting, 692
  blood, 736
  inducing, 742
  in newborns, 342
  as symptom of illness, 647–48
Vowel sounds, 351

Wading pools, 160
Wages, for housekeepers, 201
Waking at night. *See* Sleep
Walkers
  for infants three to six months old, 384
  safety and, 177
Walking, 579
  development of, 249–51 (table), 392
  social interaction and, 395
Wallerstein, Judith S., 794, 795
Washing
  newborns, 333
  See also Bathing; Cleaning; Hygiene
Water
  for infants three to six months old, 379
  purity of, 528
  requirements for, 527–28
Water pollution, 589–90
Water safety, 159–60
Watson, J. B., 224
Weaning
  from bottle-feeding, 397–98
  from breast-feeding, 397–98
  early, 355
Weddings, 98
Weight
  birth, 317
  of five-year-olds, 507
  of four-year-olds, 481
  of infants (to 14 months)
    from one to twelve weeks old, 348

from seven to fourteen months old, 390

from three to six months old, 374

of three-year-olds, 456

of toddlers (15 to 23 months), 410

of two-year-olds, 434

Weight gain

in infants one to twelve weeks old, 348

in infants seven to fourteen months old, 390

in infants three to six months old, 373

lack of, as symptom of illness, 631–32

in toddlers (15 to 23 months), 410

Weight loss

in mothers of newborns, 337

in newborns, 317, 343

as symptom of illness, 631–32

Wheezing, 643

White, Burton, 264, 390

"White lies," 501

Whole milk, 378, 398

Wife abuse, 114

Will, George, 222

Williams, Frank, 799

Window blind or drapery cords, 180

Windows

car, automatic, 179

child-proofing, 143

Winston, Stephanie, 84

Withdrawal, excessive, 260

Women

changing parenting realities for, 22

moral identities of, 237

See also Care givers

Work, 772–83

dual-worker family, 774–75

effects of maternal employment on children, 781–82

going back to, 366

parental development and, 306

reasons for working, 774

sharing household responsibilities and, 775–80

socialization and, 53

Workmen's Compensation, 201

Wounds

bleeding from, 733–36

See also Emergencies

Writing, development of, 250 (table), 252 (table), 253 (table)

Wyden, Peter, 81

X-rays, diagnostic, 591–92

Yards, safety in, 143–44, 173–74

Yates, Alayne, 79, 585

Yelling, as verbal power method, 69

"You messages," 52

Young adulthood

parental development and, 297

transition to independent, 303

Zephiran, 725